About TUSC

"Hire those who share your vision. Someone who clashes with your personality or the corporate culture will hinder your work."

—Sir Ernest Shackleton

TUSC was founded in 1988 on character and excellence just two years after Oracle went public. In 1988, the Nasdaq was only at 372, CDs outsold vinyl for the first time, the Iran/Iraq war ended, LeBron James was three years old, Brittany Spears was seven years old, and two of our employees listed in the Acknowledgments section were only six years old. (TUSC was founded at this Burger King, pictured here.) TUSC now has seven offices and continues to grow quickly.

Oracle Database 10g Performance Tuning Tips & Techniques

Richard J. Niemiec

New York   Chicago   San Francisco
Lisbon   London   Madrid   Mexico City   Milan
New Delhi   San Juan   Seoul   Singapore   Sydney   Toronto

The McGraw·Hill Companies

Cataloging-in-Publication Data is on file with the Library of Congress

McGraw-Hill books are available at special quantity discounts to use as premiums and sales promotions, or for use in corporate training programs. For more information, please write to the Director of Special Sales, Professional Publishing, McGraw-Hill, Two Penn Plaza, New York, NY 10121-2298. Or contact your local bookstore.

Oracle Database 10g Performance Tuning Tips & Techniques

1234567890 DOC DOC 01987

ISBN-13: 978-0-07-226305-3
ISBN-10:   0-07-226305-9

Sponsoring Editor Lisa McClain	**Copy Editor** Bob Campbell	**Composition** Apollo Publishing Services
Editorial Supervisor Jody McKenzie	**Proofreaders** Carolyn Welch Claire Splan	**Illustration** Apollo Publishing Services
Project Editor Carolyn Welch	**Indexer** Claire Splan	**Art Director, Cover** Jeff Weeks
Acquisitions Coordinator Mandy Canales	**Production Supervisor** George Anderson	**Cover Designer** Pattie Lee
Technical Editor Janet Stern		

"Perhaps, in order to really become free, we have to move from struggling to hear God's Voice to letting God's Voice speak through us."

—**Rabbi Jonathan Kraus**

To Regina, the love of my life…

Every person has a partner somewhere in the world who completes them perfectly.
A partner in life is finer than gold, more pleasing than success, sweeter than any words.

Greater than gold is this beautiful rose.
Greater than success is the path on the road less traveled.
Greater than praise is lasting character.

Gold glistens, but is of little refuge on a cold Chicago night.
Success is enticing, but its promises ring empty without the right person to share it with.
Praise is shallow unless it comes from the person who matters most to you.
The world offers many outwardly shiny things that prove hollow on the inside.

A partner gives you the strength to be successful when you want to give up.
It's the person who believes in you when the world gives up on you.
It's the person who walks in when the world walks out.
For me that person was always and is always Regina!

Regina is Finer than Gold, Sweeter than Praise, and Truer than Success.
She is worth more to me than the world can ever offer.
Yet she makes me a better person, and I achieve everything that I can offer the world.
Surely my cup overflowed the day I met her!

Regina is that one person in the world who completes me.
She is my helper in life and like a precious rose, she's absolutely beautiful.
She's all I ever needed in the world and is the love of my life.

Regina is still the greatest person I know in the world.
I am one of the lucky ones in the world; my partner in life is right by my side.

I love you, Regina, with all my heart!

To Jacob, Lucas, Hollyann, and Melissa

You are the other four wonderful people in my life. Thanks for your love, energy, fun, and care. You are each incredible in your own way. In your eyes, I see the love of God shine into the world and into my life. He has blessed me greatly.

Contents

Acknowledgments

"You must be the change you wish to see in the world."
—Mahatma Gandhi

I knew that any update to this book would not be a simple task. What I didn't realize when I wrote the first version of this book, was that this was really about 16 books combined into one. Only a novice writing a first book is ignorant enough to take on a task of this magnitude. You are the beneficiary of my ignorance. Between TUSC commitments and user group commitments, the complexity of getting this task accomplished would not be possible without many others from TUSC helping.

Brad Brown and Joe Trezzo are still and always will be the best two business partners I could ever have. They are always there when I need them, and they regularly display character that few have in the world today. Thanks—you guys are the best!

Janet Stern of Oracle Corporation was my primary technical editor. She is definitely one of the top Oracle gurus on the planet! Janet, you once again took the book to another level. Your tireless testing on 10gR2 as well as additional editing and proofing certainly made a difference in making this book a much better one. I can't thank you enough for all of your efforts. You continue to be one of the leaders of the Oracle pack!

Lisa McClain of McGraw-Hill managed the entire effort of the book and kept us on pace. Thanks for your efforts; this one finished in half the time of the first one. You are great to work with. Amanda Canales was my primary in-house editorial contact at McGraw-Hill. Thanks for all of your help in making this a quality book. Carolyn Welch managed the book through editorial and production. Thanks for taking me the last mile. You are wonderful. Bob Campbell was my fantastic copy editor. Bob took the book to yet another level. Scott Rogers gave me the break I needed when I suggested the Tips & Techniques line of books. Scott gets the right information into the hands of the people who build the systems that run this world. You are the man!

Kevin Aiken was an additional technical editor and helped check all of the scripts. Steve Adams of Australia was a technical editor in the past and a great contributor to the X$ scripts. Marcel Kratochvil was an additional technical editor in the past; thanks for your help. Bruce Scott – Thanks for taking the time with me in doing the Select article interview and sending me the rare Oracle founder's picture. Brad Ziola – Thanks for your help in getting the new features chapter completed. This was a very tough chapter since most of it is new. Madhu Tumma – Thanks for your great section on RAC that I added to Chapter 11. Kevin Loney – Thanks for your work in updating Chapter 2. Bill Callahan– Thanks for an outstanding job updating Chapter 3. Nitin Vengurlekar – Thanks for additions of ASM to Chapter 3. Jeff Keller – Great job in updating Chapter 4 and simplifying the key initialization parameters. Anil Khilani, Prabhaker Gongloor (GP), David LeRoy, Martin Pena, and Mughees Minhas – Thanks for your efforts in getting me screen shots as well Enterprise Manager information for Chapter 5. Warren Bakker – Thanks for the update and additions to Chapter 6. Rob Christensen – Thanks for the updates to Chapter 8. Joe Holmes of Canada – Thanks for your advanced information in Chapter 9. Thanks to Francisco Javier Moreno, Guillermo L. Ospina Romero, and Rafael I. Larios Restrepo from the University Nacional in Medellín, Colombia. Roger Schrag – Thanks for your original information on joins in Chapter 9. Bob Taylor – Another great job updating Chapter 10. Maurizio Bonomi of Italy – Thanks for your additions to Chapters 9 and 11. Murali Vallath and Richard Stroupe – Thanks for some great additions to Chapter 11. Bob Yingst – Thanks for passing along some of the V$ scripts for Chapter 12. Kevin Gilpin – Thanks for your input to Chapters 12 and 13. Graham Thornton – Thanks for your excellent additions to Chapter 13. Veljko Lavrnic – Thanks for your excellent input on block tuning in Chapter 13. Brad Nash – Thanks for a great job updating Chapter 15 and for your additions to Chapter 11. Mike Gallagher – Thanks for updating Chapter 16. Thanks to Kate Kerner and Katy Ryan for making my IOUG life easier. Chuck Phillips – You continue to take Oracle to the next plateau. Judith Sim – You are one of the Oracle leaders who puts Oracle at the top. Thanks for all your help. Rauline Ochs – You have made us true partners in the Oracle Partner Program. Tom Kyte – You are the ultimate Oracle tech guru. Ken Jacobs – Thanks for your support of the Oracle product through the eyes of the customer. Andy Mendelsohn – Thanks for getting answers to some of the really tough questions. Thomas Kurian – Thanks for putting Fusion Middleware on the map. Angelo Pruscino, Kirk McGowan, and Erik Peterson – Without you three, there would be no RAC; without Angelo, RAC would be a mess. Justin Kestelyn – You educate the world with OTN. Tirthankar Lahiri – What a job on the buffer cache! Mary Ann Davidson – Thanks for your leadership and keeping Oracle secure.

Very special thanks to these people who helped manage TUSC throughout this process (in addition to Broe): Mike Butler, Tony Catalano, Janet Dahmen, Terry Daley, Wayne Kerwood, Randy Lawson, Bill Lewkow, John Molinaro, Matt Morris, Scott Moyer, Nathan Nguyen, Burk Sherva, Dave Ventura, Barry Wiebe, and Bob Yingst.

Thanks to Sheila Reiter, Barb Dully, and Amy Horvat of TUSC, who are always there when we need them. Thanks Larry Ellison, Bob Miner, Bruce Scott, and Ed Oates for the great database.

Thanks to the following people who also contributed to this version of the book (in addition to those mentioned above): David Anstey, Eyal Aronoff, Mike Ault, Janet Bacon, Kamila Bajaria, Greg Bogode, Mike Broullette, Don Burleson, Bill Burke, Rachel Carmichael, Tony Catalano, Craig Davis, Sergio Del Rio, Dr. Paul Dorsey, Kim Floss, Mark Greenhalgh, K. Gopalakrishnan, Tim Gorman, Kent Graziano, Roman Gutfraynd, Gerry Hills, Steven Hirsch, Nguyen Hoang, Pat Holmes, Scott Heaton, Tony Jambu, Tony Jedlinski, Ron Jedlinski, Cyndi Jensen, Jeremy Judson, Dave Kaufman, Mike Killough, Peter Koletzke, Tom Kyte, Steve Lemme, Jonathan Lewis, Bill Lewkow, Steven Lu, Connor McDonald, Sean McGuire, Ronan Miles, Cary Milsap, Ken Morse, Shankar Mukherjee, Ken Naim, Frank Naude, Pradeep Navalkar, Stanley Novinsky, Albert

Nashon, Aaron Newman, Cetin Ozbutun, Tanel Poder, Venkatesh Prakasam, Greg Pucka, Heidi Ratini, Steve Rubinow, Chuck Seaks, Bert Spencer, Craig Shallahamer, Burk Sherva, Judy Sim, Felipe Teixeira de Souza, Randy Swanson, Megh Thakkar, George Trujillo, Madhu Tumma, Gaja Krishna Vaidyanatha, Jake Van der Vort, Murali Vallath, Dave Ventura, Sandra Vucinic, Lyssa Wald, Graham Wood, Tom Wood, Pedro Ybarro, Ghazi Ben Youssef, and Dr. Oleg Zhooravlev.

Thanks to the following people at TUSC who make it possible for us to write books: Andrew Abele, Derek Ahmad, Michael P. Alba, Sridhar Avantsa, Janet Bacon, Warren Bakker, Rusty Barnett, Otis Barr, Roger Behm, Monica Bigmore, Gregory Bogode, Brad Brown, Deborah Bryda, Mike "Apps Master" Butler, Steve Butterworth, William S. Callahan, Alex Campbell, Alain Campos, Brian Carignan, Mark Carlstedt, Tony "Super Bowl" Catalano, Rob Christensen, Arthur Clements, Richard Clough, Liz Coffee, Randy Cook, Bryan Cooper, Judy Corley, Matt Cox, Keith D'Agostino, Janet Dahmen, Terry Daley, Michael Day, Susan Difabio, Ernie DiLegge, Frank Dodgers, Barb Dully, Philip Ejisimekwu, James Elias, Ed Eloian, Milton Estrada, Robin Fingerson, Newton "Fletch" Fletcher, Yvonne Formel, Dave Fornalsky, Sergio "Power Surge" Frank, George Frederick, Robert Freeman, Doug Freyburger, Lowell Fryman, Steve Galassini, Mike Gallagher, Tara Gehrke, Samantha German, Brad Gibson, Kevin Gilpin, Kevin Gordon, Jason Grandy, Chelsea Graylin, Esley Gustafson, Eric Guyer, Brian Hacker, Don Hammer, Scott Heaton, Kristin Heinzel, Casey Helders, Myla Hermosura, Mark Heyvaert, Amy Horvat, Chris Hunt, Stuart Jacobs, Mohammad Jamal, Cyndi Jensen, Kim Johnson, Brad Joost, Matt Keane, Jeff Keller, Teri Kemple, Wayne Kerwood, Mike Killough, Karen King, Mike King, Bruce Kissinger, Angela Kmiec, Melissa Knight, Gillian M. Kofal, Matt Kundrat, Felix LaCap, Shari Lacey, Lynn Lafleur, Cynthia Landess, Randy Lawson, Bill Lewkow, Larry Linnemeyer, Scott Lockhart, Kevin Loney, Allen Long, Antonia Lopez, Dennis Macumber, Matt Malcheski, Ray Mansfield, JR Mariottini, Scott Martin, Dan Martino, Joe Mathew, Alexis May, Sharon Maynard, Ed McDonough, Pat McGovern, Jeff Melton, Brian Michael, Christina R. Miller, John Molinaro, Matt Morris, Scott Moyer, Dave Muehlius, Brad Nash, Nathan Nguyen, Anthony Noriega, Chris Ostrowski, John Parker, Steve Parsons, Greg Partenach, Mark Pelzel, Rob Perry, Gregg Petri, Karen Quandt, Heidi "Trinity" Ratini, Bob Reczek, Sheila Reiter, Alex Reyderman, Mark Riedel, Marie Robertson, Holly Robinson, Jamie Rocks, John Rowland, Sean Ryan, Johnny Sadkauskas, Gurdeep Saini, Alwyn "The Machine" Santos, Sabina Schoenke, Chad Scott, Burk Sherva, Jolene Shrake, Garrett Sienkiewicz, John Smiley, David Smith, Brian Sneed, Ed Stayman, Jack Stein, Jenny Tao, Kim Tate, Bob Taylor, Shashi Tewari, Chris Thoman, Graham Thornton, Jeff Tieri, Dave "Torch" Trch, Joe Trezzo, Joel Tuisl, Tom Usher, Dave Ventura, Jon Vincenzo, Barry Wiebe, Ted Williams, Nicole Wilson, Joel Wittenmyer, Lisa Wright, Bob Yingst, Ron Yount, and Brad Ziola.

Thanks to the following people who have helped out in other ways: Sandra Niemiec, Floyd and Georgia Adams, Kristen Brown, Lori Trezzo, Sohaib Abbasi, Michael Abbey, Ian Abramson, Jeff and Donna Ackerman, Steve and Becky Adams, Keith Altman, Joe Anzell, Joe Arozarena, Mike Ault, Pastor James C. Austin, Vahan Avedisian, Randy Baker, Abed Ben Brahim, John Beresniewicz, Oliver Bernhard, Hardik Bhatt, Ronny Billen, Jon & Linda Bischoff, Keith Block, George Bloom, Melanie Bock, Mike Boddy, David Bohan, A.W. Bolden, Rene Bonvanie, Gary Bradshaw, Ted Brady, Barry Brasseaux, Nicholas Bassey, Aldo Bravo, J. Birney & Julia Brown, John Brown, Karen Brownfield, Sam & Rhonda Bruner, Bill Burke, Ashley Burkholder, Jeremy Burton, Andrew Busch, Dan Cameron, Bogdan Capatina, Joe Carbonara, Dave Carey, Katie Carlson, Rachel Carmichael,

Monty Carolan, Christina Cavanna, Sheila Cepero, Bill Chappell, Edward Chu, Sonia Cillo, Joan Clark, Ray J. Clark, Rachel Cohen, Dr. Ken Coleman, Kristine Collins, Larry Collins, Lee Collins, Jim Conlon, Margarita Contreni, Mike Corey, Peter Corrigan, Jason Couchman, Stephen Covey, Shanda Cowan, Chip Coyle, Richard Daley, Sharon Daley, Nancy Daniel, Barb Darrow, Jeb Dasteel, Sudeep Datta, Mary Ann Davidson, Tom Davidson, Luis Davila, Leigh Cantrell Day, Elaine DeMeo, Tony DeMeo, Sohan DeMel, Jose DiAvilla, Bill & Barbara Dinga, Julian Dontcheff, Mary Lou Dopart, Joe Dougherty Jr., Brenda Dreier, Carl Dudley, Elonka Dunin, Matt Eberz, Kristy Edwards, Eileen Egan, Shanna Eggers, Lisa Elliot, Brian Embree, Buff Emslie, Dan Erickson, Chick Evans, Lisa Evans, Dr. Tony Evans, Darcy Evon, Mark Farnham, Tony Feisel, Jorge Ferreira, Kelly Ferris, Julie Ferry, Stephen Feurenstein, Ted & Joan File, Caryl Lee Fisher, Lee Fisher, Charlie Fishman, Tim & Jan Fleming, Flip, Joe Flores, Andy Flower, Karen Foley, Paul Ford, Heidi Fornalsky, Vicky Foster, Kate Freeman, Doug Freud, Mike Frey, Dr. Susan Friedberg, Sylvain Gagne, Hari Gandhe, Karen Gainey, Mike Gangler, Fred Garfield, Charles Gary, Julie Geer-Brown, Aydin Gencler, Len Geshan, George Gilbert, Scott Goff, Mark Gokman, Alex Golod, Laverne Gonzales, John Goodhue, Ellen Gordon, Greg Gorman, Dennis Gottlieb, Joe Graham, Cammi Granato, Tony Granato, Kent Graziano, Roxanne Gregg, Alan Greenspan, Carrie Greeter, Sarah Grigg, Ken Guion, Mark Gurry, Pasi Haapalainen, Steve Hagan, Rebecca Hahn, John Hall, Robert Hanrahan, Albrecht Haug, Jim Hawkins, Marko Hellevaara, Jeff Henley, Bob Hill, James Hobbs, Stacy Hodge, Kristin Hollins, Pat Holmes, Mike Hooper, Napoleon Hopper Jr., Rich Horbaczewski, Howard Horowitz, Dan Hotka, Rich Houle, Ellie Hurley, Laura Hurley, Bruno Ierullo, Alan Iovine, Jerry Ireland, Roger Jackson, Adam Jacobs, Jeff Jacobs, Tony Jambu, Mark Jarvis, Don Jaskulske & Dianne Innes-Jaskulske, Samantha Johns, Bobbi Jo Johnson, Steve Johnson, Jeff Jonas, Shawn Jones, Michael Jordan, Michael Josephson, Jeremy Judson, Mark Jungerman, Valerie Kane, Emily Kao, Ari Kaplan, Stephen Karniotis, Maralynn Kearney, Dan Kelleher, John Kelly, Robert Kennedy, Kate Kerner, Ann Kilhoffer-Reichert, John & Peggy King, Martin Luther King Jr., Vick Khachadourian, Jan Klokkers, George Koch, Jodi Koehn-Pike, Fran Koerner, Sergey Koltakov, James Koopman, Kaarina Koskenalusta, Larry Kozlicki, Paul C. Krause, Fred Krauss, Michael Krauss, Mark Krefta, Ron Krefta, Dave Kreines, Thomas Kurian, John Krasnick, Mark Kwasni, Paul Lam, Jennifer Lamson, Marva Land, Ray Lane, Karen Langley, Jari Lappalainen, Carl Larson, John Lartz, Brian Laskey, Deb LeBlanc, Margaret Lee, Rich Lee, Sami Lehto, Herve Lejeune, Greg Lemay, Steve Lemme, Sharon Lewis, Troy Ligon, Cheng Lim, Juan Loaiza, Quan Logan, Xavier Lopez, Senator Dick Lugar, Dave Luhrsen, Lucas Lukasiak, Barb Lundhild, Liz Macin, Tony Mack, Ann Mai, Tom Manzo, Paul Massiglia, Donna McConnell, Stephen McConnell, Kirk McGowan, Carol McGury, Amanda McLafferty, Mary Elizabeth McNeely, Gail McVey, Ehab & Andrea Mearim, Margaret Mei, Sara Mejia, Kuassi Mensah, Kelly Middleton, Regina Midkiff, Debbie Migliore, Gwen Milligan, Jeff Mills, Jal Mistri, Dr. Arnold Mitchem, John Molinaro, Congresswoman Gwen Moore, Ken Morse, Solveig Morkeberg, Bill Moses, Steve Muench, Brad Musgrave, Minelva Munoz, Scott Myers, Shyam Nath, Cassie Naval, Bill Nee, Paul Needham, Marie-Anne Neimat, Scott Nelson, Phil Newlan, Olli Niemi, Cindy Niemiec, Dr. Dave & Dawn Niemiec, Mike Niemiec, Robert & Cookie Niemiec, Dr. Ted & Paula Niemiec, Merrilee Nohr, Robin North, Stan Novinsky, Perttu Nuija, Julie O'Brian, Jon O'Connell, Barb O'Malley, Anne O'Neill, Mike Olin, Francisco Martinez Oviedo, Rita Palanov, Jeri Palmer, Jignesh Patel, Arlene Patton, Ray Payne, Ricky Penick, Monica Penshorn, Dr. Mary Peterson, Michael Pettigrew, Chuck Phillips, Mary Platt, Lisa Price, Megan Price, John Ramos, Gautham Ravi, Gary Raymond, Dick Reck, Frank Ress, Denise Rhodes, Elizabeth Richards, Dennis Richter, Arnold Ridgel, Anne Ristau, Tom Roach, George Roberts, Jerry D. Robinson Jr., Mike Rocha, Ulka Rodgers, Arden Romanillos, Charlie Rose, Chuck Rozwat, Leslie Rubin, Steve Rubin, Mike Runda, Joe Russell, Mike Russell, Katy Ryan, Theresa Rzepnicki, David Saslav, Terry Savage, Rami Savila, Nanak Sawlani, Ed Schalk, Douglas Scherer, Scott Schmidt, David Scott, Kevin Scruggs, Mike Serpe, Guner Seyhan, Allen Shaheen, Lewei Shang, Smiti Sharma, Dr. Austin Shelley, Muhammad Shuja, Julie Silverstein,

Judy Sim, Angela Sims, Dinu Skariah, Linda Smith, Mark Smith, Mary Ellen Smith, Peter Smith, Congressman Mike & Keta Sodrel, Marc Songini, Julie Sowers, Anthony Speed, Jeff Spicer, Rick Stark, Cassandra Staudacher, Leslie Steere, Albert Steidel, Carma Stewart, Thomas Stickler, Bob Strube Sr., Bob Strube Jr., Olaf Stullich, Burt & Dianna Summerfield, Cyndie Sutherland, Inna Suvorov, Matt Swann, Mary Swanson, Michael Swinarski, Ed Szofer, Matthew Szulik, Vijay Tella, David Teplow, Marlene Theriault, Margaret Tomkins, Susan Trebach, Eugene (EGBAR) & Adrienne (Sky's the Limit) Trezzo, Sean Tucker, David Tuson, Vicky Tuttle, Razi Ud-Din, Paul Ungaretti, Lisa Vaas, Lupe Valtierre, Petri Varttinen, Jussi Vira, Jarmo Viteli, Matt Vranicar, Oleg Wasynczuk, Lori Wachtman, Bill Weaver, Jim Weber, Mike Weber, Huang Wei, Erich Wessner, Steve Wilkenson, Dennie Williams, Donna Williams, John Wilmott, Marcus Wilson, Jeremiah Wilton, Oprah Winfrey, Wayne Wittenberger, Ron Wohl, Randy Womack, Marcia Wood, Jacqueline Woods, Chris Wooldridge, Don Woznicki, David Wright, Lv Xueyong, Stan Yellott, Janet Yingling Young, Tony Ziemba, Mary Ann Zirelli, Edward Zhu, Chris Zorich, and Andreas Zwimpfer.

Last, thanks to (*your name goes here*) for buying this book and being dedicated to improving your own skills (or if I forgot your name above). Father Tony once told me, **"Nothing in life is so big that God can't handle it and nothing is so small that God doesn't notice it."** Thanks to all of those above who made both big and small differences in my life and in this book!

Introduction

"The enduring impact of our choices is not what we get, but what we become."
—Michael Josephson

64-bit and Oracle Break the Space Time Continuum

Many people think the rise of the Internet in the mid-1990s was a rare event never to be repeated again in our lifetime. They are infinitely wrong! In the last version of the book, I noted that Terabyte databases would be everywhere soon; few people believed me. It's happened; Terabyte databases are now quite common. With Oracle 10*g*, Petabyte databases (1,000 Terabytes) will start to come of age, and Exabyte databases (1,000,000 Terabytes) may even make an entrance by Oracle 11*g* (almost definitely by Oracle12*g* of the database).

Few people understand that the rise of the Internet Generation was directly attributable to 32-bit computing and the ripple effect resulting from the theoretical possibilities that 32-bit computing provided. Oracle introduced 32-bit computing in 1983, yet it took until the mid to late 1990s for the hardware to catch up and for companies to take full advantage of it (roughly 12 years). The Information Age is about to take another enormous step forward. This step will be infinitely larger than the one that drove the Internet Generation. We are now embarking on an Oracle 10*g* database that functionally does everything but defy gravity, while simultaneously heading into the futuristic world of 64-bit computing. 64-bit computing was introduced in 1995 with Oracle7. Adding twelve additional years for adoption puts us at 2007 for 64-bit to start taking off. The next generation, *Generation 64*, and 64-bit computing will change the world as never before. That rise begins this year. Consider the following research from IDC/EMC and The University of California at Berkeley:

- 2K   A typewritten page
- 1M   1000K
- 1M   A small novel
- 5M   The complete works of Shakespeare
- 10M   One minute of high fidelity sound
- 100M   One meter of shelved books
- 1G   1000M
- 1G   A pickup truck filled with books (or your SGA in 2007)
- 100G   A floor of academic journals (or your new laptop hard drive in 2007)
- 1T   1000G

- 2T   An academic research library (or your Fortune 500 database in 2007)

- 2T   Information generated on YouTube in one day

- 2P   All academic research libraries (or your Grid SGA in 2010)

- 10T   530,000,000 miles of bookshelves at the Library of Congress

- 730T   Information generated on YouTube in one year

- 1P   1000T

- 20P   All hard-disk drives in 1995 (or your database in 2010)

- 700P   Combined data of 700,000 companies with revenues less than $200M

- 1E   1000P

- 1E   Combined Fortune 1000 company databases (average 1P each)

- 1E   Combined Next 9000 world-company databases (average around 100T each)

- 2E   Largest 10,000 companies in the world (total database use)

- 2E   All information generated in 1999 (fits in ONE Oracle 10g database in 2007)

- 3E   Largest 1,0000,000 companies in the world (total database use)

- 5E   New information generated in 2003 (estimated—mostly images not in DB)

- 6E   Email generated in 2006

- 8E   **Capacity of ONE Oracle10g Database (CURRENT)**

- 12E to 16E   All information generated prior to 1999 (memory resident with 64-bit)

- 16E   **Addressable memory with 64-bit (CURRENT)**

- 161E   New information generated in 2006 (estimated—mostly images not in DB)

- 246E   All hard drives built in 2007 (estimated)

- 255E   New information generated in 2007 (estimated—mostly images/video not in DB)

- 1000E   New information generated in 2010 (estimated 1 Zettabyte)

- 1Z   1000E (Zettabyte—Estimated grains of sand on all world beaches—125 Oracle DBs)

- 1Y   1000Z (Yottabytes—Estimated atoms in 1000 human bodies)

- 100TY–100 Trillion Yottabytes   **Addressable memory with 128-bit (FUTURE)**

The power of 64-bit computing can be imagined when you consider the theoretical limit for addressable memory. In unsigned 16-bit computing, we could directly address 64K (2^{16} bytes) of memory. With this huge advance in technology we saw the advent of Windows 1.0 in 1985 (a weak graphical version as was Windows 2.0 in 1987), Windows 3.0 in 1990, and the birth of the client-server soon thereafter. I remember Oracle Support telling me at the time that I "couldn't possibly need an SGA larger than 1M" when I encountered memory issues after I increased the SGA above 1M. In unsigned 32-bit computing, we could directly address 4G (2^{32} bytes) of memory (the +/- sign will cost you 2G). For a standard Oracle database, this allowed a tremendously increased System

Global Area (SGA). The SGA is where the most often used data can be stored and kept in memory for fast access. We now regularly see Gigabyte SGAs and Terabyte databases. The calls to support are from 32-bit Linux and Windows DBAs asking how to get their SGAs above 2G or 4G. The move to 64-bit computing accelerates the Information Age exponentially faster than in the Internet Generation. With 64-bit, the theoretical limit of addressable memory (2 to the power of 64) becomes 16E (Exabytes) or 18,446,744,073,709,551,616 bytes (2^{64} bytes) of directly addressable memory. Consider the following numbers to realize how big the jump we are about to make is:

Memory	Address Direct	Indirect/Extended
4 Bit	16	(640)
8 Bit	256	(65,536)
16 Bit	65,536	(1,048,576)
32 Bit	4,294,967,296	
64 Bit	18,446,744,073,709,551,616	

The Oracle 10*g* database has a maximum theoretical limit of 8 Exabytes per database (one Exabyte is a quintillion bytes or one million Terabytes). Just a few years ago (1999), it was estimated that there were only about 12-16 Exabytes of information in the entire world. All databases in the world are still only a fraction of this amount when combined together. 16 Exabytes of directly addressable memory is a pretty healthy amount. (Larry can now run every database in the entire world in a single Oracle database—World-On-Line – Memory Resident.) Imagine storing almost every single piece of information on earth in one database and IN MEMORY. Soon you may hear, "Oh the Internet, I have it on my laptop." The Internet is estimated only in Petabytes (you can fit several in your Oracle database if you remove the duplication of data). The surface web is only estimated at 167T (you can fit 50,000 of them in one Oracle database), while the deep web is estimated at 92P (you can fit a little under 100 of them in one Oracle database). And if you include all the email (440P) and instant messages (270T), it is 500P (you can still fit 16 of them in one Oracle database). When the hardware physically reaches the theoretical possibilities of 64-bit, things will change dramatically. Moving from 32-bit to 64-bit will be like moving from 1971 to 2000 overnight. It should be noted that since the 2000 study, upward revisions have estimated that all information is a bit larger than the original estimates (although there are still debates as to the exact number because of the large amount of duplication of data).

More staggering in these recent estimations is that we are now generating over 8 Exabytes (2E in 1999, 5E in 2003, and 8E in 2005) of original information per year. That's an incredible amount when you consider that 5E is equivalent to the information stored in 500,000 libraries with the information contained in the Library of Congress. With increasing amounts of video and audio, storage requirements are going through the roof, but we really don't need another million Libraries of Congress, just a bit more digital storage in the libraries we have. We may need as many as five or six Oracle databases to store everything soon versus the one that we needed just eight years ago.

I estimate that if you could stack single sheets of paper with 2K worth of text on each one, it would reach about 4.8B miles high to get 16E of information. That is, you could stack documents from the Earth so high they would pass Pluto! In one Oracle database you could fit:

- Several Internets (without duplication of data)
- 2 billion movies (4G each)

- 8 billion pickup trucks of documents
- 1 Mount Everest filled with documents
- All printed information in the world (estimated at 5E)
- All words ever spoken (estimated at 5E—often debated, though)

Oracle Will Be First

If you haven't seen the "Oracle Firsts" on oracle.com, I've listed them here so that I can add a couple of notes from Oracle's past to what I believe is a compelling vision in the Oracle future. Oracle will be the leader throughout the Information Age not only because they create the "bend in the road," but they're also willing to turn willingly when the road bends unexpectedly. Unlike Microsoft, they include Java to its fullest extent, embracing volumes of developers. Unlike IBM, they bring in every hardware solution, driving scalability to fruition and bringing choices to their customers. They embrace Linux for the future that it will bring while driving information to the Web with relentless force. They continue to support SAP and Microsoft while courting the Open Source community. I remember building the first Oracle client-server application with Brad Brown and Joe Trezzo when we were at Oracle in 1987. We wondered why it took so long for others to follow. Now, I just look at Oracle firsts and know that others will follow (in time), but I like to be part of the leading edge. Consider these Oracle firsts and get ready for a much-accelerated future:

- First commercial RDBMS
- First 32-bit database
- First database with read consistency
- First client-server database
- First SMP database
- First 64-bit RDBMS
- First Web database
- First database with Native Java Support
- First commercial RDBMS ported to Linux
- First database with XML
- First database with Real Application Clusters (RAC)
- First True Grid database
- Free Oracle Database (Oracle Express Edition)
- Unbreakable Linux Support

History Accelerates

History is accelerating, 64-bit Oracle is here, and Petabyte SGAs are on the way. You have every tuning option and every 24x7x52 option needed for availability. You have maintenance and recoverability options beyond anything imaginable. Security and auditing are at the record level if desired, and table data and database backups can be encrypted for security purposes. All of this is possible today! You will build greatness! Your job in the next year will be to learn and implement Oracle 10*g* and take the world to the next level. Your job will depend on your being more productive. Using tools like Grid Control (covered in Chapter 5) to simplify your job so that you can focus on business issues will be paramount to your success. You will also need to aggregate the tremendous amounts of data into useable datasets for your internal business customers.

The next stop after this one will be 128-bit (2^{128} bytes of addressable memory) computing or 3 with 38 zeroes (256-bit will get us to 1 with 77 zeroes in Oracle in 2019, and 512-bit will get us to over a googol or 1 with 154 zeroes in Oracle in 2031). A *googol* (not Google) was once picked as a very large unreachable number (less than infinity, but too big to ever reach). A googol is 10 to the 100th power or 1 followed by 100 zeroes. Consider that a 70 table join has over a googol of combinations (70! – 70 factorial is 1x2x3x...70). There are LESS than a googol of atoms in the known universe (10 to the 79th to 10 to the 81st), and black holes evaporate after about a googol years. Ad-hoc query users can get to a googol already if you don't watch them joining tables. Consider this dialogue from a very old (Sixties) Peanuts strip. It's a classic with the lovelorn Lucy and Schroeder at the piano. It also shows that Charles Shultz was thinking ahead of his time as do most leaders.

Lucy: Schroeder, what do you think the odds are that you and I will get married someday?

Schroeder: Oh, I'd say about a "googol" to one.

Lucy: How much is a "googol"?

Schroeder: 10,000,000,000,000,000,000,000,000,000,000,000,000,000,000,000,000,000, 000,000,000,000,000,000,000 ,000,000,000,000,000,000,000,000,000.

Carl Sagan, in the book *Cosmos*, said, "A googol is precisely as far from infinity as is the number one." We're starting to see how wrong he was and how close a googol has become in information technology. Even a googolplex is almost as close to 1 as the number 2 when compared on a number line going from 1 to infinity. With 128-bit computing, a googol won't seem so far away. Perhaps with that kind of power we'll be able to easily make things by rearranging the molecules instead of manual labor.

Technology is amazing—first we talk about it as we see it coming, then we implement it. In a 2001 "Teenage Mutant Ninja Turtles," the Gaminator video game had a "3 Googolhertz" processor. Okay, we're not there yet, but the future is coming at us much faster than most people realize. So, you're ready for the next jump: A googolplex is 1 followed by a googol of zeros. There are more digits in a googolplex than there are atoms in the universe. I think we're still a ways away from this, but remember Doc Brown in "Back to the Future III" and describing RSEN, "She's one in a googolplex."

Oracle Celebrates 30 Years

Oracle celebrates its 30th anniversary in 2007 as a multibillion-dollar company literally driving every major business. It's amazing to look back on the history of Oracle Corporation and the diverse team of people that led to its success. Larry Ellison has been the driving force behind Oracle the company, but Bob Miner was the driving force behind Oracle the product. America is all about freedom, resilience, and opportunity. Larry Ellison is one of the greatest examples of what is possible in a free society. Larry's surname is even based on Ellis Island. Larry's entrepreneurial success story shows that anything is possible where people enjoy freedom. On the Statue of Liberty it reads: *"Give me your tired, your poor, your huddled masses yearning to breathe free, the wretched refuse of your teeming shore. Send these, the homeless, tempest-tost to me, I lift my lamp beside the golden door!"* That golden door eventually led Larry to the Golden Gate Bridge and the establishment of Oracle Corporation in Silicon Valley.

The Early Years at Oracle Through the Eyes of Bruce Scott

Prior to forming Oracle, Bob Miner was Larry Ellison's manager when they worked at Ampex together on a CIA project code-named "Oracle." Larry chose Bob as his manager because he liked Bob a lot more than his original manager. Ed Oates, another founder of Oracle, happened to be walking by Bob Miner's door when Larry Ellison mentioned his (Larry's) wife's name. She turned out to be Ed Oates' lab partner from high school. Bruce Scott, who would be hired upon the formation of the company, is the "Scott" in scott/tiger (tiger was Bruce's daughter's cat).

When Larry went on to work at Precision Instruments, he discovered Precision Instruments had a need to do a $400K consulting project. For three or four engineers, that was a lot of money then since wages were about one tenth of what they are now. Larry landed the deal. Larry was not part of the new company when it was founded; he was still at Precision Instruments. The new company was called Software Development Labs (SDL). We had three employees when we started the company in August of 1977. Bob Miner was the president, and Ed Oates and I were both software engineers. We did 90 percent of the work on this two-year project in the first year, so we had the next year to work on Oracle. Ed Oates finished the other 10 percent of the project over the next year while Bob Miner and I started to write the Oracle database.

When we completed the Precision Instruments work, we had about $200,000 in the bank. We decided that we wanted to be a product company and not a consulting company. Bob wanted to build an ISAM product for the PDP11. He felt there was a need for an access layer. Larry wasn't interested in that at all. Larry had been following what IBM was doing, and in 1970 he came across Dr. Edgar Codd's paper on relational databases. It described the SQL language, which at the time was called SEQUEL/2. Larry brought us the paper and asked if we could build this. We thought that it would be easy enough to do. So we started. I was 24 years old at the time. When I left Oracle in 1982 (after working there for about five and one half years), we had just finished Version 3 of the database. Roughly half the code was mine and half was Bob's. I believe that a lot of the parser code in the current database may still be mine. Bruce Scott said

that his best day was Oracle's first users' conference. This was a customer conference we sponsored in 1982, and it drew about 25 to 50 people. It was beginning to catch on.

In a 1998 Nicole Ricci Interview, Larry Ellison said: "In fact, when I started Oracle, the goal was never to have a large company. At best, I hoped we would have fifty people in the company and make a good living. About five years into the company, it became pretty clear that the horizons were unlimited. The only limitations were us."

Oracle RDBMS History Over the Years

Here's a timeline of how things progressed:

- 1970   Dr. Edgar Codd publishes his theory of relational data modeling.

- 1977   Software Development Laboratories (SDL) formed by Larry Ellison, Bob Miner, Ed Oates, and Bruce Scott with $2,000 of startup cash. Larry and Bob come from Ampex where they were working on a CIA project code-named "Oracle." Bob and Bruce begin work on the database.

- 1978   The CIA is the first customer, but the product is not released commercially. SDL changes its name to Relational Software Inc. (RSI).

- 1979   RSI ships the first commercial version, Version 2 (there is no V1 shipped because of fears that people wouldn't buy a first version of the software) of the database written in Assembler Language. The first commercial version of the software is sold to Wright-Patterson Air Force Base. It is the first commercial RDBMS on the market.

- 1981   The first tool, Interactive Application Facility (IAF), which is a predecessor to Oracle's future SQL*Forms tool, is created.

- 1982   RSI changes its name to Oracle Systems Corporation (OSC) and then simplifies the name to Oracle Corporation.

- 1983   Version 3, written in C (which makes it portable), is shipped. Bob Miner writes half, while also supporting the Assembler based V2, and Bruce Scott writes the other half. It is the first 32-bit RDBMS.

- 1984   Version 4 is released. First tools are released (IAG –genform, IAG-runform, RPT). First database with read consistency. Oracle ported to the PC.

- 1985   Versions 5 & 5.1 are released; first Parallel Server database on VMS/VAX.

- 1986   Oracle goes public March 12th (the day before Microsoft and eight days after Sun). The stock opens at $15 and closes at $20.75. Oracle Client-Server is introduced. First client-server database. Oracle5.1 is released.

- 1987   Oracle is the largest DBMS company. Oracle Applications group started. First SMP (symmetrical multiprocessing) database introduced.

- 1987   Rich Niemiec along with Brad Brown and Joe Trezzo working at Oracle implement the first production client-server application running Oracle on a souped-up 286 running 16 concurrent client-server users for NEC Corporation.

- 1988   Oracle V6 released. First row-level locking. First hot database backup. Oracle moves from Belmont to Redwood Shores. PL/SQL introduced.

- 1992   Oracle V7 is released.

- 1993   Oracle GUI client-server development tools introduced. Oracle Applications moved from character mode to client-server.

- 1994   Bob Miner, the genius behind the Oracle database technology, dies of cancer.

- 1995   First 64-bit database.

- 1996   Oracle7.3 released.

- 1997   Oracle8 is introduced. Oracle Application Server is introduced. Applications for the Web are introduced. Oracle is the first Web database. Oracle BI tools, like Discoverer, are introduced for data warehousing. Tools have native Java support.

- 1998   First major RDBMS (Oracle8) ported to Linux. Applications 11 shipped. Oracle is the first database with XML support.

- 1999   Oracle8*i* released. Integrates Java/XML into development tools. Oracle is the first database with native Java support.

- 2000   Oracle9*i* Application Server is released at it becomes the first database with middle-tier cache. Launches E-Business Suite, wireless database with OracleMobile, Oracle9*i* Application Server Wireless, and Internet File System (iFS).

- 2001   Oracle9*i* (9.1) released. Oracle is the first database with Real Application Clusters (RAC).

- 2002   Oracle9*i* Release 2 (9.2) released.

- 2003   Oracle at France Telecom is #1 on Winter Group's Top Ten in DB size at 29T.

- 2003   Oracle 10*g* comes out—grid focused, encrypted backups, auto-tuning, and ASM.

- 2005   Oracle RAC at Amazon hits the Winter Group's Top Ten in DB size at 25T.

- 2005   Oracle buys PeopleSoft (includes JD Edwards), Oblix (Identity Management), Retek (Retail) for $630M, TimesTen (in memory DB), and Innobase (InnoDB Open Source).

- 2006   Oracle buys Siebel for $5.8B, Sleepycat Software (Open Source), and Stellant (Content Management). Oracle with an Open Source push offers "unbreakable" support for Red Hat Linux.

- 2006   Oracle 10*g* Release2 comes out in fall (this book is based on that version).

- 2007   Oracle buys Hyperion for $3.3B.

- 2007   Oracle 11*g* comes out (predicted based on prior releases).

- 2011   Oracle 12*g* comes out (predicted based on prior releases).

I asked Bruce Scott what made Oracle successful in his mind. Bruce said, "I've thought about this a lot. I really think that it was Larry. There were a lot of other databases (like Ingres) out there that we beat. It was really Larry's charisma, vision, and his determination to make this thing work no matter what. It's just the way Larry thinks. I can give you an example of what I tell people that exemplifies his thought process. We had space allocated to us and we needed to get our terminals strung to the computer room next door. We didn't have anywhere to really string the wiring. Larry picks up a hammer, crashes a hole in the middle of the wall, and says 'there you go.' It's just the way he thinks: make a hole, make it happen somehow. It was Larry, the right thing, and the right time." I always tell people that Larry Ellison is the genius behind Oracle, the company, and that Bob Miner was the genius behind Oracle, the product. Bob Miner's development spirit has continued on through Derry Kabcenell, Roger Bamford, Andy Mendelsohn, and many others. The diverse team Oracle has had over the years is the secret of their success! Happy Birthday, Oracle!

Changes Made to the Latest Version of This Book

The goal of this book is primarily focused on helping beginner and intermediate Oracle professionals understand and better tune Oracle systems. Many expert topics are also covered, but the objective is primarily to assist professionals who are frustrated and looking for simple tips to help improve performance. This book has one simple goal: to provide an arsenal of tips you can use in various situations to make your system faster. For those who read the last version of the book, here are some of the changes and/or additions for each of the chapters:

- Chapter 1: Rewritten completely for basic Oracle 10gR2 new features
- Chapter 2: Added coverage of stats collection and 10gR2 changes
- Chapter 3: Added ASM and expanded the entire chapter as I/O becomes critical
- Chapter 4: Added SGA_TARGET and updated initialization parameters for 10gR2
- Chapter 5: Added all new screen shots and rewrote for Enterprise Manager Grid Control
- Chapter 6: Updated Explain and added sections on DBMS_MONITOR and TRCSESS
- Chapter 7: Added new hints and updated others
- Chapter 8: Updated and tested for 10gR2; added SQL and Grand Unified Theory
- Chapter 9: Updated and tested for 10gR2; added block tuning and Relational vs. Object
- Chapter 10: Expanded again as PL/SQL tuning expands; added 10gR2 debugging
- Chapter 11: Added RAC to this chapter; updated Parallel Query Operations
- Chapter 12: Expanded again to show many more V$ view queries
- Chapter 13: Expanded X$ view queries, trace section, and X$ naming conventions
- Chapter 14: Updated for STATSPACK 10gR2, AWR Report, and ITL Block Tuning
- Chapter 15: Updated for 10gR2 and larger systems
- Chapter 16: Updated to include more commands
- Appendix A: Updated for 10gR2 with updated queries and new Top 25
- Appendix B: Updated for 10gR2 with updated queries
- Appendix C: Updated for 10gR2 with updated queries

In Memory

Last, I would like to remember a few of our friends that we've lost over the past couple of years in the Oracle World. Stan Yellott (November 30, 2006) made a big difference in the RMOUG, IOUG, and the Oracle World in general. Stan was dedicated to educating all of us and provided an example of how to behave and treat others in the precious time that we have here together. I remember him mostly as incredibly enthusiastic and unbelievably unselfish. I never heard him say an unkind word about anyone—EVER! I don't know too many people like that; he is someone to try to live up to and look up to. He was also, of course, the ultimate Mr. Cool!

Equally giving to the Oracle user groups was Marcia Pollard (2003), who gave her time to ODTUG and had a wonderful demeanor even with those of us who couldn't seem to get our presentations done on time. Marcia was a wonderful person! We remember the enthusiastic and bright Lex de Haan (February 1, 2006) as an Oracle expert, great teacher of Oracle, and world-class performance tuning and optimization professional. We remember Mark Beaton (August 2006), the enthusiastic

Oracle solution salesman and spectacular soccer player. We remember Ray Mansfield (November 2006), the talented Warehouse Builder consultant with the bright smile. Last, we remember the wonderful Elaine DeMeo (February 11, 2007), who was a great supporter of the MOUG and IOUG. God takes us home one day when our work is done; we'll be with them soon enough to *"run with the angels on streets made of gold."* I look forward to that day, but until that day, let's continue to make a difference and ensure that God speaks through us by our wonderful actions toward one another! By always looking to improve our Integrity, Knowledge, Physical Courage, Loyalty, Self Control, Enthusiasm, Unselfishness, Tact, Moral Courage, Respect, Humility, and Initiative we will ensure that we will have the Fortitude to face any tough challenge ahead. And of course never forget Faith, Hope, Love... and the greatest of these is Love. Make a difference in the world with character and with a heart that always brings out the best in others! This is my goal in life!

References

"How Much Information?" http://www.sims.berkeley.edu/how-much-info/summary.html
Oracle firsts are from: www.oracle.com
"A zettabyte by 2010: Corporate data grows fiftyfold in three years," Lucas Mearian, March, 2007
Roy Williams, Center of Advanced Computing Research, California Institute of Technology
"Back to the Future III," Universal Studios
Wikipedia, en.wikipedia.com (Googol, Exabyte)
"Information Inundation," Forbes.com, November 2005
"64-Bit Computing," Rich Niemiec, Oracle Magazine, 2004
"Rich Niemiec Interviews Bruce Scott," Select Magazine, 2001
"Retrospective: Still Growing after all these Years," Rich Niemiec, Oracle Magazine, 2001
"The Difference between God and Larry Ellison," Mike Wilson, November, 1998
History of Oracle, Donita Klement, 1999
"Wish You Were Here," Mark Harris, 2006

CHAPTER
1

Oracle Database 10g
New Features
(DBA and Developer)

First, I want to note that this book is primarily focused on helping beginner and intermediate Oracle professionals understand and better tune Oracle systems. Many expert topics are also covered in the later chapters, but the objective is primarily to assist professionals who are frustrated and looking for simple tips to help improve performance. This book has one simple goal: to provide an arsenal of tips you can use in various situations to make your system faster.

In the Oracle Database 10g, Oracle introduces the concept of "grid computing." A logical extension of Oracle's Real Application Clusters technology, the grid database will theoretically be able to dynamically "requisition" resources from the pool (the grid) to meet levels of peak demand. When grid computing is fully implemented, these grid resources (grids of servers) can exist on different types of hardware and operating systems, a fully heterogeneous environment. Prior versions required that the system be sized appropriately from the beginning to support peak loads. Oracle is taking its first steps toward implementing this grand plan with version 10g.

In the last edition of this book, Chapter 1 was also a New Features chapter, which many people liked. With that in mind, the first chapter of this edition focuses on what's new in Oracle 10g. The rest of the chapters gradually increase in complexity and provide a plethora of tips to help you in your tuning adventures. I am sure that you will encounter at least some information that you won't find elsewhere.

If you want a single method or an all-encompassing way of tuning a database (in a single chapter), I provide two such chapters for those who don't have the time to read the whole book. The first is Chapter 14, on Statspack and AWR Report: two incredible tools that include most of the common scripts the majority of experts use to tune a system. This chapter took a large amount of time to write. The second is Chapter 5, on Grid Control (Enterprise Manager), which is a graphical tool of the future that provides a graphical way to tune your system, including many features for both RAC systems and large-scale grid control. It gives you the incredible ability to view and tune multiple systems through one single interface.

To offer a sense of the scope of the book, let's start with the Oracle 10g new features. The chapters that follow dive deeper into the features are crucial to Oracle performance tuning. This first chapter will discuss, briefly, some of the more interesting new features, which were included in Oracle's 10g release. A boatload of new and improved features is included in this version. Oracle's goal in 10g was not only to create a more robust database management system but to simplify the installation and administration activities, thereby enhancing availability. This continues a trend that began with Oracle 9i. Oracle 10gR2 (Oracle 10g Release 2) furthers Oracle's strategic direction of providing a fully integrated set of features that replaces third-party software that DBAs typically use to help them manage their environments. Oracle formally calls this Oracle Database 10g Release 2, but I'll refer to it as 10gR2 or 10gR1 (for Release 1) or Oracle 10g (generic to the version) or even just 10g throughout the book. When the release makes a difference, I'll specify the release.

The new features covered in this chapter include

- Installation improvements

- The SYSAUX tablespace

- Automatic Storage Management (ASM)

- Cluster Ready Services (CRS)

- Automatic Workload Repository (AWR)

- Automatic Database Diagnostic Monitor (ADDM)

- SQL Tuning Advisor

- Automatic Shared Memory Management (ASMM)

- Flash recovery area and recycle bin

- Transparent Data Encryption (10gR2)

- New DBMS_STATS options

- Tracing enhancements

- Bigfile tablespaces

- Shrinking segments

- Data Pump

- Cross-platform transportable tablespaces

- Writing to an external table

- Automatic undo retention tuning

- New columns in V$SESSION

- Grid Control

CAUTION
Because these features are new, you should use them cautiously and test them completely until you are sure they work without causing your database problems. If you have access to Metalink, we strongly advise you to determine whether any known problems exist with the feature you are preparing to use. Google.com (although quite broad) is another good place to search for current information on Oracle features and functionality

Installation Improvements

The first thing you'll notice about 10g is the smaller footprint and simpler installation. The database is delivered on a single CD. Some components, such as the HTTP server and HTML DB (Application Express or APEX in the latest version) are delivered on a companion CD. The installer has fewer screens than previous versions and performs more configuration tasks automatically. For RAC installations, the installer will automatically detect that cluster ready services are installed.

Oracle advertises that installation and setup of 10g can be done a third faster, which may be fairly accurate. There are fewer basic initialization parameters to deal with, and scripting enhancements make automated deployment much simpler. Many of the pre- and post-install steps have been automated. A pre-install validation utility checks for the proper OS configuration, patches, and resource parameters prior to starting the universal installer. Configuration assistants automatically run after the install to configure many of the installed components.

Upgrades have been greatly simplified as well. Besides the Upgrade Information Tool, which performs pre-upgrade validation, and post-upgrade configuration wizards similar to those available for installs, there is a time estimator that does a fair job of determining the required upgrade window. I did not experience any problems with the upgrade I tested, but if errors do occur, the upgrade process is much more "restartable" from the point of failure than in prior versions, where the upgrade needed to be restarted from the beginning.

SYSAUX Tablespace

To simplify the administration of objects that support Oracle features, a second mandatory tablespace, the SYSAUX tablespace, has been added. It contains some objects previously contained in the SYSTEM tablespace as well as consolidating the storage of objects that support Oracle features such as LogMiner, UltraSearch, and Data Mining that were stored in other tablespaces. SYSAUX provides centralized storage for these objects. Each set of objects that support a particular feature is known as a "component" in Oracle 10g. Oracle provides a new view, V$SYSAUX_OCCUPANTS, that shows the amount of space used by each component and the name of the Oracle-supplied stored procedure that can be used to move its objects into and out of the SYSAUX tablespace. These stored procedures allow administrators to move the objects for a particular feature to a tablespace other than SYSAUX. Table 1-1 shows where some of the SYSAUX components were stored in prior versions.

Keep in mind that Table 1-1 does not show all schemas that are used. For example, OLAP also uses the OLAPSYS schema; Intermedia and Spatial use the MDDATA, MDSYS, ORDSYS, and ORDPLUGINS schemas; and EM also uses the DBSNMP schema. Using the SYSAUX tablespace will avoid fragmentation in the SYSTEM tablespace that can occur when Oracle options are installed and uninstalled.

Feature	Schema	Prior Tablespace
OLAP	CWMLITE	CWMLITE
Text	CTXSYS	DRSYS
UltraSearch	WKSYS	DRSYS
Intermedia and Spatial	ORDSYS	SYSTEM
Workspace Manager	WMSYS	SYSTEM
Data Mining	DMSYS	ODM
EM Repository	SYSMAN	OEM_REPOSITORY
LogMiner	SYSTEM	SYSTEM
StatsPack	PERFSTAT	User Specified
Job Scheduler	SYS	SYSTEM

TABLE 1-1. *SYSAUX Tablespace Component Prior Locations*

Automatic Storage Management

Automatic Storage Management (ASM) is a file system and volume manager built into the database kernel that allows the management of disk drives in place of raw or cooked file systems. It provides management across multiple nodes of a cluster for Oracle Real Application Clusters (RAC) support as well as single SMP machines. ASM does automatic load balancing and striping in parallel across all available disk drives to prevent hot spots and maximize performance. In addition, it does automatic online disk space reorganization for the incremental addition or removal of storage capacity.

It can maintain redundant copies of data to provide fault tolerance, or it can be built on top of vendor-supplied reliable storage mechanisms. Data management is done by selecting the desired reliability and performance characteristics for classes of data rather than with configuring the database on a per-file basis.

The ASM code performs its tasks through the use of a special instance called an *ASM instance.* ASM instances do not mount databases but rather manage the metadata needed to make ASM files available to database instances. Both ASM instances and database instances share the same set of disks. Multiple Oracle instances on a node share a single ASM instance. The ASM instance is started in NOMOUNT mode and must be running prior to starting any of the database instances that use ASM. The ASM instance is not backed up using RMAN or other normal database backup procedures, since it's just memory, but the ASM data is backed up. The instance can be quickly rebuilt in case of media failure, provided that the disk architecture is well documented.

Oracle has added a number of dynamic performance views to support ASM, as shown in Table 1-2.

Some of the views in Table 1-2 will display data only in the ASM instance. See Chapter 3 for detailed information on ASM.

View	Description
V$ASM_ALIAS	Shows aliases in each disk group mounted by the ASM instance
V$ASM_CLIENT	Shows database instances using a disk group
V$ASM_DISK	Shows each disk discovered by ASM even if it is not part of a disk group
V$ASM_DISKGROUP	Shows each disk group discovered by ASM
V$ASM_FILE	Shows each file in a mounted disk group
V$ASM_OPERATION	Shows long-running operations
V$ASM_TEMPLATE	Shows templates in each mounted disk group

TABLE 1-2. *Dynamic Performance Views to Support ASM*

Cluster Ready Services (CRS)

CRS (Cluster Ready Services) is a new feature for 10g Real Application Clusters (RAC) that provides a standard cluster interface on all platforms and contains new high availability features not available in previous versions. CRS is required to be installed and running prior to installing 10g RAC. It can use either vendor-supplied clusterware, such as HP Serviceguard, Sun Cluster, and Veritas Cluster, or Oracle's OCFS as its clusterware. Shared devices for the voting disk file and the OCR (Oracle Configuration Repository) file must be available *prior* to installing CRS. The voting disk file should be at least 256MB, and the OCR file should be at least 256MB (previously these were 20MB and 100MB respectively). The voting disk file is used by the CRS cluster manager in various layers. The CRS Node Monitor (NM) uses the voting disk file for a heartbeat, which is essential in the detection and resolution of cluster communication failures. If there is a network "split" (nodes lose communication with each other), one or more of the nodes may reboot automatically to prevent data corruption. The Oracle Configuration Repository (OCR) maintains dynamic information concerning cluster nodes, shared resources, and process states. CRS uses daemon processes to manage administrative cluster activities. These processes include

- **CRSD**   This process, which runs as root, maintains the OCR configuration information as well as managing "application resources" and performing starts, stops, and failovers. It is restarted automatically on failure.

- **OCSSD**   This process, which runs as the oracle user, provides access to node membership. It is the process that provides group services as well as basic cluster locking. OCSSD integrates with existing vendor clusterware when it is present, but it can also run without integration to vendor clusterware. If this process fails, it causes the server to reboot. This is to prevent data corruption in the event of internode communication failures.

- **EVMD**   This process, which runs as the oracle user, generates events when anomalous conditions occur. It spawns a permanent child process, EVMLOGGER, which spawns child processes on demand. It is restarted automatically on failure. See Chapter 11 for additional information on RAC and clustering.

Server-Generated Alerts

In an effort to provide capabilities that are typically obtained using third-party software, Oracle 10g now provides server-generated alerts directly from the Oracle Database server. These notifications act as an early warning of a potential or impending problem. They often contain suggestions for correcting the problem. Notifications are also provided when the problem condition has been addressed.

Alerts are generated when a problem occurs or when data does not match expected values for user-configurable metrics, such as

- Physical reads per second
- File system out of space
- User commits per second
- SQL response time
- Maximum extents reached

Server-generated alerts can be based on threshold levels or can be issued simply because an event has occurred. Threshold-based alerts can be configured to send notifications at both warning and critical threshold levels. Other alerts are based on conditions such as ORA- errors in the alert log. Some examples of this type of alert are

- Snapshot too old (ORA-1555)

- Resumable session suspended

- Recovery area space usage

The Oracle 10*g* database collects and stores various statistics into the workload repository. (I'll discuss the workload repository later.) Those statistics are then analyzed to produce various metrics. The server-generated alerts rely on these derived metrics. For the metrics that have thresholds defined, the MMON process verifies the thresholds and generates the alerts, if required. Then the alert is placed into the ALERT_QUE queue. Oracle Enterprise Manager reads this queue and provides notifications about outstanding server alerts and, if possible, suggests actions for correcting the problem.

Threshold alerts, also referred to as stateful alerts, are automatically cleared when the alert condition clears. The non-threshold alerts, or stateless alerts, are stored in the table accessed by the view DBA_ALERT_HISTORY. Stateless alerts are cleared through the Enterprise Manager Database Control interface.

Oracle Enterprise Manager (OEM) is typically used to configure alert thresholds, define e-mail and pager destinations and view and respond to triggered alerts. The DBMS_SERVER_ALERTS package is provided to allow manipulation of alert settings through SQL*Plus or another API.

Oracle provides a number of new views that provide information about server alerts, as shown in Table 1-3.

View	Description
DBA_THRESHOLDS	Lists the threshold settings defined for the instance
DBA_OUTSTANDING_ALERTS	Lists the triggered alerts in the database that have not been cleared
DBA_ALERT_HISTORY	Lists a history of alerts that have been cleared
V$ALERT_TYPES	Provides information such as group and type for each alert
V$METRICNAME	Contains the names, identifiers, and other information about the system metrics
V$METRIC	Contains metric threshold settings and current values (there is also a V$SYSMETRIC)
V$METRIC_HISTORY	Contains historical metric threshold settings

TABLE 1-3.   *New Views of Server Alerts*

Automatic Workload Repository (AWR)

In 10g, Automatic Workload Repository (AWR) is the primary component of the Common Manageability Infrastructure (CMI). It is the successor to StatsPack. While StatsPack is still available with 10g, a few improvements are planned to StatsPack, and therefore AWR is the preferred mechanism for diagnosing database problems. Oracle describes the Automatic Workload Repository as the "data warehouse of the Oracle 10g database." It provides the data used by other CMI components, such as system-generated alerts and the advisors. The Automatic Workload Repository consists of two main components: *in-memory statistics* and *repository snapshots.*

AWR relies on a background process, the MMON process. By default, MMON wakes up every hour and does statistics collection into the repository snapshots. This interval is configurable by the DBA. AWR snapshots provide a persistent view of database statistics. They are created in the SYS schema and stored in the SYSAUX tablespace. In-memory statistics are gathered once a second on active sessions. They are not written to the database and are aged out of memory as new statistics are gathered.

A script is provided ($ORACLE_HOME/rdbms/admin/awrrpt.sql) to generate a report using repository snapshots. There is also an awrrpti.sql report as well, which has essentially the same output but allows you to define and report on a specific instance. Automatic Database Diagnostic Monitor (discussed later) uses the snapshot information to automatically identify performance problems and make recommendations to correct them.

In-memory statistics are accessed through the view V$ACTIVE_SESSION_HISTORY, which queries the ASH buffers area of the SGA. Since this area is fixed at two megabytes per CPU, the length of time before statistics are aged out will vary by workload. See Chapter 5 for additional information on Enterprise Manager (EM) and Chapter 14 for additional information on the AWR reports as well as StatsPack.

Automatic Database Diagnostic Monitor (ADDM)

The Automatic Database Diagnostic Monitor (ADDM) feature of the CMI goes far beyond the functionality previously offered by its predecessor, the OEM Expert tool. The ADDM consists of functionality built into the Oracle kernel to assist in making tuning an Oracle instance more straightforward.

The Automatic ADDM is an integral part of the Oracle RDBMS capable of gathering performance statistics and advising on changes to solve existing performance issues.

ADDM analysis is performed every time an AWR snapshot is taken. It uses the statistics maintained in the AWR to make its diagnostic recommendations. In addition to providing suggestions for fixing problems, ADDM can automatically fix certain problems. Since the ADDM is integrated into the database server, running the analysis has a minimal impact on database performance. It nominally takes less than three seconds to complete an analysis.

To allow use of ADDM, a PL/SQL interface called DBMS_ADVISOR has been provided. This PL/SQL interface may be called directly, called through the supplied script ($ORACLE_HOME/rdbms/admin/addmrpt.sql), or used in combination with the Oracle Enterprise Manager application. Besides this PL/SQL package, a number of views allow you to retrieve the results of any actions performed with the DBMS_ADVISOR API. The preferred way of accessing ADDM is through the Enterprise Manager interface, as it shows a complete performance overview, including recommendations on how to solve bottlenecks on a single screen. When accessing ADDM manually, you should consider using the addmrpt.sql script provided with your Oracle release, as it hides the complexities involved in accessing the DBMS_ADVISOR package.

To use ADDM for advising on how to tune the instance and SQL, you need to make sure that the AWR has been populated with at least two sets of performance data. When the STATISTICS_LEVEL is set to TYPICAL or ALL the database will automatically schedule the AWR to be populated at 60-minute intervals. If you wish to create snapshots outside of the fixed intervals, then you can use the DBMS_WORKLOAD_REPOSITORY package. To be useful in diagnosing a particular problem, the snapshots need be created before and after the situation you wish to examine.

ADDM points out which events cause the performance problems to occur and suggests directions to follow to fix these bottlenecks. The findings are sorted descending by impact: the issues causing the greatest performance problems are listed at the top of the report. Solving these issues will result in the greatest performance benefits. Also, in the last section of the report ADDM indicates the areas that do not represent a problem for the performance of the instance.

Several views are available for querying ADDM information, shown in Table 1-4.

View	Description
DBA_ADVISOR_ACTIONS	Displays information about the actions associated with all recommendations in the database
DBA_ADVISOR_COMMANDS	Displays information about the commands used by all advisors in the database for specifying recommendation actions
DBA_ADVISOR_DEF_PARAMETERS	Displays the parameters and their default values for all tasks in the database
DBA_ADVISOR_DEFINITIONS	Displays the properties of all advisors in the database
DBA_ADVISOR_DIRECTIVES	Not documented
DBA_ADVISOR_FINDINGS	Displays the findings discovered by all advisors in the database
DBA_ADVISOR_JOURNAL	Displays the journal entries for all tasks in the database
DBA_ADVISOR_LOG	Displays information about the current state of all tasks in the database, as well as execution-specific data such as progress monitoring and completion status
DBA_ADVISOR_OBJECT_TYPES	Displays information about the object types used by all advisors in the database
DBA_ADVISOR_OBJECTS	Displays information about the objects currently referenced by all advisors in the database

TABLE 1-4.   *Views for Querying ADDM Information*

View	Description
DBA_ADVISOR_PARAMETERS	Displays the parameters and their current values for all tasks in the database
DBA_ADVISOR_PARAMETERS_PROJ	Not documented
DBA_ADVISOR_RATIONALE	Displays information about the rationales for all recommendations in the database
DBA_ADVISOR_RECOMMENDATIONS	Displays the result of the completed diagnostic task with action recommendations for the problems identified in each run
DBA_ADVISOR_SQLA_REC_SUM	Displays recommendation rollup information for all workload objects in the database after an Access Advisor analysis operation
DBA_ADVISOR_SQLA_WK_MAP	Displays the workload references for all tasks in the database
DBA_ADVISOR_SQLA_WK_STMTS	Displays information about all workload objects in the database after an Access Advisor analysis operation
DBA_ADVISOR_SQLW_COLVOL	Not documented
DBA_ADVISOR_SQLW_JOURNAL	Displays the journal entries for all workload objects in the database
DBA_ADVISOR_SQLW_PARAMETERS	Displays all workload parameters and their current values in the database
DBA_ADVISOR_SQLW_STMTS	Displays rows that correspond to all statements in the workload
DBA_ADVISOR_SQLW_SUM	Displays an aggregated picture of all SQLWkld workload objects in the database
DBA_ADVISOR_SQLW_TABLES	Displays cross-references between the workload statements and the tables referenced in the statement
DBA_ADVISOR_SQLW_TABVOL	Not documented
DBA_ADVISOR_SQLW_TEMPLATES	Displays an aggregated picture of all SQLWkld template objects in the database
DBA_ADVISOR_TASKS	Displays information about all tasks in the database
DBA_ADVISOR_TEMPLATES	Displays information about all templates in the database
DBA_ADVISOR_USAGE	Displays the usage information for each type of advisor in the database

TABLE 1-4. *Views for Querying ADDM Information* (continued)

SQL Tuning Advisor

This new feature automates the entire SQL tuning process. The automatic process strives to replace manual SQL tuning, but in some cases, there's no substitute for an experienced DBA or developer to get the best performance out of a query. The SQL Tuning Adviser analyzes SQL statements and executes a complete analysis of the statement, including

- Finding stale or missing statistics

- Determining better execution plan by evaluating more plans

- Detecting better access paths and objects required to satisfy them (indexes, materialized views)

- Restructuring SQL

While the primary interface for the SQL Tuning Advisor is the Oracle Enterprise Manager Database Control, the advisor can be administered with procedures in the DBMS_SQLTUNE package. To use the APIs, the user must have been granted the DBA role and the ADVISOR privilege. If using the SQL Tuning Advisor in Oracle Enterprise Manager, the user must have been granted the select_catalog_role role. All of the advisor framework privileges are part of the DBA role.

Running SQL Tuning Advisor using DBMS_SQLTUNE package is a two-step process. First you create a tuning task, and then you execute the task.

The CREATE_TUNING_TASK function returns the task name that you have provided or generates a unique task name. You can use the task name to specify this task when using other APIs.

Automatic Shared Memory Management (ASMM)

In Oracle Database 10g, the Automatic Shared Memory Management (ASMM) feature, another self-management enhancement, is introduced to automatically determine the size of the database buffer cache (default pool), shared pool, large pool, and Java pool through use of the initialization parameter SGA_TARGET. The initialization parameter STATISTICS_LEVEL must also be set to TYPICAL (default) or ALL to use ASMM.

In previous releases of Oracle, you had to manually configure the buffer cache and SGA pools. It was often challenging to properly configure these memory structures because sizing them too small could cause memory errors and sizing them too large could lead to waste of memory. You did not have exact control over the total size of the SGA, since memory was allocated by Oracle for the fixed SGA, and for other internal metadata allocations over and above the total size of the user-specified SGA parameters.

In 10g, the Oracle database periodically redistributes memory between these components according to workload requirements (sometimes it does this *poorly,* so be careful and make sure you test this under load). This feature minimizes tasks like analyzing the database workload and redistributing memory across the SGA pools. The new SGA size parameter SGA_TARGET now includes all the memory in the SGA, including all the automatically sized components, the manually sized components, and any internal allocations during startup. Setting SGA_TARGET to 0, the default value, disables Automatic Shared Memory Management and the SGA is built as in the past. ASMM does *not* automatically manage the size of the fixed SGA, the log buffer, or the KEEP, RECYCLE, or other block size caches (DB_nK_CACHE_SIZE). The ASMM feature does manage the size of the Streams Pool when the SGA_TARGET initialization parameter is set to a nonzero value in 10gR2.

The memory allocated for these areas that *are* included in the SGA_TARGET size is shared. For example, if SGA_TARGET is 1000MB and DB_KEEP_CACHE_SIZE is set to 50MB, then the memory available for automatically managed components is 950MB. The DB_KEEP_CACHE_SIZE can be increased by Oracle, but it will not be set below the set parameter of 50MB. When SGA_TARGET is set, the total size of manual SGA size parameters is subtracted from the SGA_TARGET value, and balance is available for auto-tuned SGA components.

When SGA_TARGET is not set or is equal to zero, auto-tuned SGA parameters behave as in previous releases of the Oracle Database. However, SHARED_POOL_SIZE is an exception: Internal overhead allocations for metadata (such as for data structures for processes and sessions) are now included in the value of the SHARED_POOL_SIZE parameter. As a result, you may need to increase the value of your setting for SHARED_POOL_SIZE when upgrading from Oracle 9i Database to Oracle Database 10g to account for these allocations. For example, suppose that in Oracle 9i Database you were using 256M as the value of SHARED_POOL_SIZE, and suppose that the value of the internal allocations was 32M. To get the same effective shared pool size with Oracle Database 10g, you must set SHARED_POOL_SIZE to 288M.

SGA_TARGET can be set dynamically through OEM or with the ALTER SYSTEM command. It can be increased up to the value of SGA_MAX_SIZE. It can be reduced until any one auto-tuned component reaches its minimum size (either a user-specified minimum or an internally determined minimum). If you increase the value of SGA_TARGET, the additional memory is distributed according to the auto-tuning policy across the auto-tuned components. If you reduce the value of SGA_TARGET, the memory is taken away by the auto-tuning policy from one or more of the auto-tuned components. Therefore any change in the value of SGA_TARGET affects only the sizes of the auto-tuned components.

If you dynamically disable automatic shared memory tuning by setting SGA_TARGET to zero, values of all the auto-tuned parameters are set to the current sizes of the components, even if the user had earlier specified a different non-zero value for an auto-tuned parameter. These values are written to the SPFILE to use for the next instance startup. See Chapter 4 for additional information on tuning the SGA and tuning the initialization parameters.

Automatic Shared Memory Management uses a new background process, Memory Manager (MMAN). MMAN acts as the SGA Memory Broker and coordinates the sizing of the memory components. The SGA Memory Broker keeps track of the sizes of the components and pending resize operations. The SGA Memory Broker observes the system and workload in order to determine the ideal distribution of memory. It performs the check every few minutes so that memory distributions can be adjusted in a timely manner to respond to changes in workload.

The benefits of ASMM can be significant, as many databases have workload profiles that change significantly over time. For example, consider a system that runs large OLTP jobs during the day that require large buffer caches, and runs parallel batch jobs at night that require large values for the large pool. The DBA would have to simultaneously configure both the buffer cache and the large pool to accommodate their peak requirements. With SGA auto-tuning, when the OLTP job runs, the buffer cache has most of the memory to allow for good I/O performance. When the DSS batch job starts later, the memory automatically migrates to the large pool so that it can be used by Parallel Query operations. Based on its workload analysis, ASMM tuning

- Captures statistics periodically in the background.

- Uses the different memory advisories.

- Performs "what-if" analyses to determine best distribution of memory.

- Moves memory to where it is most needed.

- Resurrects component sizes from last shutdown if SPFILE is used (component sizes are used from the last shutdown).

The following views provide information on dynamic SGA resize operations:

View	Description
V$SGA_CURRENT_RESIZE_OPS	SGA resize operations that are currently in progress
V$SGA_RESIZE_OPS	Information about the last 400 completed SGA resize operations
V$SGA_DYNAMIC_COMPONENTS	Information about the dynamic components of the SGA
V$SGA_DYNAMIC_FREE_MEMORY	Information about the amount of SGA memory available for future dynamic SGA resize operations

Flash Recovery Area

The price of disk storage has dropped in the last few years to the point where it is competitive with tape storage prices. Using disk space as the primary medium for all database recovery operations is the core feature of the flash recovery area, which provides a single storage area for all recovery-related files and recovery activities in the Oracle database. The flash recovery area can be a single directory, an entire file system, or an Automatic Storage Management (ASM) disk group. To further optimize the use of disk space for recovery operations, a flash recovery area can be shared by more than one database. All the files you need to completely recover a database from a media failure are part of the flash recovery area. The flash recovery area simplifies backup operations, and it increases the availability of the database because many backup and recovery operations using the flash recovery area can be performed when the database is open and available to users.

Flash recovery extends the functionality of Oracle Managed Files to all recovery-related files (backup sets, image copies, and archived logs). It also provides automated space management by deleting older files (based on a user-specified retention policy) to make room for newer ones. The user specifies only the location of a flash recovery area, and the amount of space that Oracle is allocated for recovery related files. All files maintained in the flash recovery area are classified as either permanent or transient. The permanent files would be multiplexed copies of the current control file and online redo logs. These cannot be deleted without causing the instance to fail. Transient files include archived redo logs, datafile copies, control file copies, control file autobackups, backup pieces, and flashback logs. Oracle manages these files automatically for deletion whenever space is required in the flash recovery area. They are deleted once they become obsolete under the retention policy or have been backed up to tape. Any transient file in the flash recovery area once backed up to tape can internally be placed on a deleted list. Until a backup of the file on disk is made to an offline storage device, it cannot be obsolete.

Flashback queries, which were introduced in Oracle version 9i, depend on undo tablespace to flash back to a prior version of the data, thereby limiting its ability to go too far into the past. Flash recovery provides an enhanced solution by creating flashback logs, which are similar to redo logs, to revert the database to a prior state. Utilizing the flashback recovery area, Oracle 10g also adds Flashback Versions Query, which allows you to see all versions of rows between two points of time, and adds Flashback Transaction Query to see all changes made by an individual transaction. This new functionality may become increasingly important in developing auditing solutions often required to assist in Sarbanes-Oxley compliance.

Flashback Database is another new feature that allows you to quickly revert the entire database to its state as of a previous point in time. Rather than restoring a backup and performing an incomplete recovery, recent changes are backed out of the current database. As databases get larger, this method becomes a more efficient method of restoring a database to a previous state.

Flashback Database uses a new background process, RVWR, to write data from the flashback buffer in the System Global Area (SGA) to flashback logs in the flash recovery area.

The new dynamic performance view, V$RECOVERY_FILE_DEST, shows information about the flash recovery area, such as its location, how much space is allocated to it, how much space is currently used in the flash recovery area, how many files are in the flash recovery area, and how much space can be freed in the flash recovery area if there are space limitations. V$FLASHBACK_DATABASE_STAT monitors the overhead of logging flashback data in the flashback logs.

Recycle Bin

Using the new features of the recycle bin and flashback table, Oracle 10g makes the revival of a dropped table as easy as the execution of few statements. The recycle bin is a logical structure within each tablespace that holds dropped tables and objects related to the tables, such as indexes. The space associated with the dropped table is not immediately available but shows up in the data dictionary view DBA_FREE_SPACE. Underneath the covers, the objects are occupying the same space as when they were created. Dropped tables and any associated objects such as indexes, constraints, nested tables, and other dependent objects are not moved; they are simply renamed with a prefix of BIN$$. When space requirements necessitate it, objects in the recycle bin are deleted in a first-in first-out (FIFO) fashion, maximizing the amount of time that the most recently dropped object remains in the recycle bin. The recycle bin can also be emptied using variations of the new PURGE command.

The dropped object still belongs to the owner and still counts against the quota for the owner in the tablespace; in fact, the table itself is still directly accessible from the recycle bin, by using a FLASHBACK TABLE...TO BEFORE DROP command.

Only non-SYSTEM locally managed tablespaces (LMT) can have a recycle bin. However, dependent objects in a dictionary managed tablespace are protected if the dropped object is in a locally managed tablespace. In addition, tables using Fine-Grained Auditing (FGA) or Virtual Private Database (VPD) policies defined on them cannot reside in a recycle bin, regardless of the type of tablespace in which they reside.

The following views are provided to view the contents of the recycle bins:

View	Description
DBA_RECYCLEBIN	Shows objects that have been dropped by all users
USER_RECYCLEBIN	Shows the current user's dropped objects

Recovery Manager Changes

RMAN has been improved to reduce the recovery time for a tablespace or the entire database using incrementally updated backups. These incremental backups can be applied to an image copy of a datafile to significantly reduce the amount of time needed to recover the datafile in case of a media failure. RMAN also provides a number of other enhancements, making it easier to back up part of the database or the entire database. You can create image copies for the entire database with just one command instead of one command for each tablespace. RMAN supports binary compression of backup sets not only to save disk space in the flash recovery area but also to potentially reduce the amount of time needed to perform the backup. The flash recovery area directory structure is used by RMAN in a very organized fashion with separate directories for each file type, such as archived logs, backup sets, image copies, control file autobackups, and so forth. In addition, each subdirectory is further divided by a datestamp, making it easy to locate backup sets or image copies based on their creation date.

A new RMAN command, BACKUP RECOVERY FILES, makes it easy to back up recovery files in the flash recovery area to offline storage. It backs up all recovery files in the flash recovery area that have not previously been backed up to tape, including full and incremental backup sets, control file autobackups, archived redo logs, and datafile copies. For manual hot backups, a new clause to the ALTER DATABASE command, BEGIN BACKUP, allows you to put all tablespaces into backup mode at once, rather than having to do each tablespace individually.

RMAN now has the ability to compress backups with the command syntax BACKUP AS COMPRESSED BACKUPSET. This command creates backup sets (rather than image copies) on the specified device type. AS BACKUPSET is the only possibility when backing up to tape, and for creating level 1 incremental backups to any destination. There is also the Oracle Secure Backup product, which allows RMAN to back up to tape (www.oracle.com/database/secure-backup.html).

Recovery Manager has already provided NULL compression for backup in previous releases. Oracle 10g has the new BINARY COMPRESSION feature added for backup set compression. This binary compression algorithm can greatly reduce the space required for disk backup storage. It is typically 2× to 4×, and greater for text-intensive databases. The RMAN list output can verify the backup is a compressed backup set. Currently, the "LIST" output in RMAN does not correctly report the actual compressed size. The work-around is to query the backup views. With the COMPRESSED option, binary compression is used. The data written into the backup set is compressed to reduce the overall size of the backup set. All backups that create backup sets can create compressed backup sets. Restoring compressed backup sets is no different from restoring uncompressed backup sets.

When storage space is more important to you than backup and restore times, you can use binary compression to reduce the size of your backup sets. The compression algorithm built into the Oracle server is tuned specifically for efficient compression of Oracle archived logs and datafiles and will generally yield better compression than general-purpose compression utilities not tuned for Oracle database files. Furthermore, because it is integrated into Oracle, compressing backups requires only that you add the AS COMPRESSED BACKUPSET argument to your BACKUP command (this could add some CPU overhead). Restoring from compressed backups requires no special action whatever. Oracle Corporation recommends that you use RMAN's integrated binary compression instead of external compression utilities when you need to make compressed backups. For more on performance considerations when using binary compression of backup sets, see the description of the AS COMPRESSED BACKUPSET option of the BACKUP command, in Oracle Database Recovery Manager Reference.

Unused Block Compression (NULL Compression is what this was called before 10g) was also used in previous versions so that blocks that were never used were not backed up (not all database blocks are backed up). Never-used data blocks in datafiles were never copied into backup sets, saving storage space and overhead during the backup process, but if used at least once empty blocks were still backed up prior to 10g. In 10g, an empty block, whether it was previously used or not, will not be backed up. Unused block compression is fundamental to how RMAN writes datafiles into backup pieces, and cannot be disabled.

An Encrypted Backup is potentially the most important new feature that Oracle has implemented in Oracle 10g Release 2. Lost tapes, smarter criminals, and security requirements are all driving the need for the encryption of backups. An encrypted backup will keep your data safe should it fall into the wrong hands. The encryption modes that are available include Transparent Encryption (this is the default that requires no DBA intervention, since the infrastructure is set up), Password Encryption (the DBA provides a password for the backup, which is needed for the recovery), and Dual-Mode Encryption (either the Password or an Oracle Encryption Wallet is used). While backup and recovery is beyond the scope of this book, I do want to mention that every DBA should investigate this Oracle ability, which is documented in the *Oracle Database Backup and Recovery Advanced Users Guide*.

Transparent Data Encryption (10gR2)

Transparent Database Encryption (TDE) is new feature in 10g Release 2 that provides an critical additional layer of security by transparently encrypting column data stored on disk. This provides an "out-of-the-box" method for protecting the data at the operating system level. Transparent Data Encryption is a key-based access control system. Even if the encrypted data is retrieved, it cannot be understood until authorized decryption occurs, which is automatic for users authorized to access the table. The keys for all tables containing encrypted columns are encrypted with the database server master key and stored in a dictionary table in the database. No keys are stored in the clear.

Encrypting INSERTs and decrypting SELECTs involves roughly an additional 20–30 percent performance penalty, but this may be an acceptable trade-off in addressing regulatory compliance issues or security restrictions. This penalty applies only when data is retrieved from or inserted into an encrypted column. No reduction of performance occurs for such operations on other columns, even in a table containing encrypted columns. The total performance effect depends on the number of encrypted columns and their frequency of access. The columns most appropriate for encryption are obviously those containing the most sensitive data.

To start using Transparent Data Encryption, the security administrator must create a wallet and set a master key. The wallet can be the default database wallet shared with other Oracle Database components or a separate wallet specifically used by Transparent Data Encryption.

You can search for a certificate identifier by querying the cert_id column of V$WALLET when the wallet is open. An ORA-28359 will be returned if you specify an invalid certificate identifier. Only certificates that can be used as master keys by transparent data encryption are displayed. The DBA_ENCRYPTED_COLUMNS and USER_ENCRYPTED_COLUMNS views are used to display information about encrypted columns.

LogMiner Changes

Oracle Database 10g introduces several enhancements to the LogMiner tool. The first of these is automatic log file determination. In 10g, when you are using the LogMiner against the same database that generated the redo log files, LogMiner scans the control file and determines the redo log files needed, based on the start time or start SCN you provide. You no longer need to map the time frame to an explicit set of redo log files. For this scan to occur, you need to use the CONTINUOUS_MINE option and specify STARTSCN or STARTTIME.

LogMiner can now also record changes made to index-organized tables. It is currently restricted to IOTs that do not contain any LOBs or overflow segments. It also now supports the mining of multibyte CLOB and NCLOB data types and also extends the support for tables containing LONG and LONG RAW columns. In addition, LogMiner provides support for the new BINARY_FLOAT and BINARY_DOUBLE data types. LogMiner in 10gR2 supports IOTs with overflow segments and LOBs.

By extending support to BINARY_FLOAT and BINARY_DOUBLE data types, as well as multibyte CLOB and NCLOB data types, the facilities such as Oracle Data Guard SQL Apply, Logical Standby, and Oracle Streams, which uses the LogMiner technology, are improved to cover more situations.

A new option (NO_ROWID_IN_STMT) for the DBMS_LOGMNR.START_LOGMNR procedure eliminates the rowid from the SQL_REDO and SQL_UNDO columns in v$logmnr_contents. Since rowids are not the same across databases, this allows SQL statements to be used on a database other than the one on which the SQL was originally generated. If this option is used and the SQL will be used on a different database, you need to ensure that the where clause of each SQL statement can uniquely identify each row that it affects.

In previous versions, to remove a log file from the current LogMiner session, the DBMS_LOGMNR.ADD_LOGFILE procedure was called with the REMOVEFILE option. Beginning in 10g, this is now accomplished by calling the procedure DBMS_LOGMNR.REMOVE_LOGFILE and passing the log file name as a parameter.

CONTINUOUS_MINE, introduced in Oracle 9i, required that at least one archive log file be added manually to the session before CONTINUOUS_MINE could be used. Now, CONTINUOUS_MINE can be used with, at a minimum, only startTime or StartSCN as parameters. LogMiner automatically determines which archived log files need to be added dynamically to the session to satisfy the requested time/scn parameters by reading the control file. The control file has a limited number of archived logs that it retains information about, based on the value of MAXLOGHISTORY specified when the database or control file is created. The dynamic view v$archived_log contains information about the available archived logs in the control file. As logs are generated, they will be automatically added to the LogMiner session and the query will return records as they are encountered.

NOTE
It is not valid to start LogMiner with only an ENDTIME specified; STARTTIME is the minimum required for continuous mining.

New DBMS_STATS Options

The optimizer statistics collection has been improved with each version of the Oracle database. Oracle 8i introduced the DBMS_STATS package, improving on the DBMS_UTILITY statistics-gathering procedures. Oracle 9i introduced the monitoring feature, which partially automated the statistics gathering process. The monitoring option had to be manually enabled, but you determined when to gather statistics. You used the GATHER AUTO option to update the statistics for the objects when the current statistics were considered stale. In Oracle 10g, the optimizer statistics collection is fully automated. You don't need to worry about statistics gathering at all, and table monitoring is enabled by default.

In 9*i*, DBMS_STATS.ALTER_SCHEMA_TABLE_MONITORING could be used to enable or disable the DML monitoring feature of all tables in the schema. This procedure is equivalent to issuing CREATE (or ALTER) TABLE...MONITORING (or NOMONITORING) individually. In 10*g*, the MONITORING and NOMONITORING keywords have been deprecated. The table-monitoring feature is controlled by the STATISTICS_LEVEL parameter. When STATISTICS_LEVEL is set to BASIC, monitoring of tables is disabled. When STATISTICS_LEVEL is set to TYPICAL or ALL, then monitoring is enabled.

By default STATISTICS_LEVEL is set to TYPICAL. That is, monitoring of tables is enabled. It is strongly recommended to keep STATISTICS_LEVEL set to TYPICAL. By setting this parameter to BASIC, you disable most of the new manageability features, including

- ASH (Active Session History)

- AWR (Automatic Workload Repository)

- ASSM (Automatic Shared Memory Management)

- ADDM (Automatic Database Diagnostic Monitor)

Statistical monitoring tracks the approximate number of INSERT, UPDATE, and DELETE operations for the table since the last time statistics were gathered. Information about how many rows are affected is maintained in the SGA until, periodically (about every 15 minutes), SMON flushes the data into the data dictionary.

This data dictionary information is made visible through the following views:

View	Description
ALL_TAB_MODIFICATIONS	Describes modifications to all accessible tables that have been modified since the last time statistics were gathered on the tables
DBA_TAB_MODIFICATIONS	Describes modifications to all tables in the database that have been modified since the last time statistics were gathered on the tables
USER_TAB_MODIFICATIONS	Describes modifications to the user's tables that have been modified since the last time statistics were gathered on the tables

Oracle uses these views to identify tables with stale statistics. Whenever there is 10 percent change in data in a table, Oracle considers its statistics to be stale.

When an Oracle 10*g* database is created or a database is upgraded to Oracle 10*g*, a job by the name of GATHER_STATS_JOB is created. The job is managed by the scheduler (discussed later) and runs when the MAINTENANCE_WINDOW_GROUP window group is opened.

Because Oracle 10*g* uses only CBO, having up-to-date statistics is very important for generating good execution plans. The automatic statistics collection job that uses the DBMS_STATS package depends on the monitoring data to determine when to collect statistics on objects with stale objects.

Tracing Enhancements

Oracle tracing has been greatly enhanced. It now has the capability of performing end-to-end tracing of transactions in multitier environments that may consist of multiple sessions. End-to-end tracing can identify problems by client identifier, service, module, action, session, or instance. This isolates the problem down to a specific user, session, or application process. In prior versions it was difficult to keep track of a client process across different database sessions. A new attribute, CLIENT_IDENTIFIER, persists across on all tiers and sessions to uniquely identify the client session. The client identifier is can be viewed as the CLIENT_IDENTIFIER column of the V$SESSION view.

Once your tracing session is completed, the generated trace files are aggregated using the TRCSESS utility. TRCSESS is a command-line tool that comes with Oracle 10g. You can use it to consolidate the information from many trace files into a single output file. The output from TRCSESS is a consolidated file consisting of raw data. It should be processed with the TKPROF utility before using it to evaluate performance problems.

You can also monitor WAITS and BINDS using the DBMS_MONITOR package. This replaces the DBMS_SUPPORT.START_TRACE_IN_SESSION procedure, or setting the 10046 event, which gave this ability to trace WAITS and BINDS on a specific session. You can enable and disable statistics aggregation using the Enterprise Manager or using the DBMS_MONITOR package.

The following data dictionary views are used to display information about tracing:

View	Description
DBA_ENABLED_TRACES	Displays information about enabled SQL traces
WK$TRACE	Internal table includes the event, source, action, description, and timestamp

DBMS_SCHEDULER

Oracle 10g includes a new scheduling mechanism to automate routine tasks. The scheduler allows you to manage the Oracle database environment by combining the tasks into components, which can be combined into larger components called *jobs*. This functionality is implemented through a collection of procedures and functions in the DBMS_SCHEDULER package. Earlier versions of Oracle included the DBMS_JOB program to schedule jobs. This utility is still available in Oracle 10g, but the new scheduler provides greatly enhanced functionality.

The primary differences between DBMS_JOB and DBMS_SCHEDULER are

- DBMS_SCHEDULER can execute stored programs, anonymous blocks, and OS executables and scripts, while DBMS_JOB can execute only stored programs or anonymous PL/SQL blocks.

- The program units for the scheduler are stored as schema objects allowing for enhanced component reuse. There is only one component to DBMS_JOB, the job. The scheduler has a hierarchy of components.

- The job or schedule intervals can be defined more descriptively using DBMS_SCHEDULER. It also has a more detailed job run status and failure handling and reporting capabilities.

A typical example of use of the scheduler is to automate database maintenance jobs such as performing database backups, loading data warehouse data, gathering database statistics, refreshing materialized views, checking for alert log errors, or generating management reports.

Jobs can either be made up of predefined parts (programs and schedules) or be completely self-contained, depending on which version of the CREATE_JOB procedure is used to create them. Jobs are normally run under the control of the job coordinator, but they can be controlled manually using the RUN_JOB and STOP_JOB procedures. The scheduler allows you to create programs that hold metadata about a task, but no schedule information. A program may relate to a PL/SQL block, a stored procedure, or an OS executable file. Programs are created using the CREATE_PROGRAM procedure. The dynamic views are shown in Table 1-5.

View	Description
DBA_SCHEDULER_PROGRAMS[1]	Displays information about all Scheduler programs in the database
DBA_SCHEDULER_JOBS[1]	Displays information about all Scheduler jobs in the database
DBA_SCHEDULER_JOB_CLASSES[2]	Displays information about all Scheduler job classes in the database
DBA_SCHEDULER_WINDOWS[2]	Displays information about all Scheduler windows in the database
DBA_SCHEDULER_PROGRAM_ARGS[1]	Displays information about the arguments of all Scheduler programs in the database
DBA_SCHEDULER_JOB_ARGS[1]	Displays information about the arguments of all Scheduler jobs in the database
DBA_SCHEDULER_JOB_LOG[1]	Displays log information for all Scheduler jobs in the database
DBA_SCHEDULER_JOB_RUN_DETAILS[1]	Displays log run details for all Scheduler jobs in the database
DBA_SCHEDULER_WINDOW_LOG[2]	Displays log information for all Scheduler windows in the database
DBA_SCHEDULER_WINDOW_DETAILS[2]	Displays log details for all Scheduler windows in the database
DBA_SCHEDULER_WINDOW_GROUPS[2]	Displays information about all Scheduler window groups in the database
DBA_SCHEDULER_WINGROUP_MEMBERS[2]	Displays the members of all Scheduler window groups in the database
DBA_SCHEDULER_SCHEDULES[1]	Displays information about all Scheduler schedules in the database
DBA_SCHEDULER_RUNNING_JOBS[1]	Displays information about all running Scheduler jobs in the database

[1,2] There are also new views beyond our scope included in 10gR2 for Scheduler Chains: DBA_SCHEDULER_CHAINS, DBA_SCHEDULER_CHAINS_RULES, DBA_SCHEDULER_CHAINS_STEPS, DBA_SCHEDULER_RUNNING_CHAINS.

TABLE 1-5. *Scheduler Dynamic Views*

Default (Permanent) Tablespace

In earlier Oracle versions, if the DEFAULT TABLESPACE and TEMPORARY TABLEPACE were not specified when a user was created, they would default to the SYSTEM tablespace. If the user did not specify a tablespace explicitly while creating a segment, it was created in the SYSTEM tablespace provided the user had a quota there, either explicitly granted or by having been granted the system privilege UNLIMITED TABLESPACE.

Oracle 9*i* began addressing this problem by allowing the DBA to specify a default TEMPORARY TABLESPACE for all users created without an explicit TEMPORARY TABLESPACE clause.

Now, in Oracle Database 10*g*, you can similarly specify a default permanent tablespace for users. During database creation, the CREATE DATABASE command can contain the clause DEFAULT TABLESPACE {tablespace}. After creation, you can make a tablespace the default one by issuing the command

```
SQL> ALTER DATABASE DEFAULT TABLESPACE {tablespace};
```

All users created without the DEFAULT TABLESPACE clause will have {tablespace} assigned as the default tablespace for permanent segments. You can change the default tablespace at any time through this ALTER command, which allows you to specify different tablespaces as the default permanent tablespace at different points in time.

If the default tablespace is not specified during the database creation, it defaults to SYSTEM. It is important to note that no existing segments are moved when the default tablespace is changed through the ALTER command. If a user is created with no default tablespace specified, and the database default tablespace is later changed, when we flash back a table that was dropped before the database default tablespace was changed, it goes to the original tablespace, not to the current default tablespace of the user.

If a user is created with a default tablespace explicitly specified during user creation time, changing the database default tablespace won't change user's default tablespace. However, all the users of the database created without a default tablespace will start using this new default tablespace. An exception to this rule is where a user has been created with a default tablespace explicitly mentioned during creation time, which is the current default tablespace of the database. In this case, changing the database default tablespace will change the default tablespace of the user even if the tablespace has been assigned during creation time.

Temporary Tablespace Groups

A tablespace *group* is a synonym pointing to one or more temporary tablespaces that provides a convenient mechanism to enable users to consume temporary space from multiple tablespaces. The rules regarding tablespace groups are as follows:

- A tablespace group must contain at least one tablespace.

- There is no explicit limit on the maximum number of tablespaces that are contained in a group.

- A tablespace group cannot use the same name as any tablespace in the instance.

- The naming rules (maximum length, etc.) for the tablespace group are the same as for tablespace names.

- A tablespace group cannot be empty. As soon as the last member tablespace is dropped, the tablespace group is dropped.

There is no explicit command to create a tablespace group. It is created referentially when you assign the first temporary tablespace to the group. You can specify the tablespace group name when a temporary tablespace is created, or using an ALTER TABLESPACE clause.

The purpose for tablespace groups is to provide a method so that a parallelizable single SQL operation can use more than one temporary tablespace for sorting. Hence you can create indexes on very large tables without being limited by the size of one tablespace, because the sort operation during index creation can be distributed across multiple tablespaces.

A tablespace group can mitigate problems caused where one tablespace is too small to hold the results of a sort, particularly on a table with many partitions. In earlier releases, if a single SQL operation needed more space within a temporary tablespace than was available, it would generate an ORA-01652 error.

Rename Tablespaces

This tablespace enhancement allows DBAs to rename tablespaces. This has been an often-requested enhancement. Besides the convenience of being able to assign more meaningful names to tablespaces, this functionality simplifies transportation of a tablespace to a target database when a tablespace with the same name exists in the target database. This powerful new command must be used with care in some cases. The following notes should be considered:

- You should not rename OMF (Oracle Managed Files) tablespaces, since the names of their respective files contain the tablespace name: Oracle does not rename the names of the associated datafiles.

- You should not rename READ ONLY tablespaces, since Oracle does not update READ ONLY datafile headers. In order to change the headers, the tablespace must be changed to READ WRITE mode.

You should be careful in renaming UNDO tablespaces, since the tablespace name is referenced in the database initialization parameter UNDO_TABLESPACE. Ensure that you change the value to reflect the new name. These changes affect both memory and SPFILE. All these changes are logged in the alert log file. If SPFILE is not being used, a specific message is added to the alert log file advising DBAs to manually change the corresponding initialization parameter file.

Also note that performing a recovery using datafile backups containing old tablespace names is not a problem: the datafiles whose headers still contain the old tablespace are recovered past the rename point, and therefore after recovery, the datafile header has the new tablespace name. You can *not* RENAME the SYSTEM tablespace or the SYSAUX tablespace. Attempting to rename these tablespaces will generate an Oracle error.

Bigfile Tablespaces

Another new change to 10g is the introduction of bigfile tablespaces. A *bigfile* tablespace is a tablespace containing a single datafile that can be as large as 128 terabytes (TB), depending on the block size, as opposed to normal tablespaces, which may contain several datafiles. A bigfile tablespace is always a locally managed tablespace, an undo tablespace, or a temporary tablespace. Using bigfile tablespaces means you never need to add datafiles to a tablespace. It simplifies the maintenance of tablespaces. Some operations that formerly were performed at the datafile level are now performed at the logical tablespace level. Bigfile tablespaces must be created as locally managed with automatic segment space management. While the default allocation policy for bigfile tablespaces is AUTOALLOCATE, you can also change the default to UNIFORM where that allocation strategy may be more efficient. To create a bigfile tablespace, use the BIGFILE keyword and specify the size of the tablespace in gigabytes (G) or terabytes (T). Bigfile tablespaces have a different format for extended ROWIDs of table rows. Since there is only one datafile to a tablespace, the ROWID does not contain a relative file number, but an expanded, encoded block identifier.

The procedures within the DBMS_ROWID package operate much as before, except for a new parameter, TS_TYPE_IN, which identifies the type of tablespace to which a particular row belongs. The value of TS_TYPE_IN is either BIGFILE or SMALLFILE. There is more information about BIGFILEs in Chapter 3.

Shrinking Segments

Another long-requested enhancement to Oracle is introduced in 10*g*, the ability to shrink a segment, which will help DBAs to manage the space in better way. Shrinking a segment compresses the data blocks in a table or index and optionally moves the high water mark (HWM) down, making the unused space available for other segments in the tablespace. In order to be eligible for shrinking a segment, it must be in a tablespace using Automatic Segment Space Management (ASSM).

By specifying ALTER TABLE...SHRINK SPACE, the storage of rows within the segment is compressed and the HWM is reduced. If SHRINK SPACE COMPACT is specified, the segment is shrunk, but the HWM remains unchanged. Specifying SPACE CASCADE shrinks the segment and the segments of all dependent objects. Segments can be shrunk for normal tables, indexes (b-tree and bit-mapped), segments containing LOBs, and materialized views. Segment shrinking is restricted for clustered tables, tables with LONG columns, and shared LOB segments, as well as for temporary and UNDO segments.

During a segment shrink, the ROWID may change for a row when it moves between blocks. Therefore, segments that rely on ROWIDs, such as a ROWID materialized view, cannot be shrunk. ROW MOVEMENT must be enabled for table segments that are to be shrunk.

Index dependencies are taken care of during segment shrink. The indexes will not be in an unusable state after shrink. The compaction of segment shrink is actually accomplished through insert/delete pairs. Segment shrink is done online, improving the availability of the object. Since during segment shrinking, data will be moved as part of the compaction phase, locks will be held on individual rows and/or blocks containing the data. This will cause the concurrent DMLs like updates and deletes to serialize on the locks. When the HWM is adjusted, the segment is locked in exclusive mode until the adjustment completes.

Data Pump

One area of Oracle that was in dire need of performance enhancement was the facility for movement of large amounts of data between Oracle tables and flat files. The primary tools for accomplishing this movement have been import (imp) and export (exp). In previous versions, incremental performance boosts were obtained by enabling parallel processing and implementing direct path methods.

In 10g, Oracle introduced a completely new architecture with Data Pump. Data Pump is available in Oracle Enterprise Edition, Standard Edition, and Personal Edition, but the parallel capability is only available in the Enterprise Edition. A major part of Data Pump replaces imp and exp. Data Pump's architecture is designed to provide significant performance increases over imp and exp. Using direct path method and parallel execution, Data Pump loads/unloads data several times faster than the traditional export/import methods. Data Pump also supports restarting jobs from the point of failure and gives you the ability to monitor the progress of your job. Data Pump is reserved for large export and import jobs because the startup time is longer for Data Pump. Data Pump has to set up jobs, queues, and the master table at the beginning of an operation, and at the end, the master table data is written to the dump file set.

In Data Pump, all of the work is performed by the database. This is a major change from the earlier functionality of export/import utilities, which ran as client applications and did the major part of the work. Because of this architecture change, the dump files for Data Pump are always stored on the server. Commonly, dump files for export/import were stored at the client.

DBMS_DATAPUMP is the PL/SQL API for the Data Pump engine. Data Pump jobs are created and monitored using this API. The DBMS_METADATA API allows you to write custom code that interfaces with the Oracle Data Pump driver. This allows you to write code that can import or export data using Data Pump, and suspend, resume, or monitor Data Pump jobs and other Data Pump–related activities.

EXPDP and IMPDP are the new client utilities that have a look and feel similar to the old export and import utilities, but EXPDP and IMPDP come with a number of new features and are much more efficient than their predecessors. The EXPDP and IMPDP new features are not available with their predecessors, such as the ability to

- Suspend an export and resume it from the point it was suspended.

- Attach or detach from running export or import jobs.

- Restart failed jobs from the point of failure.

- Use multiple threads, and control their number during the export operation.

- Use a direct path data access method.

- Load from or to another database, through a database link, directly, using network mode operations.

- Control the version of the object that is exported, and so export data from one version of Oracle Database and ensure that it is compatible with a lower-level version of Oracle Database.

NOTE
The version control feature does not apply to versions of Oracle Database prior to 10g.

- Extract metadata separately from data. You can extract only database metadata (e.g., table and index creation statements), extract only data from the database, or extract both database metadata and data at the same time.

■ Estimate the size of the files that will result from EXPDP, before actually generating the files. In addition, EXPDP can perform fine-grained object selection when exporting, such as exporting only procedures and functions, and can use external tables.

The following dynamic views are provided to support datapump jobs:

View	Description
DBA_DATAPUMP_JOBS	Displays all Data Pump jobs in the database
DBA_DATAPUMP_SESSIONS	Displays all Data pump sessions attached to a job in the database
DATAPUMP_PATHS	Displays the list of available datapump export paths

Cross-Platform Transportable Tablespaces

Oracle 8*i* introduced the transportable tablespace feature. However, the transportable tablespaces feature was supported only when the Oracle databases were running on the same architecture and operating system. Oracle 10*g* supports moving datafiles across different platforms. You can now unplug a tablespace on a Windows NT database and move it to a Sun Solaris database.

One of the possible hiccups involved in transporting tablespaces between different platforms is the datafile byte-ordering format. The OS platforms that the Oracle Database server runs on generally use one of two different byte-ordering schemes (known as the endian formats). Each operating system supports either big- or little-endian format to store numerical values. On platforms with a big-endian format, values are stored with the most significant bytes first in memory. On platforms with little-endian format, values are stored with least significant bytes first.

With 10*g* you can copy the datafiles directly when doing cross-platform transportable tablespaces, if their endian formats are the same. If the endian formats are different, you must use the CONVERT command in RMAN to convert the datafiles before importing them to the target database. The new view V$TRANSPORATABLE_PLATFORM view shows endian format for each platform. Note that there are cases where CLOB columns may need further conversion after the tablespace has been transported. This conversion is handled automatically by Oracle Database 10*g* as the data is accessed, but the conversion may have performance impacts. You can avoid these impacts by rebuilding these tables after the migration has completed.

This feature is useful in data warehouse environments, where the data marts are on smaller platforms, and the data warehouse is on a larger platform.

The databases must use the same database character set and national character set. Character set conversion is not possible in transportable tablespaces.

Write to External Table

Oracle 9*i* introduced external tables, but they were read-only from the Oracle database. In Oracle 10*g*, you can now write to them. The enhancements related to external tables in Oracle 10*g* also include the ability to perform parallel external table operations and projected column features, which can eliminate failures during external table select operations arising from data quality problems.

In Oracle 9*i*, SQL Loader was the access driver for external tables. Data could be loaded from OS files into the Oracle environment, but we couldn't write the data from Oracle to the OS files. Oracle 10g uses an external Data Pump access driver. A Data Pump–generated file is in a proprietary format (Oracle native external representation, DPAPI) that only Data Pump can read and is independent of the OS that the file is created on. Because of this, you may use this file to load to another Oracle database.

Writing to an external table is prohibited; the insert, update, and delete DML operations are not supported. However, you can use the Data Pump driver to perform transform operations on that data as you load or unload the data. Additionally, you can create joins on the data as you load or unload it, which cannot be done with the Data Pump utilities EXPDP and IMPDP. Similar to the effect of dropping a tablespace, dropping an external table does not drop the corresponding OS files.

Automatic Undo Retention Tuning

Undo retention was introduced in Oracle 9*i*. This parameter is used to support the "flashback query" feature. This parameter, however, did not completely resolve all occurrences of the ORA-1555 "snapshot too old" error. The value of the parameter UNDO_RETENTION is specified in units of seconds. This parameter determines the lower threshold value of undo retention. The system retains undo for at least the time specified in this parameter. When you set the value of UNDO_RETENTION to 0, Oracle 10g automatically tunes undo retention to reduce the chances of "snapshot too old" errors during long-running queries.

When UNDO_RETENTION is set to 0, the minimum value of UNDO RETENTION will be 900 seconds (15 minutes). The MMON background process will calculate the length of the longest running query, MAXQUERYLEN, every 30 seconds. Using the calculated value of MAXQUERYLEN, MMON will adjust TUNED_UNDORETENTION, and UNDO RETENTION will be set to TUNED_UNDORETENTION.

On systems with heavy DML, sometimes the undo retention threshold should be guaranteed, even at the expense of DML operations. Oracle 10g introduces a new RETENTION GUARANTEE clause to guarantee the minimum undo retention. This means that the database will make certain that undo will always be available for the specified undo retention period. You can specify the RETENTION GUARANTEE clause when creating the undo tablespace or later with an ALTER TABLESPACE statement. To turn the retention guarantee off, use the RETENTION NOGUARANTEE clause.

V$SESSION Include New Information

In earlier versions, to determine the sessions experiencing waits, it was necessary to join the v$session_wait dynamic performance view with the v$session view. Oracle 10g has added all wait event columns from v$session_wait to the v$session dynamic view, thus increasing performance by eliminating the overhead of joins.

The new columns in the v$session view include

■ **BLOCKING_SESSION** A new column with Oracle 10g, this column contains the session identifier of any session that is blocking the session in the current row.

- **BLOCKING_SESSION_STATUS**   Another new column, this column contains the status of the value of the blocking_session column. The valid values for the blocking session status column are

  - VALID   A valid Session ID is present in the Blocking Session column.

  - NO HOLDER   There are no holders of this resource.

  - UNKNOWN   Unable to determine the SID of the holder.

  - UNIMPLEMENTED   The callback for the event has not been implemented.

  - GLOBAL   The holder is a session in another instance.

- **SEQ#**   From the v$wait event, this column contains a sequence number that uniquely identifies this event.

- **WAIT_CLASS#**   All wait events have been classified into categories. This is the event class number. The valid values for the wait class number and name can be queried from the v$event_name dynamic view.

- **WAIT_CLASS**   This new column contains the event class name corresponding to the class number given in the WAIT_CLASS# column.

- **WAIT_TIME**   A zero value means the session is currently waiting.

- **SECONDS_IN_WAIT**   This column displays the duration of the wait event for the current session.

- **STATE**   The state of the current session's wait event. Valid values are

  - WAITING (the session is currently waiting)

  - WAITED UNKNOWN TIME (duration of last wait is unknown)

  - WAITED SHORT TIME (last wait was <1/100th of a second)

  - WAITED KNOWN TIME (WAIT_TIME = duration of last wait)

Other included columns that help (so you don't have to look to other V$ views elsewhere) include: EVENT#, EVENT, P1, P2, P3, P1TEXT, P2TEXT, P3TEXT, P1RAW, P2RAW, and P3RAW. Some enqueues and latches are now broken down by the specific type of event. You will also have the EVENT column for the enqueue in particular. The result is that instead of having only the "enqueue" wait, you will see several "enq%" types of waits.

OEM Changes

Oracle Enterprise Manager (OEM) has a completely new look and feel in 10g, integrating vastly improved functionality in an easy-to use interface. Most of the OEM screens are now architected in HTML, running on the middle tier rather than as a Java-based client application. An Apache HTTP server is included with the database server so that you can start working with the OEM out of the box, thus requiring "zero startup time." The Oracle Enterprise Manager repository, job, and event subsystems are now configured automatically, eliminating the need for manual setup.

OEM Database Control is installed at the time you install the base Oracle software. You can choose to install it into the same ORACLE_HOME location or install it in a separate ORACLE_HOME location. If you create a database using the Database Configuration Assistant (DBCA), then OEM Database Control will be installed and preconfigured along with the database.

Grid Control

Oracle's OEM Grid Control is a separate OEM version that is installed from separate media. Grid Control is used to manage multiple hardware nodes, databases, application servers, and other targets by grouping them into single logical entities. By executing jobs, enforcing standard policies, monitoring performance, and automating many other tasks across a group of targets, instead of on many systems individually, Grid Control enables your administrative abilities to scale with a growing grid. Because of this feature, you can manage the multitudes of hardware composing the grid in an efficient and affordable manner. Chapter 5 covers Grid Control in detail.

New Background Processes in 10g

Oracle 10g includes the following new background processes:

- **RVWR**   Recovery Writer supports the flashback database; this process is responsible for writing flashback logs that store pre-image(s) of data blocks.

- **CTWR**   Change Tracking Writer is a new process that works with the new block change tracking features in 10g for fast RMAN incremental backups.

- **MMNL**   Memory Monitor Light is a process that works with the Automatic Workload Repository (AWR) new features to write out full statistics buffers to disk as needed.

- **MMON**   Memory Monitor process is associated with the Automatic Workload Repository new features used for automatic problem detection and self-tuning. MMON writes out the required statistics for AWR on a scheduled basis.

- **M000**   These are MMON background slave (m000) processes.

- **RBAL**   The Rebalancing Daemon is the ASM-related process that performs rebalancing of disk resources controlled by ASM.

- **ARBx**   These processes are managed by the RBAL process and are used to do the actual rebalancing of ASM-controlled disk resources. The number of ARBx processes invoked is directly influenced by the asm_power_limit parameter.

- **ASMB**   The ASMB process is used to provide information to and from the Cluster Synchronization Services used by ASM to manage the disk resources. It is also used to update statistics and provide a heartbeat mechanism.

Version Comparison Table

The following table shows which components or options are included in the various editions of Oracle 10g (subject to change). Note that there is also a free version of Oracle called Oracle 10g

Express Edition, which allows a 4GB database, 1 CPU, and 1GB of memory (subject to change).
Please check with Oracle to verify any features.

Option or Feature	10g Standard Edition One	10g Standard Edition	10g Enterprise Edition	10g Personal Edition
Advanced Security	N	N	Y	Y
Change Mgt Pack	N	N	Y	N
Data Mining	N	N	Y	Y
Diag Pack	N	N	Y	N
Label Security	N	N	Y	Y
Oracle OLAP	N	N	Y	Y
Partitioning	N	N	Y	Y
Oracle Programmer	N	N	Y	Y
Oracle RAC	Y	N	Y	N
Oracle Spatial	N	N	Y	Y
Tuning Pack	N	N	Y	N
CM Pack	N	N	Y	Y
DB Resource Mgr	N	N	Y	Y
VLDB, Data Warehousing, Business Intelligence				
Data compression	N	N	Y	Y
Bitmapped index	N	N	Y	Y
Export transp ts	N	N	Y	Y
Import transp ts	Y	Y	Y	Y
Async change data capture	N	N	Y	Y
Summary Management	N	N	Y	Y
Analytic functions	Y	Y	Y	Y
Automated parallel query	N	N	Y	Y
Descending indexes	Y	Y	Y	Y
Direct Path Load API	Y	Y	Y	Y
External tables	Y	Y	Y	Y
Function-based indexes	Y	Y	Y	Y
Long operations monitor	Y	Y	Y	Y
Materialized views	Y	Y	Y	Y
MERGE	Y	Y	Y	Y
Optimizer stats mgt	Y	Y	Y	Y
Pipelined table functs	Y	Y	Y	Y
Sample scan	Y	Y	Y	Y
Star query optimization	Y	Y	Y	Y

Option or Feature	10g Standard Edition One	10g Standard Edition	10g Enterprise Edition	10g Personal Edition
Parallel Operations				
Parallel query	N	N	Y	Y
Parallel DML	N	N	Y	Y
Parallel idx build	N	N	Y	Y
Parallel stats gath	N	N	Y	Y
Parallel Data exp & Pump	N	N	Y	Y
Parallel text idx creation	N	N	Y	Y
Parallel backup & Rec	N	N	Y	Y
Parallel analyze	N	N	Y	Y
Parallel bitmap star query	N	N	Y	Y
Parallel index scans	N	N	Y	Y
Parallel load	Y	Y	Y	Y
High Availability				
Oracle Data Guard	N	N	Y	Y
Fast-start fault rec	N	N	Y	Y
Online operations	N	N	Y	Y
Backup and recovery	N	N	Y	Y
Oracle Flashback features	N	N	Y	Y
Content Management				
Dynamic Services	Y	Y	Y	Y
Workspace Manager	Y	Y	Y	Y
Ultra Search	Y	Y	Y	Y
Information Integration				
Oracle Streams	N	N	Y	Y
Oracle Messaging Gateway	N	N	Y	Y
Database Features				
Advanced Queuing	Y	Y	Y	Y
Database event triggers	Y	Y	Y	Y
DBMS_REPAIR package	Y	Y	Y	Y
Drop column	Y	Y	Y	Y
Flashback Query	Y	Y	Y	Y
Globalization	Y	Y	Y	Y
Index coalesce	N	N	Y	Y
Index-organized tables	Y	Y	Y	Y
Instead-of	Y	Y	Y	Y
LOB (large object) support	Y	Y	Y	Y

Option or Feature	10g Standard Edition One	10g Standard Edition	10g Enterprise Edition	10g Personal Edition
Locally managed tablespaces	Y	Y	Y	Y
LogMiner	Y	Y	Y	Y
Plan Stability	Y	Y	Y	Y
Quiesce database	N	N	Y	Y
Reverse key indexes	Y	Y	Y	Y
Temporary tables	Y	Y	Y	Y
Development				
AppWizard for Virt Studio	Y	Y	Y	Y
Autonomous transactions	Y	Y	Y	Y
COM cartridge	Y	Y	Y	Y
iSQL*Plus	Y	Y	Y	Y
Java	Y	Y	Y	Y
JDBC drivers	Y	Y	Y	Y
MS Trans Server	Y	Y	Y	Y
Object/Relational Ext	Y	Y	Y	Y
PL/SQL native compilation	Y	Y	Y	Y
PL/SQL stored procs in trgs	Y	Y	Y	Y
PL/SQL Server embedded	Y	Y	Y	Y
User-defined aggregates	Y	Y	Y	Y
XML	Y	Y	Y	Y
Distributed				
Adv Replication	N	N	Y	Y
Basic Replication	Y	Y	Y	Y
Distributed queries	Y	Y	Y	Y
Dlstributed transactions	Y	Y	Y	Y
Heterogeneous svcs	Y	Y	Y	Y
Networking				
Connection Manager	N	N	Y	Y
Multiprotocol	N	N	Y	Y
SDP for Infiniband	N	N	Y	Y
Connection pooling	Y	Y	Y	Y
Oracle Net services	Y	Y	Y	Y
System Management				
Basic Standby DB	Y	Y	Y	Y
Global index maint—DDL	Y	Y	Y	Y
Legato Storage Mgr	Y	Y	Y	Y

Option or Feature	10g Standard Edition One	10g Standard Edition	10g Enterprise Edition	10g Personal Edition
Multiple Block Size	Y	Y	Y	Y
Online backup & Rec	Y	Y	Y	Y
Standard Mgt Pack	N	N	Y	N
Oracle Enterprise Mgr	Y	Y	Y	Y
Oracle Fail Safe	Y	Y	Y	Y
Oracle Managed Files	Y	Y	Y	Y
Recovery Manager	Y	Y	Y	Y
Resumable Space Alloc	Y	Y	Y	Y
Standby Database GUI	N	N	Y	Y
Transparent Ap Failover	Y	Y	Y	Y
Unused index ident	Y	Y	Y	Y
Security				
Virtual Private DB	N	N	Y	Y
Fine-grained auditing	N	N	Y	Y
Enterprise Security	N	N	Y	Y
N-tier authentication	N	N	Y	Y
Password management	Y	Y	Y	Y
Encryption Toolkit	Y	Y	Y	Y
Proxy Authentication	Y	Y	Y	Y

This is by no means a complete list of new features in Oracle 10g. It is said there are 149 new features in 10g, although this number includes improvements on features introduced in prior versions. Overall, Oracle has made major strides in providing enhanced functionality and automating many administrative tasks, reducing the total cost of ownership. And while grid computing may not be a mature technology for several more releases, Oracle is leading the effort at making use of this technology.

New Features Review

- Installation is better and easier
- The SYSAUX Tablespace is new
- Automatic Storage Management (ASM) changing disk storage
- Cluster Ready Services (CRS) for grid technology
- Automatic Workload Repository (AWR) to store statistics
- Automatic Database Diagnostic Monitor (ADDM) for tuning
- SQL Tuning Advisor for tuning advice

- Automatic Shared Memory Management (ASMM) for auto-tuning
- Flash recovery area and recycle bin for user mistakes
- Transparent Data Encryption (10*g*R2) for security
- Data Pump for faster data movement
- Cross-platform transportable tablespaces for data movement
- Writing to an external table for dynamic data
- Automatic undo retention tuning now improved auto-undo
- V$SESSION includes new information for tuning
- Grid Control is what's next!

References

Sam Alapati, *Oracle Database* 10g: *New Features for Administrators* (Oracle Press, 2005)
Robert Freeman, *Oracle Database* 10g *New Features* (Oracle Press, 2004)
Oracle Database New Features Guide, 10g *Release 1* (Oracle Corporation, 2003)
Oracle Database Reference, 10g *Release 1* (Oracle Corporation, 2003)

Many thanks to Brad Ziola, who did an outstanding update to this chapter!

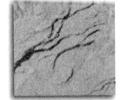

CHAPTER
2

Basic Index Principles
(Beginner Developer
and Beginner DBA)

TIPS & COVERED

This chapter is neither for the experts nor for those seeking fast answers. This is a chapter (maybe the only one) that looks at basic indexing theory. The toughest part of being a beginner is finding information that will fill in the most basic gaps and enable visualization of Oracle's indexing capabilities. This chapter is intended to serve that purpose. Although a considerable amount of material is published at the intermediate and advanced levels, information for beginners is usually scarce, yet highly desirable.

Oracle offers a variety of indexing options. Knowing which option to use in a given situation can be crucial to an application's performance. A wrong choice may cause performance to come to a grinding halt or cause processes to be terminated because of deadlock situations. Making the correct choice can make you an instant hero, by taking processes that previously took hours or even days to run and providing the resources to finish these processes in minutes. This chapter will discuss each of the indexing options and point out the benefits and limitations of each. Tips covered in this chapter include the following:

- Basic index concepts

- Finding which tables are indexed and which have concatenated indexes

- How concatenated indexes are used

- The Oracle ROWID

- How to use function-based indexes

- How to avoid comparing unmatched data types, causing index suppression

- Cluster factors as an index strategy

- Using the INDEX_STATS view

- The binary height of an index

- About histograms

- Fast full scans

- How to use the index skip-scan feature

- Explanation of b-tree indexes

- When to use bitmap indexes

- When to use hashing

- When to use the index-ordered table

- When to use reverse-key indexes

- When to use function-based indexes

- Local and global partitioned indexes

Basic Index Concepts

When accessing data from tables, Oracle has two options: to read every row in the table (also referred to as a full table scan), or to access a single row at a time by ROWID. When accessing a small percentage of the rows of a large table, you would want to use an index. For example, if you only wanted to select 5 percent of the rows in a large table, you would do fewer I/Os if you used the index to identify which blocks to read. If you don't use an index, you will read all of the blocks in the table.

The degree to which indexes help performance depends partly on the selectivity of the data and the way in which the data is distributed among the table's blocks. If the data is very selective, there will be few rows in the table that match the indexed value (such as a passport number). Oracle will be able to quickly query the index for the ROWIDs that match the indexed value, and the small number of related table blocks can be quickly queried. If the data is not very selective (such as the country name), then many ROWIDs may be returned by the index, resulting in many separate blocks being queried from the table.

If the data is selective but the related rows are not stored near each other in the table, then the benefit of indexing is further reduced. If the data that matches the indexed value is scattered throughout the table's blocks, then you may have to select many individual blocks from the table to satisfy your query. In some cases you will find that when the data is dispersed throughout the table's blocks you are better off bypassing the index and performing a full table scan instead. When doing a full table scan Oracle uses a multiblock read, enabling it to scan a table quickly. Index-based reads are single-block reads, so your goal when using an index should be to reduce the number of single blocks needed to resolve the query.

With some of the options available in Oracle, such as partitioning, parallel DML, parallel query operations, and larger I/O using the db_file_multiblock_read_count, the balance point between full table scans and index lookups is changing. Hardware is getting faster, disks cache more information in on-disk caching, and memory continues to get cheaper. At the same time, Oracle has enhanced the indexing features to include skip-scan indexes and other internal operations that reduce the time needed to retrieve your data.

TIP
As you upgrade Oracle versions, be sure to test your application's queries to determine whether the execution paths for your queries still use the indexes that were used prior to the upgrade. See if the execution plan has changed and if it is better or worse.

Indexes will generally improve performance for queries. SELECT, the WHERE clauses of UPDATE commands, and the WHERE clauses of DELETE statements (when few rows are accessed) can benefit from indexes. In general, the addition of indexes will decrease performance for INSERT statements (since inserts to both the table and the index must be performed). UPDATEs of indexed columns will be slower than if the columns were unindexed, since the database has to manage the changes to both the table and the index. Additionally, DELETEs of large numbers of rows will be slowed by the presence of indexes on the table.

A DELETE statement deleting half of a table will also need to delete half of the rows for the index (very costly for this specific situation). In general, every index on a table slows INSERTs into the table by a factor of 3; two indexes generally make the insert twice as slow (yet a two-column single index (concatenated index or two-part single index) is not much worse than a one-column single index (one-part single index). UPDATEs of the indexed columns and DELETEs may be similarly slowed. You need to balance the query performance benefits of indexes against their impact on your data manipulation performance. To get a listing of all of the indexes on a table, query the DBA_INDEXES view. Also, note that you can retrieve the indexes for your schema by accessing USER_INDEXES. To see the indexes on all tables to which you have access, query ALL_INDEXES.

For example, you can create indexes on the EMP table provided as part of the Oracle demo tables:

```
create index emp_id1 on emp(empno, ename, deptno);
create index emp_id2 on emp (sal);
```

When you issue those commands, the database will create two separate indexes on the EMP table. Each of the indexes will contain the specified values from the EMP table along with the ROWID values for the rows that match them. If you wanted to find an EMP record that had a Sal value of 1000, the optimizer could use the EMP_ID2 index to find that value, find the related ROWID in the index, and use that ROWID to find the right row(s) in the table.

The following query of USER_INDEXES shows the new indexes on the EMP table:

```
select      table_name, index_name
from        user_indexes
where       table_name = 'EMP' ;


TABLE_NAME                            INDEX_NAME
-----------------------------------   ------------------------------------

EMP                                   EMP_ID1
EMP                                   EMP_ID2
```

The output shows the two indexes, but it does not show the columns in each index. To get the specific columns that are indexed for a given table, access the USER_IND_COLUMNS view. Also note that DBAs can retrieve the columns that are indexed for all schemas by accessing DBA_IND_COLUMNS, and you can see the indexed columns for all of the tables you can access via ALL_IND_COLUMNS.

```
column index_name format a12
column column_name format a8
column table_name format a8
select      table_name, index_name, column_name, column_position
from        user_ind_columns
order       by table_name, index_name, column_position;


TABLE_NA INDEX_NAME    COLUMN_N COLUMN_POSITION
-------- ------------- -------- ----------------
EMP      EMP_ID1       EMPNO                   1
EMP      EMP_ID1       ENAME                   2
EMP      EMP_ID1       DEPTNO                  3
EMP      EMP_ID2       SAL                     1
```

The EMP table has two indexes. The first, EMP_ID1, is a concatenated index that indexes the Empno, Ename, and Deptno columns. The second, EMP_ID2, indexes the Sal column only. The Column_Position displayed in the listing shows the order of columns in a concatenated index—in this case, the Empno, then the Ename, then the Deptno.

TIP
Query DBA_INDEXES and DBA_IND_COLUMNS to retrieve a list of the indexes on a given table. Use USER_INDEXES and USER_IND_COLUMNS to retrieve information for only your schema.

Concatenated Indexes

When a single index has multiple columns that are indexed, it is called a *concatenated* or *composite* index. While Oracle 9*i*'s introduction of skip-scan index access has increased the optimizer's options when using concatenated indexes, you should be careful when selecting the order of the columns in the index. In general, the leading column of the index should be the one most likely to be used in WHERE clauses and also the most selective column of the set.

Prior to the introduction of skip-scan functionality, queries could only use the index if the leading column of the index was used in the WHERE clause. Consider the example in the following listing where the EMP table has a concatenated index on Empno, Ename, and Deptno. Note that Empno is the first part, Ename is the second part, and Deptno is the third part. If you are not making use of the skip-scan functionality, Oracle will generally not use this index unless your WHERE clause specifies a value for the leading column (Empno).

```
select      job, empno
from        emp
where       ename = 'RICH';
```

Since Ename is not the leading column of the index, the optimizer may elect not to use the index. With the introduction of the skip-scan functionality in Oracle 9*i*, the optimizer may choose to use the index even though an Empno value is not specified in the WHERE clause. Instead, the optimizer could choose to perform a fast full scan of the index or a full scan of the table.

The same holds true if the third column of the index is used in the WHERE clause:

```
select      job, empno
from        emp
where       deptno = 30;
```

In this listing, the WHERE clause specifies a value for the third column in the index. The optimizer may select to perform an index skip-scan access, an index fast full scan, or a full table scan. By creating the index, you have given the database more choices to consider when executing the query, hopefully improving the overall performance. Note that the user's code does not change; the optimizer is aware of the index and bases its decisions on the anticipated cost of each alternative.

In the following example, a part of the index is used. The leading column, Empno, is used as a limiting condition in the WHERE clause so that Oracle can use the index.

```
select      job, empno
from        emp
where       empno = 'RICH';
```

The two most common types of index scans are unique scans and range scans. In a *unique* scan, the database knows that the index contains a list of unique values. In a *range* scan, the database will be returning multiple values from the index according to the query criteria. In this example, the emp_id1 and emp_id2 indexes were not created as unique indexes. Oracle will perform a range scan when retrieving their data. To create a unique index, use the CREATE UNIQUE INDEX command when creating the index.

When you create a primary key or a UNIQUE constraint, Oracle will automatically create a unique index based on the columns you specify (unless the constraint is created with the DISABLE clause). If you create a multicolumn primary key, Oracle will create a concatenated index with the columns in the same order in which you specified them when creating the primary key.

Basic Index Concepts

Indexes like EMP_ID1 and EMP_ID2 provide Oracle with the ability to access a single row of data by supplying the ROWID of the individual row. The ROWID is a pointer directly to the physical location of the individual row.

TIP
Avoid hard-coding Oracle's ROWID into specific code. The ROWID structure in the past has changed from version to version, and will probably change again in future releases. I recommend against ever hard-coding a ROWID.

Suppressing Indexes

Suppressing indexes is one of the most common mistakes of an inexperienced developer. There are many traps within SQL that will cause indexes not to be used. Some of the most common problems will be discussed in the following sections.

The Oracle optimizer works behind the scenes to choose and exploit the most effective methods possible for retrieving your data. For example, there are multiple cases in which you don't need to specify a WHERE clause in order for Oracle to use an index. If you query the MIN or MAX value of an indexed column, Oracle will retrieve that value from the index rather than from the table. Similarly, if you perform a COUNT function on an indexed column, Oracle can use the index instead of the column. In the following sections you will see situations in which the logic of the WHERE clause prevents Oracle from using an index.

Using the NOT EQUAL Operators '<>', '!='

Indexes can only be used to find data that exists within a table. Whenever the not equal operators are used in the WHERE clause, indexes on the columns being referenced cannot be used. Consider the following query on the CUSTOMERS table, which has an index on the CUST_RATING column. The following statement would result in a full table scan (since most records would *usually* be retrieved) even though there is an index on the CUST_RATING column:

```
select      cust_id, cust_name
from        customers
where       cust_rating <> 'aa';
```

When you analyze your tables, Oracle collects statistics about the distribution of data within the table. Using that analysis, the cost-based optimizer may decide to use the index for some values in your WHERE clause but not for other values. During application development and testing you should use a representative set of rows so that you can simulate the actual distribution of data values in the production environment.

TIP
You can create your indexes and analyze them in a single step by using the COMPUTE STATISTICS clause of the CREATE INDEX command. You can also import statistics from a production database to test out execution paths (refer to section 14.5.2 in the 10gR2 Database Performance Tuning Guide (Part Number B14211-01).

Using IS NULL or IS NOT NULL

When you use IS NULL or IS NOT NULL in your WHERE clauses, index usage will be suppressed, since the value of NULL is undefined. There is no value in the database that will equal a NULL value; not even NULL equals a NULL.

NULL values pose several difficulties for SQL statements. Indexed columns that have rows containing a NULL value will not have an entry in the index (except for bitmapped indexes—which is why bitmap indexes are usually fast for NULL searches). Under normal circumstances the following statement would cause a full table scan to be performed, even if the Sal column is indexed:

```
select      empno, ename, deptno
from        emp
where       sal is null;
```

To disallow NULL values for the columns, use NOT NULL when creating or altering the table. Note that if the table already contains data, you can only set a column to NOT NULL if it has a non-NULL value for every row or if you use the DEFAULT clause of the ALTER TABLE command. The following listing shows the modification of the EMP table's Sal column to disallow NULL values:

```
alter table emp modify
(sal not null);
```

Note that an error will be returned if insertion of a NULL value is attempted for the Sal column.

TIP
Creating a table specifying NOT NULL for a column will cause NULL values to be disallowed and eliminate the performance problems associated with querying NULL values.

The following table creation statement provides a default value for the Deptno column. When a value for the column is not specified during INSERTs, the default value will be used. If a default value is specified and you *do* want a NULL value, then you need to insert a NULL into the column.

```
create table employee
(empl_id number(8) not null, first_name varchar2(20) not null,
 last_name varchar2(20) not null, deptno number(4) default 10);

insert into employee(empl_id, first_name, last_name)
values (8100, 'REGINA', 'NIEMIEC');
1 row created.

select      *
from        employee;
```

EMPL_ID	FIRST_NAME	LAST_NAME	DEPTNO
8100	REGINA	NIEMIEC	10

```
insert into employee
values (8200, 'RICH', 'NIEMIEC', NULL);

1 row created.

select     *
from       employee;

  EMPL_ID FIRST_NAME           LAST_NAME                      DEPTNO
--------- -------------------- -------------------- ----------
     8100 REGINA               NIEMIEC                            10
     8200 RICH                 NIEMIEC
```

TIP
*NULL values often cause indexes to be suppressed. Create a table
specifying NOT NULL and DEFAULT for an unspecified column and
help avoid a potential performance issue.*

Using Functions

Unless you are using function-based indexes, using functions on indexed columns in the WHERE
clause of a SQL statement will cause the optimizer to bypass indexes. Some of the most common
functions are TRUNC, SUBSTR, TO_DATE, TO_CHAR, and INSTR. All of these functions will cause
the value of the column to be altered. Therefore, the indexes and the columns being referenced will
not be used. The following statement would cause a full table scan to be performed, even if there is
an index on the hire_date column (as long as it wasn't a function-based index):

```
select     empno, ename, deptno
from       emp
where      trunc(hiredate) = '01-MAY-01';
```

Changing the statement to the following would allow for an index lookup:

```
select     empno, ename, deptno
from       emp
where      hiredate > '01-MAY-01'
and        hiredate < (TO_DATE('01-MAY-01') + 0.99999);
```

TIP
*By altering the values being compared to the column, and not the
columns themselves, the indexes become available. This is used to
eliminate full table scans.*

For further details on function-based indexes, see the "Function-Based Indexes" section later
in this chapter.

Comparing Mismatched Data Types

One of the more difficult performance issues to find results from a comparison of differing data types. Oracle does not complain about the types being incompatible—quite the opposite. For example, Oracle implicitly converts the data in the VARCHAR2 column to match the numeric data type that it is being compared to. Consider the following example where account_number is a VARCHAR2.

If the Account_Number column uses a VARCHAR2 data type, the following statement may cause a full table scan to be performed, even if the account_number column is indexed:

```
select      bank_name, address, city, state, zip
from        banks
where       account_number = 990354;
```

Oracle internally changes the WHERE clause to be

```
to_number(account_number)=990354
```

which suppresses the index. An EXPLAIN PLAN of this query only shows that the table was accessed using a "FULL SCAN" (usually to the bewilderment of the coder). To some DBAs and developers, this would appear to be a rare situation, but in many systems numeric values are zero-padded and specified as VARCHAR2. The preceding statement should be rewritten as follows to use the index on the account number by correctly using the single quote marks for the field:

```
select      bank_name, address, city, state, zip
from        banks
where       account_number = '000990354';
```

Alternatively, the Account_Number column could be defined to use the NUMBER data type, provided the leading zeros are not critical information for the column.

TIP
Comparing mismatched data types can cause Oracle to internally suppress an index. Even an EXPLAIN PLAN on the query will not help you understand why a full table scan is being performed. Only the knowledge of your data types can help you solve this problem.

Selectivity

Oracle offers several methods to determine the benefit of using an index, which depends upon both the query and the data. First, determine the number of unique or distinct keys in the index. You can determine the number of distinct values by analyzing the table or the index. You can then query the Distinct_Keys column of the USER_INDEXES view to examine the results of the analysis. By comparing the number of distinct keys to the number of rows in the table (as shown in the Num_Rows column of USER_INDEXES), you can determine the selectivity of the index. The greater the selectivity, the better the index would be for returning small numbers of rows.

TIP
*The selectivity of an index is what helps the cost-based optimizer
determine an execution path. The more selective the index is, the
fewer the number of rows that will be returned, on average, for each
distinct value. For concatenated indexes, the additional columns
added to the index do not improve the selectivity greatly, and the cost
of the additional columns may outweigh the gain.*

The Clustering Factor

The clustering factor is a measure of the ordered-ness of an index in comparison to the table that
it is based on. It is used to check the cost of a table lookup following an index access (multiplying
the clustering factor by the selectivity gives the cost of the operation). The clustering factor
records the number of blocks that will be read when scanning the index. If the index being used
has a *large* clustering factor, then more table data blocks have to be visited in order to get the
rows in each index block (because adjacent rows are in different blocks). If the clustering factor
is close to the number of *blocks* in the table, then the index is well ordered, but if the clustering
factor is close to the number of *rows* in the table, then the index is *not* well ordered. The clustering
factor is computed (briefly only):

1. The index is scanned in order.

2. The block portion of the ROWID pointed at by the current indexed value is compared to
   the previous indexed value (comparing adjacent rows in the index).

3. If the ROWID points to different TABLE blocks, the clustering factor is incremented (this
   is done for the entire index).

The Clustering_Factor column in the USER_INDEXES view gives an indication as to how
organized the data is compared to the indexed columns. If the value of the Clustering_Factor
column value is close to the number of leaf blocks in the index, the data is well ordered in the
table. If the value is *not* close to the number of leaf blocks in the index, then the data in the table
is not well ordered. The leaf blocks of an index store the indexed values as well as the ROWIDs
to which they point.

For example, say the Customer_Id for the CUSTOMERS table was generated from a sequence
generator and the Customer_Id was the primary key on the table. The index on Customer_Id
would have a clustering factor very close to the number of leaf blocks (well ordered). As the
customers are added to the database, they are stored sequentially in the table the same way the
sequence numbers are issued from the sequence generator (well ordered). However, an index on
the customer_name column would have a very high clustering factor because the arrangement of
the customer names is random throughout the table.

The clustering factor can have an impact on SQL statements that perform range scans. With
a low clustering factor (relative to the number of leaf blocks), the number of blocks needed to
satisfy the query is reduced. This increases the possibility that the data blocks would already
be in memory. A high clustering factor relative to the number of leaf blocks may increase the
number of data blocks required to satisfy a range query based on the indexed column.

TIP

The clustering of data within the table can be used to improve the performance of statements that perform range scan–type operations. By determining how the column is being used in the statements, indexing these column(s) may be a great benefit.

The Binary Height

The binary height of an index plays a major role in the amount of I/O that needs to be performed to return the ROWID to the user process. Each level in the binary height adds an extra block that needs to be read, and because the blocks are not being read sequentially, they each require a separate I/O operation. In Figure 2-1, an index with a binary height of 3 returning one row to the user would require four blocks to be read: three from the index and one from the table. As the binary height of an index increases, so will the amount of I/O required to retrieve the data.

After analyzing an index, you can query the blevel column of DBA_INDEXES to see its binary height:

```
EXECUTE DBMS_STATS.GATHER_INDEX_STATS ('SCOTT','EMP_ID1');
PL/SQL procedure successfully completed.
select      blevel, index_name
from        dba_indexes
where       index_name = 'EMP_ID1';

    BLEVEL INDEX_NAME
---------- ------------------------------
         0 EMP_ID1
```

TIP

Analyzing the index or the table will provide the binary height of the index. Use the blevel column in the USER_INDEXES view to check the binary height of the indexes.

The binary height increases mainly because of the number of non-NULL values for the indexed column in the table and the narrowness of the range of values in the indexed columns. Having a large number of deleted rows in the index can also cause the height to increase. Rebuilding the index may help to decrease the height. While these steps will reduce the number of I/Os performed against the index, the performance benefits may be small. If the number of deleted rows within an index approaches 20–25 percent, rebuild the indexes to help reduce the binary height and the amount of empty space that is being read during an I/O.

TIP

In general, the larger the database block size, the smaller the binary height of the index. Each additional level in the binary height (blevel) adds additional performance costs during DML.

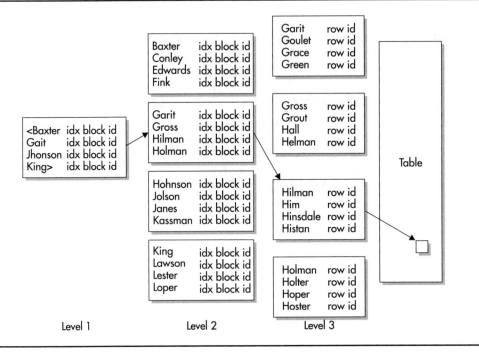

FIGURE 2-1. *Index with binary height or blevel = 3 (Level 3 is where the leaf blocks reside)*

Using Histograms

Histograms record the distribution of data when you analyze a table or index. With this information in hand, the cost-based optimizer can decide to use an index for conditions it knows will return a small number of rows and bypass the index when the condition will return many rows based on the limiting condition. The use of histograms is not limited to indexes. Any column of a table can have a histogram built on it.

The main reason for generating histograms is to help the optimizer plan properly if the data in a table is heavily skewed. For example, if one or two values make up a large percentage of a table, the related indexes may not help to reduce the number of I/Os required to satisfy the query. The creation of a histogram will let the cost-based optimizer know when using the index is appropriate, or when 80 percent of the table is going to be returned because of the value in the WHERE clause.

When creating histograms, specify a size. This size relates to the number of buckets for the histogram. Each bucket will contain information about the value of the column(s) and the number of rows.

```
EXECUTE DBMS_STATS.GATHER_TABLE_STATS
('scott','company', METHOD_OPT => 'FOR COLUMNS SIZE 10 company_code');
PL/SQL procedure successfully completed.
```

The preceding query will create a ten-bucket histogram on the COMPANY table, as shown in Figure 2-2. The values for the COMPANY_CODE column will be divided into the ten buckets as displayed in the figure. This example shows a large number (80 percent) of the company_code is equal to 1430. As is also shown in the figure, most of the width-balanced buckets contain only 3 rows; a single bucket contains 73 rows. In the height-balanced version of this distribution, each bucket has the same number of rows and most of the bucket endpoints are '1430', reflecting the skewed distribution of the data.

Oracle's histograms are height-balanced as opposed to width-balanced. Consequently, all of the buckets in the histogram contain the same number of rows. The starting and ending points for a bucket are determined by the number of rows containing those values. The width-balanced histogram would specify the range values for each bucket and then count the number of rows within that range, not an ideal option.

TIP
If the data in a table is skewed, histograms will provide the cost-based optimizer a balanced picture of the distribution (by balancing it into buckets). Using the histograms on columns that are not skewed will not provide an increase in performance.

TIP
By default, Oracle creates 75 buckets in a histogram. You can specify SIZE values ranging from 1 to 254.

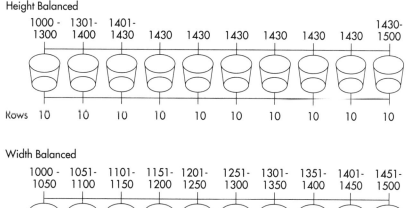

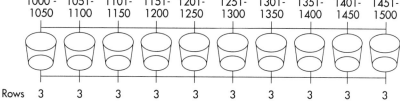

FIGURE 2-2. *A histogram is built on a Company_Code field with a size of 10 (buckets).*

Fast Full Scans

During a fast full scan of an index Oracle reads all of the leaf blocks in a b-tree index. The index is being read sequentially, so multiple blocks can be read at once. The DB_FILE_MULTIBLOCK_READ_COUNT parameter in the initialization file controls the number of blocks that can be read simultaneously. The fast full scan usually requires fewer physical I/Os than a full table scan, allowing the query to be resolved faster.

The fast full scan can be used if all of the columns in the query for the table are in the index with the leading edge of the index not part of the WHERE condition (you may need to specify the INDEX_FFS hint as detailed in Chapter 7). In the following example, the emp table is used. As shown earlier in this chapter, it has a concatenated index on the columns empno, ename, and deptno.

```
select     empno, ename, deptno
from       emp
where      deptno = 30;
```

Since all of the columns in the SQL statement are in the index, a fast full scan is available. Index fast full scans are commonly performed during joins in which only the indexed join key columns are queried. As an alternative, Oracle may perform a skip-scan access of the index; the optimizer should consider the histogram for the Deptno column (if one is available) and decide which of the available access paths yields the lowest possible performance cost.

TIP
If the indexes are relatively small in comparison to the overall size of the table, the fast full scan may provide the performance burst necessary for the application. With concatenated indexes that contain most of the columns of a table, the index may be larger than the actual table and the fast full scan could cause degradation in performance.

Skip-Scans

As discussed in the section "Concatenated Indexes" earlier in this chapter, the index skip-scan feature enables the optimizer to use a concatenated index even if its leading column is not listed in the WHERE clause. Index skip-scans are faster than full scans of the index, requiring fewer reads to be performed. For example, the following queries show the difference between a full index scan and a skip-scan. See Chapter 6 to better understand the execution plan or the statistics displayed in the following listing. In this listing, the EMP5 table has many hundreds of thousands of rows.

Following the execution of the queries, the listing shows the time the query took, its execution path within the database, and statistics showing the number of logical reads (consistent gets) and physical reads required to resolve the query.

```
create index skip1 on emp5(job,empno);
Index created.

select count(*)
from    emp5
where   empno = 7900;
```

```
Elapsed: 00:00:03.13 (Result is a single row...not displayed)

Execution Plan
   0        SELECT STATEMENT Optimizer=CHOOSE (Cost=4 Card=1 Bytes=5)
   1    0     SORT (AGGREGATE)
   2    1       INDEX (FAST FULL SCAN) OF 'SKIP1' (NON-UNIQUE)

Statistics
6826   consistent gets
6819   physical reads

select /*+ index(emp5 skip1) */ count(*)
from    emp5
where   empno = 7900;
Elapsed: 00:00:00.56

Execution Plan
   0        SELECT STATEMENT Optimizer=CHOOSE (Cost=6 Card=1 Bytes=5)
   1    0     SORT (AGGREGATE)
   2    1       INDEX (SKIP SCAN) OF 'SKIP1' (NON-UNIQUE)

Statistics
21   consistent gets
17   physical reads
```

As shown in the listing, the second option used an INDEX (SKIP SCAN) operation to read the index. That execution path required 21 logical reads, which in turn required 17 physical I/Os. The first option performed an INDEX (FAST FULL SCAN) operation, which required a significantly greater number of logical and physical I/Os.

To influence the optimizer to choose a skip-scan, you may need to use a hint in the query as shown in the listing. The hint will influence the optimizer and bias it toward the execution path you specify.

TIP

For large tables with concatenated Indexes, the index skip-scan feature can provide quick access even when the leading column of the index is not used in a limiting condition.

Types of Indexes

The following is a list of indexes discussed in this section:

- B-tree
- Bitmap
- Hash
- Index-organized table
- Reverse key

■ Function-based

■ Partitioned (local and global)

■ Bitmap join indexes

 ## B-Tree Indexes

B-tree indexes are the general-purpose indexes in Oracle. They are the default index types created when creating indexes. B-tree indexes can be single-column (simple) indexes or composite/concatenated (multicolumn) indexes. B-tree indexes can have up to 32 columns.

In Figure 2-3, a b-tree index is created on the last_name column of the employee table. This index has a binary height of three; consequently, Oracle must go through two branch blocks to get to the leaf block containing the ROWID. Within each branch block, there are branch rows containing the block ID of the next block ID within the chain.

A leaf block contains the index values, the ROWID, and pointers to the previous and next leaf blocks. Oracle has the ability to transverse the binary tree in both directions. B-tree indexes contain the ROWIDs for every row in the table that has a value in the indexed column. Oracle does not index rows that contain NULL values in the indexed column. If the index is a concatenation of multiple columns and one of the columns contains a NULL value, the row will be in the index and the column containing the NULL value will be left empty.

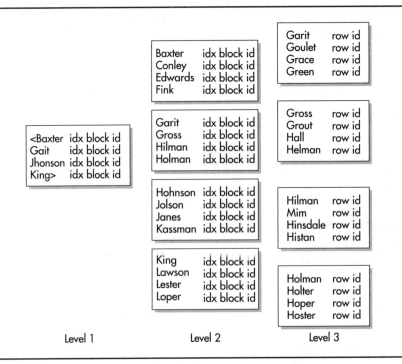

FIGURE 2-3. *Tree index creation*

TIP
The values of the indexed columns are stored in an index. For this reason, you can build concatenated (composite) indexes that can be used to satisfy a query without accessing the table. This eliminates the need to go to the table to retrieve the data, reducing I/O.

Bitmap Indexes

Bitmap indexes are ideal for decision support systems (DSS) and data warehouses. They should not be used for tables accessed via transaction processing applications. Bitmap indexes provide fast access of very large tables using low to medium cardinality (number of distinct values) columns. Although bitmap indexes can have up to 30 columns, they are generally used for a small number of columns.

For example, your table may contain a column called Sex with two possible values: male and female. The cardinality would be only 2, and it would be a prime candidate for a bitmap index if users frequently query the table by the value of the Sex column. The real power of the bitmap index is seen when a table contains multiple bitmap indexes. With multiple bitmap indexes available, Oracle has the ability to merge the result sets from each of the bitmap indexes to quickly eliminate the unwanted data.

The following listing shows an example of creating a bitmap index:

```
create bitmap index dept_idx2_bm on dept (deptno);
Index created.
```

TIP
Use bitmap indexes for columns with a low cardinality. An example would be a column called "sex" with two possible values of "male" or "female" (the cardinality is only 2). Bitmaps are very fast for low cardinality columns (few distinct values), since the size of the index is substantially smaller than a b-tree index. Since they are very small when compared to a low-cardinality b-tree index, you can often retrieve over half of the rows in the table and still use a bitmap index.

Bitmap indexes usually outperform b-trees when loading tables (INSERT operations) in batch (single-user) operation when the bulk of the entries do not add new values to the bitmap. You should not use bitmap indexes when multiple sessions will be concurrently inserting rows into the table, as occurs in most transaction-processing applications.

Bitmap Index Example
Consider a sample table called PARTICIPANT that contains surveys from individuals. Each of the columns Age_Code, Income_Level, Education_Level, and Marital_Status has a separate bitmap index built on it. The balance of the data in each histogram and the execution path for a query accessing each of the bitmap indexes are displayed in Figure 2-4. The execution path in the figure shows how the multiple bitmap indexes have been merged creating a significant performance gain.

AGE_CODE	INCOME_LEVEL	EDUCATION_LEVEL	MARITAL_STATUS
18-22 A	10,000 - 14,000 AA	High School HS	Single S
23-27 B	14,001 - 18,000 BB	Bachelor BS	Married M
28-32 C	18,001 - 22,000 CC	Masters MS	Divorced D
33-37 D	22,001 - 26,000 DD	Doctorate PhD	Widowed W
...	...	...	...

```
Select …
From Participant
Where Age_code = 'B'
   And Income_Level = 'DD'
   And Education_Level = 'MS'
   And Marital_Status = 'M'

SELECT STAEMENT Optimizer=CHOOSE
   SORT (AGGREGATE)
     BITMAP CONVERSION (RowID)
       BITMAP AND
           BITMAP INDEX (SINGLE VALUE) of 'PART_INCOME_LEVEL'
           BITMAP INDEX (SINGLE VALUE) of 'PART_AGE_CODE'
           BITMAP INDEX (SINGLE VALUE) of 'PART_EDUCATION_LEVEL'
           BITMAP INDEX (SINGLE VALUE) of 'PART_MARITAL_STATUS'
```

FIGURE 2-4.   *Bitmap index creation*

As shown in Figure 2-4, the optimizer uses each of the four separate bitmap indexes whose columns were referenced in the WHERE clause. Each of those bitmaps records pointers (like 1 or 0), indicating which rows in the table contain the known values in the bitmap. Given that, Oracle then performs a BITMAP AND operation to find which rows would be returned from all four of the bitmaps. That value is then converted into a ROWID value and the query proceeds with the rest of the processing. Note that all four of the columns had very low cardinality, yet the index allowed the matching rows to be returned very quickly.

TIP
Merging multiple bitmap indexes can lead to significant performance improvement when combined in a single query. Bitmap indexes also work better with fixed-length data types than they do with variable-length data types. Large block sizes improve the storage and read performance of bitmap indexes.

The following query displays index types. B-tree indexes are listed as 'NORMAL'; bitmap indexes will have an index_type value of 'BITMAP'.

```
select     index_name, index_type
from       user_indexes;
```

TIP
*To query a list of your bitmap indexes, query the index_type column
in the USER_INDEXES view.*

Bitmap indexes are not recommended for online transaction processing (OLTP) applications. B-tree indexes contain a ROWID with the indexed value, so Oracle has the ability to lock the index at the row level. Bitmap indexes are stored as compressed indexed values, which can contain a range of ROWIDs, so Oracle has to lock the entire range of the ROWIDs for a given value. This type of locking has the potential to cause deadlock situations with certain types of DML statements. SELECT statements are not affected by this locking problem.

Bitmap indexes have several restrictions:

- Bitmap indexes are not considered by the rule-based optimizer.

- Performing an ALTER TABLE statement and modifying a column that has a bitmap index built on it invalidates the index.

- Bitmap indexes do not contain any of the data from the column and cannot be used for any type of integrity checking.

- Bitmap indexes cannot be declared as unique.

- Bitmap indexes have a maximum length of 30.

TIP
Don't use bitmap indexes in heavy OLTP environments.

Hash Indexes

Using *hash* indexes requires the use of hash clusters. When you create a cluster or hash cluster, you define a cluster key. The cluster key tells Oracle how to store the tables in the cluster. When data is stored, all the rows relating to the cluster key are stored in the same database blocks. With the data being stored in the same database blocks, using the hash index for an exact match in a WHERE clause Oracle can access the data by performing one hash function and one I/O—as opposed to accessing the data by using a b-tree index with a binary height of four, where potentially four I/Os would need to be performed to retrieve the data. As shown in Figure 2-5, the query is an equivalence query, matching the hashed column to an exact value. Oracle can quickly use that value to determine where the row is physically stored, based on the hashing function.

Hash indexes can potentially be the fastest way to access data in the database, but they do come with their drawbacks. The number of distinct values for the cluster key needs to be known before the hash cluster can be created. This value needs to be specified at the time of creation. Underestimating the number of distinct values can cause collisions (two cluster key values with the same hash value) within the cluster, which are very costly. Collisions cause overflow buffers to be used to store the additional rows, thus causing additional I/O. If the number of distinct hash values has been underestimated, the cluster will need to be re-created to alter the value. An ALTER CLUSTER command cannot change the number of HASHKEYS.

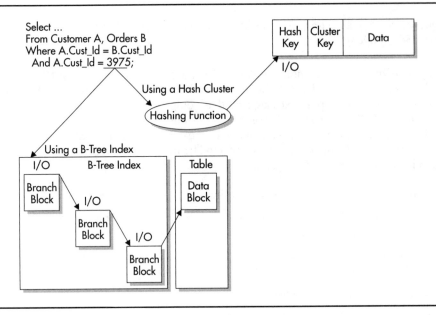

FIGURE 2-5. *Using hash indexes*

Hash clusters have a tendency to waste space. If it is not possible to determine how much space is required to hold all of the rows for a given cluster key, space may be wasted. If it is not possible to allocate additional space within the cluster for future growth, then hash clusters may not be the best option.

If the application often performs full table scans on the clustered table(s), hash clusters may not be the appropriate option. Because of the amount of empty space within the cluster to allow for future growth, full table scans can be very resource-intensive.

Caution should be taken before implementing hash clusters. The application should be reviewed fully to ensure that enough information is known about the tables and data before implementing this option. Generally, hashing is best for static data with primarily sequential values.

TIP
Hash indexes are most useful when the limiting condition specifies an exact value rather than a range of values.

Index-Organized Tables

An *index-organized table* alters the storage structure of a table to that of a b-tree index, sorted on the table's primary key. This unique type of table is treated like any other table—all DML and DDL statements are allowed. ROWIDs are not associated with the rows in the table because of the structure of the table.

Index-organized tables provide faster key-based access to the data for statements involving exact match and range searches on the primary key columns. UPDATE and DELETE statements based on the primary key values should perform better because the rows are physically ordered. The amount of storage required is reduced because values of the key columns are not duplicated in the table and then again in an index.

If you do not frequently query the data by the primary key column, then you will need to create secondary indexes on other columns in the index-organized table. Applications that do not frequently query tables by their primary keys do not realize the full benefits of using index-organized tables. Consider using index-organized tables for tables that are always accessed using exact matches or range scans on the primary key.

TIP
You can create secondary indexes on index-organized tables.

Reverse Key Indexes

When sequential data is loaded, the index may encounter I/O-related bottlenecks. During the data loads, one part of the index, and one part of the disk, may be used much more heavily than any other part. To alleviate this problem, you should store your index tablespaces on disk architectures that permit the files to be physically striped across multiple disks.

Oracle provides *reverse key* indexes as another solution to this performance problem. When data is stored in a reverse key index, its values are reversed prior to being stored in the index. Thus the values 1234, 1235, and 1236 are stored as 4321, 5321, and 6321. As a result, the index may update different index blocks for each inserted row.

TIP
If you have a limited number of disks and large concurrent sequential loads to perform, reverse key indexes may be a viable solution.

You cannot use reverse key indexes with bitmap indexes or index-organized tables.

Function-Based Indexes

You can create *function-based* indexes on your tables. Without function-based indexes, any query that performed a function on a column could not use that column's index. For example, the following query could not use an index on the Job column unless it is a function-based index:

```
select *
from   emp
where  UPPER(job) = 'MGR';
```

The following query *could* use an index on the JOB column, but it would not return rows where the job column had a value of 'Mgr' or 'mgr':

```
select *
from   emp
where  job = 'MGR';
```

Function-Based Indexes

You can create indexes that allow a function-based column or data to be supported by index accesses. Instead of creating an index on the column Job, you can create an index on the column expression UPPER(Job), as shown in the following listing:

```
create index EMP$UPPER_JOB on
emp(UPPER(job));
```

Although function-based indexes can be useful, be sure to consider the following questions when creating them:

- Can you restrict the functions that will be used on the column? If so, can you restrict all functions from being performed on the column?

- Do you have adequate storage space for the additional indexes?

- How will the increased number of indexes per column impact the performance of DML commands against the table?

Function-based indexes are useful, but you should implement them sparingly. The more indexes you create on a table, the longer all INSERTs, UPDATEs, and DELETEs will take.

NOTE
For function-based indexes to be used by the optimizer, you must set the QUERY_REWRITE_ENABLED initialization parameter to TRUE.

To see the magnitude of the benefit of function-based indexes, consider the following example that queries a table named SAMPLE that contains a million rows.

```
select      count(*)
from        sample
where       ratio(balance,limit) >.5;

Elapsed time: 20.1 minutes

create index ratio_idx1 on
sample (ratio(balance, limit));
select      count(*)
from        sample
where       ratio(balance,limit) >.5;

Elapsed time: 7 seconds!!!
```

Partitioned Indexes

A *partitioned* index is simply an index broken into multiple pieces. By breaking an index into multiple physical pieces, you are accessing much smaller pieces (faster), and you may separate the pieces onto different disk drives (reducing I/O contention). Both b-tree and bitmap indexes can be partitioned. Hash indexes cannot be partitioned. Partitioning can work several different ways. The tables can be partitioned and the indexes are not partitioned; the table is not partitioned, but the index is; or both the table and index are partitioned. Either way, the cost-based optimizer must be used. Partitioning adds many possibilities to help improve performance and increase maintainability.

There are two types of partitioned indexes: local and global. Each type has two subsets, prefixed and non-prefixed. A table can have any number or combination of the different types of indexes built on its columns. If bitmap indexes are used, they must be local indexes. The main reason to partition the indexes is to reduce the size of the index that needs to be read and to enable placing the partitions in separate tablespaces to help improve reliability and availability.

Oracle also supports parallel query and parallel DML when using partitioned tables and indexes (see Chapter 11 for more information). This will add the extra benefit of multiple processes helping to process the statement faster.

Local (Commonly Used Indexes)

Local indexes are indexes that are partitioned using the same partition key and same range boundaries as the table. Each partition of a local index will only contain keys and ROWIDs from its corresponding table partition. Local indexes can be b-tree or bitmap indexes. If they are b-tree indexes, they can be unique or non-unique.

Local indexes support partition independence, meaning that individual partitions can be added, truncated, dropped, split, taken offline, etc., without dropping or rebuilding the indexes. Oracle maintains the local indexes automatically. Local index partitions can also be rebuilt individually while the rest of the partition goes unaffected.

Prefixed   *Prefixed* indexes are indexes that contain keys from the partitioning key as the leading edge of the index. For example, let's take the participant table again. Say the table was created and range-partitioned using the survey_id and survey_date columns and a local prefixed index is created on the survey_id column. The partitions of the index are equipartitioned, meaning that the partitions of the index are created with the same range boundaries as those of the table (see Figure 2-6).

TIP
Local prefixed indexes allow Oracle to quickly prune unneeded partitions. This means that the partitions that do not contain any of the values appearing in the WHERE clause will not need to be accessed, thus improving the performance of the statement.

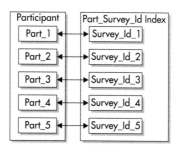

FIGURE 2-6.   *Partitioned, prefixed indexes*

Non-Prefixed   *Non-prefixed* indexes are indexes that do not have the leading column of the partitioning key as the leading column of the index. Using the same participant table with the same partitioning key (survey_id and survey_date), an index on the survey_date column would be a local non-prefixed index. A local non-prefixed index can be created on any column in the table, but each partition of the index will only contain the keys for the corresponding partition of the table (see Figure 2-7).

For a non-prefixed index to be unique, it must contain a subset of the partitioning key. In this example, we would need a combination of columns, including the survey_date and/or the survey_id columns (as long as the survey_id column was not the leading edge of the index, in which case it would be a prefixed index).

TIP
For a non-prefixed index to be unique, it must contain a subset of the partitioning key.

Global Partitioned Indexes
Global partitioned indexes contain keys from multiple table partitions in a single index partition. The partitioning key of a global partitioned index is different or specifies a different range of values from the partitioned table. The creator of the global partitioned index is responsible for defining the ranges and values for the partitioning key. Global indexes can only be b-tree indexes. Global partitioned indexes are not maintained by Oracle by default. If a partition is truncated, added, split, dropped, etc., the global partitioned indexes will need to be rebuilt unless you specify the UPDATE GLOBAL INDEXES clause of the ALTER TABLE command when modifying the table.

Prefixed   Normally, global prefixed indexes are not equipartitioned with the underlying table. Nothing prevents the index from being equipartitioned, but Oracle does not take advantage of the equipartitioning when generating query plans or executing partition maintenance operations. If the index is going to be equipartitioned, it should be created as a local index to allow Oracle to maintain the index and use it to help prune partitions that will not be needed (see Figure 2-8). As shown in the figure, the three index partitions each contain index entries that point to rows in multiple table partitions.

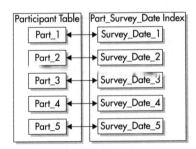

FIGURE 2-7.   *Partitioned, non-prefixed indexes*

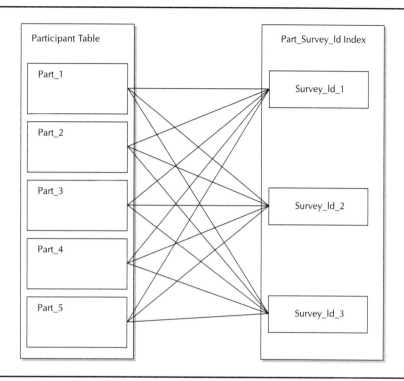

FIGURE 2-8.   *Partitioned, global prefixed index*

TIP
*If a global index is going to be equipartitioned, it should be created as
a local index to allow Oracle to maintain the index and use it to help
prune partitions that will not be needed.*

Non-prefixed   Non-prefixed global indexes are not supported by Oracle.

Bitmap Join Indexes

A *bitmap join* index is a bitmap index based on the join of two tables. Bitmap join indexes
are used in data warehousing environments to improve the performance of queries that join
dimension tables to fact tables. When creating a bitmap join index, the standard approach is to
join a commonly used dimension table to the fact table within the index. When a user queries
the fact table and the dimension table together in a query, the join does not need to be performed
because the join results are already available in the bitmap join index. Further performance
benefits are gained from the compression of ROWIDs within the bitmap join index, reducing
the number of I/Os required to access the data.

Bitmap Join Indexes

When creating a bitmap join index, you specify both tables involved. The syntax should follow this model:

```
create bitmap index FACT_DIM_COL_IDX
    on FACT(DIM.Descr_Col)
  from FACT, DIM
 where FACT.JoinCol = DIM.JoinCol;
```

The syntax for bitmap joins is unusual in that it contains both a FROM clause and a WHERE clause, and it references two separate tables. The indexed column is usually a description column within the dimension table—that is, if the dimension is CUSTOMER and its primary key is Customer_ID, you would normally index a column such as Customer_Name. If the FACT table is named SALES, you might create an index using the following command:

```
create bitmap index SALES_CUST_NAME_IDX
    on SALES(CUSTOMER.Customer_Name)
  from SALES, CUSTOMER
 where SALES.Customer_ID=CUSTOMER.Customer_ID;
```

If a user then queries the SALES and CUSTOMER tables with a WHERE clause that specifies a value for the Customer_Name column, the optimizer can use the bitmap join index to quickly return the rows that match both the join condition and the Customer_Name condition.

The use of bitmap join indexes is restricted; you can only index the columns in the dimension tables. The columns used for the join must be primary key or unique constraints in the dimension tables, and if it is a composite primary key, you must use each of the columns in your join. You cannot create a bitmap join index on an index-organized table, and the restrictions that apply to regular bitmap indexes also apply to bitmap join indexes.

Fast Index Rebuilding

The REBUILD option of the ALTER INDEX statement is executed to quickly rebuild an index using the existing index instead of the table:

```
alter index cust_idx1 rebuild parallel
tablespace cust_tblspc1
storage (pctincrease 0);
Index altered.
```

Modifications to the STORAGE clause can be made at this time and the parallel option may also be used.

TIP
Use the REBUILD option of the ALTER INDEX statement for quickly rebuilding an index using the existing index instead of the table. You must have enough space to store both indexes during this operation.

TIP

You can use the REBUILD ONLINE option to allow DML operations on the table or partition during the index rebuild. You cannot specify REBUILD ONLINE for bitmap indexes or for indexes that enforce referential integrity constraints.

Tips Review

- As you upgrade Oracle versions, be sure to test your application's queries to determine whether the execution paths for your queries still use the indexes that were used prior to the upgrade. See if the execution plan has changed and if it is better or worse.

- Query DBA_INDEXES and DBA_IND_COLUMNS to retrieve a list of the indexes on a given table. Use USER_INDEXES and USER_IND_COLUMNS to retrieve information for only your schema.

- Avoid hard-coding Oracle's ROWID into specific code. The ROWID structure in the past has changed from version to version, and it will probably change again in future releases. I recommend against *ever* hard-coding a ROWID.

- You can create your indexes and analyze them in a single step by using the COMPUTE STATISTICS clause of the CREATE INDEX command.

- Using the default values clause for a column of a table will cause NULL values to be disallowed and eliminate the performance problems associated with using NULL values.

- By using functions (such as a TO_DATE or TO_CHAR) that alter the values being compared to a column and not the columns themselves, the indexes become available for use that might have been suppressed had you used the function on the column itself.

- Comparing mismatched data types can cause Oracle to internally suppress an index. Even an EXPLAIN PLAN on the query will not help you understand why a full table scan is being performed.

- The selectivity of an index is what helps the cost-based optimizer determine an execution path. The more selective, the fewer number of rows that will be returned. Improve the selectivity by creating concatenated/composite (multicolumn) indexes.

- In general, the larger the database block size, the smaller the binary height of the index.

- Each additional level in the blevel adds additional performance costs during DML.

- The clustering of data within the table can be used to improve the performance of statements that perform range scan type operations. By determining how the column is being used in the statements, indexing these column(s) may be a great benefit.

- Analyzing the index or the table will provide the binary height of the index. Use the blevel column in the USER_INDEXES view to check the binary height of the indexes.

- If the number of deleted rows within an index approaches 20–25 percent, rebuild the indexes to help reduce the binary height and the amount of empty space that is being read during an I/O.

- If the data in a table is skewed, histograms will provide the cost-based optimizer a picture of the distribution. Using the histograms on columns that are not skewed will not provide an increase in performance but will probably degrade it.

- By default, Oracle creates 75 buckets in a histogram. You can specify SIZE values ranging from 1 to 254.

- For large tables with concatenated indexes, the index skip-scan feature can provide quick access even when the leading column of the index is not used in a limiting condition.

- The values of the indexed columns are stored in an index. For this reason, you can build concatenated (composite) indexes that can be used to satisfy a query without accessing the table. This eliminates the need to go to the table to retrieve the data, reducing I/O.

- Use bitmap indexes for columns with a low cardinality. An example is a column called Sex with two possible values of male or female (the cardinality is only 2).

- To query a list of your bitmap indexes, query the USER_INDEXES view.

- Don't use bitmap indexes on tables that are heavily inserted into primarily in heavy OLTP environments; learn the restrictions associated with bitmap indexes.

- Caution should be taken before implementing hash clusters. The application should be reviewed carefully to ensure that enough information is known about the tables and data before implementing this option. Generally speaking, hashing is best for static data with primarily sequential values.

- Hash indexes are most useful when the limiting condition specifies an exact value rather than a range of values.

- Consider using index-organized tables for tables that are always accessed using exact matches or range scans on the primary key.

- If you have a limited number of disks and large concurrent sequential loads to perform, reverse key indexes may be a viable solution.

- For function-based indexes to be used by the optimizer, you must set the QUERY_REWRITE_ENABLED initialization parameter to TRUE.

- Local prefixed indexes allow Oracle to quickly prune unneeded partitions. The partitions that do not contain any of the values appearing in the WHERE clause will not need to be accessed, thus improving the performance of the statement.

- For a non-prefixed index to be unique, it must contain a subset of the partitioning key.

- Specify the UPDATE GLOBAL INDEXES clause of the ALTER TABLE command when modifying a partitioned table. By default, you will need to rebuild global indexes when altering a partitioned table.

- ■ If a global index is going to be equipartitioned, it should be created as a local index to allow Oracle to maintain the index and use it to help prune partitions that will not be needed.

- ■ Use bitmap join indexes to improve the performance of joins within data warehousing environments.

- ■ Use the REBUILD option of the ALTER INDEX statement for quickly rebuilding an index using the existing index instead of the table.

- ■ You can use the REBUILD ONLINE option to allow DML operations on the table or partition during the index rebuild. You cannot specify REBUILD ONLINE for bitmap indexes or for indexes that enforce referential integrity constraints.

References

Greg Pucka, *Oracle Indexing* (TUSC)
Oracle7 Server Tuning (Oracle Corporation)
Oracle8 Server Tuning (Oracle Corporation)
Server Concepts (Oracle Corporation)
Server Reference (Oracle Corporation)
Kevin Loney, *Oracle8 DBA Handbook* (Oracle Press)
Rich Niemiec, Tuning Tips: You Will Be Toast! (Oracle Press)
Metalink Note: 39836.1

Greg Pucka contributed the major portion of this chapter.
Kevin Loney contributed the major portion of the update to this chapter.

CHAPTER
3

Disk Implementation Methodology and ASM (DBA)

Oracle has changed the landscape of disk access in Oracle 10g with the release of Automatic Storage Management (ASM). There will be a heavy focus in this chapter on ASM in addition to the non-ASM-specific disk implementation methodology in Oracle.

In the last several years, it has seemed that disk configuration technique was reaching the point where there wasn't much more you could do to improve the performance of your system without greatly complicating your life as a DBA. If your system operated with some unique qualities or you chose to review the I/O activity on your tablespaces on a frequent basis, you might be able to achieve slightly better performance than simply mashing all your disk use into a single logical device, but for most people out there, this just wasn't worth it. If you used RAW partitions and were diligent, you could get some performance advantages from using that "technology," but again, it didn't simplify your life as a DBA. Finally, with the enormous leap in capacity of single devices, even in the high-end Fibre Channel sector, things were further complicated, since now it was simple to restrict yourself to only four or six disks, whereas before you may have had a full array or multiple arrays of disks. In the most recent releases of the Oracle Database, you have been given a whole new toolbox.

More features are now available for managing how the data resides on disk. More has been released in the last 18 months for disk management than ever before. To make it even better, almost anyone running an Oracle database can use these new features. Don't worry, this chapter will still talk about balancing your disk and eliminating fragmentation, but it will also discuss the new features we can utilize to rid ourselves of the repeated effort these activities required in the past or very possibly prevent us from having to do them altogether.

To keep your system running at its peak, this chapter offers the following tips:

- Understanding storage hardware and its performance implications
- Understanding RAID levels
- Distributing "key" data files across file systems to minimize contention
- Moving data files to balanced file I/O
- Using Locally Managed Tablespaces (LMT) vs. dictionary-managed tablespaces
- Understanding bigfile tablespaces and getting to the eight-exabyte Oracle database
- Viewing file and tablespace information to determine problem areas
- Understanding ASM instances, installation, and SGA parameter sizing
- Understanding ASM disks, diskgroups, and multipathing
- Understanding ASM best practices and rebalancing practices
- Avoiding disk contention and managing large tables by using partitions
- Sizing extents properly to eliminate fragmentation, reduce chaining, and keep performance optimal
- Managing redo and rollbacks in the database for speed
- Using UNDO management

- Sorting only in a TEMPORARY tablespace
- Having multiple control files on different disks and controllers
- Using advance file system features and raw devices to improve performance
- Understanding issues to consider in the planning stages of your system

Disk Arrays: Not a Choice Anymore

It is now the norm to configure disks with RAID (Redundant Array of Independent/Inexpensive Disks). RAID is here to stay, and one would be hard pressed to buy even a midrange system without it. Later in this chapter, you'll see that ASM also provides levels of redundancy. Even in the personal computing area, using some hardware-based configuration of redundant disks has become more commonplace. For the DBA, this means that more than ever, care must be taken to ensure that the disk array configuration used enhances I/O while also providing appropriate protection against drive failure. Regardless of whether the RAID configuration is hardware or software based (hardware based is usually faster), the configuration should be configured properly for best performance, without sacrificing protection.

Use Disk Arrays to Improve Performance and Availability

A RAID LUN (logical unit number) is created by grouping several disks in such a way that the individual disks act as one logical disk (grouped into a volume or virtual disk). Prior to the advent of the storage area network (SAN), a LUN was exactly the address (number) for the disk drive. Therefore, during normal operation, a single logical device gets the benefit of multiple physical devices behind it. This means faster access to data (when configured properly) and the ability to have storage volumes that are significantly greater than the physical limit of an individual device. If a disk fails and all the data on the disk is destroyed, the group of disks can be structured so that the data exists in more than one place. The system never goes down because of the failure of a single disk (when the proper RAID level is employed). Users continue to operate as if nothing has happened. The system alerts the system administrator that a specific disk has failed. The administrator pulls out the disk and slides in a new disk. The hardware controller or operating system automatically writes the missing information on the new disk. The system goes on without missing a beat.

How Many Disks Do We Need?

I know the hardware vendors out there are going to love me for this, but it is true. A good rule of thumb on buying disks in today's market is "Don't buy disks on the basis of capacity alone." If you have a moderately sized database at 200GB, why would you buy a disk array with 1TB of disk? Spindles, that's why. With disk capacities hovering around 146GB and up, this can be hard to rationalize, but too often lately I have seen people make disk purchase choices on capacity alone. This leaves them with inadequate redundancy, poor performance, or both. Besides, after you configure that one-terabyte disk properly, you may only have 500GB of usable storage, and there are all sorts of nice things you can do with that extra 300GB. "What sort of things?" Using a SAN is a great first choice. Why not invest in something that can benefit more than just one system? More on this later.

How Many Disks Do We Need?

What Are Some of the RAID Levels Available?

Almost every midrange to enterprise-class server today offers a hardware RAID solution either built into the server or as an attached storage device. Using various RAID levels that have become available is pretty much standard, regardless of the type of array you buy. The following list describes some of the more common options that Oracle database administrators will want to consider:

- **RAID 0 (Striped Set)** Automatic disk striping. This means that the Oracle datafiles are automatically spread across multiple disks. The tablespace's corresponding datafile pieces can be spread across and accessed from many disks at the same time instead of one (a large savings in disk I/O). Just be wary, this isn't a solution for high availability or fault tolerance, as a loss of one disk in the group means all the data needs to be recovered.

- **RAID 1 (Mirrored Set)** Automatic disk mirroring is available on most systems today. It's usually used for the operating system itself but can be used with the Oracle database for higher availability. You need twice the storage compared to the amount of data that you have for RAID 1.

- **RAID 5 (Striped Set with Parity)** This level carries the parity on an extra disk, which allows for media recovery. Heavy read applications get the maximum advantage from this disk array distribution. It is a low-cost solution that is generally very bad for write-intensive Oracle applications. I will discuss improvements to this more in the next section.

- **RAID 1+0 (RAID 10, a Stripe of Mirrors)** Mirrored disks that are then striped. This is the most common Oracle OLTP production RAID level, also known as "RAID TEN." This incorporates the advantages of the first two RAID levels by adding the disk I/O striping benefit of RAID 0 to the mirroring provided by RAID 1. For high read/write environments such as OLTP, where sporadic access to data is the norm, this RAID level is highly recommended.

- **RAID 0+1 (RAID 01, a Mirror of Stripes)** Striped disks that are then mirrored. Often confused with RAID 10 or thought not to exist, this level incorporates the advantages of the first two RAID levels by providing the disk I/O striping benefit of RAID 0 to the mirroring provided by RAID 1. For high read/write environments such as OLTP, where sporadic access to data is the norm, this RAID level is good, but it is *not* as robust as RAID 10, and it cannot tolerate two disk failures if they are from different stripes. Also, in a rebuild after failure, all the disks in the array must participate in the rebuild, which is also not as favorable as RAID 10.

- **RAID 1+0+0 (RAID 100, a Stripe of RAID 10s)** Mirrored disks that are then striped and then striped again (usually with software, the top-level stripe is a MetaLun or soft stripe). The advantages are mainly for random read performance improvement and the elimination of hotspots.

The Newer RAID 5

Many hardware vendors configure systems with a RAID 5 configuration in order to maximize the utilization of available space on disk and reduce the overall cost of the array. While RAID 5 is a good choice for inexpensive redundancy, it is usually a poor choice for write-intensive performance. At the most general level, when a write request is made to a RAID 5 array, the modified block must be changed on disk, a "parity" block is read from disk, and using the modified block, a new parity block is calculated and then written to disk. This process, regardless of the size of the write request, can limit throughput because for every write operation, there are at least two more I/O operations. I recommend RAID 5 only for mostly read or read-only file systems. Most storage vendors realize that this parity write is a penalty and have come up with various solutions to reduce the impact of this additional operation. The most common solution is to implement a memory cache on the array to speed up the write performance of all I/O on the array. For periodic or light write activity, this may be completely suitable for your system, but you need to remember that eventually those write operations need to make it to disk. If you overload that disk cache with heavy write activity, it is possible to produce what is often referred to as a "serialized I/O" condition. This is where the array can't write to disk fast enough to clear the cache, essentially neutralizing the benefit of your cache. Be sure to check out other solutions your vendor may have implemented. Don't be afraid to ask them how they handle heavy I/O. Some solutions to look for are

- **Dynamic cache management** This is the ability for the array to adjust the way that the cache is being used. Some vendors simply split the cache down the middle—if you have 1GB of cache, 500MB is for read and 500MB is for write. Since the Oracle buffer cache is essentially already a read cache, being able to adjust the array cache so that it is primarily a write cache can give you some flexibility. This goes for other configurations other than just RAID 5.

- **Bundled writes** Generally, the maximum size of a write operation is larger than an Oracle block. Some vendors have implemented intelligence into their arrays that allows them to group multiple parity operations into a single I/O operation. Because this requires fewer round trips to the physical disk, it can greatly improve the performance and effectiveness of the cache when running RAID 5.

RAID 6 is another variant of RAID 5 that you may also see advertised. RAID 6 behaves just like RAID 5, except that it utilizes corresponding parity blocks for every set of data block stripes. While this does carry the added benefit of more fault tolerance, because you can lose two disks, it also brings with it even lower potential.

I still prefer to see RAID 1+0 (mirroring and then striping). RAID 1+0 is generally going to be faster or at least the same as RAID 5 and natively be more fault tolerant to multiple device failures. Since you may be in a situation where you have multiple physical enclosures for your disk, using striping and mirroring will allow you to build fault tolerance between enclosures too.

Setup and Maintenance of the Traditional File System

Using RAID-configured groups of physical devices and traditional file systems makes Oracle datafile setup and maintenance *much* easier for the DBA because manually balancing disks is not as arduous. With the large disk sizes in today's storage systems, dissecting file system configuration between 4 or 6 devices quickly becomes an exercise in splitting hairs. Unless you are utilizing a system where 12 or more physical disks are involved, there is only a small benefit in dividing these up into more than one logical disk device. Even if you have a case where two datafiles are heavily utilized, the cache or HBA (host bus adapter) that they share on the array may be a common avenue to the disk. Finally, depending on your expected growth, the number of file systems you could end up managing could, in time, make keeping all of this in balance a frustrating exercise.

TIP
Try to avoid splitting a logical device in a disk array into more than one file system. This action may seem to give you flexibility, but it can also increase the number of datafile locations you have to manage.

What Is the Cost?

To support disk arrays that mirror data, you need more (sometimes much more) raw disk storage (for RAID 1, you need double the space). While this can make the price of your initial system go up, the benefits are usually well worth it. For these reasons, while you are making the decision on how to configure the new storage system you are going to buy, think about the ROI (return on investment) for keeping the system up and running and also the value of great performance. This leads us to another class of storage systems that is becoming more popular. With the rising capacity of even the most basic storage array, companies are looking to leverage that storage space with multinode access technologies. Whether the implementation is as a storage area network (SAN) or network-attached storage (NAS), the initial investment and added benefit of being able to "plug in" another server to your storage system is often well worth it. So, when you are faced with the dilemma of having a 4 Gbit/sec Fibre Channel storage array with four disks and are feeling a bit like you aren't utilizing the resource to the maximum, consider expanding that purchase into an infrastructure decision that will allow your enterprise to grow and share that resource among all your important systems.

TIP
Use disk arrays to improve performance and protect your data against disk failure. Choose the proper RAID level and technology solutions that enable you to maintain the availability your organization needs. Don't go "good enough," because you will regret it at 2 A.M. when you lose a disk.

Distributing "Key" Data Files Across Hardware Disks

To operate the Oracle database efficiently on traditional file systems, special care must be taken to distribute "key" data files across available file systems. For example, heavily accessed tables should be located on file systems separate from corresponding indexes. In addition, online redo logs and archive logs should be stored separately from data files for recovery purposes when the disk configuration allows. The reality is, in most cases with the hardware available today, you want to make sure you aren't compromising the ability to effectively use your disk by resorting to overkill in dividing it up. Unless you have a lot of devices under those file systems, you will just be making more work for yourself. The files associated with the following elements should be separated when possible:

- The SYSTEM tablespace

- The TEMPORARY tablespace

- The UNDO tablespace

- The online redo log files (try to put on your fastest disks)

- The operating system disk

- Key Oracle files located in the ORACLE_HOME directory

- Data files for heavily accessed tables

- Data files for heavily accessed indexes

- Archive area (should always be separated from the data to be recovered)

The following example illustrates file distribution across 11 file systems in a Unix environment:

```
/: Operating System
/u01: Oracle software
/u02: Temporary Tablespace, Control File 1
/u03: Undo Segments, Control File 2
/u04: Redo Logs, Archive Logs, Control File 4
/u05: System and SYSAUX Tablespaces
/u06: Data1, Control File 3
/u07: Redo Log Mirror, Index3
/u08: Data2
/u09: Index2
/u10: Data3
/u11: Index1
```

Storing Data and Index Files in Separate Locations

Tables that are joined (simultaneously accessed during a query) often could also have their data and index tablespaces separated. The following example shows a table join and one possible solution for managing the data:

```
select  COL1, COL2, ....
from    CUST_HEADER, CUST_DETAIL
where   ...;
```

Here is a data management solution:

```
Disk1: CUST_HEADER Table
Disk5: CUST_HEADER Index
Disk8: CUST_DETAIL Table
Disk12: CUST_DETAIL Index
```

This solution allows the table join to be done while accessing four different disks and controllers. Separate data and index files onto different physical disk devices and controllers;

consequently, when tables and indexes are accessed at the same time, they will not be accessing the same physical devices. This could be expanded to involve a larger number of disks. We will see later in the chapter that table and index partitioning will help us to accomplish this more easily.

TIP
Separate key Oracle datafiles to ensure that disk contention is not a bottleneck. By separating tables and indexes of often-joined tables, you can ensure that even the worst of table joins do not result in disk contention.

Avoiding I/O Disk Contention

Disk contention occurs when multiple processes try to access the same physical disk simultaneously. Disk contention can be reduced, thereby increasing performance, by distributing the disk I/O more evenly over the available disks. Disk contention can also be reduced by decreasing disk I/O. To monitor disk contention, review the Database Files Metrics in Database Control. This Metric group contains two sets of metrics. The Average File Read Time and Average File Write Time apply to all datafiles associated with your database. If you find that one or two datafiles seem to have especially high values, you click one and then use the Compare Objects File Name link to view collected statistics between them. If they are both busy at the same times and are on the same disk, you may choose to relocate one datafile to another file system, if you are concerned about performance during that time.

You can also determine file I/O problems by running a query:

```
col PHYRDS   format 999,999,999
col PHYWRTS  format 999,999,999
ttitle  "Disk Balancing Report"
col READTIM   format 999,999,999
col WRITETIM   format 999,999,999
col name format a40
spool fio1.out

select  name, phyrds, phywrts, readtim, writetim
from    v$filestat a, v$datafile b
where   a.file# = b.file#
order   by readtim desc
/
spool off
```

Here is a partial query output;

```
Fri Mar 24                                          page 1
                    Disk Balancing Report
NAME                    Phyrds      Phywrts     ReadTim     WriteTim
/d01/psindex_1.dbf      48,310      51,798      200,564     903,199
/d02/psindex_02.dbf     34,520      40,224      117,925     611,121
/d03/psdata_01.dbf      35,189      36,904       97,474     401,290
/d04/undotbs01.dbf       1,320      11,725        1,214      39,892
/d05/system01.dbf        1,454          10           10         956
...
```

NOTE
You may also have sysaux01.dbf, users01.dbf, and example01.dbf.

A large difference in the number of physical writes and reads between disks may indicate that a disk is being overburdened. In the preceding example, file systems 1–3 are heavily used while file systems 4–5 are only lightly used. To get a better balance, you'll want to move some of the data files. Splitting data files across multiple disks or using partitions would also help move access to a table or an index to an additional disk.

TIP
Query V$FILESTAT and V$DATAFILE to see how effectively data files have been balanced. Note that temporary tablespaces are monitored using V$TEMPFILE and V$TEMPSTATS.

Moving Data Files to Balance File I/O

To physically move a data file that is causing file contention, follow these steps:

1. Take the tablespace corresponding to the data file offline:

```
ALTER TABLESPACE ORDERS OFFLINE;
```

2. Copy the data file to the new location on disk:

```
$cp /disk1/orders1.dbf /disk2/orders1.dbf   (UNIX copy command)
```

3. Rename the data file to the new data file location for the tablespace:

```
ALTER DATABASE ORDERS
RENAME DATAFILE '/disk1/orders1.dbf' to '/disk2/orders1.dbf';
```

4. Bring the tablespace back online:

```
ALTER TABLESPACE ORDERS ONLINE;
  Delete the old data file (when sure the moved data file can be accessed):
$rm /disk1/orders1.dbf   (UNIX delete command)
```

TIP
Solve disk contention problems by moving data files to disks that are not as heavily accessed.

Another method, useful for very large, critical files, is the following:

1. Put the tablespace in READ ONLY mode and verify the status by querying DBA_TABLESPACES.

2. Copy the data files at the OS level. Compare files sizes after the copy to make sure they are the same.

3. Alter the tablespace offline.

4. Use the ALTER TABLESPACE command to rename the datafile.

5. Alter the tablespace back ONLINE.

6. Alter the tablespace to READ WRITE.

7. Verify the control file was updated by querying V$DATAFILE.

8. Remove the old datafile at the OS level.

TIP
Use the Database Files Metrics in Enterprise Manager to determine the I/O that is taking place on each database file. Move heavily used datafiles to separate file systems to distribute I/O.

Locally Managed Tablespaces

Prior to Oracle 8*i*, all tablespace extent information for segments was maintained by the Oracle data dictionary. As a result, any operations that occurred against segments in the database that related to extent allocation, such as extending or truncating a table, would incur operations against the data dictionary. This could become very expensive from the database management point of view, since the data dictionary could become a bottleneck for these operations when many tables with many extents were involved. With Oracle 8*i*, a new extent management option was provided called *locally managed* extents. With locally managed extents, these extent management operations are relocated to a bitmap block in the header of the datafile itself. This allows for improved performance because each tablespace in the database contains only its own extent information that can be accessed using a fast hashing process instead of the slower table-based query.

When using the locally managed tablespace feature, Oracle provides two options for extent allocation to segments in addition to the traditional "user" managed extent definition available in dictionary managed tablespaces. These two options are "autoallocate" and "uniform." In an autoallocate management scheme, the database uses an internal algorithm to increase extent sizes for segments as they grow. With autoallocate, as a segment grows in a tablespace, the database determines the appropriate next extent size by use of an internal algorithm that factors in, among other things, the number of extents and the rate of extension. The advantage here is that the database will increase the next extent size of a table automatically and should therefore reduce the overall number of extents that the table would have had, if it had been defined with an inappropriately small extent size. Therefore, if you are working with a new application and are unsure of how segments may grow, there may be an advantage to using autoallocate to assure extent counts don't get out of hand.

In uniform extent management, all extents in a tablespace are allocated with an equal size that is specified when the tablespace is created, regardless of the storage clause specified in the segment create statement. When possible, usage of uniform extents is the preferred method. The principle reason for this is that when segments are moved or dropped, reuse of freed extents in the tablespace can be more efficiently achieved, since they are already the appropriate size for remaining segments. We will discuss this further in the reducing fragmentation section of the chapter.

Creating Tablespaces as Locally Managed

To create a tablespace as locally managed, use the extent management clause on the create tablespace statement to set the mode in which extents will be allocated.

```
CREATE TABLESPACE USER_256K_DAT datafile '/u01/user_256k_dat_01.dbf' SIZE 100M
extent management local uniform size 256K;
```

A good practice when creating locally managed tablespaces with uniform extents is to specify the extent size in the tablespace name. This will allow you to more easily track the tablespaces extent sizes you have defined and can make it easier to determine which tablespace a segment should be moved to or created in.

When creating segments in a locally managed tablespace, do not specify a storage clause to define parameters such as INITIAL, NEXT, and PCTINCREASE. These parameters can lead to confusion, since they will be traced in the dba_segments dictionary table, but will be ignored with respect to how extents are allocated. The following query that shows how to get more information about the extent management of tablespaces in the database can be helpful in documenting what you have:

```
SELECT tablespace_name, extent_management, allocation_type
from    dba_tablespaces;

TABLESPACE_NAME       EXTENT_MAN ALLOCATION
------------------    ---------- ----------
SYSTEM                DICTIONARY USER
TOOLS                 LOCAL      UNIFORM
TEMP                  LOCAL      UNIFORM
USERS                 LOCAL      UNIFORM
TS_SMALL_64K_DAT      LOCAL      UNIFORM
```

The default database install has allocation_type set to SYSTEM for the following tablespaces: SYSTEM, USERS, SYSAUX, EXAMPLE, and UNDOTBS1. Locally managed SYSTEM tablespaces became possible in 9.2. In 10.1 if you manually create a database using the CREATE DATABASE command, the default is to create a dictionary-managed tablespace for SYSTEM. If you use DBCA to create a new database using a template, the LOCALLY MANAGED value is the default setting in the Storage tab for all tablespaces, including the SYSTEM tablespace.

Migrating Dictionary-Managed Tablespaces to Locally Managed

It is possible to migrate dictionary-managed tablespaces to a locally managed method, but this is not recommended. When a tablespace is migrated to locally managed, the extent map is moved into the tablespace datafile header, but the second benefit, autoallocate or uniform extent size management, is not available. As a result, any benefit to reducing fragmentation is reduced, since you must now specify storage clauses for each segment in the tablespace. The extent bitmap is located at the location previously occupied by the start of the first free extent in the file. The user does not get the policy benefits from migration but can still get performance benefits: no ST (space transaction) enqueue contention and more efficient extent operations.

Migrating Dictionary-Managed
Tablespaces to Locally Managed

Whenever possible, rebuild dictionary-managed tablespaces to a locally managed uniform extent mode by exporting segments in the tablespace, dropping and re-creating the tablespace, and then importing the segments back into the tablespace. Be sure to check your segment sizes before you perform this process. It might be more beneficial to split the single tablespace into several different tablespaces with differently sized extents to accommodate segments of vastly different sizes.

The only exception to the rule with regard to tablespaces that you should migrate to locally managed, is the SYSTEM tablespace. While it is still preferred to rebuild your database using export/import, this may not always be possible. In 10g, we now have the ability to migrate the SYSTEM tablespace using the DBMS_SPACE_ADMIN.TABLESPACE_MIGRATE_TO_LOCAL package. Before this operation can be performed, there are several restrictions:

- The default temporary tablespace for all users in the database must be a tablespace other than system.

- You must migrate all of the tablespaces you intend to have read/write converted to locally managed tablespaces.

- Database must be started in restricted mode.

- You must have all tablespaces, other than undo in read-only mode for the conversion or have an online rollback segment defined in a locally managed tablespace.

 ## Oracle Bigfile Tablespaces

Oracle 10g introduced a new locally managed tablespace type for databases of extreme size. Bigfile tablespaces allow for the creation of tablespaces with one file where the size of that datafile fully incorporates the power of 64-bit systems. When implemented with Oracle Managed Files or Automatic Storage Management, bigfile tablespaces can greatly simplify the management of your storage system. Additionally, because you should have fewer datafiles, performance of database management operations such as checkpoints should improve, but be aware that recovery operation times are likely to increase in the event of datafile corruption.

Now, you may ask, "Then what is the benefit of bigfile tablespaces?" A bigfile tablespace with the typical 8K block can contain a single 32-terabyte datafile. If you're using a 32K block, it can contain a 128-terabyte datafile. This is achieved by changing the way ROWIDs are managed within the tablespace. In a traditional tablespace, three positions in the ROWID were used to identify the relative file number of the row. Since we only have one datafile in bigfile tablespaces, these three positions are instead used to lengthen the data block number for the row, thereby allowing for a much larger number of ROWIDs from traditional smallfile tablespaces.

 NOTE
To have the largest Oracle database possible of 8 Exabytes, you must use 128T datafiles.

A requirement is that you must be using locally managed tablespaces with Automatic Segment Space Management (ASSM). Also, you cannot use bigfile tablespaces for undo, temp, or system. If you are thinking of using bigfile tablespaces to reduce the amount of management of your system, consider also using Oracle Managed Files (OMF) and ASM (covered later in this chapter). Also, if you are using traditional file systems, make sure you are using a logical volume manager that provides the flexibility to map out your storage system appropriately so that the single datafile can grow as needed.

Oracle Managed Files

Oracle Managed Files (OMF) was first introduced in version 9*i* of the database. The purpose of the feature is to eliminate the need for the DBA to directly manage the names of the datafiles that belong to the database. While this sounds really great, it had some initial limitations that made it less than ideal.

If you have a big file system for all your database-related files, OMF may be for you. To implement it, you first need to specify some initialization parameters for your database.

```
DB_CREATE_FILE_DEST
```

This parameter defines the default location of new datafiles, tempfiles, redo log files, control files, and any block change tracking files.

```
DB_RECOVERY_FILE_DEST
```

This parameter defines the default location of redo logs, control files, RMAN backup files, archived logs, and flashback logs. This parameter will override the previous parameter for those file types that are in common.

```
DB_CREATE_ONLINE_LOG_DEST_n
```

This parameter defines the default location of redo log files and control files and overrides the previous two parameters for those types of files. As usual, it is suggested that you specify two locations to make sure you have multiple copies of your archive logs and control files. You specify this parameter multiple times to set mirror locations.

Now, when you need to add a datafile, you can simply run an "ALTER TABLESPACE. . .ADD DATAFILE" command. If you want to create a new tablespace, you can just run a "CREATE TABLESPACE" command, all without specifying the actual datafiles involved, because the database will do it for you.

For example, if you have six file systems you are using for the database, in order to use each of them for different files, you will need to identify the file system you need when adding a datafile to a particular tablespace as shown here:

```
SQL> ALTER SYSTEM SET DB_CREATE_FILE_DEST = '/u01/oradata';
SQL> CREATE TABLESPACE tbs_1;
```

This gives you the advantage of not needing to worry about creating a file that already exists, but it doesn't provide any advantage for capacity management or balancing I/O. To get this balance with OMF, we need to look at another technology that Oracle has provided us with, ASM.

ASM Introduction

Before we dive into the intricacies of ASM, I want to first take a moment to thank Nitin Vengurlekar from Oracle, who provided this excellent addition to this chapter.

ASM Introduction

In Oracle Database 10g Release 2, storage management and provisioning for the database has been greatly simplified using *Automatic Storage Management (ASM)*. ASM provides filesystem and volume manager capabilities built into the Oracle database kernel. With this capability, ASM simplifies storage management tasks, such as creating/laying out databases and disk space management. Since ASM allows disk management to be done using familiar create/alter/drop SQL statements, DBAs do not need to learn a new skill set or make crucial decisions on provisioning. An Enterprise Manager interface (see Chapter 5 for additional information), as well as a new command-line utility (new in Oracle Database 10g Release 2), is also available for those ASM administrators who are not familiar with SQL.

ASM is a management tool specifically built to simplify the job of the DBA. It provides a simple storage management interface across all server and storage platforms. ASM provides the DBA flexibility to manage a dynamic database environment with increased efficiency. This feature is a key component of grid computing and database storage consolidation.

The following are some key benefits of ASM:

- Spreads I/O evenly across all available disk drives to prevent hot spots and maximize performance.

- Eliminates the need for over provisioning and maximizes storage resource utilization facilitating database consolidation.

- Inherently supports large files.

- Performs automatic online redistribution after the incremental addition or removal of storage capacity.

- Maintains redundant copies of data to provide high availability, or leverage third-party RAID functionality.

- Supports Oracle Database 10g as well as Oracle Real Application Clusters (RAC).

- Can leverage third-party multipathing technologies.

For simplicity and easier migration to ASM, an Oracle Database 10g Release 2 database can contain ASM and non-ASM files. Any new files can be created as ASM files while existing files can also be migrated to ASM. Oracle Database 10g Enterprise Manager can be used to manage ASM disk and file management activities.

ASM reduces Oracle Database 10g cost and complexity without compromising performance or availability. Additionally, ASM is completely storage agnostic; thus, ASM works with a wide spectrum of storage arrays from high-end storage arrays, such as EMC DMX and HDS, to low-cost commodity storage, such as Apple XServe. ASM was primarily built to resolve configuration and layout of databases and communication across IT roles.

DBAs have a lot to consider before they deploy and create a database. They must consider and determine the following:

- Plan your file system layout and device usage

- Determine application workloads characteristics (random read/write for OLTP versus sequential I/O for DSS systems)

- Calculate storage capacity and sizing for the database

ASM addresses these concerns in the following ways:

- Traditionally, DBAs would create filesystems to store their database files, and additional filesystems would be created as needed. This can become a manageability and provisioning nightmare, since DBAs have to manage the I/O load on each filesystem. ASM presents a single storage pool (diskgroup), so there is no need to maintain several filesystem containers and no need to worry about the placement of your next datafile.

- One of the core benefits of ASM is the ability to expand storage to meet the capacity needs of the application. Thus, the ASM diskgroup that houses the database can be expanded without worrying excessively about storage capability management.

- Using ASM and applying the defined general best practices, ASM-based databases should be able to handle any workload. Additionally, since ASM inherently uses raw devices, considerations such as async I/O and direct I/O become a non-issue.

Communication Across IT Roles

There has sometimes been a disconnect between the DBA, the System Admins, and the Storage Admins. The DBA asks for a 200GB filesystem, the Storage/System Admin provides a 200GB RAID 5 device or RAID 10 device that has an improper or inefficient stripe size and performance starts to suffer. Later, the DBA finds out what was actually provisioned and isn't very happy.

DBAs and other technical IT roles will always have some inherent level of disconnect, because these groups think and operate differently. Since it is mostly a communication issue, ASM doesn't necessarily fix this disconnect. However, several things came into play with ASM that lessen this communication issue. First, Oracle published a paper called Optimal Storage Configuration Made Easy (available on technet.oracle.com). This paper proposed a stripe-and-mirror-everything (S.A.M.E.) methodology. With this paper came a standard methodology for database deployment, which made DBA–Storage Admin communication much simpler, since DBAs had a way to express what they needed.

ASM incorporates all the essentials of SAME methodology. ASM also offers a streamlined approach to storage capacity management. With ASM, database storage can be expanded as business or capacity plans dictate, all with no application downtime.

ASM Instances

In Oracle Database 10*g,* there are two types of instances: database and ASM instances. The ASM instance, which is generally named +ASM, is started with the INSTANCE_TYPE=ASM initialization parameter. This parameter, when set, signals the Oracle initialization routine to start an ASM instance, not a standard database instance. Unlike the standard database instance, the ASM instance contains no physical files, such as log files, control files, or datafiles, and requires only a few initialization parameters for startup.

Upon startup, an ASM instance will spawn all the basic background processes, plus some new ones that are specific to the operation of ASM. The STARTUP clauses for ASM instances are similar to those for database instances. For example, NOMOUNT starts up an ASM instance without mounting any diskgroup. MOUNT option simply mounts all defined diskgroups.

ASM is the volume manager for all databases that employ ASM on a given node. Therefore, only one ASM instance is required per node, regardless of the number of database instances on the node. Additionally, ASM seamlessly works with the RAC architecture to support clustered storage environments. In RAC environments, there will be one ASM instance per clustered node, and the ASM instances communicate with each other on a peer-to-peer basis using the interconnect. Here is an example to query for the instance name that you are connected to:

```
select instance_name
from   v$instance;

INSTANCE_NAME
----------------
+ASM
```

ASM init.ora Parameters

The list that follows shows the some of the basic init.ora parameters required to start ASM. Observe that all ASM processes begin with *asm,* as opposed to the database instance, whose processes begin with *ora.*

```
*.background_dump_dest='/opt/app/admin/+ASM/bdump'
*.core_dump_dest='/opt/app/admin/+ASM/cdump'
*.instance_type=asm
*.asm_diskgroups=+DATA
*.large_pool_size=12M
*.asm_diskstring='/dev/rdsk/c3t19d*s4'
*.remote_login_passwordfile='SHARED'
*.user_dump_dest='/opt/app/admin/+ASM/udump'
```

ASM Installation

In cases where a single ASM instance is managing only one database instance, it may be sufficient to maintain a single ORACLE_HOME for ASM and the database. However, for systems that have an ASM instance managing the storage for several database instances and require higher availability, it is recommended that the ASM instance be installed in a separate ORACLE_HOME (ASM_HOME) than the database ORACLE_HOME. This also gives you the ability to patch ASM separately from the Oracle Database.

In Oracle Database 10g Release 2, Oracle Universal Installer (OUI) and Database Configuration Assistant (DBCA) have been enhanced to allow the user to seamlessly create and install an ASM Instance in a separate ORACLE_HOME. OUI now has options to

■ Install and configure a database that uses ASM for storage management.

■ Install and configure an ASM instance, without creating a database.

■ Install and configure ASM on a system that already has a running database, where subsequently, the DBA can use the EM Migration Utility to migrate the database to ASM.

Additionally, in Oracle Database 10g Release 2, ASM transparently supports both older and newer software versions of the database. This new feature provides higher availability as well as the foundation for the Database Storage Consolidation Feature (covered later in this chapter).

ASM Parameters and SGA Sizing

Enabling the ASM instance requires configuring only a handful of init.ora parameters. The parameter file for ASM can be a Pfile or an Spfile. DBCA will create an ASM Pfile by default during database/ASM creation. The Spfile can be manually configured later if desired. However, if an Spfile is used in clustered ASM environments, then it must on a shared raw device. The init.ora parameters specified next are the essential parameters required to start up ASM.

The following describes the usage of SGA components:

- **db_cache_size**   This value determines the size of the cache. This buffer cache area is used to cache metadata blocks. The default value will suit most all implementations.

- **shared_pool**   Used for standard memory usage (control structures, etc.) to manage the instance. This is also used to store extent maps. The default value will suit most all implementations.

- **large_pool**   Used for large allocations. The default value will suit most all implementations.

The "processes" init.ora parameter for ASM may need to be modified. The following recommendation pertains to versions 10.1.0.3 and later of Oracle and will work for RAC and non-RAC systems. This formula can used to determine an optimal value for this parameter: *25 + 15n*, where *n* is the number of databases using ASM for their storage.

ASM and Privileges

Access to the ASM instance is comparable to a standard instance; i.e., SYSDBA and SYSOPER. Note, however, that since there is no data dictionary, authentication is done from an operating system level and/or an Oracle password file. Typically, the SYSDBA privilege is granted through the use of an operating system group. On Unix, this is typically the dba group. By default, members of the dba group have SYSDBA privileges on all instances on the node, including the ASM instance. Users who connect to the ASM instance with the SYSDBA privilege have complete administrative access to all diskgroups in the system. The SYSOPER privilege is supported in ASM instances and limits the set of allowable SQL commands to the minimum required for basic operation of an already-configured system. The following commands are available to SYSDBA users:

- STARTUP/SHUTDOWN

- ALTER DISKGROUP MOUNT/DISMOUNT

- ALTER DISKGROUP ONLINE/OFFLINE DISK

- ALTER DISKGROUP REBALANCE

- ALTER DISKGROUP CHECK

- Access to all V$ASM_* views

All other commands, such as CREATE DISKGROUP, ADD/DROP/RESIZE DISK, and so on, require the SYSDBA privilege and are not allowed with the SYSOPER privilege.

ASM and Privileges

ASM Disks

The first task in building the ASM infrastructure is to discover and associate (add) disks under ASM management. This step is best done with the coordination of Storage and Systems administrators. The Storage administrator will identify a set of disks from the storage array that will be presented to the host. The term *disk* may be used in loose terms. A disk can be a partition of a physical spindle, the entire spindle, or a RAID group set (defined in the storage array); this depends on how the storage array presents the logical unit number (LUN) to the operating system (OS). In this chapter we will refer generically to LUNs or disks presented to the OS as simply *disks*. On Solaris systems, disks will generally have the following SCSI name format: *CwTxDySz*, where C is the controller number, T is the target, D is the LUN/disk number, and S is the partition. Note that each OS will have its unique representation of SCSI disk naming.

ASM must use only character devices as disks and not block devices. According to the Oracle Admin Guide for 10.2, you can use ASMLib to access block devices: "The purpose of ASMLib, which is an optional add-on to ASM, is to provide an alternative interface for the ASM-enabled kernel to discover and access block devices." On most Unix systems character devices are shown as /dev/rdsk or /dev/raw/raw on Linux. The only exception to this case is when ASM uses NAS filesystem files as disks.

For example, it is a best practice on a Solaris system to create a partition on the disk; such as slice 4 or 6, that skips the first 1MB into the disk. Creating a partition serves several purposes. A partition creates a placeholder to identify that the disk is being used. An unpartitioned disk could be accidentally misused or overwritten. Skipping 1MB into the disk is done to skip the OS label/VTOC (volume table of contents), as well as to preserve alignment between ASM striping and storage array internal striping. Different operating systems will have varying requirements for the OS label; i.e., some may require an OS label before it is used while others will not. The same principles apply for different operating systems, although the procedures may be different.

In SAN environments, it assumed that the disks are identified and configured; i.e., they are appropriately zoned or LUN masked within the SAN fabric and can be seen by the OS. Once the disks are identified, they will need to be discovered by ASM. This requires that the disk devices (Unix filenames) have their ownership changed from root to the OS user that owns the ASM software, for example, oracle.

Throughout this chapter, a running example consisting of diskgroup DATA will be used to procedurally outline the steps for creating a diskgroup and other ASM objects. In our example, disks c3t19d5s4, c3t19d16s4, c3t19d17s4, c3t19d18s4 are identified, and their ownership set to the correct "*oracle:dba*" ownership. Now, these disks can be defined in the init.ora parameter, asm_diskstring. In our example, we will use the following wildcard setting:

```
*.asm_diskstring='/dev/rdsk/c3t19d*s4'.
```

When ASM scans for disks, it will use that string and find any devices that it has permissions to open. Upon successful discovery, the V$ASM_DISK view on the ASM instance will now reflect which disks were discovered. Note, henceforth, all views, unless otherwise stated, are examined from the ASM instance and not from the database instance. In the example that follows, notice that the NAME column is empty and the group_number is set to 0. Disks that are discovered but not yet associated with a diskgroup have a null name and a group number of 0.

```
select name, path, group_number
from   v$asm_disk;
```

NAME	PATH	GROUP_NUMBER
	/dev/rdsk/c3t19d5s4	0
	/dev/rdsk/c3t19d16s4	0
	/dev/rdsk/c3t19d17s4	0
	/dev/rdsk/c3t19d18s4	0

Disks have various *header statuses* that reflect its membership state with a diskgroup. Disks can have the following header statuses:

- **Former**   This state declares that the disk was formerly part of a diskgroup.

- **Candidate**   When a disk is in this state, it indicates that it is available to be added to a diskgroup.

- **Member**   This state indicates that a disk is already part of a diskgroup.

- **Provisioned**   This state is similar to candidate, in that it is available to diskgroups.

However, the provisioned state indicates that this disk has been configured or made available using ASMLib. ASMLib is a support library for ASM. ASMLib allows an Oracle database using ASM more efficient and capable access to the diskgroups that it is using.

There may be cases in RAC environments where disk paths are not identical on all nodes. For example, node1 will have /dev/rdsk/c3t1d4s4 that points to a disk, and node2 will present /dev/rdsk/c4t1d4s4 for the same device. This is typical and should not be considered an issue. ASM does not require the disks have the same names on every node. However, ASM does require that the same disks are visible to each ASM instance via that instance's discovery string. The instances can have different discovery strings if necessary.

ASM and Multipathing

An I/O path generally consists of an initiator port, a fabric port, a target port, and an LUN. Each permutation of this I/O path is considered an independent path. Dynamic Multipathing/failover tools aggregate these independent paths into a single logical path. This path abstraction provides I/O load balancing across the host bus adapters (HBA), as well as non-disruptive failovers on I/O path failures. Multipathing (MP) software requires all the required disks to be visible on each available and eligible HBA. An MP driver will detect multipaths by performing a SCSI inquiry command. Multipathing software also provides multipath software drivers. To support multipathing, a physical HBA driver must comply with the multipathing services provided by this driver. Please ensure that the configuration that you are considering is certified by the vendor. A multipathing tool provides the following benefits:

- Provides a single block device interface for a multipathed LUN.

- Detects any component failures in the I/O path; e.g., fabric port, channel adapter, or HBA.

- When a loss of path occurs, ensures that I/Os are re-routed to the available paths, with no process disruption.

- Reconfigures the multipaths automatically when events occur.

ASM and Multipathing

- Ensures that failed paths get revalidated as soon as possible and provides auto-failback capabilities.

- Configures the multipaths to maximize performance using various load balancing methods; e.g., round robin, least I/Os queued, or least service time.

Examples of multipathing software include EMC PowerPath, Veritas DMP, Sun Traffic Manager, Hitachi HDLM, and IBM SDDPCM. Linux 2.6 has a kernel-based multipathing driver called Device Mapper. Additionally, some HBA vendors also provide multipathing solutions. Oracle Corporation does not certify or qualify these multipathing tools.

TIP
Although ASM does not provide multipathing capabilities, ASM does leverage multipathing tools, as long the path or device produced by the Multipathing tool returns a successful return code from an fstat system call. Metalink Note 294869.1 provides more details on ASM and multipathing.

ASM DiskGroups

Once the disks are discovered, a diskgroup can be created that will encapsulate one or more of these disks. A diskgroup, which is the highest-level data structure in ASM, is comparable to a LVM's volume group. However, there are differences between typical LVM volume groups and ASM diskgroups. An ASM filesystem layer is implicitly created within a diskgroup. This filesystem is transparent to users and only accessible through ASM, interfacing databases, and the 10.2 ASM command-line tool. There are inherent automatic file-level striping and mirroring capabilities. A database file created within an ASM diskgroup will have its file extents (not to be confused with its database extents) distributed equally across all online disks in the diskgroup, which provides an even I/O load.

The creation of a diskgroup involves the validation of the disks to be added. These disks must have the following attributes:

- Cannot already be in use by another diskgroup

- Must not have a pre-existing ASM header

- Cannot have an Oracle file header

This check and validation prevents ASM from destroying any in-use data device. Disks with a valid header status, candidate, former, or provisioned are the only ones allowed to be diskgroup members. The diskgroup is created using SQL commands.

```
create diskgroup DATA external redundancy disk
'/dev/rdsk/c3t19d5s4',
'/dev/rdsk/c3t19d16s4',
'/dev/rdsk/c3t19d17s4',
'/dev/rdsk/c3t19d18s4';
```

The output that follows, from V$ASM_DISKGROUP, shows the newly created diskgroup.

```
select name, state, type, total_mb, free_mb
from   v$asm_diskgroup;

NAME                                 STATE        TYPE    TOTAL_MB   FREE_MB
------------------------------------ ------------ ------  ---------- ----------
DATA                                 MOUNTED      EXTERN      34512      34101
```

In the preceding example, a DATA diskgroup is created using four disks, which reside in a storage array, with the redundancy being handled externally via the storage array. The query that follows shows how the V$ASM_DISK view reflects the disk state change after being incorporated into the diskgroup.

```
SQL> select name, path, mode_status, state, disk_number
from v$asm_disk

NAME          PATH                     MODE_ST STATE    DISK_NUMBER
------------- ------------------------ ------- -------- -----------
DATA_0000     /dev/rdsk/c3t19d5s4      ONLINE  NORMAL             0
DATA_0001     /dev/rdsk/c3t19d16s4     ONLINE  NORMAL             1
DATA_0002     /dev/rdsk/c3t19d17s4     ONLINE  NORMAL             2
DATA_0003     /dev/rdsk/c3t19d18s4     ONLINE  NORMAL             3
```

ASM will generate and assign a disk name with a sequence number to each disk added to the diskgroup. However, if you omit the NAME clause and you assigned a label to a disk through ASMLib, then that label is used as the disk name. If you omit the NAME and you did not assign a label through ASMLib, then Automatic Storage Management creates a default name of the form `diskgroup_name_####`, where #### is the disk number. The disk name is used when performing any disk management activities. The ASM disk name is different from the disk/device name. This allows for consistent naming across RAC nodes and protects from disk/device name changes due to array re-configurations. In 10.2, disk names are now unique only within diskgroups, whereas in 10.1, disk names were unique to an ASM instance (or clustered ASM instances in RAC).

After the diskgroup is successfully created, metadata information, which includes creation date, diskgroup name, and redundancy type, is stored in the SGA and in the disk header of each disk in the DATA diskgroup. The V$ASM_DISK view will now reflect this disk header information. Once these disks are under ASM management, all subsequent mounts of the diskgroup will cause ASM to re-read and validate the ASM disk headers. When mounting diskgroups, either at ASM startup or for subsequent mounts, it is advisable to mount all required diskgroups at once. This is done to minimize the overhead of multiple ASM disk discovery scans. When a diskgroup becomes mounted, ASM registers the diskgroup name, the instance name, and the corresponding Oracle Home path name with Cluster Synchronization Services (CSS). This registered data is then used by the database instance to build the TNS connect string. This connect string is subsequently used by the database instance to connect to the ASM instance for volume management activities.

The ASM instance also houses I/O statistics in the V$ASM_DISK and V$ASM_DISK_STAT views. These views include reads/writes processed, read/write blocks handled, and read/write errors incurred. An ASM-based utility similar to *iostat,* called asmiostat, can be used to show I/O statistics for ASM-based disks. This utility from Oracle can be copied into a file and executed against any 10.2 ASM instance.

ASM DiskGroups

In 10.1, querying V$ASM_DISK and V$ASM_DISKGROUP was an expensive operation because each execution involved a disk discovery. To minimize overhead and allow lightweight access to this dataset, 10.2 introduces two new views: V$ASM_DISK_STAT and V$ASM_DISKGROUP_STAT. These two views are identical to V$ASM_DISK and V$ASM_DISKGROUP; however, V$ASM_DISK_STAT and V$ASM_DISKGROUP_STAT views are polled from memory and therefore do not require disk discovery. Since these new views provide efficient lightweight access, EM (Enterprise Manager) can periodically query performance statistics at the disk level and aggregate space usage statistics at the diskgroup level, without incurring significant overhead.

TIP
To get accurate real-time statistics, it may be prudent to query the V$ASM_DISK and V$ASM_DISKGROUP views, but caution should be exercised when running queries against these views during peak workloads.

 ## ASM Diskgroups and Databases

A single ASM instance can service one or more single-instance databases on a stand-alone server. Each ASM diskgroup can be shared among all the databases on the server. Thus, the databases cannot reside on different servers. However, a disk and a database file can be part of only one diskgroup. Alternatively, one Oracle database may also store its files in multiple diskgroups managed by the same ASM instance. Allowing multiple databases to share a diskgroup provides greater potential for improved disk utilization and greater overall throughput.

TIP
To reduce the complexity of managing ASM and its diskgroups, Oracle recommends that generally no more than two diskgroups be maintained and managed per RAC cluster or single ASM instance.

The Database Area is where active database files such as datafiles, control files, online redo logs, and change tracking files used in incremental backups are stored. The flash recovery area is where recovery-related files are created, such as multiplexed copies of the current control file and online redo logs, archived redo logs, backup sets, and flashback log files. To provide higher availability for the database, when a flash recovery area is chosen at database creation time, an active copy of the control file and one member set of the redo log group is stored in the flash recovery area.

NOTE
Additional copies of the control file or extra log files can be created and placed in either diskgroup as desired. Also note that these "areas" are really diskgroups.

ASM Redundancy and Failure Groups

For systems that do not use external redundancy, ASM provides its own internal redundancy mechanism and additional high availability by way of *failure groups.* A failure group, which is a subset of a diskgroup, is by definition a collection of disks that can become unavailable due to a failure of one of its associated components; e.g., controllers or entire arrays. Thus, disks in two separate failure groups (for a given diskgroup) must not share a common failure component. If you define failure groups for your diskgroup, ASM can tolerate the simultaneous failure of multiple disks in a single failure group.

ASM uses a unique mirroring algorithm. ASM does not mirror disks; rather, it mirrors extents. As a result, to provide continued protection in event of failure, only spare capacity in your diskgroup is needed rather than having to provision a hot spare disk. It is not advisable to create failure groups of different sizes, as this will create problems when allocating secondary extents. When ASM allocates a primary extent of a file to one disk in a diskgroup, it allocates a mirror copy of that extent to another disk in the diskgroup. Primary extents on a given disk will have their respective mirror extents on one of several partner disks in the diskgroup. ASM ensures that a primary extent and its mirror copy never reside in the same failure group. Redundancy for diskgroups can be either *normal redundancy* (the default); where files are two-way mirrored (requiring at least two failure groups), or *high redundancy,* which provides a higher degree of protection using three-way mirroring (requiring at least three failure groups). Once a diskgroup has been created, its redundancy level cannot be changed. To change the redundancy of a diskgroup, another diskgroup must be created with the appropriate redundancy desired, and then the datafiles must be moved (using RMAN restore or DBMS_FILE_TRANSFER) to this newly created diskgroup.

The following example shows how to create a diskgroup using failure groups. In this example, ASM normal redundancy is being deployed over a storage array that has four internal trays, with each tray having four disks. The failing component to isolate is the storage tray, and thus the failure group boundary is the storage tray; i.e., each storage tray will be associated with a failure group.

```
SQL> create diskgroup DATA_NRML normal redundancy
FAILGROUP flgrp1 disk
'/dev/rdsk/c3t19d3s4','/dev/rdsk/c3t19d4s4','/dev/rdsk/c3t19d5s4',
'/dev/rdsk/c3t19d6s4'
FAILGROUP flgrp2 disk
'/dev/rdsk/c4t20d3s4','/dev/rdsk/c4t20d4s4','/dev/rdsk/c4t20d5s4',
'/dev/rdsk/c4t19ds4'
FAILGROUP flgrp3 disk
/dev/rdsk/c5t21d3s4','/dev/rdsk/c5t21d4s4','/dev/rdsk/c5t21d5s4',
'/dev/rdsk/c5t21ds4'
FAILGROUP flgrp4 disk
/dev/rdsk/c6t22d3s4','/dev/rdsk/c6t22d4s4','/dev/rdsk/c6t22d5s4',
'/dev/rdsk/c6t22ds4';
```

Diskgroups created with normal or high redundancy contain files that are double or triple mirrored; respectively. The first file extent allocated is chosen as primary extent, and the mirrored extent is called the secondary extent. In the case of high redundancy there will two secondary extents. This logical grouping of primary and secondary extents is called an *extent set.* An extent set always contains the exact same data, since they are mirrored versions of each other. Thus when a block is written to a file, each extent in the extent set is written in parallel. However, when a block is read from disk, it is always read from the primary extent, unless the primary extent cannot be read. Keep in mind that each disk in a diskgroup (and failure groups) contains nearly the same number of primary and secondary extents. This provides an even distribution of read I/O activity across all the disks. This is different than most logical volume managers, which have primary and mirrored disk sets.

As stated, failure groups are used to isolate component failures, and thus failing components needs to be understood. If this failing component cannot be determined or the failing component is the disk itself (as opposed to the array controller or storage tray), then it may be advisable not to specify any failure groups when defining normal or high redundancy diskgroups. This results in every ASM disk being in its own failure group, with ASM internally determining the disk mirroring partnership. If the storage array has fully redundant components with dual paths to the disk, it is best not to specify failure groups but to let ASM manage the disk mirroring partnerships.

In the previous example, consider the event of a disk failure in failure group flgrp1, which will induce a rebalance—the contents (data extents) of the failed disk are reconstructed using the redundant copies of the extents from the partnered disk. This partnered disk can be from either failure group flgrp2 or flgrp3. Let's say that the partnered disk is c5t21d3s4 from failure group 3. During the rebalance, if the database instance needs to access an extent whose primary extent was on the failed disk, then the database will read the mirror copy from the appropriate disk in failure group flgrp3. Once the rebalance is complete, and the disk contents fully reconstructed, the database instance will return to reading primary copies only.

Since disk drives are mechanical devices, they have a tendency to fail. As drives begin to fail or have sporadic I/O errors, the probability for database corruption increases. ASM takes proactive measures with regard to I/O errors. This is done irrespective of using failure groups. A permanent I/O error is only signaled to the caller (Oracle I/O process) after several retries in the device driver. If a permanent disk IO error is incurred during an Oracle write operation, then the affected disk is removed from the diskgroup by ASM, thus preventing more application failures. If the loss of a disk results in data loss, ASM will automatically dismount the diskgroup to protect the integrity of the diskgroup data.

New Space-Related Columns in Oracle Database 10g Release 2

There are two new columns for ASM introduced in Oracle Database 10g Release 2 that provide more accurate information on free space usage:

- **USABLE_FREE_SPACE** In 10.1, the FREE_MB value that is reported in V$ASM_DISKGROUP does not take into account mirroring. 10.2 introduces a new column in V$ASM_DISKGROUP called USABLE_FREE_SPACE to indicate the amount of free space that can be "safely" utilized taking mirroring into account. The column provides a more accurate view of usable space in the diskgroup.

- **REQUIRED_MIRROR_FREE_MB** Along with *usable_free_space,* a new column has been added to V$ASM_DISKGROUP to more accurately indicate the amount of space that is required to be available in a given diskgroup in order to restore redundancy after one or more disk failures. The amount of space displayed in this column takes mirroring into account.

Cluster Synchronization Services

ASM was designed to work with single instances as well as with RAC 10g clusters. ASM, even in single-instance form, requires that Cluster Synchronization Services (CSS) be installed and started before ASM becomes available. In a single instance, CSS maintains synchronization between the ASM and database instances. CSS, which is a component of Oracle's Cluster Ready Services (CRS), is automatically installed on every node that runs Oracle Database 10g ASM and starts up automatically on server boot-up. In RAC 10g environments, the full Oracle Clusterware (CRS) is installed on every RAC node.

Since CSS provides cluster management and node monitor management, it inherently monitors ASM and its shared storage components (disks and diskgroups). Upon startup, ASM will register itself and all diskgroups it has mounted, with CSS. This allows CSS to keep diskgroup metadata in sync across all RAC nodes. Any new diskgroups that are created are also dynamically registered and broadcasted to other nodes in the cluster. As with the database, internode communication is used to synchronize activities in ASM instances. CSS is used to heartbeat the health of the ASM instances. ASM internode messages are initiated by structural changes that require synchronization, e.g., adding a disk. Thus, ASM uses the same integrated lock management infrastructure that is used by the database for efficient synchronization.

Database Instances and ASM

A database instance is the standard Oracle instance and is the client of the ASM instance. The database-to-ASM communication is always intra-node; i.e., the database will not contact the remote (in case of RAC) ASM instance for servicing database requests. After the ASM diskgroup is created, DBCA can now be used to create the database. DBCA has three options for database file structures: filesystem, raw, or ASM.

If ASM is selected, then all available diskgroups, if already created for that ASM instance, will be listed. Selecting ASM and a diskgroup will instruct DBCA to create a database within ASM. If no diskgroups exist or a new diskgroup is desired, then DBCA offers the opportunity to create a new diskgroup.

NOTE
An ASM diskgroup can house all of the Oracle physical files, ranging from control files, datafiles, spfiles, and RMAN backup files. However, Oracle executables, CRS files (OCR and voting disks), and non-database files cannot be housed in ASM diskgroups. Throughout this chapter all Oracle physical files will be generically referred to as database files.

An active database instance that uses ASM storage can then operate just like a typical database instance; i.e., all file access is directly performed without extensive ASM intervention. Database instances interact with the ASM instance when files are created, deleted, or opened. At this time the file layout is read from the ASM instance and all subsequent I/Os are done using the extent map stored in the database instance. ASM and DB instances also interact if the storage configuration changes; e.g., when disks are added, dropped, or fail.

Although the ASM layer is transparent to the database clients and users on the server, all datafile access can only be done via the database instance and its utilities. For example, database backups of ASM-based files can only be performed with RMAN. Note, utilities like the Unix *dd* command are not recommended for backing up or restoring ASM diskgroups.

The database file level access (read/write) of ASM files is similar to pre-10g, except that any database filename that begins with a "+", will automatically be handled and managed using the ASM code path. However, with ASM files, the database file access inherently has the characteristics of raw devices—i.e., un-buffered (direct I/O) with kernelized asynchronous I/O (KAIO).

Database Consolidation and Clustering with ASM

In Oracle Database 10g Release 1, RAC and single-instance databases could not be managed by the same ASM instance. This created challenges in implementing storage grid architectures and consolidated database solutions. Oracle Database 10g Release 2 enhances the ASM functionality in a clustered environment, allowing one ASM instance per node to manage all database instances in the cluster. Therefore, an ASM instance on a given node can now manage storage simultaneously for a single instance or many RAC database instances and one or more single-instance databases. This feature relieves the customer from maintaining more than one ASM instance needed to serve the different database types that might exist in the cluster, thus avoiding the need for DBAs to manage separate storage pools. This new feature leverages Oracle Clusterware to economically consolidate multiple islands of databases into a single clustered pool of storage managed by ASM. This essentially allows customers to optimize their storage utilization by eliminating wasted, over-provisioned storage and save money by reducing their overall footprint of database storage.

Once the database is created and the instance is active, the database instance will become a client of ASM. This is reflected in the V$ASM_CLIENT view. V$ASM_CLIENT contains one row for every ASM diskgroup that is opened by a database instance. In the example that follows, V$ASM_CLIENT displays two databases connected to ASM, with each instance using two diskgroups.

> **NOTE**
> *Instance cubs1 is a 10.2 RAC–enabled database and sox1 is a*
> *10.1.0.4 single instance.*

```
select  instance,name,  status, software_version, compatible_version
from    v$asm_client;

INSTANCE STATUS        SOFTWARE_VRSN COMPATIBLE_VRSN
-------- ------------  ------------- ---------------
cubs1    CONNECTED     10.2.0.1.0    10.2.0.1.0
cubs1    CONNECTED     10.2.0.1.0    10.2.0.1.0
sox1     CONNECTED     10.1.0.3.0    10.1.0.2.0
sox1     CONNECTED     10.1.0.3.0    10.1.0.2.0
```

Database Processes to Support ASM

In a database instance three sets of processes are added to support the ASM diskgroups and infrastructure:

■ **RBAL** This process performs global opens of all the disks in the diskgroup.

■ **ASMB** This process contacts CSS using the diskgroup name and acquires the associated ASM connect string. This connect string is then used to connect into the ASM instance. Using this persistent connection, periodic messages are exchanged to update statistics and provide a heartbeat mechanism. During operations that require ASM intervention, such as a file creation by a database foreground, the database foreground connects directly to the ASM instance to perform the operation. Upon successful completion of file creation, database file extent maps are sent by ASM to ASMB. Additionally, ASMB also sends database I/O statistics to the ASM instance.

■ **O00x** A group of slave processes establish connections to the ASM instance, where x is a number from 1 to 10. Through this connection pool, database processes can send messages to the ASM instance. For example, opening a file sends the open request to the ASM instance via a slave. However, slaves are not used for long-running operations such as creating a file. The slave (pool) connections eliminate the overhead of logging in to the ASM instance for short requests. These slaves are shut down when not in use.

Bigfile and ASM

The bigfile feature (as stated earlier in this chapter) is a perfect fit for VLDB (very large databases) and ASM. Instead of managing several hundred datafiles, using bigfiles will reduce the number datafiles significantly. This improves checkpointing, and database opens become significantly faster, as fewer file opens have to be performed. Bigfile usage reduces internal overhead to manage large number of datafiles. With ASM, bigfiles can be 32TB for external redundancy and 12TB for normal/high redundancy. This is considering an 8K block size. When using bigfiles, you'll have to carefully review your backup and recovery strategy. Obviously, you can't do full datafile backup for a 36TB datafile, so things like RMAN incremental and cumulative backups become an integral part of bigfile management.

Database Init.ora Parameters to Support ASM

The SGA parameters for database instance need slight modification to support ASM extent maps and other ASM information. If the 10g Automatic Memory Management feature is being used on the database instance, then the following sizing data can be treated as informational only or as supplemental data in gauging appropriate values for the SGA. The following are guidelines for SGA sizing on the database instance:

■ **Processes** Add 16.

■ **Large_pool** Add an additional 600K.

■ **Shared_pool** Additional memory is required to store extent maps. Add the values from the following queries to obtain current database storage size that is either already on ASM or will be stored in ASM. Then determine the redundancy type that is used (or will be used) and calculate the shared_pool, using the total value as input:

```
connect user/pass@<SID> as sysdba
select sum(bytes)/(1024*1024*1024)
from   v$datafile;
```

```
select sum(bytes)/(1024*1024*1024)
from   v$logfile a, v$log b
where  a.group#=b.group#;

select sum(bytes)/(1024*1024*1024)
from   v$tempfile
where  status='ONLINE';
```

- **For diskgroups using external redundancy** Every 100GB of space needs 1MB of extra shared pool + 2M.

- **For diskgroups using normal redundancy** Every 50GB of space needs 1MB of extra shared pool + 4M.

- **For diskgroups using high redundancy** Every 33GB of space needs 1MB of extra shared pool + 6M.

ASM and Database Deployment Best Practices

ASM provides out-of-the-box enablement of redundancy and optimal performance. However, the following items should be considered to increase performance and/or availability:

- Implement multiple access paths to the storage array using two or more HBAs (host bus adaptors) or initiators.

- Deploy multipathing software over these multiple HBAs to provide I/O load-balancing and failover capabilities.

- Use diskgroups with disks of similar size and performance. A diskgroup containing a large number of disks provides a wide distribution of data extents, thus allowing greater concurrency for I/O and reducing the occurrences of hotspots. Since a large diskgroup can easily sustain various I/O characteristics and workloads, a single (database area) diskgroup can be used to house database files, log files, and control files.

- Use diskgroups with four or more disks, and make sure these disks span several back-end disk adapters.

As stated earlier, Oracle generally recommends no more than two diskgroups. For example, a common deployment can be four or more disks in a database diskgroup (DATA diskgroup for example) spanning all back-end disk adapters/directors, and 8–10 disks for the flash recovery area diskgroup. The size of the flash recovery area will depend on what is stored and how much; i.e., full database backups, incremental backups, flashback database logs, and archive logs. An active copy of the control file and one member of each of the redo log group are stored in the flash recovery area. See the Oracle's *High Availability Architecture and Best Practices Manual* for more details on these topics.

ASM Storage Management and Allocation

A database created under the constructs of ASM will be striped by default and mirrored as specified in the SAME methodology (i.e., the I/O load is evenly distributed and balanced across all disks within the diskgroup). The striping is done on a file-by-file basis, using a 1MB stripe size, as opposed to other LVMs (logical volume managers) that do striping and mirroring at a disk-volume level. Oracle states that an ASM 1MB stripe depth has proved to be the best stripe depth for Oracle databases. This optimal stripe depth, coupled with even distribution of extents in the diskgroup, prevents the occurrence of hot spots.

ASM allocates space in units called allocation units (AUs). ASM always creates one-AU extents (not the same as tablespace extents) across all of the disks in a diskgroup. For diskgroups with similarly sized disks, there should be an equal number of AU extents on every disk. A database file is broken up into file extents. There are two types of AU extent distributions: coarse and fine. For coarse distribution, each coarse-grain file extent is mapped to a single allocation unit. With fine-grain distribution, each grain is interleaved 128K across groups of eight AUs. Fine distribution breaks up large I/O operations into multiple 128K I/O operations that can execute in parallel, benefiting sequential I/Os. Coarse- and fine-grain attributes are predefined, as part of system templates, for all system-related files.

TIP
Redo and archive log files are defined as fine-grained, whereas datafiles are coarse.

ASM Rebalance and Redistribution

With traditional volume managers, expansion/growth or shrinkage of striped filesystems has typically been difficult. With ASM, these disk/volume changes now include seamless redistribution (rebalancing) of the striped data and can be performed online. Any change in the storage configuration will trigger a rebalance. The main objective of the rebalance operation is to always provide an even distribution of file extents and space usage across all disks in the diskgroup. Rebalancing is performed on all database files on a per-file basis; however, some files may not require a rebalance.

The Oracle background process, RBAL, from the ASM instance manages this rebalance. The Rebalance process examines each file extent map, and the new AU extents are re-plotted on to the new storage configuration. For example, consider an eight-disk diskgroup, with a datafile with 40 AU extents (each disk will house 5 AU extents). When two new drives of same size are added, that datafile is rebalanced and spread across ten drives, with each drive containing 4 AU extents. Only 8 AU extents need to move to complete the rebalance; i.e., a complete redistribution of AU extents is not necessary; only the minimum number of AU extents are moved to reach equal distribution. The following is a typical process flow for ASM rebalancing:

- On the ASM instance, a DBA adds (or drops) a disk to (from) a diskgroup.

- This invokes the RBAL process to create the rebalance plan and then begin coordination of the redistribution.

- RBAL will calculate estimation time and work required to perform the task and then message the ARB*x* processes to actually handle the request. The number of ARB*x* processes invoked is directly determined by the asm_power_limit parameter.

- The Continuing Operations Directory (metadata) will be updated to reflect a rebalance activity.

ASM Rebalance and Redistribution

- Each extent to be relocated is assigned to an ARBx process.

- ARBx performs rebalance on these extents. Each extent is locked, relocated, and unlocked. This is shown as Operation *REBAL* in V$ASM_OPERATION.

Rebalancing involves physical movement of AU extents. This impact is generally low because the rebalance is done one AU extent at a time; therefore, there will only be one outstanding I/O at any given time, per ARBx processes. This should not adversely affect online database activity. However, it is generally advisable to schedule the rebalance operation during off-peak hours.

TIP
The init.ora parameter asm_power_limit is used to influence the throughput and speed of the rebalance operation. The range of values for the asm_power_limit is 0 to 11, where a value of 11 is full throttle and a value of 1 is low speed. A value of 0, which turns off automatic rebalance, should be used with caution.

The power limit value can also be set for a specific rebalance activity using the *alter diskgroup* command. This value is only effective for the specific rebalance task. In the example that follows, using a *power limit value of 0* would indicate that no rebalance should occur for this rebalance, but we will use 11, which is full-throttle rebalancing. This setting is particularly important when adding or removing storage (that has external redundancy), and then deferring the rebalance to a later scheduled time.

```
"Session1 SQL"> alter diskgroup DATA add disk '/dev/rdsk/c3t19d39s4' rebalance
power 11;

From another session:
"Session2 SQL"> select * from v$asm_operation
```

GROUP	OPERA	STAT	POWER	ACTUAL	SOFAR	EST_WORK	EST_RATE	EST_MINUTES
1	REBAL	WAIT	11	0	0	0	0	0
1	DSCV	WAIT	11	0	0	0	0	0

```
time passes.............)
```

OPERA	STAT	POWER	ACTUAL	SOFAR	EST_WORK	EST_RATE	EST_MINUTES
1 REBAL	REAP	11	2	25	219	485	0

TIP
If removing or adding several disks with ASM, it is a best practice to add or remove drives all at once. This will reduce the number rebalance operations that are needed for storage changes.

An ASM diskgroup rebalance is an asynchronous operation, in that the control is returned immediately to DBA after the operation is sent in the background, with the status of the ongoing operation query-able from V$ASM_OPERATION. However, there are situations when the diskgroup operation needs to synchronous; i.e., wait until rebalance is completed. In Oracle Database 10g Release 2, ASM alter diskgroup commands that result in a rebalance now have the option of specifying the option to wait. This allows for accurate (sequential) scripting that may rely on the space change from a rebalance completing before any subsequent action is taken. For example, if you add 100GB of storage to a completely full diskgroup, you won't be able to use all 100GB of storage until the rebalance completes. If a new rebalance command is entered while one is already in progress in wait mode, the prior command will not return until the diskgroup is in a balanced state or the rebalance operation encounters an error.

The example that follows illustrates how the WAIT option can be used in SQL scripting. The script adds a new disk, /dev/raw/raw6, and waits until the *add* and *rebalance* operations complete, returning the control back to the script. The subsequent step adds a large tablespace.

```
#An example script to test WAIT option
alter diskgroup data add disk '/dev/raw/raw6' rebalance power 2 wait;
#login into database and create a tablespace for the next month's
#Order Entry data
sqlplus  oe_dba/oe1@proddb  << EOF
create BIGFILE tablespace May_OE  datafile size 800 Gb;
<< EOF
```

With external redundancy, the dropping and adding of disks in the diskgroup is very seamless, and becomes more of an exercise of scheduling the rebalancing. However, with failure groups, some planning and forethought maybe required with respect to how disks are removed and added.

Avoiding Disk Contention by Using Partitions

Partitioning is probably the single best option available for increasing the performance related to large tables. Partitioning is a way to increase efficiency by accessing smaller pieces of a table or index instead of accessing the full table or index. This can be particularly useful when one or more users are accessing multiple parts of the same table. If these partitions (pieces) of the table reside on different devices, the throughput is greatly increased. Partitions can also be backed up and recovered independently of each other (even while they are in use), eliminating potential disk I/O issues during backup times. Only when partitions are properly implemented are the best performance-enhancing features of Oracle realized. The best way to understand partitioning is to look at an example. Consider the following simple example, where we partition the dept table into three partitions (pieces) using the deptno column.

The table dept is created with three partitions:

```
create table dept
  (deptno       number(2),
   dept_name    varchar2(30))
   partition    by range(deptno)
(partition d1 values less than (10) tablespace dept1,
 partition d2 values less than (20) tablespace dept2,
 partition d3 values less than (maxvalue) tablespace dept3);
```

In the preceding example, we built three distinct partitions on the dept table. The key to getting better throughput is to ensure that each partition is placed on a different physical disk so that all three partitions can be accessed simultaneously if you are not using ASM. The tablespaces dept1, dept2, and dept3 must have physical files that are located on different physical disks. Remember that the tablespace is the logical holder of information where the data file is the physical disk. You can have one tablespace that includes multiple data files, but a data file can only relate to a single tablespace. The key to partitioning to improve disk I/O is to ensure that the partitions that will be accessed simultaneously are located on different physical disks or use ASM.

Data is entered into all three partitions of the table:

```
insert into dept values (1, 'ADMIN');
insert into dept values (7, 'MGMT');
insert into dept values (10, 'MANUF');
insert into dept values (15, 'ACCT');
insert into dept values (22, 'SALES');
```

The dept table still looks like a single table when we select from it:

```
select  *
from    dept;

DEPTNO    DEPT_NAME
1         ADMIN
7         MGMT
10        MANUF
15        ACCT
22        SALES
```

We selected all records from all of the partitions in the preceding example. In the next three examples, we select individually from each partition.

We select from a single partition and access only a *single* partition:

```
select  *
from    dept partition (d1);

DEPTNO    DEPT_NAME
1         ADMIN
7         MGMT

select  *
from    dept partition (d2);

DEPTNO    DEPT_NAME
10        MANUF
15        ACCT

select  *
from    dept partition (d3);

DEPTNO    DEPT_NAME
22        SALES

select  *
```

```
from     dept
where    deptno = 22;

DEPTNO    DEPT_NAME
22        SALES
```

Note that in the final example, we are eliminating the need to access the first or second partition (partition elimination). Partitioning indexes and using the parallel option along with partitions make partitioning even more powerful.

TIP

To minimize disk I/O on a single large table, you can break the table into multiple partitions that reside in tablespaces on different physical disks.

Getting More Information about Partitions

We can retrieve the information regarding partitions by accessing user_tables, dba_part_tables, and user_segments. Example queries to these three tables are displayed next with corresponding output for the examples in the preceding section.

```
select   table_name, partitioned
from     dba_tables
where    table_name in ('DEPT','EMP');

TABLE_NAME    PAR
DEPT          YES
EMP           NO
```

In the preceding example, the par column indicates whether a table is partitioned.

```
select   owner, table_name, partition_count
from     dba_part_tables
where    table_name = 'DEPT';

OWNER     TABLE_NAME    PARTITION_COUNT
KEVIN     DEPT          3
```

In the preceding and following examples, there are three partitions on the dept table.

```
select   segment_name, partition_name, segment_type, tablespace_name
from     user_segments;

SEGMENT_NAME    PARTITION_NAME    SEGMENT_TYPE        TABLESPACE_NAME
EMP                               TABLE               USER_DATA
DEPT            D1                TABLE PARTITION     DEPT1
DEPT            D2                TABLE PARTITION     DEPT2
DEPT            D3                TABLE PARTITION     DEPT3
```

TIP
Tables can be easily partitioned for individual pieces to be accessed and/or manipulated; you can still access the entire table of a partitioned table. Accessing the tables dba_tables, dba_part_table, and dba_segments provides additional information concerning tables that have been partitioned. See Chapter 2 for additional information on index partitioning.

Other Types of Partitions

There are several types of partitioning. The main ones are range, hash, composite, and list partitioning. There are also multiple index types associated with partitions. We've covered range partitioning in the preceding section, but there is also multicolumn range partitioning as well.

Multicolumn Range Partitioning

Multicolumn partitioning is the same as range partitioning except when using multiple columns to define the ranges. In the following example, the data is segmented into quarters so that we can eliminate the quarters that are not needed when a single quarter is accessed, but also so that the data can be archived one quarter at a time without interfering with another quarter. The data can also be segmented into multiple tablespaces as well so that better I/O is achieved.

```
create table cust_sales
(acct_no      number(5),
 cust_name    char(30),
 item_id      number(9),
 sale_day     integer not null,
 sale_mth     integer not null,
 sale_yr      integer not null)
partition by range (sale_yr, sale_mth, sale_day)
(partition cust_sales_q1 values less than (1998, 04, 01) tablespace users,
 partition cust_sales_q2 values less than (1998, 07, 01) tablespace users2,
 partition cust_sales_q3 values less than (1998, 10, 01) tablespace users,
 partition cust_sales_q4 values less than (1999, 01, 01) tablespace users2,
 partition cust_sales_qx values less than (maxvalue, maxvalue, maxvalue)
 tablespace users2);
```

TIP
You can also partition tables using multiple columns as the criteria. You must specify "maxvalue" for all columns that are part of the partition key.

Hash Partitioning

Hash partitioning is usually used when you are unsure where to put the breakpoints as you do in range partitioning. It breaks up data into the number of partitions specified based on the hash of the partition key specified. To get an even distribution, you should always specify a power of 2 as the number of hash partitions. Hash partitioning only supports local indexes. You can specify the names of the index and table partition names, and you can later add or reduce the number of partitions if you find you have to many or too few. An example follows that shows a table with four hash partitions that is built on the partitioning key ACCT_NO and distributed across four tablespaces.

```
create table cust_sales_hash (
acct_no    number(5),
cust_name char(30),
sale_day  integer not null,
sale_mth  integer not null,
sale_yr    integer not null)
partition by hash (acct_no)
partitions 4
store in (users1, users2, users3, users4);
```

TIP
*When you don't know how to break up a table, but you know that it
needs to be partitioned and spread out, use hash partitioning.*

Composite Partitioning
There are times when a table is so large and accessed so frequently that you need a much better
way to "slice and dice it." Composite partitioning is the combination of using range and hash
partitioning. You use range to allow partition elimination and then hash the partitions further
to distribute I/O. Composite partitioning supports local indexes and range partitioned global
indexes. The following is an example of composite partitioning that could lead to incredible
job security due to the non-intuitive complexity.

```
create table orders(
ordid      number,
acct_no    number(5),
cust_name char(30),
orderdate date,
productid number)
 partition by range(orderdate)
 subpartition by hash(productid) subpartitions 8
   (partition q1 values less than  (to_date('01-APR-1998', 'dd-mon-yyyy')),
    partition q2 values less than  (to_date('01-JUL-1998', 'dd-mon-yyyy')),
    partition q3 values less than  (to_date('01-OCT-1998', 'dd-mon-yyyy')),
    partition q4 values less than(maxvalue));
```

This example will build partitions based on the range of values listed for the ORDERDATE
column and put them into partitions q1, q2, q3, and q4. It will then subpartition each of these
range partitions into eight subpartitions based on a hash of the PRODUCTID column.

List Partitioning
Oracle 9*i* added list partitioning for the DBA or developer who really knows their data well. List
partitioning allows you to assign the individual column values associated with each of the partitions.
There are a several restrictions on list partitioning that are displayed after the following code listing.

```
create table dept_part
(deptno     number(2),
 dname      varchar2(14),
 loc        varchar2(13))
partition by list (dname)
```

Other Types of Partitions

```
(partition d1_east  values ('BOSTON', 'NEW YORK'),
 partition d2_west  values ('SAN FRANCISCO', 'LOS ANGELES'),
 partition d3_south values ('ATLANTA', 'DALLAS'),
 partition d4_north values ('CHICAGO', 'DETROIT'));
```

Restrictions on list partitioning are as follows:

- You can specify only one partitioning key in the column list, and it cannot be a LOB column. If the partitioning key is an object-type column, you can partition on only one attribute of the column type.

- Each partition value in the VALUES clause must be unique among all partitions of the table.

- You cannot list partition an index-organized table.

- The string comprising the list of values for each partition can be up to 4K bytes.

- The total number of partition values for all partitions cannot exceed 64K–1.

Partitionwise Joins

Oracle also allows two partitioned tables to be joined by only their partitions. Instead of joining many rows to many rows, you can now perform partition elimination on each table and then join the results. To join on partitions the tables must be equi-partitioned tables, which means

- Tables are partitioned using the same partition key.

- Tables must be partitioned with the same partition breakpoints.

Other Partitioning Options

This section covers some of the many options that can be used when managing partitions. You will see that many of the options that are available for operations on tables are also available for partitions:

- *MODIFY PARTITION partition_name* Modifies the real physical attributes of a table partition. You can specify any of the following as new physical attributes for the partition: LOGGING, ATTRIBUTE, PCTFREE, PCTUSED, INITRANS, MAXTRANS, STORAGE.

- *RENAME PARTITION partition_name TO new_partition_name* Renames table partition PARTITION_NAME to NEW_PARTITION_NAME.

- *MOVE PARTITION partition_name* Moves table partition PARTITION_NAME to another segment. You can move partition data to another tablespace, recluster data to reduce fragmentation, or change a create-time physical attribute:

  ```
  alter table dept move partition d3 tablespace dept4 nologging;
  ```

  In the preceding example, the d3 partition with all corresponding data is moved from the dept3 tablespace, where it originally resided, to the dept4 tablespace.

TIP
When moving a partition, use the nologging option (if possible) for speed.

■   ***ADD PARTITION new_partition_name***   Adds a new partition new_partition_name to the "high" end of a partitioned table. You can specify any of the following as new physical attributes for the partition: logging, attribute, PCTFREE, PCTUSED, INITRANS, MAXTRANS, STORAGE.

■   ***VALUES LESS THAN (value_list)***   Specifies the upper bound for the new partition. The value_list is a comma-separated, ordered list of literal values corresponding to column_list. The value_list must collate greater than the partition bound for the highest existing partition in the table.

■   ***EXCHANGE PARTITION***   This powerful option allows you to convert a partition or subpartition into a non-partitioned table or convert a non-partitioned table into a partition. This is very useful if you are archiving old range partitions and want to export them off as stand-alone tables before you drop them. Also, it can be very useful for quickly loading incremental data into an already-existing partitioned table.

■   ***DROP PARTITION partition_name***   Removes partition partition_name, and the data in that partition, from a partitioned table:

```
alter table dept drop partition d3;
```

TIP
Dropping a table partition causes its local index (but not the other local partition indexes) to be dropped and a global index (one that exists on the entire table) to be unavailable (unless your are willing to rebuild the indexes afterward). Don't use global indexes if you desire to drop partitions of a table.

■   ***TRUNCATE PARTITION partition_name***   Removes all rows from a partition in a table. The example that follows shows the truncation of the D1 partition. Note that you must also rebuild the indexes after this operation.

```
Alter table dept truncate partition d1;
Alter index dept_idx rebuild partition d1;
```

■   ***SPLIT/MERGE PARTITION partition_name_old***   Creates two new partitions, each with a new segment, new physical attributes, and new initial extents. The segment associated with the old partition is discarded. The example that follows shows *splitting* the D1 partition into a D1A partition and D1B partition at deptno=5. Note that you must also rebuild the indexes after this operation.

```
Alter table dept split partition d1 at (5) into
   (partition d1a tablespace dept1,
    partition d1b tablespace dept2);
```

```
SEGMENT_NAME  PARTITION_NAME  SEGMENT_TYPE
------------  --------------  ----------------
DEPT          D1A             TABLE PARTITION
DEPT          D1B             TABLE PARTITION
DEPT          D2              TABLE PARTITION
```

Other Partitioning Options

```
Alter index dept_idx rebuild partition d1a;
Alter index dept_idx rebuild partition d1b;
```

You can take two partitions and combine them into one partition using the *merge*. The example that follows shows *merging* the D1A and D1B partition back into the partition named D1. Note that you must also rebuild the indexes after this operation.

```
Alter table dept merge partition d1a, d1b
into partition d1;


SEGMENT_NAME  PARTITION_NAME  SEGMENT_TYPE
------------  --------------  ----------------
DEPT          D1              TABLE PARTITION
DEPT          D2              TABLE PARTITION


Alter index dept_idx rebuild partition d1;
```

- **UNUSABLE LOCAL INDEXES** Marks all the local index partitions associated with partition_name as unusable.

- **REBUILD UNUSABLE LOCAL INDEXES** Rebuilds the unusable local index partitions associated with partition_name.

- **UNUSABLE** Marks the index or index partition(s) as unusable. An unusable index must be rebuilt, or dropped and re-created, before it can be used. While one partition is marked unusable, the other partitions of the index are still valid, and you can execute statements that require the index if the statements do not access the unusable partition. You can also split or rename the unusable partition before rebuilding it.

- **REBUILD PARTITION** Rebuilds one partition of an index. You can also use this option to move an index partition to another tablespace, or to change a create-time physical attribute.

Index Partitioning

Partitioned indexes have the same advantages as partitioned tables. Accessing smaller pieces instead of one index on the entire table increases performance when properly executed. There are local and global indexes, and prefixed or non-prefixed indexes. A local index has been partitioned; each piece is a local index. A global index is a non-partitioned index, used before partitioning existed. A prefixed index is when the leftmost part of the index is the partition key, whereas a nonprefixed index can be costly to access, since the partition key is not indexed. If a partition of a table with a global index is dropped, then the corresponding global index is invalidated. If a partition of a table with a local index is dropped, then the local index is also dropped.

In Release 9i and earlier the session parameter SKIP_UNUSABLE_INDEXES was provided to allow the user to disable error reporting of indexes and index partitions marked unusable. In Release 10g, this is now an initialization parameter and defaults to TRUE. If you do not want the database to choose a new execution plan to avoid using unusable segments, you should set this parameter to false.

The following is an example of a local partitioned index (the most common type). The index name is dept_index, and the index is on the deptno column of the dept table. The index is split into three pieces (d1, d2, and d3) that are located in three tablespaces (dept1, dept2, and dept3) that are striped differently from the location of the corresponding data. This will ensure that accessing information from a partition of a table and its corresponding index partition will result in accessing two physical disk drives instead of one—given that dept1–dept3 are tablespaces that correspond to data files on different physical disks.

```
create index dept_index on dept (deptno)
  local
 (partition d1 tablespace dept2,
  partition d2 tablespace dept3,
  partition d3 tablespace dept1);

Index Created.
```

We can get the information regarding partitioned indexes by accessing dba_indexes:

```
select    index_name, partition_name, tablespace_name
from      dba_indexes
where     index_name = 'DEPT_INDEX'
order by  partition_name;


INDEX_NAME     PARTITION_NAME     TABLESPACE_NAME
DEPT_INDEX              D1              DEPT2
DEPT_INDEX              D2              DEPT3
DEPT_INDEX              D3              DEPT1
```

TIP
Indexes that are partitioned (local indexes) should also be prefixed; the partitioning key is the leading edge of the index.

Exporting Partitions

Partitions can be effortlessly exported. If the data in your table is segmented carefully, it is possible to keep all new information in a single partition to export. This is only true for certain data sets, which use some sort of increasing column value for partition key. For example, if you partition on date, all new data goes into the latest partition. However, if your data is partitioned by username, or some other generic identifier, then this is not always true. This potentially could eliminate the need to export data from partitions that have not changed and have been previously exported. By using the EXPORT command and giving the owner.table.partition_name for the table to be exported, only the partition is exported.

```
exp user/pass file=tab.dmp tables=(owner.table.partition_name)
```

TIP
If you are archiving old data, consider exchanging the partition to a table name that is more verbose before exporting it. This way, you could import just that table back for reference later and potentially avoid even having to return it to the partitioned table.

Eliminating Fragmentation

Fragmentation can hamper space management operations in the database, but it is a long-enduring myth that overall the number of extents in a segment *always* impacts performance against the database. It is an equally long-enduring myth that the number of extents *never* impacts performance. Bitmap indexes with many non-contiguous extents spanning multiple datafiles can be a big performance problem. Generally, locally managed tablespaces can minimize most extent-related issues. The need for repeated reorganizations should be a thing of the past for most DBAs (but not all DBAs), if you have set up your storage properly. Unfortunately, if you do still need to deal with the occasional reorganization, you now have several ways of performing this activity while minimizing down time.

To avoid performance issues with extent management, you can do the following:

- Use locally managed uniform-extent tablespaces when you know how big a segment will grow.

- Use uniform extent sizes in dictionary-managed tablespaces, except the SYSTEM tablespace.

- Use extent sizes that are multiples of the database block size.

- Move tables to tablespaces with an appropriate extent size when they grow too large.

- Avoid FREELIST contention by using ASSM.

- Rebuild or split tablespaces with uniform extent sizes.

It is recommended that you regularly monitor your database to find segments that are growing to extreme numbers of extents (over a thousand) and then manage those segments appropriately.

```
select    segment_name, segment_type, extents, bytes
from      dba_segments a, dba_tablespaces b
where     a.extents > 1000;
```

SEGMENT_NAME	SEGMENT_TYPE	EXTENTS	BYTES
ORDER	TABLE	2200	220000000
ORDER_IDX1	INDEX	1200	120000000
CUSTOMER	TABLE	7000	70000000

TIP
Query DBA_SEGMENTS on a regular basis to ensure that objects are not building up too many extents (when not using ASM). Catching problems early is the key to avoiding performance issues later. Correctly locating objects in tablespaces with uniform extent sizes that are appropriate based on the growth of the object is the key.

Using the Correct Extent Size

When data is read from a table, it is either accessed by a ROWID operation via an index or by a full table scan (except for index-organized tables). In most cases, access by ROWID is the preferred method. This is because the ROWID method allows the database to determine the exact block that a record resides in and therefore bypasses any extent allocation information in the segment. The short answer is that ROWID operations do not care how many extents are in the segment. Database block sizes generally range from 4K to 32K. So, regardless of the number of extents in a segment, a full table scan will always perform the same number of reads as long as the extent size is a multiple of the database block size. So do we still need to worry about extent counts if we are using extents that are multiples of the block size? Yes we do, but we aren't as driven by it as we used to be. Think of it this way, the more extents you have, the more you have to manage, even if it is managed via faster methods. Therefore, my rule of thumb is, if you have a segment growing over 4096 extents (assuming you are using locally managed tablespaces), consider moving it to a tablespace where the extent size is more appropriate for the size of the segment. If you have a 15GB table, using a 200M extent size is probably more efficient than using a 1M extent size. For the purposes of loading data alone, you will save back-end processing time because the database does not have to allocate as many extents during the load process.

Create a New Tablespace and Move the Segments to It

If a table is getting very large, you can reduce the number of extents by creating a new tablespace and moving the data to the new location. In our example, the customer table is fragmented into 100 extents of 1M each, which can be found by querying the DBA_EXTENTS view:

```
select   SEGMENT_NAME, BYTES
from     DBA_EXTENTS
where    SEGMENT_NAME = 'CUSTOMER';


SEGMENT_NAME          BYTES
CUSTOMER              1048576
CUSTOMER              1048576
CUSTOMER              1048576
CUSTOMER              1048576
..etc.
```

First, create a tablespace and then create a new customer table called customer1 into the new_10M_dat tablespace (this tablespace has 10M extents that will better accommodate its growth):

```
CREATE TABLE CUSTOMER1
TABLESPACE NEW_10M_DAT
AS SELECT * FROM CUSTOMER;
```

After ensuring that the customer1 table was created, then drop the original table and all of its indexes:

```
DROP TABLE CUSTOMER;
```

You can now rename your new table and build its corresponding indexes (rebuilding indexes can be time consuming depending on the size of the table):

```
RENAME CUSTOMER1 TO CUSTOMER;
```

The new customer table now occupies only 10 extents that are 10M in size. If the customer table is growing even faster, you will want to move it to a tablespace with an even larger uniform extent size to accommodate this growth. While you will still have to rebuild the indexes on the customer table (one of the drawbacks to this method), it does ensure that the table is never physically gone from the database until the new table is created. You can also use the COPY command to avoid the rollback segment requirements. You can also use the NOLOGGING option (as of version 8) to avoid redo issues. An example of using the NOLOGGING feature is displayed in the two examples listed next.

The following is an example of creating a table with NOLOGGING:

```
create table orders_temp
as select * from orders
nologging;

Table created.
```

Here's an example of creating an index with NOLOGGING:

```
Create index ot_idx1 on orders_temp (order_no) nologging;

Index created.
```

TIP
Use NOLOGGING option when rebuilding a problem table to avoid the redo.

Exporting and Then Re-Importing the Table

You can also relocate the table by exporting, manually creating the table in the new tablespace, and then re-importing the table with the ignore=y option. Don't forget to include your indexes, grants, and constraints (set their import parameters to Y when you export and import) and make sure you create a large enough rollback segment (not if using Automatic UNDO) for the import. You can also use this method to move your indexes to tablespaces with a larger extent size by creating an indexfile and modifying it to change the tablespace location. You can minimize the rollback or undo area needed by setting COMMIT=Y (to commit during the table import) and you can set the buffer setting higher to increase the speed of the import. The following procedure describes the operation:

```
Export the CUSTOMER Table
Import the CUSTOMER table with indexfile=[file name]
Modify indexfile file to create table in new location.
(Optional: Modify index locations also)
Drop the CUSTOMER Table

Create the table from the modified script.
Import the CUSTOMER Table (Ignore=y)
```

Do *not* use the compress option (compress=y) when you export. This used to be the method of reducing fragmentation, but while it could still be used, it shouldn't. First of all, if you are still using dictionary-managed tablespaces, it will ruin your uniform extent allocation. Second, if you are using locally managed tablespaces this will just confuse things, since the object views in the database will report the initial extent value as much larger, probably, than it actually is. Using export/import is faster than recreating the table using SQL as described in the preceding section, but it could be a problem if something were to happen to the export file before you have a chance to do the import. Pre-creating the table in the new tablespace is a critical step, since the import will normally want to put the table back where you exported it from.

TIP
To speed up the actual import of the table, use the indexes=n option to not create the indexes at import time. Since you have the indexfile script created for changing the table location, you can run this script after the import to recreate the indexes.

To Avoid Chaining, Set Percents Correctly

When a row is created in a table, the data is written to a block and is given a ROWID. The ROWID identifies the data's location on disk. If a row is updated, the changes are written to the same location on disk. The ROWID for the row does not change. Row chaining can occur when there isn't enough room in the data blocks to store a single row or the most recent changes made to a row. A chained row is one that exists in multiple blocks instead of a single block. Accessing multiple blocks for the same row can be costly in terms of performance. To see if you have chaining problems, run the utlchain.sql script that Oracle provides to create the "chained_rows" table. The utlchain.sql file is a file that comes with Oracle and is in the /rdbms/admin subdirectory of your ORACLE_HOME. You can also use Enterprise Manager or look for "fetch by continued row" in STATSPACK or AWR Report to detect chained rows. You should check for chaining on a weekly basis and fix any problems immediately. To analyze the amount of chaining in a table (customer in this example) run the following query:

```
ANALYZE TABLE CUSTOMER
LIST CHAINED ROWS;
```

Then, run the following query accessing the CHAINED_ROWS table to check the customer table for chaining:

```
select   HEAD_ROWID
from     CHAINED_ROWS
where    TABLE_NAME = 'CUSTOMER';
```

If no rows are returned, then you don't have a chaining problem. If there is a chaining problem, then the query will return the head_rowid for all chained rows. You can also use select "count(*)" against the CHAINED_ROWS table to find the number of chained rows. In V$SYSSTAT, the "table fetch continued row" is an indicator of chained rows as well.

To avoid row chaining, set PCTFREE (the amount of space reserved in a block for updates) correctly. This parameter is set when the table is created. The default value is set to 10 (10 percent free for updates), but this needs to be much higher in a table where there is a large frequency of update activity to rows in the table.

Incidentally, if you have a table where update activity will be very low to non-existent, you can set the PCTFREE to a slightly lower value to assure more rows will fit into the block and therefore conserve space in your table.

TIP
Find chaining problems by accessing the CHAINED_ROWS table.
Avoid chaining problems by correctly setting PCTFREE.

Automatic Segment Space Management

In version 9*i* of the database, Oracle introduced Automatic Segment Space Management, as an alternative to using free lists, in locally managed tablespaces. This system of managing free space in segments utilizes bitmaps to track the amount of free space in blocks that is available for inserting rows. Since free lists are no longer used when ASSM is enabled, the overall time and resource needed by the database is greatly minimized.

In 10*g*, the database has expanded the feature set of ASSM further and provided a new clause to the ALTER TABLE and ALTER INDEXES statements. The "SHRINK SPACE" clause essentially coalesces the free space in the segment, releasing unused space so that the segment can be smaller. This can improve the performance of queries on this segment, and it is much easier to implement than reducing a segment size through export/import or move/rename operations. Refer to the documentation on this feature for restrictions and limitations.

ASSM should improve overall performance of block management within segments, but there is a circumstance where the architecture of using a free space bitmap for the block usage can slow performance. Full table scans of small tables (<1000 rows) will actually require more buffer gets than a non-ASSM tablespace. Therefore, if you have your tablespaces organized by the size of segments, ASSM should probably be used only on those tablespaces with medium to large segments.

ASSM has the potential to make a dramatic improvement to block management performance, but do your research, as there are several bugs scattered across different versions of the database that can affect you in specific situations. Before implementing ASSM on your system, be sure to research the types of segments you will have in your tablespace and check for issues related to operations against those types of segments for your version of the database. Most of these bugs have patches that can be applied to resolve the issues.

TIP
Use ASSM instead of FREELISTS, FREELIST GROUPS, and PCTUSED.

Rebuilding the Database

While you should rarely need to do this, it seems that more and more people are looking to this as a necessary step to move forward. Sometimes it is because they have decided to move the database to a new platform like Linux. In other cases, there are new features in release 10*g* that are best implemented in a "new" database. However, be aware that this is a very large step to take and can be very time-consuming (e.g., take up an entire weekend) and should be done only by an advanced DBA. It is not guaranteed to bring you any performance benefit. Therefore, it should be planned in advance, tested, and done only when absolutely necessary. To rebuild the database, an advanced DBA should complete the following steps in the order presented:

1. Complete a full-database export.

2. Complete a full-image backup, which includes the following:

   ■ The database files

   ■ The control files

   ■ The online redo log files

   ■ The init.ora(s)

3. Run a rebuild on the database by using the CREATE DATABASE command.

4. Make sure you have a large enough rollback segment and large enough temporary tablespace to handle importing the database and the creation of indexes.

5. Import the entire database.

Refer to the *DBA Administrators Guide* for a more detailed approach.

Increasing the Log File Size and LOG_CHECKPOINT_INTERVAL for Speed

If you want to speed up large numbers of INSERTs, UPDATEs, and DELETEs, increase the sizes of your log files and make sure that they are on the fastest disk. Previously, you could also increase the LOG_CHECKPOINT_INTERVAL if it was set such that it would checkpoint prior to a log switch, but this parameter is being deprecated and currently defaults to zero (which indicates switching based on the redo log being full). Increasing the size of your log files can increase the time needed for media recovery.

Oracle relies on online redo log files to record transactions. Each time a transaction takes place in the database, an entry is added to the online redo log file. If you increase the size allocated for the log, you can increase performance. Uncommitted transactions generate redo entries, too, because they generate undo records and these undo records are also written to the redo logs. You can watch the logs spin during a large batch transaction. But keep the following characteristics in mind when you make modifications to the size of your log files:

■ A log file must be online and available while the database is up or the database will halt (one of the few things that stop the database immediately).

■ Online redo log files are recycled and offline redo log files are created automatically (if archiving is activated).

■ Offline logs are the ones that have been closed for archiving or backup.

■ Minimum is two online redo log files. Online redo log file multiplexing (additional copies) is recommended if an online redo log file is lost.

■ The number of initial log files and their sizes are determined when the database is created.

■ Archive logging can be turned on and off by the ALTER DATABASE command.

■ Checkpoints are points when committed transactions in redo logs get written to the database.

Determining If Redo Log File Size Is a Problem

Two potential problems are possible that should be addressed. The first concerns batch jobs that do not have enough total redo space to complete or are so fast that the online redo logs wrap (cycle through all the logs and start writing to the first one again) before they are archived to the offline redo logs. Because an online redo log cannot be overwritten until it is archived (when archiving is enabled), DML and DDL activity has to wait until an online log becomes available. By listing the online redo logs with their last update date and time at the operating system level, you can determine how often they are switching. You can also query V$LOG_HISTORY for the last 100 log switches. If you increase the size of the online redo logs, it may provide the space for large batch jobs doing large INSERT, UPDATE, and DELETE transactions. A better solution may be to increase the number of online redo logs so that the additional space is provided while also having a frequent log switch (smaller but more online redo logs).

The second concern is for very long-running jobs that are spending a large amount of time switching online redo logs. Long-running jobs are often much faster when the entire job fits into a single online redo log. For the online transaction processing (OLTP) type of environment, smaller online redo logs are usually better. My rule of thumb is for online redo logs to switch every half hour (not counting the long-running batch jobs that shorten this time). By monitoring the date and time of the online redo logs at the operating system level (or querying v$log_history), you can make a determination to increase the size or number of online redo logs to reach an optimum switching interval.

Here is a query that will show you the time between log switches. It can be handy in determining if you have a problem:

```
select  b.recid,
        to_char(b.first_time,'dd-mon-yy hh:mi:ss') start_time, a.recid,
        to_char(a.first_time,'dd-mon-yy hh:mi:ss') end_time,
        round(((a.first_time-b.first_time)*25)*60,2) minutes
from    v$log_history a, v$log_history b
where   a.recid = b.recid+1
order   by a.first_time asc
/
```

Determining the Size of Your Log Files and Checkpoint Interval

You can determine the size of your online redo log files by checking the size at the operating system level or querying the V$LOG and V$LOGFILE tables. Displaying information about redo logs is shown in the query listed here:

```
select  a.member, b.*
from    v$logfile a, v$log b
where   a.group# = b.group#;
```

MEMBER	GRP#	THRD#	BYTES	MEMBERS	STATUS
/disk1/log1a.ora	1	1	2048000	2	INACTIVE
/disk1/log2a.ora	2	1	2048000	2	CURRENT

```
/disk2/log1b.ora   1     1      2048000   2        INACTIVE
/disk2/log2b.ora   2     1      2048000   2        CURRENT
(partial columns listed only...)
```

The query output shows two groups of logs. Each group has two log files in it (one primary file and one multiplexed file). The data in /disk1/log1a.ora and in /disk2/log1b.ora is exactly the same (multiplexing log files is for availability and recoverability purposes).

TIP
Increase the size of your log files to increase the rate at which large INSERTS, DELETES, and UPDATES (DMLs) are processed.

Other Helpful Redo Log Commands

You can add additional logs by using the ALTER DATABASE ADD LOGFILE. . . command to create larger logs and then drop the smaller ones. Keep in mind that the checkpoint interval will force a checkpoint based on the number of blocks specified for the CHECKPOINT_INTERVAL in the init.ora file. So, if you increase the size of your online redo logs, make sure that you also increase your checkpoint interval. To multiplex online redo log files (create a mirrored copy) use this command to add a log file to an existing group:

```
alter database add logfile member '/disk2/log1b.ora' to group 1;
alter database add logfile member '/disk2/log2b.ora' to group 2;
```

To drop an online redo log member, use this command:

```
alter database drop logfile member '/disk2/log2b.ora';
```

To add a new online redo log group, use this command:

```
alter database add logfile group 3 ('/disk1/log3a.ora') size 10M;
```

To drop an entire online redo log group (all copies), use this command:

```
alter database drop logfile group 1;
```

NOTE
You cannot drop a redo log file group if doing so would cause the redo thread to contain less than two redo log file groups.

To switch log files, use this command:

```
alter system switch logfile;
```

TIP
Put the redo logs on the fastest disk if you plan to do write a lot of information. Try to use the outer edge of the disk (the fastest part on many disk types) for the redo logs.

Determine the Size of Log Files and Checkpoint Interval

TIP
Increase the size of online redo logs if log switches are occurring less than every half hour during normal business conditions (excluding infrequent large batch jobs). Increase the number of online redo logs if you are wrapping during large batch jobs.

Additional init.ora Parameters

The following init.ora parameters can have an effect on the performance of your online log files:

- **LOG_ARCHIVE_DUPLEX_DEST** Directory location with archive prefix (arch). This is a location to write an additional copy of archive logs (as redo logs are filled and are archived in ARCHIVELOG mode only). If you have the space, this is a nice safety net to save you if archiving errors occur.

- **LOG_ARCHIVE_MIN_SUCCEED_DEST** Can be set to 1 to 10 if you are using LOG_ARCHIVE_DEST_*n*. Values of 1 or 2 if you are using LOG_ARCHIVE_DEST and LOG_ARCHIVE_DUPLEX_DEST. This is the minimum number of successful archives written for a redo log. If you set it to 2, then you have two mandatory archiving destinations, similar to setting LOG_ARCHIVE_DEST1 and LOG_ARCHIVE_DEST2. If you set it to 1, then the LOG_ARCHIVE_DUPLEX_DEST is an optional best-effort archive site, not a mandatory site.

- **DB_WRITER_PROCESSES** This is the number of database writers to write data from the SGA to disk when one database writer isn't enough.

- **DBWR_IO_SLAVES** If you can't use multiple processes (or if you don't have asynch I/O and want to emulate it), then you can use DBWR_IO_SLAVES to distribute the load over multiple I/O slaves. This can't be used if DB_WRITER_PROCESSES > 1.

Flash Recovery

The flash recovery area is a new mechanism for maintaining recovery information on disk to improve recovery time. This new feature in 10g greatly improves the ability to recover more quickly from an issue in your database, but it can take a lot of extra disk space to implement. For this reason, many people may be inclined to utilize slower, less expensive storage for maintaining the flash recovery area. This introduces some potential performance implications to your environment, depending on how you implement it. Oracle suggests you have an equal size group of disk on another disk array for your flash recovery:

- If you are using a slower-performing disk for your flash recovery area, redo performance will be negatively affected, since all redo activity is governed by the slowest performing device.

- Consider whether you want to have a very large flash recovery area, and find out what size is the most appropriate for your recovery needs or budget.

- A large flash recovery area can slow down your write performance when backups and other activities utilize the flash recovery area.

Instead of implementing flash recovery on a large scale, consider using a smaller flash recovery area with two groups of disk for redo. This would look more like having two archive log destinations. This configuration has these advantages:

- Because the flash recovery area is most often used only for archive and flashback db writes, it doesn't overburden the disk.

- This configuration still maintains redundant redo areas.

Increasing Chances of Recovery: Committing after Each Batch

To increase your chances of recovering large batch processes, COMMIT after each batch process. While this will slow processing, it will save time if a recovery is necessary. A large batch process really depends on how large your system is, but a job that takes several hours to complete should be broken into smaller jobs that have periodic COMMITs so that the entire job doesn't need to be rerun in its entirety, in the event of a failure during the job.

Using Rollback Segments

Rollback segments hold the data snapshot (before image) during an update or delete. With the initialization parameter UNDO_MANAGEMENT=MANUAL, rollback segments are used as in previous versions of Oracle (covered in this section). With the initialization parameter UNDO_MANAGEMENT=AUTO, undo tablespace management is used, which is covered in the section following those on rollback segments.

When a transaction is rolled back, a snapshot of the data is applied. When setting up your database using rollback segments, reserve multiple tablespaces for rollback segments so that users do not contend with each other in the same tablespace (which usually means the same physical disk):

```
Tablespace1/disk1: rbseg1
Tablespace2/disk2: rbseg2
Tablespace3/disk3: rbseg3
Tablespace4/disk4: rbseg4
Tablespace1/disk1: rbseg5
Tablespace2/disk2: rbseg6
Tablespace3/disk3: rbseg7
Tablespace4/disk4: rbseg8
```

Avoiding Contention among Rollback Segments

As a rule of thumb, you don't want more than one user *using* a rollback segment at a given time, although a general recommendation for the number of rollback segments is based on four concurrent transactions per rollback segment. You should base the number of rollback segments on the needs of your system, not this guideline.

Avoiding Contention among Rollback Segments

Monitoring Rollback Segment Waits and Contention

You can use Oracle's Enterprise Manager to check rollback fragmentation and use. The v$ tables are also a good way to monitor rollback segment waits and contention. SQL statements like the following one can also be used to display rollback information:

```
select   a.name, b.extents, b.rssize, b.xacts, b.waits, b.gets,
         optsize, status
from     v$rollname a, v$rollstat b
where    a.usn = b.usn;
```

NAME	EXTENTS	RSSIZE	XACTS	WAITS	GETS	OPTSIZE	STATUS
SYSTEM	4	540672	1	0	51		ONLINE
RB1	2	10240000	0	0	427	10240000	ONLINE
RB2	2	10240000	1	0	425	10240000	ONLINE
RB3	2	10240000	1	0	422	10240000	ONLINE
RB4	2	10240000	0	0	421	10240000	ONLINE

Examine the results to determine if you need to add rollback segments. If the xacts (active transactions) are regularly above 1 (or your chosen threshold of users per rollback segment) for any of the rollback segments, then increase the number of rollback segments to eliminate potential contention. If the wait is greater than 0, then increase the number of rollback segments to eliminate contention.

Increasing Rollback Segments

If demand is high, you can increase the number of rollback segments by adding a rollback segment; for example, you could create a rollback segment named rb9 into the rollback2 tablespace, as shown here:

```
Create rollback segment rb9
tablespace rollback2
storage (initial 1M next 2M);
```

TIP
Try to keep the number of users per rollback segment to one. This can be accomplished by monitoring the number of users per rollback segment and adding rollback segments if needed. This will keep waits and contention to a minimum.

Isolating Large Transactions to Their Own Rollback Segments

When using rollback segments, keep in mind that batch processes may require a single large rollback segment. Use the "set transaction use rollback segment rollbig" for large transactions (you can't do this if you are using automatic undo mode). An example is displayed next. Also, note that you must precode the "set transaction" with a COMMIT even if it is the first command for your session.

```
commit;
set transaction use rollback segment rb_big;
delete from big_table;
commit;
```

TIP
Failure to use the "set transaction use rollback segment rollbig"
command for a given UPDATE, INSERT, DELETE, or BATCH program
could cause the rollback segments to become fragmented and
potentially too large for the corresponding tablespace. The "set
transaction…" command must be reissued after each COMMIT or
rollback process.

A rollback segment is dynamically extended as needed by a transaction up to the total available space in the tablespace (transactions cannot span rollback segments) in which it resides. The OPTIMAL storage option for a rollback segment will dynamically shrink extended rollback segments to a specified size. While large transactions should be preceded with the "set transaction…" statement, it is still a good idea to set the OPTIMAL option so that rollback segments that have been extended are returned to their original size, releasing the disk space. Use this statement to alter a rollback segment to OPTIMAL:

```
alter rollback segment rb1
storage (optimal 15M);
```

Note that you may also use the OPTIMAL storage setting at rollback creation time.
You can also force a rollback segment to shrink to its optimal setting or a specified size using these commands:

```
alter rollback segment rb1 shrink;
alter rollback segment rb1 shrink to 15M;
```

TIP
Do not depend on the OPTIMAL setting to constantly shrink rollback
segments as this is a costly process in terms of performance. The
OPTIMAL setting should be activated infrequently. Also, note that
you cannot shrink a rollback segment to a size that is less than the
combined value of its first two extents.

The Simpler Approach: UNDO Tablespace
In 9*i*, Oracle offers a new approach for managing rollback or "undo" data in the database. This approach is creation of "undo" tablespaces in the database, which greatly simplifies the management of these transactions. With rollback segments, undo blocks are overwritten by newer transactions

as required. This leads to the "juggling" by the DBA to ensure that large enough rollback segments are available for large transactions to avoid a "snapshot too old" error as well as to ensure that enough rollback segments are available for the regular activity on the database and to keep rollback header contention minimized.

To utilize Automatic Undo management, create a tablespace in the database of type UNDO.

```
create undo tablespace UNDOTBS1 datafile '/u01/oradata/prod/undotbs1_01.dbf'
extent management local uniform size 256k;
```

Next, modify your initialization file to specify three new parameters:

- UNDO_MANAGEMENT=AUTO

- UNDO_TABLESPACE=UNDOTBS1

- UNDO_RETENTION = <# of minutes>

CAUTION
*If UNDO_MANAGEMENT is set to AUTO and the UNDO_*
TABLESPACE is not set, then the SYSTEM tablespace is used.
(Don't do this.)

The initialization parameter UNDO_RETENTION is used to specify the amount of time (in seconds) that undo data is retained in the undo tablespace after it is committed. This is the real advantage of using undo tablespaces, since unlike with traditional rollback segments, the database will at least make an attempt to maintain the older version of the data for long-running queries. Another advantage is that if you are running into issues where you aren't maintaining enough undo information, you can simply add more space to the tablespace and increase the value of UNDO_RETENTION.

Be aware, though, that if the tablespace does not have enough room for all of the undo records, it will reuse unexpired undo space as necessary regardless of the UNDO_RETENTION setting. One thing that you can't do if you are using Automatic Undo Management is to use a particular rollback segment.

Monitoring Undo Space

The V$UNDOSTAT view can be used to monitor the utilization of undo space by current transactions in the instance. Each row in this view lists statistics collected in the instance for ten-minute intervals. Each row represents one snapshot of the statistics for undo space utilization, transaction volume, and query length, every ten minutes for the last 24 hours.

A database can have either UNDO segments or rollback segments. The V$ROLLSTAT view will show information on the undo segments in the undo tablespace when in automatic undo management mode. Information on the actual extents for the undo tablespace can be retrieved from the DBA_UNDO_EXTENTS view in the database. If you set UNDO_MANAGEMENT to AUTO, DBAs cannot manage undo segments at all. If you create an UNDO tablespace, you can create rollback segments in UNDO tablespaces, but it is strongly recommended *not* to do it. When using UNDO segments, they are implemented as rollback segments in the UNDO tablespace. This is why V$ROLLSTAT works.

Killing Problem Sessions

If the demand for resources on your system is at a temporary peak, you can stop a low priority, problem session by using the operating system KILL command. But first, you must find the user who's running the job that is draining system resources. The following commands will help you find and KILL the problematic users:

```
select   sid, serial#
from     v$session
where    username = 'BADUSER'
```

Here is the query output:

```
SID    SERIAL#
5      33
```

The following command is used to KILL the session:

```
alter system kill session '5,33';
```

You can also use the following code to determine which rollback segment is processing each transaction, along with the corresponding user and SQL statement. The output has been slightly modified for readability):

```
select   a.name, b.xacts, c.sid, c.serial#, c.username, d.sql_text
from     v$rollname a, v$rollstat b, v$session c, v$sqltext d,
         v$transaction e
where    a.usn = b.usn
and      b.usn = e.xidusn
and      c.taddr = e.addr
and      c.sql_address = d.address
and      c.sql_hash_value = d.hash_value
order by a.name, c.sid, d.piece;
```

name	xacts	sid	serial#	username	sql_text
RB1	1	5	33	USER1	delete from test1;
RB2	1	7	41	USER9	update orders
					set items = 5
					where orderno = 555;

The preceding output shows which users are currently using rollback segments. This query could also show how many users are utilizing or waiting for the same rollback segment if the WAITS column is also selected.

TIP
Isolate large transactions to their own rollback segment, but in 10g, use undo tablespaces (automatic undo) to simplify your undo management.

Don't Sort in the SYSTEM or SYSAUX Tablespaces

Having the initialization parameters SORT_AREA_SIZE or HASH_AREA_SIZE or else the parameter PGA_AGGREGATE_TARGET set too small to accommodate sorts in memory can be a cause of fragmentation in the SYSTEM tablespace. The fragmentation occurs because the temporary tablespace gets used for disk sorting instead of in memory. When setting up your system, be aware that the temporary tablespace adheres to the following characteristics:

- If you do not specify a temporary tablespace or tablespace group, then the user's temporary segments are stored in the database default temporary tablespace, or if none has been specified, in the SYSTEM tablespace. This can be changed with an ALTER USER command or during the CREATE USER command.

- It is used when the available memory is not large enough to process the entire data set.

- It stores the temporary segments generated by the following statements:

```
Create Index
select.... Order By
select.... Distinct
select.... Group By
select.... Union
select.... Intersect
select.... Minus
Unindexed Joins
Some Correlated Subqueries
```

To lower your chances of fragmentation, set the initialization parameters SORT_AREA_SIZE or PGA_AGGREGATE_TARGET (you should be using this in 10g) to eliminate disk sorts related to the preceding SQL commands. (See Chapter 4 for more information on tuning the initialization parameters.) Also, make sure that you create a separate temporary tablespace that has a uniform extent size. Then, direct users to that temporary tablespace using the following statement:

```
SQL> ALTER USER username TEMPORARY TABLESPACE temp1;
```

Also, use ALTER DATABASE to set the default temporary tablespace to TEMP1 for all users created in the future.

Temporary tablespaces can also be locally managed. If you are on a version of the database that supports locally managed tablespaces, your temporary tablespaces should be locally managed to reduce disk contention during disk sorting operations. Tablespaces of type temporary use tempfiles. Tempfiles carry some special characteristics that improve performance, but they can require some additional attention. If you use the command CREATE TEMPORARY TABLESPACE, the temp tablespace is locally managed; it cannot be dictionary managed. You can have dictionary-managed temporary tablespaces only if you put the TEMPORARY keyword after the tablespace name. However, this syntax has been deprecated.

Locally managed temporary tablespaces

- Do not generate undo information and therefore do not require the disk impact of those operations.

■ Do not carry the same dictionary extent overhead caused by dictionary-managed temporary tablespaces.

■ Do not allocate the entire "tempfile" when created. This means that you may add a 2GB tempfile, but it will not show up as 2GB on disk until it is utilized.

■ Are not maintained in the control file the same way other datafiles are. Therefore, some utilities such as RMAN will not address them. But who cares? If the temp tablespace is not backed up and gets corrupted or damaged, just create a new one!

Have Multiple Control Files on Different Disks and Controllers

Control files store information regarding startup, shutdown, and archiving. Because your system is useless without at least one good control file, you should store three copies of the control files on separate disks and controllers (if possible). If you do happen to remove *all* the control files while the database is open, you can use the ALTER DATABASE BACKUP CONTROLFILE command to generate a new one. If the database is closed and the control file is missing, you can use the CREATE CONTROLFILE statement to re-create a control file. However, recreating the control file from scratch is a lot of work and prone to error. And lots of valuable, possibly critical, information is lost (for example, most recent backup information for RMAN backups). To view current control files, run the following query:

```
select   name, value
from     v$parameter
where    name = 'control_files';


NAME                  VALUE
control_files         /disk1/ora10/ctl1.ora,  /disk2/ora10/ctl2.ora,
                      /disk3/ora10/ctl3.ora
```

Using Raw Devices to Improve I/O for Write-Intensive Data

A *raw* device is an unformatted disk slice (a portion of a physical disk) that Oracle can read and write without the overhead of Unix I/O buffering (the content of a raw device is not managed by the operating system). While raw devices may improve performance, they are becoming less attractive as other options become prevalent. Most claims of substantial performance improvements resulting from using raw devices come from hardware sales representatives. Raw devices are not currently in wide-scale use, since there is little evidence that they offer substantial performance gains. In my tests, raw devices have increased performance from 5–10 percent, but with an increased cost in maintenance. For large data warehouses, however, raw devices can provide excellent performance and should definitely be explored. Now that clustered file systems are available, Oracle RAC no longer needs raw devices in Oracle 9.2, but raw devices are supported in 10gR2 if desired.

Reasons for Using Raw Devices

There are several reasons you may choose to use raw devices (especially for a data warehouse):

- If I/O is the problem on your system *and* the CPU sits relatively idle.

- If asynchronous I/O is available on your platform.

- If you have variable disk partitioning (and are able to "slice" the disk easily), then raw devices become a choice for write-intensive, sequentially accessed data and redo log files not included in backup procedures.

Drawbacks

While there are a number of advantages to using raw devices, there are some drawbacks:

- Administration of raw devices is more costly. Many common operating system backup utilities provided by the hardware vendor cannot be used with raw devices.

- If I/O is not the bottleneck, then raw devices will probably not help much.

- If variable disk partitioning is not available, you will often allocate far more space than is needed for a given file, causing space to be wasted (very common).

- If raw devices are used in a production environment, Oracle recommends that backup and recovery be thoroughly tested before employing the raw devices.

Other Disk I/O Precautions and Tips

Here are a few further miscellaneous notes pertaining to disk I/O:

- Heavy batch processing may need much larger rollback, redo, and temp tablespace sizes.

- Heavy DML (INSERT, UPDATE, and DELETE) processing may need much larger rollback, redo, and temporary tablespace sizes.

- Heavy user access to large tables will require more CPU and memory, and larger temporary tablespace sizes.

- Poorly tuned systems will require more CPU and memory, and larger temporary tablespace sizes.

- A greater number of well-balanced disks and controllers will always increase performance (by reducing I/O contention).

- If you increase in the disk capacity, you can speed backup and recovery time by keeping a copy of the backup on disk instead of tape.

- Finally, if you can afford it, EMC and/or solid state disks and solutions are still one of the absolute best ways to improve Oracle I/O performance.

Issues to Consider in the Planning Stages

If you're planning a new system or an upgrade, here are some things you'll want to consider:

- What is the maximum possible disk capacity for the hardware?
- What disk sizes are available?
- What will be the initial size of the database?
- What will be the future size of the database and what is the rate of growth?
- Will there be a RAID (striping) level for database files or OS?
- What recovery methods will be employed?
- What archiving methods will be used to store historical information?
- How often will report output be kept on the system?
- What development space will be needed?
- What software will be installed, and how much space will it need to function efficiently?
- What system utilities will be installed, and how much space will they need to function efficiently?
- What type of mail system is going to be installed?
- What data transfer methods are going to be employed?
- Is ASM a possibility? Learn and plan for it if it is.
- What are the batch processing requirements, and will there be ad hoc user queries?
- How will the data be accessed that may cause potential hot spots?

TIP

When you are in the system planning stage, ensure that you find out all of the information related to the current and future use of the system. Don't just think about the Oracle database needs—investigate the other software and applications that will have performance implications for your Oracle database.

Tips Review

- Try to avoid splitting a logical device in a disk array into more than one file system. This action may seem to give you flexibility, but it can also increase the number of datafile locations you have to manage.

- Use disk arrays to improve performance and protect your data against disk failure. Choose the proper RAID level and technology solutions that enable you to maintain the availability your organization needs. Don't just go "good enough," because you will regret it at 2 A.M. when you lose a disk.

- Separate key Oracle data files to ensure that disk and disk cache contention is not a bottleneck. By separating tables and indexes of often-joined tables, you can ensure that even the worst of table joins do not result in disk contention.

- Query V$FILESTAT and V$DATAFILE to see how effectively data files have been balanced. Temporary tablespaces are monitored using V$TEMPFILE and V$TEMPSTATS.

- Solve disk contention problems by moving data files to disks that are not as heavily accessed or moving tables to different tablespaces on different disks.

- Use the Database Files Metrics in Enterprise Manager to determine the I/O that is taking place on each database file. Move heavily used datafiles to separate file systems to distribute I/O. See Chapter 5 for addition information.

- Dictionary-managed tablespaces are obsolete. We have so many new options, they generally shouldn't even be used anymore.

- To minimize disk I/O on a single large table, break the table into multiple partitions that reside on different physical disks.

- Although ASM does not provide multipathing capabilities, ASM does leverage multipathing tools, as long the path or device produced by the multipathing tool returns a successful return code from an fstat system call. Metalink Note 294869.1 provides more details on ASM and multipathing.

- To get accurate real-time statistics, it maybe be prudent to query the V$ASM_DISK and V$ASM_DISKGROUP views, but caution should be exercised when running queries against these views during peak workloads.

- The init.ora parameter asm_power_limit is used to influence the throughput and speed of the rebalance operation. The range of values for asm_power_limit is 0 to 11, where a value of 11 is full throttle and a value of 1 is low speed. A value of 0, which turns off automatic rebalance, should be used with caution.

- If removing or adding several disks with ASM, it is a best practice to add or remove drives all at once. This will reduce the number rebalance operations that are needed for storage changes.

- Accessing DBA_TABLES, DBA_PART_TABLE, and DBA_SEGMENTS provides additional information concerning tables that have been partitioned.

- You can also partition tables using multiple columns as the partitioning criteria.

- Dropping a table partition causes its local index (but not the other local partition indexes) to be dropped and a global index (one that exists on the entire table) to be unavailable. Don't use global indexes if you desire to drop partitions of a table.

- Indexes that are partitioned (local indexes) should also be prefixed (the partitioning key is the leading edge of the index).

- Use NOLOGGING when rebuilding a problem table. Examples using NOLOGGING are covered in Chapter 11.

■   Find chaining problems by accessing the CHAINED_ROWS table. Avoid chaining problems by correctly setting PCTFREE.

■   Add larger log files and drop the smaller log files to increase the speed of large INSERT, UPDATE, and DELETE statements.

■   Try to keep the number of concurrent users per rollback segment to one. This can be accomplished by monitoring the number of users per rollback segment and adding rollback segments if needed. This will keep waits and contention to a minimum.

■   When you are in the system planning stage, ensure that you find out all of the information related to the current and future use of the system. Don't just think about the Oracle database needs, investigate the other software and applications that will have performance implications on your Oracle database.

References

TUSC DBA Guide, 1988–2006
DBA Reference Guide (Oracle Corporation)

Many thanks to Bill Callahan, who once again did a wonderful update to this chapter, and Nitin Vengurlekar, who contributed the massive amount of ASM knowledge to this chapter.

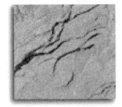

CHAPTER
4

Tuning the Database with Initialization Parameters (DBA)

The init.ora file (and spfile) determines many Oracle operating system environment attributes, such as memory allocated for data, memory allocated for statements, resources allocated for I/O, and other crucial performance-related parameters. Each version of Oracle continues to add to the total number of initialization parameters. In Oracle 10*g* Release 2 there are now 1381 (257 documented and 1124 hidden) different initialization parameters (these numbers vary slightly on different versions of Oracle and platforms). As you might expect, an entire book could be written on how to set and tune each parameter; this book focuses on the key parameters that affect database performance. The key to an optimized Oracle database is often the architecture of the system and the parameters that set the environment for the database. Setting four key initialization parameters (SGA_MAX_SIZE, PGA_AGGREGATE_TARGET, DB_CACHE_SIZE, and SHARED_POOL_SIZE) can be the difference between sub-second queries and queries that take several minutes. There is also a new SGA_TARGET parameter that can replace some of the key parameter that can be set as well that is covered in this chapter. This chapter will focus on the crucial initialization parameters but also list the top 25 initialization parameters near the end of the chapter. The chapter concludes with a look at typical server configurations for various database sizes.

This chapter contains the following tips and techniques designed to achieve the greatest performance gain with the least effort by focusing on the parameters that yield the biggest impact:

- Crucial initialization parameters in Oracle

- Modifying the initialization parameter file without a restart

- Viewing the initialization parameters via Enterprise Manager

- Tuning DB_CACHE_SIZE and monitoring hit ratios

- Tuning the SHARED_POOL_SIZE

- Checking library cache and dictionary cache

- Querying the X$KSMSP table to get another picture of SHARED_POOL_SIZE

- Using multiple buffer pools

- Tuning the PGA_AGGREGATE_TARGET

- User, session, and system memory use

- Cost- vs. rule-based optimization

- The top 25 performance-related initialization parameters to consider

- Undocumented initialization parameters (more in Appendix A)

- Typical server setups with different size databases

Identifying Crucial Initialization Parameters

While tuning specific queries alone can lead to performance gains, the system will still be slow if the parameters for the initialization file are not set correctly because the initialization file plays such an integral role in the overall performance of an Oracle database. While you can spend time setting all the initialization parameters, there are just four main parameters that need to be set correctly to realize significant performance gains:

- SGA_MAX_SIZE
- PGA_AGGREGATE_TARGET
- DB_CACHE_SIZE
- SHARED_POOL_SIZE

TIP
The key initialization parameters in Oracle are SGA_MAX_SIZE, PGA_AGGREGATE_TARGET, DB_CACHE_SIZE, and SHARED_POOL_SIZE.

There is also a new parameter, SGA_TARGET, which can be set so that Oracle manages the shared memory on your system (Automatic Shared Memory Management); Metalink Note 295626.1 describes this in detail. While this is a new parameter, the Oracle Application Development team recommends this for 10*g* (I included these recommendations at the end of this chapter). I would like to see this mature a bit more before I hand the "keys to the car" to Oracle, but I like the approach to simplicity, especially for beginners. The following query can be used to find the current settings of the key initialization parameters on your database (if SGA_TARGET is set to a non-zero value, then some of these parameters will be set to zero):

```
Col name for a25
Col value for a50

select    name, value
from      v$parameter
where     name in ('sga_max_size', 'pga_aggregate_target',
                   'db_cache_size', 'shared_pool_size');


NAME                     VALUE
------------------------ -------------------- ---

shared_pool_size         50331648
sga_max_size             135338868
db_cache_size            25165824
pga_aggregate_target     25165824
```

Changing the Initialization Parameters Without a Restart

With each version of Oracle, more and more parameters can be altered without needing to restart the database. This has greatly reduced the need for scheduled downtime to implement system tuning changes. The next example shows changing the SHARED_POOL_SIZE to 128M while the database is running:

```
SQL> ALTER SYSTEM SET SHARED_POOL_SIZE = 128M;
```

In addition to being able to dynamically change parameters, Oracle 10g provides for the use of a SPFILE to persistently store dynamic changes to the instance parameters. Prior to Oracle 9i, any dynamic changes were lost when the database was restarted unless the parameters were added to the initialization parameter file manually. As of Oracle 9i and continuing into Oracle 10g Release 2, dynamic changes can be stored in a server parameter file (spfile). The default order of precedence when an instance is started is to read parameter files in the following order:

1. spfile<SID>.ora

2. spfile.ora

3. init<SID>.ora

Parameters can be dynamically modified at a system-wide or session-specific scope. In addition, parameters can be changed in memory only or persist across restarts via an SPFILE.

TIP
If you can't figure out why your system isn't using the value in your init.ora file, you probably have an spfile overriding it. And, don't forget, you can also use a hint to override parameters at the query level in 10gR2.

Finally, in a Real Application Cluster environment, parameters can be changed for a single node or for all nodes in a cluster.

There are two key fields in the V$PARAMETER view:

- **ISSES_MODIFIABLE**   Indicates if a user with the ALTER SESSION privilege can modify this initialization parameter for their session.

- **ISSYS_MODIFIABLE**   Indicates if someone with ALTER SYSTEM privilege can modify this particular parameter.

The following query illustrates a list of initialization parameters that can be set without shutting down and restarting the database. This query displays the initialization parameters that can be modified with an ALTER SYSTEM or ALTER SESSION command (partial result displayed):

```
select     name, value, isdefault, isses_modifiable, issys_modifiable
from       v$parameter
where      issys_modifiable <> 'FALSE'
or         isses_modifiable <> 'FALSE'
order by   name;
```

The result of the query is all of the initialization parameters that may be modified:

NAME	VALUE	ISDEFAULT	ISSES	ISSYS_MOD
aq_tm_processes	0	TRUE	FALSE	IMMEDIATE
archive_lag_target	0	TRUE	FALSE	IMMEDIATE
background_dump_dest	C:\oracle\admin\orcl9ir2\bdump	FALSE	FALSE	IMMEDIATE
backup_tape_io_slaves	FALSE	TRUE	FALSE	DEFERRED

Be careful granting the ALTER SESSION privilege to users, as knowledgeable developers can set individual parameters that positively affect their session at the expense of others on the system.

TIP
Changing initialization parameters dynamically is a powerful feature for both developers and DBAs. Consequently, a user with the ALTER SESSION privilege is capable of irresponsibly allocating 100M+ for the SORT_AREA_SIZE for a given session, if it is not restricted.

Viewing the Initialization Parameters with Enterprise Manager

You can also use Enterprise Manager to view the initialization parameter settings in the Configuration screen under the Instance option. The section of Enterprise Manager displayed in Figure 4-1 shows the initialization parameters. It shows the current settings for the parameters and also shows if the parameters can be modified (dynamic=Y) without shutting down the database. Oracle Enterprise Manager is covered in detail in Chapter 5.

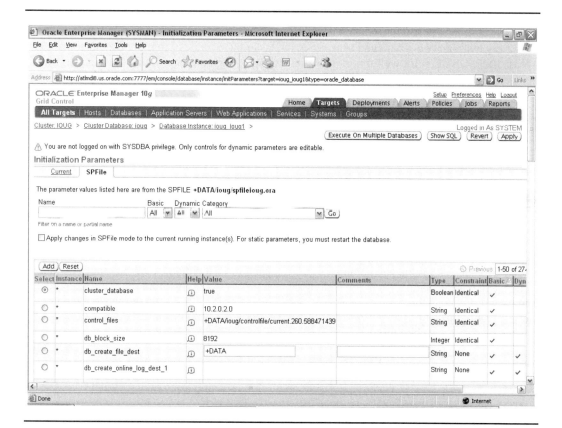

FIGURE 4-1. *Enterprise Manager—initialization parameters in the SPFILE*

Increasing Performance by Tuning the DB_CACHE_SIZE

Long-time users of Oracle and readers of prior editions of this book will notice that some familiar parameters have not been mentioned. This is because parameters such as DB_BLOCK_BUFFERS have been deprecated (a parameter _DB_BLOCK_BUFFERS is set behind the scenes for backward compatibility). While many of the familiar parameters from prior version of Oracle are still valid, using them disables many Oracle 10g Release 2 features, including automatic cache memory management. This chapter focuses on the Oracle 10g Release 2 parameters for tuning your system.

DB_CACHE_SIZE is the first parameter to look at in the initialization parameter file because it's the most crucial parameter in Oracle. If the DB_CACHE_SIZE is set too low, Oracle won't have enough memory to operate efficiently and the system may run poorly, no matter what else you do to it. If DB_CACHE_SIZE is too high, your system may begin to swap and may come to a halt. DB_CACHE_SIZE makes up the area of the SGA that is used for storing and processing data in memory. As users request information, data is put into memory. If the DB_CACHE_SIZE parameter is set too low, then the least recently used data will be flushed from memory. If the flushed data is recalled with a query, it must be reread from disk (causing I/O and CPU resources to be used).

Retrieving data from memory can be over 10,000 times faster than disk (depending on the speed of memory and disk devices). Even if you take into consideration disk caching (memory on disk) and Oracle inefficiencies, retrieving data from memory is still about 100 times faster than reading data from disk. Therefore, the higher the percentage of frequency that records are found in memory (without being retrieved from disk), the faster the overall system performance (usually at least 100 times faster for well-tuned queries). Having enough memory allocated to store data in memory depends on the value used for DB_CACHE_SIZE (or for SGA_TARGET if used).

TIP
Retrieving data from physical memory is generally substantially faster than retrieving it from disk, so make sure that the SGA is large enough. One Oracle study showed Oracle memory access as averaging about 100 times faster than disk access. However, this takes into account disk caching advances, which you may or may not have on your system. The same study also showed an individual case where Oracle memory access was well over 10,000 times faster than disk (which was hard for me to believe), but it shows how important it is to measure this on your own unique system.

DB_CACHE_SIZE is the key parameter to use when tuning the data cache hit ratio. The data cache hit ratio is the percentage of the data block accesses that occur without requiring a physical read from disk. While there are several situations that can artificially inflate or deflate the data cache hit ratio, this ratio is a key indicator of system efficiency. The following query can be used to view the data cache hit ratio:

```
column phys          format 999,999,999   heading 'Physical Reads'
column gets          format 999,999,999   heading ' DB Block Gets'
column con_gets      format 999,999,999   heading 'Consistent Gets'
column hitratio format 999.99 heading ' Hit Ratio '
  select    sum(decode(name,'physical reads',value,0)) phys,
            sum(decode(name,'db block gets',value,0)) gets,
```

```
            sum(decode(name,'consistent gets', value,0)) con_gets,
            (1 - (sum(decode(name,'physical reads',value,0)) /
            (sum(decode(name,'db block gets',value,0)) +
            sum(decode(name,'consistent gets',value,0)))))) * 100 hitratio
from        v$sysstat;


Physical Reads  DB Block Gets Consistent Gets  Hit Ratio
--------------  ------------- ---------------  -----------
     1,671          39,561          71,142        98.49
```

While there are exceptions for every application, a data cache hit ratio of 95 percent or greater should be achievable for a well-tuned transactional application with the appropriate amount of memory. Because there is such a performance difference between some disk devices and memory access, improving the data cache hit ratio from 90 to 95 percent can nearly double system performance when reading disk devices that are extremely slow. Improving the cache hit ratio from 90 to 98 percent could yield nearly a 500 percent improvement where disks are extremely slow and under the right (or should I say wrong) architectural setup.

Poor joins and poor indexing can also yield very high hit ratios due to reading many index blocks, so make sure that your hit ratio isn't high for a reason other than a well-tuned system. An unusually high hit ratio may indicate the introduction of code that is poorly indexed or includes join issues.

TIP
Hit ratios are useful to experienced DBAs but can be misleading for inexperienced DBAs. The best use of hit ratios is still to compare over time to help alert you to a substantial change to a system on a given day. While there are some that have deprecated hit ratios, they are usually tool vendors who don't see the value of tracking hit ratios over time, since their tools are point-in-time or reactive-based tuning solutions. Hit ratios should never be your only tool, but they should definitely be one of many proactive tools in your arsenal.

Oracle continues to downplay the importance of hit ratios by reducing the discussions on hit ratio tuning. Oracle is beginning to focus on analyzing system performance in terms of work done (CPU or service time) versus time spent waiting for work (wait time). Areas where hit ratios are still the primary tuning method are library cache and dictionary cache. See Chapter 14 on STATSPACK for more information on balancing the entire tuning arsenal including hit ratios.

Using V$DB_CACHE_ADVICE in tuning DB_CACHE_SIZE
V$DB_CACHE_ADVICE is a view introduced in Oracle 9*i* to assist in tuning DB_CACHE_SIZE. The view can be queried directly, and the data in the view is used by the Oracle kernel (or database engine) to make automatic cache management decisions. Here is an Oracle 10*g* Release 2 query (note that Oracle 9*i* Release 1 does not have the column size_factor) to view the effect of changing DB_CACHE_SIZE on the data cache hit ratio:

```
select name, size_for_estimate, size_factor, estd_physical_read_factor
from   v$db_cache_advice;
```

NAME	SIZE_FOR_ESTIMATE	SIZE_FACTOR	ESTD_PHYSICAL_READ_FACTOR
DEFAULT	4	.1667	1.8136
DEFAULT	8	.3333	1.0169
DEFAULT	12	.5	1.0085
DEFAULT	16	.6667	1
DEFAULT	20	.8333	1
DEFAULT	24	1	1

Reading these results, we see the following:

- The current cache size is 24MB (size_factor = 1).

- We can decrease the cache size to be 16MB and maintain the current cache hit ratio, since the physical_read_factor remains at 1 up to a decrease to 16MB.

While this view provides an estimate of the effect of changing the cache size on the cache hit ratio, any changes should be tested to validate that the results are as forecasted. Oracle Enterprise Manager provides a graphical view of the data in V$DB_CACHE_ADVICE.

Keeping the Hit Ratio for the Data Cache Above 95 Percent

The hit ratio for the data cache should generally be above 95 percent for transactional systems. But, the best use for a hit ratio is to study your system over time to see major changes that should warrant further investigation. Usually, if your hit ratio is below 95 percent, you may need to increase the value of DB_CACHE_SIZE. In some instances, you can increase performance substantially by increasing the hit ratio from 95 to 98 percent—especially if the last 5 percent of the hits going to disk are the main lag on the system.

Monitoring the V$SQLAREA View to Find Bad Queries

Although hit ratios below 95 percent are usually a sign that your DB_CACHE_SIZE is set too low or that you have poor indexing, distortion of the hit ratio numbers is possible and needs to be taken into account while tuning. Hit ratio distortion and non-DB_CACHE_SIZE issues include the following:

- Recursive calls

- Missing or suppressed indexes

- Data sitting in memory

- Rollback segments

- Multiple logical reads

- Physical reads causing the system to use CPU

To avoid being misled, locate bad queries by monitoring the V$SQLAREA view. Once you isolate the queries that are causing performance hits, tune the queries or modify how the information is stored to solve the problem. Using the Performance page of Enterprise Manager

Grid Control, a DBA can generate the TopSQL for their system. The TopSQL section of Enterprise Manager Grid Control (Figure 4-2) displays a list of the worst SQL statements in the current cache based on Activity and also the Top Sessions by Activity. The DBA can then click on the problem SQL to begin the process of analyzing and tuning the problem SQL statement. Chapter 5 discusses the benefits of Oracle's Enterprise Manager in detail and how to tune the SQL statements using Enterprise Manager Grid Control.

TIP
In Oracle 10g Release 2, use the Enterprise Manager Grid Control to find problem queries.

Hit Ratios Are Not Always Accurate

If you are utilizing hit ratios to measure performance, note that within Performance Manager, during peak times the number of disk reads is larger than the number of in-memory reads and thus the negative hit ratio is being computed in terms of the deltas between physical reads and logical reads.

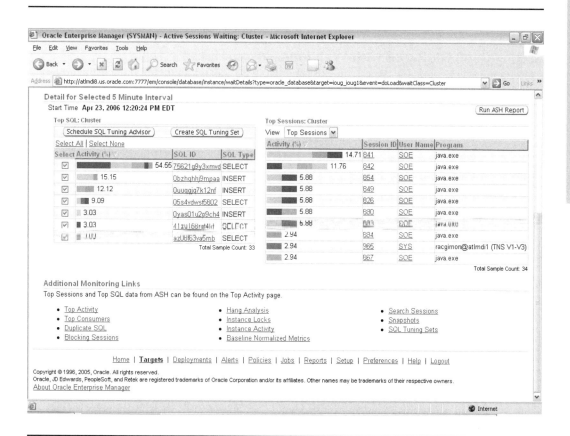

FIGURE 4-2. *Use Oracle's Enterprise Manager Grid Control to find problem queries.*

Bad Hit Ratios Can Occur When an Index Is Suppressed

Consider the following query where the CUSTOMER table is indexed on the unique custno column. It is *not* optimal to have this index suppressed by using the NVL, because it results in a poor hit ratio.

```
select     custno, name
from       customer
where      nvl(custno,0)   = 5789;

Tries (Logical Reads) = 105        Physical = 100
% hit ratio     =     (1    -       Physical/Tries) x 100
% hit ratio     =     (1 - 100/105) x 100%
% hit ratio     =        4.8%  (A very low/bad hit ratio)
```

If you are looking at this in Enterprise Manager, there is an index missing on a query that is being executed at the current time. Focus on the query that is causing this problem and fix the query. The query can be found by accessing the V$SQLAREA view as shown in Chapter 8.

TIP
A low hit ratio for a query is an indication of a missing or suppressed index.

Getting Good Hit Ratios with Well-Indexed Queries

Consider the following query, where the customer table is indexed on the unique custno column. In this situation, it is optimal to utilize the custno index because it results in an excellent hit ratio.

```
select     custno, name
from       customer
where      custno = 5789;

Tries (Logical Reads) = 105 Physical = 1
% hit ratio     =     (1 - Physical/Tries) x 100
% hit ratio     =     (1 - 1/105) x 100%
% hit ratio     =        99% (A very high/usually good hit ratio)
```

If you are looking at this in the Enterprise Manager, there is usually an index on the query that is being executed.

Bad Queries Executing a Second Time Can Result in Good Hit Ratios

When a full table scan is completed for the second time and the data is still in memory, you may see a good hit ratio even though the system is trying to run a bad query.

```
Tries (Logical Reads) = 105        Physical = 1
% hit ratio     =     (1 - Physical/Tries) x 100
% hit ratio     =     (1 - 1/105) x 100%
% hit ratio     =        99% (A very high/usually good hit ratio)
```

If you are looking at this in the Enterprise Manager, it appears that there is an index on the query being executed when in fact the data is in memory from the last time it was executed. The result is that you are "hogging up" a lot of memory even though it appears that an indexed search is being done.

TIP
Bad (slow) queries show in V$SQLAREA view with poor hit ratios the first time they are executed. Make sure your tune them at that time. The second time that they execute, they may not show a poor hit ratio.

Other Hit Ratio Distortions

There are several other hit distortions to consider:

- **Oracle Forms distortion**   Systems that use Oracle Forms (screens) frequently might use the same information over and over. This reuse by some of the users of the system will drive up the hit ratio. Other users on the system may not be experiencing hit ratios that are as good as the Forms users, yet the overall system hit ratio may look very good. The DBA must take into consideration that the Forms users can be boosting the hit ratio to an artificially high level.

- **Rollback segment distortion**   Because the header block of the rollback segment is usually cached, the activity to the rollback segment gives a falsely high hit ratio impact when truly there is no significant impact on the hit ratio.

- **Index distortion**   An index range scan results in multiple logical reads on a very small number of blocks. Hit ratios as high as 86 percent can be recorded when none of the blocks are cached prior to the query executing. Make sure you monitor the hit ratio of individual poorly tuned queries in addition to monitoring the big picture (overall hit ratio).

- **I/O distortion**   Physical reads that appear to be causing heavy disk I/O may be actually causing you to be CPU bound. In tests, the same amount of CPU was used for 89 logical reads as it was to process 11 physical reads. The result is that the physical reads are CPU costly because of BUFFER MANAGEMENT. Fix the queries causing the disk I/O problems and you will usually free up a large amount of CPU as well. Performance degradation can be exponentially downward spiraling, but the good news is that when you begin to fix your system, it is often an exponentially upward-spiraling event. It's probably the main reason why some people live to tune; tuning can be exhilarating.

Setting DB_BLOCK_SIZE to Reflect the Size of Your Data Reads

The DB_BLOCK_SIZE is the size of the default data block size when the database is created. With Oracle 10g Release 2, each tablespace can have a different block size, thus making block size selection a *less* critical selection before the database is created. That said, a separate cache memory allocation must be made for each different database block size. But, it is still very important to choose wisely. While you can have different block size tablespaces, this is not truly a performance feature, as the non-default buffer caches are not optimized for performance. So, you still want to put the bulk of your data in the default buffer cache. The database must be rebuilt if you want to increase the DB_BLOCK_SIZE.

The data block cache for the default block size is set using the DB_CACHE_SIZE initialization parameter. Cache is allocated for other database block sizes by using the DB_nK_CACHE_SIZE, where *n* is the block size in KB. The larger the DB_BLOCK_SIZE, the more that can fit inside a

Setting DB_BLOCK_SIZE to Reflect Size of Data Reads

single block and the more efficient large amounts of data can be retrieved. A small DB_BLOCK_SIZE actually lets you retrieve single records faster and saves space in memory. In addition, a smaller block size can improve transactional concurrency and reduce log file generation rates. As a rule of thumb, a data warehouse should use the maximum block size available for your platform (either 16KB or 32KB), while a transaction processing system should use an 8KB block size. Rarely is a block size smaller than 8KB beneficial. If you have an extremely high transaction rate system or very limited system memory, you might consider a block size smaller than 8KB.

Full table scans are limited to the maximum I/O of the box (usually 64K, but as high as 1M on many systems). You can up the amount of data read into memory in a single I/O by increasing DB_BLOCK_SIZE to 8K or 16K. You can also increase the DB_FILE_MULTIBLOCK_READ_COUNT to the value of (max I/O size)/DB_BLOCK_SIZE.

Environments that run a lot of single queries to retrieve data could use a smaller block size, but "hot spots" in those systems will still benefit from using a larger block size. Sites that need to read large amounts of data in a single I/O read should increase the DB_FILE_ MULTIBLOCK_READ_ COUNT. Setting the DB_FILE_MULTIBLOCK_READ_COUNT higher is especially important for data warehouses that retrieve lots of records. If the use of DB_FILE_MULTIBLOCK_READ_COUNT starts to cause many full table scans (since the optimizer now decides it can perform full table scans much faster and decides to do more of them) then set OPTIMIZER_INDEX_COST_ADJ between 1 and 10 (I usually use 10) to force index use more frequently.

TIP

The database must be rebuilt if you increase the DB_BLOCK_SIZE. Increasing the DB_FILE_MULTIBLOCK_READ_COUNT will allow more block reads in a single I/O, giving a benefit similar to a larger block size.

The general rule of thumb is to start with an SGA_MAX_SIZE parameter at 25 percent of the size allocated to your main memory. A large number of users (300+) or a small amount of available memory may force you to make this 15–20 percent of physical memory. A small number of users (less than 100) or a large amount of physical memory may allow you to make this 30–50 percent of physical memory. If you set the SGA_MAX_SIZE less than 128M, then the _ksm_granule_size will be 4M. If the SGA_MAX_SIZE is greater or equal to 128M, then the _ksm_granule_size will be 16M. This granule size will determine the multiples for other initialization parameters. A granule size of 4M means that certain initialization parameters will be rounded up to the nearest 4M. Therefore, if I set SGA_MAX_SIZE to 64M and DB_CACHE_SIZE to 9M, then the DB_CACHE_SIZE will be rounded to 12M (since the granule size is 4M). If I set SGA_MAX_SIZE to 200M and DB_CACHE_SIZE to 9M, then the DB_CACHE_SIZE will be rounded to 16M (since the granule size is 16M).

TIP

The SGA_MAX_SIZE determines the granule size for other parameters. An SGA_MAX_SIZE<128M means a 4M granule, whereas an SGA_MAX_SIZE>=128M means a 16M granule size.

Tuning the **SHARED_POOL_SIZE** for Optimal Performance

Sizing the SHARED_POOL_SIZE correctly will make sharing SQL statements that are identical possible. Getting the statement parsed is priority #1. If the query never makes it into memory, it can never request the data to be accessed; that's where the SHARED_POOL_SIZE comes in. SHARED_POOL_SIZE specifies the memory allocated in the SGA for data dictionary caching and shared SQL statements.

The data dictionary cache is very important because that's where the data dictionary components are buffered. Oracle references the data dictionary several times when a SQL statement is processed. Therefore, the more information (database and application schema and structure) that's stored in memory, the less information that'll have to be retrieved from disk. While the dictionary cache is part of the shared pool, Oracle also caches SQL statements and their corresponding execution plans in the library cache portion of the shared pool (see next section for how the shared SQL area works).

The data dictionary cache portion of the shared pool operates in a manner similar to the DB_CACHE_SIZE when caching information. For the best performance, it would be great if the entire Oracle data dictionary could be cached in memory. Unfortunately, this usually is not feasible, so Oracle uses a least recently used algorithm for deciding what gets to stay in the cache.

Using Stored Procedures for Optimal Use of the Shared SQL Area

Each time a SQL statement is executed, the statement is searched for in the shared SQL area and, if found, used for execution. This saves parsing time and improves overall performance. Therefore, to ensure optimal use of the shared SQL area, use stored procedures as much as possible, since the SQL parsed is exactly the same every time and therefore shared. However, keep in mind the only time the SQL statement being executed can use a statement already in the shared SQL area is if the statements are identical (meaning they have the same content exactly—the same case, the same number of spaces, etc.). If the statements are not identical, the new statement will be parsed, executed, and placed in the shared SQL area (exceptions to this are possible when the initialization parameter CURSOR_SHARING has been set to SIMILAR or FORCE).

In the following example, the statements are identical in execution, but the word *from* causes Oracle to treat the two statements as if they were different, thus *not* reusing the original cursor that was located in the shared SQL area:

```
SQL>    select name, customer from customer_information;
SQL>    select name, customer FROM customer_information;
```

TIP
SQL must be written exactly the same to be reused. Case differences and any other differences will cause a reparse of the statement.

In the following example, we are using different values for ENAME, which is causing multiple statements to be parsed.

```
declare
     temp VARCHAR2(10);
```

```
begin
     select ename into temp
     from   rich
     where  ename = 'SMITH';
     select ename into temp
     from   rich
     where  ename = 'JONES';
end;
```

A query of V$SQLAREA shows that two statements were parsed even though they were very close to the same thing. Note, however, that PL/SQL converted each SQL statement to uppercase *and* trimmed spaces *and* carriage returns (which is a benefit of using PL/SQL).

```
select sql_text
from   v$sqlarea
where  sql_text like 'SELECT ENAME%';

SQL_TEXT
-----------------------------------------------------
SELECT ENAME   FROM RICH   WHERE ENAME = 'JONES'
SELECT ENAME   FROM RICH   WHERE ENAME = 'SMITH'
```

In the following example, we see a problem with third-party applications that do not use bind variables (they do this to keep the code "vanilla" or capable of working on many different databases without modification). The problem with this code is that the developer has created many statements that fill the shared pool and these statements can't be shared (since they're slightly different). We can build a smaller shared pool so that there is less room for cached cursors and thus fewer cursors to search through to find a match (this is the band-aid inexperienced DBAs use). If the following is your output from v$sqlarea, you may benefit from lowering the SHARED_POOL _SIZE, but using CURSOR_SHARING is a better choice.

```
SQL_TEXT
-----------------------------------------------------
select empno from rich778 where empno =451572
select empno from rich778 where empno =451573
select empno from rich778 where empno =451574
select empno from rich778 where empno =451575
select empno from rich778 where empno =451576
etc. . .
```

Set CURSOR_SHARING=FORCE and the query to V$SQLAREA will change to the one listed next, because Oracle builds a statement internally that can be shared by all of the preceding statements. Now the shared pool is not inundated with all of these statements; only one simple statement that can be shared by all of them:

```
SQL_TEXT
-----------------------------------------------------
select empno from rich778 where empno =:SYS_B_0
```

Setting the SHARED_POOL_SIZE High Enough to Fully Use the DB_CACHE_SIZE

If the SHARED_POOL_SIZE is set too low, then you will not get the full advantage of your DB_CACHE_SIZE (since statements that can't be parsed can't be executed). The queries that can be performed against the Oracle V$ views to determine the data dictionary cache hit ratio and the shared SQL statement usage are listed in the sections that follow. These will help you determine if increasing the SHARED_POOL_SIZE will improve performance.

The SHARED_POOL_SIZE parameter is specified in bytes. The default value for the SHARED_POOL_SIZE parameter varies per system but is generally lower than necessary for large production applications.

Keeping the Data Dictionary Cache Hit Ratio at or above 95 Percent

The data dictionary cache is a key area to tune because the dictionary is accessed so frequently, especially by the internals of Oracle. At startup, the data dictionary cache contains no data. But as more data is read into cache, the likelihood of cache misses decreases. For this reason, monitoring the data dictionary cache should be done only after the system has been up for a while and stabilized. If the dictionary cache hit ratio is below 95 percent, then you'll probably need to increase the size of the SHARED_POOL_SIZE parameter in the initialization parameter file. Implementing Locally Managed Tablespaces (LMT) can also help your dictionary cache (see Metalink Note 166474.1, "Can We Tune the Row Cache!") However, keep in mind that the shared pool also includes the library cache (SQL statements) and Oracle decides how much the distribution will be for the library cache versus the row cache.

Use the following query against the Oracle V$ view to determine the data dictionary cache hit ratio:

```
select      ((1 - (Sum(GetMisses) / (Sum(Gets) + Sum(GetMisses)))) * 100) "Hit Rate"
from        V$RowCache
where       Gets + GetMisses <> 0;

 Hit Rate
---------
 91.747126
```

TIP

Measure hit ratios for the row cache (data dictionary cache) of the shared pool with the V$ROWCACHE view. A hit ratio of over 95 percent should be achieved. However, when the database is initially started, hit ratios will be around 85 percent.

Using Individual Row Cache Parameters to Diagnose Shared Pool Use   To diagnose a problem with the shared pool or the overuse of the shared pool, use a modified query to the V$ROWCACHE view. This will show how each individual parameter makes up the data dictionary cache, also referred to as the row cache.

```
column parameter       format a20            heading 'Data Dictionary Area'
column gets            format 999,999,999    heading 'Total|Requests'
column getmisses       format 999,999,999    heading 'Misses'
```

```
column modifications   format 999,999    heading 'Mods'
column flushes         format 999,999    heading 'Flushes'
column getmiss_ratio   format 9.99       heading 'Miss|Ratio'
set pagesize 50
ttitle 'Shared Pool Row Cache Usage'

select   parameter, gets, getmisses, modifications, flushes,
         (getmisses / decode(gets,0,1,gets)) getmiss_ratio,
         (case when (getmisses / decode(gets,0,1,gets)) > .1 then '*' else ' ' end) " "
from     v$rowcache
where    Gets + GetMisses <> 0;
```

Tue Aug 27   page   1
                         Shared Pool Row Cache Usage
                           Total   Miss
Data Dictionary Area   Requests   Misses   Mods Flushes Ratio
--------------------   ------------   ----------- ------- -------- ----- -

Data Dictionary Area	Total Requests	Misses	Mods	Flushes	Miss Ratio	
dc_segments	637	184	0	0	.29	*
dc_tablespaces	18	3	0	0	.17	*
dc_users	126	25	0	0	.20	*
dc_rollback_segments	235	21	31	30	.09	
dc_objects	728	167	55	0	.23	*
dc_global_oids	16	6	0	0	.38	*
dc_object_ids	672	164	55	0	.24	*
dc_sequences	1	1	1	1	1.00	*
dc_usernames	193	10	0	0	.05	
dc_histogram_defs	24	24	0	0	1.00	*
dc_profiles	1	1	0	0	1.00	*
dc_user_grants	24	15	0	0	.63	*

This query places an asterisk (*) for any query that has misses greater than 10 percent. It does this by using the CASE expression to limit the miss ratio to the tenth digit, and then analyzes that digit for any value greater than 0 (which would indicate a hit ratio of 10 percent or higher). A 0.1 miss or higher returns an *. Explanations of each of the columns are listed in the next section.

Keeping the Library Cache Reload Ratio at 0 and the Hit Ratio Above 95 Percent

For optimal performance, you'll want to keep the library cache reload ratio [sum(reloads) / sum(pins)] at zero and the library cache hit ratio above 95 percent. If the reload ratio is not zero, then there are statements that are being "aged out" that are later needed and brought back into memory. If the reload ratio is zero (0), that means items in the library cache were never aged or invalidated. If the reload ratio is above 1 percent, the SHARED_POOL_SIZE parameter should probably be increased. Likewise, if the library cache hit ratio comes in below 95 percent, then the SHARED_POOL_SIZE parameter may need to be increased. Also, if you are using ASMM, the SGA_TARGET includes both auto-tuned and manual parameters. When you decide to raise a parameter specifically (such as SHARED_POOL_SIZE), it will influence the auto-tuned part. (Other parameters will be affected; see Metalink Note 295626.1, "How to Use Automatic Shared Memory Management (ASMM) in Oracle 10g.")

There are a couple of ways to monitor the library cache. The first method is to execute the STATSPACK report (STATSPACK is covered in detail in Chapter 14). The second is to use the

V$LIBRARYCACHE view. The following query uses the V$LIBRARYCACHE view to examine the reload ratio in the library cache:

```
select    Sum(Pins) "Hits",
          Sum(Reloads) "Misses",
          ((Sum(Reloads) / Sum(Pins)) * 100)"Reload %"
from      V$LibraryCache;


Hits         Misses    Reload %
1969             50    0.253936
```

The next query uses the V$LIBRARYCACHE view to examine the library cache's hit ratio in detail:

```
select    Sum(Pins) "Hits",
          Sum(Reloads) "Misses",
          Sum(Pins) / (Sum(Pins) + Sum(Reloads)) "Hit Ratio"
from      V$LibraryCache;


HITS        MISSES     HIT RATIO
1989             5     .99749248
```

This hit ratio is excellent (over 99 percent) and does not require any increase in the SHARED_POOL_SIZE parameter.

Using Individual Library Cache Parameters to Diagnose Shared Pool Use   Using a modified query on the same table, we can see how each individual parameter makes up the library cache. This may help diagnose a problem or show overuse of the shared pool.

```
set numwidth 3
set space 2
set newpage 0
set pagesize 58
set linesize 80
set tab off
set echo off
ttitle 'Shared Pool Library Cache Usage'
column namespace     format a20                  heading 'Entity'
column pins          format 999,999,999          heading 'Executions'
column pinhits       format 999,999,999          heading 'Hits'
column pinhitratio   format 9.99                 heading 'Hit|Ratio'
column reloads       format 999,999              heading 'Reloads'
column reloadratio   format .9999                heading 'Reload|Ratio'
spool cache_lib.lis
select    namespace, pins, pinhits, pinhitratio, reloads, reloads
          /decode(pins,0,1,pins) reloadratio
from      v$librarycache;

Sun Mar 19                                                 page      1
                       Shared Pool Library Cache Usage
                                       Hit            Reload
```

Entity	Executions	Hits	Ratio	Reloads	Ratio
SQL AREA	1,276,366	1,275,672	1.00	2	.0000
TABLE/PROC	539,431	539,187	1.00	5	.0000
BODY	0	0	1.00	0	.0000
TRIGGER	0	0	1.00	0	.0000
INDEX	21	0	.00	0	.0000
CLUSTER	15	5	.33	0	.0000
OBJECT	0	0	1.00	0	.0000
PIPE	0	0	1.00	0	.0000
JAVA SRCE	0	0	1.00	0	.0000
JAVA RES	0	0	1.00	0	.0000
JAVA DATA	0	0	1.00	0	.0000

11 rows selected.

Use the following list to help interpret the contents of the V$LIBRARYCACHE view:

- **namespace**   The object type stored in the library cache. The values SQL AREA, TABLE/PROCEDURE, BODY, and TRIGGER show the key types.

- **gets**   Shows the number of times an item in library cache was requested.

- **gethits**   Shows the number of times a requested item was already in the library cache.

- **gethitratio**   Shows the ratio of gethits to gets.

- **pins**   Shows the number of times an item in the library cache was executed.

- **pinhits**   Shows the number of times an item was executed where that item was already in the library cache.

- **pinhitratio**   Shows the ratio of pinhits to pins.

- **reloads**   Shows the number of times an item had to be reloaded into the library cache because it aged out or was invalidated.

Keeping the Pin Hit Ratio for Library Cache Items Close to 100 Percent
The pin hit ratio for all library cache items "sum(pinhits) / sum(pins)" should be close to one (or a 100 percent hit ratio). A pin hit ratio of 100 percent means that every time the system needed to execute something, it was already allocated and valid in the library cache. While there will always be some misses the first time a request is made, misses can be reduced by writing identical SQL statements.

TIP

Measure hit ratios for the library cache of the shared pool with the V$LIBRARYCACHE view. A hit ratio of over 95 percent should be achieved. However, when the database is initially started, hit ratios will be around 85 percent.

Keeping the Miss Ratio Less Than 15 Percent
The miss ratio for data dictionary cache "sum(getmisses) / sum(gets)" should be less than 10 to 15 percent. A miss ratio of zero (0) means that every time the system went into the data dictionary cache, it found what it was looking for and did not have to retrieve the information from disk.

If the miss ratio "sum(getmisses) / sum(gets)" is greater than 10–15 percent, the initialization SHARED_POOL_SIZE parameter should be increased.

Using Available Memory to Determine if the SHARED_POOL_SIZE is Set Correctly

The main question that people usually want answered is: "Is there any memory left in the shared pool?" To find out how fast memory in the shared pool is being depleted (made noncontiguous or in use) and also what percent is unused (and still contiguous), run the following query after starting the database and running production queries for a short period of time (for example, after the first hour of the day):

```
col value for 999,999,999,999 heading "Shared Pool Size"
col bytes for 999,999,999,999 heading "Free Bytes"
select to_number(v$parameter.value) value, v$sgastat.bytes,
       (v$sgastat.bytes/v$parameter.value)*100 "Percent Free"
from   v$sgastat, v$parameter
where  v$sgastat.name = 'free memory'
and    v$parameter.name = 'shared_pool_size'
and    v$sgastat.pool = 'shared pool';


Shared Pool Size      Free Bytes Percent Free
---------------   ---------------- ------------
     50,331,648       46,797,132   92.9775476
```

If there is plenty of contiguous free memory (greater than 2MB) after running most of the queries in your production system (you'll have to determine how long this takes), then there is no need to increase the SHARED_POOL_SIZE parameter. I have never seen this parameter go all of the way to zero (Oracle saves a portion for emergency operations via the SHARED_POOL_RESERVED_SIZE parameter).

TIP
The V$SGASTAT view shows how fast the memory in the shared pool is being depleted. Remember that it is only a rough estimate. It shows you any memory that has never been used combined with any piece of memory that has been reused. Free memory will go up and down as the day goes on, depending on how the pieces are fragmented.

Using the X$KSMSP Table to Get a Detailed Look at the Shared Pool

The X$KSMSP table can be queried to get total breakdown for the shared pool. This table will show the amount of memory that is free, memory that is freeable, and memory that is retained for large statements that won't fit into the current shared pool. Consider the following query for a more accurate picture of the shared pool. Refer to Chapter 13 for an in-depth look at this query and how it is adjusted as Oracle is started and as the system begins to access shared pool memory.

```
select     sum(ksmchsiz) Bytes, ksmchcls Status
from       x$ksmsp
group by   ksmchcls;


     BYTES    STATUS
 ----------   ------
 50,000,000   R-free
```

```
              40    R-freea
     888,326,956    free
         837,924    freeabl
      61,702,380    perm
         359,008    recr
```

Oracle does not state anywhere what the values for status in the X$KSMSP table indicate. In the following table, I offer the following possible descriptions based on the behavior of these values as researched in Chapter 13.

Status	Possible Meaning
Free	This is the amount of contiguous free memory available.
Freeabl	Freeable but not flushable shared memory; currently in use.
Perm	I have read that this is permanently allocated and non-freeable memory, but in testing this, I find that it behaves as free memory not yet moved to the free area for use.
Recr	Allocated memory that is flushable when the shared pool is low on memory.
R-free	This is SHARED_POOL_RESERVED_SIZE (default 5 percent of SP).
R-freea	This is probably reserved memory that is freeable but not flushable.
R-recr	Recreatable chucks of memory in the reserved pool.
R-perm	Permanent chucks of memory in the reserved pool.

TIP
The general rule of thumb is to make the SHARED_POOL_SIZE parameter 50–150 percent of the size of your DB_CACHE_SIZE. In a system that makes use of a large amount of stored procedures or Oracle supplied packages but has limited physical memory, this parameter could make up as much as 150 percent the size of DB_CACHE_SIZE. In a system that uses no stored procedures but has a large amount of physical memory to allocate to DB_CACHE_SIZE, this parameter may be 10–20 percent of the size of DB_CACHE_SIZE. I have worked on larger systems where the DB_CACHE_SIZE was set as high as 100G. Note that in a shared server configuration (previously known as MTS) items from the PGA are allocated from the shared pool rather than the session process space.

Points to Remember about Cache Size

Here are some quick further notes about setting your cache and share pool sizes:

- If the dictionary cache hit ratio is low (below 95 percent), then consider increasing SHARED_POOL_SIZE.

- If the library cache reload ratio is high (>1 percent), then consider increasing SHARED_POOL_SIZE.

■   Size the data cache and shared pool appropriately for your systems in terms of workload requirements.

Waits Related to Initialization Parameters

Setting initialization parameters incorrectly will often result in various types of performance issues that will show up as general "waits" or "latch waits" in a STATSPACK report. In Chapter 14, we cover every type of wait and latch issue related to this. The following tables identify some waits and latch waits and their potential fixes.

Wait Problem	Potential Fix
Free buffer	Increase the DB_CACHE_SIZE; shorten the checkpoint; tune the code
Buffer busy	Segment Header — Add freelists or freelist groups or use ASSM
Buffer busy	Data Block — Separate hot data; use reverse key indexes; small block sizes
Buffer busy	Data Block — Increase initrans and/or maxtrans
Buffer busy	Undo Header —Use automatic undo management
Buffer busy	Undo Block — Commit more; use automatic undo management
Latch free	Investigate the detail (listing in next table of this chapter for fixes)
Log buffer space	Increase the log buffer; use faster disks for the redo logs
Scattered read	Indicates many full table scans — tune the code; cache small tables
Sequential read	Indicates many index reads — tune the code (especially joins)
Write complete waits	Adds database writers; checkpoint more often; buffer cache too small

Latch Problem	Potential Fix
Library cache	Use bind variables; adjust the shared_pool_size
Shared pool	Use bind variables; adjust the shared_pool_size
Row cache objects	Increase the shared pool. This is not a common problem.
Cache buffers chain	If you get this latch wait, it means you need to reduce logical I/O rates by tuning and minimizing the I/O requirements of the SQL involved. High I/O rates could be a sign of a hot block (meaning a block highly accessed). Cache *buffer lru chain* latch contention can be resolved by increasing the size of the buffer cache and thereby reducing the rate at which new blocks are introduced into the buffer cache. You should adjust DB_BLOCK_BUFFERS, and possible DB_BLOCK_SIZE. Multiple buffer pools can help reduce contention on this latch. You can create additional *cache buffer lru chain* latches by adjusting the configuration parameter DB_BLOCK_LRU_LATCHES. You may be able to reduce the load on the *cache buffer chain* latches by increasing the configuration parameter. _DB_BLOCK_HASH_BUCKETS may need to be increased or set to a prime number (in pre-9i versions).

Tuning the SHARED_POOL_SIZE for Optimal Performance

Some latch problems have often been bug related in the past, so make sure that you check Metalink for issues related to latches. Any of the latches that have a hit ratio below 99 percent should be investigated.

Using Oracle Multiple Buffer Pools

There are pools for the allocation of memory. They relate to the DB_CACHE_SIZE and SHARED_POOL_SIZE. Each of these parameters, which were all-inclusive of the memory they allocate, now has additional options for memory allocation within each memory pool. I will cover each of the two separately.

Pools Related to DB_CACHE_SIZE and Allocating Memory for Data

In this section, we will focus on the Oracle pools that are used to store the actual data in memory. The initialization parameters DB_CACHE_SIZE, DB_KEEP_CACHE_SIZE, and DB_RECYCLE_CACHE_SIZE will be the determining factors for memory used to store data. DB_CACHE_SIZE refers to the total size in bytes of the main buffer cache (or memory for data) in the SGA. Two additional buffer pools are DB_KEEP_CACHE_SIZE and DB_RECYCLE_CACHE_SIZE. These additional two pools serve the same purpose as the main buffer cache (DB_CACHE_SIZE), with the exception that the algorithm to maintain the pool is different for all three available pools. Note that the BUFFER_POOL_KEEP, DB_BLOCK_BUFFERS, and BUFFER_POOL_RECYCLE parameters have been deprecated and should no longer be used. Unlike BUFFER_POOL_KEEP and BUFFER_POOL_RECYCLE, DB_KEEP_CACHE_SIZE and DB_RECYCLE_CACHE_SIZE are not subtracted from DB_CACHE_SIZE; they are allocated in addition to DB_CACHE_SIZE.

The *main buffer cache* (defined by *DB_CACHE_SIZE*) maintains the LRU (least recently used) list and flushes the oldest buffers in the list. While all three pools utilize the LRU replacement policy, the goal for the main buffer cache is to fit most data being used in memory.

The *keep pool* (defined by *DB_KEEP_CACHE_SIZE*) is hopefully never flushed; it is intended for buffers that you want to be "pinned" indefinitely (buffers that are very important and need to stay in memory). Use the keep pool for small tables (that will fit in their entirety in this pool) that are frequently accessed and need to be in memory at all times.

The *recycle pool* (defined by *DB_RECYCLE_CACHE_SIZE*) is a pool from which you expect the data to be regularly flushed, since there is too much data being accessed to stay in memory. Use the recycle pool for large, less important data that is usually accessed only once in a long while (usually ad hoc user tables for inexperienced users are put here).

The following examples provide a quick look on how information is allocated to the various buffer pools. Remember, if no pool is specified, then the buffers in the main pool are used.

1. Create a table that will be stored in the keep pool upon being accessed:

   ```
   Create table state_list (state_abbrev varchar2(8), state_desc varchar2(25))
   Storage (buffer_pool keep);
   ```

2. Alter the table to the recycle pool:

   ```
   Alter table state_list storage (buffer_pool recycle);
   ```

3. Alter the table back to the keep pool:

   ```
   Alter table state_list storage (buffer_pool keep);
   ```

4. Find the disk and memory reads in the keep pool:

```
select    physical_reads "Disk Reads",
          db_block_gets + consistent_gets "Memory Reads"
from      v$buffer_pool_statistics
where     name = 'KEEP';
```

Modifying the LRU Algorithm

In this section, we're going to go over the deep edge for experts only. Skip this section if you've used Oracle for only a decade or less. There are five undocumented initialization parameters (defaults are in parentheses) that can be used to alter the LRU algorithm for greater efficiency when you really have studied and understand your system buffer usage well:

- **_db_percent_hot_default (50)**   The percent of buffers in the hot region

- **_db_aging_touch_time (3)**   Seconds that must pass to increment touch count again

- **_db_aging_hot_criteria (2)**   Threshold to move a buffer to the MRU end of LRU chain

- **_db_aging_stay_count (0)**   Touch count reset to this when moved to MRU end

- **_db_aging_cool_count (1)**   Touch count reset to this when moved to LRU end

We can see that by decreasing the value of the first of these parameters, we allow buffers to remain longer; setting it higher will cause a flush sooner. Setting parameter 2 lower will give higher value to buffers that are executed a lot in a short period of time. Parameters 3, 4, and 5 all relate to how quickly to move things from the hot end to the cold end and how long they stay on each end.

Pools Related to SHARED_POOL_SIZE and Allocating Memory for Statements

In this section, we will focus on the pools that are used to store the actual statements in memory. Unlike the pools related to the data, the LARGE_POOL_SIZE is allocated outside the memory allocated for SHARED_POOL_SIZE, but it is still part of the SGA.

The LARGE_POOL_SIZE is a pool of memory used for the same operations as the shared pool. Oracle defines this as the size set aside for large allocations of the shared pool. You'll have to do your own testing to ensure where the allocations are coming from in your system and version of Oracle. The minimum setting is 300K, but the setting must also be as big as the _LARGE_POOL_MIN_ALLOC, which is the minimum size of shared pool memory requested that will force an allocation in the LARGE_POOL_SIZE memory. Unlike the shared pool, the large pool does not have an LRU list. Oracle does not attempt to age memory out of the large pool.

You can view your pool settings by querying the V$PARAMETER view:

```
select    name, value, isdefault, isses_modifiable, issys_modifiable
from      v$parameter
where     name like '%pool%'
and       isdeprecated <> 'TRUE'
order by 1;
```

Using Oracle Multiple Buffer Pools

```
NAME                          VALUE ISDEFAULT ISSES ISSYS_MOD
----------------------------- ----------- --------- ----- ---------
java_pool_size                54525952    FALSE     FALSE IMMEDIATE
large_pool_size                2516582    FALSE     FALSE IMMEDIATE
olap_pool_size                 8388608    FALSE     FALSE DEFERRED
shared_pool_reserved_size      4613734    FALSE     FALSE FALSE
shared_pool_size             134217728    TRUE      FALSE IMMEDIATE
streams_pool_size                        TRUE      FALSE IMMEDIATE
6 rows selected.
```

TIP
The additional buffer pools (memory for data) available in Oracle are initially set to zero.

Tuning the **PGA_AGGREGATE_TARGET** for Optimal Use of Memory

The PGA_AGGREGATE_TARGET specifies the total amount of session PGA memory that Oracle will attempt to allocate across all sessions. PGA_AGGREGATE_TARGET was introduced in Oracle 9*i* and should be used in place of the *_SIZE parameters such as SORT_AREA_SIZE. Also, in Oracle 9*i*, the PGA_AGGREGATE_TARGET parameter does not automatically configure ALL *_SIZE parameters. For example, both the LARGE_POOL_SIZE and JAVA_POOL_SIZE parameters are not affected by PGA_AGGREGATE_TARGET. The advantage of using PGA_AGGREGATE_TARGET is the ability to cap the total user session memory to minimize OS paging.

When PGA_AGGREGATE_TARGET is set, WORKAREA_SIZE_POLICY must be set to AUTO. Like the V$DB_CACHE_ADVICE view, the V$PGA_TARGET_ADVICE (Oracle 9.2 and later versions) and V$PGA_TARGET_ADVICE_HISTOGRAM views exist to assist in tuning the PGA_AGGREGATE_TARGET. Oracle Enterprise Manager provides graphical representations of these views.

The PGA_AGGREGATE_TARGET should be set to attempt to keep the ESTD_PGA_CACHE_HIT_PERCENTAGE greater than 95 percent. By setting this appropriately, more data will be sorted in memory that may have been sorted on disk. The next query returns the minimum value for the PGA_AGGREGATE_TARGET that is projected to yield a 95 percent or greater cache hit ratio:

```
select  min(pga_target_for_estimate)
from    v$pga_target_advice
where   estd_pga_cache_hit_percentage > 95;

MIN(PGA_TARGET_FOR_ESTIMATE)
----------------------------
                    12582912
```

Modifying the Size of Your SGA to Avoid Paging and Swapping

Before you increase the size of your SGA, you must understand the effects on the physical memory of your system. If you increase parameters that use more memory than what is available on your system, then serious degradation in performance may occur. When your system processes jobs, if it doesn't have enough memory, it will start paging or swapping to complete the active task.

When *paging* occurs, information that is *not currently* being used is moved from memory to disk. This allows memory to be used by a process that *currently* needs it. If paging happens a lot, the system will experience decreases in performance, causing processes to take longer to run.

When *swapping* occurs, an *active* process is moved from memory to disk temporarily so that another *active* process that also desires memory can run. Swapping is based on system cycle time. If swapping happens a lot, your system is dead. Depending on the amount of memory available, an SGA that is too large can cause swapping.

Understanding the Cost-Based Optimizer

The cost-based optimizer was built to make your tuning life easier by choosing better paths for your poorly written queries. Rule-based optimization was built on a set of rules on how Oracle processes statements. Oracle 10*g* Release 2 now only supports the use of the cost-based optimizer; the rule-based optimizer is no longer supported. Oracle 10*g* Release 2 has automatic statistics gathering turned on to aid the effectiveness of the cost-based optimizer. In Oracle, many features are only available when using cost-based optimization. The cost-based optimizer now has two modes of operation, normal mode, and tuning mode. Normal mode should be used in production and test environments; tuning mode can be used in development environments to aid developers and DBAs in testing specific SQL code.

How Optimization Looks at the Data

Rule-based optimization is *Oracle-centric,* while cost-based optimization is *data-centric.* The optimizer mode under which the database operates is set via the initialization parameter OPTIMIZER_MODE. The possible optimizer modes are as follows:

- **CHOOSE**   Uses cost-based optimization for all analyzed tables. This is a good mode for well-built and well-tuned systems (for advanced users). This option is not documented for 10*g*R2 but is still usable.

- **RULE**   Always uses rule-based optimization. If you are still using this, you need to start using cost-based optimization, as rule-based optimization is no longer supported under Oracle 10*g* Release 2.

- **FIRST_ROWS**   Gets the first row faster (generally forces index use). This is good for untuned systems that process lots of single transactions (for beginners).

- **FIRST_ROWS (1 | 10 | 100 | 1000)**   Gets the first *n* rows faster. This is good for applications that routinely display partial results to users such as paging data to a user in a web application.

- **ALL_ROWS**   Gets all rows faster (generally forces index suppression). This is good for untuned, high-volume batch systems (usually not used).

The default optimizer mode for Oracle 10*g* Release 2 is ALL_ROWS. Also, cost-based optimization will be used even if the tables are not analyzed.

NOTE
The optimizer in Oracle 10g Release 2 uses cost-based optimization regardless of whether the tables have been analyzed or not.

TIP
There is no OPTIMIZER MODE called COST (a misconception). If you are using Oracle Database 9i Release 2 or an earlier version and are not sure what optimizer mode to use, then use CHOOSE or FIRST_ROWS and analyze all tables. By doing this, you will be using cost-based optimization. As the data in a table changes, tables need to be re-analyzed at regular intervals. Oracle 10g Release 2 automatically does this right out of the box.

Creating Enough Dispatchers

When using a shared server, some of the things you need to watch for are high busy rates for the existing dispatcher processes and increases in wait times for response queues of existing dispatcher processes. If the wait time increases, as the application runs under normal use, you may wish to add more dispatcher processes, especially if the processes are busy more than 50 percent of the time.

Use the following statement to determine the busy rate:

```
select    Network,
          ((Sum(Busy) / (Sum(Busy) + Sum(Idle))) * 100) "% Busy Rate"
from      V$Dispatcher
group by Network;


NETWORK          % Busy Rate
TCP1                       0
TCP2                       0
```

Use the following statement to check for responses to user processes that are waiting in a queue to be sent to the user:

```
select    Network Protocol,
          Decode (Sum(Totalq), 0, 'No Responses',
          Sum(Wait) / Sum(TotalQ) || ' hundredths of a second')
          "Average Wait Time Per Response"
from      V$Queue Q, V$Dispatcher D
where     Q.Type = 'DISPATCHER'
and       Q.Paddr = D.Paddr
group by Network;

PROTOCOL         Average Wait Time Per Response
TCP1             0 hundredths of a second
TCP2             1 hundredths of a second
```

Use the following statement to check the requests from user processes that are waiting in a queue to be sent to the user:

```
select     Decode (Sum(Totalq), 0, 'Number of Requests',
           Sum(Wait) / Sum(TotalQ) || 'hundredths of a second')
           "Average Wait Time Per Request"
from       V$Queue
where      Type = 'COMMON';


Average Wait Time Per Request
12 hundredths of a second
```

Open Cursors

If you don't have enough open cursors, then you will receive errors to that effect. The key is to stay ahead of your system by increasing the OPEN_CURSORS initialization parameter before you run out of open cursors.

25 Important Initialization Parameters to Consider

1. **DB_CACHE_SIZE**   Initial memory allocated to data cache or memory used for data itself.

2. **SGA_TARGET**   If you use Oracle's Automatic Shared Memory Management, this parameter is used to automatically determine the size of your data cache, shared pool, large pool, and Java pool (see Chapter 1 for more information). Setting this to 0 disables it.

3. **PGA_AGGREGATE_TARGET**   Soft memory cap for total of all users' PGAs.

4. **SHARED_POOL_SIZE**   Memory allocated for data dictionary and SQL and PL/SQL.

5. **SGA_MAX_SIZE**   Maximum memory that the SGA can dynamically grow to.

6. **OPTIMIZER_MODE**   CHOOSE, RULE, FIRST_ROWS, FIRST_ROWS_*n* or ALL_ROWS. Although RULE is definitely desupported and obsolete and people are often scolded for even talking about it, I was able to set the mode to RULE in 10*g*.

7. **CURSOR_SHARING**   Converts literal SQL to SQL with bind variables, reducing parse overhead.

8. **OPTIMIZER_INDEX_COST_ADJ**   Coarse adjustment between the cost of an index scan and the cost of a full table scan. Set between 1 and 10 to force index use more frequently. Setting this parameter to a value between 1 and 10 would pretty much guarantee index use, even when not appropriate, so be careful, since it is highly dependent on the index design and implementation being correct. Please note that if you using Applications 11i: Setting OPTIMIZER_INDEX_COST_ADJ to any value other than the default (100) is not supported (see Note 169935.1). Also, see bug 4483286.

9. **QUERY_REWRITE_ENABLED**   Used to enable Materialized View and Function-Based-Index capabilities and other features in some versions.

10. **DB_FILE_MULTIBLOCK_READ_COUNT**   For full table scans to perform I/O more efficiently, this reads this many blocks in a single I/O.

11. **LOG_BUFFER**   Buffer for uncommitted transactions in memory (not dynamic; set in pfile).

12. **DB_KEEP_CACHE_SIZE**   Memory allocated to keep pool or an additional data cache that you can set up outside the buffer cache for very important data that you don't want pushed out of the cache.

13. **DB_RECYCLE_CACHE_SIZE**   Memory allocated to a recycle pool or an additional data cache that you can set up outside the buffer cache and in addition to the keep cache described in the preceding item. Usually, DBAs set this up for ad hoc user query data that has queries that are poorly written.

14. **DBWR_IO_SLAVES**   (also DB_WRITER_PROCESSES if you have async I/O)   Number of writers from SGA to disk for simulated async I/O. If you have async I/O, then you use DB_WRITER_PROCESSES to set up multiple writers to more quickly write out dirty blocks during a database write (DBWR).

15. **LARGE_POOL_SIZE**   Total blocks in the large pool allocation for large PL/SQL and a few other Oracle options less frequently used.

16. **STATISTICS_LEVEL**   Used to enable advisory information and optionally keep additional OS statistics to refine optimizer decisions. TYPICAL is the default.

17. **JAVA_POOL_SIZE**   Memory allocated to the JVM for Java stored procedures.

18. **JAVA_MAX_SESSIONSPACE_SIZE**   Upper limit on memory that is used to keep track of user session state of JAVA classes.

19. **MAX_SHARED_SERVERS**   Upper limit on shared servers when using shared servers.

20. **WORKAREA_SIZE_POLICY**   Used to enable automatic PGA size management.

21. **FAST_START_MTTR_TARGET**   Bounds time to complete a crash recovery. This is the time (in seconds) that the database will take to perform crash recovery of a single instance. If you set this parameter, LOG_CHECKPOINT_INTERVAL should *not* be set to 0. If you don't set this parameter, you can still see your estimated MTTR (mean time to recovery) by querying V$INSTANCE_RECOVERY for ESTIMATED_MTTR.

22. **LOG_CHECKPOINT_INTERVAL**   Checkpoint frequency (in OS blocks—most OS blocks are 512 bytes) where Oracle performs a database write of all dirty (modified) blocks to the datafiles in the database. Oracle will also perform a checkpoint if more the one quarter of the data buffers are dirty in the db cache and also on any log switch. The LGWR (log writer) also updates the SCN in the control files and datafiles with the SCN of the checkpoint.

23. **OPEN_CURSORS**   Specifies the size of the private area used to hold (open) user statements. If you get "ORA-01000: maximum open cursors exceeded," you may need to increase this parameter, but make sure you are *closing* cursors that you no longer need. Prior to 9.2.0.5, these open cursors were also cached and at times caused issues (ORA-4031) if OPEN_CURSORS was set too high. In 9.2.05, SESSION_CACHED_CURSORS now controls the setting of the PL/SQL cursor cache. Do *not* set the parameter SESSION_CACHED_CURSORS as high as you set OPEN_CURSORS or you may experience ORA-4031 or ORA-7445 errors.

24. **DB_BLOCK_SIZE**   Default block size for the database. A smaller block size will reduce contention by adjacent rows, but a larger block size will lower the number of I/Os needed to pull back more records. A larger block size will also help in range scans where the blocks desired are sequentially stored.

25. OPTIMIZER_DYNAMIC_SAMPLING Controls the number of blocks read by the dynamic sampling query. Very useful with systems that are using Global Temporary Tables.

TIP
Setting certain initialization parameters correctly could be the difference between a report taking two seconds and two hours. Test changes on a test system thoroughly before implementing those changes in a production environment.

Initialization Parameters over the Years

Oracle has moved from a point where there were over four times as many documented parameters as undocumented in Oracle 6 to where the undocumented parameters exceeded the documented in Oracle 8*i* to where there are four times as many undocumented as documented parameters in Oracle 10*g*. Clearly, we have moved to a place where there are more dials to set in 10*g* for the experts (undocumented), but the number of dials to set for the standard database setup (documented parameters) is not increasing any more and is becoming standardized. The following table charts the changing numbers of documented and undocumented parameters:

Version	Documented	Undocumented	Total
6	111	19	130
7	117	68	185
8.0	193	119	312
8.1	203	301	504
9.0	251	436	687
9.2	257	540	797
10.2	257 (+0%)	1124 (+108%)	1381 (+73%)

Finding Undocumented Initialization Parameters

Querying the table X$KSPPI shows you documented as well as undocumented initialization parameters. The query may only be done as user SYS, so be careful. See Chapter 13 for a complete look at the X$ tables. My top 13 undocumented initialization parameters are listed in Appendix A. Appendix C gives a complete listing as of the writing of this book of the X$ tables.

```
select ksppinm, ksppstvl, ksppstdf
from    x$ksppi a, x$ksppcv b
where   a.indx = b.indx
order   by ksppinm;
```

The following is a brief description of the columns in the x$ksppi & x$ksppcv tables:

- **KSPPINM**   Parameter name
- **KSPPSTVL**   Current value for the parameter
- **KSPPSTDF**   Default value for the parameter

A partial output listing of the initialization parameters is shown here:

```
KSPPINM                         KSPPSTVL                KSPPSTDF
------------------------------  ----------------------  ----------
...
_write_clones                   3                       TRUE
_yield_check_interval           100000                  TRUE
active_instance_count                                   TRUE
aq_tm_processes                 1                       FALSE
archive_lag_target              0                       TRUE
...
```

TIP
*Using undocumented initialization parameters can cause corruption.
Never use these if you are not an expert and you are not directed by
Oracle Support! Ensure that you work with Oracle Support before
setting these parameters.*

Understanding the Typical Server

The key to understanding Oracle is to understand its dynamic nature. Oracle continues to have
many attributes of previous versions while also leading the way by implementing the future of
distributed database and object-oriented programming. Experience from earlier versions of Oracle
always benefits the DBA in future versions of Oracle. Here are some of the future changes to
consider as you build your system:

- Oracle can be completely distributed and maintained at a single point. (Many databases
  and locations with one DBA managing the system looks like the corporate future.)

- Database maintenance is becoming completely visual (all point-and-click maintenance
  as in the Enterprise Manager). The V$ views are still your lowest-performance cost access
  method, but Enterprise Manager is easier to use for more complex inquiries that may
  require multiple V$ views to get the same result.

- Network throughput continues to be an issue that looks to be solved by technology (next
  three or so years).

- CPUs will continue to get faster, eliminating the CPU as a system resource issue. (I/O and
  correct design will continue to be the issues.)

- Object-oriented development will be crucial to rapid system development.

- Current database design theory is being rewritten to focus more on denormalization.

- Graphics are causing the sizes of databases to become increasingly large. Also, the fact that disk space is getting cheaper and cheaper has made businesses more willing to keep data around longer.

Modeling a Typical Server

This section contains rough estimates designed as setup guidelines. However, it is important to emphasize that these are only guidelines and that the reality is that every system is different and must be tuned to meet the system's demands. (CPU speed will depend on the type of processor, e.g., RISC vs. Intel.) The following table does not include guidelines for Oracle Applications. Oracle Applications tends to have unique issues that are addressed by Oracle in the application documentation and on Metalink.

Database Size	Up to 25GB	100–200GB	500–1,000GB
Number of users	100	200	500
Number of CPUs	4	8	16+
System memory	8GB	16GB	32GB+
SGA_MAX_SIZE	2GB	4GB	8GB
PGA_AGGREGATE_TARGET	512MB	1GB	2GB
Total disk capacity	100GB	500–1000GB	1–50TB
Percentage of query	75 percent	75 percent	75 percent
Percentage of DML	25 percent	25 percent	25 percent
Number of redo logs multiplexed?	4–8 Yes	6–10 Yes	6–12 Yes
Number of control files	4	4	4
Percent batch	20 percent	20 percent	20 percent
Percent online	80 percent	80 percent	80 percent
Archiving used?	Yes	Yes	Yes
Buffer hit ratio	95 percent +	95 percent +	95 percent +
Dictionary hit ratio	95 percent +	95 percent +	95 percent +
Library hit ratio	95 percent +	95 percent +	95 percent +
Other system software (other than Oracle)	Minimum	Minimum	Minimum

Modeling a Typical Server

Database Size	Up to 25GB	100–200GB	500–1,000GB
Use raw devices?	No	No	No
Use parallel query?	Depends on queries	Depends on queries	Probably in many queries

The following variables can be reason to deviate from the typical server configuration:

- Heavy batch processing may need much larger rollback or undo, redo, and temp tablespace sizes.

- Heavy DML processing may need much larger rollback or undo, redo, and temp tablespace sizes.

- Heavy user access to large tables requires more CPU and memory, and larger temp tablespace sizes.

- Poorly tuned systems require more CPU and memory, and larger temp tablespace sizes.

- A greater number of disks and controllers always increase performance by reducing I/O contention.

- An increase in the disk capacity can speed backup and recovery time by going to disk and not tape.

Sizing the Oracle Applications Database

Oracle recommends via Metalink Note 216205.1 (written by Oracle Applications Development) the SGA settings shown in Table 4-1. This is also a nice guideline for sizing systems. Note that the SGA_TARGET takes the place of the other memory parameters and allows Oracle to allocate memory where needed. I don't think this should necessarily be used in all cases (in the Metalink note it is recommended for 10g); be careful to test this well if you use it as it is a new parameter. If you do set the initialization parameter SGA_TARGET to allow Oracle to use Automatic Shared Memory Management (ASMM), you can query the view V$SGA_DYNAMIC_COMPONENTS to see where (i.e., buffer cache, shared pool, etc.) the memory is being allocated. The SGA_TARGET parameter cannot be set larger than the SGA_MAX_SIZE or you will receive the ORA-00823 error.

The CSP and NOCSP options of the shared pool–related parameters refer to the use of cursor_space_for_time, which is documented in the common database initialization parameters section. The use of cursor space for time results in much larger shared pool requirements.

The Development / Test instance refers to a small instance used for only development or testing in which no more than 10 users exist. The range of user counts provided in the table refers to active Applications users, not total or named users. For example, if you plan to support a maximum of 500 active Oracle Applications users, then you should use the sizing per the range 101–500 users. The parameter values provided in this document reflect a development / test instance configuration, and you should adjust the relevant parameters according to the Applications user counts (refer to the table).

Parameter Name	Development / Test Instance	11–100 Users	101–500 Users	501–1,000 Users	1001–2000 Users[1]
Processes	200	200	800	1200	2500
Sessions	400	400	1600	2400	5000
db_block_buffers	20000	50000	150000	250000	400000
db_cache_size[2]	156M	400M	1G	2G	3G
sga_target[3]	1G	1G	2G	3G	14G
undo_retention[4]	1800	3600	7200	10800	14400
Shared_pool_size (csp)	N/A	N/A	N/A	1800M	3000M
Shared_pool_reserved_size (csp)	N/A	N/A	N/A	180M	300M
Shared_pool_size (no csp)	400M	600M	800M	1000M	2000M
Shared_pool_reserved_size (no csp)	40M	60M	80M	100M	100M
pga_aggregate_target[5]	1G	2G	4G	10G	20G
Total Memory Required[6]	~ 2GB	~ 3GB	~ 6GB	~ 13GB	~ 25GB

[1]For instances supporting a minimum of 1000 Oracle Applications users, you should use the Oracle 64-bit Server for your platform in order to support large SGAs.

[2]The parameter db_cache_size should be used for 9*i*-based environments in place of db_block_buffers.

[3]The parameter sga_target should be used for 10*g*-based environments (I suggest that if you use this parameter, you test this well before handing over full memory management to Oracle).

[4]The values for undo_retention are recommendations only, and this parameter should be adjusted according to the elapsed times of the concurrent jobs and corresponding commit windows. It is not required to set undo_retention for 10*g*-based systems, as undo retention is automatically set as part of automatic undo tuning.

[5]pga_aggregate_target should only be used with a 9*i*- or 10*g*-based database instances. This parameter should not be set in 8*i*-based instances.

[6]The total memory required refers to the amount of memory required for the data server instance and associated memory, including the SGA and the PGA. You should ensure that your system has sufficient available memory in order to support the values provided in the table. The values provided should be adjusted in accordance with available memory so as to prevent swapping and paging.

TABLE 4-1. *SGA Settings*

Tips Review

- The key initialization parameters in Oracle are SGA_MAX_SIZE, PGA_AGGREGATE_TARGET, DB_CACHE_SIZE, and SHARED_POOL_SIZE. If you use ASMM, then SGA_TARGET is the key initialization parameter.

- If you can't figure out why your system isn't using the value in your init.ora file, you probably have an spfile overriding it. And don't forget, you can also use a hint to override parameters at the query level in 10*g*R2.

■ Changing initialization parameters dynamically is a powerful feature for both developers and DBAs. Consequently, a user with the ALTER SESSION privilege is capable of irresponsibly allocating 100M+ for the SORT_AREA_SIZE for a given session, if it is not restricted.

■ In Oracle 10g Release 2, use the Enterprise Manager Grid Control to find problem queries.

■ Physical memory is generally much faster than retrieving data from disk, so make sure that the SGA is large enough to accommodate memory reads when it is effective to do so.

■ Poor joins and poor indexing also yield very high hit ratios, so make sure that your hit ratio isn't high for a reason other than a well-tuned system. An unusually high hit ratio may indicate the introduction of code that is poorly indexed or includes join issues.

■ Hit ratios are useful to experienced DBAs but can be misleading to inexperienced DBAs. The best use of hit ratios is still to compare over time to help alert you to a substantial change to a system on a given day. While there are those who don't like using hit ratios, they are usually tool vendors who don't see the value of tracking hit ratios over time, since their tools are point-in-time or reactive-based tuning solutions. Hit ratios should never be your only tool, but they should definitely be one of many proactive tools in your arsenal.

■ In Oracle 10g Release 2, use the TopSQL monitor of Oracle's SQL Analyze to find problem queries.

■ A low hit ratio for a query is an indication of a missing or suppressed index.

■ Bad (slow) queries show in V$SQLAREA view with poor hit ratios the first time they are executed. Make sure you tune them at that time. The second time that they execute, they may not show a poor hit ratio.

■ The database must be rebuilt if you increase the DB_BLOCK_SIZE. Increasing the DB_FILE_MULTIBLOCK_READ_COUNT will allow more block reads in a single I/O, giving a benefit similar to a larger block size.

■ SQL must be written *exactly* the same to be reused. Case differences and any other differences will cause a reparse of the statement.

■ Measure hit ratios for the data dictionary row cache of the shared pool with the V$ROWCACHE view. A hit ratio of over 95 percent should be achieved. However, when the database is initially started, hit ratios will be around 85 percent.

■ Measure hit ratios for the library cache of the shared pool with the V$LIBRARYCACHE view. A hit ratio of over 95 percent should be achieved. However, when the database is initially started, hit ratios will be around 85 percent.

■ The V$SGASTAT view shows how fast the memory in the shared pool is being depleted. Remember that it is only a rough estimate. It shows you any memory that has never been used combined with any piece of memory that has been reused. Free memory will go up and down as the day goes on according to how the pieces are fragmented.

■ The general rule of thumb is to make the SHARED_POOL_SIZE parameter 50–150 percent of the size of your DB_CACHE_SIZE.

- The additional buffer pools (memory for data) available in Oracle are initially set to zero.

- The optimizer in Oracle 10g Release 2 uses cost-based optimization regardless of whether the tables have been analyzed or not.

- Setting certain initialization parameters correctly could be the difference between a report taking two seconds and two hours. Test changes on a test system thoroughly before implementing those changes in a production environment.

- Using undocumented initialization parameters can cause corruption. Never use these if you are not an expert and you are not directed by Oracle Support! Ensure that you work with Oracle Support before setting these parameters.

References

Craig Shallahamer, *All about Oracle's Touch-Count Data Block Buffer Algorithm* (OraPub, excellent)
Rich Niemiec, *DBA Tuning; Now YOU are the Expert* (TUSC)
Performance Tuning Guide, Oracle Corporation

Thanks to Randy Swanson, who did the update for this chapter in the 9*i* version of the book. (Where were you this time around?)

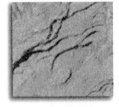

CHAPTER
5

Enterprise Manager
and Grid Control
(DBA and Developer)

Oracle Enterprise Manager Grid Control finally matches or exceeds the market's answer to monitoring and tuning the Oracle 10g database. Oracle has usually been behind the market with an okay-to-good product over the years. No longer is this the case; Oracle has stepped up to the plate and delivered one of the best products ever. This chapter provides a quick tour of why Oracle's Enterprise Manager Grid Control (EM) is now at the next level. The tour will not explore the entire product, nor will it teach you how to use all of the features (it would take an entire book). Rather, this chapter exposes you to some of the tools and tuning features that will be helpful in your tuning endeavors. With Oracle's focus on the grid in Oracle 10g, many screen shots show multiple instances so that either a single-instance or multi-instance cluster can be seen with the product. Oracle Enterprise Manager is an excellent tuning tool for all levels of DBAs and is especially valuable as we head into the decade of the grid. There are two versions of EM in 10g. There is Grid Control, which is a separate product, and EM Database Control, which is installed along with the database (unless you specify that you do not want to use it for monitoring your database). You can do most of the functions for RAC with Database Control, but I personally prefer using Grid Control when monitoring Oracle RAC databases.

One way to ensure great performance for your system is to monitor your system for potential performance issues before they become major problems. One vehicle that provides a GUI (graphical user interface) for tuning is the Oracle Enterprise Manager, along with related performance tuning add-on products. The Oracle Enterprise Manager product suite continues to change over time, but this particular version (10gR2) has taken a giant leap forward. With the statistics from the Automatic Workload Repository (AWR), this tool is now tremendously powerful. AWR snapshots are taken every hour by default, and once the AWR snapshot is taken, the Automatic Database Diagnostic Monitor (ADDM) analysis occurs immediately (STATISTICS_LEVEL must be TYPICAL or ALL) via the MMON background process. The results of ADDM are also stored in the AWR and accessible via EM.

In addition to monitoring, there are spectacular screens that will show you where a problem is, down to the "latch wait" or "global cache cr transfer wait." The tools for running the AWR Report (covered in detail in Chapter 14) are included, as are tools to change the init.ora or spfile.ora file. The tools for monitoring the grid are equally spectacular (yes, they are that good). There are screens showing the performance on every instance (each in a different color) where you can click the graph to branch to an individual instance. You can look into performance at the database, host, application server, network, or disk (ASM or non-ASM) level. Of all the Oracle products I have seen hit a home run over time, this one hit a grand slam with the Oracle 10gR2 Grid Control release.

Oracle's Enterprise Manager standard applications include a central management console and additional packs, and many products have an additional cost (please check with Oracle for any price implications of different modules). Accessing the AWR requires the Diagnostics Pack, and running SQL Tuning Sets requires the Tuning Pack.

The following tips are covered in this chapter:

- ■ Enterprise Manager Basics
- ■ Policies and Alerts
- ■ Monitoring the Database
- ■ Tuning the Oracle Database using EM and ADDM
- ■ The Database Maintenance Tab

- Viewing the Oracle Topology

- Monitoring and Tuning the Hosts

- Monitoring and Tuning the Web Applications

- Monitoring and Tuning the Application Servers

- Monitoring and Tuning ASM

- Deployments and Patching Advisories

- Viewing and Scheduling Jobs

- Reports That Are Available, including the ASH and AWR Reports

The Enterprise Manager (EM) Basics

Once EM is installed, the login screen (shown in Figure 5-1) is displayed. Depending on how security is set up, the username, password, or database information may need to be entered at login screens, depending on which screens are accessed within the product.

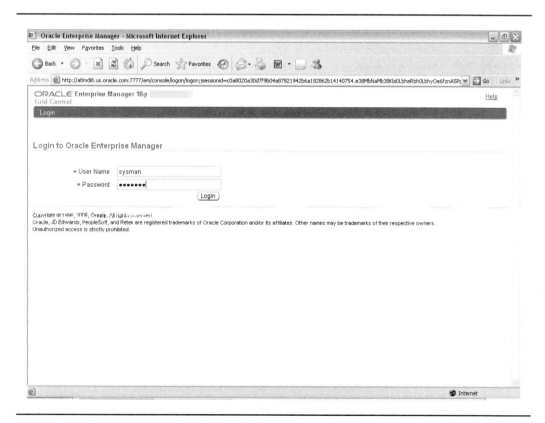

FIGURE 5-1. *Oracle Enterprise Manager (EM) Login screen*

Shortly after logging in to EM, it is worth checking some of the Setup options that exist for customization of the product. In the upper-right corner of the screen, the word "Setup" can be clicked to display the setup screen in Figure 5-2.

Some of the setup options that available including Patching, Notification Methods, Blackout Periods, and access to various tools and other configuration items available. For example: If "Blackouts" is clicked from the screen in Figure 5-2, the screen shown in Figure 5-3 will be displayed. Blackouts are periods of time that allow the system to suspend monitoring for the performance of maintenance activities. This is done to eliminate the skewing of the data during normal operating hours. Even though statistics gathering is suspended, the period is still recorded to ensure too many blackouts aren't scheduled by a DBA.

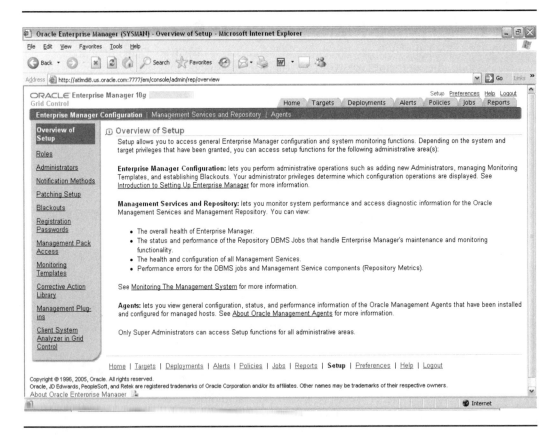

FIGURE 5-2. *Setup & Configuration Screen*

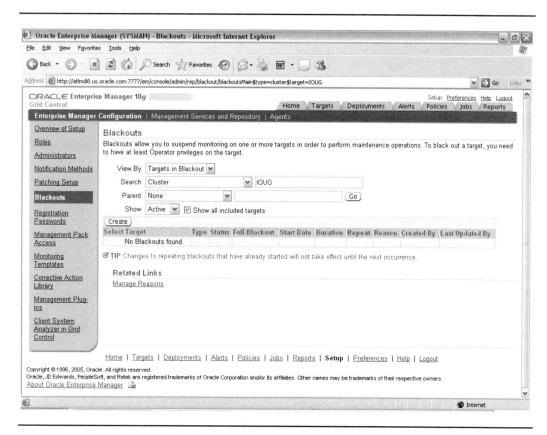

FIGURE 5-3. *Setup & Configuration – Blackouts*

After becoming familiar with EM, the DBA should set up the preferences that are deemed best for the environment being monitored. At any time while using the product, you can click Preferences (located at the upper-right part of the screen) to see the screen in Figure 5-4 displayed with all the preference options. Several preferences should be set, including the e-mail addresses for sending various alerts or messages as well as notification rules. Even the tabs on the screen can be changed to be exactly what is most intuitive for the environment. It is best to stay within the standard that Oracle has so that another DBA can easily follow what's been done.

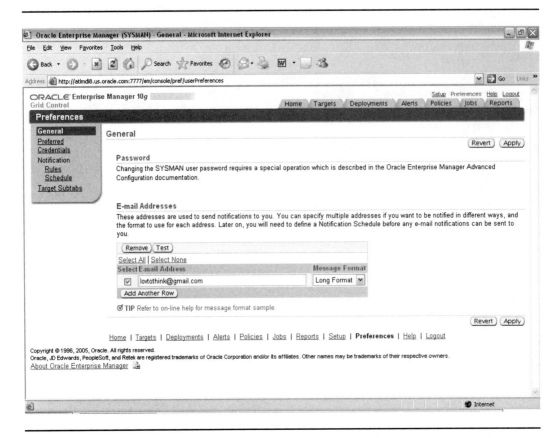

FIGURE 5-4. *Setting Preferences*

One of the best parts of EM is the great Help that is provided. Throughout the product, there is always a "help" tab or button to get specific help on any screen or item. The help can be either a very general area like "monitoring database performance" or something very specific like the "histogram for wait event page" (see Figure 5-5). There is substantial help included in the product on how to tune the various areas of Oracle at the host, database, application server, ASM, O/S, or network levels. The key is to take advantage of this and learn something every time EM is accessed.

TIP
In Oracle 10gR2, the online help is spectacular. Learn something every day by clicking the Help button.

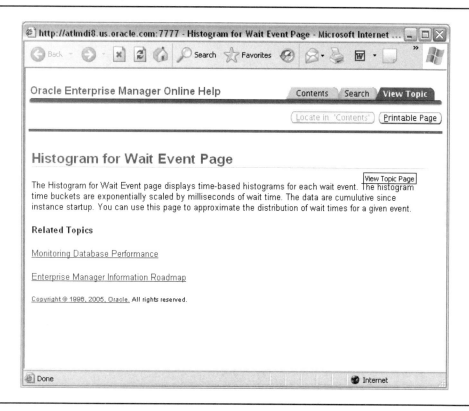

FIGURE 5-5. *Online Help*

Starting with All Targets and Other Groupings

The first thing displayed when logging into EM is the Home screen (Figure 5-6). This shows All Targets (by default) and shows everything that's being monitored. It instantly shows how many things are up or down. The View pull-down tab can also be changed to Databases, Hosts, or any other monitored target. This is the screen that I want to see first thing in the morning so that I know that every part of the system is up and running. It also shows if there are any Security Policy Violations (covered a bit later in this section), Patch Advisories (covered in the section "Deployments Tab: Patching Options" of this chapter), as well as other links.

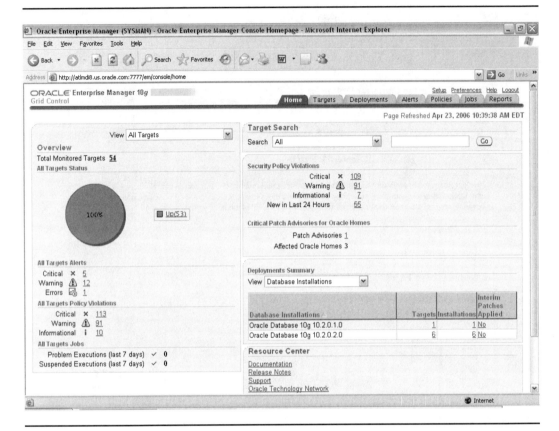

FIGURE 5-6. *EM Home tab*

There is also a tabular version of all the targets. By clicking the Targets tab, all targets being monitored are listed. The list in Figure 5-7 includes ASM (Automatic Storage Management), Application, System, Server, OC4J, and Web Cache Monitoring. There are also numerous databases, cluster databases, and hosts (further down the page) that are monitored by this system; they will be shown throughout this chapter.

A nice feature that was also available in the Oracle 9*i* version of EM is the ability to group common areas together. For instance, you can group all databases together into a group called prod_db so that the group can be monitored together to see if they are all up. The same can be done for development databases (call them dev_db). A DBA will usually configure things so that

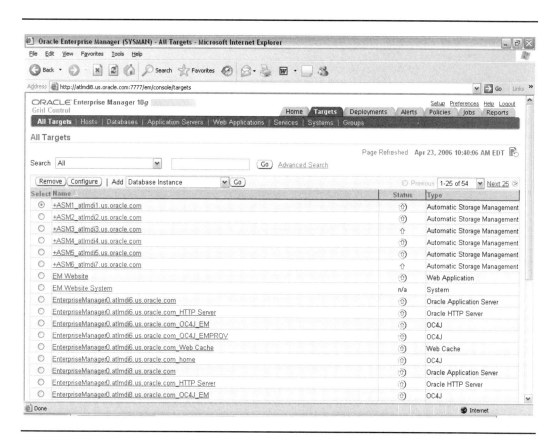

FIGURE 5-7. *All Targets listing*

the prod_db group will be more proactive in sending alerts, pages, or e-mails than the dev_db group. Figure 5-8 shows the screen for Groups with the four different groups that have been set up. There is a Listener group (RAC_SIG_Listeners), a Database Instance group (ggroup), a Host group (groupvanzandt), and a Database Instance Group (ioug_cluster, with six instances). It is easy to see any alerts that are critical (in red) or cautionary (yellow) as well as take a quick look at Policy Violations.

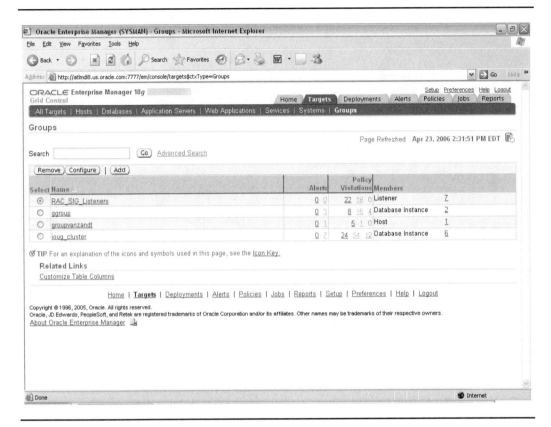

FIGURE 5-8. *All Groups listing*

If you click the RAC_SIG_listeners Group, only information for that group (Figure 5-9) is displayed. In this screen, the information is much more detailed, but only for the group that has been chosen.

Clicking the Alert tab or clicking any alert is also a quick way to see the alerts that have been set up or to see Oracle's default alert settings. It's easy to see any triggered alerts, shown as red (critical), yellow (caution), or blue (informational). These are alerts (that are throughout the product) that Oracle has set defaults for, but alerts can also be tailored to an environment's specific system. The key is to set them so that there is an alert when a problem comes up.

For instance, if the buffer cache hit ratio is usually 95 percent, the DBA may want to be alerted when it drops to 50 percent to see what happened to cause this drop. If CPU is usually running at 60 percent, the DBA may want a cautionary note when it hits 80 percent and a critical alert when it goes over 90 or 95 percent. This built-in alerting methodology that the DBA builds into the product is useful for both new and experienced DBAs who may be able to leverage the

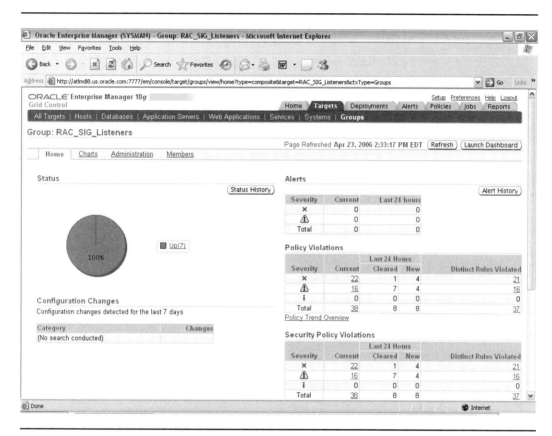

FIGURE 5-9. *Status of the RAC_SIG_Listeners group*

experience of the Oracle Master that sets it up for that particular system. There are also alerts for policy violations that work in a similar manner; they are covered in the next section.

Policies (Violations) Tab

By clicking the Policy tab, you can view the violations and other related policy information (Figure 5-10). The policies are Oracle's general policy guidelines for the product; however, for the DBA, the environment may dictate a more rigid or less rigid standard than those specified by Oracle. Oracle puts these out as a general guideline. If a system has an application on the Internet, it may require a very rigid policy. If the system is a single-user accounting system on a single PC, the policies may be less stringent. Always employ the highest level of security required for the situation.

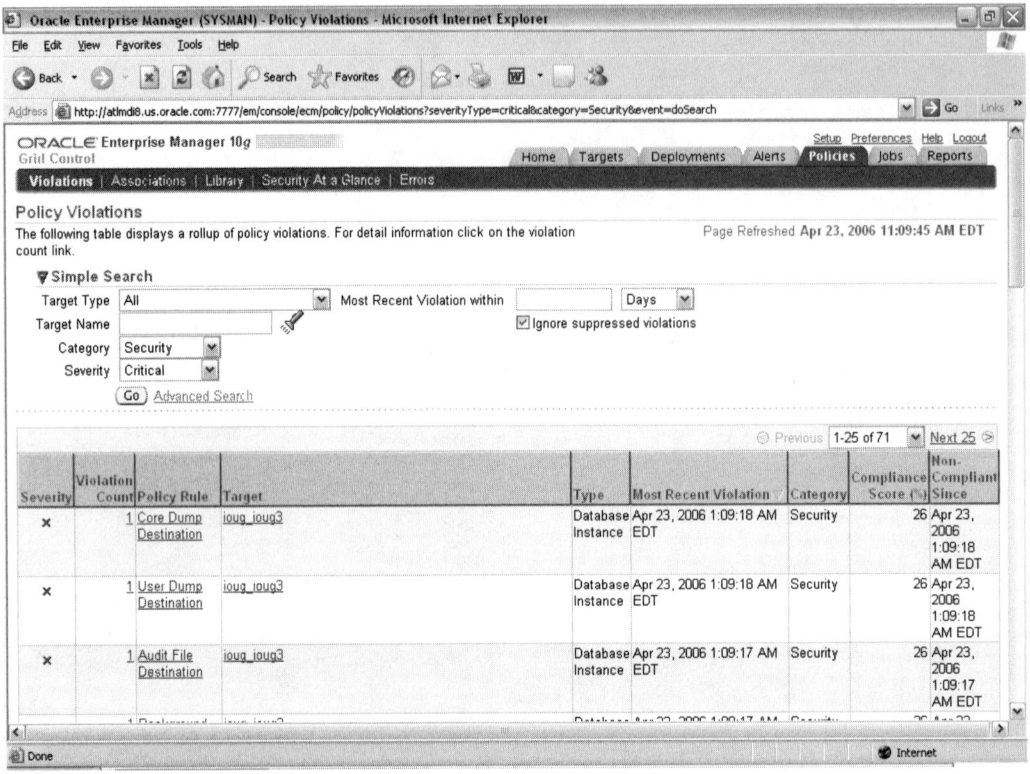

FIGURE 5-10. *Policy violations*

Monitoring the Database

The database is an area where the DBA will spend much a lot of time either monitoring or tuning. Once things are running well, the DBA may set up things so that he or she is notified only under certain conditions. Getting the system to a stable setting is the first milestone a DBA must achieve. By clicking the Targets tab and then the Databases tab underneath it, you can view the databases that are included as in Figure 5-11. Two databases, "orcl" and "ioug," are included in this listing. The "ioug" database is a six-instance cluster database, while the "orcl" database is a single-instance database.

The "ioug" cluster database is clicked to display the monitored information for this cluster database (Figure 5-12). This screen shows that there are six instances that are all up at this time. There is some CPU being used (around 25 percent) and just under 20 active sessions (we'll find out why so many are waiting later in the chapter). This cluster database has a 99.36 percent

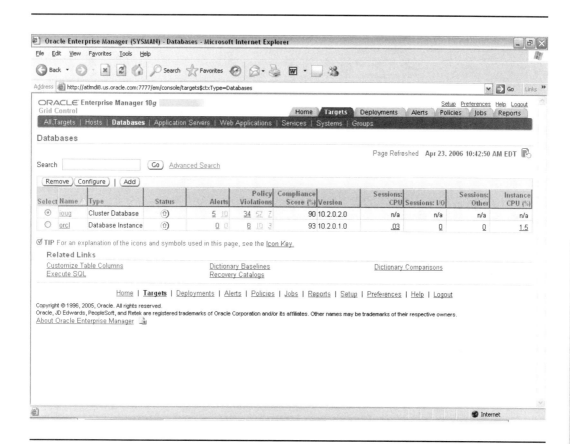

FIGURE 5-11. *Databases tab*

availability. There is also specific information as to the exact location of the Oracle Home, the exact version, the time zone, and a plethora of links to other screens.

A *very* important section of this page is the Diagnostic Summary section. This will include any ADDM (Automatic Database Diagnostic Monitor) findings. In this case, there are four interconnect findings. If there are performance findings from ADDM, they will be listed here. Oracle is taking periodic snapshots of data, and ADDM performs an analysis.

TIP
AWR runs every hour by default, and ADDM runs just after the AWR snapshot. The Diagnostic Summary that ADDM provides should be viewed regularly.

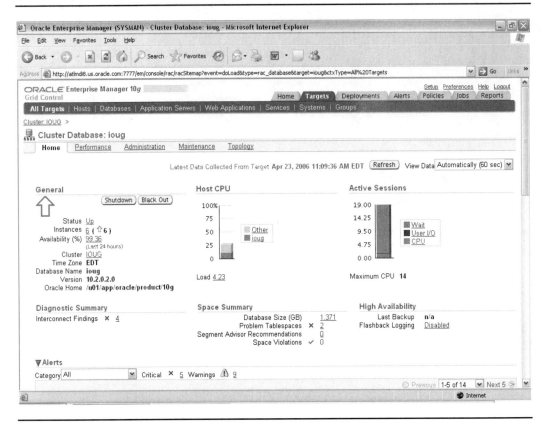

FIGURE 5-12. *Performance information for the "ioug" six-instance cluster database*

Further down this same page, there appear all of the current Oracle-generated alerts for the database that are being monitoring. Since this is a display for the "ioug" cluster database, there are alerts that are specific to individual instances. In Figure 5-13, there are alerts specific to the cluster database "ioug" related to the tablespace being almost full, but also alerts on instances "ioug_ioug1," "ioug_ioug2," "ioug_ioug5," and "ioug_ioug6" for using an interconnect that is public rather than a private connection.

Further yet down the page (at the bottom), we find some of the most useful links and information for a cluster database (Figure 5-14). This includes all of the instances associated with the cluster database. It also includes links to the corresponding alerts, policy violations, and ASM (Automatic Storage Management) statistics (if used). There is also information showing what percent of the CPU the given instance is using (Instance %CPU) at that point in time. The six instances (ioug_ioug1 through ioug_ioug6) are also displayed here, making it very easy to see information for an individual instance by clicking through to that instance.

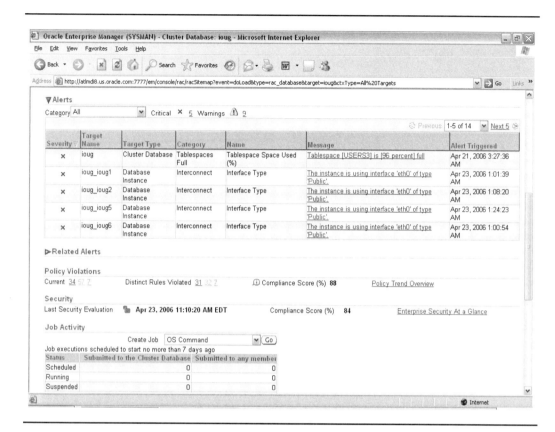

FIGURE 5-13. *Performance Information for the "ioug" six-instance cluster database (mid-page)*

By clicking one of the instances (ioug_ioug1 in this example), the main informational screen for an instance is displayed (Figure 5-15). This is the master screen where much of the DBA's time is spent looking at performance; it also serves as a starting point to branch to other places. This screen includes critical performance information such as CPU, active sessions, SQL response time, and whether the instance is up or down. Although this chapter is in black and white, this screen is very colorful. The Host CPU section shows a dark green for ioug1 and light green for other. The Active sessions show green for CPU, blue for User I/O, but bright red for waits (begging the DBA to look there). The alerts show up in red, the cautionary notes in yellow, and informational in blue. There is also additional helpful information, including availability, version of the database, host, ASM (if applicable), uptime, and any alerts. The refresh rate is every 60 seconds automatically, but this value can be changed with the View Data pull-down in the upper-right portion of the screen. There is also a pull-down just above that one that allows a quick switch to another database instance.

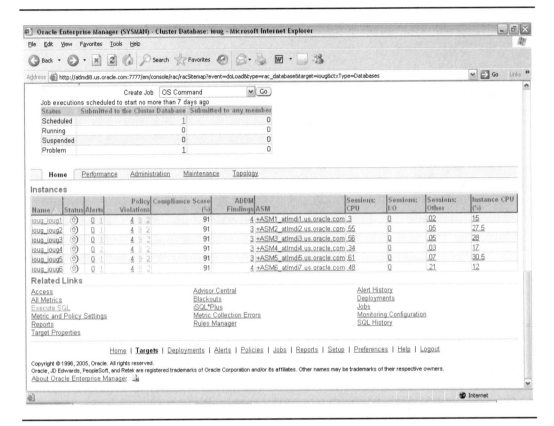

FIGURE 5-14. *Performance information for the "ioug" six-instance cluster database (bottom)*

Note also that there are four ADDM findings related to SQL in Figure 5-15. ADDM runs automatically in the database to make recommendations for improving performance. We will see in the next section that just below the ADDM findings are the SQL recommendations.

Further down this same page, there are all of the current Oracle-generated alerts for the instance that are being monitored. Since this screen is for the "ioug_ioug1" instance, there are alerts that are specific to this instance only. In Figure 5-16, we can see that there is only one alert (the SYS user logged on). The Alerts section now has specific SQL to this instance as well with recommended action. There is a SQL statement listed with significant wait time and another with row locks that should be tuned. We'll look at some tuning options later in this chapter. Note also that the four ADDM findings related to SQL are listed with recommendations listed in the Performance Analysis section. Clicking the SQL displays the Performance Finding Details

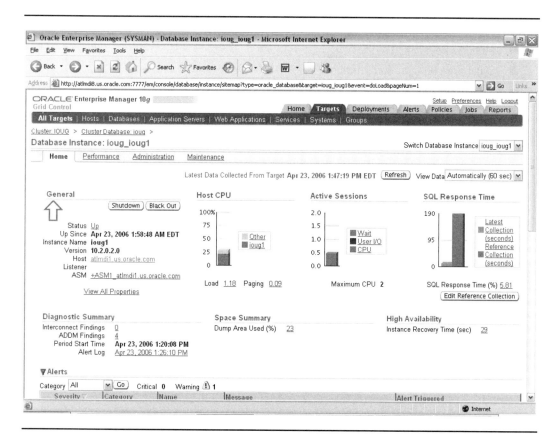

FIGURE 5-15. *Performance information for the "ioug1" instance*

Screen to see suggested actions based on the ADDM task. The DBA can also schedule the Tuning Advisor (note that this is part of the SQL Tuning Pack) to investigate the SQL in greater detail and make recommendations for changes in the SQL. You can go directly to ADDM through the Advisor Central (ADDM information can also be accessed via the various DBA_ADVISOR_* data dictionary views). You can also run an ADDM Report (addmrpt.sql) to see these findings. In an effort to increase performance, ADDM analyzes a number of different database-related problems, including

■ Memory-related issues such as shared pool latch contention, log buffer issues, or database buffer cache–related problems

- CPU bottlenecks

- Disk I/O performance issues

- Database configuration problems

- Space-related issues, such as tablespaces running out of space

- Application and SQL tuning issues such as excessive parsing and excessive locking

Also note an Oracle 10gR2 enhancement for the SQL Tuning Advisor. In Oracle 10.2, Oracle recommends using the SQL Tuning Advisor only for those SQL statements that will benefit from SQL Tuning (e.g., it will not help to run the SQL Tuning Advisor to analyze row lock waits with an update statement).

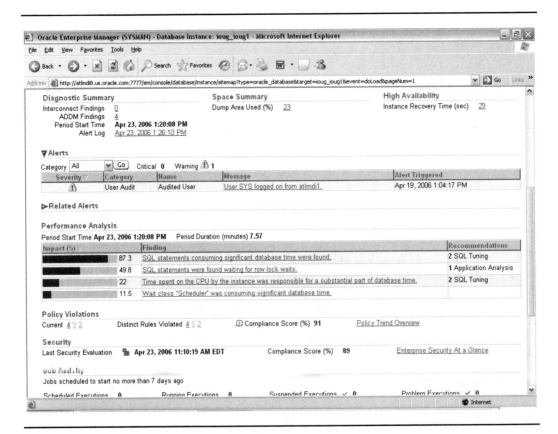

FIGURE 5-16. *Performance information for the "ioug1" instance (mid-page)*

TIP
In Oracle 10gR2, use the SQL Tuning Advisor only to tune SQL
statements, not conditions such as row locks.

By clicking a piece of problem SQL, the Performance Findings Detail for ADDM screen is displayed. This will display the SQL in question as well as offer solutions for fixing the SQL. In the example in Figure 5-17, the Top SQL is causing a lot of CPU consumption.

By clicking the Schedule SQL Tuning Advisor button, Oracle's Tuning Advisor is employed to tune the SQL in question and offer suggestions. In Figure 5-18, the recommendations are displayed for the worst SQL. The worst SQL seems like it will benefit from employing a SQL Profile.

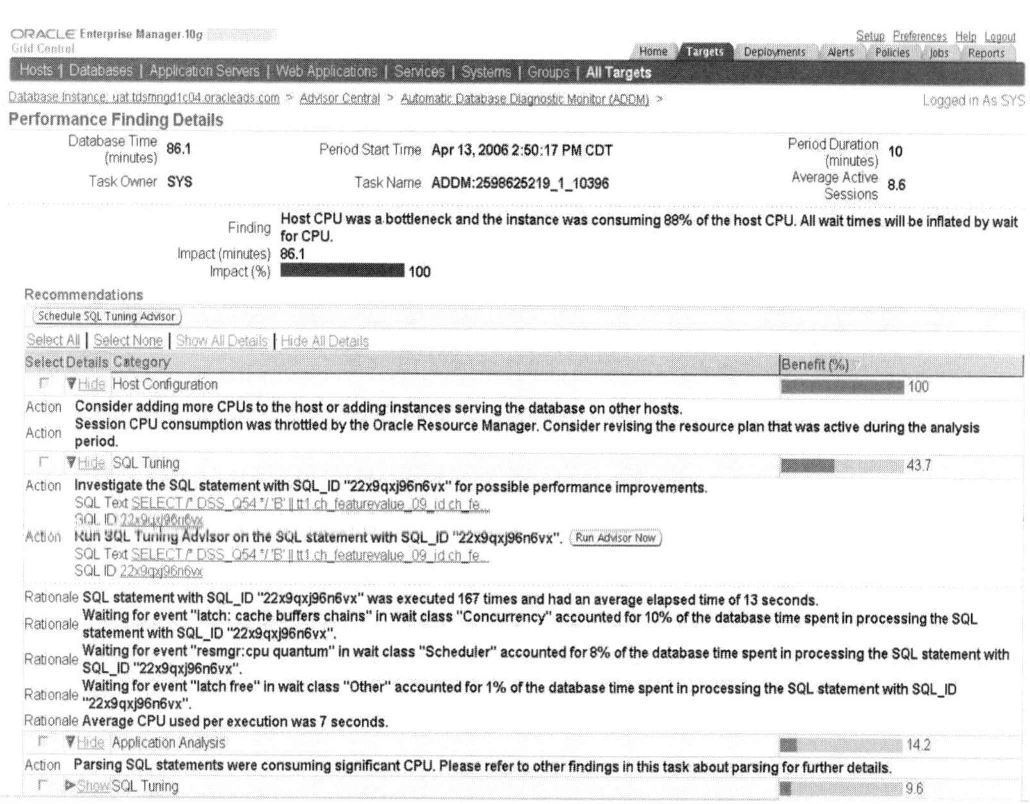

FIGURE 5-17.   *ADDM performance finding details for SQL*

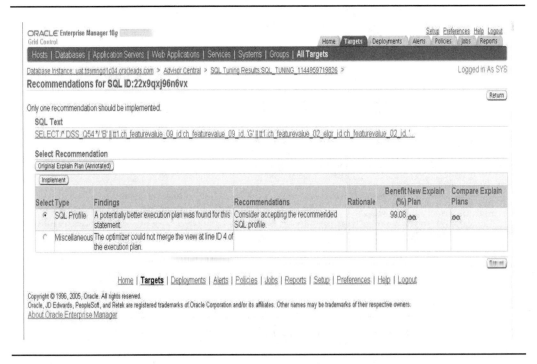

FIGURE 5-18. *SQL Tuning Advisor – Tuning Results*

By clicking the worst SQL, the details of the recommendations can be viewed (Figure 5-19). Employing the SQL Profile should help by 99.08 percent according to the recommendations. There is also a link to compare the Explain Plans side by side to see what is being changed and what the benefit will be.

FIGURE 5-19. *SQL Tuning Advisor recommends a SQL profile.*

The side-by-side Explain Plan shows that the order of table access has been changed as well as some of the joining methods. A Hash Join Inlist Iterator replaced a Nested Loops Cartesian Merge Join as seen in Figure 5-20.

TIP
The Explain Plan Comparison is a great SQL Tuning tool built into EM.

In Figure 5-21, the SQL Statement statistics can be checked after the profile is employed. The system shows that the new SQL Profile substantially reduced the impact to the system that this particular SQL statement was having.

In Figure 5-22, it is evident that the SQL statement that is now tuned is no longer causing the negative impact previously felt. The entire system is now running much better, with fewer users waiting in the queue.

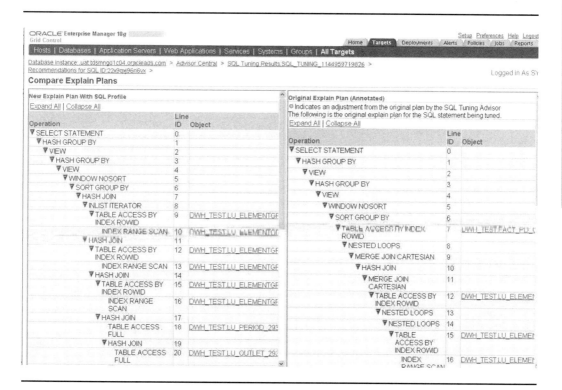

FIGURE 5-20. *Side-by-Side Explain Plan Comparison*

Monitoring the Database

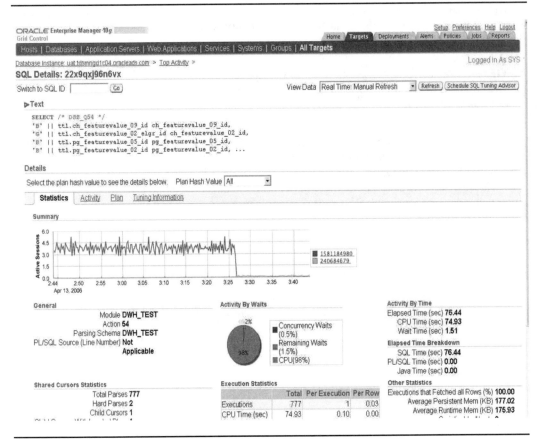

FIGURE 5-21. *Top SQL Details – much better after tuning*

Database Administration Tab

There are several tabs under the database instance or cluster database (depending on which one you select). These selections include: Home (default), Performance, Administration, Maintenance, and Topology. Clicking the Administration tab will display some very nice options. The scope of these options is well beyond this chapter, but it can be seen from the screen in Figure 5-23 that there are some wonderful built-in tools to help the DBA work more effectively and efficiently. A couple of these frequently used options are displayed in this section of the chapter.

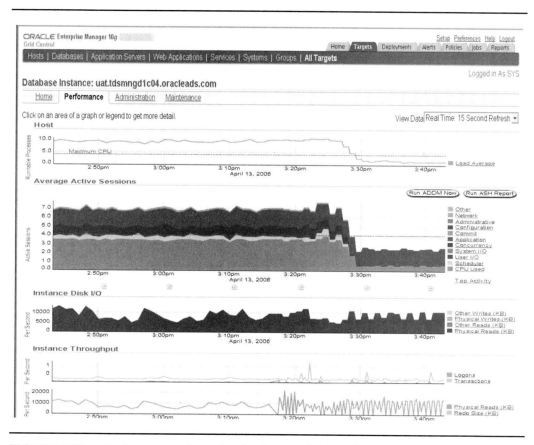

FIGURE 5-22.   *Performance Information for the "oracleads" – better now!*

Under the Schema heading, there is information showing an individual schema (within a given instance) and the objects associated with that schema. This includes information about clusters, database links, functions, indexes, package bodies, packages, procedures, refresh groups (for snapshots), snapshots, synonyms, tables, triggers, and views. There are multiple screens associated with each choice. All of the columns for the given table can be displayed. All the storage information for the table (initial extent, next extent, pctincrease, minextents, maxextents, pctfree, and pctused) are also listed. The constraints, as well as options for adding or removing constraints, are available. There are options to allow for the enabling or disabling of constraints. Note that the number of rows and last analyzed date for all tables are displayed;

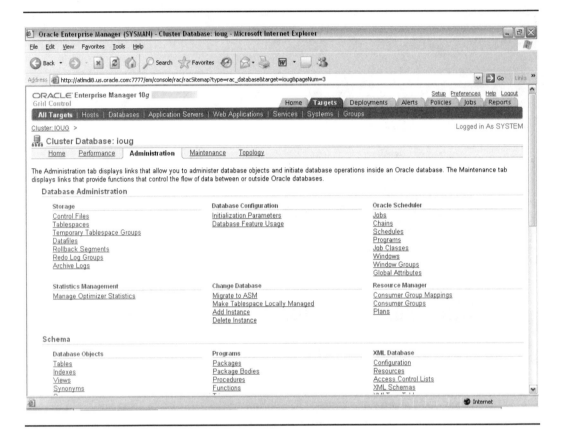

FIGURE 5-23. *Database Administration links*

this information shows up only if the table has been analyzed. The Show Object DDL option generates the create statement for a table or other object. Viewing the general information about an index such as the columns that are indexed and the index storage information is listed in this section.

TIP
The Schema information within the Oracle Enterprise Manager is a very quick way to look at tables and indexes when tuning the Oracle database.

A new source of performance bottlenecks arrived with the advent of functions, packages, procedures, and triggers. At times, it is difficult to find the source code for a function, package, procedure, or trigger. With the EM, the process is simplified by using the schema links to select the code that is in question.

TIP
Use the schema information to quickly find code to tune that is related to packages, procedures, and triggers for a given schema.

Database Administration Tab: Tablespaces

By clicking the Database Storage option "Tablespaces" while in the administration screen, the Tablespaces screen in Figure 5-24 will be displayed. This screen lists all of the tablespaces for

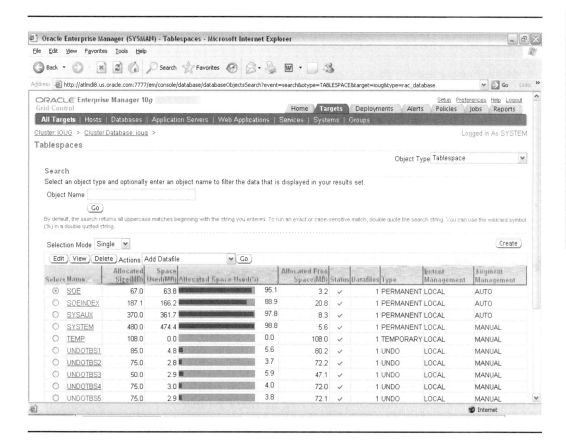

FIGURE 5-24. *Database Administration links – Tablespaces*

this cluster database (or single instance if only a single instance was specified). Note the advancements in the product since Oracle 9*i* including information on allocated and used space, what type of tablespace it is, the extent management, and the segment management.

By clicking a specific tablespace (SOE in this example), the View Tablespace screen in Figure 5-25 is displayed. This screen includes additional information, including the actual database file(s) underlying the tablespace. Also notice all the pull-down Actions that are available for the tablespace screen. Some of these are *very* powerful and huge time savers.

By choosing the Show Tablespace Contents from the pull-down menu, the screen in Figure 5-26 is displayed. This shows all of the segments that are contained in the given tablespace. This can be an excellent way to view objects that correspond to a heavily accessed tablespace.

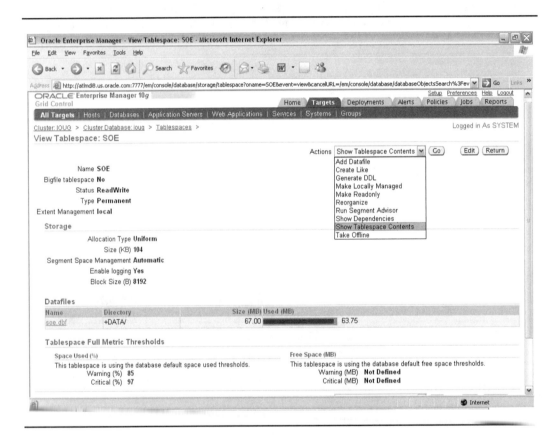

FIGURE 5-25. *Database Administration links – Specific Tablespace*

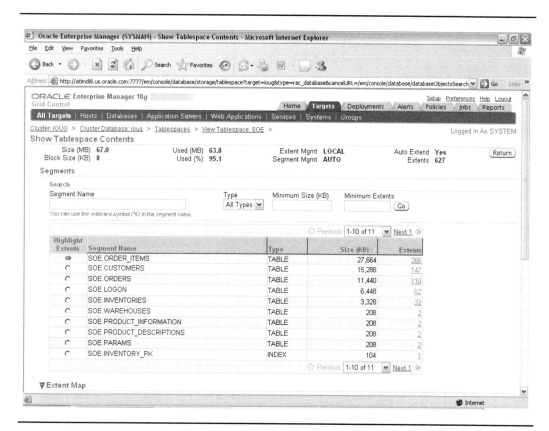

FIGURE 5-26. *Database Administration links – Specific Tablespace Contents*

Something more difficult to discover is the Extent Map. Clicking the Extent Map "+" sign (shown at the bottom of Figure 5-26) will expand the Tablespace to show a very cool Extent Map displayed in Figure 5-27. This Tablespace Map provides graphical view of all tablespaces, datafiles, segments, total data blocks, free data blocks, and percentage of free blocks available in the tablespace current storage allocation. The tool provides the option of displaying all segments for a tablespace or all segments for a datafile. The Tablespace Map also provides additional information for each segment, including average free space per block, chained rows, and the last date that the object was analyzed.

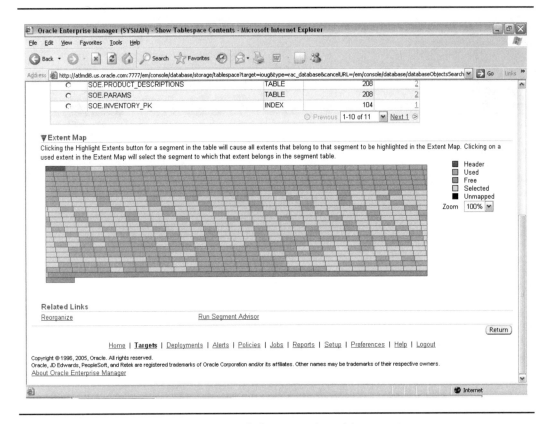

FIGURE 5-27. *Database Administration links – Specific Tablespace Contents*

TIP
The Extent Map, which displays the information in a Tablespace block by block in a graphical manner, is a super-cool feature that's hard to find in EM.

Database Administration Tab: Instance Level

The Database Administration tab can also be useful at the instance level (Figure 5-28). Items such as Manage Optimizer Statistics and Initialization parameters are included at the cluster or instance level. But at the instance level, there are also additional options, including the Automatic Workload Repository (AWR).

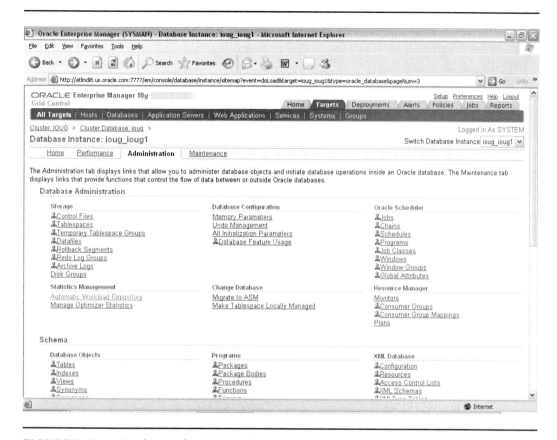

FIGURE 5-28. *Database Administration links instance level*

Database Administration Tab: All Initialization Parameters

Another option from Administration screen is the link to the initialization parameters. By clicking the All Initialization Parameters link under the Database Configuration heading, the screen in Figure 5-29 is displayed. Viewing the current initialization parameters and altering them can be done from this screen. In the example, there is a change to the statistics level to TYPICAL in the pull-down menu. Other databases and/or instances can be checked for any current values or recent changes.

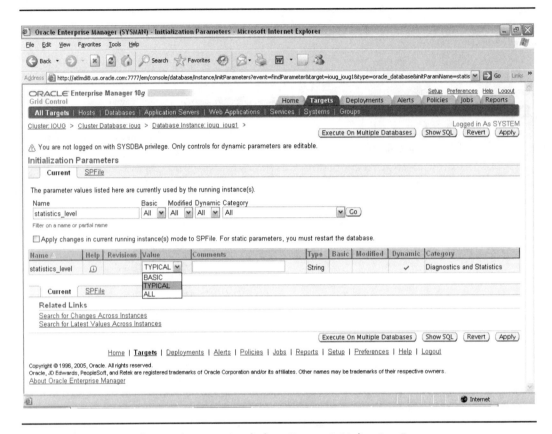

FIGURE 5-29. *Database Administration links – Current Initialization Parameters*

Clicking the SPFILE tab will display the contents (see more information in Chapter 4) if the SPFILE is being used. Figure 5-30 shows an example of viewing the initialization parameters from the SPFILE, which is located in +DATA/ioug/spfileioug.org.

Database Administration Tab: Manage Optimizer Statistics

Another option from Administration screen is the link to the Manage Optimizer Statistics Job screen (Figure 5-31). Keeping statistics up to date for dynamic tables can be a chore (worse if done for static tables too—don't do that). The gather statistics job (GATHER_STATS_JOB) can

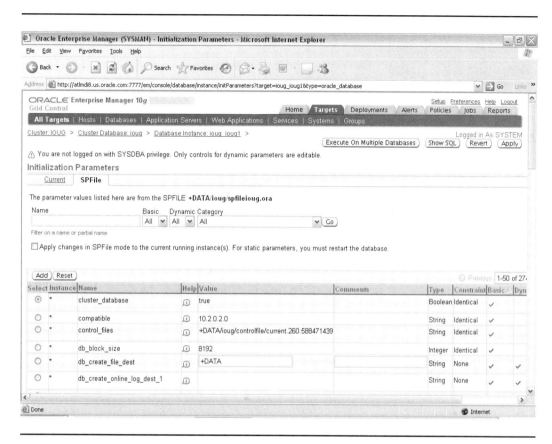

FIGURE 5-30.   *Database Administration links – SPFile Initialization Parameters*

help in this endeavor. Many different optimizer statistics gathering options can be specified from this screen, as well as the scheduling and managing of specific jobs.

An option from Administration screen only at the instance level is the link to the Automatic Workload Repository (AWR). Once the AWR option from the Administration screen is clicked, the AWR General information is displayed. This screen includes information on all snapshots and collection levels. (See more in Chapter 14 on how snapshots work.) In the example in Figure 5-32, there are 40 snapshots with a retention of 25 days and an interval of 10 minutes (way too often—an hour may be a better interval).

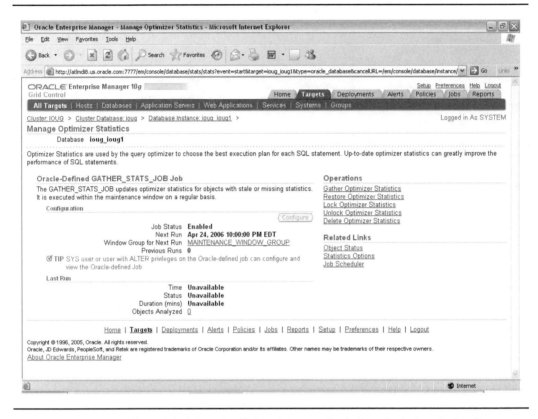

FIGURE 5-31. *Database Administration links – Manage Optimizer Statistics; Gather Stats*

By clicking the Edit button (see Figure 5-33), the interval or retention of the information may be changed. The collection level can also be edited here.

By clicking the number of snapshots displayed in the AWR General information screen (the number 40 as shown in Figure 5-32), the 40 snapshots will then be displayed one at a time as shown in Figure 5-34. The time that the snapshot was generated is listed along with the collection level.

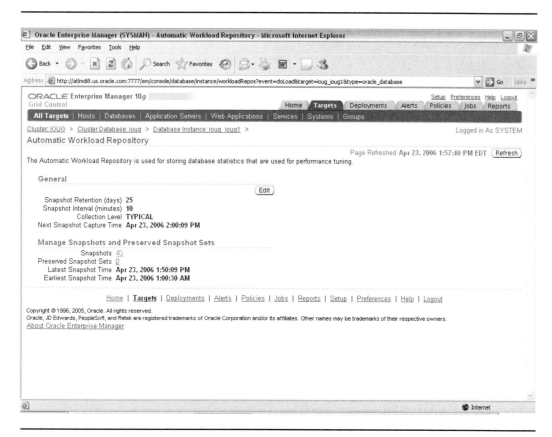

FIGURE 5-32.   *Automatic Workload Repository (AWR)*

Clicking any specific snapshot to begin and end with will generate some basic snapshot details listed in Figure 5-35 (like a very mini-statspack), or we can run a report by clicking Report. This will run and display the AWR Report (covered in detail in Chapter 14—see that chapter for full display output).

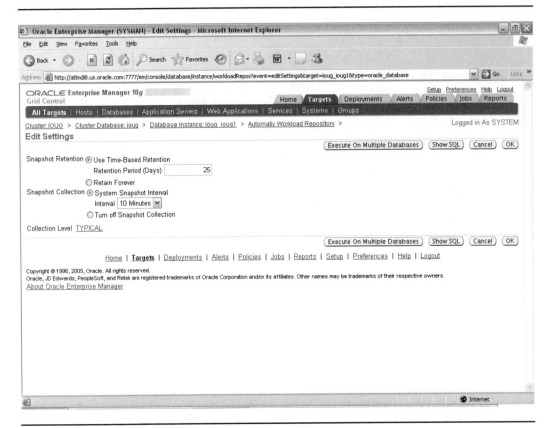

FIGURE 5-33. *Automatic Workload Repository (AWR) Edit settings*

Database Administration Tab, Instance Level: Resource Manager (Consumer Groups)

Another option from Administration screen is the link to the Consumer Groups under the Resource Management heading. This screen will display pie charts that group things into Services (if set up) and also by Modules as displayed in Figure 5-36. A system that includes users in AR

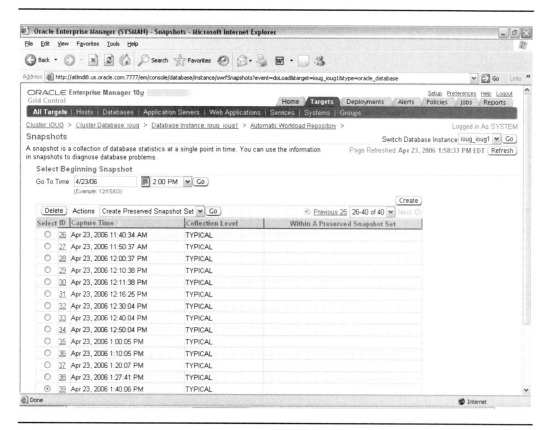

FIGURE 5-34. *Automatic Workload Repository (AWR) Snapshot listing*

(Accounts Receivable), CRM (Customer Relationship Management), and BI (Business Intelligence) can be better visualized when there are services set up for each of them (now it's easy to see who is using all of the resources).

TIP
If you take the time to set up Services, the Top Consumers screen can be used to quickly see which business areas are consuming the most resources.

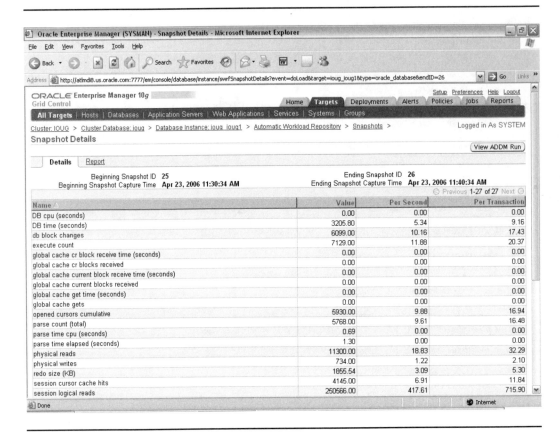

FIGURE 5-35. *Automatic Workload Repository (AWR) Snapshot listing*

Database Maintenance Tab

The Maintenance tab also has several administration links that are associated with maintenance, including Backup and Recovery, Data Guard, and Import/Export (see Figure 5-37). Once again, Oracle creates an excellent option to help make the DBA more productive.

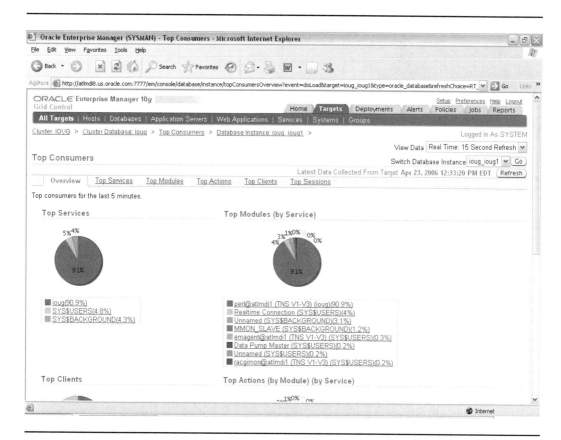

FIGURE 5-36. *Database Administration – Instance Level – Consumer Groups*

Database Topology Tab

The Database Topology tab is something newer in the Oracle product, but I've seen it in other software maintenance products. Figure 5-38 shows the topology for the six-node cluster that we've been working with in this chapter. Notice that all tiers are shown for each of the nodes on the right part of the screen (Listener, ASM, Database, etc.) with detail information for the selected

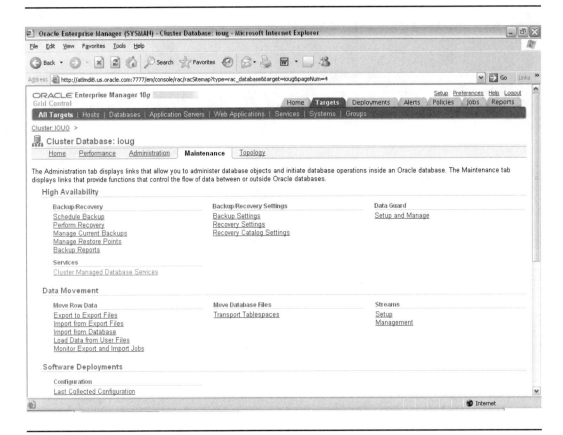

FIGURE 5-37. *Database Maintenance links*

node on the left side of the screen. Something nice (not displayed) is information about the node, which pops up when the mouse rolls over one of the pictures in the right pane.

When at the cluster level (note that Figure 5-38 is at the cluster database level), clicking the Interconnects tab shows information related to interconnect(s) between the nodes of a cluster (Figure 5-39). All six nodes and the corresponding interconnects are listed (complete with the subnet IP address). When there are interconnect performance issues, this is a very helpful screen in identifying slow I/O transfer rates and/or errors.

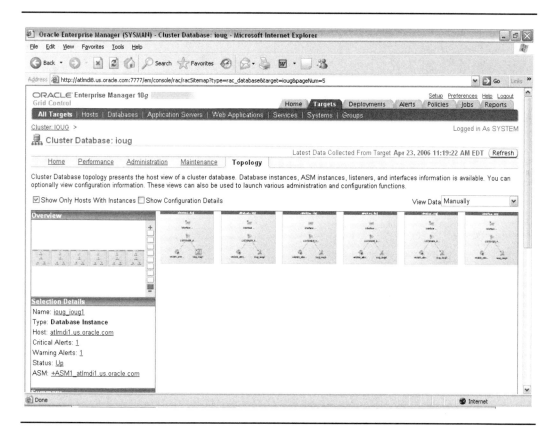

FIGURE 5-38. *Database Topology*

Database Performance Tab

Click the Targets tab and then All Targets to select the ioug Cluster Database as shown in the earlier part of this chapter. Clicking the Performance tab displays the insightful graphs for this cluster and one of the main screens that can be used for tuning. The refresh rate can be set to 15 seconds (default), 1 minute, a manually specified time ,or Historical (to see a week's worth of data—great stuff). This screen will provide graphs for all major metrics related to tuning. Figure 5-40 shows the upper part of this screen. Clicking any individual graph will display a more

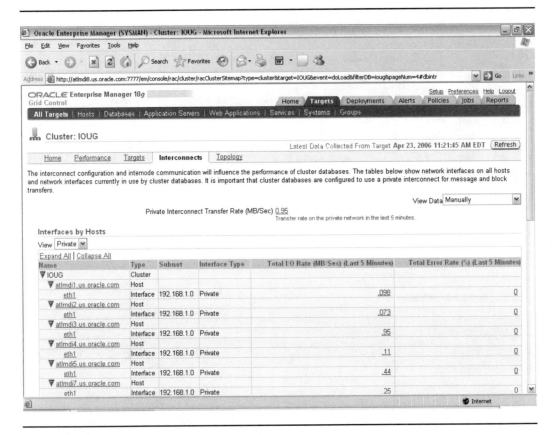

FIGURE 5-39. *Cluster Interconnects detail*

detailed graph for the given performance metric. For example, Figure 5-42 will display the screen that results when the load average graph (first graph displayed in Figure 5-40) is selected. Note that in the Active Sessions, we can see a spike in Network Activity at about 11:10 A.M.

 TIP
The Database or Cluster Performance Screen within EM is the quickest way to find where performance problems are in your system.

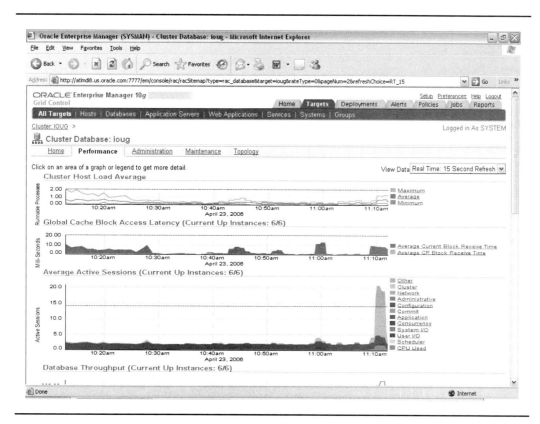

FIGURE 5-40.   *Cluster Database Performance*

Moving to the middle of the screen displayed in Figure 5-40 will display additional graphs and also many additional performance links (Figure 5-41). These include Database Locks, Top Sessions, Top Consumers, Cluster Cache Coherence, and Top Segments. Each of these is used to drill into a specific problem. Below that, there are additional instance-level links, including Top Activity, Duplicate SQL, Blocking Sessions, Hang Analysis, Instance Activity, Search Sessions, Snapshots (quick link), and SQL Tuning Sets. Below those links are yet more links to the individual instances or directly to ASM. There are also links for each instance to Alerts, Policy Violations, and other Performance Statistics (I/O, CPU, etc.).

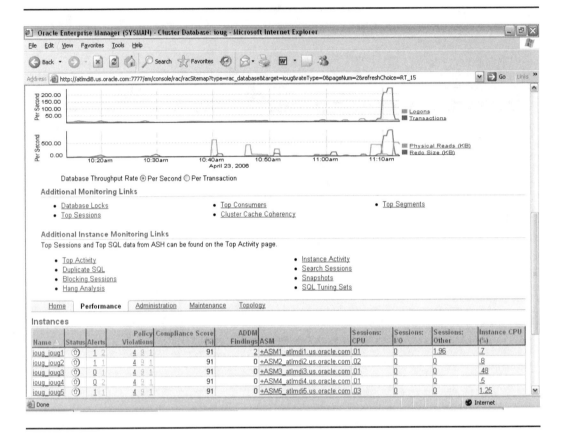

FIGURE 5-41. *Cluster Database Performance (mid-page)*

By clicking the load average graph in Figure 5-40, we display a larger version of that graph, which has a color for each of the nodes listed. In the example in Figure 5-42, there are four instances (on four physical nodes) in the ioug cluster that are displayed in the graph. Note that the instances are ioug3, ioug4, ioug5, and ioug6 and that the physical nodes that the instances reside on are atlmdi3, atlmdi4, atlmdi5, and atlmdi7. There could have been additional instances on these nodes from another database (but there was not in my test). The graph can show a maximum of four instances at one time, but you can choose which instances are displayed. The performance spike in this example at 11:10 A.M. occurred on all nodes.

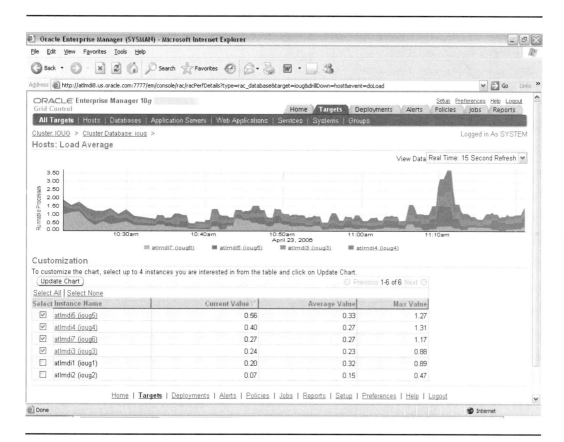

FIGURE 5-42. *Cluster Database Performance – Load Average*

Clicking the second graph of Figure 5-40 will show interconnect issues. The global cache block access latency and transfers have to do with sending blocks from one instance to another instance. Clicking the Cluster Cache Coherency link on the Cluster Database performance screen (Figure 5-40) will also display this screen. In Figure 5-43, the amount of block transfers increases greatly at about 11:10 A.M. Any block access latency over 20 ms should be cause to investigate further. Fixing this issue could involve tuning the query that is causing a lot of blocks to be either read or transferred, getting a faster interconnect, eliminating any locking that is slowing the transfer (one instance hanging on to the block), or ensuring that you are using the private (not the public) interconnect.

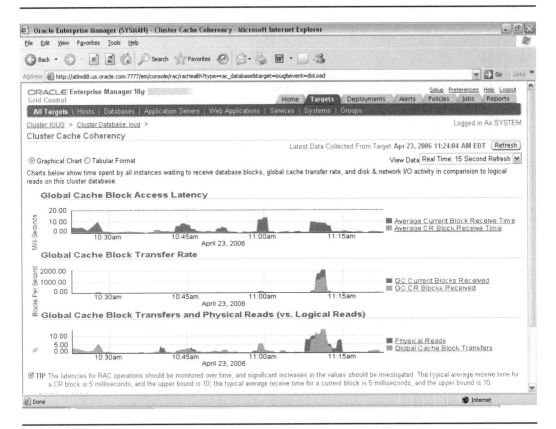

FIGURE 5-43. *Cluster cache coherency*

In the third graph of Figure 5-40, the Active Sessions graph shows a large number of cluster waits. By clicking the Cluster link to the right of the graph, the detailed graph of all cluster waits is displayed (Figure 5-44). We can see many Global Cache (or gc)–type waits associated with this graph at a couple of times during the hour displayed. Below the graph, we can see the actual Top SQL queries that are being run as well as the Top Sessions of the users that are running the queries. Note that this screen shows *only* the Top SQL and Top Sessions for Cluster waits. Once again, this is a very colorful screen showing each wait in a different color to make it very intuitive to use for tuning.

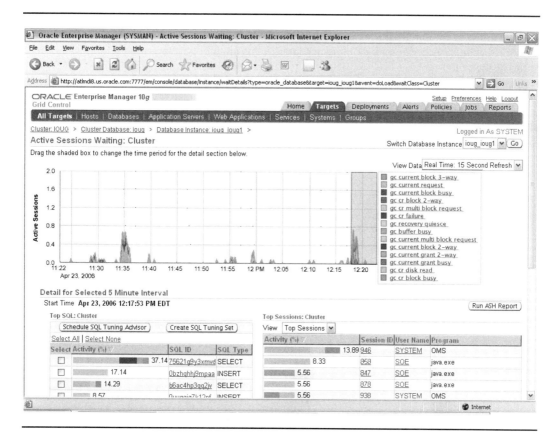

FIGURE 5-44.   *Active Session Waiting – Cluster*

TIP
The Top SQL and Top Sessions section of the Database/Cluster
Performance screen instantly tells where the performance issues are
and which users are consuming all of the resources.

By clicking the link to the right of the graph on "gc current block busy" wait, we are instantly transferred to the Histogram for this wait to see if the waits are many short waits or fewer long waits. In this case, some of the waits are short (1–2 ms) and others are long (32 ms and higher).

Some are short and others are longer in the histogram of Figure 5-45. Later in this chapter, you will see a histogram for "db file sequential read" waits where most waits are very short in duration, while a histogram of locking issues later in this chapter will reveal only long waits in the histogram.

At the bottom of the Active Sessions Screen the Top SQL statement (SQL ID = 75621g9y3xmvd) can be selected and the SQL statement for this query and the associated waits for it are displayed (Figure 5-46). We can see that this SQL statement is causing most of the global cache activity. The Top SQL section is a powerful tool to quickly find the most troublesome users and/or queries on a given system.

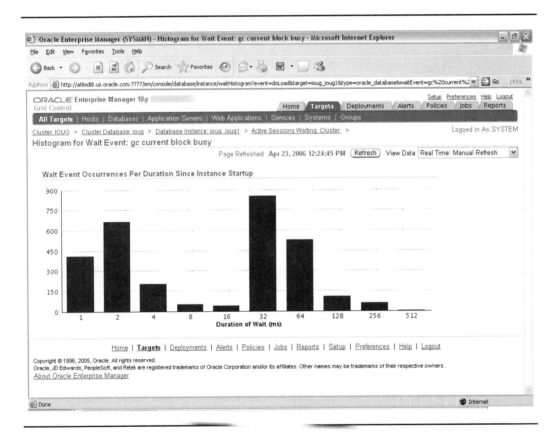

FIGURE 5-45. *Wait Events histogram for "gc current block busy" waits*

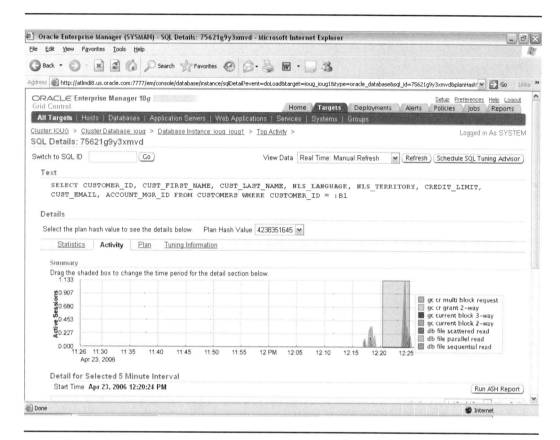

FIGURE 5-46.   *Top SQL – SQL Details for worst SQL (SQL ID = 75621g9y3xmvd)*

The second worst SQL statement listed is also a potential problem. Figure 5-47 shows the second worst statement (SQL ID = 0bzhqhhj9mpaa) listed in the Top SQL section. Perhaps a look at the link to the "db file sequential reads" to the right of the graph to see the histogram for these waits will provide some insight to the query.

TIP
Use the Top SQL section to find the sessions that are using the most resources on a system. By investigating a problem session in more detail, it is easy to free up resources for other processes.

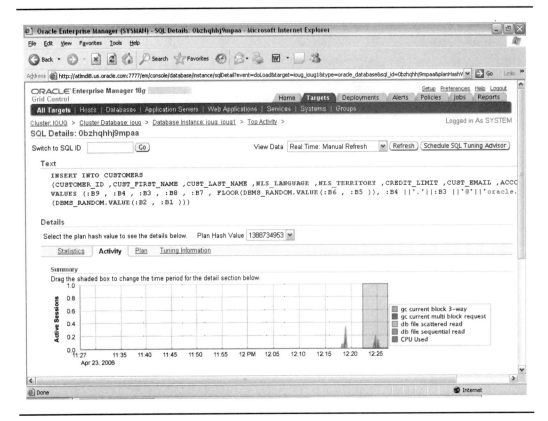

FIGURE 5-47. *Top SQL – SQL Details for second worst SQL (SQL ID = 0bzhqhhj9mpaa)*

By clicking the "db file sequential read" link, the histogram in Figure 5-48 is displayed. This shows that most of the waits are very fast. If these were slow, it would be worth checking the I/O or the size of the cache (to see if it can cache all needed blocks or if it is too small, causing additional I/O). Tuning the query that is causing the waits may limit the number of reads required (see Chapter 14 for detail on how to fix different types of wait events).

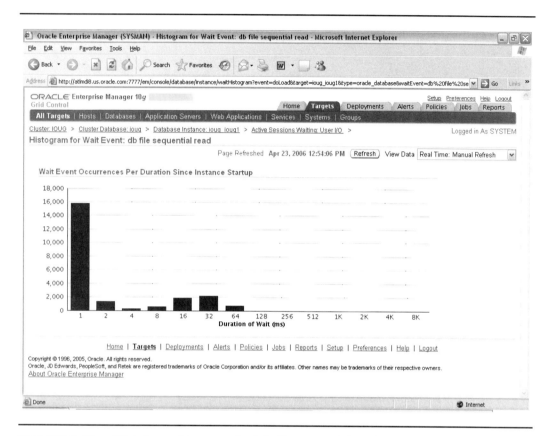

FIGURE 5-48. *Wait Events histogram for "db file sequential read" waits*

You can click the Active Sessions of Figure 5-40 on the CPU link to view the graph that displays CPU USED for each of the four instances that are up and running (Figure 5-49). Since the ioug_ioug2 instance seems to be the worst one, clicking *either* the color of the graph that shows this instance *or* the instance name in the list below the graph will take us to an individual CPU graph for that given instance.

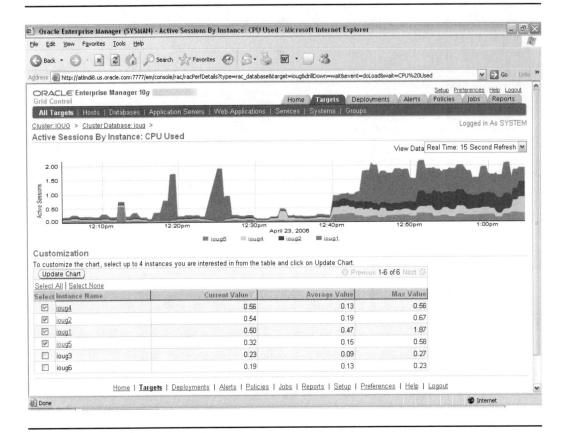

FIGURE 5-49. *Active Sessions by Instance – CPU Used*

Figure 5-50 displays the CPU used by instance ioug_ioug2 in the ioug cluster. The graph shows that the amount of CPU is rising quickly over the past hour. The Top SQL shows clearly that a single statement is using most of the CPU. The rectangle in the graph may be placed/moved anywhere for the period (there may also be a slide bar below that allows you to move the rectangle—depending on the version) and the Top SQL is only for that given five-minute interval.

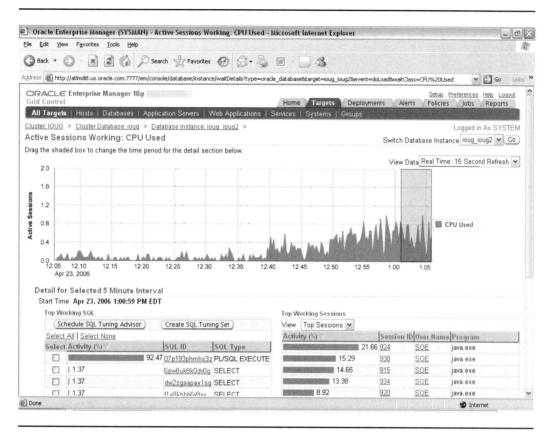

FIGURE 5-50. *Active Sessions by Instance – CPU Used on the ioug_ioug2 instance*

By clicking the Top SQL statement (SQL ID − 07p193phmhx3z), you can see, as in Figure 5-51, that this is the PL/SQL that is using up all of the CPU. Our tuning efforts should focus directly on this statement to fix this CPU issue.

Database Performance Tab

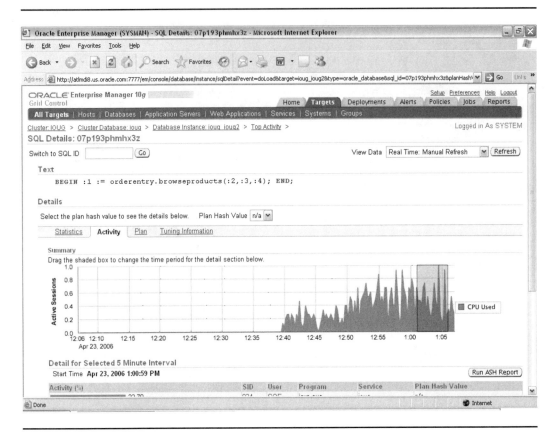

FIGURE 5-51. *Active Sessions by Instance – CPU Used for SQL ID = 07p193phmhx3z*

Monitoring the Hosts

While the Top SQL is usually the problem, digging into other areas of the infrastructure can quickly reveal issues. The Hosts tab under Targets displays all of the hosts that are out there. In this example, there are eight different hosts in the listing in Figure 5-52.

Clicking just one of the hosts (atlmdi1) displays all of the detailed information about that host. This includes the IP address, the OS (operating system), the number of CPUs, the amount of memory, the available disk space, how many users are logged on, and the availability of the system. It also shows any Alerts or Policy violations as it did at the database or instance level. Figure 5-53 shows that the host is currently UP.

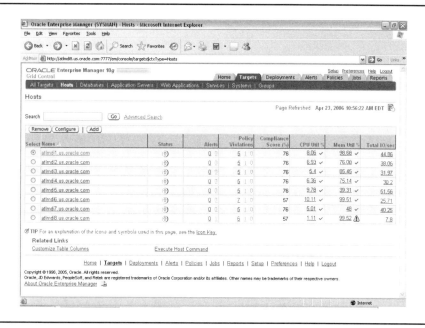

FIGURE 5-52. *The Hosts tab*

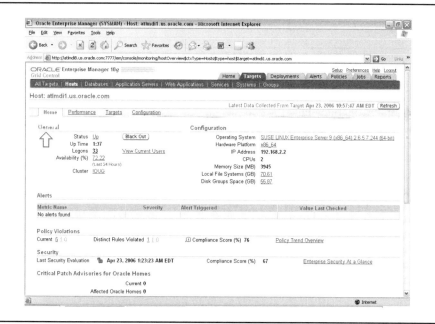

FIGURE 5-53. *The Hosts tab – Viewing Information about a host*

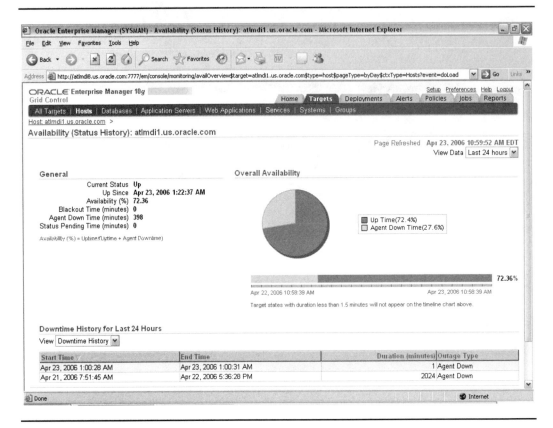

FIGURE 5-54. *The Hosts tab – Viewing Information about Host Availability*

By clicking the Availability link, the complete availability of this host is displayed over a period of time. In Figure 5-54, the host shown has been down over 27 percent of the time, yet the down time occurred during the night (perhaps a maintenance window that requires a blackout to be set up).

Monitoring the Application Servers

While the database and host monitoring was crucial to performance of client/server systems in the 90s, the Internet and web applications have driven performance issues at the application server level. Finding issues at the application server level (usually where the actual code is running) is critical to good performance. EM offers an Application Server tab to monitor all App Servers as displayed in Figure 5-55. The Application Server name as well as CPU and

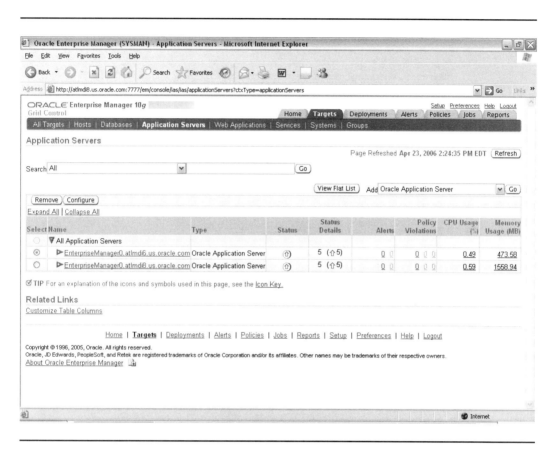

FIGURE 5-55.   *Targets – Applications Servers*

Memory usage is displayed. As at the database and host levels, alerts and policy violations are also listed.

By clicking a specific application server (atlmdi6.us.oracle.com), the response time as well as component-level information is displayed in a screen specific to the application server chosen (Figure 5-56).

Perhaps the best information comes from clicking the Performance tab for a specific component. In Figure 5-57, the EM Application OC4J (Oracle Components for Java) performance is displayed showing Servlet and JSP (Java Server Pages) performance.

The Performance tab for the entire Application Server is displayed in Figure 5-58 and Figure 5-59. These screens are absolutely outstanding to get a glimpse of CPU, memory, web cache, HTTP response, HTTP active connections, and servlet response time.

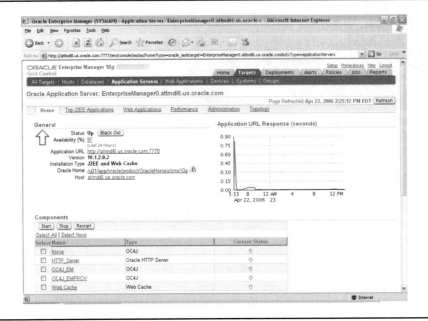

FIGURE 5-56. *Targets – Applications Servers – Specific Server Information*

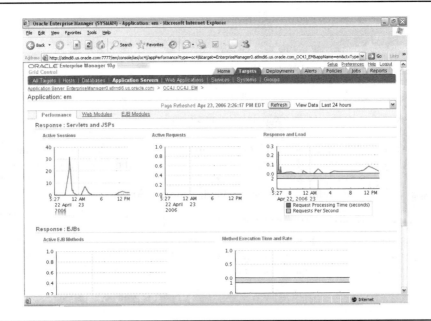

FIGURE 5-57. *Targets – Applications Servers – OC4J Performance*

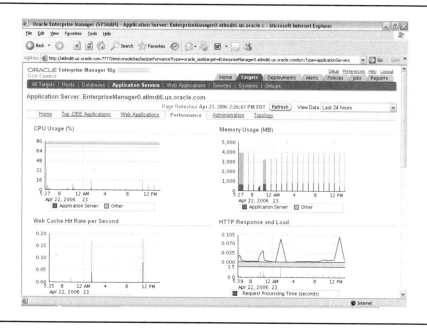

FIGURE 5-58. *Targets – Specific Application Server Performance*

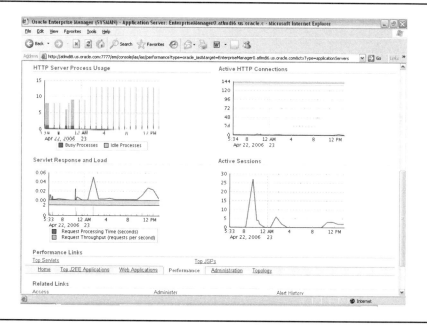

FIGURE 5-59. *Targets – Specific Application Server Performance (lower page)*

Monitoring the
Application Servers

TIP
The Application Server is the new hiding area for performance problems. EM has many tools to view Application Server and Web Application performance.

There is an Administration tab for the Application Server displaying a plethora of options for configuration as well as maintenance (Figure 5-60). There is also a Topology tab that can be selected to display a topology diagram similar to that in the database section.

Figure 5-61 shows a potential problem on the Application Server with the amount of memory usage rising exponentially over the past hour. This could be due to a number of rising connections or just one bad user eating up a lot of memory.

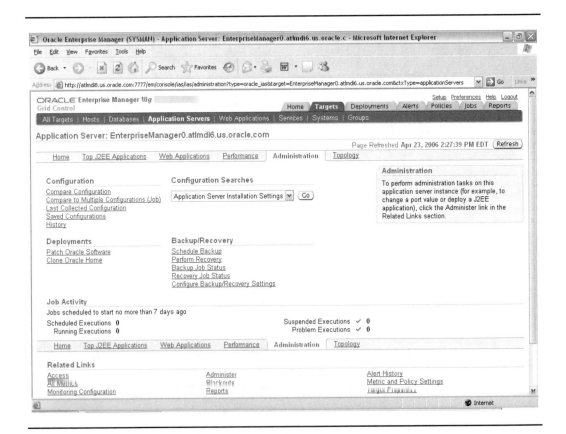

FIGURE 5-60. *Targets – Specific Application Server Administration*

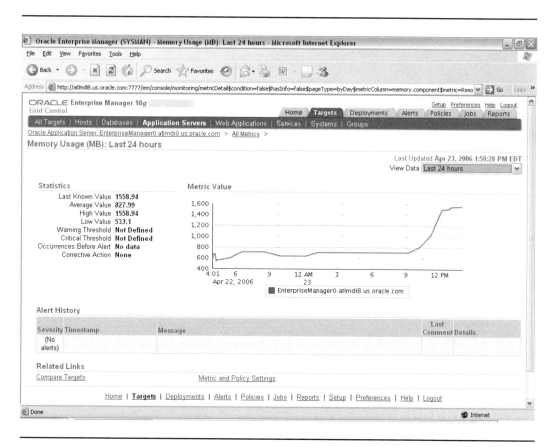

FIGURE 5-61. *Specific Application Server "All Metrics" – Memory Usage*

Monitoring the Web Applications

One of the nicest aspects to EM is that a piece of the infrastructure can be monitored or a specific program that is causing performance issues can be investigated. In this section, viewing the Web Application itself will be investigated. By clicking the Targets tab and then the Web Applications tab, all of the information about a given Web Application is displayed. EM shows whether it is up or down, how long it's been up, the availability, related topology, alerts, and a variety of performance information as displayed in Figure 5-62.

EM also tests the performance of a given Web Application by allowing beacons to run at various times to measure that performance. These beacons are representative queries of what a user may be do on a regular basis. Now the DBA knows when an application is slow because the

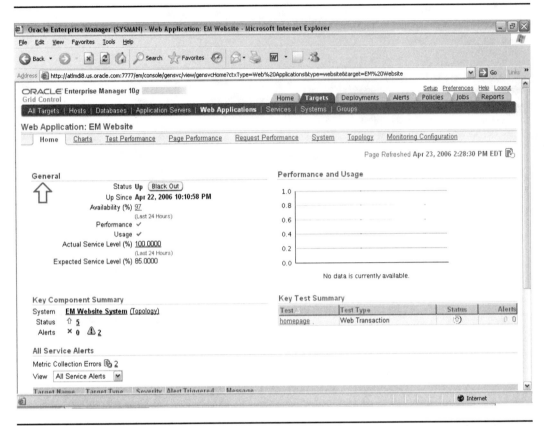

FIGURE 5-62. *Targets – Specific Web Application*

DBA will also be running a query that is similar to the user's query on a regular basis. Figure 5-63 shows the EM screen that displays the test performance of the beacon over a period of several hours. Not only can the performance of the application be measured, but spikes in performance can be pinpointed for future evaluation.

Another way to look at an application's performance or to solve performance problems is to go directly to a given instance and view the Active Sessions Waiting for the Application. In Figure 5-64 the Targets tab is selected, All Targets is clicked, and then the Cluster IOUG is selected. After that, the specific database in the cluster is selected "ioug." Finally, the specific instance of that database is selected, "ioug_ioug1" in this case. Going to the "Active Sessions Waiting: Application" gives the performance for this specific instance. In Figure 5-64, there is an Enqueue (locking) problem. Also note, that the rectangle can be "dragged" to any part of the graph and the corresponding Top SQL for that five-minute period will be displayed.

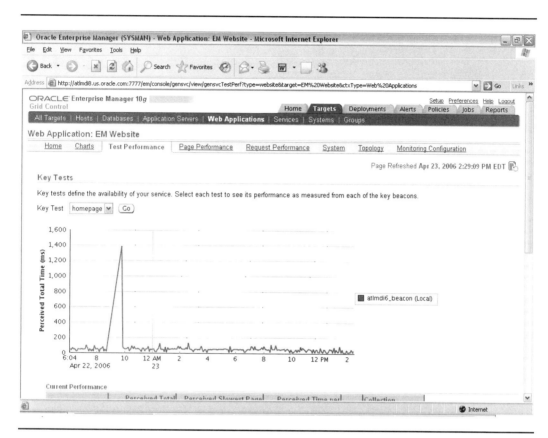

FIGURE 5-63.   *Targets – Specific Web Application Test Performance*

Clicking the specific Enqueue (lock) wait by clicking that part of the screen (enq: TX – row lock contention) will display the histogram associated with this particular enqueue so that it can be seen if it is very few short waits with a few long waits or a lot of long waits. In this case, the waits are *very* long—512 ms per wait as seen in the histogram in Figure 5-65.

As seen earlier, click the Top SQL to show which query is causing all the problems. Clicking the very Top SQL (33ctvpdstwb25), which is the actual SQL that is causing the enqueue waits to be displayed, will show that it is an Update statement (Figure 5-66). It is also locking several rows, and this is the cause for all the waits. At this point, tune the statement, remove the user, or employ the Tuning Advisor to help out.

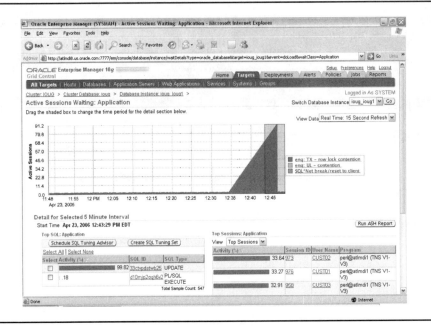

FIGURE 5-64. *Active Sessions Waiting: Application*

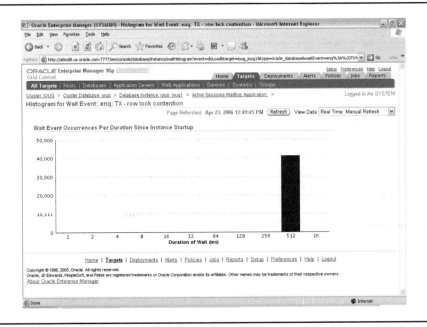

FIGURE 5-65. *Application – Enqueue Wait Histogram*

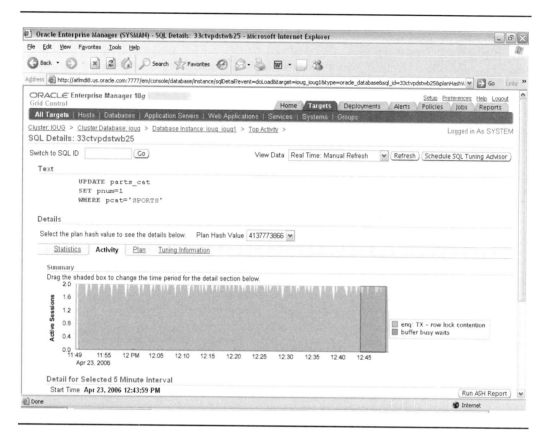

FIGURE 5-66. *Active Session by Instance: Application – Specific SQL Issue*

TIP
When a user finds that he or she has executed a problem query and needs the DBA to end it, the kill session screen is an excellent tool for the DBA to use.

Deployments Tab (Patching Options)

I've often received e-mails from DBAs that say they have a machine that runs an application well, but when they move it a machine that is set up *exactly* the same, the performance changes and they don't know why. Of course the answer is that something is different on one of the systems. So I end up doing a line-by-line comparison of the two environments to find out what actually is different. Despite their claim that things were exactly the same, many things are usually different (so many that I am often amazed that anyone claimed they were the same). Now there is a wonderful EM screen under the Deployments tab where two deployments of Oracle can be compared to find out how they measure up against each other. The screen shows what's different in the hardware (all the way down to the chipset), the OS version, and the Oracle database version, as well as any other software such as one of the Agents or Clusterware versions. In Figure 5-67, the Oracle versions are both 10.2, but one is version 10.2.0.1.0 and the other is version 10.2.0.2.0. One machine is using dual x86_64 CPUs, while the other is using a single i686 CPU. One is Red Hat Linux, while the other is SUSE. These differences are not uncommon when someone tells me two systems are exactly the same!

Also under the Deployments tab is the Patch Advisory section of EM. Depending on how this is set up, it allows notifications of Oracle patches as they become available for a specific environment. This includes patch upgrades to the product as well as Oracle Security Patches often referred to as CPUs (critical patch updates), which come out quarterly on a prespecified day. One cool feature in the Patch Advisory is that you can set up a connection to Oracle MetaLink and scan for all patches that can be applied to your system. Then you can have the patches downloaded and staged in the Oracle Home directory for EM automatically. In Figure 5-68, the Critical Patch Advisories for Oracle Homes is displayed.

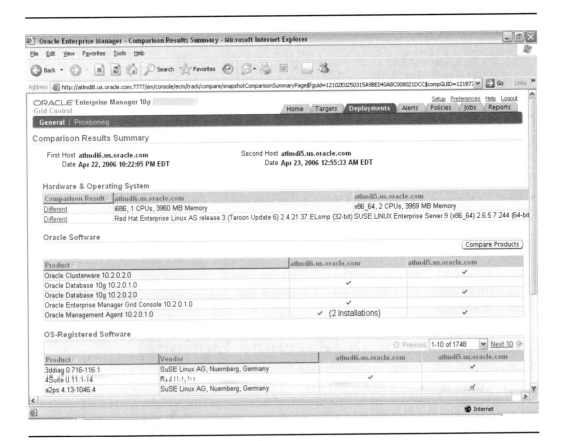

FIGURE 5-67. *Deployments – Comparing two hosts*

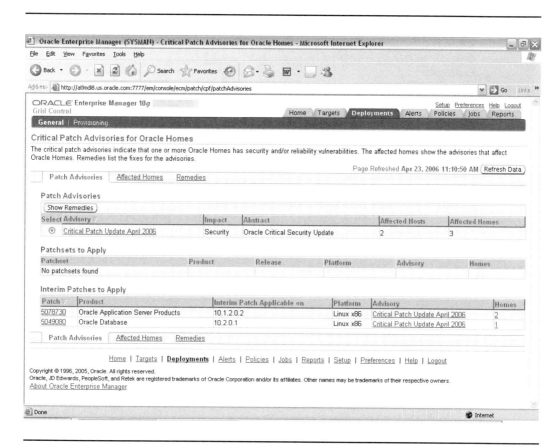

FIGURE 5-68.   *Deployments – Critical Patch Advisories*

Jobs Tab

By clicking the Jobs tab, the job activity and all jobs are listed. In Figure 5-69, there are two jobs listed. One is an RMAN backup script, and the other is an OS command testing script. The time that each job will execute, as well as the target system on which the job will execute, is displayed.

By clicking the IG_RMAN_BACKUP job, the Job Run screen is displayed showing all information related to this specific job (Figure 5-70). Note that one confusing thing about jobs is that there are EM jobs and then there are database jobs (Scheduler). The two job systems are separate.

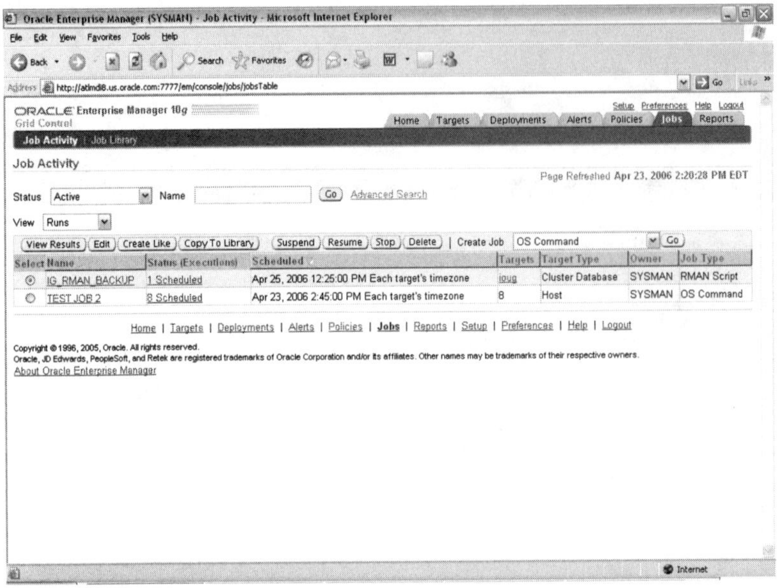

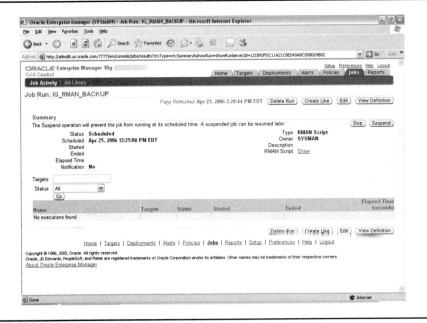

FIGURE 5-69. *Jobs – Job Activity*

FIGURE 5-70. *Jobs – Job Activity for the IG_RMAN_BACKUP job*

Reports Tab

The last part of EM to see is perhaps the best section of all, and that is the Reports section of EM. Many DBAs spend a lot of time writing reports when Oracle has already written almost all of the reports that are needed. From the Reports tab, there are reports for pretty much anything ever required. There are about five to six pages of reports included within the product (the first page is shown in Figure 5-71).

The best report IMHO (in my humble opinion) is the AWR Report (Automatic Workload Repository) covered in detail in Chapter 14. The AWR Report is the best generation statspack report. The next best report is a mini-AWR report (as I call it). It is the Active Session History Report (ASH Report). It shows in a very quick way the key sections found in a statspack or AWR report. Figure 5-72 shows the main choices for running the ASH Report.

Once the ASH Report is generated, by clicking the Generate Report button, the ASH Report is displayed on the screen (Figure 5-73). The output looks very similar to the AWR Report, but it's a much smaller report.

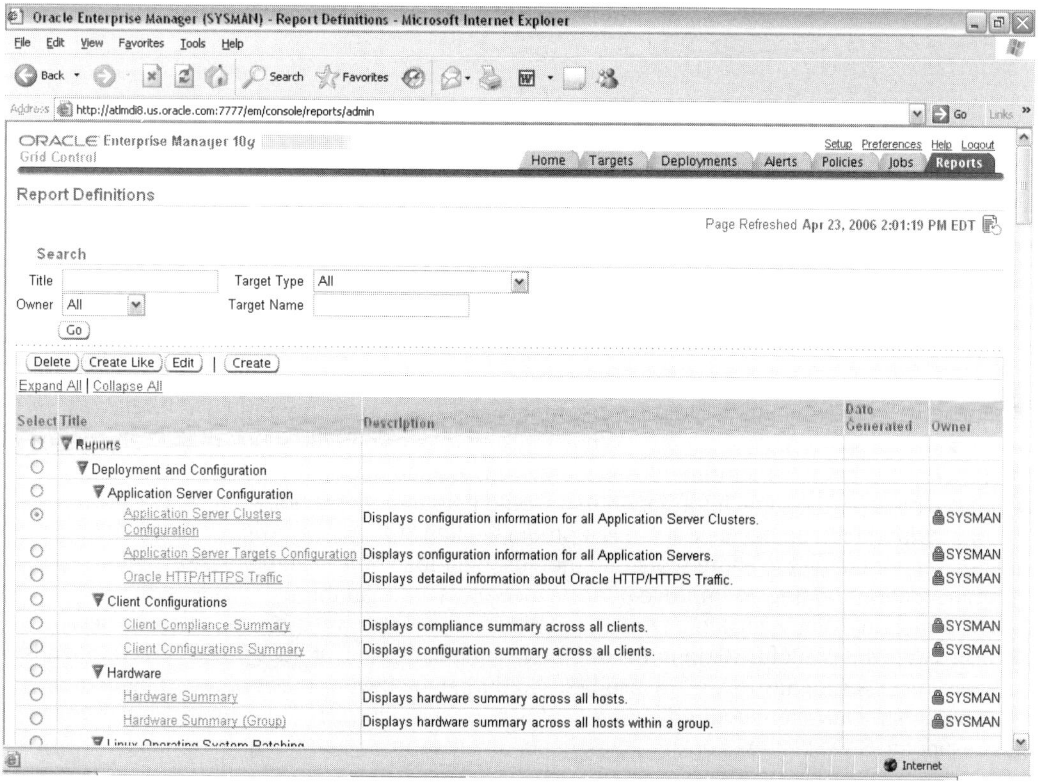

FIGURE 5-71. *The Reports tab*

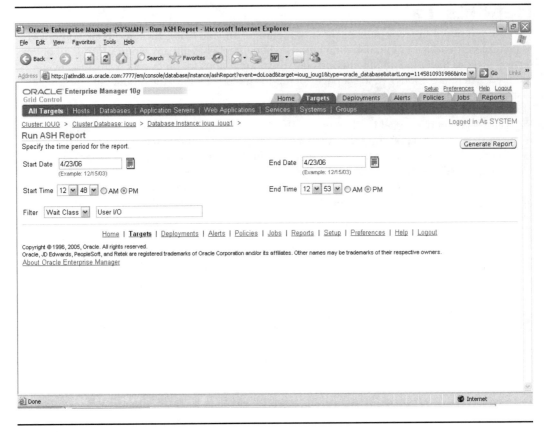

FIGURE 5-72. *Running the ASH (Active Session History) Report*

Some of the information in the ASH Report includes the Top Events and Load Profile (Figure 5-74) as in a statspack or AWR Report. While this report is beyond the scope of the chapter, please refer to Chapter 14 for tuning wait events and detailed information on the AWR Report, which has much of the same information that would help in understanding the ASH Report.

Also, within the Tuning Pack, there is a product called SQL Access Advisor (SAA). SAA can be used for tuning the entire workload (not just high-load SQL statements). SAA gives recommendations on how to improve performance of a workload through indexes (Bitmap, B-Tree, Functional, and Concatenated), materialized views/logs, and a combination of these. SAA considers the cost of DML in terms of index maintenance and storage when it recommends additional access structure. SAA can also be used during the development phase to figure out what access structures are required before deployment in production. You can use SQL Tuning Sets as input to SAA. Please check the Oracle documentation for additional information.

TIP
The Active Session History (ASH) report is a new and simple report that can be used to quickly find and diagnose performance problems.

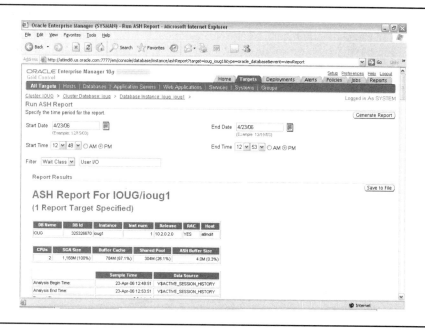

FIGURE 5-73. *The ASH Report output*

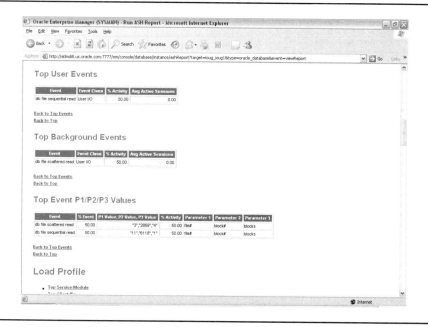

FIGURE 5-74. *The ASH Report output further down the page*

Reports Tab

Automatic Storage Management Performance

With the advent of Oracle's Automatic Storage Management (ASM), Oracle added many EM screens to assist in the management of this new feature. ASM is covered in detail in Chapter 3, but showing a couple of the screens for ASM is certainly helpful. In Figure 5-75, the main ASM home for a node (atlmdi1.us.oracle.com) shows that this instance of ASM is servicing the ioug_ioug1 instance with a little over 12G of space used and about 52G still free. The ASM instance is UP.

By clicking a specific disk group (DATA in this case), detailed information on disk usage is displayed, as well as information for all disks (DISK1, DISK2, DISK3) in the disk group (Figure 5-76).

By clicking a specific member disk (DISK1), the performance information, including I/O response time, I/O Operations, and Disk Throughput, is displayed (Figure 5-77). All reads, writes, and other I/O are displayed clearly.

TIP
The quickest and easiest way to monitor ASM is through EM.

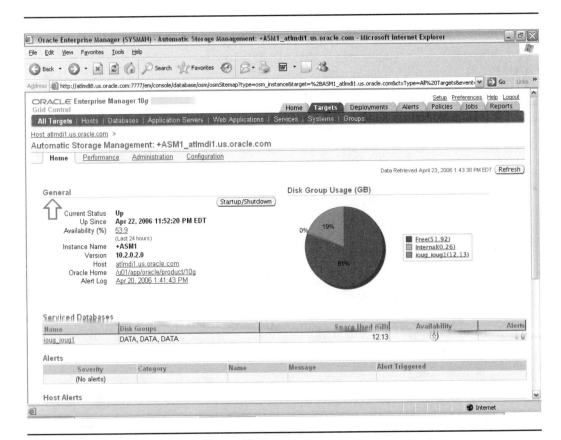

FIGURE 5-75. *The Automatic Storage Management (ASM) home*

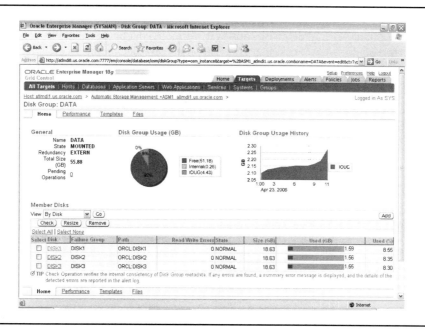

FIGURE 5-76.   *The ASM Disk Group home*

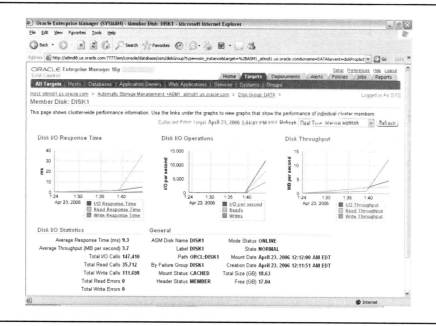

FIGURE 5-77.   *The ASM Disk Performance screen*

Summary

DBAs are able to manage more databases and systems more effectively using this versatile tool, which now extends into Grid Computing. This comprehensive knowledge of system health and performance also enables businesses to plan and trend out for future growth. EM is the most powerful Oracle utility available. It's not just for beginners; the better you are, the better this tool is.

Tips Review

- In Oracle 10gR2, the online help is spectacular. Learn something every day by clicking the Help button.

- AWR runs every hour by default, and ADDM runs just after the AWR snapshot. The Diagnostic Summary that ADDM provides should be viewed regularly.

- In Oracle 10gR2, use the SQL Tuning Advisor only to tune SQL statements, not to monitor conditions like row locks.

- The Explain Plan Comparison is a great SQL Tuning tool built into EM.

- The schema information within the Oracle Enterprise Manager is a very quick way to look at tables and indexes when tuning the Oracle database.

- The Extent Map, which displays the information in a tablespace block by block in a graphical manner, is a super-cool feature that's hard to find in EM.

- If you take the time to set up Services, the Top Consumers screen can be used to quickly see which business areas are consuming the most resources.

- The Database or Cluster Performance screen within EM is the quickest way to find where performance problems are in your system.

- The Top SQL and Top Sessions section of the Database/Cluster Performance screen instantly tells where the performance issues are and which users are consuming all of the resources.

- The Application Server is the new hiding area for performance problems. EM has many tools to view Application Server and Web Application performance.

- The Active Session History (ASH) report is a new and simple report that can be used to quickly find and diagnose performance problems.

- The quickest and easiest way to monitor ASM is through EM.

References

Anil Khilani, *Oracle Troubleshooting Script*
Rich Niemiec, *Tuning the Oracle Grid* (IOUG Collaborate 2006)
Rich Niemiec, *Tuning the Oracle Grid* (–Oracle Open World 2005)
Oracle Enterprise Manager Reference Manual (Oracle Corporation)
Tuning Pack 2.0 (Oracle White Paper)

Many thanks to Anil Khilani, Prabhaker Gongloor (GP), Valerie K. Kane, and David LeRoy of Oracle, who contributed a couple of the screen shots and a bit of the verbiage to this chapter. I want to also thank Ken Morse of Oracle who contributed the majority of the screen shots and verbiage in the first tuning book on SQL Analyze, Oracle Expert, and Tuning Pack 2.0. Ken was a tremendous help to completing this chapter the first time around, while Valerie and David were instrumental the second time around.

CHAPTER
6

Using EXPLAIN and STORED OUTLINES (Developer and DBA)

F inding and fixing problem queries has a lot to do with using the tools that are available. Different tools need to be used for different situations. The tools covered in this chapter are Oracle's provided utilities: SQL TRACE, TKPROF, EXPLAIN PLAN, and STORED OUTLINES (also known as PLAN STABILITY). With Oracle 10g, these tools have been enhanced, including the addition of the DBMS_MONITOR package and TRCSESS. The SQL tracing options have been centralized and extended using the DBMS_MONITOR package. TRCSESS is a command-line tool that allows developers and DBAs to consolidate the information from more than one trace file into a single output file.

The topics covered in this chapter include the following:

- Simple steps for using SQL TRACE/TKPROF

- Sections of the SQL TRACE output

- A more complex query traced, and what to look for to help performance

- DBMS_MONITOR – *10g new feature*

- TRCSESS – *10g new feature*

- Using EXPLAIN PLAN

- Reading EXPLAIN PLAN; top to bottom or bottom to top?

- Using DBMS_XPLAN

- Yet another EXPLAIN PLAN method; the parent/child tree structure method

- Tracing in developer tools

- Important columns in the PLAN_TABLE table

- Tracing for errors and the undocumented init.ora parameters

- Building and using STORED OUTLINES

- Using STORED OUTLINES (PLAN STABILITY) to migrate SQL from the rule-based optimizer

The Oracle SQL TRACE Utility

You use the Oracle SQL TRACE utility to measure timing statistics for a given query, a batch process, and an entire system. It is a thorough method of finding where potential bottlenecks on the system reside. SQL TRACE has the following functionality:

- SQL TRACE runs the query and generates statistics about an Oracle query (or series of queries) that is executed.

- SQL TRACE helps developers analyze every section of a query.

Generally, the Oracle SQL TRACE utility records all database activity (particularly queries) in a *trace* file. The trace file is generated by Oracle SQL TRACE; however, it is very hard to read and should be changed into a readable format using the TKPROF utility.

Simple Steps for SQL TRACE with a Simple Query

The steps for setting up and running Oracle's SQL TRACE utility are listed here:

1. Set the following init.ora parameters (SPFILE users will need to use the ALTER SYSTEM command to change these parameters):

```
TIMED_STATISTICS = TRUE
MAX_DUMP_FILE_SIZE = unlimited (also see metalink article 108723.1)
USER_DUMP_DEST = /oracle/admin/ora9i/udump
```

The TIMED_STATISTICS parameter allows tracing to occur on the system. The USER_DUMP_DEST specifies the location for the files, and the MAX_DUMP_FILE_SIZE specifies the maximum file size in "minimum physical block size at device level" blocks. This is the largest size that the file will grow to; any further data to be recorded will be ignored, will not be written to the trace file, and might be missed. All three of these parameters may also be set via an ALTER SYSTEM (for the entire system) command and take effect when the next user logs in, but they will not affect those currently logged in to the system. You may also set the TIMED_STATISTICS and MAX_DUMP_FILE_SIZE at the session level using the ALTER SESSION (for an individual session) command.

2. Enable SQL TRACE for a SQL*Plus session (this starts tracing for an individual session):

```
alter session set SQL_TRACE true;
```

There are actually several different ways of starting and stopping trace sessions, which will be discussed later in this chapter.

3. Run the query to be traced:

```
Select table_name, owner, initial_extent, uniqueness
from    ind2
where   owner || '' = 'SCOTT' ; --Note: An index on "OWNER" is suppressed
```

4. Disable SQL TRACE for the SQL*Plus session:

```
alter session set SQL_TRACE false;
```

You do not actually have to stop the trace to examine the trace file, but it is a good idea. After running SQL TRACE, your output filename will look something like the following (the SID is usually included in the trace filename):

```
orcl_ora_3372.trc
```

TIP
Setting TIMED_STATISTICS = TRUE in the init.ora will enable the collection of time statistics. Also, in 10g, the initialization parameter SQL_TRACE has been deprecated (see Appendix A for more information).

Finding the generated trace file may be the trickiest part of this whole process. The generated file should be named for the process ID of the trace session and will include that number in the filename. Looking for the date and time of the file makes it easy to find if you are the only one tracing something. In the previous example, 19544 is the process ID of the session being traced. The trace filenames may vary between ora% and ora_%, depending on the operating system on which the trace was performed, and the file should appear in the location specified by the USER_DUMP_DEST init.ora parameter. Another way of finding the file is to put a marker inside (such as issuing a query like SELECT 'Rich1' FROM DUAL;) and then use a file search utility like *grep* or Windows search to find the text.

You can use the following query, running from the same session, to obtain the number included in the trace filename (assuming you can see the v$ views).

```
Select  spid, s.sid,s.serial#, p.username, p.program
from    v$process p, v$session s
where   p.addr = s.paddr
and     s.sid = (select sid from v$mystat where rownum=1);
```

NOTE
Don't forget to grant select on v_$process, v_$session and v_$mystat to the user if not already granted.

Run TKPROF at the command line to put the TRACE file into readable format (this command will create the file rich2.prf in the current directory from the ora_19554.trc trace file and will also log in to the database as system/manager to get the EXPLAIN Plan output):

```
tkprof ora_19554.trc rich2.prf explain=system/manager
```

The TKPROF utility translates the TRACE file generated by the SQL TRACE facility to a readable format. You can run TKPROF against a TRACE file that you have previously created, or you can run it while the program that is creating the TRACE file is still running. Table 6-1 lists options for TKPROF.

The syntax for TKPROF is as follows:

```
tkprof tracefile output_file [sort = parameters] [print=number]
[explain=username/password] [waits=yes|no] [aggregate=yes|no] [insert=filename]
[sys=yes|no] [table=schema.table] [record=filename]
```

The following are some quick examples using these options.
Run TKPROF and list only the top five CPU (fetch + execute + parse) results:

```
tkprof ora_19554 rich2 explain=system/manager sort=(FCHCPU,EXECPU,PRSCPU) print=5
```

Run TKPROF and omit all recursive statements:

```
tkprof ora_19554 rich2 explain=system/manager sys=no
```

Run TKPROF and create a file that will create a table and insert records from the trace:

```
tkprof ora_19554.trc rich2.prf explain=system/manager insert=insert1.ins
```

Variable	Definition
Tracefile	This is the name of the SQL TRACE file containing the statistics by SQL_TRACE.
Output_file	This is the name of the file where TKPROF writes its output.
print = number	This is the number of statements to include in the output. If this statement is not included, TKPROF will list all statements in the output.
Explain = username/password	Run the EXPLAIN PLAN on the user's SQL statements in the TRACE file. This option creates a plan_table of its own, so the user will need to have privileges to create the table and space in which to create it. When TKPROF is finished, this table is dropped. Ensure that you use the username/password of the user that parsed the cursor (ran the query) to ensure the explain is by the correct user. See Metalink note: 199081.1 for more information.
insert = filename	This option creates a script to create a table and store the TRACE file statistics for each SQL statement traced.
record = filename	This option produces a file of all the user's SQL statements.
Sys = yes|no	This option allows the user to request that the recursive SQL statements (issued by the SYS user) not be displayed in the output. The default is YES. Recursive SQL usually includes internal calls and any table maintenance, such as adding an extent to a table during an insert.
sort = parameters	A tremendous number of sorting options are available. My favorites are FCHCPU (CPU time of fetch); FCHDSK (disk reads for fetch); FCHCU and FCHQRY (memory reads for fetch); FCHROW (number of rows fetched); EXEDSK (disk reads during execute); EXECU and EXEQRY (memory reads during execute); EXEROW (rows processed during execute); EXECPU (execute CPU time); PRSCPU (parse CPU); and PRSCNT (times parsed).
waits=yes/no	Record summary for any wait events.
aggregate=yes/no	If no, then tkprof does not combine multiple users of the same SQL text.
table=schema.table	The table in which tkprof temporarily put execution plans before writing them to the output file.

The Oracle SQL TRACE Utility

TABLE 6-1. *Command-Line Options*

The partial output of insert1.ins is shown here:

```
REM  Edit and/or remove the following CREATE TABLE
REM  statement as your needs dictate.
CREATE TABLE  tkprof_table
(date_of_insert                    DATE
,cursor_num                        NUMBER
,depth                             NUMBER
,user_id                           NUMBER
,parse_cnt                         NUMBER
...etc...
,sql_statement                     LONG );
INSERT INTO tkprof_table VALUES
(SYSDATE, 1, 0, 5, 0, 0, 0, 0, 0, 0, 0 , 1, 0, 0, 0, 0, 0, 1, 0
, 0, 0, 0, 0, 0, 0, 0, 4294877296 , 'alter session set sql_trace true');
INSERT INTO tkprof_table VALUES
(SYSDATE, 1, 0, 5, 1, 450648, 471000, 0, 46, 2, 1 , 1, 0, 0, 0, 0, 0, 0, 0
, 2, 10015, 10000, 0, 685, 4, 1, 50000, 'select count(*) from emp');
INSERT INTO tkprof_table VALUES
(SYSDATE, 1, 0, 5, 1, 0, 0, 0, 0, 0, 1 , 1, 0, 0, 0, 0, 0, 0, 0
, 0, 0, 0, 0, 0, 0, 0, 7481000, 'alter session set sql_trace false');
```

Run TKPROF and create a file that shows your trace session:

```
tkprof ora_19554.trc rich2.prf explain=system/manager record=record1.sql
```

The output of record1.sql is shown here:

```
alter session set sql_trace true ;
select count(*) from emp ;
alter session set sql_trace false ;
```

TIP
The TKPROF utility puts a traced output into a readable format. Without running TKPROF, it would be difficult to read the output of a TRACE. By specifying explain = username/password (as shown in the accompanying examples), we are able to get the EXPLAIN execution path, in addition to the execution statistics of the query.

TIP
To use multiple sort parameters, you can just repeat the sort = parameter on the command line, as tkprof source_file out_file sort = parm1 sort = parm2.

```
select    TABLE_NAME, OWNER, INITIAL_EXTENT, UNIQUENESS
from      IND2
where     OWNER = 'SCOTT';
```

	count	cpu	elapsed	disk	query	current	rows
Parse:	1	1	2	0	0	0	
Execute:	1	0	0	0	0	2	0
Fetch:	2	69	113	142	430	0	36

Here is the execution plan (no index used):

```
TABLE ACCESS (FULL) OF 'IND2'
```

The preceding output shows 142 disk reads (physical reads) and 430 total reads (query + current). The number of memory reads is the total reads less the disk reads, or 288 memory reads (430 – 142). Having such a high number of disk reads compared to query reads is certainly a potential problem unless you are running a data warehouse or queries that often do require a full table scans. The execution path shows a full table scan, confirming that we may have a potential problem.

TIP

A traced query with a large number of physical reads may indicate a missing index. The disk column indicates the physical reads (usually when an index is not used), and the query column added to the current column is the total number of block reads (the physical reads are included in this number). A query with a large number of query reads and a low number of disk reads may indicate the use of an index, but if the query reads are overly high, it could indicate a bad index or bad join order of tables. A query with a large number of current reads usually indicates a large DML (UPDATE, INSERT, DELETE) query.

The next listing shows what happens when we rerun the query (after restarting the system) to be traced, now using an index on the OWNER column:

```
select    table_name, owner, initial_extent, uniqueness
from      ind2
where     owner = 'SCOTT' ;   (The index on "OWNER" is not suppressed)
```

The following listing shows the output of the file rich2.prf. Often there are 0 disk reads for queries that have frequently accessed data. The first time a query is run, there will always be disk reads.

```
select    table_name, owner, initial_extent, uniqueness
from      ind2
where     owner = 'SCOTT' ;
```

	count	cpu	elapsed	disk	query	current	rows
Parse:	2	0	0	0	0	0	0
Execute:	2	0	0	0	0	0	0
Fetch:	4	6	6	0	148	0	72

The following shows the Execution plan (index used):

```
TABLE ACCESS (BY ROWID) OF 'IND2'
  INDEX (RANGE SCAN) OF 'IND2_1' (NON-UNIQUE)
```

A traced query output with only memory reads (query-consistent reads) indicates that an index is likely being used.

TIP
There is currently a bug in 10gR1 (fixed in 10gR2); it results in an "ORA-922: missing or invalid option" error and the following message being logged into the TKPROF report file: "Error in CREATE TABLE of EXPLAIN PLAN table: SCOTT.prof$plan_table." A work-around is described in Metalink Note 293481.1. To implement the solution for this problem, follow these steps:

1. Run the $ORACLE_HOME/rdbms/admin/utlxplan.sql script in the schema you want to place the explain table in.

2. Run tkprof with the TABLE option.

```
SQL> @?/rdbms/admin/utlxplan.sql
...
tkprof <tracefile> <outfile> EXPLAIN = ... TABLE = PLAN_TABLE ...
```

The Sections of a TRACE Output

The TRACE utility has multiple sections, including the SQL statements, statistics, information, and EXPLAIN PLAN. Each of these is discussed in the following text sections.

The SQL Statement

The first section of a TKPROF statement is the *SQL statement.* This statement will be exactly the same as the statement that was executed. If there were any hints or comments in the statement, they would be retained in this output. This can be helpful when you are reviewing the output from multiple sessions. If you find a statement that is causing problems, you can search for the exact statement. Remember, some of the statements from Oracle Forms are generated dynamically, so parts of the query (particularly WHERE clause predicates) may be displayed as bind variables (:1) and not actual text.

The Statistics Section

The *statistics* section contains all the statistics for this SQL statement and all the recursive SQL statements generated to satisfy this statement. This section has eight columns, the first being the type of call to the database. There are three types of calls: Parse, Execute, and Fetch. Each call type generates a separate line of statistics. The Parse is where the SQL statement itself is put into memory (library cache of the shared pool), or it can also reuse an exact cursor. The Execute is where the statement is actually executed, and the fetch goes and gets the data that results from the execute. The other seven columns are the statistics for each type of call. Table 6-2 explains each column and its definition.

Information Section

The *information* section contains information about the number of library cache misses from parse and execute calls. If the number of misses is high, there may be a problem with the size of the shared pool. You should check the hit ratio and the reload rate of the library cache. This section also shows the username of the last user to parse this statement. There is also information about the current optimizer mode setting.

Column	Definition
Count	The number of times this type of call was made.
Cpu	The total CPU time for all of the calls of this type for this statement. If the TIMED_STATISTICS parameter in the init.ora file is not set to TRUE, this statistic and the elapsed statistic will be 0.
Elapsed	The total elapsed time for this call.
Disk	The total number of data blocks retrieved from disk to satisfy this call. This is the number of physical reads.
Query	The total number of data buffers retrieved from memory for this type of call. SELECT statements usually retrieve buffers in this mode. This is the number of consistent gets.
Current	The total number of data buffers retrieved from memory for this type of call. UPDATE, INSERT, or DELETE usually access buffers in this mode, although SELECT statements may use a small number of buffers in this mode also. This is the number of db block gets.
Rows	The total number of rows processed by this statement. The rows processed for SELECT statements will appear in the row of Fetch statistics. Inserts, updates, and deletes will appear in the Execute row.

TABLE 6-2. *Statistics for Each Type of Call*

Sections of a TRACE Output

The Row Source Operation Section

The *row source operation* section lists the number of rows cross-referenced with the operation that used the rows. The output looks something like this:

```
Rows     Row Source Operation
-------  ------------------------------------------------------
      1  TABLE ACCESS FULL DUAL
```

TIP
Note that the trace file is a point-in-time picture of what happened on the system at a given moment. In contrast, the explain plan (detailed next) is generated when the TKPROF listing is analyzed, which could be some time later. The row source operation listing is generated as part of the trace file and can be used to see if the database objects have changed since the trace was performed.

The EXPLAIN PLAN

I find this section of the TKPROF to be the most useful. The first column of this section is the number of rows processed by each line of the execution plan. Here, you will be able to see how slow a statement is. If the total number of rows in the fetch statistics is low compared to the number of rows being processed by each line of the EXPLAIN PLAN, you may want to review the statement.

It is also possible that only one line of the execution plan is processing a large number of rows compared to the rest of the statement. This can be caused by full table scans or the use of a bad index.

A More Complex TKPROF Output

The following listing illustrates a TRACEd query with a slightly higher complexity:

```
select   Item_Item_Id, InitCap(Item_Description)
from     Item
where    Item_Classification = 1
and      Item_Item_Id Between 1000000 And 2700000
and      Item_Item_Id Not In (Select Invitem_Item_Id
from     Inventory_Item
where    Invitem_Location_Id = '405')
```

call	count	cpu	elapsed	disk	query	current	rows
Parse	1	0.00	0.00	0	0	0	0
Execute	1	0.00	0.00	0	0	0	0
Fetch	27	20.87	21.24	0	4408	0	399
Totals	29	20.87	21.24	0	4408	0	399

```
Misses in library cache during parse: 0
Optimizer hint: CHOOSE
Parsing user id: 106   (C12462)
```

Rows	Execution Plan
0	SELECT STATEMENT OPTIMIZER HINT: CHOOSE
572	FILTER
598	TABLE ACCESS (BY ROWID) OF 'ITEM'
599	INDEX (RANGE SCAN) OF 'ITEM_PK' (UNIQUE)
278790	INDEX (RANGE SCAN) OF 'INVITEM_PK' (UNIQUE)

Table 6-3 lists some of the problems to look for in the TKPROF output.

Digging into the TKPROF Output

When we compare the TKPROF output to the actual object's physical characteristics, we start to see how Oracle is really working. Consider a CUSTOMER table with over 100,000 records contained in over 1000 blocks. By querying DBA_TABLES and DBA_EXTENTS, we can see the blocks that are both allocated (1536) and being used (1382), as shown in the following listing:

```
select sum(blocks)
from dba_segments
where segment_name = 'CUSTOMER';
```

```
SUM(BLOCKS)
-----------
       1536


select blocks, empty_blocks
from dba_tables
where table_name = 'CUSTOMER';


    BLOCKS EMPTY_BLOCKS
---------- ------------
   1382        153
```

If we look at the TKPROF output of a query that counts all records in the CUSTOMER table (shown in the next listing), we see that it performs a full table scan because this is the first access after a startup. Also note that the number of blocks accessed (mostly physical disk access) is slightly higher than the total number of blocks in the physical table (seen in the previous queries).

Problem	Solution
The parsing numbers are high.	The SHARED_POOL_SIZE may need to be increased.
The disk reads are very high.	Indexes are not being used or may not exist.
The query and/or current (memory reads) are very high.	Indexes may be on columns with low cardinality (columns where an individual value generally makes up a large percentage of the table; like a y/n field). Removing/suppressing the index or using histograms or a bitmap index may increase performance. A poor join order of tables or bad order in a concatenated index may also cause this.
The parse elapse time is high.	There may be a problem with the number of open cursors.
The number of rows processed by a row in the EXPLAIN PLAN is high compared to the other rows.	This could be a sign of an index with a poor distribution of distinct keys (unique values for a column). This could also be a sign of a poorly written statement.
The number of misses in the library cache during parse is greater than 1.	This indicates that the statement had to be reloaded. You may need to increase the SHARED_POOL_SIZE in the init.ora file or do a better job of sharing SQL.

TABLE 6-3. *Problems to Look for in the TKPROF Output*

Digging into the TKPROF Output

All but 4 of the 1387 query blocks read are disk reads. (Disk reads are a subset of the query, which are the sum of disk and memory reads in consistent mode.)

```
SELECT COUNT(*)
FROM CUSTOMER;

call      count       cpu    elapsed        disk       query     current        rows
-------  ------  --------  ----------  ----------  ----------  ----------  ----------
Parse         1   3505.04    3700.00           0           0           0           0
Execute       1      0.00       0.00           0           0           0           0
Fetch         2   1101.59   18130.00        1383        1387          15           1
-------  ------  --------  ----------  ----------  ----------  ----------  ----------
total         4   4606.63   21830.00        1383        1387          15           1

Misses in library cache during parse: 1
Optimizer goal: ALL_ROWS
Parsing user id: 5


Rows       Row Source Operation
-------    ---------------------------------------------------------
      1    SORT AGGREGATE
 114688      TABLE ACCESS FULL CUSTOMER
```

If we run this query a second time (shown in the following listing), a big change occurs. If we look at the TKPROF output of a query that counts all records in the CUSTOMER table this time, we see that it still performs a full table scan, but now there are many fewer disk reads because most of the blocks needed are already cached in memory. Most of the 1387 query blocks read are memory reads. (Only 121 are disk reads.)

```
SELECT COUNT(*)
FROM CUSTOMER

call      count       cpu    elapsed        disk       query     current        rows
-------  ------  --------  ----------  ----------  ----------  ----------  ----------
Parse         1      0.00       0.00           0           0           0           0
Execute       1      0.00       0.00           0           0           0           0
Fetch         2    901.29    2710.00         121        1387          15           1
-------  ------  --------  ----------  ----------  ----------  ----------  ----------
total         4    901.29    2710.00         121        1387          15           1

Misses in library cache during parse: 0
Optimizer goal: ALL_ROWS
Parsing user id: 5


Rows       Row Source Operation
-------    ---------------------------------------------------------
      1    SORT AGGREGATE
 114688      TABLE ACCESS FULL CUSTOMER
```

TIP
Full table scans are one of the first things directed by Oracle to be pushed out of memory (become least recently used as soon as you run them) because they are so inefficient, usually using a lot of memory.

Using DBMS_MONITOR (10g New Feature)

In a multitier environment with connection pooling or a shared server, a session can span multiple processes and even multiple instances. DBMS_MONITOR is a built-in package introduced in Oracle 10g that allows any user's session to be traced from client machine to middle tier to back end database. This makes it easier to identify the specific user who is creating a large workload. DBMS_MONITOR replaces trace tools such as DBMS_SUPPORT. The DBA role is required to use DBMS_MONITOR.

End-to-end application tracing can be based on the following:

- **Session**   Based on session ID (SID) and serial number.

- **Client Identifier**   Allows trace to be set across multiple sessions. Specifies the end user based on the logon ID. Set this using the DBMS_SESSION.SET_IDENTIFIER procedure.

- **Instance**   Specifies a given instance based on the instance name.

- **Service Name**   Specifies a group of related applications. Set using the DBMS_SERVICE.CREATE_SERVICE procedure.

- **Module Name**   Set by developers in their application code using procedure DBMS_APPLICATION_INFO.SET_MODULE. This name is used to represent the module or code being executed.

- **Action Name**   Set by developers in their application code using procedure DBMS_APPLICATION_INFO.SET_ACTION. This name is used to represent the action being performed by the module.

The last three tracing options are associated hierarchically; you can't specify an action name without specifying the module name and the service name, but you can specify only the service name, or only the service name and module name.

Setting Trace Based on Session ID and Serial Number

To set the trace based on session ID and serial number, first determine the SID and serial number of the session you want to trace:

```
Select sid,serial#,username
from   v$session;

SID    SERIAL# USERNAME
---------- ---------- --------------------------------
       156       3588 SCOTT
       142       1054 SYS
```

To enable the trace,

```
SQL> exec dbms_monitor.session_trace_enable(156,3588,TRUE,FALSE);
```

The third parameter is for waits (default is TRUE), and the fourth parameter is for bind variables (default is FALSE).

To turn off the trace,

```
SQL> exec dbms_monitor.session_trace_disable(156,3588);
```

To trace the current session, set the SID and SERIAL# to null:

```
SQL> exec dbms_monitor.session_trace_enable(null,null);
```

Setting Trace Based on Client Identifier

To set the trace based on client identifier as the user, run the following:

```
SQL> exec dbms_session.set_identifier('bryan id');
```

To verify the client identifier,

```
select sid,serial#,username, client_identifier
from   v$session
where  client_identifier is not null;

    SID    SERIAL# USERNAME                            CLIENT_IDENTIFIER
---------- ---------- ------------------------------- ------------------
    156      3588 SCOTT                               bryan id
```

Now we can set the trace for this client identifier:

```
SQL> exec dbms_monitor.client_id_trace_enable('bryan id',true,false);
```

The second parameter is for waits (default is TRUE), and the third parameter is for bind variables (default is FALSE).

To disable this client identifier trace,

```
SQL> exec dbms_monitor.client_id_trace_disable('bryan id');
```

Setting Trace for the Service Name/Module Name/Action Name

In order to use the action name, the module name and the service name must be present. In order to use the module name, the service name must be present. Tracing will be enabled for a given combination of service name, module name, and action name globally for a database unless an instance name is specified for a procedure. The service name is determined by the connect string used to connect to a service.

An Oracle database is represented to clients as a service; that is, the database performs work on behalf of clients. A database can have one or more services associated with it. For example, you could have one database with two different services for web clients: book.us.acme.com for clients making book purchases and soft.us.acme.com for clients making software purchases. In this example, the database name is sales.acme.com, so the service name isn't even based on the database name. The service name is specified by the SERVICE_NAMES parameter in the initialization parameter file. The service name defaults to the global database name, a name comprising the database name (DB_NAME parameter) and the domain name (DB_DOMAIN parameter).

To enable tracing for a service name,

```
SQL> exec dbms_monitor.serv_mod_act_trace_enable(service_name=>'ebk2');
```

This will trace all sessions with a service name of ebk2.

To enable tracing for a combination service, module, and action,

```
SQL> exec dbms_monitor.serv_mod_act_trace_enable(service_name=>'ebk2', -
module_name=>'salary_update', action_name=>'insert_item');
```

To disable tracing in the preceding code, use the procedure
SERV_MOD_ACT_TRACE_DISABLE, as shown here:

```
SQL> exec dbms_monitor.serv_mod_act_trace_disable(service_name=>'ebk2', -
module_name=>'salary_update', action_name=>'insert_item');
```

To trace for entire db or instance (not recommended),

```
execute DBMS_MONITOR.DATABASE_TRACE_ENABLE(waits => TRUE, binds => FALSE, -
instance_name => 'ebk1');
```

TIP
*When using DBMS_MONITOR, be sure to disable tracing when you
are done; otherwise, every session that meets the criteria specified
will be traced.*

Enabled Tracing Views
DBA_ENABLED_TRACES and DBA_ENABLED_AGGREGATIONS are the views to look at to see
what enabled tracing and statistics gathering is in place. You can use these views to make sure all
the tracing options have been disabled.

TRCSESS Multiple Trace Files into One File (10g New Feature)
This Oracle 10g new feature allows trace data to be selectively extracted from multiple trace
files and saved into a single trace file based on criteria such as session ID or module name. This
command-line utility is especially useful in connection pooling and shared server configurations,
where each user request could end up in a separate trace file. TRCSESS lets you obtain consolidated
trace information pertaining to a single user session.

This consolidated trace file can be created according to several criteria:

- session id
- client id
- service name
- action name
- module name

The command syntax is as follows:

```
trcsess [output=] [session=] [clientid=] [service=] [action=] [module=] [trace_file}

output= output destination default being standard output.
```

```
session= session to be traced. (SID and SERIAL#)
clientid= clientid to be traced.
service= service to be traced.
action= action to be traced.
module= module to be traced.

trace_file = list of trace file names, separated by spaces, which need to searched by the
trcsess command. If no files are listed, then all the files in the current directory will
be searched. The wild card character, *, may be used in the file names.
```

Example 1

This is from one of the examples in the earlier section "Using DBMS_MONITOR," where
service_name = ebk2, module= salary_update, and action = insert_item. Go to the user_
dump_dest directory and run the following command:

```
trcsess output=combo.trc service="ebk2" module="salary_update" - action="insert_item"
```

This will search all the trace files which meet the preceding criteria and will create a
consolidated trace file named combo.trc.

Now TKPROF can be run against combo.trc:

```
tkprof combo.trc output=combo_report sort=fchela
```

Example 2

Set the client ID:

```
SQL> exec dbms_session.set_identifier('ebk3');
```

Enable tracing for the client ID:

```
SQL> EXECUTE DBMS_MONITOR.CLIENT_ID_STAT_ENABLE(ebk3);
```

Trace by this client ID, and then issue this command (from the user_dump_dest directory):

```
trcsess output=combo2.trc clientid=ebk3    *.trc
```

Trcsess will check all the trace files for the specified client ID. Now tkprof can be run against
combo2.trc (the combined trace file).

Example 3

In the first case, all the trace file in the current directory as used as input, and a single trace file
(combo3.trc) will be created with all session=17.1988 trace information.

```
trcsess output=combo3.trc session=17.1988
trcsess output=combo4.trc session=17.1988 ebk2_ora_0607.trc ebk2_ora_0125.trc
```

In this case, only the 2 trc files listed are used as input and a single trace file (combo4.trc) will be
created with all session=17.1988 (note that 17.1988 is the <SID>.<Serial#>) trace information
from the two trace files listed.

Using **EXPLAIN PLAN** Alone

The EXPLAIN PLAN command allows developers to view the query execution plan that the Oracle optimizer will use to execute a SQL statement. This command is very helpful in improving performance of SQL statements, because it does not actually execute the SQL statement—it only outlines the plan to use and inserts this execution plan in an Oracle table. Prior to using the EXPLAIN PLAN command, a file called utlxplan.sql (located in the same directory as catalog.sql, which is usually located in the ORACLE_HOME/rdbms/admin directory) must be executed under the Oracle account that will be executing the EXPLAIN PLAN command.

The script creates a table called PLAN_TABLE that the EXPLAIN PLAN command uses to insert the query execution plan in the form of records. This table can then be queried and viewed to determine if the SQL statement needs to be modified to force a different execution plan. Oracle supplies queries to use against the plan table, too: utlxpls.sql and utlxplp.sql. Either will work, but utlxplp.sql is geared toward parallel queries. An EXPLAIN PLAN example is shown next (executed in SQL*Plus):

Q. Why use EXPLAIN without TRACE?

A. The statement is *not* executed; it only shows what will happen if the statement is executed.

Q. When do you use EXPLAIN without TRACE?

A. When the query will take exceptionally long to run.

The procedures for running TRACE vs. EXPLAIN are demonstrated here:

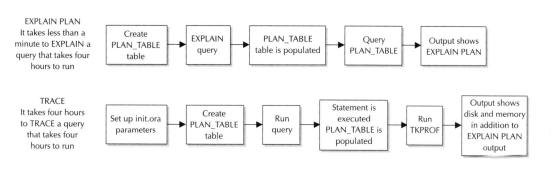

Q. How do I use EXPLAIN by itself?

1. Find the script; it is usually in the ORACLE_HOME/rdbms/admin:

```
"utlxplan.sql"
```

2. Execute the script utlxplan.sql in SQLPLUS:

```
@utlxplan (run this as the user who will be running the EXPLAIN plan)
```

This creates the PLAN_TABLE for the user executing the script. You can create your own PLAN_TABLE, but use Oracle's syntax—or else!

3. Run EXPLAIN PLAN for the query to be optimized:

```
explain plan for
select     CUSTOMER_NUMBER
```

```
from        CUSTOMER
where       CUSTOMER_NUMBER = 111;
Explained.
```

4. Run EXPLAIN PLAN for the query to be optimized (using a tag for the statement):

```
explain plan
set statement_id = 'CUSTOMER' for
select      CUSTOMER_NUMBER
from        CUSTOMER
where       CUSTOMER_NUMBER = 111;
```

TIP
Use the SET STATEMENT_ID = 'your_identifier' when the PLAN_TABLE will be populated by many different developers. I rarely use the SET STATEMENT_ID statement. Instead, I EXPLAIN a query, look at the output, and then delete from the PLAN_TABLE table. I continue to do this (making changes to the query), until I see an execution plan that I think will be favorable. I then run the query to see if the performance has improved. If multiple developers/DBAs are using the same PLAN_TABLE, the SET STATEMENT_ID (case sensitive) will be essential to identifying a statement.

5. Select the output from the PLAN_TABLE:

```
select      operation, options, object_name, id, parent_id
from        plan_table
where       statement_id = 'CUSTOMER';
```

Operation	Options	Object_Name	ID	Parent
select statement			0	
Table Access	By ROWID	Customer	1	
Index	Range Scan	CUST_IDX	2	1

TIP
Use EXPLAIN instead of TRACE so that you don't have to wait for the query to run. EXPLAIN shows the path of a query without actually running the query. Use TRACE only for multiquery batch jobs to find out which of the many queries in the batch job are slow.

TIP
You can use the utlxpls.sql and utlxplp.sql queries provided by Oracle to query the plan table without having to write your own query and without having to format the output.

An Additional EXPLAIN Example for a Simple Query

This section shows a simple process of running a query and then checking the explain plan for the information about how the query will be processed.

1. Run the query with the EXPLAIN syntax embedded prior to the query:

```
explain plan
set statement_id = 'query 1' for
select    customer_number, name
from      customer
where     customer_number = '111';
```

2. Retrieve the output of EXPLAIN by querying the PLAN_TABLE.

To retrieve the information for viewing, a SQL statement must be executed. Two scripts provided in the Oracle documentation are displayed in Steps 2 and 3, along with the results of each based on the previous EXPLAIN PLAN command. Note that this example varies from the last example. The customer_number column is an indexed number field, which in the second example is suppressed because of a data type mismatch (111 is in quotes forcing a to_char operation). In the first example, I treated the customer_number column correctly as a number field (111 is not in quotes). At times the optimizer is smart enough *not* to do this to you, but when you use Pro*C or other similar coding, the optimizer may not be able to translate this for you.

```
select    operation, options, object_name, id, parent_id
from      plan_table
where     statement_id = 'query 1'
order by  id;
Operation              Options      Object_Name          ID      Parent_ID
select Statement                                          0
Table Access           Full    Customer_Information       1            0
```

3. Retrieve a more intuitive and easy-to-read output of EXPLAIN:

```
select    lpad(' ', 2*(level-1)) || operation || ' ' || options || ' ' ||
          object_name || ' ' || decode(id, 0, 'Cost = ' || position)
"Query Plan"
from      plan_table
start     with id = 0
and       statement_id = 'query 1'
connect by prior id   parent_id
and       statement_id = 'query 1';
```

The output is shown here:

```
Query Plan
select statement     Cost=220
    Table Access Full Customer
```

EXPLAIN PLAN—Read It Top to Bottom or Bottom to Top?

Whether you should read from top to bottom or bottom to top depends on how you write the query that retrieves the information from the PLAN_TABLE table. That is probably why many people disagree about which way to read the result. (All methods may be correct.) The following listing shows the order of execution based on the query that retrieves the information. In this example, the output is read top to bottom with one caveat: you must read it from the innermost to the outermost. This listing shows a method that should clear up any questions.

The SQL statement should be placed after the FOR clause of the EXPLAIN PLAN statement.

```
delete     from plan_table;
explain plan
set        statement_id = 'SQL1' for
select     to_char(sysdate, 'MM/DD/YY HH:MI AM'), to_char((trunc((sysdate -4 -1),
           'day') +1), 'DD-MON-YY')
from       bk, ee
where      bk_shift_date >= to_char((trunc(( sysdate - 4 - 1), 'day') + 1), 'DD-
           MON-YY')
and        bk_shift_date <= to_char((sysdate - 4), 'DD-MON-YY')
and        bk_empno = ee_empno(+)
and        substr(ee_hierarchy_code, 1, 3) in ('PNA', 'PNB', 'PNC', 'PND', 'PNE',
           'PNF')
order by   ee_job_group, bk_empno, bk_shift_date
/
select     LPad(' ', 2*(Level-1)) || Level || '.' || Nvl(Position,0)|| ' ' ||
           Operation || ' ' || Options || ' ' || Object_Name || ' ' || Object_Type
           || ' ' || Decode(id, 0, Statement_Id ||' Cost = ' || Position) || cost
           || ' ' || Object_Node "Query Plan"
from       plan_table
start      with id = 0 And statement_id = 'SQL1'
connect by prior id = parent_id
and        statement_id = 'SQL1'
/
 Query Plan
1.0 SELECT STATEMENT    SQL1  Cost =
    2.1 SORT ORDER BY (7th)
        3.1 FILTER (6th)
            4.1 NESTED LOOPS OUTER (5th)
                5.1 TABLE ACCESS BY ROWID BK (2nd)
                    6.1 INDEX RANGE SCAN I_BK_06 NON-UNIQUE (1st)
                5.2 TABLE ACCESS BY ROWID EE (4th)
                    6.2 INDEX UNIQUE SCAN I_EE_01 UNIQUE (3rd)
```

Reading the EXPLAIN PLAN

Using the previous EXPLAIN PLAN, I will elucidate the steps. The numbers in the left column in Table 6-4 identify each step. They are listed in the order in which they are executed.

TIP
Whether the EXPLAIN PLAN is read from top to bottom or from bottom to top depends entirely on the query used to select information from the PLAN_TABLE. Both methods of reading the query may be correct, given that the query selecting the information is correctly structured.

Step	Action
6.1	This is the index range scan of I_BK_06. This is the first step. This index is on the BK_SHIFT_DATE column. This step performs a scan of this index to produce a list of ROWIDs that fall between the two dates.
5.1	This retrieves the rows from the BK table.
6.2	This scans the I_EE_01 index. This index is on the EE_EMPNO column. Using the BK_EMPNO retrieved from the previous step, this index is scanned to retrieve the ROWIDs to produce a list of the EE_EMPNOs that match the BK_EMPNOs.
5.2	This retrieves the rows from the EE table.
4.1	This is a nested loop. The two lists are joined, producing one list.
3.1	This is a filter. The rest of the conditions of the WHERE clause are applied.
2.1	This is SORT_ORDER_BY. The remaining rows are sorted according to the ORDER BY clause.
1.0	This tells which type of statement it is.

TABLE 6-4. *Reading the EXPLAIN PLAN*

Setting AUTOTRACE On

There is also an easier method for generating an EXPLAIN PLAN and statistics about the performance of a query with SQL*Plus. The main difference between AUTOTRACE and EXPLAIN PLAN is that AUTOTRACE actually executes the query (in the way TRACE does) and automatically queries the plan table, whereas EXPLAIN PLAN does neither. The AUTOTRACE command generates similar information, as shown in the next listing. To use AUTOTRACE, the user must possess the PLUSTRACE role (by running plustrce.sql, which is usually located in the ORACLE_HOME/sqlplus/admin directory).

```
SET AUTOTRACE ON
select     count(last_name)
from       emp
where      name = 'branches';
```

The output is as follows:

```
COUNT(LAST_NAME)
----------------
               0


Execution Plan
----------------------------------------------------------
Plan hash value: 141239332
----------------------------------------------------------------
```

```
| Id  | Operation          | Name        | Rows | Bytes | Cost (%CPU)| Time|
-------------------------------------------------------------------------------
|   0 | SELECT STATEMENT   |             |    1 |     8 |    1  (0)| 00:00:01|
|   1 |  SORT AGGREGATE    |             |    1 |     8 |          ||
|*  2 |   INDEX RANGE SCAN | EMP_NAME_IX |    1 |     8 |    1  (0)| 00:00:01|
-------------------------------------------------------------------------------

Predicate Information (identified by operation id):
---------------------------------------------------
   2 - access("LAST_NAME"='BRANCHES')


Statistics
----------------------------------------------------------
         0  recursive calls
         0  db block gets
         0  consistent gets
         0  physical reads
         0  redo size
         0  bytes sent via SQL*Net to client
         0  bytes received via SQL*Net from client
         0  SQL*Net roundtrips to/from client
         0  sorts (memory)
         0  sorts (disk)
         1  rows processed
```

The AUTOTRACE option provides an EXPLAIN PLAN and statistics for a query. The AUTOTRACE provides many of the TRACE and TKPROF statistics such as disk reads (physical reads) and total reads (consistent reads + db block gets).

TIP
If the error "Unable to verify plan table format or existence" occurs when enabling AUTOTRACE, you must create a plan table using the script utlxplan.sql.

CAUTION
AUTOTRACE may fail when querying system views because the user may not have permission to view underlying objects.

Table 6-5 shows other AUTOTRACE options.

Option	Function
SET AUTOT ON	Short way of turning on AUTOTRACE
SET AUTOT ON EXP	Shows only the explain plan
SET AUTOTRACE ON STAT	Shows only the statistics
SET AUTOT TRACE	Does not show the output of the query

TABLE 6-5. *AUTOTRACE Options*

EXPLAIN PLAN When Using Partitions

Table partitions yield different outputs for their EXPLAIN PLANs (as shown in the following listing). Here, we create a table with three partitions and a partitioned index. Broadly speaking, partitions are tables stored in multiple places in the database. For more information on partitioning tables, refer to Chapter 3.

```
create table dept1
      (deptno      number(2),
      dept_name        varchar2(30))
      partition by range(deptno)
      (partition d1 values       less than (10),
      partition d2 values        less than (20),
      partition d3 values        less than (maxvalue));

insert into dept1 values (1, 'DEPT 1');
insert into dept1 values (7, 'DEPT 7');
insert into dept1 values (10, 'DEPT 10');
insert into dept1 values (15, 'DEPT 15');
insert into dept1 values (22, 'DEPT 22');

create index dept_index
      on dept1 (deptno)
      local
      (partition  d1,
      partition  d2 ,
      partition  d3 );
```

We now generate an EXPLAIN PLAN that forces a full table scan to access the first two partitions.

```
explain plan for
select      dept_name
from        dept1
where       deptno  || '' = 1
or          deptno  || '' = 15;
```

When selecting from the plan table, you must select the additional columns partition_start (starting partition) and partition_stop (ending partition). For a full table scan, all partitions will be accessed:

```
select      operation, options, id, object_name, partition_start,
            partition_stop
from        plan_table;
```

The output (for the full table scan) is shown here:

OPERATION	OPTIONS	ID	OBJECT_NAME	PARTITION_START	PARTITION_STOP
SELECT STATEMENT					
PARTITION	CONCATENATED	1		1	3
TABLE ACCESS	FULL	2	DEPT1	1	3

The preceding example shows that a full table scan on the DEPT1 table is performed. All three partitions are scanned. The starting partition is 1 and the ending partition is 3.

Steps to Read the
EXPLAIN PLAN

Next, an EXPLAIN PLAN is generated in the following listing for an index range scan of partition 2 only (ensure that you delete from the plan table to clear it).

```
explain plan for select dept_name
from       dept1
where      deptno   = 15;

Explained.
```

We now generate an EXPLAIN PLAN for an index range scan accessing only the second partition:

```
select     operation, options, id, object_name, partition_start,
           partition_stop
from       plan_table;
```

The output (for the index range scan) is shown here.

OPERATION	OPTIONS	ID	OBJECT_NAME	PARTITION_START	PARTITION_STOP
SELECT STATEMENT					
TABLE ACCESS	BY LOCAL INDEX ROWID	1	DEPT1	2	2
TABLE ACCESS	RANGE SCAN	2	DEPTIDX	2	2

This output shows that the only partition of the table OR index that is accessed is the second partition. This is because the value for deptno = 15 is within the second partition of the DEPT1 table. The DEPTNO column is also indexed, and this value is also within the second partition of the index.

TIP
Partitions can also be viewed by the EXPLAIN PLAN by accessing the columns PARTITION_STOP and PARTITION_STOP in the PLAN_TABLE table.

Finding High Disk and/or Memory Reads Without Using TRACE

Is there another method for retrieving problem disk and memory read information without tracing everything? Yes! By using V$sqlarea, you can find the problem queries on your system. This next listing shows how to find the problem queries. In this query, we are searching for queries where the disk reads are greater than 10,000 (missing or suppressed index potentials). If your system is much larger, you may need to set this number higher.

```
select     disk_reads, sql_text
from       v$sqlarea
where      disk_reads > 10000
order by   disk_reads desc;
```

DISK_READS	SQL_TEXT	
12987	select	order#,columns,types from orders
	where	substr(orderid,1,2)=:1
11131	select	custid, city from customer
	where	city = 'CHICAGO'

This output suggests that there are two problem queries causing heavy disk reads. The first has the index on ORDERID suppressed by the SUBSTR function; the second shows that there is a missing index on CITY.

In the query in the following listing, we are searching for queries where the memory reads are greater than 200,000 (overindexed query potentials). If your system is much larger, you may need to set this number higher.

```
select     buffer_gets, sql_text
from       v$sqlarea
where      buffer_gets > 200000
order by   buffer_gets desc;


BUFFER_GETS     SQL_TEXT
    300219      select order#,cust_no, from orders
                where division = '1'
```

The output suggests that one problem query is causing substantially heavy memory reads (300,219 blocks of data read into memory). The index on DIVISION appears to have a cardinality of 1, since there was only a single division in this table. What's happening here is that the entire index is being read and then the entire table is being read. The index should be suppressed for this statement to improve the performance (and perhaps should be removed permanently if additional divisions will not be added).

TIP
Accessing the V$SQLAREA table can give statistics that are often found when tracing a query. See Chapter 12 for additional information on accessing the V$sqlarea table.

Using DBMS_XPLAN

With Oracle 9*i* and later, Oracle gave us an easier way yet to look at the Explain Plan. You can now use DBMS_XPLAN to query the execution plan. Some notes on using this package.

- It automatically queries the last plan in PLAN_TABLE.

- It uses a TABLE() function with another pipelined function.

- A text truncation operation might be a problem.

- It will give additional information after the plan, such as the following:

  - Highlights filter vs. join conditions, if the plan table is current

  - Displays a warning message when the old version of the plan table is being used

The following is an example of DBMS_XPLAN:

```
Select *
from   table (dbms_xplan.display);
```

```
PLAN_TABLE_OUTPUT
-------------------------------------------------------------------------------
-------------------------------------------------------------------------------
| Id | Operation            | Name         | Rows | Bytes | Cost | Pstart| Pstop |
-------------------------------------------------------------------------------
|  0 | UPDATE STATEMENT     |              |  328 |  2296 |   2  |       |       |
|  1 |  UPDATE              | JOURNAL_LINE |      |       |      |       |       |
|  2 |   PARTITION RANGE ALL|              |      |       |      |   1   |   4   |
|  3 |    TABLE ACCESS FULL | JOURNAL_LINE |  328 |  2296 |   2  |   1   |   4   |
-------------------------------------------------------------------------------

11 rows selected
```

Yet Another EXPLAIN PLAN Output Method: Building the Tree Structure

Although many people find the earlier EXPLAIN PLAN methods sufficient, others require a more theoretical approach that ties to the parent/child relationships of a query and the corresponding tree structure. For some people, this makes using EXPLAIN easier to visualize, and it is included here for that audience.

1. The following is the query to be explained:

```
explain plan
set statement_id = 'SQL2' for
select    cust_no ,cust_address ,cust_last_name, cust_first_name ,cust_mid_init
from      customer
where     cust_phone = '3035551234';
```

2. Here is the query used for this approach:

```
select    LPAD(' ',2*(LEVEL-1))||operation "OPERATION", options "OPTIONS",
          DECODE(TO_CHAR(id),'0','COST = ' || NVL(TO_CHAR(position),'n/a'),
          object_name) "OBJECT NAME", id ||'-'|| NVL(parent_id, 0)||'-'||
          NVL(position, 0) "ORDER", SUBSTR(optimizer,1,6) "OPT"
from   plan_table
start      with id = 0
and    statement_id = 'SQL2'
connect by prior id = parent_id
and        statement_id = 'SQL2';
```

3. Here is the output for this approach:

```
OPERATION            OPTIONS          OBJECT NAME    ORDER      OPT
--------------       --------         -----------    --------   ----------
SELECT STATEMENT                      COST = 2       0-0-1      ALL_RO
  TABLE ACCESS       BY INDEX ROWID   CUSTOMER       1-0-1
    INDEX            RANGE SCAN       IX_CUST_PHONE  2-1-1      ANALYZ
```

Note that two new columns are introduced:

■ **ORDER** This column contains the ID, the parent ID, and the position of the step in the execution plan. The ID identifies the step but does not imply the order of execution. The parent ID identifies the parent step of the step. The position indicates the order in which children steps are executed that have the same parent ID.

■ **OPT**   This column contains the current mode of the optimizer.

4. The execution tree is constructed.
   Based on the execution plan in the illustration, an execution tree can be constructed to get a better feel for how Oracle is going to process the statement. To construct the tree, simply start with Step 1, find all other steps whose parent step is 1, and draw them in. Repeat this procedure until all the steps are accounted for. The execution tree for the execution plan for the query in this example is displayed here.

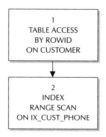

5. The execution plan is interpreted.

To understand how Oracle is going to process a statement, you must understand in what sequence Oracle is going to process the steps and what Oracle is doing in each step.

The sequence is determined by the parent/child relationship of the steps. Basically, the child step is always performed first, at least once, and feeds the parent steps from there. When a parent has multiple children, child steps are performed in the order of the step position, which is the third number displayed in the ORDER column of the execution plan. When the execution tree is constructed, if the lower-position children for a parent are arranged left to right, the execution tree reads left to right, bottom to top.

Another Example Using the Tree Approach

This section shows the simple process of using the tree approach and then viewing the information about how the query will be processed.

1. The following is the query to be explained:

```
select      a.cust_last_name, a.cust_first_name, a.cust_mid_init, b.order_desc,
            b.order_create_dt
from        order_hdr b, customer a
where       cust_phone = :host1
and         b.cust_no = a.cust_no
and         b.order_status = 'OPEN';
```

2. Here is the execution plan:

OPERATION	OPTIONS	OBJECT NAME	ORDER	OPT
SELECT STATEMENT		COST = n/a	0-0-0	ALL_RO
NESTED LOOPS			1-0-1	
TABLE ACCESS	BY ROWID	ORDER_HDR	2-1-1	

```
    INDEX            RANGE SCAN   IX_ORDER_STATUS 3-2-1
TABLE ACCESS         BY ROWID     CUSTOMER        4-1-2
    INDEX            UNIQUE SCAN  PK_CUSTOMER     5-4-1
```

3. The following illustration shows the multi-table execution tree.

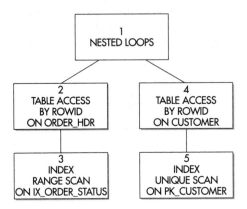

4. The execution plan sequence is determined for the query.
   This statement has five steps. Child Step 3 is executed first. Because it is a range scan, it returns 0, 1, or many ROWIDs to Step 2. For each ROWID returned, Step 2 accesses the order table by ROWID, gets the requested data, and returns the data to Step 1. For each row of data received from Step 2, Step 1 sends the CUST_NO to Step 5. Step 5 uses the customer number to perform a unique scan to get the ROWID. The ROWID is then returned from Step 5 to Step 4. If no ROWID is found, Step 4 tells Step 1 to eliminate that particular row. If a ROWID is found, Step 4 accesses the table by ROWID and retrieves the data. Once it gets the data, if the phone number is correct, it returns the data to Step 1, where it is merged with the result from Steps 2 and 3 for that row and returned to the user. If the phone number is incorrect, Step 4 returns no row and Step 1 throws out the row.

5. The performance is reviewed.
   Is this a good table access order? In most order-entry systems where there are lots of customers and many open orders at a given time, why would you want to spin through all open orders first, get the data for each one, go to the CUSTOMER table for each of those, and then throw out all but the one open order for the customer with the right phone number? To correct this situation, we want to first go to the customer table based on phone number because most of the rows will be filtered out in the first step, thus improving performance. How do we do this? Consider the changes made next.

6. Performance changes occur (the driving table is changed):

```
select     /*+ ORDERED */ a.cust_last_name, a.cust_first_name,
           a.cust_mid_init, b.order_desc, b.order_create_dt
from       customer a, order_hdr b
where      cust_phone = :host1
and        b.cust_no = a.cust_no
and        b.order_status = 'OPEN';
```

7. The *new* execution plan is determined:

OPERATION	OPTIONS	OBJECT NAME	ORDER	OPT
SELECT STATEMENT		COST = n/a	0-0-0	ALL_RO
NESTED LOOPS			1-0-1	
TABLE ACCESS	BY ROWID	CUSTOMER	2-1-1	
INDEX	RANGE SCAN	IX_CUST_PHONE	3-2-1	
TABLE ACCESS	BY ROWID	ORDER_HDR	4-1-2	
AND-EQUAL			5-4-1	
INDEX	RANGE SCAN	IX_ORDER_CUST	6-5-1	
INDEX	RANGE SCAN	IX_ORDER_STATUS	7-5-2	

8. The performance of the semi-tuned query is reviewed.
   Why did the table order change? Because we forced the table driving order with the ORDERED hint. Usually, the cost-based optimization will figure the best driving order based on table and index statistics. If not, the ORDERED hint can be used to force a driving order.
   Is this a good table access order? The table order is good because the CUSTOMER half of the query is executed first and will probably return only one row to the ORDER half of the query. Is the AND-EQUAL optimal? In this case, no. Why churn through 1000 ROWIDs in the ORDER_STATUS index and all the ROWIDs in the CUST_NO index and keep only the ones that match? What we should do is either pick the most selective index of the two and use it, or create a composite index on CUST_NO and ORDER status. Changing the driving table was the right thing to do. Now, we must stop Oracle from using the order status index to completely tune the query.

9. The *tuned* query is shown next (the index on ORDER_STATUS is suppressed):

```
select      /*+ ORDERED */ a.cust_last_name, a.cust_first_name,
            a.cust_mid_init, b.order_desc, b.order_create_dt
from        customer a, order_hdr b
where       cust_phone = :host1
and         b.cust_no = a.cust_no
and         b.order_status || '' = 'OPEN';
```

10. The *tuned* execution plan is shown next.

OPERATION	OPTIONS	OBJECT NAME	ORDER	OPT
SELECT STATEMENT		COST = n/a	0-0-0	RULE
NESTED LOOPS			1-0-1	
TABLE ACCESS	BY ROWID	CUSTOMER	2-1-1	
INDEX	UNIQUE SCAN	PK_CUSTOMER	3-2-1	
TABLE ACCESS	BY ROWID	ORDER_HDR	4-1-2	
INDEX	RANGE SCAN	IX_ORDER_STATUS	5-4-1	

To determine how Oracle is going to process a SQL statement, you must generate and interpret an execution plan for the statement. With access to the tools that can generate execution plans for SQL, along with a rudimentary understanding of the information that is an execution plan and the knowledge of how to construct an execution tree, a developer or DBA can begin exploring the vast variety of EXPLAIN PLANs that the diverse SQL code produces and learn fairly quickly how to tune and develop quality SQL.

Using the Tree Approach

Tracing/Explaining Problem Queries in Developer Products

Although you can issue the ALTER SESSION SET SQL_TRACE TRUE command on the SQL*Plus command line to TRACE SQL statements, this is tough when it comes to using developer products. One drawback to this option is that you are not able to trace a form or report; you need to cut the code out of the form or report and run it from SQL*Plus. This process can be very time-consuming if you do not know which statements you need to trace.

There is another way to produce a trace of the execution of a form. If you are using an earlier version of Oracle Forms, such as Forms 3.0, you can include -s on the command line; when using Forms (versions 4–6), you can include statistics = yes on the command line. This way, you are able to trace individual forms. Later versions of Oracle Forms and Oracle Reports allow tracing from inside a form or report. Please refer to the Forms and/or Reports documentation for an explanation of how to use these options. Oracle Applications often has a menu item to do this as well. You could also use DBMS_MONITOR to trace these products as well.

TIP
You can also use TRACE within the Developer products. You simply need to set statistics = yes on the command line for some products, or you may embed the tracing within an actual trigger to turn tracing on and off.

Important Columns in the PLAN_TABLE Table

The descriptions for *some* of the more important columns available in the PLAN_TABLE table are as follows:

- **STATEMENT_ID**   The value of the option STATEMENT_ID parameter specified in the EXPLAIN PLAN statement.

- **TIMESTAMP**   The date and time when the EXPLAIN PLAN statement was issued.

- **REMARKS**   Any comment (of up to 80 bytes) you wish to associate with each step of the EXPLAIN PLAN. If you need to add or change a remark on any row of the PLAN_TABLE table, use the UPDATE statement to modify the rows of the PLAN_TABLE table.

- **OPERATION**   The name of the internal operation performed in this step. In the first row generated for a statement, the column contains one of four values: DELETE, INSERT, SELECT, or UPDATE, depending on the type of the statement.

- **OPTIONS**   A variation on the operation described in the OPERATION column. See Appendix A of *Oracle Server Tuning* for information on the contents of this column.

TIP
The OPERATION and OPTIONS columns of the PLAN_TABLE are the most important columns for tuning a query. The OPERATION column shows the actual operation performed (including type of join), and the OPTIONS column tells you when there is a full table scan being performed (that may need an index).

■   **OBJECT_NODE**   The name of the database link used to reference the object (a table name or view name). For local queries using the parallel query option, this column describes the order in which output from operations is consumed.

■   **OBJECT_OWNER**   The name of the user who owns the schema containing the table or index.

■   **OBJECT_NAME**   The name of the table or index.

■   **OBJECT_INSTANCE**   A number corresponding to the ordinal position of the object as it appears in the original statement. The numbering proceeds from left to right, outer to inner, with respect to the original statement text. Note that view expansion results in unpredictable numbers.

■   **OBJECT_TYPE**   A modifier that provides descriptive information about the object, for example, NON-UNIQUE for indexes.

■   **OPTIMIZER**   The current mode of the optimizer.

■   **ID**   A number assigned to each step in the execution plan.

TIP
The ID column shows the order in which a statement is processed. One of the basic rules of tuning a SQL statement is to change the query such that the ID of the order in which steps in the query execute is changed. Changing the order in which steps execute in a query will usually change the performance of a query either positively or negatively. Using HINTS (see Chapter 7) will force a query to execute in a different statement order and will usually make a query faster or slower.

■   **PARENT_ID**   The ID of the next execution step that operates on the output of the ID step.

TIP
The PARENT_ID column is very important because it shows the dependencies of two steps in an EXPLAIN PLAN. If a section of the EXPLAIN PLAN has a PARENT_ID, it implies that this statement must run prior to the PARENT_ID that is specified.

■   **POSITION**   The order of processing for steps that all have the same PARENT_ID.

■   **OTHER**   Other information that is specific to the execution step that a user may find useful.

■   **OTHER_TAG**   The contents of the OTHER column.

■   **COST**   The cost of the operation as *estimated* by the optimizer's cost-based approach. The value of this column does not have any particular unit of measurement; it is merely a weight value used to compare costs of execution plans.

■   **CARDINALITY**   The cost-based approach's *estimate* of the number of rows accessed by the operation.

■   **BYTES**   The cost-based approach's *estimate* of the number of bytes accessed by the operation.

Important Columns in the PLAN_TABLE Table

TIP
The BYTES column is extremely important when evaluating how to tune a query. When an index is used and the number of bytes is great, it implies that doing a full table scan would perhaps be more efficient (i.e., reading the index and data is more costly than just reading the data in a full table scan). Also, the number of bytes helps us to determine which table should be accessed first in the query (driving table), because one table may limit the number of bytes needed from another. See Chapter 9 for tips on choosing the driving table.

TIP
Remember that both the COST and BYTES values in a query are estimates; it is quite possible for a version of a query with a higher estimated cost or bytes to run faster than another with a lower value.

Helpful Oracle-Supplied Packages

You can also TRACE the sessions of other users by using their session information within the DBMS_SYSTEM package. First, you must get the user's information from the V$session. You then pass that information to the procedure to begin tracing, as shown in the following listing:

```
select    sid, serial#
from      v$session
where     username = 'SCOTT';
```

The output is shown here:

```
SID       SERIAL#
  9           190

1 row selected.
```

Begin tracing the username by using the following package (the SID and SERIAL# for the user's session must be entered):

```
execute dbms_system.set_sql_trace_in_session(9,190,TRUE);
PL/SQL procedure successfully completed.
```

You can also initiate a TRACE for the session that you are in using the DBMS_SESSION package. This package is particularly helpful for tracing queries within stored procedures, as well as for use within PL/SQL code.

```
execute DBMS_SESSION.SET_SQL_TRACE (TRUE);
PL/SQL procedure successfully completed.
```

Initialization Parameters for Undocumented TRACE

One area that the experts can investigate is the X$KSPPI table. A brief listing for undocumented TRACE parameters (there are nine more in 10g than there were in 9i) in init.ora is shown here (see

Appendix A for additional information). Note that Oracle does not support the use of undocumented features of the product.

```
select ksppinm "Parameter Name", ksppstvl "Value",ksppstdf "Default"
from   x$ksppi x, x$ksppcv y
where  x.indx = y.indx
and    ksppinm like '/_%trace%' escape '/';
```

Parameter Name	Value	Default
_trace_files_public	FALSE	TRUE
_ksi_trace		TRUE
_trace_processes	ALL	TRUE
_trace_archive	FALSE	TRUE
_trace_events		TRUE
_trace_buffers	ALL:256	TRUE
_trace_flush_processes	ALL	TRUE
_trace_file_size	65536	TRUE
_trace_options	text,multiple	TRUE
_dump_trace_scope	global	TRUE
_trace_navigation_scope	global	TRUE
_dlmtrace		TRUE
_ges_trace	TRUE	TRUE
_db_block_trace_protect	FALSE	TRUE
_trace_buffer_flushes	FALSE	TRUE
_trace_multi_block_reads	FALSE	TRUE
_trace_cr_buffer_creates	FALSE	TRUE
_trace_buffer_gets	FALSE	TRUE
_trace_pin_time	0	TRUE
_trace_buffer_wait_timeouts	0	TRUE
_db_mttr_sim_trace_size	256	TRUE
_db_mttr_trace_to_alert	FALSE	TRUE
_kkfi_trace	FALSE	TRUE
_px_trace	0	TRUE
xt_trace	none	TRUE
_ku_trace	none	TRUE
_smm_trace	0	TRUE
_px_compilation_trace	0	TRUE
_stn_trace	0	TRUE
_olap_continuous_trace_file	FALSE	TRUE
_optimizer_trace	none	TRUE
_xpl_trace	0	TRUE
_kql_subheap_trace	0	TRUE
_rowsrc_trace_level	0	TRUE
_xsolapi_source_trace	FALSE	TRUE

```
35 rows selected
```

Initialization Parameters for Undocumented TRACE

TIP

The X$ksppi table can be accessed only by the SYS user. See Chapter 13 for tips on accessing the X$ tables and using some of these parameters. Do not use any undocumented parameters without consulting Oracle Corporation. Also, the layout and column names of these views have been known to change between Oracle releases.

Tracing Errors Within Oracle for More Information

This section explains the use of one of the undocumented features of TRACE. Before using undocumented init.ora parameters, please contact Oracle Corporation. To TRACE errors for a session, you can alter and monitor the session (shown next) or set an event in the init.ora file (see Chapter 13 for more information). Sessions can be traced for errors by running the query shown next (used to TRACE a 4031 error). These queries build a TRACE file in your user_dump_dest that will contain a dump of the full error text.

Use the following command:

```
alter session set events='4031 trace name errorstack level 4';
```

TIP

Tracing queries can help performance, but using the TRACE facility built within the undocumented TRACE init.ora parameters (discussed previously) can give great insight into solving errors within Oracle.

Tracing by Enabling Events

Trace sessions can also be initiated by using this command:

```
SQL> Alter session set events '10046 trace name context forever, level 1';
Session altered.
```

The value of the level (1 in the previous command) can be 1 (regular trace), 4 (trace bind variables), 8 (trace wait states), or 12 (regular trace, plus bind variables and wait states). Information about bind variables and wait states can then appear in the trace file but will be ignored by TKPROF when formatting the report. Output in the trace file for the previous command could look like that shown here:

```
SELECT SYSDATE   FROM DUAL  WHERE SYSDATE IN ( :b1  )
END OF STMT
PARSE #4:c=0,e=0,p=0,cr=0,cu=0,mis=0,r=0,dep=1,og=4,tim=0
BINDS #4:
 bind 0: dty=12 mxl=07(07) mal=00 scl=00 pre=00 oacflg=03 oacfl2=1 size=8 offset=0
   bfp=0ddcc774 bln=07 avl=07 flg=05
   value="11/19/2000 19:25:47"
WAIT #1: nam='SQL*Net message to client' ela= 0 p1=1413697536 p2=1 p3=0
```

To turn event tracing off, use the following command:

```
SQL> Alter session set events '10046 trace name context off';
Session altered.
```

Using Stored Outlines

Up until recently, the chief use for execution plans was to determine what Oracle was doing with queries at run time as a tuning tool. A fairly new facility called *STORED OUTLINES* allows a query to use a predetermined execution plan every time that query is run, no matter where the query is run from. People sometimes speak of the STORED OUTLINES as storing an execution plan, but this is not really what happens. Instead, Oracle stores a series of *hints*—instructions to the database to execute a query in a precise way—to duplicate the execution plan as saved during a recording session.

Oracle can replicate execution plans for queries using stored outlines through a process similar to using the EXPLAIN PLAN functionality in SQL*PLUS. First, you set up the STORED OUTLINE session by telling Oracle to save outlines for queries you are about to run using the ALTER SESSION command. Next, you execute the query for which you want the outline stored. (This is usually done on a session-only basis so as not to affect other users.) Finally, if the execution plan is acceptable, it can be saved to the database and used by everyone everywhere. The following sections describe each of these steps in greater detail.

TIP
Oracle Corporation likes to refer to STORED OUTLINES as PLAN STABILITY. For further information on using STORED OUTLINES, see the Oracle documentation on PLAN STABILITY.

Setting Up STORED OUTLINES

Unfortunately, as with most of the spectacular new features that Oracle provides, the setup process for using STORED OUTLINES is complex. Many user *and* session privileges must set up properly before outlines can be stored, or stored ones can be used.

The following privileges are required to use STORED OUTLINES:

- CREATE ANY OUTLINE
- EXECUTE_CATALOG (to use the DBMS OUTLN package)
- PLUSTRACE (to use AUTOTRACE, if applicable)

Beyond permissions, STORED OUTLINES further require the use of several specific session parameters (environment settings):

- QUERY_REWRITE _ENABLED = TRUE
- STAR_TRANSFORMATION_ENABLED = TRUE
- OPTIMIZER_FEATURES_ENABLE = 10.1.0 (for example)
- USE_STORED_OUTLINES = TRUE (to use existing STORED OUTLINES)
- CREATE_STORED_OUTLINES = TRUE (to create or edit STORED OUTLINES)
- USE_PRIVATE_OUTLINES = TRUE (to use private outlines, current session only)

How OUTLINES Are Stored

As with most other features, Oracle stores OUTLINES in internal database tables whose contents are available though the usual distribution of system views (USER_*, ALL_*, and DBA_*). Of course, only the DBA privileged few can see the DBA views, while the ALL_* views display information about objects the user can see (but may not own), and the USER_* views show information about those objects the current user actually owns. For brevity, we will consider the USER_* views. The views chiefly used by STORED OUTLINES are

- USER_OUTLINES
- USER_OUTLINE_HINTS

The contents of USER_OUTLINES look something like the following:

```
NAME                              CATEGORY                          USED
--------------------------------- --------------------------------- ---------
TIMESTAMP VERSION
--------- ---------------------------------------------------------------------
SQL_TEXT
---------------------------------------------------------------------------
SIGNATURE
-------------------------------
SYS_OUTLINE_020213193254787    DEFAULT                           UNUSED
13-FEB-02 9.0.1.2.0
select id
from s_emp
where id = 1

NAME                              CATEGORY                          USED   TIMESTAMP
--------------------------------- --------------------------------- ------ ---------
VERSION
------------------------------------------------------------------
SQL_TEXT
--------------------------------------------------------------------------
SIGNATURE                         COMPATIBLE   ENABLED   FORMAT
--------------------------------- ------------ --------- ------
KGB_OUTLINE                       DEFAULT                           UNUSED 02-JAN-06
10.2.0.1
select * from emp
E64F36A7F73BECFE2C61CBAA5781982F COMPATIBLE   ENABLED   NORMAL
```

A small listing from the USER_OUTLINE_HINTS table (multiple rows would probably be displayed) looks like this:

```
NAME                              NODE       STAGE    JOIN_POS
--------------------------------- ---------- ---------- ----------
HINT
--------------------------------- ---------- ---------- ----------
SYS_OUTLINE_020213193254787          1          3          0
NO_EXPAND
SYS_OUTLINE_020213193254787          1          3          0
```

```
ORDERED
SYS_OUTLINE_020213193254787           1          3          0
NO_FACT(S_EMP)


NAME                                  NODE       STAGE      JOIN_POS
--------------------------------      ---------- ---------- ----------
HINT
---------------------------------------------------------------------------
KGB_OUTLINE                           1          1          0
NO_EXPAND(@"SEL$1" )

KGB_OUTLINE                           1          1          0
LEADING(@"SEL$1"   "EMP"@"SEL$1")

KGB_OUTLINE                           1          1          0
NO_STAR_TRANSFORMATION(@"SEL$1" )
```

You should create the outline tables in your own schema (which is a good idea); if you don't, the outlines will be stored in the SYSTEM tablespace (which is almost always a mistake). The outline tables can be created in the current schema by running the DBMS_OUTLN_EDIT.CREATE_EDIT_TABLES procedure with the following command:

```
exec dbms_outln_edit.create_edit_tables
```

Creating and Using Stored Outlines

There are two kinds of stored outlines: *private,* which are session-specific, and *public,* which can affect the entire database. Which kind is being used is controlled by the USE_PRIVATE_OUTLINES session parameter setting. If this setting is TRUE, then private outlines are used. Generally, it's best to use private outlines until an optimal execution plan is generated. Private outlines can be saved publicly using the CREATE OR REPLACE PRIVATE OUTLINE command; public outlines can be created from private ones using the CREATE OR REPLACE OUTLINE. . .FROM PRIVATE. . .command. This process is called *editing* and is used to copy an existing private outline to a public one. When the stored outlines are in place, Oracle uses them automatically and this process is invisible to the user executing the command.

TIP
Oracle applies STORED OUTLINES to query execution on a per-query basis. To be used on a given query, the query must match its stored equivalent perfectly. The slightest variation will cause Oracle to decide that the queries are different and the outline is not to be used. The rules are like the cursor-sharing that Oracle uses to parse queries with the shared pool.

Although outlines can be edited using SQL*PLUS to update them, this isn't really recommended because it's difficult. An easier and better way to update them is to use the outline editor provided with Oracle Enterprise Manager. For more information on Oracle Enterprise Manager, see Chapter 5.

Using Stored Outlines

Outlines can initially be created in a couple of different ways. Setting the CREATE STORED_ OUTLINES session parameter to TRUE (if everything is set up correctly, of course) causes an outline (with a cryptic SYS-prefixed name for each generated outline) to be generated for *every* query executed, similar to using TRACE to monitor an entire session. A more precise (and controllable) way is to create an outline for a specific query using the CREATE OUTLINE command, as shown here:

```
create or replace outline pb_outline on
  select e.last_name, e.salary
  from   s_emp e
  where  userid = 'lngao';
```

In this example, pb_outline is the outline created. This method has the big advantage of giving you control over what's happening *and* the ability to give the outline a usable name.

Oracle provides some helpful packages that you can use to work with STORED OUTLINES. The DBMS_OUTLN and DBMS_OUTLN_EDIT packages may be investigated for additional possibilities when using stored outlines. Unlike most Oracle packages, these don't belong to the SYS user, and although they can be described in SQL*PLUS, their source code is not available from the USER_SOURCE view (unlike most packages, where at least the headers are visible). The tables underlying the views cannot be directly maintained either. (They are system tables.)

Dropping Stored Outlines

How do you get rid of stored outlines when you don't want them anymore or when they cause performance to be worse? Use the DROP_UNUSED procedure in the DBMS_OUTLN package. The following command shows how to drop all unused outlines:

```
execute dbms_outln.drop_unused
```

To remove outlines that *have* been used, first apply the DBMS_OUTLN.CLEAR_USED procedure, which accepts an outline name (available from the USER_OUTLINES view) and can be run against only one outline at a time. A short PL/SQL program could be written to clear outlines en masse.

To determine whether an outline is actually being used, examine the USED column in USER_OUTLINES. You can also query the OUTLINE_CATEGORY column in the V$SQL view to see things that are still in the cache.

```
SELECT OUTLINE_CATEGORY, OUTLINE_SID
FROM   V$SQL
WHERE  SQL_TEXT = 'portion of query%'
```

Using Plan Stability (Stored Outlines)

For applications developed using the Rule-Based Optimizer (RBO), considerable effort usually has gone into ensuring that the performance of the application is acceptable. Plan Stability can be used to ensure that going from RBO to query optimization is a smooth transition by preserving the performance of the SQL running under RBO in stored outlines. These stored outlines can be used, if necessary, in the new environment to maintain the performance of SQL statements. Follow these steps to set this up:

I. As SYS, run the following for each schema involved:

```
GRANT CREATE ANY OUTLINE TO schema;
```

2. As each schema, run the following:

```
ALTER SESSION SET CREATE_STORED_OUTLINES = rbo;
```

Run the application long enough to create the stored outlines of the important SQL statements.

3. When you are finished with Step 2, then run this:

```
ALTER SESSION SET CREATE_STORED_OUTLINES = FALSE:
```

You can then use the stored outline for any of the SQL that was run in Step 2. If there are only some SQL statements that are problematic under query optimization, you can selectively use the stored outlines only for those problematic SQL statements. For each problematic statement, change the category of the stored outline:

```
ALTER OUTLINE outline_name CHANGE CATEGORY TO keepoutline;
```

and then alter the session to use this category of outlines:

```
ALTER SESSION SET USE_STORED_OUTLINE = keepoutline;
```

Use the user_outlines view to get the outline_name for a specific stored outline.

Stored Outlines Example

This chapter closes with a short demonstration of using STORED OUTLINES. The following code section is the code; the second one is the spooled result when it was run.

```
--table s_emp contains the following structure
--and contains a unique index on userid
/*

SQL> desc s_emp;
 Name                    Null?    Type
 ------------------------------------------------------
 ID                      NOT NULL NUMBER(7)
 LAST_NAME               NOT NULL VARCHAR2(25)
 FIRST_NAME                       VARCHAR2(25)
 USERID                           VARCHAR2(8)
 START_DATE                       DATE
 COMMENTS                         VARCHAR2(255)
 MANAGER_ID                       NUMBER(7)
 TITLE                            VARCHAR2(25)
 DEPT_ID                          NUMBER(7)
 SALARY                           NUMBER(11,2)
 COMMISSION_PCT                   NUMBER(4,2)
*/

analyze table s_emp compute statistics;

alter session set query_rewrite_enabled       = true;
```

```
alter session set use_stored_outlines          = true;
alter session set star_transformation_enabled = true;

--first create the public outline without a hint (user the index on userid)
create or replace outline pb_outline on
select e.last_name,
       e.salary
  from s_emp e
 where userid = 'lngao';

--create storage tables for private outlines
--OL$, OL$HINTS and OL$NODES
exec dbms_outln_edit.create_edit_tables;

create private outline pr_outline from pb_outline;

--edit the ol$hints table
--use a full table scan rather than the index just to see if this works
update ol$hints
    set hint_text = 'FULL(E)'
 where hint# = 6;

commit;

--resynch stored outline definition
--alter system flush shared_pool;    --or
create private outline pr_outline from private pr_outline;
--this is probably a better option

--to test the new private outline
alter session set use_private_outlines = true;

set autotrace on;

select e.last_name,
       e.salary
  from s_emp e
 where userid = 'lngao';

set autotrace off;

--make your changes permanent
create or replace outline pb_outline from private pr_outline;

--use the new public outline
alter session set use_private_outlines = false;
```

When run, the preceding code produces this output:

```
SQL> @outlines
DOC>SQL> desc s_emp;
```

```
DOC>
DOC> Name               Null?    Type
DOC> ------------------------------------------------
DOC> ID                 NOT NULL NUMBER(7)
DOC> LAST_NAME          NOT NULL VARCHAR2(25)
DOC> FIRST_NAME                  VARCHAR2(25)
DOC> USERID                      VARCHAR2(8)
DOC> START_DATE                  DATE
DOC> COMMENTS                    VARCHAR2(255)
DOC> MANAGER_ID                  NUMBER(7)
DOC> TITLE                       VARCHAR2(25)
DOC> DEPT_ID                     NUMBER(7)
DOC> SALARY                      NUMBER(11,2)
DOC> COMMISSION_PCT              NUMBER(4,2)
DOC>*/

Table analyzed.
Session altered.
Session altered.
Session altered.
Outline created.
Table created.
Outline created.
1 row updated.
Commit complete.
Session altered.

LAST_NAME                   SALARY
------------------------    ----------
LNGAO                          1450
```

Autotrace output in 10.2 looks like this:

```
Execution Plan
----------------------------------------------------------
Plan hash value: 79371356


---------------------------------------------------------------------------
| Id  | Operation          | Name  | Rows  | Bytes | Cost (%CPU)| Time     |
---------------------------------------------------------------------------
|   0 | SELECT STATEMENT   |       |     1 |    17 |     3   (0)| 00:00:01 |
|*  1 |  TABLE ACCESS FULL | S_EMP |     1 |    17 |     3   (0)| 00:00:01 |
---------------------------------------------------------------------------


Predicate Information (identified by operation id):
---------------------------------------------------

   1 - filter("USERID"='lngao')

Note
-----
   - outline "PR_OUTLINE" used for this statement
```

```
Statistics
----------------------------------------------------------------
        96  recursive calls
       173  db block gets
        40  consistent gets
         0  physical reads
      6188  redo size
       334  bytes sent via SQL*Net to client
       370  bytes received via SQL*Net from client
         1  SQL*Net roundtrips to/from client
         2  sorts (memory)
         0  sorts (disk)
         0  rows processed

Outline created.
Session altered.
SQL> spool off
```

Tips Review

- Setting TIMED_STATISTICS = TRUE in the init.ora will *enable the collection of time statistics.* Also, in 10g, the initialization parameter SQL_TRACE has been deprecated.

- The TKPROF utility puts a traced output into a readable format. Without running TKPROF, it would be difficult to read the output of a TRACE. By specifying explain = username/password, we are able to get the EXPLAIN execution path, in addition to the execution statistics of the query.

- To use multiple sort parameters, just repeat the sort = parameter on the command line, as tkprof source_file out_file sort = parm1 sort = parm2.

- A traced query with a large number of physical reads usually indicates a missing index.

- A traced query output with only memory reads usually indicates that an index is being used.

- There is currently a bug in 10gR1 (fixed in 10gR2): "ORA-922: missing or invalid option" and the following message being logged into the TKPROF report file: "Error in CREATE TABLE of PLAN table: SCOTT.prof$plan_table. ORA-922: missing or invalid option."

- When using DBMS_MONITOR, be sure to disable tracing when you are done; otherwise, every session that meets the criteria specified will be traced.

- The trace file is a point-in-time picture of what happened on the system at a given moment. In contrast, the explain plan is generated when the TKPROF listing is analyzed, which could be some time later. The row source operation listing is generated as part of the trace file and can be used to see if the database objects have changed since the trace was performed.

- If multiple developers/DBAs are using the same PLAN_TABLE, SET STATEMENT_ID is essential to identifying a statement.

■ Use EXPLAIN instead of TRACE so that you don't have to wait for the query to run. EXPLAIN shows the path of a query without actually running the query. Use TRACE only for multiquery batch jobs to find out which of the many queries in the batch job is slow.

■ You can use the utlxpls.sql and utlxplp.sql queries provided by Oracle to query the plan table without having to write your own query and format the output.

■ Whether the EXPLAIN PLAN is read from top to bottom or from bottom to top depends entirely on the query used to select information from the PLAN_TABLE.

■ The AUTOTRACE option also provides an EXPLAIN PLAN for a query. AUTOTRACE also provides many of the TRACE and TKPROF statistics, such as disk reads (physical reads) and memory reads (consistent reads + db block gets).

■ If the error "Unable to verify plan table format or existence" occurs when enabling AUTOTRACE, a plan table must be created using utlxplan.sql.

■ AUTOTRACE may fail when querying system views because the user may not have permission to view underlying objects.

■ Partitions can also be viewed by the EXPLAIN PLAN by accessing the columns PARTITION_START and PARTITION_STOP in the PLAN_TABLE table.

■ Accessing the V$sqlarea table can give statistics that are often found when tracing a query.

■ You can also use TRACE within the Developer/2000 products. You simply need to set statistics = yes on the command line for Oracle Forms.

■ The OPERATION and OPTIONS columns of the PLAN_TABLE are the most important columns for tuning a query. The OPERATION column shows the actual operation performed (including type of join), and the OPTIONS column tells you when there is a full table scan being performed that may need an index.

■ The ID column of the PLAN_TABLE shows the order in which a statement is processed. One of the primary rules of tuning a SQL statement is to change the query such that the ID of the order in which the steps in the query execute is changed. Changing the order in which steps execute in a query usually changes the performance of a query, either positively or negatively.

■ The PARENT_ID column of the PLAN_TABLE is very important because it shows the dependencies of two steps in an EXPLAIN PLAN. If a section of the EXPLAIN PLAN has a PARENT_ID, it implies that this statement *must* run prior to the PARENT_ID that is specified.

■ The BYTES column of the PLAN_TABLE is extremely important when evaluating how to tune a query. When an index is used and the number of BYTES is great, it implies that perhaps doing a full table scan would be more efficient (i.e., reading the index and data is more costly than just reading the data in a full table scan). Also, the number of bytes helps us to determine which table should be accessed first in the query, because one table may limit the number of bytes needed from another.

■ Both the COST and BYTES values in a query are estimates; it is quite possible for a version of a query with a higher estimated cost or bytes to actually run faster than another with a lower value.

- The X$KSPPI table can be accessed only by the SYS user. See Chapter 15 for tips on accessing the X$ tables and using some of these parameters. Do not use *any* undocumented parameters without consulting Oracle Corporation. Note that the layout and column names of these views have been known to change between releases of Oracle.

- Tracing queries can help performance, but using the TRACE facility built into the undocumented TRACE init.ora parameters can give great insight to (and better information for) solving errors within Oracle.

- Oracle Corporation likes to refer to STORED OUTLINES as PLAN STABILITY.

- Oracle applies STORED OUTLINES to query executions on a per-query basis. To be applied, a query must match its stored equivalent perfectly. The slightest variation could cause Oracle to decide that the queries are different and the outline should not be used. The rules are like those Oracle uses to parse queries when running them in the database.

References

Many thanks to Warren Bakker for upgrading this chapter to Oracle 10g. Thanks to Mark Riedel for upgrading this chapter to Oracle 9*i*, and to Dave Hathway, Greg Pucka, and Roger Behm for their contributions to this chapter.

CHAPTER
7

Basic Hint Syntax
(Developer and DBA)

While the optimizer is incredibly accurate in choosing the correct optimization path and use of indexes for thousands of queries on your system, it is not perfect. Oracle provides hints that you can specify for a given query so that the optimizer is overridden, hopefully achieving better performance for a given query. This chapter focuses on the basic syntax and use of hints. The chapters following this one (Chapters 8 and 9) have more complex examples, using various hints covered in this chapter.

The most useful hints that you use for your system may not be the same ones that I have found to be best, because of the diversity of every system. Common to most systems is the use of the FULL, INDEX, and ORDERED hints. A system with the parallel option may use the PARALLEL hint most often. Tips covered in this chapter include the following:

- The top hints used, the available hints and groupings, and specifying multiple hints
- That when using an alias, you *must* use the alias, *not* the table in the hint
- Using the FIRST_ROWS hint to generally force the use of indexes
- Using the ALL_ROWS hint to generally force a full table scan
- Using the FULL hint to force a full table scan
- Using the INDEX hint to force the use of an index
- Using the NO_INDEX hint to disallow a specified index from being used
- Using the INDEX_JOIN hint to allow the merging of indexes on a single table
- Using the INDEX_ASC hint to use an index ordered in ascending order
- Using the INDEX_DESC hint to use an index ordered in descending order
- Using the AND_EQUAL hint to access multiple b-tree indexes
- Using the INDEX_COMBINE hint to access multiple bitmap indexes
- Forcing fast full scans with the INDEX_FFS hint
- Using the ORDERED hint to specify the driving order of tables
- Using the LEADING hint to specify just the first driving table
- Using the NO_EXPAND hint to eliminate OR expansion
- Queries involving multiple locations and the DRIVING_SITE hint
- Using the USE_MERGE hint to change how tables are joined internally
- Forcing the subquery to process earlier with PUSH_SUBQ
- Using the parallel query option and using PARALLEL and NO_PARALLEL
- Using APPEND and NOAPPEND with parallel options
- Caching and pinning a table into memory with the CACHE hint
- Forcing clustering with the CLUSTER hint
- Forcing cluster hashing with the HASH hint
- Overriding the CURSOR_SHARING setting with the CURSOR_SHARING_EXACT hint

Top Hints Used

I did an informal survey at TUSC to see which hints both DBAs and developers use in their day-to-day tuning. I asked them to give me only the top three that they used. The results were not surprising to me, but if you've never used hints, this is quite helpful in determining where to start. Here is the list of TUSC's top hints, in the order in which they are used:

1. INDEX

2. ORDERED

3. PARALLEL

4. FIRST_ROWS

5. FULL

6. LEADING

7. USE_NL

8. APPEND

9. USE_HASH

NOTE
The top three in this list are also the top three that I've used the most since hints were introduced. I've frequently used all of these in my tuning, so they are a great place to start.

Use Hints Sparingly

Hints fall into two primary categories, usage directives and compiler directives. Usage directives are those that can be set at the init.ora or system parameter file (spfile) level in addition to the statement level (i.e., FIRST_ROWS, ALL_ROWS). If you have an OLTP database, setting the optimizer (at the instance level) from ALL_ROWS to FIRST_ROWS immediately focuses the optimizer on returning the first few rows faster (best response time for most OLTP applications). Setting the optimizer (at the instance level) to ALL_ROWS immediately focuses the optimizer on returning all rows faster (best throughput for all rows, which may be preferred for batch operations or data warehouses). The hints you give the optimizer will influence its choices for join operations and the order of operations. In both database cases (OLTP and data warehouse), the goal is to solve performance issues system-wide instead of needing to tune individual queries.

When there are queries inside a data warehouse that behave more like OLTP queries or vice versa, you may need to use hints for those specific statements. As you begin to use hints, you may find yourself tuning the same type of problem over and over, indicating that there are improper instance-level settings or improper database structures (missing indexes or I/O contention, for example) that are impacting performance. Tuning the symptoms (using compiler directives in the short term) will lead you to the pattern that can be fixed for the long term. You will hopefully be able to then use a usage directive to fix the problem system-wide. Try to use hints with this in mind and you'll use them only rarely.

Fix the Design First

In a three-table join, depending on the column order of the index on the intersection table, the query usually accesses the tables in a particular order. By correctly indexing the intersection table and the joined columns of the other tables, you will eliminate many of your performance problems before they happen. If you are using an ORDERED or LEADING hint over and over for joins, review the indexes on the joined tables to help you change how the optimizer is looking at the problem. Rewriting SQL statements so that they correctly use indexes will also solve many of your problems, eliminating the need for a hint. Putting a function on an indexed column may suppress the index and cause the tables to drive differently. Always use hints when you have exhausted the other avenues for tuning a query. If you find that you are using the same hint for the same problem over and over, you almost certainly have a problem that can be fixed system wide instead. Always try to unlock the system problem inside each query level issue. This will also help you avoid the pain caused by hints working differently when you upgrade to a new version.

For example, consider a typical three-table join between STUDENT, CLASS, and STUDENT_CLASS tables. The STUDENT table contains one row for each student, the class table contains one row for each CLASS, and the STUDENT_CLASS table is the intersection table, as multiple students attend multiple classes. The primary keys for the tables look like this:

STUDENT primary key Student_ID
CLASS primary key Class_ID
STUDENT_CLASS concatenated primary key of (Class_ID, Student_ID)

When the primary keys are defined in this manner, Oracle will automatically create indexes to support them. The intersection table, STUDENT_CLASS, will have a concatenated index on two columns, Class_ID and Student_ID, with Class_ID as the leading column. Is this the best column order for all of the application's queries? Unless you can forecast all of the queries that will join these tables, you should create a second index on the STUDENT_CLASS table's primary key columns:

STUDENT_CLASS secondary index on (Student_ID, Class_ID)

When processing a join of these three tables, the optimizer can now choose to begin at either the STUDENT or CLASS table and will have an available index on STUDENT_CLASS that will support its needs. You may find that the secondary index is rarely used—but it is there when it is needed to support the application users and their related business processes. By designing the indexing structures to support multiple access paths, you give the optimizer the tools it needs to choose the best execution path.

Available Hints and Groupings

The available hints vary according to the version of the database installed. While this chapter focuses on the hints that are used frequently, many of these hints that are not covered in detail may give great performance gains for someone with a particular system.

Hints are separated into the different categories described in the following sections according to which type of operation is being modified by the hint. Each hint is discussed in detail, including syntax and examples, in the sections that follow.

Execution Path

Hints modify the execution path when an optimizer processes a particular statement. The instance-level parameter OPTIMIZER_MODE can be used to modify all statements in the database to follow a specific execution path, but a hint to a different execution path overrides anything that is specified in the instance parameter file. If a SQL statement has a hint specifying an optimization approach and goal, then the optimizer uses the specified approach regardless of the presence or absence of statistics, the value of the OPTIMIZER_MODE initialization parameter, and the OPTIMIZER_MODE parameter of the ALTER SESSION statement. Oracle also notes in its documentation that: If these statistics have not been gathered, or if the statistics are no longer representative of the data stored within the database, then the optimizer does not have sufficient information to generate the best plan. Hints that change the execution path include the following:

- ALL_ROWS
- FIRST_ROWS(n)

Access Methods

The hints that are grouped into access methods allow the coder to vary the way the actual query is accessed. This group of hints is most frequently used, especially the INDEX hint. It provides direction as to whether and how indexes are used, and how the corresponding indexes will be merged to get the final answer. The access method hints are listed here and described later in this chapter:

- CLUSTER
- FULL
- HASH
- INDEX
- INDEX_ASC
- INDEX_COMBINE
- INDEX_DESC
- INDEX_JOIN
- INDEX_FFS
- INDEX_SS
- INDEX_SSX_ASC
- INDEX_SS_DESC
- NO_INDEX
- NO_INDEX_FFS
- NO_INDEX_SS

Access Methods

Query Transformation Hints

Query transformation hints are especially helpful in a data warehouse where you are familiar with using fact and dimension tables. The FACT hint can force a given table to be the FACT or driving table for a query. The NO_FACT hint does the opposite. The STAR_TRANSFORMATION hint is used to efficiently access the fact table when joining multiple tables. The NO_STAR_TRANSFORMATION hint instructs the optimizer *not* to perform a star query transformation when you may have a schema whose structures appear to be a data warehouse schema, but is not actually a data warehouse.

The query transformation hints are

- FACT
- MERGE
- NO_EXPAND
- NO_FACT
- NO_MERGE
- NO_QUERY_TRANSFORMATION
- NO_REWRITE
- NO_STAR_TRANSFORMATION
- NO_UNNEST
- REWRITE
- STAR_TRANSFORMATION
- UNNEST
- USE_CONCAT

Join Operations

The join operations group of hints controls how joined tables merge data together. A join operation may direct the optimizer to choose the best path for retrieving all rows for a query (throughput) or for retrieving the first row (response time).

Two hints are available to directly influence join order. LEADING specifies a table to start with for the join order to use, while ORDERED tells the optimizer to join the tables based on their order in the FROM clause using the first table listed as the driving table (accessed first).

Additional hints available to direct the use of join operations are

- NO_USE_HASH
- NO_USE_MERGE
- NO_USE_NL

- USE_HASH
- USE_MERGE
- USE_NL
- USE_NL_WITH_INDEX

Parallel Execution

The parallel execution group of hints applies to databases using the Parallel Option. These hints override the table specification for the degree of parallelism.

- NO_PARALLEL
- NO_PARALLEL_INDEX
- PARALLEL
- PARALLEL_INDEX
- PQ_DISTRIBUTE

Other Hints

The APPEND and NOAPPEND hints can be used without the parallel option, but they are frequently used with it. The cache grouping pertains to the hints that will put items as most recently used (CACHE) or least recently used (NOCACHE). Like APPEND and CACHE, the following hints are available to influence the ways in which the optimizer processes the table accesses.

- APPEND
- CACHE
- CURSOR_SHARING_EXACT
- DRIVING_SITE
- DYNAMIC_SAMPLING
- MODEL_MIN_ANALYSIS
- NOAPPEND
- NOCACHE
- NO_PUSH_PRED
- NO_PUSH_SUBQ
- NO_PX_JOIN_FILTER
- PUSH_PRED

- PUSH_SUBQ
- PX_JOIN_FILTER
- QB_NAME

Specifying a Hint

If you incorrectly specify a hint in any way, it becomes a comment and is ignored. Be very careful to get the hint syntax *exactly* correct. The best way to ensure that a hint has been correctly specified is to run an EXPLAIN PLAN, or set AUTOTRACE to ON in SQL*Plus to see if the hint was used. Some hints are overridden by Oracle despite the fact that a hint is primarily to override decisions made by the Oracle optimizer. The basic hint syntax (in this example, it is for a FULL hint) is shown here:

```
select      /*+ FULL(table) */ column1,…
```

The *table* in the preceding code snippet is the table name to perform a full table scan on, or the alias for the table if you specified an alias in the FROM clause, as shown here:

```
select      /*+ FULL(emp) */ empno, ename, deptno
from        emp
where       deptno = 1;
```

In this example, if there were an index on the DeptNo column, a full table scan would be performed. The hint is not required to be uppercase.

```
select      /* FULL(emp) */ empno, ename, deptno
from        emp
where       deptno = 1;
```

In this query, if there were an index on the deptno column, the index would be used, since the hint is missing the plus sign (**+**).

TIP
Incorrect hint syntax leads to the hint being interpreted as a comment.
If there is an additional hint that is specified correctly, it will be used.

By default, hints only affect the code block in which they appear. If you hint the access of the EMP table in a query that is part of a UNION operation, the other queries within the UNION will not be affected by your hint. If you want all of the unioned queries to use the same hint, you will need to specify the hint in each of the queries.

You can specify the query block name in hints to specify the query block to which the hint applies. Thus, in an outer query you can specify a hint that applies to a subquery. The syntax for the *queryblock* argument of the hint syntax is in the form

```
@queryblock
```

where *queryblock* is a user-specified or system-generated identifier. Use the QB_NAME hint to specify the name for the query block. If you are using system-generated hints, you can view the query block names via the explain plan for the query (an example is given later in this chapter).

Specifying Multiple Hints

You can use more than one hint at a time, although this may cause some or all of the hints to be ignored. Separate hints with spaces, are shown here:

```
select      /*+ FULL(table) CACHE(table)*/ column1,…
```

The (*table*) in this code snippet is the table name to perform the full scan and cache on.

```
select      /*+ FULL(emp) CACHE(emp)*/ empno, ename, deptno
from        emp
where       deptno = 1;
```

TIP
Multiple hints are separated with a space. Specifying multiple hints that conflict with each other causes the query to use none of the hints that are conflicting.

When Using an Alias, Hint the Alias, Not the Table

When you use aliases on a given table that you want to use in a hint, you must specify the alias and *not* the table name in the hint. If you specify the table name in the hint when an alias is used, the hint is *not* used.

```
select      /*+ FULL(table) */ column1,…
```

The (*table*) in this code snippet has to be replaced with the alias that follows, since the query uses an alias. If an alias is used, the alias *must* be used in the hint or the hint will *not* work.

```
select      /*+ FULL(A) */ empno, ename, deptno
from        emp A
where       deptno = 1;
```

TIP
If an alias is used, the alias must be used in the hint or the hint will not work.

The Hints

The hints discussed here are available as of Oracle Database 10g Release 2. Consult the Oracle documentation for more information on these or other hints.

TIP
If the database does not have statistics about the tables accessed by a command, the optimizer will use default statistical values based on the physical storage allocated to the tables and indexes. Instead of using those default values, you should use the DBMS_STATS package to gather statistics on the database objects.

The FIRST_ROWS Hint

The FIRST_ROWS hint directs the optimizer to optimize a query on the basis of retrieving the first rows the fastest. This approach is especially helpful when users of the system are using online transaction processing systems to retrieve a single record on their screen. This approach would be a poor choice for a batch-intensive environment where a lot of rows are generally retrieved by a query. The FIRST_ROWS hint generally forces the use of indexes, which under normal circumstances may not have been used. The FIRST_ROWS or ALL_ROWS hint (the optimizer will make a best-guess effort to choose the better of the two) is used, even when statistics are not gathered when using cost-based optimization.

The FIRST_ROWS hint is ignored in UPDATE and DELETE statements, since all rows of the query must be updated or deleted. It is also ignored when any grouping statement is used (GROUP BY, DISTINCT, INTERSECT, MINUS, UNION), since all of the rows for the grouping have to be retrieved for the grouping to occur. The optimizer may also choose to avoid a sort when there is an ORDER BY in the statement if an index scan can do the actual sort. The optimizer may also choose NESTED LOOPS over a SORT MERGE when an index scan is available and the index is on the inner table. The inner table shortens the result set that is joined back to the outside table in the query, and specifying access paths overrides this hint.

You may also specify the number of rows (as in the second example that follows) that you want FIRST_ROWS to optimize getting (the default is one). Note that this is specified in powers of ten up to 1000. Using FIRST_ROWS (n) is totally based on costs, and is sensitive to the value of n. With small values of n, the optimizer tends to generate plans that consist of nested loop joins with index lookups. With large values of n, the optimizer tends to generate plans that consist of hash joins and full table scans (behaving more like ALL_ROWS).

Syntax

```
select      /*+ FIRST_ROWS(n) */ column1, …
```

Example

```
select      /*+ FIRST_ROWS */ empno, ename, deptno
from        emp
where       deptno = 1;
```

Example

```
select      /*+ FIRST_ROWS(10) */ empno, ename, deptno
from        emp
where       deptno = 1;
```

TIP
The FIRST_ROWS hint causes the optimizer to choose a path that retrieves the first row (or a specified number of rows) of a query fastest, at the cost of retrieving multiple rows slower. The FIRST_ ROWS hint may be set as the default for the entire database by setting OPTIMIZER_MODE= FIRST_ROWS in the system parameter file; query-level hints will override the default setting for a given query.

The ALL_ROWS Hint

The ALL_ROWS (best throughput) hint directs a query to optimize a query on the basis of retrieving all of the rows the fastest. This approach is especially helpful when users of the system are in a heavy batch report environment and running reports that retrieve a lot of rows. This would be a poor choice for a heavy transaction processing environment where users are trying to view a single record on a screen. The ALL_ROWS hint may suppress the use of indexes that under normal circumstances would have been used. Specifying access path hints overrides the use of this hint.

Syntax

```
select      /*+ ALL_ROWS */ column1, …
```

Example

```
select      /*+ ALL_ROWS */ empno, ename, deptno
from        emp
where       deptno = 1;
```

TIP
The ALL_ROWS hint causes the optimizer to choose a path that will retrieve all the rows of a query fastest, at the cost of retrieving one single row slower. The ALL_ROWS hint may be set as the default for the entire database by setting OPTIMIZER_MODE= ALL_ROWS in the system parameter file; query-level hints will override the default setting for a given query.

The FULL Hint

The FULL hint directs a query to override the optimizer and perform a full table scan on the specified table in the hint. The FULL hint has different functionality based on the query that you are tuning. You can use it to force a full table scan when a large portion of the table is being queried. The cost of retrieving the index *and* the rows may be larger than just retrieving the entire table. The full hint may also cause an unexpected result. Causing a full table scan may cause tables to be accessed in a different order, because a different driving table is used. This may lead to better performance, leading one to believe that the full table scan was the key benefit, when changing the order of the driving table was the real cause of the increased performance. The syntax for the FULL hint is as follows:

Syntax

```
select      /*+ FULL(table) */ column1,…
```

Here, *(table)* is the table name to perform the full scan on. If an alias is used, the alias *must* be used in the hint or it will *not* work.

Note that you should only specify the table name in the hint, not the schema name.

Example

```
select      /*+ FULL(emp) */ empno, ename, deptno
from        emp
where       deptno = 1;
```

The FULL hint in this example would be particularly helpful if the only department in the company was one (1). Going to an index on deptno and the emp table would be slower than simply performing a full table scan on the emp table.

The FULL hint is also a necessary part of using some of the other hints. The CACHE hint can cache a table in memory only when the full table is accessed. Some of the hints in the parallel grouping also necessitate the use of a full table scan. We look at each of these hints later in this chapter.

TIP
The FULL hint performs a full table scan on the table that is specified, and not all tables in the query. The FULL hint may also lead to better performance, which is attributable to causing a change in the driving table of the query and not the actual full table scan.

If there are multiple tables with the same name in the same query, assign aliases to them in the FROM clause and then reference the aliases in the hints.

The INDEX Hint

The INDEX hint is frequently used to force one or more indexes to be executed for a given query. Oracle generally chooses the correct index or indexes with the optimizer, but when the optimizer chooses the wrong index or no index at all, this hint is excellent. You may also use multiple indexes with this hint and Oracle will choose one or more of the indexes specified based on the best plan. If you only specify one index, the optimizer considers only one index.

Syntax

```
select      /*+ INDEX (table index1, index2…) */ column1, …
```

Example

```
select    /*+ INDEX (emp deptno_idx) */ empno, ename, deptno
from      emp
where     deptno = 1;
```

In this example, the deptno_idx index on the emp table will be used.

Example

```
select    /*+ INDEX (emp deptno_idx, empno_idx) */ empno, ename, deptno
from      emp
where     deptno = 1
and       empno = 7750;
```

In the second example, Oracle may use the deptno_idx index, or the empno_idx index, or a merge of both of them. We have placed these choices in the optimizer's hands to decipher the best choice. It would have been best to only specify the index on the empno column (empno_idx) if this were the most restrictive statement (usually much more restrictive than the department).

TIP
The INDEX hint causes the optimizer to choose the index specified in the hint. Multiple indexes for a single table can be specified, but it is usually better to specify only the most restrictive index on a given query (avoiding the merging of the result of each index). If multiple indexes are specified, Oracle chooses which (one or more) to use, so be careful or your hint could potentially be overridden.

Example

```
select    /*+ INDEX */ empno, ename, deptno
from      emp
where     deptno = 1
and       empno = 7750;
```

In this example, no index is specified. Oracle now weighs all of the possible indexes that are available and chooses one or more to be used. Since we have not specified a particular index, but we have specified the INDEX hint, the optimizer will *not* do a full table scan.

TIP
The INDEX hint, without a specified index, will not consider a full table scan, even though no indexes have been specified. The optimizer will choose the best index or indexes for the query.

As of Oracle Database 10g, you can specify column names as part of the INDEX hint. The columns can be prefixed with the table names (not table aliases). Each column listed in the hint must be a physical column in the table, not an expression or calculated column.

The INDEX Hint

Syntax

```
select      /*+ INDEX ([table.]column1 [[table2.]column2]) */ column1, ...
```

Example

```
select      /*+ INDEX (emp.deptno) */ empno, ename, deptno
from        emp
where       deptno = 1;
```

The NO_INDEX Hint

The NO_INDEX hint disallows the optimizer from using a specified index. This is a great hint for tuning queries with multiple indexes. While you may not know which of multiple indexes to drive the query with, you might know which ones that you *don't* want the optimizer to use. You may also want to disallow an index for many queries prior to dropping an index that you don't think is necessary.

Syntax

```
select      /*+ NO_INDEX (table index1, index2...) */ column1, ...
```

Example

```
select      /*+ NO_INDEX (emp deptno_idx) */ ename, deptno
from        emp
where       deptno = 1;
```

In this example, the deptno_idx index on the emp table will *not* be used. If the NO_INDEX hint is used and no index is specified, a full table scan will be performed. If the NO_INDEX and a conflicting hint (such as INDEX) are specified for the same index, then both hints are ignored (as in the example that follows).

Example

```
select      /*+ NO_INDEX (emp deptno_idx) INDEX (emp deptno_idx) */ ename, deptno
from        emp
where       deptno = 1;
```

TIP
The NO_INDEX hint must be in the tuning expert's toolkit. It is used to remove an index from consideration by the optimizer so that you may evaluate the need for the index prior to dropping it or so that you can evaluate other indexes. Be careful not to conflict with other index hints.

The INDEX_JOIN Hint

The INDEX_JOIN hint merges separate indexes from a single table together so that *only* the indexes need to be accessed. This approach saves a trip back to the table.

Syntax

```
select      /*+ INDEX_JOIN (table index1, index2…) */ column1, …
```

Example

```
select      /*+ index_join(test2 year_idx state_idx) */ state, year
from        test2
where       year = '1972'
and         state = MA;
```

In this query, the optimizer will merge the year_idx and state_idx indexes and will *not* need to access the test2 table. All information is contained in these two indexes when they are merged together. For a more detailed example, see Chapter 8.

TIP

The INDEX_JOIN hint not only allows us to access only indexes on a table, which is a scan of fewer total blocks, but it is also five times faster than using an index and scanning the table by ROWID.

The INDEX_COMBINE Hint

The INDEX_COMBINE hint is used to specify multiple bitmap indexes when you want the optimizer to use *all* indexes that you specify. You can also use the INDEX_COMBINE hint to specify single indexes (this is preferred over using the INDEX hint for bitmaps). For b-tree indexes, use the INDEX hint instead of this one.

Syntax

```
select     /*+ INDEX_COMBINE (table index1, index2…) */ column1, …
```

Example

```
select     /*+ INDEX_COMBINE (emp deptno_bidx, mgr_bidx) */ empno, ename, deptno
from       emp
where      deptno = 1
and        mgr = 7698;
```

In this example, Oracle uses a merge of both the deptno_bidx index AND the mgr_bidx bitmap indexes.

TIP
The INDEX_COMBINE hint causes the optimizer to merge multiple bitmap indexes for a single table instead of choosing which one is better (as with the INDEX hint).

The INDEX_ASC Hint

The INDEX_ASC hint currently does *exactly* the same thing as the INDEX hint. Since indexes are already scanned in ascending order, this does nothing more than the current INDEX hint. So what is it good for? Oracle does not guarantee that indexes will be scanned in ascending order in the future, but this hint will guarantee that an index will be scanned in ascending order.

Syntax

```
select      /*+ INDEX_ASC (table index1, index2...) */ column1, ...
```

Example

```
select      /*+ INDEX_ASC (emp deptno_idx) */ empno, ename, deptno
from        emp
where       deptno = 1;
```

In this example, the deptno_idx index on the emp table will be used.

TIP
As of Oracle8i, the INDEX_ASC does exactly what the INDEX hint does, since indexes are already scanned in ascending order. It is used to guarantee this to be true, as Oracle may change this default in the future. As of Oracle9i, descending indexes are actually sorted in descending order. Oracle treats descending indexes as function-based indexes. The columns marked DESC are sorted in descending order.

The INDEX_DESC Hint

The INDEX_DESC hint causes indexes to be scanned in descending order (of their indexed value or order), which is the opposite of the INDEX and INDEX_ASC hints. This hint is overridden when the query has multiple tables, because the index needs to be used in the normal ascending order to be joined to the other table in the query. Some restrictions for this include that it does not work for bitmap indexes or for descending indexes, that it causes the index to be scanned in ascending order, and that it does not work across partitioned index boundaries but performs a descending index scan of each partition.

Syntax

```
select      /*+ INDEX_DESC (table index1, index2…) */ column1, …
```

Example

```
select      /*+ INDEX_DESC (emp deptno_idx) */ empno, ename, deptno
from        emp
where       deptno = 1;
```

TIP
The INDEX_DESC processes an index in descending order of how it was built. This hint will not be used if more than one table exists in the query.

The INDEX_FFS Hint

The INDEX_FFS hint indicates a fast full scan of the index should be performed. This hint accesses only the index and *not* the corresponding table. The fast full scan of the index will be used only if all of the information that the query needs to retrieve is in the index. This hint can give great performance gains, especially when the table has a large number of columns.

Syntax

```
select      /*+ INDEX_FFS (table index) */ column1, …
```

Example

```
select      /*+ INDEX_FFS (emp deptno_idx) */ deptno, empno
from        emp
where       deptno = 1;
```

The INDEX_FFS hint will be used only if the deptno_idx index contains both the *deptno* and *empno* columns as a part of it. The NO_INDEX_FFS has the same syntax, but this hint tells the optimizer *not* to perform fast full index scans of the specified indexes. You must specify both the table and index in both of these hints.

TIP
The INDEX_FFS processes only the index and does not take the result and access the table. All columns that are used and retrieved by the query must be contained in the index.

The ORDERED Hint

The ORDERED hint causes tables to be accessed in a particular order, based on the order of the tables in the FROM clause of the query, which is often referred to as the driving order for a query. Before cost-based optimization, the last table in the FROM clause was the driving table in queries;

however, using the ORDERED hint causes the first table in the FROM clause to be the driver. The ORDERED hint also guarantees the driving order. When the ORDERED hint is not used, Oracle may internally switch the driving table when compared to how tables are listed in the FROM clause (EXPLAIN PLAN can show how tables are accessed). The complexity of possibilities when this hint is used is so great that much of the next chapter is focused on this subject (please see Chapter 8 for more information regarding tuning joins). This chapter briefly covers this hint, mainly for syntactical purposes.

Syntax

```
select      /*+ ORDERED */ column1, …
```

Example

```
select      /*+ ORDERED */ empno, ename, dept.deptno
from        emp, dept
where       emp.deptno = dept.deptno
and         dept.deptno = 1
and         emp.empno = 7747;
```

If both tables (emp and dept) have been analyzed (using the cost-based optimizer) *and* there are *no* indexes on either table, the emp table is accessed first and the dept table is accessed second. There are a lot of possible variations (covered in the next two chapters) that cause this to work differently.

Example

```
select      /*+ ORDERED */ emp.empno, ename, dept.deptno, itemno
from        emp, dept, orders
where       emp.deptno = dept.deptno
and         emp.empno = orders.empno
and         dept.deptno = 1
and         emp.empno = 7747
and         orders.ordno = 45;
```

If all three tables (emp, dept, and orders) have been analyzed *and* there are *no* indexes on any of the tables, the emp table would be accessed first and then joined to the dept table, which would be accessed second. The result would be joined with the orders table, which is accessed last. There are a lot of possible variations (covered in the next chapter) that cause this to work differently.

 TIP
The ORDERED hint is one of the most powerful hints available. It processes the tables of the query in the sequential order that they are listed in the FROM clause. There are many variations that cause this to work differently. The version of Oracle, the existence of indexes on the tables, and which tables have been analyzed all cause this to work differently. However, when a multitable join is slow and you don't know what to do, this is one of the first hints you should try!

The LEADING Hint

As the complexity of queries becomes greater, it becomes more difficult to figure out the order of *all* of the tables using the ORDERED hint. You can often figure out which table should be accessed *first* (driving table), but you may not know which table to access after that one. The LEADING hint allows you to specify *one* table to drive the query; the optimizer figures out which table to use after that. If you specify more than one table with this hint, it is ignored. The ORDERED hint overrides the LEADING hint.

Syntax

```
select      /*+ LEADING (table1) */ column1, …
```

Example

```
select      /*+ LEADING(DEPT) */ emp.empno, ename, dept.deptno, itemno
from        emp, dept, orders
where       emp.deptno = dept.deptno
and         emp.empno = orders.empno
and         dept.deptno = 1
and         emp.empno = 7747
and         orders.ordno = 45;
```

If all three tables (emp, dept, and orders) have been analyzed *and* there are *no* indexes on any of the tables, the DEPT table would be accessed first (driving the query). The optimizer would figure out the rest (probably accessing the intersection table EMP next).

TIP
The LEADING hint works similar to the ORDERED hint. The LEADING hint is used to specify a single table to drive a query while allowing the optimizer to figure out the rest.

Be sure you have properly configured the indexes to support the join order you specify.

The NO_EXPAND Hint

The NO_EXPAND hint is used to keep the optimizer from "going off the deep end" when it is evaluating IN-lists that are combined with an OR. It disallows the optimizer from using OR expansion. Without the NO_EXPAND hint, the optimizer may create a very long explain plan.

Syntax

```
select      /*+ NO_EXPAND */ column1, …
```

Example

```
select /*+ FIRST_ROWS NO_EXPAND */ col1, col2...
from    members
```

```
where   (memb_key between 205127 and 205226
or       memb_key between 205228 and 205327
or       memb_key between 205330 and 205429
or       memb_key between 205431 and 205530);
```

I have used the NO_EXPAND hint and was able to get performance that was almost 50 times faster than without the hint.

Example (Using Oracle's Sample Schema tables)

```
select  /*+ FIRST_ROWS NO_EXPAND */ product_id, translated_name
from    oe.product_descriptions
where   language_id = 'US'
and     (product_id between 2187 and 2193
or       product_id between 2326 and 2330
or       product_id between 3176 and 3177
or       product_id between 3245 and 3249);
```

TIP
The NO_EXPAND hint prevents the optimizer from using OR expansion and is used when the query will become substantially more complex as a result of the expansion.

The DRIVING_SITE Hint

The DRIVING_SITE hint is identical to the ORDERED hint, except this hint is for processing data by driving it from a particular database. The table specified in the hint will be the driving site that will be used to process the actual join.

Syntax

```
select    /*+ DRIVING_SITE (table) */ column1, …
```

Example

```
select    /*+ DRIVING_SITE (deptremote) */ empno, ename, deptremote.deptno
from      emp, dept@oratusc deptremote
where     emp.deptno = deptremote.deptno
and       deptremote.deptno = 10
and       empno = 7747;
```

Oracle normally would retrieve the rows from the remote site and join them at the local site if this hint was not specified. Since the "empno = 7747" limits the query greatly, we would rather pass the small number of rows from the emp table to the remote site instead of pulling an entire dept table department back to our local site to process.

Limiting the rows that are retrieved from a remote site can also be achieved by creating a view locally for the remote table. The local view should have the WHERE clause that will be used, so that the view will limit the rows returned from the remote database before they are sent back to the local database. I have personally tuned queries from hours to seconds using this method.

The location is not specified in the hint (just the table name). However, if an alias were used, the alias would have to be used instead of the table name in the hint.

TIP
The DRIVING_SITE hint is extremely powerful, as it will potentially limit the amount of information that will be processed over your network. The table specified with the DRIVING_SITE hint will be the location for the join to be processed. Using views for remote tables can also lead to better performance by limiting the number of rows passed from the remote site before the records are sent to the local site.

The USE_MERGE Hint

The USE_MERGE hint is a hint that tells the optimizer to use a MERGE JOIN operation when performing a join. A MERGE JOIN operation may be useful when queries perform set operations on large numbers of rows. Assume you are joining two tables together. In a MERGE JOIN, the row set returned from each table is sorted and then merged to form the final result set. Since each result is sorted and then merged together, this action is most effective when retrieving all rows from a given query. If you wanted the first row faster instead, the USE_NL would be the hint to use (to force a nested loops join). In the following illustration, the emp and dept tables are joined, and that result set is then joined to the orders table via a MERGE JOIN operation.

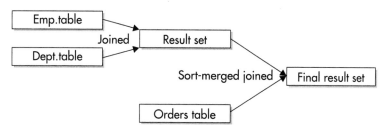

Syntax

```
select      /*+ USE_MERGE (table) */ column1, …
```

Example

```
select      /*+ USE_MERGE(orders) */ emp.empno, ename, dept.deptno, itemno
from        emp, dept, orders
where       emp.deptno = dept.deptno
and         emp.empno = orders.empno
and         dept.deptno = 1
and         emp.empno = 7747
and         orders.ordno = 45;
```

The USE_MERGE hint in this query causes the orders table to be joined in a *sort-merge join* to the returned row source resulting from the join of the emp and dept tables. The rows are sorted and then merged together to find the final result. The NO_USE_MERGE hint uses the same syntax but instructs the optimizer to not use merge joins when selecting execution paths for a query. The optimizer will instead favor other join methods such as hash joins and nested loops joins. See Chapter 9 for a more detailed discussion of joins.

TIP
In a join of three or more tables, the USE_MERGE hint causes the table(s) specified in the hint to be sort-merge joined with the resulting row set from a join of the other tables in the join.

The USE_NL Hint

The USE_NL (use nested loops) hint is usually the fastest way to return a single row (response time); thus, it may be slower at returning all the rows. This hint causes a statement to be processed using nested loops, which takes the first matching row from one table based on the result from another table. This is the opposite of a merge join, which retrieves rows that match the conditions from each table and then merges them together.

Syntax

```
select     /*+ USE_NL (table1, table2,...) */ column1, ...
```

Example

```
select     /*+ ORDERED USE_NL(dept) */ empno, ename, dept.deptno
from       emp, dept
where      emp.deptno = dept.deptno
and        dept.deptno = 1
and        emp.empno = 7747;
```

The USE_NL hint causes the optimizer to take the resulting rows returned from the emp table and process them with the matching rows from the dept table (the specified nested loop table). The first row that matches from the dept table can be returned to the user immediately (as in a web-based application), as opposed to waiting until all matching rows are found. The ORDERED hint guarantees that the emp table is processed first.

TIP
The USE_NL hint usually provides the best response time (first row comes back faster) for smaller result sets; whereas the USE_MERGE hint usually provides the best throughput when the USE_HASH hint can't be used.

The NO_USE_NL hint uses the same syntax, but instructs the optimizer not to use nested loops joins, but to use a different join execution plan. A related hint, USE_NL_WITH_INDEX, takes two parameters—the name of the inner table for the join along with the name of the index to use when performing the join.

The USE_HASH Hint

The USE_HASH hint is usually the fastest way to join many rows together from multiple tables if you have adequate memory for this operation. The USE_HASH <hint or method> is similar to the nested loops where one result of one table is looped through the result from the joined table. The difference here is that the second table (the one being looped through) is put into memory. You must have a large enough HASH_AREA_SIZE or PGA_AGGREGATE_TARGET (see Chapter 4) for this to work properly; otherwise, the operation will occur on disk.

Syntax

```
select      /*+ USE_HASH (table1, table2,...) */ column1, …
```

Example

```
select      /*+ USE_HASH (dept) */ empno, ename, dept.deptno
from        emp, dept
where       emp.deptno = dept.deptno
and         emp.empno = 7747;
```

The USE_HASH hint causes the optimizer to take the rows returned from the emp table and process them with the matching rows from the dept table (the specified hash table), which are hashed into memory. The first row that matches from the dept table can be returned to the user immediately, as opposed to waiting until all matching rows are found. There are cases where the optimizer will override this hint. In the preceding query, if we added the condition "and dept.deptno=1", the optimizer would override the USE_HASH hint and do the more efficient nested loops join (since the dept table has been narrowed down by this condition). The NO_USE_HASH hint has a similar syntax but instructs the optimizer to not use hash joins when selecting execution paths for a query. The optimizer will instead use other join methods such as nested loops or merge joins.

> **TIP**
> *The USE_HASH hint usually provides the best response time for larger result sets.*

The PUSH_SUBQ Hint

The PUSH_SUBQ hint can lead to dramatic performance gains (an increase of over 100 times in performance) when used in the appropriate situation. The best situation to use this hint is when the subquery will return a relatively small number of rows (quickly); those rows can then be used to substantially limit the rows in the outer query. PUSH_SUBQ causes the subquery to be evaluated at the earliest possible time. This hint cannot be used when the query uses a merge join and cannot be used with remote tables. Moving the subquery to be part of the main query (when possible) can lead to the same gains when the tables are driven in the correct order (accessing the former subquery table first).

The PUSH_SUBQ Hint

Syntax

```
select      /*+ PUSH_SUBQ */ column1, …
```

Example

```
select      /*+ PUSH_SUBQ */ emp.empno, emp.ename, itemno
from        emp, orders
where       emp.empno = orders.empno
and         emp.deptno =
(select     deptno
 from       dept
 where      loc = 'BELMONT');
```

This query processes the subquery to be used by the outer query at its earliest possible time.

> **TIP**
> *The PUSH_SUBQ hint can improve performance greatly when the*
> *subquery will return only a few rows very fast, and those rows can*
> *be used to limit the rows returned in the outer query.*

The PARALLEL Hint

The PARALLEL hint causes the optimizer to break a query into pieces (the *degree of parallelism*) and process each piece with a different process. The degree of parallelism is applied to each parallelizable operation of a SQL statement. A query that requires a sort operation causes the number of processes used to be double the degree specified, as both the table accesses and the sorts are parallelized. A query coordinator process is also invoked, so if you set the degree of parallelism for a query to 4, it may use four processes for the query plus four *more* processes for the sorting, plus one *more* process for the breaking up and putting together of the four pieces, or nine (9) total processes.

The PARALLEL hint allows you to specify the desired number of concurrent servers that can be used for a parallel operation. The hint can be applied to the INSERT, UPDATE, and DELETE portions of a statement (you have to commit immediately after if you use this) as well as to SELECT commands. You should create tables with the PARALLEL clause where you plan to use this option. See Chapter 11 for a detailed look at all of the requirements and rules associated with this powerful option.

Syntax

```
/*+ PARALLEL (table, DEGREE) */
```

The *degree* is the number of pieces into which the query is broken.

Example

```
select      /*+ PARALLEL (order_line_items) */ invoice_number, invoice_date
from        order_line_items
order by    invoice_date;
```

This statement does not specify a degree of parallelism. The default degree of parallelism is dictated by the table definition when the table was created.

Example

```
select     /*+ PARALLEL (order_line_items, 4) */  invoice_number, invoice_date
from       order_line_items
order by   invoice_date;
```

This statement specifies a degree of parallelism of four. Per previous discussion, as many as nine query servers may be allocated or created to satisfy this query.

Example

```
select     /*+ PARALLEL (oli, 4) */ invoice_number, invoice_date
from       order_line_items oli
order by   invoice_date;
```

In this example, an alias is used and now must be used in the hint instead of using the table name.

TIP
Using the PARALLEL hint will enable the use of parallel operations. If the degree is not specified with the hint, the default degree specified during the table creation will be used.

The NO_PARALLEL Hint

If a table is created with a parallel degree set, the table will use that degree for all full table scan queries. However, you may also "turn off" the use of parallel operations in any one given query on a table that has been specified to use parallel operations using the NO_PARALLEL hint. The NO_PARALLEL hint results in a query with a degree of one (1).

NOTE
The NO_PARALLEL hint used to be NOPARALLEL before they standardized the naming.

Syntax

```
select     /*+ NO_PARALLEL (table) */ ...
```

Example

```
select     /*+ NO_PARALLEL (oli) */ invoice_number, invoice_date
from       order_line_items oli
order by   invoice_date;
```

The NO_PARALLEL hint results in a query with a degree of one (1).

TIP
Using the NO_PARALLEL hint disables parallel operations in a statement that would otherwise use parallel processing due to a parallel object definition.

The APPEND Hint

The APPEND hint improves the performance of INSERTs, but with a potential cost in terms of space. The APPEND hint does not check to see if there is space within currently used blocks for inserts, but instead appends the data into new blocks. You might potentially waste space, but you will gain speed in return. If you never delete rows from a table, you should definitely use the APPEND hint.

If an INSERT is parallelized using the PARALLEL hint, APPEND will be used by default. You can use the NOAPPEND hint (next section) to override this behavior. Also note that before you can use this example, you must first enable parallel DML.

Syntax

```
insert /*+ APPEND */ …
```

Example

```
insert /*+ APPEND */
into     emp (empno, deptno)
values   (7747, 10);
```

TIP
The APPEND hint inserts values into a table without checking the free space in the currently used blocks, but instead appends the data into new blocks.

The NOAPPEND Hint

The NOAPPEND hint is used to override the default for the PARALLEL inserts (the default, of course, is APPEND). The NOAPPEND hint is the opposite of the APPEND hint and checks for free space within current blocks before using new ones.

Syntax

```
insert     /*+ NOAPPEND */ …
```

Example

```
insert     /*+ PARALLEL(emp) NOAPPEND */
into     emp (empno, deptno)
values   (7747, 10);
```

TIP
The NOAPPEND hint overrides a PARALLEL hint, which normally uses the APPEND hint by default.

The CACHE Hint

The CACHE hint causes a full table scan to be cached (pinned) into memory, so future users accessing the same table find it in memory instead of going to disk. This creates one potentially large problem. If the table is very large, it is taking up an enormous amount of memory (data block buffer cache space in particular). For small lookup tables, however, this is an excellent option to use. Tables can be created with the CACHE option to be cached the first time they are accessed.

Syntax

```
select      /*+ CACHE(table) */ column1, …
```

Example

```
select      /*+ FULL(dept) CACHE(dept) */ deptno, loc
from        dept;
```

The entire dept table is now cached in memory and is marked as a most recently used object (MRU).

TIP
The CACHE hint should be used with small lookup tables that are often accessed by users. This ensures the table remains in memory.

The NOCACHE Hint

The NOCACHE hint causes a table that is specified to be CACHED at the database level to *not* get cached when you access it.

Syntax

```
select      /*+ NOCACHE(table) */ column1, …
```

Example

```
alter       table dept cache;
select      deptno, loc
from        dept;
```

In this example, the table is cached because the table was altered to use this option.

Example

```
alter     table dept cache;
select    /*+ NOCACHE(dept) */ deptno, loc
from      dept;
```

In this example, the table is not cached despite the ALTER statement and is put on the Least Recently Used (LRU) list.

TIP
The NOCACHE hint should be used to prevent caching a table specified with the CACHE option—basically, when you want to access the table but you don't want to cache it.

The CLUSTER Hint

The CLUSTER hint is used only for clusters. A cluster is usually created when tables are joined so often that it is faster to create an object containing information about the joined tables that is accessed most often. A cluster is identical to denormalizing a table or group of tables. The CLUSTER hint forces the use of the cluster. If hashing is used for the cluster (see the next section), the HASH hint should be considered. I have not had much luck with using clusters and gaining performance.

Syntax

```
select    /*+ CLUSTER (table) */ column1, …
```

TIP
The CLUSTER hint forces the use of a cluster. It is good to have clusters if the joined tables are frequently accessed but not frequently modified.

The HASH Hint

HASH indexes require the use of hash clusters. When a cluster or hash cluster is created, a cluster key is defined. The cluster key tells Oracle how to identify the rows stored in the cluster and where to store the rows in the cluster. When data is stored, all of the rows relating to the cluster key are stored in the same database blocks. With the data being stored in the same database blocks, using the hash index, Oracle can access the data by performing one hash function and one I/O—as opposed to accessing the data by using a b-tree index. Hash indexes can potentially be the fastest way to access data in the database, but they don't come without their drawbacks. Note that you can even create a hash cluster that contains a single table. This hint is *not* related to the USE_HASH hint in any way.

Syntax

```
select      /*+ HASH(table) */ column1, …
```

Example

```
select      /*+ HASH(emp) */ empno, dept.deptno
from        emp, dept
where       emp.deptno = dept.deptno
where       empno = 7747;
```

In this query, Oracle uses the hash key to find the information in the emp table (note that you must create a hash cluster prior to using this). I've not had a lot of luck tuning things with hash clusters.

TIP
Be careful implementing HASH clusters. The application should be reviewed fully to ensure that enough information is known about the tables and data before implementing this option. Generally speaking, hashing is best for static data with primarily sequential values.

The CURSOR_SHARING_EXACT Hint

The CURSOR_SHARING_EXACT hint is used to ensure that literals in SQL statements are not replaced with bind variables. This hint can be used to correct any minor issues when you *don't* want to use cursor sharing even though instance-level CURSOR_SHARING parameter is set to either FORCE or SIMILAR.

Syntax

```
select      /*+ CURSOR_SHARING_EXACT */ column1, …
```

Example

```
select      /*+ CURSOR_SHARING_EXACT */ empno, ename
from        emp
where       empno = 123;
```

In this example, Oracle will not be able to reuse a current statement in the shared pool unless it is *exactly* as this one is. It will not try to create a bind variable. Additional examples related to cursor sharing are in Chapter 4.

TIP
The CURSOR_SHARING_EXACT hint overrides the system parameter file setting of CURSOR_SHARING to either FORCE or SIMILAR.

CURSOR_SHARING_EXACT
Hint

The QB_NAME Hint

The QB_NAME hint is used to assign a name to a query block within a statement. You can then assign a hint elsewhere in the statement that references the query block. For example, if you have a query that contains a subquery, you can assign a query block name to the subquery and then provide the hint at the outermost query level. If two or more query blocks are given the same QB_NAME value, the optimizer will ignore the hints.

If you have a complex query, with subqueries, in the explain plan, it appears that the optimizer generates a name for these query blocks, such as emp@sel$4. By using the QB_NAME hint, you can specify the name to be used instead. This would be very helpful when trying to tune extremely complex queries that contain more than one subquery.

```
select      /*+ FULL(@deptblock dept) */ empno
from        emp
where       emp.deptno IN
  (select      /*+ QB_NAME(deptblock) */ dept.deptno
      from        dept
      where       loc = 'CHICAGO');
```

Some Miscellaneous Hints and Notes

In this section, I wanted to list "the best of the rest" of the hints that are available for use. Each hint is listed with a brief explanation of the hint. Please see the Oracle documentation if you're looking to use one of them.

- **USE_NL_WITH_INDEX**   The USE_NL hint instructs the optimizer to use a nested loops join with the specified table as the non-driving table (or as the inner table that is *looped* through with the result of the driving table). The USE_NL_WITH_INDEX hint allows you to also specify the index that is used during the access. However, the optimizer must be able to use that index with at least one join.

  ```
  Select /*+ USE_NL_WITH_INDEX (table index1, index2,...) */
  ```

- **INDEX_SS**   The INDEX_SS hint instructs the optimizer to use the "skip scan" option for an index on the specified table. A skip scan is where in a concatenated index Oracle skips the first column of the index and uses the rest of the index. This hint works well with a two-part concatenated index where you often use both parts but infrequently need only the second part (at times you don't have any condition for the first part). You need to specify both the table and the index.

  ```
  Select /*+ INDEX_SS(table index1, index2,,,) */
  ```

- **INDEX_SS_ASC**   The INDEX_SS_ASC hint is the same as the INDEX_SS hint, but this could change in a future version of Oracle.

- **INDEX_SS_DESC**   The INDEX_SS_DESC hint uses the same syntax as the INDEX_SS hint but instructs the optimizer to scan the index skip scan in descending order.

- **MODEL_MIN_ANALYSIS**   The MODEL_MIN_ANALYSIS hint instructs the optimizer to omit some compile-time optimizations of spreadsheet rules. This hint can reduce the compilation time required during spreadsheet analysis and is used with SQL Modeling queries.

■ **REWRITE_OR_ERROR** The REWRITE_OR_ERROR hint in a query produces the following error if the query did not rewrite: "ORA-30393: a query block in the statement did not rewrite".

■ **OPT_PARAM** This is a new hint in 10gR2 that allows you to modify the parameter setting in effect for the duration of the query. The syntax is

```
opt_param(<parameter_name> [,] <parameter_value>)
```

where parameter_name is the name of a parameter and parameter_value is its value. If the parameter contains a numeric value, the parameter value has to be specified without quotes. For example, the following hint sets parameter star_transformation_enabled to true for the statement where it is added:

```
OPT_PARAM('star_transformation_enabled' 'true')
```

Notes on Hints and Stored Outlines

Stored outlines are covered in Chapter 6, but a note here is relevant for the discussion on hints. Stored outlines allow a query to use a predetermined execution plan every time that query is run, no matter where the query is run from. People sometimes speak of the STORED OUTLINES as storing an execution plan, but this is not really what happens. Instead, Oracle stores a series of *hints* or instructions to the database to execute a query in a precise way to duplicate the execution plan as saved during a recording session. If you want to query the hints for a stored outline, the following query to USER_OUTLINE_HINTS can be used:

```
Select      hint
from        user_outline_hints
where       name = 'your_outline_name';
```

Why Isn't My Hint Working?

Often we find that a hint won't behave like we want it to. There are times when the optimizer overrides the hint, but usually people have a problem related to one of the following:

■ The hint syntax is incorrect.

■ The table(s) is not analyzed.

■ There is a conflict with another hint.

■ The hint requires a system parameter to be set for it to work.

■ The table name was aliased in the query, but you used the table name, not the alias, in the hint.

■ The hint requires a different version of Oracle than you have.

■ You don't understand the correct application for the hint.

■ You haven't slept lately; it is for many of the reasons cited here.

■ There is a software bug.

Hints at a Glance

The following table lists each hint discussed in this chapter and the use of the hint.

Hint	Use
FIRST_ROWS	Generally force the use of indexes
ALL_ROWS	Generally force a full table scan
FULL hint	Force a full table scan
INDEX	Force the use of an index
NO_INDEX	Disallow a specified index from being used
INDEX_JOIN	Allow the merging of indexes on a single table
INDEX_ASC	Use an index ordered in ascending order
INDEX_DESC	Use an index ordered in descending order
INDEX_COMBINE	Access multiple bitmap indexes
INDEX_FFS	Force fast full scans
ORDERED	Specify the driving order of tables
LEADING	Specify just the first driving table
NO_EXPAND	Help eliminate OR expansion
STAR_TRANSFORMATION	Force a star query transform
DRIVING_SITE	Process data by driving it from a particular database
USE_MERGE	Change how tables are joined internally
PUSH_SUBQ	Force the subquery to process earlier
PARALLEL	Cause full table scan queries to break query into pieces and process each piece with a different process
NO_PARALLEL	Turn off use of parallel operations in any one given query
APPEND	Append data into new blocks
NOAPPEND	Check for free space within current blocks before using new ones
CACHE	Cause a full table scan to be pinned into memory
NOCACHE	Cause a table that is specified to be cached at database level to not get cached when you access it
CLUSTER	Force clustering
HASH	Force cluster hashing
CURSOR_SHARING_EXACT	Override the CURSOR_SHARING setting
QB_NAME	Assign a name to a query block

Tips Review

- Incorrect hint syntax leads to the hint being interpreted as a comment.

- Multiple hints are separated with a space between each. At times, specifying multiple hints can cause the query to use *none* of the hints.

- If an alias is used, the alias *must* be used in the hint or it will *not* work.

- If the database does not have statistics about the tables accessed by a command, the optimizer will use default statistical values based on the physical storage allocated to the tables and indexes. Instead of using those default values, you should use the DBMS_STATS package to gather statistics on the database objects.

- The FIRST_ROWS hint causes the optimizer to choose a path that retrieves the first row of a query fastest, at the cost of retrieving multiple rows slower.

- The ALL_ROWS hint causes the optimizer to choose a path that retrieves all rows of a query fastest, at the cost of retrieving one single row slower.

- The FULL hint performs a full table scan on the table that is specified (not all tables in the query).

- The INDEX hint causes the optimizer to choose the index specified in the hint.

- The INDEX_JOIN hint allows you to access and merge together only indexes on a table, which is a scan of fewer total blocks and often faster than scanning the table by ROWID.

- The NO_INDEX hint is used to disallow the optimizer from using the specified index.

- The INDEX_COMBINE hint causes the optimizer to merge multiple *bitmap* indexes for a single table instead of choosing which one is better (as in the INDEX hint).

- The INDEX_ASC does exactly what the INDEX hint does, since indexes are already scanned in ascending order. It is used to guarantee this to be true, as Oracle may change this default in the future.

- The INDEX_DESC processes an index in the descending order of how it was built. This hint will not be used if more than one table exists in the query.

- The INDEX_FFS processes *only* the index and does not take the result and access the table. All columns that are used and retrieved by the query *must* be contained in the index.

- The ORDERED hint is one of the most powerful hints provided. It processes the tables of the query in the order that they are listed in the FROM clause (the *first* table in the FROM is processed first). There are, however, many variations that cause this to work differently.

- The LEADING hint is used to specify a single table to drive a query with while allowing the optimizer to figure out the rest of the query. The ORDERED hint overrides LEADING.

- The NO_EXPAND hint prevents the optimizer from using OR expansion.

- The DRIVING_SITE hint is extremely powerful, as it will potentially limit the amount of information to be processed over your network. The table specified with the DRIVING_SITE hint will be the location for the join to be processed.

- Using views for remote tables can also lead to better performance by limiting the number of rows passed from the remote site *before* the records are sent to the local site.

- In a three or more table join, the USE_MERGE hint causes the table(s) specified in the hint to merge the resulting row set from a join to the other tables in the join.

- The USE_NL hint *usually* provides the best response time (first row comes back faster), whereas the USE_MERGE hint *usually* provides the best throughput.

- The PUSH_SUBQ hint can improve performance greatly when the subquery returns only a few rows very fast and those rows can be used to limit the rows returned in the outer query.

- The PARALLEL hint enables the use of parallel operations. If the degree is not specified with the hint, the default degree specified during the table creation is used.

- The use of the NO_PARALLEL hint disables parallel operations in a statement that would otherwise use parallel processing due to a parallel object definition.

- The APPEND hint inserts values into a table without checking the free space in the currently used blocks, but instead appending the data into new blocks.

- The CACHE hint should be used with small lookup tables that are often accessed by users. This ensures that the table remains in memory.

- The NOCACHE hint should be used to prevent caching a table specified with the CACHE option—basically, when you want to access the table but you *don't* want to cache it.

- The CLUSTER hint forces the use of a cluster scan to access the table(s). It is good to have clusters if the joined tables are frequently accessed but *not* frequently modified.

- Caution should be taken before implementing hash clusters. The application should be reviewed fully to ensure that enough information is known about the tables and data before implementing this option. Generally speaking, hashing is best for static data with primarily sequential values.

- The CURSOR_SHARING_EXACT hint overrides the instance-level setting of CURSOR_SHARING to either FORCE or SIMILAR.

References

Oracle10gR2 Performance Tuning Guide
Oracle10gR2 Reference
Performance Tuning Guide (Oracle Corporation)
Kevin Loney and Bob Bryla, *Oracle Database 10g DBA Handbook* (McGraw-Hill, 2005)
Rich Niemiec, *Tuning Tips: You Will Be Toast!* (presentation from www.tusc.com)

One final note from the "Oracle Database Sample Schemas 10g Release 1 (10.1) – Part No. B10771-01." During a complete installation of Oracle Database, the Sample Schemas can be installed automatically with the seed database. If for some reason the seed database is removed from your system, you will need to reinstall the Sample Schemas before you can duplicate the examples you find in Oracle documentation and training materials. Using DBCA is by far the most intuitive and simple way to install the Sample Schemas. During Step 9 of the database creation process, the check box "Example Schemas" needs to be checked for any Sample Schema to be created. DBCA installs all five schemas (HR, OE, PM, IX, SH) in your database. You can also create Sample Schemas manually by running SQL scripts, rather than using DBCA. The scripts are included in the companion directory on the installation medium. (Thanks to Janet Stern for this note.)

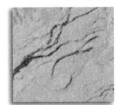

CHAPTER
8

Query Tuning:
Developer and
Beginner DBA

TIPS & COVERED

This chapter will focus on specific queries that you may encounter and some general information for tuning those specific queries, but it has also been updated to include some basic information on Oracle's 10g Automatic SQL Tuning and some queries to access Oracle's 10g Automatic Workload Repository (AWR). There are examples of query tuning spread throughout this book as well as instructions to make them more effective in terms of the architecture of your system. This chapter will focus on some of the most common queries that can be tuned on *most* systems. There are several variations in behavior that can be displayed by a query, depending on the architecture of the system, the distribution of data in the tables, the specific version of Oracle Database, and a variety of other exceptions to the rules. Your results will vary; use your own testing to come up with the most favorable performance.

This chapter will use strictly cost-based examples for timings (except where noted). No other queries were performed at the time of the tests in this chapter. Many hints are used throughout this chapter. For a detailed look at hints and the syntax and structure of hints, please refer to Chapter 7. Multiple table queries will be the focus of the next chapter and are not covered here.

Please note that this is not an all-inclusive chapter. There are many other queries throughout the book, which need to be investigated when trying to increase performance for a given query. Some of the most dramatic include using the parallel features of Oracle Database (Chapter 11), using partitioned tables and indexes (Chapter 3), and using PL/SQL to improve performance (Chapter 10). Note the benefits of using EXPLAIN and TRACE for queries (Chapter 6). Oracle Database 10g provides the Automatic Workload Repository (AWR) and Automatic Database Diagnostic Monitor (ADDM). The Enterprise Manager views of these new features are shown in Chapter 5. Tips covered in this chapter include the following:

- What queries do I tune? Querying the V$SQLAREA and V$SQL views
- Some useful new 10g views for locating resource-intensive sessions and queries
- When an index should be used
- What if I forget the index?
- Creating and checking an index
- What if you create a bad index?
- Dropping an index and caution to be exercised
- Increasing performance by indexing the SELECT and WHERE columns
- Use the Fast Full Scan feature to guarantee success
- Making queries "magically" faster
- Caching a table into memory
- Choosing between multiple indexes on a table (use the most selective)
- Indexes that get suppressed
- Using the EXISTS clause and the nested subquery

- That table is a view!
- SQL and the Grand Unified Theory

What Queries Do I Tune? Querying V$SQLAREA

V$SQLAREA and V$SQL are great views that can be queried to find the worst-performing SQL statements that need optimization. The value in the disk_reads column signifies the volume of disk reads that are being performed on the system. This, combined with the executions (disk_reads/executions), returns the SQL statements that have the most disk hits per statement execution. Any statement that makes the top of this list is most likely a problem query that needs to be tuned. Statspack also lists the resource-intensive queries; see Chapter 14 for detailed information.

Selecting from the V$SQLAREA View to Find the Worst Queries

The following query can be used to fix the worst queries existing in your database. This query alone is worth the price of this book if you've not heard of V$SQLAREA yet.

```
select      b.username username, a.disk_reads reads,
            a.executions exec, a.disk_reads /decode
            (a.executions, 0, 1,a.executions) rds_exec_ratio,
            a.sql_text Statement
from        V$sqlarea a, dba_users b
where       a.parsing_user_id = b.user_id
and         a.disk_reads > 100000
order       by a.disk_reads desc;


USERNAME    READS EXEC RDS_EXEC_RATIO STATEMENT
--------    ------- ---- -------------- ---------------- ----
ADHOC1      7281934    1       7201934 select custno, ordno
from cust, orders


ADHOC5      4230044    4       1057511 select ordno
from orders where trunc(ordno) = 721305


ADHOC1      801716     2        400858 select custno,
ordno from cust where substr(custno,1,6) = '314159'
```

The disk_reads column in the preceding statement can be replaced with the buffer_gets column, to provide information on SQL statements requiring the largest amount of memory.

TIP
Query V$SQLAREA to find your problem queries that need to be tuned.

Selecting from the V$SQL View to Find the Worst Queries

Querying V$SQL allows us to see the shared SQL area statements individually versus grouped together (as V$SQLAREA does). Here is a faster query to get the top statements from V$SQL (this query can also access V$SQLAREA by only changing the view name):

```
select * from
  (select address,
   rank() over ( order by buffer_gets desc ) as rank_bufgets,
    to_char(100 * ratio_to_report(buffer_gets) over (), '999.99') pct_bufgets
from   V$sql )
where  rank_bufgets < 11;


ADDRESS  RANK_BUFGETS PCT_BUF
-------- ------------ -------
131B7914            1   66.36
131ADA6C            2   24.57
131BC16C            3    1.97
13359B54            4     .98
1329ED20            5     .71
132C7374            5     .71
12E966B4            7     .52
131A3CDC            8     .48
131947C4            9     .48
1335BE14           10     .48
1335CE44           10     .48
```

You can alternatively select sql_text instead of address if you want to see the SQL:

```
COL SQL_TEXT FOR A50
select * from
  (select sql_text,
   rank() over ( order by buffer_gets desc ) as rank_bufgets,
    to_char(100 * ratio_to_report(buffer_gets) over (), '999.99') pct_bufgets
from   V$sql )
where  rank_bufgets < 11;
```

TIP
You can also query V$SQL to find your problem queries that need to be tuned.

New 10g Views for Locating Resource-Intensive Sessions and Queries

Oracle 10g provides many new views giving access to a wealth of information from the OS (Operating System) and the Automatic Workload Repository (AWR). The AWR provides metric-based information, which is useful for monitoring and diagnosing performance issues. Metrics are "a set of statistics for certain system attributes as defined by Oracle." Essentially, they are context defined statistics that are collated into historical information within the AWR.

Accessing the AWR and ADDM information via the DBCONSOLE and Enterprise Manager Grid Control are covered in Chapter 5 as well as in the Oracle documentation. In this section, we will only be looking at pulling some specific information out of these views using SQL to locate queries that may need tuning.

Selecting from V$SESSMETRIC to Find Current Resource-Intensive Sessions

This query shows the sessions that are heaviest in physical reads, CPU usage, or logical reads over a defined interval (15 seconds by default). You may want to adjust the thresholds as appropriate for your environment.

```
select
TO_CHAR(m.end_time,'DD-MON-YYYY HH24:MI:SS') e_dttm,       -- Interval End Time
m.intsize_csec/100 ints,                       -- Interval size in sec
s.username usr,
m.session_id sid,
m.session_serial_num ssn,
ROUND(m.cpu) cpu100,                            -- CPU usage 100th sec
m.physical_reads prds,                          -- Number of physical reads
m.logical_reads lrds,                           -- Number of logical reads
m.pga_memory pga,                               -- PGA size at end of interval
m.hard_parses hp,
m.soft_parses sp,
m.physical_read_pct prp,
m.logical_read_pct lrp,
s.sql_id
from v$sessmetric m, v$session s
where (m.physical_reads > 100
or     m.cpu > 100
or     m.logical_reads > 100)
and    m.session_id = s.sid
and    m.session_serial_num = s.serial#
order by m.physical_reads DESC, m.cpu DESC, m.logical_reads DESC;


E_DTTM               INTS USR SID SSN  CPU100 PRDS  LRDS PGA     HP SP PRP
LRP        SQL_ID
-------------------- ---- --- --- ---- ------ ----- ---- ------ -- -- ---
---------- --------------
20-NOV-2005 00:11:07  15  RIC 146 1501   1758 41348    1 781908  0  0 100
.512820513 03ay719wdnqz1
```

Viewing Available AWR Snapshots

The next few queries will be accessing AWR snapshot information. The DBA_HIST_SNAPSHOT view may be queried to find more information about specific AWR snapshots.

```
select snap_id,
       TO_CHAR(begin_interval_time,'DD-MON-YYYY HH24:MI:SS') b_dttm,
       TO_CHAR(end_interval_time,'DD-MON-YYYY HH24:MI:SS') e_dttm
```

```
from    dba_hist_snapshot
where   begin_interval_time > TRUNC(SYSDATE);

SNAP_ID                      B_DTTM      E_DTTM
----------------------       ----------- --------
36    19-NOV-2005 19:27:03 19-NOV-2005 19:37:25
37    19-NOV-2005 19:37:25 19-NOV-2005 21:00:39
38    19-NOV-2005 21:00:39 19-NOV-2005 22:01:01
39    19-NOV-2005 22:01:01 19-NOV-2005 23:00:28
```

Selecting from the DBA_HIST_SQLSTAT View to Find the Worst Queries

SQL statements that have exceeded predefined thresholds are kept in the AWR for a predefined time (seven days by default). You can query the DBA_HIST_SQLSTAT view to find the worst queries. The equivalent statement to the V$SQLAREA query earlier in this chapter is:

```
select snap_id, disk_reads_delta reads_delta,
       executions_delta exec_delta, disk_reads_delta /decode
       (executions_delta, 0, 1,executions_delta) rds_exec_ratio,
       sql_id
from   dba_hist_sqlstat
where  disk_reads_delta > 100000
order  by disk_reads_delta desc;

SNAP_ID READS_DELTA EXEC_DELTA RDS_EXEC_RATIO     SQL_ID
------- ----------- ---------- --------------  -------------
     38     9743276          0        9743276  03ay719wdnqz1
     39     9566692          0        9566692  03ay719wdnqz1
     37     7725091          1        7725091  03ay719wdnqz1
```

Note that the same sql_id appears in three different AWR snapshots. (In this case, it was executed during the first one and is still running). You could also choose to filter on other criteria, including cumulative or delta values for disk_reads, buffer_gets, rows_processed, cpu_time, elapsed_time, iowait, clwait (cluster wait), etc. Run a DESC command of the view dba_hist_sqlstat to get a full list of its columns.

Selecting Query Text from the dba_hist_sqlstat View

The query text for the offending queries retrieved by the previous select statement may be obtained from the dba_hist_sqltext view with the following query:

```
select command_type,sql_text
from   dba_hist_sqltext
where  sql_id='03ay719wdnqz1';

COMMAND_TYPE    SQL_TEXT
------------    -------------------------
         3      select count(1) from t2, t2
```

Selecting Query Explain Plan from the DBA_HIST_SQL_PLAN View

The explain plan for the offending SQL is also captured. You may view information about the execution plan through the DBA_HIST_SQL_PLAN TABLE. If you want to display the explain plan, the simplest way is to use the DBMS_XPLAN package with a statement such as this one:

```
select *
from   table(DBMS_XPLAN.DISPLAY_AWR('03ay719wdnqz1'));

PLAN_TABLE_OUTPUT
-----------------------------------------------------------------------------------
-----------------------------------------------------------------------------------

SQL_ID 03ay719wdnqz1
--------------------
select count(1) from t2, t2

Plan hash value: 1163428054
-----------------------------------------------------------------------------------
| Id | Operation             | Name  | Rows  | Cost (%CPU)| Time      |
-----------------------------------------------------------------------------------
|  0 | SELECT STATEMENT      |       |       | 10G(100)  |           |
|  1 | SORT AGGREGATE        |       |     1 |           |           |
|  2 | MERGE JOIN CARTESIAN  |       | 6810G | 10G (2)   |999:59:59  |
|  3 | INDEX FAST FULL SCAN  | T2_I1 | 2609K | 3996 (2)  | 00:00:48  |
|  4 | BUFFER SORT           |       | 2609K | 10G (2)   |999:59:59  |
|  5 | INDEX FAST FULL SCAN  | T2_I1 | 2609K | 3994 (2)  | 00:00:48  |
-----------------------------------------------------------------------------------
```

As can be seen, this particular query is a Cartesian join. This is normally not a valid table join and can lead to the massive resource consumption observed. This query was used to show how to take advantage of some of the new 10g functionality for identifying and collecting information about poorly performing SQL.

When Should an Index Be Used?

In Oracle version 5, many DBAs called the indexing rule the 80/20 Rule; you needed to use an index if less than 20 percent of the rows were being returned by a query. In version 7, this number was reduced to about 7 percent on average, and in versions 8i and 9i, the number is closer to 4 percent. In version 10, Oracle is better at retrieving the entire table, so the value continues to be in the 5 percent range, although it depends not only on the number of rows but on how the blocks are distributed as well (see Chapter 2 for additional information). Figure 8-1 shows when an index should generally be used (in V5 and V6 for rule-based optimization and in V7, V8i, V9i, and V10g for cost-based optimization). However, based on the distribution of data, parallel query or partitioning can be used and other factors need to be considered. In Chapter 9, you will see how to make this graph for your own queries. If the table has fewer than 1000 records (small tables), then the graph is also different. For small tables, Oracle's cost-based optimizer will generally use the index when only less than 1 percent of the table is queried. This graph shows you the progress of Oracle. The lower the percentage of rows returned, the more likely you would use an index. This shows the speed of a full table scan becoming faster. Because of the many variables with Oracle 9*i*, the graph could continue to go down as the trend is showing from V5 to V8*i*, or it could go up slightly, depending on how you architect the database. Oracle 9*i* and Oracle 10*g* make you creator of where the graph goes; your choice may depend on how the data and indexes are architected, how the data is distributed within the blocks, and how it is accessed.

> **TIP**
> *When a small number of rows ("small" is version dependent) are to be returned to meet a condition in a query, you generally want to use an index on that condition (column), given that the small number of rows also returns a small number of individual blocks (usually the case).*

What Happens When I Forget the Index?

While it seems obvious that columns, which are generally restrictive, require indexes, it is not always such common knowledge. I once went to a job where they were from suffering incredibly poor performance. When I asked for a list of tables and indexes, they replied, "We have a list of tables, but we haven't figured out what indexes are yet and if we should use them—do you think you can help our performance." My first thought was "Wow, can I ever—my dream tuning job." My second thought was that I had been training experts too long and had forgotten that not everyone is as far along in their performance education. While basic index principles and structure are covered in Chapter 2, this section will focus on query-related issues surrounding indexes.

Even if you have built indexes correctly for most columns needing them, you may miss a crucial column here and there. If you forget to put an index on a column that is restrictive, then the speed of those queries will not be optimized. Consider the following example where the percent of rows returned by any given CUST_ID is less than 1 percent. Under these circumstances,

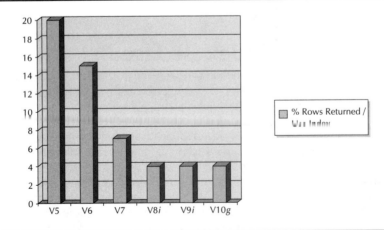

FIGURE 8-1. *When to generally use an index based on the percentage of rows returned by a query*

an index on the CUST _ID column should normally be implemented. The next query does *not* have an index on CUST_ID:

```
select count(*)
from    sales2
where   cust_id = 22340;


  COUNT(*)
----------
     25750


Elapsed: 00:04:47.00 (4 minutes, 47 seconds)

Execution Plan
------------------------------------------------------------
   0       SELECT STATEMENT Optimizer=CHOOSE
   1    0    SORT (AGGREGATE)
   2    1      TABLE ACCESS (FULL) OF 'SALES2'

121,923 consistent gets (memory reads)
121,904 physical reads (disk reads)
```

Not only is the query extremely slow (5000 times slower than using an index), but it also uses a tremendous amount of memory and CPU to perform the query. This results in an impatient user and a frustrating wait for other users due to the lack of system resources. (Sound familiar?)

Creating an Index

To accelerate the query in the last example, I build an index on the CUST_ID column. The storage clause must be based on the size of the table and the column. The table is over 25 million rows (the space for the index is about 461M). If you specify automatic segment-space management for the underlying tablespace, this allows Oracle to automatically manage segment space for best performance. I could also perform an alter session set sort_area_size=500000000 (if I had the OS memory needed) and the index creation would be much faster.

```
create index sales2_idx1 on sales2(cust_id)
tablespace rich
storage (initial 400M next 10M pctincrease 0);
Index Created.
```

Check the Index on a Table

Before creating indexes, check for current indexes that exist on that table to ensure there will not be conflicts. Once you have created the index, verify that it exists by querying the DBA_IND_COLUMNS view, as shown here.

```
select    table_name, index_name, column_name, column_position
from      dba_ind_columns
where     table_name = 'SALES2'
```

```
and        table_owner = 'SH'
order      by index_name, column_position;

TABLE_NAME INDEX_NAME_ COLUMN_NAME COLUMN_POSITION
---------- ----------- ----------- ---------------
SALES2     SALES2_IDX1 CUST_ID                   1
```

The table_name is the table that is being indexed, the index_name is the name of the index, the column_name is the column being indexed, and the column_position is the order of the columns in a multipart index. Since our index involves only one column, the column_position is '1' (CUST_ID is the first and only column in the index). In the concatenated index section (later in this chapter), we will see how a multipart index will appear.

Rerun the same query now that the CUST_ID column is properly indexed. The query is dramatically faster, and more important, it will no longer "flood" the system with a tremendous amount of data to the SGA (low number of memory reads) and subsequently reduce the physical reads.

```
select  count(*)
from    sales2
where   cust_id = 22340;

  COUNT(*)
----------
     25750

Elapsed: 00:00:00.06 (0.06 seconds)

Execution Plan
-----------------------------------------------------------
    0       SELECT STATEMENT Optimizer=CHOOSE
    1    0    SORT (AGGREGATE)
    2    1      INDEX (RANGE SCAN) OF 'SALES_IDX' (NON-UNIQUE)

89 consistent gets (memory reads)
64 physical reads (disk reads)
```

TIP
The first tip concerning slow queries is that you'll have a lot of them if you don't index columns that are restrictive (return a small percentage of the table). Building indexes on restrictive columns is the first step toward better system performance.

What If I Create a Bad Index?

In the PRODUCT table, I also have a company_no column. Since this company's expansion has not occurred, all rows in the table have a company_no = 1. What if I am a beginner and I have heard that indexes are good, and have decided to index the company_no column?

The cost-based optimizer will analyze the index as bad and will suppress it. The table *must* be reanalyzed after the index is created for the cost-based optimizer to make the informed choice. The index created on company_no is correctly suppressed by Oracle internally (since it would access the entire table and index):

```
select      product_id, qty
from        product
where       company_no = 1;

Elapsed time: 405 seconds (all records are retrieved via a full table scan)

OPERATION                  OPTIONS              OBJECT NAME
------------------         --------------       -----------
SELECT STATEMENT
TABLE ACCESS               FULL                 PRODUCT

49,825 consistent gets (memory reads)
41,562 physical reads (disk reads)
```

An originally suppressed index can be forced to be used (bad choice), as follows:

```
select      /*+ index(product company_idx1) */ product_id, qty
from        product
where       company_no = 1;

Elapsed time: 725 seconds   (all records retrieved using the index on company_no)

OPERATION                  OPTIONS              OBJECT NAME
------------------         --------------       -----------
SELECT STATEMENT
TABLE ACCESS               BY ROWID             PRODUCT
     INDEX                 RANGE SCAN           COMPANY_IDX1

4,626,725 consistent gets (memory reads)
80,513 physical reads (disk reads)
```

Indexes can also be suppressed when they cause poorer performance by using the FULL hint:

```
select      /*+ FULL(PRODUCT) */ product_id, qty
from        product
where       company_no = 1;

Elapsed time: 405 seconds (all records are retrieved via a full table scan)

OPERATION                  OPTIONS              OBJECT NAME
------------------         --------------       -----------
SELECT STATEMENT
TABLE ACCESS               FULL                 PRODUCT

49,825 consistent gets (memory reads)
41,562 physical reads (disk reads)
```

TIP
Bad indexes (indexing the wrong columns) can cause as much trouble as forgetting to use indexes on the correct columns. While Oracle's cost-based optimizer generally suppresses poor indexes, problems can still develop when a bad index is used at the same time as a good index.

Caution Should Be Exercised When Dropping Indexes

For some people, their first reaction when they find a query that is using a poor index is to drop the index. Suppressing the index should be the first reaction, and investigating the impact of the index on other queries should be the next action. Unless your query was the only one being performed against the given table, changing/dropping an index might be a detrimental solution. The next section will investigate indexing columns that are both in the SELECT and WHERE clauses of the query.

Indexing the Columns Used in the SELECT and WHERE

The preceding section described how dropping an index can hurt performance for a query. Consider the following query where the index was created to help. I build a million-row employees table from the famous scott.emp table. This query does not have indexed columns:

```
select  ename
from    employees
where   deptno = 10;

Elapsed time: 55 seconds (a full table scan is performed)

OPERATION              OPTIONS           OBJECT NAME
-----------------      --------------    -----------
SELECT STATEMENT
TABLE ACCESS           FULL              EMPLOYEES
```

First, we place an index on the deptno column to try to improve performance:

```
Create index dept_idx1 on employees (deptno)
Tablespace test1
Storage (initial 20M next 5M pctincrease 0);

select    ename
from      employees
where     deptno = 10;

Elapsed time: 70 seconds (the index on deptno is used but made things worse)

OPERATION              OPTIONS           OBJECT NAME
-----------------      --------------    -----------
SELECT STATEMENT
TABLE ACCESS           BY INDEX ROWID    EMPLOYEES
      INDEX            RANGE SCAN        DEPT_IDX1
```

This situation is now worse. In this query, only the ename is selected. If this is a crucial query on the system, choose to index both the SELECT and the WHERE columns. By doing this, a concatenated index is created:

```
Drop index dept_idx1;

Create index emp_idx1 on employees (deptno, ename)
Tablespace test1
Storage (initial 20M next 5M pctincrease 0);
```

The query is now tremendously faster:

```
select     ename
from       employees
where      deptno = 10;
```

Elapsed time: Less than 1 second (the index on deptno AND ename is used)

```
OPERATION                 OPTIONS        OBJECT NAME
------------------        ----------     -----------
SELECT STATEMENT
INDEX                     RANGE SCAN     EMP_IDX1
```

The table itself did not have to be accessed, which increases the speed of the query. Indexing both the column in the SELECT clause and the column in the WHERE clause allows the query to only access the index.

TIP
For crucial queries on your system, consider concatenated indexes on the columns contained in both the SELECT and the WHERE clauses so that only the index is accessed.

The Fast Full Scan

The preceding section demonstrated that if we index both the SELECT and the WHERE columns, the query is much faster. Oracle does not guarantee that only the index will be used under these circumstances. However, there is a hint that guarantees that only the index will be used under these circumstances. The INDEX_FFS hint is a fast full scan of the index. This hint will access only the index and not the corresponding table. Using the query from the preceding section with the index on emp_name and dept_no yields the following:

```
select     /*+ index_ffs(employees emp_idx1) */ ename
from       employees
where      deptno = 10;
```

Elapsed time: Less than 1 second (only the index is accessed)

```
OPERATION                 OPTIONS        OBJECT NAME
------------------        ----------     -----------
SELECT STATEMENT
INDEX                     RANGE SCAN     EMP_IDX1
```

The query is now guaranteed to only access the index. Also note, however, that sometimes your queries will scan the ENTIRE index, which is often not as good, so be careful.

The Fast Full Scan

TIP
The INDEX_FFS (available since Oracle 8) will process only the index and will not access the table. All columns that are used and retrieved by the query must be contained in the index.

A "Magically" Faster Query

Consider the following query from the last example in which the user adds a hint called "richs_secret_hint." The user overheard a conversation about this hint at a recent user group and believes this hint (buried deep in the X$ tables) is the hidden secret to tuning. First, the query is run and no index can be used:

```
select     ename, job
from       employees
where      deptno = 10
and        ename = 'ADAMS';

Elapsed time: 50 seconds (one record is retrieved in this query)

OPERATION                 OPTIONS        OBJECT NAME
-----------------         ----------     -----------
SELECT STATEMENT
TABLE ACCESS              FULL           EMPLOYEES
```

There is *no* index that can be used on this query. A full table scan is performed.
The user now adds Rich's secret hint to the query:

```
select     /*+ richs_secret_hint */ ename, job
from       employees
where      deptno = 10
and        ename = 'ADAMS';

Elapsed time: 3 seconds (one record is retrieved in this query)

OPERATION                 OPTIONS        OBJECT NAME
-----------------         ----------     -----------
SELECT STATEMENT
TABLE ACCESS              FULL           EMPLOYEES
```

The hint worked and the query is "magically" faster, although a full table scan was still performed. Actually, the data is now stored in memory and querying the data from memory is now much faster than going to disk for the data—so much for the magic!

TIP
When a query is run multiple times in succession, it becomes faster, since you have now cached the data in memory (although full table scans are aged out of memory quicker than indexed scans). At times, people are tricked into believing that they have made a query faster, when in actuality they are accessing data stored in memory.

Caching a Table in Memory

While it is disappointing that there is no "secret hint" for tuning, we can use the last section to learn, and we can use this knowledge to our advantage. In the last section, the query ran faster the second time because it was cached in memory. What if the tables used most often were cached in memory all the time? Well, the first problem is that if we cannot cache every table in memory, we must focus on the smaller and more often used tables to be cached. We can also use multiple buffer pools as discussed in Chapter 4. The following query is an unindexed customer table to return one of the rows:

```
select      cust_no, name
from        customer
where       cust_no = 1;
```

Elapsed time: 5 seconds (one record is retrieved in this query without an index)

```
OPERATION                OPTIONS        OBJECT NAME
-----------------        ----------     -----------
SELECT STATEMENT
TABLE ACCESS             FULL           CUSTOMER
```

The database is then stopped and restarted so as to not influence the timing statistics. The table is altered to cache the records:

```
Alter table customer cache;
```

Table altered.

Query the unindexed but now cached customer table to return one of the rows:

```
select      cust_no, name
from        customer
where       cust_no = 1;
```

Elapsed time: 5 seconds (one record is retrieved in this query without an index)

```
OPERATION                OPTIONS        OBJECT NAME
-----------------        ----------     -----------
SELECT STATEMENT
TABLE ACCESS             FULL           CUSTOMER
```

Still five seconds? The table has been altered to be cached, but the data is not in memory yet. Every subsequent query will now be faster. I query the unindexed (but now cached) customer table to return one of the rows:

```
select      cust_no, name
from        customer
where       cust_no = 1;
```

Elapsed time: 1 second (one record is retrieved in this query without an index)

```
OPERATION              OPTIONS      OBJECT NAME
-------------------    ----------   -----------
SELECT STATEMENT
TABLE ACCESS           FULL         CUSTOMER
```

The query is faster because the table is now cached in memory; in fact, all queries to this table are now fast regardless of the condition used. A cached table is "pinned" into memory and will be placed at the "most recently used" end of the cache; it will be pushed out of memory only after other full table scans to tables that are not cached are pushed out. Running a query multiple times places the data in memory so that subsequent queries are faster—only caching a table will ensure that the data is not later pushed out of memory.

TIP
Caching an often-used but relatively small table into memory will ensure that the data is not pushed out of memory by other data. Also, be careful—cached tables can alter the execution path normally chosen by the optimizer, leading to an unexpected execution order for the query (it can affect the driving table in nested loop joins).

Using Multiple Indexes (Use the Most Selective)

Having multiple indexes on a table can cause problems when you execute a query where there are choices that include using more than one of the indexes. The optimizer will almost always choose correctly. Consider the following example where the percent of rows returned by any given product_id is less than 1 percent where the data is equally distributed between the blocks. Under these circumstances, place an index on the product_id column. The following query has a single index on product_id:

```
select     product_id, qty
from       product
where      company_no = 1
and        product_id = 167;

Elapsed time: 1 second (one record is retrieved; the index on product_id is used)

OPERATION              OPTIONS      OBJECT NAME
-------------------    ----------   -----------
SELECT STATEMENT
TABLE ACCESS           BY ROWID     PRODUCT
     INDEX             RANGE SCAN   PROD_IDX1

107 consistent gets (memory reads)
1 physical reads (disk reads)
```

Now create an additional index on the company_no column. In this example, all of the records have a company_no =1, an extremely poor index. Rerun the query with both indexes (one on product_id and one on company_no) existing on the table.

```
select     product_id, qty
from       product
where      company_no = 1
and        product_id = 167;
```

Elapsed time: 725 seconds (one record is returned; a full table scan is performed)

```
OPERATION               OPTIONS        OBJECT NAME
-----------------       ----------     -----------
SELECT STATEMENT
TABLE ACCESS            FULL           PRODUCT
```

4,626,725 consistent gets (memory reads)
80,513 physical reads (disk reads)

Oracle has chosen not to use either of the two indexes (perhaps because of a multiblock initialization parameter), and the query performed a full table scan. Depending on the statistical data stored and version of Oracle used, I have seen this same query use the right index, the wrong index, no index at all, or a merge of both indexes. The correct choice is to force the use of the correct index. The correct index is the most restrictive. Rewrite the query to force the use of the most restrictive index, as follows, or better yet, fix the real initialization parameter issue.

```
select     /*+ index(product prod_idx1) */ product_id, qty
from       product
where      company_no = 1
and        product_id = 167;
```

Elapsed time: 1 second (one record is retrieved)

```
OPERATION               OPTIONS        OBJECT NAME
-----------------       ----------     -----------
SELECT STATEMENT
TABLE ACCESS            BY ROWID       PRODUCT
    INDEX               RANGE SCAN     PROD_IDX1
```

107 consistent gets (memory reads)
1 physical reads (disk reads)

TIP

When multiple indexes on a single table can be used for a query, use the most restrictive index when you need to override an optimizer choice. While Oracle's cost-based optimizer will generally force the use of the most restrictive index, variations will occur, depending on the version of Oracle used, the structure of the query, and the initialization parameters that you may use. Fix the larger issue if you see this as a trend.

TIP

Bitmap indexes will usually behave differently, since they will usually be much smaller. See Chapter 2 for more information on the differences.

Using Multiple Indexes (Use the Most Selective)

The Index Merge

The index merge feature of Oracle allows you to merge two separate indexes and use the result of the indexes instead of going to the table from one of the indexes. Consider the following example: The following statistics are based on 1,000,000 records. The table is 210MB.

```
create   index year_idx on test2 (year);
create   index state_idx on test2 (state);

select   /*+ rule index(test2) */ state, year
from     test2
where    year = '1972'
and      state = 'MA'

SELECT STATEMENT Optimizer=HINT: RULE
   TABLE ACCESS (BY INDEX ROWID) OF 'TEST2'
      INDEX (RANGE SCAN) OF 'STATE_IDX' (NON-UNIQUE)

Elapsed time: 23.50 seconds

select   /*+ index_join(test2 year_idx state_idx) */
         state, year
from     test2
where    year = '1972'
and      state = 'MA'

SELECT STATEMENT Optimizer=CHOOSE
   VIEW OF 'index$_join$_001'
      HASH JOIN
         INDEX (RANGE SCAN) OF 'YEAR_IDX' (NON-UNIQUE)
         INDEX (RANGE SCAN) OF 'STATE_IDX' (NON-UNIQUE)

Elapsed time: 4.76 seconds
```

In the first query, we test the speed of using just one of the indexes and then going back to the table (under certain scenarios, Oracle will tune this with an AND-EQUAL operation to access data from the indexes). We then use the INDEX_JOIN hint to force the merge of two separate indexes and use the result of the indexes instead of going back to the table. When the indexes are both small compared to the size of the table, this can lead to better performance.

Indexes That Get Suppressed

Building the perfect system with all of the correctly indexed columns does not guarantee success in the performance of the system. With the prevalence In business of the bright-eyed ad hoc query user comes a variety of tuning challenges. One of the most common is the suppression of perfectly good indexes. Any modification of the column side of a WHERE clause will result in the suppression of that index (unless function-based indexes are utilized). Alternative methods for writing the same query do not modify the column that is indexed. A couple of those examples are listed next.

A math function is performed on the column

```
select   product_id, qty
from     product
where    product_id+12 = 166;
```

```
Elapsed time: 405 second

OPERATION              OPTIONS        OBJECT NAME
---------------        -------        -----------
SELECT STATEMENT
TABLE ACCESS           FULL           PRODUCT
```

The math function is performed on the other side of the clause

```
select     product_id, qty
from       product
where      product_id = 154;

Elapsed time: 1 second

OPERATION              OPTIONS        OBJECT NAME
---------------        -------        -----------
SELECT STATEMENT
TABLE ACCESS           BY ROWID       PRODUCT
      INDEX            RANGE SCAN     PROD_IDX1
```

A function is performed on the column

```
select     product_id, qty
from       product
where      substr(product_id,1,1) = 1;

Elapsed time: 405 second

OPERATION              OPTIONS        OBJECT NAME
---------------        -------        -----------
SELECT STATEMENT
TABLE ACCESS           FULL           PRODUCT
```

The function is rewritten so that the column is not altered

```
select     product_id, qty
from       product
where      product_id like '1%';

Elapsed time: 1 second

OPERATION              OPTIONS        OBJECT NAME
---------------        ----------     -----------
SELECT STATEMENT
TABLE ACCESS           BY ROWID       PRODUCT
      INDEX            RANGE SCAN     PROD_IDX1
```

TIP
*Any modification to the column side of the query results in the
suppression of the index unless a function-based index is used.*

Function-Based Indexes

One of the largest problems with indexes, as seen in the previous section, is that indexes are often suppressed by developers and ad hoc users. Developers using functions often suppress indexes. There is a way to combat this problem. Function-based indexes allow you to create an index based on a function or expression. The value of the function or expression is specified by the person creating the index and is stored in the index. Function-based indexes can involve multiple columns, arithmetic expressions, or maybe a PL/SQL function or C callout. The following example shows how to create a function-based index.

```
CREATE INDEX emp_idx ON emp (UPPER(ename));
```

An index that uses the UPPER function has been created on the ename column. The following example queries the EMP table using the function-based index:

```
select ename, job, deptno
from   emp
where  upper(ename) = 'ELLISON';
```

The function-based index (emp_idx) can be used for this query. For large tables where the condition retrieves a small amount of records, the query yields substantial performance gains over a full table scan. See Chapter 2 for additional details and examples.

The following initialization parameters must be set (subject to change with each version) to use function-based indexes (the optimization mode must be cost-based as well). When a function-based index is not working, this is often the problem.

```
query_rewrite_enabled = true
query_rewrite_integrity = trusted (or enforced)
```

TIP
Function-based indexes can lead to dramatic performance gains when used to create indexes on functions often used on selective columns in the WHERE clause.

To check the details for function based indexes on a table, you may use a query similar to this.

```
select table_name, index_name, column_expression
from   dba_ind_expressions
where  table_name = 'SALES2'
and    table_owner = 'SH'
order  by index_name, column_position;
```

The "Curious" OR

It seems that the cost-based optimizer often has problems when the OR clause is used. The best way to think of the OR clause is as multiple queries that are then merged. Consider the following example where there is a single primary key on col1, col2, and col3. Prior to Oracle 9*i*, the Oracle Database performed this query in the following way:

```
select *
from    table_test
where   pk_col1 = 'A'
and     pk_col2 in ('B', 'C')
and     pk_col3 = 'D';


2       Table Access By Rowid TABLE_TEST
1       Index Range Scan TAB_PK
```

NOTE
pk_col2 and pk_col3 were not used for the index access.

Since Oracle 9*i*, Oracle improved how the optimizer handles this query (internally performing an OR-expansion). In Oracle 10*g*, the optimizer uses the full primary key and concatenates the results (as shown next), which is much faster than using only part of the primary key (as in the preceding access path). Even though the access path for preceding query looks better because there are less lines, don't be tricked, less lines in the explain plan doesn't mean a more efficient query.

```
5 Concatenation
2   Table Access By Rowid TAB
1   Index Unique Scan TAB_PK
4   Table Access By Rowid TAB
3   Index Unique Scan TAB_PK
```

To get this desired result prior to 9*i*, you would have needed to break up the query as shown here:

```
select *
from    table_test
where   (pk_col1 = 'A'
and      pk_col2 = 'B'
and      pk_col3 = 'D')
or       (pk_col1 = 'A'
and      pk_col2 = 'C'
and      pk_col3 = 'D');


5   Concatenation
2   Table Access By Rowid TAB
1   Index Unique Scan TAB_PK
4   Table Access By Rowid TAB
3   Index Unique Scan TAB_PK
```

TIP
Oracle has improved the way that it performs the OR clause. The NO_EXPAND hint can still be helpful, as it prevents the optimizer from using OR expansion, as described in Chapter 7.

The "Curious" OR

The EXISTS Function

Another helpful tip to remember is to use the EXISTS function instead of the IN function in most circumstances. The EXISTS function checks to find a single matching row to return the result in a subquery. Because the IN function retrieves and checks all rows, it is slower. Oracle has also improved the optimizer so that it will often perform this optimization for you as well. Consider the following example, where the IN function leads to very poor performance. This query is faster only if the ITEMS table is extremely small:

```
select     product_id, qty
from       product
where      product_id = 167
and        item_no in
(select    item_no
from       items);

Elapsed time: 25 minutes (The items table is 10 million rows)

OPERATION                OPTIONS         OBJECT NAME
------------------       ----------      -----------
SELECT STATEMENT
NESTED LOOPS SEMI
   TABLE ACCESS          BY ROWID        PRODUCT
      INDEX              RANGE SCAN      PROD_IDX1
      SORT
         TABLE ACCESS    FULL            ITEMS
```

In this query, the entire items table is retrieved.

This query is faster when the condition PRODUCT_ID = 167 substantially limits the outside query:

```
select     product_id, qty
from       product a
where      product_id = 167
and        exists
  (select  'x'
   from    items b
   where   b.item_no = a.item_no);

Elapsed time: 2 seconds (The items table query search is limited to 3 rows)

OPERATION                OPTIONS         OBJECT NAME
------------------       ----------      -----------
SELECT STATEMENT
  NESTED LOOPS SEMI
    TABLE ACCESS         BY ROWID        PRODUCT
       INDEX             RANGE SCAN      PROD_IDX1
       INDEX             RANGE SCAN      ITEM_IDX1
```

In this query, only the records retrieved in the outer query (from the PRODUCT table) are checked against the ITEMS table. This query can be substantially faster than the first query if the item_no in the ITEMS table is indexed or if the ITEMS table is very large, yet the items are limited by the condition product_id = 167 in the outer query.

TIP
Using the nested subquery with an EXISTS clause may make queries dramatically faster, depending on the data being retrieved from each part of the query. Oracle 9i provided a much-improved optimizer that will often perform some semblance of this transformation for you. Oracle 10g is even better!

That Table Is Actually a View!

Views can hide the complexity of SQL but can add to the complexity of optimization. When looking at a SELECT statement, unless there is some kind of naming convention for views, you cannot tell if an object is a table or a view from the SELECT statement alone. You must examine the object in the database to tell the difference. Views can join multiple tables. Be careful about joining views or using a view designed for one purpose for a different purpose, or you may pay a heavy performance price. Ensure that all tables involved in the view are actually required by your query.

SQL and Grand Unified Theory

Many physicists have searched for a single theory that explains all aspects of how the universe works. Many theories postulated have worked well in certain circumstances and break down in others. This is fine for theoretical physics, but it can spell disaster in a database. When writing SQL, one should not attempt to write the "Grand Unified SQL" statement that will do all tasks, depending on the arguments passed to it. This typically results in suboptimal performance for most tasks performed by the statement. It is better to write separate, highly efficient statements for each task that needs to be performed.

Tuning Changes in Oracle Database 10g

The general SQL tuning principles remain the same in 10g, but there are some significant optimizer changes that should be noted.

- The RULE optimizer_mode has been deprecated in 10g. (The only way to get rule-based behavior in 10g is by using the RULE hint in a query). In general, this is not recommended, but for individual queries that need it, it is there.

- There are two modes for the cost-based optimizer in 10g—NORMAL and TUNING:

  - In the NORMAL mode of the cost-based optimizer, the CBO considers a very small subset of possible execution plans to determine which one to choose. The number of plans considered is far smaller than in 9i in order to keep the time to generate the execution plan within strict limits. SQL profiles can be used to influence which plans are considered.

  - The TUNING mode of the cost-based optimizer can be used to perform more detailed analysis of SQL statements and make recommendations for actions to be taken and for auxiliary statistics to be accepted into a SQL profile for later use when running under NORMAL mode.

Oracle states that the NORMAL mode should provide an acceptable execution path for most SQL statements. SQL statements that do not perform well in NORMAL mode may be tuned in TUNING mode for later use in NORMAL mode. This should provide a better balance of performance for queries that have SQL profiles defined, with the majority of the optimizer work for complex queries being performed in TUNING mode once, rather than repeatedly each time the SQL statement is parsed.

10g Automatic SQL Tuning

The 10g Automatic SQL Tuning analysis includes statistics analysis, SQL profiling, access path analysis, and SQL structure analysis and can be performed through the SQL Tuning Advisor. The SQL Tuning Advisor uses input from the ADDM, from resource-intensive SQL statements captured by the AWR, from the cursor cache, or from SQL Tuning Sets. Since this is a chapter on query tuning, we will look at how to pass specific SQL to the SQL Tuning Advisor in the form of a SQL Tuning Set. The Oracle recommended interface for the SQL Tuning Advisor is Oracle Enterprise Manager, but you can use the APIs via the command line in SQL*Plus. We will look at a command-line session to better understand the analysis procedure of a single query. This is only a small glance into the functionality of the SQL Tuning Advisor. There is also the capability of creating SQL Tuning Sets and SQL Profiles, as well as the ability to transport SQL Tuning sets from one database to another.

Ensure That the Tuning User Has Access to the API

Access to these privileges should be restricted to authorized users in a production environment. The privileges are granted by SYS. "ADMINISTER SQL TUNING SET" only allows access to its own tuning sets.

```
GRANT ADMINISTER SQL TUNING SET to &TUNING_USER;    -- or
GRANT ADMINISTER ANY SQL TUNING SET to &TUNING_USER;
GRANT ADVISOR TO &TUNING_USER
GRANT CREATE ANY SQL PROFILE TO &TUNING_USER;
GRANT ALTER ANY SQL PROFILE TO &TUNING_USER;
GRANT DROP ANY SQL PROFILE TO &TUNING_USER;
```

Create the Tuning Task

If we want to tune a single SQL statement, for example

```
select  COUNT(*)
from    t2
where   UPPER(owner) = 'RIC';
```

we must first create a tuning task using the DBMS_SQLTUNE package.

```
DECLARE
 tuning_task_name VARCHAR2(30);
```

```
  tuning_sqltext    CLOB;
BEGIN
  tuning_sqltext :=       'SELECT COUNT(*) '        ||
                          'FROM t2 '                ||
                          'WHERE UPPER(owner) = :owner';
  tuning_task_name := DBMS_SQLTUNE.CREATE_TUNING_TASK(
        sql_text     => tuning_sqltext,
        bind_list    => sql_binds(anydata.ConvertVarchar2(100)),
        user_name    => 'RIC',
        scope        => 'COMPREHENSIVE',
        time_limit   => 60,
        task_name    => 'first_tuning_task13',
        description  => 'Tune T2 count');
END;
/
```

The Task Can Be Seen in the Advisor Log

To see the task, query the user_advisor log:

```
select task_name
from   user_advisor_log;

TASK_NAME
------------------
first_tuning_task13
```

Execute the SQL Tuning Task

To execute the tuning task, we use the DBMS_SQLTUNE package, as shown here.

```
BEGIN
  DBMS_SQLTUNE.EXECUTE_TUNING_TASK( task_name => 'first_tuning_task13' );
END;
/
```

Check Status of the Tuning Task

To see the specific tuning task, query the user_advisor log:

```
select status
from   user_advisor_tasks
where  task_name = 'first_tuning_task13';

STATUS
---------
COMPLETED
```

Check Status of the Tuning Task

Displaying the SQL Tuning Advisor Report

To see the SQL Tuning Advisor Report, we also use the DBMS_SQLTUNE package:

```
SET LONG 8000
SET LONGCHUNKSIZE 8000
SET LINESIZE 100
SET PAGESIZE 100


select dbms_sqltune.report_tuning_task('first_tuning_task13')
from   dual;
```

Reviewing the Report Output

The report output shown next is lengthy, but it essentially recommends creating a function-based index on the owner column of table T2. Had the SQL Tuning Advisor recommended the use of a SQL Profile, this could have been accepted by using the DBMS_SQLTUNE.ACCEPT_SQL_PROFILE package.

```
DBMS_SQLTUNE.REPORT_TUNING_TASK('FIRST_TUNING_TASK13')
-------------------------------------------------------------------------------
-----------
GENERAL INFORMATION SECTION
-------------------------------------------------------------------------------
Tuning Task Name            : first_tuning_task13
Tuning Task Owner           : RIC
Scope                             : COMPREHENSIVE
Time Limit(seconds)         : 60
Completion Status             : COMPLETED
Started at                        : 11/20/2005 20:49:56
Completed at                    : 11/20/2005 20:49:56
Number of Index Findings      : 1
Number of SQL Restructure Findings: 1

DBMS_SQLTUNE.REPORT_TUNING_TASK('FIRST_TUNING_TASK13')
-------------------------------------------------------------------------------
-----------
-------------------------------------------------------------------------------
Schema Name: RIC
SQL ID     : 8ubrqzjkkyj3g
SQL Text   : SELECT COUNT(*) FROM t2 WHERE UPPER(owner) = 'RIC'
-------------------------------------------------------------------------------
FINDINGS SECTION (2 findings)
-------------------------------------------------------------------------------
1- Index Finding (see explain plan section below)

DBMS_SQLTUNE.REPORT_TUNING_TASK('FIRST_TUNING_TASK13')
-------------------------------------------------------------------------------
----------
-------------------------------------------------------
  The execution plan of this statement can be improved by creating one or more
  indices.

  Recommendation (estimated benefit: 100%)
  ----------------------------------------
  - Consider running the Access Advisor to improve the physical schema design
```

```
    or creating the recommended index.
    create index RIC.IDX$$_00CF0001 on RIC.T2(UPPER('OWNER'));

  Rationale

DBMS_SQLTUNE.REPORT_TUNING_TASK('FIRST_TUNING_TASK13')
-------------------------------------------------------------------------
-----------
  ---------
    Creating the recommended indices significantly improves the execution plan
    of this statement. However, it might be preferable to run "Access Advisor"
    using a representative SQL workload as opposed to a single statement. This
    will allow to get comprehensive index recommendations which takes into
    account index maintenance overhead and additional space consumption.

2- Restructure SQL finding (see plan 1 in explain plans section)
-----------------------------------------------------------------
  The predicate UPPER("T2"."OWNER")='RIC' used at line ID 2 of the execution
  plan contains an expression on indexed column "OWNER". This expression

DBMS_SQLTUNE.REPORT_TUNING_TASK('FIRST_TUNING_TASK13')
-------------------------------------------------------------------------
-----------
  prevents the optimizer from selecting indices on table "RIC"."T2".

  Recommendation
  --------------
  - Rewrite the predicate into an equivalent form to take advantage of
    indices. Alternatively, create a function-based index on the expression.

  Rationale
  ---------
    The optimizer is unable to use an index if the predicate is an inequality
    condition or if there is an expression or an implicit data type conversion

DBMS_SQLTUNE.REPORT_TUNING_TASK('FIRST_TUNING_TASK13')
-------------------------------------------------------------------------------
-----------
    on the indexed column.

------------------------------------------------------------------------------
EXPLAIN PLANS SECTION
------------------------------------------------------------------------------

1- Original
-----------
Plan hash value: 1374435053
-------------------------------------------------------------------------------

DBMS_SQLTUNE.REPORT_TUNING_TASK('FIRST_TUNING_TASK13')
-------------------------------------------------------------------------------
-----------
| Id  | Operation              | Name  | Rows  | Bytes | Cost (%CPU)|
Time       |
-------------------------------------------------------------------------------
|   0 | SELECT STATEMENT       |       |     1 |     6 |  4049   (3) |
00:00:49 |
|   1 |  SORT AGGREGATE        |       |     1 |     6 |            |
|         |                    |       |       |       |            |
|*  2 |   INDEX FAST FULL SCAN| T2_I1 | 26097 |  152K|  4049   (3) | 00:00:49 |
-------------------------------------------------------------------------------
```

```
Predicate Information (identified by operation id):
---------------------------------------------------
   2 - filter(UPPER("OWNER")='RIC')

DBMS_SQLTUNE.REPORT_TUNING_TASK('FIRST_TUNING_TASK13')
------------------------------------------------------------------------------
----------

2- Using New Indices
--------------------
Plan hash value: 2206416184


------------------------------------------------------------------------------
--------------------------
| Id  | Operation            | Name            | Rows  | Bytes  |
Cost (%CPU)| Time         |
------------------------------------------------------------------------------
--------------------------
|   0 | SELECT STATEMENT     |                 |     1 |     6  |
524   (2)      | 00:00:07 |
|   1 |   SORT AGGREGATE     |                 |     1 |     6  |
|*  2 |    INDEX RANGE SCAN  | IDX$$_00CF0001  |  237K| 1390K| 524   (2)      | 00:00:07
|
```

Tips Review

- Query V$SQLAREA and V$SQL to find problem queries that need to be tuned.

- In 10g, take advantage of the new views and AWR information.

- When a small number of rows ("small" is version dependent) are to be returned based on a condition in a query, you generally want to use an index on that condition (column), given that the rows are not skewed within the individual blocks.

- The first tip concerning slow queries is that you will have a lot of them if you are missing indexes on columns that are generally restrictive. Building indexes on restrictive columns is the first step toward better system performance.

- Bad indexes (indexing the wrong columns) can cause as much trouble as forgetting to use indexes on the correct columns. While Oracle's cost-based optimizer generally suppresses poor indexes, problems can still develop when a bad index is used at the same time as a good index.

- For crucial queries on your system, consider concatenated indexes on the columns contained in both the SELECT and the WHERE clauses.

- The INDEX_FFS will process *only* the index and will not take the result and access the table. All columns that are used and retrieved by the query *must* be contained in the index. This is a much better way to guarantee that the index will be used.

- When a query is run multiple times in succession, it becomes faster, since you have now cached the data in memory. At times, people are tricked into believing that they have actually made a query faster when in actuality they are accessing data stored in memory.

- Caching an often-used but relatively small table into memory will ensure that the data is not pushed out of memory by other data. Also, be careful—cached tables can alter the execution path normally chosen by the optimizer, leading to an unexpected execution order for the query (it can affect the driving table in nested loop joins).

- When multiple indexes on a single table can be used for a query, use the most restrictive index. While Oracle's cost-based optimizer will generally force the use of the most restrictive index, variations occur, depending on the version of Oracle used and the structure of the query.

- Any modification to the column side of the query results in the suppression of the index unless a function-based index is created. Function-based indexes can lead to dramatic performance gains when used to create indexes on functions often used on selective columns in the WHERE clause.

- Oracle's optimizer now performs OR-expansion, which improves the performance of certain queries that ran poorly in prior versions.

- Write separate highly efficient SQL statements for individual tasks rather than suboptimally efficient statements for multiple tasks.

- In 10g, the SQL Tuning Advisor may be used to analyze SQL statements and make recommendations.

References

Deb Dudek, *DBA Tips, or a Job Is a Terrible Thing to Waste* (TUSC)
Rich Niemiec, *DBA Tuning Tips: Now YOU Are the Expert* (TUSC)
Oracle® Database Performance Tuning Guide 10g Release 2 (10.2)
Query Optimization in Oracle 9i, An Oracle Whitepaper (Oracle)

Thanks to Connor McDonald for his feedback on V$SQLAREA. Rob Christensen contributed the major portion of the update to this chapter.

CHAPTER
9

Table Joins and Other
Advanced Tuning (Advanced
DBA and Developer)

his chapter was the most painful to write because the complexities of Oracle joins and block level tuning come to light here. The driving table or the first table accessed in a query is an important aspect of superior performance. Using the Tuning Pack and the Automatic Workload Repository (AWR) statistics, Oracle can do a lot to help you tune things (see Chapter 5 for more information). If the optimizer has designated the wrong table as the driving table in a query, this choice can make the difference between hours and seconds. Usually, the cost-based optimizer chooses the correct table, but your indexing on tables affects how this works. If you need to change the driving table using a hint on the same table over and over, this symptom often indicates an indexing plan that still needs work. When you have to tune multiple tables using hints, it gets progressively harder to tune increasing numbers of tables. With only two or three tables, it's easy enough to use an ORDERED hint (guaranteeing the order of the tables) and then try variations of the order of the tables until the fastest outcome

is achieved. However, in a ten-table join, there are 3,628,800 possible combinations, which makes trying all combinations slightly time-consuming. Using a LEADING hint (you specify the first or leading table to drive the query with) simplifies this chore, but it is still far more daunting than building the correct indexing scheme in the first place.

One of the greatest challenges of this book was trying to put driving tables into a useful format for readers. The optimizer's complexity and all the potential paths for joining and optimizing a query can be mind-boggling. Suppressing a single index in a query can affect the driving table, how Oracle joins tables in a query, and how Oracle uses or suppresses other indexes. This chapter focuses on helping you make better decisions when choosing a driving table. Although I have a good understanding of how Oracle performs these complexities, putting that understanding into words was the challenging task for the first half of this chapter. The challenge for the second half was relating performance tuning to mathematical equations and also comparing join performance of relational to object-relational queries.

The tips covered in this chapter include the following:

- Join methods
- Table join initialization parameters
- Comparing the primary join methods
- A two-table join: equal-sized tables (cost-based)
- A two-table INDEXED join: equal-sized tables (cost-based)
- Forcing a specific join method
- Eliminating join records (candidate rows) in multitable joins
- A two-table join between a large table and a small table
- Three table joins: not as much fun (cost-based)
- Bitmap join indexes
- Third-party product tuning
- Tuning distributed queries
- When you have everything tuned
- Miscellaneous tuning snippets

- Tuning at the block level
- Tuning using simple mathematical techniques
- Join tuning: relational vs. object-relational performance

Join Methods

Since the days of Oracle 6, the optimizer has used three different ways to join row sources together: the NESTED LOOPS join, the SORT-MERGE join, and the CLUSTER join. (There is also the favorite of the ad hoc query user, the CARTESIAN join.) In Oracle 7.3, the HASH join was introduced, and in Oracle 8i, the INDEX join was introduced, making for a total of five primary join methods. Each has a unique set of features and limitations. Before you attack a potential join issue, you need to know the following:

- Which table will drive the query (first table accessed), and when will other tables be accessed given the path that is chosen for the query? What are the alternate driving paths?

- What are the Oracle join possibilities (described in this section)? Remember, each join possibility for Oracle can yield different results, depending on the join order, the selectivity of indexes, and the available memory for sorting and/or hashing.

- Which indexes are available, and what is the selectivity of the indexes? The selectivity of an index cannot only cause the optimizer to use or suppress an index, but it can also change the way the query drives and may determine the use or suppression of other indexes in the query.

- Which hints provide alternate paths, and which hints suppress or force an index to be used? These hints change the driving order of the tables, and they change how Oracle performs the join and which indexes it uses or suppresses.

- Which version of Oracle are you using? Your choices vary, depending on the version and release of Oracle you are using. The optimizer also works differently, depending on the version.

NESTED LOOPS Joins

Suppose somebody gave you a telephone book and a list of 20 names to look up, and asked you to write down each person's name and corresponding telephone number. You would probably go down the list of names, looking up each one in the telephone book one at a time. This task would be pretty easy because the telephone book is alphabetized by name. Moreover, somebody looking over your shoulder could begin calling the first few numbers you write down while you are still looking up the rest. This scene describes a NESTED LOOPS join.

In a NESTED LOOPS join, Oracle reads the first row from the first row source and then checks the second row source for matches. All matches are then placed in the result set and Oracle goes on to the next row from the first row source. This continues until all rows in the first row source have been processed. The first row source is often called the outer or *driving* table, whereas the second row source is called the *inner* table. Using a NESTED LOOPS join is one of the fastest methods of receiving the first records back from a join.

NESTED LOOPS Joins

NESTED LOOPS joins are ideal when the driving row source (the records you are looking for) is small and the joined columns of the inner row source are uniquely indexed or have a highly selective non-unique index. NESTED LOOPS joins have an advantage over other join methods in that they can quickly retrieve the first few rows of the result set without having to wait for the entire result set to be determined. This situation is ideal for query screens where an end user can read the first few records retrieved while the rest are being fetched. NESTED LOOPS joins are also flexible in that any two-row sources can always be joined by NESTED LOOPS—regardless of join condition and schema definition.

However, NESTED LOOPS joins can be very inefficient if the inner row source (second table accessed) does not have an index on the joined columns or if the index is not highly selective. If the driving row source (the records retrieved from the driving table) is quite large, other join methods may be more efficient.

Figure 9-1 illustrates the method of executing the query shown next where the dept table is accessed first and the result is then looped through the emp table with a NESTED LOOPS join. The type of join that is performed can be forced with a hint and will vary by different variables on your system.

```
select    /*+ ordered */ ename, dept.deptno
from      dept, emp
where     dept.deptno = emp.deptno
```

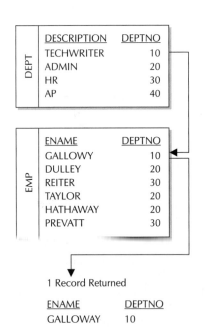

NESTED LOOPS Join

The loop would continue until each of the DEPTNOs in the DEPT table have been checked against those in the EMP table. The subseqent loop results are (for DEPTNOs 20, 30, 40):

The second loop:
3 Records Returned

ENAME	DEPTNO
DULLEY	20
TAYLOR	20
HATHAWAY	20

The third loop:
2 Records Returned

ENAME	DEPTNO
REITER	30
PREVATT	30

FIGURE 9-1. *NESTED LOOPS (DEPT is the driving table)*

SORT-MERGE Joins

Suppose two salespeople attend a conference and each collect over 100 business cards from potential new customers. They now each have a pile of cards in random order, and they want to see how many cards are duplicated in both piles. The salespeople alphabetize their piles, and then they call off names one at a time. Because both piles of cards have been sorted, it becomes much easier to find the names that appear in both piles. This example describes a SORT-MERGE join.

In a SORT-MERGE join, Oracle sorts the first row source by its join columns, sorts the second row source by its join columns, and then merges the sorted row sources together. As matches are found, they are put into the result set.

SORT-MERGE joins can be effective when lack of data selectivity or useful indexes render a NESTED LOOPS join inefficient, or when both of the row sources are quite large (greater than 5 percent of the blocks accessed). However, SORT-MERGE joins can be used only for equijoins (WHERE D.deptno = E.deptno, as opposed to WHERE D.deptno >= E.deptno). SORT-MERGE joins require temporary segments for sorting (if PGA_AGGREGATE_TARGET or SGA_TARGET, if used, is set too small). This can lead to extra memory utilization and/or extra disk I/O in the temporary tablespace.

Figure 9-2 illustrates the method of executing the query shown next when a SORT-MERGE join is performed.

```
select      /*+ ordered */ ename, dept.deptno
from        emp, dept
where       dept.deptno = emp.deptno;
```

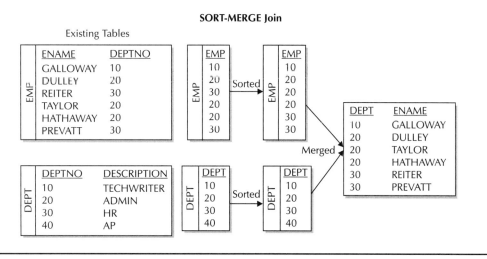

FIGURE 9-2. *SORT-MERGE join*

CLUSTER Joins

A CLUSTER join is really just a special case of the NESTED LOOPS join that is not used very often. If the two row sources being joined are actually tables that are part of a cluster, and if the join is an equijoin between the cluster keys of the two tables, then Oracle can use a CLUSTER join. In this case, Oracle reads each row from the first row source and finds all matches in the second row source by using the CLUSTER index.

CLUSTER joins are extremely efficient because the joining rows in the two row sources will actually be located in the same physical data block. However, clusters carry certain caveats of their own, and you cannot have a CLUSTER join without a cluster. Therefore, CLUSTER joins are not very commonly used.

HASH Joins

HASH joins are the usual choice of the Oracle optimizer when the memory is set up to accommodate them. In a HASH join, Oracle accesses one table (usually the smaller of the joined results) and builds a hash table on the join key in memory. It then scans the other table in the join (usually the larger one) and probes the hash table for matches to it. Oracle uses a HASH join efficiently only if the parameter PGA_AGGREGATE_TARGET is set to a large enough value. If you set the SGA_TARGET, you must set the PGA_AGGREGATE_TARGET as the SGA_TARGET does not include the PGA. The HASH join is similar to a NESTED LOOPS join in the sense that there is a nested loop that occurs—Oracle first builds a hash table to facilitate the operation and then loops through the hash table. When using an ORDERED hint, the first table in the FROM clause is the table used to build the hash table.

HASH joins can be effective when the lack of a useful index renders NESTED LOOPS joins inefficient. The HASH join might be faster than a SORT-MERGE join, in this case, because only one row source needs to be sorted, and it could possibly be faster than a NESTED LOOPS join because probing a hash table in memory can be faster than traversing a b-tree index. As with SORT-MERGE joins and CLUSTER joins, HASH joins work only on equijoins. As with SORT-MERGE joins, HASH joins use memory resources and can drive up I/O in the temporary tablespace if the sort memory is not sufficient (which can cause this join method to be extremely slow). Finally, HASH joins are available only when cost-based optimization is used (which should be 100 percent of the time for your application running on Oracle 10g).

Figure 9-3 illustrates the method of executing the query shown in the listing that follows when a HASH join is used.

```
select    /*+ ordered */ ename, dept.deptno
from      emp, dept
where     dept.deptno = emp.deptno;
```

Index Joins

Prior to Oracle 8i, you always had to access the table unless the index contained all of the information required. As of Oracle 8i, if a set of indexes exists that contains all of the information required by the query, then the optimizer can choose to generate a sequence of HASH joins between the indexes. Each of the indexes are accessed using a range scan or fast full scan, depending on the conditions available in the WHERE clause. This method is extremely efficient when a table

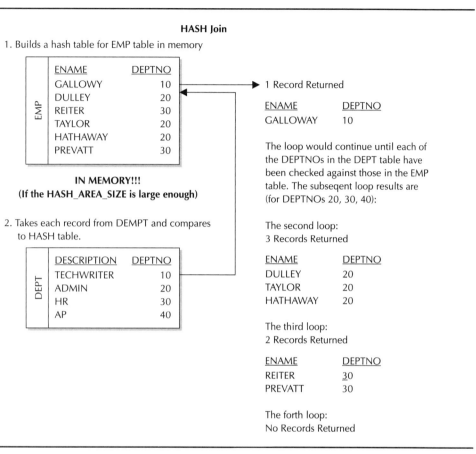

HASH Join

1. Builds a hash table for EMP table in memory

ENAME	DEPTNO
GALLOWY	10
DULLEY	20
REITER	30
TAYLOR	20
HATHAWAY	20
PREVATT	30

EMP

IN MEMORY!!!
(If the HASH_AREA_SIZE is large enough)

2. Takes each record from DEMPT and compares to HASH table.

DESCRIPTION	DEPTNO
TECHWRITER	10
ADMIN	20
HR	30
AP	40

DEPT

1 Record Returned

ENAME	DEPTNO
GALLOWAY	10

The loop would continue until each of the DEPTNOs in the DEPT table have been checked against those in the EMP table. The subseqent loop results are (for DEPTNOs 20, 30, 40):

The second loop:
3 Records Returned

ENAME	DEPTNO
DULLEY	20
TAYLOR	20
HATHAWAY	20

The third loop:
2 Records Returned

ENAME	DEPTNO
REITER	30
PREVATT	30

The forth loop:
No Records Returned

FIGURE 9-3. *HASH join*

has a large number of columns, but you want to access only a limited number of those columns. The more limiting the conditions in the WHERE clause, the faster the execution of the query. The optimizer evaluates this as an option when looking for the optimal path of execution.

You must create indexes on the appropriate columns (those that will satisfy the entire query) to ensure that the optimizer has the INDEX join as an available choice. This task usually involves adding indexes on columns that may not be indexed or on columns that were not indexed together previously. The advantage of INDEX joins over fast full scans is that fast full scans have a *single* index satisfying the entire query. INDEX joins have multiple indexes satisfying the entire query.

Two indexes (one on ENAME and one on DEPTNO) have been created prior to the execution of the corresponding query in this next listing. The query does not need to access the table! Figure 9-4 shows this index merge in graphical format.

```
select    ENAME, DEPTNO
from      EMP
where     DEPTNO = 20
and       ENAME = 'DULLY';
```

Index Joins

INDEX-MERGE Join

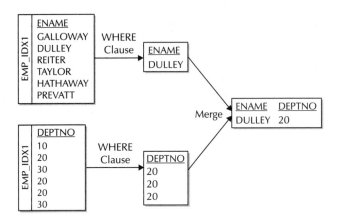

FIGURE 9-4. *An INDEX MERGE join of EMP_IDX1 and EMP_IDX2*

The statistics shown here are based on one million records. The table is 210MB. Indexes were created on doby, state, and dobmsy.

```
create    index doby on test2    ( doby );
create    index state on test2     ( state );
create    index dobmsy on test2  (state, doby );
```

Neither doby nor state individually are very limiting; consequently, the first indication is to execute a full table scan, as shown in this listing:

```
select    /*+ FULL(test2) */   state, doby
from      test2
where     doby = '1972'
and       state = MA

SELECT STATEMENT Optimizer=CHOOSE
    TABLE ACCESS (FULL) OF 'TEST2'

Elapse time: 12.6 seconds
```

Using a single index on doby is slower than the full table scan.

```
select    /*+ rule index(test2 doby) */ state, doby
from      test2
where     doby = '1972'
and       state = MA

SELECT STATEMENT Optimizer=HINT: RULE
```

```
   TABLE ACCESS (BY INDEX ROWID) OF 'TEST2'
      INDEX (RANGE SCAN) OF 'DOBY' (NON-UNIQUE)
```

Elapsed time: 13:45 seconds

Using a single index on state is also slower than a full table scan.

```
select    /*+ rule index(test2 state) */ state, doby
from      test2
where     doby = '1972'
and       state = MA
SELECT STATEMENT Optimizer=HINT: RULE
   TABLE ACCESS (BY INDEX ROWID) OF 'TEST2'
      INDEX (RANGE SCAN) OF 'STATE' (NON-UNIQUE)
```

Elapsed time: 23.50 seconds

However, using an index join of doby and state is quicker than a full table scan because the table does not need to be accessed, as in this listing:

```
select    /*+ index_join(test2 doby state) */ state, doby
from      test2
where     doby = '1972'
and       state = MA

SELECT STATEMENT Optimizer=CHOOSE
   VIEW OF 'index$_join$_001'
      HASH JOIN
         INDEX (RANGE SCAN) OF 'DOBY' (NON-UNIQUE)
         INDEX (RANGE SCAN) OF 'STATE' (NON-UNIQUE)
```

Elapsed time: 4.76 seconds

However, the INDEX_FFS (if a single index on all needed columns exists) is still the most efficient method, as shown here:

```
select    /*+ index_ffs(test2 dobmsy) */ state, doby
from      test2
where     doby = '1972'
and       state = MA

SELECT STATEMENT Optimizer=CHOOSE
   INDEX (FAST FULL SCAN) OF 'DOBMSY' (NON-UNIQUE)
```

Elapsed time: 3.6 seconds

Although fast full scan is the most efficient option in this case, the index join accommodates more situations. Also, an INDEX_FFS is *very* often a problem as it scans through a lot of index blocks and shows up as a severe amount of 'db file sequential read' waits (so try to tune it so that it doesn't need to scan the whole index by using a better index or having a more selective query).

Index Joins

Table Join Initialization Parameters

Performance of SORT-MERGE joins and HASH joins is strongly impacted by certain initialization parameters. Join performance can be crippled if certain parameters are not set properly.

SORT-MERGE and HASH Join Parameters

The initialization parameter DB_FILE_MULTIBLOCK_READ_COUNT specifies how many blocks Oracle should read at a time from disk when performing a sequential read such as a full table scan. Because SORT-MERGE joins often involve full table scans, setting this parameter will reduce overhead when scanning large tables.

The initialization parameter PGA_AGGREGATE_TARGET specifies how much memory can be used for sorting, and this has a strong impact on performance of all sorts. Because SORT-MERGE joins require sorting of both row sources, allocated memory for sorting can greatly impact SORT-MERGE join performance. If an entire sort cannot be completed in the amount of memory specified by this parameter, then a temporary segment in the temporary tablespace is allocated. In this case, the sort is performed in memory one part at a time, and partial results are stored on disk in the temporary segment. If memory allocated for sorting is set very small, then excessive disk I/O is required to perform even the smallest of sorts. If it is set too high, then the operating system may run out of physical memory and resort to swapping. The same is true for HASH joins. If the HASH table can't be built because of insufficient memory, a HASH join could be excessively slow using disk I/O instead.

Table 9-1 provides a quick view of the primary join types.

Category	NESTED LOOPS Join	SORT-MERGE Join	HASH Join
Optimizer hint	USE_NL.	USE_MERGE.	USE_HASH.
When you can use it	Any join.	Any join.	Equijoins only.
Resource concerns	CPU, disk I/O.	Memory, temporary segments.	Memory, temporary segments.
Features	Efficient with highly selective indexes and restrictive searches. Used to return the first row of a result quickly.	Better than NESTED LOOPS when an index is missing or the search criteria are not very selective. Can work with limited memory.	Better than NESTED LOOPS when an index is missing or the search criteria are not very selective. It is usually faster than a SORT-MERGE.
Drawbacks	Very inefficient when indexes are missing or if the index criteria are not limiting.	Requires a sort on both tables. It is built for best optimal throughput and does not return the first row until all rows are found.	Can require a large amount of memory for the hash table to be built. Does not return the first rows quickly. Can be extremely slow if it must do the operation on disk.

TABLE 9-1. *Primary Join Methods*

A Two-Table Join: Equal-Sized Tables (Cost-Based)

Consider the following tables (they have been analyzed) that will be used for this example:

```
SMALL1    10000  rows    No Indexes
SMALL2    10000  rows    No Indexes
```

This section of examples is important as we look at how the cost-based optimizer works, with all conditions being equal in a join (same size tables/no indexes).

Example 1

Neither table has an index and there aren't any other noteworthy conditions on the tables. Oracle uses a HASH join if the initialization parameters have been set up to allow a HASH join; otherwise, it uses a SORT-MERGE join. The first table accessed will be SMALL1, which is important for a HASH join but irrelevant for a SORT-MERGE join. A HASH join typically chooses the smaller result set to access first to build the hash table. In this example, both tables are equal, so the first one in the FROM clause is used.

```
select    small1.col1, small2.col1
from      small1, small2
where     small1.col1 = small2.col1;
```

Join Method: HASH-Join   The SMALL1 table is accessed first and used to build a hash table. Oracle accesses the SMALL1 table and builds a hash table on the join key (COL1) in memory. It then scans SMALL2 and probes the hash table for matches to SMALL2.

Join Method: SORT-MERGE Join (If Hash Initialization Parameters Are Not Set Up)
Although SMALL1 would normally be the driving table (because it is first in the FROM clause and we are in cost-based optimization), a SORT-MERGE join forces the sorting of each of the tables before they are merged together (because there are no indexes). A full table scan is needed on both tables, and the order in the FROM clause has no impact, as shown here:

```
select    small1.col1, small2.col1
from      small2, small1
where     small1.col1 = small2.col1;
```

Join Method: HASH-Join   The SMALL2 table is accessed first and used to build a hash table. Oracle accesses the SMALL2 table and builds a hash table on the join key (COL1) in memory. It then scans SMALL1 and probes the hash table for matches to SMALL1.

Join Method: SORT-MERGE Join (If Hash Initialization Parameters Are Not Set Up)
Although SMALL2 would normally be the driving table (because it is first in the FROM clause and we are in cost-based optimization), a SORT-MERGE join forces the sorting of each of the tables before they are merged together (because there are no indexes). A full table scan is needed on both tables, and the order in the FROM clause has no impact.

Example 1 Outcomes

If you have set up the initialization parameters for hashing, Oracle builds a hash table from the join values of the *first* table, and then it probes that table for values from the second table. If you have not set up the initialization parameters for hashing, the *first* table in the FROM clause in cost-based optimization is the driving table. However, in a SORT-MERGE join, this has no impact because each table must be sorted and then all results must be merged together. Also note that the order of tables cannot be guaranteed when all conditions are *not* equal (when you have tables of different sizes or with different indexes) because the optimizer chooses the order unless you specify the ORDERED hint.

Finally, if neither table was analyzed in Example 1, Oracle resorts to previous version behavior by accessing the last table in the FROM clause and using a SORT-MERGE join (yes, even in Oracle 10g). This is noted here so that you will realize this behavior may indicate that you haven't analyzed your tables.

Example 2

Neither table has an index, and you will use the ORDERED hint, as in this listing:

```
select     /*+ ORDERED */ small1.col1, small2.col1
from       small1, small2
where      small1.col1 = small2.col1;
```

Join Method: HASH-Join   The SMALL1 table is accessed first and used to build a hash table. Oracle accesses the SMALL1 table and builds a hash table on the join key (COL1) in memory. It then scans SMALL2 and probes the hash table for matches to SMALL2.

Join Method: SORT-MERGE Join (If Hash Initialization Parameters Are Not Set Up)
Although SMALL1 would normally be the driving table (because it is first in the FROM clause and we are in cost-based optimization), a SORT-MERGE join forces the sorting of each of the tables before they are merged together (because there are no indexes). A full table scan is needed on both tables, and the order in the FROM clause has no impact.

```
select     /*+ ORDERED */ small1.col1, small2.col1
from       small2, small1
where      small1.col1 = small2.col1;
```

Join Method: HASH-Join   The SMALL2 table is accessed first and used to build a hash table. Oracle accesses the SMALL2 table and builds a hash table on the join key (COL1) in memory. It then scans SMALL1 and probes the hash table for matches to SMALL1.

Join Method: SORT-MERGE Join (If Hash Initialization Parameters Are Not Set Up)
Although SMALL2 would normally be the driving table (because it is first in the FROM clause and we are in cost-based optimization), a SORT-MERGE join forces the sorting of each of the tables before they are merged together (because there are no indexes). A full table scan is needed on both tables, and the order in the FROM clause has no impact.

Example 2 Outcomes

If hash initialization parameters are set up, Oracle builds a hash table from the join values of the *first* table listed and then probes that hash table for values from the *second* table listed. If hash initialization parameters are not set up, the *first* table in the FROM clause in cost-based optimization is the driving table when an ORDERED hint is used; but in a SORT-MERGE join, this has no impact because each table must be sorted and then all tables must be merged together.

TIP
Using cost-based optimization, the first table in the FROM clause is the driving table when the ORDERED hint is used. This overrides the optimizer from choosing the driving table. If a SORT-MERGE join is used, then the order of the tables has no impact because neither will drive the query. Knowing which table is generally the driving table when using an ORDERED hint in small joins can help you solve larger table join issues and also help you find indexing problems.

TIP
When hash initialization parameters are set up, the optimizer uses HASH joins in lieu of SORT-MERGE joins. With HASH joins, the first table is used to build a hash table (in memory if available), and the second table in the FROM clause then probes for corresponding hash table matches. The first table in the FROM clause (using the ORDERED hint) is the first table accessed in a HASH join.

A Two-Table INDEXED Join: Equal-Sized Tables (Cost-Based)

To get a better understanding of the driving table and how Oracle processes a query, it is instructive to have an example where all conditions are equal in both tables. Although the queries in this section look strange because we are trying to keep all conditions equal, they are helpful in understanding the way joins work. Consider the following tables (they have been analyzed) that will be used for this example:

```
SMALL1    10000 rows    Index on COL1
SMALL2    10000 rows    Index on COL1
```

NOTE
This section of examples is important as we look at how the cost-based optimizer works using indexes. Although the query in this section wouldn't normally be written, it shows how the driving table works with a two-table join, all conditions being equal. In other words, it is only for instructional purposes.

Example I
Both tables have an index on the COL1 column, as in this example.

```
select    small1.col1, small2.col1
from      small1, small2
```

```
where      small1.col1 = small2.col1
and        small1.col1 = 77
and        small2.col1 = 77;
```

EXPLAIN PLAN output

```
SELECT STATEMENT Optimizer=CHOOSE
  NESTED LOOPS (Cost=2 Card=3 Bytes=90)  (small1 result checks small2 matches)
    INDEX (RANGE SCAN) OF 'SMALL1_IDX'   (This is first/gets first row to check)
    INDEX (RANGE SCAN) OF 'SMALL2_IDX'   (This is second/checks for matches)
```

Join Method: NESTED LOOPS Join   The SMALL1 table (first table in the FROM clause) is the driving table of the query. Oracle retrieves the records from the index on SMALL1 and then takes each record and checks for matches in the SMALL2 index. A NESTED LOOPS join will be faster when the source rows from the SMALL1 table are a small set and there is a reasonably selective index on the SMALL2 joining column.

```
select     small1.col1, small2.col1
from       small2, small1
where      small1.col1 = small2.col1
and        small1.col1 = 77
and        small2.col1 = 77;
```

EXPLAIN PLAN output

```
SELECT STATEMENT Optimizer=CHOOSE
  NESTED LOOPS (Cost=2 Card=3 Bytes=90)   (small2 result checks small1 matches)
    INDEX (RANGE SCAN) OF 'SMALL2_IDX'   (This is first/gets first row to check)
    INDEX (RANGE SCAN) OF 'SMALL1_IDX'   (This is second/checks for matches)
```

Join Method: NESTED LOOPS Join   The SMALL2 table (first table in the FROM clause) is the driving table of the query. Oracle retrieves the records from the index on SMALL2 and then takes each record and checks for matches in the SMALL1 index. A NESTED LOOPS join will be faster when the source rows from the SMALL2 table are a small set and there is a reasonably selective index on the SMALL1 joining column.

Example 1 Outcomes

All conditions being equal, the *first* table in the FROM clause in cost-based optimization is the driving table. The index is used on the join condition for the second table. In Example 1, Oracle used a NESTED LOOPS join to join the queries, but a HASH join or MERGE join was also possible, depending on the number of records in the table and index.

Example 2

Both tables have an index on the COL1 column and we use the ORDERED hint, as shown next.

```
select     /*+ ORDERED */ small1.col1, small2.col1
from       small1, small2
where      small1.col1 = small2.col1
and        small1.col1 = 77
and        small2.col1 = 77;
```

EXPLAIN PLAN output

```
SELECT STATEMENT Optimizer=CHOOSE
  NESTED LOOPS  (Each result from small1 is checked for matches in small2)
    INDEX (RANGE SCAN) OF 'SMALL1_IDX'  (This is first/gets first row to check)
    INDEX (RANGE SCAN) OF 'SMALL2_IDX'  (This is second/checks for matches)
```

Join Method: NESTED LOOPS Join   The SMALL1 table (first table in the FROM clause) is the driving table of the query. Oracle retrieves the records from the index on SMALL1 and then takes each record and checks for matches in the SMALL2 index. A NESTED LOOPS join will be faster when the source rows from the SMALL1 table are a small set and there is a reasonably selective index on the SMALL2 joining column, as shown next:

```
select   /*+ ORDERED */ small1.col1, small2.col1
from     small2, small1
where    small1.col1 = small2.col1
and      small1.col1 = 77
and      small2.col1 = 77;
```

EXPLAIN PLAN output

```
SELECT STATEMENT Optimizer=CHOOSE
  NESTED LOOPS  (Each result from small2 is checked for matches in small1)
    INDEX (RANGE SCAN) OF 'SMALL2_IDX'  (This is first/gets first row to check)
    INDEX (RANGE SCAN) OF 'SMALL1_IDX'  (This is second/checks for matches)
```

Join Method: NESTED LOOPS Join   The SMALL2 table (first table in the FROM clause) is the driving table of the query. Oracle retrieves the records from the index on SMALL2 and then takes each record and checks for matches in the SMALL1 index. A NESTED LOOPS join will be faster when the source rows from the SMALL2 table are a small set and there is a reasonably selective index on the SMALL1 joining column.

Example 2 Outcomes
All conditions being equal, the *first* table in the FROM clause in cost-based optimization using a NESTED LOOPS join is the driving table with or without the ORDERED hint. Only the ORDERED hint guarantees the order in which the tables will be accessed. The index is used on the join condition for the second table.

TIP
Using cost-based optimization and a NESTED LOOPS join as the means of joining, the first table in the FROM clause is the driving table (all other conditions being equal), but only the ORDERED hint guarantees this. In NESTED LOOPS joins, choosing a driving table that is the smaller result set (not always the smaller table) makes fewer loops through the other result set (from the nondriving table) and usually results in the best performance.

A Two-Table
INDEXED Join

Forcing a Specific Join Method

When choosing an execution plan for a query involving joins, the Oracle optimizer considers all possible join methods and table orders. The optimizer does its best to evaluate the merits of each option and to choose the optimal execution plan, but sometimes the optimizer does not choose the best solution because of poor indexing strategies.

In these situations, you can use the USE_NL, USE_MERGE, and USE_HASH hints to request a specific join method, and you can use the ORDERED hint to request a specific join order. The optimizer does its best to observe the wishes of these hints, but if you ask for something impossible (such as a SORT-MERGE join on an antijoin), the hint will be ignored.

NOTE
There is no hint to request a CLUSTER join.

When tuning SQL that uses joins, you should run benchmark comparisons between different join methods and table execution order. For example, if a report joins two tables that form a master-detail relationship and the proper primary-key and foreign-key indexes are in place, the optimizer will probably choose to use a NESTED LOOPS join. However, if you know that this particular report joins all of the master records to all of the detail records, you might think it's faster to use a SORT-MERGE join or HASH join instead. Run a benchmark to ensure that you have the best solution.

In the following three listings, the first listing shows an example query and its TKPROF output, the second listing shows the same query with a USE_MERGE hint, and the third listing shows it with a USE_HASH hint. In this example, the indexes were built so that a full table scan must be executed on the PURCHASE_ORDER_LINES table. (Using an index would have been the better choice but not as instructive.) You can see that in this situation the HASH join cut CPU time by almost 40 percent and logical I/Os by about 98 percent. The goal is not to demonstrate how to tune this type of query, but how to use different types of joining.

Forcing a NESTED LOOPS join

```
select      /*+ USE_NL (a b) */
            b.business_unit,b.po_number,b.vendor_type,a.line_number,
            a.line_amount,a.line_status,a.description
from        purchase_order_lines a, purchase_orders b
where       b.business_unit = a.business_unit
and         b.po_number = a.po_number
order by    b.business_unit,b.po_number,a.line_number
```

TKPROF output

call	count	cpu	elapsed	disk	query	current	rows
Parse	1	0.01	0.01	0	0	0	0
Execute	1	0.04	0.12	0	0	1	0
Fetch	73370	23.47	23.55	2071	298667	2089	73369
total	73372	23.52	23.68	2071	298667	2090	73369

```
Rows     Execution Plan
0         SELECT STATEMENT    GOAL: CHOOSE
73369      SORT (ORDER BY)
73369       NESTED LOOPS
73726         TABLE ACCESS    GOAL: ANALYZED (FULL) OF 'PURCHASE_ORDER_LINES'
73369         TABLE ACCESS    GOAL: ANALYZED (BY ROWID) OF 'PURCHASE_ORDERS'
73726           INDEX    GOAL: ANALYZED (UNIQUE SCAN) OF 'PURCHASE_ORDERS_PK' (UNIQUE)
```

The PURCHASE_ORDER_LINES table is the driving table. Each record (one at a time) is taken from the PURCHASE_ORDER_LINES table, and for each one, you loop through for matches in the PURCHASE_ORDER table. This is slow because the driving table list is large. (PURCHASE_ORDER_LINES has a large number of rows.)

Forcing a SORT-MERGE join

```
select      /*+ USE_MERGE (a b) */
            a.business_unit,a.po_number,a.vendor_type,b.line_number,
            b.line_amount,b.line_status,b.description
from        purchase_orders a,purchase_order_lines b
where       b.business_unit = a.business_unit
and         b.po_number = a.po_number
order by    a.business_unit,a.po_number,b.line_number
```

TKPROF output

call	count	cpu	elapsed	disk	query	current	rows
Parse	1	0.01	0.01	0	0	0	0
Execute	1	0.02	0.15	0	0	2	0
Fetch	73370	17.49	19.57	3772	4165	3798	73369
total	73372	17.52	19.73	3772	4165	3800	73369

```
Rows     Execution Plan
0         SELECT STATEMENT    GOAL: CHOOSE
73369      SORT (ORDER BY)
73369       MERGE JOIN
886          SORT (JOIN)
886            TABLE ACCESS    GOAL: ANALYZED (FULL) OF 'PURCHASE_ORDERS'
73726        SORT (JOIN)
73726          TABLE ACCESS    GOAL: ANALYZED (FULL) OF 'PURCHASE_ORDER_LINES'
```

For the SORT-MERGE case, Oracle sorts both tables and then merges the result. This method is still not an efficient way to perform the query.

Forcing a HASH join

```
select      /*+ USE_HASH (a b) */
            a.business_unit,a.po_number,a.vendor_type,b.line_number,
            b.line_amount,b.line_status,b.description
from        purchase_orders a,purchase_order_lines b
where       b.business_unit = a.business_unit
```

Forcing a Specific
Join Method

```
and        b.po_number = a.po_number
order by   a.business_unit,a.po_number,b.line_number
```

TKPROF output

call	count	cpu	elapsed	disk	query	current	rows
Parse	1	0.00	0.00	0	0	0	0
Execute	1	0.05	0.13	0	0	1	0
Fetch	73370	14.88	14.95	2071	4165	2093	73369
total	73372	14.93	15.08	2071	4165	2094	73369

Rows	Execution Plan
0	SELECT STATEMENT GOAL: CHOOSE
73369	SORT (ORDER BY)
137807	HASH JOIN
886	TABLE ACCESS GOAL: ANALYZED (FULL) OF 'PURCHASE_ORDERS'
73726	TABLE ACCESS GOAL: ANALYZED (FULL) OF 'PURCHASE_ORDER_LINES'

The HASH join has proved to be the most efficient because it puts the PURCHASE_ORDERS table into a hash table and then scans to retrieve the corresponding records from PURCHASE_ ORDER_LINES. If you cannot get the correct order of access, you can use the SWAP_JOIN_INPUTS hint as well.

Oracle chose to do a NESTED LOOPS method of joining the tables, but this method was not the most efficient way of joining in this case. Using the USE_HASH hint, you can cut CPU time by almost 40 percent and logical I/Os by about 98 percent. Although the CPU reduction is impressive, the reduction in logical I/Os (memory reads) is saving SGA memory for other users. Sometimes when you are retrieving a large amount of data, access using a full table scan is the most efficient method.

TIP
To change the method that Oracle uses to join multiple tables, use the USE_MERGE, USE_NL, and USE_HASH hints. Multiple tables may need to be specified for the hint to work, and the driving order will usually be from first to last in the FROM clause.

Eliminating Join Records (Candidate Rows) in Multitable Joins

Suppose you have a list of 1000 residents of your town along with each resident's street address, and you are asked to prepare an *alphabetized* list of residents who have the newspaper delivered to their home. (Only 30 get the newspaper.) You could first alphabetize the list of 1000 names (all residents in the town), and then look up each street address in the list of 50 residents who get the newspaper. (Sort the 1000 and then find the 50.) A faster method would be to look up each street address of those who get the newspaper first, and then get the names of the residents at that street and do the alphabetization last. (Find the 50 who get the newspaper from the list of 1000 and then sort the 50 matches.) Either way, you will need to look at the 1000 street addresses. However, these lookups will eliminate many names from the list, and the sorting will be faster when you have a list of only 50 to sort.

You can apply the same concept when writing SQL joining tables together. The Oracle optimizer is pretty smart about choosing the most efficient order in which to perform tasks, but how a query is written can constrain the options available to the optimizer.

The query in this next listing leaves the optimizer no choice but to read all of Acme's invoice lines (the large table/the intersection table), when in fact, only the unpaid invoices (the small table) are of interest:

```
select     v.vendor_num, i.invoice_num, sum (l.amount)
from       vendors v, invoices i, invoice_lines l
where      v.vendor_name = 'ACME'
and        l.vendor_num = v.vendor_num
and        i.vendor_num = l.vendor_num
and        i.invoice_num = l.invoice_num
and        i.paid = 'N'
group by   v.vendor_num, i.invoice_num
order by   i.invoice_num
```

You could rewrite this query, as shown here:

```
select     v.vendor_num, i.invoice_num, sum (l.amount)
from       vendors v, invoices i, invoice_lines l
where      v.vendor_name = 'ACME'
and        i.vendor_num = v.vendor_num
and        i.paid = 'N'
and        l.vendor_num = i.vendor_num
and        l.invoice_num = i.invoice_num
group by   v.vendor_num, i.invoice_num
order by   i.invoice_num
```

In the rewritten query in this listing, the optimizer eliminates all of the paid invoices (the new intersection table) before joining to the INVOICE_LINES table. If most of the invoices in the database have already been paid, then the rewritten query will be significantly faster. (The schema design in this example is dubious and is used only for illustrative purposes.)

TIP

In a three-table join, the driving table is the intersection table or the table that has a join condition to each of the other two tables in the join. Try to use the most limiting table as the driving table (or intersection table) so that your result set from the join of the first two tables is small when you join it to the third table.

A Two-Table Join Between a Large and Small Table

Consider the following tables that will be used for this example:

```
PRODUCT          70 thousand rows     Index on PRODUCT_ID
PRODUCT_LINES    4 million rows       Index on PRODUCT_ID
```

A Two-Table Join Between a Large and Small Table

This section uses only cost-based optimization. This is an important section of examples because it looks at a situation often encountered. It involves a two-table join between a small (business small) table and a large table. The subsequent conditions (beyond the join itself) are on the column that we are joining. At times, the index on this column in the subsequent condition is suppressed. Unfortunately, this situation leads to seven possible situations, based on various conditions. This section covers three of the main situations, and the results are summarized at the end.

Example 1

Neither table can use an index (they are suppressed), and there are no other conditions, shown in this example.

```
select      product.name, product_lines.qty
from        product, product_lines
where       product.product_id || ''  = product_lines.product_id || '';
```

EXPLAIN PLAN output

```
SELECT STATEMENT Optimizer=CHOOSE
  HASH JOIN
    TABLE ACCESS FULL OF 'PRODUCT'
    TABLE ACCESS FULL OF 'PRODUCT_LINES'
```

The order of the tables in the FROM clause can be reversed, as shown here:

```
select      product.name, product_lines.qty
from        product_lines, product
where       product.product_id || ''  = product_lines.product_id || '' ;
```

EXPLAIN PLAN output

```
SELECT STATEMENT Optimizer=CHOOSE
  HASH JOIN
    TABLE ACCESS FULL OF 'PRODUCT'
    TABLE ACCESS FULL OF 'PRODUCT_LINES'
```

Example 1 Outcome

All conditions being equal, the *first* table in the FROM clause in cost-based optimization is the driving table. However, because these tables are different sizes, Oracle chooses the smaller table to be the driving table regardless of the order in the FROM clause. The product table is used to build a hash table on the join key (PRODUCT_ID), and then the PRODUCT_LINES table is scanned, probing the hash table for join key matches.

TIP
Using cost-based optimization, when a large table and a small table are joined, the smaller table is used to build a hash table in memory on the join key. The larger table is scanned and then probes the hash table for matches to the join key. Also note that if there is not enough memory for the hash, the operation can become extremely slow because the hash table may be split into multiple partitions that could be paged to disk. If the ORDERED hint is specified, then the first table in the FROM clause will be the driving table and it will be the one used to build the hash table.

Example 2

A subsequent clause allows the large table to use the PRODUCT_ID index.

```
select      product.name, product_lines.qty
from        product, product_lines
where       product.product_id = product_lines.product_id
and         product_lines.product_id = 4488;
```

EXPLAIN PLAN output

```
SELECT STATEMENT Optimizer=CHOOSE
  MERGE JOIN
    TABLE ACCESS BY INDEX ROWID PRODUCT
      INDEX RANGE SCAN PRODUCT_ID1
    BUFFER SORT
      TABLE ACCESS BY INDEX ROWID PRODUCT_LINES
        INDEX RANGE SCAN PRODUCT1
```

The order of the tables in the FROM clause can be reversed, as shown here:

```
select      product.name, product_lines.qty
from        product_lines, product
where       product.product_id = product_lines.product_id
and         product_lines.product_id = 4488;
```

EXPLAIN PLAN output

```
SELECT STATEMENT Optimizer=CHOOSE
  MERGE JOIN
    TABLE ACCESS BY INDEX ROWID PRODUCT
      INDEX RANGE SCAN PRODUCT_ID1
    BUFFER SORT
      TABLE ACCESS BY INDEX ROWID PRODUCT_LINES
        INDEX RANGE SCAN PRODUCT1
```

Example 2 Outcomes

When a subsequent condition on PRODUCT_ID on the large table exists, the larger table is always the driving table regardless of the order in the FROM clause. The order of the tables in the FROM clause will not alter the order in which Oracle performs this join unless an ORDERED hint is used. In Example 2 a SORT-MERGE join is executed.

TIP
Using cost-based optimization, when a large and small table are joined, the larger table is the driving table if an index can be used on the large table. If the ORDERED hint is specified, then the first table in the FROM clause will be the driving table.

Example 3

A subsequent clause, shown in the following listing, allows the small table to use the PRODUCT_ID index. The large table will still drive the query after getting this condition (on PRODUCT_ID) passed to it by the join. Oracle is smart enough to figure out that PRODUCT_ID exists in both tables and it is more efficient to limit the PRODUCT_LINES table. In the section "Three-Table Joins: Not as Much Fun (Cost-Based)" of this chapter, Oracle's excellent internal processing to improve queries will become more evident.

```
select      product.name, product_lines.qty
from        product, product_lines
where       product.product_id = product_lines.product_id
and         product.product_id = 4488;
```

EXPLAIN PLAN output

```
SELECT STATEMENT Optimizer=CHOOSE
  MERGE JOIN
    TABLE ACCESS BY INDEX ROWID PRODUCT
      INDEX RANGE SCAN PRODUCT_ID1
    BUFFER SORT
      TABLE ACCESS BY INDEX ROWID PRODUCT_LINES
        INDEX RANGE SCAN PRODUCT1
```

```
select      product.name, product_lines.qty
from        product_lines, product
where       product.product_id = product_lines.product_id
and         product.product_id = 4488;
```

EXPLAIN PLAN output

```
SELECT STATEMENT Optimizer=CHOOSE
  MERGE JOIN
    TABLE ACCESS BY INDEX ROWID PRODUCT
      INDEX RANGE SCAN PRODUCT_ID1
    BUFFER SORT
      TABLE ACCESS BY INDEX ROWID PRODUCT_LINES
        INDEX RANGE SCAN PRODUCT1
```

Example 3 Outcomes
When a subsequent condition on PRODUCT_ID on the small table exists, the larger table gets this condition passed to it via the join and is *still* the driving table. The order of the tables in the FROM clause will not alter the procedure unless an ORDERED hint is used.

Summary
The examples in this section demonstrate the value of some of the optimizer's behavior. It almost always chooses how to drive a query correctly, but sometimes it must be corrected for a given query. It chooses the right path in most situations.

Three-Table Joins: Not as Much Fun (Cost-Based)

In a three-table join, Oracle joins two of the tables and joins the result with the third table.

When the query in the following listing is executed, the EMP, DEPT, and ORDERS tables will be joined together, as illustrated in Figure 9-5.

```
select    /*+ ORDERED */ ENAME, DEPT.DEPTNO, ITEMNO
from      EMP, DEPT, ORDERS
where     emp.deptno = dept.deptno
and       emp.empno = orders.empno;
```

Which table is the driving table in a query? People often give different answers, depending on the query that accesses the PLAN_TABLE. This next listing shows a query that has only one possible way to be accessed (the subqueries must be accessed first) and a query to the PLAN_TABLE that will be used for the remainder of this chapter. This listing is provided to ensure that you understand how to read the output effectively.

```
explain plan for
 select     name
 from       customer
 where      cust_no =
  (select   cust_no
   from     product_lines
   where    qty = 1
   and      product_id =
    (select  product_id
     from    product
     where   product.product_id = 807
     and     description = 'test'));
```

The following listing is quick and simple EXPLAIN PLAN query (given the PLAN_TABLE is empty).

```
select    lpad(' ',2*level)||operation oper, options, object_name
from      plan_table
connect   by prior id = parent_id
start     with id = 1
order by  id;
```

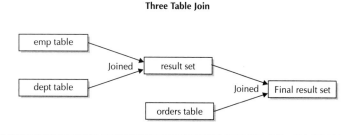

Three Table Join

FIGURE 9-5. *A three-table join*

Three-Table Joins

Next, you can see an abbreviated EXPLAIN PLAN output. (Additional EXPLAIN PLAN information can be found in Chapter 6.)

OPER	OPTIONS	OBJECT_NAME
TABLE ACCESS	BY INDEX ROWID	CUSTOMER
INDEX	RANGE SCAN	CUST1
TABLE ACCESS	BY INDEX ROWID	PRODUCT_LINES
INDEX	RANGE SCAN	PRODUCT_ID1
TABLE ACCESS	BY INDEX ROWID	PRODUCT
INDEX	RANGE SCAN	PRODUCT1

The order of access is PRODUCT, PRODUCT_LINES, and CUSTOMER. The innermost subquery (to the product table) must execute first so that it can return the PRODUCT_ID to be used in the PRODUCT_LINES table (accessed second), which returns the CUST_NO that the CUSTOMER table (accessed third) needs.

TIP
To ensure that you are reading your EXPLAIN PLAN correctly, run a query in which you are sure of the driving table (with nested subqueries).

One exception to the previous subquery is shown here:

```
explain plan for
 select    name
 from      customer
 where     cust_no =
  (select  cust_no
   from    product_lines
   where   product_lines.product_id = 807
   and     qty = 1
   and     product_id =
    (select   product_id
     from     product
     where    product.product_id = 807
     and      description = 'test'));
```

EXPLAIN PLAN output

OPER	OPTIONS	OBJECT_NAME
TABLE ACCESS	BY INDEX ROWID	CUSTOMER
INDEX	RANGE SCAN	CUST1
FILTER		
TABLE ACCESS	BY INDEX ROWID	PRODUCT_LINES
INDEX	RANGE SCAN	PRODUCT_ID1
TABLE ACCESS	BY INDEX ROWID	PRODUCT
INDEX	RANGE SCAN	PRODUCT1

The expected order of table access is based on the order in the FROM clause: PRODUCT, PRODUCT_LINES, and CUSTOMER. The actual order of access is PRODUCT_LINES, PRODUCT, and CUSTOMER. The PRODUCT_LINES query takes the PRODUCT_ID from the subquery to the PRODUCT table and executes first.

Bitmap Join Indexes

Oracle changes the boundaries of relational database design and implementation with the addition of new indexing features. The bitmap join index allows you to build a single index across the joined columns of two tables. The ROWIDs from one table are stored along with the other table. Both of these features are incredible performance gold mines, which was also the case of the function-based index, and they are as powerful as the designer, developer, or DBA who implements them. This section focuses on the bitmap join index.

Bitmap Indexes

To fully appreciate where a bitmap join index is helpful, it is important to understand a bitmap index. Bitmap indexes are most helpful in a data warehouse environment because they are generally great (fast) when you are only selecting data. A bitmap index is smaller than a b-tree index because it stores only the ROWID and a series of bits. In a bitmap index, if a bit is set, it means that a row in the corresponding ROWID (also stored) contains a key value. For example, consider the EMP table with two new columns, gender and marital status:

Empno	Gender (M/F)	Married (Y/N)
1001	F	Y
1002	F	Y
1003	F	N
1004	M	N
1005	M	Y

The bitmaps stored may be the following (the actual storage depends on the algorithm used internally, which is more complex than this example):

Empno=	Gender=F	Married=Y
1001	1	1
1002	1	1
1003	1	0
1004	0	0
1005	0	1

As you can tell from the preceding example, it would be easy to find all of the females by searching for the gender bit set to a '1' in the example. You can similarly find all of those married or even quickly find a combination of gender and marital status. Oracle stores ranges of rows for each bitmap as well, which is why bitmaps don't do well when you update the bitmap-indexed column (can lock an entire range of rows).

You should use b-tree indexes when columns are unique or near-unique; you should at least consider bitmap indexes in all other cases. Although you generally would *not* use a b-tree index when retrieving 40 percent of the rows in a table, using a bitmap index usually makes this task faster than doing a full table scan. This is seemingly in violation of the 80/20 or 95/5 rules, which are generally to use an index when retrieving 5–20 percent or less of the data and to do a full table scan when retrieving more. Bitmap indexes are smaller and work differently than b-tree indexes. You can use bitmap indexes even when retrieving large percentages (20–80 percent) of a table. You can also use bitmaps to retrieve conditions based on NULLs (because NULLs are also indexed), and can be used for not equal conditions for the same reason. The best way to find out is to test!

Bitmap Index Caveats

Bitmap indexes do not perform well in a heavy DML (UPDATE, INSERT, DELETE) environment and generally are not used in certain areas of an OLTP environment. There is a heavy cost if you are doing a lot of DML, so be very careful with this. Also, be careful if you are still using the rule-based optimization; bitmap indexes are *not* considered by the rule-based optimizer. Using NOT NULL constraints and fixed-length columns helps bitmaps use less storage, so a good designer is once again worth his or her weight in gold. Use the INDEX_COMBINE hint instead of the INDEX or AND_EQUAL hints for bitmap indexes. Like b-tree indexes, bitmap indexes should be rebuilt (alter index . . . rebuild) if there is a lot of DML (UPDATE, INSERT, DELETE) activity. Bitmaps are very good for multicolumn read-only indexes that together make a reasonably selective value but separately do not. These columns indexed together, if often used together in a WHERE clause, are a good choice for a bitmap.

Bitmap Join Index

In a typical business relational database, you are often joining the same two or three tables over and over. The bitmap join index can give you substantial gains when properly applied to many of these circumstances. In a bitmap join index, the ROWIDs from one table are stored along with the indexed column from the joined table. The bitmap join index in Oracle is a lot like building a single index across two tables. You must build a primary key or unique constraint on one of the tables. When you are looking for information from just the columns in the index or a count, then you will be able to access the single join index. Let's look at a very simplistic example to learn how to use it. Then we'll look at how you can apply it to multiple columns and multiple tables.

Example 1

Let's create two sample tables to use from our friendly EMP and DEPT tables, as shown in this listing.

```
create table emp1
as select * from scott.emp;

create table dept1
as select * from scott.dept;
```

You must then add a unique constraint (or have a primary key) to the DEPT1 table to use this type of index. You can then create the bitmap index on the EMP1 table that includes the columns of both tables.

```
alter table dept1
add constraint dept_constr1 unique (deptno);
```

```
create bitmap index empdept_idx
 on emp1(dept1.deptno)
 from emp1, dept1
 where emp1.deptno = dept1.deptno;
```

You are now storing the ROWID to the DEPT1 table in the bitmap index that maps to the DEPTNO column in the EMP1 table. To test how well this works, you can perform a simple count(*) of the intersection rows between the two tables (you would usually have additional limiting conditions), forcing the use of the bitmap index with an INDEX hint.

```
select /*+ index(emp1 empdept_idx) */ count(*)
from    emp1, dept1
where   emp1.deptno = dept1.deptno;


    COUNT(*)
---------------
          14

Elapsed: 00:00:00.67

Execution Plan

----------------------------------------------------------------
   0        SELECT STATEMENT Optimizer=CHOOSE
   1    0   SORT (AGGREGATE)
   2    1     BITMAP CONVERSION (COUNT)
   3    2       BITMAP INDEX (FULL SCAN) OF 'EMPDEPT_IDX'
```

You can see from the AUTOTRACE output (using SET AUTOTRACE ON while in SQL*Plus) that the bitmap index was used. Although this simplistic example shows how to count an index (instead of the table) and uses some benefits of the bitmap join index, the next section explores better uses by manipulating columns outside the join in the index.

Best Uses for the Bitmap Join Index
Example 1 showed a basic use of the bitmap join index focusing on just the joined columns. The next three sections show targeted areas where you may find the best use of the bitmap join index.

Bitmap Join Indexes on Columns Other Than the Join
Consider this example where EMP1 and DEPT1 tables are once again joined on the DEPTNO column. In this example, you want to index the LOC column instead of the join column. This allows you to select the location column from the DEPT1 table by directly accessing only the index and the EMP1 table. Remember, the join condition must be on the primary key or unique column. The example in the following listing assumes that the unique constraint on dept1.deptno from the example in the earlier listing (where we added a unique constraint to the DEPT1 table) exists.

```
Create bitmap index emp_dept_location
on     emp1 (dept1.loc)
from   emp1, dept1
where  emp1.deptno = dept1.deptno;
```

Bitmap Indexes

The query shown next can now use the bitmap join index appropriately.

```
select emp1.empno, emp1.ename, dept1.loc
from    emp1, dept1
where   emp1.deptno = dept1.deptno;
```

Bitmap Join Indexes on Multiple Columns

Consider an example where you want an index on multiple columns. The syntax is still the same, but now you include multiple columns in the index. The next example assumes that the unique constraint on dept1.deptno from the example in the earlier listing (where we added a unique constraint to the DEPT1 table) exists.

```
create bitmap index emp_dept_location_deptname
on      emp1 (dept1.loc, dept1.dname)
from    emp1, dept1
where   emp1.deptno = dept1.deptno;
```

The query in the following listing would now be able to use the bitmap join index appropriately:

```
select emp1.empno, emp1.ename, dept1.loc, dept1.dname
from    emp1, dept1
where   emp1.deptno = dept1.deptno;
```

Bitmap Join Indexes on Multiple Tables

As you become more familiar with using the bitmap join index, you will be able to solve complex business problems that involve multiple tables. The following example shows how to apply the bitmap join index to multiple tables. The syntax is still the same, but it has now been expanded to include multiple columns in the index and multiple tables being joined for the index. The example shown next assumes that the unique constraint on dept1.deptno from the example in the earlier listing (where we added a unique constraint to the DEPT1 table) exists and additionally on sales1.empno (creation not shown).

```
Create bitmap index emp_dept_location_ms
on      emp1 (dept1.loc, sales1.marital_status)
from    emp1, dept1, sales1
where   emp1.deptno = dept1.deptno
and     emp1.empno = sales1.empno;
```

The query in this next listing would now be able to use the bitmap join index appropriately:

```
select emp1.empno, emp1.ename, dept1.loc, sales1.marital_status
from    emp1, dept1, sales1
where   emp1.deptno = dept1.deptno
and     emp1.empno = sales1.empno;
```

Bitmap Join Index Caveats

Because the result of the join is stored, only one table can be updated concurrently by different transactions, and parallel DML is supported only on the fact table. Parallel DML on the dimension table marks the index as unusable. No table can appear twice in the join, and you can't create a bitmap join index on an index-organized table (IOT) or a temporary table.

Another Nice Use for the Join Index

A nice tuning trick when you are counting rows is to try to count the index instead of the table. Consider the following large table example used for counting. These tables each contain roughly two million rows each, so that you can see the impact that is possible on a larger scale. The new tables, EMP5 and EMP6, each have 2 million rows with empno indexes on them.

```
alter table emp5
add constraint emp5_constr unique (empno);

select count(*)
from emp5, emp6
where emp5.empno=emp6.empno;
```

Adding the constraint and running a join without the bitmap index

```
  COUNT(*)

-------------------
   2005007
Elapsed: 00:01:07.18


Execution Plan


-----------------------------------------------------------
   0        SELECT STATEMENT Optimizer=CHOOSE
   1    0     SORT (AGGREGATE)
   2    1       NESTED LOOPS
   3    2         TABLE ACCESS (FULL) OF 'EMP6'
   4    2         INDEX (RANGE SCAN) OF 'EMP5I_EMPNO' (NON-UNIQUE)

Statistics


-----------------------------------------------------------
6026820  consistent gets
7760  physical reads
```

There is an index on the EMP5 table, but there is no correlation or index back to the EMP6 table because the index on EMP6 has only empno as the second part of a concatenated index. The result is a relatively slow query.

If you make empno the only part or the leading part of the concatenated index, you will solve this problem. Instead, use the new bitmap join index, as shown here:

```
create bitmap index emp5_j6
 on emp6(emp5.empno)
 from emp5,emp6
 where emp5.empno=emp6.empno;
```

Bitmap Indexes

```
Index created.

Elapsed: 00:02:29.91

select /*+ index(emp6 emp5_j6) */ count(*)
from emp5, emp6
where emp5.empno=emp6.empno;
```

Creating and using the bitmap join index

```
          COUNT(*)
------------------
           2005007

Elapsed: 00:00:00.87

Execution Plan


-----------------------------------------------------------
   0       SELECT STATEMENT Optimizer=CHOOSE
   1    0     SORT (AGGREGATE)
   2    1       BITMAP CONVERSION (COUNT)
   3    2         BITMAP INDEX (FULL SCAN) OF 'EMP5_J6'

Statistics


-----------------------------------------------------------
970   consistent gets
967   physical reads
```

Performing a count of the bitmap join index makes this very fast. I chose this example for a reason. The real problem with the original slow query was not that it took a minute to execute, but that it performed over six million memory block reads and over seven thousand disk block reads. You may not receive any wait events, but you have a poorly written query that will cause problems when you begin to have volumes of users on the system. Take a step up to expert level by finding queries with large memory and disk reads and do proactive tuning so that you don't get to wait states and need to reactively tune things. Using a bitmap join index is one way to improve performance.

Third-Party Product Tuning

Sometimes, you are at the mercy of a third-party product. Although you cannot modify the code, you can often modify the use of indexes. The following three examples are from a financials third-party product.

Example 1

This query was taking 22 minutes to run. By providing a hint to a more efficient index, the query execution time was reduced to 15 seconds.

This next listing shows the query before the hint is added:

```
update PS_COMBO_DATA_TBL
set     EFFDT_FROM = TO_DATE ('1990-01-01', 'YYYY-MM-DD'),
        EFFDT_TO = TO_DATE ('2099-01-01', 'YYYY-MM-DD')
where   SETID = 'RRD'
and     PROCESS_GROUP = 'GROUP1'
and     COMBINATION = 'ACCT/NOLOC'
and     VALID_CODE = 'V'
and     EFFDT_OPEN = 'Y'
and     EXISTS
  (select    'X'
   from      PS_JRNL_LN
   where     BUSINESS_UNIT = '00003'
   and       PROCESS_INSTANCE = 0000085176
   and       JRNL_LINE_STATUS = '3'
   and       ACCOUNT = PS_COMBO_DATA_TBL.ACCOUNT
   and       PRODUCT = PS_COMBO_DATA_TBL.PRODUCT );
```

Now, we can see the query after the Index hint is added:

```
update PS_COMBO_DATA_TBL
set     EFFDT_FROM = TO_DATE ('1990-01-01', 'YYYY-MM-DD'),
        EFFDT_TO = TO_DATE ('2099-01-01', 'YYYY-MM-DD')
where   SETID = 'RRD'
and     PROCESS_GROUP = 'GROUP1'
and     COMBINATION = 'ACCT/NOLOC'
and     VALID_CODE = 'V'
and     EFFDT_OPEN = 'Y'
and     EXISTS
  (select    /*+ INDEX(PS_JRNL_LN PSGJRNL_LN) */  'X'
   from      PS_JRNL_LN
   where     BUSINESS_UNIT = '00003'
   and       PROCESS_INSTANCE = 0000085176
   and       JRNL_LINE_STATUS = '3'
   and       ACCOUNT = PS_COMBO_DATA_TBL.ACCOUNT
   and       PRODUCT = PS_COMBO_DATA_TBL.PRODUCT );
```

Example 2

The query in the next listing was taking 33 minutes to run. By creating a concatenated index on the PS_GROUP_CONTROL table (columns: DEPOSIT_BU, DEPOSIT_ID, PAYMENT_SEQ_NUM), the query execution time was reduced to 30 seconds, as shown here:

```
select  C.BUSINESS_UNIT, C.CUST_ID, C.ITEM,
        C.ENTRY_TYPE, C.ENTRY_REASON, C.ENTRY_AMT,
        C.ENTRY_CURRENCY, C.ENTRY_AMT_BASE,
        C.CURRENCY_CD, C.POSTED_FLAG, D.PAYMENT_SEQ_NUM
from    PS_PENDING_ITEM C,
        PS_GROUP_CONTROL D
where   D.DEPOSIT_BU = :1
and     D.DEPOSIT_ID = :2
and     D.PAYMENT_SEQ_NUM = :3
```

```
and          D.GROUP_BU = C.GROUP_BU
and          D.GROUP_ID = C.GROUP_ID
order by  D.PAYMENT_SEQ_NUM;
```

EXPLAIN PLAN before index is added

```
Execution Plan
RULE SELECT STATEMENT
      SORT ORDER BY
         NESTED LOOPS
           ANALYZED TABLE ACCESS FULL PS_GROUP_CONTROL
           ANALYZED TABLE ACCESS BY ROWID PS_PENDING_ITEM
              ANALYZED INDEX RANGE SCAN PS_PENDING_ITEM
```

EXPLAIN PLAN after index is added

```
Execution Plan
RULE SELECT STATEMENT
      SORT ORDER BY
         NESTED LOOPS
           ANALYZED TABLE ACCESS BY ROWID PS_GROUP_CONTROL
              INDEX RANGE SCAN PSAGROUP_CONTROL
           ANALYZED TABLE ACCESS BY ROWID PS_PENDING_ITEM
              ANALYZED INDEX RANGE SCAN PS_PENDING_ITEM
```

Example 3

The query shown next was taking 20 minutes to run and was reduced to 30 seconds. You create a concatenated unique index on the PS_CUST_OPTION table (columns: CUST_ID, EFFDT) instead of the current index, which is only on CUST_ID. This forces Oracle to use a concatenated unique index rather than a single-column index, as shown here:

```
INSERT INTO PS_PP_CUST_TMP  (PROCESS_INSTANCE,
 DEPOSIT_BU, DEPOSIT_ID, PAYMENT_SEQ_NUM, CUST_ID,
 PAYMENT_AMT, PAYMENT_DT, PP_METHOD, SETID,
 SUBCUST_QUAL1, SUBCUST_QUAL2, PP_HOLD, PP_MET_SW,
 PAYMENT_CURRENCY)
select    DISTINCT P.PROCESS_INSTANCE, P.DEPOSIT_BU,
          P.DEPOSIT_ID, P.PAYMENT_SEQ_NUM, C.CUST_ID,
          P.PAYMENT_AMT, P.PAYMENT_DT, O.PP_METHOD,
          O.SETID, C.SUBCUST_QUAL1, C.SUBCUST_QUAL2,
          O.PP_HOLD, 'N', P.PAYMENT_CURRENCY
from      PS_CUST_OPTION O, PS_CUSTOMER C, PS_ITEM I,
          PS_SET_CNTRL_REC S, PS_PAYMENT_ID_ITEM X,
          PS_PP_PAYMENT_TMP P
where     P.PROCESS_INSTANCE = 85298
and       S.SETCNTRLVALUE = I.BUSINESS_UNIT
and       I.CUST_ID = C.CUST_ID
and       I.ITEM_STATUS = 'O'
and       (X.REF_VALUE = I.DOCUMENT
or        SUBSTR (X.REF_VALUE, 3, 7)
```

```
              = SUBSTR (I.DOCUMENT, 4, 7))
and       S.RECNAME = 'CUSTOMER'
and       S.SETID = C.SETID
and       O.SETID = C.REMIT_FROM_SETID
and       O.CUST_ID = C.REMIT_FROM_CUST_ID
and       O.EFFDT =
    (select   MAX (X.EFFDT)
     from      PS_CUST_OPTION X
     where     X.SETID = O.SETID
     and       X.CUST_ID = O.CUST_ID
     and       X.EFF_STATUS = 'A'
     and       X.EFFDT <= P.PAYMENT_DT)
and       O.PP_METHOD <> ' '
and       P.DEPOSIT_BU = X.DEPOSIT_BU
and       P.DEPOSIT_ID = X.DEPOSIT_ID
and       P.PAYMENT_SEQ_NUM = X.PAYMENT_SEQ_NUM
and       X.REF_QUALIFIER_CODE = 'D';
```

EXPLAIN PLAN before index is added

```
Execution Plan
RULE INSERT STATEMENT
    SORT UNIQUE
        NESTED LOOPS
            NESTED LOOPS
                NESTED LOOPS
                    NESTED LOOPS
                        NESTED LOOPS
                            ANALYZED TABLE ACCESS BY ROWID PS_PP_PAYMENT_TMP
                                ANALYZED INDEX RANGE SCAN PSAPP_PAYMENT_TMP
                                ANALYZED INDEX RANGE SCAN PSAPAYMENT_ID_ITEM
                            ANALYZED INDEX RANGE SCAN PSDSET_CNTRL_REC
                        ANALYZED INDEX RANGE SCAN PSEITEM
                    ANALYZED TABLE ACCESS BY ROWID PS_CUSTOMER
                        ANALYZED INDEX UNIQUE SCAN PS_CUSTOMER
                ANALYZED TABLE ACCESS BY ROWID PS_CUST_OPTION
                    ANALYZED INDEX RANGE SCAN PSACUST_OPTION
            SORT AGGREGATE
                ANALYZED TABLE ACCESS BY ROWID PS_CUST_OPTION
                    ANALYZED INDEX RANGE SCAN PSACUST_OPTION
```

EXPLAIN PLAN after index is added

```
Execution Plan
RULE INSERT STATEMENT
    SORT UNIQUE
        NESTED LOOPS
            NESTED LOOPS
                NESTED LOOPS
                    NESTED LOOPS
                        NESTED LOOPS
```

```
              ANALYZED TABLE ACCESS BY ROWID PS_PP_PAYMENT_TMP
                ANALYZED INDEX RANGE SCAN PSAPP_PAYMENT_TMP
                ANALYZED INDEX RANGE SCAN PSAPAYMENT_ID_ITEM
              ANALYZED INDEX RANGE SCAN PSDSET_CNTRL_REC
            ANALYZED INDEX RANGE SCAN PSEITEM
          ANALYZED TABLE ACCESS BY ROWID PS_CUSTOMER
            ANALYZED INDEX UNIQUE SCAN PS_CUSTOMER
        ANALYZED TABLE ACCESS BY ROWID PS_CUST_OPTION
          ANALYZED INDEX RANGE SCAN PS_CUST_OPTION
      SORT AGGREGATE
        ANALYZED TABLE ACCESS BY ROWID PS_CUST_OPTION
          ANALYZED INDEX RANGE SCAN PS_CUST_OPTION
```

TIP
You may not be able to modify actual code for some third-party products, but you can often add, force, or suppress indexes to improve the performance.

Tuning Distributed Queries

When improperly written, distributed queries can sometimes be disastrous and lead to poor performance. In particular, a NESTED LOOPS join between two row sources on separate nodes of a distributed database can be very slow because Oracle moves all the data to the local machine (depending on how the query is written). The following listing shows a simple distributed query and its execution plan. This query is slow because for each row retrieved from the CUSTOMERS table, a separate query is dispatched to the remote node to retrieve records from the bookings table. This results in many small network packets moving between the two nodes of the database, and the network latency and overhead degrade performance.

```
select    customer_id, customer_name, class_code
from      customers cust
where     exists
(select   1
 from     bookings@book bkg
 where    bkg.customer_id = cust.customer_id
 and      bkg.status = 'OPEN' )
order by  customer_name;
```

TKPROF Output

call	count	cpu	elapsed	disk	query	current	rows
Parse	1	0.00	0.01	0	0	0	0
Execute	1	0.00	0.00	0	0	0	0
Fetch	156	0.41	11.85	0	476	2	155
total	158	0.41	11.86	0	476	2	155

Rows	Execution Plan
0	SELECT STATEMENT GOAL: CHOOSE
155	SORT (ORDER BY)

```
467         FILTER
467           TABLE ACCESS   GOAL: ANALYZED (FULL) OF 'CUSTOMERS'
0               REMOTE [BOOK.WORLD]
                  SELECT "CUSTOMER_ID","STATUS" FROM "BOOKINGS" BKG WHERE
                    "STATUS"='open' AND "CUSTOMER_ID"=:1
```

The query in the preceding listing can be rewritten in a form that causes less network traffic. In the next listing, one query is sent to the remote node to determine all customers with open bookings. The output is the same, but performance is greatly improved. Both versions of the query use roughly the same CPU time and logical I/Os on the local node, but the elapsed time is about 97 percent better here. This gain is attributable to reduced network overhead.

```
select    customer_id, customer_name, class_code
from      customers
where     customer_id in
(select   customer_id
 from     bookings@book
 where    status = 'OPEN' )
order by  customer_name;
```

TKPROF Output

call	count	cpu	elapsed	disk	query	current	rows
Parse	1	0.00	0.01	0	0	0	0
Execute	1	0.00	0.00	0	0	0	0
Fetch	156	0.07	0.27	0	467	0	155
total	158	0.07	0.28	0	467	0	155

```
Rows    Execution_Plan
0       SELECT STATEMENT   GOAL: CHOOSE
155       SORT (ORDER BY)
155         NESTED LOOPS
156           VIEW
1000            SORT (UNIQUE)
1000              REMOTE [BOOK.WORLD]
                    SELECT "CUSTOMER_ID","STATUS" FROM "BOOKINGS" BOOKINGS WHERE
                      "STATUS"='open'
155           TABLE ACCESS   GOAL: ANALYZED (BY ROWID) OF 'CUSTOMERS'
156             INDEX   GOAL: ANALYZED (UNIQUE SCAN) OF 'SYS_C002109'
                  (UNIQUE)
```

When distributed queries cannot be avoided, use IN clauses, set operators such as UNION and MINUS, and use everything else you can to reduce the network traffic between nodes of the database. Using views that limit the records in a table can also improve performance by reducing what is sent from the remote client to the local client. With Oracle 8, you can use the DRIVING_SITE hint to control which node of the distributed database drives the distributed query. In Oracle 7, the driving site is always the local node where the query originated. From the 10.2 Admin Guide, Chapter 31, "Rewriting your query to access the remote database once is achieved by using collocated inline views."

Tuning Distributed Queries

TIP
When distributed queries cannot be avoided, use IN clauses, set operators such as UNION and MINUS, and use everything else you can to reduce the network traffic between nodes of the database. Queries written in a manner that causes looping between distributed nodes (distributed databases) can be extremely slow.

When You Have Everything Tuned

If you successfully tune all of *your* queries, then you can start working on those that go to the data dictionary views. The next example shows that even Oracle's own views have some highly complex joining schemes.

```
select     *
from       dba_ind_columns
where      table_name = 'PRODUCT_LINES';
```

Execution plan output

Id	Operation	Name
0	SELECT STATEMENT	
1	NESTED LOOPS OUTER	
2	TABLE ACCESS BY INDEX ROWID	COL$
* 3	INDEX UNIQUE SCAN	I_COL3
* 4	TABLE ACCESS CLUSTER	ATTRCOL$
5	NESTED LOOPS	
6	NESTED LOOPS	
7	NESTED LOOPS OUTER	
8	NESTED LOOPS	
9	NESTED LOOPS	
10	NESTED LOOPS	
11	NESTED LOOPS	
12	TABLE ACCESS BY INDEX ROWID	OBJ$
* 13	INDEX SKIP SCAN	I_OBJ2
14	TABLE ACCESS CLUSTER	ICOL$
* 15	INDEX UNIQUE SCAN	I_OBJ#
16	TABLE ACCESS BY INDEX ROWID	OBJ$
* 17	INDEX UNIQUE SCAN	I_OBJ1
* 18	TABLE ACCESS BY INDEX ROWID	IND$
* 19	INDEX UNIQUE SCAN	I_IND1
* 20	TABLE ACCESS CLUSTER	COL$
* 21	TABLE ACCESS CLUSTER	ATTRCOL$
22	TABLE ACCESS CLUSTER	USER$
* 23	INDEX UNIQUE SCAN	I_USER#
24	TABLE ACCESS CLUSTER	USER$
* 25	INDEX UNIQUE SCAN	I_USER#

Miscellaneous Tuning Snippets

The issues covered in this section will help the advanced DBA. We'll look at external tables, consider the Snapshot Too Old issue along with how to set the event to dump every wait, and explore what's really going on by performing block dumps.

External Tables

External tables allow you to access data that is not inside the database. Relational databases took off in the 1980s because of the ability to access data through relational tables. This was the first move away from mainframes and legacy systems that stored information in flat files or some facsimile of that. Oracle 10*g* will be the next paradigm in relational database technology. External tables extend the relational model beyond the database. Now we have a means by which to access all of the legacy data. We have a way to access all of that information dumped into flat files (perhaps, via third-party products).

One of the most costly parts of the extract, transform, load (ETL) process used for data warehousing and business intelligence is loading data into temporary tables so that it can be used with other tables already in the database. Although external tables were introduced primarily to assist in the ETL process, Pandora's box cannot be closed. I have seen a plethora of uses for external tables, and I believe it's just the beginning. If Java and XML were minor aspects integrated into the relational model, the use of external tables brings the entire machine into the database and forever changes the rules of engagement.

This simple example shows you exactly how to use external tables. First, you need a flat file of data to access for the examples. You do this by simply spooling some data from our familiar friend, the EMP table.

```
set head off
set verify off
set feedback off
set pages 0
spool emp4.dat
select empno||','||ename ||','|| job||','||deptno||','
from    scott.emp;
spool off
```

Output of the emp4.dat file

```
7369,SMITH,CLERK,20,
7499,ALLEN,SALESMAN,30,
7521,WARD,SALESMAN,30,
7566,JONES,MANAGER,20,
7654,MARTIN,SALESMAN,30,
```

Then you need to create a directory from within SQL*Plus so that Oracle knows where to find your external tables.

```
SQL> create directory rich_new as '/u01/home/oracle/rich';

Directory created.
```

External Tables

You then create the actual table definition that will reference the flat file that resides externally. Note that even if you successfully create the table, access to the external table may not necessarily result in a successful query. If the data is not stored in the column definition of your table, you will get an error when you select the actual data. An example of the create table command is shown here.

```
create table emp_external4
(empno char(4), ename char(10), job char(9), deptno char(2))
organization external
(type oracle_loader
 default directory rich_new
 access parameters
 (records delimited by newline
  fields terminated by ','
  (empno , ename, job, deptno ))
 location ('emp4.dat'))
reject limit unlimited;

SQL> desc emp_external4
Name                                          Null? Type
--------------------------------------------- -------- --------------
EMPNO                                               CHAR(4)
ENAME                                               CHAR(10)
JOB                                                 CHAR(9)
DEPTNO                                              CHAR(2)
select  *
from    emp_external4;
EMPNO       ENAME          JOB           DEPTNO
--------    --------------  -----------   --------------
7369        SMITH          CLERK         20
7499        ALLEN          SALESMAN      30
7521        WARD           SALESMAN      30
...
```

There is currently no support for DML (insert, update, delete) commands, but you can always do this outside the database because the data is in a flat file. Using shell scripting as shown next, you can certainly replicate those commands. Although you can't create an index currently, external tables are pleasantly and surprisingly fast.

```
SQL> insert into emp_external4 ...;

ERROR at line 1:
ORA-30657: operation not supported on external organized table
SQL> create index emp_ei on emp_external4(deptno);
               *
ERROR at line 1:
ORA-30657: operation not supported on external organized table
```

To count records, you can either use the Unix command or do it within the database. Either way, you have a means to work with data that is in flat files that are not within the database. This next listing is the wc (word count) command with the –l option, which indicates to count the lines. This is a simple Unix command for counting records in a flat file. I created a file with 200,020 rows for the next more intensive test.

```
$ wc -l emp4.dat
  200020  200020 4400400 emp4.dat
$ ls -l emp4.dat
-rwxr-xr-x  1 oracle  oinstall 4400400 Aug  9 06:31 emp4.dat
```

You can also count the records in the flat file using SQL, since you've now built an external table. The command shown next takes less than one second to return its result.

```
select count(*)
from   emp_external4;

   COUNT(*)
------------------
     200020
Elapsed: 00:00:00.63
```

Once you know you can count records in less than one second, you press on to look for specific information. Can you count selective pieces of data that fast? Yes. The code in the next listing looks for specific employee numbers (empno) from the flat file, which is now referenced via an external table. The result is returned to once again in less than one second.

```
select count(*)
from   emp_external4
where  empno=7900;

COUNT(*)
------------------
     20
Elapsed: 00:00:00.82
```

Once you know you can scan through 200,000 records in less than one second (on a single-processor machine in my case), you want to see how fast you can scan through millions of records. The example shown next builds a second table and joins it with the first so you can test scanning through four million rows. The result is less than three seconds to scan through this massive amount of data using only modest hardware.

```
create table emp_external5
(empno char(4), ename char(10), job char(9), deptno    char(2))
organization external
  ...
location ('emp5.dat'));
```

Now you join the two 200-thousand-row tables to create a join that merges the 20 rows in the first result set with the 20 rows of the second table, as shown here. This results in a join accessing 4 million rows with a result set of 400 rows. The result is an answer in less than three seconds.

```
select a.empno, b.job, a.job
from   emp_external4 a, emp_external5 b
```

External Tables

```
where   a.empno = b.empno
and     a.empno = 7900
and     b.empno = 7900;

400 rows selected.
Elapsed: 00:00:02.46
```

The execution plan for the previous join is shown here:

```
Execution Plan
----------------------------------------------------------
    0        SELECT STATEMENT Optimizer=CHOOSE
    1    0     MERGE JOIN
    2    1       SORT (JOIN)
    3    2         EXTERNAL TABLE ACCESS (FULL) OF 'EMP_EXTERNAL5'
    4    1       SORT (JOIN)
    5    4         EXTERNAL TABLE ACCESS (FULL) OF 'EMP_EXTERNAL4'
```

You can also use hints with external tables, and you can join external tables with regular tables. You can parallelize the operation, and you can even insert the data from the external table directly into the database at any time. The possibilities are endless. External tables are not just a serious advantage of using Oracle: they are one of the largest benefits to relational technology in the past decade. They give you the window into the data that is *not* in your database. They allow you to access those legacy systems that have data stored in a multitude of flat files. They provide you the path to consolidate those legacy systems by moving step-by-step into the future.

Consider the quick use for an external table to read the alert file shown in the following listing. The original script for this was written by Dave Moore and passed to me by Howard Horowitz. The following is an alteration of those scripts.

```
SQL> Create directory BDUMP as 'f:\ora\admin\ora\bdump';
Directory created.
SQL> Create table alert_log (text varchar2(200))
Organization EXTERNAL
(Type oracle_loader
Default directory BDUMP
Access parameters
(Records delimited by newline
Badfile 'rich1.bad'
Logfile 'rich1.log')
Location ('alert_ora.log'))
Reject limit unlimited;
Table created.
select *
from    alert_log
where   rownum < 4;

TEXT
----------------------------------------------------------------------------------
Dump file d:\software\10.2.0.2/admin/orcl/bdump\alert_orcl.log
Thu Jan 05 11:33:51 2006
ORACLE V10.2.0.1.0 - Production vsnsta=0
alter database rename global_name to ora.world
Completed: alter database rename global_name to ora.world
```

CAUTION
External tables are one of the best Oracle inventions in many versions. Your innovative mind will drive you to new heights using external tables. But be careful: data residing outside the database is not subject to the same Oracle backups and security as data inside the database.

Snapshot Too Old: Developer Coding Issue

Oracle holds rollback information in case of the need to roll back a transaction, and also to keep a read-consistent version of data. Long-running queries may need the read-consistent versions of the data in the undo tablespace in undo segments because they may not be the same System Change Number (SCN) as the ones currently in memory. (They may have been changed since the start of the query.) If the rollback segment holding the original data is overwritten, the user receives the dreaded Snapshot Too Old error. With advances in Oracle 9*i* and Oracle 10*g*, this error would be rare indeed (using automatic undo management), but there is another, more frequent occurrence in the later versions of Oracle.

In their infinite wisdom, developers find wonderful ways to update information that they are querying within the same piece of code causing this problem. They are the ones both querying and updating, and causing the Snapshot Too Old error to occur. One flawed developer method is known as the Fetch Across Commit. In this method, the developer first selects a large number of rows from a table into a cursor and then fetches the rows to use for an update to the table, committing after a select number (say, every 1000 records) based on a counter. What happens is that the cursor needs a read-consistent image of the table, yet the developer is committing 1000 records within the same code to the table. The result is a Snapshot Too Old error.

NOTE
See an excellent paper by Dave Wotton (listed in the references) on understanding Snapshot Too Old for a detailed explanation of this esoteric problem.

TIP
In addition to the more typical reasons, when developers modify the data as it is being selected, fetching across commits, the Snapshot Too Old error can occur. To fix this problem, close and reopen the cursor causing the issue.

Set Event to Dump Every Wait

In Chapter 14, you learned that STATSPACK and AWR are excellent tuning tools that Oracle offers. These are great for showing everything in a single report for you to analyze. But what if you have a burning issue and you directly need to dump exactly what the system is doing so that you can see every wait on the system? If the compilation of all waits in the V$ views is not enough to solve problems and you need to see the waits in real time, the answer is the very dangerous Set

Set Event to Dump Every Wait

Event 10046 at the system level. You can also do this at the session level (see Chapter 13 for additional settings beyond this section).

This event dumps every single wait that occurs so that you can search through and see exactly what's causing the problem. You should use this strategy only as a last resort, and you should rarely use it. You need a lot of disk space to use it when you have a lot of waits.

When you're ready to dump the problem, here's how to turn it on:

```
Alter system set events '10046 trace name context forever, level 12';
```

The following listing shows what you'll get (in your USER_DUMP_DEST).

```
Dump file f:\ora\admin\ora\udump\ora_ora_240.trc
Mon Feb 17 00:31:47 2003
...etc...
PARSING IN CURSOR #1 len=69 dep=0 uid=49 oct=42 lid=49 tim=189871918082 hv=3799341816
ad='12954910'
Alter session set events '10046 trace name context forever, level 12'
END OF STMT
EXEC #1:c=10014,e=51216,p=0,cr=0,cu=0,mis=1,r=0,dep=0,og=4,tim=189871484620
WAIT #1: nam='SQL*Net message to client' ela= 64 p1=1111838976 p2=1 p3=0
*** 2003-02-17 00:32:00.000
WAIT #1: nam='SQL*Net message from client' ela= 12734591 p1=1111838976 p2=1 p3=0
====================
PARSE ERROR #1:len=55 dep=0 uid=49 oct=42 lid=49 tim=189884741177 err=1756
Alter session set events '10046 trace name context off
WAIT #1: nam='SQL*Net break/reset to client' ela= 255 p1=1111838976 p2=1 p3=0
WAIT #1: nam='SQL*Net break/reset to client' ela= 258 p1=1111838976 p2=0 p3=0
WAIT #1: nam='SQL*Net message to client' ela= 13 p1=1111838976 p2=1 p3=0
*** 2003-02-17 00:32:16.000
WAIT #1: nam='SQL*Net message from client' ela= 16306602 p1=1111838976 p2=1 p3=0
====================
PARSING IN CURSOR #1 len=55 dep=0 uid=49 oct=42 lid=49 tim=189901104969 hv=1730465789
ad='129530c8'
Alter session set events '10046 trace name context off'
END OF STMT
```

Although this output shows some irrelevant waits that came up when you quickly turn this on and off, when you have a real problem, the waits will be clear. You will be looking for a section with something like the following, which shows a latch free issue. (See Chapter 14 for how to resolve this issue.) When you don't know what you're waiting for, this gives you a slightly more "at the street" level understanding of exactly what's going on than the V$ views.

```
WAIT #2: nam='latch free' ela= 0 p1=-2147423252 p2=105 p3=0
WAIT #2: nam='latch free' ela= 0 p1=-2147423252 p2=105 p3=1
WAIT #2: nam='latch free' ela= 0 p1=-1088472332 p2=106 p3=0
WAIT #2: nam='latch free' ela= 0 p1=-2147423252 p2=105 p3=0
WAIT #2: nam='latch free' ela= 0 p1=-2147423252 p2=105 p3=1
WAIT #2: nam='latch free' ela= 1 p1=-2147423252 p2=105 p3=2
WAIT #2: nam='latch free' ela= 0 p1=-2147423252 p2=105 p3=0
WAIT #2: nam='latch free' ela= 1 p1=-2147423252 p2=105 p3=1
WAIT #2: nam='latch free' ela= 0 p1=-2147423252 p2=105 p3=0
WAIT #2: nam='latch free' ela= 0 p1=-2147423252 p2=105 p3=1
```

When you have a nice dump of the problem, here's how you turn it off.

```
Alter system set events '10046 trace name context off';
```

CAUTION
Using the event 10046 at the system level can give a real-time dump of waits. Be careful because you can quickly use a lot of space on a very busy system. Only an expert who has the help of Oracle Support should use this method.

14 Hours to 30 Seconds with the Exists Operator

Although the Oracle optimizer is very good at ensuring a query is efficient, you can change a multitable join into a query with a sub-query using the EXISTS operator. You can only do this if the table to put into the subquery doesn't have anything being selected from it in the SELECT statement. In this example, the goal was to pull one row back to use for test data in a test system.

```
--query with table join
explain plan for
SELECT MEMBER_NO
  , CONTRACT
  , DEP
  , SBSB_CK
  , SBSB_ID
  , GRGR_ID
  , MEME_BIRTH_DT
  , x.MEME_CK
  , MEME_REL
  , MEME_SFX
  , MEME_LAST_NAME
  , MEME_FIRST_NAME
  , to_timestamp('06/01/2006','mm/dd/yyyy')
  , 'PHASE 3'
  , CREATE_WHO
  , CREATE_DT
  , UPDATE_WHO
  , UPDATE_DT FROM PROD_PH.XREF_MEME x
      , PROD.CMC_MEPE_PRCS_ELIG
WHERE x.meme_ck = e.meme_ck
  and rownum = 1;

--Star query plan with B-TREE indexes!
-------------------------------------------------------------------------
| Id | Operation              | Name            | Rows  | Bytes | Cost  |
-------------------------------------------------------------------------
|  0 | SELECT STATEMENT       |                 | 1272G |  123T |  274M |
|  1 |  MERGE JOIN CARTESIAN  |                 | 1272G |  123T |  274M |
|  2 |   TABLE ACCESS FULL    | XREF_MEME       |  638K |   65M |   757 |
|  3 |   BUFFER SORT          |                 | 1991K |       |  274M |
|  4 |    INDEX FAST FULL SCAN| CMCX_MEPE_SECOND| 1991K |       |   429 |
-------------------------------------------------------------------------

--exists subquery
explain plan for
SELECT MEMBER_NO
  , CONTRACT
  , DEP
  , SBSB_CK
  , SBSB_ID
  , GRGR_ID
  , MEME_BIRTH_DT
```

```
  , x.MEME_CK
  , MEME_REL
  , MEME_SFX
  , MEME_LAST_NAME
  , MEME_FIRST_NAME
  , to_timestamp('06/01/2006','mm/dd/yyyy')
  , 'PHASE 3'
  , CREATE_WHO
  , CREATE_DT
  , UPDATE_WHO
  , UPDATE_DT
FROM PROD_PH.XREF_MEME x
WHERE exists(
        select 0
          from prod.cmc_mepe_prcs_elig e
         where e.meme_ck = x.meme_ck
      )
  and rownum = 1;
```

```
--------------------------------------------------------------------------------
| Id | Operation              | Name            | Rows  | Bytes |TempSpc| Cost |
--------------------------------------------------------------------------------
|  0 | SELECT STATEMENT       |                 |     1 |   112 |       | 5067 |
|* 1 |  COUNT STOPKEY         |                 |       |       |       |      |
|* 2 |   HASH JOIN SEMI       |                 |  635K |   67M |   72M | 5067 |
|  3 |    TABLE ACCESS FULL   | XREF_MEME       |  638K |   65M |       |  757 |
|  4 |    INDEX FAST FULL SCAN| CMCX_MEPE_CLUSTER| 1991K| 9726K |       |  464 |
--------------------------------------------------------------------------------
```

You can see from this example that using the EXISTS instead of joining the tables can be very beneficial. Thanks to Mark Riedel of TUSC for sending this; as he puts it: "the TUSC patented EXISTS statement." We first discovered this around 1990.

Tuning at the Block Level (Advanced)

While block tuning is covered briefly in Chapter 14, here we will cover it in a bit more depth. An internal table called the buffer hash table (x$bh) holds block headers. There is a hash chain to which blocks are linked that are protected by a CBC latch (cache buffers chains latch). This links to the actual address located in memory (the memory set up with DB_CACHE SIZE, which is the cache used for data). For a given block in Oracle, only one version of a block is CURRENT, and there are no more than five other CR versions of the block (as of V9). Thus there are only six versions of a given block (maximum) in memory at a time (forming a hash chain of six), although different blocks can be hashed to the same chain (depending on the hashing algorithm). When you perform a DML (data manipulation lock) transaction, which is an INSERT, UPDATE, or DELETE, you always need the CURRENT version of a block. In some versions of Oracle 8, you had to set _DB_BLOCK_HASH_BUCKETS to a prime number to keep the dba blocks evenly balanced in the hash buckets (more information on this in Chapter 14) and avoid a long hash chain arising from the way the hash was calculated. If you didn't set this to a prime number, you could get a very long hash chain (as many blocks were hashed to the same chain) and then get major cbc (cache buffers chains) latch waits (cbc latches are shared in 10g, although not under all conditions). This was fixed in 9i and 10g. I am told that the hashing algorithm changed in certain versions of Oracle 10g and this will not need to be prime in the future (so don't change it).

Also note that Oracle 10g has something called "in-memory undo" (IMU), which can give you some hard-to-understand results when you are viewing information at the block level. If you are familiar with IMU, which is new in 10*g*, you will find that blocks don't show up as dirty when you query x$bh and they have been dirtied. This is because updates are made *inside the actual block,* as opposed to in the undo block, before images are taken. I found out that this happens only for certain retention settings, though. There is a parameter _IN_MEMORY_ IMU=TRUE in the init.ora file that is set to false for some tpc benchmarks. Other parameters include _IMU_POOLS and _DB_WRITER_FLUSH_IMU. If you access the block trying to update a different row in the block, the IMU will be flushed to the undo block and the block will show as dirty (in my tests anyway, although I was told this depends on what the undo retention is set to). IMU writes the undo and redo to memory instead of to disk (which is what the IMU_POOLS parameter is for). IMU transactions always have room reserved in the current log file for writing out their redo. They also acquire an ITL in the block header and reserve space in the UNDO segment.

When you are querying a block for the first time, you always use the CURRENT version of a block. It the block is being used, you will build a *CLONE* of the block called a CONSISTENT READ (CR) version by applying any undo needed to the CURRENT version of the block to get it to a point in time that makes it useful to you (perhaps you need a version of the block before the DML was performed and not committed by another user). This complex and Oracle-patented process may include reading the ITL (the interested transaction list, which is populated when someone does a DML on a block), mapping the record to the UNDO HEADER, or directly to the UNDO BLOCK, and then applying the UNDO to get the correct CR version that you need. So let's take a look at how this happens:

- User 1 updates a record in block 777 (user1 has not committed).

- User 2 queries the same block and sees that the lock byte is set for a row being queried.

- User 2 goes to the ITL portion of the block and get the XID (transaction ID).

- The XID maps to the UNDO block, which holds the information before the update was done.

- A clone of the block is done (call it block 778).

- The UNDO information is applied to the block, rolling it forward, but to where it used to be (versus how most people think of it—rolling it back).

- Block 777 is a CURRENT block.

- Block 778 is a CONSISTENT READ block before the User 1 update occurred.

- If another user wants to do a query before the commit, that user can also read the CR version.

Note *especially* the fact that the block is not *rolled back* to what it was, but it is *rolled forward* to what it used to be. While the result is the same, how Oracle performs this operation is *critical* to understanding how Oracle works. They are always moving forward in time (this is why the REDO works—it's always applying things forward sequentially). There are also links to all blocks for the LRU (least recently used) and LRU-W (least recently used–write) to help make buffer replacement and writing much faster. This is also maintained in the buffer headers.

If nothing has been advanced enough for you so far, this section will be worth the price of the book and should keep you busy for the next decade tuning your system to perfection (if you'd like). Oracle often has perplexing new features: either I can't seem to get them working, or there's

Tuning at the Block Level (Advanced)

simply a bug in the program that I am unaware of. How do you find out if a problem is yours or Oracle's? Dump the blocks one at a time.

Consider the intense example in the listing that follows. Find the table/index block information that you want to dump, as shown here:

```
SELECT FILE_ID, BLOCK_ID, BLOCKS FROM DBA_EXTENTS
WHERE SEGMENT_NAME = 'EMP'
AND OWNER = 'SCOTT';

   FILE_ID         BLOCK_ID           BLOCKS
---------     --------------      ------------
         1             50465                 3
```

Dump the table/index block information, as demonstrated here:

```
ALTER SYSTEM DUMP DATAFILE 5 BLOCK 50465;
ALTER SYSTEM DUMP DATAFILE 5 BLOCK 50466;
ALTER SYSTEM DUMP DATAFILE 5 BLOCK 50467;

-- You could also issue the following command to dump the range of blocks:

ALTER SYSTEM DUMP DATAFILE 5 BLOCK MIN 50465 BLOCK MAX 50467;
```

The ALTER SYSTEM command shown here selects and then dumps the data blocks for the EMP table owned by SCOTT to the USER_DUMP_DEST. The information that is dumped is very cryptic, but it can be helpful for tuning purposes.

The information in the listing that follows compares portions of the block dumps of two different bitmap join indexes. One is on the DEPTNO column, where the tables are also being joined by DEPTNO. The other is on the LOCATION column, where the table is being joined by DEPTNO. By comparing index information, you can see that the LOCATION column was included in the stored part of the index, even though the query was going back to the table to retrieve the location column in the query. The problem was an Oracle bug that you would discover only by performing this dump (partially shown in this next listing; only the first record is displayed for each).

```
DUMP OF BITMAP JOIN INDEX ON location JOINING deptno ON EMP1/DEPT1
row#0[3912] flag: -----, lock: 0
col 0; len 7; (7): 43 48 49 43 41 47 4f
col 1; len 6; (6): 00 40 f3 31 00 00
col 2; len 6; (6): 00 40 f3 31 00 0f
col 3; len 3; (3): c9 36 0a

----- end of leaf block dump
End dump data blocks tsn: 0 file#:
DUMP OF BITMAP JOIN INDEX ON deptno JOINING deptno ON EMP1/dept1 TABLE ***
row#0[3917] flag: -----, lock: 0
col 0; len 2; (2): c1 0b
col 1; len 6; (6): 00 40 f3 31 00 00
col 2; len 6; (6): 00 40 f3 31 00 0f
col 3; len 3; (3): c9 40 21
...
----- end of leaf block dump -----
End dump data blocks tsn: 0 file#:
```

The best use for dumping blocks is to see how Oracle really works. Get ready for a long night if you plan to use this tip; I spent a weekend playing with this the first time I used it.

TIP
Dumping data blocks can be a valuable tool to understand how Oracle works and to investigate problem-tuning areas. Only a tuning expert should use block dumps, and even an expert should use the help of Oracle Support.

Now let's look at an example to show you how to interpret some of the output that you get from a block dump as well as some other helpful queries that you can do when you do the deep dive into block dumps.

This query will give you the block number for *every* record of a table:

```
select  rowid,empno,
        dbms_rowid.rowid_relative_fno(rowid) fileno,
        dbms_rowid.rowid_block_number(rowid) blockno,
        dbms_rowid.rowid_row_number(rowid)   rowno, rownum,
        rpad(to_char(dbms_rowid.rowid_block_number(rowid), 'FM0xxxxxxx') || '.' ||
             to_char(dbms_rowid.rowid_row_number  (rowid), 'FM0xxx'    ) || '.' ||
             to_char(dbms_rowid.rowid_relative_fno(rowid), 'FM0xxx'    ), 18) myrid
from    emp1;
```

ROWID	EMPNO	FILENO	BLOCKNO	ROWNO	ROWNUM
MYRID					
AAAMfcAABAAAN0KAAA	7369	1	56586	0	1
0000dd0a.0000.0001					
AAAMfcAABAAAN0KAAB	7499	1	56586	1	2
0000dd0a.0001.0001					
AAAMfcAABAAAN0KAAC	7521	1	56586	2	3
0000dd0a.0002.0001					

Most of the information found in block dumps can be found in the data dictionary or can be accessed using a built-in package such as DBMS_SPACE. In certain scenarios, however, knowing how to read a block dump might benefit you; for instance, it may help you determine exactly why a transaction is blocked. You will probably use other tools prior to dumping a block, utllockt.sql, for instance, or EM (Enterprise Manager), but if you want to see exactly what is holding a lock on a row in a block, and how many rows are blocked, the block dump output can be quite useful. You may also want to look at row chaining or to look at the space utilization in the block for each row or simply to look at the block because a block is corrupted and you want to take a closer look at it.

Key Sections of a Block Dump
Sections to note within the block dump include the block dump ITL, the flag section, and the block dump data section. Each section is discussed in the text that follows.

The Block Dump ITL Section

One of the key sections of a block dump is the interested transaction list (ITL). The ITL section shown next appears in the early part of the dump. This one shows *two* ITL slots (two is the *minimum* number of ITL slots for both tables and indexes—if you don't believe what you read, you can dump it yourself to make sure). The XID is the Transaction ID. The UBA is the Undo Block Address, I'll discuss the Flag in a moment, the lock shows the number of records locked (four records are locked in the first ITL slot, since I deleted four rows for this example), and the SCN/FSC is either the SCN for committed information (Flag is a C) or FSC (Free Space Credit), which is the amount of bytes that will be recovered within the block if the transaction is committed. This number is in hex. For our example it is 9d, which is 157 bytes recovered if the transaction to delete four records is committed.

```
Itl              Xid              Uba            Flag     Lck         Scn/Fsc
0x01   0x0004.010.00000fba   0x0080003d.08b5.10   ----      4   fsc 0x009d.00000000
0x02   0x0004.016.00000fae   0x008000cc.08af.34   C---      0   scn 0x0000.003deb5b
```

The Flag Section

The Flag section is a bit complex. It tells you what state the transaction is in (CBUT):

- **----**   The transaction is active, or it is committed pending block cleanout.

- **C---**   The transaction has been committed and the row locks have been cleaned out.

- **B---**   The Undo Block Address contains undo for this block.

- **--U-**   The transaction is committed (the SCN is the upper bound), but block cleanout has not occurred (a fast commit).

- **---T**   This transaction was still active when the SCN for block cleanout was recorded.

- **C-U-**   The block was cleaned by delayed block cleanout, and the rollback segment information has been overwritten. The SCN will show the lowest SCN that could be regenerated by the rollback segment.

The Block Dump Data Section

The next block dump shows output from udump. This is the first part (the header section) of the block dump data section.

```
tab 0, row 13, @0x1b0b
tl: 39 fb: --H-FL-- lb: 0x0  cc: 8
```

Following is the description of this header information:

```
tab = this data is for table 0
row 13 = 14th Row (0-13 total rows)
Offset: 1b0b (in Hex) - Offset from header
tl: Total bytes of row plus the header = 39
fb: --H-FL-- = flag byte; ( -KCHDFLPN)
H = Head of row piece, F = First data piece, L=Last piece
D = Deleted; P= First column continues from previous piece (chaining) ; N= Last column
continues in next piece; K = Cluster Key; C = Cluster table member
lb: lock byte is 1+ if this row is locked = 0 (unlocked)
cc: Column count = 8
```

The data part of the block dump data section is shown in the block dump that follows:

```
col  0: [ 3]   c2 50 23
col  1: [ 6]   4d 49 4c 4c 45 52
col  2: [ 5]   43 4c 45 52 4b
col  3: [ 3]   c2 4e 53
col  4: [ 7]   77 b6 01 17 01 01 01
col  5: [ 2]   c2 0e
col  6: *NULL*
col  7: [ 2]   c1 0b...
```

Following is the output from the block dump data section EMPNO:

```
col  0: [ 3]   c2 50 23

Hex to Decimal:      Col0 = EMPNO = 7934
50 (Hex) = 80 (Decimal) - 1 = 79
23 (Hex) = 35 (Decimal) - 1 = 34
c2: Number in the thousands (c2 is exponent)
```

Following is the dump output from the block dump data section ENAME:

```
col  1: [ 6]   4d 49 4c 4c 45 52

Hex to Character:     Col1 = ENAME = MILLER
4d (Hex) = M (Character)
49 (Hex) = I (Character)
4c (Hex) = L (Character)
4c (Hex) = L (Character)
45 (Hex) = E (Character)
52 (Hex) = R (Character)
```

Also note that the hex values correspond to the character mapping tables (which depend upon the NLS settings for your database). For example, if you search "ASCII code character" on Google, you get a table of hex/decimal ASCII codes, in which 4d/77 corresponds to M.

The dump output from the block dump data HIREDATE section is shown next:

```
col  4: [ 7]   77 b6 01 17 01 01 01

Hex to Decimal: Col4 = HIREDATE = 23-JAN-82
77 (Hex) = 119 (Decimal) - 100 = 19
B6 (Hex) = 182 (Decimal) - 100 = 82
01(Hex) = 1 (Decimal) <month>
17 (Hex) = 23 (Decimal) <day>
01 01 01 (Hex) = This is the Hour, Minute, Second
(The Default time is 00:00:00)
```

You may want to select the Hex data from the table. The next block dump uses SELECT dump() and gets the ename from the Hex:

```
select  dump(ename,16), ename
from  emp1
where  dump(ename,16) like '%4d,49,4c,4c,45,52';
```

```
DUMP(ENAME,16)                                          ENAME
------------------------------------------------        --------------
Typ=1 Len=6: 4d,49,4c,4c,45,52                          MILLER
```

Let's query a new block (56650) from EMP1 and watch the EMP1 buffer header change (so far it's clean—the dirty bit is N—and consists of only 1 copy (or record), and it's the current version, with state=1):

```
select lrba_seq, state, dbarfil, dbablk, tch, flag, hscn_bas,cr_scn_bas,
      decode(bitand(flag,1), 0, 'N', 'Y') dirty,  /* Dirty bit */
      decode(bitand(flag,16), 0, 'N', 'Y') temp, /* temporary bit */
      decode(bitand(flag,1536),0,'N','Y') ping, /* ping (to shared or null) bit */
      decode(bitand(flag,16384), 0, 'N', 'Y') stale,    /* stale bit */
      decode(bitand(flag,65536), 0, 'N', 'Y') direct,   /* direct access bit */
      decode(bitand(flag,1048576), 0, 'N', 'Y') new   /* new bit */
from   x$bh
where dbablk = 56650
order by dbablk;
```

LRBA_SEQ	STATE	DBARFIL	DBABLK	TCH	FLAG	HSCN_BAS
CR_SCN_BAS	D	T	P	S	D	N
0	1	1	56650	0	35659776	4294967295
0	N	N	N	N	N	N

Let's watch the EMP1 buffer header when we delete a row (two copies of the block):

```
delete from emp1
where comm = 0;
```

1 row deleted.

Let's query the block (56650) and watch the EMP1 buffer header. There are now two copies (or records); one copy is the current version (state=1), and one is a clone (CR, state=3):

```
select lrba_seq, state, dbarfil, dbablk, tch, flag, hscn_bas,cr_scn_bas,
      decode(bitand(flag,1), 0, 'N', 'Y') dirty,    /* Dirty bit */
      decode(bitand(flag,16), 0, 'N', 'Y') temp,    /* temporary bit */
      decode(bitand(flag,1536),0,'N','Y') ping, /* ping (to shared or null) bit */
      decode(bitand(flag,16384), 0, 'N', 'Y') stale,    /* stale bit */
      decode(bitand(flag,65536), 0, 'N', 'Y') direct,   /* direct access bit */
      decode(bitand(flag,1048576), 0, 'N', 'Y') new   /* new bit */
from   x$bh
where dbablk = 56650
order by dbablk;
```

LRBA_SEQ	STATE	DBARFIL	DBABLK	TCH	FLAG	HSCN_BAS
CR_SCN_BAS	D	T	P	S	D	N
0	1	1	56650	1	8200	4294967295
0	N	N	N	N	N	N
0	3	1	56650	2	524288	0
4347881	N	N	N	N	N	N

Note that V$Transaction now has our record (created when transactions have undo):

```
SELECT  t.addr, t.xidusn USN, t.xidslot SLOT, t.xidsqn SQN, t.status,
               t.used_ublk UBLK, t.used_urec UREC, t.log_io LOG,
               t.phy_io PHY, t.cr_get, t.cr_change CR_CHA
FROM    v$transaction t, v$session s
WHERE   t.addr = s.taddr;
```

ADDR	USN	SLOT	SQN	STATUS	UBLK
--------	----------	----------	----------	----------------	----------

UREC	LOG	PHY	CR_GET	CR_CHA
----------	----------	----------	----------	----------

ADDR	USN	SLOT	SQN	STATUS	UBLK
69E50E5C	5	42	652 ACTIVE		1
1	3	0	3	0	

The column names in the output have these meanings:

- USN is the Undo Segment Number (rollback segment ID).

- SLOT is the slot number in the rollback segment's transaction table.

- SQN (Wrap) is the sequence number for the transaction.

- USN+SLOT+SQN are the three values that uniquely identifiy a transaction XID.

- UBAFIL is the file for the last undo entry.

- UBLK is the block for the last undo entry (it tells you how many undo blocks there are).

- UBASQN is the sequence number of the last entry.

- UREC is the record number of the block (it shows how many table and index entries the transaction has inserted, updated, or deleted).

If you are doing an INSERT or DELETE, then you will see that UREC is set to <number of indexes for this table> + how many rows you insert/delete. If you UPDATE a column, then UREC will be set to <number of indexes that his column belongs to> * 2 + number of updated rows (so if the column belongs to no index, then UREC is set to the number of rows that were updated). If UBLK and UREC are decreasing each time you query, then the transaction is rolling back. When UREC reaches zero, the rollback is finished.

If you dump the block at this time, you see the locked record in the ITL section:

```
Itl           Xid                  Uba              Flag  Lck      Scn/Fsc
0x01   0x0005.02a.0000028c   0x008000af.02b6.01   ----     1   fsc 0x0029.00000000
0x02   0x0004.016.00000fae   0x008000cc.08af.34   C---     0   scn 0x0000.003deb5b
```

Now let's do an INSERT in three other sessions to get x$bh up to the max of six versions of the block. There are now six copies; one copy is the current version (state=1), and five are clones (CR, state=3):

LRBA_SEQ	STATE	DBARFIL	DBABLK	TCH	FLAG	HSCN_BAS
----------	----------	----------	----------	----------	----------	----------

CR_SCN_BAS	D	T	P	S	D	N
----------	-	-	-	-	-	-

LRBA_SEQ	STATE	DBARFIL	DBABLK	TCH	FLAG	HSCN_BAS
0	3	1	56650	1	524416	0

```
4350120 N N N N N N
      0              3         1       56650      1      524416             0
4350105 N N N N N N
    365              1         1       56650      7    33562633      4350121
      0 Y N N N N N
      0              3         1       56650      1      524416             0
4350103 N N N N N N
      0              3         1       56650      1      524416             0
4350089 N N N N N N
      0              3         1       56650      1      524288             0
4350087 N N N N N N
```

NOTE
The LRBA (least redo block address) is set for the current block.

Can we get more than six versions of a block? Probably, but this is unsupported. In the following listing, we're selecting the maximum allowed CR buffers per data block address (dba).

```
select a.ksppinm, b.ksppstvl, b.ksppstdf, a.ksppdesc
from   x$ksppi a, x$ksppcv b
where a.indx = b.indx
and    substr(ksppinm,1,1) = '_'
and    ksppinm like '%&1%'
order by     ksppinm;


KSPPINM          KSPPSTVL      KSPPSTDF  KSPPDESC
------------------------------------------------------------------------------------
_db_block_max_cr_dba        6  TRUE     Maximum Allowed Number of CR buffers per dba
```

A deeper dive into block tuning is beyond the scope of this book. However, some of the queries we present in this section will allow you to investigate what is going on at the block level in the very rare case that you need to see it. The best reason to perform block dumps is to see what's going on inside of Oracle.

Tuning Using Simple Mathematical Techniques

This section discusses some simple but effective mathematical techniques you can use to significantly improve the performance of some Oracle SQL–based systems. These techniques can leverage the effectiveness of Oracle performance diagnostic tools and uncover hidden performance problems that can be overlooked by other methods. Using these techniques also helps you make performance predictions at higher loads.

NOTE
Joe A. Holmes provided the material for this section. I am extremely grateful for his contribution because I believe it ties all the chapters of this book together.

The methodology called Simple Mathematical Techniques involves isolating and testing the SQL process in question under ideal conditions, graphing the results of rows processed versus time, deriving equations using simple methods (without regression), predicting performance, and interpreting and applying performance patterns directly to tuning SQL code.

Traditional Mathematical Analysis

First of all, do not be intimidated by this section. You *will* be able to understand this, and the information provided will help you predict response times for your queries as the tables grow.

Traditional mathematical methods are very useful for analyzing performance. These may include graphing performance metrics on an *x-y* coordinate axis to obtain a picture of what a process is really doing and applying Least Squares Regression or Polynomial Interpolation to derive equations for predicting performance at higher loads. Computer science academics and specialists use these techniques extensively for performance analysis, which is laden with problems. First, textbook notation and explanations are often very complex and difficult to understand. Most math textbooks I have encountered that treat approximation and interpolation, for example, are steeped in theory rather than providing clear and practical examples.

Second, little or no information is available on how to apply this kind of analysis directly to tuning SQL code. This is probably because SQL analysis requires more specific interpretations to be useful rather than something broader or more general.

Seven-Step Methodology

The following are seven steps in the methodology. Note that deriving performance equations and interpreting patterns are discussed in more detail in the sections that follow.

- **Step 1**   Isolate the SQL code in question.
  The SQL code in question is isolated from surrounding system code and placed in a SQL*PLUS or PL/SQL script that can be run independently to duplicate the production process.

- **Step 2**   Run tests under ideal conditions.
  In this context, "ideal" is defined as one SQL process running on a dedicated machine with hardware processing power fixed and executed under high-volume data.

- **Step 3**   Graph performance observations on an *x-y* coordinate axis.
  From tests, the number of rows processed (*x*) versus time (*y*) for each SQL statement within a process is graphed on an *x-y* coordinate axis. We refer to this as a *row-time metric*. Ideally, the optimizer is for the most part more mechanical and less random, creating a more clearly defined and predictable trendline. The basic line shape can provide clues to the cause of underlying performance problems.

- **Step 4**   Use simple equation determination.
  Once points are plotted on a graph, you assume that what appears straight is a linear function and what appears curved upward is a quadratic function. (Other shapes may appear, but they are beyond the scope of this section.) From these observations, you can use either a simple two-point linear or three-point quadratic method to determine the equations. You can perform both methods easily by hand or with a basic calculator. You can also use spreadsheets like Microsoft Excel with graphing and trendline (regression) capabilities. Each separate SQL statement is graphed and analyzed individually.

- **Step 5** Predict performance.
  You can use derived equations to predict performance at much higher loads than are practical to test. Because the accuracy of the predictions may decrease as the predicted load increases, it is suggested that you make only ballpark predictions.
  It may be advantageous to calculate two performance lines: the first as a lower bound if the performance line is truly linear, and the second as an upper bound if the performance line might turn out to be a quadratic curve. The predicated value would therefore lie somewhere in between. Later, you may want to try a test to see how close your prediction was to the actual time. Also be aware that it is not as important whether a slow-running process is predicted to take 20 or 24 hours, but rather, whether it can be improved to, say, 1 hour.

- **Step 6** Interpret performance patterns and experiment.
  The shape of the performance lines and the nature of the equations can provide clues about the cause of underlying performance problems and support (or sometimes contradict) the interpretations of diagnostic tools. You can conduct experiments on SQL code based on pattern clues and the correction applied to production code. You can graph tests of an improved process again and compare the results with the original process.

- **Step 7** Keep a record of results to build expertise.
  To build up your expertise at using both these mathematical methods and your interpretation of Oracle diagnostic tools, keep a record of before and after performance graphs, the true cause of performance problems, and the effective solutions you found. Graphs provide hard evidence of performance problems that you can present in a clear visual form to management and end users.

Deriving Performance Equations

The following discusses two simple methods for equation determination based on simplified versions of Newton's Divided Difference Interpolating Polynomial. You can use these methods if you assume that what appears as a straight line is linear and what appears as upward sloping is quadratic.

Simple Linear Equation Determination

The following is a simple two-point method for determining a linear best-performance line equation:

$y = a_0 + a_1x$ (This is the final equation to use for linear queries.)

y = the number of rows in the table

x = the time to process the query

a_1 = the slope of the line (Calculate this with two query tests.)

a_0 = the y-intercept of the line (Calculate this with two query tests.)

Figure 9-6 shows points from an ideal test that appears linear. You visually select two points (x_1, y_1) and (x_2, y_2) that define a straight line of minimum slope, where

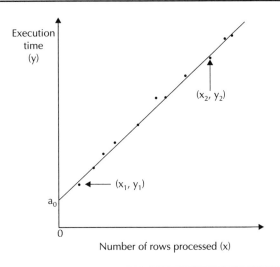

FIGURE 9-6.   *Linear best-performance line*

slope: $a_1 = (y_2 - y_1)/(x_2 - x_1)$

y-intercept: $a_0 = y_1 - a_1 x_1$

A Simple Example   These equations look great, but let's look at a real-life query (using a basic query to the EMP table). You must time the query on the basis of two different table sizes to get an equation for the line.

```
select ename, deptno
from   emp
where  deptno = 10;
```

For a very small system, consider the response for two tests:

- When 1000 records were in the EMP table, this query took 2 seconds.

- When 2000 records were in the EMP table, this query took 3 seconds.

Therefore, you know that

$y_1 = 2$ (seconds)

$x_1 = 1000$ (records)

$y_2 = 3$ (seconds)

$x_2 = 2000$ (records)

■ **Step 1** Find the slope of the line.

$a_1 = (y_2 - y_1)/(x_2 - x_1)$

$a_1 = (3 - 2)/(2000 - 1000)$

$a_1 = 0.001$ (The slope of the line is 0.001.)

■ **Step 2** Get the y-intercept.

$a_0 = y_1 - a_1 x_1$

$a_0 = 2 - (0.001)(1000)$

$a_0 = 2 - 1$

$a_0 = 1$ (The y-intercept is 1.)

■ **Step 3** Now you can calculate response for any size EMP table.

You now have everything you need for this query, so you can figure out how long this query will take as the number of rows in the EMP table increases.

What will the response time be for 3000 rows?

$y = a_0 + a_1 x$ (The response time is y and x is the number of rows in the table.)

$y = 1 + (0.001)(3000)$

$y = 1 + 3$

$y = 4$ seconds (The response time for this query in a 3000-row EMP table will be 4 seconds.)

What will the response time be for 100,000 rows?

$y = a_0 + a_1 x$

$y = 1 + (0.001)(100,000)$

$y = 101$ seconds (The response time for a 100,000-row EMP table will be 1 minute and 41 seconds.)

Simple Quadratic Equation Determination

Unfortunately, many queries don't behave linearly. Consequently, the preceding section doesn't always help you. But never fear—a simple method for curved lines is next. Once again, do not be intimidated by this section. You *will* be able to understand this, and with this information, you will be able to predict query scaling (predict any response time for an increased number of rows). The following is a simple three-point method for determining a quadratic best-performance equation. This is the equation you will use:

$y = a_0 + a_1 x + a_2 x^2$ (This is the final equation to use for nonlinear queries.)

y = response time for a query

x = number of rows

a_0, a_1, a_2 = constants derived from the curve the query creates

Figure 9-7 shows points from an ideal test.
You visually select three points, $(0, y_0)$, (x_1, y_1), and (x_2, y_2), that appear to be of minimum slope on a quadratic-like curve. The midpoint between 0 and x_1 is x_a, and the midpoint between x_1 and x_2 is x_b, such that

$$x_a = (x_1 + 0)/2 \text{ and } x_b = (x_2 + x_1)/2$$

When joined, $(0, y_0)$ and (x_1, y_1) form a secant (a straight line that connects two points on a curve) with slope S_a, and (x_1, y_1) and (x_2, y_2) form a secant with slope S_b. The x midpoints (x_a, y_a) and (x_b, y_b) lie on the desired curve with tangents having slopes S_a and S_b, respectively. From the derivative of a quadratic equation, which gives the slope of the curve at the midpoints, we have

$$S_a = (y_1 - y_0)/(x_1 - 0) = a_1 + 2a_2x_a$$

S_a = slope of the lower part of the curve

$$S_b = (y_2 - y_1)/(x_2 - x_1) = a_1 + 2a_2x_b$$

S_b = slope of the upper part of the curve

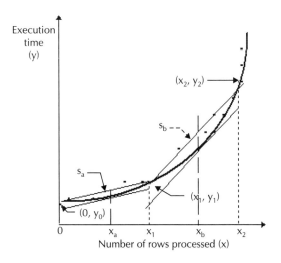

FIGURE 9-7. *Quadratic best-performance curve*

Seven-Step Methodology

Using Gauss elimination, you solve for the a_i coefficients, such that

$$a_2 = (S_b - S_a)/[2(x_b - x_a)] = (S_b - S_a)/x_2$$

$$a_1 = S_a - 2a_2x_a = S_a - a_2x_1$$

$$a_0 = y_0$$

You'll have to use these three equations to get a_0, a_1, and a_2 and then you can use the final equation. These will be the constants in the equation that will give you the response time of a query as you vary the number of rows in the table.

NOTE
This method will not work in all cases. If any a_i coefficients are negative, the equation may dip below the X axis and something else must be used. Often, the origin or $a_0 = y_0 = 0$ works best with this method.

A Simple Example   All of these equations look great, but let's look at a real-life query. You must time the query using two different table sizes to get an equation for the line. The ORDERS table has an index on ORDNO, but it is suppressed by the NVL function (causing the nonlinear response time). The real solution to this problem is to eliminate NULLs in the ORDERS table and remove the NVL function from the query. However, this example is for instructional purposes to generate a quadratic equation.

```
select     ordno, total
from       orders
where      nvl(ordno,0)  = 7777;
```

For your system, consider the response of this query for two tests:

- When there were 100 records in the ORDERS table, this query took 5 seconds.
- When there were 2000 records in the ORDERS table, this query took 1000 seconds.

You want to know how bad this query will be when you have 10,000 rows in the ORDERS table. Therefore, you know that

y_1 = 5 (seconds)

x_1 = 100 (records)

y_2 = 1000 (seconds)

x_2 = 2000 (records)

$y_0 = 1$ (second – estimate); this is the y-intercept

You could calculate y_0 by using two points near the lower part of the curve (near 100 rows using the linear equations from the preceding section), but because the lower part of the curve is small (5 seconds for 100 rows), you can guesstimate this to be 1 second. (You should calculate it.)

■ **Step 1**   Calculate S_a and S_b.

$S_a = (y_1 - y_0)/(x_1 - 0)$

$S_a = (5 - 1)/(100 - 0)$

$S_a = 0.04$ (The slope of the lower part of the curve is almost horizontal.)

$S_b = (y_2 - y_1)/(x_2 - x_1)$

$S_b = (1000 - 5)/(2000 - 100)$

$S_b = 0.52$ (The slope of the upper part of the curve is much higher than the lower part.)

■ **Step 2**   Calculate a_0, a_1, and a_2.

$a_2 = (S_b - S_a)/x_2$

$a_2 = (0.52 - 0.04)/2000$

$a_2 = 0.00024$

$a_1 = S_a - a_2 x_1$

$a_1 = 0.04 - (0.00024)(100)$

$a_1 = 0.016$

$a_0 = y_0$

$a_0 = 1$ (The y-intercept is 1.)

■ **Step 3**   Create the equation to use as the table grows.

$y = a_0 + a_1 x + a_2 x_2$

$y = 1 + (0.016)x + (0.00024)x^2$ (This is your equation to calculate future responses.)

■ **Step 4**   Calculate the *expected* response for 10,000 rows.

$y = 1 + (0.016)x + (0.00024)x^2$

$y = 1 + (0.016)(10,000) + (0.00024)(10,000^2)$

$y = 24,161$ (The query will take 24,161 seconds, or just under seven hours; you have a problem.)

You'll have to fix the NVL problem soon so the users don't have to wait seven hours. But in reality, you have calculated only a couple of points, and this should be extended out further to get a better future estimate of performance.

Seven-Step Methodology

TIP
Spreadsheets like Microsoft Excel are very useful tools for graphing performance metrics and automatically deriving trendline equations. For example, to create a graph using Excel, list the observed (x,y) data in cells. Highlight the cells, and select Chart Wizard | XY (Scatter) | Chart Sub-type. Select a Line subtype and click Next | Next | Finish to create the graph. To derive a trendline equation, click the graph line once, and select Chart | Add Trendline. On the Type tab, select Linear, Polynomial Order=2 (for quadratic) or other model type. To show the trendline equation, on the Options tab, select Display Equation On Chart. Then click OK to complete the graph. The solution equation can be programmed back into the spreadsheet and used to predict values at higher volumes.

Pattern Interpretation

Graphical performance patterns provide clues to underlying SQL problems and solutions, as seen in Figure 9-8. The ultimate goal in using these methods is to convert a steep linear or quadratic best-performance line to one that is both shallow and linear by optimizing the SQL process. This may involve experiments with indexes, temporary tables, optimizer hint commands, or other methods of Oracle SQL performance tuning.

With pattern interpretation, it is important to perform your own application-specific SQL experiments to develop expertise at using these methods. Table 9-2 shows more specific interpretations—based on my personal experience—that provide a general idea of how you can apply what you observe directly to tuning SQL code. Assuming the scale is correct, pattern

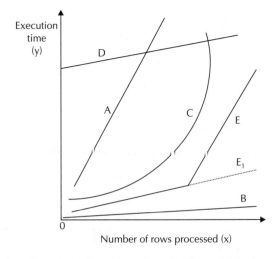

FIGURE 9-8. *Examples of performance patterns*

Pattern in Figure 9-8	Possible Problem	Possible Solution
A	Missing index on a query SELECTing values.	Create an index. Fix a suppressed index.
A	Over-indexed table suffering during DML statements.	Drop some of the indexes or index fewer columns (or smaller columns) for the current indexes.
B	No problem.	Don't touch it!
C	Missing index on a query SELECTing values.	Create an index. Fix a suppressed index.
C	Over-indexed table suffering during an INSERT.	Drop some of the indexes or index fewer columns (or smaller columns) for the current indexes.
D	Doing a full table scan or using the ALL_ROWS hint when you shouldn't be.	Try to do an indexed search. Try using the FIRST_ROWS hint to force the use of indexes.
E	The query was fine until some other limitation (such as disk I/O or memory) was encountered.	Find out which ceiling you hit caused this problem. Increasing the SGA may solve the problem, but this could be many things.
E_1	If the limitation in line E is corrected, processing should continue along a straight line.	Further tuning may improve the process to line B.

TABLE 9-2.   *Graphical Representations of Various Tuning Situations*

interpretation often provides a more accurate picture of what is actually happening to a process and may support or even contradict what a diagnostic tool tells you.

General Linear and Quadratic Interpretations

A shallow linear performance line usually indicates a relatively efficient process compared to something much steeper or curved. The slope a_1 indicates the rate y increases for a given x. Scale is important because a shallow line on one scale can look steep on another, and vice versa. A large a_0 coefficient always indicates an inefficient process.

An upward-sloping (concave) quadratic curve almost always indicates a problem with the process because as more rows are added, the time to process each additional row increases. Coefficient a_2 affects the bowing of the curve. If it is very small, the equation may be more linear. However, even a very slight bowing may be an indicator of something more insidious under much higher volumes.

In rare cases, a quadratic curve might appear downward sloping (convex), indicating a process where as more rows are added, the time to process each additional one decreases (i.e., economies of scale). This is desirable and may occur at a threshold, where a full table scan is more efficient than using an index.

Pattern Interpretation

Indexing

Missing indexes commonly cause poor SQL performance. In Figure 9-8, line *A* or *C* could result from a missing index, depending on code complexity and data volume. Proper indexing improves performance to line *B*. Over indexing can be as bad as missing indexes. Line *A* or *C* could be a process that is forced to use an index, whereas a full table scan would improve the process to *B*. Inserting into an indexed table is always slower than into an index-free table. Line *A* or *C* could be from an INSERT into a heavily indexed table versus line *B* with no indexing.

Indexing Example   This listing illustrates what can happen with indexing analysis. Suppose you have two tables, TABLE_A and TABLE_B, and there is a one-to-many relationship between them using KEY_FIELD. There does not have to be a join between the two tables.

```
TABLE_A
KEY_FIELD       NUMBER
TOTAL           NUMBER


TABLE_B
KEY_FIELD       NUMBER
AMOUNT          NUMBER
```

You want to perform the following update within a KEY_FIELD:

```
table_a.total = table_a.total + sum(table_b.amount)
```

The SQL statement shown next will do this. Note that the EXISTS subquery must be used to prevent the NULLing out of any table_a.total fields, where table_a.key_field does not match total_b.key_field.

```
update    table_a ta  set ta.total =
(select    ta.total + sum(tb.amount)
 from      table_b tb
 where     tb.key_field = ta.key_field
 group by  ta.total)
where     exists
(select    null
 from      table_b tb2
 where     tb2.key_field = ta.key_field);
```

If there is a unique index on table_a.key_field and a non-unique index on table_b.key_field, then the performance will be similar to line *B* in Figure 9-8. However, if there is no index on table_b.key_field or the cost-based optimizer decides to shut it off, a line will be generated similar to *A* or *C*. The reason is that the EXISTS subquery heavily depends on indexing.

I have seen cases where the number of rows in TABLE_A was small (< 2000) but the cost-based optimizer shut off the index on TABLE_B and reported a small EXPLAIN PLAN cost. This was regardless of the number of rows in TABLE_B (which was up to 800,000 rows). Actual tests showed a steep performance line that contradicted the EXPLAIN PLAN cost. This is an example of uncovering a problem that may have been overlooked by a diagnostic tool.

When the optimizer (cost-based) finds a query to retrieve less than 5–6 percent (based on the average distribution) of the data in a table, the optimizer generally drives the query with an index if one exists. Figure 9-9 shows how Oracle has evolved through the past years prior to Oracle 9*i*. In Oracle 10*g*, the optimizer is so good at analyzing not only the number of rows, but also the distribution of data as well and also knows if the query has been run previously. The first time a query is executed is different from the second time even if this was weeks ago. While the response time still depends on the percentage of blocks (better than looking at the percentage of rows) retrieved by the query, what kind of disks, cache for the disks, cache for the operating system and previous queries change the upper part of the graph greatly (where you retrieve most of the table). Everything starts depending more on your hardware and access patterns. I have left the following graph in Figure 9-9 in this version of the book to show where Oracle has been in the past.

Optimizer Execution Plan
You can graph performance patterns to leverage available diagnostic tools. For example, you analyzed a slow and complex SQL statement that used views, and ran high-volume data under the Oracle cost-based optimizer. Results showed a very high performance line identical to D in Figure 9-8. The Oracle EXPLAIN PLAN also showed an inefficient execution plan. Once an effective optimizer hint command was found (i.e., FIRST_ROWS) and added directly to the SQL statements that defined the views, performance improved dramatically to line B.

Multiple Table Joins
Complex multiple-table join statements often run poorly regardless of the conventional tuning used and may be similar to lines A or C in Figure 9-8. From past experience, rather than trying to tune only the statement with conventional techniques, a more effective solution is to decompose it into a series of simple SQL statements using temporary tables. The final result would be the same but at much faster speed, represented by a composite line at B.

Jackknifing
Jackknifing is a pattern where a performance line starts off shallow but then veers steeply upward at a certain threshold point, similar to E in Figure 9-8. Two linear equations may define the behavior; its cause could be anything from disk I/O or memory limitations to a switch in the optimizer execution plan due to changing data volumes. Possible solutions are to increase the system's limitations, run fresh optimizer statistics, use the rule-based optimizer, or break the statement into selection ranges. Proper tuning might either straighten out the line to L, or improve it further to line B.

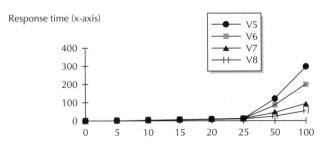

FIGURE 9-9. *Optimum percentage of rows for index for older versions of Oracle*

Riding the Quadratic Curve

Often, a poorly performing SQL process is designed and tested on low-volume data, but in production under higher volumes, its true and degrading quadratic nature is revealed, as shown by curve A in Figure 9-10. In this example, a process was created and tested up to x_1. Performance was believed to be close to line B, but once in production and when the volume was increased to x_3, the line really turned out to be curve A.

If a proper tuning solution cannot be found, a quadratic process of unknown cause can still be improved by breaking the original statement into lower-volume selection ranges and riding the shallow part of the quadratic curve. Suppose in Figure 9-10, you break the process into three selection ranges: [from 0 to x_0] that rides the lower part of curve A, [from x_1 to x_2] that rides the lower part of curve A_1, and [from x_2 to x_3] that rides the lower part of curve A_2. The overall result is something closer to line B [from 0 to x_3] with y_3' taking a lot less time than the original y_3. Although this technique may not be the best solution, it could still solve the problem.

Instead of running everything all at once, breaking up the process using a SQL loop and commit mechanism can sometimes buy better overall performance for processes like updates and deletes that use rollback segments.

Volatility Effects

Running under ideal conditions and graphing the results makes it much easier to analyze the effects of outside traffic and its resulting volatility. For example, line A in Figure 9-11 is from an inefficient linear process run under ideal conditions. Suppose a controlled amount of traffic from another process is then run at the same time. It could be a large query, insert, update, or backup, etc. This second test moves line A by 100 percent to A_1. In other words, the process with added traffic on the system is twice as slow.

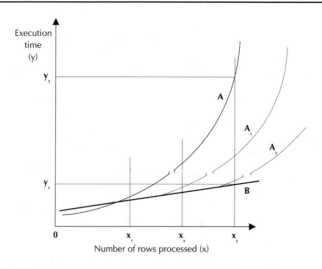

FIGURE 9-10. *Example of riding the quadratic curve*

Now suppose you optimize the original process. Under an ideal test of the new process, the best performance line shifts down to *B.* If you were to predict what would happen if you applied the same controlled traffic to the new process, you might predict a 100 percent shift to B_1. However, since the slopes between *A* and *B* differ (with *A* being much steeper than *B*), the 100 percent time increase from *B* to B_1 would be much less than from *A* to A_1. In fact, an actual traffic test on line *B* might prove to be much less than even the predicted 100 percent due to the overall efficiency of the line *B* process. In general, more efficient SQL processes are less susceptible to added traffic effects than less efficient processes.

Mathematical Techniques Conclusions

Simple Mathematical Techniques is an effective Oracle SQL performance analysis and tuning methodology that involves running tests under ideal conditions, graphing performance observations, and using simple linear and quadratic equation determination for predicting performance at higher loads. It also includes the interpretation of performance patterns that can be applied directly to tuning SQL code.

The methodology acts as a catalyst by combining the use of some traditional mathematical analysis with Oracle diagnostic tools to aid in their interpretation and to leverage their effectiveness. It can also help you identify hidden problems that may be overlooked by other diagnostic methods by providing a broad picture of performance. The technique can also help you overcome performance-tuning barriers such as inexperience with Oracle, lack of hard evidence, or difficulties with diagnostic tool interpretation that may prevent effective performance tuning. You can also analyze volatility effects from outside traffic. Graphs provide a visual picture of performance for presentation to management and end users. And you can use spreadsheets such as Microsoft Excel with these techniques for quick and easy performance analysis.

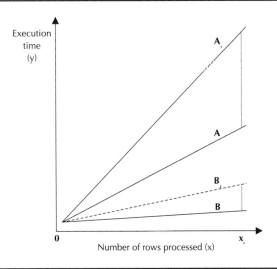

FIGURE 9-11. *Example of volatility effects*

TIP
If you want an Oracle symphony as great as one of Beethoven's, you must learn and know how to apply mathematical techniques to your tuning efforts. You don't have to learn everything that you learned in college calculus; merely apply the simple equations in this chapter to tie everything in this book together. Thank you Joe Holmes for doing the math for us!

Join Tuning: Relational vs. Object-Relational Performance

Searching for query optimization to reduce response time or avoid excessive use of system resources has become an important direction over the past few years. In many queries, joins between tables are necessary to obtain required business information. This section will demonstrate cases where it is better to use a particular join method for the relational and object-relational models supported by Oracle. In order to accomplish this, we will work with Oracle's tkprof tool (see Chapter 6 for more information on tkprof). In the listing that follows, we can see the result structure of the TKPROF tool, and how the tkprof output looks (without the data for each column). We will use some of the key columns to calculate metrics.

call	count	cpu	elapsed	disk	query	current	rows
Parse(a)	(d)	--	--	--	--	--	--
Execute(b)	(e)	--	--	--	--	--	--
Fetch(c)	(j)	--	--	--	--	--	(i)
Total	---	--	--	(k)	(f)	(g)	(h)

According to this listing, which shows a result of a typical file obtained through the tkprof tool, we will analyze the following rates, which will serve as criteria for the optimization process:

- **Blocks read (f+g) to rows processed (h)**   This rate indicates the relative cost of the query. While more blocks have to be accessed in relation to the returned rows, the fetched row will be more expensive. A similar relation can be deduced from the rate: read blocks over executions (f+g)/e. The procured value for this rate should be less than 10; however, values in the range of 10 to 20 are acceptable. Values above 20 could indicate some possibility for optimization in this field.

- **Parse count (d) over execute count (e)**   Ideally, the parsing count should be close to one. If this value is high in relation to the execution count, then the statement has been parsed several times. This indicates that there could be problems in the shared pool size (too small). Poor use of bind variables can be another reason for unnecessary parsing.

- **Rows fetched (i) to fetches (j)**   This rate indicates the level in which the array fetch capability has been used. Array Fetch is an Oracle feature that permits fetching more than one row for every fetch executed. A value close to one indicates that there was no array processing, which signifies that there is a good possibility for optimization.

■   **Disk reads (k) to logical reads (f+g)**   This is (generally) a miss rate for data in the cache buffer. It shows the percentage of the times when the engine could not find the solicited rows in the buffer cache and therefore had to bring the data blocks from the disk. Generally, the values of this rate should represent less than 10 percent (ideally under 5 percent, depending on the query mix).

The join methods that will be analyzed in this section are Hash, Sort Merge, and Nested Loops. To force the Oracle optimizer to execute a specific join, method hints are necessary. The hints to use include the following:

■   **USE_MERGE** (*table_name*)   Forces the optimizer to use the Sort Merge method.

■   **USE_HASH** (*table_name*)   Forces the optimizer to use the Hash method.

■   **USE_NL** (*table_name*)   Forces the optimizer to use the Nested Loops method.

■   **INDEX** (*table_name*)   Forces the optimizer to use a table index.

However, in some object-relational queries, especially when REFs are used, this *table_name* is not available; that's why in our queries the internal table name (alias) provided by Oracle will be used. This internal name can be obtained in this way (it only works since Oracle 10*g*):

1. Run an explain plan for the specific query.

2. Run the query utilizing DBMS_XPLAN.

```
SELECT plan_table_output
FROM TABLE(DBMS_XPLAN.DISPLAY ('PLAN_TABLE', NULL,'ALL'));
```

The DBMS_XPLAN.DISPLAY function accepts three parameters, in this order:

■   **Table_name**   The table name where the explain plan data is saved. The default value is PLAN_TABLE.

■   **Statement id**   The ID of the sentence plan to be shown. The default value is NULL unless you set a value to identify this particular statement.

■   **Format**   Controls the detail level to be shown. The default value is TYPICAL. Others values include BASIC, ALL, and SERIAL.

The following query retrieves (in addition to a lot of other columns and data) the alias of the involved tables in the statements found in the execution plan table. In our case, the table is the PLAN_TABLE. For example, if we have tables whose aliases are B@SEL$1 and P000003$@SEL$1, and we desire to join these tables through the Sort Merge method, the query to use will be

```
SELECT /*+ USE_MERGE (B@SEL$1 P000003$@SEL$1)*/ [columns]
FROM...
```

If two or more joins are needed in a query in order to achieve the possible combinations of these methods, several hints must be used.

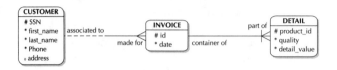

FIGURE 9-12. *Entity-relation model for the test*

Models Used

The relational and object-relational models will be analyzed as they apply to a particular case of three tables, where customer, invoice, and detail data could be found, as shown in Figure 9-12.

In the object-relational model, "detail" will be a nested table located in "invoice." See the code listing at the end of this section (preceding the Tips Review), which shows the creation of the tables in both models. For both models, tables with many and few rows will be used. The smaller tables will be about 10 percent of the size of the larger tables. Table 9-3 shows the table sizes for both models.

Note the presence of indexes in the tables on the joining columns. Special attention should be placed on the indexing of the "nested_table_id" pseudo-column in the nested table "detail."

Results

First, the results for the join between invoice and detail tables will be executed, and then the join between three tables (customer, invoice, and detail) will be executed.

Two-Table Join (Invoice and Detail)

In the following, we use queries with both large and small tables. For the relational model:

```
SELECT   /*+ ORDERED USE_HASH(d) INDEX(i) INDEX(d)*/
         i.invoice_date, d.quantity, d.detail_value
FROM     invoice i, detail d
WHERE    i.id = d. invoice_id;
```

Tables	Many Rows	Few Rows
Customer	3375	343
Invoice	12,000	1200
Detail	23,481	2363

TABLE 9-3. *Table Sizes*

For the object-relational model:

```
SELECT /*+ ORDERED USE_HASH(D@SEL$1) INDEX(I@SEL$1) INDEX(D@SEL$1)*/
       i.invoice_date, d.quantity, d.detail_value
FROM    invoice i, TABLE(i.detail) d;
```

In this case the Hash join method is used; however, for the Sort Merge and Nested Loops methods the same syntax is applied.

Joins with Large Tables   In Figure 9-13 results are presented corresponding to the join of two tables with many rows using indexes in both.

In Figures 9-14 and 9-15 the EXPLAIN PLANs made with the Hash method are presented using a screen shot from JDeveloper. Note that the EXPLAIN PLANs for both models are the same, even though the object-relational model has a nested table, as it is internally treated as a typical relational table.

Figures 9-16 and 9-17 show that in every join method, in terms of the ratio of blocks read (logical reads) to rows processed, the object-relational model behaves better than the relational model. The number of logical reads is *much* smaller for the object-relational model than the relational. The performance gets slightly better in the Sort Merge method than the Hash; worst by far is the performance of the Nested Loops method.

RATE	(f + g) / h	d / e	i / j	k / (f + g)	JOIN METHOD
NORMAL VALUE	Less than 10	1 (or close to 1)	The bigger the better	1 (or close to 1)	
	1,063966611	1	14,98353148	0,00872593	HASH
RELATIONAL MODEL	1,12976449	1	14,98353148	0	MERGE
	48,38222393	1	14,98353148	0	NL
	0,160877053	1	14,98353148	0,0751958	HASH
OBJECT-RELATIONAL MODEL	0,02801697	1	14,98353148	0	MERGE
	0,863527534	1	14,98353148	0	NL

FIGURE 9-13.   *Results for the test with large tables in both models*

Results

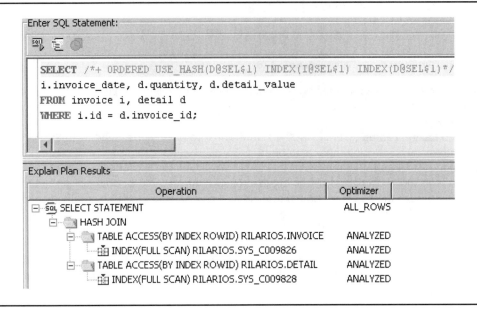

FIGURE 9-14. *Explain plan for the HASH method in the relational model*

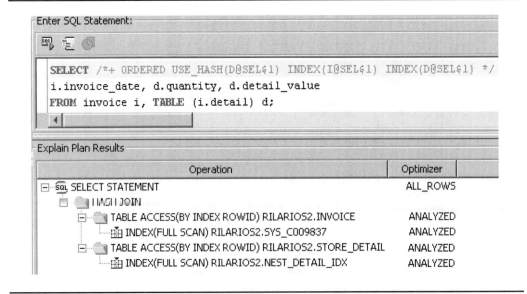

FIGURE 9-15. *Explain plan for the HASH method in the Object-relational model (JDev)*

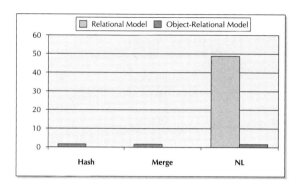

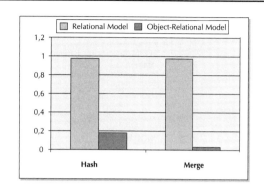

FIGURE 9-16. *Blocks read (f+g) to rows processed (h) for large tables*

FIGURE 9-17. *Blocks read (f+g) to rows processed (h) without NL for large tables*

In Figure 9-18, it is observed that in general, all models behave well; the Hash method shows a bit worse performance in the object-relational model, but the difference is negligible compared with the Hash performance in the relational model.

Joins with Small Tables   Figure 9-19 shows results for the same queries tested before, but now, it represents tests with small tables.

Again, the object-relational model has an advantage over the relational model in the ratio of blocks read (logical reads) to rows processed, and it is observed that in every join method, especially in Sort Merge, the performance is better (see Figure 9-20).

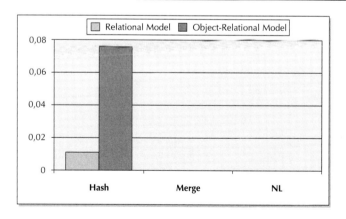

FIGURE 9-18. *Disk reads (k) to logical reads (f+g) for large tables*

Results

RATE	(f + g) / h	d / e	i / j	k / (f + g)	JOIN METHOD
NORMAL VALUE	Less than 10	1 (or close to 1)	While bigger the better	Less than 10%	
RELATIONAL MODEL	0,977147694	1	14,8710692	0,01299263	**HASH**
	1,035548032	1	14,8710692	0	**MERGE**
	5,424883623	1	14,87106918	0	**NL**
OBJECT-RELATIONAL MODEL	0,171174979	1	14,87106918	0,07654321	**HASH**
	0,038038884	1	14,87106918	0	**MERGE**
	0,875739645	1	14,87106918	0	**NL**

FIGURE 9-19. *Results for test with small tables in both models*

According to Figure 9-21, good results are obtained in both models. Though the Hash method in the object-relational model shows the worst performance, the difference is low compared with the performance drawbacks of the relational model.

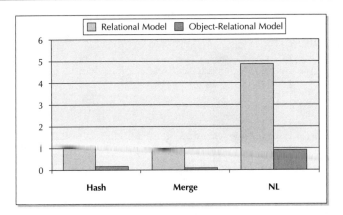

FIGURE 9-20. *Blocks read (f+g) to rows processed (h) for small tables*

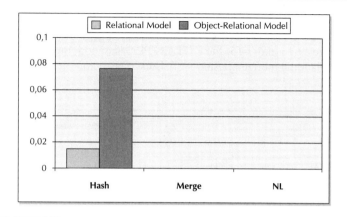

FIGURE 9-21. *Disk reads (k) to logical reads (f+g) for small tables*

Three-Table Join (Customer, Invoice, and Detail)

I have not followed through with the same analysis for three tables. It is possible to perform combinations between join methods; that is to say, two tables can be joined with the Hash method, and the result can be joined with a third table through a Sort Merge method. It should be noted that, in this case, the detail table is a nested table in the object-relational model. The queries to use for this part of the study are (in this case, the Hash-Merge join is):

For the relational model

```
SELECT /*+ ORDERED  USE_MERGE(i) USE_HASH(d) INDEX(c) INDEX(d) INDEX(i) */
       c.first_name, c.last_name, f.invoice_date, d.quantity, d.detail_value
FROM   customer c, invoice i, detail d
WHERE  c.ssn = i.sn_cust
AND    i.id = d.invoice_id;
```

For the object-relational model

```
SELECT /*+ ORDERED USE_MERGE(P000004$@SEL$1 I@SEL$1) USE_HASH(D@SEL$1)
          INDEX(P000004$@SEL$1) INDEX(I@SEL$1) INDEX(D@SEL$1)          */
       i.ref_cust.first_name, i.ref_cust.last_name, i.invoice_date,
       d.quantity, d.valor_detalle
FROM   invoice i, TABLE(i.detail) d;
```

It should be noted that the table names for the object-relational model (object alias) are obtained through the DBMS_XPLAN.DISPLAY function as explained before. It should also be noted that in the query for the object-relational model, the "customer" table is not in the FROM clause, due to the use of pointers (REF) to that specific table. Those pointers are located in the invoice table.

Results

Join with Large Tables   In Figure 9-22, results are presented corresponding to the three-table join using indexes (for the three) with many data.

In Figures 9-23 and 9-24 the EXPLAIN PLANs for the joins with the Hash-Merge method are presented. As in Figures 9-14 and 9-15, the EXPLAIN PLANs in both models are the same, even when in the object-relational model a nested table is used (as before, it is treated as a typical relational table).

RATE	(f + g) / h	d / e	i / j	k / (f + g)	JOIN METHOD
NORMAL VALUE	Less than 10	One	The bigger the better	Less than 10%	
RELATIONAL MODEL	1,131255057	1	14,98353148	0,01299263	HASH-HASH
	0,998552021	1	14,98353148	0	HASH-MERGE
	48,38371449	1	14,98353148	0	HASH-NL
	1,128060985	1	14,98353148	0	MERGE-HASH
	0,998552021	1	14,98353148	0	MERGE-MERGE
	48,84749372	1	14,98353148	0	MERGE-NL
	12,10297687	1	14,98353148	0	NL-HASH
	11,77539287	1	14,98353148	0	NL-MERGE
	59,82053575	1	14,98353148	0	NL-NL
OBJECT-RELATIONAL MODEL	0,1622632	1	14,98353148	0,01087237	HASH-HASH
	0,030327215	1	14,98353148	0	HASH-MERGE
	1,324106355	1	14,98353148	0	HASH-NL
	0,030327215	1	14,98353148	0	MERGE-HASH
	0,030327215	1	14,98353148	0	MERGE-MERGE
	1,195782753	1	14,98353148	0	MERGE-NL
	1,236107027	1	14,98353148	0,00070156	NL-HASH
	1,036711891	1	14,98353148	0	NL-MERGE
	1,938883522	1	14,98353148	0	NL-NL

FIGURE 9-22.   *Results for test with large tables in both models*

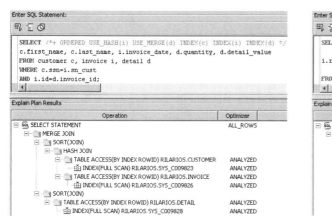

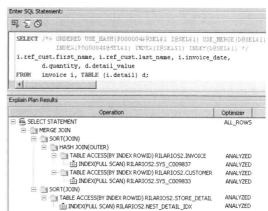

FIGURE 9-23. *Explain plan for the HASH-MERGE method in the relational model*

FIGURE 9-24. *Explain plan for the HASH-MERGE method in the object-Relational model*

In Figures 9-25 and 9-26 it can be observed again that the object-relational model is better than the relational model (on the ratio of blocks read to rows processed), especially when the Sort Merge method is involved. In the disk reads (k) to logical reads (f+g) rate (Figure 9-27), it is observed that in general both models are efficient. While the worst-performing join method is the one that involved the Hash method in the object-relational model, the difference is not significant.

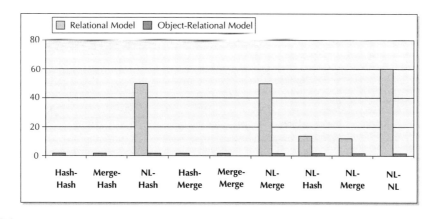

FIGURE 9-25. *Blocks Read read (f+g) to Rows rows Processed processed (h) for large tables*

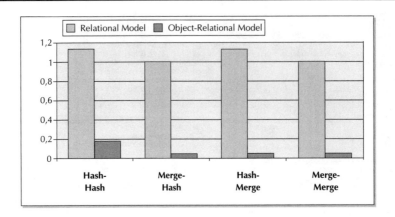

FIGURE 9-26. *Blocks Read read (f+g) to Rows rows Processed processed (h) without NL for large tables*

Join with Small Tables   In Figures 9-28 and 9-29 the performance advantage presented by the object-relational model over the relational model is again observed in the ratio of blocks read to rows processed.

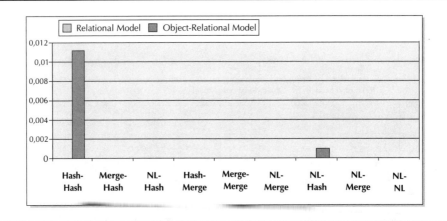

FIGURE 9-27. *Disk reads (k) to logical reads (f+g) for large tables*

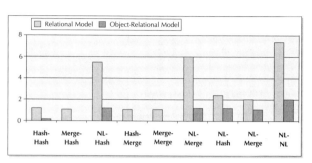

FIGURE 9-28.   *Blocks read (f+g) to rows processed (h) for small tables*

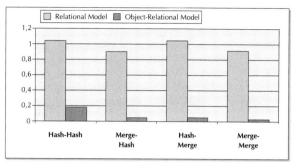

FIGURE 9-29.   *Blocks read (f+g) to rows processed (h) without NL for small tables*

On the disk reads (k) to logical reads (f+g) ratio (Figure 9-30) it is observed that in general, both models are similar, but as seen in previous tests the joins that involve the Hash method in the object-relational model have the lower performance.

Results for the join with few rows can be seen in Figure 9-31.

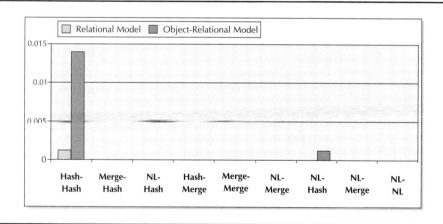

FIGURE 9-30.   *Disk reads (k) to logical reads (f+g) for small tables*

Results

RATE	(f + g) / h	d / e	i / j	k / (f + g)	JOIN METHOD
NORMAL VALUE	Less than 10	One	The bigger the better	Less than 10%	
RELATIONAL MODEL	1,037663986	1	14,8710692	0,00163132	HASH-HASH
	0,904782057	1	14,8710692	0	HASH-MERGE
	5,426999577	1	14,8710692	0	HASH-NL
	1,035548032	1	14,8710692	0	MERGE-HASH
	0,904782057	1	14,8710692	0	**MERGE-MERGE**
	5,837917901	1	14,8710692	0	MERGE-NL
	2,392297926	1	14,8710692	0	NL-HASH
	2,063055438	1	14,8710692	0	NL-MERGE
	7,318662717	1	14,8710692	0	NL-NL
OBJECT-RELATIONAL MODEL	0,176669484	1	14,8710692	0,01196172	HASH-HASH
	0,045646661	1	14,8710692	0	HASH-MERGE
	1,307269653	1	14,8710692	0	HASH-NL
	0,045646661	1	14,8710692	0	MERGE-HASH
	0,026627219	1	14,8710692	0	**MERGE-MERGE**
	1,195266272	1	14,8710692	0	MERGE-NL
	1,256551141	1	14,8710692	0,00100908	NL-HASH
	1,058326289	1	14,8710692	0	NL-MERGE
	1,96238377	1	14,8710692	0	NL-NL

FIGURE 9-31   *Results for test with small tables in both models*

Conclusion

It is clear that the object-relational model performed better than the relational model in all of these tests, especially when ratio of the blocks read (logical reads) to rows processed is the measured value and when the Sort Merge join is involved. However, in the ratio of disk reads (k) to logical reads (f+g), the object-relational model turns out to be slightly more expensive, especially when the Hash join is involved. Such cost differences were reduced significantly when other join methods were used. In general, the object-relational model offers good performance, surpassing the relational model. Since there are a variety of variables that can be encountered in an application, readers should do their own testing to validate any potential gains. However, the results suggest that the object-relational model offers great performance that at a minimum should be considered where needed. Listed next are the creation scripts for both the relational and object-relational objects used in this section.

For the relational model

```
-- CUSTOMER table
CREATE TABLE customer
(
  ssn          NUMBER(8)    PRIMARY KEY,              --Social Security Number
  first_name   VARCHAR2(20) NOT NULL,
  last_name    VARCHAR2(30) NOT NULL,
  phone        NUMBER(7)    NOT NULL,
  address      VARCHAR2(40)
);

-- INVOICE table
CREATE TABLE invoice
(
  id             NUMBER(8) PRIMARY KEY,               -- Invoice Number
  invoice_date   DATE NOT NULL,                       -- Invoice Date
  sn_cust        NUMBER(8) REFERENCES customer NOT NULL
);

-- Detail table
CREATE TABLE detail
(
  quantity       NUMBER(3), -- Quantity of Prduct
  detail_value   NUMBER(8),
  product_id     VARCHAR2(20),
  invoice_id     NUMBER(8) REFERENCES invoice,
  PRIMARY KEY(invoice_id, product_id)
);
```

For the object-relational model

```
-- Customer type and its respective table
CREATE TYPE customer_type AS OBJECT
(
  ssn          NUMBER(8),
  first_name   VARCHAR2(20),
  last_name    VARCHAR2(30),
  phone        NUMBER(7),
  address      VARCHAR2(40)
);
/
```

```
CREATE TABLE customer OF customer_type
(
  ssn          PRIMARY KEY,
  first_name   NOT NULL,
  last_Name    NOT NULL,
  phone        NOT NULL
);
/


--Detail type
CREATE TYPE detail_type AS OBJECT
(
  product_id     VARCHAR2(20),
  quantity       NUMBER(3),
  detail_value   NUMBER(8) --Valor del detalle.
);
/


--Nested table type based on detail type
CREATE TYPE nest_detail AS TABLE OF detail_type;
/


--Invoice type and its respective table
CREATE TYPE invoice_type AS OBJECT
(
  id             NUMBER(8),
  invoice_date   DATE,
  detail         nest_detail,                      --Nested table of details
  ref_cust       REF customer_type
);
/

CREATE TABLE invoice OF invoice_type
(
  id             PRIMARY KEY,
  invoice_date   NOT NULL,
  ref_cust       NOT NULL,
  SCOPE FOR (ref_cust) IS customer
) NESTED TABLE detail STORE AS store_detail;
/

--Index on nested table.
CREATE INDEX nest_detail_idx on store_detail(nested_table_id);
```

 # Tips Review

- The optimizer often uses HASH joins in lieu of SORT-MERGE joins if the correct initialization parameters are set. With HASH joins, the driving table is used to be a hash table; on the join key, the other table is scanned and the result probes the hash table for matches. If there is not enough memory, the hash table could be split into multiple partitions and it may also be swapped to disk. Be careful: HASH joins can be slow when memory is low or the tables are poorly indexed.

- If the ORDERED hint is used, then the first table in the FROM clause is also the driving table. The LEADING hint is also helpful in tuning multitable joins. Oracle Enterprise Manager and the Tuning Pack are directly helpful as well and are covered in Chapter 5.

- Using cost-based optimization and NESTED LOOPS joins as the means of joining, the first table in the FROM clause is the driving table (all other conditions being equal), but only the ORDERED hint guarantees this. In NESTED LOOPS joins, choosing a driving table that is the smaller result set (not always the smaller table) means making fewer loops to the other result set (from the non-driving table) and usually results in the best performance.

- The columns that are retrieved can change which indexes Oracle uses and also change the way Oracle joins the tables in the query.

- To change the way Oracle joins multiple tables, use the USE_MERGE, USE_NL, and USE_HASH hints.

- In a three-table join, the driving table is the intersection table or the table that has a join condition to each of the other two tables in the join. Try to use the most limiting table as the driving table (or intersection table), so that your result set from the join of the first two tables is small when you join it to the third table. Also, ensure that all join conditions on all tables are indexed!

- To ensure that you are reading your EXPLAIN PLAN correctly, run a query for which you are sure of the driving table (with nested subqueries).

- You may not be able to modify actual code for some third-party products, but you can often add, force, or suppress indexes to improve the performance.

- When distributed queries cannot be avoided, use IN clauses, use set operators such as UNION and MINUS, and do whatever else you can to reduce the network traffic between nodes of the database. Queries written in a manner that causes looping between distributed nodes (distributed databases) can be extremely slow.

- If you want an Oracle symphony as great as Beethoven's, you must learn how to tune at the block level and know how to apply mathematical techniques to your tuning efforts. You don't have to learn everything you learned in college calculus; merely apply the simple equations in this chapter to tie everything in this book together.

- If you've read and understood this entire chapter, you're probably among the top-tuning professionals and you will see the heights and joys that I've seen with tuning Oracle.

References

Oracle10g Documentation (Oracle Corporation)
Guy Harrison, *Oracle SQL High-Performance Tuning 2/e* (Prentice Hall, 2000)
Block Level Reading Tool from Terlingua Software (www.tlingua.com)
Scott Marin, *The Machinations of Oracle* (Terlingua Software)

Craig Schallahamer, "All about Oracle's Touch Count Algorithm" (orapub.com)

Kevin Gilpin, Mark Bobak, Jonathon Lewis, Metalink Notes

"EM Grid Control 10g" (otn.oracle.com, Oracle Corporation)

Jay Rossiter, "Oracle Enterprise Manager 10g: Making the Grid a Reality" (Oracle Corporation)

Oracle 10g and Oracle 9i documentation

James Morle, *Scaling Oracle8i* (Addison-Wesley, 1999)

Janet Bacon, "Reading a Block Dump" (TUSC)

Roger Schrag, "Tuning Joins" (Database Specialists)

J.A. Holmes, "Leveraging Oracle Performance Tuning Tools Using Simple Mathematical Techniques," *SELECT Magazine*, Vol. 5, No. 4, July 1998, IOUG-A, pp. 36–42

J.A. Holmes, "Seven Deadly SQL Traps and How to Avoid Them," *SELECT Magazine*, Vol. 6, No 4, July 1999, IOUG-A, pp. 22–26.

J.A. Holmes, "Amazing SQL*Plus Tricks," *SELECT Magazine*, Vol. 7, No. 4, July 2000, IOUG-A, pp 26–33.

E. Aronoff, K. Loney, and N. Sonawalla, *Advanced Oracle Tuning and Administration*, (Oracle Press, Osborne McGraw-Hill, 1997)

S. Chapra, and R. Canale, *Numerical Methods for Engineers; with Programming and Software Applications, 3/e* (McGraw-Hill, 1998)

J.A. Holmes, "SQL Performance Analysis and Tuning Using Simple Mathematical Techniques," *The Carleton Journal of Computer Science*, No. 2, 1998, Carleton University Press Inc., Ottawa, ON, pp. 9–14.

R. Jain, *The Art of Computer Systems Performance Analysis: Techniques for Experimental Design, Measurement, Simulation and Modeling* (John Wiley & Sons, Inc., 1991)

Dave Wotton, "Understanding 'Snapshot Too Old'" (http://home.clara.net/dwotton/dba/snapshot.htm)

The tips and techniques section of www.ioug.org

Bradley Brown, *Oracle Web Development* (McGraw-Hill, 1999).

Dave Moore, article in *Oracle Professional,* February 2002

"Managing Oracle9i Real Application Clusters: An Oracle White Paper," March 2001

"Oracle RAC—Cache Fusion delivers Scalability: An Oracle White Paper," May 2001

"Building Highly Available Database Servers using RAC: An Oracle White Paper," May 2001

Real Application Cluster Documentation Set: technet.oracle.com

Rich Niemiec, "Oracle10g New Features" (TUSC Presentation)

Mike Ault, "Advantages of Oracle9i Real Application Clusters" (TUSC, 2002)

Randy Swanson, "Oracle10g new features" (www.tusc.com)

www.tusc.com, www.oracle.com, www.ixora.com, www.laoug.org, www.ioug.org, technet.oracle.com, www.lookuptables.com

Special thanks to Francisco Javier Moreno, Guillermo L. Ospina Romero, and Rafael I. Larios Restrepo from the University Nacional in Medellín, Colombia, Maurizio Bonomi of Italy, Joe Holmes of Canada, Roger Schrag, Joe Trezzo, Sean McGuire, Judy Corley, Greg Pucka, Randy Swanson, Bob Taylor, and Mark Greenhalgh for their contributions to this chapter.

In addition, Francisco Javier Moreno, Guillermo L. Ospina Romero, and Rafael I. Larios Restrepo contributed the excellent section "Join Tuning: Relational vs. Object-Relational Performance" earlier in this chapter.

CHAPTER
10

Using PL/SQL to
Enhance Performance
(Developer and DBA)

TIPS & COVERED

Oracle 10g takes PL/SQL to the next level. We'll focus on helpful tips that are new with 10g (up to 10gR2) as well as tips that continue to be useful from older versions in this chapter. Once you have all of the great queries to monitor your system, you need to automate all of them. PL/SQL gives you the ability to do so while also providing some great packages and procedures that can be used for tuning. The PL/SQL engine processes all PL/SQL requests and passes the statements onto Oracle for execution. When PL/SQL is passed to Oracle, it is placed in Oracle's System Global Area (SGA), more particularly in the shared pool. In Oracle, PL/SQL source code can be stored in the database in the form of procedures, functions, packages, and triggers. Once these objects are stored in the database in compiled format, they can be executed from any Oracle tool by any user who has been granted EXECUTE privilege on that object. Upon execution, the p-code (executable code) is loaded into the shared pool and executed by Oracle. A PL/SQL object remains in the shared pool until the object is aged out with a Least Recently Used (LRU) algorithm. If any process calls the object, it does not have to be reloaded into the SGA shared pool as long as it has not been aged out. Therefore, Oracle will look in the shared pool (which is very efficient) for the object prior to going to disk (which is not as efficient) to load the object. How well the SQL within the PL/SQL is tuned is probably the biggest driving factor of performance, yet there are also other tuning considerations that will be covered in this chapter. The first portion of this chapter is dedicated to understanding and being able to locate the PL/SQL. These are among the tips covered in this chapter:

- Use DBMS_APPLICATION_INFO for real-time monitoring.

- Use a custom replacement of DBMS_APPLICATION_INFO for real-time monitoring in a RAC environment.

- Log timing information in a database table.

- Reduce PL/SQL program unit iterations and iteration time.

- Use ROWID for iterative processing.

- Standardize on data types, IF statement order, and PLS_INTEGER.

- Reduce the calls to SYSDATE.

- Reduce the use of the MOD function.

- Find specific objects in the shared pool.

- Flush the shared pool when errors occur.

- Pin objects in the shared pool.

- Identify the PL/SQL that needs to be pinned.

- Use PL/SQL to pin all packages into the shared pool.

- Use and modify DBMS_SHARED_POOL.SIZES.

- Get detailed object information from DBA_OBJECT_SIZE.

- Find invalid objects.

- Find disabled triggers.

- Use PL/SQL associative arrays for fast reference table lookups.

- Access USER_SOURCE, USER_TRIGGER, and USER_DEPENDENCIES.

- Use PL/SQL with Oracle's Date data type.

- Use PL/SQL to tune PL/SQL.

- Understand the implications of PL/SQL location.

- Specify a rollback segment for a large cursor.

- Use temporary database tables for increased performance.

- Integrate a user tracking mechanism to pinpoint execution location.

- Limit the use of dynamic SQL.

- Use pipelined table functions to build complex result sets.

- Suppress debugging commands with conditional compilation.

- Take advantage of the samples just for the beginners (beginners start here).

Use **DBMS_APPLICATION_INFO** for **Real-Time Monitoring**

The DBMS_APPLICATION_INFO package provides a powerful mechanism for communicating point-in-time information about the execution in an environment. This is illustrated in the following example, enabling a long-running PL/SQL program unit to provide information on the progress of the routine every 1000 records. The PL/SQL code segment updates the application information with the number of records processed and the elapsed time every 1000 records.

The following is an example illustrating the update of all employees' salaries:

```
DECLARE
    CURSOR cur_employee IS
       SELECT employee_id, salary, ROWID
       FROM   s_employee_test;
    lv_new_salary_num NUMBER;
    lv_count_num       PLS_INTEGER := 0;
    lv_start_time_num PLS_INTEGER;
BEGIN
    lv_start_time_num := DBMS_UTILITY.GET_TIME;
    FOR cur_employee_rec IN cur_employee LOOP
       lv_count_num := lv_count_num + 1;
       -- Determination of salary increase
       lv_new_salary_num := cur_employee_rec.salary;
       UPDATE s_employee_test
       SET     salary       = lv_new_salary_num
       WHERE   rowid = cur_employee_rec.ROWID;
       IF MOD(lv_count_num, 1000) = 0 THEN
          DBMS_APPLICATION_INFO.SET_MODULE('Records Processed: ' ||
             lv_count_num, 'Elapsed: ' || (DBMS_UTILITY.GET_TIME -
```

```
          lv_start_time_num)/100 || ' sec');
    END IF;
  END LOOP;
  COMMIT;
  DBMS_APPLICATION_INFO.SET_MODULE('Records Processed: ' ||
    lv_count_num, 'Elapsed: ' || (DBMS_UTILITY.GET_TIME -
    lv_start_time_num)/100 || ' sec');
END;
/
```

To monitor the progress, the V$SESSION view can be queried, as shown in the following example:

```
SELECT username, sid, serial#, module, action
FROM    V$SESSION
WHERE   username = 'SCOTT';
```

Please note that this query needs to be run in a separate session than the one executing the PL/SQL block.

The following is the output from the V$SESSION view, when queried three different times. The last is when the PL/SQL program unit was completed.

```
USERNAME    SID SERIAL# MODULE                     ACTION
---------- --- ------- ------------------------- ------------------
SCOTT         7       4 SQL*Plus
SCOTT        10      10 Records Processed: 1000    Elapsed: 0.71 sec


USERNAME    SID SERIAL# MODULE                     ACTION
---------- --- ------- ------------------------- ------------------
SCOTT         7       4 SQL*Plus
SCOTT        10      10 Records Processed: 10000   Elapsed: 4.19 sec


USERNAME    SID SERIAL# MODULE                     ACTION
---------- --- ------- ------------------------- ------------------
SCOTT         7       4 SQL*Plus
SCOTT        10      10 Records Processed: 25000   Elapsed: 9.89 sec
```

Your response time for this will depend on how fast your system and how well it is architected. The reason for the two records being returned for each query in the preceding output is both the execution of the PL/SQL program unit to update employees' salary and the SQL statement to monitor the progress via the V$SESSION view are executed under the SCOTT schema in two different SQL*Plus sessions. The preceding example illustrates a valuable technique to deploy in an environment and provides a real-time monitoring mechanism. It becomes easier to accurately determine how long a program has been running and to estimate how long a program has to complete.

If DBAs do not want users' queries against the V$SESSION view to return information for all users, they can create a view based on the V$SESSION view that limits the retrieval to only the executing user's session information. This can be accomplished by executing the commands as the SYS user. The following syntax creates the new view (session_log was used for the new view name, but any name could have been used). Using "USER" in the query that follows returns the name of the session user (the user who logged on) with the datatype VARCHAR2.

```
CREATE VIEW session_log AS
SELECT *
FROM    V$SESSION
WHERE   username = USER;
```

The following syntax creates a public synonym:

```
CREATE PUBLIC SYNONYM session_log FOR session_log;
```

The following syntax grants SELECT permission to all users:

```
GRANT SELECT ON session_log TO PUBLIC;
```

Once the session_log view is set up, as shown in the preceding statements, the preceding V$SESSION view query can be changed to SELECT from the session_log view, as in the following query, to limit the output to only the user executing the query.

```
SELECT username, sid, serial#, module, action
FROM    session_log;
```

TIP
Use the Oracle-supplied package DBMS_APPLICATION_INFO package to log point-in-time information to the V$SESSION view to enable monitoring of long-running processes.

Use a Custom Replacement of DBMS_APPLICATION_INFO for Real-Time Monitoring in a RAC Environment

The preceding tip applies only to a RAC environment because instance-specific tables (the V$ tables) become an inappropriate mechanism for providing application-wide real-time feedback. In a RAC environment one has multiple Oracle instances servicing a single Oracle database. At any given moment each instance will be carrying some of the load of the system. Thus, a process running on one instance will not be able to see (via V$SESSION and V$SESSION_LONGOPS) runtime feedback being provided by sessions running on the other instances of the RAC.

This limitation can be overcome by introducing a custom package that mimics the calls and behavior of DBMS_APPLICATION_INFO. In a nutshell this is accomplished by using a physical table (T$SESSION) to provide a persistent display of information at the database level across all instances servicing that database. This custom package contains a majority of the common setters that are available in DBMS_APPLICATION_INFO (set_action, set_client_info, and set_module). When the setters in this package are called, they will initially hand off the call to the DBMS_APPLICATION_INFO package so that the instance-specific V$ tables are updated; then this package will replicate the session's V$ record in the T$SESSION table. The result is that if you are only interested in what is running on the instance servicing your session (or you are not in a RAC environment), you can continue to query the V$SESSION table to see real-time feedback being provided by custom application code. If you are in a RAC environment and you want to see what real-time feedback information is being provided by running processes, regardless of the instance that is servicing those processes, you should query the T$SESSION table.

Note that the tip that is being presented here is specific to the basic monitoring capabilities provided by DBMS_APPLICATION_INFO and does not cover the long operations support provided by that package. However, the techniques presented here can be easily expanded to cover long operations so that they too can be monitored from any instance in a RAC environment.

First we will start with a physical table that mimics some of the columns of interest within V$SESSION.

```
create table t$session
(
instance          varchar2(100) not null,
audsid            number        not null,
sid               number,
serial#           number,
program           varchar2(100),
module            varchar2(100),
action            varchar2(100),
client_info       varchar2(100),
osuser            varchar2(100),
username          varchar2(100),
machine           varchar2(100),
terminal          varchar2(100),
logon_time        date,
last_update_time date not null
)
pctfree 50
pctused 40
initrans 10
maxtrans 255
storage (initial 1M
        next 1M
        minextents 1
        maxextents unlimited
        pctincrease 0)
nologging;

comment on table t$session is 'SessionInfo Persistent Storage Table.';
comment on column t$session.instance is 'The Instance Name.';
comment on column t$session.audsid is 'The Auditting SID (from V$SESSION).';
comment on column t$session.sid is 'The SID (from V$SESSION).';
comment on column t$session.serial# is 'The Serial# (from V$SESSION).';
comment on column t$session.program is 'The Program (from V$SESSION).';
comment on column t$session.module is 'The Module (specfied by the user in the api
call).';
comment on column t$session.action is 'The Action (specfied by the user in the api
call).';
comment on column t$session.client_info is 'The Client Info (specfied by the user in the
api call).';
comment on column t$session.osuser is 'The OS User (from V$SESSION).';
comment on column t$session.username is 'The User Name (from V$SESSION).';
comment on column t$session.machine is 'The Machine (from V$SESSION).';
comment on column t$session.terminal is 'The Terminal (from V$SESSION).';
comment on column t$session.logon_time is 'The Logon Time (from V$SESSION).';
comment on column t$session.last_update_time is 'The last update time of this record.';
```

```
create  index t$session_idx1 on t$session
(
instance,
audsid
)
pctfree 10
initrans 100
maxtrans 255
storage (initial 500K
        next 500K
        minextents 1
        maxextents unlimited
        pctincrease 0)
nologging;
```

Note the following points of interest regarding the design of this table:

- To facilitate "value too large" protections in the API package, all varchar2 columns have been made the same length.

- To maintain maximum performance in a highly concurrent environment, this table does not utilize any PK or UK constraints. However, the columns that should be considered logically bound by such constraints are

   - PK = instance, audsid

   - UK = instance, sid, serial#

Next, we will introduce a custom version of DBMS_APPLICATION_INFO that supports the same call specifications. Before we present the source code, let's provide an outline of the necessary procedures:

- **init_sessinfo_record (procedure, internal)**   Initializes the Session Info Record that will be used to write the V$SESSION contents for the current session to the persistent storage tables.

- **persistence_cleanup_session (procedure, internal)**   Synchronizes the SessionInfo Persistent Storage Table with the V$SESSION records of the Instance in which the code is executing.

- **persistence_cleanup (procedure, internal)**   Coordinates the synchronization of persistent Session records with the Instance in which they originated.

- **write_sessinfo_record (procedure, internal)**   Writes the Session Info Record to the persistent table.

- **release_session_records (procedure)**   Removes the persistent records associated with this session.

- **set_action (procedure)**   Updates the "Action" of both V$SESSION and the persistent table for the Instance and Session in which the calling code is executing.

- **set_client_info (procedure)**   Updates the "Client Info" of both V$SESSION and the persistent table for the Instance and Session in which the calling code is executing.

- **set_module (procedure)**   Updates the "Module" and "Action" of both V$SESSION and the persistent table for the Instance and Session in which the calling code is executing.

Customize
DBMS_APPLICATION_INFO

Here is the actual source code:

```
CREATE OR REPLACE PACKAGE tsc_appinfo_pkg is
  --A custom procedure to provide cleanup operations.
  procedure release_session_records;
  --Setter calls that mimic DBMS_APPLICATION_INFO.
  procedure set_action (p_action_name_c in varchar2);
  procedure set_client_info (p_client_info_c in varchar2);
  procedure set_module (p_module_name_c in varchar2,
                        p_action_name_c in varchar2);
 END tsc_appinfo_pkg;
/
CREATE OR REPLACE PACKAGE BODY tsc_appinfo_pkg is
 --*************************
 --Declare package variables.
 --*************************
 --The name of the Instance servicing the current session.
 pg_session_instance_name_c varchar2(100);
 --The AUDSID of the current session.
 --This is needed to find the appropriate record in V$SESSION.
 pg_session_audsid_n number;
 --The earliest time when the next persistence table cleanup can occur.
 --The default will be in the past so that the first call to this package
 --within a session will drive a cleanup operation.
 pg_next_cleanup_time date := sysdate - 1;
 --This SessionInfo Record.
 --This record is used to replicate the updates being performed against
 --V$SESSION so that they can be written to the SessionInfo Persistent
 --Storage Table without the need to read V$SESSION.
 --Important Note: A given session has one and only one record in
 --               V$SESSION.
 pg_max_length_i constant integer := 100;
 type pg_sessinfo_type is record
    (arowid         rowid,
     sid            t$session.sid%type,
     serial#        t$session.serial#%type,
     program        t$session.program%type,
     module         t$session.module%type,
     action         t$session.action%type,
     client_info    t$session.client_info%type,
     osuser         t$session.osuser%type,
     username       t$session.username%type,
     machine        t$session.machine%type,
     terminal       t$session.terminal%type,
     logon_time     t$session.logon_time%type,
     last_update_time t$session.last_update_time%type);
 pg_sir pg_sessinfo_type;
 --Reuseable cursors.
 cursor pg_current_sessions_cur is
   select audsid
```

```
      from V$SESSION;
--*****************************
--Declare package exceptions.
--*****************************
PU_FAILURE exception;
pragma exception_init (PU_FAILURE, -20000);
INVALID_COLUMN exception;
pragma exception_init (INVALID_COLUMN, -904);
PRECISION_ERROR exception;
pragma exception_init (PRECISION_ERROR, -1438);
RESOURCE_LOCKED exception;
pragma exception_init (RESOURCE_LOCKED, -54);
UNIQUE_VIOLATION exception;
pragma exception_init (UNIQUE_VIOLATION, -1);
--*****************************
--Declare local program units.
--*****************************
--init_sessinfo_record procedure.
--
--Description: Initializes the SessionInfo Record that will be used to
--             persist, in this package, the contents of the sessions's
--             V$SESSION information.
--
--Technical: This procedure should only be called once at package
--             instantiation.
--
--Notes:  This is a supporting program unit that is NOT exposed to the
--        user. As such, this program unit must push exceptions up
--        through the call stack.
--
--Syntax: init_sessinfo_record;
PROCEDURE init_sessinfo_record is
  cursor v_session_cur(p_audsid_i      IN number,
                       p_text_length_i IN integer) is
    select /*+ FIRST_ROWS */
           sid,
           serial#,
           substr(program, 1, p_text_length_i),
           substr(module, 1, p_text_length_i),
           substr(action, 1, p_text_length_i),
           substr(client_info, 1, p_text_length_i),
           substr(osuser, 1, p_text_length_i),
           substr(username, 1, p_text_length_i),
           substr(machine, 1, p_text_length_i),
           substr(terminal, 1, p_text_length_i),
           logon_time
    from V$SESSION
   where audsid = p_audsid_i;
BEGIN
  --Retrieve V$SESSION information and store it in the SessionInfo Record.
```

Customize DBMS_APPLICATION_INFO

```
        open v_session_cur(pg_session_audsid_n,
                            pg_max_length_i);
        fetch v_session_cur into pg_sir.sid,
                                pg_sir.serial#,
                                pg_sir.program,
                                pg_sir.module,
                                pg_sir.action,
                                pg_sir.client_info,
                                pg_sir.osuser,
                                pg_sir.username,
                                pg_sir.machine,
                                pg_sir.terminal,
                                pg_sir.logon_time;
        close v_session_cur;
EXCEPTION
    when PU_FAILURE then
        raise PU_FAILURE;
    when OTHERS then
        --Error logging goes here.
        NULL;
END init_sessinfo_record;

--persistence_cleanup_session procedure.
--Description: Synchronizes the SessionInfo Persistent Storage Table with
--             the V$SESSION records of the  Instance in which the code
--             is executing. The goal is to remove from the persistence
--             tables those records whose parent session is no longer
--             running in the Instance from which it originated.
--Notes: Do not send an exception back to the caller.
--Syntax: persistence_cleanup_session;
PROCEDURE persistence_cleanup_session is
    pragma autonomous_transaction;
    type v_audsid_table is table of number;
    v_current_array     v_audsid_table;
    v_persistent_array  v_audsid_table;
    v_purge_array       v_audsid_table := v_audsid_table();
    v_found_b boolean;
    cursor v_persistent_sessions_cur(p_instance_c IN varchar2) is
        select audsid
            from t$session
        where instance = p_instance_c;
BEGIN
    --Obtain a list of all currently active sessions in the current
    --instance.
    open pg_current_sessions_cur;
    fetch pg_current_sessions_cur bulk collect into v_current_array;
    close pg_current_sessions_cur;
    --Obtain a list of all sessions for the current instance appearing
    --in the persistent table.
    open v_persistent_sessions_cur(pg_session_instance_name_c);
    fetch v_persistent_sessions_cur bulk collect into v_persistent_array;
```

```
      close v_persistent_sessions_cur;
      --Transfer to the Purge Array those records from the Persistent Array
      --that are still in the current array.
      for x in 1..v_persistent_array.count loop
        v_found_b := false;
        for y in 1..v_current_array.count loop
          if (v_current_array(y) = v_persistent_array(x)) then
            v_found_b := true;
            exit;
          end if;
        end loop;
        if ( not v_found_b ) then
          v_purge_array.extend();
          v_purge_array(v_purge_array.count) := v_persistent_array(x);
        end if;
      end loop;
      --Purge from the persistent table those records that are still in the
      --persistent array as these are records that no longer have a
      --counterpart in V$SESSION.
      if (v_purge_array.count > 0) then
        forall i in 1..v_purge_array.count
          delete from t$session
            where instance = (select instance from v$instance)
              and audsid = v_purge_array(i);
      end if;
      commit;
EXCEPTION
  when PU_FAILURE then
    rollback;
  when OTHERS then
    rollback;
    --Error logging goes here.
END persistence_cleanup_session;


--persistence_cleanup procedure.
--Description: Coordinates the synchronization of persistent Session
--             records with the Instance in which they originated.
--Syntax: persistence_cleanup;

PROCEDURE persistence_cleanup is
BEGIN
  --For performance reasons, Persistence Cleanup will never occur more
  --than once per minute.
  if ( sysdate > pg_next_cleanup_time ) then
    persistence_cleanup_session;
    pg_next_cleanup_time := sysdate + 1/1440;
  end if;
END;


--write_sessinfo_record procedure.
--Description: Writes the SessionInfo Record to the persistent table.
```

Customize
DBMS_APPLICATION_INFO

```
--Technical: For performance reasons, this subroutine will generate a
--            single insert per package instantiation. The new rowid will
--            be captured during the insert. From that point forward the
--            captured rowid will be used to perform subsequent updates to
--            the inserted record.
--Notes: Do not send an exception back to the caller.
--Syntax: write_sessinfo_record;
PROCEDURE write_sessinfo_record is
  pragma autonomous_transaction;
BEGIN
  --If we have a RowID for the SessionInfo Record then we will use it to
  --perform an update.
  if ( pg_sir.arowid is not null ) then
    update t$session
       set module          = pg_sir.module,
           action          = pg_sir.action,
           client_info     = pg_sir.client_info,
           last_update_time = pg_sir.last_update_time
     where rowid = pg_sir.arowid;
    --It would be odd to have updated zero rows by rowid.
    --This would most likely be an incorrect cleanup operation being
    --performed by another instance or by a user. We will record an
    --error and then nullify the rowid of the SessionInfo Record so that
    --it will be treated as a new record needing an insert.
    if ( sql%rowcount = 0 ) then
      pg_sir.arowid := null;
      --Error logging goes here.
    end if;
  end if;
  --If we do not have a RowID for the SessionInfo Record then we must
  --insert a new record and captures its rowid for use in future updates.
  if ( pg_sir.arowid is null ) then
    --Just in case there is already a record in the table.
    --Normally, this shouldn't be necessary but we should compensate
    --for packages that may have been flushed from memory.
    --The primary concern here is to maintain the logical PK and UK
    --constraints on the table.
    delete from t$session
     where instance = pg_session_instance_name_c
       and audsid   = pg_session_audsid_n;
    commit;
    delete from t$session
     where instance = pg_session_instance_name_c
       and sid      = pg_sir.sid
       and serial#  = pg_sir.serial#;
    commit;
    insert /*+ append */
           into t$session(instance,           audsid,
                          sid,                 serial#,
                          program,             module,
                          action,              client_info,
```

```
                        osuser,                    username,
                        machine,                   terminal,
                        logon_time,                last_update_time)
    values (pg_session_instance_name_c,  pg_session_audsid_n,
            pg_sir.sid,                pg_sir.serial#,
            pg_sir.program,            pg_sir.module,
            pg_sir.action,             pg_sir.client_info,
            pg_sir.osuser,             pg_sir.username,
            pg_sir.machine,            pg_sir.terminal,
            pg_sir.logon_time,         pg_sir.last_update_time)
    returning rowid into pg_sir.arowid;
  end if;
  commit;
EXCEPTION
  when PU_FAILURE then
    rollback;
  when OTHERS then
    rollback;
    --Error logging goes here.
END write_sessinfo_record;
--****************************
--Declare global program units.
--****************************
--release_session_records procedure.
--Description: Removes the persistent records associated with this session.
--             Since the Session data is being persisted in a
--             physical table we don't have the convenience of the records
--             going away when the session disconnects(as is the case with
--             V$SESSION). Normally, this should
--             not pose a major issue since other calls to this package
--             will eventually perform the persistence_cleanup operation.
--             However, in the event that you are annoyed by lingering
--             persistence information you can force the records to be
--             purged immediately with this procedure.
--Notes: Do not send an exception back to the caller.
--Syntax: release_session_records;
procedure release_session_records is
  pragma autonomous_transaction;
BEGIN
  delete from t$session
   where instance = pg_session_instance_name_c
     and audsid   = pg_session_audsid_n;
  commit;
EXCEPTION
  when PU_FAILURE then
    rollback;
  when OTHERS then
    rollback;
    --Error logging goes here.
END release_session_records;
```

```
--set_action procedure.
--Description: Updates the "Action" of both V$SESSION and the persistent
--              table for the Instance and Session in which the calling
--              code is executing.
--Notes: Do not send an exception back to the caller.
--Syntax: set_action (p_action_name_c in varchar2);
--Where: p_action_name_c = The Action value to be set.
PROCEDURE set_action (p_action_name_c in varchar2) is
BEGIN
  --Perform cleanup operations on the Persistent Storage Tables.
  persistence_cleanup;
  --Update V$SESSION. Remember, this data will only be visible to
  --sessions connected to the same Instance.
  DBMS_APPLICATION_INFO.set_action(p_action_name_c);
  --Update the SessionInfo Record to reflect the same change just made
  --to V$SESSION.
  pg_sir.last_update_time := sysdate;
  pg_sir.action := substr(p_action_name_c, 1, pg_max_length_i);
  --Update the SessionInfo Persistent Storage Table. Remember, this will
  --be visible to all connections to the database, regardless of the
  --Instance the connection is coming through.
  write_sessinfo_record;
EXCEPTION
  when PU_FAILURE then
    NULL;
  when OTHERS then
    --Error logging goes here.
    NULL;
END set_action;

--set_client_info procedure.
--Description: Updates the "Client Info" of both V$SESSION and the
--              persistent table for the Instance and Session in which
--              the calling code is executing.
--Notes: Do not send an exception back to the caller.
--Syntax: set_client_info (p_client_info_c in varchar2);
--Where: p_client_info_c = The Client Info value to be set.
PROCEDURE set_client_info (p_client_info_c in varchar2) is
BEGIN
  --Perform cleanup operations on the Persistent Storage Tables.
  persistence_cleanup;
  --Update V$SESSION. Remember, this data will only be visible to
  --sessions connected to the same Instance.
  DBMS_APPLICATION_INFO.set_client_info(p_client_info_c);
  --Update the SessionInfo Record to reflect the same change just made
  --to V$SESSION.
  pg_sir.last_update_time := sysdate;
  pg_sir.client_info := substr(p_client_info_c, 1, pg_max_length_i);
  --Update the SessionInfo Persistent Storage Table. Remember, this will
  --be visible to all connections to the database, regardless of the
```

```
      --Instance the connection is coming through.
      write_sessinfo_record;
   EXCEPTION
      when PU_FAILURE then
         NULL;
      when OTHERS then
         --Error logging goes here.
         NULL;
   END set_client_info;

   --set_module procedure.
   --Description: Updates the "Module" and "Action" of both V$SESSION and
   --             the persistent table for the Instance and Session in which
   --             the calling code is executing.
   --Notes: Do not send an exception back to the caller.
   --Syntax: set_action (p_module_name_c in varchar2,
   --                     p_action_name_c in varchar2);
   --Where: p_module_name_c = The Module value to be set.
   --       p_action_name_c = The Action value to be set.
   PROCEDURE set_module (p_module_name_c in varchar2,
                         p_action_name_c in varchar2) is
   BEGIN
      --Perform cleanup operations on the Persistent Storage Tables.
      persistence_cleanup;
      --Update V$SESSION. Remember, this data will only be visible to
      --sessions connected to the same Instance.
      DBMS_APPLICATION_INFO.set_module(p_module_name_c, p_action_name_c);
      --Update the SessionInfo Record to reflect the same change just made
      --to V$SESSION.
      pg_sir.last_update_time := sysdate;
      pg_sir.module := substr(p_module_name_c, 1, pg_max_length_i);
      pg_sir.action := substr(p_action_name_c, 1, pg_max_length_i);
      --Update the SessionInfo Persistent Storage Table. Remember, this will
      --be visible to all connections to the database, regardless of the
      --Instance the connection is coming through.
      write_sessinfo_record;
   EXCEPTION
      when PU_FAILURE then
         NULL;
      when OTHERS then
         --Error logging goes here.
         NULL;
   END set_module;

BEGIN
   --Retrieve the AUDSID of the current session.
   BEGIN
      pg_session_audsid_n := sys_context('userenv', 'sessionid');
   EXCEPTION
      when OTHERS then
```

```
            pg_session_audsid_n := to_number(to_char(sysdate, 'yyyydddsssss'));
    END;
    --Retrieve the name of the Oracle Instance in which the code is executing.
    DECLARE
      cursor v_instance_cur(p_text_length_i IN integer) is
        select substr(instance_name, 1, p_text_length_i)
          from v$instance;
    BEGIN
      open v_instance_cur(pg_max_length_i);
      fetch v_instance_cur into pg_session_instance_name_c;
      close v_instance_cur;
    EXCEPTION
      when OTHERS then
        pg_session_instance_name_c := 'Error: '||user;
    END;
    --Initialize the SessionInfo record.
    init_sessinfo_record;
EXCEPTION
  when OTHERS then
    --Error logging goes here.
    NULL;
END tsc_appinfo_pkg;
/
```

The primary purpose of this package (and its supporting table) is to store in physical tables information that typically only exists in memory tables (V$SESSION and V$SESSION_LONGOPS) for the purpose of using familiar calls (DBMS_APPLICATION_INFO) to provide real-time feedback of executing processes in a RAC environment. The simple introduction of physical storage tables imposes a severe performance penalty that was recognized in the creation of this package and must be recognized by the developer when interacting with the setters of this package.

Here are the specific things that have been done in this package to offset the performance impact of using physical tables:

- The T$SESSION table does not utilize any PK or UK constraints. The logical constraints that are enforced by this package are

  - PK = instance, audsid

  - UK = instance, sid, serial#

- The V$SESSION record of the current session is read only once, at package instantiation. From that point forward only the module, action, and client_info values being changed via the setters in this package will be updated in the physical tables. Because of the significant overhead in continually reading V$SESSION, it was decided that it would only be read once. Normally, this will be okay because a majority of the columns in V$SESSION are static. Where we can run into trouble is if the developer intermixes calls to the setters in the package with calls to the setters in DBMS_APPLICATION_INFO. In such a scenario, the physical tables will not reflect any of the change made by the direct call to DBMS_APPLICATION_INFO.

- Transactions must be kept as short as possible to avoid contention.

Here are the specific things you can do as a developer when incorporating this package into your custom modules:

- Do not intermix setter calls from this package with setter calls from DBMS_APPLICATION_ INFO. Doing so will result in the physical storage table being out of sync with V$SESSION.

- Use the calls judiciously. A call to a setter in this package will take two orders or magnitude longer to execute than a call to a setter in DBMS_APPLICATION_INFO. In rapidly executing, iterative code you should provide logic to only call these setters every Xth iteration. Failure to take these precautions could have drastic performance impacts on iterative code.

The following script can be used to exercise this custom package:

```
set timing on;

BEGIN
  tsc_appinfo_pkg.set_module(user, 'Working...');
  for i in 1..10000 loop
    tsc_appinfo_pkg.set_client_info('Iteration: '||i);
  end loop;
  tsc_appinfo_pkg.set_action('Done');
END;
/
```

Another session, whether or not it is being serviced by the same RAC node, can monitor the progress of this script by querying the T$SESSION table. If the second session knew that it was being serviced by the same RAC node as the first, it could alternately monitor V$SESSION as well.

TIP
Use a custom replacement of DBMS_APPLICATION_INFO for real-time monitoring in a RAC environment.

Log Timing Information in a Database Table

Monitoring performance is an ongoing process. Many variables in an environment can change and affect performance over time; therefore, performance should be monitored continuously. Some of the variables include user growth, data growth, reporting growth, application modification/enhancement deployment, and additional load on the system from other applications. With this in mind, an Oracle system must be regularly monitored to ensure performance remains at, or above, an acceptable level.

One method of monitoring the system performance is to create a mechanism for logging timing statistics for certain aspects of an application. Batch programs are good candidates for this monitoring procedure. The monitoring procedure can be accomplished by inserting timing statistics into a database table. The following example provides the database table logging method by creating a database table, and then integrating INSERT statements for the timing of the process into the table. The important information to log in the database table are the program identifier (some unique method of identifying the program), the date and time the program is executed, and the elapsed time of the execution. One column has been added for this application, namely, the number of records updated. This additional column is important for this application to monitor the growth of employee records being processed. When creating a timing log table for your application, add columns to store additional important processing information that may affect your timing results. Therefore, the following table can be created to log the timing information.

```
CREATE TABLE process_timing_log
    (program_name       VARCHAR2(30),
     execution_date     DATE,
     records_processed  NUMBER,
     elapsed_time_sec   NUMBER);
```

Once the table is created, PL/SQL program units can be enhanced to log the timing information into the process_timing_log table as illustrated in the following program.

```
CREATE OR REPLACE PROCEDURE update_salary AS
    CURSOR cur_employee IS
        SELECT employee_id, salary, ROWID
        FROM   s_employee_test;
    lv_new_salary_num NUMBER;
    lv_count_num       PLS_INTEGER := 0;
    lv_start_time_num PLS_INTEGER;
    lv_total_time_num NUMBER;
BEGIN
    lv_start_time_num := DBMS_UTILITY.GET_TIME;
    FOR cur_employee_rec IN cur_employee LOOP
        lv_count_num := lv_count_num + 1;
        -- Determination of salary increase
        lv_new_salary_num := cur_employee_rec.salary;
        UPDATE s_employee_test
        SET     salary      = lv_new_salary_num
        WHERE   rowid = cur_employee_rec.ROWID;
    END LOOP;
    lv_total_time_num := (DBMS_UTILITY.GET_TIME -
        lv_start_time_num)/100;
    INSERT INTO process_timing_log
        (program_name, execution_date, records_processed,
         elapsed_time_sec)
    VALUES
        ('UPDATE SALARY', SYSDATE, lv_count_num,
         lv_total_time_num);
    COMMIT;
END update_salary;
/
```

As shown in the preceding code segment, the timer is started at the beginning of the program unit and then stopped at the end of the program unit. The difference between the start and ending timers is logged into the process_timing_log for each execution of the update_salary program. If the update_salary program unit is executed three times, as shown in the following syntax, then three timing records will be inserted into the process_timing_log table.

Another method is to use the DBMS_PROFILER package to get timing statistics per line of PL/SQL code. See Metalink article 104377.1, "Performance of New PL/SQL Features" for more information.

```
EXECUTE update_salary
EXECUTE update_salary
EXECUTE update_salary
```

The following script retrieves the information from the process_timing_log table:

```
SELECT program_name,
       TO_CHAR(execution_date,'MM/DD/YYYY HH24:MI:SS') execution_time,
       records_processed, elapsed_time_sec
FROM   process_timing_log
ORDER BY 1,2;

PROGRAM_NAME   EXECUTION_TIME        RECORDS_PROCESSED ELAPSED_TIME_SEC
-------------  -------------------   ----------------- ----------------
UPDATE_SALARY  07/02/2002 19:43:57              25252             8.89
UPDATE_SALARY  07/02/2002 19:44:07              25252             9.11
UPDATE_SALARY  07/02/2002 19:44:15              25252             8.62
```

This output shows one possible result. There is a difference in the elapsed time for the same program execution. If the difference increases over time, this may indicate a need to analyze the program unit further or the application to determine what caused the execution time increase. With logging mechanisms in place, the elapsed time can be monitored at any point in time because the timing information is being logged to a database table.

In the preceding example, the time logged was per program unit. If the program is complex and executed for an extended period of time, it may be desirable to change the logging of timing statistics in the program. The INSERT into the process_timing_log table could be performed after a certain number of iterations or to log timing for certain functionality in a program unit.

TIP

Log (INSERT) execution timing information into a database table for long-running PL/SQL program units to integrate a proactive performance monitoring mechanism into your system. The database table can be reviewed at any point in time to determine if performance has decreased over time.

TIP

System load in terms of number of active sessions can have a large impact on the performance of program execution; therefore, it would be helpful to modify the database table logging method to include a column for the number of active sessions. This column can be filled by adding one additional query to the program unit being executed to retrieve the count from the V$SESSION view.

Reduce PL/SQL Program Unit Iterations and Iteration Time

Any PL/SQL program unit involving looping logic is a strong candidate for performance improvements. Potential improvements for these types of programs can be accomplished in two ways. The first is to reduce the number of iterations by restructuring the logic to accomplish the same functional result. The second is to reduce the time per iteration. Either reduction often improves performance dramatically.

To bring this point into perspective, think of the following scenario: We need to process 9000 employee records in a PL/SQL routine, and to process each employee takes two seconds. This equates to 18,000 seconds, which equates to five hours. If the processing per employee is reduced to one second, the time to process the 9000 employees is reduced by 9000 seconds, or 2.5 hours . . . quite a difference!

The following example shows a minor restructuring of a PL/SQL program unit to illustrate reducing per-loop processing and overall processing. The program unit processes a loop 1,000,000 times. Each iteration adds to the incremental counter used to display a message each 100,000 iterations and adds to the total counter used to check for loop exiting. To view DBMS_OUTPUT, make sure you issue the SET SERVEROUTPUT ON command first.

```
CREATE OR REPLACE PACKAGE stop_watch AS
    pv_start_time_num     PLS_INTEGER;
    pv_stop_time_num      PLS_INTEGER;
    pv_last_stop_time_num PLS_INTEGER;
-- This procedure creates a starting point for the timer routine and
-- is usually called once at the beginning of the PL/SQL program unit.
PROCEDURE start_timer;
--
This procedure retrieves a point in time and subtracts the current
-- time from the start time to determine the elapsed time. The
-- interval elapsed time is logged and displayed. This procedure is
-- usually called repetitively for each iteration or a specified
-- number of iterations.
PROCEDURE stop_timer;
END stop_watch;
/
Package created.
CREATE OR REPLACE PACKAGE BODY stop_watch AS
PROCEDURE start_timer AS
BEGIN
    pv_start_time_num     := DBMS_UTILITY.GET_TIME;
    pv_last_stop_time_num := pv_start_time_num;
END start_timer;
PROCEDURE stop_timer AS
BEGIN
    pv_stop_time_num := DBMS_UTILITY.GET_TIME;
    DBMS_OUTPUT.PUT_LINE('Total Time Elapsed: ' ||
        TO_CHAR((pv_stop_time_num - pv_start_time_num)/100,
        '999,999.99') || ' sec   Interval Time: ' ||
        TO_CHAR((pv_stop_time_num - pv_last_stop_time_num)/100,
```

```
               '99,999.99')  ||  ' sec');
      pv_last_stop_time_num := pv_stop_time_num;
END stop_timer;
END;
/
```
Package body created.

```
SET SERVEROUTPUT ON

DECLARE
   lv_counter_num        PLS_INTEGER := 0;
   lv_total_counter_num PLS_INTEGER := 0;
BEGIN
   stop_watch.start_timer;
   LOOP
      lv_counter_num        := lv_counter_num + 1;
      lv_total_counter_num := lv_total_counter_num + 1;
      IF lv_counter_num >= 100000 THEN
         DBMS_OUTPUT.PUT_LINE('Processed 100,000 Records. ' ||
            'Total Processed ' || lv_total_counter_num);
         lv_counter_num := 0;
         EXIT WHEN lv_total_counter_num >= 1000000;
      END IF;
   END LOOP;
   stop_watch.stop_timer;
END;
/

Processed 100,000 Records. Total Processed 100000
Processed 100,000 Records. Total Processed 200000
Processed 100,000 Records. Total Processed 300000
Processed 100,000 Records. Total Processed 400000
Processed 100,000 Records. Total Processed 500000
Processed 100,000 Records. Total Processed 600000
Processed 100,000 Records. Total Processed 700000
Processed 100,000 Records. Total Processed 800000
Processed 100,000 Records. Total Processed 900000
Processed 100,000 Records. Total Processed 1000000
Total Time Elapsed:        .71 sec   Interval Time:        .71 sec

PL/SQL procedure successfully completed.
```

By changing the program to only add to the lv_total_counter_num variable each time the incremental counter reaches 100,000, the overall execution time is reduced.

```
DECLARE
   lv_counter_num        PLS_INTEGER := 0;
   lv_total_counter_num PLS_INTEGER := 0;
BEGIN
   stop_watch.start_timer;
   LOOP
```

```
      lv_counter_num          := lv_counter_num + 1;
   IF lv_counter_num >= 100000 THEN
      DBMS_OUTPUT.PUT_LINE('Processed 100,000 Records. Total ' ||
          'Processed ' || lv_total_counter_num);
      lv_total_counter_num := lv_total_counter_num +
          lv_counter_num;
      lv_counter_num := 0;
      EXIT WHEN lv_total_counter_num >= 1000000;
   END IF;
 END LOOP;
 stop_watch.stop_timer;
END;
/
```

The DBMS_OUTPUT.PUT_LINE output for each batch of processed records was not included in the following output.

```
Total Time Elapsed:        .47 sec   Interval Time:        .47 sec

PL/SQL procedure successfully completed.
```

The preceding example illustrates the performance difference by changing the iteration logic to reduce the timing per iteration. The example is basic and shows a 34 percent increase on one million iterations. Based on the restructuring and the iterations, this improvement can make a large difference.

TIP
When a PL/SQL program unit involves extensive looping or recursion, concentrate on reducing the execution time per iteration. This adds up fast, and it is easy to do the math to determine the overall improvement potential. The looping or recursion should also be reviewed for restructuring to reduce the number of iterations, while keeping the functionality. With the extreme flexibility of PL/SQL and SQL, typically a variety of ways exist to accomplish the same result. If a PL/SQL program unit is not performing optimally, sometimes you have to rewrite the logic another way.

Use ROWID for Iterative Processing

The ROWID variable can help improve PL/SQL programs that retrieve records from the database, perform manipulation on the column values, and then complete with an UPDATE to the retrieved record. When retrieving each record, the ROWID can be added to the selected column list. When updating each record, the ROWID can be used in the predicate clause. The ROWID is the fastest access path to a record in a table, even faster than a unique index reference.

The performance improvement of using the ROWID is illustrated in the following example. The example retrieves each of the 25,000 employee records, calculates a new salary for each employee, and then updates the employees' salary. The actual salary calculation is not shown in this example. The first PL/SQL code segment shows the timing results with the UPDATE using the employee_id column, which has a unique index on the column.

```
DECLARE
   CURSOR cur_employee IS
      SELECT employee_id, salary
      FROM   s_employee_test;
   lv_new_salary_num NUMBER;
BEGIN
   stop_watch.start_timer;
   FOR cur_employee_rec IN cur_employee LOOP
      -- Determination of salary increase
      lv_new_salary_num := cur_employee_rec.salary;
      UPDATE s_employee_test
      SET    salary      = lv_new_salary_num
      WHERE  employee_id = cur_employee_rec.employee_id;
   END LOOP;
   COMMIT;
   stop_watch.stop_timer;
END;
/
```

The following output shows the timing of two executions of the preceding code segment.

```
Total Time Elapsed:        1.71 sec   Interval Time:       1.71 sec
PL/SQL procedure successfully completed.

Total Time Elapsed:        1.59 sec   Interval Time:       1.59 sec
PL/SQL procedure successfully completed.
```

In the following procedure, the same functionality is maintained while changing the UPDATE to perform the UPDATE based on the ROWID. This involves adding the ROWID in the SELECT statement and changing the UPDATE predicate clause.

```
DECLARE
   CURSOR cur_employee IS
      SELECT employee_id, salary, ROWID
      FROM   s_employee_test;
   lv_new_salary_num NUMBER;
BEGIN
   stop_watch.start_timer;
   FOR cur_employee_rec IN cur_employee LOOP
      -- Determination of salary increase
      lv_new_salary_num := cur_employee_rec.salary;
      UPDATE s_employee_test
      SET    salary = lv_new_salary_num
      WHERE  rowid  = cur_employee_rec.ROWID;
   END LOOP;
   COMMIT;
   stop_watch.stop_timer;
END;
/
```

Use ROWID

The following output shows the timing of two executions of the preceding code segment.

```
Total Time Elapsed:          1.45 sec    Interval Time:        1.45 sec
PL/SQL procedure successfully completed.

Total Time Elapsed:          1.48 sec    Interval Time:        1.48 sec
PL/SQL procedure successfully completed.
```

As evidenced from the timings, the execution is faster by using the ROWID. The first PL/SQL code segment UPDATE statement retrieves the result by using the index on employee_id to get the ROWID, and then goes to the table to search by ROWID. The second PL/SQL code segment UPDATE statement goes directly to the table to search by ROWID, thus eliminating the index search. The performance improvement increases when more records are involved and when the index used does not refer to a unique index.

TIP
Use the ROWID variable to enhance performance when SELECTing a record in a PL/SQL program unit and then manipulating the same record in the same PL/SQL program unit. Also, one caveat to this technique is that it cannot be used for Index Organized Tables (IOT).

Standardize on Data Types, IF Statement Order, and PLS_INTEGER

Several minor programming modifications can be introduced into your standard PL/SQL development that can improve performance. Three of these techniques are outlined in this section.

- Ensure the same data types in comparison operations.

- Order IF conditions based on the frequency of the condition.

- Use the PLS_INTEGER PL/SQL data type for integer operations.

Ensure the Same Data Types in Comparison Operations

When variables or constant values are compared, they should have the same data type definition. If the comparison does not involve the same data types, then Oracle implicitly converts one of the values, thus introducing undesired overhead. Any time values are compared in a condition, the values should be the same data type. This should be a standard used when developing PL/SQL program units and is good programming style.

The following procedure illustrates the cost of comparing different data types, namely a numeric data type to a character value in the IF statement.

```
CREATE OR REPLACE PROCEDURE test_if (p_condition_num NUMBER) AS
   lv_temp_num          NUMBER := 0;
   lv_temp_cond_num     NUMBER := p_condition_num;
BEGIN
   stop_watch.start_timer;
   FOR lv_count_num IN 1..100000 LOOP
      IF lv_temp_cond_num = '1' THEN
```

```
            lv_temp_num := lv_temp_num + 1;
        ELSIF lv_temp_cond_num = .'2' THEN
            lv_temp_num := lv_temp_num + 1;
        ELSIF lv_temp_cond_num = '3' THEN
            lv_temp_num := lv_temp_num + 1;
        ELSIF lv_temp_cond_num = '4' THEN
            lv_temp_num := lv_temp_num + 1;
        ELSIF lv_temp_cond_num = '5' THEN
            lv_temp_num := lv_temp_num + 1;
        ELSIF lv_temp_cond_num = '6' THEN
            lv_temp_num := lv_temp_num + 1;
        ELSIF lv_temp_cond_num = '7' THEN
            lv_temp_num := lv_temp_num + 1;
        ELSE
            lv_temp_num := lv_temp_num + 1;
        END IF;
    END LOOP;
    stop_watch.stop_timer;
END;
/
```

The following illustrates the execution of the test_if procedure:

```
EXECUTE test_if(8)
```

The following output is the execution result of the test_if procedure:

```
Total Time Elapsed:          .26 sec   Interval Time:          .26 sec
PL/SQL procedure successfully completed.
```

Unnecessary overhead is introduced with the different data types. If the procedure is changed to the same data type comparisons, the following execution is much faster:

```
CREATE OR REPLACE PROCEDURE test_if (p_condition_num NUMBER) AS
    lv_temp_num         NUMBER := 0;
    lv_temp_cond_num    NUMBER := p_condition_num;
BEGIN
    stop_watch.start_timer;
    FOR lv_count_num IN 1..100000 LOOP
        IF lv_temp_cond_num = 1 THEN
            lv_temp_num := lv_temp_num + 1;
        ELSIF lv_temp_cond_num = 2 THEN
            lv_temp_num := lv_temp_num + 1;
        ELSIF lv_temp_cond_num = 3 THEN
            lv_temp_num := lv_temp_num + 1;
        ELSIF lv_temp_cond_num = 4 THEN
            lv_temp_num := lv_temp_num + 1;
        ELSIF lv_temp_cond_num = 5 THEN
            lv_temp_num := lv_temp_num + 1;
        ELSIF lv_temp_cond_num = 6 THEN
            lv_temp_num := lv_temp_num + 1;
```

```
      ELSIF lv_temp_cond_num = 7 THEN
          lv_temp_num := lv_temp_num + 1;
      ELSE
          lv_temp_num := lv_temp_num + 1;
      END IF;
   END LOOP;
   stop_watch.stop_timer;
END;
/
```

The following code listing illustrates the execution of the new test_if procedure:

```
EXECUTE test_if(8)

Total Time Elapsed:            .17 sec    Interval Time:           .17 sec
PL/SQL procedure successfully completed.
```

As shown in the preceding examples, the execution is 23 percent faster. The improvement increases as the frequency of execution increases.

TIP
Ensure all conditional comparisons compare the same data types. Additionally, it helps to ensure the data types within the numeric family are comparing the same subtype. Therefore, in the final example, the comparison in the IF statement to a 1,2,3, and so forth is comparing a NUMBER to a PLS_INTEGER. There is still some internal Oracle conversion overhead taking place. To eliminate this overhead, the 1,2,3 . . . should be changed to 1.0, 2.0, 3.0 . . . . When this change is made to the final example, the timing is reduced to 0.16 seconds.

Order IF Conditions Based on the Frequency of the Condition

The natural programming method when developing IF statements with multiple conditions is to order the conditional checks by some sequential order. This order is typically alphabetical or numerically sequenced to create a more readable segment of code, but it usually is not the most optimal. Especially, when using the ELSIF condition several times in an IF statement, the most frequently met condition should appear first, followed by the next frequent match, and so forth.

In the preceding section, the execution of the procedure was always carried out by passing an 8, which meant every loop had to check all eight conditional operations of the IF logic to satisfy the condition. If we pass a 1, which is equivalent to saying the first condition satisfies all IF executions, we get a more optimized result, as shown in the following example:

```
EXECUTE test_if(1)

Total Time Elapsed:            .05 sec    Interval Time:           .05 sec
PL/SQL procedure successfully completed.
```

The preceding output illustrates a performance improvement from the preceding section with the correct ordering of IF conditions. Therefore, take the extra step of analyzing IF condition order before coding them.

TIP
Ensure the string of PL/SQL IF conditions appear in the order of most frequently satisfied, not a sequential order based numerically or alphanumerically.

Use the PLS_INTEGER PL/SQL Data Type for Integer Operations

The typical standard for declaring a numeric data type is to use the data type of NUMBER. In PL/SQL release 2.2, Oracle introduced the PLS_INTEGER data type. This data type can be used in place of any numeric family data type declaration, as long as the content of the variable is an integer and remains within the bounds of –2147483647 and +2147483647. Therefore, most counters and operations with integers can use this data type. The PLS_INTEGER involves fewer internal instructions to process, thus increasing performance when using this numeric data type. The more references to this variable, the more improvement realized.

This improvement is illustrated in the following PL/SQL code segment. The code segment is the same example as the previous two sections, with the data type declarations being changed to PLS_INTEGER from NUMBER.

```
CREATE OR REPLACE PROCEDURE test_if (p_condition_num PLS_INTEGER) AS
    lv_temp_num          PLS_INTEGER := 0;
    lv_temp_cond_num     PLS_INTEGER := p_condition_num;
BEGIN
    stop_watch.start_timer;
    FOR lv_count_num IN 1..100000 LOOP
        IF lv_temp_cond_num = 1 THEN
            lv_temp_num := lv_temp_num + 1;
        ELSIF lv_temp_cond_num = 2 THEN
            lv_temp_num := lv_temp_num + 1;
        ELSIF lv_temp_cond_num = 3 THEN
            lv_temp_num := lv_temp_num + 1;
        ELSIF lv_temp_cond_num = 4 THEN
            lv_temp_num := lv_temp_num + 1;
        ELSIF lv_temp_cond_num = 5 THEN
            lv_temp_num := lv_temp_num + 1;
        ELSIF lv_temp_cond_num = 6 THEN
            lv_temp_num := lv_temp_num + 1;
        ELSIF lv_temp_cond_num = 7 THEN
            lv_temp_num := lv_temp_num + 1;
        ELSE
            lv_temp_num := lv_temp_num + 1;
        END IF;
    END LOOP;
```

Use PLS_INTEGER PL/SQL

```
    stop_watch.stop_timer;
END;
/
```

The following illustrates the execution of the test_if procedure:

```
EXECUTE test_if(1)
```

The following performance improvement is evident based on the results of the execution:

```
Total Time Elapsed:          .03 sec   Interval Time:        .03 sec
PL/SQL procedure successfully completed.
```

TIP
Use the PLS_INTEGER type when processing integers to improve performance.

TIP
If a number with precision is assigned to a PLS_INTEGER variable, the value will be rounded to a whole number as if the ROUND function had been performed on the number.

Reduce the Calls to SYSDATE

The SYSDATE variable is a convenient method of retrieving the current date and time. Calls to SYSDATE involve some overhead; therefore, if this variable is needed to log the date of certain processing, the call to this variable should be made once at the start of the program rather than at each iteration. This technique of calling SYSDATE once at the start of the program assumes the date logging is desired at the point in time the program started.

The reduction of SYSDATE calls is illustrated in the following example. The example loops through 10,000 iterations, calling SYSDATE (only the date portion of the variable because the TRUNC function is used to truncate the time portion) every iteration.

```
DECLARE
    lv_current_date       DATE;
BEGIN
    stop_watch.start_timer;
    FOR lv_count_num IN 1..10000 LOOP
        lv_current_date := TRUNC(SYSDATE);
    END LOOP;
    stop_watch.stop_timer;
END;
/
```

The following output shows the timing of two executions of the preceding code segment:

```
Total Time Elapsed:          .04 sec   Interval Time:        .04 sec
PL/SQL procedure successfully completed.
```

```
Total Time Elapsed:          .01 sec   Interval Time:        .01 sec
PL/SQL procedure successfully completed.
```

The following PL/SQL code segment is modified to retrieve the SYSDATE only once, at the beginning of the program, and set to another variable each iteration.

```
DECLARE
    lv_current_date     DATE := TRUNC(SYSDATE);
    lv_final_date       DATE;
BEGIN
    stop_watch.start_timer;
    FOR lv_count_num IN 1..10000 LOOP
        lv_final_date := lv_current_date;
    END LOOP;
    stop_watch.stop_timer;
END;
/
```

The following output shows the timing of two executions of the preceding code segment:

```
Total Time Elapsed:          .00 sec   Interval Time:        .00 sec

PL/SQL procedure successfully completed.

Total Time Elapsed:          .01 sec   Interval Time:        .01 sec
PL/SQL procedure successfully completed.
```

As evident in the preceding example, overhead is associated with the SYSDATE call, and the number of calls to SYSDATE should be reduced, if possible.

TIP
Attempt to limit the calls to SYSDATE in iterative or recursive loops because overhead is associated with this variable. Set a PL/SQL DATE variable to SYSDATE in the declaration and reference the PL/SQL variable to eliminate the overhead.

Reduce the Use of the MOD Function

Certain PL/SQL functions are more costly to use than others. MOD is one function that is better performed with additional PL/SQL logic to improve the overall performance. This is illustrated in the following example. This is a useful function, but if it is executed in an IF statement as illustrated in the following example, additional overhead is introduced.

```
BEGIN
    stop_watch.start_timer;
    FOR lv_count_num IN 1..10000 LOOP
        IF MOD(lv_count_num, 1000) = 0 THEN
            DBMS_OUTPUT.PUT_LINE('Hit 1000; Total: ' || lv_count_num);
        END IF;
```

```
   END LOOP;
   stop_watch.stop_timer;
END;
/
```

The following output shows the timing of two executions of the preceding code segment:

```
Hit 1000; Total: 1000
Hit 1000; Total: 2000
Hit 1000; Total: 3000
Hit 1000; Total: 4000
Hit 1000; Total: 5000
Hit 1000; Total: 6000
Hit 1000; Total: 7000
Hit 1000; Total: 8000
Hit 1000; Total: 9000
Hit 1000; Total: 10000
Total Time Elapsed:          .04 sec   Interval Time:          .04 sec
PL/SQL procedure successfully completed.

Total Time Elapsed:          .04 sec   Interval Time:          .04 sec
```

The preceding PL/SQL code segment is modified to eliminate the MOD function use and perform the same check with additional PL/SQL logic, as illustrated in the following code segment:

```
DECLARE
   lv_count_inc_num PLS_INTEGER := 0;
BEGIN
   stop_watch.start_timer;
   FOR lv_count_num IN 1..10000 LOOP
      lv_count_inc_num := lv_count_inc_num + 1;
      IF lv_count_inc_num = 1000 THEN
         DBMS_OUTPUT.PUT_LINE('Hit 1000; Total: ' || lv_count_num);
         lv_count_inc_num := 0;
      END IF;
   END LOOP;
   stop_watch.stop_timer;
END;
/

Hit 1000; Total: 1000
Hit 1000; Total: 2000
Hit 1000; Total: 3000
Hit 1000; Total: 4000
Hit 1000; Total: 5000
Hit 1000; Total: 6000
Hit 1000; Total: 7000
Hit 1000; Total: 8000
Hit 1000; Total: 9000
Hit 1000; Total: 10000
Total Time Elapsed:          .01 sec   Interval Time:          .01 sec
```

```
PL/SQL procedure successfully completed.

Total Time Elapsed:          .00 sec    Interval Time:          .00 sec
```

As shown from the two preceding examples, the MOD function adds overhead and has better performance with PL/SQL IF statements.

TIP
The MOD function is one function that is faster to perform with additional PL/SQL logic. While this is minor, it is a standard technique to introduce into your PL/SQL standard programming techniques.

Shared Pool and Pinning PL/SQL Objects

The SHARED_POOL_SIZE parameter sets the amount of shared pool allocated in the SGA (see Chapter 4 and Appendix A for a detailed look at SHARED_POOL_SIZE and closely related shared pool parameters). The shared pool stores all SQL statements and PL/SQL blocks executed in the Oracle database. Given the method by which Oracle manages the shared pool, as far as aging, the shared pool can become fragmented. In addition, since Oracle will not age any objects that are currently being processed by a session, there is the possibility that you can get an Oracle error indicating that the shared pool does not have enough memory for a new object. The exact error message that a user will receive is "ORA-4031: unable to allocate XXX bytes of shared memory" (where XXX is the number of bytes it is attempting to allocate). If this error is ever received, it means that your SGA shared pool should be increased in size as soon as possible. The method prior to Oracle 9*i* was to modify the initialization parameter SHARED_POOL_SIZE and then shut down and start up the database. The quick but costly method of eliminating this error until the next database shutdown was to flush the SGA shared pool. This was accomplished with the following command (only allowed if ALTER SYSTEM privilege is assigned to a user):

```
alter system flush shared_pool;
```

As of Oracle 9*i,* you can modify the SHARED_POOL_SIZE parameter without shutting down the database as long as you don't exceed the SGA_MAX_SIZE. This will eliminate the need to do things that you had to do in previous versions. You still will want to pin the large objects into the shared pool when the database has started and make sure that the shared pool is large enough for all of these statements to be cached.

TIP
As of Oracle 9i, the SHARED_POOL_SIZE parameter may be modified while the database is up as long as you don't exceed the SGA_MAX_SIZE. See Chapter 4 for additional information about setting initialization parameters.

Pinning (Caching) PL/SQL Object Statements into Memory

In the event that you cannot maintain a sufficient SHARED_POOL_SIZE to keep all statements in memory, it may become important to keep the most important objects cached (pinned) in memory.

The following example shows how to pin PL/SQL object statements (the procedure PROCESS_DATE is pinned in the example that follows) in memory using the DBMS_SHARED_POOL.KEEP procedure:

```
begin
dbms_shared_pool.keep('process_date','p');
end;
/
```

or

```
execute sys.dbms_shared_pool.keep ('SYS.STANDARD');
```

By pinning an object in memory, the object will not be aged out or flushed until the next database shutdown. Also consider Metalink note 61760.1: DBMS_SHARED_POOL should be created as user SYS. No other user should own this package. Any user requiring access to the package should be granted execute privileges by SYS. If you create the package in the SYS schema, and run the sample code in a different schema, you first need to (a) grant the EXECUTE_CATALOG_ROLE role to the user running the example (i.e., TEST) and grant EXECUTE privilege on DBMS_SHARED_POOL to TEST, and (b) fully qualify the package, as in SYS.DBMS_SHARED_POOL.KEEP, because the dbmspool.sql script does *not* create a public synonym for this package.

TIP
Use the DBMS_SHARED_POOL.KEEP procedure to pin PL/SQL objects into the shared pool.

NOTE
To use this procedure, you must first run the DBMSPOOL.SQL script. The PRVTPOOL.PLB script is automatically executed after DBMSPOOL.SQL runs. These scripts are not run by CATPROC.SQL.

Pinning All Packages

To pin all packages in the shared pool, execute the following as the SYS user (this code comes from Oracle's Metalink):

```
declare
own varchar2(100);
nam varchar2(100);
cursor pkgs is
    select      owner, object_name
    from        dba_objects
    where       object_type = 'PACKAGE';
begin
    open pkgs;
    loop
        fetch pkgs into own, nam;
        exit when pkgs%notfound;
        dbms_shared_pool.keep(own || '.' || nam, 'P');
    end loop;
```

```
end;
/
```

A more targeted approach, pinning only packages which needed to be reloaded, would be better than pinning *all* packages, especially because most DBA interfaces since Oracle 8*i* involve PL/SQL packages. At the very least you should check to make sure you are not trying to pin invalid packages as well. Common packages that are shipped with Oracle (that should be kept) include STANDARD, DBMS_STANDARD, and DIUTIL.

TIP
Use the DBMS_SHARED_POOL.KEEP procedure in PL/SQL to pin all packages when the database is started (if memory/shared pool permits) and to avoid errors involving loading packages in the future.

Identifying PL/SQL Objects That Need to Be Pinned

Fragmentation that causes several small pieces to be available in the shared pool, and not enough large contiguous pieces, is a common occurrence in the shared pool. The key to eliminating shared pool errors (as noted in the preceding section) is to understand which of the objects will be large enough to cause problems when you attempt to load them. Once you know the problem PL/SQL, you can then pin this code when the database has started (and the shared pool is completely contiguous). This will ensure that your large packages are already in the shared pool when they are called, instead of searching for a large contiguous piece of the shared pool (which may not be there later as the system is used). You can query the V$DB_OBJECT_CACHE view to determine PL/SQL that is both large and currently not marked "kept." These are objects that may cause problems (due to their size and need for a large amount of contiguous memory) if they need to be reloaded at a later time. This will only show the current statements in the cache. The example that follows searches for those objects requiring greater than 100K.

```
select    name, sharable_mem
from      v$db_object_cache
where     sharable_mem > 100000
and       type in ('PACKAGE', 'PACKAGE BODY', 'FUNCTION',
          'PROCEDURE')
and       kept = 'NO';
```

TIP
Query the V$DB_OBJECT_CACHE table to find objects that are not pinned and are also large enough to potentially cause problems.

Using and Modifying DBMS_SHARED_POOL.SIZES

An alternative and very precise indication of shared pool allocation can be viewed through the DBMS_SHARED_POOL.SIZES package procedure. This call accepts a MINIMUM SIZE parameter and will display all cursors and objects within the shared pool of a size greater than that provided. The actual statement issued to retrieve this information follows:

```
select     to_char(sharable_mem / 1000 ,'999999') sz, decode
           (kept_versions,0,' ',rpad('yes(' || to_char(kept_versions)
           || ')' ,6)) keeped, rawtohex(address) || ',' || to_char
           (hash_value)  name, substr(sql_text,1,354) extra, 1 iscursor
from       v$sqlarea
where      sharable_mem > &min_ksize * 1000
union
select     to_char(sharable_mem / 1000 ,'999999') sz, decode(kept,'yes',
           'yes   ','') keeped, owner || '.' || name || lpad(' ',29 -
           (length(owner) + length(name) ) ) || '(' || type || ')'
           name, null  extra, 0 iscursor
from       v$db_object_cache v
where      sharable_mem > &min_ksize * 1000
order by   1 desc;
```

The preceding query can be placed into a procedure package, of your own construction, to display a formatted view of cursors and objects within the shared pool.

Finding Large Objects

You can use DBMS_SHARED_POOL.SIZES package procedure (*DBMS_SHARED_POOL* is the package and *sizes* is the procedure within the package) to view the objects using shareable memory higher than a threshold that you set. Execute this package as displayed next for a threshold of 100K (the output follows):

```
Set serveroutput on size 10000;

begin
sys.dbms_shared_pool.sizes(100);
end;
/

SIZE(K)    KEPT        NAME
118        YES         SYS.STANDARD        (PACKAGE)
109                    SELECT    DT.OWNER,DT.TABLE_NAME,DT.TABLESPACE_NAME,
                                 DT.INITIAL_EXTTENT,DT.NEXT_EXTENT,DT.NUM_ROWS,
                                 DT.AVG_ROW_LEN,
                                 SUM(DE.BYTES) PHY_SIZE
                       FROM      DBA_TABLES DT,DBA_SEGMENTS DE
                       WHERE     DT.OWNER = DE.OWNER
                       AND       DT.TABLE_NAME = DE.SEGMENT_NAME
                       AND       DT.TABLESPACE_NAME = DE.TABLESPACE_NAME
                       GROUP BY  DT.OWNER,DT.TABLE_NAME,DT.TABLESPACE_NAME,
                                 DT.INITIAL_EXTENT,DT.NEX
                                 (0B14559C,3380846737)    (CURSOR)
22                     RDBA.RDBA_GENERATE_STATISTICS (PACKAGE)
PL/SQL procedure successfully completed.
```

TIP
Use the DBMS_SHARED_POOL.SIZES package procedure to find specific information about an object.

Get Detailed Object Information from DBA_OBJECT_SIZE

Query the DBA_OBJECT_SIZE view to show the memory used by a particular object that will include much more detailed information concerning the object.

```
Compute sum of source_size on report
Compute sum of parsed_size on report
Compute sum of code_size on report
Break on report
select   *
from     dba_object_size
where    name = 'RDBA_GENERATE_STATISTICS';
```

OWNER	NAME	TYPE	SOURCE_SIZE	PARSED_SIZE	CODE_SIZE
RDBA	RDBA_GENERATE_STATISTICS	PACKAGE	5023	4309	3593
RDBA	RDBA_GENERATE_STATISTICS	PACKAGE BODY	85595	0	111755
SUM			90618	4309	115348

(partial display only...not all columns shown)

Getting Contiguous Space Currently in the Shared Pool

Why does the shared pool return errors when an object is loaded? The answer is that a large enough piece of the shared pool is not available to fit the piece of code. We saw in the last section how to find the size of the code that you have. We also saw in a previous section how to pin pieces of code into the shared pool. Now, we must look at the query that will tell you which code, that has made it into the shared pool, is either very large and should be pinned or should be investigated and shortened if possible.

The following query accesses an x$ table (see Chapter 15), and you must be the SYS user to access these tables:

```
select   ksmchsiz, ksmchcom
from     x$ksmsp
where    ksmchsiz > 10000
and      ksmchcom like '%PL/SQL%';
```

This query shows that the packages that have been accessed are very large and should be pinned at the time that the database has started. If the last line of this query is eliminated, it will also show the large pieces of free memory (KSMCHCOM = 'free memory' and KSMCHCOM = 'permanent memory') that are still available (unfragmented) for future large pieces of code to be loaded. See Chapter 13 for more details on the x$ tables and example output.

TIP
Query x$ksmsp to find all large pieces of PL/SQL that have appeared in the shared pool. These are candidates to be pinned when the database has started.

Finding Invalid Objects

Developers often change a small section of PL/SQL code that fails to compile upon execution, forcing an application failure. A simple query, reviewed daily, will help you spot these failures before the end user does:

```
col       "Owner" format a12
col       "Object" format a20
col       "OType" format a12
col       "Change DTE" format a20
select    substr(owner,1,12) "Owner", substr(object_name,1,20)
          "Object", object_type "OType", to_char(last_ddl_time,
          'DD-MON-YYYY HH24:MI:SS') "Change Date"
from      dba_objects
where     status <> 'VALID'
order by  1, 2;
```

The preceding example will display any objects that are INVALID, meaning they were never compiled successfully or changes in dependent objects have caused them to become INVALID. If we had a procedure PROCESS_DATE, for example, found to be INVALID, we could manually recompile this procedure with the following command:

```
alter procedure PROCESS_DATE compile;
```

Once this command is executed and the PROCESS_DATE passes the recompile, the procedure would be changed by Oracle automatically from INVALID to VALID. Another manual method that exists is to call the DBMS_UTILITY.COMPILE_SCHEMA package procedure as outlined next to recompile all stored procedures, functions, and packages for a given schema:

```
begin
dbms_utility.compile_schema('USERA');
end;
/
```

To find the state of all PL/SQL objects for your schema, execute the following:

```
column    object_name format a20
column    last_ddl_time heading 'last ddl time'
select    object_type, object_name, status, created, last_ddl_time
from      user_objects
where     object_type in ('PROCEDURE', 'FUNCTION', 'PACKAGE',
          'PACKAGE BODY', 'TRIGGER');


OBJECT_TYPE          OBJECT_NAME          STATUS   CREATED    last ddl
-------------------- -------------------- -------- ---------- ---------
PACKAGE              DBMS_REPCAT_AUTH     VALID    12-MAY-02  12-MAY-02
PACKAGE BODY         DBMS_REPCAT_AUTH     VALID    12-MAY-02  12-MAY-02
```

```
TRIGGER                DEF$_PROPAGATOR_TRIG VALID   12-MAY-02 12-MAY-02
PROCEDURE              ORA$_SYS_REP_AUTH    VALID   12-MAY-02 12-MAY-02
TRIGGER                REPCATLOGTRIG        VALID   12-MAY-02 12-MAY-02
```

TIP

Query DBA_OBJECTS (for system-wide objects) or USER_OBJECT (for your schema only) to find the state of objects and avoid errors and reloading by the user. You can recompile individual objects or an entire schema with DBMS_UTILITY.COMPILE_SCHEMA.

Finding Disabled Triggers

In some respects, a disabled trigger is far more dangerous than an invalid object because it doesn't fail—*it just doesn't execute!* This can have severe consequences for applications, and consequently business processes, that depend on business logic stored within procedural code. The following script identifies disabled triggers:

```
col       "Owner/Table" format a30
col       "Trigger Name" format a25
col       "Event" format a15
col       "Owner" format a10
select    substr(owner,12) "Owner", trigger_name "Trigger Name",
          trigger_type "Type", triggering_event "Event",
          table_owner||'.'||table_name "Owner/Table"
from      dba_triggers
where     status <> 'ENABLED'
order by  owner, trigger_name;
```

If we modify the preceding query to check only the SYS schema and certain columns, as shown next, we will get a list of disabled triggers that were provided by Oracle:

```
Select    trigger_name "Trigger Name",STATUS,
          trigger_type "Type", triggering_event "Event"
from      dba_triggers
where     status <> 'ENABLED'
and       owner = 'SYS'
order     by owner, trigger_name;
```

Trigger Name	STATUS	Type	Event
AURORA$SERVER$SHUTDOWN	DISABLED	BEFORE EVENT	SHUTDOWN
AURORA$SERVER$STARTUP	DISABLED	AFTER EVENT	STARTUP
NO_VM_CREATE	DISABLED	BEFORE EVENT	CREATE
NO_VM_DROP	DISABLED	BEFORE EVENT	DROP
SYS_LOGOFF	DISABLED	BEFORE EVENT	LOGOFF
SYS_LOGON	DISABLED	AFTER EVENT	LOGON

To find all triggers for your schema, execute the following code:

```
column    trigger_name        format a15
column    trigger_type        format a15
```

Finding Disabled Triggers

```
column    triggering_event  format a15
column    table_name        format a15
column    trigger_body      format a25
select    trigger_name, trigger_type, triggering_event,
          table_name, status, trigger_body
from      user_triggers;


TRIGGER_NAME  TRIGGER_TYPE      TRIGGERING_EVENT  TABLE_NAME STATUS   TRIGGER_BODY
UPDATE_TOTAL  AFTER STATEMENT   INSERT OR UPDATE  ORDER_MAIN ENABLED  begin
                                OR DELETE                             update
                                                                      total_orders
                                                                      set
                                                                      order_total =
                                                                      10;
                                                                      end;
```

> **TIP**
> *Query DBA_TRIGGERS (for system-wide objects) or USER_TRIGGERS*
> *(for your schema only) to find the state of triggers and avoid errors*
> *with disabled triggers. Disabled triggers can have fatal results for an*
> *application; they don't fail, they just don't execute.*

Use PL/SQL Associative Arrays for Fast Reference Table Lookups

Programs that are designed to process data coming into a system usually incorporate numerous reference table lookups to properly validate and/or code the incoming data. When the reference tables are searched, using a unique key that is a numerical data type, the query performance against the reference tables can be drastically increased by loading the reference tables into PL/SQL associative arrays (formerly known as index-by tables). Consider an incoming data set that contains a single numerical column that must be translated to a coded string using a reference table. Here is a program to handle this task using the classic approach of repeated searches against the reference table:

```
DECLARE
  v_code_c ref_table.ref_string%type;
  cursor v_lookup_cur (p_code_n IN number) is
    select ref_string
      from ref_table
     where ref_num = p_code_n;
  cursor v_inbound_cur is
    select *
      from incoming_data;
BEGIN
  --Open a cursor to the incoming data.
  for inbound_rec in v_inbound_cur loop
    BEGIN
      --Calculate the reference string from the reference data.
      open v_lookup_cur(inbound_rec.coded_value);
```

```
      fetch v_lookup_cur into v_code_c;
      if v_lookup_cur%notfound then
        close v_lookup_cur;
        raise NO_DATA_FOUND;
      end if;
      close v_lookup_cur;
      dbms_output.put_line(v_code_c);
      --processing logic...
      --Commit each record as it is processed.
      commit;
    EXCEPTION
      when NO_DATA_FOUND then
        null;--Appropriate steps...
      when OTHERS then
        null;--Appropriate steps...
    END;
  end loop;
END;
/
```

While this program may appear to be written efficiently, it is in fact hampered by the repeated queries against the reference table. Even though Oracle may have the entire reference table in memory, due to pinning or prior queries, there is still a certain amount of overhead involved with processing the queries.

A more efficient technique is to load the entire reference table into a PL/SQL associative array. The numerical column (that the searches are performed against) is loaded as the array index. When a lookup against the reference data is required, the array is used instead of the actual reference table—the code in the incoming data that must be translated is used as the array index. The inherent nature of working with PL/SQL associative arrays is that if an INVALID array index is used (meaning the code in the incoming data does not match any value in the reference table), the NO_DATA_FOUND exception will be raised. Here is the same processing program rewritten using an associative array to store the reference data:

```
DECLARE
  type v_ref_table is table of ref_table.ref_string%type index by binary_integer;
  v_ref_array v_ref_table;
  v_code_c ref_table.ref_string%type;
  cursor v_lookup_cur is
    select *
      from ref_table;
  cursor v_inbound_cur is
    select *
      from incoming_data;
BEGIN
  --First, load the reference array with data from the reference table.
  for lookup_rec in v_lookup_cur loop
    v_ref_array(lookup_rec.ref_num) := lookup_rec.ref_string;
  end loop;
  --Open a cursor to the incoming data.
  for inbound_rec in v_inbound_cur loop
    BEGIN
```

```
        --Calculate the reference string from the reference data.
        v_code_c := v_ref_array(inbound_rec.coded_value);
        dbms_output.put_line(v_code_c);
        --processing logic...
        --Commit each record as it is processed.
        commit;
      EXCEPTION
        when NO_DATA_FOUND then
          null;--Appropriate steps...
        when OTHERS then
          null;--Appropriate steps...
      END;
    end loop;
END;
/
```

The result should be a drastic increase in the processing speed due to the reduced overhead in working with the PL/SQL associative arrays in comparison to the actual database table.

Finally, quite some time ago, the requirement that an associative array be indexed by a numeric value was lifted. Thus, the index of an associative array can be a string value. This capability makes it possible for the same solution to be used when the coded values to be resolved are not necessarily of a numerical nature. Consider the traditional example that some inbound data is carrying a two-character representation of a state code that needs to be resolved and validated. A slight modification to the previous procedure, as shown next, makes this possible. The index type for the array must be a VARCHAR2 type.

```
DECLARE
    type v_ref_table is table of states_table.state_name%type
      index by states_table.state_code%type;
    v_ref_array v_ref_table;
    v_state_c states_table.state_name%type;
    cursor v_lookup_cur is
      select state_code,
             state_name
        from states_table;
    cursor v_inbound_cur is
      select *
        from incoming_data;
BEGIN
    --First, load the reference array with data from the reference table.
    for lookup_rec in v_lookup_cur loop
      v_ref_array(lookup_rec.state_code) := lookup_rec.state_name;
    end loop;
    --Open a cursor to the incoming data.
    for inbound_rec in v_inbound_cur loop
      BEGIN
        --Calculate the reference string from the reference data.
        v_state_c := v_ref_array(inbound_rec.coded_value);
        dbms_output.put_line(v_state_c);
        --processing logic...
```

```
        --Commit each record as it is processed.
        commit;
      EXCEPTION
        when NO_DATA_FOUND then
            null;--Appropriate steps...
        when OTHERS then
            null;--Appropriate steps...
      END;
    end loop;
END;
/
```

TIP
Load reference tables into PL/SQL associative arrays for faster lookups.
This takes advantage of the performance of array indexes in PL/SQL.

Finding and Tuning the SQL When Objects Are Used

At times, the hardest part of tuning stored objects is finding the actual code that is stored in the database. This section looks at queries that retrieve the SQL that can be tuned. In this section, we query views that retrieve information about the actual source code that exists behind the stored objects.

Retrieve the code for a procedure you created called PROCESS_DATE:

```
column    text  format a80
select    text
from      user_source
where     name = 'PROCESS_DATE'
order by  line;
```

This query works procedures, triggers, or functions. For packages, change the last line in the query to

```
order by type, line;

TEXT
procedure process_date is
  test_num number;
 begin
 test_num := 10;
 if test_num = 10 then
  update order_main
  set       process_date = sysdate
  where    order_num = 12345;
 end if;
 end;
```

The following example retrieves the code for the familiar DBMS_RULE package:

```
column   text format a80
select   text
from     dba_source
where    name = 'DBMS_RULE'
and      type = 'PACKAGE'
order by line;

TEXT
--------------------------------------------------------------------------------
PACKAGE dbms_rule AUTHID CURRENT_USER AS

  PROCEDURE evaluate(
          rule_set_name         IN      varchar2,
          evaluation_context    IN      varchar2,
          event_context         IN      sys.re$nv_list := NULL,
          table_values          IN      sys.re$table_value_list := NULL,
          column_values         IN      sys.re$column_value_list := NULL,
          variable_values        IN      sys.re$variable_value_list := NULL,
          attribute_values      IN      sys.re$attribute_value_list := NULL,
          stop_on_first_hit     IN      boolean := FALSE,
          simple_rules_only     IN      boolean := FALSE,
          true_rules            OUT     sys.re$rule_hit_list,
          maybe_rules           OUT     sys.re$rule_hit_list);

  PROCEDURE evaluate(
          rule_set_name         IN      varchar2,
          evaluation_context    IN      varchar2,
          event_context         IN      sys.re$nv_list := NULL,
          table_values          IN      sys.re$table_value_list := NULL,
          column_values         IN      sys.re$column_value_list,
          variable_values       IN      sys.re$variable_value_list := NULL,
          attribute_values      IN      sys.re$attribute_value_list := NULL,
          simple_rules_only     IN      boolean := FALSE,
          true_rules_iterator   OUT     binary_integer,
          maybe_rules_iterator  OUT     binary_integer);
  FUNCTION get_next_hit(
          iterator              IN      binary_integer)
  RETURN sys.re$rule_hit;
  PROCEDURE close_iterator(
          iterator              IN      binary_integer);
END dbms_rule;
35 rows selected.
```

The following example attempts to retrieve the package body for the DBMS_JOB package:

```
column   text  format a80
select   text
from     dba_source
where    name = 'DBMS_JOB'
and      type = 'PACKAGE BODY'
```

```
order by  line;

TEXT
PACKAGE BODY dbms_job wrapped
0
abcd
abcd
...
:2 a0 6b d a0 ac :3 a0 6b b2
ee :2 a0 7e b4 2e ac e5 d0
b2 e9 93 a0 7e 51 b4 2e
:2 a0 6b 7e 51 b4 2e 6e a5
57 b7 19 3c b0 46 :2 a0 6b
ac :2 a0 b2 ee ac e5 d0 b2
e9 :2 a0 6b :3 a0 6e :4 a0 :5 4d a5
57 :2 a0 a5 57 b7 :3 a0 7e 51
```

In this example, the package was wrapped (protected) using the WRAP command, and the output is unreadable. If you find yourself tuning the preceding code, you need sleep!

You can use the following query to retrieve the source code for a trigger:

```
column    trigger_name       format a15
column    trigger_type       format a15
column    triggering_event   format a15
column    table_name         format a15
column    trigger_body       format a25
select    trigger_name, trigger_type, triggering_event, table_name, trigger_body
from      user_triggers;
```

TRIGGER_NAME	TRIGGER_TYPE	TRIGGERING_EVEN	TABLE_NAME	TRIGGER_BODY

UPDATE_TOTAL	AFTER STATEMENT	INSERT OR UPDATE OR DELETE	ORDER_MAIN	begin
				  update order_main
				  set order_total = 10;
				end;

The following example shows how to find the dependencies for PL/SQL objects:

```
column    name               format a20
column    referenced_owner   format a15 heading R_OWNER
column    referenced_name    format a15 heading R_NAME
column    referenced_type    format a12 heading R_TYPE
select    name, type, referenced_owner, referenced_name, referenced_type
from      user_dependencies
order by  type, name;
```

NAME	TYPE	R_OWNER	R_NAME	R_TYPE
INSERT_RECORD	PROCEDURE	USERA	ORDER_MAIN	TABLE
INSERT_RECORD	PROCEDURE	SYS	STANDARD	PACKAGE
PROCESS_DATE	PROCEDURE	SYS	STANDARD	PACKAGE
PROCESS_DATE	PROCEDURE	USERA	ORDER_MAIN	TABLE

TIP
*Finding the source code behind PL/SQL package procedures involves
querying the USER_SOURCE and DBA_SOURCE views. Finding the
source code behind a trigger involves querying the USER_TRIGGERS
and DBA_TRIGGERS views. You can find dependencies among
PL/SQL object by querying the USER_DEPENDENCIES and the
DBA_DEPENDENCIES views.*

The Time Component When Working with DATE Data Types

When working with the Oracle DATE data type, it is more accurate to think of it as a TIME data
type. This is because the DATE data type always stores a complete temporal value, down to the
second. It is impossible to insert a date value only into either a PL/SQL variable or database
column that is defined as a DATE. If this behavior is not kept in mind during the design of an
application, it is possible that the finished product will exhibit undesirable side effects. One
of the most common side effects of improper date management within an application is when
reports, which filter the data by a date value, return different results across multiple executions.

When a column or variable of this type (DATE) is initialized with a value, any missing
component (if any) will be automatically supplied by Oracle. If the initialization value contains
only the date component, only then Oracle will supply the time component, and vice versa. This
begs the question of how can one tell which component, if any, is missing during the initialization?
Quite simply, both components are automatically present only when a date variable is initialized
from another date variable. The system variable SYSDATE is one such date variable. Thus,
whenever a column or variable is initialized from SYSDATE, it will contain a value representing
the date and time when the initialization occurred.

If it is January 10, 1998 at 3:25:22 A.M., and you execute the following command:

```
Date_Var_1 date := SYSDATE;
```

the value contained in the variable Date_Var_1 will be

```
10-JAN-1998 03:25:22.
```

It is also possible to initialize a date variable using a text string. For example,

```
Date_Var_2 date := '10-JAN-98';
```

The value contained in the variable Date_Var_1 will be

```
10-JAN-98 00:00:00
```

Here is a simple PL/SQL block that will allow you to see this for yourself:

```
DECLARE
  date_var_2 DATE;
BEGIN
```

```
   date_var_2 := '10-JAN-98';
   DBMS_OUTPUT.PUT_LINE('Selected date is '|| to_char(date_var_2, 'DD-MON-YYYY
HH24:MI:SS'));
END;
/

10-JAN-1998 00:00:00
```

TIP
*A DATE data type always stores a complete temporal value, down to
the second. It is impossible to insert a date value only into either a
PL/SQL variable or database column that is defined as a DATE.*

At this point, it should be clear that Date_Var_1 and Date_Var_2 are not equal. Even though
they both contain a date component of 10-JAN-98, they are not equal because their time
components differ by almost three and a half hours. Herein lies the problem with a program that
does not anticipate the time component that is inherent with date values. Consider an application
that uses the SYSDATE variable to initialize the accounting date of records inserted into a database
table. If a PL/SQL processing program (or a simple SQL SELECT statement) does not take the time
component of the records into account, then records will be missed during processing.

Given that the date values in a table *contain time values* other than 12:00 midnight, the
following statements would miss records. The problem is the time is not the same and these
statements all miss records:

```
select    *
from      table
where     date_column = SYSDATE;
select    *
from      table
where     date_column = trunc(SYSDATE);
select    *
from      table
where     date_column = '10-JAN-98';
select    *
from      table
where     date_column between '01-JAN-98' and '10-JAN-98';
```

The solution is to truncate the time on both sides of the WHERE clause.

One way to prevent this problem is to negate the difference in time components on both
sides of the conditional test.

```
select    *
from      table
where     trunc(date_column) = trunc(SYSDATE);
select    *
from      table
where     trunc(date_column) = '10-JAN-98';
```

DATE Data Types

```
select     *
from       table
where      trunc(date_column) between '01-JAN-98' and '10-JAN-98';
```

One note on these examples: If you modify the NLS_DATE_FORMAT to a different value than the default, these examples might not work. I used "dd-mon-yy hh:mi:ss" as my format, and the modified queries returned no rows. When I logged out and back in to reset the NLS_DATE_FORMAT setting, the same queries then returned rows.

The tuned solution is where the time is truncated on the non-column side of the WHERE clause. This technique has the undesired affect of suppressing any indexes that might otherwise improve query performance—the TRUNC function on the column_name suppresses the index on the column. The desired technique would be to adjust the filter conditions to include all possible times within a given date. Also note in the example that follows that .000011574 of one day is one second.

```
select     *
from       table
where      date_column between trunc(SYSDATE) and
           trunc(SYSDATE + 1) - .000011574;


select     *
from       table
where      date_column between to_date('10-JAN-98') and
           to_date('11-JAN-98') - .000011574;


select     *
from       table
where      date_column between to_date('01-JAN-98') and
           to_date('11-JAN-98') - .000011574;
```

TIP
The Oracle DATE data type has both date and time included in it. Avoid suppressing indexes when trying to match dates. The key is to never modify the column side in the WHERE clause. Do all modifications on the non-column side. As we saw in Chapter 2, you can add a function-based index to overcome this issue.

Tuning and Testing PL/SQL

You can also use PL/SQL to time your PL/SQL and ensure that it is performing to your standards. Here is a simple example of how you can write a script that would allow you to test and tune your procedures (a procedure called "get_customer" in this example) directly from SQL*Plus (or PL/SQL within SQL*Plus):

```
set serveroutput     on
declare
cust_name char(100);
```

```
begin
dbms_output.put_line('Start Time:
    '||to_char(sysdate,'hh24:mi:ss'));
    get_customer(11111,cust_name);
    dbms_output.put_line('Complete Time:
    '||to_char(sysdate,'hh24:mi:ss'));
    dbms_output.put_line(cust_name);
end;
/
```

TIP
*Use PL/SQL to display the start and end times for your PL/SQL.
Basically, don't forget to use PL/SQL to tune your PL/SQL. Use things
like the package DBMS_PROFILER (mentioned earlier in this chapter)
to get timing statistics per line of PL/SQL code.*

PL/SQL Object Location Implications

At TUSC, we generally recommend storing the PL/SQL objects on the server side, for many of the
obvious reasons. The server is usually much more powerful and objects are reused much more
often (especially when pinned into the shared pool). The security methods employed are also
more straightforward. Sending the PL/SQL to be processed on the client side can be dependent
on the power of the client and can lessen the number of round trips from client to server. But,
when written correctly, the calls may be limited back to the server (see the next section for an
example). There is certainly a continuing debate on this one, but with the evolving thin client, the
server will probably be the only place to store the PL/SQL. Figure 10-1 diagrams how PL/SQL is
executed when stored on the server side. Some additional reasons for storing code on the server
are listed here:

- Performance is improved, since the code is already compiled code (p-code).

- You can pin objects in the Oracle SGA.

- It enables transaction-level security at the database level.

- You have less redundant code and fewer version control issues.

- You can query the source code online, since it is stored in the data dictionary.

- It is easier to perform impact analysis, since the code is stored in the data dictionary.

- It uses less memory, since only one copy of the code is in memory.

- If packages are used, then the entire package is loaded upon initially being referenced.

TIP
*Where to store the PL/SQL code is an ongoing debate. Generally, the
server side is the preferred place to store the code, and it may become
the only choice as thin clients become more prevalent.*

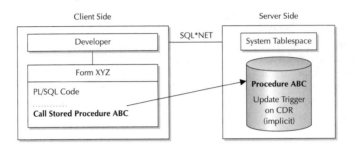

FIGURE 10-1. *Executing an object on the Server Side*

Use Rollback Segments to Open Large Cursors

This section is intended for developers and DBAs not using Oracle's automatic undo management. Any skilled PL/SQL developer should be familiar with the need to properly size and use rollback segments when attempting large INSERTS/UPDATES/DELETES to the database. If a rollback segment of the appropriate size is not explicitly set prior to the performance of a large data manipulation operation, the operation may fail. The error code usually returned is "ORA-01562: failed to extend rollback segment." The reason for the failure is that transactions that do not explicitly set the rollback segment use one that is randomly assigned by Oracle. If this randomly assigned rollback segment is insufficiently sized to hold the entire transaction, the operation will fail. Errors of this type can be eliminated by anticipating the amount of data that will be changed, choosing an appropriately sized rollback segment (the DBA_ROLLBACK_SEGS view is helpful in this regard), and setting this rollback segment just prior to the DML statement. The following example demonstrates the proper set of statements:

```
commit;
set transaction use rollback segment rbs1;
update big_table
set column_1 = column_1 * 0.234;
commit;
```

It is a little known fact that Oracle uses rollback segments when cursors are used, even if DML statements are not being issued from within the cursor loop. The rollback segments are used as a type of work area as a cursor loop is being executed. Thus, it is quite possible that a cursor loop will fail if a rollback segment of insufficient size is used to read the cursor. The failure does not occur immediately—only after numerous iterations of the cursor loop have been performed. Because the error message that is returned is the same as what would be returned when a single DML statement fails, many developers are fooled into thinking that the error lies elsewhere in their code. Valiant efforts are made to properly manage transaction sizes *within* the cursor loops, but to no avail. To successfully open a large cursor, it is imperative that a large rollback segment be set just prior to the opening of the cursor.

```
commit;
set transaction use rollback segment rbs_big;
for C1_Rec in C1 loop
```

```
-- your processing logic goes here ...
end loop;
```

If large amounts of data are being manipulated within the cursor loop, the code should be setting rollback segments within the cursor loop as well. This prevents the DML statements from utilizing the same rollback segment that is being used to ensure that the large cursor can be read.

TIP

If you are not using automatic undo management (see Chapter 3 for more information), then you may need to specify a large enough rollback segment when opening a large cursor.

Use Active Transaction Management to Process Large Quantities of Data

When coding procedures that will process large quantities of data, remember to take into account the size of the rollback segments. The rollback segments are the weak link in a program that performs mass data manipulation. A procedure that performs a single COMMIT statement at the end just won't do if it is processing millions of rows of data. It could be argued that a single transaction could be used to process mass quantities of data, provided the rollback segments were large enough. There are two flaws in this logic: 1) rarely is it feasible to devote gigabytes of valuable drive space to serve as rollback space; and 2) should a hardware or software error occur, then the entire data set would have to be reprocessed. Thus, active transaction management is always the desired technique when processing large quantities of data; it yields efficient utilization of drive space (devoted to rollback segments) and provides for automatic recovery in the event of hardware/software failures.

Active transaction management is a coding technique that consists of three components: setting transactions for cursor and DML statements, performing intermittent database COMMITs, and utilizing a table column as a processing flag to indicate which records have been processed. Consider the following database procedure:

```
declare
  counter number;
  cursor C1 is
    select     rowid,column_1,column_2,column_3
    from       big_table
    where      process_time is NULL;
begin
  Counter := 0;
  commit;
  set transaction use rollback segment rbs_big;
  for C1_Rec in C1 loop
    -- Commit every 1000 records processed.
    if (Counter = 0) or (Counter >= 1000)
      then
        commit;
        set transaction use rollback segment rbs_medium;
```

```
      Counter := 0;
   else
      Counter := Counter + 1;
   end if;
   -- Processing logic...

   update big_table
   set process_time = sysdate
   where rowid = C1_Rec.rowid;
 end loop;
 commit;
end;
/
```

The set transaction statements ensure that an appropriately sized rollback segment is used for both cursor reading and DML statements. The database COMMIT for every 1000 records processed does two things: prevents the DML statements from exceeding the capacity of the rollback segment and divides the records being processed into discrete units in the event that there is a hardware/software failure. Finally, the process_time column serves as the processing flag that allows the procedure to identify records that have not yet been processed.

TIP
Specify the correct size of rollback segment for transactional processing. Limiting the amount of data manipulated between COMMITs is key to avoiding rollback segment errors.

Use Temporary Database Tables for Increased Performance

PL/SQL tables are great for specific cases, especially when repeated iterations are involved and the amount of data is relatively small. As outlined earlier in this chapter, the memory cost (per session) can add up fast if not used properly. When a temporary storage area is needed to house large volumes of records for a short period of time, the method of creating, indexing, and querying a temporary database table should be viewed as a viable and useful option. I have seen far too many developers abandon the common method of temporary database tables after the introduction and expansion of PL/SQL tables; remember, PL/SQL tables are not the preferred method in all cases.

Oracle writes undo data for temporary tables to facilitate transaction recovery, rollback to savepoints, read consistency, and reclaiming of space. Thus, transactions in temporary tables will generate redo because we need to log the changes made to the rollback or undo segments. The redo generated should be less than the redo generated for DML on permanent tables.

Integrate a User Tracking Mechanism to Pinpoint Execution Location

Oracle-developed applications continue to become increasingly more complicated from a development standpoint, with all the products available and being used, as well as the location flexibility of PL/SQL program unit source code. When users express their displeasure over performance or inform the DBA that they are stuck, it is important to know what the users were executing at that point in time and the location in the source code of the actual processing logic.

The Oracle-supplied DBMS_APPLICATION_INFO package, described earlier in this chapter and in Chapter 12, provides a mechanism for logging the location of processing logic execution. Developers can integrate calls to this package to log the current location of the process executing. A standard practice is to call the DBMS_APPLICATION_INFO.SET_MODULE procedure to identify the product the user is currently executing (for example, this can be accomplished in a startup trigger of Oracle Forms by logging the fact that the user is in Forms, including the Form name, and upon exiting the Form by nulling these values). In procedures or functions, the DBMS_APPLICATION_INFO.SET_MODULE procedure can be called to identify the procedure name and, optionally, the time—down to the second—of when they entered the procedure. Upon exiting the procedures or functions, the same procedure can be called to NULL these values.

Limit the Use of Dynamic SQL

Oracle provides the Oracle-supplied package DBMS_SQL and the native dynamic SQL command EXECUTE IMMEDIATE, both of which provide [or allow] for the creation of dynamic SQL and PL/SQL commands. These are extremely powerful features, but also dangerous if not used appropriately. When designing and developing Oracle applications, one of the hardest decisions that must be made is where to draw the line on building in dynamic capabilities and flexibility. Developing dynamic and flexible applications is extremely helpful from a functional perspective. However, the more dynamic and flexible an application, the more potential for performance degradation.

A completely accurate and functional application is considered a failure if it does not perform at acceptable levels. Users will reject an application if they have to wait to do their job. I am not advocating the elimination of dynamic or flexible applications, but a balance must exist. Build flexibility into applications when necessary, not just to make every application module more flexible for the future, just in case business rules may change. Only build flexibility into applications when you are sure the flexibility is needed and the performance impact will be negligible.

Both the DBMS_SQL package and the EXECUTE IMMEDIATE command provide the dynamic and flexible means in PL/SQL program units. Use these features when needed, but do not abuse them, unless you want to set yourself up for failure.

TIP
If you integrate the DBMS_SQL package into a PL/SQL program unit to create SQL statements dynamically for a production application, remember optimizing the generated SQL statements will be difficult.

TIP
Use bind variables with dynamic SQL to minimize resource contention and maximize performance.

Use Pipelined Table Functions to Build Complex Result Sets

Occasionally, we encounter situations in which a DML select statement is incapable of providing the necessary information. Typically this occurs when the data doesn't reside in a database table(s) or the amount of transformations necessary to get table data into a usable form exceeds the capabilities of SQL and inline functions. Historically, the solution to such a problem would have been the creation of a preprocessor that, when called, would accumulate the data in some type of intermediate table, perhaps a global temporary table, for subsequent extraction using a simple DML select. However, pipelined table functions not only allow us to combine these two steps but also allow us to eliminate the overhead associated with maintaining the data in an intermediate table.

Pipelined table functions are functions that produce a collection of rows (such as a nested table) that can be queried like a physical database table or assigned to a PL/SQL collection variable. You can use a table function in place of the name of a database table in the FROM clause of a query or in place of a column name in the SELECT list of a query.

To demonstrate, we will start with the assumption that this simple table is the only table in our schema.

```
create table states
(
state_code varchar2(2)    not null,
state_name varchar2(100) not null,
constraint states_pk  primary key (state_code),
constraint states_uk1 unique (state_name),
constraint states_chk1 check (state_code = upper(state_code))
);
```

The problem to be solved is that we need a way to create a SQL script to reproduce all of the custom constraints in our schema subject to the following requirements:

- The script is to be created on an application server, not the database server, using a Java Server Pages (JSP) approach.

- The script needs to ensure that dependencies between constraints are taken into account.

- The script should leave disabled constraints in a disabled state when they are reproduced.

- The script should protect against revalidation of existing data when enabled check and foreign key restraints are reproduced.

Now, it *might* be possible to solve this problem with a huge SQL query using multiple table joins and several UNION clauses and a healthy dose of DECODE statements, but the end result would most likely be a monstrosity that would be difficult to maintain. So we will opt for a more elegant solution that involves pipelined table functions that, as we will see, are founded in some very basic PL/SQL functionality. By using a pipelined table function, we simplify what the JSP needs to do to get the desired information from the database . . . issue a simple DML SELECT statement. The pipelined table function will return the DDL commands to the JSP in the proper format adhering to all the rules of the requirements. From the JSP's perspective the pipelined table function looks and behaves like a table, so it can simply issue the query and iterate over the returning result set, writing the commands to a file as they are fetched.

A pipelined table function is declared by specifying the PIPELINED keyword. The PIPELINED keyword indicates that the function returns rows iteratively. The return type of the pipelined table function must be a supported collection type, such as a nested table or a varray. This collection type can be declared at the schema level or inside a package. Inside the function, you return individual elements of the collection type. Here is the package header for the solution to the problem. Note that the *get_contstraint_ddl* function returns a collection type and uses the PIPELINED keyword.

```
CREATE OR REPLACE PACKAGE ddl_extract_pkg is

  --Record and array types to support pipelined tabled functions.
  type sg_constraint_ddl_rec is record (ddl_name varchar2(100),
                                        ddl_text varchar2(1000));
  type sg_constraint_ddl_array is table of sg_constraint_ddl_rec;

  --Public routines.
  FUNCTION get_constraint_ddl return sg_constraint_ddl_array pipelined;

END ddl_extract_pkg;
/
```

In PL/SQL, the PIPE ROW statement causes a pipelined table function to return a row and continue processing. The statement enables a PL/SQL table function to return rows as soon as they are produced. The PIPE ROW statement may be used only in the body of pipelined table functions; an error is raised if it is used anywhere else. The PIPE ROW statement can be omitted for a pipelined table function that returns no rows. A pipelined table function may have a RETURN statement that does not return a value. The RETURN statement transfers the control back to the consumer and ensures that the next fetch gets a NO_DATA_FOUND exception.

Before looking at the package body, we will briefly discuss some of the key components of the solution:

- First, to avoid the tedious assembly of reconstructive DDL from various dictionary tables, the DBMS_METADATA package will be utilized. The DBMS_METADATA package is a supplied package that does the work of building DDL from the dictionary for us. It requires some initial PL/SQL-based configuration calls that would have invalidated its use in the "do it in a monstrous SQL statement" approach. By using the DBMS_METADATA package we ensure that we will capture all of the nuances of reconstructive DDL (such as storage parameters, tablespaces, and segment attributes) if desired.

- Once the base reconstructive DDL has been obtained from DBMS_METADATA it will be processed using string commands to implement the specified functionality.

- The internal processing of the pipelined function is where the dependency order of the constraints must be taken into account. The order in which records are returned by the function (via the PIPE ROW statement) defines the order in which the calling DML SELECT statement will receive them.

```
CREATE OR REPLACE PACKAGE BODY ddl_extract_pkg is

  --scrub_raw_ddl function.
  --
  --Description: This function performs basic scrubbing routines on a
```

```
--              DDL command returned by dbms_metadata.get_ddl.
--
--Syntax: scrub_raw_ddl(p_status_c, p_cons_type_c, p_ddl_c);
--
--Where: p_status_c     = The current status (Enabled/Disabled).
--       p_cons_type_c  = The constraint type (P, U, C, R).
--       p_ddl_c        = The constraint reconstruction DDL.
--
FUNCTION scrub_raw_ddl (p_status_c      IN varchar2,
                        p_cons_type_c   IN varchar2,
                        p_ddl_c         IN varchar2) return varchar2 is
  v_new_ddl_c varchar2(1000);
BEGIN
  --Capture the passed DDL.
  v_new_ddl_c := p_ddl_c;
  --Trim off any carriage returns.
  v_new_ddl_c := replace(v_new_ddl_c, chr(10), null);
  --Trim off any whitespace.
  v_new_ddl_c := trim(v_new_ddl_c);
  --For Check and Relational constraints, if the constraint is
  --currently disabled then we will leave it that way.
  --Otherwise, we will enable it but without the re-validation of existing data.
  if ( p_cons_type_c in ('C', 'R') ) then
    if ( ( p_status_c = 'ENABLED' ) ) then
      if ( instr(v_new_ddl_c, ' NOVALIDATE') = 0 ) then
        v_new_ddl_c := v_new_ddl_c||' NOVALIDATE';
      end if;
    end if;
  end if;
  --Properly terminate the command.
  v_new_ddl_c := v_new_ddl_c||';';
  --Return.
  return(v_new_ddl_c);
END scrub_raw_ddl;

--get_constraint_ddl function.
--
--Description: Pipelined table function returning proper DDL commands to
--             reconstruct the custom constraints (PK, UK, CHK, FK) for all
--             tables within the current schema.
--
FUNCTION get_constraint_ddl return sg_constraint_ddl_array pipelined is

  v_mdc_i     integer;
  v_raw_sql_c varchar2(1000);

  --The function returns a collection of records of type X.
  --So, in the code we will return single records of type X.
```

```
v_out_record sg_constraint_ddl_rec;

--Cursor to control the extraction order to prevent dependency errors.
--Check constraints, then PK, then UK, then FK.
--We do this to prevent dependencies errors.
cursor v_extract_order_cur is
  select 1          as a_cons_order,
         'C'        as a_cons_type,
         'CONSTRAINT' as a_cons_group
    from dual
   union all
  select 2, 'P', 'CONSTRAINT'
    from dual
   union all
  select 3, 'U', 'CONSTRAINT'
    from dual
   union all
  select 4, 'R', 'REF_CONSTRAINT'
    from dual
   order by 1;

--Cursor to access the custom constraints from the data dictionary.
cursor v_constraints_cur (p_type_c   IN varchar2) is
  select owner,            table_name,
         constraint_name,  constraint_type,
         status,           validated
    from user_constraints
   where table_name      = 'STATES'
     and constraint_type = p_type_c
     and generated       <> 'GENERATED NAME';

BEGIN

  --Configure the dbms_metadata package.
  v_mdc_i := dbms_metadata.session_transform;
  dbms_metadata.set_transform_param(v_mdc_i, 'PRETTY',             false);
  dbms_metadata.set_transform_param(v_mdc_i, 'SEGMENT_ATTRIBUTES', false);
  dbms_metadata.set_transform_param(v_mdc_i, 'STORAGE',            false);
  dbms_metadata.set_transform_param(v_mdc_i, 'TABLESPACE',         false);
  dbms_metadata.set_transform_param(v_mdc_i, 'CONSTRAINTS_AS_ALTER', true);
  dbms_metadata.set_transform_param(v_mdc_i, 'CONSTRAINTS',        true);
  dbms_metadata.set_transform_param(v_mdc_i, 'REF_CONSTRAINTS',    true);
  dbms_metadata.set_transform_param(v_mdc_i, 'SQLTERMINATOR',      false);

  --Open the cursor that controls the extraction order...
  for extract_order_rec in v_extract_order_cur loop
    --Open the cursor to access the constraints of the
    --current type (PK, UK, etc).
```

```
    for constraints_rec in v_constraints_cur(extract_order_rec.a_cons_type) loop
      --Initialize the next pipeline record to be returned.
      v_out_record.ddl_name := constraints_rec.constraint_name;
      v_out_record.ddl_text := null;
      --Get the raw DDL for the current constraint.
      v_raw_sql_c := dbms_metadata.get_ddl(extract_order_rec.a_cons_group,
                                           constraints_rec.constraint_name,
                                           constraints_rec.owner);
      --Scrub the raw DDL.
      --The cleaned DDL will be placed into the record
      --being returned to the pipeline.
      v_out_record.ddl_text := scrub_raw_ddl(constraints_rec.status,
                                             extract_order_rec.a_cons_type,
                                             v_raw_sql_c);
      --Return the constructed command to the pipeline.
      pipe row(v_out_record);
    end loop;
  end loop;
  return;
 END get_constraint_ddl;
END ddl_extract_pkg;
/
```

After the package is installed, executing it is as simple as issuing a DML SELECT statement . . . almost. There are a couple of minor nuances to remember when accessing a PIPELINED table function from SQL:

■ The SQL TABLE collection expression must be used to inform Oracle that the collection being returned from a pipelined table function should be treated as a table for purposes of query and DML operations.

■ The desired columns to be accessed from the collection must be explicitly enumerated. The column list wildcard (*) cannot be used.

```
select x.ddl_name,
       x.ddl_text
  from table(ddl_extract_pkg.get_constraint_ddl) x
 order by 1;

DDL_NAME      DDL_TEXT
------------  ------------------------------------------------------

STATES_CHK1   ALTER TABLE "TRS3_PROC"."STATES" ADD CONSTRAINT "S
              TATES_CHK1" CHECK (state_code = upper(state_code))
               ENABLE NOVALIDATE;

STATES_PK     ALTER TABLE "TRS3_PROC"."STATES" ADD CONSTRAINT "S
              TATES_PK" PRIMARY KEY ("STATE_CODE") ENABLE;
```

```
STATES_UK1    ALTER TABLE "TRS3_PROC"."STATES" ADD CONSTRAINT "S
              TATES_UK1" UNIQUE ("STATE_NAME") ENABLE;
```

TIP
Avoid intermediate tables by using pipelined table functions to build complex result sets.

TIP
Use DBMS_METADATA to create reconstructive DDL from the data dictionary.

Leave Those Debugging Commands Alone!

During the development of nearly any PL/SQL module it inevitably becomes littered with a plethora of debugging commands. More important than the debugging commands themselves is the strategic location chosen by the developer to maximize the benefit of the debugging. For complex algorithms, effective debugging often becomes artistic in nature, and only someone intimately familiar with the code knows the precise location of debug statements to yield maximum benefit. Unfortunately, prior to putting the code into production those strategically placed debugging statements must be either removed or disabled (commented out) because PL/SQL lacks the conditional compilation that is a given in many programming languages. Until now, that is! Oracle Database 10g Release 2 has given the PL/SQL developer the power to leave those debugging commands in place so that they can be reactivated on the fly should an issue arise.

With conditional compilation we can enter an if-then control structure that is only evaluated at compile time. The intent is to use the if-then control structure to control which textual statements (from the THEN or ELSE clauses) will be included in the program as it compiles. The conditional compilation control structure is identified by the conditional compilation trigger character ($) pre-pended to the keywords (IF, THEN, ELSE, ELSIF, END) of a standard if-then block (the exception being that the block terminator is END in lieu of END IF). The Oracle PL/SQL compiler performs a preliminary scan of the source code looking for the conditional compilation trigger character, $. If any valid trigger characters are found, then the compiler will evaluate the compilation condition to determine which code text, if any, should be included in the actual compilation of the code. Here is the basic structure of the conditional compilation block:

```
$if test_expression $then text_to_include
  [ $elsif test_expression $then text_to_include ]
  [ $else text_to_include ]
$end
```

Conditional compilation uses either a *selection directive* or an *inquiry directive* to determine which text is to be included in the compiling program. The selection directive allows a static expression to be evaluated at compile time. Here is the simplest form of a conditional compilation command that uses the selection directive:

```
$if static_boolean_expression $then text_to_include; $end
```

At compile time, if *static_boolean_expression* evaluates to TRUE, then the *text_to_include* will be included in the compiling program; otherwise, the *text_to_include* will be skipped. To demonstrate, we'll start with a package specification that will be used exclusively to store conditional compilation constants for debugging purposes.

```
CREATE OR REPLACE PACKAGE debug_pkg IS
   debug constant boolean := true;
END debug_pkg;
/
```

Next, we'll create the package specification for some fictional component of a business application.

```
CREATE OR REPLACE PACKAGE worker_pkg as
   PROCEDURE run_prc;
END worker_pkg;
/
```

We'll follow that with the package body that includes a conditional compilation command referencing the static constant in the debugging package.

```
CREATE OR REPLACE PACKAGE BODY worker_pkg as
   PROCEDURE run_prc is
   BEGIN
     dbms_output.put_line('Processing started.');
     $if debug_pkg.debug $then dbms_output.put_line('Debugging is on.'); $end
     dbms_output.put_line('Processing completed.');
   END;
END worker_pkg;
/
```

Since the static constant was set to TRUE at the time we compiled this package body, the extra DBMS_OUTPUT command will be included in the compiled program. This can be verified by executing the run_prc procedure.

```
set serverout on;
exec worker_pkg.run_prc;

Processing started.
Debugging is on.
Processing completed.
PL/SQL procedure successfully completed
```

Changing the debug_pkg package will cause all dependent objects to recompile and as that occurs the current value of the conditional compilation control constant will be used to determine if the debugging statements are compiled into the recompiled code.

```
CREATE OR REPLACE PACKAGE debug_pkg IS
   debug constant boolean := false;
END debug_pkg;
/
```

This time around since the static constant was set to FALSE, the extra DBMS_OUTPUT command will not be included in the compiled program as the worker_pkg package automatically recompiles. This can be verified by executing the *run_prc* procedure again.

```
set serverout on;
exec worker_pkg.run_prc;

Processing started.
Processing completed.
PL/SQL procedure successfully completed
```

Let's pause for a moment and perform a traditional activity of querying the data dictionary to retrieve the source of a stored package.

```
select text
  from user_source
 where name = 'WORKER_PKG'
   and type = 'PACKAGE BODY'
 order by line;

TEXT
------------------------------------------------------------------------------
PACKAGE BODY worker_pkg as
  PROCEDURE run_prc is
  BEGIN
    dbms_output.put_line('Processing started.');
    $if debug_pkg.debug $then dbms_output.put_line('Debugging is on.'); $end
    dbms_output.put_line('Processing completed.');
  END;
END worker_pkg;

8 rows selected
```

What we discover is that the _source (such as USER_SOURCE, DBA_SOURCE) dictionary tables can no longer be relied upon to reveal the precise code that is executing within the database. The _source dictionary tables are, after all, just that . . . the source code. To ascertain the exact code that has been compiled, taking into account conditional compilation, Oracle now provides the DBMS_PREPROCESSOR package.

```
set serverout on

BEGIN
  dbms_preprocessor.print_post_processed_source('PACKAGE BODY',
                                                USER,
                                                'WORKER_PKG');
END;
/

PACKAGE BODY worker_pkg as
  PROCEDURE run_prc is
```

```
BEGIN
  dbms_output.put_line('Processing started.');

  dbms_output.put_line('Processing completed.');
  END;
END worker_pkg;
```

```
PL/SQL procedure successfully completed
```

Now back to the debugging package. To have a bit more granularity over which procedures are debugged, we simply need to introduce some procedure-specific control constants.

```
CREATE OR REPLACE PACKAGE debug_pkg IS
  debug_run_prc constant boolean := true;
  debug_xxx_prc constant boolean := false;
  debug_yyy_prc constant boolean := false;
  debug_zzz_prc constant boolean := false;
END debug_pkg;
/
```

And then we update the worker package to utilize the new constants.

```
CREATE OR REPLACE PACKAGE BODY worker_pkg as
  PROCEDURE run_prc is
  BEGIN
    dbms_output.put_line('Processing started.');
    $if debug_pkg.debug_run_prc $then
      dbms_output.put_line('Debugging is on.');
    $end
    dbms_output.put_line('Processing completed.');
  END;
END worker_pkg;
/
```

Let's make sure that everything is still working as expected.

```
set serverout on;
exec worker_pkg.run_prc;

Processing started.
Debugging is on.
Processing completed.
PL/SQL procedure successfully completed
```

Keep in mind that a physical dependency exists between the package containing the static constants and the packages referencing them for conditional compilation. Thus, if you alter the debug_pkg package to change the setting for a single constant, it is still going to cause a cascading recompilation of all procedures/functions that are dependent upon that package regardless of whether or not the changed constant is referenced in the dependent package. In an application with a large population of stored code this may be undesirable behavior. In such scenarios we can disperse the static constants across more packages, or with Oracle Database 10*g* Release 2 we can switch to another method of controlling conditional compilation, *inquiry directives.*

First, we'll start by cleaning up a bit.

```
drop package debug_pkg;
```

```
Package dropped
```

The conditional compilation inquiry directive allows the test conditions to be tied to the compilation environment via the following predefined directive names:

- Any of the Oracle PL/SQL compilation initialization parameters, such as PLSQL_CCFLAGS, PLSQL_CODE_TYPE, or PLSQL_WARNINGS

- The module line number from PLSQL_LINE

- The current source unit name from PLSQL_UNIT. Note that this directive name will return NULL for anonymous blocks

- A custom name-value pair introduced via PLSQL_CCFLAGS

For this example we will construct a custom name-value pair via the PLSQL_CCFLAGS initialization parameter.

```
alter session set PLSQL_CCFLAGS = 'MyDebugMode:TRUE';
```

Next we'll modify the test procedure to switch to an inquiry directive.

```
CREATE OR REPLACE PACKAGE BODY worker_pkg as
  PROCEDURE run_prc is
  BEGIN
    dbms_output.put_line('Processing started.');
    $if $$MyDebugMode $then
      dbms_output.put_line('Debugging is on.');
    $end
    dbms_output.put_line('Processing completed.');
  END;
END worker_pkg;
/
```

And a quick test reveals that everything is working per expectations.

```
set serverout on;
exec worker_pkg.run_prc;
```

```
Processing started.
Debugging is on.
Processing completed.
```

```
PL/SQL procedure successfully completed.
```

Unlike when we were using selection directives tied to a static constant, altering the value of our custom inquiry directive does not cause automatic recompilation of the package.

```
alter session set PLSQL_CCFLAGS = 'MyDebugMode:FALSE';

Session altered.

set serverout on;
exec worker_pkg.run_prc;

Processing started.
Debugging is on.
Processing completed.
PL/SQL procedure successfully completed.
```

Until another stimulus causes the package to recompile the change in the custom inquiry directive will not be realized.

```
alter package worker_pkg compile;

Package altered.

set serverout on;
exec worker_pkg.run_prc;

Processing started.
Processing completed.
PL/SQL procedure successfully completed.
```

Optionally, to adjust the behavior of a specific package without altering the session, the PL/SQL persistent compiler parameters can be specified during a forced recompilation of the module.

```
alter package worker_pkg compile PLSQL_CCFLAGS = 'MyDebugMode:TRUE' reuse settings;

Package altered.

set serverout on;
exec worker_pkg.run_prc;

Processing started.
Debugging is on.
Processing completed.
PL/SQL procedure successfully completed.
```

The REUSE SETTINGS clause is used to bypass the normal compiler behavior of dropping and reloading (from the session) all the persistent compiler parameters. Thus, the only compiler parameter that will be updated during the forced recompile is the one that was specified as part of the ALTER command.

TIP
Suppress debugging commands with conditional compilation.

TIP
Use the static constants defined in DBMS_DB_VERSION as selection directives to control conditional compilation. The DBMS_DB_VERSION package specifies the Oracle version numbers and other information, which is useful for simple conditional compilation selections based on Oracle versions.

The "Look and Feel" Just for the Beginners

Since many developers and DBAs that may read this book are beginners at PL/SQL, I am also including examples of a piece of PL/SQL code, a procedure, a function, a package, and a trigger. I feel it is important that you have a feel for what these objects look like and how they differ, especially if you haven't seen some of them before. This section is intentionally placed as the last section of this chapter as a short reference section only and to give you a feel for how each looks. The goal is not to teach you how to write PL/SQL (please refer to Joe Trezzo's *PL/SQL Tips and Techniques* [McGraw-Hill, 1999] for that).

Both procedures and functions can take parameters and can be called from PL/SQL. However, procedures typically perform an action. The parameters used in procedures can be in(put), out(put), and/or in(put)/out(put) parameters, whereas functions typically compute a value and the parameters can only be in(put) parameters. As a matter of fact, you can't even specify the "direction" of the parameters. Functions only permit the passing of one return value. Functions are "selectable," so you can create your own user-defined functions that return information. As of Oracle Database release 7.2 (or Oracle 7 Server Release 2), developers can create user-defined functions that can be used to process through a standard SQL-type function.

Functions can also be used when creating indexes so the index key is sorted in a fashion that matches your queries.

PL/SQL Example

Here is an example of a piece of PL/SQL code.

```
declare
   acct_balance      NUMBER(11,2);
   acct              CONSTANT NUMBER(4)  := 3;
   debit_amt         CONSTANT NUMBER(5,2)  := 500.00;
begin
  select  bal into acct_balance
  from    accounts
  where   account_id = acct
  for     update of bal;
    if acct_balance >= debit_amt THEN
    update       accounts
    set   bal = bal - debit_amt
    where        account_id = acct;
    else
    insert into temp values
         (acct, acct_balance, 'Insufficient funds');
             -- insert account, current balance, and message
```

```
      end if;
   commit;
end;
/
```

Create a Procedure Example

Here is an example of how to create a procedure. I have listed it here in case you have never witnessed one before:

```
create or replace procedure
    get_cust (in_cust_no in char, out_cust_name out char,
    out_cust_addr1 out char, out_cust_addr2 out char,
    out_cust_city out char, out_cust_st out char,
    out_cust_zip out char, out_cust_poc out char) IS
begin
  select  name, addr1, addr2, city, st, zip, poc
  into     out_cust_name, out_cust_addr1, out_cust_addr2,
           out_cust_city, out_cust_st, out_cust_zip,
           out_cust_poc
  from     customer cust, address addr
  where    cust.cust_no = addr.cust_no
  and      addr.primary_flag  = 'Y'
  and      cust.cust_no = in_cust_no;
end      get_cust;
/
```

Execute the Procedure from PL/SQL Example

Here is an example of how to execute a PL/SQL procedure from within a block of PL/SQL code. As before, I have listed it here in case you have never witnessed one before:

```
get_cust (12345, name, addr1, addr2, city, st, zip, poc);
```

Create a Function Example

Here is an example of how to create a function. Once again, I have listed it here in case you have never witnessed one before:

```
create or replace function  get_cust_name (in_cust_no number)
return char
IS
  out_cust_name cust.cust_last_name%type;
begin
  select  cust_last_name
  into     out_cust_name
  from     cust
  where    customer_id = in_cust_no;
```

```
      return  out_cust_name;
end get_cust_name;
```

Execute the get_cust_name Function from SQL

Here is an example of how to execute the GET_CUST_NAME function.

```
select    get_cust_name(12345)
from      dual;
```

A Package Example

Here is an example of how to create a package.

```
Create or replace package emp_actions IS  -- package specification

   procedure hire_employee
        (empno NUMBER, ename CHAR, ...);
   procedure retired_employee (emp_id NUMBER);
end emp_actions;
/

Create or replace package body emp_actions IS  -- package body

   procedure hire_employee
        (empno NUMBER, ename CHAR, ...)
is
   begin
      insert into emp VALUES (empno, ename, ...);
   end hire_employee;
   procedure fire_employee (emp_id NUMBER) IS
   begin
      delete from emp WHERE empno = emp_id;
   end fire_employee;
end emp_actions;
/
```

Database Trigger Example Using PL/SQL

Here is an example of how to create a trigger using PL/SQL.

```
create trigger audit_sal
   after update of sal ON emp
   for each row
begin
   insert into emp_audit VALUES( ...)
end;
```

DatabaseTrigger Example
Using PL/SQL

Tips Review

- Use DBMS_APPLICATION_INFO for real-time monitoring.

- Use a custom replacement of DBMS_APPLICATION_INFO for real-time monitoring in a RAC environment.

- Log (INSERT) execution timing information into a database table for long-running PL/SQL program units to integrate a proactive performance monitoring mechanism into your system. The database table can be reviewed at any point in time to determine if performance has decreased over time.

- System load in terms of number of active sessions can have a large impact on the performance of program execution; therefore, it would be helpful to modify the database table logging method to include a column for the number of active sessions. This column can be filled by adding one additional query to the program unit being executed to retrieve the count from the V$SESSION view.

- When a PL/SQL program unit involves extensive looping or recursion, concentrate on reducing the execution time per iteration. This adds up fast, and it is easy to do the math to determine the overall improvement potential. The looping or recursion should also be reviewed for restructuring to reduce the number of iterations, while keeping the functionality. With the extreme flexibility of PL/SQL and SQL, typically a variety of ways exist to accomplish the same result. If a PL/SQL program unit is not performing optimally, sometimes you have to rewrite the logic another way.

- Use the ROWID variable to enhance performance when SELECTing a record in a PL/SQL program unit and then manipulating the same record in the same PL/SQL program unit. Also, one caveat to this technique is that it cannot be used for Index Organized Tables (IOT).

- Ensure that all conditional comparisons compare the same data types. Additionally, it helps to ensure that the data types within the numeric family are comparing the same subtype. Therefore, in the final example, the comparison in the IF statement to a 1,2,3, and so forth is comparing a NUMBER to a PLS_INTEGER. There is still some internal Oracle conversion overhead taking place. To eliminate this overhead, the 1,2,3 . . . should be changed to 1.0, 2.0, 3.0 . . . . When this change was made to our example in the chapter, the timing was reduced.

- Ensure the string of PL/SQL IF conditions appear in the order of most frequently satisfied, not a sequential order based numerically or alphanumerically.

- If a number with precision is assigned to a PLS_INTEGER variable, the value will be rounded to a whole number as if the ROUND function had been performed on the number.

- Attempt to limit the calls to SYSDATE in iterative or recursive loops because overhead is associated with this variable. Set a PL/SQL DATE variable to SYSDATE in the declaration and reference the PL/SQL variable to eliminate the overhead.

- As of Oracle 9i, the SHARED_POOL_SIZE parameter may be modified while the database is up as long as you don't exceed the SGA_MAX_SIZE. See Chapter 4 for additional information about setting initialization parameters.

- Use the DBMS_SHARED_POOL.KEEP procedure to pin PL/SQL objects.

- Query the V$DB_OBJECT_CACHE view to find objects that are not pinned and are also large enough to potentially cause problems.

- Use the DBMS_SHARED_POOL.SIZES package procedure to find specific information about an object.

- Query x$ksmsp to find all large pieces of PL/SQL that have appeared in the shared pool. These are candidates to be pinned when the database has started.

- Query DBA_OBJECTS (for system-wide objects) *or* USER_OBJECT (for your schema only) to find the state of objects and avoid errors and reloading by the user.

- Query DBA_TRIGGERS (for system-wide objects) *or* USER_TRIGGERS (for your schema only) to find the state of triggers and avoid errors with disabled triggers. Disabled triggers can have fatal results for an application; they don't *fail,* they just don't execute.

- Load reference tables into PL/SQL associative arrays for faster lookups.

- Finding the source code behind PL/SQL objects involves querying the USER_SOURCE, DBA_SOURCE, USER_TRIGGERS, and DBA_TRIGGERS views. Find dependencies by querying the USER_DEPENDENCIES and the DBA_DEPENDENCIES views.

- A DATE data type always stores a complete temporal value, down to the second. It is impossible to insert a date value only into either a PL/SQL variable or database column that is defined as a DATE.

- The Oracle DATE has both date and time included in it. Avoid suppressing indexes when trying to match dates. The key is to never modify the column side in the WHERE clause. Do all modifications on the non-column side.

- Use PL/SQL to display the start and end times for your PL/SQL.

- Generally, the server side is the preferred place to store the PL/SQL.

- Specify the correct size of rollback segment within the PL/SQL for large cursors.

- Use pipelined table functions to build complex result sets.

- If you integrate the DBMS_SQL package into a PL/SQL program unit to create SQL statements dynamically for a production application, remember that optimizing the generated SQL statements will be difficult.

- Use bind variables with dynamic SQL to minimize resource contention and maximize performance.

- Use DBMS_METADATA to create reconstructive DDL from the data dictionary.

- Suppress debugging commands with conditional compilation.

- Use the static constants defined in DBMS_DB_VERSION as selection directives to control conditional compilation.

References

Joe Trezzo, *PL/SQL Tips and Techniques* (Oracle Press, 1999)

Joe Trezzo, *Procedures, Functions, Packages, and Triggers* TUSC, 1999

SQL Language Reference Manual (Oracle Corporation)

Application Developer's Guide (Oracle Corporation)

Frank Naude's underground Oracle Web page (www.oraclefaq.com)

Bradley Brown, "OOPs-Objected Oriented PL/SQL," *Select Magazine,* April 1996

Scott Urman and Tim Smith, *Oracle PL/SQL Programming* (Oracle Press, 1996)

Kevin Loney and Bob Bryla, *Oracle Database 10g DBA Handbook* (McGraw-Hill, 2005)

Steven Feuerstein, *Oracle PL/SQL Programming, 4/e* (O'Reilly & Associates, 2005)

Steven Feuerstein, "Using SQL to Examine Stored Code," *Integrator,* February 1996

Oracle Database PL/SQL User's Guide and Reference 10g Release 2 (Oracle Corporation)

Thanks to Joe Trezzo, Bob Taylor, and Dave Ventura of TUSC for contributions to this chapter. Bob Taylor did the outstanding Oracle 10g update to the chapter. Thanks Bob!

CHAPTER
11

Tuning RAC and Using Parallel Features

Oracle's Parallel Server was first introduced in Oracle 6.1 (beta) and Oracle 6.2 (limited customer release production) but widely used only on VAX/VMS. Not until Oracle 9*i* did Oracle truly have a clustering product (Real Application Clustering—RAC) when they rewrote the code for the product almost completely (95 percent, I am told). In Oracle 10*g*, RAC has not only has matured but has become the cornerstone for grid computing (entire grids of servers using the Oracle RAC or clustering architecture).

In addition to using many servers to help increase availability and improve performance, Oracle also has improved the parallel query technology that was first introduced with Oracle release 7.1. The Parallel Query Option (PQO), which is now called the Parallel Executions Option (PEO), makes query operations and DML statements parallel, generating potentially significant performance benefits. Enhancements have been added to the PEO for each release of the RDBMS kernel. In Oracle 10*g*, most operations can be parallelized, including queries (Parallel SQL Execution), DML, DDL operations, intra-partition parallelism, parallelism for data replication and recovery, and data loading; multiple parallel query server processes can even execute against the same partition.

The tips covered in this chapter include the following:

- Real Application Clusters (RAC) overview and architecture
- Tuning the RAC interconnect
- Finding RAC wait events
- Tuning the grid (large-scale RAC implementations) using Enterprise Manager Grid Control
- Basic concepts of parallel operations
- Parallel DML and DDL statements and operations
- Parallel DML statements and operations since Oracle 9*i*
- Parallelism and partitions
- Inter- and intraoperation parallelization
- Creating table and index examples using parallel operations
- Parallel DML statements and examples
- Monitoring parallel operations via the V$ views
- Using EXPLAIN PLAN and AUTOTRACE on parallel operations
- Tuning parallel execution and the Oracle 9*i* initialization parameters
- Parallel loading
- Performance comparisons and monitoring parallel operations
- Other parallel notes

Real Application Clusters (RAC)

High performance and high availability of information systems constitute a key requirement for day-to-day operations of the business. As the dependence on stored information grew in last couple of decades, large amounts of data are being accumulated and analyzed. There is an ever-increasing demand for high-performance databases, and at the same time, awareness and requirement for keeping such databases online all the time has increased. Global operations and e-business growth depend very much on the highly available stored data. With uneven and unpredictable loads on the database systems, it became imperative for many business groups to search for high-performance systems and suitable parallel systems to support complex and large database systems. Scalability is another important feature. As the business grows, data accumulation and data interaction increase. More and more users and applications begin to use the database systems. The database systems should be able to support the increased demand for data without losing ground in performance and scope of availability. Oracle 9i introduced Real Application Clusters (RAC) to solve these issues. This section by no means covers all aspects of the RAC functioning. It merely highlights some important concepts and inner workings of RAC. This scope of this book does not cover RAC specifically.

Parallel Databases

A *parallel clustered database* is a complex application that provides access to the same database (group of data tables, indexes, and other objects) from any server in the cluster concurrently without compromising data integrity. Parallel databases typically contain multiple instances (nodes/servers) accessing same physical storage or data concurrently. In terms of storage access type, parallel systems are implemented in two ways: a shared-nothing model or a shared-disk model.

In a *shared-nothing* model, also termed as data-partitioning model, each system owns a portion of the database and each partition can only be read or modified by the owning system. Data partitioning enables each system to locally cache its portion of the database in processor memory without requiring cross-system communication to provide data access concurrency and coherency controls. Both IBM's and Microsoft's databases can operate this way and have in the past. Perhaps Oracle's adoption of the shared-disk model is what gave them a huge lead in grid computing.

In a *shared-disk* model, all the disks containing data are accessible by all nodes of the cluster. Disk sharing architecture requires suitable lock management techniques to control the update concurrency control. Each of the nodes in the cluster has direct access to all disks on which shared data is placed. Each node has a local database buffer cache. Oracle's RAC database operates this way.

With due emphasis on high availability and high performance, Oracle has provided Oracle Parallel Server (OPS) for a long time. With Oracle 9i, it drove into the next generation and rebuilt OPS as Real Application Clusters (RAC). RAC follows the shared disk model and thus has access to all the shared disks as well as an extensive mechanism to coordinate the resources across the nodes. Shared-disk technology has advanced rapidly over the past few years, giving RAC added advantages. Storage area network (SAN) technology hides much of the complexity of hardware units, controllers, disk drives, and interconnects from the servers and provides just *storage volumes.* In the same way, a group of servers together in a cluster provide a single system image and computing resource. In another recent development, there has been increased interest in the processing area network (PAN) as popularized by some of the new technology firms like Egenera (see www.egenera.com/pdf/system_data.pdf). BladeFrame computing provides hassle-free scalability in terms of adding extra nodes and management. All of these hardware advancements only strengthen an already-compelling RAC story.

Architecture of Oracle RAC

At a very high level, RAC is multiple Oracle instances (nodes) accessing a single Oracle database. The database is a single physical database stored on a shared storage system. Each of the instances resides on separate host (also called node or server). All the nodes are clustered through a private

Architecture of Oracle RAC

interconnect, and all nodes have access to the shared storage. All the nodes concurrently execute transactions against the same database. The cluster manager software, usually supplied by the cluster vendor, provides a single system image, controls node membership, and monitors the node status. Broadly, the major components include

- Nodes/servers

- High-speed private interconnect (connects the nodes together)

- Cluster Manager or OSD (Operating system–dependent layer)

- Shared disk or storage

- Cluster file system or raw devices

- Volume Manager

- Public network

Cluster Interconnect

If a block of data is on one node and the user asks for it on another node, Oracle uses cache fusion to pass one block through the interconnect (a wire connecting the nodes, or it could be some sort of switch/fabric) to the other node. Parallel processing relies on passing messages among multiple processors. Processors running parallel programs call for data and instructions, and then perform calculations. Each processor checks back periodically with the other nodes or a master node to plan its next move or to synchronize the delivery of results. These activities rely on message-passing software, such as industry-standard Message Passing Interface (MPI).

In parallel databases, there is a great deal of message passing and data blocks, or pages, transferring to the local cache of another node. Much of the functionality and performance depends on the efficiency of the transport medium or methodology. It becomes very critical for the overall performance of the cluster and usage of the parallel application. As the parallel databases do not impose any constraints on the nodes to which users can connect and access, users have a choice to connect to any node in the cluster. Irrespective of the nature of the application, OLTP, or data warehousing databases, the movement of data blocks from one node to another using the interconnect is widely practiced. The role of the cluster interconnect to provide some kind of extended cache encompassing the cache from all the nodes is one of the most significant design features of the cluster. In general, the cluster interconnect is used for the following high-level functions:

- Health, status, and synchronization of messages

- Distributed lock manager (DLM) messages

- Accessing remote file systems

- Application-specific traffic

- Cluster alias routing

High performance, by distributing the computations across an array of nodes in the cluster, requires the cluster interconnect to provide a high data transfer rate and low latency communication between nodes. Also, the interconnect needs to be capable of detecting and isolating faults, and using alternative paths. Some of the essential requirements for the interconnect are

- Low latency for short messages

- High speed and sustained data rates for large messages

- Low host-CPU utilization per message

- Flow control, error control, and heartbeat continuity monitoring

- Host interfaces that execute control programs to interact directly with host processes (OS bypass)

- Switch networks that scale well

Many of the cluster vendors have designed very competitive technology. Many of the interconnect products described next come close to the latency levels of a SMP (symmetric multiprocessing) bus. Table 11-1 summarizes the various interconnect capabilities (they will be faster yet by the time you read this).

- **The HP Memory Channel** Memory channel interconnect is a high-speed network interconnect that provides applications with a cluster-wide address space. Applications map portions of this address space into their own virtual address space as 8KB pages and then read from or write into this address space just like normal memory.

- **Myrinet** Myrinet is a cost-effective, high-performance packet communication and switching technology. It is widely used in Linux clusters. Myrinet software supports most common hosts and operating systems. The software is supplied open source.

- **Scalable Interconnect (SCI)** SCI is the Sun's best-performing cluster interconnect because of its high data rate and low latency. Applications that stress the interconnect will scale better using SCI compared to using lower-performing alternatives. Sun SCI implements Remote Shared Memory (RSM), a feature that bypasses the TCP/IP communication overhead of Solaris. This improves cluster performance.

- **Veritas** Database Edition/Advanced Cluster (DBE/AC) communications consist of LLT (low-latency transport) and GAB (Group Membership and Atomic Broadcast) services. LLT provides kernel-to-kernel communications and functions as a performance booster for the IP stack. Use of LLT rather than IP reduces latency and overhead with the IP stack. This is now known as Storage Foundation.

- **HP HyperFabric Hyper Messaging Protocol (HMP)** HP HyperFabric supports both standard TCP/UDP over IP and HP's proprietary Hyper Messaging Protocol. HyperFabric extends the scalability and reliability of TCP/UDP by providing transparent load balancing of connection traffic across multiple network interface cards. HMP coupled with OS bypass capability and the hardware support for protocol offload provides low latency and extremely low CPU utilization.

For building a high-performance Oracle Real Application Cluster, selecting the right interconnect is important. Care should be taken to select the appropriate technology suitable for your environment. Check with your vendor to get the most up-to-date hardware that is available.

Architecture of Oracle RAC

Measurement	Typical SMP Bus	Memory Channel	Myrinet	SCI	Gigabit Ethernet
Latency (µs)	0.5	3	7 to 9	9	100
CPU overhead (µs)	< 1	< 1	< 1		
Messages per sec (millions)	> 10	> 2			
Hardware Bandwidth (MB/sec)	> 500	> 100	~ 250		~ 50

TABLE 11-1. *Some Interconnect Products and Their Capabilities*

The key here is that going to disk is in the millisecond range, whereas going through the interconnect is in the microsecond or single-digit millisecond range.

Internal Workings of the Oracle RAC System

In 9*i* RAC, we no longer talk about DLM, PCM, non-PCM, Lock Monitor, etc. Most of the functionality is replaced in Oracle 10g or performed in the name of Global Cache Services. A lock is now treated as a held resource. The background processes in the previous versions still exist but serve different functions.

RAC Instances and Processes

RAC is a multi-instance database. Multiple instances access the same database concurrently. There is not much of a difference in terms of structure between a RAC instance and a stand-alone Oracle instance. Besides all the usual Oracle processes like PMON, SMON, LGWR, and DBWR, there are many special processes spawned to coordinate inter-instance communication and to facilitate resource sharing among nodes in a cluster. Because of the inter-instance buffer movement and the new set of blocks, called Past Image Blocks (to preserve data integrity), additional resources from the SGA are used.

- **LMON**   The Global Enqueue Service Monitor (LMON) monitors the entire cluster to manage global enqueues and resources. LMON manages instance and process expirations and the associated recovery for the Global Cache Service.

- **LMD**   The Global Enqueue Service Daemon (LMD) is the lock agent process that manages enqueue manager service requests for Global Cache Service enqueues to control access to global enqueues and resources. The LMD process also handles deadlock detection and remote enqueue requests.

- **LMSn**   These Global Cache Service processes (LMSn) are processes for the Global Cache Service (GCS). RAC software provides for up to ten Global Cache Service processes. The number of LMSn varies depending on the amount of messaging traffic among nodes in the cluster. The LMSn processes do these things:

■ Handle blocking interrupts from the remote instance for Global Cache Service resources.

■ Manage resource requests and cross-instance call operations for shared resources.

■ Build a list of invalid lock elements and validate lock elements during recovery.

■ Handle global lock deadlock detection and monitor lock conversion timeouts.

■ **LCK process**   Manages global enqueue requests and cross-instance broadcast.

■ **DIAG**   The Diagnosability Daemon monitors the health of the instance. It captures data for instance process failures.

Global Cache Resources (GCS) and Global Enqueue Services (GES)

The key role is played by GCS and GES (which are basically RAC processes). GCS ensures a single system image of the data even though the data is accessed by multiple instances. The GCS and GES are integrated components of Real Application Clusters that coordinate simultaneous access to the shared database and to shared resources within the database and database cache. GES and GCS together maintain a Global Resource Directory (GRD) to record information about resources and enqueues. GRD remains in memory and is stored on all the instances. Each instance manages a portion of the directory. This distributed nature is a key point for fault tolerance of the RAC.

Coordination of concurrent tasks within a shared cache server is called synchronization. Synchronization uses the private interconnect and heavy message transfers. The following types of resources require synchronization: data blocks and enqueues. GCS maintains the modes for blocks in the global role and is responsible for block transfers between the instances. LMS processes handle the GCS messages and do the bulk of the GCS processing.

An *enqueue* is a shared memory structure that serializes access to database resources. It can be local or global. Oracle uses enqueues in three modes 1) Null (N) mode, 2) Share (S) mode, and 3) Exclusive (X) mode. Blocks are the primary structures for reading and writing into and out of buffers. It is often the most requested resource.

GES maintains or handles the synchronization of the dictionary cache, library cache, transaction locks, and DDL locks. In other words, GES manages enqueues other than data blocks. To synchronize access to the data dictionary cache, latches are used in exclusive mode and in single-node cluster databases. Global enqueues are used in cluster database mode.

Cache Fusion and Resource Coordination

Since each node in Real Application Cluster has its own memory (cache) that is not shared with other nodes, RAC must coordinate the buffer caches of different nodes while minimizing additional disk I/O that could reduce performance. Cache Fusion is the technology that uses high-speed interconnects to provide cache-to-cache transfers of data blocks between instances in a cluster. Cache Fusion functionality allows direct memory writes of dirty blocks to alleviate the need to force a disk write and re-read (or ping) the committed blocks. However, this is not to say that disk writes do not occur. Disk writes are still required for cache replacement and when a checkpoint occurs. Cache Fusion addresses the issues involved in concurrency between instances: concurrent reads on multiple nodes, concurrent reads and writes on different nodes, and concurrent writes on different nodes.

Oracle only reads data blocks from disk if they are not already present in the buffer caches of any instance. Because data block writes are deferred, they often contain modifications from multiple transactions. The modified data blocks are written to disk only when a checkpoint occurs. Before we go further, we need to be familiar with a couple of concepts introduced in Oracle 9i RAC: resource modes and resource roles. Because the same data blocks can concurrently exist in multiple instances, there are two identifiers that help to coordinate these blocks:

- **Resource mode**   The modes are null, shared, and exclusive. The block can be held in different modes, depending on whether a resource holder intends to modify data or merely read them.

- **Resource role**   The roles are locally managed and globally managed.

Global Resource Directory (GRD) is *not* a database. It is a collection of internal structures and is used to find the current status of the data blocks. Whenever a block is transferred out of a local cache to another instance's cache, GRD is updated. The following information about a resource is available in GRD:

- Data Block Identifiers (DBA)

- Location of most current versions

- Modes of the data blocks (N, S, X)

- The roles of the blocks (local or global)

Past Image

To maintain the data integrity, a new concept of past image was introduced in 9i Version of RAC. A *past image (PI)* of a block is kept in memory before the block is sent and serves as an indication of whether or not it is a dirty block. In the event of failure, GCS can reconstruct the current version of the block by reading PIs. This PI is different from a CR block, which is needed to reconstruct read-consistent images. The CR version of a block represents a consistent snapshot of the data at a point in time.

As an example, Transaction-A of Instance-A has updated row-2 on block-5, and later another Transaction-B of Inst-B has updated row-6 on same block-5. Block-5 has been transferred from Inst-A to B. At this time, Past Image (PI) for block-5 is created on Inst-A.

SCN Processing

System change numbers (SCNs) uniquely identify a committed transaction and the changes it makes. An SCN is a logical time stamp that defines a committed version of a database at one point in time. Oracle assigns every committed transaction a unique SCN.

Within RAC, since you have multiple instances that perform commits, the SCN changes need to be maintained within an instance, but at the same time, they must also be synchronized across all instances with a cluster. Therefore, SCN is handled by the Global Cache Service using the Lamport SCN generation scheme, or by using a hardware clock or dedicated SCN server. SCNs are recorded in the redo log so that recovery operations can be synchronized in Oracle 9i Real Application Clusters.

Is RAC Unbreakable?

Can it be brought down? Sure it can. Any bad design or choice will bring it down. There are many components involved in providing database service, besides the database itself. RAC may be up and running, but clients cannot reach it. There are intermediate network components involved between client machines and database servers. They may fail. Natural outages that destroy all of the hardware, like fire, flood, and earthquake, will make the cluster and database inoperable.

Assuming that failures are localized or contained, however, RAC provides maximum protection and provides continuous database service. Even with the loss of many of the components, a RAC cluster can still function. But it calls for redundant design in terms of all the components involved. Design is the key word. Just setting up two or more nodes will not be enough; dual interconnects, dual paths to storage units, dual storage units, dual power supplies, dual public network interfaces, etc. will create a robust Real Application Cluster. As an example, this table shows the effects of individual component failures:

Result	Component	Effect of Failure
Okay	CPU panic/crash	Node Failed, other node still active
Okay	Memory crash	Node Failed, other node still active
Okay	Interconnect	With dual interconnects, Okay
Down	Interconnect switch	Nodes cannot communicate
Okay	OS failure / freeze	Node failed, other node still active
Down	Cluster Manager s/w	Custer freezes, all nodes go down
Okay	DB instance crash	Instance running on other node provides database service
Okay	Control file (corrupt / lost)	Multiplexed control file will be used
Okay	Redo log file	Multiplexed redo file
Down	Lost data file	Requires media recovery
Down	Human error	Depends on type of mistake
Down	Dropped object	DB is available, but applications stall
Down	DB software bug	DB may stall on all instances

As long as one of the Oracle instances is available in the cluster, client applications have data access and can execute their applications without any problems.

Summary

This section by no means covers all aspects of the RAC internal functioning. It merely highlights some important concepts and some of the inner workings of RAC (subject to change, of course). Understanding special RAC requirements and implementation of global shared cache helps in proper planning of RAC and its usage appropriately. An entire book would be needed to cover RAC fully, but the next few sections should help you with tuning RAC.

SCN Processing

RAC Performance Tuning Overview

Performance issues related to a RAC implementation should focus on the following areas *in the order listed*:

- Traditional database tuning and monitoring (most of this book)

- RAC cluster interconnect performance (this chapter and Chapter 5)

- Monitoring workload performance (most of this book, especially Chapter 5)

- Monitoring contention uniquely associated with RAC (this chapter)

- Prior to tuning RAC specific operations, each instance should be tuned separately:

    - APPLICATION tuning

    - DATABASE tuning

    - OS tuning

- Then, begin tuning RAC. Normal or traditional database monitoring is covered in other areas of this book (especially Chapter 5). Aspects of database performance related to RAC are covered in this chapter. After tuning each instance individually, then focus on the processes that communicate through the cluster interconnect.

RAC Cluster Interconnect Performance

The most complex aspect of RAC tuning involves monitoring and the subsequent tuning of processes associated with the Global Services Directory (GSD). The group of processes associated with the GSD is the Global Enqueue Service (GES) and the Global Cache Service (GCS). The GSD processes communicate through the cluster interconnects. If the cluster interconnects are not configured to process data packets efficiently, then the entire RAC implementation will perform poorly. This is true regardless of performance-related tuning and configuration efforts in other areas.

Interconnect Traffic – Sessions Waiting

Sessions that wait on non-idle wait events that impact interconnect traffic can be monitored by a query that lists GCS waits using the global dynamic performance view gv$session_wait. You may also see these waits in a STATSPACK or AWR Report. The major waits that are being monitored are as follows:

Wait	Wait Description
global cache busy	A wait event that occurs whenever a session has to wait for an ongoing operation on the resource to complete.
gc buffer busy	A wait event that is signaled when a process has to wait for a block to become available because another process is obtaining a resource for this block.
buffer busy global CR	Waits on a consistent read (block needed for reading) via the global cache.

To identify the sessions experiencing waits on the system, perform the following tasks. Query V$SESSION_WAIT to determine whether or not any sessions are experiencing RAC-related waits (at the current time). Identify the objects that are causing contention for these sessions. Try to modify the object or query to reduce contention. For example, query v$session_wait to determine whether or not any sessions are experiencing RAC cache–related waits. Note that the GV$ views are used much more to show statistics for the entire cluster, whereas the V$ views still show statistics from a single node. If you plan to use RAC, you must extend the V$ views and queries to the GV$ views for multiple nodes. This section is only an initial guide to help you see all of the components. This scope of this book does not cover RAC specifically, but some things that will help you tune RAC.

```
SELECT   inst_id, event, p1 FILE_NUMBER, p2 BLOCK_NUMBER, WAIT_TIME
FROM     gv$session_wait
WHERE    event IN ('buffer busy global cr', 'global cache busy',
         'buffer busy global cache');
```

The output from this query should look something like this:

```
INST_ID EVENT                                       FILE_NUMBER BLOCK_NUMBER WAIT_TIME
------- ----------------------------------------- ----------- ------------ ----------
      1 global cache busy                                   9          150         15
      2 global cache busy                                   9          150         10
```

Run this query to identify objects that are causing contention for these sessions and identifying the object that corresponds to the file and block for each file_number/block_number combination returned (this query is a bit slower):

```
SELECT owner, segment_name, segment_type
FROM   dba_extents
WHERE  file_id = 9
AND    150 BETWEEN block_id AND block_id+blocks-1;
```

The output will be similar to

```
OWNER       SEGMENT_NAME                    SEGMENT_TYPE
-------     ---------------------------     ----------------

SYSTEM      MOD_TEST_IND                    INDEX
```

Modify the object to reduce the chances for application contention by doing the following:

- Reduce the number of rows per block.

- Adjust the block size to a smaller block size.

- Modify INITRANS and FREELISTS.

RAC Wait Events and Interconnect Statistics

The RAC events are listed next in the report if you are running RAC (multiple instances). As stated earlier, you need to run STATSPACK or AWR Report for *each* instance that you have. For statspack, you run the statspack.snap procedure and the spreport.sql script on each node you want to monitor to compare to other instances. One of the best methods to see if a node is operating efficiently is to compare the report from that node to one from another node that accesses the same database. Grid control tuning is covered in Chapter 5. It's very important to remember that single-instance tuning should be performed before attempting to tune the processes that communicate via the cluster interconnect. In other words, tune the system in single instance before you move it to RAC.

Some of the top wait events that you may encounter are listed briefly next, and wait events are covered in more detail in Chapter 14. The top global cache (gc) waits to look out for include

- **gc current block busy** Happens when an instance requests a CURR data block (wants to do some DML) and the block to be transferred is in use.

- **gc buffer busy** A wait event that occurs whenever a session has to wait for an ongoing operation on the resource to complete because the block is in use. The process has to wait for a block to become available because another process is obtaining a resource for this block.

- **gc cr request** This happens when one instance is waiting for blocks from another instance's cache (sent via the interconnect). This wait says that the current instance can't find a consistent read (CR) version of a block in the local cache. If the block is not in the remote cache, then a db file sequential read wait will also follow this one. Tune the SQL that is causing large amounts of reads that get moved from node to node. Try to put users that are using the same blocks on the same instance so that blocks are not moved from instance to instance. Some non-Oracle application servers will move the same process from node to node looking for the fastest node (unaware that they are moving the same blocks from node to node). Pin these long processes to the same node. Potentially increase the size of the local cache if slow I/O combined with a small cache is the problem. Monitor V$CR_BLOCK_SERVER to see if there is an issue like reading UNDO segments. Correlated to the waits the values for P1,P2,P3=file, block, lenum (look in V$LOCK_ELEMENT for the row where lock_element_addr has the same value as lenum). Happens when an instance requests a CR data block and the block to be transferred hasn't arrived at the requesting instance. This is the one I see the most, and it's usually because the SQL is poorly tuned and *many* index blocks are being moved back and forth between instances.

Figure 11-1 shows the AWR Report RAC section. You can see that there are six instances (nodes) in this cluster. You can also see things like the number of blocks sent and received as well as how many of the blocks are being accessed in the local cache (93.1 percent) versus the disk or another instance. As you would guess, it is faster to access blocks in the local cache, but accessing one of the remote caches on one of the other nodes is almost always faster (given a fast enough interconnect and no saturation of the interconnect) than going to disk.

The following is another valuable query to derive session wait information. The INSTANCE_ID lists the instance where the waiting session resides. The SID is the unique identifier for the waiting session (gv$session). The p1, p2, and p3 columns list event-specific information that may be useful for debugging. LAST_SQL lists the last SQL executed by the waiting session.

```
SET NUMWIDTH 10
COLUMN STATE FORMAT a7 tru
COLUMN EVENT FORMAT a25 tru
COLUMN LAST_SQL FORMAT a40 tru
SELECT sw.inst_id INSTANCE_ID, sw.sid SID, sw.state STATE, sw.event EVENT,
```

```
          sw.seconds_in_wait SECONDS_WAITING, sw.p1, sw.p2, sw.p3,
          sa.sql_text LAST_SQL
FROM      gv$session_wait sw, gv$session s, gv$sqlarea sa
WHERE     sw.event NOT IN ('rdbms ipc message','smon timer','pmon timer',
           'SQL*Net message from client','lock manager wait for remote message',
           'ges remote message', 'gcs remote message', 'gcs for action',
           'client message', 'pipe get', 'null event', 'PX Idle Wait',
           'single-task message', 'PX Deq: Execution Msg',
           'KXFQ: kxfqdeq - normal deqeue', 'listen endpoint status',
           'slave wait','wakeup time manager')
AND       sw.seconds_in_wait > 0
AND       (sw.inst_id = s.inst_id and sw.sid = s.sid)
AND       (s.inst_id = sa.inst_id and s.sql_address = sa.address)
ORDER BY seconds_waiting DESC;
```

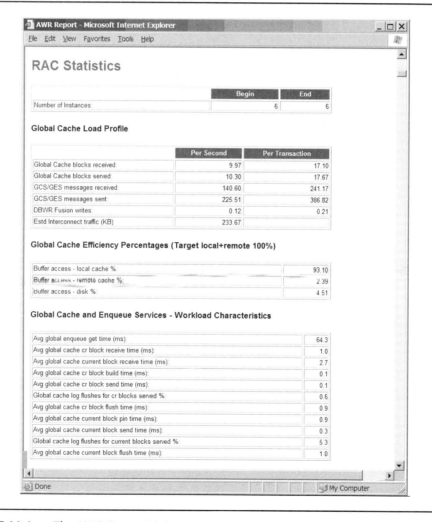

FIGURE 11-1. *The AWR Report RAC statistics*

Here is a query that gives a description of the parameter names of the events seen in the last section.

```
COLUMN EVENT  FORMAT a30 tru
COLUMN p1text FORMAT a25 tru
COLUMN p2text FORMAT a25 tru
COLUMN p3text FORMAT a25 tru
SELECT DISTINCT event EVENT, p1text, p2text, p3text
FROM   gv$session_wait sw
WHERE sw.event NOT IN ('rdbms ipc message','smon timer','pmon timer',
       'SQL*Net message from client','lock manager wait for remote message',
       'ges remote message', 'gcs remote message', 'gcs for action',
       'client message','pipe get', 'null event', 'PX Idle Wait',
       'single-task message', 'PX Deq: Execution Msg',
       'KXFQ: kxfqdeq - normal dequeue','listen endpoint status',
       'slave wait','wakeup time manager')
AND    seconds_in_wait > 0
ORDER BY event;
```

Contents of the GV$SESSION_WAIT View are as follows:

Column	Data Type	Description
INST_ID	NUMBER	Number of the instance in the RAC configuration
SID	NUMBER	Session identifier
SEQ#	NUMBER	Sequence number that uniquely identifies this wait, incremented for each wait
EVENT	VARCHAR2(64)	Resource or event for which the session is waiting
P1TEXT	VARCHAR2(64)	Description of the first additional parameter
P1	NUMBER	First additional parameter
P1RAW	RAW(4)	First additional parameter
P2TEXT	VARCHAR2(64)	Description of the second additional parameter
P2	NUMBER	Second additional parameter
P2RAW	RAW(4)	Second additional parameter
P3TEXT	VARCHAR2(64)	Description of the third additional parameter
P3	NUMBER	Third additional parameter
P3RAW	RAW(4)	Third additional parameter
WAIT_CLASS_ID	NUMBER	Identifier of the wait class
WAIT_CLASS#	NUMBER	Number of the wait class
WAIT_CLASS	VARCHAR2(64)	Name of the wait class

Column	Data Type	Description
WAIT_TIME	NUMBER	A nonzero value is the session's last wait time. A zero value means the session is currently waiting.
SECONDS_IN_WAIT	NUMBER	If WAIT_TIME = 0, then SECONDS_IN_WAIT is the seconds spent in the current wait condition. If WAIT_TIME > 0, then SECONDS_IN_WAIT is the seconds since the start of the last wait, and SECONDS_IN_WAIT – WAIT_TIME / 100 is the active seconds since the last wait ended.
STATE	VARCHAR2(19)	State

New with 10g is the WAIT_CLASS column, which represents 12 basic wait classes. One of the primary wait classes is the cluster wait class.

TIP
Use V$SESSION_WAIT or GV$SESSION_WAIT, Statspack, or the AWR Report to find RAC Wait Events.

GES Lock Blockers and Waiters

Sessions that are holding global locks that persistently block others can be problematic to a RAC implementation and are in many instances associated with application design. Sessions waiting on a lock to release hang and are required to poll the blocked object to determine the status. Large numbers of sessions holding global locks will create substantial interconnect traffic and inhibit performance.

```
-- GES LOCK BLOCKERS:
--INSTANCE_ID    The instance on which a blocking session resides
--SID            Unique identifier for the session
--GRANT_LEVEL Lists how GES lock is granted to user associated w/ blocking session
--REQUEST_LEVEL  Lists the status the session is attempting to obtain
--LOCK_STATE     Lists current status the lock has obtained
--SEC            Lists how long this session has waited

SET numwidth 10
COLUMN LOCK_STATE FORMAT a16 tru;
COLUMN EVENT FORMAT a30 tru;

SELECT dl.inst_id INSTANCE_ID, s.sid SID ,p.spid SPID,
    dl.resource_name1 RESOURCE_NAME,
    decode(substr(dl.grant_level,1,8),'KJUSERNL','Null','KJUSERCR','Row-S (SS)',
    'KJUSERCW','Row-X (SX)','KJUSERPR','Share','KJUSERPW','S/Row-X (SSX)',
    'KJUSEREX','Exclusive',request_level) AS GRANT_LEVEL,
    decode(substr(dl.request_level,1,8),'KJUSERNL','Null','KJUSERCR','Row-S (SS)',
    'KJUSERCW','Row-X (SX)','KJUSERPR','Share','KJUSERPW','S/Row-X (SSX)',
    'KJUSEREX','Exclusive',request_level) AS REQUEST_LEVEL,
    decode(substr(dl.state,1,8),'KJUSERGR','Granted','KJUSEROP','Opening',
    'KJUSERCA','Canceling','KJUSERCV','Converting') AS LOCK_STATE,
```

```
      s.sid, sw.event EVENT, sw.seconds_in_wait SEC
FROM   gv$ges_enqueue dl, gv$process p, gv$session s, gv$session_wait sw
WHERE  blocker = 1
AND    (dl.inst_id = p.inst_id and dl.pid = p.spid)
AND    (p.inst_id = s.inst_id and p.addr = s.paddr)
AND    (s.inst_id = sw.inst_id and s.sid = sw.sid)
ORDER BY sw.seconds_in_wait DESC;


GES LOCK WAITERS:
--INSTANCE_ID    The instance on which a blocking session resides
--SID            Unique identifier for the session
--GRANT_LEVEL Lists how GES lock is granted to user associated w/ blocking session
--REQUEST_LEVEL  Lists the status the session is attempting to obtain
--LOCK_STATE     Lists current status the lock has obtained
--SEC            Lists how long this session has waited


SET numwidth 10
COLUMN LOCK_STATE FORMAT a16 tru;
COLUMN EVENT FORMAT a30 tru;

SELECT dl.inst_id INSTANCE_ID, s.sid SID, p.spid SPID,
    dl.resource_name1 RESOURCE_NAME,
    decode(substr(dl.grant_level,1,8),'KJUSERNL','Null','KJUSERCR','Row-S (SS)',
    'KJUSERCW','Row-X (SX)','KJUSERPR','Share','KJUSERPW','S/Row-X (SSX)',
    'KJUSEREX','Exclusive',request_level) AS GRANT_LEVEL,
    decode(substr(dl.request_level,1,8),'KJUSERNL','Null','KJUSERCR','Row-S (SS)',
    'KJUSERCW','Row-X (SX)','KJUSERPR','Share','KJUSERPW','S/Row-X (SSX)',
    'KJUSEREX','Exclusive',request_level) AS REQUEST_LEVEL,
    decode(substr(dl.state,1,8),'KJUSERGR','Granted','KJUSEROP','Opening',
    'KJUSERCA','Canceling','KJUSERCV','Converting') AS LOCK_STATE,
    s.sid,sw.event EVENT, sw.seconds_in_wait SEC
FROM   gv$ges_enqueue dl, gv$process p,gv$session s,gv$session_wait sw
WHERE  blocked = 1
AND    (dl.inst_id = p.inst_id and dl.pid = p.spid)
AND    (p.inst_id = s.inst_id and p.addr = s.paddr)
AND    (s.inst_id = sw.inst_id and s.sid = sw.sid)
ORDER BY sw.seconds_in_wait DESC;
```

Fusion Reads and Writes

Fusion writes occur when a block previously changed by another instance needs to be written to disk in response to a checkpoint or cache aging. When this occurs, Oracle sends a message to notify the other instance that a fusion write will be performed to move the data block to disk. Fusion writes do not require an additional write to disk and are a subset of all physical writes incurred by an instance. The ratio DBWR fusion writes / physical writes shows the proportion of writes that Oracle manages with fusion writes. Here is a query to determine ratio of Cache Fusion Writes:

```
SELECT A.inst_id "Instance",
       A.VALUE/B.VALUE "Cache Fusion Writes Ratio"
FROM   GV$SYSSTAT A, GV$SYSSTAT B
WHERE  A.name='DBWR fusion writes'
AND    B.name='physical writes'
AND    B.inst_id=a.inst_id
ORDER  BY A.INST_ID;
```

Here is some sample output:

```
Instance Cache Fusion Writes Ratio
--------- ------------------------
        1             .216290958
        2             .131862042
```

A high large value for Cache Fusion Writes ratio may indicate

- Insufficiently large caches

- Insufficient checkpoints

- Large numbers of buffers written due to cache replacement or checkpointing

Cluster Interconnect Tuning – Hardware Tier

Cluster interconnect tuning is a very important piece of the clustered configuration. Oracle depends on the cluster interconnect for movement of data between the instances. It is extremely important that a dedicated private network is used for the interconnect. The following query will help determine if the instances have the correct network address registered:

```
SQL> SELECT * FROM GV$CLUSTER_INTERCONNECTS;

   INST_ID NAME   IP_ADDRESS         IS_ SOURCE
---------- ------ ------------------ --- --------------------------------
         1 eth1   10.16.0.168        NO  Oracle Cluster Repository
         2 eth1   10.16.0.170        NO  Oracle Cluster Repository
```

The column SOURCE indicates that the interconnect is registered with the OCR (Oracle Cluster Repository). The possible values for this column are as follows:

- **Oracle Cluster Repository**   The interconnect information is configured using the OCR.

- **Cluster Interconnect**   The interconnect information is configured using the parameter CLUSTER_INTERCONNECT.

- **Operating system dependent**   A third-party cluster manager is configured, and Oracle Clusterware is only a bridge between Oracle RDBMS and the third-party cluster manager.

The important test on the cluster interconnect should start with a test of the hardware configuration. Tests to determine the transfer rate versus the actual implemented packet size should be undertaken to ensure the installation has been made per specification. Starting with Oracle Database 10g Release 2, using a crossover cable when configuring interconnects between two nodes is *not* supported. Hence a switch would be required to act as a bridge between the nodes participating in the cluster. Now as you determine the performance of the system, the speed of the switch has to be determined independent of the speed of the interconnect to determine the true latency of the switch and the interconnect.

The speed of the cluster interconnect solely depends on the hardware vendor (noted in earlier Table 11-1) and the layered operating system. Oracle in the current version depends on the operating system and the hardware for sending packets of information across the cluster interconnect. For example, one type of cluster interconnect supported between SUN 4800s is UDP (the User Datagram Protocol). However, Solaris on this specific version of the interconnect protocol has an OS limitation of a 64K packet size used for data transfer. To transfer 256K worth of data across this interconnect protocol would take this configuration over four round trips. On a high-transaction system where there is a large amount of interconnect traffic, this could cause a serious performance issue.

After the initial hardware and operating system level tests to confirm the packet size across the interconnect, subsequent tests could be done from the Oracle database to ensure that there is not any significant added latency using cache-to-cache data transfer or the cache fusion technology. The query that follows provides the average latency of a consistent block request on the system. The data in these views are a cumulative figure since the last time the Oracle instance was bounced. The data from these views do not reflect the true performance of the interconnect or give a true picture of the latency in transferring data. To get a more realistic picture of the performance, it would be good to bounce all the Oracle instances and test again. To obtain good performance, it is important that the latency across the cluster interconnect be as low as possible. Latencies on the cluster interconnect could be caused by

- Large number of processes in the run queues waiting for CPU or scheduling delays
- Platform-specific OS parameter settings that affect IPC buffering or process scheduling
- Slow, busy, or faulty interconnects

Oracle recommends that the average latency of a consistent block request typically should not exceed 15 milliseconds, depending on the system configuration and volume. When you are sending many blocks across the interconnect, this is really too high (especially since going to disk is this fast usually). For a high-volume system, it should be in the single-digit millisecond-to-microsecond range. The average latency of a consistent block request is the average latency of a consistent read request round-trip from the requesting instance to the holding instance and back to the requesting instance.

```
set numwidth 20
column "AVG CR BLOCK RECEIVE TIME (ms)" format 9999999.9
select b1.inst_id, b2.value "GCS CR BLOCKS RECEIVED",
       b1.value "GCS CR BLOCK RECEIVE TIME",
       ((b1.value / b2.value) * 10) "AVG CR BLOCK RECEIVE TIME (ms)"
from   gv$sysstat b1, gv$sysstat b2
where  b1.name = 'gc cr block receive time'
and    b2.name = 'gc cr blocks received'
and    b1.inst_id = b2.inst_id;

INST_ID GCS CR BLOCKS RECEIVED GCS CR BLOCK RECEIVE TIME  AVG CR BLOCK RECIVE TIME (ms)
------- ---------------------- ------------------------- -----------------------------
      1                   2758                    112394                        443.78
      2                   1346                      1457                          10.8

2 rows selected.
```

In the preceding output, notice that the AVG CR BLOCK RECEIVE TIME is 443.78 (ms); this is significantly high when the expected average latency as recommended by Oracle should not exceed 15 (ms). A high value is possible if the CPU has limited idle time and the system typically processes long-running queries. However, it is possible to have an average latency of less than one millisecond with user-mode IPC. Latency can also be influenced by a high value for the DB_MULTI_BLOCK_READ_COUNT parameter. This is because a requesting process can issue more than one request for a block, depending on the setting of this parameter. Correspondingly, the requesting process may have to wait longer. This kind of high latency requires further investigation of the cluster interconnect configuration and that tests be performed at the operating system level. When such high latencies are experienced over the interconnect, another good test is to perform a test at the operating system level by checking the actual ping time. This will help to determine if there are any issues at the OS level. After all, the performance issue may not be from data transfers within the RAC environment.

Apart from the basic packet transfer tests that can be performed at the OS level, there are other checks and tests that can be done to ensure that the cluster interconnect has been configured correctly. There are redundant private high-speed interconnects between the nodes participating in the cluster. Implementing NIC (network interface card) bonding or pairing will help interconnect load balancing and failover when one of the interconnects fails. The user network connection does not interfere with the cluster interconnect traffic. That is, they are isolated from each other.

At the operating system level, the netstat and ifconfig commands display network-related data structures. The output that follows, from netstat-i, indicates that there are four network adapters configured and NIC pairing is implemented.

```
[oracle@oradb3 oracle]$ netstat -i
Kernel Interface table
Iface       MTU Met    RX-OK RX-ERR RX-DRP RX-OVR    TX-OK TX-ERR TX-DRP TX-OVR Flg
bond0      1500   0     3209      0      0      0     4028      0      0      0 BMmRU
bond0:1    1500   0     4390      0      0      0     6437      0      0      0 BMmRU
bond1      1500   0     7880      0      0      0    10874      0      0      0 BMmRU
eth0       1500   0     1662      0      0      0     2006      0      0      0 BMsRU
eth1       1500   0     1547      0      0      0     2022      0      0      0 BMsRU
eth2       1500   0     4390      0      0      0     6437      0      0      0 BMRU
eth3       1500   0     3490      0      0      0     4437      0      0      0 BMRU
lo        16436   0     7491      0      0      0     7491      0      0      0 LRU
```

The values in the Iface column have these meanings:

■ **bond0**   This is the public interconnect created using the bonding functionality (bonds eth0 and eth1).

■ **bond0:1**   This is the VIP (Virtual IP) assigned to bond0.

■ **bond1**   This is a private interconnect alias created using bonding functionality (bonds eth2 and eth3).

■ **eth0 and eth1**   These are the physical public interfaces, which are bonded/paired together (bond0).

■ **eth2 and eth3**   These are the physical private interfaces, which are bonded/paired together (bond1).

- **lo**   This is the loopback; that is, the output also indicates that there is a loopback option configured. Whether Oracle is using the loopback option should also be verified using the ORADEBUG command, which is discussed later in this section. The use of the loopback IP depends on the integrity of the routing table defined on each of the nodes. Modification of the routing table can result in the inoperability of the interconnect.

Also found in the preceding netstat output is the MTU (maximum transmission unit), which is set at 1500 bytes (this is a standard setting for UDP). MTU definitions do not include the data-link header. However, packet size computations include data-link headers. Maximum packet size displayed by the various tools is MTU plus the data-link header length. To get the maximum benefit from the interconnect, MTU should be configured to the highest possible value supported. For example, a setting as high as 9K using jumbo frames would help in improved interconnect bandwidth and data transmission.

Apart from the basic packet transfer tests that could be performed at the OS level, there are other checks and tests that could be done to ensure that the cluster interconnect has been configured correctly. Checks could also be done from the Oracle instance to ensure proper configuration of the interconnect protocol. If the following commands are executed as user 'SYS', a trace file is generated in the user dump destination directory that contains certain diagnostic information pertaining to the UDP /IPC configurations. (See Chapter 13 for more on the DEBUG functionality.) Please do not use this until you read the Oracle Documentation on it.

```
SQL> ORADEBUG SETMYPID
        ORADEBUG IPC
        EXIT
```

The following is the extract from the trace file pertaining to the interconnect protocol. The output confirms that the cluster interconnect is being used for instance-to-instance message transfer.

```
SSKGXPT 0x3671e28 flags SSKGXPT_READPENDING      info for network 0
socket no 9     IP 172.16.193.1         UDP 59084
sflags SSKGXPT_WRITESSKGXPT_UP
        info for network 1
        socket no 0     IP 0.0.0.0      UDP 0
        sflags SSKGXPT_DOWN
context timestamp 0x4402d
        no ports
```

The preceding output is from a Sun 4800 and indicates the IP address and that the protocol used is UDP. On certain operating systems such as Tru64 the trace output does not reveal the Cluster interconnect information. The following NDD Unix command at the operating system level will confirm the actual UDP size definition. The following output is from a SUN environment:

```
oradb1:RAC1:oracle # ndd -get /dev/udp
name to get/set ? udp_xmit_hiwat
value ?
length ?
8192
name to get/set ? udp_recv_hiwat
value ?
length ?
8192
```

This output reveals that the UDP has been configured for an 8K packet size. Applying this finding to the data gathered from the Oracle's views indicates that it would take 14050 trips for all the blocks to be transferred across the cluster interconnect (112394/8 =14050). If this were set to be 64K, then the number of round trips would be significantly reduced (112394/64 = 1756 trips).

Another parameter that affects the interconnect traffic is the DB_FILE_MULTIBLOCK_READ_COUNT. This parameter helps read certain number of blocks at a time from disk. When data needs to be transferred across the cluster interconnect, this parameter determines the size of the block that each instance would request from the other during read transfers. Sizing this parameter should be based on the interconnect latency and the packet sizes as defined by the hardware vendor and after considering the operating system limitations (for example, the SUN UDP max setting is only 64K). The following kernel parameters define the udp parameter settings:

- udp_recv_hiwat
- udp_xmit_hiwat

Setting these parameters to 65536 each increased the udp buffer size to 64K.

Another parameter, CLUSTER_INTERCONNECTS, provides Oracle information on the availability of additional cluster interconnects that could be used for cache fusion activity across the cluster interconnect. The parameter overrides the default interconnect settings at the operating system level with a preferred cluster traffic network. While this parameter does provide certain advantages on systems where high interconnect latency is noticed by helping reduce such latency, configuring this parameter could affect the interconnect high availability feature. In other words, an interconnect failure that is normally unnoticeable could instead cause an Oracle cluster failure as Oracle still attempts to access the network interface.

Resource Availability

Resources available on any machine or node or to an Oracle instance are limited, meaning they are not available in abundance and that if a process on the system needs them, they may not be immediately available. There is a physical limit on the amount of resources available on any system. For example, the processor resources are limited by the number of CPUs available on the system, and the amount of memory or cache area is limited by the amount of physical memory available on the system. Now for an Oracle process this is further limited by the actual amount of memory allocated to the SGA. Within the SGA, the shared pool, the buffer cache, etc., are again preallocated from the shared pool area. These are memory allocations used by a regular single-instance configuration.

In a RAC environment, there are no parameters to allocate any global specific resources, for example, global cache size or global shared pool area. Oracle allocates a certain portion of the available resources from the SGA for global activity. The availability of global resources can be monitored using the view GV$RESOURCE_LIMIT. For example, the following query displays the current number of resources available for global activity. In the output that follows, the availability of resources is limited by the column "LIMIT_VALUE," and when these resources are low, the method to increase the limit is to increase the SHARED_POOL_SIZE.

The following query generates the output containing the current utilization of resources:

```
SELECT RESOURCE_NAME, CURRENT_UTILIZATION CU, MAX_UTILIZATION MU,
       INITIAL_ALLOCATION IA, LIMIT_VALUE LV
FROM   GV$RESOURCE_LIMIT
WHERE  MAX_UTILIZATION > 0
```

```
ORDER BY INST_ID, RESOURCE_NAME;

RESOURCE_NAME                     CU           MU IA          LV
-------------------------  ----------  ----------  ----------  ----------
cmtcallbk                          0           1         187  UNLIMITED
dml_locks                          2          59         748  UNLIMITED
enqueue_locks                     19          27        2261        2261
enqueue_resources                 22          45         968  UNLIMITED
gcs_shadows                     2259        2579       18245       18245
ges_big_msgs                      27          28         964  UNLIMITED
ges_cache_ress                   338        1240           0  UNLIMITED
ges_procs                         35          36         320         320
ges_reg_msgs                      44          81        1050  UNLIMITED
max_rollback_segments             11          11         187       65535
max_shared_servers                 1           1   UNLIMITED  UNLIMITED
processes                         31          34         150         150
sessions                          37          40         170         170
sort_segment_locks                 0           1   UNLIMITED  UNLIMITED
transactions                       2           4         187  UNLIMITED
(truncated output)
```

When the SHARED_POOL_SIZE is increased by 10M, the global resource allocation also changes to the following new values.

```
gcs_resources              2553        2553       19351       19351
gcs_shadows                1279        1279       19351       19351
```

The rule should be, when the MAX_UTILIZATION (MU) gets close to the LIMIT_VALUE (LV) and remains constant at this value for a considerable amount of time, consider increasing the SGA.

Oracle also maintains several global areas within its memory that are specifically related to Oracle. While allocation sizes are constant for these areas, they are also included in the SHARED_POOL_SIZE parameter; for example, the following query will list memory areas maintained specially for a RAC environment:

```
SELECT *
FROM    v$sgastat
where   name like 'g%';

POOL            NAME                                BYTES
-----------     --------------------------     ----------
shared pool     ges enqueue rum usage pe           16
shared pool     ges deadlock xid hash tab        11036
shared pool     ges recovery domain table          108
shared pool     ges process hash table            9504
shared pool     gcs res hash bucket              65536
shared pool     gcs close obj                     4104
shared pool     ges lmd process descripto         2684
```

```
shared pool   gcs scan queue array            216
shared pool   ges process array            281600
shared pool   gcs resources              7379392
shared pool   grplut_kfgsg                   256
shared pool   generic process shared st      448
shared pool   ges enqueue max. usage pe       16
shared pool   ges reserved msg buffers   2897860
shared pool   gcs mastership buckets        4608
shared pool   ges scan queue array           108
shared pool   groups_kfgbsg                 4096
shared pool   gcs shadows                5241536
shared pool   gcs resource freelist dyn       32
shared pool   gcs shadow locks dyn seg        32
shared pool   ges resource hash seq tab    16384
shared pool   gcs I/O statistics struct       32
shared pool   ges deadlock xid freelist     7040
shared pool   gcs resource freelist arr      272
shared pool   ges regular msg buffers     609004
shared pool   gcs opaque in                 4028
shared pool   grptab_kfgsg                  3592
shared pool   ges enqueues               3870184
shared pool   ges res mastership bucket     3072
shared pool   ges resource hash table     442368
shared pool   ges ipc instance maps          384
shared pool   ges big msg buffers        3979396
shared pool   gcs res latch table          15360
shared pool   gcs affinity                  4108
shared pool   ges resource              3105300
shared pool   gcs shadow locks freelist      272
shared pool   ges enqueue multiple free      400
shared pool   ges lms process descripto     5368
shared pool   ges shared global area       22724
shared pool   gcs commit sga state         67596

41 rows selected.
```

Tuning RAC Using Enterprise Manager Grid Control

The Oracle Enterprise Manager Grid Control, the AWR Report, and the STATSPACK report are also a good source of information to determine the interconnect latency. The best RAC tuning tool is Oracle Enterprise Manager Grid Control. While this is covered in detail in Chapter 3, the interconnect portion is worth investigating here as well. To look at a clustered database (or RAC/Grid database), we must go to the Targets/All Targets screen and click the cluster database to view. In this example, the "ioug" cluster database is clicked to display the monitored information for this cluster database (see Figure 11-2). This screen shows that there are six instances that are all up at this time. There is some CPU being used (around 25 percent) and just under 20 active sessions.

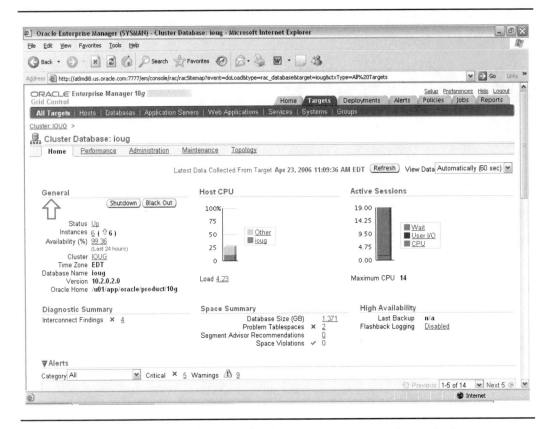

FIGURE 11-2. *Performance information for the "ioug" six-instance cluster database*

A *very* important section of this page is the Diagnostic Summary section, which in this example shows that there are four interconnect findings.

TIP
Find Interconnect issues using Enterprise Manager Grid Control.

At the bottom of the same screen, we find some of the most useful links and information for a cluster database (see Figure 11-3). This includes all of the instances associated with the

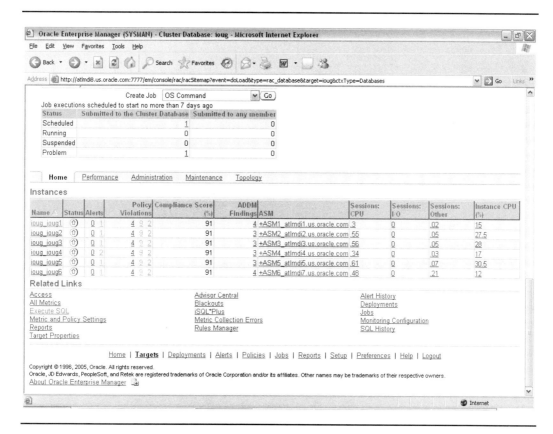

FIGURE 11-3. *Performance information for the "ioug" six-instance cluster database (bottom)*

cluster database. The six instances (ioug_ioug1 through ioug_ioug6) are also displayed here, making it very easy to see information for an individual instance by clicking through to that instance.

By clicking one of the Instances (ioug_ioug1 in this example), the main informational screen for an instance is displayed (Figure 11-4). There is also a pull-down menu in Figure 11-4 in the upper-right corner that allows you to quickly switch to another database instance.

Tuning RAC with Enterprise
Manager Grid Control

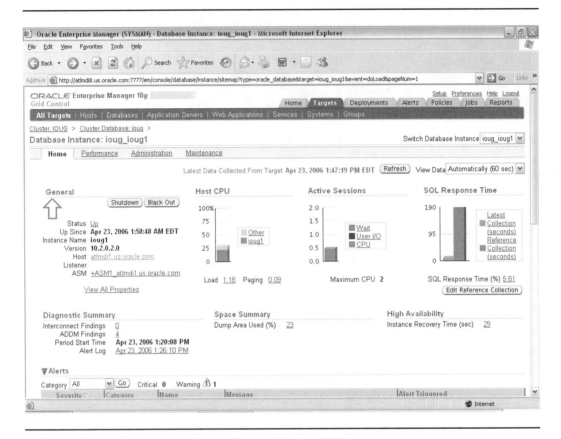

FIGURE 11-4. *Performance information for the "ioug1" instance*

Database Performance Tab

Clicking the Performance tab displays the insightful graphs for this cluster and one of the main screens that can be used for tuning the interconnect. Figure 11-5 shows the upper part of this screen. Clicking any individual graph will display a more detailed graph for the given performance metric. Moving to the middle of this screen will display additional graphs.

TIP
The Database or Cluster Performance screen within OEM is the quickest way to find where performance problems are in your system.

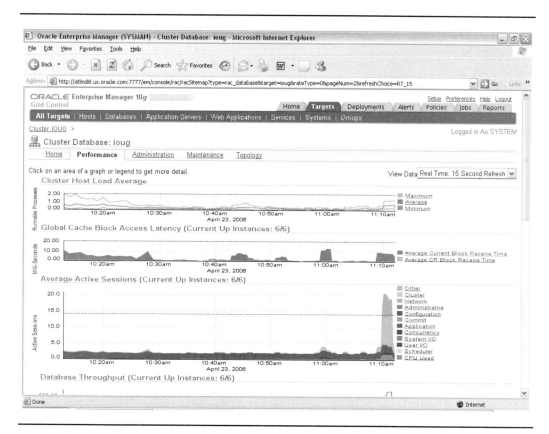

FIGURE 11-5.   *Cluster database performance*

Figure 11-6 shows many additional performance links These include Database Locks, Top Sessions, Top Consumers, Cluster Cache Coherence, and Top Segments. Each of these is used to drill into a specific problem.

By clicking the Cluster Host Load Average graph shown earlier in Figure 11-5, we display a larger version of that graph, which has a color for each of the nodes listed. In the example in Figure 11-7, four instances (on four physical nodes) in the ioug cluster are displayed in the graph. The instances are ioug3, ioug4, ioug5, and ioug6, and the physical nodes the instances reside on are atlmdi3, atlmdi4, atlmdi5, and atlmdi7.

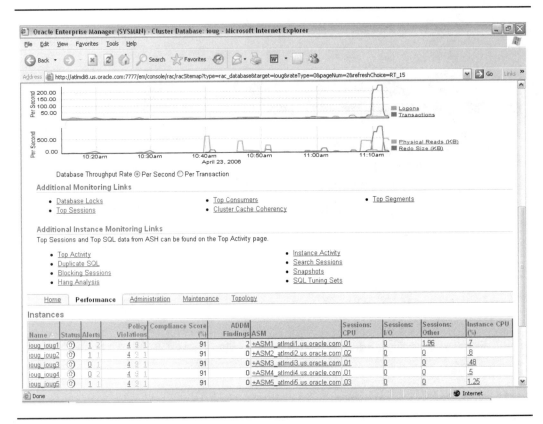

FIGURE 11-6. *Cluster database additional performance links*

Clicking the second graph of Figure 11-5 will show interconnect issues. The global cache block access latency and transfers have to do with sending blocks from one instance to another instance. Clicking the Cluster Cache Coherency link on the Cluster Database Performance screen (Figure 11-8) will also display this screen. In Figure 11-8, the number of block transfers increases greatly at about 11:10 A.M. Any block access latency over 20 ms should be cause to investigate further. Fixing this issue could involve tuning the query that is causing a lot of blocks to be either read or transferred, getting a faster interconnect, eliminating any locking that is slowing the transfer (one instance hanging on to the block) or using the public (instead of private) interconnect.

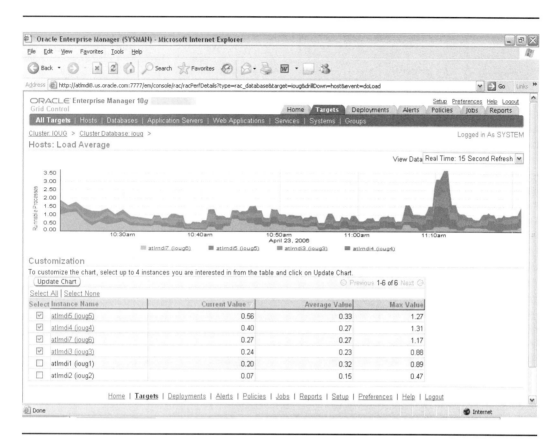

FIGURE 11-7. *Cluster database performance load average*

In the third graph of Figure 11-5, the Active Sessions graph shows a large number of Cluster waits. By clicking the "Cluster" link to the right of the graph (but at the instance level), the detailed graph of all cluster waits is displayed (Figure 11-9). We can see many Global Cache (or gc) type of waits associated with this graph at a couple of times during the hour displayed. Below the graph, we can see the actual Top SQL queries that are being run as well as the Top Sessions of the users that are running the queries. This screen shows *only* the Top SQL and Top Sessions for Cluster waits. Once again, this is a very colorful screen showing each wait in a different color to make it very intuitive to use for tuning.

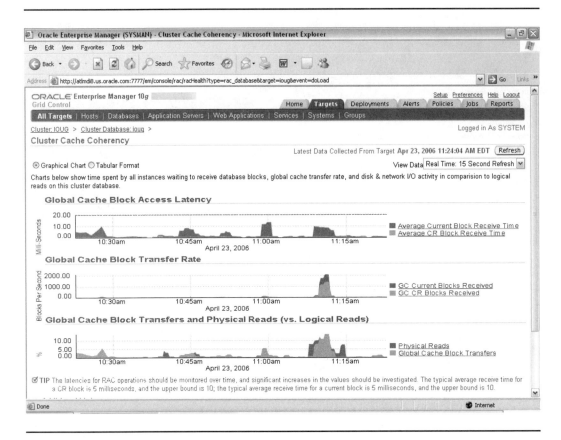

FIGURE 11-8. *Cluster cache coherency*

TIP
You can investigate specific Global Cache wait events in Enterprise Manager.

By clicking the link to the right of the graph on the "gc current block busy" wait, we are instantly transferred to the histogram for this wait to see if the waits are many short waits or fewer long waits. In this case, some of the waits are short (1–2 ms) and others are long (32 ms and higher), as the histogram in Figure 11-10 shows.

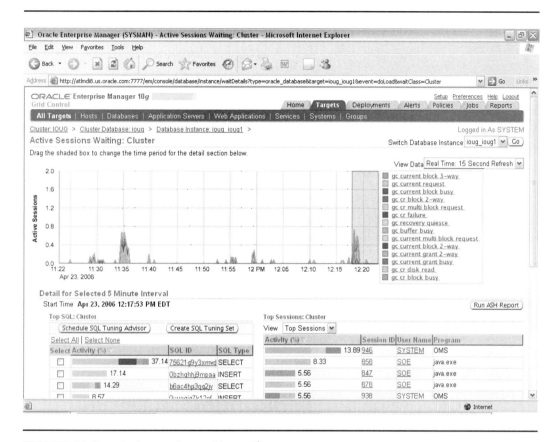

FIGURE 11-9. *Active session waiting—Cluster*

Tuning RAC with Enterprise Manager Grid Control

NOTE
Chapter 5 provides a more detailed look at how to use Enterprise Manager Grid Control as well as many more screen shots than those listed here. Chapter 5 also shows you how to find specific SQL statements causing problems and how to tune them with the Enterprise Manager Grid Control tuning features.

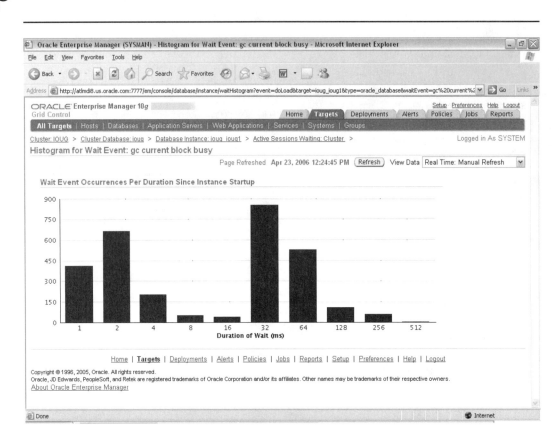

FIGURE 11-10. *Wait events histogram for "gc current block busy" waits*

Basic Concepts of Parallel Operations

Using parallel operations enables multiple processes (and potentially processors) to work together simultaneously to resolve a single SQL statement. This feature improves data-intensive operations, is dynamic (the execution path is determined at run time), and (when wisely implemented) makes use of all of your processors and disk drives. There are some overhead costs and administrative requirements, but the PEO can improve the performance of many operations.

Consider a full table scan. Rather than have a single process execute the table scan, Oracle can create multiple processes to scan the table in parallel. The number of processes used to perform the scan is called the *degree of parallelism (DOP)*. The degree can be set in a hint at table creation time or as a hint in the query. Figure 11-11 shows a full table scan of the EMP table broken into four separate parallel query server processes. (The degree of parallelism is 4.) A fifth process, the query coordinator, is created to coordinate the four parallel query server processes.

TIP
Parallel processes commonly involve disk accesses. If the data is not distributed across multiple disks, using the PEO may lead to an I/O bottleneck.

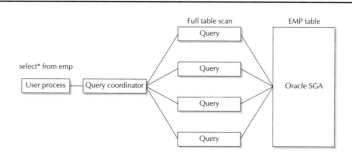

FIGURE 11-11. *A simple full table scan with parallel execution (disk access not shown)*

If the rows returned by the full table scan shown in Figure 11-11 also need to be sorted, the resulting operation will look like Figure 11-12 instead. Now Oracle may use one process to coordinate the query, four processes to run the query, and four processes to sort the query. The total is now nine processes, although the degree of parallelism is still 4. If you have nine processors (CPUs), your machine can use all nine processors for the operation (depending on the setup of your system and other operations that are being performed at the same time). If you have fewer than nine processors available, you may encounter some CPU bottleneck issues as Oracle manages the query.

Because the query coordination parts of the operation take resources, fast-running queries are not usually enhanced (and may be degraded) with the use of parallel operations.

TIP
Using parallel operations on very small tables or very fast queries can also degrade performance because the query coordination may also cost performance resources. You should evaluate whether the parallel cost exceeds the nonparallelized cost.

Both queries in Figure 11-11 and Figure 11-12 require access to the physical disks to retrieve data, which is then brought into the SGA. Balancing data on those disks based on how the query is "broken up" makes a large I/O difference.

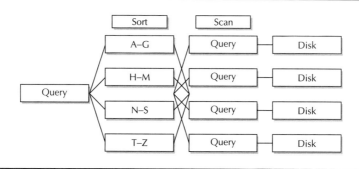

FIGURE 11-12. *A simple full table scan requiring a sort with parallel execution (SGA not shown)*

TIP
*When the parallel degree is set to N, it is possible to use (2*N) + 1
total processes for the parallel operation. Although parallel operations
deal with processes and not processors, when a large number of
processors are available, Oracle usually uses the additional processors
to run parallel queries, usually enhancing the performance of the query.*

Parallel DML and DDL Statements and Operations

Oracle supports parallelization of both DDL and DML operations. Oracle can parallelize the following operations on tables and indexes:

- SELECT
- UPDATE, INSERT, DELETE
- MERGE
- CREATE TABLE AS
- CREATE INDEX
- REBUILD INDEX
- MOVE/SPLIT/COALESCE PARTITION
- ENABLE CONSTRAINT

The following operations can also be parallelized within a statement:

- SELECT DISTINCT
- GROUP BY
- ORDER BY
- NOT IN
- UNION and UNION ALL
- CUBE and ROLLUP
- Aggregate functions such as SUM and MAX
- NESTED LOOPS joins
- SORT/MERGE joins
- Star transformations

TIP
*As of Oracle 8i, parallel DML statements are allowed. This
functionality applies to partitioned tables and indexes.*

Oracle uses the cost-based optimizer to determine whether to parallelize a statement and to determine the degree of parallelism applied.

Parallel DML Statements and Operations Since Oracle 9i

In Oracle 9i, most operations can be parallelized, including queries, DML, and DDL operations. As of Oracle 9i, intrapartition parallelism is supported; multiple parallel query server processes can execute against the same partition.

The degree of parallelism may be limited by a number of factors. Although the partitioning strategy does not play as significant a role for parallelism in Oracle 9i, you should still be aware of other limiting factors:

- ■ The number of processors available on the server

- ■ That you still have to have the partition option enabled, and UPDATE, DELETE, and MERGE are parallelized only for partitioned tables

- ■ The number of parallel query server processes allowed for the instance, set via the PARALLEL_MAX_SERVERS initialization parameter

- ■ The parallel degree limit supported for your user profile, if you use the Database Resource Manager

- ■ The number of parallel query server processes used by other users in the instance

- ■ The setting for the PARALLEL_ADAPTIVE_MULTI_USER parameter, which may limit your parallelism in order to support other users

It is important to monitor your parallel operations in multiuser environments to guarantee they are allocated the resources that you planned for them to use. The Database Resource Manager can help allocate resources.

Parallelism and Partitions

Oracle's partitioning feature can have a significant impact on parallel operations in Oracle 10g. *Partitions* are logical divisions of table data and indexes, and partitions of the same table or index can reside in multiple tablespaces. Given this architecture, the following important distinctions exist with Oracle 8i parallel operations on partitions:

- ■ Operations are performed in parallel on partitioned objects *only* when more than one partition is accessed.

- ■ In Oracle 8i, if a table is partitioned into 12 logical divisions and a query executed against the table will access only 6 of those partitions (because the dimension of the data dictates the partition in which the data is stored), a maximum of 6 parallel server processes will be allocated to satisfy the query.

NOTE
As of Oracle 9i and in 10g, these restrictions are no longer in effect.

Inter- and Intraoperation Parallelization

Due to the distribution of data, the processor allocated to each parallel server process, and the speed of devices servicing the parallel server data request, each parallel query server process may complete at a different time. As each server process completes, it passes its result set to the next lower operation in the statement hierarchy. Any single parallel server process may handle or service statement operation requests from any other parallel execution server at the next higher level in the statement hierarchy.

TIP
Any server process allocated for a statement may handle any request from a process within the same statement. Therefore, if some processes are faster than others, the ones that are faster can consume the rows produced by the child set of parallel execution processes as soon as they are available instead of waiting for the ones that are slower (but only at the next higher statement hierarchy level).

The optimizer evaluates a statement and determines how many parallel query server processes to use during its execution. This intraoperation parallelization is different from interoperation parallelization. *Intraoperation parallelization* is dividing a single task within a SQL statement, such as reading a table, among parallel execution servers. When multiple parts of a SQL statement are performed in parallel, the results from one set of parallel execution servers are passed to another set of parallel execution servers. This is known as *interoperation parallelization.*

The degree of parallelism is applied to each operation of a SQL statement that can be parallelized, including the sort operation of data required by an ORDER BY clause. As shown earlier in Figure 11-12, a query with a degree of parallelism of 4 may acquire up to nine processes.

Examples of Using Inter- and Intraoperations (PARALLEL and NO_PARALLEL Hints)

You can parallelize SQL statements via a SQL hint or by the object-level options declared for the table or index. The following listing illustrates a statement hint:

```
select     /*+ parallel (ORDER_LINE_ITEMS) */
           Invoice_Number, Invoice_Date
from       ORDER_LINE_ITEMS
order by   Invoice_Date;
```

The preceding statement does *not* specify a degree of parallelism. The default degree of parallelism dictated by the table definition or the initialization parameters will be used. When you create a table, you can specify the degree of parallelism to use for the table, as shown here:

```
create table ORDER_LINE_ITEMS
           (Invoice_Number  NUMBER(12) not null,
            Invoice_Date    DATE not null)
parallel 4;
```

When you execute queries against the ORDER_LINE_ITEMS table without specifying a degree of parallelism for the query, Oracle uses 4 as the default degree. To override the default, specify the new value within the PARALLEL hint, as shown in this next listing. Also shown in the listing is the PARALLEL_INDEX hint, whose only difference from the PARALLEL hint is that the index name is also specified.

```
select      /*+ parallel (ORDER_LINE_ITEMS, 6) */
            Invoice_Number, Invoice_Date
from        ORDER_LINE_ITEMS
order by    Invoice_Date;

select      /*+ parallel_index (ORDER_LINE_ITEMS, invoice_number_idx, 6) */
            Invoice_Number, Invoice_Date
from        ORDER_LINE_ITEMS
where       Invoice_Number = 777
order by    Invoice_Date;
```

This listing specifies a degree of parallelism of 6. As many as 13 parallel execution servers may be allocated or created to satisfy this query.

To simplify the hint syntax, use table aliases, as shown in the following listing. If you assign an alias to a table, you must use the alias, not the table name, in the hint.

```
select      /*+ parallel (oli, 4) */
            Invoice_Number, Invoice_Date
from        ORDER_LINE_ITEMS oli
order by    Invoice_Date;
```

TIP
Using the PARALLEL hint enables the use of parallel operations. If you use the PARALLEL hint but do not specify the degree of parallelism with the hint or set it at the table level, the query still executes in parallel, but the DOP is calculated from the initialization parameters CPU_COUNT and PARALLEL_THREADS_PER_CPU.

You can also "turn off" the use of parallel operations in a given query on a table that has been specified to use parallel operations. The ORDER_LINE_ITEMS table has a default degree of parallelism of 4, but the query shown here overrides that setting via the NO_PARALLEL hint.

```
select      /*+ no_parallel (oli) */
            Invoice_Number, Invoice_Date
from        ORDER_LINE_ITEMS oli
order by    Invoice_Date;
```

TIP
The use of the NO_PARALLEL hint disables parallel operations in a statement that would otherwise use parallel processing due to a parallel object definition.

To change the default degree of parallelism for a table, use the PARALLEL clause of the alter table command, shown here:

```
alter table order_line_items
parallel (degree 4);
```

To disable parallel operations for a table, use the NO_PARALLEL clause of the alter table command, shown here:

```
alter table order_line_items
no_parallel;
```

The coordinator process evaluates the following in determining whether to parallelize the statement:

- Hints contained in the SQL statement
- Session values set via the alter session force parallel command
- Tables/indexes defined as parallel as well as table/index statistics

You are advised to specify an explicit degree of parallelism either in the SQL statement itself or in the table definition. You can rely on default degrees of parallelism for many operations, but for performance management of time-sensitive operations, you should specify the degree of parallelism using a hint.

TIP
Specify the degree of parallelism using a hint instead of relying on the table definition to ensure that all operations are tuned for the given query.

Creating Table and Index Examples Using Parallel Operations

To further illustrate the application of parallel operations in SQL statements, consider the implementations of parallel operations for table and index creation shown in the following listings.

Using parallel operations for table creation

```
create table ORDER_LINE_ITEMS
tablespace tbsp1
storage (initial 75m next 75m pctincrease 0)
parallel (degree 4)
as
select    /*+ parallel (OLD_ORDER_LINE_ITEMS,4) */ *
from      OLD_ORDER_LINE_ITEMS;
```

Using parallel operations for index creation

```
create index ORDER_KEY on ORDER_LINE_ITEMS (Order_Id, Item_Id)
tablespace idx1
```

```
storage (initial 10m next 1m pctincrease 0)
parallel (degree 5) NOLOGGING;
```

The CREATE INDEX statement creates the ORDER_KEY index using parallel sort operations. The CREATE TABLE statement creates a new table ORDER_LINE_ITEMS with a degree of parallelism of 4 by selecting from an existing OLD_ORDER_LINE_ITEMS table using a parallel operation. In the preceding table creation listing, two separate operations within the CREATE TABLE command are taking advantage of parallelism: the query of the OLD_ORDER_LINE_ITEMS table is parallelized, and the insert into ORDER_LINE_ITEMS is parallelized.

NOTE
Although parallel queries increase the performance of operations that modify data, the redo log entries are written serially and could cause a bottleneck. By using the NOLOGGING option introduced in Oracle 8, you can avoid this bottleneck during the table and index creations.

Because the writes to the redo log files are serial, redo log writes may effectively eliminate the parallelism you have defined for your statements. Using NOLOGGING forces the bulk operations to avoid logging, but individual INSERT commands will still be written to the redo log files. If you use the NOLOGGING option, you must have a way to recover your data other than via the archived redo log files.

TIP
Use NOLOGGING to remove the I/O bottleneck caused by serial writes to the redo logs.

Up to this point, we have ignored the physical location of the data queried in the example SELECT statements. If a full-scanned table's data is all contained on a single disk, you may succeed only in creating a huge I/O bottleneck on the disk. An underlying principle of the performance gains that you can achieve using parallel operations is that the data is stored on different devices, all capable of being addressed independently of one another.

Not only that, but using the PEO may make your system perform *worse*. If your system has processing power to spare but has an I/O bottleneck, using PEO will generate more I/O requests faster, creating a larger queue for the I/O system to manage. If you already have an I/O bottleneck, creating more processes against that same bottleneck will not improve your performance. You need to redesign your data distribution across your available I/O devices.

TIP
Make sure your data is properly distributed, or the parallel query server processes may add to existing I/O bottleneck problems.

Returning to the create index statement shown earlier in the "Using parallel operations for index creation" listing, consider the following tips:

■   Index creation will use temporary tablespace if there is not enough memory available to perform the sort in memory (SORT_AREA_SIZE). Construct the temporary tablespace in such a way that the physical data files are striped across at least as many disks as the degree of parallelism of the CREATE INDEX statement.

- When adding/enabling a primary or unique key for a table, you cannot create the associated index in parallel. Instead, create the index in parallel first and then use ALTER TABLE to add/enable the constraint and specify the USING INDEX clause. For this to work, the index must have the same name as the constraint.

Real-World Example of Distributing Data for Effective Parallel Operations

Returning to the CREATE TABLE statement example, the following conditions/sequence of events might be pursued if this were an initial data load of a small but growing data warehouse:

1. A tablespace (TBSP1) is created comprising four data files, each 100MB in size, on separate disks.

2. The CREATE TABLE statement is then executed specifying MINEXTENTS 4, creating four extent allocations of 75MB each (and thus on four separate disks/devices) because extents cannot span datafiles.

3. The table storage definition is subsequently changed to a NEXT allocation of 25MB for subsequent, smaller data loads/population.

4. The temporary tablespace definition in this instance uses at least four data files to physically compose the tablespace.

This method illustrates that careful planning and management of table and temporary tablespace construction can provide the underlying physical data distribution necessary to extract the most performance from parallel DDL operations. But all this is not necessary if you use ASM.

TIP
Effective parallel operations depend greatly on how the data is physically located. Avoid introducing I/O bottlenecks into your database.

As of Oracle 9i, you can use the Oracle-Managed File (OMF) feature to create datafiles for your tablespaces. If you use this feature, all of the OMF datafiles created will be placed in the directory specified via the DB_CREATE_FILE_DEST initialization parameter. To avoid creating I/O conflicts, you should point that parameter to a logical volume spanning multiple disks. You can move OMF datafiles after they have been created, following the standard procedures for moving datafiles and renaming them internally via the ALTER DATABASE or ALTER TABLESPACE command.

Parallel DML Statements and Examples

The Oracle 8 RDBMS introduced the capability to perform DML operations in parallel. Parallel DML support must be enabled within a SQL session to perform a parallelized DML statement operation. The following conditions apply to parallel DML:

- You cannot enable a parallel DML session without first completing your transaction. You must first perform a commit or rollback.

- The session must be enabled via the alter session enable parallel dml command.

■   You cannot access a table modified by parallel DML until the parallel transaction has ended (via commit or rollback).

NOTE
Parallel DML mode does not affect parallel DDL or parallel queries.

The following statements prevent parallel DML:

■   SELECT for UPDATE

■   LOCK TABLE

■   EXPLAIN PLAN

NOTE
Statement failure does not disable parallel DML within your session.

Parallel DML Restrictions

Consider the following restrictions when using parallel DML:

■   UPDATE, MERGE, and DELETE operations cannot be parallelized on nonpartitioned tables.

■   After a table has been modified by a parallel DML command, no DML operation or query can access the same table again within the same transaction. You need to execute a commit or rollback command between such transactions.

■   If a table has triggers on it, parallel DML operations are not supported. Likewise, tables involved in replication cannot be the subject of parallel DML operations.

■   Deletes on tables having a foreign key with DELETE CASCADE will not be parallelized; nor will deletes on tables having deferred constraints or self-referencing foreign keys if the primary keys are involved in the DML.

■   Parallel DML is not supported on object or LOB columns but can be performed on other columns of the same table.

■   DML against clustered tables cannot be parallelized.

■   Any INSERT/UPDATE/MERGE/DELETE statement referencing a remote object will not be parallelized.

■   Prior to Oracle 9*i*, recovery from a system failure during parallel DML was performed serially, but in Oracle 9*i*, Oracle can parallelize both the rolling forward stage and the rolling back stage of transaction recovery.

TIP
Parallel DML is limited to specific types of tables, and sometimes only certain columns within them. You must manage your tables to properly enable parallel DML operations.

Parallel DML Restrictions

Parallel DML Statement Examples

The next two listings illustrate the use of parallel DML statements. In the first listing, a new transaction is created for the session and parallel DML is enabled.

```
commit;
alter session enable parallel dml;
```

In the second listing, shown next, a table named COSTS (a partitioned table from the Oracle sample schema) is updated, with a degree of parallelism of 4, and the table is then queried.

```
update      /*+ PARALLEL (costs, 4) */ COSTS
set         Unit_Price = Unit_Price * 1.15
where       Prod_Id > 40000;
27041 rows updated.

select      COUNT(*)
from        COSTS;
select COUNT(*) from COSTS
*
ERROR at line 1:
ORA-12838: cannot read/modify an object after modifying it in parallel

commit;
Commit complete.
```

The query failed because the parallel transaction had not been committed on this table. But if you do the same select, but for a different table, you will not get this error.

TIP
You must issue a commit or rollback after using parallel DML statements. Otherwise, you will receive an error doing a SELECT statement on the same table that follows a parallel DML statement on that table.

The next listing shows a parallel DDL statement. Note that in this example, two different sections are parallelized: the query, with a degree of 6, and the population of the table, with a degree of 4.

```
create table COST_SUMMARY
parallel 4
as    select /*+ PARALLEL (COSTS, 6) */
      Prod_Id, Time_Id, SUM(Unit_Cost) Cost
from   COSTS
group by Prod_Id, Time_Id;
```

Instead of using the CREATE TABLE AS SELECT syntax, you could have created the table first and then parallelized an INSERT, as shown here. The APPEND hint fills only new blocks and is used here only for the purpose of showing you the syntax for it:

```
insert    /*+ APPEND PARALLEL (COST_SUMMARY,4) */
into      COST_SUMMARY (Prod_Id, Time_Id, Cost)
select    /*+ PARALLEL (COSTS, 6) */
          Prod_Id, Time_Id, SUM(Unit_Cost) Cost
from      COSTS
group by Prod_Id, Time_Id;

27041 rows created.
```

TIP
You can use the PARALLEL hint in multiple sections of an INSERT AS SELECT. Inserting with a degree of parallelism of 4 requires MAXTRANS on a table to be set to at least 4 and also requires four rollback segments large enough to handle each transaction. (The set transaction use rollback segment command does not work with parallel.)

NOTE
Rollback segment resources should not be a problem if you are using Automatic Undo Management.

Monitoring Parallel Operations via the V$ Views

The V$ dynamic performance views are always a great place for instance monitoring and evaluating the current performance of the database; parallel operations are no exception. The key performance views for monitoring parallel execution at a system level are V$PQ_TQSTAT and V$PQ_SYSSTAT. In general, V$ views beginning with *V$PQ* views give statistics and DBA information (mostly tuning information) while the *V$PX* views give details at the process level about parallel sessions and operations (mostly the mechanics). In the following sections you will see examples of the most commonly used V$ views for monitoring parallel operations.

V$PQ_TQSTAT

Detailed statistics on all parallel server processes and the producer/consumer relationship between them are presented in the V$PQ_TQSTAT view. Additional information is presented on the number of rows and bytes addressed by each server process. V$PQ_TQSTAT is best used by the DBA tuning long-running queries that require very specific tuning and evaluation of data distribution between server processes. The following listing shows an example of the data available from V$PQ_TQSTAT. This view is good for locating uneven distribution of work between parallel execution servers.

```
select    DFO_Number, TQ_ID, Server_Type,
          Num_Rows, Bytes, Waits, Process
from      V$PQ_TQSTAT;

DFO_NUMBER TQ_ID SERVER_TYPE NUM_ROWS   BYTES WAITS TIMEOUTS PROCE
---------- ----- ----------- -------- ------- ----- -------- -----
         1     0 Consumer       14315  123660    14        0 P000
         2     0 Producer       23657  232290     7        0 P003
```

2	0 Producer	12323	90923	7	0 P002
2	0 Producer	12321	92300	7	0 P001
2	0 Consumer	190535	2234322	48	2 QC

In this example, the results for two parallel operations can be seen. The first parallel operation involved only one parallel execution server. The second parallel operation involved three parallel execution servers (P001, P002, and P003) and a coordinator process, QC. For the second parallel operation (DFO_Number = 2), you can see that process P003 did more work than any other process. More testing is required to determine if a problem exists. Also note that the last record in the output is for a query coordinator process. It has a higher-than-average number of waits because it needs to communicate with all the other query server processes.

V$PQ_SYSSTAT

V$pq_sysstat provides parallel statistics for all parallelized statement operations within the instance. V$pq_sysstat is ideal for evaluating the number of servers executing currently high-water mark levels, and the frequency of startup and shutdown of parallel servers, as shown here:

```
select      Statistic, Value
from        V$PQ_SYSSTAT;


STATISTIC                   VALUE
--------------------        -------
Servers Busy                   12
Servers Idle                    0
Servers Highwater              12
Server Sessions                39
Servers Started                13
Servers Shutdown                7
Servers Cleaned Up              0
Queries Initiated               5
DML Initiated                   3
DDL Initiated                   0
DFO Trees                       5
Sessions Active                 3
Local Msgs Sent             91261
Distr Msgs Sent                 0
Local Msgs Recv'd           91259
Distr Msgs Recv'd               0
```

TIP
To easily determine if parallel DML is being used, query the DML Initiated statistic before and after executing a parallel DML statement.

This next listing illustrates the statistics found on a freshly started instance. These statistics show parallel servers executing during the UPDATE statement in the section "Parallel DML Statements and Examples" earlier in this chapter, where there was a degree of parallelism of 4.

```
select      Statistic, Value
from        V$PQ_SYSSTAT;
```

```
STATISTIC                VALUE
--------------------     -------
Servers Busy                 4
Servers Idle                 0
Servers Highwater            4
Server Sessions              4
Servers Started              0
Servers Shutdown             0
Servers Cleaned Up           0
Queries Initiated            0
DML Initiated                1
DDL Initiated                0
DFO Trees                    1
Sessions Active              1
Local Msgs Sent              8
Distr Msgs Sent              0
Local Msgs Recv'd           12
Distr Msgs Recv'd            0
```

As you can see, four parallel execution servers were used and no new processes were started. Next, query V$PQ_SYSSTAT after an INSERT operation specifying a parallel degree of 4. The subsequent execution of the INSERT statement produces the statistics from the V$PQ_SYSSTAT view.

```
STATISTIC                VALUE
--------------------     -------
Servers Busy                 4
Servers Idle                 0
Servers Highwater            8
Server Sessions             16
Servers Started              4
Servers Shutdown             4
Servers Cleaned Up           0
Queries Initiated            0
DML Initiated                2
DDL Initiated                0
DFO Trees                    3
Sessions Active              2
Local Msgs Sent            108
Distr Msgs Sent              0
Local Msgs Recv'd          122
Distr Msgs Recv'd            0
```

Query V$PQ_SYSSTAT after a SELECT on a table defined with a hint specifying a parallel degree of 5. The following listing illustrates V$PQ_SYSSTAT output following the query. Note the values for Servers Busy and Servers Highwater.

```
select     Statistic, Value
from       V$PQ_SYSSTAT;

STATISTIC                VALUE
--------------------     -------
Servers Busy                 5
```

```
Servers Idle                    0
Servers Highwater               8
Server Sessions                20
Servers Started                 5
Servers Shutdown                4
Servers Cleaned Up              0
Queries Initiated               1
DML Initiated                   2
DDL Initiated                   0
DFO Trees                       4
Sessions Active                 2
Local Msgs Sent               117
Distr Msgs Sent                 0
Local Msgs Recv'd             136
Distr Msgs Recv'd               0
```

In this case, the hint has overridden the default degree of parallelism defined for the table, using five parallel query server processes.

TIP
If the number of servers started consistently increases, consider increasing the PARALLEL_MIN_SERVERS initialization parameter. However, if a parallel execution server is started through the PARALLEL_MIN_SERVERS parameter, it does not exit until the database shuts down, the parallel process aborts, or the process is killed. This can lead to process memory fragmentation, so increase this number only when you are sure it is needed.

TIP
A PARALLEL hint overrides the degree of parallelism defined for a table when determining the degree of parallelism for an operation.

V$PQ_SESSTAT

To provide the current session statistics, query the V$PQ_SESSTAT view. Use this view to see the number of queries executed within the current session, as well as the number of DML operations parallelized. Here's a sample output of a simple query from this view.

```
select Statistic, Last_Query, Session_Total
from   V$PQ_SESSTAT;

STATISTIC               LAST_QUERY  SESSION_TOTAL
----------------------  ----------  -------------
Queries Parallelized             0              1
DML Parallelized                 1              2
DDL Parallelized                 0              0
DFO Trees                        1              3
Server Threads                   6              0
```

```
Allocation Height          6              0
Allocation Width           0              0
Local Msgs Sent           27            171
Distr Msgs Sent            0              0
Local Msgs Recv'd         27            167
Distr Msgs Recv'd          0              0
```

The output shown in V$PQ_SESSTAT refers only to the current session, so it is most useful when performing diagnostics during testing or problem resolution processes. Note that V$PX_ SESSTAT has a similar name but a completely different set of columns. V$PX_SESSTAT joins session information from V$PX_SESSION with the V$SESSTAT table. V$PX_SESSION can also give information on the process requested degree (req_degree) as compared to the actual degree (degree) that ended up being used. A listing of V$ views related to parallel operations is given in the section "Other Parallel Notes" at the end of this chapter.

The next listing shows a simple example of querying V$PX_SESSTAT. In this example, if you tried to execute a parallel query where the specified degree of parallelism (12) is greater than PARALLEL_MAX_SERVERS (10), you might see the following:

```
Select       DISTINCT Req_Degree, Degree
from         V$PX_SESSTAT;


REQ_DEGREE           DEGREE
------------------   ------------------
          12               10
```

The V$PX_SESSTAT view is populated only while a parallel operation is executing; as soon as the parallel operation finishes, the contents of this view are cleared.

Using **EXPLAIN PLAN** and **AUTOTRACE** on Parallel Operations

You can use the Explain plan command to see tuned parallel statements. When you create a PLAN_TABLE for your database (via the utlxplan.sql script in the /rdbms/admin subdirectory under the Oracle software home directory), Oracle includes columns that allow you to see how parallelism affects the query's execution path. The information about the parallelization of the query is found in the Object_Node, Other_Tag, and Other columns in PLAN_TABLE.

TIP
New columns may be added to the PLAN_TABLE with each new release of Oracle. You should drop and recreate your PLAN_TABLE following each upgrade of the Oracle kernel. If you upgrade an existing database to a new version of Oracle, you should drop your old PLAN_TABLE and re-execute the utlxplan.sql script to see all of the new PLAN_TABLE columns. You can also view the plan using Oracle Enterprise Manager in the SQL Details page.

The Object_Node column is the name of the database link used to reference the object. The Other column provides information about the query server processes involved. The Other_Tag column describes the function of the Other column's entries. The Other column contains a derived SQL statement—either for a remote query or for parallel query operations.

Table 11-2 shows the possible values for Other_Tag and their associated Other values.

When an operation is parallelized, it may be partitioned to multiple query server processes based on ranges of ROWID values; the ranges are based on contiguous blocks of data in the table. You can use the Other_Tag column to verify the parallelism within different operations of the query, and you can see the parallelized query in the Other column. For example, the query in this next listing forces a MERGE JOIN to occur between the COMPANY and SALES tables; because a MERGE JOIN involves full tablescans and sorts, multiple operations can be parallelized. You can use the Other_Tag column to show the relationships between the parallel operations.

```
select /*+ FULL(company) FULL(sales) USE_MERGE(company sales)*/
       COMPANY.Name, Sales.Sales_Total
  from COMPANY, SALES
 where COMPANY.Company_ID = SALES.Company_ID
   and SALES.Period_ID = 3;
```

Next, you can see the EXPLAIN PLAN for the MERGE JOIN query.

```
MERGE JOIN
  SORT JOIN
    TABLE ACCESS FULL COMPANY
  SORT JOIN
    TABLE ACCESS FULL SALES
```

Value	Description
PARALLEL_COMBINED_WITH_CHILD	The parent of this operation performs the parent and child operations together; Other is NULL.
PARALLEL_COMBINED_WITH_PARENT	The child of this operation performs the parent and child operations together; Other is NULL.
PARALLEL_TO_PARALLEL	The SQL in the Other column is executed in parallel, and results are returned to a second set of query server processes.
PARALLEL_TO_SERIAL	The SQL in the Other column is executed in parallel, and the results are returned to a serial process (usually the query coordinator).
PARALLEL_FROM_SERIAL	The SQL operation consumes data from a serial operation and outputs it in parallel; Other is NULL.
SERIAL	The SQL statement is executed serially (the default); the Other column is NULL.
SERIAL_FROM_REMOTE	The SQL in the Other column is executed at a remote site.

TABLE 11-2.   *Possible Values for PLAN_TABLE.OTHER_TAG for Parallel Operations*

As shown in the plan, Oracle performs a full table scan (TABLE ACCESS FULL) on each table, sorts the results (using the SORT JOIN operations), and merges the result sets. The query of PLAN_TABLE in the next listing shows the Other_Tag for each operation. The query shown in the listing following the Other_Tag for each operation generates the EXPLAIN PLAN listings.

```
select
  LPAD(' ',2*Level)||Operation||' '||Options
                ||' '||Object_Name   Q_Plan, Other_Tag
from PLAN_TABLE
where Statement_ID = 'TEST'
connect by prior ID = Parent_ID and Statement_ID = 'TEST'
start with ID=1;
```

The result of the query for the MERGE JOIN example is shown here.

```
Q_PLAN                          OTHER_TAG
------------------------------  ------------------------------
MERGE JOIN                      PARALLEL_TO_SERIAL
  SORT JOIN                     PARALLEL_COMBINED_WITH_PARENT
    TABLE ACCESS FULL COMPANY   PARALLEL_TO_PARALLEL
  SORT JOIN                     PARALLEL_COMBINED_WITH_PARENT
    TABLE ACCESS FULL SALES     PARALLEL_TO_PARALLEL
```

You can see (by their Other_Tag values of PARALLEL_TO_PARALLEL) that each of the TABLE ACCESS FULL operations is parallelized and provides data to a parallel sorting operation. Each of the TABLE ACCESS FULL operations' records in PLAN_TABLE will have the parallel query text in their Other column values. The Other column values for the TABLE ACCESS FULL operations will show that the table will be scanned according to ranges of ROWID values. The SORT JOIN operations, which are PARALLEL_COMBINED_WITH_PARENT (their "parent" operation is the MERGE JOIN) will have NULL values for their Other column values. The MERGE JOIN operation, which is PARALLEL_TO_SERIAL (the merge is performed in parallel; output is provided to the serial query coordinator process), will have an Other column value that shows how the merge occurs.

The Object_Node column values display information about the query server processes involved in performing an operation. The following listing shows the Object_Node and Other columns for the TABLE ACCESS FULL of COMPANY operation performed for the MERGE JOIN query.

```
set long 1000
select Object_Node, Other
  from PLAN_TABLE
 where Operation||' '||Options = 'TABLE ACCESS FULL'
   and Object_Name = 'COMPANY';

OBJECT_NODE OTHER
----------- -------------------------------------------------
:Q15000     SELECT /*+ ROWID(A1) */ A1."COMPANY_ID" C0,
                   A1."NAME" C1
               FROM "COMPANY" A1
               WHERE ROWID BETWEEN :1 AND :2
```

As shown in this listing, the Object_Node column references a parallel query server process. (Q15000 is an internal identifier Oracle assigned to the process for this example.) The Other column shows that the COMPANY table is queried for ranges of ROWID values. Each of the query server processes performing the full tablescan performs the query for a different range of ROWIDs. The SORT JOIN and MERGE JOIN operations sort and merge (in parallel) the results of the tablescans.

TIP
When using the explain plan command for a parallelized query, you cannot rely on querying just the operations-related columns to see the parallelized operations within the explain plan. At a minimum, you should query the Other_Tag column to see which operations are performed in parallel. If an operation is not performed in parallel and you think it should be, you may need to add hints to the query, set a degree of parallelism for the tables, or check the size of the query server pool to make sure query server processes are available for use by the query. Also, there are Consumer Group limitations and settings for PARALLEL_ADAPTIVE_MULTI_USER and PARALLEL_MIN_ PERCENT. These could also prevent parallelism from occurring.

Oracle provides a second script, utlxplp.sql, also located in the /rdbms/admin subdirectory under the Oracle software home directory. The utlxplp.sql script queries the PLAN_TABLE, with emphasis on the parallel query data within the table. You must create the PLAN_TABLE (via the utlxplan.sql script) and populate it (via the explain plan command) prior to running the utlxplp.sql script.

TIP
When using explain plan for parallel operations, use the utlxplp.sql script to view the PLAN_TABLE.

Using the set autotrace on Command
You can have the explain plan automatically generated for every transaction you execute within SQL*Plus. The set autotrace on command will cause each query, after being executed, to display both its execution path and high-level trace information about the processing involved in resolving the query.

To use the set autotrace on command, you must have first created the PLAN_TABLE table within your account. When using the set autotrace on command, you do not set a Statement_ID and you do not have to manage the records within the PLAN_TABLE. To disable the autotrace feature, use the set autotrace off command.

If you use the set autotrace on command, you will not see the explain plan for your queries until *after* they complete, unless you specify TRACEONLY. The explain plan command shows the execution paths without running the queries first. Therefore, if the performance of a query is unknown, use the explain plan command before running it. If you are fairly certain that the performance of a query is acceptable, use set autotrace on to verify its execution path.

The next listing shows the effect of the set autotrace on command. When a MERGE JOIN query is executed, the data is returned from the query, followed by the explain plan. The explain plan is in two parts; the first part shows the operations involved, and the second part shows the parallel-related actions. Here, you can see the first part of the autotrace output.

```
set autotrace on

rem
rem for this example, disable hash joins
rem to force merge joins to occur.
rem
alter session set hash_join_enabled=FALSE;
rem
select
 /*+ FULL(company) FULL(sales) USE_MERGE(company sales)*/
     COMPANY.Name, Sales.Sales_Total
 from COMPANY, SALES
where COMPANY.Company_ID = SALES.Company_ID
  and SALES.Period_ID = 3;

<records returned here>

Execution Plan
----------------------------------------------------------
   0      SELECT STATEMENT Optimizer=CHOOSE (Cost=10 Card=1 Bytes=59)
   1    0   MERGE JOIN* (Cost=10 Card=1 Bytes=59)                    :Q17002
   2    1     SORT* (JOIN)                                           :Q17002
   3    2       TABLE ACCESS* (FULL) OF 'COMPANY' (Cost=1 Card=1 Bytes :Q17000
        =20)
   4    1     SORT* (JOIN)                                           :Q17002
   5    4       TABLE ACCESS* (FULL) OF 'SALES' (Cost=1 Card=1 Bytes=3 :Q17001
        9)
```

The AUTOTRACE output shows the ID column of each row, along with the operations and the objects on which they act. The information at the far right (:*Q17002* and so on) identifies the parallel query servers used during the query.

The second portion of the AUTOTRACE output for the MERGE JOIN example uses the step ID values to describe the parallelism of the execution path's operations, as shown here.

```
1 PARALLEL_TO_SERIAL          SELECT /*+ ORDERED NO_EXPAND USE_MERGE(A2) *
                              / A1.C1,A2.C1,A2.C2 FROM :Q17000 A1,:Q17001
                              A2 WHERE A1.C0=A2.C0

2 PARALLEL_COMBINED_WITH_PARENT
3 PARALLEL_TO_PARALLEL        SELECT /*+ ROWID(A1) */ A1."COMPANY_ID" C0,A
                              1."NAME" C1 FROM "COMPANY" A1 WHERE ROWID BE
                              TWEEN :1 AND :2

4 PARALLEL_COMBINED_WITH_PARENT
5 PARALLEL_TO_PARALLEL        SELECT /*+ ROWID(A1) */ A1."COMPANY_ID" C0,A
                              1."SALES_TOTAL" C1,A1."PERIOD_ID" C2 FROM "S
                              ALES" A1 WHERE ROWID BETWEEN :1 AND :2 AND A
                              1."PERIOD_ID"=3
```

The first column in this listing is the step's ID value, which allows you to find the operation it refers to (from the first portion of the AUTOTRACE output). The second value is the Other_Tag value for the step. The third column is the Other value for the step, showing the parallelized SQL. Also note that just setting autotrace on will also list statistics at the end.

Tuning Parallel Execution and the Oracle Initialization Parameters

Parameters related to physical memory are generally set much higher in a database that uses parallel operations than in a nonparallel environment. The settings shown in Table 11-3 are general parameter settings, but your settings must be based on your unique business environment. Also note that OPTIMIZER_PERCENT_PARALLEL is obsolete as of Oracle 9i.

TIP
Be sure your environment is properly configured to support the increase in processes and transactions generated by parallel operations.

Initialization Parameter	Meaning	Suggested Values
COMPATIBLE	Setting this parameter to the release level of the instance allows you to take advantage of all of the functionality built into the RDBMS engine. Oracle recommends backing up the database *before* changing this parameter!	Generally set to the default value for the database version. Standby databases must use a consistent setting for both the primary and standby.
*DB_BLOCK_SIZE	Sets the database block size for the database.	In general, use the largest supported size for data warehousing and smaller sizes for OLTP. As of Oracle 9i, you can create caches and tablespaces with differing database block sizes.
*DB_CACHE_SIZE (This was DB_BLOCK_BUFFERS times DB_BLOCK_SIZE in previous versions of Oracle.)	To support a larger number of processes performing parallel queries and DML operations, increase the memory available.	Increase to support parallel operations.
*DB_FILE_MULTIBLOCK_READ_COUNT	Determines how many blocks are read at once during a full table scan. Improves the performance of parallel operations using table scans.	OS-dependent.
*DISK_ASYNCH_IO	Supports asynchronous writes to the operating system, reducing a potential I/O bottleneck.	Whether DISK_ASYNCH_IO should be set to TRUE depends on whether the OS supports asynchronous I/O, and how stable it is on that platform.
*DML_LOCKS	Sets the maximum number of DML locks acquired for the database. The default value assumes an average of four tables referenced per transaction.	Default value is 4*TRANSACTIONS. Increase to support parallel DML.

TABLE 11-3. *Oracle 10g Parallel Initialization Parameters*

Initialization Parameter	Meaning	Suggested Values
*ENQUEUE_RESOURCES	Specifies the number of distinct database structures that can be locked concurrently within the database. If parallel DML is used, increase beyond the default value.	Default value is derived from SESSIONS. An enqueue resource is a memory structure that stores the lock ID, information about locks held against the object, and locks requested. So, the setting of ENQUEUE_RESOURCES minus the number of enqueues taken up by the background processes is the total number of other locks you can have active concurrently on your system.
*HASH_AREA_SIZE	Specifies the maximum amount of memory, in bytes, to use for hash joins.	Increase if hash joins are frequently used by parallel queries. Increase this parameter only if you do not have a larger than average SORT_AREA_SIZE or PGA_AGGREGATE_TARGET, because the default value is derived from SORT_AREA_SIZE.
LARGE_POOL	The large pool allocation heap is used by parallel execution for message buffers. In 10g, Parallel execution allocates buffers out of the large pool only when SGA_TARGET is set.	Default value should be okay, but if you increase the value of PARALLEL_EXECUTION_MESSAGE _SIZE, you should set this parameter to a higher value.
*LOG_BUFFER	Increase to support the transaction volume generated by parallel DML.	Default value is 524288, set to 512KB minimum. Increase if parallel DML is used extensively.
PARALLEL_ADAPTIVE_MULTI_USER	Reduces the degree of parallelism based on number of active parallel users.	Set this to FALSE and control parallel resources with the Database Resource Manager instead if needed.
PARALLEL_EXECUTION_MESSAGE_SIZE	Specifies the size of messages for all parallel operations. Larger values than the default will require a larger shared pool size.	Operating system-dependent; values range from 2148 to 65535. Setting this parameter to a larger value than the default leads to better throughput for parallel operations but uses more memory, which may cause performance problems for nonparallel operations or applications.
PARALLEL_MAX_SERVERS	Maximum number of parallel query server processes allowed to exist simultaneously.	Default value is derived from the values of CPU_COUNT, PARALLEL_THREADS_PER_CPU, and PGA_AGGREGATE_TARGET.

TABLE 11-3. *Oracle 10g Parallel Initialization Parameters* (continued)

Initialization Parameter	Meaning	Suggested Values
PARALLEL_MIN_PERCENT	If this percentage of the degree of parallelism (number of servers) required by the query is not available, statement will terminate with an error (ORA-12827). This is effective when a serial execution of the statement is undesired.	Default value is 0, range of values is 0–100. If 0, parallel operations will always execute in parallel. If 100, operations execute in parallel only if all servers can be acquired.
PARALLEL_MIN_SERVERS	Minimum number of servers created when instance originates. As servers idle out or terminate, the number of servers never falls below this number.	0–OS limit. Realistically, start with 10–24. Consider changing if V$ views show heavy use of parallel queries. *Set this parameter!*
PARALLEL_THREADS_PER_CPU	Specifies the default degree of parallelism for the instance, based on the number of parallel execution processes a CPU can support during parallel operations.	Any nonzero number; default is OS-dependent. This "number times CPUs" is the number of threads used in parallel operations.
PGA_AGGREGATE_TARGET	Enables the automatic sizing of SQL working areas used by memory-intensive SQL operators such as a sort and hash join.	A useful parameter to help control paging, because you set the PGA target to the total memory on your system that is available to the Oracle instance and subtract the SGA. It is used for sorting operations as well as others as discussed in Chapter 4.
RECOVERY_PARALLELISM	Number of recovery processes that will be devoted to instance or media recovery.	A value between 2 and PARALLEL_MAX_SERVERS. A value of 0 or 1 indicates that serial recovery will be performed.
*ROLLBACK_SEGMENTS	Names the rollback segments for the instance.	Increase the number of rollback segments if parallel DML is extensively used. Using UNDO Management may be a better idea. See Chapter 3 for more info.
*SHARED_POOL_SIZE	Size of Oracle shared pool. Portion of shared pool is used for query server communication.	Increase existing parameter value by 5–10 percent for heavy, concurrent PQ use, but this is needed only if you are setting PARALLEL_AUTOMATIC_TUNING (deprecated in 10g) to FALSE. This parameter does not need to be set if SGA_TARGET is used and set properly.

TABLE 11-3. *Oracle 10g Parallel Initialization Parameters* (continued)

The parameters in the initialization file define and shape the environment used by parallel operations. You enable parallel operations for your commands by using a PARALLEL hint on a SQL statement or using the PARALLEL clause during a create/alter table command. When you are considering adjusting any initialization parameter (or removing deprecated parameters), fully

Initialization Parameter	Meaning	Suggested Values
*TAPE_ASYNCH_IO	Supports asynchronous writes to the operating system, reducing a potential I/O bottleneck.	This parameter affects writes only to serial devices. This is useful for parallel backup operations or for use with RMAN, but not important for parallel query or DML. The default is TRUE.
*TRANSACTIONS	Specifies the number of concurrent transactions, which will increase if parallel DML is extensively used.	Default value is derived from SESSIONS setting. Increase to support parallel DML.

* Has an indirect effect on parallel options

TABLE 11-3.   *Oracle 10g Parallel Initialization Parameters* (continued)

investigate the *Oracle 10g Database Administrator's Guide,* the *Database Upgrade Guide,* or the appropriate server installation guide for your system *prior* to experimenting with an Oracle database.

Parallel Loading

To use Parallel Data Loading, start multiple SQL*Loader sessions using the PARALLEL keyword. Each session is an independent session requiring its own control file. This listing shows three separate Direct Path loads, all using the PARALLEL=TRUE parameter on the command line:

```
sqlldr USERID=SCOTT/PASS CONTROL=P1.CTL DIRECT=TRUE PARALLEL=TRUE
sqlldr USERID=SCOTT/PASS CONTROL=P2.CTL DIRECT=TRUE PARALLEL=TRUE
sqlldr USERID=SCOTT/PASS CONTROL=P3.CTL DIRECT=TRUE PARALLEL=TRUE
```

Each session creates its own log, bad, and discard files (p1.log, p1.bad, etc.) by default. You can have multiple sessions loading data into different tables, but the APPEND option is still required. APPEND is very fast because it fills only unused blocks. The SQL*Loader REPLACE, TRUNCATE, and INSERT options are not allowed for Parallel Data Loading. If you need to delete the data using SQL commands, you must manually delete the data.

TIP
*If you use Parallel Data Loading, indexes are not maintained by the SQL*Loader session, unless you are loading a single table partition. Before starting a parallel loading process, you must drop all indexes on the table and disable all of its PRIMARY KEY and UNIQUE constraints. After the parallel loads complete, you need to recreate or rebuild the table's indexes. Inserting data using APPEND and UNRECOVERABLE is the fastest way to insert data into a table without an index. External tables may provide faster extract, transform, load (ETL) operations yet.*

In Parallel Data Loading, each load process creates temporary segments for loading the data; the temporary segments are later merged with the table. If a Parallel Data Load process fails before the load completes, the temporary segments will not have been merged with the table. If the temporary segments have not been merged with the table being loaded, no data from the load will have been committed to the table.

You can use the SQL*Loader FILE parameter to direct each data loading session to a different datafile. By directing each loading session to its own database datafile, you can balance the I/O load of the loading processes. Data loading is very I/O-intensive and must be distributed across multiple disks for parallel loading to achieve significant performance improvements over serial loading.

> **TIP**
> *Use the FILE parameter to direct the writes generated by parallel data loads.*

After a Parallel Data Load, each session may attempt to re-enable the table's constraints. As long as at least one load session is still under way, attempting to re-enable the constraints will fail. The final loading session to complete should attempt to re-enable the constraints, and should succeed. You should check the status of your constraints after the load completes. If the table being loaded has PRIMARY KEY and UNIQUE constraints, you should first recreate or rebuild the associated indexes in parallel and then manually enable the constraints.

> **TIP**
> *The PARALLEL option for data loading improves performance of loads, but it can also cause space to be wasted when not properly used.*

Performance Comparisons and Monitoring Parallel Operations

To show the performance difference between a nonparallel operation and a parallel operation, we performed the following tests:

- Started the database with 12 parallel server processes and checked the background processes that were created

- Ran a query without PARALLEL and checked the speed

- Ran a query with PARALLEL that required sorting with a degree of 6

- Checked the output of V$PQ_SYSSTAT and V$PQ_SESSTAT

The next listing shows the pc of output (ps -ef is a Unix or Linux OS command) for 12 parallel servers running. We started the database with the parameter PARALLEL_MIN_SERVERS = 12. The name of the database is fdr1.

```
#ps -ef
oracle  2764   1  0 17:08:30  ?  0:00 ora_pmon_fdr1
oracle  2766   1  0 17:08:34  ?  0:00 ora_lgwr_fdr1
oracle  2768   1  0 17:08:38  ?  0:00 ora_reco_fdr1
oracle  2770   1  0 17:08:42  ?  0:00 ora_d000_fdr1
oracle  2769   1  0 17:08:40  ?  0:00 ora_s000_fdr1
```

```
oracle  2767     1   0 17:08:36     ?    0:00 ora_smon_fdrl
oracle  2771     1   4 17:08:44     ?    0:33 ora_p000_fdrl
oracle  2772     1   5 17:08:46     ?    0:42 ora_p001_fdrl
oracle  2773     1   4 17:08:48     ?    0:33 ora_p002_fdrl
oracle  2774     1   4 17:08:50     ?    0:32 ora_p003_fdrl
oracle  2775     1   5 17:08:52     ?    0:40 ora_p004_fdrl
oracle  2776     1  14 17:08:54     ?    1:26 ora_p005_fdrl
oracle  2819  2802  13 17:12:39     ?    1:44 ora_p006_fdrl
oracle  2820  2802   1 17:12:41     ?    0:05 ora_p007_fdrl
oracle  2821  2802   0 17:12:43     ?    0:01 ora_p008_fdrl
oracle  2822  2802   0 17:12:45     ?    0:01 ora_p009_fdrl
oracle  2825  2802   2 17:12:47     ?    0:11 ora_p010_fdrl
oracle  2826  2802  10 17:12:49     ?    1:18 ora_p011_fdrl
```

Next, run the query *without* using parallel execution servers. A partial result set is shown here. (You can time this in a variety of ways shown in Chapter 6 or by just selecting sysdate from dual.)

```
select     Job_Sub_Code job, SUM(Amount_Cost), SUM(Amount_Credit),
           SUM(Amount_Debit)
from       JOB_ORDER_LINE_ITEMS
group by   Job_Sub_Code;

JOB SUM(AMOUNT_COST) SUM(AMOUNT_CREDIT) SUM(AMOUNT_DEBIT)
--- --------------- ------------------ -----------------
02         9834013.62         20611471.9                 0
04         38670782.7         43440986.1                 0
05         1252599.77         7139753.85                 0
07            8899.66                  0                 0
12         1689729.94         3355174.16                 0
14          103089.64         3287384.45                 0
```

For this test, the elapsed time was 2 minutes, 30 seconds.

Next, run the query using PARALLEL:

```
select     /*+ PARALLEL (JOB_ORDER_LINE_ITEMS, 6) */
           Job_Sub_Code, SUM(Amount_Cost), SUM(Amount_Credit),
           SUM(Amount_Debit)
from       JOB_ORDER_LINE_ITEMS
group by   Job_Sub_Code;
```

For this test, the elapsed time was just over 1 minute. The query completes over twice as fast, with a degree of 6.

TIP
Increasing the degree of a parallel operation does not always decrease the time of execution. It depends on the complete setup of the system that you have. The degree specifies only the number of parallel execution servers that should be used for the operation. The number of parallel execution servers used depends on the parameter settings and the Database Resource Manager settings.

Performance Comparisons of Parallel Operations

The following listing shows the V$ view data when executing the preceding query using PARALLEL with a degree of 12.

```
select      Statistic, Value
from        V$PQ_SYSSTAT;

STATISTIC                   VALUE
--------------------        -----
Servers Busy                   12
Servers Idle                    0
Servers Highwater              12
Server Sessions                39
Servers Started                13
Servers Shutdown                7
Servers Cleaned Up              0
Queries Initiated               5
DML Initiated                   0
HARD RETURNDDL Initiate         0
HARD RETURNDFO Trees            5
Local Msgs Sent             91261
Distr Msgs Sent                 0
Local Msgs Recv'd           91259
Distr Msgs Recv'd               0


select      *
from        V$PQ_SESSTAT;

STATISTIC                   LAST_QUERY  SESSION_TOTAL
------------------------    ----------  -------------
Queries Parallelized                1              4

DML Parallelized                    0              0
HARD RETURNDDL Parallelized         0              0
HARD RETURNDFO Trees                1              4
Server Threads                     12              0
Allocation Height                   6              0
Allocation Width                    1              0
Local Msgs Sent                 20934          83722
HARD RETURNDistr Msgs Sent          0              0
Local Msgs Recv'd               20934          83722
Distr Msgs Recv'd                   0              0
```

Optimizing Parallel Operations in RAC

The benefits of using parallel operations with an Oracle Database have been well established, with the feature first being offered in version 7.1. Parallel execution of SQL statements on traditional Unix-based symmetric multiprocessor (SMP) architectures greatly increased utilization of the server and the speed of large resource-intensive operations. In a Real Application Clusters (RAC) architecture, the equivalent of a parallel SMP deployment is placed into effect and utilizes all the available servers (nodes) in the cluster. Use of parallel operations with RAC greatly enhances the scale-out cluster architecture.

Objectives of Parallel Operations

The objective of a parallel implementation is to use all available resources of the database platform architecture to increase overall processing potential. Resources included in this type of deployment are memory, processor, and I/O. Parallel operations that can be performed in any scale-up or single-system SMP image environment can also be performed in the scale-out RAC cluster environment. Operations that are included are as follows:

- Queries (based on full table scan)
- Create Table As
- Index Builds/Re-builds
- DML Operations (insert, update, delete) on partitioned tables
- Data Loads

The first four operations referenced in this list can be performed with the use of SQL hints or by setting degree of parallelism at the object level. Node groups can be configured to restrict parallel operations to specific nodes. Therefore, when implementing a large RAC architecture (more than two servers), named servers can be allocated to named groups to restrict or enable parallel operations.

RAC Parallel Usage Models

There are several usage models for parallel execution with RAC. Since splitting a query across multiple nodes could cause worse performance as well, care must be taken when using PARALLEL Query with RAC! The models included are the following:

- **Standard**   Use of parallel query for large data sets. In this deployment, the degree of parallelism is usually defined to utilize all of the available resources in the cluster.
- **Restricted**   This deployment restricts processing to specific nodes in the cluster. The referenced nodes can be logically grouped for specific types of operations.
- **Parallel index builds/rebuilds**   In cases where large index builds are required, parallelism can be utilized to maximize the use of cluster node resources.

Initialization Parameters

There are several standard parameters that can be set to implement parallel processes at the server level as discussed earlier in the chapter. The two general parallel parameters to consider are as follows:

Parameter Name	Type	Description
parallel_max_servers	Integer	Maximum number of parallel processes per instance
parallel_min_servers	Integer	Minimum number of server processes per instance

Initialization Parameters

The RAC-specific parameter is as follows:

Parameter Name	Type	Description
Instance_groups	Integer	Defines the logical groups for enabling processing of specific servers

V$ Views for Viewing Parallel Statistics

There are several database views used to obtain parallel operation statistics. The view names referenced here are prefaced with the GV$ identifier, which depicts the RAC level statistics:

View Name	Description
GV$PQ_SYSSTAT	All parallel-related statistics for the entire RAC configuration
GV$PQ_SESSTAT	Session-specific parallel statistics by session ID

Parallel Configuration and Associated Baseline Test

The Initialization parameters set in a test environment are listed next. For the examples outlined in this section, a two-node RAC architecture running under Red Hat Advanced Server was utilized. The "*" identifies these as global across all of the RAC instances.

```
*.parallel_max_servers=5
*.parallel_min_servers=2
```

The listing that follows indicates that the TEST1 and TEST2 instances each initiated two parallel background processes at database startup.

```
UID        PID     PPID  C STIME TTY       TIME CMD
oracle     39414   1     0 11:18 ?     00:00:00 ora_p000_TEST1
oracle     39418   1     0 11:18 ?     00:00:00 ora_p001_TEST1
oracle       520   1     0 11:19 ?     00:00:00 ora_p000_TEST2
oracle       523   1     0 11:19 ?     00:00:00 ora_p001_TEST2
```

A query of the GV$PQ_SYSSTAT table shows the base status of the parallel processes within the Oracle kernel.

```
SELECT inst_id,statistic,value
FROM   gv$pq_sysstat
WHERE  value > 0
order by 1, 2;

INST_ID   STATISTIC                                VALUE
--------  ---------------------------------------  ---------
      1   Servers Busy                                 1
          Servers Idle                                 1
          Servers Highwater                            1
```

```
            Server Sessions                    1
    2   Servers Busy                           1
        Servers Idle                           1
        Servers Highwater                      1
        Server Sessions                        1
```

Parallel Query Test Examples

In this section, we will examine the use of parallel query with the two-node RAC architecture referenced in the preceding section. The two tests performed are

- Unbounded test where the query is executed using both RAC nodes

- Bound test where the query is restricted to a single RAC node

Test 1: Unbounded Test

In the unbounded test, a simple query is run utilizing standard SQL with parallel hints. As with any query, to utilize parallel operations a full table scan must be part of the statement.

```
select /*+ full(c_test) parallel(c_test,6) */ sum(s_test_quantity) testcnt
from   q_test;
```

When executing the query using a parallel hint that requests six parallel workers, three processes are initiated on each of the server nodes.

```
UID        PID        PPID  C STIME TTY      TIME CMD
oracle     15888      1     0 11:13 ?        00:00:03 ora_p000_TEST1
oracle     15879      1     0 11:13 ?        00:00:03 ora_p001_TEST1
oracle     15956      1     1 11:23 ?        00:00:02 ora_p002_TEST1
oracle     17811      1     0 11:23 ?        00:00:01 ora_p000_TEST2
oracle     17620      1     0 11:22 ?        00:00:01 ora_p001_TEST2
oracle     17621      1     3 11:24 ?        00:00:01 ora_p002_TEST2
```

Statistics obtained from the GV$PQ_SYSSTAT view demonstrate that each of the instances started additional servers.

```
INST_ID    STATISTIC                              VALUE
---------- -------------------------------------- ----------
1          DFO Trees                                  7
           Distr Msgs Recv'd                         80
           Distr Msgs Sent                           80
           Local Msgs Recv'd                        204
           Local Msgs Sent                          116
           Queries Initiated                          6
           Server Sessions                           10
           Servers Busy                               1
           Servers Highwater                          3
           Servers Idle                               1
           Servers Shutdown                           1
           Servers Started                            1
```

```
         Sessions Active                    1

2        Distr Msgs Recv'd                 12
         Distr Msgs Sent                    6
         Server Sessions                    6
         Servers Busy                       1
         Servers Highwater                  3
         Servers Idle                       1
         Servers Shutdown                   1
         Servers Started                    1
```

Test 2: Bounded Test

To restrict parallel processing to specific cluster nodes, instance groups are employed to create logical server groupings. Control is via the INIT.ORA with the parameter INSTANCE_GROUPS. INSTANCE_GROUPS is a RAC-related parameter that is specified only in parallel mode. Used in conjunction with the runtime parameter PARALLEL_INSTANCE_GROUP, it allows for the restriction of parallel query operations to a limited number of instances. For the tests in this section, the INSTANCE_GROUPS identified here will be used:

```
# Init.ora Parameter Setting for Parallel Options
SALES1.INSTANCE_GROUPS='test1'
SALES2.INSTANCE_GROUPS='test2'
```

The session that follows is altered prior to the execution of the query to be assigned to the FINANCE group. Even though the query is initiated on the test1 node, based on the INSTANCE_GROUP setting all of the processing will be executed on test2.

```
alter session set parallel_instance_group = 'test2';

select /*+ full(q_amount) parallel(q_stock,6) */ sum(q_quant) ocnt
from   q_stock;
```

Note in the process listing that all of the parallel workers requested are indeed run only on the test2 node, as there is no CPU time being utilized by the processes on test1.

```
UID       PID     PPID  C STIME TTY    TIME CMD
oracle    29994   1     0 14:13 ?      00:00:00 ora_p000_TEST1
oracle    29996   1     0 14:13 ?      00:00:00 ora_p001_TEST1
oracle    2631    1     0 14:51 ?      00:00:01 ora_p000_TEST2
oracle    2633    1     0 14:51 ?      00:00:01 ora_p001_TEST2
oracle    2676    1     4 14:57 ?      00:00:01 ora_p002_TEST2
oracle    2678    1     J 14.57 ?      00:00:01 ora_p003_TEST2
oracle    2680    1     4 14:57 ?      00:00:01 ora_p004_TEST2
```

A query of the GV$PQ_SYSSTAT table also shows that an additional three servers were started on the second test2 instance. Why only three servers and not four? Remember the setting of the INIT.ORA parameter parallel_max_servers. The value of the parameter is five, thus only an additional three are added to the initial two (although the high-water mark did hit 6).

```
INST_ID   STATISTIC                          VALUE
--------- ------------------------------ ----------
1         DFO Trees                          3
```

```
          Distr Msgs Recv'd              74
          Distr Msgs Sent               74
          Local Msgs Recv'd              2
          Local Msgs Sent                1
          Queries Initiated              3
          Server Sessions                1
          Servers Busy                   1
          Servers Highwater          1
          Servers Idle                   1
          Sessions Active                2

2         Distr Msgs Recv'd             22
          Distr Msgs Sent               11
          Server Sessions               11
          Servers Busy                   6
          Servers Highwater          6
          Servers Started                3
```

In the preceding example, the query was restricted to the test node by using the TEST_10 instance group. The INIT.ORA example that follows allows for the TEST_10 instance group to now run across both the test1 and test2 nodes. Note that the INIT.ORA parameter INSTANCE_GROUPS must be entered explicitly for each of the groups.

```
# Init.ora Parameter Setting for Parallel Options
TEST1.instance_groups='TEST_20'
TEST1.instance_groups='TEST_10'
TEST2.instance_groups='TEST_10'
```

Create Table As

Using the Create Table As (CTAS) feature within Oracle can be extremely useful for making copies of table objects. For large tables, the operation can be performed in parallel in the same manner as with the parallel query examples in the prior section. The SQL statement that follows is an example of the use of CTAS with the parallel option. Instance groups can also be used to restrict processing to specific nodes. Thus, based on the INSTANCE_GROUPS parameter, the execution of the query would be performed only on the TEST1 node.

```
alter session set parallel_instance_group = 'TEST_20';

create table c_district_backup parallel (degree 3)
as
select *
from   c_district;
```

Index Builds

Performing index creates or rebuilds for large tables is another resource-intensive operation where performance can be greatly improved with parallel operations. The index create statement requests a parallel degree of six for the operation. Similar to the previous examples, this operation can also utilize the INSTANCE_GROUPS parameter to restrict the operation to specific nodes.

```
alter session set parallel_instance_group = 'TEST_20';

create unique index C_STOCK_I1 on C_STOCK (s_i_id, s_w_id)
tablespace stock_indx
parallel (degree 6);
```

Performance Considerations and Summary

The downside of parallel operations is the exhaustion of server resources. The easiest server resource to monitor is CPU utilization. If normal CPU utilization were relatively high, deploying a large number of parallel processes would not be advisable. Exceeding the total number of CPUs would cause performance degradation as well. Data layout is another immediate consideration. If I/O bottlenecks currently exist, use of parallel operations may exacerbate this condition. Ensure that data files for parallel target objects are spread across a reasonable number of disk spindles.

The use of parallel operations within a RAC deployment provides for the flexibility to utilize all server hardware included in the cluster architecture. Utilizing instance groups, database administrators can further control the allocation of these resources based on application requirements or service level agreements.

Other Parallel Notes

Planning (or reengineering) the physical location of data files is key to successful parallel data access. Determine an appropriate degree of parallelism for each parallelized SQL statement and parallelize the creation of your physical design. Don't let the initialization parameters dictate how the degree of parallelism is determined. Remember, you're usually trying to optimize a small number of slow queries, not every table access. Experiment with conservative parameters; use parallel operations for table or index creations and hint the degree of parallelism you identify as optimal. Use proper syntax for the parallel hints or they will be ignored. Other V$ views that may be helpful to you include V$px_session (session performing parallel operations), V$px_sesstat (statistics for sessions performing parallel operations), V$px_process (parallel processes), V$px_process_sysstat (statistics for parallel execution servers), V$sesstat (user session statistics), V$filestat (file I/O statistics), V$parameter (init.ora parameters), and V$pq_tqstat (workload statistics for parallel execution servers).

The parallel features offered in Oracle are incredibly powerful tools when used in a targeted fashion—most databases can be tuned to place indexes in the right quantity and location to deliver acceptable performance. Use parallel operations for those statements that cannot be written any other way but to scan an entire table or address a partitioned large table/index. Parallelized operations are powerful tools for managing data warehouses or performing periodic maintenance activities. The database environment must be configured to take full advantage of the benefits parallelism offers.

Oracle Documentation Is Online

Don't forget that all of the Oracle documentation (multiple Oracle versions) for all of the products is online at http://tahiti.oracle.com.

For the complete archives of all Oracle documentation (back to Oracle 7.3.4), visit www.oracle.com/technology/documentation/index.html.

TIPS Tips Review

REVIEW

- RAC is the next generation of Relational Database Architecture. Get ready for it!

- Use V$SESSION_WAIT, Statspack, or the AWR Report to find RAC Wait Events.

- Find Interconnect issues using Enterprise Manager Grid Control.

- The Database or Cluster Performance Screen within OEM is the quickest way to find where performance problems are in your system.

- You can investigate specific Global Cache wait events in Enterprise Manager.

- Parallel processes commonly involve disk accesses. If the data is not distributed across multiple disks, using parallel operations may lead to an I/O bottleneck.

- When the parallel degree is set to N, it is possible to use $(2*N) + 1$ total processes for the parallel operation. Although parallel operations deal with processes and *not* processors, when a large number of processors are available, Oracle usually uses the additional processors to run parallel queries, usually enhancing the performance of the query.

- Using parallel operations on very small tables or very fast queries can also degrade performance because the query coordination also uses performance resources. You should evaluate whether the parallel cost exceeds the nonparallelized cost.

- As of Oracle 9*i*, parallelized INSERT does not require a partitioned table.

- As of Oracle 9*i*, intrapartition parallelism restrictions are no longer in effect.

- Using the PARALLEL hint enables the use of parallel operations. If the degree is not specified with the hint, the default degree during the table creation is used, or the degree is calculated from various initialization parameters.

- The use of the NO_PARALLEL hint disables parallel operations in a statement that would otherwise use parallel processing due to a parallel object definition.

- Specify the degree of parallelism using a hint instead of relying on the table definition to ensure that all operations are tuned for the given query.

- Effective parallel operations depend greatly on how the data is physically located. Avoid introducing I/O bottlenecks into your database.

- To use parallel DML, you must first enable a parallel DML session.

- Statement failure does not disable parallel DML within your session.

- Parallel DML is limited to specific types of tables—and sometimes only certain columns within them. You must manage your tables to properly enable parallel DML operations.

- You *must* issue a commit or rollback after using parallel DML statements. Otherwise, you will receive an error doing a SELECT statement on the same table that follows a parallel DML statement on that table.

■ The PARALLEL hint may be used in multiple sections of an INSERT . . . AS SELECT.

■ If the number of servers started consistently increases, you may consider increasing the PARALLEL_MIN_SERVERS initialization parameter. However, if a parallel execution server is started through the PARALLEL_MIN_SERVERS parameter, it does not exit until the database shuts down, the parallel process aborts, or the process is killed. This can lead to process memory fragmentation, so increase this only when you are sure it's needed.

■ A PARALLEL hint overrides the parallel object definition when it comes to which degree of parallelism the operation will use. The degree of parallelism specified in the hint is applied to all statement operations that can be parallelized, when possible.

■ New columns may be added to the PLAN_TABLE with each new release of Oracle. You should drop and recreate your PLAN_TABLE following each upgrade of the Oracle kernel. If you upgrade an existing database to a new version of Oracle, you should drop your old PLAN_TABLE and re-execute the utlxplan.sql script to see all of the new PLAN_TABLE columns.

■ When using the explain plan command for a parallelized query, you cannot rely on querying just the operations-related columns to see the parallelized operations within the explain plan. At a minimum, you should query the Other_Tag column to see which operations are performed in parallel. If an operation is not performed in parallel and you think it should be, you may need to add hints to the query, set a degree of parallelism for the tables, or check other factors that limit parallel resources.

■ You can use the utlxplp.sql script to query the parallel-related columns from PLAN_TABLE following an EXPLAIN PLAN.

■ Be sure your environment is properly configured to support the increase in processes and transactions generated by parallel operations.

■ If you use Parallel Data Loading, indexes are not maintained by the SQL*Loader session. Before starting a parallel loading process, you must drop all indexes on the table and disable all of its PRIMARY KEY and UNIQUE constraints. After the loads complete, you can recreate the table's indexes.

■ Use the FILE parameter to direct the writes generated by parallel data loads.

■ The PARALLEL option for data loading improves performance of loads, but can also cause space to be wasted when not properly used.

■ The degree of a parallel operation does not always decrease the time of execution. It depends on the complete setup of the system you have. The degree specifies only the number of parallel execution servers that should be used for the operation. The number of parallel execution servers used depends on the parameter settings and the Database Resource Manager settings.

■ Go to http://tahiti.oracle.com for a quick Internet connection to Oracle Documentation.

References

Rich Niemiec, *Oracle RAC Tuning* (Collaborate and Oracle World Conference Paper)
Oracle Server Tuning (Oracle Corporation)

Oracle Server Concepts (Oracle Corporation)
Oracle Server Reference (Oracle Corporation)
Oracle Data Warehousing Guide (Oracle Corporation)
Jake Van der Vort, *Oracle Parallel Query* (TUSC)

Special thanks go to Madhu Tumma of Credit Suisse First Boston for writing the section "Real Application Clusters" of this chapter. Jake Van der Vort did a major portion of the original parallel query chapter. Kevin Loney did the update to Oracle 9*i* for the original parallel query chapter. Brad Nash did most of the Oracle 10*g* update and added the RAC information. Special thanks to Murali Vallath for many contributions to this chapter and his great book on RAC.

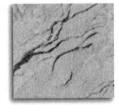

CHAPTER
12

The V$ Views
(Developer and DBA)

S enior DBAs often tell junior DBAs that back in version 6 they used to know every V$ view by heart. In version 6, there were only 23 V$ views, and the DBAs from the old days had it pretty easy. Oracle 9*i* had 259 V$ views and almost 400 X$ tables. Oracle 10gR2 (10.2.0.1.0) now has 372 V$ views and 613 X$ tables.

Almost every great tuning or DBA product has one aspect in common. Most of them access the V$ view information to get the insightful information that is retrieved about the database, individual queries, or an individual user. Accessing the V$ views has become quite prevalent due to the numerous presentations by Joe Trezzo and other V$ gurus. If you currently don't look at the V$ views, you don't know what you're missing. The V$ views look into the heart of the Oracle database. They are the link to moving from the average to the expert DBA.

Chapter 13 more extensively explores the X$ tables, which are the underlying part of the V$ views. Appendixes B and C provide information about the V$ views and also the creation scripts from the X$ tables. Unfortunately, I can't show every great V$ script due to space limitations, and I'll try not to duplicate things that are covered in depth in other chapters. Please check our web site (www.tusc.com) for the latest V$ scripts available.

Topics covered in this chapter include the following:

- Creating V$ views and granting access to them

- Getting a listing of all V$ views

- Getting a listing of the X$ scripts that make up the V$ views

- Examining the underlying objects that make up the DBA_ views

- Querying V$DATABASE to get database creation time and archiving information

- Learning about the Automatic Workload Repository (AWR)

- Querying V$LICENSE to view licensing limits and warning settings

- Accessing V$OPTION to view all options that have been installed

- Querying V$SGA to allocate basic memory for Oracle

- Querying V$SGASTAT to allocate detailed memory for Oracle

- Finding init.ora settings in V$PARAMETER

- Determining hit ratio for data (V$SYSSTAT)

- Determining hit ratio for the data dictionary (V$ROWCACHE)

- Determining hit ratio for the shared SQL and PL/SQL (V$LIBRARYCACHE)

- Deciding which objects need to be pinned and whether there is contiguous free memory (V$DB_OBJECT_CACHE)

- Finding the problem queries accessing V$SQLAREA, V$SQLTEXT, V$SESSION, and V$SESS_IO

- Finding out what users are doing and which resources they are using

- Identifying locking problems and killing the corresponding session

- Finding users with multiple sessions

- Balancing I/O using the views V$DATAFILE, V$FILESTAT, and DBA_DATA_FILES

- Checking to see if freelists is sufficient

- Checking for roles and privileges

- Finding Waits with V$SESSION, V$SESSION_WAIT, V$SESSION_EVENT, V$SESSION_WAIT_CLASS, V$SESSION_WAIT_HISTORY, V$SYSTEM_EVENT, and V$SYSTEM_WAIT_CLASS

- Using a table grouping the V$ views by category to match the poster

V$ View Creation and Access

The V$ views are created by the catalog.sql script. As of Oracle 10g, there are approximately 372 V$ views. The actual number varies by the version and platform. Here is the number of each from Oracle 6 to Oracle 10gR2:

Version	V$ Views	X$ Tables
6	23	(?)
7.1	72	126
8.0	132	200
8.1	185	271
9.0	227	352
9.2	259	394
10.1	340	543
10.2	372	613

They are all created with the prefix of $v\_\$$. Two of the views are created by the catldr.sql script, which is used for SQL*Loader direct load statistical information. The underlying view definitions (technically, these views are never created; their definitions are hard-coded into the binary) for each V$ view can be seen in the V$ view named V$FIXED_VIEW_DEFINITION. The views are created by selecting from one or more X$ tables. A view is created for each $v\_\$$ view to allow users to access the view. Users cannot access the actual $v\$$ views (they actually access the $v\_\$$ views; the $v\$$ objects are only visible to SYS), and therefore, this method provides access to these views via a view on a view. The view name changes the prefix of each view to *V$*. Lastly, a public synonym is created on each view because the SYS user owns the tables. The following listing shows an example of a V$ view creation in the catalog.sql script.

```
create or replace view gv_$datafile as
select *
from    gv$datafile;

create or replace public synonym gv$datafile for gv_$datafile;
```

The complete sequence of events is detailed in the following steps.

1. The GV$ view definitions are created from the X$ tables when the database is created:

```
create  or replace view gv$fixed_table as
select  inst_id,kqftanam, kqftaobj, 'TABLE', indx
from    X$kqfta
union all
select  inst_id,kqfvinam, kqfviobj, 'VIEW', 65537
from    X$kqfvi
union all
select  inst_id,kqfdtnam, kqfdtobj, 'TABLE', 65537
from    X$kqfdt;
```

2. The version-specific catalog script is executed:

```
SQL> @catalog
```

3. A v_$ view is created from the V$ view:

```
create or replace view v_$fixed_table
as
select *
from   v$fixed_table;
```

4. A new V$ synonym is created on the v_$ view:

```
create or replace public synonym v$fixed_table for v_$fixed_table;
```

TIP
The V$ views that are accessed by SYSTEM are actually synonyms that point to the v_$ views that are views of the original V$ views based on the X$ tables. (Better read that one again!)

The only operation that can be performed on these views is a SELECT. To provide access to the V$ views, you must grant access to the underlying v_$ view.
You cannot grant access to the V$ views (even as the SYS user):

```
connect     sys/change_on_install as sysdba
Grant select on v$fixed_table to richn;
ORA-02030: can only select from fixed tables/views.
```

Although the error message (following the preceding code) for attempting to grant access to V$FIXED_TABLE is erroneous, the grant will not be allowed. You may, however, grant access to the underlying v_$ view that is behind the V$ view.
To connect to the SYS superuser, use the following:

```
Connect sys/change_on_install as sysdba

Connected.
```

To grant access to an underlying view to the desired user, use the following:

```
grant select on v_$fixed_table to richn;

Grant succeeded.
```

To connect as the desired user, use this:

```
conn    richn/tusc

Connected.
```

Access the V$FIXED_TABLE view via the synonym V$FIXED_TABLE created for V_$FIXED_TABLE with the following:

```
select count(*)
from    v$fixed_table;

COUNT(*)
--------

    1224
```

You still *can't* access the v_$fixed_table even though that was the grant made:

```
select count(*)
from    v_$fixed_table;

ORA-00942: table or view does not exist.
```

You *can* access the v_$fixed_view if you preface it with SYS:

```
conn    richn/tusc

select count(*)
from    SYS.v_$fixed_table;

COUNT(*)
--------
    1224
```

To avoid confusion, it is better to give access to the v_$ tables and notify the DBA that he or she has access to the V$ views. Using this method, you may give access to the V$ view information without giving out the password for the SYS or SYSTEM accounts. The key is granting SELECT access to the original SYS owned v_$ view.

TIP

When other DBAs need access to the V$ view information, but not the SYS or SYSTEM passwords, grant the user access to the v_$ views. The user may then access the V$ views that have public synonyms to the v_$ views. However, scripts should always be written to query the SYS.V_$ views directly, to avoid the performance cost of de-referencing the public synonym.

CAUTION
You should grant non-DBA users privileges to the V$ views only as needed, and use caution. Remember, performance costs come with querying the V$ views, and the larger your environment, the greater those costs.

Obtaining a Count and Listing of All V$ Views

To get a count of all V$ views for a given version of Oracle, query the V$FIXED_TABLE view. The number of V$ views continues to change even within the same version. The examples that follow display the V$ view queries for Oracle 10g. The frontier in the world of the V$ views continues to expand with each version of Oracle.

Query to get a count of V$ views, as shown here:

```
select  count(*)
from    v$fixed_table
where   name like 'V%';


COUNT(*)
--------
     372
```

Many of the V$ views continue to be undocumented. The methods of exploring information are continually growing in Oracle because the number of views continues to expand. In Oracle 8, the GV$ views were introduced. The GV$ (global V$) views are the same as the V$ views with an additional column for the instance ID.

Get a list of GV$ views, as shown here (partial listing; you'll find a complete list in Appendix B).

```
select    name
from      v$fixed_table
where     name like 'GV%'
order by  name;


NAME

----------------------------------
GV$ACCESS
GV$ACTIVE_INSTANCES
GV$ACTIVE_SERVICES
GV$ACTIVE_SESSION_HISTORY
GV$ACTIVE_SESS_POOL_MTH
GV$ADVISOR_PROGRESS
GV$ALERT_TYPES
GV$AQ1
GV$ARCHIVE
GV$ARCHIVED_LOG
GV$ARCHIVE_DEST
GV$ARCHIVE_DEST_STATUS
GV$ARCHIVE_GAP
GV$ARCHIVE_PROCESSES
...
```

TIP
Query V$FIXED_TABLE to obtain a listing of all GV$ and V$ views in the database. The GV$ views are the exact same as the V$ views, except the instance ID contains an identifier.

Finding the X$ Tables Used to Create the V$ Views

To understand where the V$ view information comes from, query the underlying X$ tables (see Chapter 13 for X$ table information). At times, it may be advantageous to query the underlying X$ tables because the V$ views are often the join of several X$ tables. The X$ tables are very cryptic because they are similar to the underlying table constructs of the Oracle Data Dictionary. Oracle creates V$ views in the SGA to allow users to examine the information stored in the X$ tables in a more readable format. In fact, when SELECTs are performed against the V$ views, the SELECTs are actually retrieving information out of the SGA—and more specifically, out of the X$ tables.

With the knowledge of the V$ view underlying a given SELECT statement, you have the capability to create customized views; simply copy the existing V$ view underlying the SELECT statement and modify it or create a new customized SELECT on the X$ tables. This technique allows more selective and more optimized queries. The next listing is used to access the underlying query to the X$ tables. To get a listing of the X$ tables that make up the V$ views, you must access the V$FIXED_TABLE_DEFINITION view (output formatted for readability).

```
select   *
from     v$fixed_view_definition
where    view_name = 'GV$FIXED_TABLE';
```

Output

```
VIEW_NAME           VIEW_DEFINITION

--------------      -------------------------------------------------------
GV$FIXED_TABLE      select  inst_id,kqftanam, kqftaobj, 'TABLE', indx
                    from    X$kqfta
                    union all
                    select  inst_id,kqfvinam, kqfviobj, 'VIEW', 65537
                    from    X$kqfvi
                    union all
                    select  inst_id,kqfdtnam, kqfdtobj, 'TABLE', 65537
                    from    X$kqfdt
```

TIP
Access the V$FIXED_VIEW_DEFINITION view to get all of the information of the underlying X$ tables that make up a V$ view.

Also note that as of Oracle 8, there are indexes on the underlying X$ tables to provide faster execution of queries performed on the V$ views. You can view the index information on the underlying X$ tables through the V$INDEXED_FIXED_COLUMN view (see Chapter 13 for more information).

Finding the Underlying Objects That Make Up the DBA_ views

Some people think the DBA_ views also come from the X$ tables and/or the V$ views. They actually come from Oracle's underlying database tables (although some access the X$ tables as well). To look at the objects that make up the DBA_ views, access DBA_VIEWS, as shown in this listing:

NOTE
You may need to set long 2000000 to see all of this output.

```
select text
from   dba_views
where  view_name='DBA_IND_PARTITIONS';

TEXT
-------------------------------------------------------------------------------
select u.name, io.name, 'NO', io.subname, 0, ip.hiboundval, ip.hiboundlen

SQL> set long 2000000
(RUN IT AGAIN)

select text
from   dba_views
where  view_name='DBA_IND_PARTITIONS';

TEXT

-------------------------------------------------------------------------------
select u.name, io.name, 'NO', io.subname, 0,  ip.hiboundval,ip.hiboundlen,
       ip.part#,decode(bitand(ip.flags, 1), 1, 'UNUSABLE', 'USABLE'), ts.name,
       ip.pctfree$,ip.initrans, ip.maxtrans, s.iniexts * ts.blocksize,
       decode(bitand(ts.flags, 3), 1, to_number(NULL),  s.extsize * ts.blocksize),
       s.minexts, s.maxexts, decode(bitand(ts.flags,3),1,to_number(NULL),s.extpct),
       decode(bitand(ts.flags, 32), 32, to_number(NULL),
          decode(s.lists, 0, 1, s.lists)),
       decode(bitand(ts.flags, 32), 32, to_number(NULL),
          decode(s.groups, 0, 1, s.groups)),
       decode(mod(trunc(ip.flags / 4), 2), 0, 'YES', 'NO'),
       decode(bitand(ip.flags, 1024), 0, 'DISABLED', 1024, 'ENABLED', null),
       ip.blevel, ip.leafcnt, ip.distkey, ip.lblkkey, ip.dblkkey,
       ip.clufac, ip.rowcnt, ip.samplesize, ip.analyzetime,
       decode(s.cachehint, 0, 'DEFAULT', 1, 'KEEP', 2, 'RECYCLE', NULL),
       decode(bitand(ip.flags, 8), 0, 'NO', 'YES'), ip.pctthres$,
       decode(bitand(ip.flags, 16), 0, 'NO', 'YES'),'',''
from   obj$ io, indpart$ ip, ts$ ts, sys.seg$ s, user$ u
where  io.obj# = ip.obj# and ts.ts# = ip.ts# and ip.file#=s.file# and
       ip.block#=s.block# and ip.ts#=s.ts# and io.owner# = u.user#
     union all
select u.name, io.name, 'YES', io.subname, icp.subpartcnt,
       icp.hiboundval, icp.hiboundlen, icp.part#, 'N/A', ts.name,
       icp.defpctfree, icp.definitrans, icp.defmaxtrans,
       icp.definiexts, icp.defextsize, icp.defminexts, icp.defmaxexts,
       icp.defextpct, icp.deflists, icp.defgroups,
       decode(icp.deflogging, 0, 'NONE', 1, 'YES', 2, 'NO', 'UNKNOWN'),
       'N/A', icp.blevel, icp.leafcnt, icp.distkey, icp.lblkkey, icp.dblkkey,
       icp.clufac, icp.rowcnt, icp.samplesize, icp.analyzetime,
       decode(icp.defbufpool, 0, 'DEFAULT', 1, 'KEEP', 2, 'RECYCLE', NULL),
```

```
        decode(bitand(icp.flags, 8), 0, 'NO', 'YES'), TO_NUMBER(NULL),
        decode(bitand(icp.flags, 16), 0, 'NO', 'YES'),'',''
from    obj$ io, indcompart$ icp, ts$ ts, user$ u
where   io.obj# = icp.obj# and icp.defts# = ts.ts# (+) and u.user# = io.owner#
        union all
select u.name, io.name, 'NO', io.subname, 0,
        ip.hiboundval, ip.hiboundlen, ip.part#,
        decode(bitand(ip.flags, 1), 1, 'UNUSABLE',
                decode(bitand(ip.flags, 4096), 4096, 'INPROGRS', 'USABLE')),
        null, ip.pctfree$, ip.initrans, ip.maxtrans,
        0, 0, 0, 0, 0, 0, 0,
        decode(mod(trunc(ip.flags / 4), 2), 0, 'YES', 'NO'),
        decode(bitand(ip.flags, 1024), 0, 'DISABLED', 1024, 'ENABLED', null),
        ip.blevel, ip.leafcnt, ip.distkey, ip.lblkkey, ip.dblkkey,
        ip.clufac, ip.rowcnt, ip.samplesize, ip.analyzetime,
        'DEFAULT',
        decode(bitand(ip.flags, 8), 0, 'NO', 'YES'), ip.pctthres$,
        decode(bitand(ip.flags, 16), 0, 'NO', 'YES'),
        decode(i.type#,
        9, decode(bitand(ip.flags, 8192), 8192, 'FAILED', 'VALID'),''),
        ipp.parameters
from    obj$ io, indpartv$ ip,  user$ u, ind$ i, indpart_param$ ipp, tab$ t
where   io.obj# = ip.obj# and io.owner# = u.user# and
        ip.bo# = i.obj# and ip.obj# = ipp.obj# and i.bo# = t.obj# and
        bitand(t.trigflag, 1073741824) != 1073741824
        and io.namespace = 4 and io.remoteowner IS NULL and iolinkname IS NULL
```

Never modify the underlying objects; many DBAs have corrupted their database in this manner. Do *not* do the following here, but note that it is possible:

```
Connect sys/change_on_install as sysdba
Connected.
DELETE FROM OBJAUTH$;   -- Don't do this! If you commit this, your database is over!
13923 rows deleted.
Rollback;
Rollback complete.
```

TIP
The DBA_ views are not derived from the X$ tables or V$ views. The fact that you can delete rows from obj$ is a great reason to never be the SYS superuser.

Using Helpful V$ Scripts

The rest of this chapter is dedicated to scripts that are very helpful in analyzing different areas of the Oracle database. Many of these scripts are dynamic and provide valuable insight into areas of the database that may need to be analyzed to determine resource contention at a point in time. Typically, the result is that the DBA performs some operation to immediately eliminate the contention by tuning a query or increasing an init.ora parameter to reduce the resource contention in the future. Revoking access to a given ad hoc query user, or restricting his or her system resource use with profiles, could be an emergency option as well. The next three sections include scripts that retrieve the following:

- Basic database information
- Information about the Automatic Workload Repository (AWR)

- Basic licensing information

- Database options installed in your database

Basic Database Information

Getting the basic information about your instance is usually as easy as logging in to SQL*Plus, because all of the information shows in the banner at that time. If you would like to see the full banner header, you can access the V$VERSION view to display the banner. The following listing shows a quick way to see the version you are using as well as other information:

```
Version Information:
SQL> select * from v$version;


BANNER
----------------------------------------------------------------
Oracle Database 10g Enterprise Edition Release 10.2.0.1.0 - Prod
PL/SQL Release 10.2.0.1.0 - Production
CORE    10.2.0.1.0      Production
TNS for 32-bit Windows: Version 10.2.0.1.0 - Production
NLSRTL Version 10.2.0.1.0 - Production


Database Information:
select name, created, log_mode
from    v$database;


NAME      CREATED       LOG_MODE
--------- ---------     ---------------
ORCL      03-DEC-04     ARCHIVELOG
```

Accessing V$DATABASE gives you basic information concerning the database. The most important information in the output is to ensure that you are in the desired ARCHIVELOG mode. Another way to view the archive log status for the database is to simply use the ARCHIVE LOG LIST command as the SYS user in SQL*Plus. The output also gives you the exact date when the database was created, as you can see in the preceding listing.

TIP
Query V$VERSION and V$DATABASE to view basic database information such as the version, to find out when your database was created, and to find out basic archiving information.

Basic Automatic Workload Repository (AWR) Information

With the advent of the Automatic Workload Repository (AWR), there are many areas to watch. By default, the repository is populated every hour and the retention period is seven days. Here are some queries that are worth knowing for the AWR (the MMON background process is used to flush AWR data from memory to disk). See Chapter 5 for detailed information on AWR, licensing related to the V$ views based on the AWR, and using information from the AWR for tuning purposes.

How much space is the AWR using?

select occupant_name, occupant_desc, space_usage_kbytes

```
from    v$sysaux_occupants
where   occupant_name like '%AWR%';

OCCUPANT_NAME OCCUPANT_DESC                                         SPACE_USAGE_KBYTES
------------- ----------------------------------------------------- ------------------
SM/AWR        Server Manageability - Automatic Workload Repository               44352
```

What's the oldest AWR information on the system?

```
select dbms_stats.get_stats_history_availability from dual;

GET_STATS_HISTORY_AVAILABILITY
---------------------------------------------------------------------
03-NOV-06 09.30.34.291000000 AM -06:00
```

What's the retention period for AWR information?

```
select dbms_stats.get_stats_history_retention from dual;

GET_STATS_HISTORY_RETENTION
---------------------------
                         31
```

Change the retention period for AWR information to 15 days?

```
EXEC dbms_stats.alter_stats_history_retention(15);

GET_STATS_HISTORY_RETENTION
---------------------------
                         15
```

TIP
*Query V$SYSAUX_OCCUPANTS to ensure that the Automatic
Workload Repository (AWR) isn't taking up too much space. Use
DBMS_STATS to check history and retention.*

Basic Licensing Information

The V$LICENSE view allows a DBA to monitor the system activity in terms of overall database numbers at any time. It provides a DBA with a log of the maximum number of concurrent sessions at any time, which allows a company to ensure they are licensed properly. The current number of sessions is displayed along with the session warning level and session maximum level. A session warning level of 0 indicates that the init.ora session warning parameter was not set; therefore, no warning message displays. A session maximum level of 0 indicates that the init.ora session maximum parameter was not set; therefore, there is no limit on the number of sessions.

The script should be executed periodically to provide a DBA with the actual number of sessions on the system throughout the day and to ensure proper licensing. Setting the init.ora parameter LICENSE_MAX_SESSIONS = 110 limits the sessions to 110. Setting the init.ora parameter LICENSE_SESSIONS_WARNING = 100 gives every user past the one-hundredth a warning message so that they will (hopefully) notify the DBA that the system is closing in on a problem. The LICENSE_MAX_USERS init.ora parameter is used to set the number of named users that can be created in the database. In this next listing, there is no limit and the value is set to 0.

```
select *
from   v$license;
```

SESS_MAX	SESS_WARNING	SESS_CURRENT	SESS_HIGHWATER	USERS_MAX
110	100	44	105	0

(selected columns listed above)

TIP
*Query the V$LICENSE view to see the maximum sessions that you are
allowed. You can also set warnings when you get close to the maximum.*

Database Options Installed in Your Database

The script shown next describes what options are installed on your database and are available for
use. If you have purchased a product that does not show up in this list, you may have incorrectly
installed it. Query the V$OPTION view to check for installed products or log on to SQL*Plus to
see the products that are installed (does your open source database do all this?).

```
select *
from   v$option;
```

To get the following output, you need to order by PARAMETER.

Output

PARAMETER	VALUE
Partitioning	TRUE
Objects	TRUE
Real Application Clusters	FALSE
Advanced replication	TRUE
Bit-mapped indexes	TRUE
Connection multiplexing	TRUE
Connection pooling	TRUE
Database queuing	TRUE
Incremental backup and recovery	TRUE
Instead-of triggers	TRUE
Parallel backup and recovery	TRUE
Parallel execution	TRUE
Parallel load	TRUE
Point-in-time tablespace recovery	TRUE
Fine-grained access control	TRUE
Proxy authentication/authorization	TRUE
Change Data Capture	TRUE
Plan Stability	TRUE
Online Index Build	TRUE
Coalesce Index	TRUE
Managed Standby	TRUE
Materialized view rewrite	TRUE
Materialized view warehouse refresh	TRUE
Database resource manager	TRUE
Spatial	TRUE
Visual Information Retrieval	TRUE

```
Export transportable tablespaces          TRUE
Transparent Application Failover           TRUE
Fast-Start Fault Recovery                  TRUE
Sample Scan                                TRUE
Duplexed backups                           TRUE
Java                                       TRUE
OLAP Window Functions                      TRUE
Block Media Recovery                       TRUE
Fine-grained Auditing                      TRUE
Application Role                           TRUE
Enterprise User Security                   TRUE
Oracle Data Guard                          TRUE
Oracle Label Security                      FALSE
OLAP                                       TRUE
Table compression                          TRUE
Join index                                 TRUE
Trial Recovery                             TRUE
Data Mining                                TRUE
Online Redefinition                        TRUE
Streams Capture                            TRUE
File Mapping                               TRUE
Block Change Tracking                      TRUE
Flashback Table                            TRUE
Flashback Database                         TRUE
Data Mining Scoring Engine                 FALSE
Transparent Data Encryption                FALSE
Backup Encryption                          FALSE
Unused Block Compression                   TRUE

54 rows selected.
```

The previous database has the Partitioning option, but it does not have Real Application Clusters (RAC) installed.

TIP
Query the V$OPTION view to retrieve the Oracle options you have installed. The V$VERSION view will give the versions of the base options that are installed.

Summary of Memory Allocated (V$SGA)

V$SGA gives the summary information for the System Global Area (SGA) memory structures of your system, as shown in this next listing. The "Database Buffers" is the number of bytes allocated to memory for data. It comes from the init.ora parameter DB_CACHE_SIZE. The "Redo Buffers" comes primarily from the value of the init.ora parameter LOG_BUFFER, which is used to buffer changed records and flushed to the redo logs whenever a COMMIT is issued.

```
COLUMN value FORMAT 999,999,999,999
select *
from   v$sga;
```

Summary of Memory Allocated (V$SGA)

```
NAME                              VALUE
-------------------------------   ----------------
Fixed Size                                 734,080
Variable Size                          352,321,536
Database Buffers                     2,667,577,344
Redo Buffers                             1,335,296

If SGA_TARGET is used - it is dynamically resizing internally:
select (
    (select sum(value) from v$sga) -
    (select current_size from v$sga_dynamic_free_memory)
    ) "SGA_TARGET"
from dual;


SGA_TARGET
----------
 138412032
```

This output indicates a relatively large SGA with a buffer cache that includes DB_CACHE_SIZE, DB_KEEP_CACHE_SIZE, and DB_RECYCLE_CACHE_SIZE of over 2.5GB. As discussed in Chapters 1 and 4, I could have just set the SGA_TARGET to something like 3G and set the other parameters to enforce minimum sizes only. The predominant part of the Variable Size category is the shared pool. (The shared pool for this SGA was slightly over 200MB.) This SGA is using about 3GB of the actual physical system memory in the preceding listing. This information is also given in the Statspack report (see Chapter 14) and can be displayed by issuing an SHOW SGA command as the SYS superuser.

TIP
Access the V$SGA view to get a baseline idea of the system's physical memory allocated for data, shared pool, large pool, java pool, and log buffering of Oracle.

Detail of Memory Allocated (V$SGASTAT)

A more detailed V$ view query to retrieve the information about memory allocation for the SGA is in the V$SGASTAT view. This view provides dynamic information about SGA and memory resources. (It changes as the database is accessed.) This statement describes the SGA sizes at a detailed level. The records FIXED_SGA, BUFFER_CACHE, and LOG_BUFFER are the same values for both the V$SGA and V$SGASTAT. The remaining records in V$SGASTAT make up the only other V$SGA record (the Variable Size or Shared Pool record).

Fixed Size (V$SGA)	= fixed_sga (V$SGASTAT)
Database Buffers (V$SGA)	= buffer_cache (V$SGASTAT)
Redo Buffers (V$SGA)	= log_buffer (V$SGASTAT)
Variable Size (V$SGA)	= 39 Other Records (V$SGASTAT)

In Oracle 9.2, the V$SGASTAT has 43 total records as shown here:

```
select  *
from    v$sgastat;

POOL            NAME                            BYTES
-----------     -------------------------   ----------
                fixed_sga                       787828
                buffer_cache                  16777216
                log_buffer                      262144
shared pool     KQR L SO                         76800
shared pool     KQR M PO                       1414752
shared pool     KQR M SO                        242688
shared pool     KQR S PO                        157508
shared pool     KQR S SO                           512
shared pool     KTI-UNDO                       1235304
shared pool     sessions                        781324
shared pool     sql area                      11719164
...etc.

597 rows selected
```

This information is also given in the Statspack report (see Chapter 14), along with the starting and ending values over the duration of the Statspack report.

TIP
Accessing V$SGASTAT gives you a detailed breakdown for the Oracle SGA and breaks down all buckets for the Shared Pool allocation.

Finding Initialization Settings in V$PARAMETER

The script in the next listing displays the init.ora parameters for your system. It also provides information on each parameter that identifies whether the current value was the default value (ISDEFAULT=TRUE). It further shows whether the parameter is modifiable with the alter session command, and with the alter system command (ISSYS_MODIFIABLE=IMMEDIATE). These can be modified with the alter session and alter system commands instead of by modifying the init.ora file and shutting down and restarting the instance. The example in this listing displays some of the init.ora parameters that can be modified with one of the alter commands. (IMMEDIATE means it can be modified and it will take effect immediately.) Note that you can use an ALTER command, but for some parameters, such as o7_dictionary_accessibility, you can only use an ALTER SYSTEM . . . SCOPE=SPFILE command to modify it, and *then* you have to bounce the database for it to take effect.

```
select    name, value, isdefault, isses_modifiable,
          issys_modifiable
```

```
from       v$parameter
order by   name;
```

Query of V$PARAMETER

NAME	VALUE	ISDEFAULT	ISSES	ISSYS_MOD
O7_DICTIONARY_ACCESSIBILITY	FALSE	TRUE	FALSE	FALSE
__db_cache_size	16777216	FALSE	FALSE	IMMEDIATE
__shared_pool_size	58720256	FALSE	FALSE	IMMEDIATE
active_instance_count		TRUE	FALSE	FALSE
aq_tm_processes	0	TRUE	FALSE	IMMEDIATE
archive_lag_target	0	TRUE	FALSE	IMMEDIATE
asm_diskgroups		TRUE	FALSE	IMMEDIATE
asm_diskstring		TRUE	FALSE	IMMEDIATE
asm_power_limit	1	TRUE	TRUE	IMMEDIATE

...partial output listing)

Version-dependent columns are also available.

TIP
Query V$PARAMETER and find out the current values for the init.ora parameters. It also shows which init.ora parameters have been changed from their original defaults: ISDEFAULT = FALSE. It also shows which parameters may be changed only for a given session, if ISSES_MODIFIABLE = TRUE. Lastly, it shows which parameters may be changed without shutting down and restarting the database for ISSYS_MODIFIABLE = IMMEDIATE as well as ISSYS_MODIFIABLE = DEFERRED for a parameter that is enforced for all new logins but not currently logged on sessions. If the parameter ISSYS_MODIFIABLE = FALSE, then the instance must be shut down and restarted for the parameter to take effect.

Determining Hit Ratio for Data (V$SYSSTAT)

Query V$SYSSTAT (as shown in the next listing) to see how often your data is being read from memory. It gives the hit ratio for the setting of the database block buffers. This information can help you identify when your system needs more data buffers (DB_CACHE_SIZE) or when a system is not tuned very well. (Both lead to low hit ratios.) Generally, you should ensure the read hit ratio is greater than 95 percent. Increasing the hit ratio on your system from 98 percent to 99 percent could mean performance that is 100+ percent faster (depending on what is causing the disk reads).

```
select 1-(sum(decode(name, 'physical reads', value,0))/
          (sum(decode(name, 'db block gets', value,0)) +
          (sum(decode(name, 'consistent gets', value,0))))))
          "Read Hit Ratio"
from      v$sysstat;
```

```
Read Hit Ratio
--------------
    .996558641
```

In 10g, you can also go directly to AWR information in V$SYSMETRIC:
```
select metric_name, value
from   v$sysmetric
where  metric_name = 'Buffer Cache Hit Ratio';
```

```
METRIC_NAME                                                        VALUE
------------------------------------------------------------- ----------
Buffer Cache Hit Ratio                                               100
```

The hit ratio in this listing is very good, but that does not mean the system is perfectly tuned. A high hit ratio could mean that overly indexed queries are being used. If this hit ratio is well below 95 percent, you may need to increase the init.ora parameter, DB_CACHE_SIZE, or tune some of the queries that are causing disk reads (if possible and efficient to do so). One exception to this is when the distribution of data within the individual blocks is greatly skewed. Despite this possibility, hit ratios below 90 percent almost always involve systems that are poorly tuned, other than those that are built in a Petri dish by someone who has built an extremely rare balance of data within each block (see Chapter 4 for additional information on data hit ratios).

You can also use the new V$DB_CACHE_ADVICE view to help you resize the data cache if you feel it is necessary. The next listing creates a list of values that shows you the effects of larger and smaller data caches:

```
column buffers_for_estimate format 999,999,999 heading 'Buffers'
column estd_physical_read_factor format 999.90 heading 'Estd Phys|Read Fact'
column estd_physical_reads format 999,999,999 heading 'Estd Phys| Reads'

SELECT  size_for_estimate, buffers_for_estimate,
        estd_physical_read_factor, estd_physical_reads
FROM    V$DB_CACHE_ADVICE
WHERE   name = 'DEFAULT'
AND     block_size =
            (SELECT value
             FROM   V$PARAMETER
             WHERE  name = 'db_block_size')
AND     advice_status = 'ON';
```

```
                               Estd Phys    Estd Phys
SIZE_FOR_ESTIMATE     Buffers Read Fact        Reads
----------------- ----------- --------- ------------
                4         501     63.59  243,243,371
                8       1,002     45.65  174,614,755
               12       1,503      2.61    9,965,760
               16       2,004      1.00    3,824,900
               20       2,505       .76    2,909,026
               24       3,006       .57    2,165,817
               28       3,507       .41    1,555,860
               32       4,008       .33    1,253,696
```

Determining Hit Ratio for the Data Dictionary (V$ROWCACHE)

You use the V$ROWCACHE view (as in this next listing) to find how often the data dictionary calls are effectively hitting the memory cache allocated by the SHARED_POOL_SIZE init.ora parameter. This is discussed in Chapter 4 in detail. The only goal here is to review the V$ view access. If the dictionary hit ratio is not adequate, the overall system performance suffers greatly.

```
select    sum(gets), sum(getmisses),(1 - (sum(getmisses) / (sum(gets)
          + sum(getmisses)))) * 100 HitRate
from      v$rowcache;


SUM(GETS)    SUM(GETMISSES)       HITRATE
---------    --------------       ----------
   110673               670    99.3982558


In 10g, you can also go directly to AWR information in V$SYSMETRIC:
select metric_name, value
from    v$sysmetric
where   metric_name = 'Library Cache Hit Ratio';


METRIC_NAME                                                      VALUE
--------------------------------------------------------------- ----------
Library Cache Hit Ratio                                            99
```

The recommended hit ratio is 95 percent or higher. If the hit ratio falls below this percentage, it indicates that the SHARED_POOL_SIZE init.ora parameter may need to be increased. But remember, you saw in the V$SGASTAT view that the shared pool is made up of many pieces, of which this is only one. Note: Environments that make heavy use of public synonyms may struggle to get their dictionary cache hit rate above 75 percent even if the shared pool is huge. This is because Oracle must often check for the existence of non-existent objects.

Determining Hit Ratio for the Shared SQL and PL/SQL (V$LIBRARYCACHE)

Accessing the V$LIBRARYCACHE view shows how well the actual statements (SQL and PL/SQL) are accessing memory. If the SHARED_POOL_SIZE in init.ora is too small, enough room may not be available to store all of the statements into memory. If the shared pool becomes extremely fragmented, large PL/SQL routines may not fit into the shared pool. If statements are not reused effectively, an enlarged shared pool may cause more harm than good (see Chapter 4 for additional details).

There is an execution ratio (pinhitratio) and a reload hit ratio. The recommended hit ratio for pin hits is 95+ percent, and the reload hit ratio should be 99+ percent (less than 1 percent reloads). Reloads occur when a statement has been parsed previously, but the shared pool is usually not large enough to hold it in memory as other statements are parsed. The body of the statement is pushed out of memory (the head is still there); when the statement is again needed, a reload is recorded to reload the body. This could also occur if the execution plan for the statement changes. If either of the hit ratios falls below these percentages, it indicates that the shared pool should be investigated in greater detail. The following listing shows how to query for all of the information discussed:

Query v$librarycache to see if SQL is being reused:
```
select   sum(pins) "Executions", sum(pinhits) "Hits",
         ((sum(pinhits) / sum(pins)) * 100) "PinHitRatio",
         sum(reloads) "Misses", ((sum(pins) / (sum(pins)
         + sum(reloads))) * 100)  "RelHitRatio"
from     v$librarycache;


Executions      Hits PinHitRatio    Misses RelHitRatio
---------- ---------- ----------- ---------- -----------
   7002504   6996247  99.9106462       327  99.9953305
```

Query v$sql_bind_capture to see if binds per SQL statement is greater than 20 (issue):
```
select sql_id, count(*) bind_count
from    v$sql_bind_capture
where   child_number = 0
group  by sql_id
having count(*) > 20
order  by count(*);


SQL_ID        BIND_COUNT
------------- ----------
9qgtwh66xg6nz         21
```

Find the Problem SQL to fix:
```
select sql_text, users_executing, executions, users_opening, buffer_gets
from    v$sqlarea
where   sql_id =  '9qgtwh66xg6nz'
order  by buffer_gets;


SQL_TEXT
--------------------------------------------------------------------------------
USERS_EXECUTING EXECUTIONS USERS_OPENING BUFFER_GETS
--------------- ---------- ------------- -----------
update seg$ set type#=:4,blocks=:5,extents=:6,minexts=:7,maxexts=:8,extsize=:9,e
xtpct=:10,user#=:11,iniexts=:12,lists=decode(:13, 65535, NULL, :13),groups=decod
e(:14, 65535, NULL, :14), cachehint=:15, hwmincr=:16, spare1=DECODE(:17,0,NULL,:
17),scanhint=:18 where ts#=:1 and file#=:2 and block#=:3
              0         90             0         690
```

Query v$sql_bind_capture to see if average binds is greater than 15 (issue):
```
select avg(bind_count) AVG_NUM_BINDS from
      (select sql_id, count(*) bind_count
       from    v$sql_bind_capture
       where   child_number = 0
       group  by sql_id);


AVG_NUM_BINDS
-------------
   3.35471698
```

TIP
Query V$LIBRARYCACHE to see how often your SQL and PL/SQL are being read from memory. The pinhitratio should generally be 95 percent or higher, and the number of reloads should not be greater than 1 percent. Query V$SQL_BIND_CAPTURE to see if binds per SQL is too high and CURSOR_SHARING is needed.

Identifying PL/SQL Objects That Need to Be Kept (Pinned)

Fragmentation that causes several small pieces to be available in the shared pool, and not enough large contiguous pieces, is a common occurrence in the shared pool. The key to eliminating shared pool errors (see Chapters 4 and 13 for more information) is to understand which objects can cause problems. Once you know the potential problem PL/SQL objects, you can then pin this code when the database is started (and the shared pool is completely contiguous). You can query the V$DB_OBJECT_CACHE view to determine PL/SQL that is both large and currently not marked *kept*. This query shows only the current statements in the cache. The example in this listing searches for those objects requiring greater than 100KB.

```
select  name, sharable_mem
from    v$db_object_cache
where   sharable_mem > 100000
and     type in ('PACKAGE', 'PACKAGE BODY',
        'FUNCTION', 'PROCEDURE')
and     kept = 'NO';

NAME                                    SHARABLE_MEM
-----------------------------------     ------------
MGMT_JOB_ENGINE                               238590
DBMS_STATS_INTERNAL                           220939
STANDARD                                      435820
DBMS_RCVMAN                                    354875
WK_CRW                                         183688
DBMS_BACKUP_RESTORE                            258495
DBMS_STATS                                     446886
```

TIP
Query the V$DB_OBJECT_CACHE view to find objects that are not pinned and are also potentially large enough to cause problems.

Finding Problem Queries by Querying V$SQLAREA

V$SQLAREA provides a means of identifying the *potential* problem SQL statements or SQL statements needing optimization to improve overall database optimization by reducing disk access. The disk_reads signify the volume of disk reads that are being performed on the system. This, combined with the executions (disk_reads/executions), returns the SQL statements that have the most disk hits per statement execution. The disk_reads value was set to 100000, but it could be set much larger or smaller on production systems (depending on the database) to reveal only the greater problem statements on your system. Once identified, the top statements should be reviewed and optimized to improve overall performance. Typically, the statement is not using an index or the execution path is forcing the statement not to use the proper indexes.

One potentially misleading part of the query in the following listing is the rds_exec_ratio. This is the number of disk reads divided by the executions. In reality, a statement may be read once using 100 disk reads and then forced out of memory (if memory is insufficient). If it is read again, then it will read 100 disk reads again and the rds_exec_ratio will be 100 (or 100 + 100 reads divided by 2 executions). But if the statement happens to be in memory the second time (memory is sufficient), the disk reads will be zero (the second time) and the rds_exec_ratio will be only 50 (or 100 + 0 divided by 2 executions). Any statement that makes the top of this list is a problem and needs to be tuned—period!

NOTE
The following code was formatted for ease of reading.

```
select      b.username username, a.disk_reads reads,
            a.executions exec, a.disk_reads /decode
            (a.executions, 0, 1,a.executions) rds_exec_ratio,
            a.command_type, a.sql_text Statement
from        v$sqlarea a, dba_users b
where       a.parsing_user_id = b.user_id
and         a.disk_reads      > 100000
order by    a.disk_reads desc;

USERNAME   READS      EXEC   RDS_EXEC_RATIO   STATEMENT
--------   -------    ----   --------------   ----------------------------------
ADHOC1     7281934    1             7281934   select   custno, ordno
                                              from     cust, orders
ADHOC5     4230044    4             1057511   select   ordno
                                              from     orders
                                              where    trunc(ordno) = 721305
ADHOC1     801715     2              499858   select   custno, ordno
                                              from     cust
                                              where    decode(custno,1,6) = 314159
```

The DISK_READS column in the preceding statement can be replaced with the BUFFER_GETS column, to provide information on SQL statements that may not possess the large disk hits (although they usually do) but possess a large number of memory hits (higher than normally desired). These are statements that are using a large amount of memory that is allocated for the data (DB_CACHE_SIZE). The problem is not that the statement is being executed in memory (which is good), but that the statement is hogging a lot of the memory. Many times, this problem is attributable to a SQL statement using an index when it should be doing a full tablescan or a join. These types of SQL statements can also involve a join operation that is forcing the path to use a different index than desired, or using multiple indexes and forcing index merging or volumes of data merging. Remember, the bulk of system performance problems are attributable to poorly written SQL and PL/SQL statements.

TIP
Query the V$SQLAREA to find problem queries (and users).

Finding Out What Users Are Doing and Which Resources They Are Using

Joining V$SESSION and V$SQLTEXT displays the SQL statement that is currently being executed by each session, as shown here. It is extremely useful when a DBA is trying to determine what is happening in the system at a given point in time.

```
select    a.sid, a.username, s.sql_text
from      v$session a, v$sqltext s
where     a.sql_address    = s.address
and       a.sql_hash_value = s.hash_value
order by a.username, a.sid, s.piece;


SID  USERNAME       SQL_TEXT
---  ----------     -----------------------------------------
 11  PLSQL_USER     update s_employee set salary = 10000
  9  SYS            select a.sid, a.username, s.sql_text
  9  SYS            from v$session a, v$sqltext
  9  SYS            where a.sql_address    = s.address
  9  SYS            and a.sql_hash_value   = s.hash_value
  9  SYS            order by a.username, a.sid, s.piece
(...partial output listing)
```

The SQL_TEXT column displays the entire SQL statement, but the statement is stored in the V$SQLTEXT view as a VARCHAR2(64) data type and therefore spans multiple records. The PIECE column is used to order the statement. To view the resources being used by each of the users, simply use the query in the next listing. The goal of this statement is to highlight the physical disk and memory hits for each session. It is very easy to recognize users who are performing a large number of physical disk or memory reads.

```
select    a.username, b.block_gets, b.consistent_gets,
          b.physical_reads, b.block_changes, b.consistent_changes
from      v$session a, v$sess_io b
where     a.sid = b.sid
order by  a.username;
```

USERNAME	BLOCK_GETS	CONSISTENT_GETS	PHYSICAL_READS	BLOCK_ CHANGES	CONSISTENT_CHANGES
PLSQL_USER	39	72	11	53	1
SCOTT	11	53	12	0	0
OXC	14	409	26	0	0
SYSTEM	8340	10197	411	2558	419

TIP
Query V$SESSION, V$SQLTEXT, and V$SESS_IO to find the problem users and what they are executing at a given point in time.

Finding Out Which Objects a User Is Accessing

Querying V$ACCESS can point you to potential problem objects (potentially missing indexes) once you have found the problem user or query on your system. It can also be helpful when you want to modify a particular object and need to know who is using it at a given point in time, as shown here:

```
select a.sid, a.username, b.owner, b.object, b.type
from   v$session a, v$access b
where  a.sid = b.sid;
```

```
SID   USERNAME   OWNER    OBJECT                    TYPE
---   --------   -----    --------------------      -------
  8   SCOTT      SYS      DBMS_APPLICATION_INFO     PACKAGE
  9   SYS        SYS      DBMS_APPLICATION_INFO     PACKAGE
  9   SYS        SYS      X$BH                      TABLE
 10   SYSTEM     PUBLIC   V$ACCESS                  SYNONYM
 10   SYSTEM     PUBLIC   V$SESSION                 SYNONYM
 10   SYSTEM     SYS      DBMS_APPLICATION_INFO     PACKAGE
 10   SYSTEM     SYS      V$ACCESS                  VIEW
 10   SYSTEM     SYS      V$SESSION                 VIEW
 10   SYSTEM     SYS      V_$ACCESS                 VIEW
```

This script displays all objects being accessed, including synonyms, views, and stored source code.

TIP
Query V$ACCESS to find all objects that are being accessed by a user at a given time. This can help to pinpoint problem objects, while also being helpful when modifying a particular object (find out who is accessing it). However, this would be a very expensive operation on a system with a large shared pool and hundreds of users.

Getting Detailed User Information

A method for analyzing user statistics is extremely valuable when a new or updated application module is being tested to determine the overhead. It also provides a window to a user who is having performance problems, because it provides statistics on a variety of areas for each user. In addition, it can serve as a guideline for setting profiles to limit a particular user. The script in this next listing limits the statistics only to areas that have a value (b.value != 0). Note the IMUs are only listed and only exist in 10g.

```
select    a.username, c.name, sum(b.value) value
from      v$session a, v$sesstat b, v$statname c
where     a.sid        = b.sid
and       b.statistic# = c.statistic#
and       b.value      != 0
group by  name, username;
```

Find Out Which Objects a User Is Accessing

```
USERNAME                            NAME                                    VALUE
-----------------------------       ------------------------------     ----------
SYS                                 DB time                                  3690
                                    redo size                             2143640
SYS                                 redo size                               98008
                                    user calls                                 28
SYS                                 user calls                                337
                                    IMU Flushes                                 1
SYS                                 IMU Flushes                                 2
                                    IMU commits                                19
SYS                                 IMU commits                                 1
                                    redo writes                              4443
                                    redo entries                             8728
...etc.
```

Using Indexes

Oracle 9*i* introduced the ability to monitor the use of indexes. This new view signifies whether the index was used but not how often it was used. Indexes that you want to monitor need to be individually turned ON and OFF. You initiate monitoring with the alter index command, and index use is then tracked by querying the V$OBJECT_USAGE view. Here is a description of the V$OBJECT_USAGE view:

```
SQL> desc v$object_usage

Name                      Null?     Type
----------------------    --------  ------------------------------
INDEX_NAME                NOT NULL  VARCHAR2(30)
TABLE_NAME                NOT NULL  VARCHAR2(30)
MONITORING                          VARCHAR2(3)
USED                                VARCHAR2(3)
START_MONITORING                    VARCHAR2(19)
END_MONITORING                      VARCHAR2(19)
```

Before any index is monitored, the view has no records:

```
select   *
from     v$object_usage;

no rows selected
```

You start monitoring on four indexes:

```
alter index HRDT_INDEX1 monitoring usage;
alter index HRDT_INDEX2 monitoring usage;
alter index HRDT_INDEX3 monitoring usage;
alter index HRDT_INDEX4 monitoring usage;
```

The view now shows the four indexes with a start time but no use yet:

```
select index_name, table_name, monitoring, used,
       start_monitoring, end_monitoring
from   v$object_usage;

INDEX_NAME   TABLE_NAME MON USE START_MONITORING    END_MONITORING
-----------  ---------- --- --- ------------------  ------------------
HRDT_INDEX1  HRS_DETAIL YES NO  10/13/2002 03:11:34
HRDT_INDEX2  HRS_DETAIL YES NO  10/13/2002 03:11:38
HRDT_INDEX3  HRS_DETAIL YES NO  10/13/2002 03:11:46
HRDT_INDEX4  HRS_DETAIL YES NO  10/13/2002 03:11:52
```

If you query using HRDT_INDEX1, the view now shows that this index has been used:

```
select index_name, table_name, monitoring, used,
       start_monitoring, end_monitoring
from   v$object_usage;

INDEX_NAME   TABLE_NAME MON USE START_MONITORING    END_MONITORING
-----------  ---------- --- --- ------------------  ------------------
HRDT_INDEX1  HRS_DETAIL YES YES 10/13/2002 03:11:34
HRDT_INDEX2  HRS_DETAIL YES NO  10/13/2002 03:11:38
HRDT_INDEX3  HRS_DETAIL YES NO  10/13/2002 03:11:46
HRDT_INDEX4  HRS_DETAIL YES NO  10/13/2002 03:11:52
```

You end the monitoring on HRDT_INDEX4 and the view now shows an end monitoring time:

```
alter index HRDT_INDEX4 nomonitoring usage;
select index_name, table_name, monitoring, used,
       start_monitoring, end_monitoring
from   v$object_usage;

INDEX_NAME   TABLE_NAME MON USE START_MONITORING    END_MONITORING
-----------  ---------- --- --- ------------------  ------------------
HRDT_INDEX1  HRS_DETAIL YES YES 10/13/2002 03:11:34
HRDT_INDEX2  HRS_DETAIL YES NO  10/13/2002 03:11:38
HRDT_INDEX3  HRS_DETAIL YES NO  10/13/2002 03:11:46
HRDT_INDEX4  HRS_DETAIL NO  NO  10/13/2002 03:11:52 10/13/2002 03:16:01
```

TIP
Use V$OBJECT_USAGE view to find out if indexes are being used.
Perhaps some indexes are not needed.

Identifying Locking Issues

Identifying locking issues is instrumental in locating the user who is waiting for someone or
something else. You can use this strategy to identify users who are currently being locked in the
system. This allows DBAs to ensure whether an Oracle-related process is truly locked or just
running slow. You can also identify the current statement that the locked user(s) are currently
executing. The next listing provides an example of identifying locking issues.

Identifying Locking Issues

NOTE
These statements were not tuned in the previous version of the book.
(Now that's embarrassing!)

```
select     /*+ ordered */ b.username, b.serial#, d.id1, a.sql_text
from       v$lock d, v$session b, v$sqltext a
where      b.lockwait   = d.kaddr
and        a.address    = b.sql_address
and        a.hash_value = b.sql_hash_value;


USERNAME      SERIAL#          ID1   SQL_TEXT
--------   ----------   ----------   ------------------------------------------
AUTHUSER           53       393242   update emp set salary = 5000
```

You also need to identify the user in the system who is causing the problem of locking the
previous user, as shown in this listing. (Usually this is the user/developer who presses
CTRL-ALT-DEL as you approach his or her desk.)

```
select     /*+ ordered */ a.serial#, a.sid, a.username, b.id1, c.sql_text
from       v$lock b, v$session a, v$sqltext c
where      b.id1 in
(select    /*+ ordered */ distinct e.id1
from       v$lock e, v$session d
where      d.lockwait   = e.kaddr)
and        a.sid        = b.sid
and        c.hash_value = a.sql_hash_value
and        b.request    = 0;


SERIAL#   SID   USERNAME      ID1   SQL_TEXT
-------   ---   --------   ------   ------------------------------------------
     18    11   JOHNSON    393242   update authuser.emp set salary=90000
```

JOHNSON will make everyone happy by forgetting a crucial WHERE clause. Unfortunately,
JOHNSON has locked the authorized user of this table.

You can also look at locking in more detail to see exactly what's running and blocking. In
Chapter 9, we look at block-level tuning; there we describe some of these columns and also
perform queries to V$TRANSACTION (which shows all DML [update/insert/delete] transactions
currently running). In the following listing, we can see four transactions all running at the same
time to the same block of information. There is no blocking because the initrans is set to handle
(at least set to 4 ITL slots) all four changes within the same block at the same time. If there was a
problem, the LMODE would have been 0 and the REQUEST would have been 6 (TX6) as in the
third query that follows.

```
Four Users are updating different rows in the same block:
select /*+ ordered */ username, v$lock.sid, trunc(id1/power(2,16)) rbs,
       bitand(id1,to_number('ffff','xxxx'))+0 slot,
       id2 seq, lmode, request
from   v$lock, v$session
where  v$lock.type = 'TX'
and    v$lock.sid = v$session.sid;
```

USERNAME	SID	RBS	SLOT	SEQ	LMODE	REQUEST
SCOTT	146	6	32	85	6	0
SCOTT	150	4	39	21557	6	0
SCOTT	151	5	34	1510	6	0
SCOTT	161	7	24	44	6	0

```
select xid, xidusn, xidslot, xidsqn, status, start_scn
from    v$transaction
order by start_scn;
```

XID	XIDUSN	XIDSLOT	XIDSQN	STATUS	START_SCN
0600200055000000	6	32	85	ACTIVE	16573480
0400270035540000	4	39	21557	ACTIVE	16573506
05002200E6050000	5	34	1510	ACTIVE	16573545
070018002C000000	7	24	44	ACTIVE	16574420

Three Users are trying to update the exact same row:

```
select /*+ ordered */ username, v$lock.sid, trunc(id1/power(2,16)) rbs,
       bitand(id1,to_number('ffff','xxxx'))+0 slot,
       id2 seq, lmode, request
from   v$lock, v$session
where  v$lock.type = 'TX'
and    v$lock.sid = v$session.sid;
```

USERNAME	SID	RBS	SLOT	SEQ	LMODE	REQUEST
SCOTT	146	4	47	21557	0	6
SCOTT	150	4	47	21557	6	0
SCOTT	161	4	47	21557	0	6

```
select xid, xidusn, xidslot, xidsqn, status, start_scn
from    v$transaction
order by start_scn;
```

XID	XIDUSN	XIDSLOT	XIDSQN	STATUS	START_SCN
04002F0035540000	4	47	21557	ACTIVE	16575501

Two Users are blocked:

```
SELECT sid, blocking_session, username, blocking_session_status
FROM   v$session
WHERE  username='SCOTT'
ORDER BY blocking_session;
```

      SID BLOCKING_SESSION USERNAME   BLOCKING_SESSION_STATUS

```
---------- ----------------  ----------  ------------------------
    146              150  SCOTT        VALID
    161              150  SCOTT        VALID
    150                   SCOTT        NO HOLDER
```

Killing the Problem Session

A user may have run something that he or she really didn't want to run, or a problem query may need to be eliminated during business hours and rerun at night. If the operation in the preceding section needed to be aborted, you could execute the statements in the next listing (to find and then kill the session).

```
select username, sid, serial#, program, terminal
from   v$session;

alter system kill session '11,18';

You can't kill your own session though:

alter system kill session '10,4';
*
ERROR at line 1:
ORA-00027: cannot kill current session
```

The order of the parameters is SID, and then SERIAL#. Make sure you DESCribe V$SESSION, because it has many columns that are helpful. In previous versions of Oracle, you could kill the current user session. Thankfully, you can no longer kill your own session accidentally, as just shown in the preceding listing.

TIP
Identify users who are locking others and kill their session (if necessary).

Finding Users with Multiple Sessions

At times, users enjoy using multiple sessions to accomplish several tasks at once, and this can be a problem. The problem may also be a developer who has built a poor application that begins spawning multiple processes. Either of these could degrade the system's overall performance. The usernames that are null are background processes. The query to the V$SESSION view in this listing displays these types of issues:

```
select    username, count(*)
from      v$session
group by  username;

USERNAME        COUNT(*)
----------      --------
PLSQL_USER             1
```

```
SCOTT               1
JOHNSON             9
SYS                 4
SYSTEM              1
                   14
```

On certain OS platforms, if a user starts a session and reboots his or her PC, oftentimes the process will continue in the background as the user starts another session. If the user is running multiple reports on multiple terminals or PCs, this could also affect the system's overall performance.

NOTE
The rows in V$SESSION that have NULL values for username are the Oracle background processes.

TIP
Identify users who are holding multiple sessions and determine whether it is an administrative problem (the user is using multiple terminals) or a system problem (sessions are not being cleaned or are spawning runaway processes).

Querying for Current Profiles

Profiles are limits on a given schema (user). To view the profiles for your system, execute the query shown here.

```
select     substr(profile,1,10) Profile,
           substr(resource_name,1,30) "Resource Name",
           substr(limit,1,10) Limit
from       dba_profiles
group by   substr(profile,1,10), substr(resource_name,1,30),
           substr(limit,1,10);
```

```
PROFILE      Resource Name                    LIMIT
----------   ------------------------------   ----------
DEFAULT      IDLE_TIME                        UNLIMITED
DEFAULT      PRIVATE_SGA                      UNLIMITED
DEFAULT      CONNECT_TIME                     UNLIMITED
DEFAULT      CPU_PER_CALL                     UNLIMITED
DEFAULT      COMPOSITE_LIMIT                  UNLIMITED
DEFAULT      CPU_PER_SESSION                  UNLIMITED
DEFAULT      SESSIONS_PER_USER                UNLIMITED
DEFAULT      PASSWORD_LIFE_TIME               UNLIMITED
DEFAULT      PASSWORD_LOCK_TIME               UNLIMITED
DEFAULT      PASSWORD_REUSE_MAX               UNLIMITED
DEFAULT      PASSWORD_GRACE_TIME              UNLIMITED
DEFAULT      PASSWORD_REUSE_TIME              UNLIMITED
DEFAULT      FAILED_LOGIN_ATTEMPTS            10
DEFAULT      LOGICAL_READS_PER_CALL           UNLIMITED
DEFAULT      PASSWORD_VERIFY_FUNCTION         NULL
```

```
DEFAULT    LOGICAL_READS_PER_SESSION       UNLIMITED
MONITORING IDLE_TIME                       DEFAULT
MONITORING PRIVATE_SGA                     DEFAULT
MONITORING CONNECT_TIME                    DEFAULT
MONITORING CPU_PER_CALL                    DEFAULT
MONITORING COMPOSITE_LIMIT                 DEFAULT
MONITORING CPU_PER_SESSION                 DEFAULT
MONITORING SESSIONS_PER_USER               DEFAULT
MONITORING PASSWORD_LIFE_TIME              DEFAULT
MONITORING PASSWORD_LOCK_TIME              DEFAULT
MONITORING PASSWORD_REUSE_MAX              DEFAULT
MONITORING PASSWORD_GRACE_TIME             DEFAULT
MONITORING PASSWORD_REUSE_TIME             DEFAULT
MONITORING FAILED_LOGIN_ATTEMPTS           UNLIMITED
MONITORING LOGICAL_READS_PER_CALL          DEFAULT
MONITORING PASSWORD_VERIFY_FUNCTION        DEFAULT
MONITORING LOGICAL_READS_PER_SESSION       DEFAULT

32 rows selected.
```

Finding Disk I/O Issues

The views V$DATAFILE, V$FILESTAT, and DBA_DATA_FILES provide file I/O activity across all datafiles and disks of your database. Ideally, the physical reads and writes should be distributed equally. If the system is not configured properly, overall performance suffers. The script in this next listing identifies the actual distribution and makes it easy to identify where an imbalance exists. Chapter 3 looks at this topic in great detail; this section just shows the quick-hit query to get a baseline.

```
select    a.file#, a.name, a.status, a.bytes,
          b.phyrds, b.phywrts
from      v$datafile a, v$filestat b
where     a.file# = b.file#;
```

The queries in the following listings provide an improved formatted report for file and data distribution issues. The first listing gets the data file I/O, and the second listing gets the disk I/O:

```
Set TrimSpool On
Set Line      142
Set Pages     57
Set NewPage   0
Set FeedBack Off
Set Verify    Off
Set Term      On
TTitle        Off
BTitle        Off
Clear Breaks
Break On Tablespace_Name
Column TableSpace_Name For A12     Head "Tablespace"
Column Name     For A45            Head "File Name"
Column Total    For 999,999,990    Head "Total"
Column Phyrds   For 999,999,990    Head "Physical|Reads  "
```

```
Column Phywrts  For 999,999,990    Head "Physical| Writes "
Column Phyblkrd For 999,999,990    Head "Physical |Block Reads"
Column Phyblkwrt For 999,999,990   Head "Physical |Block Writes"
Column Avg_Rd_Time  For 90.9999999 Head "Average |Read Time|Per Block"
Column Avg_Wrt_Time For 90.9999999 Head "Average |Write Time|Per Block"
Column Instance         New_Value _Instance   NoPrint
Column Today            New_Value _Date       NoPrint
select   Global_Name Instance, To_Char(SysDate, 'FXDay, Month DD, YYYY HH:MI') Today
from     Global_Name;
TTitle On
TTitle Left 'Date Run: ' _Date Skip 1-

Center 'Data File I/O' Skip 1 -
     Center 'Instance Name: ' _Instance Skip 1

select   C.TableSpace_Name, B.Name, A.Phyblkrd +
         A.Phyblkwrt Total, A.Phyrds, A.Phywrts,
         A.Phyblkrd, A.Phyblkwrt
from     V$FileStat A, V$DataFile B, Sys.DBA_Data_Files C
where    B.File# = A.File#
and      B.File# = C.File_Id
order by TableSpace_Name, A.File#
/

select object_name, statistic_name, value
from v$segment_statistics
where value > 100000
order by value;

OBJECT_NAME   STATISTIC_NAME    VALUE
-----------------------------------------
ORDERS        space allocated   96551
ORDERS        space allocated   134181
ORDERS        logical reads     140976
ORDER_LINES   db block changes  183600
```

This second listing gets the disk I/O:

```
Column TableSpace_Name For A12     Head "Tablespace"
Column Total       For 9,999,999,990 Head "Total"
Column Phyrds      For 9,999,999,990 Head "Physical|Reads   "
Column Phywrts     For 9,999,999,990 Head "Physical| Writes "
Column Phyblkrd    For 9,999,999,990 Head "Physical |Block Reads"
Column Phyblkwrt   For 9,999,999,990 Head "Physical |Block Writes"
Column Avg_Rd_Time    For 9,999,990.9999   Head "Average |Read Time|Per Block"
Column Avg_Wrt_Time   For 9,999,990.9999   Head "Average |Write Time|Per Block"
Clear Breaks
Break on Disk Skip 1
Compute Sum Of Total On Disk
Compute Sum Of Phyrds On Disk
Compute Sum Of Phywrts On Disk
Compute Sum Of Phyblkrd On Disk
Compute Sum Of Phyblkwrt On Disk
TTitle Left 'Date Run: ' _Date Skip 1-
     Center 'Disk I/O' Skip 1 -
     Center 'Instance Name: ' _Instance Skip 2

select    SubStr(B.Name, 1, 13) Disk, C.TableSpace_Name,
```

```
              A.Phyblkrd + A.Phyblkwrt Total, A.Phyrds, A.Phywrts,
              A.Phyblkrd, A.Phyblkwrt, ((A.ReadTim /
              Decode(A.Phyrds,0,1,A.Phyblkrd))/100) Avg_Rd_Time,
              ((A.WriteTim / Decode(A.PhyWrts,0,1,A.PhyblkWrt)) /
              100) Avg_Wrt_Time
from          V$FileStat A, V$DataFile B, Sys.DBA_Data_Files C
where         B.File# = A.File#
and           B.File# = C.File_Id
order by      Disk,C.Tablespace_Name, A.File#
/

Set FeedBack On
Set Verify   On
Set Term     On
Ttitle       Off
Btitle       Off
```

TIP
The views V$DATAFILE, V$FILESTAT, and DBA_DATA_FILES provide file I/O activity across all datafiles and disks of your database. Ensure that both datafiles and disks are properly balanced for optimal performance.

Finding Rollback Segment Contention

This helpful query shows the actual waits on a rollback segment. You can display rollback information (including automatic undo). Shrinks and wraps can also be queried from the views shown here.

NOTE
Automatic or system-managed UNDO is used in this database.

```
select   a.name, b.extents, b.rssize, b.xacts,
         b.waits, b.gets, optsize, status
from     v$rollname a, v$rollstat b
where    a.usn = b.usn;
```

File Name	EXTENTS	RSSIZE	XACTS	WAITS	GETS	OPTSIZE	STATUS
_SYSSMU	6	385024	0	0	164		ONLINE
_SYSSMU1$	6	4317184	0	0	3947		ONLINE
_SYSSMU2$	6	3334144	0	0	2985		ONLINE
_SYSSMU3$	7	450560	1	0	204		ONLINE
_SYSSMU4$	4	253952	0	0	244		ONLINE
_SYSSMU5$	17	2088960	0	1	5426		ONLINE
_SYSSMU6$	7	450560	0	0	1070		ONLINE
_SYSSMU7$	3	188416	0	0	275		ONLINE
_SYSSMU8$	2	122880	0	0	182		ONLINE
_SYSSMU9$	2	122880	0	0	182		ONLINE
_SYSSMU10$	2	122880	0	0	182		ONLINE

TIP

Querying V$ROLLNAME, V$ROLLSTAT, and V$TRANSACTION can provide information on how users are using rollback segments and your UNDO Tablespace. Generally, more than one person should not be accessing a rollback segment at one time (although this is allowed).

NOTE

If using Automatic Undo Management, the previous query is really not needed.

The query in this listing shows the waits on the entire system as a whole.

```
Set TrimSpool On
Set NewPage    0
Set Pages     57
Set Line      132
Set FeedBack Off
Set Verify    Off
Set Term      On
TTitle        Off
BTitle        Off
Clear Breaks
Column Event      For A40 Heading "Wait Event"
Column Total_Waits For 999,999,990 Head "Total Number| Of Waits  "
Column Total_Timeouts For 999,999,990 Head "Total Number|Of TimeOuts"
Column Tot_Time    For 999,999,990 Head "Total Time|Waited  "
Column Avg_Time    For  99,990.999 Head "Average Time|Per Wait  "
Column Instance New_Value _Instance    NoPrint
Column Today    New_Value _Date        NoPrint

select    Global_Name Instance, To_Char(SysDate,
          'FXDay DD, YYYY HH:MI') Today
from      Global_Name;

TTitle On
TTitle Left 'Date Run: ' _Date Skip 1-
       Center 'System Wide Wait Events' Skip 1 -
       Center 'Instance Name: ' _Instance Skip 2

select    event, total_waits, total_timeouts,
          (time_waited / 100)  tot_time, (average_wait / 100)
          Avg_time
from      v$system_event
order by  total_waits desc
/

Date Run: Friday    01, 2006 09:24
                                    System Wide Wait Events
                                      Instance Name: ORCL

                                  Total Number Total Number   Total Time Average
Time
Wait Event                          Of Waits    Of TimeOuts    Waited   Per Wait
-------------------------------------- ------------ ------------ ------------ ---------
db file sequential read             2,376,513          0        30,776
```

```
0.010
db file scattered read               136,602          0        6,069
0.040
rdbms ipc message                    103,301     99,481      276,659
2.680
latch: redo writing                   57,488          0            0
0.000
...etc...
```

Determining Whether Freelists Are Sufficient

If you have multiple processes doing large inserts, using the default value of 1 for freelists (list
of free database blocks) may not be enough. If you are not using Automatic Space Segment
Management (ASSM), you may need to increase freelists and/or freelist groups (see Chapter 14
for additional information). To check if the freelist groups storage parameter is sufficient, run the
report shown in this listing:

```
Set TrimSpool On
Set Line 132
Set Pages 57
Set NewPage  0
Set FeedBack Off
Set Verify Off
Set Term Off
TTitle Off
BTitle Off

Column Pct Format 990.99 Heading "% Of      |Free List Waits"
Column Instance New_Value _Instance NoPrint
Column Today   New_Value _Date NoPrint

select    Global_Name Instance, To_Char
          (SysDate, 'FXDay DD, YYYY HH:MI') Today
from      Global_Name;

TTitle On
TTitle Left 'Date Run: ' _Date Skip 1-
       Center 'Free list Contention' Skip 1 -
       Center 'If Percentage is Greater than 1%' Skip 1 -
       Center 'Consider increasing the number of free lists' Skip 1 -
       Center 'Instance Name: ' _Instance

select    ((A.Count / (B.Value + C.Value)) * 100) Pct
from      V$WaitStat A, V$SysStat B, V$SysStat C
where     A.Class = 'free list'
and       B.Statistic# = (select  Statistic#
                          from    V$StatName
                          where   Name = 'db block gets')
and       C.Statistic# = (select  Statistic#
                          from    V$StatName
                          where   Name = 'consistent gets')
/

Date Run: Friday    01, 2006 09:26
                                      Free list Contention
                              If Percentage is Greater than 1%
                          Consider increasing the number of free lists
                                      Instance Name: ORCL
```

```
       % Of
Free List Waits
---------------
          0.00
(of course... I'm using ASSM)
```

If the activity rate is greater than 1 percent, then freelist groups need to be increased.

TIP
*Ensure that freelists and freelist groups are sufficient when using
multiple processes to do inserts. The default storage value for freelists
is only 1. If you use ASSM, Oracle manages this for you, but a
high-transaction environment should be well tested prior to employing
ASSM. Nonetheless, it is generally good practice to use ASSM.*

Checking Privileges and Roles

This section contains several V$ scripts that show various security privileges. The titles of each
script in the following listings give you a quick idea of what it would retrieve for you. The output
can be *very large,* depending on your system, so run with caution.

Object-level privileges that have been granted by username

```
select b.owner || '.' || b.table_name obj,
       b.privilege what_granted, b.grantable,
       a.username
from   sys.dba_users a, sys.dba_tab_privs b
where  a.username = b.grantee
order by 1,2,3;
```

Object-level privileges that have been granted by grantee

```
Select   owner || '.' || table_name obj,
         privilege what_granted, grantable, grantee
from     sys.dba_tab_privs
where    not exists
         (select 'x'
         from sys.dba_users
         where  username = grantee)
order by 1,2,3;
```

System-level grants by username

```
select   b.privilege what_granted,
         b.admin_option, a.username
from     sys.dba_users a, sys.dba_sys_privs b
where    a.username = b.grantee
order by 1,2;
```

System-level grants by grantee

```
select    privilege what_granted,
          admin_option, grantee
from      sys.dba_sys_privs
where     not exists
          (select  'x' from sys.dba_users
           where username = grantee)
order by 1,2;
```

Roles granted by username

```
select    b.granted_role ||
          decode(admin_option, 'YES',
        ' (With Admin Option)',
          null) what_granted, a.username
from      sys.dba_users a, sys.dba_role_privs b
where     a.username = b.grantee
order by  1;
```

Roles granted by grantee

```
select    granted_role  ||
          decode(admin_option, 'YES',
        ' (With Admin Option)', null) what_granted,
          grantee
from      sys.dba_role_privs
where     not exists
          (select 'x'
           from sys.dba_users
           where username = grantee)
order by 1;
```

Usernames with corresponding granted privileges

```
select a.username,

 b.granted_role || decode(admin_option,'YES',
    ' (With Admin Option)',null) what_granted
from   sys.dba_users a, sys.dba_role_privs b
where  a.username = b.grantee

UNION

select a.username,

b.privilege || decode(admin_option,'YES',
    ' (With Admin Option)', null) what_granted
from   sys.dba_users a, sys.dba_sys_privs b
where  a.username = b.grantee
```

```
UNION

select   a.username,
         b.table_name || ' - ' || b.privilege
         || decode(grantable,'YES',
      ' (With Grant Option)',null) what_granted
from     sys.dba_users a, sys.dba_tab_privs b
where    a.username = b.grantee
order by 1;
```

TIP
*Document the privileges that you have for your system so that you
can be ready for any type of security situation.*

Usernames with corresponding profile, default tablespace, and temporary tablespace

```
Select   username, profile, default_tablespace,
         temporary_tablespace, created
from     sys.dba_users
order by username;
```

Wait Events V$ Views

This section contains several V$ scripts that show wait events. Personally, I prefer using the
STATSPACK Report, the AWR Report, or the Enterprise Manager to find wait events. That said,
here are some nice views to look at wait events. Several new views have been added for Oracle
10gR2, but the *best* thing is that everything you found in V$SESSION_WAIT is now in V$SESSION.

Who is waiting right now – Query V$SESSION_WAIT / V$SESSION

```
select event, sum(decode(wait_time,0,1,0)) "Waiting Now",
       sum(decode(wait_time,0,0,1)) "Previous Waits",
       count(*) "Total"
from v$session_wait
group by event
order by count(*);


WAIT_TIME = 0 means that it's waiting
WAIT_TIME > 0 means that it previously waited this many ms
```

EVENT	Waiting Now	Previous Waits	Total
db file sequential read	0	1	1
db file scattered read	2	0	2
latch free	0	1	1
enqueue	2	0	2
SQL*Net message from client	0	254	480

```
...
select event, sum(decode(wait_time,0,1,0)) "Waiting Now",
       sum(decode(wait_time,0,0,1)) "Previous Waits",
       count(*) "Total"
from v$session
group by event
order by count(*);


EVENT                       Waiting Now      Previous Waits     Total
-------------------------   ------------     --------------     --------
db file sequential read     0                1                  1
db file scattered read      2                0                  2
latch free                  0                1                  1
enqueue                     2                0                  2
SQL*Net message from client 0                254                480
...
```

Who is waiting right now; SPECIFIC Waits – Query V$SESSION_WAIT

```
SELECT /*+ ordered */ sid, event, owner, segment_name, segment_type,p1,p2,p3
FROM    v$session_wait sw, dba_extents de
WHERE   de.file_id = sw.p1
AND     sw.p2 between de.block_id and de.block_id+de.blocks - 1
AND     (event = 'buffer busy waits' OR event = 'write complete waits')
AND     p1 IS NOT null
ORDER BY event,sid;
```

Who is waiting – Last 10 Waits – Query V$SESSION_WAIT_HISTORY

```
SELECT /*+ ordered */ sid, event, owner, segment_name, segment_type,p1,p2,p3
FROM    v$session_wait_history sw, dba_extents de
WHERE   de.file_id = sw.p1
AND     sw.p2 between de.block_id and de.block_id+de.blocks - 1
AND     (event = 'buffer busy waits' OR event = 'write complete waits')
AND     p1 IS NOT null
ORDER BY event,sid;
```

Finding what P1, P2, P3 stand for – Query V$EVENT_NAME

```
col name for a20
col p1 for a10
col p2 for a10
col p3 for a10
select event#,name,parameter1 p1,parameter2 p2,parameter3 p3
from    v$event_name
where   name in ('buffer busy waits', 'write complete waits');


EVENT#          NAME                   P1           P2          P3
-------------   --------------------   ----------   ---------   ----------
```

```
                  143 write complete waits   file#        block#
                  145 buffer busy waits      file#        block#        id
```

All waits since the session started – Query V$SESSION_EVENT

```
select  sid, event, total_waits, time_waited, event_id
from    v$session_event
where   time_waited > 0
order   by time_waited;
```

```
SID       EVENT                                TOTAL_WAITS TIME_WAITED
--------- ------------------------------------ ----------- -----------
      159 process startup                                2           1
      167 latch: redo allocation                         4           1
      168 log buffer space                               2           3
      166 control file single write                      5           4
...
```

All SESSION waits by Class – Query V$SESSION_WAIT_CLASS

```
select  sid, wait_class, total_waits
from    v$session_wait_class;
```

```
    SID WAIT_CLASS           TOTAL_WAITS
--------- -------------------- -----------
    168 Other                          2
    168 Concurrency                    1
    168 Idle                       12825
    168 User I/O                      12
    168 System I/O                  4448
    169 Other                          1
    169 Idle                       12812
    170 Idle                       13527
```

ALL waits since the system started – Query V$SYSTEM_EVENT

```
select  event, total_waits, time_waited, event_id
from    v$system_event
where   time_waited > 0
order   by time_waited;
```

```
EVENT                               TOTAL_WAITS TIME_WAITED    EVENT_ID
----------------------------------- ----------- ----------- ----------
enq: TX - row lock contention              1196      366837  310662678
enq: TM - contention                        170       52074  668627480
db file sequential read                   17387       31630 2652584166
control file parallel write               12961       23117 4078387448
db file scattered read                     4706       15762  506183215
class slave wait                             20       10246 1055154682
```

SYSTEM waits by Class – Query V$SYSTEM_WAIT_CLASS

Wait Events V$ Views

```
select wait_class, total_waits
from   v$system_wait_class
order  by total_waits desc;

WAIT_CLASS           TOTAL_WAITS
-------------------- -----------
Idle                      161896
Other                      65308
System I/O                 24339
User I/O                   22227
Application                 1404
Commit                       524
Network                      522
Concurrency                  221
Configuration                 55
...
```

SYSTEM waits by Class – Query V$ACTIVE_SESSION_HISTORY

```
-- In the query below, the highest count session is leader in non-idle wait events.

select session_id,count(1)
from   v$active_session_history
group  by session_id
order by 2;

-- In the query below, find the SQL for the leader in non-idle wait events.

select c.sql_id, a.sql_text
from v$sql a, (select   sql_id,count(1)
                        from v$active_session_history b where sql_id is not null
                        group by sql_id
                        order by 2 desc) c
where rownum <= 5
order by rownum;
```

TIP
In 10g, all wait event columns that are in V$SESSION_WAIT are now in V$SESSION. So make sure you query V$SESSION for wait information since it's a faster view. V$ACTIVE_SESSION_HISTORY (ASH) rolls many of the great statistics into one view as well as one report (ASH Report).

Some of the Major V$ View Categories

The views in this section are categorized according to their primary function. Not all are listed (please see Appendix B for a complete listing with the V$ views complete with X$ table queries). You will often need to join one category to another category to retrieve the desired information. The V$ views can be queried the same as any other Oracle view, but keep in mind that the information in these tables changes rapidly. You can insert the information from the V$ views into a precreated table to allow for the compilation of data over a period of time, to be analyzed later or to build statistical reports and alerts based on different conditions in your database.

The V$ view (and X$ table) information is used by most DBA monitoring tools on the market today. Querying this database information without a DBA monitoring tool requires that you have an in-depth understanding of the information stored in each view and how to query the view properly. Table 12-1 contains a list of V$ views categorized according to their primary function. The views are listed in categories related to the operation that they monitor. This list is not exhaustive. It contains only the most commonly used views. Some views have changed from version to version of Oracle. This is the information that is contained on the TUSC V$ Poster.

Category	Description and Associated V$ Views
Advisors	Information related to cache advisors **V$ Views:** VPGA_TARGET_ADVICE, VPGA_TARGET_ADVICE_HISTOGRAM, V$MTTR_TARGET_ADVICE, V$PX_BUFFER_ADVICE, VDB_CACHE_ADVICE, VSHARED_POOL_ADVICE, V$JAVA_POOL_ADVICE, V$STREAMS_POOL_ADVICE (10.2), V$SGA_TARGET_ADVICE (10.2), and V$ADVISOR_PROGRESS (10.2)
ASM	V$ASM_ALIAS (10.1), V$ASM_CLIENT(10.1), V$ASM_DISK(10.1), V$ASM_DISK_STAT(10.2), V$ASM_DISKGROUP(10.1), V$ASM_DISKGROUP_STAT(10.2), V$ASM_FILE(10.1), V$ASM_OPERATION(10.1), V$ASM_TEMPLATE(10.1)
Backup/recovery	Information related to database backups and recovery, including last backup, archive logs, state of files for backup, and recovery **V$ Views:** V$ARCHIVE, V$ARCHIVED_LOG, V$ARCHIVE_DEST, V$ARCHIVE_DEST_STATUS , V$ARCHIVE_GAP , V$ARCHIVE_PROCESSES, V$BACKUP, V$BACKUP_ASYNC_IO, V$BACKUP_CORRUPTION, V$BACKUP_DATAFILE, V$BACKUP_DEVICE, V$BACKUP_PIECE, V$BACKUP_REDOLOG, V$BACKUP_SET, V$BACKUP_SYNC_IO, V$BLOCK_CHANGE_TRACKING, V$COPY_CORRUPTION, V$DATABASE_BLOCK_CORRUPTION, V$DATABASE_INCARNATION, V$DATAFILE_COPY, V$DELETED_OBJECT, V$FAST_START_SERVERS, V$FAST_START_TRANSACTIONS, V$INSTANCE_RECOVERY, V$MTTR_TARGET_ADVICE, V$PROXY_ARCHIVEDLOG, V$PROXY_DATAFILE, V$RMAN_CONFIGURATION , V$RECOVERY_FILE_STATUS, V$RECOVERY_LOG, V$RECOVERY_PROGRESS, V$RECOVERY_STATUS, V$RECOVER_FILE, V$BACKUP_ARCHIVELOG_DETAILS(10.2), V$BACKUP_ARCHIVELOG_SUMMARY(10.2), V$BACKUP_CONTROLFILE_DETAILS(10.2), V$BACKUP_CONTROLFILE_SUMMARY(10.2), V$BACKUP_COPY_DETAILS(10.2), V$BACKUP_COPY_SUMMARY(10.2), V$BACKUP_FILES(10.1), V$BACKUP_PIECE_DETAILS(10.2), V$BACKUP_SET_DETAILS(10.2), V$BACKUP_SET_SUMMARY(10.2), V$BACKUP_SPFILE, V$BACKUP_SPFILE_DETAILS(10.2), V$BACKUP_SPFILE_SUMMARY(10.2), V$DATAFILE_HEADER, V$FLASH_RECOVERY_AREA_USAGE(10.2), V$FLASHBACK_DATABASE_LOG(10.1), V$FLASHBACK_DATABASE_STAT(10.1), V$OBSOLETE_BACKUP_FILES, V$OFFLINE_RANGE, V$PROXY_ARCHIVELOG_DETAILS(10.2), V$PROXY_ARCHIVELOG_SUMMARY(10.2), V$PROXY_COPY_DETAILS(10.2), V$PROXY_COPY_SUMMARY(10.2), V$RECOVERY_FILE_DEST(10,1), V$RESTORE_POINT(10.2), V$RMAN_BACKUP_JOB_DETAILS(10.2), V$RMAN_BACKUP_SUBJOB_DETAILS(10.2), V$RMAN_BACKUP_TYPE(10.2), V$RMAN_ENCRYPTION_ALGORITHMS(10.2), V$RMAN_OUTPUT(10.1), V$RMAN_STATUS(10.1), V$UNUSABLE_BACKUPFILE_DETAILS(10.2)

TABLE 12-1. *V$ Views Categories*

Category	Description and Associated V$ Views
Caches	Information related to the various caches, including objects, library, cursors, and the dictionary **V$ Views:** V$ACCESS, V$BUFFER_POOL, V$BUFFER_POOL_STATISTICS, VDB_CACHE_ADVICE, VDB_OBJECT_CACHE, V$JAVA_POOL_ADVICE, V$LIBRARYCACHE, V$LIBRARY_CACHE_MEMORY, V$PGASTAT, VPGA_TARGET_ADVICE, VPGA_TARGET_ADVICE_HISTOGRAM, V$ROWCACHE, V$ROWCACHE_PARENT, V$ROWCACHE_SUBORDINATE, V$SESSION_CURSOR_CACHE, VSGA, VSGASTAT, V$SGA_CURRENT_RESIZE_OPS, V$SGA_DYNAMIC_COMPONENTS, V$SGA_DYNAMIC_FREE_MEMORY, VSGA_RESIZE_OPS, VSGAINFO, V$SHARED_POOL_ADVICE, V$SHARED_POOL_RESERVED, V$SYSTEM_CURSOR_CACHE, V$SUBCACHE, V$JAVA_LIBRARY_CACHE_MEMORY(10.1), V$PROCESS_MEMORY(10.2), V$SGA_TARGET_ADVICE(10.2)
Cache Fusion/RAC	V$ACTIVE_INSTANCES, V$BH, V$CLUSTER_INTERCONNECTS(10.2), V$CONFIGURED_INTERCONNECTS(10.2), VCR_BLOCK_SERVER, VCURRENT_BLOCK_SERVER(10.1), V$GC_ELEMENT, VGCSHVMASTER_INFO, V$GCSPFMASTER_INFO, V$GES_BLOCKING_ENQUEUE, V$GES_CONVERT_LOCAL, V$GES_CONVERT_REMOTE, V$GES_ENQUEUE, V$GES_LATCH, V$GES_RESOURCE, V$GES_STATISTICS, V$HVMASTER_INFO, V$INSTANCE_CACHE_TRANSFER, V$RESOURCE_LIMIT
Control files	Information related to instance control files **V$ Views:** V$CONTROLFILE, V$CONTROLFILE_RECORD_SECTION
Cursors/SQL statements	Information related to cursors and SQL statements, including the open cursors, statistics, and actual SQL text **V$ Views:** V$OPEN_CURSOR, V$SQL, V$SQLAREA, V$SQLTEXT, V$SQLTEXT_WITH_NEWLINES, V$SQL_BIND_DATA, V$SQL_BIND_METADATA, V$SQL_CURSOR, V$SQL_OPTIMIZER_ENV, V$SQL_PLAN, V$SQL_PLAN_STATISTICS, V$SQL_PLAN_STATISTICS_ALL, V$SQL_REDIRECTION, V$SESSION_CURSOR_CACHE, VSQL_SHARED_CURSOR, VSQL_SHARED_MEMORY, V$SQL_WORKAREA, V$SQL_WORKAREA_ACTIVE, V$SQL_WORKAREA_HISTOGRAM, V$SYSTEM_CURSOR_CACHE V$MUTEX_SLEEP(10.2), V$MUTEX_SLEEP_HISTORY(10.2) (for those dubious shared latches), V$SQL_BIND_CAPTURE(10.1), V$SQL_JOIN_FILTER(10.2), V$SQL_AREA_PLAN_HASH(10.2), V$SQLSTATS(10.2), V$SYS_OPTIMIZER_ENV(10.1), V$VPD_POLICY
Database instances	Information related to the actual database instance **V$ Views:** V$ACTIVE_INSTANCES, V$BGPROCESS, V$DATABASE, V$INSTANCE, V$PROCESS, V$SGA, V$SGASTAT, V$BLOCKING_QUIESCE(10.2), V$CLIENT_STATS(10.1) **RAC Views:** VBH, VACTIVE_INSTANCES
Direct Path Operations	Information related to the SQL*Loader direct load option **V$ Views:** V$LOADISTAT, V$LOADPSTAT
Distributed/Heterogeneous Services	**V$ Views:** V$DBLINK, V$GLOBAL_TRANSACTION, V$GLOBAL_BLOCKED_LOCKS, V$HS_AGENT, V$HS_PARAMETER, V$HS_SESSION
Fixed view	Information related to the v$ tables themselves **V$ Views:** V$FIXED_TABLE, V$FIXED_VIEW_DEFINITION, V$INDEXED_FIXED_COLUMN
General	General information related to various system information **V$ Views:** V$DBPIPES, V$CONTEXT, V$GLOBALCONTEXT, V$LICENSE, V$OPTION, V$RESERVED_WORDS, V$TIMER, V$TIMEZONE_NAMES, V$TYPE_SIZE, V$_SEQUENCES, and V$VERSION. V$DB_TRANSPORTABLE_PLATFORM(10.2), V$TRANSPORTABLE_PLATFORM(10.1), and V$SCHEDULER_RUNNING_JOBS(10.2)

TABLE 12-1. *V$ Views Categories* (continued)

Category	Description and Associated V$ Views
I/O	Information related to I/O, including files and statistics **V$ Views:** V$DBFILE, V$FILESTAT, V$WAITSTAT, V$TEMPSTAT, V$FILE_HISTOGRAM(10.1), V$FILEMETRIC(10.1), V$FILEMETRIC_HISTORY(10.1), V$SYSAUX_OCCUPANTS(10.1). V$TABLESPACE, V$TEMP_HISTOGRAM(10.1), V$TEMP_SPACE_HEADER, V$TEMPFILE, V$TEMPSEG_USAGE
Latches/locks	Information related to latches and locks **V$ Views:** V$ENQUEUE_LOCK, V$ENQUEUE_STAT, V$EVENT_NAME, V$FILE_CACHE_TRANSFER, V$GLOBAL_BLOCKED_LOCKS, V$LATCH, V$LATCHHOLDER, V$LATCHNAME, V$LATCH_CHILDREN, V$LATCH_MISSES, V$LATCH_PARENT, V$LOCK, V$LOCKED_OBJECT, V$RESOURCE, V$RESOURCE_LIMIT, V$TRANSACTION_ENQUEUE, V$_LOCK, V$_LOCK1, V$ENQUEUE_STATISTICS. **RAC Views:** VCR_BLOCK_SERVER, VGCSHVMASTER_INFO, V$GCSPFMASTER_INFO, V$GC_ELEMENT, V$GES_BLOCKING_ENQUEUE, V$GES_ENQUEUE, V$HVMASTER_INFO, V$GES_LATCH, V$GES_RESOURCES
Log Miner	Information related to Log Miner **V$ Views:** V$LOGMNR_CALLBACK, V$LOGMNR_CONTENTS, V$LOGMNR_DICTIONARY, V$LOGMNR_LATCH, V$LOGMNR_LOGFILE, V$LOGMNR_LOGS, V$LOGMNR_PARAMETERS, V$LOGMNR_PROCESS, V$LOGMNR_REGION, V$LOGMNR_SESSION, V$LOGMNR_STATS, V$LOGMNR_TRANSACTION, V$LOGMNR_DICTIONARY_LOAD(10.2)
Metrics	Information related to Metrics (ALL New in 10*g*!) **V$ Views:** V$METRICNAME, V$SERVICEMETRIC, V$EVENTMETRIC, V$FILEMETRIC, V$FILEMETRIC_HISTORY, V$SERVICEMETRIC_HISTORY, V$SESSMETRIC, V$SYSMETRIC, V$SYSMETRIC_HISTORY, V$SYSMETRIC_SUMMARY, V$THRESHOLD_TYPES, V$WAITCLASSMETRIC, V$WAITCLASSMETRIC_HISTORY
Multithreaded/ shared servers	Information related to multithreaded and parallel servers, including connections, queues, dispatchers, and shared servers **V$ Views:** V$CIRCUIT, V$DISPATCHER, V$DISPATCHER_RATE, V$QUEUE, V$QUEUEING_MTH, V$REQDIST, V$SHARED_SERVER, V$SHARED_SERVER_MONITOR, V$DISPATCHER_CONFIG(10.1)
Object Usage	Information related to object use and dependencies **V$ Views:** V$OBJECT_DEPENDENCY, V$OBJECT_USAGE
Overall system	Information related to the overall system performance **V$ Tables:** V$GLOBAL_TRANSACTION, V$SHARED_POOL_RESERVED, V$RESUMABLE, V$SORT_SEGMENT, V$TEMPSEG_USAGE, V$STATNAME, V$SYS_OPTIMIZER_ENV, V$SYS_TIME_MODEL, V$SYSSTAT, V$SYSTEM_CURSOR_CACHE, V$SYSTEM_EVENT, V$TEMPFILE, V$TEMPORARY_LOBS, V$TEMP_EXTENT_MAP, V$TEMP_EXTENT_POOL, V$TEMP_SPACE_HEADER, V$TRANSACTION, V$ALERT_TYPES(10.1), V$EVENT_HISTOGRAM(10.1), V$OSSTAT(10.1), V$SYSTEM_WAIT_CLASS(10.1), V$TEMP_HISTOGRAM(10.1), V$XML_AUDIT_TRAIL
Parallel Query	Information related to the Parallel Query option **V$ Views:** V$EXECUTION, V$PARALLEL_DEGREE_LIMIT_MTH, V$PQ_SESSTAT, V$PQ_SLAVE, V$PQ_SYSSTAT, V$PQ_TQSTAT, V$PX_PROCESS, V$PX_PROCESS_SYSSTAT, V$PX_SESSION, V$PX_SESSTAT
Parameters	Information related to various Oracle parameters, including initialization and NLS per session **V$ Views:** V$NLS_PARAMETERS, V$NLS_VALID_VALUES, V$OBSOLETE_PARAMETER, V$PARAMETER, V$PARAMETER2, V$SPPARAMETER, V$SYSTEM_PARAMETER, V$SYSTEM_PARAMETER2, V$PARAMETER_VALID_VALUES(10.2)
Redo logs	Information related to redo logs, including statistics and history **V$ Views:** VLOG, VLOGFILE, V$LOGHIST, V$LOG_HISTORY, V$THREAD (RAC related)

TABLE 12-1. *V$ Views Categories* (continued)

Some of the Major V$ View Categories

Category	Description and Associated V$ Views
Replication and materialized views	Information related to replication and materialized views **V$ Views:** V$MVREFRESH , V$REPLPROP, V$REPLQUEUE
Resource Manager	Information related to resource management **V$ Views:** V$ACTIVE_SESSION_POOL_MTH, V$ACTIVE_SESSION_POOL_HISTORY, V$RSRC_CONS_GROUP_HISTORY(10.2), V$RSRC_CONSUMER_GROUP, V$RSRC_CONSUMER_GROUP_CPU_MTH, V$RSRC_PLAN, V$RSRC_PLAN_CPU_MTH, V$RSRC_PLAN_HISTORY(10.2), V$RSRC_SESSION_INFO(10.2)
Rollback segments And Undo	Information on rollback segments, including statistics and transactions **V$ Views:** V$ROLLNAME, V$ROLLSTAT, V$TRANSACTION, V$UNDOSTAT
Security/privileges	Information related to security **V$ Views:** V$ENABLEDPRIVS, V$PWFILE_USERS, VVPD_POLICY, VWALLET(10.2), and V$XML_AUDIT_TRAIL(10.2)
Sessions (includes some replication information and heterogeneous services)	Information related to a session, including object access, cursors, processes, and statistics **V$ Views:** V$ACTIVE_SESSION_HISTORY, V$MYSTAT, V$PROCESS, V$SESS_TIME_MODEL, V$SESSION, V$SESSION_CONNECT_INFO, V$SESSION_CURSOR_CACHE, V$SESSION_EVENT, V$SESSION_LONGOPS, V$SESSION_OBJECT_CACHE, V$SESSION_WAIT, V$SESSION_WAIT_CLASS, V$SESSION_WAIT_HISTORY, V$SESSTAT, V$SESS_IO, V$SES_OPTIMIZER_ENV, V$SESSMETRIC, and V$CLIENT_STATS, and V$TSM_SESSIONS(10.2)
Services (all new for 10.1)	V$ACTIVE_SERVICES, V$SERV_MOD_ACT_STATS, V$SERVICE_EVENT, V$SERVICE_STATS, V$SERVICE_WAIT_CLASS, V$SERVICES
Sorting	Information related to sorting **V$ Views:** V$SORT_SEGMENT, V$TEMPSEG_USAGE, V$TEMP_EXTENT_MAP, V$TEMP_EXTENT_POOL, V$TEMP_HISTOGRAM(10.1), V$TEMP_SPACE_HEADER, V$TEMPFILE, V$TEMPSTAT
Standby databases (Data Guard)	Information related to standby databases **V$ Views:** V$DATAGUARD_STATUS, V$LOGSTDBY, V$LOGSTDBY_STATS, V$MANAGED_STANDBY, V$STANDBY_LOG, V$DATAGUARD_CONFIG(10.1), V$DATAGUARD_STATS(10.2), V$LOGSTDBY_PROCESS(10.2), V$LOGSTDBY_PROGRESS(10.2), V$LOGSTDBY_STATE(10.2), V$LOGSTDBY_TRANSACTION(10.2)
File mapping interface	Information related to file mapping **V$ Views:** VMAP_COMP_LIST, VMAP_ELEMENT, V$MAP_EXT_ELEMENT, V$MAP_FILE, VMAP_FILE_EXTENT, VMAP_FILE_IO_STACK, V$MAP_LIBRARY, and V$MAP_SUBELEMENT
Streams	Information related to streams **V$ Views:** VAQ,VSTREAMS_APPLY_COORDINATOR, V$STREAMS_APPLY_READER, V$STREAMS_APPLY_SERVER, V$STREAMS_CAPTURE, V$BUFFERED_PUBLISHERS(10.1), V$BUFFERED_QUEUES(10.1), V$BUFFERED_SUBSCRIBERS(10.1), V$PROPAGATION_RECEIVER(10.1), V$PROPAGATION_SENDER(10.1), V$RULE(10.1), V$RULE_SET(10.1), V$RULE_SET_AGGREGATE_STATS(10.1), V$STREAMS_TRANSACTION(10.2)
Statistics	Information related to statistics in general **V$ Views:** V$SEGMENT_STATISTICS, V$SEGSTAT, V$SEGSTAT_NAME, V$STATISTICS_LEVEL, V$STATNAME, V$WAITSTAT
Transactions	Information related to transactions in general **V$ Views:** V$GLOBAL_TRANSACTION, V$LOGSTDBY_TRANSACTION, V$RESUMABLE, V$STREAMS_TRANSACTION, V$TRANSACTION, V$TRANSACTION_ENQUEUE

TABLE 12-1. *V$ Views Categories* (continued)

NOTE
The V$ROLLNAME view is created slightly differently than the other V$ views. The V$ROLLNAME is a join of an X$ table and the undo$ table. Some of the V$ timing fields are dependent on the TIMED_ STATISTICS init.ora parameter being set to TRUE; otherwise, there will be no timing in these fields.

TIPS   Tips Review

REVIEW

- The V$ views that are accessed by SYSTEM are actually synonyms that point to the v_$ views that are views of the original V$ views based on the X$ tables. (Better read that one again.)

- When other DBAs need access to the V$ view information, but *not* the SYS or SYSTEM passwords, grant the user access to the v_$ views. The user may then access the V$ views that have public synonyms to the v_$ views.

- In Oracle 10g, query V$FIXED_TABLE to get a listing of all GV$ and V$ views in the database. The GV$ views are exactly the same as the V$ views, except the instance ID contains an identifier.

- Query V$FIXED_VIEW_DEFINITION to retrieve the query that creates the V$ and GV$ views from the X$ tables.

- The DBA_ views are *not* derived from the X$ tables or V$ views. The fact that you can delete rows from obj$ is a great reason to *never* be the SYS superuser.

- Query the V$DATABASE view to find out when your database was created and also to determine basic archiving information.

- Query V$SYSAUX_OCCUPANTS to ensure that the Automatic Workload Repository (AWR) isn't taking up too much space. Use DBMS_STATS to check history and retention.

- Query the V$LICENSE view to see the maximum sessions you are allowed. You can also set warnings when you get close to the maximum.

- Query the V$OPTION view to retrieve the Oracle options you have installed. The V$VERSION view gives you the actual versions of products installed.

- Access the V$SGA view to get a baseline idea of the system's physical memory that is allocated for Data, Shared Pool, and Log Buffering of Oracle.

- Accessing V$SGASTAT gives you a detailed breakdown for the Oracle SGA and breaks down all buckets for the Shared Pool allocation.

- Query V$PARAMETER and find out the current values for the initialization parameters. It also shows which init.ora parameters have been changed from their original defaults (ISDEFAULT = FALSE) and which parameters may be changed without shutting down and restarting the database.

- Query V$LIBRARYCACHE to see how often your SQL and PL/SQL is being read from memory. The pinhitratio should optimally be at 95 percent or better, and the number of reloads should not be greater than 1 percent.

- Query V$SQL_BIND_CAPTURE to see if binds per SQL is too high and CURSOR_SHARING is needed.

- Query the V$DB_OBJECT_CACHE view to find objects that are not pinned and are also large enough to potentially cause problems.

- Query the V$SQLAREA to find problem queries (and users).

- Query V$SESSION, V$SQLTEXT, and V$SESS_IO to find the problem users and what they are executing at a given point in time.

- Query V$ACCESS to find all objects that are being accessed by a user at a given time. This can help to pinpoint problem objects, while also being helpful when modifying a particular object (find out who is accessing it).

- Identify users who are locking others and kill their session (if necessary).

- Identify users who are holding multiple sessions and determine whether it is an administrative problem (the user is using multiple terminals) or a system problem (sessions are not being cleaned or they are spawning runaway processes).

- The views V$DATAFILE, V$FILESTAT, and DBA_DATA_FILES provide file I/O activity across all data files and disks of your database.

- Querying V$ROLLNAME, V$ROLLSTAT, and V$TRANSACTION can provide information on how users are using rollback segments. V$UNDOSTAT gives you UNDO information. (Rollback segments are quickly becoming passé.)

- Ensure that the freelists value is sufficient or use ASSM when using multiple processes to do inserts. The default storage value is 1.

- Document the privileges that you have for your system so that you can be ready for any type of security situation.

References

Joe Trezzo, "The V$ Arsenal: Key V$ Scripts Every DBA Should Use Regularly" (TUSC, 1997)
Oracle Corporation, *Oracle Server: SQL Language Reference Manual*
Oracle Corporation, *Oracle Server: Application Developer's Guide*
Joe Trezzo, "The V$ Views—A DBA's Best Friend" *IOUG-A Proceedings* (TUSC, 1997)
Rich Niemiec and Kevin Loney, *How I Broke into Your Database* (COUG, 2001)
asktom.oracle.com
Metalink Notes: 276103.1, 296765.1, 287679.1, 1019592.6 (Script Library), 243132.1, 245055.1

Many thanks to Joe Trezzo, who wrote most of this chapter for the original book. Also, thanks to Kevin Gilpin who supplied a lot of material for this update, and to Robert Freeman, Bob Yingst, and Greg Pucka, who contributed to this chapter in some way. To obtain a poster that contains the V$ view definitions grouped by category, call TUSC at (630) 960-2909 and request one.

CHAPTER
13

The X$ Tables
(Advanced DBA)

TIPS

&

COVERED

W hy do people climb mountains? Because they are there!
Why do people open the hood of their car and look at what's inside? Because they can!
Why do DBAs look at the X$ tables? Because they are there and they can!

There are now 613 X$ tables, and they are the last frontier for the expert DBA to explore and analyze the deepest cavern of the Oracle database. Querying the X$ tables can give secrets to undocumented features and parameters, information about future Oracle versions, and shorter or faster routes to database information. The X$ tables are rarely mentioned in the Oracle documentation or the Oracle user community. Therefore, I am including them in this book as one of the only references available. The queries in this chapter were tested accessing version 10.2 of the database.

The topics covered in this chapter include

- Introducing the X$ tables

- Creating V$ views and X$ tables

- Obtaining a list of all the X$ tables

- Obtaining a list of all the X$ indexes

- Using hints with X$ tables and indexes

- Shared pool

- Queries to monitor the shared pool

- Redo

- Initialization parameters

- Buffer cache/data blocks

- Instance/database

- Effective X$ Table Use and Strategy

- Related Oracle internals topics

- X$ table groups

- X$ table and non-V$ fixed view associations

- Common X$ table joins

Introducing the X$ Tables

The X$ tables are intriguing to mischievously curious DBAs. There are 613 X$ tables in 10gR2 (10.2.0.1) compared to only 394 in Oracle 9i Release 2 (9.2.0.1.0); a staggering 55 percent increase. There are also 440 indexes on the X$ tables. Appendix C has a list of all of these. The Oracle dynamic tables are designed like many robust Oracle application data models are. A set of tables is available to users (DBAs) via a set of synonyms on a set of views based on these tables. The synonym names start with V$ and are the object names published in the reference manual of the Oracle documentation set. These synonyms on the V$ views are used as the primary method of querying data from these tables. Interested DBAs, however, keep and use a toolkit of practical X$ table queries that supplement their V$ view queries.

The X$ tables contain instance-specific information spanning a variety of areas. They contain information about the current configuration of the instance, information about the sessions connected to the instance, and a gold mine of performance information. The X$ tables are platform-specific. The documented column definitions of the V$ views may be consistent from platform to platform, but the underlying SQL statements referencing the X$ tables may differ. The Oracle kernel consists of layers. The X$ table names contain an abbreviation for the particular kernel layer to which they pertain.

The X$ tables are not permanent or even temporary tables that reside in database datafiles. The X$ tables reside only in memory. When you start up your instance, they are created. They exist even before you create your control file. When you shut down your instance, they are destroyed. All 613 X$ tables are defined right after the instance is started (before mount). They are defined, but they cannot all be queried. Many of them require at least a mounted, if not open, database. To observe this, query the X$KQFTA & X$KQFDT table after starting your instance with the nomount option.

The X$ tables are owned by the SYS database user and are read-only, which is why they are referred to as *fixed tables* and the V$ views are referred to as *fixed views*. This statement might be a juicy invitation for you to try to verify this read-only property. Any attempt to alter these tables with a DDL or DML statement is met with an ORA-02030 error.

Oracle has extensively used the decode function in the underlying SQL statements of the data dictionary views. If you compare the V$ view underlying SQL statements from version to version, you will likely find differences in the implementation of some V$ views. The columns of the V$ views may stay more constant in their name and meaning, which allows Oracle RDBMS engineers to change the X$ tables from version to version while not disrupting too much of the Oracle user community's use of the V$ views. The fact that the V$ views are accessed through synonyms allows another level of flexibility for Oracle engineers to alter the underlying structures, also with little or no impact on the user community's use of the V$ views. Oracle's extensive use of the decode function in the underlying V$ view SQL statements also facilitates the platform-specific implementation of a query returning the generic data that a user of a particular V$ view expects from platform to platform. Consequently, it is important to run the correct scripts when upgrading a database—to make sure the dictionary views are created in a way that matches the underlying X$ tables.

Misconceptions About the X$ Tables

NOTE
Application designers and developers may save themselves some development and maintenance pain by adopting a similar strategy. They can employ views and synonyms for application software access to an application's underlying tables and stored programmatic objects (Java, PL/SQL). DBAs should investigate whether designers and developers can benefit from using this strategy. In some cases, the costs will be higher than the benefits.

Although this section is by no means a complete treatment of useful X$ table queries, it introduces some of the commonly used X$ table queries, grouped by the major tuning areas to which they pertain. Because X$ table queries are a supplement to queries of fixed views rather than a replacement for them, this section includes queries of both X$ tables and related fixed views.

Misconceptions about the X$ Tables

Do not use the X$ tables if you have a heart condition or are an inexperienced DBA, or you may ruin the entire database. (At least this is what some people will tell you. Sounds pretty scary.)

The most common misconception about the X$ tables is that the DBA can drop one or update one, thus ruining the database. However, X$ tables cannot be ruined. The only user who can select from these tables is the SYS user. A SELECT statement is the only command available to be performed on these X$ tables. An error occurs if you attempt to grant SELECT access to a user. Consider the following attempts to drop or alter an X$ table in the following listings. In the first listing, you will not be able to drop any of the X$ tables (even as the SYS user).

```
connect sys/change_on_install as sysdba
drop table X$ksppi;
ORA-02030: can only select from fixed tables/views
```

In this next listing, you will not be able to update, insert, or delete any data in the X$ tables (even as the SYS user).

```
update  X$ksppi
set     ksppidf = 'FALSE'
where   ksppidf = 'TRUE';
ORA-02030: can only select from fixed tables/views
```

NOTE
When you mention the X$ tables, most people say, "Ooh, pretty scary. I would never touch those tables." The fact is, DML commands (UPDATE, INSERT, DELETE) are not allowed on the X$ tables, even as the SYS superuser.

TIP
Only the SYS superuser can select from the X$ tables. An error occurs if an attempt is made to grant SELECT access to a user. But, the X$ tables are not completely harmless. Since they are not documented, they could lead to misinterpretation of data. For example, if a V$ view definition is modified to use a brand new X$ table, but the DBA has created his own view on the X$ tables, he might not have accurate information following an upgrade.

 ## Granting Access to View the X$ Tables

You cannot grant access to the X$ tables even if you are the SYS user. You will get the error in the following listing if you try to make grants to the X$ tables.

```
connect sys/change_on_install as sysdba
grant select on X$ksppi to richn;
ORA-02030: can only select fixed from fixed tables/views
```

Although the error message for attempting to grant access to X$KSPPI in the previous code is a little cryptic at first, it clarifies that you can perform only a SELECT and that the grant will not be allowed. However, you may build your own X$ views from the original X$ tables and then grant access to those views. Consider the examples in the following six listings, which give access to the X$KSPPI table via a view called X$_KSPPI and a synonym called X$KSPPI.

Connecting to the SYS superuser

```
Connect sys/change_on_install as sysdba
Connected.
```

Creating a view mirroring the X$KSPPI table

```
create view rich$_ksppi as
select      *
from        X$ksppi;

View created.
```

Creating a synonym for the newly created view

```
create public synonym X$_ksppi for x$_ksppi;
Synonym created.
```

Granting to the desired user access to the newly created view

```
grant select on X$_ksppi to richn;
Grant succeeded.
```

Connecting as the desired user

```
conn richn/tusc
Connected.
```

Accessing the X$_KSPPI view via the synonym created for X$_ksppi

```
select      count(*)
from        X$_ksppi;
COUNT(*)
1381
```

> **NOTE**
> *In Oracle 10g Release 1, Oracle made a mistake in the creation of
> the X$KSFMLIB view. It includes two columns named CAP_ELEM.
> Therefore you cannot create a custom view on this X$ view using
> the "as select *" clause. This does not appear in 10g Release2.*

You can now give access to the X$ table information without giving the password to the SYS
account. The key is creating a view that references the original SYS-owned X$ tables.

> **TIP**
> *A DBA may need access to the X$ table information, but not the
> SYS password. Create a view under a different name that mirrors
> the desired tables. Name these tables according to the appropriate
> synonyms of the original tables.*

Creating V$ Views and X$ Tables

The X$ tables are virtual or fixed tables, which are created in memory at database startup and maintained real-time in memory. These tables store up-to-date information on the current activity of the database at the current point in time, or since the last database startup. In the SGA, V$ views are created (see Chapter 12) on these X$ tables to allow users to view this information in a more readable format. The X$ tables are fixed tables, and because they have been created in memory, access to these tables is very limited.

The V$ views are known as the virtual tables, fixed tables, v$ tables, dynamic performance tables, and a half-dozen other names. The first hurdle to understanding the X$ tables is to become familiar with their creation, security, content, and relationship to the V$ views.

In addition, these X$ tables are very cryptic in nature. They are similar to the underlying table construction of the Oracle Data Dictionary. Therefore, Oracle creates V$ views that are more readable and practical. In addition, Oracle has built other views (USER, DBA, ALL) within the catalog.sql script for easier use. Oracle has also created a public synonym on V_$ views in the catalog.sql file that changes the name back to a view with a prefix of v$. An example of a V_$ view and v$ public synonym creation in the CATALOG.SQL is shown here:

```
create or replace view v_$datafile
as select * from v$datafile;
create or replace public synonym v$datafile for v_$datafile;
```

TIP
See Chapter 12 and Appendix B for detailed V$ view information and Appendix C for detailed X$ information.

Once the catalog.sql file has been executed, the V$ views are available only to the SYS user. At this point, access can be granted to V$ views by granting SELECT on the V$ view. Therefore, all SELECTs performed against the V$ views are actually retrieving information out of the SGA, more specifically out of the X$ tables. DBAs cannot modify X$ tables in any manner, and they cannot create indexes on these tables. Oracle began providing indexes on the X$ tables in version 8. In addition, the V$ views are the underlying views that are used for Oracle monitoring tools. Here you can see how to get a listing of all V$ views:

```
select    kqfvinam name
from      x$kqfvi
order by  kqfvinam;
```

Here is the partial output:

```
NAME
GV$ACCESS
GV$ACTIVE_INSTANCES
GV$ACTIVE_SESS_POOL_MTH
GV$AQ1
GV$ARCHIVE
GV$ARCHIVED_LOG
GV$ARCHIVE_DEST
```

```
GV$ARCHIVE_DEST_STATUS
GV$ARCHIVE_GAP
...
V$ACCESS
V$ACTIVE_INSTANCES
V$ACTIVE_SESS_POOL_MTH
V$AQ1
V$ARCHIVE
...
```

Note that the GV$ views are the same as the V$ tables except that you can see multiple instances with Oracle Real Application Clusters (RAC). The only difference between the GV$ and V$ tables is a column that shows the instance ID.

Obtaining a List of the X$ Tables That Make Up the V$ Views

To obtain a list of the X$ tables that make up the V$ views, you must access the V$FIXED_VIEW_DEFINITION view. This view shows how the V$ views were created. By knowing which X$ tables make up a V$ view, you may be able to build a faster query that goes directly to the X$ tables, as shown here:

```
select    *
from      v$fixed_view_definition
where     view_name = 'GV$FIXED_TABLE';
```

Here is the output:

```
VIEW_NAME          VIEW_DEFINITION
GV$FIXED_TABLE     select  inst_id,kqftanam, kqftaobj, 'TABLE', indx
                   from    X$kqfta
                   union all
                   select  inst_id,kqfvinam, kqfviobj, 'VIEW', 65537
                   from    X$kqfvi
                   union all
                   select  inst_id,kqfdtnam, kqfdtobj, 'TABLE', 65537
                   from    X$kqfdt
```

TIP
Access the X$KQFVI table for a listing of all V$ and GV$ views. Access the V$FIXED_VIEW_DEFINITION view to get all of the information of the underlying X$ tables that make up a V$ view.

Obtaining a List of All the X$ Tables

The names of the X$ tables are in the X$KQFTA table (contains 597 of the X$ V9.2 tables) and X$KQFDT table (contains another 13 of the X$ V9.2 tables). The v$ names can be found in the X$KQFDT table. The V$FIXED_TABLE view combines all three of these tables so that you can obtain a listing of any desired grouping. The query in this next listing shows how to obtain a listing of the X$ tables.

```
select      name
from        v$fixed_table
where       name like 'X%'
order by    name;
```

Following is the partial output (for a complete listing, see Appendix C):

```
NAME
X$ABSRACT_LOB
X$ACTIVECKPT
X$ASH
X$BH
X$BUFFER
X$BUFFER2
X$BUFFERED_PUBLISHERS
X$BUFFERED_SUBSCRIBERS
X$CKPTBUF
... (there are 613 in Oracle 10gR2)
```

The following query shows output from X$KQFDT, which is a partial listing of the X$ tables:

```
select      kqfdtnam, kqfdtequ
from        x$kqfdt;

KQFDTNAM                                KQFDTEQU
--------------------------------------- ---------
X$KCVFHONL                              X$KCVFH
X$KCVFHMRR                              X$KCVFH
X$KCVFHALL                              X$KCVFH
X$KGLTABLE                             X$KGLOB
X$KGLBODY                             X$KGLOB
X$KGLTRIGGER                          X$KGLOB
X$KGLINDEX                            X$KGLOB
X$KGLCLUSTER                          X$KGLOB
X$KGLCURSOR                           X$KGLOB
X$KGLCURSOR_CHILD_SQLID               X$KGLOB
X$KGLCURSOR_CHILD_SQLIDPH             X$KGLOB
X$KGLCURSOR_CHILD                     X$KGLOB
X$JOXFS                               X$JOXFT
X$JOXFC                               X$JOXFT
X$JOXFR                               X$JOXFT
X$JOXFD                               X$JOXFT
16 rows selected.
```

TIP
Query V$FIXED_TABLE for the names of the X$ tables, or you can also access the two X$ tables X$KQFTA and X$KQFDT for partial listings that when combined make up the full list.

Obtaining a List of All the X$ Indexes

If you often query the V$ views or X$ tables for information, it is helpful to understand which indexes are being used, as shown here:

```
select     table_name, index_number, column_name
from       v$indexed_fixed_column
order by   table_name, index_number, column_name, column_position;
```

Here is the partial output:

```
TABLE_NAME                                 INDEX_NUMBER COLUMN_NAME

--------------------------------- ------------ -----------
X$ASH                                         1 SAMPLE_ADDR
X$ASH                                         1 SAMPLE_ID
X$BUFFER                                      1 OBJNO
X$BUFFER2                                     1 OBJNO
X$DUAL                                        1 ADDR
X$DUAL                                        2 INDX
X$JOXFM                                       1 OBN
X$JOXFT                                       1 JOXFTOBN
X$KAUVRSTAT                                   1 ADDR
X$KAUVRSTAT                                   2 INCX
X$KCBBES                                      1 ADDR
X$KCBBES                                      2 INDX
... (there are 440 X$ indexes in Oracle 10gR2)
```

Only two X$ tables have multicolumn indexes, as shown in this listing:

```
SELECT   DISTINCT a.table_name, a.index_number,
         a.column_name,a.column_position
FROM     v$indexed_fixed_column a, v$indexed_fixed_column b
WHERE    a.table_name = b.table_name
AND      a.index number = b.index_number
AND      a.column_name != b.column_name
ORDER BY a.table_name,a.index_number, a.column_position;
```

```
TABLE_NAME   INDEX_NUMBER COLUMN_NAME             COLUMN_POSITION
----------- ------------ -------------------- ----------------
X$ASH                   1 SAMPLE_ADDR                        0
X$ASH                   1 SAMPLE_ID                          1
X$KTFBUE                1 KTFBUESEGTSN                       0
X$KTFBUE                1 KTFBUESEGFNO                       1
X$KTFBUE                1 KTFBUESEGBNO                       2
```

To see the data concerning from which X$ tables the information is retrieved, perform this query to the V$FIXED_VIEW definition table:

```
select   *
from     v$fixed_view_definition
where    view_name = 'GV$INDEXED_FIXED_COLUMN';
```

Here is the output:

```
VIEW_NAME                       VIEW_DEFINITION
V$INDEXED_FIXED_COLUMN          select    c.inst_id,    kqftanam,    kqfcoidx,
                                          kqfconam,     kqfcoipo
                                from      X$kqfco c,    X$kqfta t
                                where     t.indx = c.kqfcotab
                                and       kqfcoidx != 0
```

TIP
Access the V$INDEXED_FIXED_COLUMN view for a listing of all X$TABLE indexes.

Using Hints with X$ Tables and Indexes

As with other tables, you can also use hints with the X$ tables to achieve greater performance. The queries in the next two listings show the explain plan and statistics while changing the driving table using an ORDERED hint. Note that I am using aliases for the tables and would need to hint the alias (and not the table) if I used a hint requiring the table (such as the index hint). The ORDERED hint does not require the table name but accesses tables in the order listed in the FROM clause.

Forcing the X$KSBDP table as the driving table

```
select    /*+ ordered */ p.ksbdppro, p.ksbdpnam,
          d.ksbdddsc,p.ksbdperr
from      X$ksbdd d, X$ksbdp p
where     p.indx = d.indx;

Execution Plan
-----------------------------------------------------------
| Id | Operation              | Name          | Rows | Bytes | Cost (%CPU)
| Time       |

|  0 | SELECT STATEMENT       |               |  100 | 8100 |    0    (0)
| 00:00:01 |

|  1 |  NESTED LOOPS          |               |  100 | 8100 |    0    (0)
| 00:00:01 |

|  2 |   FIXED TABLE FULL     | X$KSBDD       |  100 | 4700 |    0    (0)
| 00:00:01 |

|* 3 |   FIXED TABLE FIXED INDEX| X$KSBDP (ind:1) |  1 |  34 |    0    (0)
| 00:00:01 |
```

Using the ordered hint to force the driving table to be X$KSBDP

```
select    /*+ ordered */ p.ksbdppro, p.ksbdpnam,
          d.ksbdddsc,p.ksbdperr
from      X$ksbdp p, X$ksbdd d
where     p.indx = d.indx;
```

```
Execution Plan
------------------------------------------------------------------
| Id  | Operation              | Name          | Rows  | Bytes | Cost (%CPU)
| Time       |

|   0 | SELECT STATEMENT       |               |   100 |  8100 |    0    (0)
| 00:00:01 |

|   1 |  NESTED LOOPS          |               |   100 |  8100 |    0    (0)
| 00:00:01 |

|   2 |   FIXED TABLE FULL     | X$KSBDP       |   100 |  3400 |    0    (0)
| 00:00:01 |

|*  3 |   FIXED TABLE FIXED INDEX| X$KSBDD (ind:2) |    1 |    47 |    0    (0)
| 00:00:01 |
```

TIP
*Oracle generally uses the indexes as needed, but from time to time,
you may use hints to achieve a desired result.*

Shared Pool

You can use the X$KSMLRU table to monitor space allocations in the shared pool that may be
causing space allocation contention. The *relevant* columns in this table are as follows:

Column	Definition
ADDR	Address of this row in the array of fixed tables
INDX	Index number of this row in the array of fixed tables
INST_ID	Oracle instance number
KSMLRCOM	Description of allocation type
KSMLRSIZ	Size in bytes of the allocated chunk
KSMLRNUM	Number of items flushed from the shared pool to allocate space
KSMLRHON	Name of the object being loaded
KSMLROHV	Hash value of the object being loaded
KSMLRSES	Session performing the allocation, joins to V$SESSION.SADDR

You can use the X$KSMSP table to examine the current contents of the shared pool. Each row
represents a chunk of memory in the shared pool. The *relevant* columns in this table are as follows:

ADDR	Address of this row in the array of fixed tables
INDX	Index number of this row in the array of fixed tables
INST_ID	Oracle instance number
KSMCHCOM	Description of the allocated chunk of memory

KSMCHPTR	Physical address of this chunk of memory
KSMCHSIZ	The size of this chunk of allocated shared memory
KSMCHCLS	The class of this chunk of allocated shared memory, which has the following possible values:

recr   An allocated chunk of shared memory that is flushable if the shared pool is low on memory

freeabl   A freeable, but not flushable, chunk of shared memory that is currently in use

free   A free chunk of shared memory

perm   A permanently allocated, nonfreeable chunk of shared memory

R-free   Free memory in the reserved pool

R-freea   A freeable chunk in the reserved pool

R-recr   A recreatable chunk in the reserved pool

R-perm   A permanent chunk in the reserved pool

Queries to Monitor the Shared Pool

The shared pool is often a key area of performance impact. This section will focus on queries that will help you investigate the shared pool.

ORA-04031 Errors

V$SHARED_POOL_RESERVED.REQUEST_FAILURES (or X$KGHLU.KGHLUNFU) gives the number of ORA-04031 errors that have occurred since the instance was started. If any ORA-04031 errors are occurring, then SHARED_POOL_SIZE and/or JAVA_POOL_SIZE are too small, the shared pool is fragmented, or application code may not be being shared optimally. The query in this listing checks the ORA-04031 errors that have occurred since the instance was started.

```
-- Number of ORA-04031 errors since instance startup.
SELECT request_failures
  FROM v$shared_pool_reserved;
```

If any ORA-04031 errors have occurred, then some SHARED_POOL_SIZE, JAVA_POOL_SIZE, and/or application tuning is in order. Consider one or more of the following:

- Pin large, high-use (high values for X$KSMLRU.KSMLRSIZ, COUNT(X$KSMLRU.KSMLRHON), and/or X$KSMLRU.KSMLRNUM) PL/SQL packages in memory with DBMS_SHARED_POOL.KEEP:

  ```
  EXECUTE dbms_shared_pool.keep('PACKAGENAME');
  ```

- Pin large, high-use Java classes, also with DBMS_SHARED_POOL.KEEP. You can pin a Java class by enclosing it in double quotes:

  ```
  EXECUTE dbms_shared_pool.keep('"FullJavaClassName"', 'JC');
  ```

TIP
Enclose the class in double quotes if it contains a slash (/); otherwise,
you will get an ORA-00995 error.

- Increase the size of the shared pool by increasing the shared_pool_size initialization parameter if the percentage of SHARED_POOL free memory is low *and* there is contention for library cache space allocation and/or more than zero occurrences of the ORA-04031 error. The section "Shared Pool" later in this chapter notes that increasing the shared pool is *not* always recommended if a low amount of shared pool memory is observed. If you are increasing the size of the shared pool, you might also need to raise the value of the parameter SGA_MAX_SIZE.

- Increase the size of the shared pool reserved area by increasing the SHARED_POOL_RESERVED_SIZE initialization parameter (the default is 5 percent of shared_pool_size).

- Promote the sharing of SQL, PL/SQL, and Java code by application developers.

Large Allocations Causing Contention

The object being loaded (X$KSMLRU.KSMLRHON) is a *keep* candidate (consider keeping it with DBMS_SHARED_POOL.KEEP) if the X$KSMLRU.KSMLRCOM value is MPCODE or PLSQL%.

If you use features such as Shared Servers (previously called MTS), Recovery Manager, or Parallel Query, you should configure a larger shared pool and also configure a large pool that is bigger than the default. These features will create large allocations in the shared pool. These features will use the large pool instead if it is large enough. Contention on the shared pool latch (as shown in this next listing) will be reduced if the large pool is used because the shared pool latch is not used for allocations in the large pool.

```
        -- Amount of each type of shared pool allocation causing contention.

SELECT    ksmlrcom, SUM(ksmlrsiz)
FROM      x$ksmlru
GROUP BY  ksmlrcom;


KSMLRCOM                 SUM(KSMLRSIZ)
-------------------- -------------
kgghteInit                    4152
object level s                4240
qeeOpt: qeesCreate             236
seg:kggfaAllocSeg             5116
                                 0
```

TIP
If X$KSMLRU.KSMLRCOM is similar to Fixed UGA, then a high
amount of session-specific allocation is occurring, which suggests
that OPEN_CURSORS may be set too high. This is relevant only
in cases where shared servers are being used.

(Large Allocations Causing Contention — side tab)

Shared Pool Fragmentation

This section takes a closer look at the shared pool with a plethora of queries to help you investigate in detail when needed. (The shared pool is also discussed in detail in Chapter 4.) The shared pool may be fragmented if you observe a large number of entries in X$KSMLRU, particularly a large number of them with small KSMLRSIZ values, or if there are a lot of chunks of type "free" in X$KSMSP. This may be contrasted with a large number of entries in X$KSMLRU with medium to high values of KSMLRSIZ, which is not likely to be a symptom of the shared pool being too fragmented; rather, it indicates that large PL/SQL packages and/or Java classes need to be kept in the shared pool, and possibly also that the shared pool itself is too small, and perhaps that application code is not being effectively shared (or some combination thereof). In identifying the problem, take the time to monitor the application code use over time to find out which code the user sessions are attempting to load. It is beneficial to network with application users, developers, designers, and application vendors. The queries in the following listings will help you find contention and fragmentation issues.

Finding contention and fragmentation issues

```
   -- Names of and sessions for shared pool allocations causing contention.
 SELECT ksmlrhon, ksmlrsiz, ksmlrses
   FROM x$ksmlru
  WHERE ksmlrsiz > 1000
ORDER BY ksmlrsiz;
Shared Pool Memory Allocated
   -- Shared pool memory allocated.
SELECT sum(ksmchsiz)||' bytes' "TotSharPoolMem"
  FROM x$ksmsp;


TotSharPoolMem
--------------------------------------------
58719640 bytes
```

Fragmentation of shared pool

```
    -- Fragmentation of Shared Pool.
   SET VERIFY off
 COLUMN PctTotSPMem for a11
 SELECT ksmchcls       "ChnkClass",
        SUM(ksmchsiz)  "SumChunkTypeMem",
        MAX(ksmchsiz)  "LargstChkofThisTyp",
        COUNT(1)       "NumOfChksThisTyp",
        ROUND((SUM(ksmchsiz)/tot_sp_mem.TotSPMem),2)*100||'%' "PctTotSPMem"
   FROM x$ksmsp,
        (select sum(ksmchsiz) TotSPMem from x$ksmsp) tot_sp_mem
GROUP BY ksmchcls, tot_sp_mem.TotSPMem
ORDER BY SUM(ksmchsiz);
```

```
ChnkClas SumChunkTypeMem LargstChkofThisTyp NumOfChksThisTyp PctTotSPMem
-------- --------------- ------------------ ---------------- -----------
R-freea             672                 24               28 0%
free             282088               9004             1333 0%
R-free          2980600             212900               14 5%
recr            9229668              17656            15411 16%
freeabl        16767416             299612            13077 29%
perm           29459196            3980612               15 50%

6 rows selected.
```

Information about SHARED_POOL_RESERVED_SIZE

```
    -- Information regarding shared_pool_reserved_size.
SELECT free_space,free_count,max_free_size,max_used_size,
       request_misses,max_miss_size
  FROM v$shared_pool_reserved;


FREE_SPACE FREE_COUNT MAX_FREE_SIZE MAX_USED_SIZE REQUEST_MISSES MAX_MISS_SIZE
---------- ---------- ------------- ------------- -------------- -------------
   2980600         14        212900             0              0             0
```

Low Free Memory in Shared and Java Pools

If a low percentage of the shared or java pools' memory is free, then the shared and/or java pools may have crossed the fine line between an optimal amount of free memory and not enough free memory. To determine this, consider how many free chunks exist, what the largest one is, whether there is a high number of reloads, and whether there have been any ORA-04031 errors. The two queries shown here will help.

Amount of shared pool free memory

```
    -- Amount of shared pool free memory.
SELECT *
  FROM v$sgastat
 WHERE name = 'free memory'
   AND pool = 'shared pool';


POOL        NAME                       BYTES
----------- -------------------------- ----------
shared pool free memory                 3819124
```

Amount of java pool free memory

```
    -- Amount of java pool free memory.
SELECT *
  FROM v$sgastat
 WHERE name = 'free memory'
   AND pool = 'java pool';
```

```
POOL          NAME                           BYTES
-----------   --------------------------   ----------
java pool     free memory                    44626368
```

Library Cache Hit Ratio

A low library cache hit ratio is a symptom of one of several problems. The shared and/or java pools may be too small, the SHARED_POOL_RESERVED_SIZE may be too small, CURSOR_SHARING may need to be set to FORCE, there may be inefficient sharing of SQL, PL/SQL, or Java code, or there may be insufficient use of bind variables. Investigate which application code is being used over time and how efficiently it is used (code sharing). Monitor the shared and java pool freespace over time. If the amount of free memory in the shared and java pools is relatively high, no ORA-04031 errors are occurring, and the library cache hit ratio is low, then poor code sharing is probably occurring. The queries in the following listings will help you investigate this area. I included some V$ view queries here because of the applicable nature to this subject.

Library cache hit ratio

```
    -- Library cache hit ratio.
  SELECT ROUND(SUM(pinhits)/SUM(pins),2)*100||'%' "Library Cache Hit Ratio"
    FROM v$librarycache
ORDER BY namespace;

Library Cache Hit Ratio
-----------------------
90%
```

Library cache reload ratio

```
    -- Library cache reload ratio.
SELECT namespace,
       ROUND(DECODE(pins,0,0,reloads/pins),2)*100||'%' "Reload Ratio"
  FROM v$librarycache;

NAMESPACE         Reload Ratio
---------------   -------------
SQL AREA          0%
TABLE/PROCEDURE   0%
BODY              0%
TRIGGER           0%
INDEX             0%
CLUSTER           0%
OBJECT            0%
PIPE              0%
JAVA SOURCE       0%
JAVA RESOURCE     0%
JAVA DATA         0%
```

Library cache high-use objects (make this a top-10 list by adding "WHERE ROWNUM<11")

```
      -- Library cache high-use objects (You may want to limit listing).
   SELECT name,type
     FROM v$db_object_cache
ORDER BY executions;
```

Library cache object sizes

```
    -- Library cache object sizes (you may want to limit listing).
   SELECT *
     FROM v$db_object_cache
ORDER BY sharable_mem;
```

Shared pool object sharing efficiency (you many want to limit these)

```
Column name format a40
Column type format a15

      -- Execute counts for currently cached objects.
   SELECT name, type, COUNT(executions) ExecCount
     FROM v$db_object_cache
GROUP BY name, type
ORDER BY ExecCount;

      -- Currently cached objects that have execute counts of just 1.
      -- Consider converting these objects to use bind variables.
   SELECT distinct name, type
     FROM v$db_object_cache
GROUP BY name, type
  HAVING COUNT(executions) = 1;

      -- Currently unkept, cached objects that have execute counts > 1.
      -- Consider pinning these objects.
   SELECT distinct name, type, COUNT(executions)
     FROM v$db_object_cache
    WHERE kept = 'NO'
GROUP BY name, type
  HAVING COUNT(executions) > 1
ORDER BY COUNT(executions);

-- Currently unkept, cached objects that are similar. Each of these
-- statements has at least 10 versions currently cached, but has only
-- been executed less than 5 times each. Consider converting these
-- objects to use bind variables and possibly also pinning them.
   SELECT SUBSTR(sql_text,1,40) "SQL", COUNT(1) , SUM(executions) "TotExecs"
     FROM  v$sqlarea
    WHERE executions < 5
```

```
      AND kept_versions = 0
GROUP BY SUBSTR(sql_text,1,40)
  HAVING COUNT(1) > 10
ORDER BY COUNT(1) ;
Clear columns
```

A high percentage of reloads indicates that the shared and/or java pools are too small, code sharing is insufficient, and possibly also large code objects are repeatedly being used. Monitor the application code used over time. If particular large code objects are identified as frequently used, consider pinning them and/or increasing the size of the SHARED_POOL_RESERVED_SIZE. If features such as Shared Servers, Recovery Manager, or Parallel Query are used, consider a larger SHARED_POOL_SIZE and/or larger LARGE_POOL_SIZE.

High Number of Hard Parses

You should review similar queries with low numbers of executions to uncover opportunities to combine them into statements using bind variables. A high ratio of hard parses may mean that the shared pool itself is too small or perhaps a SQL statement is repeatedly nudging other code out of the precious shared pool or java pool cache space. Identify these statements and consider pinning. Consider also setting the CURSOR_SHARING parameter = FORCE. The next listing shows various queries to view parse activity:

```
    -- Overall Parse Activity.
SELECT name, value
  FROM v$sysstat
 WHERE name = 'parse count (total)'
    OR name = 'parse count (hard)';
```

```
NAME                                                              VALUE
---------------------------------------------------------------- ----------
parse count (total)                                               11357
parse count (hard)                                                  924
```

```
    -- Ratio of hard parses to total parses.
SELECT ROUND((b.value/a.value),2)*100||'%' HardParseRatio
  FROM v$sysstat a, v$sysstat b
 WHERE a.name = 'parse count (total)'
   AND b.name = 'parse count (hard)';
```

```
HARDPARSERATIO
----------------
8%
```

```
    -- SQL Statements experiencing a high amount of parse activity.
SELECT sql_text, parse_calls, executions
  FROM v$sqlarea
 WHERE parse_calls > 100
   AND kept_versions = 0
   AND executions < 2*parse_calls;
```

```
SQL_TEXT
--------------------------------------------------------------------------------
PARSE_CALLS EXECUTIONS
----------- ----------
lock table sys.mon_mods$ in exclusive mode nowait
        126        126
lock table sys.col_usage$ in exclusive mode nowait
        269        269
(...partial listing only)
```

Latch Waits and/or Sleeps

If latch waits are high but shared and java pool freespace is also high, consider reducing the size of the shared and/or java pools. This could indicate that sessions are spending time scanning the unnecessarily large list of free shared pool chunks. Monitor the amount of shared and java pool freespace over time. If ample freespace is available in these pools and no ORA-04031 errors are occurring, consider reducing the sizes of these pools. Investigate when the miss ratio and sleeps are high for any of the latches in the following list:

- Row cache objects
- Library cache
- Shared pool
- Shared java pool

If freespace in the shared and java pools is low, then you should consider the other tuning areas, such as increasing the shared and/or java pools, pinning objects, and combining similar SQL statements to use bind variables. The query in this listing will help you acquire some of these metrics.

```
Column name for a20
     -- Shared pool latch efficiency.
SELECT name,
       ROUND(misses/decode(gets,0,1,gets),2)*100||'%' as "WillToWaitMissRatio",
       ROUND(immediate_misses/decode(immediate_gets,0,1,
       immediate_gets),2)*100 ||'%' "ImmMissRatio",
       sleeps
  FROM v$latch
 WHERE name in ('library cache', 'row cache objects', 'shared pool', 'shared java pool');
Clear columns

NAME                 WillToWaitMissRatio
-------------------- ----------------------------------------
ImmMissRatio                                         SLEEPS
---------------------------------------------------- ----------
row cache objects    0%
0%                                                        0
shared pool          0%
0%                                                        3
library cache        0%
0%                                                        1
```

Remember that before increasing the SHARED_POOL_SIZE, you should consider whether there are any shared pool latch waits. Depending on what you observe, it may actually be more appropriate to reduce the size of the shared pool. This will be the case if there is a sufficient amount of free shared pool memory available, a low number of reloads, and a high number of shared pool latch waits. The reason to consider reducing the shared pool in this case is that with an oversized shared pool, sessions will hold the shared pool latch slightly longer than would be needed otherwise because the shared pool needs to scan a larger amount of space to determine exactly where to allocate the space it is requesting.

Miscellaneous

After exhausting previously discussed shared and java pool tuning options, you should consider increasing the _KGL_LATCH_COUNT parameter. This undocumented parameter sets the number of library cache latches: the latches that allow protected access to library cache objects for execution. Although only one shared pool latch existed prior to Oracle 9i, seven shared pool latches are available in Oracle 9i and later. These enable Oracle to perform a protected memory allocation on behalf of a session. With this parameter you can create additional latches, allowing increased concurrent library cache object execution access. Consider prime values between 1 and the smallest prime number greater than twice the number of database server CPUs for the _KGL_LATCH_COUNT parameter. The maximum allowed value for this parameter is 66.

Adjusting this parameter is, as with all undocumented parameters, unsupported by Oracle. Implement such changes only under the direction of Oracle Support and after thoroughly testing under direct simulation of production conditions.

Note that any particular database may experience conditions that are a combination of two or more of the previous conditions. Frequently, you must evaluate multiple conditions and decide on two or more potential corrective measures.

Also note that after each query on X$KSMLRU, the values in this table are reset back to zero. To effectively monitor the table, consider capturing the contents of it to a permanent table with an INSERT INTO . . . AS SELECT . . . statement or by simply spooling the output to a file. Furthermore, whenever you query X$KSMLRU, you might want to always select all of the columns instead of just one or a few you might be interested in at a particular moment; otherwise, you may miss some information that you later decide you wanted to see.

CAUTION
When "resetting" the X$KSMLRU table, there may still be rows in this table after each query. Do not interpret the remaining rows appearing after each query as entries pertaining to contention-causing code, but rather to preallocated entries in this table. If no problem statements are in X$KSMLRU, then the KSMLRITON and KSMLRSIZ values will be NULL and zero, respectively. If they are non-NULL, then these rows pertain to contention-causing code. Make sure multiple DBAs do not simultaneously query X$KSMLRU because each of them may observe misleading results.

Remember that when you decide to alter initialization parameters to remedy performance problems, you can now alter many of them by using an alter system command in Oracle 9i. Despite the ease of doing this, you should first test such changes on a test system. For example, if you attempt to alter the SHARED_POOL_SIZE too small, the SQL*Plus session may hang and/or consume a large amount of memory and CPU resources during the execution of the alter system command. Or, prior to Oracle 9*i*, if you set the _KGL_LATCH_COUNT parameter too high, you will get an ORA-600 [17038] error when you next try to start up the database.

Redo

The X$KCCCP table contains information about the current redo log file. The X$KCCLE table contains information about all redo log files, as shown here:

```
    -- Percentage full of the current redo log file.
SELECT ROUND((cpodr_bno/lesiz),2)*100||'%' PctCurLogFull
  FROM X$kcccp a, X$kccle b
 WHERE a.cpodr_seq = leseq;


PCTCURLOGFULL
---------------
35%
```

If you are observing in V$LOG_HISTORY or in the "log file space waits" statistic that log switches are occurring more frequently than is appropriate for your database, you may decide to alter the redo log file configuration. This task can be performed while the database is open to users and all tablespaces are online. If you want to minimize the impact on database performance while this or other similar maintenance is performed that involves a DBA-induced log switch with the alter system switch log file command, you can use the query in the preceding listing to measure how much redo log information will have to be copied to complete the archive of the current log file. This is particularly relevant in cases of databases with large redo log files (100MB or larger).

You can also use this query as a tuning aid to measure how much redo activity is created by a particular transaction or process, if it is possible to isolate a particular database to one session that will be guaranteed as the only creator of redo records, other than Oracle itself. It may be useful to capture before and after results of this query when testing such a transaction.

Initialization Parameters

Oracle 9*i* introduced the concept of the server parameter file, or spfile. This file allows DBAs to make persistent initialization parameter changes with the alter system command without having to manually incorporate these changes into a traditional parameter file, or pfile, to implement the persistence of the parameter change. This also allows the DBA to instantaneously save the current instance configuration to a file for archival or backup purposes. This flexibility introduces a bit of initialization parameter management complexity in that the Oracle instance can be started with either a pfile or an spfile. This complexity raises a few questions for the DBA when managing initialization parameters. The DBA must know what Oracle will use as an initialization parameter file at instance startup time, where the initialization parameters will be saved when an alter system . . . scope=spfile or alter system . . . scope=both command is issued, and whether a currently running Oracle instance was started using a pfile, an spfile, or both.

If the spfile in the platform-specific default location with the platform-specific default name exists, then Oracle will use it to start the instance. To get Oracle to use an spfile other than the one residing in the default location with the default filename, you must first rename, relocate, or delete this default spfile and then relocate and/or rename the desired spfile from the nondefault location to the default location and name. Alternatively, you can specify this nondefault spfile in the spfile initialization parameter in a pfile that is used to start up the instance.

Note that there is still the concept of the platform-specific default name and location for the pfile, which is used if no spfile is in the spfile default location and name. As in pre–Oracle 9*i* versions, a nondefault pfile can be used to start an instance with the pfile option of the startup command. These are the only ways that Oracle will use a nondefault parameter file to start up the instance. There is no startup spfile command. Spfiles and pfiles are not interchangeable. Spfiles are (mostly) binary files that can be altered only with alter system commands and can be created only with create spfile commands.

As in pre–Oracle 9*i* versions, pfiles are simply text files that may be created and altered with a text editor. An attempt to use an spfile in the startup pfile command will be met with an ORA-01078 error. If an instance was started with an spfile, then any changes made using the alter system . . . scope=spfile or alter system . . . scope=both commands will be saved to the spfile that was used to start the instance, even if the default spfile exists and was not used to start the instance. If both a pfile and an spfile are used to start an Oracle instance, Oracle overrides any parameters specified in the pfile with those specified in the spfile, if there are any conflicts.

The question of which file was used to start an Oracle instance has five possible answers:

- On startup, the database first looks for spfile<SID>.ora in the default location, and then looks for spfile.ora in the default location. Spfile in the default location is used with the default name and no pfile was used.

- A pfile in the default location with the default name was used and a nondefault spfile was used.

- A nondefault pfile was used and a nondefault spfile was used.

- A pfile in the default location with the default name was used and no spfile was used.

- A nondefault pfile was used and no spfile was used.

> **NOTE**
> *It is possible that both an spfile and a pfile may have been used to start an instance. Check the following queries in the order listed to answer the question of which files may have been used for the initialization parameters to start the instance.*

Case 1

Run the query in this listing to check for spfile-specified initialization parameters.

```
    -- Check for spfile-specified initialization parameters.
SELECT count(1)
  FROM v$spparameter
 WHERE isspecified = 'TRUE';
```

```
COUNT(1)
----------
        29
```

Or, just use the SQL*Plus command show parameter spfile. This will show you exactly which spfile is used to start the database (gets set automatically when the database is started without specifying a pfile or spfile). If you start the database with the PFILE option, then this parameter is NULL. This is the equivalent to the query in the preceding listing but involves less typing.

```
SQL> SHOW PARAMETER SPFILE
```

Case 2

Run this query to determine which spfile was used to start the instance.

```
    -- Determine which spfile was used to start the instance.
SELECT value
  FROM v$parameter
 WHERE name = 'spfile';
```

Look for a pfile in the default location. If the spfile parameter value from the query in the preceding listing (to V$PARAMETER) is non-NULL and the value is not the default value for the spfile, then a pfile was used and it specified an alternate spfile in the spfile parameter. If this is the case and if the default pfile exists, then it was used to start the instance.

Case 3

If the spfile parameter value from the query in the Case 2 listing (to V$PARAMETER) is non-NULL and the value is not the default value for the spfile, then a pfile was used and it specified an alternate spfile in the spfile parameter. If this is the case and if the default pfile does not exist, then you must determine the location of the nondefault pfile. See Case 5.

Case 4

If the spfile parameter value from the query in the listing in Case 2 (to V$PARAMETER) is NULL, then a pfile was used and no spfile was used. If this is the case and if the default pfile exists, then it was used to start the instance.

Case 5

If it is determined from Cases 1 through 3 that no spfile was used at all, and that the default pfile was not used, then the remaining possibility is that a nondefault pfile was used and no spfile was used. There are many site-specific possibilities for a nondefault pfile. A database startup, shutdown, or backup script, a third-party backup or database management software package, or a site-specific Oracle software directory structure may give a clue to what this file is. If there is uncertainty about this file, you can save the existing configuration initialization parameters by querying some of the Oracle X$ tables pertinent to initialization parameters. There is also the possibility that OEM, which can store a local copy of the parameter file, started the database.

Initialization Parameters

Several X$ tables are relevant to initialization parameters: X$KSPSPFILE, X$KSPPSV, X$KSPPSV2, X$KSPPCV, X$KSPPCV2, X$KSPPI, and X$KSPPO. The X$KSPSPFILE table lists the contents of the spfile. The V$SPPARAMETER view, which is based on the X$KSPSPFILE table, excludes parameter names that start with an underscore, unless such "underscore" or "undocumented" parameters were explicitly specified in an spfile, in a pfile, or with an alter system command and/or Oracle had to modify the DBA-specified value to fit a functional requirement of the parameter, such as a requirement that a particular parameter value be a prime number or a multiple of another DBA-specified parameter value, for example. To see all the parameter names, including those that the V$SPPARAMETER view excludes, query the X$KSPSPFILE table.

Note that if an spfile was not used to start an instance, then all of the values in the KSPSPFFTCTXSPVALUE column of X$KSPSPFILE will be NULL and all of the values in the KSPSPFFTCTXISSPECIFIED column will be FALSE. Conversely, if an spfile was used to start an instance, the values in the KSPSPFFTCTXISSPECIFIED column for which the particular parameter was specified in the spfile will be TRUE and the value in the KSPSPFFTCTXSPVALUE column for such parameters will be a non-NULL value.

The X$KSPPSV table lists the parameter names and values that are currently in effect for the instance. The V$SYSTEM_PARAMETER view, which is based on the X$KSPPSV table, excludes parameters that start with an underscore and have not been modified from their default value.

The X$KSPPSV2 table is very similar to the X$KSPPSV table. The difference is in how parameter values are stored that consist of lists of values. This table, like the X$KSPPSV table, lists parameters and parameter values that are currently in effect for this Oracle instance. A new session inherits parameter values from the system values. Each list parameter value appears as a separate row in the table. Presenting the list parameter values in this format enables you to quickly determine the values for a list parameter. For example, if a parameter value is "a,b" looking at X$KSPPSV does not tell you whether the parameter has two values ("a" and "b") or one value ("a, b"). X$KSPPSV2 makes the distinction between the list parameter values clear. Correspondingly, the V$SYSTEM_PARAMETER2 view is based on the X$KSPPSV2 table.

The X$KSPPCV and X$KSPPCV2 tables are similar to the X$KSPPSV and X$KSPPSV2 tables, except that the X$KSPPCV and X$KSPPCV2 tables apply to the current session, not necessarily the whole instance. If a parameter is changed with an alter session command, the change is reflected in the X$KSPPCV and X$KSPPCV2 tables. The V$PARAMETER and V$PARAMETER2 fixed views are based on the X$KSPPCV and X$KSPPCV2 tables, respectively.

The X$KSPPI table lists the initialization parameter names, types, and statuses. The V$PARAMETER, V$PARAMETER2, V$SYSTEM_PARAMETER, and V$SYSTEM_PARAMETER2 fixed views are based on the X$KSPPCV, X$KSPPCV2, X$KSPPSV, and X$KSPPSV2 tables; each of these X$ tables is joined with the X$KSPPI table in these fixed views to get the associated parameter names and other information. The query in this next listing is the query on which V$SYSTEM_PARAMETER is based, excluding the line in V$SYSTEM_PARAMETER that excludes parameter names that start with an underscore. The underlying SQL statements of the V$PARAMETER, V$PARAMETER2, and V$SYSTEM_PARAMETER2 fixed views have the same structure as the query in the listing in Case 2 described previously.

```
-- All initialization parameter settings in effect for the instance.
SELECT x.indx+1 InstanceNum,
       ksppinm ParamName,
       ksppity ParamType,
       ksppstvl ParamValue,
       ksppstdf IsDefaultVal,
       DECODE(bitand(ksppiflg/256,1),
```

```
               1,'TRUE',
                 'FALSE') IsSessModifiable,
        DECODE (bitand(ksppiflg/65536,3),
               1,'IMMEDIATE',
               2,'DEFERRED',
                 'FALSE') IsSysModifiable,
        DECODE (bitand(ksppstvf,7),
               1,'MODIFIED',
                 'FALSE') IsModified,
        DECODE (bitand(ksppstvf,2),
                 2,'TRUE',
                   'FALSE') IsAdjusted,
        ksppdesc Description,
        ksppstcmnt UpdateComment
    FROM X$ksppi x, X$ksppsv y
    WHERE (x.indx = y.indx)
ORDER BY ParamName;
```

The V$OBSOLETE_PARAMETER fixed view, which is based on the X$KSPPO table, lists obsolete initialization parameters. For some of these, such as SPIN_COUNT, you may note that they are now undocumented parameters.

Buffer Cache/Data Blocks

Four key performance-related buffer cache topics are the current buffer statuses, the identification of segments that are occupying the block buffers, the detection of hot (popular, or high contention) data blocks, and the cause of buffer-cache-related latch contention and wait events. These topics are relevant to buffer cache tuning in all Oracle versions, but there are additional considerations in Oracle 8, 8*i*, and 9*i*. Oracle 8 introduced the concept of multiple buffer pools. Oracle 9*i* introduced the concept of multiple data block sizes and therefore the need for multiple buffer cache buffer sizes.

The X$ tables are used in the buffer-cache-related queries that follow:

X$ Table	Definition
X$BH	Status and number of pings for every buffer in the SGA
X$KCBWDS	Statistics on all buffer pools available to the instance
X$KCBWBPD	Statistics on all buffer pools available to the instance, including buffer pool names
X$KCBWAIT	Number of and time spent in waits for buffer pool classes
X$KCBFWAIT	Buffer cache wait count and time

The following queries are relevant to these topics.

Buffer Statuses

A low number of buffers with a status of "Free" in X$BH does not necessarily mean that the buffer cache is undersized. It may, in fact, mean that the buffer cache is optimally sized such that Oracle will not have to perform frequent organization and maintenance on a superfluous number of buffers. Unfortunately, this same thought process leads many DBAs to undersize the buffer cache and leave memory sitting idle on their system. Similarly, if a large percentage of buffers are consistently free, then perhaps the buffer cache is oversized. See the subsequent sections discussing buffer cache contents, latches, and wait events for a better indication of the proper sizing and configuration of the buffer cache as it relates to the segments that are being used. Tuning and looking at Oracle at the block level is covered in detail in Chapter 9. The query in this listing shows how to see the state of the buffers in the buffer cache:

```
        -- Buffer cache buffer statuses.
      SET VERIFY off
  COLUMN PctTotBCMem for a11
  SELECT /*+ ordered */
         tot_bc_mem.TotBCMem,
         decode(state,
                   0,'Free',
                   1,'Exclusive',
                   2,'SharedCurrent' ,
                   3,'ConsistentRead',
                   4,'BeingRead',
                   5,'InMediaRecoveryMode',
                   6,'InInstanceRecoveryMode',
                   7,'BeingWritten',
                   8,'Pinned',
                   9,'Memory',
                  10,'mrite',
                  11,'Donated') "BlockState",
         SUM(blsiz) "SumStateTypeMem",
         COUNT(1)   "NumOfBlksThisTyp",
         ROUND(SUM(blsiz)/tot_bc_mem.TotBCMem,2)*100||'%' "PctTotBCMem"
     FROM (SELECT sum(blsiz) TotBCMem
           FROM X$bh) tot_bc_mem,
          X$bh
  GROUP BY tot_bc_mem.TotBCMem,
           decode(state,
                   0,'Free',
                   1,'Exclusive',
                   2,'SharedCurrent' ,
                   3,'ConsistentRead',
                   4,'BeingRead',
                   5,'InMediaRecoveryMode',
                   6,'InInstanceRecoveryMode',
                   7,'BeingWritten',
                   8,'Pinned',
                   9,'Memory',
                  10,'mrite',
                  11,'Donated')
  ORDER BY SUM(blsiz);
  CLEAR COLUMNS


    TOTBCMEM BlockState                SumStateTypeMem NumOfBlksThisTyp PctTotBCMem
  ---------- ----------------------    --------------- ---------------- -----------
    16416768 ConsistentRead                     253952               31 2%
    16416768 Exclusive                        16162816             1973 98%
```

Here is a quick reference for the states of the buffers in X$BH:

Buffer State	Meaning
0	Free
1	Exclusive
2	Shared Current
3	Consistent Read
4	Being Read
5	In Media Recovery Mode
6	In Instance Recovery Mode
7	Being Written
8	Pinned
9	Memory
10	mwrite
11	Donated

Segments Occupying Block Buffers

It is useful to note the distribution of segment owners, types, and names among the occupied buffers. Note in particular which objects occupy the most buffers. Observe the indexes currently in the cache. Question whether these indexes are appropriate. If they are nonselective indexes being used by selective queries (or vice versa), these indexes could be occupying precious buffers that could be used more effectively by the corresponding table blocks or by the blocks of other segments experiencing "buffer busy waits" wait events. Query V$SQLTEXT to observe the SQL statements currently using the segments occupying the highest percentages of the buffers and determine whether index usage in these statements is appropriate. The two queries in the following listings show the segments occupying block buffers and also the percentage of buffers occupied by segments in the buffer cache.

All segments occupying block buffers

```
    -- Segments Occupying Block Buffers (long listing / for testing usually).
SELECT o.*, d_o.owner, d_o.object_name, object_type, o.buffers, o.avg_touches
FROM (     SELECT obj object, count(1) buffers, AVG(tch) avg_touches
                   FROM X$bh
          GROUP BY obj) o,
dba_objects d_o
WHERE o.object = d_o.data_object_id
ORDER BY owner, object_name;
```

Percentage of buffers occupied by segments in the buffer cache

```
    -- Percentage of Buffers Occupied by Segments in the Buffer Cache.
    -- Note that this percentage is the percentage of the number of
```

```
    -- occupied buffers, not the percentage of the number of allocated
    -- buffers.
SELECT tot_occ_bufs.TotOccBufs,o.*,d_o.owner, d_o.object_name, object_type,
       ROUND((o.buffers/tot_occ_bufs.TotOccBufs)*100,2) || '%' PctOccBufs
FROM   (SELECT obj object, count(1) buffers, AVG(tch) avg_touches
          FROM X$bh
       GROUP BY obj) o,
        (SELECT COUNT(1) TotOccBufs
           FROM X$bh
          WHERE  state != 0) tot_occ_bufs,
        dba_objects d_o
 WHERE o.object = d_o.data_object_id
ORDER BY round((o.buffers/tot_occ_bufs.TotOccBufs)*100,2),owner, object_name;
```

Note also that only segments that are of the same block size as the block size of the default pool (the default block size) may be assigned to the keep or recycle pools. As of the first release of Oracle 9*i*, the keep and recycle pools are not available for use by segments that are not the default block size. This defeats some of the strategy involved with tuning segments that are either high or low access and are not the default block size. However, other tuning options are available for such segments, such as partitioning.

Pool-specific buffer cache buffer occupation

```
    -- Pool Specific Buffer Cache Buffer Occupation
SELECT DECODE(wbpd.bp_id,1,'Keep',
                         2,'Recycle',
                         3,'Default',
                         4,'2K Pool',
                         5,'4K Pool',
                         6,'8K Pool',
                         7,'16K Pool',
                         8,'32K Pool',
                           'UNKNOWN') Pool,
       bh.owner,
       bh.object_name object_name,
       count(1) NumOfBuffers
  FROM X$kcbwds wds, X$kcbwbpd wbpd,
       (SELECT set_ds,x.addr,o.name object_name,
               u.name owner
          fROM sys.obj$ o,
               sys.user$ u,
               X$bh x
         WHERE o.owner# = u.user#
           AND o.dataobj# = x.obj
           AND x.state !=0
           AND o.owner# !=0 ) bh
 WHERE wds.set_id >= wbpd.bp_lo_sid
   AND wds.set_id <= wbpd.bp_hi_sid
   AND wbpd.bp_size != 0
   AND wds.addr=bh.set_ds
 GROUP BY
   DECODE(wbpd.bp_id,1,'Keep',
```

```
                              2,'Recycle',
                              3,'Default',
                              4,'2K Pool',
                              5,'4K Pool',
                              6,'8K Pool',
                              7,'16K Pool',
                              8,'32K Pool',
                               'UNKNOWN'),
        bh.owner,
        bh.object_name
ORDER BY 1,4,3,2;
```

Hot Data Blocks/Latch Contention and Wait Events

The blocks of the segments returned by the query in the next listing are ones that are being accessed frequently, particularly if the value of the tch (count) column changes (higher *and* lower) between consecutive executions of this query. The tch column value is incremented every time a particular buffer is "touched" or "visited" by a transaction. This value can fluctuate as a buffer is moved up and down the LRU list. The reason for the fluctuation is that Oracle internally adjusts the tch value according to its position in the LRU list and other factors, such as how long it has been since the buffer was last touched. In some scenarios of this algorithm, Oracle internally resets the tch value back to 1.

```
    -- Segments Occupying Hot Buffers (could be slow for a large cache / test).
    -- This query defines a "hot" buffer as a buffer that has
    -- a touch count greater than 10.
COL NAME FOR A35
SELECT /*+ ordered */ u.username ||'.'|| o.name  name,
       so.object_type type, bh.dbablk, bh.tch touches
FROM   x$bh  bh, dba_users u, sys.obj$ o, sys.sys_objects so
WHERE  bh.obj = o.obj#
and    bh.obj = so.object_id
and    o.owner# = u.user_id
AND    bh.tch  > 10
ORDER  BY bh.tch desc;
```

NAME	TYPE	DBABLK	TOUCHES
SYS.FILE$	TABLE	114	807
SYS.I_FILE#_BLOCK#	INDEX	82	804
SYS.C_USER#	CLUSTER	92	746
SYS.C_USER#	CLUSTER	90	737
SYS.I_FILE#_BLOCK#	INDEX	88	612
SYS.JOB$	TABLE	1473	506
SYS.JOB$	TABLE	1474	505
SYS.I_JOB_NEXT	INDEX	1490	485
SYS.I_FILE#_BLOCK#	INDEX	85	396
SYS.C_USER#	CLUSTER	91	344
SYS.I_OBJ1	INDEX	54721	340

(Output truncated...)

```
    -- Segments Occupying Hot Buffers (could be slow for a large cache / test).
```

Hot Data Blocks and Wait Events

```
      -- This query defines a "hot" buffer as a buffer that has
      -- a touch count greater than 10 and groups by OBJECT.
COL NAME FOR A35
SELECT /*+ ordered */ u.username ||'.'|| o.name  name,
       so.object_type type, count(bh.dbablk) blocks, sum(bh.tch) touches
FROM   X$bh  bh, dba_users u, sys.obj$ o, sys.sys_objects so
WHERE  bh.obj = o.obj#
and    bh.obj = so.object_id
and    o.owner# = u.user_id
AND    bh.tch  > 10
group  by u.username ||'.'|| o.name, so.object_type
ORDER  BY touches desc;


NAME                                 TYPE                 BLOCKS    TOUCHES
---------------------------------    -------------        --------  --------
SYS.C_FILE#_BLOCK#                   CLUSTER                 131      20263
SYS.OBJ$                             TABLE                    75      10407
SYS.I_FILE#_BLOCK#                   INDEX                    20       6063
SYS.I_OBJ1                           INDEX                    28       5453
SYS.C_USER#                          CLUSTER                   4       1984
SYS.JOB$                             TABLE                     2       1017
SYS.FILE$                            TABLE                     1        811
SYS.I_JOB_NEXT                       INDEX                     1        488
(Output truncated...)
```

Capture the SQL statements involving these segments by querying V$SQLTEXT for SQL_TEXT lines that contain these segment names, and analyze their execution plans with the explain plan as described in Chapter 6. Consider the number of sessions accessing these blocks using the queries in this section, and whether these blocks are tables or appropriate indexes. Table blocks appearing in this list that are being accessed by multiple sessions are candidates for the keep pool. Table segments in this list that incur frequent full table scans are candidates for being recreated in tablespaces that are configured for large block sizes (16K or larger). Conversely, table segments that incur single-row accesses are candidates for being recreated in tablespaces that are configured for smaller block sizes (2K, 4K, or 8K).

Note that you should balance rebuilding such single-row access tables in small block tablespaces with data locality considerations. If such a single-row access table is accessed *frequently* for similar data that is likely to be stored consecutively, then you should consider storing such segments in large block tablespaces instead of a small block tablespace. As a result, a lower number of physical block reads occurs because of the increased chance that the block containing the desired rows already resides in a buffer cache buffer from other recent queries.

Deciding how to size such objects depends on the default block size of the database and the amount of physical memory and SGA space available for creating a keep pool. Segments in buffers with a consistently low touch count should be candidates for the recycle pool, depending on the block size of the particular table versus the default block size. You should review the application SQL code, particularly the indexing strategy, to reconsider the logic of accessing such blocks frequently, in an effort to reduce contention on them. The following queries will help. (Note that in 10gR2, the cache buffers chain latch can be shared—but not all the time. Also, in-memory undo [IMU] will lessen issues with the buffer cache.) While Oracle does in-memory updates *all* the time , this happens in the buffer cache. IMU is new because UNDO and REDO in Oracle 9i had to be written out to disk quickly to protect the data.

Segments experiencing waits on the cache buffers chains latch

```
     -- Segments Experiencing Waits on the Cache Buffers Chains Latch (slow - test)
 SELECT  /*+ ordered */
         de.owner ||'.'|| de.segment_name  segment_name,
         de.segment_type  segment_type,
         de.extent_id  extent#,
         bh.dbablk - de.block_id + 1  block#,
         bh.lru_flag,
         bh.tch,
         lc.child#
  FROM   (SELECT MAX(sleeps) MaxSleeps
          FROM   v$latch_children
          WHERE  name='cache buffers chains') max_sleeps,
          v$latch_children  lc,
          X$bh  bh,
          dba_extents  de
   WHERE  lc.name     = 'cache buffers chains'
     AND  lc.sleeps  > (0.8 * MaxSleeps)
     AND  bh.hladdr   = lc.addr
     AND  de.file_id = bh.file#
     AND  bh.dbablk between de.block_id and de.block_id + de.blocks - 1
 ORDER BY bh.tch;
```

Segments experiencing waits on the cache buffers LRU chain latch

```
     -- Segments Experiencing Waits on Cache Buffers LRU Chain Latch (slow - test)
 SELECT  /*+ ordered */
         de.owner ||'.'|| de.segment_name  segment_name,
         de.segment_type  segment_type,
         de.extent_id  extent#,
         bh.dbablk - de.block_id + 1  block#,
         bh.lru_flag,
         bh.tch,
         lc.child#
  FROM   (SELECT MAX(sleeps) MaxSleeps
          FROM v$latch_children
          WHERE name='cache buffers lru chain') max_sleeps,
          v$latch_children  lc,
          X$bh  bh,
          dba_extents  de
 WHERE   lc.name     = 'cache buffers lru chain'
   AND   lc.sleeps  > (0.8 * MaxSleeps)
   AND   bh.hladdr   = lc.addr
   AND   de.file_id = bh.file#
   AND   bh.dbablk between de.block_id and de.block_id + de.blocks - 1
 ORDER BY bh.tch;
```

Sessions experiencing waits on the buffer busy waits or write complete waits events

```
     -- Sessions Experiencing Waits on the Buffer Busy Waits or Write
     -- Complete Waits Events. Note that the values returned by the p1, p2,
```

```
    -- and p3 parameters disclose the file, block, and reason for the wait.
    -- The cause disclosed by the p3 parameter is not externally published.
    -- The p3 parameter is a number that translates to one of several
    -- causes, among which are the buffer being read or written by
    -- another session.
  SELECT /*+ ordered */
         sid,event,owner,segment_name,segment_type,p1,p2,p3
    FROM v$session_wait sw, dba_extents de
   WHERE de.file_id = sw.p1
     AND sw.p2 between de.block_id and de.block_id + de.blocks - 1
     AND (event = 'buffer busy waits' OR event = 'write complete waits')
     AND p1 IS NOT null
ORDER BY event,sid;
```

Problem segments returned by queries in this section are likely to be the same as those returned by the query returning hot buffers earlier in this section. If they're not, a possible explanation may be that such a segment is accessed frequently by one session, as shown by the hot buffer query, but there may be no contention for it by other sessions, as may be shown by the absence of that segment from the result set of the other queries in this section. Other than that scenario, the segments returned by a hot buffers query are likely to also be returned by the other queries in this section that show the problem segment. Each of these queries conveniently includes the blocks of the particular segments associated with the latches or waits in question.

For table segments, you can use the DBMS_ROWID PL/SQL package to map the file and block numbers returned by these queries to the corresponding table rows. If one or a set of segments consistently shows up in the result sets of the queries in this section, then these are highly used segments. Investigate the application to reconsider the use of these popular segments. Ask questions like the following:

- Is the indexing scheme appropriate?

- Are there PL/SQL (or Java) loop exit conditions where they should be?

- Are superfluous tables included in join queries?

- Can any SQL code be reengineered to alter a join strategy, either with reengineered subqueries, inline views, or similar alternatives?

- Should some hints, like ordered, USE_HASH, etc., be used?

- Are statistics up to date?

- Do any of the involved tables have a high watermark that is well beyond the actual blocks that contain rows?

- Could a table or index make advantageous use of partitioning or histograms?

- Should a keep pool be used?

If a variety of different segments are repeatedly showing up in the result of the buffer-busy query, the buffer cache is probably undersized or the disk subsystem is not writing changed (dirty) buffers out to the datafiles fast enough for them to be reused (or both). If there does not seem to be contention on particular segments, but rather on a varying set of segments, this problem indicates that Oracle is having trouble in general satisfying requests to load blocks into free buffers.

If rollback segment blocks show up in the result sets of the queries in this section, then more rollback segments are probably needed due to rollback segment header block contention. Confirm this with a query on V$ROLLSTAT (check the WAITS column). Alternatively, you should consider whether the application is performing too many rollbacks and whether the physical rollback segment placement is optimal. Another option is to determine whether the rollback segment datafiles reside on physical disks with other high I/O datafiles or whether the physical disk configuration, such as a RAID5 configuration, will hinder rollback segment write performance and exacerbate these types of waits. A better option is to switch to Automatic Undo Management and avoid all of this.

You should also review the storage parameter configuration of the problem segments returned by the queries in this section. Consider whether there are sufficient freelists for the tables and indexes that can be classified as high concurrent update (multiple sessions updating them concurrently). You should probably set freelists to 2 or higher for these segments, but do not set freelists higher than the number of CPUs in the database server or use Automatic Segment Space Management (ASSM). You should review the data block size and PCT_FREE because different conditions call for blocks of a table or index to contain more rows or fewer rows. In situations in which a particular segment block is popular, you may want to reconstruct the segment with a higher PCT_FREE; thus, interblock contention for rows that were previously stored in the same block is reduced because the chance of those rows being stored in the same block has been reduced by simply reducing the number of rows that can be inserted into a block.

Obviously, more buffer cache buffers are required to accommodate a table reconstructed to have a larger pct_free and therefore consist of more row-containing blocks. The trade-off is that this can reduce the performance of full table scan operations on such tables because more blocks must be visited to complete a full table scan. In general, you must consider the overall use of these tables and indexes to judge whether it is more advantageous to have more or fewer rows in the blocks of the particular table or index. These points can be summarized as follows:

- **Condition** Higher PCT_FREE and therefore fewer rows per block.

  - **Advantage** Less contention on updates of popular blocks.

  - **Disadvantage** The segment will consist of more blocks and therefore reduce full table scan performance.

- **Condition** Lower PCT_FREE and therefore more rows per block.

  - **Advantage** There is a better chance that the block containing a requested row is already in a buffer cache buffer from a recent query. Full tablescans will need to visit fewer blocks.

  - **Disadvantage** There may be more contention on blocks being updated. If a block contains a row to be updated, all the other rows (more of them) in that block are now in a copy of the block that is incompatible with other sessions requesting a read of other rows in that block; thus, another read-consistent copy of the block must be read into another buffer cache buffer.

Hot Data Blocks and Wait Events

Instance/Database

You can obtain some database- and instance-specific information from the X$KCCDI table. Consider the following queries, which you can use to find overall instance- and database-specific information:

MAXLOGMEMBERS setting for a database

```
-- MAXLOGMEMBERS setting for a database.
SELECT dimlm
  FROM X$KCCDI;
```

Datafile creation times

```
-- Datafile creation times.
SELECT indx file_id,
       fecrc_tim creation_date,
       file_name,
       tablespace_name
  FROM X$kccfe int,
       dba_data_files dba
  WHERE dba.file_id = int.indx + 1
ORDER BY file_name;
```

Background process names and process IDs

```
-- Background process names and process ids.
SELECT ksbdpnam ProcessName, ksbdppro OSPid
  FROM X$ksbdp
  WHERE  ksbdppro != '00' ;

PROCE OSPID
----- --------
PMON  6A4ED064
MMAN  6A4ED4E4
DBW0  6A4ED964
LGWR  6A4EDDE4
CKPT  6A4EE264
CMON  6A4EE6E4
RECO  6A4EEB64
CJQ0  6A4EEFE4
QMNC  6A4EFD64
MMON  6A4F0664=
MMNL  6A4F0AE4

11 rows selected.
```

Various instance resources

```
-- Various instance resources (very cool).
SELECT kviival ResourceValue, kviidsc ResourceName
   FROM X$kvii;
```

Note that the last query has different values returned for the resource values on different platforms.

Effective X$ Table Use and Strategy

Consider creating a separate X$ query user that has its own X$ views on the SYS X$ tables as described earlier in the chapter. This user could manually or with DBMS_JOB perform periodic queries to capture X$ table data into some other tables so that the contents of the X$ tables can be examined over time. If you do this, keep in mind that the data in the X$ tables is highly transient. Some scripts or jobs written to capture such information will likely miss a lot of it. On the other hand, you do not want to query these tables so frequently that these queries themselves and their associated activity information are a non-negligible percentage of the data in the tables.

In monitoring the X$KSMLRU table (and perhaps X$KSMSP and others), it may be prudent to capture the contents of the table to a permanent table for analysis and comparison over time.

Related Oracle Internals Topics

Alas, more toys for the mischievously curious DBAs. Except for traces, you should not use the utilities described in the following sections in production without the guidance of Oracle Support. You can take them and run with them in a sandbox database to learn what useful information they provide.

Traces

Database sessions can be traced to collect session information about the work performed in the session, and to diagnose problems. Traces can be turned on by a variety of methods:

- Set SQL_TRACE = TRUE with an alter session command.

- Set SQL_TRACE = TRUE in the initialization parameter file (deprecated).

- Execute the DBMS_SYSTEM.SET_SQL_TRACE_IN_SESSION( ) PL/SQL package for another session.

- Create them with the $ORACLE_HOME/rdbms/admin/dbmssupp.sql script.

- Execute the DBMS_SYSTEM.SET_EV( ) PL/SQL package to set tracing events in another session.

- Use the ORADEBUG command.

CAUTION
If you set SQL_TRACE = TRUE in the parameter file, it generates traces for every process connected to the database, including the background processes.

Traces

The simplest method to invoke a trace of a session is for the session itself to enable tracing with the following command:

```
SQL> alter session set sql_trace=true;

Session altered.
```

Developers may do this themselves from SQL*Plus, and may also include it in PL/SQL code using the execute immediate facility. The DBA may optionally decide to make the trace files in the user dump destination world-readable (Unix and OpenVMS) by setting the hidden parameter _trace_files_public to TRUE on instance startup. See Note 210317.1 if setting this to TRUE as nondefault values poses a security risk.

Having users generate traces for themselves is simple but not always practical. Third-party applications usually do not permit the code to be modified for the insertion of trace-start commands, and there is usually no SQL prompt from where the trace can be started. We could use system logon triggers to identify the user connecting and optionally start a trace, but there are easier methods at our disposal.

In these situations we need to be able to invoke a trace for another session. As the DBA we have a number of methods to do this. In each case however we need to know the SID and the SERIAL# of the session we want to trace. We can find this information in the V$SESSION view as follows:

```
select sid, serial#
from   v$session where username = 'NICOLA';

     SID    SERIAL#
---------- ----------
     540         11
```

Once we have this information, we can use the SET_SQL_TRACE_IN_SESSION procedure of the DBMS_SYSTEM package to invoke the trace. The procedure takes three arguments: SID, SERIAL# and a Boolean argument to start or stop the tracing. It is invoked as follows:

```
SQL> exec dbms_system.set_sql_trace_in_session(540,11,TRUE);
PL/SQL procedure successfully completed.
```

When sufficient tracing information has been collected, the trace can be disabled as follows:

```
SQL> exec dbms_system.set_sql_trace_in_session(540,11,FALSE);
PL/SQL procedure successfully completed.
```

Alternatively, we can use the DBMS_SUPPORT package to start the trace. The DBMS_SUPPORT package is an option that can be loaded into the database from the rdbms/admin directory. To load the package, you must be connected to the database as a SYSDBA privileged user and then run the dbmssupp.sql script.

The DBMS_SUPPORT package offers much of the same functionality for tracing as the DBMS_SYSTEM package but with these additional features:

- It allows bind variables and session wait information to be optionally included in the trace file.

■ It verifies the SID and SERIAL# specified for tracing, rejecting invalid combinations. This can be useful in critical situations. It can be very frustrating to have spent an hour believing you have collected useful trace information only to find that you mis-typed something and the user dump destination directory is empty.

The START_TRACE_IN_SESSION procedure of the DBMS_SUPPORT package is used to start the trace. The procedure takes four arguments: SID, SERIAL#, a Boolean specifying if wait information is recorded (default TRUE). and a Boolean specifying if bind variables are recorded (default FALSE). It is invoked as follows:

```
SQL> exec dbms_support.START_TRACE_IN_SESSION(540,13,TRUE,TRUE);
PL/SQL procedure successfully completed.
```

To stop tracing, the STOP_TRACE_IN_SESSION procedure is used:

```
SQL> exec dbms_support.stop_trace_in_session(540,13);
```

Another method to invoke tracing for another session is to use the DBMS_SYSTEM.SET_EV method. This procedure allows database events to be set in any session in the database. By setting the 10046 event, we can gather complete tracing information about any session. As before, we need the SID and SERIAL# of the session we want to monitor. We can then set the event as follows:

```
SQL> exec dbms_system.set_ev(537,21,10046,12,'');
PL/SQL procedure successfully completed.
```

The first two arguments are the SID and SERIAL# of the session. The next argument is the event we want to set which in this case is event 10046 to trace the session. The fourth argument sets the level of the event. We have set the level to 12 to gather all wait and bind variable information in addition to the basic trace. The available levels are as follows:

Level	Information Gathered
0	All tracing disabled
1	Standard tracing enabled
2	Same as level 1
4	Standard trace plus bind variable information
8	Standard trace plus wait information
12	Standard trace plus bind and wait information

To stop tracing, we need to set the event level to zero as follows:

```
SQL> exec dbms_system.set_ev(537,21,10046,0,'');
PL/SQL procedure successfully completed.
```

Finally, we could use the ORADEBUG facility to invoke the required trace. This will be explored further later in this chapter.

Traces

Once a trace file has been generated, you can use the standard TKPROF utility to interpret the contents of the trace. (The TKPROF tool is covered in detail in Chapter 6.) Oracle also offers the more advanced TRCANLZR tool, which can be downloaded from Metalink (see Note 224270.1). The more adventurous DBA may wish to examine the raw trace file, which can sometimes yield information not shown by TKPROF.

The Trace Analyzer takes the trace files generated by the methods described previously and produces an HTML format report. The report will be written to the user dump destination directory and will have the filename format *trcanlzr_<PROCESS_ID>_1.html*. The report is very detailed and can take an extended period of time to produce, especially if your server is running poorly to begin with. To generate the report, you need to know the name of the trace file generated. and then you can invoke the analyzer as follows:

```
SQL> exec trca$i.trace_analyzer('lwdb_ora_5818.trc');
PL/SQL procedure successfully completed.
```

The finished HTML report summarizes the trace file (see Figure 13-1). The report includes all of the details found on TKPROF, plus additional information normally requested and used for a transaction performance analysis.

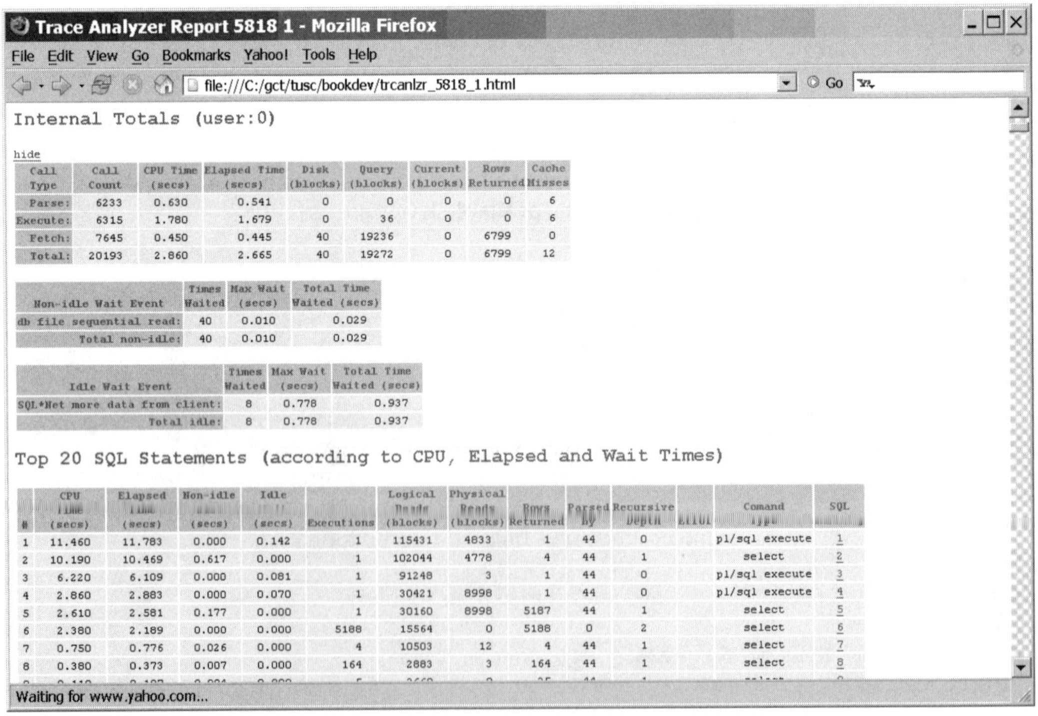

FIGURE 13-1. *Sample trace analyzer report*

DBMS_TRACE Package

The DBMS_TRACE package is another method of tracing, but unlike the preceding examples, it is designed specifically to trace PL/SQL rather than individual sessions. It can be extremely useful when trying to debug PL/SQL programs. To use the DBMS_TRACE package, the DBA must first load the following scripts from the rdbms/admin directory as a SYSDBA user:

```
TRACETAB.SQL
DBMSPBT.SQL
PRVTPBT.PLB
```

Once the packages are loaded, PL/SQL can be traced. There are two methods of doing this:

```
SQL> alter session set plsql_debug=true;
```

All PL/SQL code created by the session after this point will have the additional hooks to allow it to be traced. This includes anonymous PL/SQL blocks. However, code created before this point cannot be traced with the DBMS_TRACE package. Alternatively, any existing PL/SQL package, procedure, or function can be re-compiled using the following command:

```
SQL> alter [PROCEDURE | FUNCTION | PACKAGE BODY] <procedure name> compile debug;
```

TIP
Anonymous PL/SQL blocks cannot be traced using the "compile debug" method. PL/SQL tracing for the entire session must be enabled with the "alter session set plsql_debug=true" command.

Now to trace the PL/SQL code execution, you can start with the following command:

```
SQL> execute dbms_trace.set_plsql_trace(dbms_trace.trace_all_lines);
```

The argument here specifies which lines of PL/SQL to trace. The options are TRACE_ALL_LINES to trace every line executed, TRACE_ENABLED_LINES to trace only PL/SQL that was explicitly compiled with the debug option, TRACE_ALL_EXCEPTIONS to trace only exceptions, and TRACE_ENABLED_EXCEPTIONS to trace only exceptions of PL/SQL that was explicitly compiled with the debug option. When the tracing is complete, it can be disabled with the following command:

```
SQL> execute dbms_trace.clear_plsql_trace();
```

The results of the trace can be seen in the PLSQL_TRACE_EVENTS table owned by the SYS schema.

```
select event_seq as seq, stack_depth, event_kind as kind,
       event_unit as unit, event_line as line, event_comment
from   sys.plsql_trace_events;

  SEQ STACK_DEPTH  KIND UNIT                     LINE EVENT_COMMENT
------- ----------- ----- -------------------- ----- --------------------------------
 270001           7    51 RDBA_MONITOR_C         108 New line executed
 270002           7    51 RDBA_MONITOR_C         110 New line executed
```

270003	8	51	RDBA_UTILITY	174	New line executed
270004	8	51	RDBA_UTILITY	183	New line executed
270005	8	51	RDBA_UTILITY	192	New line executed
270006	8	51	RDBA_UTILITY	195	New line executed
270007	9	51	DBMS_SQL	9	New line executed
270008	10	51	DBMS_SYS_SQL	882	New line executed
270009	10	51	DBMS_SYS_SQL	883	New line executed
270010	9	51	DBMS_SQL	9	New line executed
270011	9	51	DBMS_SQL	10	New line executed
270012	8	51	RDBA_UTILITY	195	New line executed
270013	8	51	RDBA_UTILITY	196	New line executed

Events

An *event* is similar to a system trigger in an Oracle instance. A trigger can capture pertinent information about the instance and individual database sessions to trace files. If an event is set in an initialization parameter file or with an alter system or alter session setting, then Oracle captures information to a trace file based on the conditions set in the event. Several events can be set. These can be described with the oerr command-line facility. Try the following command (in Unix only):

```
oerr ora 10046
```

A particularly useful tuning tool is event 10046 (described in Chapter 9 in detail). This event can be enabled in the initialization parameter file with the following line (although this is not something that you generally want to set at the database level):

```
event = '10046 trace name context forever, level 8'
```

Or, it is more likely to be used at the session level with an alter session command:

```
alter session set events '10046 trace name context forever,level 12';
```

The trace information is captured to a file in the USER_DUMP_DEST directory specified in the initialization parameter file. This event is equivalent to setting SQL_TRACE = TRUE in the initialization parameter file. At level 12, this event setting includes the values of bind variables and the occurrences of wait events. Other events are useful in troubleshooting database and performance issues. Do not set events in production databases without first consulting with Oracle Support and testing them in a test database.

You can use the oradebug command (covered later in this chapter in the oradebug section) or DBMS_SUPPORT PL/SQL package to set events in sessions other than the current session. Also, to UNSET this event you use

```
alter session set events '10046 trace name context off';
```

Dumps

Several structures in an Oracle instance or database can be dumped to a trace file for low-level analysis, such as these:

- Control files

- Datafile headers
- Redo log file headers
- Instance state
- Process state
- Library cache
- Data blocks
- Redo blocks

These dumps can be created with these commands:

```
alter session set events 'immediate trace name CONTROLF level 10';
alter session set events 'immediate trace name FILE_HDRS level 10';
alter session set events 'immediate trace name REDOHDR level 10';
alter session set events 'immediate trace name SYSTEMSTATE level 10';
alter session set events 'immediate trace name PROCESSSTATE level 10';
alter session set events 'immediate trace name library_cache level 10';
alter system dump datafile 10 block 2057;
alter system dump logfile '<logfilename>';
```

The trace files containing this dump information are in the USER_DUMP_DEST directory.

ORADEBUG

You use the oradebug command for troubleshooting the instance or sessions. Oradebug can capture current instance state information, set events in sessions, and perform other low-level diagnostics. Type **oradebug help** from SQL*Plus to get the usage list shown next.

NOTE
*You must be connected AS SYSDBA to be able to access ORADEBUG
(version dependent listing—run this for your own version).*

```
SQL> oradebug help
HELP              [command]                   Describe one or all commands
SETMYPID                                      Debug current process
SETOSPID          <ospid>                     Set OS pid of process to debug
SETORAPID         <orapid> ['force']          Set Oracle pid of process to debug
DUMP              <dump_name> <level>         Invoke named dump
DUMPSGA           [bytes]                     Dump fixed SGA
DUMPLIST                                      Print a list of available dumps
EVENT             <text>                      Set trace event in process
SESSION_EVENT     <text>                      Set trace event in session
DUMPVAR           <p|s|uga> <name> [level]    Print/dump a fixed PGA/SGA/UGA variable
SETVAR            <p|s|uga> <name> <value>    Modify a fixed PGA/SGA/UGA variable
PEEK              <addr> <len> [level]        Print/Dump memory
POKE              <addr> <len> <value>        Modify memory
WAKEUP            <orapid>                     Wake up Oracle process
```

```
SUSPEND                                      Suspend execution
RESUME                                       Resume execution
FLUSH                                        Flush pending writes to trace file
CLOSE_TRACE                                  Close trace file
TRACEFILE_NAME                               Get name of trace file
LKDEBUG                                      Invoke global enqueue service debugger
NSDBX                                        Invoke CGS name-service debugger
-G             <Inst-List | def | all>      lkdebug cluster database command prefix
-R             <Inst-List | def | all>      lkdebug cluster database command prefix
SETINST        <instance# .. | all>         Set instance list in double quotes
SGATOFILE      <SGA dump dir>          Dump SGA to file; dirname in double quotes
DMPCOWSGA      <SGA dump dir> Dump & map SGA as COW; dirname in double quotes
MAPCOWSGA      <SGA dump dir>          Map SGA as COW; dirname in double quotes
HANGANALYZE    [level]                       Analyze system hang
FFBEGIN                                      Flash Freeze the Instance
FFDEREGISTER                                 FF deregister instance from cluster
FFTERMINST                                   Call exit and terminate instance
FFRESUMEINST                                 Resume the flash frozen instance
FFSTATUS                                     Flash freeze status of instance
SKDSTTPCS      <ifname>  <ofname>            Helps translate PCs to names
WATCH          <address> <len> <self|exist|all|target>  Watch a region of memory
DELETE         <local|global|target> watchpoint <id>    Delete a watchpoint
SHOW           <local|global|target> watchpoints        Show  watchpoints
CORE                                         Dump core without crashing process
UNLIMIT                                      Unlimit the size of the trace file
PROCSTAT                                     Dump process statistics
CALL           <func> [arg1] ... [argn]     Invoke function with arguments
```

The following example shows using the ORADEBUG command to invoke a trace of another session. A user might be complaining of slow performance on a database, or we might have identified the process ID from the operation system. To get the SPID, use the following query:

```
select spid
from    v$process
where   addr = (select paddr from v$session where username = 'NICOLA';);
```

You use the SETOSPID command to attach to the process and invoke the trace:

```
select spid
from    v$process
where   addr = (select paddr from v$session where username = 'NICOLA';);
SQL> oradebug setospid 6943
Oracle pid: 11  Unix process pid: 6943, image: oraclelwdb@dc-mvndb3
```

Now that we are attached, we can invoke the trace by setting the 10046 event. We select a level 12 to force all bind variables and wait information to be written to the trace file:

```
SQL> oradebug event 10046 trace name context forever, level 12
Statement processed.
```

The session is now tracing. If we want to see the name of the trace file being generated, we use the TRACEFILE_NAME option as follows:

```
SQL> oradebug tracefile_name
/u01/app/oracle/admin/lwdb/udump/lwdb_ora_6943.trc
```

This shows us the name and location of the trace file. This file can then be processed with the TKPROF analysis tool to obtain detailed information about the operations of the monitored process.

If your Oracle database has trace file size limitation specified in the SPFILE or INIT.ORA file, you can override this from ORADEBUG using the following command:

```
SQL> oradebug unlimit
Statement processed.
```

The DBA should remember, however, that Oracle buffers its writes to the trace file, and so the information contained in the file might not be completely up to date. Fortunately the ORADEBUG command gives us the ability to flush the trace file write buffer as follows:

```
SQL> oradebug flush
Statement processed.
```

The ORADEBUG can also be used to suspend the execution of a process. For example you might have a long-running database job that is about to fail due to space, or an intensive update job that you want to disable during a backup. The ORADEBUG command allows specific sessions to be suspended as follows:

```
SQL> oradebug setospid 6943
Oracle pid: 11, Unix process pid: 6943, image: oraclelwdb@dc-mvndb3

SQL> oradebug suspend
Statement processed.
```

The Oracle operating system process 6943 is now suspended and will remain that way until you issue the ORADEBUG RESUME command.

TIP
Do not use ORADEBUG SUSPEND on the Microsoft Windows platform. Due to the thread-based processing model of Windows, the whole database will be suspended, not just the process you are attached to.

When you want to disable tracing for the specified session, you can use the following ORADEBUG command:

```
SQL> oradebug event 10046 trace name context off
Statement processed.
```

trcsess Utility

With the 10g release of the database, Oracle provided us with another tracing utility: *trcsess*. The utility can be found in the bin directory under the Oracle Home. The tool is designed to read database trace files and extract information the DBA is interested in. Trace information can be located based on session identifier (SID and serial number), client identifier, service name, action name, or module name. The tool is primarily designed for use in shared server or connection pooling environments where multiple processes may have to be traced to capture all relevant information. The tool does not interpret the trace information; it simply aggregates multiple traces files into a single one based on the criteria provided. The result is a combined trace file that can be analyzed using TKPROF, TRCANLZR, or another tool. For additional information on this tool, see Metalink Note 280543.1.

Reading the Trace File

The preceding section showed several methods that can be used to generate a trace of a session. Once the session being traced has completed, the DBA will need to locate, read, and interpret the trace file. The trace file is written to the directory pointed to by the user dump destination parameter. You can see from SQL*Plus with the following command:

```
SQL> show parameter user_dump_dest

NAME                                 TYPE        VALUE
------------------------------------ ----------- ------------------------------
user_dump_dest                       string      /u01/app/oracle/admin/lwdb/udump
```

The trace file will have the filename format <sid>_ora_<process id>.trc. The process ID can be found in the V$PROCESS view as follows:

```
select  spid
from    gv$process vp, gv$session vs
where   vs.sid = userenv('SID')
and     vs.paddr = vp.addr
and     vs.inst_id = vp.inst_id;

SPID
------------
4508
```

So, in this example our trace file name will be

```
/u01/app/oracle/admin/lwdb/udump/lwdb_ora_2173.trc
```

Once located, the trace file can be read with the TKPROF tool (see Chapter 6) or the TRZANLZR tool shown earlier in this chapter. However, the curious DBA might be interested to see the contents of the trace file for himself or herself. Since the raw trace file is written in ANSI format, this can be accomplished with any standard file browser or editor. The trace file will show the traced session as a series of blocks. Each block represents a database call and is separated by a single line. At the top of the trace file is the standard trace file header that many DBAs will already be familiar with:

```
/u01/app/oracle/admin/lwdb/udump/lwdb_ora_12287.trc
Oracle Database 10g Enterprise Edition Release 10.1.0.2.0 - 64bit Production
With the Partitioning, OLAP and Data Mining options
```

```
ORACLE_HOME = /u01/app/oracle/product/10.1
System name:    SunOS
Node name:      dc-mvndb3
Release:        5.9
Version:        Generic_117171-07
Machine:        sun4u
Instance name: lwdb
Redo thread mounted by this instance: 1
Oracle process number: 11
Unix process pid: 12287, image: oracle@dc-mvndb3 (TNS V1-V3)
```

The trace file then shows each database call that was executed in the traced session in sequential order. The following example shows a simple SELECT statement:

```
======================
PARSING IN CURSOR #1 len=51 dep=0 uid=44 oct=3 lid=44 tim=4640811701949 hv=3771583942
ad='df845680'
select birthday from sprogs where name = :"SYS_B_0"
END OF STMT
PARSE #1:c=0,e=741,p=0,cr=0,cu=0,mis=1,r=0,dep=0,og=4,tim=4640811701937
BINDS #1:
 bind 0: dty=1 mxl=32(04) mal=00 scl=00 pre=00 oacflg=10 oacfl2=0100 size=32 offset=0
   bfp=ffffffff7ba79e98 bln=32 avl=04 flg=09
   value="Jake"
EXEC #1:c=0,e=1834,p=0,cr=0,cu=0,mis=1,r=0,dep=0,og=4,tim=4640811703910
WAIT #1: nam='SQL*Net message to client' ela= 4 p1=1413697536 p2=1 p3=0
FETCH #1:c=0,e=277,p=0,cr=14,cu=0,mis=0,r=1,dep=0,og=4,tim=4640811704358
WAIT #1: nam='SQL*Net message from client' ela= 63976 p1=1413697536 p2=1 p3=0
FETCH #1:c=0,e=63,p=0,cr=2,cu=0,mis=0,r=0,dep=0,og=4,tim=4640811798402
WAIT #1: nam='SQL*Net message to client' ela= 2 p1=1413697536 p2=1 p3=0
*** 2006-01-20 14:57:28.470
WAIT #1: nam='SQL*Net message from client' ela= 28379958 p1=1413697536 p2=1 p3=0
STAT #1 id=1 cnt=1 pid=0 pos=1 obj=57668 op='TABLE ACCESS FULL SPROGS (cr=16 pr=0 pw=0
time=251 us)'
```

The first line shows information about the statement being executed. The tags can be interpreted as follows:

Tag	Meaning
Len	Length of SQL statement.
Dep	Recursive depth of the cursor. Blocks where dep is not zero are recursive calls made by the database on the user's behalf. Time spent here will contribute to the "recursive CPU" usage recorded in V$SYSSTAT.
Uid	Schema user ID of parsing user—see USER_ID in DBA_USERS.
Oct	Oracle command type.
Lid	Privilege user ID—may not be the sane as parsing user if executing another user's PL/SQL code.
Tim	Timestamp—the value is the value in V$TIMER when the line was written. Pre–Oracle 9*i*, the times recorded by Oracle are centiseconds (10 mS). As of Oracle 9*i* some times are microseconds (1/1,000,000ths of a second).

Reading the Trace File

Tag	Meaning
Hv	SQL Hash—maps to SQL_HASH in V$SQLAREA.
Ad	SQL Address—maps to SQL_ADDRESS in V$SQLAREA.

The trace file then shows the text of the SQL statement being executed. In this case we are selecting a value from the SPROGS table. We can also see from the trace file that this statement has been assigned cursor number 1.

TIP
Cursors may be re-assigned if the cursor is closed and released. Therefore, when reading a long trace file, it is important to remember that a cursor number referenced at one part of the trace file may not represent the same SQL statement as it does elsewhere in the trace file.

The trace file now shows the operations Oracle performs to actually satisfy the query. This basically amounts to a series of executions (EXEC) and fetches (FETCH). Both the EXEC and FETCH trace lines report the following tracing information:

Tag	Meaning
C	CPU time (100ths of a second).
E	Elapsed time (100ths of a second in Oracle 7, 8, microseconds in Oracle 9 onward).
P	Number of physical reads.
Cr	Number of buffers retrieved for CR reads.
Cu	Number of buffers retrieved in current mode.
Mis	Cursor missed in the cache.
R	Number of rows processed.
Dep	Recursive call depth (0 – user SQL, >0 – recursive).
Og	Optimizer goal: 1 – all rows, 2 – first rows, 3 – rule, 4 – choose.
Tim	Timestamp (large number in 100ths of a second).

Applying this knowledge to the EXEC line from our trace, we can determine the following:

```
EXEC #1:c=0,e=1834,p=0,cr=0,cu=0,mis=1,r=0,dep=0,og=4,tim=4640811703910
```

- A total of 0 ms of CPU was used for this exec.
- Total elapsed time was 1834 ms.
- Physical reads was zero.

- Buffers retrieved in CR (consistent read) mode was zero.

- Buffers retrieved in current mode was zero.

- Library cache misses was 1 (this statement was not found in the cache).

- Rows processed was zero.

- Recursive call depth was 0 (this was a user call).

- Optimizer goal was choose.

Wait Information and Response Time

The trace file also includes Wait (WAIT) information. This shows time Oracle spent waiting for certain items between parsing, executing, and fetching data. In our trace file we can see this wait event:

```
WAIT #1: nam='SQL*Net message to client' ela= 4 p1=1413697536 p2=1 p3=0
```

The NAM column shows the event that was waited on. The ELA column shows the time waited. The meaning of the P1, P2, and P3 columns depends on the event. The information shown can also be observed by inspecting the GV$SESSION_WAIT view during statement execution. In this example, we can also see that Oracle waited on a "SQL*Net message to client" event for 4 ms. The wait is followed by this:

```
FETCH #1:c=0,e=277,p=0,cr=14,cu=0,mis=0,r=1,dep=0,og=4,tim=4640811704358
```

The FETCH step takes 277 ms, reads 14 buffers in CR mode, and processes 1 row. The 277 ms includes the 4 ms from the WAIT step. Elapsed times for all WAIT events immediately preceding an EXEC or FETCH operation are incorporated in the total elapsed time shown for that event:

```
WAIT #9: nam='db file sequential read' ela= 6388 p1=6 p2=12892 p3=1
WAIT #9: nam='db file sequential read' ela= 3390 p1=6 p2=8286 p3=1
WAIT #9: nam='db file sequential read' ela= 7345 p1=6 p2=8500 p3=1
WAIT #9: nam='db file sequential read' ela= 4606 p1=7 p2=5828 p3=1
WAIT #9: nam='db file sequential read' ela= 7224 p1=6 p2=8822 p3=1
FETCH #9:c=10000,e=44951,p=8,cr=17,cu=0,mis=0,r=1,dep=1,og=4,tim=1077249917950
FETCH #9:c=0,e=249,p=0,cr=7,cu=0,mis=0,r=1,dep=1,og=4,tim=1077249918691
WAIT #9: nam='db file sequential read' ela= 2088 p1=6 p2=8285 p3=1
WAIT #9: nam='db file sequential read' ela= 91 p1=6 p2=8821 p3=1
FETCH #9:c=0,e=2698,p=2,cr=9,cu=0,mis=0,r=1,dep=1,og=4,tim=1077249921635
```

In the preceding example, the elapsed time for the FETCH operation shown on line 6 includes the elapsed times from lines 1 through 5. The elapsed wait time shown for the FETCH operation on line 10 includes 2088 ms from the WAIT operation on line 8 and 91 ms from the WAIT operation on line 9.

Recursive Calls

The trace file identifies recursive calls by showing the call depth of each call. In the following extract we see a user call (cursor #50) being serviced by a recursive call (cursor #54), which itself is serviced by two recursive calls (cursor #35).

```
EXEC #35:c=0,e=71,p=0,cr=0,cu=0,mis=0,r=0,dep=2,og=4,tim=4232475308506
FETCH #35:c=0,e=48,p=0,cr=3,cu=0,mis=0,r=1,dep=2,og=4,tim=4232475308664
EXEC #54:c=0,e=4986,p=0,cr=9,cu=0,mis=0,r=1,dep=1,og=4,tim=4232475309925
EXEC #50:c=30000,e=31087,p=0,cr=9,cu=0,mis=0,r=0,dep=0,og=4,tim=4232475335361
```

The CPU time, Elapsed time, OS Blocks reads and CR and current blocks reads for all recursive calls are added to the totals for the originating call. In the preceding example, the total elapsed time for cursor #50 of 31,087ms includes the 4,986 ms elapsed time for cursor #54, which itself includes the 71 ms spent executing in cursor #35 and the 48 ms spent fetching.

Module Information

The raw trace file includes module information recorded by calls to the DBMS_APPLICATION_INFO package.

```
APPNAME mod='SES' mh=3264509754 act='Job ID: 3407193' ah=1464295440
```

The entry includes the following tags:

Tag	Meaning
Mod	Module
Mh	Module hash value (see V$SESSION)
Act	Action
Ah	Action hash (see V$SESSION)

Commit

Commit operations are shown in the trace file as XCTEND (Transaction END) calls.

```
XCTEND rlbk=0, rd_only=0
```

The rlbk tag is listed as one if a rollback is performed or zero if it is committed. The rd_only tag is listed as one if the transaction was read-only or zero if blocks were changed.

Unmap

The unmap operation records when temporary tables are cleaned up.

```
UNMAP #1:c=0,e=0,p=0,cr=0,cu=0,mis=0,r=0,dep=0,og=4,tim=2559434286
```

The flag records the same information as for EXEC and FETCH operations.

Bind Variables

One of the most powerful features of the 10046 trace with a level of 8 or 12, is that bind variable information is captured in the trace. This can be seen in the raw trace file as a series of BIND operations. The following example is taken from a 10*g* database with cursor sharing set to FORCE.

```
PARSING IN CURSOR #1 len=53 dep=0 uid=44 oct=3 lid=44 tim=1515557761996 hv=1439846314
ad='df3f6420'
select birthday from sprogs where name = :"SYS_B_0"
END OF STMT
PARSE #1:c=0,e=727,p=0,cr=0,cu=0,mis=1,r=0,dep=0,og=4,tim=1515557761984
BINDS #1:
 bind 0: dty=1 mxl=32(04) mal=00 scl=00 pre=00 oacflg=10 oacfl2=0100 size=32 offset=0
   bfp=ffffffff7b95e390 bln=32 avl=04 flg=09
   value="Alex"
```

In the preceding example the SQL statement is shown as we see it in the V$SQLTEXT, with the bind variable represented as SYS_B_0. However the BIND operation listed shows that bind variable zero of cursor #1 is being bound to the value "Alex". Note that we must be careful when interpreting the BIND information. Oracle replaces all static values with dynamically generated variable names such as SYS_B_*n*. However, named variables are *not* replaced. The BIND statements are listed in strict sequential order, with each value being bound to the next variable in the statement. Consider the following statement:

```
select *
from    SPROGS
where   name != 'Nicola'
and     birthday > ( to_date(:BIRTHDAY,'DDMONYY'));
```

If CURSOR_SHARING is set to FORCE or SIMILAR, the value 'Nicola' will be replaced with the variable SYS_B_0 and the value 'DDMONYY' will be replaced with SYS_B_1. For the purposes of binding, however, SYS_B_0 will be treated a variable 0, BIRTHDAY will be treated as variable 1, and SYS_B_1 will be treated as variable 2:

```
PARSE #10:c=0,e=1397,p=0,cr=0,cu=0,mis=1,r=0,dep=0,og=4,tim=4646278930704
BINDS #10:
 bind 0: dty=1 mxl=32(06) mal=00 scl=00 pre=00 oacflg=10 oacfl2=0100 size=32 offset=0
   bfp=ffffffff7b957de8 bln=32 avl=06 flg=09
   value="Nicola"
 bind 1: dty=1 mxl=2000(200) mal=00 scl=00 pre=00 oacflg=03 oacfl2=0010 size=2000 offset=0
   bfp=ffffffff7ba79980 bln=2000 avl=07 flg=05
   value="03APR73"
 bind 2: dty=1 mxl=32(07) mal=00 scl=00 pre=00 oacflg=10 oacfl2=0100 size=32 offset=0
   bfp=ffffffff7b957d98 bln=32 avl=07 flg=09
   value="DDMONYY"
```

When tracing larger more complex queries, it is important to remember that SYS_B_*n* does not necessarily bind to variable *n*.

Errors

The raw trace file will include errors that occur during the period of the trace. Two types of errors are recorded: execution errors and parsing errors. Parsing errors occur when the SQL statement could not be parsed due to problems such as syntax or object permissions.

```
PARSE ERROR #7:len=50 dep=0 uid=44 oct=3 lid=44 tim=1515543106413 err=936
select date from birthday where name = :"SYS_B_0"
```

The preceding trace line shows error ORA-936 when parsing cursor #7. The information includes all of the same information as a successful parse operation, expect for the SQL hash and address, as the failed statement is not stored in the library cache.

Execution errors simply list the error code and the time of the error.

```
ERROR #76:err=1555 tim=54406123
```

The preceding trace line shows that error ORA-1555 was raised during the execution of cursor #76.

Some Common X$ Table Groups

Some of the X$ tables can be logically grouped as shown in Tables 13-1 through 13-44. This is by no means a complete list. The descriptions for these are updated to the best of my knowledge. I am unsure of the value where the description or other field is missing or blank. Oracle Corporation does not provide a full description list. In the final section of the chapter, I include a *very nice* definition tree structure that was provided for an earlier version the X$ tables that can certainly be used with most versions to help you understand the naming conventions much better.

X$ Tables	Description
X$KCKCE	Features in use by the database instance that may prevent downgrading to a previous release
X$KCKFM	Some sort of information about the version of database or database parts
X$KCKTY	Features in use by the database instance that may prevent downgrading to a previous release
X$KSULL	Information about license limits
X$OPTION	Installed options
X$VERSION	Oracle RDBMS software version

TABLE 13-1. *Version/Installation*

X$ Tables	Description
X$KSUSGSTA	Instance statistics
X$KCCDI	Main source of information for V$DATABASE
X$KSMSD	SGA component sizes ("show sga")
X$KSMSS	Detailed SGA statistics (38 rows on Solaris and NT, 39 on Linux)
X$KSPPCV	Parameters and values that are in effect for the session
X$KSPPCV2	Parameters and values that are in effect for the session. List parameter values appear as separate rows.
X$KSPPI	Parameters and values that are currently in effect for the session
X$KSPPO	Obsolete parameters
X$KSPPSV	Parameters and values that are in effect for the instance
X$KSPPSV2	Parameters and values that are in effect for the instance. List parameter values appear as separate rows.
X$KSPSPFILE	Parameter names specified with an spfile (808 rows on Linux and Solaris, 799 rows on NT)
X$KSQDN	Database name
X$OPTION	Installed options
X$KVII	Instance limits and other instance metadata (includes miscellaneous information)
X$KVIS	Platform-specific block space information
X$KVIT	State of various buffer cache conditions
X$KSUXSINST	Main source of information for V$INSTANCE
X$QUIESCE	Quiescent state of the instance

TABLE 13-2. *Instance/Database*

X$ Tables	Description
X$KSULV	Valid values of NLS parameters
X$NLS_PARAMETERS	Current values of NLS parameters

TABLE 13-3. *NSL*

X$ Table Groups

X$ Table	Description
X$TIMEZONE_NAMES	Time zone names

TABLE 13-4. *Time Zones*

X$ Tables	Description
X$KCCAL	Information about archive log files from the control file
X$KCRRARCH	Information about the ARCH processes for the current instance
X$KCRRDEST	Describes, for the current instance, all the archive log destinations, their current value, mode, and status
X$KCRRDSTAT	Archive destination status

TABLE 13-5. *Archive Log Files/Destinations/Processes*

X$ Tables	Description
X$KCCFE	File creation and other metadata
X$KCCTF	Temp file I/O information
X$KCVFH	Information source of V$DATAFILE
X$KCFIO	File I/O information
X$KCFTIO	Temp file I/O information
X$KCVFHALL	Datafile information similar to information in V$DATAFILE
X$KTFBFE	Free extents in files (ktfb free extents)
X$KTFBHC	Transaction information

TABLE 13-6. *Data Files*

X$ Tables	Description
X$KCCCF	Control file information
X$KCCOR	Datafile offline information from the control file
X$KCCRS	Information about the control file record sections
X$KCCRT	Log file information from the control files

TABLE 13-7. *Control Files*

X$ Tables	Description
X$KCCCP	Redo log block information
X$KCCFN	Information about redo log files
X$KCCLE	Information about redo log files in need of archiving

TABLE 13-8. *Redo Log Files*

X$ Table	Description
X$KCCTS	Tablespace information

TABLE 13-9. *Tablespaces*

X$ Tables	Description
X$KTFTHC	Space usage in each temp tablespace
X$KTFTME	Status of each unit of all temp tablespaces (temp map extents/blocks)
X$KTSSO	Sort segment activity by session
X$KTSTFC	Temp segment usage: blocks used, cached, etc.
X$KTSTSSD	System temporary sort segment data

TABLE 13-10. *Sort/Temp Segments*

X$ Tables	Description
X$KTFBUE	Rollback/undo segment block/extent usage
X$KTTVS	Rollback/undo segment stats
X$KTUGD	Global rollback/undo data
X$KTURD	Rollback/undo segment stats
X$KTUSMST	Rollback/undo segment stats
X$KTUXE	Rollback/undo segment activity: wraps, etc.

TABLE 13-11. *Rollback/Undo Segments*

X$ Table Groups

X$ Tables	Description
X$KCVFHTMP	Tempfile information
X$KDLT	Temporary LOB information

TABLE 13-12. *Temporary Objects*

X$ Table	Description
X$UGANCO	Database link information

TABLE 13-13. *Database Links*

X$ Table	Description
X$KNSTMVR	Materialized view information

TABLE 13-14. *Materialized Views*

X$ Tables	Description
X$KNSTRPP	Replication information
X$KNSTRQU	Replication information

TABLE 13-15. *Replication*

X$ Tables	Description
X$KCCBF	Information from the control file about datafiles and control files in backup sets (RMAN)
X$KCCBL	Information from the control file about archived logs in backup sets (RMAN)

TABLE 13-16. *Backup*

X$ Tables	Description
X$KCCBP	Backup piece information from the control file (RMAN)
X$KCCBS	Backup set information from the control file (RMAN)
X$KCCCC	Datafile copy corruptions from the control file (RMAN)
X$KCCDC	Datafile copy information from the control file (RMAN)
X$KCCFC	Corruption in datafile backups (RMAN)
X$KCVFHONL	Backup status of all online datafiles
X$KSFHDVNT	Supported backup devices (RMAN)
X$KSFQP	Performance information about ongoing or recently completed backups
X$KSFVQST	Backup information
X$KSFVSL	Backup information
X$KSFVSTA	Backup information

TABLE 13-16. *Backup* (continued)

X$ Tables	Description
X$KCRFX	Statistics about the current recovery process
X$KCRMF	Statistics and status of files involved in recovery
X$KCRMX	Statistics and status of files involved in recovery
X$KCVFHMRR	Displays status of files during media recovery
X$KRVSLV	Recovery slave status
X$KRVSLVS	Recovery slave statistics
X$KTPRXRS	Information about recovery slaves performing parallel recovery
X$KTPRXRT	Information about transactions Oracle is currently recovering
X$ESTIMATED_MTTR	Estimates on the I/O work required if an instance recovery is needed right now
X$TARGETRBA	Target recovery block accesses or target redo block accesses

TABLE 13-17. *Recovery*

X$ Table Groups

X$ Tables	Description
X$KCCDL	Information about deleted objects. Recovery catalog resync operation uses this to speed its optimize operation.
X$KCCPA	Descriptions of archivelog backups taken with proxy copy
X$KCCPD	Descriptions of datafile and control file backups taken with proxy copy
X$KCCRM	RMAN configuration

TABLE 13-18. *RMAN*

X$ Table	Description
X$KCRRMS	Standby database status information
X$kccsl	Undetermined standby information
X$NKSTACR	Standby database information: log standby coordinator
X$KNSTASL	Standby database information

TABLE 13-19. *Standby Databases*

X$LOGMNR_ATTRIBUTE

X$LOGMNR_CALLBACK

X$LOGMNR_COL$

X$LOGMNR_COLTYPE$

X$LOGMNR_CONTENTS

X$LOGMNR_DICT$

X$LOGMNR_DICTIONARY

X$LOGMNR_ENCRYPTED_OBJ$

X$LOGMNR_ENCRYPTION_PROFILE$

TABLE 13-20. *LogMiner*

X$LOGMNR_IND$

X$LOGMNR_INDPART$

X$LOGMNR_LOGFILE

X$LOGMNR_LOGS

X$LOGMNR_PARAMETERS

X$LOGMNR_PROCESS

X$LOGMNR_OBJ$

X$LOGMNR_REGION

X$LOGMNR_SESSION

X$LOGMNR_TAB$

X$LOGMNR_TABCOMPART$

X$LOGMNR_TABSUBPART$

X$LOGMNR_TRANSACTION

X$LOGMNR_TS$

X$LOGMNR_TYPE$

X$LOGNNR_TABPART$

X$LOGMNR_TABSUBPART$

X$LOGMNR_USER$

TABLE 13-20. *LogMiner* (continued)

X$ Tables	Description
X$MESSAGES	Messages that each background process processes
X$QESMMSGA	Limits, use, estimates, etc., of memory use by PGAs

TABLE 13-21. *Sessions/Processes*

X$ Tables	Description
X$KOCST	Object cache statistics for the current session
X$KSLES	Waits on event by sessions
X$KSQRS	Session resource usage
X$KSUSIO	I/O statistics for each session
X$KSULOP	Session information about long-running operations
X$KSUMYSTA	Statistics for the current session
X$KSUPL	Session information
X$KSUPR	Main source of information for V$PROCESS
X$KSUSE	Information in V$SESSION
X$KSUSECON	Information about how each session connected and authenticated
X$KSUSECST	Session waits, including wait parameters
X$KSUSESTA	Session performance statistics

TABLE 13-22. *Session Performance*

X$ Table	Description
X$KTCXB	Transaction information, including locks requested and held, rollback segments used by the transaction, and the type of transaction

TABLE 13-23. *Transactions*

X$ Tables	Description
X$K2GTE	Information on the currently active global transactions
X$K2GTE2	Information on the currently active global transactions

TABLE 13-24. *Global Transactions*

X$ Tables	Description
X$KGSKASP	All available active session pool resource allocation methods
X$KGSKCFT	Data related to currently active resource consumer groups
X$KGSKCP	All resource allocation methods defined for resource consumer groups
X$KGSKDOPP	Available parallel degree limit resource allocation methods
X$KGSKPFT	Names of all currently active resource plans
X$KGSKQUEP	Available queue resource allocation methods
X$KSRMSGDES	Queue messages
X$KSRMSGO	Queue publisher/subscriber information
X$KWQSI	Read/write statistics on queues

TABLE 13-25. *Advanced Queuing (AQ)*

X$ Tables	Description
X$KCLCRST	Information about block server background processes used in cache fusion
X$KJBL	RAC DLM information
X$KJBLFX	RAC information
X$KJBR	RAC DLM information
X$KJDRHV	RAC instance information
X$KJDRPCMHV	RAC instance information
X$KJDRPCMPF	RAC instance information
X$KJICVT	RAC DLM information
X$KJILKFT	RAC DLM information
X$KJIRFT	RAC DLM information
X$KJISFT	RAC DLM information
X$KJITRFT	RAC DLM information
X$KJMDDP	RAC information
X$KJMSDP	RAC information
X$KJXM	RAC information

TABLE 13-26. *Real Application Clusters*

X$ Table Groups

X$ Tables	Description
X$KSIMAT	RAC information
X$KSIMAV	RAC information
X$KSIMSI	Map of instance names to instance numbers for all instances mounting a particular database
X$LE	RAC lock element statistics (mode, blocks, releases, acquisitions, etc.)
X$LE_	RAC lock element status and activity

TABLE 13-26. *Real Application Clusters* (continued)

X$ Tables	Description
X$KGLCLUSTER	Likely currently loaded or recently referenced clusters
X$KGLCURSOR	Statistics on shared SQL area without the GROUP BY clause and contains one row for each child of the original SQL text entered
X$KGLNA	Text of SQL statements belonging to shared SQL cursors
X$KGLNA1	Text of SQL statements belonging to shared SQL cursors: newlines and tabs not replaced with spaces
X$KGLOB	Database objects that are cached in the library cache. Objects include tables, indexes, clusters, synonym definitions, PL/SQL procedures and packages, and triggers.
X$KGLST	Library cache performance and activity information
X$KKSBV	Bind variable data (depending on setting of CURSOR_SHARING) for cursors owned by the current session
X$KKSCS	Information about why nonshared child cursors are nonshared
X$KKSSRD	Redirected SQL statements
X$KQFVI	SQL statements of all the fixed views
X$KQLFXPL	Execution plan for each child cursor loaded in the library cache
X$KQLSET	Information about subordinate caches currently loaded in the library cache
X$KSLEI	Wait statistics (totals) for each event
X$KXSBD	SQL or session bind data

TABLE 13-27. *Library Cache*

X$ Tables	Description
X$KXSCC	Shared cursor cache. V$SQL_CURSOR debugging information for each cursor associated with the session querying this view. Memory use by each cursor of a session SQL cursor cache.
X$QESMMIWT	Shared memory management instantaneous working. Join to X$QKSMMWDS.
X$QKSMMWDS	Shared memory management working data size. Library cache memory use by child cursors.

TABLE 13-27. *Library Cache* (continued)

X$ Tables	Description
X$KGHLU	Shared pool reserved list performance information
X$KGICC	Session cursor usage statistics: opens, hits, count, etc.
X$KGICS	Systemwide cursor usage statistics: opens, hits, count, etc.
X$KSMFSV	Shared memory information
X$KSMGV	SGA component names: buffer cache, java pool, large pool, shared pool
X$KSMHP	Shared memory information
X$KSMLRU	Shared memory: specific, loaded objects and their sizes, pin candidates
X$KSMFS	SGA sizes: fixed SGA, DB_BLOCK_BUFFERS, LOG_BUFFER
X$KSMSS	SGA size: shared pool (also listed in the "Instance/Database" section)
X$KSMJS	SGA size: java pool
X$KSMLS	SGA size: large pool
X$KSMPP	Very similar to X$KSMSP, without DUR and IDX columns varying numbers on Linux, Solaris, and NT
X$KSMSP	Shared pool section sizes/values, etc.
X$KSMSPR	Shared pool reserved memory statistics/sizes
X$KSMSPR	Shared pool section sizes/values, etc.
X$KSMSP_DSNEW	Shared memory information
X$KSMSP_NWEXT	Shared memory information
X$KSMUP	Instance and memory structure sizes/statistics

TABLE 13-28. *Shared Memory*

X$ Table Groups

X$ Tables	Description
X$ACTIVECKPT	Checkpoint statistics information
X$BH	Status and number of pings for every buffer in the SGA
X$CLASS_STAT	Number of blocks pinged per block class
X$KCBBHS	DBWR histogram statistics
X$KCBFWAIT	Buffer cache wait count and time
X$KCBKPFS	Buffer cache block prefetch statistics
X$KCBLSC	Buffer cache read/write/wait performance statistics
X$KCBSC	Buffer cache set read performance statistics
X$KCBWAIT	Number of and time spent in waits for buffer pool classes
X$KCBWBPD	Statistics on all buffer pools available to the instance, including buffer pool names
X$KCBWDS	Statistics on all buffer pools available to the instance

TABLE 13-29. *Buffer Cache*

X$ Tables	Description
X$KQRFP	Information about parent objects in the data dictionary
X$KQRFS	Information about subordinate objects in the data dictionary
X$KQRPD	Rowcache information
X$KQRSD	Rowcache information
X$KQRST	Rowcache performance statistics

TABLE 13-30. *Rowcache*

X$ Tables	Description
X$KGLINDEX	Object names with currently held locks and other information about these locks
X$KGLLK	DDL locks currently held and requested
X$KSQEQ	Locks held by sessions
X$KSQST	Enqueue type, number of requests, number of waits, wait time, etc.
X$KTADM	Locks requested and held by sessions

TABLE 13-31. *Locks/Enqueues*

X$ Tables	**Description**
X$KSLLD	Latch names and levels
X$KSLLT	Parent and child latch statistics
X$KSLLW	Statistics on latch waits, plus latch names
X$KSLPO	Latch posting
X$KSLWSC	Statistics on latch wait sleeps, plus latch names
X$KSUPRLAT	Information about current latch holders

TABLE 13-32. *Latches*

X$ Tables	**Description**
X$KDXHS	Index histogram information
X$KDXST	Index statistics from the last analyze index validate structure command

TABLE 13-33. *Optimizer*

X$ Tables	**Description**
X$KMCQS	Multithread message queue information
X$KMCVC	Virtual circuit connection message transport statistical information
X$KMMDI	MTS dispatcher performance information
X$KMMDP	MTS dispatcher performance information
X$KMMRD	MTS dispatcher information
X$KMMSG	Shared servers process performance information
X$KMMSI	Shared servers process information

TABLE 13-34. *MTS*

X$ Table Groups

X$ Tables	Description
X$KSTEX	Information about parallel execution
X$KXFPCDS	PQ information very similar to X$KXFPSDS
X$KXFPCMS	PQ information very similar to X$KXFPSMS
X$KXFPCST	Performance statistics for all PQ sessions combined
X$KXFPDP	X$KXFPDP: metadata about current PQ sessions, such as number of degree of parallelism, etc.
X$KXFPPFT	Parallel query information
X$KQFPSDS	Selects a.type,b.reason from X$KXFPSMS a, X$KXFPSDS b, where a.indx = b.indx
X$KXFPSMS	Parallel query information
X$KXFPSST	Session statistics for parallel queries
X$KXFPYS	Parallel query system statistics
X$KXFPNS	Performance statistics for sessions running parallel execution
X$KXFQSROW	Statistics on parallel execution operations, query statistics row

TABLE 13-35. *Parallel Query*

X$ Tables	Description
X$KZDOS	Role-related security
X$KZRTPD	Fine-grained security policies and predicates associated with the cursors currently in the library cache
X$KZSPR	Privileges
X$KZSRO	Roles
X$KZSRT	List of users who have been granted SYSDBA and SYSOPER privileges

TABLE 13-36. *Security-Granted Privileges and Roles, Fine-Grained Security Policies*

X$ Tables	Description
X$KGSKPP	Available CPU resource allocation methods defined for resource plans
X$KGSKQUEP	Available queuing resource allocation methods
X$KGSKTE	Possibly rcg names
X$KGSKTO	Possibly rcg types and attributes

TABLE 13-37.   *Resource/Consumer Groups*

X$ Tables	Description
X$CONTEXT	Context information
X$GLOBALCONTEXT	Context information

TABLE 13-38.   *Contexts*

NOTE
"Contexts" has nothing to do with Oracle Text, which used to be called "Context."

X$ Tables	Description
X$HOFP	Init parameters in use by the hs server and agent

TABLE 13-39.   *Heterogeneous Services*

X$ Table	Description
X$KWDDEF	PL/SQL reserved words

TABLE 13-40.   *PL/SQL*

X$ Tables	Description
X$KLCIE	SQL*Loader load performance information
X$KLPT	SQL*Loader load performance information

TABLE 13-41. *SQL*Loader*

X$ Tables	Description
X$JOXFC	Compile, resolve, reference information
X$JOXFD	Compile, resolve, reference information
X$JOXFR	Compile, resolve, reference information
X$JOXFS	Source name and/or code
X$JOXFT	Reference names, resolve information, compile information, class name information

TABLE 13-42. *Java Source*

X$ Tables	Description
X$DUAL	Everybody loves the permanent table DUAL, including Oracle. When the database is in a nomount or mount state, the permanent table DUAL is not available. For some operations, such as recovery, which Oracle needs to do when the database is in a nomount or mount state, Oracle queries X$DUAL.
X$KQFCO	Indexed columns of dynamic performance tables
X$KQFDT	Fixed dynamic or derived tables
X$KQFP	Fixed object names
X$KQFSZ	Stores the sizes of various database component types
X$KQFTA	Names of all the fixed tables
X$KQFVI	Names of all the fixed views
X$KSBDD	Descriptions of the background processes
X$KSBDP	Background process names

TABLE 13-43. *Miscellaneous*

X$ Tables	Description
X$KSLED	Wait event names
X$KSURLMT	System resource limits
X$KSUSD	Statistics descriptions
X$KSUTM	Lists the elapsed time in hundredths of seconds since the beginning of the epoch

TABLE 13-43.   *Miscellaneous* (continued)

Table Name	Probable Use
X$VINST	Unknown
X$RFMTE	Unknown
X$RFMP	Unknown
X$TRACE_EVENTS	Available events try to enable some of these events and see what shows up in X$TRACE. It seems that there are 1000 available events in 901 on NT, Linux, and Solaris.
X$TRACE	Enabled trace events
X$LCR	RAC lock/enqueue information
X$KZMAIE	Security
X$KZEMAEA	Information about security encryption algorithm
X$KTSPSTAT	Undo/rollback information
X$KSXRSG	Unknown
X$KSRREPQ	Unknown
X$KSXRMSG	Unknown
X$KSXRCONQ	Unknown
X$KSXRCH	Unknown
X$KSXAFA	Unknown
X$KSUSEX	Session information
X$KSURU	Resource usage
X$KSUPGS	Unknown

X$ Table Groups

TABLE 13-44.   *Other X$ Tables*

Table Name	Probable Use
X$KSUPGP	Unknown
X$KSUCF	Unknown
X$KSRMPCTX	Unknown
X$KSRCHDL	Unknown
X$KSRCDES	Unknown
X$KSRCCTX	Unknown
X$KSMNS	Shared memory information
X$KSMNIM	Shared memory information
X$KSMMEM	Shared memory information
X$KSMJCH	Shared memory information
X$KSMGST	Shared memory information
X$KSMGOP	Shared memory information
X$KSMDD	Shared memory information
X$KRBAFF	Unknown
X$KQDPG	Dynamic performance information
X$KKSAI	Unknown
X$KGLXS	Library cache information
X$KGLTRIGGER	System trigger information
X$KGLTR	Library cache information
X$KGLTABLE	Table information
X$KGLSN	Unknown
X$KGLLC	Unknown
X$KGLAU	Unknown
X$KGLRD	Unknown
X$KDNSSF	Lock information
X$KCRMT	Cache fusion information
X$KCLQN	Cache fusion information
X$KCLLS	Cache fusion information
X$KCLFX	Cache fusion information

TABLE 13-44.   *Other X$ Tables* (continued)

Table Name	Probable Use
X$KCLFI	Cache fusion information
X$KCLCURST	Cache fusion information
X$KCBWH	Information about functions pertaining to the buffer cache
X$KCBSW	Buffer cache information
X$KCBSH	Buffer cache information
X$KCBSDS	Buffer cache information
X$KCBLDRHIST	Buffer cache information
X$KCBKWRL	Buffer cache write list
X$KCBBF	Unknown
X$KCBBES	Unknown
X$CKPTBUF	Checkpoint information

TABLE 13-44. *Other X$ Tables* (continued)

Some Common X$ Table and Non-V$ Fixed View Associations

Table 13-45 lists non-V$ fixed views (V$ views listed in Appendixes B and C) that are based on at least one X$ table. Many of the fixed views are based on one or more X$ tables, plus other fixed views. You can use this list with the Oracle Reference manual and the $ORACLE_HOME/rdbms/admin/sql.bsq and $ORACLE_HOME/rdbms/admin/migrate.bsq as an aid in deciphering the meaning of X$ table and column contents and in constructing queries that join X$ tables to other X$ tables or to fixed views.

Fixed View	Base X$ Tables and/or Fixed Views
COLUMN_PRIVILEGES	OBJAUTH$, COL$, OBJ$, USER$, X$KZSRO
DBA_BLOCKERS	V$SESSION_WAIT, X$KSQRS, V$_LOCK, X$KSUSE
DBA_DATA_FILES	FILE$, TS$, V$DBFILE, X$KTFBHC
DBA_DDL_LOCKS	V$SESSION, X$KGLOB, X$KGLLK
DBA_DML_LOCKS	V$_LOCK, X$KSUSE, X$KSQRS
DBA_EXTENTS	UET$ SYS_DBA_SEGS, FILE$, X$KTFBUE, FILE#
DBA_FREE_SPACE	TS$, FET$, FILE$, X$KTFBFE

TABLE 13-45. *X$ Table and Non-V$ Fixed View Associations*

Fixed View	Base X$ Tables and/or Fixed Views
DBA_FREE_SPACE_COALESCED	X$KTFBFE
DBA_KGLLOCK	X$KGLLK, X$KGLPN
DBA_LMT_FREE_SPACE	X$KTFBFE
DBA_LMT_USED_EXTENTS	X$KTFBUE
DBA_LOCK_INTERNAL	V$LOCK, V$PROCESS, V$SESSION, V$LATCHHOLDER, X$KGLOB, DBA_KGLLOCK
DBA_SOURCE	OBJ$, SOURCE$, USER$, X$JOXFS
DBA_TEMP_FILES	X$KCCFN, X$KTFTHC, TS$
DBA_UNDO_EXTENTS	UNDO$, TS$, X$KTFBUE, FILE$
DBA_WAITERS	V$SESSION_WAIT, X$KSQRS, V$_LOCK, X$KSUSE
DICTIONARY	V$ENABLED_PRIVS, OBJ$, COM$, SYN$, OBJAUTH$, X$KZSRO
DISK_AND_FIXED_OBJECTS	OBJ$, X$KQFP, X$KQFTA, X$KQFVI
EXU7FUL	X$KZSRO, USER$
EXU8FUL	X$KZSRO, USER$
EXU9FIL	FILE$, V$DBFILE, DBFILE$, X$KTFBHC, TS$, X$KCCFN, X$KTFTHC
EXU9TNEB	X$KTFBUE
IMP9TVOID	OBJ$, USER$, TYPE$, SESSION_ROLES, OBJAUTH$, X$KZSRO
INDEX_HISTOGRAM	X$KDXST, X$KDXHS
INDEX_STATS	OBJ$, IND$, SEG$, X$KDXST, INDPART$, INDSUBPART$
LOADER_DIR_OBJS	OBJ$, DIR$, V$ENABLEDPRIVS, X$KZSRO
LOADER_TAB_INFO	OBJ$, V$ENABLEDPRIVS, X$KZSRO, TAB$, USER$, OBJAUTH$
LOADER_TRIGGER_INFO	OBJ$, USER$, TRIGGER$, OBJAUTH$, V$ENABLED_PRIVS, X$KZSRO
LOADER_TRIGGER_INFO	OBJ$, USER$, TRIGGER$, X$KZSRO
ORA_KGLR7_DEPENDENCIES	OBJ$, DEPENDENCY$, USER$, X$KZSRO, V$FIXED_TABLE, OBJAUTH$

TABLE 13-45. *X$ Table and Non-V$ Fixed View Associations* (continued)

Fixed View	Base X$ Tables and/or Fixed Views
ORA_KGLR7_IDL_CHAR	ORA_KGLR7_OBJECTS, IDL_CHAR$, OBJAUTH$, X$KZSRO
ORA_KGLR7_IDL_SB4	ORA_KGLR7_OBJECTS, IDL_SB4$, OBJAUTH$, X$KZSRO, SYSAUTH$
ORA_KGLR7_IDL_UB1	ORA_KGLR7_OBJECTS, IDL_UB1$, OBJAUTH$, X$KZSRO, SYSAUTH$
ORA_KGLR7_IDL_UB2	ORA_KGLR7_OBJECTS, IDL_UB1$, OBJAUTH$, X$KZSRO, SYSAUTH$
QUEUE_PRIVILEGES	OBJAUTH$, OBJ$, USER$, X$KZSRO
ROLE_SYS_PRIVS	USER$, SYSTEM_PRIVILEGE_MAP, SYSAUTH$, X$KZDOS
ROLE_ROLE_PRIVS	USER$, SYSAUTH$, X$KZDOS
ROLE_TAB_PRIVS	USER$, TABLE_PRIVILEGE_MAP, OBJAUTH$, OBJ$, COL$, X$KZDOS, SYSAUTH$
SESSION_ROLES	X$KZSRO

TABLE 13-45. *X$ Table and Non-V$ Fixed View Associations* (continued)

Common X$ Table Joins

Table 13-46 contains the X$ table column joins used in fixed views.

X$ Table and Column	Associated X$ Table and Column
X$BH.LE_ADDR	X$LE.LE_ADDR
X$KCCFN.FNFNO	X$KTFTHC.KTFTHCTFNO
X$HS_SESSION.FDS_INST_ID	X$HOFP.FDS_INST_ID
X$KCBSC.BPID	X$KCBWBPD.BP_ID
X$KCBSC.INST_ID	X$KCBWBPD.INST_ID
X$KCBWDS.SET_ID	X$KCBWBPD.BP_LO_SID
X$KCBWDS.SET_ID	X$KCBWBPD.BP_HI_SID
X$KCCFE.FEFNH	X$KCCFN.FNNUM
X$KCCFE.FENUM	X$KCCFN.FNFNO

TABLE 13-46. *Common Table Joins*

X$ Table and Column	Associated X$ Table and Column
X$KCCFE.FENUM	X$CFIO.KCFIOFNO
X$KCCFE.FENUM	X$KCCFN.FNFNO
X$KCCFE.FEPAX	X$KCCFN.FNNUM
X$KCCFN.FNFNO	X$KCVFHTMP.HTMPXFIL
X$KCCFN.FNFNO	X$KCVFH.HCFIL
X$KCCFN.FNFNO	X$KTFTHC.KTFTHCTFNO
X$KCCLE.INST_ID	X$KCCRT.INST_ID
X$KCCLE.LETHR	X$KCCRT.RTNUM
X$KCCTF.TFFNH	X$KCCFN.FNNUM
X$KCCTF.TFNUM	X$KCCFN.FNFNO
X$KCFTIO.KCFTIOFNO	X$KCCTF.TFNUM
X$KCRMF.FNO	X$KCCFN.FNFNO
X$KCRMF.FNO	X$KCCFN.FNFNO
X$KCRMX.THR	X$KCRFX.THR
X$KGLCRSOR.KGLHDADR	X$KZRTPD.KZRTPDAD
X$KGLCRSOR.KGLHDPAR	X$KZRTPD.KZRTPDPA
X$KGLCURSOR.KGLHDPAR	X$KZRTPD.KZRTPDPA
X$KGLCURSOR.KGLHDPAR	X$KKSSRD.PARADDR
X$KGLCURSOR.KGLOBHD6	X$KSMHP.KSMCHDS
X$KGLCURSOR.KGLOBHD6	X$KSMHP.KSMCHDS
X$KGLLK.KGLLKHDL	X$KGLDP.KGLHDADR
X$KGLLK.KGLLKUSE	X$KSUSE.ADDR
X$KGLLK.KGLNAHSH	X$KGLDP.KGLNAHSH
X$KGLOB.KGLHDADR	X$KGLDP.KGLRFHDL
X$KGLOB.KGLHDADR	X$KGLLK.KGLLKHDL
X$KGLOB.KGLNAHSH	X$KGLDP.KGLRFHDL
X$KQFVI.INDX	X$KQFVT.INDX
X$KSBDP.INDX	X$KSBDD.INDX
X$KSLEI.INDX	X$KSLED.INDX
X$KSLEI.INDX	X$KSLED.INDX

TABLE 13-46. *Common Table Joins* (continued)

X$ Table and Column	Associated X$ Table and Column
X$KSLES.KSLESENM	X$KSLED.INDX
X$KSLLD.INDX	X$KSLLT.LATCH#
X$KSLLT.KSLLTNUM	X$KSLLD.INDX
X$KSLLT.LATCH#	X$KSLLD.INDX
X$KSLLW.INDX	X$KSLWSC.INDX
X$KSLWSC.INDX	X$KSLLW.INDX
X$KSPPI.INDX	X$KSPPSV.INDX
X$KSPPI.INDX	X$KSPPCV.INDX
X$KSPPI.INDX	X$KSPPCV2.INDX
X$KSPPI.INDX	X$KSPPSV2.KSPFTCTXPN
X$KSQEQ.KSQLKRES	X$KSQRS.ADDR
X$KSQEQ.KSQLKSES	X$KSUSE.ADDR
X$KSUSE.INDX	X$KXUSESTA.INDX
X$KSUSE.KSUSEPRO	X$KXFPDP.KXFPDPPRO
X$KSUSECST.KSUSSOPC	X$KSLED.INDX
X$KSUSECST.KSUSSOPC	X$KSLED.INDX
X$KSUXSINST	Joined with X$KVIT and X$QUIESCE to create V$INSTANCE, but with no specific column joins
X$KSXTMPT.KGLHDADR	X$KGLCURSOR.KGLHDADR
X$KSXTMPT.KGLNAHSH	X$KGLCRSOR.KGLNAHSH
X$KTCXB.KSQLKRES	X$KSQRS.ADDR
X$KTCXB.KSQLKRES	X$KSQRS.DDR
X$KTCXB.KSQLKSES	X$KSUSE.ADDR
X$KTCXB.KSQLKSES	X$KSUSE.ADDR
X$KTCXB.KTCXBSES	X$KSUSE.ADDR
X$KTCXB.KTCXBSES	X$KSUSE.ADDR
X$KTCXB.KTCXBXBA	X$KTADM.KSSOBOWN
X$KTCXB.KTCXBXBA	X$KTADM.KSSOBOWN
X$TARGETRBA.INST_ID	X$SUSGSTA.INST_ID
X$TARGETRBA.INST_ID	X$ESTIMATED_MTTR.INST_ID

Common X$ Table Joins

TABLE 13-46. *Common Table Joins* (continued)

New Oracle 10gR1 X$ Tables

The following X$ tables are new in Oracle 10gR1:

- X$ABSTRACT_LOB
- X$ASH
- X$BUFFER
- X$BUFFERED_PUBLISHERS
- X$BUFFERED_QUEUES
- X$BUFFERED_SUBSCRIBERS
- X$INSTANCE_CACHE_TRANSFER
- X$KCCFLE
- X$KCCRDI
- X$KCCRSR
- X$KCCTIR
- X$KCFIOHIST
- X$KCFTIOHIST
- X$KCPXPL
- X$KCRRDGC
- X$KCTICW
- X$KCTLAX
- X$KELRTD
- X$KELTGSD
- X$KELTOSD
- X$KELTSD
- X$KEWASH
- X$KEWECLS
- X$KEWESMAS
- X$KEWESMS
- X$KEWMDRMV
- X$KEWMDSM
- X$KEWMEVMV
- X$KEWMFLMV
- X$KEWMGSM
- X$KEWMSEMV

- X$KEWMSMDV
- X$KEWMSVCMV
- X$KEWSSESV
- X$KEWSSMAP
- X$KEWSSVCV
- X$KEWSSYSV
- X$KEWXOCF
- X$KFALS
- X$KFDSK
- X$KFFIL
- X$KFGMG
- X$KFGRP
- X$KFKID
- X$KFNCL
- X$KFTMTA
- X$KGLJMEM
- X$KGLJSIM
- X$KMGSCT
- X$KMGSOP
- X$KQLFBC
- X$KQLFSQCE
- X$KRBMROT
- X$KRBMRST
- X$KRCFH
- X$KRFBLOG
- X$KRFGSTAT
- X$KSFQDVNT
- X$KSIRESTYP
- X$KSLCS
- X$KSLSCS
- X$KSLSESHIST

- X$KSMSGMEM
- X$KSMSTRS
- X$KSQEQTYP
- X$KSUCPUSTAT
- X$KSUSEH
- X$KSUVMSTAT
- X$KSWSASTAB
- X$KSWSCLSTAB
- X$KSWSEVTAB
- X$KTTEFINFO
- X$KTURHIST

- X$KUPVA
- X$KUPVJ
- X$KWRSNV
- X$LOGMNR_DICTIONARY_LOAD
- X$LOGMNR_LATCH
- X$QKSCESES
- X$QKSCESYS
- X$TIMEZONE_FILE
- X$XSAGOP
- X$XSLONGOPS

New Oracle 10gR2 X$ Tables

The following X$ tables are new in Oracle 10gR2:

- X$JSKSLV
- X$KCCNRS
- X$KCCRSP
- X$KCRRPTDGSTATS
- X$KCRRPVRS
- X$KFDSK_STAT
- X$KFGRP_STAT
- X$KGSKSCS
- X$KGSKVFT
- X$KKSSQLSTAT
- X$KMGSBSADV
- X$KNLAROW
- X$KNSTTXN
- X$KRBZA
- X$KRFSTHRD
- X$KRVSLVAS
- X$KRVSLVPG
- X$KRVSLVST
- X$KRVXTX
- X$KSKPLW

- X$KSMPGDP
- X$KSMPGDST
- X$KSMPGST
- X$KSPVLD_VALUES
- X$KSUSM
- X$KTATL
- X$KTATRFIL
- X$KTATRFSL
- X$KTSTUSC
- X$KTSTUSG
- X$KTSTUSS
- X$KZEKMFVW
- X$LOGMNR_LOG
- X$MUTEX_SLEEP
- X$MUTEX_SLEEP_HISTORY
- X$QESBLSTAT
- X$RULE
- X$RULE_SET
- X$XML_AUDIT_TRAIL

New Oracle 10gR2 X$ Tables

NOTE

See Appendixes B and C for detailed listings of all V$ views and X$ tables. There are 613 X$ tables in Oracle 10.2. Appendix C lists all X$ tables along with all indexes. There is also a cross-listing of X$ to V$ tables, and the X$ tables used in the V$ creation scripts are also detailed in Appendix C.

X$ Table Naming Conventions

This is a summary list of X$ Table Definitions. The last revision was in 7.3.2 from Oracle, and the main purpose of this note was to show the naming conventions.

```
[K]ernel Layer
  [2]-Phase Commit
    [G]lobal [T]ransaction [E]ntry
      X$K2GTE  - Current 2PC tx
      X$K2GTE2 - Current 2PC tx

  [C]ache Layer
    [B]uffer Management
      Buffer [H]ash
        X$BH - Hash Table

      Buffer LRU Statistics
        X$KCBCBH - [C]urrent [B]uffers (buckets) - lru_statistics
        X$KCBRBH - [R]ecent [B]uffers (buckets) - lru_extended

      Buffer [WAIT]s
        X$KCBWAIT  - Waits by block class
        X$KCBFWAIT - Waits by File

      [W]orking Sets - 7.3 or higher
        X$KCBWDS - Set [D]escriptors

    [C]ontrol File Management
      [C]ontrol [F]ile List - 7.0.16 or higher
        X$KCCCF - Control File Names & status

      [D]atabase [I]nformation
        X$KCCDI - Database Information

      Data [F]iles
        X$KCCFE - File [E]ntries ( from control file )
        X$KCCFN - [F]ile [N]ames

      [L]og Files
        X$KCCLE - Log File [E]ntries
        X$KCCLH - Log [H]istory ( archive entries )

      Thread Information
        X$KCCRT - [R]edo [T]hread Information
```

```
     [F]ile Management
       X$KCFIO - File [IO] Statistics

     [L]ock Manager Component ( LCK )
       [H]ash and Bucket Tables - 7.0.15 to 7.1.1, and 7.2.0 or higher
         X$KCLFH - File [H]ash Table
         X$KCLFI - File Bucket Table

       X$LE - Lock [E]lements
       X$LE_STAT - Lock Conversion [STAT]istics
       X$KCLFX - Lock Element [F]ree list statistics - 7.3 or higher
       X$KCLLS - Per LCK free list statistics - 7.3 or higher
       X$KCLQN - [N]ame (hash) table statistics - 7.3 or higher

     [R]edo Component
       [M]edia recovery  - kcra.h - 7.3 or higher
         X$KCRMF - [F]ile context
         X$KCRMT - [T]hread context
         X$KCRMX - Recovery Conte[X]t

       [F]ile read
         X$KCRFX - File Read Conte[X]t -  7.3 or higher

     Reco[V]ery Component
       [F]ile [H]eaders
         X$KCVFH - All file headers
         X$KCVFHMRR - Files with [M]edia [R]ecovery [R]equired
         X$KCVFHONL - [ONL]ine File headers

     [K]ompatibility Management - 7.1.1 or higher
       X$KCKCE - [C]ompatibility Segment [E]ntries
       X$KCKTY - Compatibility [TY]pes
       X$KCKFM - Compatibility [F]or[M]ats ( index into X$KCKCE )

[D]ata Layer
  Sequence [N]umber Component
     X$KDNCE - Sequence [C]ache [E]ntries - 7.2 or lower

     [S]equence Enqueues - common area for enqueue objects
       X$KDNSSC - [C]ache Enqueue Objects - 7.2 or lower
       X$KDNSSF - [F]lush Enqueue Objects - 7.2 or lower
     X$KDNST - Cache [ST]atistics - 7.2 or lower

  Inde[X] Block Component
    X$KDXHS - Index [H]i[S]togram
    X$KDXST - Index [ST]atistics

[G]eneric Layer
  [H]eap Manager
    X$KGHLU - State (summary) of [L]R[U] heap(s) - defined in ksmh.h

  [I]nstantiation Manager
    [C]ursor [C]ache
      X$KGICC - Session statistics - defined in kqlf.h
```

```
            X$KGICS - System wide statistics - defined in kqlf.h

     [L]ibrary Cache Manager  ( defined and mapped from kqlf )
        Bind Variables
           X$KKSBV - Library Object [B]ind [V]ariables

        Object Cache
           X$KGLOB - All [OB]jects
           X$KGLTABLE   - Filter for [TABLE]s
           X$KGLBODY    - Filter for [BODY] ( packages )
           X$KGLTRIGGER - Filter for [TRIGGER]s
           X$KGLINDEX   - Filter for [INDEX]es
           X$KGLCLUSTER - Filter for [CLUSTER]s
           X$KGLCURSOR  - Filter for [CURSOR]s

        Cache Dependency
           X$KGLDP - Object [D]e[P]endency table
           X$KGLRD - [R]ead only [D]ependency table - 7.3 or higher

        Object Locks
           X$KGLLK - Object [L]oc[K]s

        Object Names
           X$KGLNA - Object [NA]mes (sql text)
           X$KGLNA1 - Object [NA]mes (sql text) with newlines - 7.2.0 or higher

        Object Pins
           X$KGLPN - Object [P]i[N]s

        Cache Statistics
           X$KGLST - Library cache [ST]atistics

        Translation Table
           X$KGLTR - Address [TR]anslation

        Access Table
           X$KGLXS - Object Access Table

        Authorization Table - 7.1.5 or higher
           X$KGLAU - Object Authorization table

        Latch Cleanup - 7.0.15 or higher
           X$KGLLC - [L]atch [C]leanup for Cache/Pin Latches
  [K]ompile Layer
     [S]hared Objects
        X$KKSAI - Cursor [A]llocation [I]nformation - 7.3.2 or higher

  [L]oader
     [L]ibrary
        X$KLLCNT - [C]o[NT]rol Statistics
        X$KLLTAB - [TAB]le Statistics

  [M]ulti-Threaded Layer
     [C]ircuit component
```

```
      X$KMCQS - Current [Q]ueue [S]tate
      X$KMCVC - [V]irtual [C]ircuit state

  [M]onitor Server/dispatcher
    [D]ispatcher
      X$KMMDI - [D]ispatcher [I]nfo (status)
      X$KMMDP - [D]ispatcher Config ( [P]rotocol info )

    [S]erver
    X$KMMSI - [S]erver [I]nfo ( status )
    X$KMMSG - [SG]a info ( global statistics)
    X$KMMRD - [R]equest timing [D]istributions

s[Q]l Version and Option Layer
  Kernel [V]ersions
    X$VERSION - Library versions

  Kernel [O]ptions - 7.1.3 or higher
    X$OPTION - Server Options

[Q]uery Layer
  [D]ictionary Cache Management
    X$KQDPG - [PG]a row cache cursor statistics

  [F]ixed Tables/views Management
    X$KQFCO - Table [CO]lumn definitions
    X$KQFDT - [D]erived [T]ables
    X$KQFSZ - Kernel Data structure type [S]i[Z]es
    X$KQFTA - Fixed [TA]bles
    X$KQFVI - Fixed [VI]ews
    X$KQFVT - [V]iew [T]ext definition - 7.2.0 or higher

  [R]ow Cache Management
    X$KQRST - Cache [ST]atistics
    X$KQRPD - [P]arent Cache [D]efinition - 7.1.5 or higher
    X$KQRSD - [S]ubordinate Cache [D]efinition - 7.1.5 or higher

[S]ervice Layer
  [B]ackground Management
    [D]etached Process
      X$KSBDD - Detached Process [D]efinition (info)
      X$KSBDP - Detached [P]rocess Descriptor (name)
      X$MESSAGES - Background Message table

  [I]nstance [M]anagement - 7.3 or higher
    X$KSIMAT - Instance [AT]tributes
    X$KSIMAV - [A]ttribute [V]alues for all instances
    X$KSIMSI - [S]erial and [I]nstance numbers

  [L]ock Management
    [E]vent Waits
      X$KSLED - Event [D]escriptors
      X$KSLEI - [I]nstance wide statistics since startup
      X$KSLES - Current [S]ession statistics
```

```
   [L]atches
     X$KSLLD - Latch [D]escriptor (name)
     X$KSLLT - Latch statistics [ + Child latches @ 7.3 or higher ]
     X$KSLLW - Latch context ( [W]here ) descriptors - 7.3+
     X$KSLPO - Latch [PO]st statistics - 7.3 or higher
     X$KSLWSC- No[W]ait and [S]leep [C]ount stats by Context -7.3+

 [M]emory Management
   [C]ontext areas
     X$KSMCX - E[X]tended statistics on usage - 7.3.1 or lower

   Heap Areas
     X$KSMSP - SGA Hea[P]
     X$KSMPP - [P]GA Hea[P] - 7.3.2 and above
     X$KSMUP - [U]GA Hea[P] - 7.3.2 and above
     X$KSMHP - Any [H]ea[P] - 7.3.2 and above
     X$KSMSPR- [S]hared [P]ool [R]eserved List - 7.1.5 or higher

   [L]east recently used shared pool chunks
     X$KSMLRU - LR[U] flushes from the shared pool

   [S]GA Objects
     X$KSMSD - Size [D]efinition for Fixed/Variable summary
     X$KSMSS - Statistics (lengths) of SGA objects

   SGA [MEM]ory
     X$KSMMEM - map of the entire SGA - 7.2.0 or higher
     X$KSMFSV - Addresses of [F]ixed [S]GA [V]ariables - 7.2.1+

 [P]arameter Component
     X$KSPPI  - [P]arameter [I]nfo ( Names )
     X$KSPPCV - [C]urrent Session [V]alues - 7.3.2 or above
     X$KSPPSV - [S]ystem [V]alues - 7.3.2 or above

 En[Q]ueue Management
   X$KSQDN - Global [D]atabase [N]ame
   X$KSQEQ - [E]n[Q]ueue Object
   X$KSQRS - Enqueue [R]e[S]ource
   X$KSQST - Enqueue [S]tatistics by [T]ype

 [U]ser Management
   [C]ost
     X$KSUCF - Cost [F]unction (resource limit)

   [L]icence
     X$KSULL - Licence [L]imits

   [L]anguage Manager
     X$NLS_PARAMETERS - NLS parameters
     X$KSULV - NLS [V]alid Values - 7.1.2 or higher

   [MY] [ST]atistics
     X$KSUMYSTA - [MY] [ST]atisics (current session)
```

```
   [P]rocess Info
     X$KSUPL - Process (resource) [L]imits
     X$KSUPRLAT - [LAT]ch Holder
     X$KSUPR - Process object

   [R]esource
     X$KSURU - Resource [U]sage

   [S]tatistics
     X$KSUSD - [D]escriptors (statistic names)
     X$KSUSGSTA - [G]lobal [ST]atistics

   [SE]ssions
     X$KSUSECST - Session status for events
     X$KSUSESTA - Session [STA]tistics
     X$KSUSECON - [CON]nection Authentication - 7.2.1 or higher
     X$KSUSE - [SE]ssion Info
     X$KSUSIO - [S]ystem [IO] statistics per session

   [T]imer
     X$KSUTM - Ti[M]e in 1/100th seconds

   Instance [X]
     X$KSUXSINST - [INST]ance state

   [T]race management
     X$TRACE - Current traced events
     X$TRACES - All possible traces
     X$KSTEX - Code [EX]ecution - 7.2.1 or higher

 E[X]ecution Management
   Device/Node [A]ffinity - 7.3.2 and above
     X$KSXAFA - Current File/Node Affinity

[T]ransaction Layer
 Table [A]ccess [D]efinition
   X$KTADM - D[M]L lock

 [C]ontrol Component
   X$KTCXB - Transaction O[B]ject

 [S]or[T] Segments - 7.3 or higher
   X$KTSTSSD - [S]ort [S]egment [D]escriptor - per tablespace stats

 [T]ablespace
   X$KTTVS - [V]alid [S]aveundo

 [U]ndo
   X$KTURD - Inuse [D]escriptors
   X$KTUXE - Transaction [E]ntry (table) - 7.3.2 or above

Performance Layer [V] - 7.0.16 or higher
   [I]nformation tables
   X$KVII - [I]nitialisation Instance parameters
```

```
        X$KVIS - [S]izes of structure elements
        X$KVIT - [T]ransitory Instance parameters

    Security Layer [Z]
      [D]ictionary Component
        X$KZDOS - [OS] roles

      [S]ecurity State
        X$KZSPR - Enabled [PR]ivileges
        X$KZSRO - Enabled [RO]les

      [R]emote Logins - 7.1.1 or higher
        X$KZSRT - [R]emote Password File [T]able entries

    E[X]ecution Layer
      Parallel Query (Execute [F]ast) - 7.1.1 or higher
        [P]rocess and Queue Manager
          Statistics - 7.1.3 or higher
            X$KXFPYS - S[YS]tem Statistics
            X$KXFPDP - [D]etached [P]rocess (slave) statistics
            X$KXFQSROW - Table [Q]ueue Statistics - 7.3.2 or higher

          [C]oordinator Component
            X$KXFPCST - Query [ST]atistics
            X$KXFPCMS - [M]essage [S]tatistics
            X$KXFPCDS - [D]equeue [S]tatistics

          [S]lave Component
            X$KXFPSST - Query [ST]atistics
            X$KXFPSMS - [M]essage [S]tatistics
            X$KXFPCDS - [D]equeue [S]tatistics

        [S]hared Cursor
          X$KXSBD - [B]ind [D]ata - 7.3.2 and above
          X$KXSCC - SQL [C]ursor [C]ache Data - 7.3.2 and above

    [N]etwork Layer - 7.0.15 or higher
      Network [CO]nnections
        X$UGANCO - Current [N]etwork [CO]nnections
```

Future Version Impact

As noted several times in this chapter, the V$ views and X$ tables are constantly being enhanced as more and more features are added to Oracle. Performance of SELECTs on V$ views and X$ tables has improved as Oracle has added indexes (in V8) on the underlying X$ tables. More changes will certainly come in the future!

Why do I climb mountains? I don't have the time—I'm a DBA!

Why do I open the hood of my car and look at what's inside? To impress my wife!

Why do I look at the X$ tables? Because I don't spend a lot of time climbing mountains and I don't know what's *really* under the hood of my car, but I do know how to use these to my advantage! Now you do, too!!

TIPS Tips Review

REVIEW

- When you mention the X$ tables, most people say, "Ooh, pretty scary, I would never touch those tables." The fact is that DML commands (UPDATE, INSERT, DELETE) are not allowed on the X$ tables, even as the SYS superuser.

- Only the SYS superuser can SELECT from the X$ tables. An error occurs if an attempt is made to grant SELECT access to a user. A DBA may need access to the X$ table information, but *not* the SYS password. Create a view under a different name that mirrors the desired tables. Name these tables according to the appropriate synonyms of the original tables.

- Access the X$KQFVI table for a listing of all V$ and GV$ views.

- Access the V$FIXED_VIEW_DEFINITION view to obtain all of the information of the underlying X$ tables that make up a V$ view.

- Query V$FIXED_TABLE for the names of the X$ tables, or you may also access the two X$ tables X$KQFTA and X$KQFTD for partial listings, which when combined, make up the full list.

- Access the V$INDEXED_FIXED_COLUMN view for a listing of all X$TABLE indexes.

- Oracle generally uses the indexes and uses the correct driving table as needed for accessing the X$ tables, but from time to time, you may use hints to achieve a desired result.

- Anonymous PL/SQL blocks cannot be traced using the "compile debug" method. PL/SQL tracing for the entire session must be enabled with the "alter session set plsql_debug=true" command.

- Do not use ORADEBUG SUSPEND on the Microsoft Windows platform. Due to the thread-based processing model of Windows, the whole database will be suspended, not just the process you are attached to.

- Cursors may be re-assigned if the cursor is closed and released. Therefore when reading a long trace file it is important to remember that a cursor number referenced at one part of the trace file may not represent the same SQL statement as it does elsewhere in the trace file.

References

Joe Trezzo, *Journey to the Center of the X$ tables* (TUSC)

Steve Adams, *Oracle8i Internal Services for Waits, Latches, Locks, and Memory* (O'Reilly, 1999)

Miladin Modrakovic, "ORADEBUG – Undocumented Oracle Utility" (www.evdbt.com/Oradebug_Modrakovic.pdf)

Oracle Server: SQL Language Reference Manual (Oracle Corporation)

Oracle Server: Application Developer's Guide (Oracle Corporation)

Joseph Trezzo, *Get the Most out of Your Money: Utilize the v$ Tables* (IOUG, 1994)

Eyal Aronoff & Noorali Sonawalla, "Monitoring Oracle Database: The Challenge" (IOUG 1994)

Frank Naude's underground Oracle web page (www.orafaq.com/)

Tony Jambu, *Select* Magazine column
Rich Niemiec, *Oracle Performance Tuning Tips & Techniques* (McGraw-Hill, 1999)
Tip of the Week, oracle.com, Wolfgang Genser (for an idea on making touch counts faster)
Tanel Poder, "Memory Management and Latching Improvements inOracle9*i* and 10*g*" (http://integrid.info/)
www.ixora.com.au (Oracle dump information)
www.orafaq.com/faqdbain.htm
Metalink Notes: 186859.995, 1066346.6, 153334.995, 258597.999, 235412.999, 135223.1, 221860.999, 104933.1, 83222.996, 43600.1, 129813.999, 10630.996, 86661.999, 4256.997, 2497.997, 102925.1, 95420.1, 14848.997, 235412.999, 62172.1, 135223.1, 221860.999, 83222.996, 163424.1, 104397.1, 33883.1, 346576.999, 96845.1, 73582.1, 221860.999, 212629.995, 162866.1, 138119.1, 137483.1, 186859.995, 1066346.6, 153334.995, 258597.999, 235412.999, 135223.1, 221860.999, 104933.1, 83222.996, 43600.1, 129813.999, 10630.996, 86661.999, 4256.997, 2497.997, 102925.1, 210375.995, 39366.1, 62294.1, 187913.1, 171647.1, 39817.1, 224270.1, 62294.1, 39817.1, 104239.1, 280543.1

Graham Thornton and Kevin Gilpin helped with the incredible job of updating this chapter. (Please read it quietly and with an English accent.)

CHAPTER
14

Using STATSPACK and the AWR Report to Tune Waits and Latches

I f you could choose just two Oracle utilities to monitor and find performance problems of your system, those two utilities would be Enterprise Manager (Chapter 5) and the new AWR (Automatic Workload Repository) Report and/or STATSPACK (both covered in this chapter). In Oracle 10gR2, the new AWR Report has everything that is in STATSPACK and a whole lot more! STATSPACK also remains in 10g and has a few great improvements. The STATSPACK utility has been available since Oracle 8.1.6 to monitor the performance of your database. STATSPACK originally replaced the UTLBSTAT/UTLESTAT scripts available with earlier versions of Oracle. The AWR Report leverages the Automatic Workload Repository statistics and can be executed within Enterprise Manager Grid Control if desired and will probably replace STATSPACK for good in the future. Although the AWR Report has some very nice things in it that STATSPACK doesn't have, you must license the Oracle Diagnostics Pack to access the AWR dictionary views necessary for the AWR Report (STATSPACK is still a free utility).

In this chapter, you will see how to install the AWR Report and STATSPACK, how to manage them, and how to run and interpret the reports generated by the AWR Report and/or STATSPACK. STATSPACK includes data for both proactive and reactive tuning and is probably the best way to query most of the relevant V$ views and X$ tables and view the results in a single report. The AWR Report is the great way to mine the AWR for aggregate performance data in a report similar to STATSPACK.

Tips covered in this chapter include the following:

- What's new in 10gR2 and 10gR1

- Finding the files needed to create, manage, and drop the STATSPACK objects

- Creating a tablespace to hold the STATSPACK data apart from your application and SYSTEM objects

- Changing the PERFSTAT password and locking the account when it is no longer in use

- Selecting the proper level for your reporting

- Times to avoid running STATSPACK reports

- Using Grid Control to run the AWR Report

- Running the AWR Report and STATSPACK together: cautionary notes

- The top 10 things to look for in the AWR Report and STATSPACK output

- Managing the STATSPACK data, analyzing and purging it as needed

- Tuning the top wait events

- Tuning latches

- Issues revealed using the Segment Statistics sections of the reports

- Monitoring STATSPACK space usage

- Including STATSPACK data in your backup and upgrade plans

- Tuning at the block level to find hot blocks and ITL problems

- Using the ADDM Report (text) as a stand-alone tool

What's New in 10gR2 (10.2) STATSPACK

There are many new features in Oracle 10g Release 2. I have listed the ones here that I've seen as important and helpful. Please see the Oracle document listed in the References at the end of the chapter for a complete STATSPACK reference. New features in 10gR2 include

- Added Average (Ave) Wait (ms) for Top 5 Timed Events section
- Added OS statistics (not all features on all platforms) to identify if the OS is CPU bound and if it's due to Oracle
- File I/O histogram (added in 10.1) has new bucket of <= 2 ms bucket
- Buffer Pool Stats now shows K, M, or G instead of all the zeros
- Rollstat section omitted if using Auto Undo unless specified in sprepcon.sql
- SQL ordered by CPU and SQL ordered by Elapsed Time added
- SGA Target Advisory (from v$sga_target) added
- RAC Stats section now computes interconnect traffic in KB/s
- Sleeps 1–3 are made obsolete for latches (you can still get this by going to v$latch_parent, v$latch_children, v$latch)
- You use spup92.sql and spup101.sql to upgrade to 10.2 from 9.2
- You use spup101.sql to upgrade only from 10.1 to 10.2

New Features in 10gR2 (10.2) STATSPACK

There are also many new features in Oracle 10g Release 1. I have listed the ones here that I think are important or helpful. Please see the Oracle document listed in the References at the end of the chapter for a complete list. New features in 10gR1 include

- You can identify "baseline snapshots" that will not be purged.
- The algorithm to get HASH_VALUE from V$SQL is changed from 9i to 10g. STATSPACK shows both the old value and the new value for backward compatibility.
- When you make an error running STATSPACK, you now see the error message in the output and the actual values that caused the errors.
- SQL ordered by Gets, Reads, and Parse Calls all only show when they exceed 1 percent of total resources for the interval reported on (and only if above report thresholds set).
- The title for SQL ordered by Gets now includes the percentage of all gets that the listing has. If the SQL listed in this section includes 80 percent of *all* Gets for the period, then it will let you know in the title that "Captured SQL accounts for 80% of total Buffer Gets" (sweet!).
- Top SQL by Cluster Wait Time has been added for RAC.
- A new report, sprsqins.sql, has been added to report on a *single* SQL statement for an instance that includes the SQL stats and optimizer execution plan.

- Stats$sql_plan has new columns: projection, time, object_alias, object_type, qblock_name, and remarks.

- You use spup92.sql to upgrade to 10.1 from 9.2 and spup10.sql to upgrade to 10.2.

Installing STATSPACK

STATSPACK must be installed in every database to be monitored. Prior to installing STATSPACK, you should create a tablespace to hold the STATSPACK data. During the installation process, you will be prompted for the name of the tablespace to hold the STATSPACK database objects. You should also designate a temporary tablespace that will be large enough to support the large inserts and deletes STATSPACK may perform.

The installation script, named spcreate.sql, is found in the /rdbms/admin subdirectory under the Oracle software home directory. The spcreate.sql script creates a user named PERFSTAT and creates a number of objects under that schema.

TIP
Allocate at least 120M for the initial creation of the PERFSTAT schema's objects. Oracle 10g requires about 20M more space than Oracle 9i.

To start the spcreate.sql script, change your directory to the ORACLE_HOME/rdbms/admin directory and log in to SQL*Plus in an account with SYSDBA privileges:

```
SQL> connect system/manager as SYSDBA
SQL> @spcreate
```

During the installation process, you will be prompted for a password for the PERSTAT user (there is no longer a default for security purposes); then you are prompted for a default tablespace for the PERFSTAT user (a list of available tablespaces will be displayed along with this prompt). You will also be asked to specify a temporary tablespace for the user. Once you have provided default and temporary tablespaces for the PERFSTAT account, the account will be created and the installation script will log in as PERFSTAT and continue to create the required objects. If there is not sufficient space to create the PERFSTAT objects in the specified default tablespace, the script will return an error.

The spcreate.sql script calls three scripts: spcusr.sql to create the user, spctab.sql to create the underlying tables, and spcpkg.sql to create the packages. When run, each of these scripts generates a listing file (spcusr.lis, etc.). Although you start the installation script while logged in as a SYSDBA-privileged user, the conclusion of the installation script will leave you logged in as the PERFSTAT user. If you want to drop the PERFSTAT user at a later date, you can run the spdrop.sql script (which calls spdusr.sql and spdtab.sql) located in the ORACLE_HOME/rdbms/admin directory.

Security of the PERFSTAT Account

The spcusr.sql script creates the PERFSTAT account and asks you to supply a password (the default was PERFSTAT in previous versions). The STATSPACK utility does not need to use the PERFSTAT default password; change the password after the installation process completes.

The PERFSTAT user is granted the SELECT_CATALOG_ROLE. The PERFSTAT user is granted several system privileges (CREATE/ALTER SESSION, CREATE TABLE, CREATE/DROP PUBLIC SYNONYM, CREATE SEQUENCE, and CREATE PROCEDURE). Any user who can access your PERFSTAT account can select from all of the dictionary views. For example, such a user could query all of the database account usernames from DBA_USERS, all the segment owners from DBA_SEGMENTS, and the currently logged in sessions from V$SESSION. The PERFSTAT account, if left unprotected, provides a security hole that allows intruders to browse through your data dictionary and select targets for further intrusion.

In addition to the privileges it receives during the installation process, the PERFSTAT account will also have any privileges that have been granted to PUBLIC. If you use PUBLIC grants instead of roles for application privileges, you must secure the PERFSTAT account. You can lock database accounts and unlock them as needed. To lock the PERFSTAT account when you are not using STATSPACK, use the alter user command, as shown in the following listing:

```
alter user PERFSTAT account lock;
```

When you need to gather statistics or access the STATSPACK data, you can unlock the account:

```
alter user PERFSTAT account unlock;
```

Post-Installation

Once the installation process is complete, the PERFSTAT account will own 67 tables, 68 indexes, a synonym, a sequence, and a package (with body). In 9*i*, there were only 36 tables, 37 indexes, a sequence, and a package. You will use the package, named STATSPACK, to manage the statistics collection process and the data in the tables. The collection tables, whose names all begin with "STATS$," will have column definitions based on the V$ view definitions. For example, the columns in STATS$WAITSTAT are the columns found in V$WAITSTAT with three identification columns added at the top:

```
desc stats$waitstat
```

Name	Null?	Type
SNAP_ID	NOT NULL	NUMBER(6)
DBID	NOT NULL	NUMBER
INSTANCE_NUMBER	NOT NULL	NUMBER
CLASS	NOT NULL	VARCHAR2(18)
WAIT_COUNT		NUMBER
TIME		NUMBER

The Class, Wait_Count, and Time columns are based on the Class, Count, and Time columns from V$WAITSTAT. STATSPACK has added three identification columns:

SNAP_ID	An identification number for the collection. Each collection is called a "snapshot" and is assigned an integer value.
DBID	A numeric identifier for the database.
INSTANCE_NUMBER	A numeric identifier for the instance, for Real Application Cluster installations.

Installing STATSPACK

TIP
Do not use both STATSPACK and UTLBSTAT/UTLESTAT in the same database. The UTLBSTAT/UTLESTAT scripts provided with earlier versions of Oracle also created a table named STATS$WAITSTAT, and you may encounter errors if you attempt to use both unless UTLESTAT is run as the PERFSTAT user.

Each collection you perform is given a new Snap_ID value that is consistent across the collection tables. You will need to know the Snap_ID values when executing the statistics report provided with STATSPACK.

Gathering Statistics

Each collection of statistics is called a *snapshot*. Snapshots of statistics have no relation to snapshots or materialized views used in replication. Rather, they are a point-in-time collection of the statistics available via the V$ views and are given a Snap_ID value to identify the snapshot. You can generate reports on the changes in the statistics between any two snapshots. This is a significant advantage over the UTLBSTAT/UTLESTAT reports available with prior releases of Oracle. With STATSPACK, you can collect as many snapshots as you need and then generate reports against any combination of them. As with the UTLBSTAT/UTLESTAT reports, the STATSPACK report will only be valid if the database was *not* shut down and restarted between the snapshots evaluated.

TIP
Be sure the TIMED_STATISTICS database initialization parameter is set to TRUE prior to gathering statistics.

To generate a snapshot of the statistics, execute the SNAP procedure of the STATSPACK package, as shown in the following listing. You must be logged in as the PERFSTAT user to execute this procedure.

```
execute STATSPACK.SNAP;
PL/SQL procedure successfully completed.
```

When you execute the SNAP procedure, Oracle populates your STATS$ tables with the current statistics. You can then query those tables directly, or you can use the standard STATSPACK report (to see the change in statistics between snapshots).

Snapshots should be taken in one of two ways:

■   To evaluate performance during specific tests of the system. For these tests, you can execute the SNAP procedure manually, as shown in the prior example.

■   To evaluate performance changes over a long period of time. To establish a baseline of the system performance, you may generate statistics snapshots on a scheduled basis. For these snapshots, you should schedule the SNAP procedure execution via the Oracle Scheduler or via an operating system scheduler.

For the snapshots related to specific tests, you may wish to increase the collection level, which lets you gather more statistics. As noted in the section "Managing the STATSPACK Data" later in this chapter, each snapshot has a cost in terms of space usage and query performance. For example, since V$SYSSTAT has 255 rows (in Oracle 9.0.1 on NT), every snapshot generates 255 rows (232 on Windows) in STATS$SYSSTAT. Avoid generating thousands of rows of statistical data with each snapshot unless you plan to use them. In 10.2.01, there are 347 rows on Windows XP.

To support differing collection levels, STATSPACK provides a level parameter (_i_snap_level). By default, the level value is set to 5. Prior to changing the level value, generate several snapshots and evaluate the reports generated. The default level value is adequate for most reports. Alternative level values are listed in the following table:

Level	Description
0–4	General performance statistics on all memory areas, latches, pools, and events, and segment statistics, such as rollback and undo segments.
5	Same statistics from the lower levels, plus the most resource-intensive SQL statements.
6	Introduced in Oracle 9.0.1, level 6 includes the level 5 results plus SQL plans.
7–9	Introduced in Oracle 10g, level 7 includes level 6 results plus additional Segment Level statistics, including logical reads, physical reads/writes, global cache cr/current served and buffer busy, ITL, and row lock waits.
10 and greater	Same statistics from level 6 plus parent/child latch data.

The greater the collection level, the longer the snapshot will take. The default value (5) offers a significant degree of flexibility during the queries for the most resource-intensive SQL statements. The parameters used for the resource-intensive SQL portion of the snapshot are stored in a table named STATS$STATSPACK_PARAMETER. You can query STATS$STATSPACK_PARAMETER to see the settings for the different thresholds during the SQL statement gathering. Its columns include Snap_Level (the snapshot level), Executions_Th (threshold value for the number of executions), Disk_Reads_Th (threshold value for the number of disk reads), and Buffer_Gets_Th (threshold value for the number of disk reads).

For a level 5 snapshot using the default thresholds, SQL statements are stored if they meet any of the following criteria:

- The SQL statement has been executed at least 100 times.
- The number of disk reads performed by the SQL statement exceeds 1000.
- The number of parse calls performed by the SQL statement exceeds 1000.
- The number of buffer gets performed by the SQL statement exceeds 10,000.
- The sharable memory used by the SQL statement exceeds 1MB.
- The version count for the SQL statement exceeds 20.

When evaluating the snapshot's data and the performance report, keep in mind that the SQL threshold parameter values are cumulative. A very efficient query, if executed enough times, will exceed 10,000 buffer gets. Compare the number of buffer gets and disk reads to the number of executions to determine the activity each time the query is executed.

Gathering Statistics

To modify the default settings for the thresholds, use the MODIFY_STATSPACK_PARAMETER procedure of the STATSPACK package. Specify the snapshot level via the i_snap_level parameter, along with the parameters to change. Table 14-1 lists the available parameters for the MODIFY_ STATSPACK_PARAMETER procedure.

Parameter Name	Range of Values	Default	Description
i_snap_level	0, 5, 6, 7, 10	5	Snapshot level
i_ucomment	Any text	Blank	Comment for the snapshot
i_executions_th	Integer >= 0	100	Threshold for the cumulative number of executions
i_disk_reads_th	Integer >= 0	1000	Threshold for the cumulative number of disk reads (physical reads)
i_parse_calls_th	Integer >= 0	1000	Threshold for the cumulative number of parse calls
i_buffer_gets_th	Integer >= 0	10000	Threshold for the cumulative number of buffer gets (logical reads)
i_sharable_mem_th	Integer >= 0	1048576	Threshold for the amount of sharable memory allocated
i_version_count_th	Integer >= 0	20	Threshold for the number of versions of the SQL statement
i_seg_buff_busy_th	Integer >= 0	100	Threshold for the number of buffer busy waits on a SEGMENT
i_seg_rowlock_w_th	Integer >= 0	100	Threshold for the number of row lock waits on a SEGMENT
i_seg_itl_waits_th	Integer >=0	100	Threshold for the number of ITL waits on a SEGMENT
i_seg_cr_bks_sd_th	Integer >= 0	1000	Threshold for the number of Consistent Read (CR) blocks served for a SEGMENT
i_seg_ cu_bks_sd _th	Integer >= 0	1000	Threshold for the number of Current (CU) blocks served for a SEGMENT
i_seg_phy_reads_th	Integer >= 0	1000	Threshold for the number of physical reads on a SEGMENT
i_seg_log_reads_th	Integer >= 0	10000	Threshold for the number of logical reads on a SEGMENT
i_session_id	Valid SID from V$SESSION	0	Session ID of an Oracle session, if you wish to gather session-level statistics
i_modify_parameter	True or False	False	Set to True if you wish to save your changes for future snapshots

TABLE 14-1. *Modification Parameters*

To increase the Buffer_Gets threshold for a level 5 snapshot to 100,000, issue the following command:

```
EXECUTE STATSPACK.MODIFY_STATSPACK_PARAMETER -
  (i_snap_level=>5, i_buffer_gets_th=>100000, -
  i_modify_parameter=>'true');
```

If you plan to run the SNAP procedure on a scheduled basis, you should pin the STATSPACK package following database startup. The following listing shows a trigger that will be executed each time the database is started. The KEEP procedure of the DBMS_SHARED_POOL package pins the STATSPACK package in the shared pool. As an alternative to pinning, you can use the SHARED_POOL_RESERVED_SIZE initialization parameter to reserve shared pool area for large packages.

```
create or replace trigger PIN_ON_STARTUP
after startup on database
begin
    DBMS_SHARED_POOL.KEEP ('PERFSTAT.STATSPACK', 'P');
end;
/
```

TIP
Pin the STATSPACK package following database startup if you plan to run the SNAP procedure on a scheduled basis.

Running the Statistics Report

If you have generated more than one snapshot, you can report on the statistics for the period between the two snapshots. The database must not have been shut down between the times the two snapshots were taken. When you execute the report, you will need to know the Snap_ID values for the snapshots. If you run the report interactively, Oracle will provide a list of the available snapshots and the times they were created.

To execute the report, go to the /rdbms/admin directory under the Oracle software home directory. Log in to SQL*Plus as the PERFSTAT user and run the spreport.sql file found there.

```
SQL> @ORACLE_HOME/rdbms/admin/spreport
```

Oracle will display the database and instance identification information from V$INSTANCE and V$DATABASE and will then call a second SQL file, sprepins.sql.

The sprepins.sql script generates the report of the changes in the statistics during the snapshot time interval. The available snapshots will be listed, and you will be prompted to enter beginning and ending snapshot IDs. Unless you specify otherwise, the output will be written to a file named sp_*beginning_ending*.lst (sp_1_2.lst for a report between Snap_ID values of 1 and 2).

TIP
A second report, sprepsql.sql, can be used for additional research into the problem SQL statements identified via the spreport.sql report.

The Automatic Workload Repository (AWR) and the AWR Report

We covered the AWR in Chapter 1 as an introduction to this topic. The AWR Report reports on the AWR stored data and is definitely the next generation of the STATSPACK Report. It does require additional licensing, so ensure that you are licensed to use it. AWR collects database statistics every 60 minutes out of the box (this is configurable), and this data is maintained for a week and then purged. The statistics collected by AWR are stored in the database. The AWR Report accesses the AWR to report statistical performance information similar to how STATSPACK always did. Since the AWR schema was originally based on the STATSPACK schema, you will find much of what is in STATSPACK in the AWR Report. Learning the AWR Report if you are familiar with STATSPACK is easy, *but* you will not find everything in STATSPACK that you find in the AWR Report. There are some newer/cooler parts of the AWR Report that STATSPACK users will definitely value. The AWR data is stored separately from the STATSPACK data, so running both is a bit superfluous. If you choose to run *both,* ensure that you stagger the data collection of AWR from the collection for STATSPACK (by at least 30 minutes) to avoid a performance hit as well as conflicts. You should also run both as you switch from one to the other for overlap to ensure that you have coverage that shows comparison reports.

The Oracle database uses AWR for problem detection and analysis as well as for self-tuning. A number of different statistics are collected by the AWR, including wait events, time model statistics, active session history statistics, various system- and session-level statistics, object usage statistics, and information on the most resource-intensive SQL statements. To properly collect database statistics, the initialization parameter STATISTICS_LEVEL should be set to TYPICAL (the default) or ALL. Other Oracle Database 10g features use the AWR, such as ADDM and other Enterprise Manager Grid Control features as discussed in Chapter 5.

If you want to explore the AWR, feel free to do so. The AWR consists of a number of tables owned by the SYS schema and typically stored in the SYSAUX tablespace (currently no method exists that I know of to move these objects to another tablespace). All AWR table names start with the identifier "WR." AWR tables come with three different type designations:

- Metadata (WRM$)
- Historical data (WRH$)
- AWR tables related to advisor functions (WRI$)

Most of the AWR table names are pretty self-explanatory, such as WRM$_SNAPSHOT or WRH$_ACTIVE_SESSION_HISTORY (a very valuable view to check out). Also Oracle Database 10g offers several DBA tables that allow you to query the AWR repository. The tables start with DBA_HIST and are followed by a name that describes the table. These include tables such as DBA_HIST_FILESTATS, DBA_HIST_DATAFILE, or DBA_HIST_SNAPSHOT.

TIP
If you choose to run both, ensure that you stagger the data collection of AWR from the collection for STATSPACK (by at least 30 minutes) to avoid a performance hit as well as conflicts.

Manually Managing the AWR

While AWR is meant to be automatic, provisions for manual operations impacting the AWR are available. You can modify the snapshot collection interval and retention criteria, create snapshots, and remove snapshots from the AWR. We will look at this process in more detail in the next few sections, but please refer to the Oracle documentation for full coverage of the AWR.

You can modify the snapshot collection interval using the dbms_workload_repository package. The procedure dbms_workload_repository.modify_snapshot_settings is used in this example to modify the snapshot collection so that it occurs every 15 minutes, and retention of snapshot data is fixed at 20160 minutes (exactly 14 days):

```
-- This causes the repository to refresh every 15 minutes
-- and retain all data for 2 weeks.
exec dbms_workload_repository.modify_snapshot_settings -
(retention=>20160, interval=> 15);
```

Setting the interval parameter to 0 will disable all statistics collection.

To view the current retention and interval settings of the AWR, use the DBA_HIST_WR_CONTROL view. Here is an example of how to use this view:

```
select *
from    dba_hist_wr_control;

      DBID SNAP_INTERVAL            RETENTION
---------- -------------------- --------------------
2139184330 +00000 01:00:00.0    +00007 00:00
```

In the preceding example, we see that the snapshot interval is every hour (the default), and the retention is set for seven days.

You can use the dbms_workload_repository package to create or remove snapshots. The dbms_workload_repository.create_snapshot procedure creates a manual snapshot in the AWR as seen in this example:

```
exec dbms_workload_repository.create_snapshot;
```

You can see what snapshots are currently in the AWR by using the DBA_HIST_SNAPSHOT view as seen in this example:

```
select snap_id, begin_interval_time, end_interval_time
from    dba_hist_snapshot
order   by 1;

   SNAP_ID END_INTERVAL_TIME
---------- -------------------------
      1107 03-OCT-04 01.24.04.449 AM
      1108 03-OCT-04 02.00.54.717 AM
      1109 03-OCT-04 03.00.23.138 AM
      1110 03-OCT-04 10.58.40.235 PM
```

Manually Managing the AWR

Each snapshot is assigned a unique snapshot ID that is reflected in the SNAP_ID column. If you have two snapshots, the earlier snapshot will always have a smaller SNAP_ID than the later snapshot. The END_INTERVAL_TIME column displays the time that the actual snapshot was taken.

Sometimes you might want to drop snapshots manually. The dbms_workload_repository.drop_snapshot_range procedure can be used to remove a range of snapshots from the AWR. This procedure takes two parameters, low_snap_id and high_snap_id, as seen in this example:

```
exec dbms_workload_repository.drop_snapshot_range -
(low_snap_id=>1107, high_snap_id=>1108);
```

AWR Automated Snapshots

Oracle Database 10g uses a scheduled job, GATHER_STATS_JOB, to collect AWR statistics. This job is created and enabled automatically when you create a new Oracle database under Oracle Database 10g. To see this job, use the DBA_SCHEDULER_JOBS view as seen in this example:

```
select a.job_name, a.enabled, c.window_name,
       c.repeat_interval
from   dba_scheduler_jobs a, dba_scheduler_wingroup_members b,
       dba_scheduler_windows c
where  job_name='GATHER_STATS_JOB'
and    a.schedule_name=b.window_group_name
and    b.window_name=c.window_name;

(you can also add c.schedule_name, c.start_date to the Select if desired):
JOB_NAME                        ENABL WINDOW_NAME
------------------------------- ----- -------------------------------
REPEAT_INTERVAL
--------------------------------------------------------------------------
GATHER_STATS_JOB                TRUE  WEEKEND_WINDOW
freq=daily;byday=SAT;byhour=0;byminute=0;bysecond=0

GATHER_STATS_JOB                TRUE  WEEKNIGHT_WINDOW
freq=daily;byday=MON,TUE,WED,THU,FRI;byhour=22;byminute=0; bysecond=0
```

You can disable this job using the dbms_scheduler.disable procedure as seen in this example:

```
exec dbms_scheduler.disable('GATHER_STATS_JOB');
```

And you can enable the job using the dbms_scheduler.enable procedure as seen in this example:

```
exec dbms_scheduler.enable('GATHER_STATS_JOB');
```

AWR Snapshot Reports

Oracle provides reports that you can run to analyze the data in the AWR. These reports are much like the STATSPACK reports prior to Oracle Database 10g. There are two reports: awrrpt.sql (the main AWR Report) and awrrpti.sql, which are available in the directory $ORACLE_HOME/ rdbms/admin. The output of these reports (run from SQL*Plus) is essentially the same, except that awrrpti.sql script allows you to define a specific instance to report on. The reports are much like the STATSPACK reports of old, in that you define beginning and ending snapshot IDs, along with the output filename of the report. Additionally, you can opt to produce the report in either text format or HTML format. As you will see when you run awrrpt.sql, the following simple example shows how this is similar to STATSPACK other than the text (STATSPACK looking output) or HTML (the screen shots in this chapter are the HTML) output:

```
SQL> @C:\oracle\product\10.1.0\Db_1\RDBMS\ADMIN\awrrpt

Current Instance
~~~~~~~~~~~~~~~~

   DB Id     DB Name      Inst Num Instance
---------- ------------ -------- ------------
 1071709215 ORCL              1 orcl

Specify the Report Type
~~~~~~~~~~~~~~~~~~~~~~~~~
Would you like an HTML report, or a plain text report?
Enter 'html' for an HTML report, or 'text' for plain text
Defaults to 'html'
Enter value for report_type: html
```

TIP
With the new AWR Report you can choose to get text (like STATSPACK output) or the new HTML format when you run awrrpt.sql. The HTML format is much better, as you can click on various links within the report to navigate between sections easily. You can also run the AWR Report within Grid Control.

As when using STATSPACK, it is a good idea to create a baseline in the AWR. A baseline is defined as a range of snapshots that can be used to compare with other pairs of snapshots. The Oracle database server will exempt the snapshots assigned to a specific baseline from the automated purge routine. Thus, the main purpose of a baseline is to preserve typical runtime statistics in the AWR repository, allowing you to run the AWR snapshot reports on the preserved baseline snapshots at any time and compare them to recent snapshots contained in the AWR. This allows you to compare current performance (and configuration) to established baseline performance, which can assist in determining database performance problems.

You can use the create_baseline procedure contained in the dbms_workload_repository stored PL/SQL package to create a baseline as seen in this example:

```
exec dbms_workload_repository.create_baseline -
(start_snap_id=>1109, end_snap_id=>1111, -
baseline_name=>'EOM Baseline');
```

Baselines can be seen using the DBA_HIST_BASELINE view as seen in the following example:

```
select baseline_id, baseline_name, start_snap_id, end_snap_id
from   dba_hist_baseline;

BASELINE_ID BASELINE_NAME   START_SNAP_ID END_SNAP_ID
----------- --------------- ------------- -----------
          1 EOM Baseline             1109        1111
```

In this case, the column BASELINE_ID identifies each individual baseline that has been defined. The name assigned to the baseline is listed, as are the beginning and ending snapshot IDs.

You can remove a baseline using the dbms_workload_repository.drop_baseline procedure as seen in this example, which drops the EOM Baseline that we just created:

```
EXEC dbms_workload_repository.drop_baseline -
(baseline_name=>'EOM Baseline', Cascade=>FALSE);
```

Note that the cascade parameter will cause all associated snapshots to be removed if it is set to TRUE; otherwise, the snapshots will be cleaned up automatically by the AWR automated processes.

Run the AWR Report in Oracle Enterprise Manager Grid Control

While we have demonstrated how to use the dbms_workload_repository package to manage the AWR repository, Oracle also provides the ability to manage AWR from the Oracle Enterprise Manager Grid Control. Enterprise Manager is covered in detail in Chapter 5, but some of the AWR Report screens are covered in this chapter. Grid Control provides a nice interface into the management of AWR (under the Workload section) and also provides an easy method for creating the AWR Report (under the Statistics Management section). Navigate to the database you wish to report on and then go to the administration page as seen in the screen displayed in Figure 14-1. You can then click Automatic Workload Repository under the Statistics Management section.

The next AWR screen (Figure 14-2) provides a summary of the current AWR settings and gives you an option to modify them. You can also look at details about the snapshots in the AWR and create baseline AWR snapshots (called preserved snapshot sets in Grid Control). Some of the important things you'll see on the settings page include snapshot retention, how often snapshots are collected (or if collection is turned off), and the collection level.

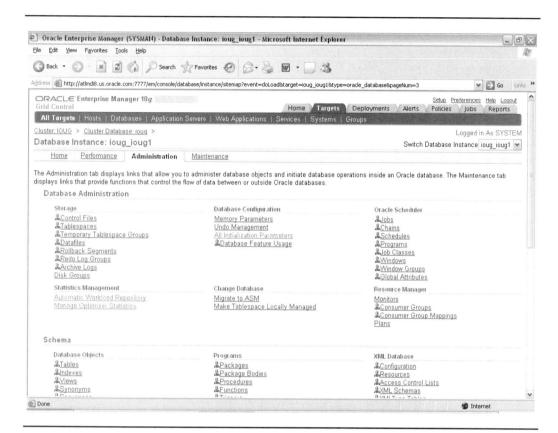

FIGURE 14-1.   *Statistics management and the Automatic Workload Repository*

If you click the snapshots, the Snapshots page (Figure 14-3) displays the last several snapshots in the AWR and allows you to review older snapshots if you wish. You can click a specific snapshot number if you want detail information on that snapshot or if you want a printable report based on the snapshot you selected. You can also get snapshot details by clicking the snapshots link on the AWR page, which takes you directly to this same snapshots page seen in Figure 14-3.

In this screen (Figure 14-3) you will see the snapshot ID, which you can then use for starting and ending snapshots for running your AWR Report. You also see the capture date and time for each of these snapshots. As long as there is a snapshot, you can run a report starting with any snapshot and ending with any snapshot. If you take snapshots every hour, you can either run a report for an hour or you can run a report spanning 24 hours (as long as the instance is not shut down). If you are running RAC (Real Application Clusters), you must run the report for each instance individually. You can also click Create Preserved Snapshot from the Action list, and then

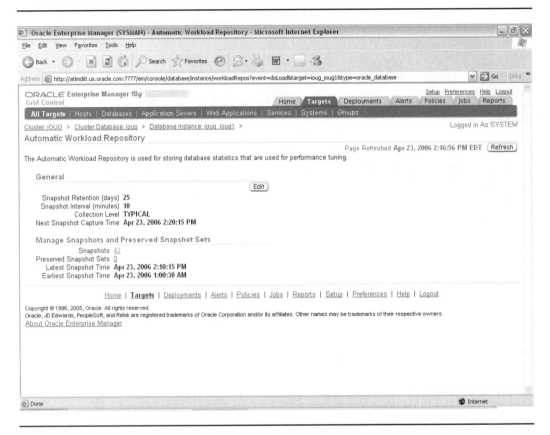

FIGURE 14-2. *AWR collection settings and snapshots*

click Go. Oracle will then prompt you for the beginning and ending snapshots to assign to the preserved snapshot set. Once you have created snapshots, you can use the Actions pull-down box to perform many actions; for instance, you can create SQL tuning sets, create reports much like STATSPACK reports from earlier versions of Oracle, and create an ADDM task that will analyze the snapshot set and produce an analysis report. You can also use the pull-down box to delete preserved snapshot sets, and you can compare two sets of snapshot pairs. Comparing snapshots allows you to determine if differences exist between a baseline snapshot and a recent set of snapshots. Using the report generated from this action, you can determine if the current system performance is diverging from the baseline performance in some way.

To run the AWR Report, you now need to choose beginning and ending snapshot IDs and run the report as discussed in the preceding section. You will see the snapshot details for this

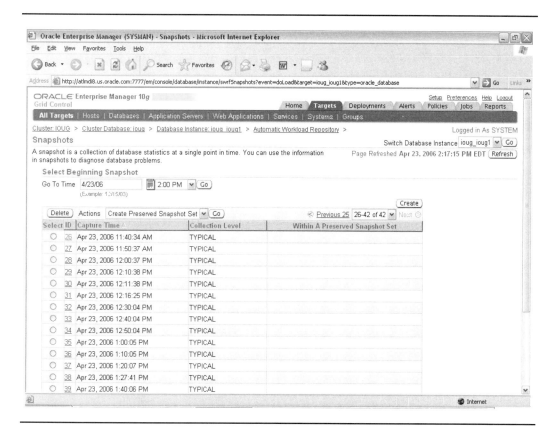

FIGURE 14-3.   *Viewing the snapshots collected in AWR*

particular period (ID 25 to ID 26) in Figure 14-4. Note that much of the statistical information contained in the AWR Report (and STATSPACK) is shown in this particular screen.

TIP
If you use Grid Control, you can run the AWR Report directly from Grid Control.

Next, you will click the Report tab to run the AWR Report. When you click this, you will probably see a little clock (this screen is not displayed here), which tells you that the report is being generated. Next you will see the actual report (listed in Figure 14-5) in the Enterprise Manager browser. You can also generate the report (awr_report_25_26.html in my case) in a file

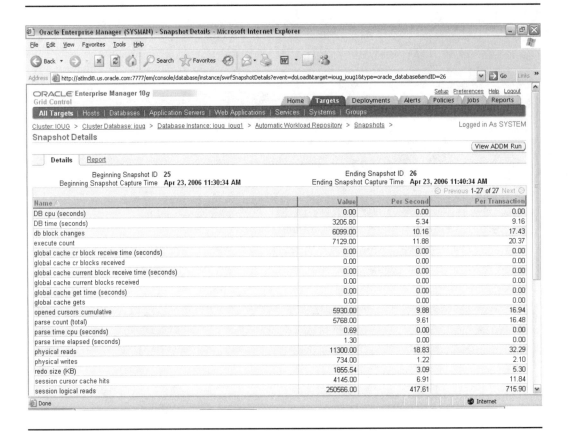

FIGURE 14-4. *The Snapshot Details section*

that can be viewed at any time by clicking Save To File. Many of the AWR Report screenshots in this chapter come from this report, but I also show a higher-volume example at times. You can see from Figure 14-5 that the AWR Report looks exactly like the STATSPACK report at the top of the report.

Interpreting the STATSPACK Output

Several sections are included in a STATSPACK output report. We'll cover each of the main sections and information on what to look for and how to use information that appears to be a problem. Most information must be combined with additional research to solve an issue and lead to an optimal system.

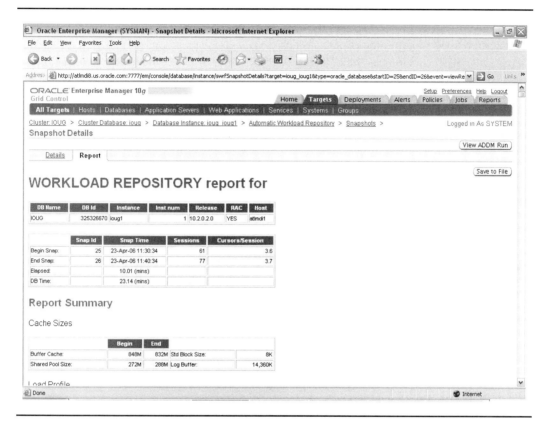

FIGURE 14-5.   *The actual AWR Report is browsable or savable in a file.*

The Header Information

The first section of the report includes information about the database itself, including information on the database name, ID, release number, and host. Following this information is information on when the snapshot was started and ended and how many sessions were active. Always check to ensure the snapshot interval is what you were trying to measure, and make sure that it's a long enough interval to make it representative. If your interval is five minutes, that is just not long enough unless you are measuring something very short in duration. If your interval is five days, then you have all kinds of peaks and valleys that average out, so it may be too long. But, it is great to have one-day, one-hour (at peak), and one-hour (at non-peak) STATSPACKs handy to compare for any given day when an anomaly occurs on your system. Generally, a STATSPACK report should cover at least an hour of time and should be timed strategically to measure periods of time that are problematic. You may also want to look at an entire day so that you can compare days over a period of time. The cache sizes section shows the values of the Buffer Cache (DB_CACHE_SIZE in the initialization file), Shared Pool Size (SHARED_POOL_SIZE), Std Block Size (DB_BLOCK_SIZE), and the Log Buffer (LOG_BUFFER). An example of the header information is displayed next. The equivalent information is displayed in Figure 14-6 for the AWR Report.

```
DB Name        DB Id      Instance      Inst Num Release      RAC Host
----------- ------------- ------------- -------- ----------- --- ----------
ORCL         1050469182 orcl                    1 10.1.0.2.0  NO  RJNMOBILE5

               Snap Id    Snap Time       Sessions Curs/Sess Comment
               --------- ----------------- -------- --------- ------------
Begin Snap:       458 28-Nov-03 00:15:00      814     179.1
  End Snap:       505 28-Nov-03 23:45:00      816     211.4
  Elapsed:             1,410.00 (mins)


Cache Sizes (end)
~~~~~~~~~~~~~~~~~~
              Buffer Cache:   32,773M      Std Block Size:        8K
         Shared Pool Size:    2,048M         Log Buffer:     1,024K
```

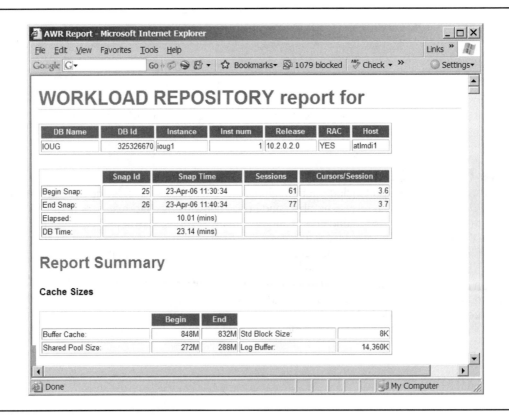

FIGURE 14-6. *The AWR Report header information*

The Load Profile

The next portion of the report output, following the basic information, provides per-second and per-transaction statistics of the load profile. This is an excellent section for monitoring throughput and load variations on your system. As the load on the system increases, you will see larger numbers per second. As you tune the system for maximum efficiency, you will usually receive lower numbers for the per-transaction statistic. The following listing shows sample output for the load profile section:

```
Load Profile
~~~~~~~~~~~~                                Per Second         Per Transaction
                                          ---------------      ---------------
                 Redo size:               1,409,245.79               36,596.21
             Logical reads:                 157,472.47                4,089.35
             Block changes:                   4,061.85                  105.48
             Physical reads:                  5,965.05                  154.90
            Physical writes:                    587.76                   15.26
                User calls:                   5,922.08                  153.79
                    Parses:                      92.11                    2.39
               Hard parses:                       0.17                    0.00
                     Sorts:                      93.88                    2.44
                    Logons:                       0.25                    0.01
                  Executes:                   5,686.76                  147.68
              Transactions:                      38.51

  % Blocks changed per Read:    2.58     Recursive Call %:     2.38
  Rollback per transaction %:   1.22     Rows per Sort:      114.10
```

The load profile helps to identify both the load and type of activity being performed. In this example, the activity recorded included a large amount of both logical and physical activity.

Things to look for include

- An increase in Redo size, Block changes, and % Blocks changed per Read: indicates increased DML (insert/update/delete) activity.

- A hard parse occurs when a SQL statement is executed and is *not* currently in the shared pool. A hard parse rate greater than 100/second could indicate that bind variables are not being used effectively, the CURSOR_SHARING initialization parameter should be used, or there is a shared pool sizing problem. (See Chapter 4 on sizing the shared pool and a detailed discussion related to this.)

- A soft parse occurs when a SQL statement is executed and it *is* currently in the shared pool. A soft parse rate greater than 300/second could indicate program inefficiencies where statements are being parsed over and over again instead of the program efficiently parsing the statement only once per session.

Figure 14-7 shows the equivalent AWR Report information for a heavily used system (especially heavy DML).

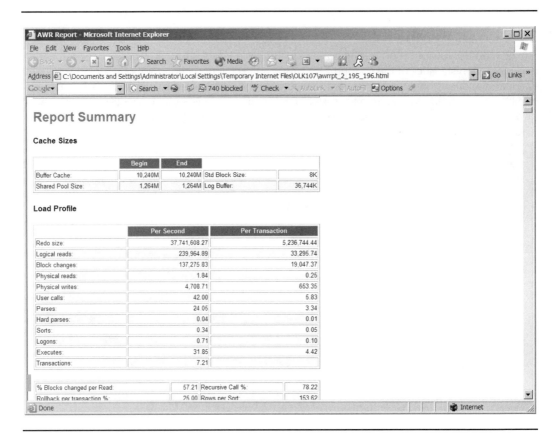

FIGURE 14-7. *The AWR Report load profile*

TIP
*Get to know your system by reviewing and knowing the regular Load
Profile of your system. Significant changes to the Load Profile during
what should be similar workloads or common times during the day
may warrant further investigation.*

Instance Efficiency

The Instance Efficiency section shows information for many of the common hit ratios. DBAs
generally measure these so that they can be alerted of significant changes in system behavior
when compared historically. Hit ratios (when managed regularly) are a great way to be alerted
of general potential problems or specific potential problems, such as bad SQL, that has been
introduced recently into the system. This can give you the opportunity to find the issue and have
it addressed before having a serious/noticeable effect on the system. Waits (covered in depth later

in this chapter) are another excellent way to find major problems, but waits usually show up after the problem becomes a large issue. Unfortunately, by that time, the business users will often raise it as a problem.

Monitoring hit ratios are just one part of the thousands of pieces of your tuning arsenal. The reason that so many tuning tips are provided in this book is that in writing about tuning, I am writing about all of the turns that the optimizer will make and how to compensate for any issues. While I don't believe you could capture everything in a book (you'd be *un*-writing the hardest part of Oracle—the optimizer), I do believe this compilation helps solve many of them. Some DBAs (usually those trying to sell you a tuning product) minimize the importance of hit ratios (proactive tuning) and focus completely on waits (reactive tuning), since focusing on waits is a great way to quickly solve the current burning problems. By monitoring the Instance Efficiency section (and using all of STATSPACK and Enterprise Manager), the DBA will combine reactive and proactive tuning and will find some problems before the users scream or wait events hit the top 5 list. Hit ratios are one important piece of the puzzle (so are waits). The listing that follows shows how well this STATSPACK section shows you all of the common hit ratios at once.

```
Instance Efficiency Percentages (Target 100%)
~~~~~~~~~~~~~~~~~~~~~~~~~~~~~~~~~~~~~~~~~~~~~~~~~~~~~
            Buffer Nowait %:   99.99        Redo NoWait %: 100.00
            Buffer  Hit   %:   95.27     In-memory Sort %: 100.00
            Library Hit   %:   99.67         Soft Parse %:  97.24
        Execute to Parse %:   91.82          Latch Hit %:  99.60
  Parse CPU to Parse Elapsd %:  73.48      % Non-Parse CPU:  99.82
```

Things to look for include

- The Buffer NoWait % of less than 99 percent. This is ratio of hits on a request for a specific buffer where the buffer was immediately available in memory. If the ratio is low, then there is a (hot) block(s) being contended for that should be found in the Buffer Wait section.

- A Buffer Hit % of less than 95 percent. This is the ratio of hits on a request for a specific buffer when the buffer was in memory and no physical I/O was needed. While originally one of the few methods of measuring memory efficiency, it still is an excellent method for showing how often you need to do a physical I/O, which merits further investigation as to the cause. Unfortunately, if you have unselective indexes that are frequently accessed, that will drive your hit ratio higher, which can be a misleading indication of good performance to some DBAs. When you effectively tune your SQL and have effective indexes on your entire system, this issue is not encountered as frequently and the hit ratio is a better performance indicator. A high hit ratio is not a measure of good performance, but a low hit ratio is often a sign of performance that can be improved or should at least be looked into. A hit ratio that is steadily at 95 percent and then one day goes to 99 percent should be checked for bad SQL or a bad index that is causing a surge of logical reads (check the load profile and top buffer gets SQL). A hit ratio that is steadily at 95 percent and then drops to 45 percent should be checked for bad SQL (check the top physical reads SQL) causing a surge in physical reads that are not using an index or an index that has been dropped (I've seen this more often than you can imagine).

- A Library Hit % of less than 95 percent. A lower library hit ratio usually indicates that SQL is being pushed out of the shared pool early (could be due to a shared pool that is too small). A lower ratio could also indicate that bind variables are not used or some other issue is causing SQL not to be reused (in which case a smaller shared pool may only be a band-aid that will potentially fix a library latch problem that may result). Despite the rants about lowering your shared pool all the time to fix library cache and shared pool latching issues, most multi-terabyte systems I've seen with heavy usage have shared pools in the gigabytes without any issues because they've fixed the SQL issues. You must fix the problem (use bind variables or CURSOR_SHARING) and then appropriately size the shared pool. I'll discuss this further when we get to latch issues.

- In-Memory Sort % of less than 95 percent in OLTP. In an OLTP system, you really don't want to do disk sorts. Setting the PGA_AGGREGATE_TARGET (or SORT_AREA_SIZE in previous versions) initialization parameter effectively will eliminate this problem.

- Soft Parse % of less than 95 percent. As covered in the Load Profile section (last section), a soft parse ratio that is below around 80 percent indicates that SQL is not being reused and needs to be investigated.

- A Latch Hit % of less than 99 percent is usually a big problem. Finding the specific latch will lead you to solving this issue. I will cover this in detail when discussing the Latch Wait section.

Figure 14-8 shows how the Load Profile section looks in the AWR Report (essentially the same as STATSPACK).

If you regularly run STATSPACK, comparing hit ratios from one day to another can be a great barometer as to whether something drastic has changed. If an index was dropped on a frequently accessed column, the buffer hit ratio could drop greatly, giving you something to investigate. If an index was added to a table, it could cause the buffer hit ratio to soar if it causes a table join to occur in the wrong order, causing massive buffers to be read. A library hit ratio that rises or falls greatly from one day to the next will give you indications of changing SQL patterns. Latch hit ratio changes can indicate contention issues that need to be investigated more.

Hit ratios can be a very proactive tool for a DBA who regularly monitors and understands a given production system, whereas many of the other tuning tools are reactive to problems that have already occurred.

TIP

Hit ratios are a great barometer of the health of your system. A large increase or drop from day to day is an indicator of a major change that needs to be investigated. Investigating waits is like investigating an accident that has already occurred, while investigating a change in hit ratios is like looking into the intersection with a changing traffic pattern that may cause an accident in the future if something is not adjusted. Generally, buffer and library cache hit ratios should be greater than 95 percent for OLTP, but they could be lower for a data warehouse that may perform many full table scans.

It is also important to remember that a system with very high ratios in this section of the report may still have performance problems. As described previously, a poorly written query can cause volumes of index searches to join to other indexes, causing a high hit ratio (with lots of buffer gets), which is not good in this case. The database is doing most of its work in memory, but it shouldn't be doing so much work. Good hit ratios don't show the whole picture either. There are always cases where the database is working very efficiently, but this report only shows the database operations, not the application operations, server actions, or networking issues that also impact the performance of the application.

The Shared Pool statistics that follow the Instance Efficiency section show the percentage of the shared pool in use and the percentage of SQL statements that have been executed multiple

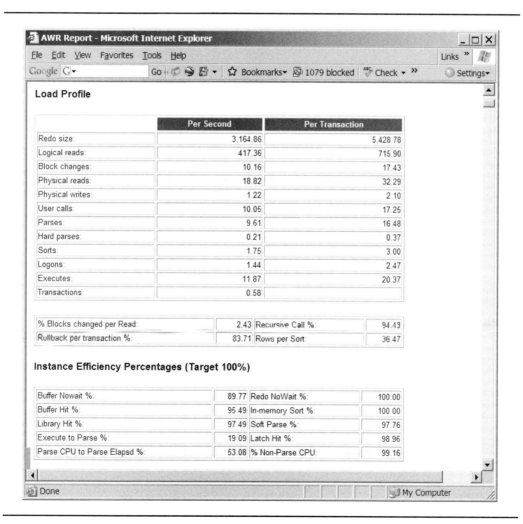

FIGURE 14-8. *The AWR Report load profile and hit ratios*

times (as desired). Combining this data with the library, parse, and latch data will help you to size the shared pool. The following listing shows sample shared pool statistics from the report:

```
Shared Pool Statistics        Begin    End
                              ------   ------
          Memory Usage %:     28.37    29.17
  % SQL with executions>1:    27.77    30.45
% Memory for SQL w/exec>1:    56.64    67.74
```

As shown by the data in the preceding listing, at the time of the second snapshot, 29.17 percent of the shared pool's memory was in use. Of the statements in the shared pool, only 30 percent had been executed more than once, indicating a potential need to improve cursor sharing in the application. The section of the report showing the percentage of shared pool memory in use is new with the Oracle 9*i* version of STATSPACK.

Top Wait Events

The Top Wait Events section of STATSPACK is probably the most revealing section in the entire report when you are trying to quickly eliminate bottlenecks on your system. This section of the report shows the Top 5 Wait Events, the full list of Wait Events, and the Background Wait Events. Identifying major wait events may help to target your tuning efforts to the most burning issues on your system. If TIMED_STATISTICS is true, then the events are ordered in time waited; if false, then the events are ordered by the number of waits (in testing Microsoft Windows this still was ordered by wait time).

For example, the following listing shows the top 5 wait events for a report interval:

```
Top 5 Timed Events
~~~~~~~~~~~~~~~~~~~~~
                                                      % Total
Event                          Waits     Time (s)   Ela Time
----------------------------  ----------  ----------  --------
db file sequential read       399,394,399  2,562,115    52.26
CPU time                                     960,825    19.60
buffer busy waits             122,302,412    540,757    11.03
PL/SQL lock timer                   4,077    243,056     4.96
log file switch                   188,701    187,648     3.83
(checkpoint incomplete)
```

In the preceding example, the db file sequential read waits show an incredible number of waits (almost 400,000,000) and an incredible amount time spent waiting on db file sequential reads. This wait event was due to poor SQL using too many indexes and reading many more blocks than it should have. Slow disk access also contributed to slow performance, as many blocks needed to be read in, but the issue was the SQL itself (as usual). After tuning the code for a single day, well over five terabytes of reads were eliminated in a 24-hour period. Consider the following top 5 wait events for a system:

```
Top 5 Wait Events
~~~~~~~~~~~~~~~~~~~
                                                    Wait     % Total
Event                                      Waits  Time (cs)  Wt Time
----------------------------------------  -------  ---------  -------
```

```
db file sequential read                      18,977,104   22,379,571   82.29
latch free                                    4,016,773    2,598,496    9.55
log file sync                                 1,057,224      733,490    2.70
log file parallel write                       1,054,006      503,695    1.85
db file parallel write                        1,221,755      404,230    1.49
```

In the preceding listing, we see a large number of waits related to reading a single block (db file sequential reads) and also waits for latches (latch free). We also see some pretty high waits for some of the writing to both datafiles and log files, as well as other potential issues with log file contention. To solve these issues (to identify which are truly major issues), we must narrow down these issues by investigating the granular reports within other sections of STATSPACK.

In the listing that follows, we see a sample listing of waits on this very intense system (not as bad as the preceding one, though). After the listing, we will investigate some of the common events that cause problems. This is only a partial listing, but I've tried to include many of the most common problems.

Top Wait Events

Event	Waits	Timeouts	Total Wait Time (cs)	Avg wait (ms)	Waits /txn
db file sequential read	18,977,104	0	22,379,571	12	17.4
latch free	4,016,773	2,454,622	2,598,496	6	3.7
log file sync	1,057,224	10	733,490	7	1.0
enqueue	90,140	1,723	67,611	8	0.1
library cache pin	3,062	0	29,272	96	0.0
db file scattered read	21,110	0	26,313	12	0.0
buffer busy waits	29,640	2	22,739	8	0.0
log file sequential read	31,061	0	18,372	6	0.0
row cache lock	22,402	0	3,250	1	0.0
LGWR wait for redo copy	4,436	45	183	0	0.0
SQL*Net more data to client	15,937	0	156	0	0.0
file identify	125	0	12	1	0.0
wait for inquiry response	76	0	10	1	0.0
SQL*Net message to client	35,427,781	0	6,599	0	32.5

Next are some of the most common problems; explanations and potential solutions are given as well. These sections are very important and worth their weight in gold!

DB File Scattered Read

The DB File Scattered Read wait event generally indicates waits related to full table scans or fast full index scans. As full table scans are pulled into memory, they are scattered throughout the buffer cache, since it is usually unlikely that they fall into contiguous buffers. A large number indicates that there may be missing or suppressed indexes. This could also be preferred, since it may be more efficient to perform a full table scan than an index scan. Check to ensure full table scans are necessary when you see these waits. Try to cache small tables to avoid reading them into memory over and over again. Locate the data on disk systems that have either more disk caching or are buffered by the OS file system cache. DB_FILE_MULTIBLOCK_READ_COUNT can make full scans faster (but it could also influence Oracle to do more of them). You can also partition tables and indexes so that only a portion is scanned. Slow File I/O (slow disks) can cause these waits. Correlated to each of the waits are the values for P1,P2,P3=file, block, blocks.

DB File Sequential Read

The DB File Sequential Read wait event generally indicates a single block read (an index read, for example). A large number could indicate poor joining orders of tables or unselective indexing. This number will certainly be large (normally) for a high-transaction, well-tuned system. You should correlate this wait with other known issues within the STATSPACK report such as inefficient SQL. Check to ensure index scans are necessary and check join orders for multiple table joins. The DB_CACHE_SIZE will also be a determining factor in how often these waits show up; hash-area joins causing problems should show up in the PGA memory but similarly are memory hogs that can cause high wait numbers for sequential reads or can also show up as direct path read/write waits. Range scans can read a lot of blocks if the data is spread in many different blocks (density within blocks could cause issues with range scans, and reverse key indexes could be problematic with range scans). Loading data in a sorted manner can help range scans and reduce the number of blocks read. Partitioning can help, as it can eliminate some blocks. Look for unselective indexes that are causing a lot of these. Locate the data on disk systems that either have more disk caching and/or are buffered by OS file system cache. Correlated to the waits are the values for P1,P2,P3=file, block, blocks.

Buffer Busy Waits IDs and Meanings

A buffer busy wait is a wait event for a buffer that is being used in an unsharable way or is being read into the buffer cache. Buffer busy waits should not be greater than 1 percent. Check the buffer wait statistics section (or V$WAITSTAT) to find out where the wait is. Follow the solution in this section for buffer busy waits associated with Segment Header, Undo Header, Undo Block, Data Block, and Index Block. Correlated to the waits are the values for P1,P2,P3=file, block, id (see the list in the following table). Some people argue that buffer busy waits can be helped by adding more ITL slots (initrans), but the information shown in the following table makes it evident that initrans can help in the appropriate situation (based on the correlated TX enqueue wait).

Reason Code (Id)		Reason
<=8.0.6	>=8.1.6	
0	0	A block is being read.
1003	100	We want to NEW the block, but the block is currently being read by another session (most likely for undo).
1007	200	We want to NEW the block, but someone else has is using the current copy, so we have to wait for them to finish.
1010	230	Trying to get a buffer in CR/CRX mode, but a modification has started on the buffer that has not yet been completed.
1012		A modification is happening on a SCUR or YCUR buffer but has not yet completed
1012 (dup.)	231	CR/CRX scan found the CURRENT block, but a modification has started on the buffer that has not yet been completed.
1013	130	The block is being read by another session and no other suitable block image was found, so we wait until the read is completed. This may also occur after an assumed buffer cache deadlock. The kernel can't get a buffer in a certain amount of time and assumes a deadlock. Therefore, it will read the CR version of the block.
1014	110	We want the CURRENT block as either shared or exclusive, but the block is being read into cache by another session, so we have to wait until their read() is completed.

Reason Code (Id)		Reason
1014 (duplicate)	120	We want to get the block in current mode, but someone else is currently reading it into the cache. We wait for them to complete the read. This occurs during buffer lookup.
1016	210	The session wants the block in SCUR or XCUR mode. If this is a buffer exchange or the session is in discrete TX mode, the session waits for the first time; the second time, it escalates the block as a deadlock, and so this does not show up as waiting for very long. In this case the statistic "exchange deadlocks" is incremented and we yield the CPU for the "buffer deadlock" wait event.
1016 (duplicate)	220	During buffer lookup for a CURRENT copy of a buffer, we have found the buffer, but someone holds it in an incompatible mode so we have to wait.

Buffer Busy/Segment Header

If the wait is on a segment header, you can increase the freelists or freelist groups (this can even help single instances) or increase the PCTUSED-to-pctfree gap. Use Automatic Segment Space Management (ASSM). If you are using ASSM, Oracle does this for you by using bitmap freelists. This also removes the need to set PCTUSED.

Buffer Busy/Undo Header

If the wait is on an undo header, you can address this by adding rollback segments or increase the undo area.

Buffer Busy/Undo Block

If the wait is on an undo block, you should try to commit more often (but not too often, or you'll get "log file sync" waits) or use larger rollback segments or undo areas. You may need to reduce the data density on the table driving this consistent read or increase the DB_CACHE_SIZE.

Buffer Busy/Data Block

If the wait is on a data block, you can move "hot" data to another block to avoid this hot block or use smaller blocks (to reduce the number of rows per block, making it less "hot"). Check for scanning unselective data and fix queries that are causing this or partition the table to eliminate unnecessary scans of data. You can also increase initrans for a hot block (where users are simultaneously accessing the same block). Don't set initrans too high, as this takes 24 bytes per ITL slot and you only need enough for the number of users accessing the *exact* same block for DML at the same time (usually something like five is more than enough). When a DML (insert/update/delete) occurs on a block, the lock byte is set in the block and any user accessing the record(s) being changed must check the ITL for information regarding building the before image of the block. The Oracle Database writes information into the block, including all users who are "interested" in the state of the block, in the Interested Transaction List (ITL). To decrease waits in this area, you increase the initrans, which will create the space in the block to allow multiple ITL slots (for multiple DML user access). The default is two ITL slots per index or data block. You can also increase the pctfree value on the table where this block exists. Oracle will use space in pctfree to add ITL slots up to the number specified by maxtrans in 9*i* (maxtrans is not set in 10*g* and defaults to 255) when there are not enough slots pre-built with the initrans that is specified. Check for correlated TX4 enqueue waits as well.

Top Wait Events

Buffer Busy/Index Block

Use reverse key indexes and or smaller blocks (to reduce the number of rows per block). Note that reverse key indexes can slow down range scans where you want the data to be sequentially located in the same block. Check for scanning unselective indexes (bad code / bad indexes). You may want to rebuild the index or partition the index to lessen accesses to it. Increase initrans for a hot block (not too high, as this takes 24 bytes per slot) where multiple users are accessing the same block for DML (see the "Tuning and Viewing at the Block Level" section for more information on ITL). Check for correlated TX4 enqueue waits as well.

Latch Free

Latches are low-level queueing mechanisms (they're accurately referred to as mutually exclusive mechanisms) used to protect shared memory structures in the System Global Area (SGA). Latches are like locks on memory that are very quickly obtained and released. Latches are used to prevent concurrent access to a shared memory structure. If the latch is not available, a latch free miss is recorded. Most latch problems are related to the failure to use bind variables (library cache latch and shared pool latch), redo generation issues (redo allocation latch), buffer cache contention issues (cache buffers lru chain), and hot blocks in the buffer cache (cache buffers chain). There are also latch waits related to bugs; check MetaLink for bug reports if you suspect this is the case (oracle.com/support). When latch miss ratios are greater than 0.5 percent, you should investigate the issue.

Enqueue

An *enqueue* is a lock that protects a shared resource. Locks protect shared resources such as data in a record, to prevent two people from updating the same data at the same time. It includes a queueing mechanism, which is FIFO (first in, first out). Note that Oracle's latching mechanism is not FIFO. Enqueue waits usually point to the *ST* enqueue, the *HW* enqueue, and the *TX4* enqueue. The ST enqueue is used for space management and allocation for dictionary-managed tablespaces. Use LMTs (Locally Managed Tablespaces), or try to preallocate extents or at least make the next extent larger for problematic dictionary-managed tablespaces. HW enqueues are used with the high water mark of a segment; manually allocating the extents can circumvent this wait. TX4 is one of the most common enqueue waits. TX4 enqueue waits are usually the result of one of three issues. The first issue involves duplicates in a unique index; you need to commit/roll back to free the enqueue. The second concerns multiple updates to the same bitmap index fragment. Since a single bitmap fragment may contain multiple ROWIDs, you need to issue a commit or a rollback to free the enqueue when multiple users are trying to update the same fragment. The third and most likely issue arises when multiple users are updating the same block. If there are no free ITL slots when multiple users want to perform DML on a different row of the same block, a block-level lock could occur. You can easily avoid this scenario by increasing the initrans to create multiple ITL slots and/or by increasing the pctfree on the table (so that Oracle can create the ITL slots as needed). You could also use a smaller block size so that there are fewer rows in the block, and thus greater concurrency on the data is allowed. There are also two other TX4 waits that are less prevalent: waiting for a prepared statement and inserting a row into an index where another transaction is splitting the index block. When users want to change the exact same record in a block, a TX6 lock is the result. Lastly, while you no longer get TM locks, which are table locks when you don't index foreign keys, be sure to still index them to avoid a performance issue. Correlated to the waits are the values for P1,P2,P3=lock type and mode, lockid1, lockid2 (there are also a p2raw and a p3raw that show p2/p3 in hex).

Log File Switch

All commit requests are waiting for 'logfile switch (archiving needed)' or 'logfile switch (chkpt. Incomplete)'. Ensure that the archive disk is not full or slow. DBWR may be too slow due to I/O. You may need to add more or larger redo logs, and you may also need to add database writers if the DBWR is the problem.

Log Buffer Space

When a change is made, the changed block is copied to the log buffer. If the log buffer doesn't get written fast enough to the redo logs, it can cause log buffer space issues (things get backed up). This can also be a problem when you commit a very large amount of data at once (make this larger for these types of transactions). This wait usually occurs because you are writing the log buffer faster than LGWR can write it to the redo logs, or because log switches are too slow, but *usually* not because the log buffer is too small (although this is also the case at times). To address this problem, increase the size of the log files, or get faster disks to write to, but as a last resort increase the size of the log buffer (in very large systems, it is not uncommon to see the Log Buffer in the tens of megabytes). You might even consider using solid-state disks, for their high speed for redo logs.

Log File Sync

When a user changes a record, the record is copied to the log buffer. When a commit or rollback is issued, the log buffer is flushed (copied) to the redo logs by LGWR (Log Writer). The process when committing of writing the changed data from the log buffer to the redo and getting a confirmation that the write successfully occurred is called a *log file sync*. To reduce Log File Sync waits, try to commit more records (try to commit a batch of 50 instead of one at a time if possible). If you commit 50 records one at a time, 50 log file syncs need to occur. Put Redo Logs on a faster disk or alternate Redo Logs on different physical disk arrays to reduce the archiving effect on LGWR. Don't use RAID 5, since it is very slow for applications that write a lot; potentially consider using filesystem direct I/O or raw devices, which are very fast at writing information. Correlated to the waits are the values for P1,P2,P3=buffer#, unused, unused.

Global Cache CR Request

When using multiple instances (RAC/Grid), a global cache CR request occurs when one instance is waiting for blocks from another instance's cache (sent via the interconnect). This wait says that the current instance can't find a consistent read (CR) version of a block in the local cache. If the block is not in the remote cache, then a db file sequential read wait will also follow this one. Tune the SQL that is causing large amounts of reads that get moved from node to node. Try to put users who are using the same blocks on the same instance so that the blocks are not moved from instance to instance. Some non-Oracle application servers will move the same process from node to node looking for the fastest node (unaware that they are moving the same blocks from node to node). Pin these long processes to the same node. Potentially increase the size of the local cache if slow I/O combined with a small cache is the problem. Monitor V$CR_BLOCK_SERVER to see if there is an issue like reading UNDO segments. Correlated to the waits are the values for P1,P2,P3=file, block, lenum (look in V$LOCK_ELEMENT for the row where lock_element_addr has the same value as lenum).

Log File Parallel Write

Put redo logs on fast disks and don't use RAID5. Separate redo logs from other data that might slow them down and ensure tablespaces are not left in hot backup mode. Correlated to the waits are the values for P1,P2,P3=files written to, blocks, requests.

DB File Parallel Write

Fix and/or speed up the Operating System I/O and/or file system I/O doing the database writing to database files. Correlated to the waits are the values for P1,P2,P3=files, blocks, requests/timeouts.

Direct Path Read

Oracle usually does direct path reads to directly read blocks into the PGA. This is used for things such as sorting, parallel query, and read ahead. The time here does not always reflect the true wait time. This is usually an issue with the file I/O (see if any disks are I/O bound using OS utilities, as described in Chapter 16). Check for sorting on disk instead of in memory. Using async I/O could reduce the elapsed time, although it may not reduce the wait time. Correlated to the waits are the values for P1,P2,P3=file, start block, number of blocks.

Direct Path Write

Direct path writes used for such things as direct load operations, parallel DML, and writes to uncached LOBs (Large Objects). The time here does not always reflect the true wait time. This is usually an issue with the file I/O (see if any disks are I/O bound using OS utilities, as described in Chapter 16). Check for sorting on disk. Using async I/O could reduce the elapsed time, although it may not reduce the wait time. Correlated to the waits are the values for P1,P2,P3=file, start block, number of blocks.

Async Disk I/O

Oracle is waiting for the completion of an async write or for an async slave to write. The problem could arise from I/O issues with the DBWR (Database Writer), the LGWR (Log Writer), the ARCH (Archiver), and/or the CKPT (checkpoint process) but is usually some file I/O issue.

Idle Events

There are also several idle wait events listed after the output that can be ignored. Idle events are generally listed at the bottom of each section and include things like SQL*Net messages to or from the client and other background-related timings. Idle events are listed in the stats$idle_event table.

Some of the most common wait problems and potential solutions are outlined here:

Wait Problem	Potential Fix
Sequential Read	Indicates many index reads—tune the code (especially joins)
Scattered Read	Indicates many full table scans—tune the code; cache small tables
Free Buffer	Increase the DB_CACHE_SIZE; shorten the checkpoint; tune the code
Buffer Busy	Segment header—add freelists or freelist groups
Buffer Busy	Data block—separate "hot" data; use reverse key indexes, use smaller blocks; increase initrans (debatable); reduce block popularity; make I/O faster
Buffer Busy	Undo header—add rollback segments or areas
Buffer Busy	Undo block—commit more; larger rollback segments or areas
Latch Free	Investigate the detail (a listing later in this chapter includes fixes)
Enqueue – ST	Use LMTs or preallocate large extents

Wait Problem	Potential Fix
Enqueue – HW	Preallocate extents above the high water mark
Enqueue – TX4	Increase initrans or use a smaller block size on the table or index
Enqueue – TX6	Fix the code that is making the block unsharable (use v$lock to find)
Enqueue – TM	Index foreign keys; check application locking of tables
Log Buffer Space	Increase the log buffer; use faster disks for the redo logs
Log File Switch	Archive destination slow or full; add more or larger redo logs
Log file sync	Commit more records at a time; use faster redo log disks; use raw devices
Write complete waits	Add database writers; checkpoint more often; buffer cache too small
Idle Event	Ignore it

Following are some common idle events (by type of idle event):

- Dispatcher timer (shared server idle event)

- Lock manager wait for remote message (RAC idle event)

- Pipe get (user process idle event)

- Pmon timer (background process idle event)

- PX Idle Wait: (parallel query idle event)

- PX Deq Credit: need buffer (parallel query idle event)

- PX Deq: Execution Msg (parallel query idle event)

- Rdbms ipc message (background process idle event)

- Smon timer (Background process idle event)

- SQL*Net message from client (user process idle event)

- Virtual circuit status (shared server idle event)

In Oracle 10g, there is also a Wait Event Histogram that shows how many of the waits fall into various buckets (0–1 ms, 1–4 ms, 4–8 ms, 8–16 ms, and 32+ ms). This type of histogram is also provided for file I/O by tablespace to show if you are waiting on mostly short waits with a few very long waits or a lot of medium length waits.

In 10g, the enqueue section actually spells out the type of enqueue. For instance, if it is a TX Enqueue, it will now say TX Transaction. If that wasn't good enough, it goes one step further and even tells you the type of TX. For instance, for a TX4, it will show that it is a TX Transaction (row lock contention) and then it will give the Requests, Gets, Waits, and a few other bits of helpful information. See Figure 14-9 for a look at this through the AWR Report.

TIP
Tuning by wait events is one of the best possible reactive tuning methods.

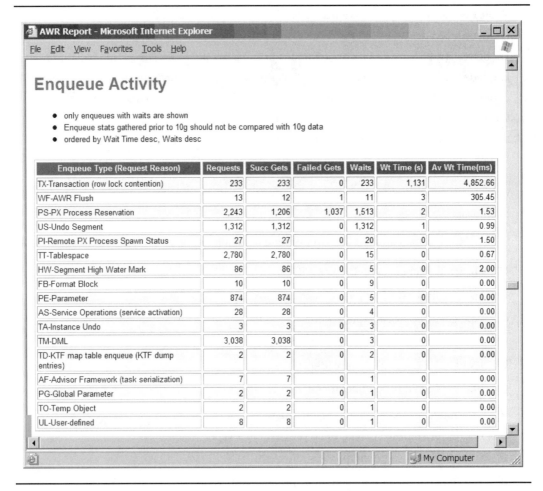

Enqueue Activity

- only enqueues with waits are shown
- Enqueue stats gathered prior to 10g should not be compared with 10g data
- ordered by Wait Time desc, Waits desc

Enqueue Type (Request Reason)	Requests	Succ Gets	Failed Gets	Waits	Wt Time (s)	Av Wt Time(ms)
TX-Transaction (row lock contention)	233	233	0	233	1,131	4,852.66
WF-AWR Flush	13	12	1	11	3	305.45
PS-PX Process Reservation	2,243	1,206	1,037	1,513	2	1.53
US-Undo Segment	1,312	1,312	0	1,312	1	0.99
PI-Remote PX Process Spawn Status	27	27	0	20	0	1.50
TT-Tablespace	2,780	2,780	0	15	0	0.67
HW-Segment High Water Mark	86	86	0	5	0	2.00
FB-Format Block	10	10	0	9	0	0.00
PE-Parameter	874	874	0	5	0	0.00
AS-Service Operations (service activation)	28	28	0	4	0	0.00
TA-Instance Undo	3	3	0	3	0	0.00
TM-DML	3,038	3,038	0	3	0	0.00
TD-KTF map table enqueue (KTF dump entries)	2	2	0	2	0	0.00
AF-Advisor Framework (task serialization)	7	7	0	1	0	0.00
PG-Global Parameter	2	2	0	1	0	0.00
TO-Temp Object	2	2	0	1	0	0.00
UL-User-defined	8	8	0	1	0	0.00

FIGURE 14-9. *The AWR Report enqueue activity (enqueues spelled out)*

TIP
The top 5 wait events reveal to you the largest issues on your system at the macro level. Rarely do they point you to a specific problem. Other parts of STATSPACK or the AWR Report will tell you why you are receiving the top 5 waits.

Oracle Bugs

There are also Oracle bugs (undocumented features?) related to wait events. The first diagnostic step to resolve this behavior is to apply the latest patchset available in your platform. Most of the buffer cache issues related to bugs can be avoided by applying these patchsets. The following table summarizes the most common bugs related to buffer cache problems, possible workarounds, and the patchset that fixes the problem.

Bug	Description	Workaround	Fix
Bug: 2079526	Free buffer waits / LRU latch contention possible on write-intensive systems.	Not available	8174, 9013, 9201, 10*g*
Bug: 1967363	Increased index block gets / "cache buffer chains" contention in 8*i*/9*i*.	Not available	8173, 9013, 9201, 10*g*
Bug: 2268098	If you shrink a buffer pool by a certain amount and later try to grow the shared pool by the same amount, the attempt may fail with an "insufficient memory" error.	Not available	9014, 9201, 10*g*

The Life of an Oracle Shadow Process

Here is a breakdown of the life of an Oracle shadow process and where it might be waiting as it lives. This comes from Oracle Doc ID 61998.1 and shows what's happening in less than one second within Oracle.

State	Notes
IDLE	Waits for "SQL*Net message from client" (waiting for the user). Receives the SQL*Net packet requesting "parse/execute" of a statement.
ON CPU	Decodes the SQL*Net packet.
WAITING	Waits for "latch free" to obtain the "library cache" latch. Gets the library cache latch.
ON CPU	Scans the shared pool for the SQL statement, finds match, frees latch, sets up links to the shared cursor, etc., and begins to execute.
WAITING	Waits for "db file sequential read"; we need a block not in the cache (wait for I/O).
ON CPU	Block read from disk complete. Execution continues. Construct SQL*Net packet with first row of data to send to client and sends.
WAITING	Waits on "SQL*Net message from client" for acknowledgment packet received.
IDLE	Waits for next SQL*Net message from client.

RAC Wait Events and Interconnect Statistics

The RAC events are listed next in the report if you are running RAC (multiple instances). As stated earlier, you need to run STATSPACK or the AWR Report for *each* instance that you have. For STATSPACK, you run statspack.snap procedure and spreport.sql script on each node you want to monitor to compare to other instances. The greatest comparison report is one from another node that accesses the same database. I cover more on tuning RAC in Chapter 11 and will not repeat that information it here. It's very important to remember that single-instance tuning should be performed before attempting to tune the processes that communicate via the cluster interconnect. In other words, tune the system in single-instance mode before you move it to RAC.

Some of the top wait events that you may encounter are listed briefly next and covered in more detail in Chapter 11. The top global cache (gc) waits to look out for include:

- **gc current block busy** Happens when an instance requests a CURR data block (wants to do some DML) and the block to be transferred is in use.

- **gc buffer busy** A wait event that occurs whenever a session has to wait for an ongoing operation on the resource to complete because the block is in use.

- **gc (global cache) buffer busy** A wait event that is signaled when a process has to wait for a block to become available because another process is obtaining a resource for this block.

- **gc cr request** Happens when an instance requests a CR data block and the block to be transferred hasn't arrived at the requesting instance. This is the one I see the most, and it's usually because the SQL is poorly tuned and *many* index blocks are being moved back and forth between instances.

Figure 14-10 shows the AWR Report RAC section. You can see that there are six instances (nodes) in this cluster. You can also see things like the number of blocks sent/received as well as how many of the blocks are being accessed in the local cache (93.1 percent) as opposed to on the disk or in another instance. As you would guess, it is faster to access blocks in the local cache, but accessing one of the remote caches on one of the other nodes is almost always faster (given a fast enough interconnect and no saturation of the interconnect) than going to disk (more on this in Chapter 11).

Top SQL Statements

The most resource-intensive SQL statements in the database are listed next, in descending order of buffer gets. Since the buffer gets statistic is cumulative, the query with the most buffer gets may not be the worst-performing query in the database; it may just have been executed enough times to earn the highest ranking. Compare the cumulative number of buffer gets to the cumulative number of disk reads for the queries; if the numbers are close, then you should

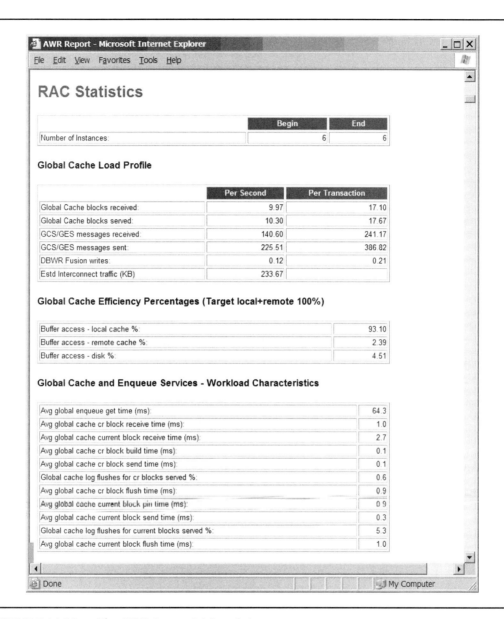

FIGURE 14-10. *The AWR Report RAC statistics*

evaluate the explain plan for the query to find out why it is performing so many disk reads. If the disk reads are not high but the buffer gets are high and the executions are low, then the query is either using a bad index or performing a join in the wrong order. This is also a problem for your system, since you are using a lot of your memory unnecessarily. Here is an example of this listing:

```
SQL ordered by Gets for DB
-> End Buffer Gets Threshold:  10000
-> Note that resources reported for PL/SQL includes the resources used by
   all SQL statements called within the PL/SQL code. As individual SQL
   statements are also reported, it is possible and valid for the summed
   total % to exceed 100

  Buffer Gets    Executions  Gets per Exec  % Total  Hash Value
--------------- ------------ -------------- ------- ------------
  166,697,520         6,514       25,590.7     2.5   1577170159

SELECT DISTINCT USERNAME   FROM USER_TEST A, SALES B,CUSTOMER C
WHERE A.USERNAME_TYPE = :b1  AND A.ITEMNO = :b2 C.NAME =
A.NAME  AND B.TYPE = C.TYPE  AND NVL(C.STARTDATE,'31-DEC-2002')
> :b3 ORDER BY NAME
  101,306,038         6,510       15,561.6     1.5   613844091

SELECT A.ITEMNO, B.LINEITEM, C.LINEITEM_AMT FROM LINES A, LINE_ITEMS B, LINE_ORDERS C
WHERE A.LINENO = B.LINENO AND A.LINENO = C.LINENO AND A.ORDERDATE = '31-DEC-2002' AND
B.TYPE = 'CURRENT' ORDER BY CUSTOMERNO
```

After listing the SQL commands with the most cumulative buffer gets, a second listing of the commands is provided, this time ordered by the greatest number of physical reads. A third listing of commands orders the executions, and then a fourth orders by parse calls.You may also see the internal Oracle data dictionary operations listed as part of these sections. Your application commands commonly account for the great majority of the buffer gets and disk reads performed by the database. If the shared pool is flushed between the execution times of the two snapshots, the SQL portion of the output report will not necessarily contain the most resource-intensive SQL executed during the period. In 10g, V$SQL now shows SQL for multiple users with same statement and shows child cursors, V$SQL_PLAN_STATISTICS show the execution stats for each cached cursor, and V$SQL_PLAN_STATISTICS_ALL shows the joins plan and stats and many other performance-related statistics. In the AWR Report, there are many Top SQL sections. An example is shown in Figure 14-11. They include the following:

- SQL ordered by Elapsed Time

- SQL ordered by CPU Time

- SQL ordered by Gets

- SQL ordered by Reads

- SQL ordered by Executions

- SQL ordered by Parse Calls

- SQL ordered by Sharable Memory

- SQL ordered by Version Count

- SQL ordered by Cluster Wait Time

- Complete List of SQL Text

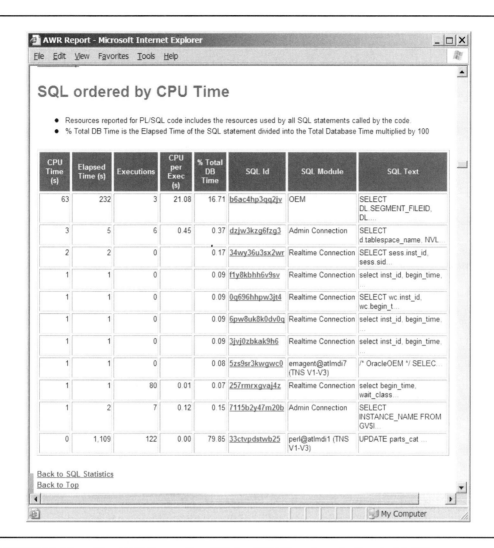

FIGURE 14-11. *The AWR Report Top SQL by CPU Time (new in Oracle 10gR2)*

TIP
Tuning the top 25 buffer get and top 25 physical get queries has yielded system performance gains of anywhere from 5 percent to 5000+ percent in my tuning. The SQL section of the STATSPACK report tells you which queries to consider tuning first. The top 10 SQL statements should not be substantially more than 10 percent of your buffer gets or disk reads.

Instance Activity Statistics

Following the SQL statement listing, you will see the list of changes to statistics from V$SYSSTAT, entitled "Instance Activity Stats." The V$SYSSTAT statistics are useful for identifying performance issues not shown in the prior sections. Here is a partial listing with some of the key sections listed:

```
Instance Activity Stats
Statistic                              Total    per Second    per Trans
------------------------------  ----------------  ------------  ------------
CPU used by this session               3,876,875       110.8           3.6
DBWR buffers scanned                   6,775,741       193.6           6.2
consistent gets                      366,674,801    10,476.4         336.5
db block changes                      19,788,834       565.4          18.2
db block gets                         41,812,892     1,194.7          38.4
dirty buffers inspected                1,204,544        34.4           1.1
enqueue waits                             87,613         2.5           0.1
free buffer requested                 20,053,136       573.0          18.4
index fast full scans (full)              28,686         0.8           0.0
leaf node splits                          21,066         0.6           0.0
logons cumulative                            186         0.0           0.0
parse count (hard)                        54,681         1.6           0.1
parse count (total)                    1,978,732        56.5           1.8
physical reads                        19,320,574       552.0          17.7
physical writes non checkpoint         2,027,920        57.9           1.9
recursive calls                        5,020,246       143.4           4.6
sorts (disk)                                   2         0.0           0.0
sorts (memory)                         1,333,831        38.1           1.2
sorts (rows)                          14,794,401       422.7          13.6
```

These statistics can also be found in the AWR Report. In Figure 14-12, you can see a shortened version of these statistics from a 10gR2 RAC database instance.

Things to Look for in the Instance Statistics Section

Compare the number of sorts performed on disk to the number performed in memory; increase the PGA_AGGREGATE_TARGET (or SORT_AREA_SIZE for earlier versions) to reduce disk sorts (see Chapter 4 for more information). If physical reads are high, you are probably performing full table scans. If there are a significant number of full table scans of large tables, evaluate the most-used queries and try to reduce this inefficiency by using indexes. A large number for consistent gets signals potentially over indexed or non colective index use. If dirty buffers inspected is high (over 5 percent) relative to free buffers requested, the DB_CACHE_SIZE may be too small or you may not be checkpointing often enough. If leaf node splits are high, consider rebuilding indexes that have grown and fragmented. The following sections will look at a few of these scenarios.

The following listing shows the four applicable rows from this section of the report:

```
Statistic                   Total    per Second    per Trans
------------------------  ------  ------------  ------------
sorts (disk)                  89           0.3          44.5
sorts (rows)               7,659          26.1       3,829.5
```

```
table scans (long tables)          0        0.0        0.0
table scans (short tables)        10        0.0        5.0
```

In the preceding example, the database performed 89 sorts on disk during the reporting interval. Of the table scans performed, all were of very small tables. The table scans (short tables) are tables that are smaller than 2 percent of the buffer cache in Oracle 10*g* (in V7 it was 5 blocks, in V8 it was 20 blocks, and in V9 it was also 2 percent). In the high-volume example that follows, we see a well-tuned memory sorting area where almost 15 million records were sorted in memory while only 2 sorts were done on disk.

```
Statistic                    Total   per Second    per Trans
-------------------------  ---------  -----------  -----------
sorts (disk)                     2         0.0          0.0
sorts (memory)           1,333,831        38.1          1.2
sorts (rows)            14,794,401       422.7         13.6
```

TIP
If there are many sorts being performed to disk (greater than 1–5 percent of the total number of rows being sorted), you may need to increase the initialization parameters associated with sorting. See Chapter 4 for more information on these.

Instance Activity Statistics

Instance Activity Stats

Statistic	Total	per Second	per Trans
CPU used by this session	8,420	14.02	24.06
CPU used when call started	2,223	3.70	6.35
CR blocks created	147	0.24	0.42
Cached Commit SCN referenced	497	0.83	1.42
Commit SCN cached	1	0.00	0.00
DB time	320,580	533.97	915.94
DBWR checkpoint buffers written	623	1.04	1.78
DBWR checkpoints	0	0.00	0.00
DBWR fusion writes	72	0.12	0.21
DBWR transaction table writes	115	0.19	0.33
DBWR undo block writes	282	0.47	0.81
DFO trees parallelized	22	0.04	0.06
IPC CPU used by this session	957	1.59	2.73
PX local messages recv'd	155	0.26	0.44
PX local messages sent	162	0.27	0.46
PX remote messages recv'd	4,109	6.84	11.74
PX remote messages sent	2,708	4.51	7.74

FIGURE 14-12. *The AWR Report instance activity stats*

Key Areas to Consider

A few key areas to consider are explained in this section:

- **Consistent gets** The number of blocks read from the buffer cache for queries without the SELECT FOR UPDATE clause. The value for this statistic plus the value of the "db block gets" statistic constitute what is referred to as logical reads (all reads cached in memory). These are usually the CURRENT version of the block, but it can also be a Consistent Read (CR) version.

- **DB block gets** The number of blocks read in the buffer cache that were accessed for INSERT, UPDATE, DELETE, or SELECT FOR UPDATE statements. These are CURRENT versions of the block. When these are changed, they are reflected in the 'db block changes' value.

- **Physical reads** The number of data blocks that were not read from the cache. This could be reads from disks, OS cache, or disk cache to satisfy a SELECT, SELECT FOR UPDATE, INSERT, UPDATE, or DELETE statement.

By adding the "consistent gets" and "db block gets," you get the number of Logical Reads (memory reads). Using the following equation, you can calculate the Data Cache Hit Ratio:

```
Hit Ratio = (Logical Reads - Physical Reads) / Logical Reads
```

TIP
The buffer hit ratio should be above 95 percent. If it is less than 95 percent, you should consider increasing the size of the data cache by increasing the DB_CACHE_SIZE initialization parameter (given that physical memory is available to do this).

- **Dirty buffers inspected** This is the number of dirty (modified) data buffers that were aged out on the LRU list. A value here indicates that the DBWR is not keeping up. You may benefit by adding more DBWRs.

TIP
If the dirty buffers inspected is greater than 0, consider increasing the database writes as detailed in Chapter 3.

- **Enqueue timeouts** The number of times that an enqueue (lock) was requested and the specific one that was requested was not available. If this statistic is above 0 investigate the locking issues.

- **Free buffer inspected** 'Free buffers inspected' includes buffers that were skipped because they were dirty, pinned, or busy. If you subtract those values ('dirty buffers inspected' and 'buffer is pinned count') from this statistic, it will leave the buffers that could not be reused due to latch contention. A large number would be a good indicator of a too-small buffer cache.

- **Parse count** The number of times a SQL statement was parsed (total count).

- **Recursive calls** The number of recursive calls to the database. This type of call occurs for a few reasons—misses in the Dictionary Cache, dynamic storage extension, and when PL/SQL statements are executed. Generally, if the number of recursive calls is more than 4 per process, you should check the Dictionary Cache Hit Ratio, and see if there are tables or indexes with a large number of extents. Unless there is a significant use of PL/SQL, the ratio of recursive calls to user calls should be 10 percent or less.

- **Redo size** The size in bytes of the amount of redo information that was written to the redo logs. This information can be used to help size the redo logs. There is additional information for redo sizing in Chapter 3.

- **Sorts (disk)** The number of sorts that were unable to be performed in memory and therefore required the creation of a temp segment in the temporary tablespace. This statistic divided by the sorts (memory) should not be above 5 percent. If it is, you should increase the SORT_AREA_SIZE or PGA_AGGREGATE_TARGET parameter in the init.ora file.

- **Sorts (memory)** The number of sorts that were performed in memory.

- **Sorts (rows)** The total number of rows that were sorted.

TIP
The "sorts (disk)" statistic divided by the "sorts (memory)" should not be above 1–5 percent. If it is, you should increase the PGA_AGGREGATE_TARGET (or SORT_AREA_SIZE) parameter in the initialization file (given that physical memory is available to do this). Remember that the memory allocated for Sort_Area_Size is a per-user value and PGA_AGGREGATE_TARGET is across all sessions.

- **Table fetch by rowid** Indicates the number of rows that were accessed by using a ROWID. This ROWID came from either an index or a 'where rowid = ' statement. A high number *usually* indicates a well-tuned application as far as fetching the data goes.

- **Table fetch continued row** The number of rows that were fetched that were chained or migrated.

TIP
If chained rows are indicated, the problem needs to be fixed as soon as possible. Chained rows can cause severe degradation of performance if a large number of rows are chained. See Chapter 3 for tips on chaining.

- **Table scans (long tables)** A long table is one that is larger than _SMALL_TABLE_THRESHOLD (hidden) with no CACHE clause. The default value of _SMALL_TABLE_THRESHOLD is 2 percent of the buffer cache in Oracle 10g and Oracle 9i. _SMALL_TABLE_THRESHOLD is a dangerous parameter to modify without careful benchmarking of the effects. As this affects all tables accessing it, is unwise to increase this significantly, if at all, as it can cause blocks to age more quickly and reduce your hit ratio. In Oracle, this parameter is the number of db blocks up to which the table is considered small. This threshold is used to determine the cutover point for direct-read operations. Any object that is smaller than it will not be worth performing direct reads for and thus will be read through the buffer cache. If the number of table scans per transaction is above 0, you may wish to review the application SQL statements and try to increase the use of indexes.

NOTE
The table scans (long tables) parameter has a different meaning in Oracle 10g (less than 2 percent of the buffer cache), Oracle 9i (less than 2 percent of the buffer cache), Oracle 8i (fewer than 20 blocks), and Oracle 7 (fewer than 5 blocks).

TIP
If full table scans are being performed, serious performance issues may result and data hit ratios will be distorted. These tables need to be identified so that the appropriate indexes are created or used. See Chapters 8 and 9 on query tuning for more information.

- **Table scans (short tables)** A short table is one that is shorter than 2 percent of the buffer cache in 10g. Full table scans on short tables are preferred by Oracle.

Tablespace and File I/O Statistics

The next section of the report provides the I/O statistics first listed by I/Os and then listed by tablespace and by datafile. If the I/O activity is not properly distributed among your files, you may encounter performance bottlenecks during periods of high activity. As a rule of thumb, you don't want more than 100 I/Os per second per 10,000 RPM disk (even with a RAID array). If the 'Av Rd(ms)' column (reads per millisecond) is higher than 14 ms (given a fair amount of reading is being done), you may want to investigate, since most disks should provide at least this much performance. If this column shows 1000 ms or more, you probably have some type of I/O problem, and if it shows ######, then you have a serious I/O problem of some kind (this can also be a formatting problem, but anything greater than 1000 is a problem when there are a fair number of reads being done). I have seen I/O issues that are related to other problems but show up as an I/O problem. For disks with a lot of memory cached on the disk, the I/O time is often less than 1 ms for a disk where heavy reading is being done. You should use this section of the report to identify such bottlenecks and to measure how effectively you have resolved those problems.

The parameter that can be set in the init.ora to help improve the read time is the DB_FILE_MULTIBLOCK_READ_COUNT parameter, which controls the number of blocks that can be read in one I/O when a full table scan is being performed. This can reduce the number of I/Os needed to scan a table, thus improving the performance of the full table scan. Unfortunately, the optimizer might do more full table scans as a result of setting DB_FILE_MULTIBLOCK_READ_COUNT (you don't want this behavior), so you may also need to set the OPTIMIZER_INDEX_COST_ADJ to a number, such as 10, to eliminate this problem and drive the use of indexes. Here is an example listing from this section of the report:

```
Tablespace IO Stats for DB: ORA10  Instance: ora10  Snaps: 1 -2
->ordered by IO's (Reads + Writes) desc
Tablespace
-----------------------------

                Av     Av     Av                        Av     Buffer Av Buf
        Reads Reads/s Rd(ms) Blks/Rd       Writes Writes/s   Waits Wt(ms)
------------- ------- ------ ------- ------------ -------- ---------- ------
TS_ORDERS
    1,108,981      32   12.1     1.0    1,006,453       29      6,445    4.9
```

```
TS_ORDER_SUM
      967,108      28    12.5      1.0      675,647      19        51    7.6
TS_ORDER_LINES
    1,389,292      40    10.1      1.0       22,930       1     1,753    3.9
```

Here are descriptions of some of the columns appearing in this output:

Tablespace	The name of the tablespace.
Reads	The number of physical reads that were performed on the data file to retrieve data.
Av Blks/Rd	The number of blocks per read that were read from the data file to satisfy an average read.
Writes	The number of writes to the data file.

An example of the AWR Report Tablespace I/O is displayed in Figure 14-13. We can also see from this figure that Oracle also gives file I/O information as well in this section.

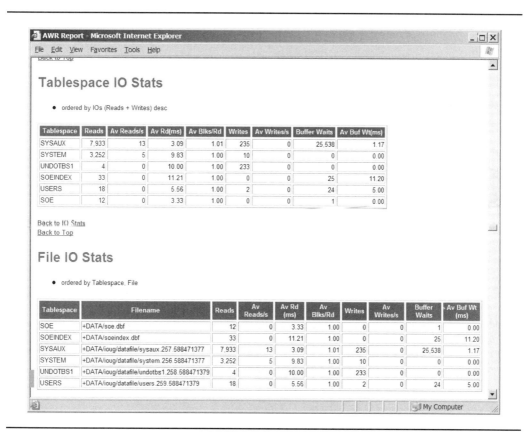

FIGURE 14-13.   *The AWR Report tablespace and file I/O stats*

Following the tablespace I/O statistics is a file I/O section breakdown. This is a very granular look at how the I/O is being distributed across the data files. If one of the data files is getting a majority of the reads and writes, you may be able to improve performance by creating multiple data files on separate disks or by striping the data file across multiple disks. Also, stay away from RAID 5 (Chapter 3 has more on this) or you'll get very slow write times.

TIP
If the number of physical reads is heavier on one physical disk, proper balancing of data will probably increase performance. See Chapter 3 for tips on fixing I/O problems with either data files or tablespaces.

Segment Statistics

One of the new data dictionary views that Oracle provided in Oracle 9*i* was V$SEGMENT_STATISTICS. This view quickly became a DBA favorite. Now, Oracle 10*g* takes this approach to the next level with Segment Statistics for everything you would ever need. Here are the sections that the AWR Report now shows in Oracle 10gR2:

- Segments by Logical Reads
- Segments by Physical Reads
- Segments by Row Lock Waits
- Segments by ITL Waits
- Segments by Buffer Busy Waits
- Segments by Global Cache Buffer Busy
- Segments by CR Blocks Received
- Segments by Current Blocks Received

Figure 14-14 shows the section of the AWR Report dedicated to Segment Statistics. This is particularly useful for finding what specific INDEX or DATA segment is causing a bottleneck of some kind. It was also very difficult to find specific ITL (interested transaction list) waits. Now in the Segment Statistics section you can see the exact number of ITL waits by owner, tablespace name, object name, and subobject name (such as an index partition subobject name).

TIP
Segment statistics are a great way to pinpoint performance problems to a given table, index, or partition. Oracle 10gR2 contains many segment-level statistics in both the AWR Report and STATSPACK.

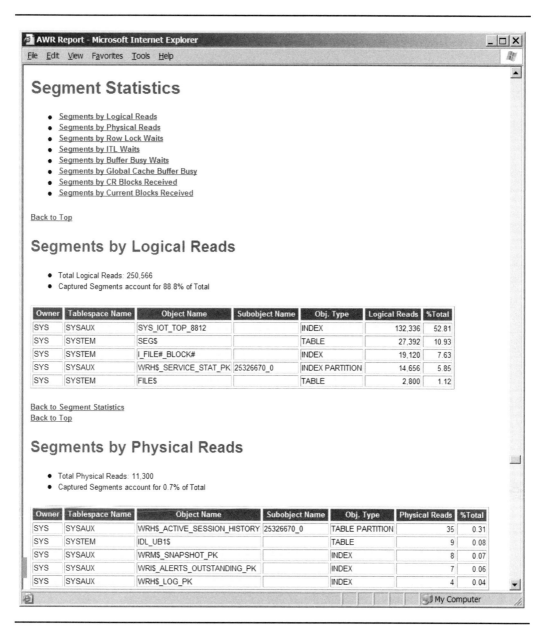

FIGURE 14-14. *The AWR Report segment statistics*

Additional Memory Statistics

Following the I/O statistics, the report lists the buffer cache statistics by pool (default, keep, and recycle), instance recovery statistics (the number of redo blocks), and the PGA memory statistics. A sample listing of these three sections is shown here:

```
Buffer Pool Statistics for DB: ORA10  Instance: ora10  Snaps: 1 -2
-> Standard block size Pools  D: default, K: keep, R: recycle
-> Default Pools for otherblock sizes: 2k, 4k, 8k, 16k, 32k

                                                 Free    Write   Buffer
           Number of Cache    Buffer   Physical Physical Buffer Complete  Busy
P          Buffers  Hit %     Gets      Reads    Writes   Waits   Waits   Waits
---       --------- -----  ----------- --------- -------- ------ -------- ------
D           5,898  100.0      4,721         0      208      0       0       0
          -------------------------------------------------------------------

Instance Recovery Stats for DB: ORA10  Instance: ora10  Snaps: 1 -2
-> B: Begin snapshot, E: End snapshot
   Targt Estd                                   Log File  Log Ckpt  Log Ckpt
   MTTR  MTTR   Recovery   Actual     Target      Size     Timeout   Interval
   (s)   (s)   Estd IO's  Redo Blks  Redo Blks  Redo Blks Redo Blks Redo Blks
 ----- ----- ---------- ---------- ---------- ---------- ---------- ----------
B   33    18     5898       706       13546      184320     13546   ##########
E   33    24     5898       717       14524      184320     14524   ##########
          -------------------------------------------------------------------


PGA Memory Stats for DB: ORA10  Instance: ora10  Snaps: 1 -2
-> WorkArea (W/A) memory is used for: sort, bitmap merge, and hash join ops
Statistic                            Begin (M)        End (M)      % Diff
----------------------------------- ---------------- ---------------- ----------
maximum PGA allocated                  10.587          10.587         .00
```

While much of this information is shown in other sections, the section on buffer pool statistics is very detailed in this section of the report. It shows individual buffer pools for the keep and recycle pools if they are used (Chapter 4 includes more information on buffer pools). It also shows information for the different block sizes if you use multiple block sizes. The AWR Report shows statistics on the following advisories (see the SGA Target Advisory in Figure 14-15):

- Instance Recovery Stats
- Buffer Pool Advisory
- PGA Aggr Summary
- PGA Aggr Target Stats
- PGA Aggr Target Histogram
- PGA Memory Advisory
- Shared Pool Advisory
- SGA Target Advisory
- Streams Pool Advisory
- Java Pool Advisory

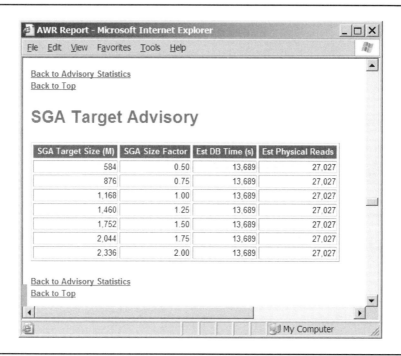

FIGURE 14-15. *The AWR Report SGA Target Advisory*

TIP
*In Oracle 10g, multiple data block sizes are allowed, and
STATSPACK shows statistics for each of these block sizes individually.
There are many advisories to help you size things that both the AWR
Report (see Figure 14-15) and Enterprise Manager (graphically, see
Chapter 5) provide. These suggestions should be tested and are not
always best. As Robert Freeman would say, "Your mileage may vary."*

UNDO Statistics

The next section provides undo segment statistics. The first part of this section shows the undo
tablespace and the number of transactions and undo blocks for the entire tablespace. Next it gives
information about how many undo blocks utilized and the number of transactions have occurred
for a given segment (undostat row). The AWR Report in Oracle 10g provides a summary and undo
segment stats that were not available in Oracle 9i. This new output is shown in Figure 14-16.

While I have eliminated the ROLLSTAT information from this version of the book (since most
people now use AUTO UNDO), this information can still be reported in STATSPACK. By using
the configuration file, sprepcon.sql, you can modify the display_rollstat parameter.

UNDO Statistics

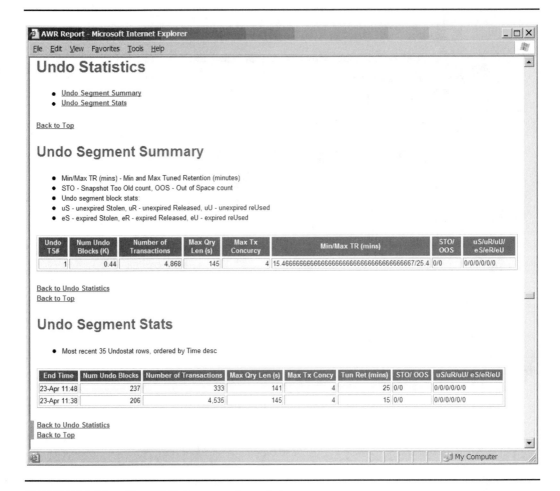

FIGURE 14-16. *The AWR Report undo statistics*

Latch Statistics

Latches are low-level queueing mechanisms (they're accurately referred to as mutual exclusion mechanisms) used to protect shared memory structures in the SGA (memory). Latches are like locks on memory that are very quickly gotten and released, consuming roughly 32 bytes. Latches are used to prevent concurrent access to a shared memory structure. If the latch is not available, then a latch free miss is recorded. Most latch problems are related to *not* using bind variables (library cache latch), redo generation issues (redo allocation latch), buffer cache contention issues (cache buffers lru chain), and hot blocks in the buffer cache (cache buffers chain). There are also latch waits related to bugs, so check MetaLink as well. When latch miss ratios are greater than 0.5 percent, you should investigate the issue. In Oracle 10gR2, the Cache Buffers Chains (CBC) latch can be shared to some degree.

There are two types of latches: "willing to wait" latches (example is a library cache latch) and "not willing to wait" latches (an example is a redo copy latch). A process that is willing to wait will try to acquire a latch. If none are available, it will spin and then request the latch again. It will continue to do this up to the _SPIN_COUNT initialization parameter (note that spinning costs CPU). If it can't get a latch after spinning up to the _SPIN_COUNT, it will go to sleep, not do anything for a while, and then will wake up after one centisecond (one hundredth of a second). It will do this twice. It will then start this process again, spinning up to the _SPIN_COUNT and then sleeping for twice as long (two centiseconds). After doing this again, it will double again. So the pattern is 1, 1, 2, 2, 4, 4, etc. It will do this until it gets the latch. Every time the latch sleeps, it will create a latch sleep wait. An example of a "willing to wait" latch is a library cache latch. Some latches are "not willing to wait." A latch of this type does not wait for the latch to become available. It immediately times out and retries to obtain the latch. A redo copy latch is an example of a "not willing to wait" latch. A "not willing to wait" latch will generate information for the immediate_gets and the immediate_misses columns of the V$LATCH view and also in the STATSPACK report. The hit ratio for these latches should also approach 99 percent, and the misses should never fall below 1 percent misses.

By viewing this section of STATSPACK or querying the V$LATCH view, you can see how many processes had to wait (a latch miss) or sleep (a latch sleep) and the number of times they had to sleep. If you see ##### in any field, it usually means bad news, as the value exceeds the length of the field. V$LATCHHOLDER, V$LATCHNAME, and V$LATCH_CHILDREN are also helpful in investigating latch issues. Here is a partial listing of the latch activity section; there are three sections (latch activity, latch sleep, and latch miss) of the STATSPACK report (this one has a library cache problem—partial display latches only):

```
Latch Activity for DB: ORA10  Instance: ora10  Snaps: 1 -2
->"Get Requests", "Pct Get Miss" and "Avg Slps/Miss" are statistics for
  willing-to-wait latch get requests
->"NoWait Requests", "Pct NoWait Miss" are for no-wait latch get requests
->"Pct Misses" for both should be very close to 0.0
-> ordered by Wait Time desc, Avg Slps/Miss, Pct NoWait Miss desc
                                    Pct    Avg   Wait                  Pct
                          Get       Get    Slps  Time     NoWait    NoWait
Latch                     Requests  Miss   /Miss  (s)     Requests  Miss
-----------------------   --------  -----  -----  ------  --------  ------
KCL freelist latch           4,924   0.0                          0
cache buffer handles       968,992   0.0   0.0                    0
cache buffers chains   761,708,539   0.0   0.4          21,519,841   0.0
cache buffers lru chain  8,111,269   0.1   0.8          19,834,466   0.1
library cache           67,602,665   2.2   2.0             213,590   0.8
redo allocation         12,446,986   0.2   0.0                    0
redo copy                      320   0.0               10,335,430   0.1
user lock                    1,973   0.3   1.2                    0
                       -----------------------------------------------------

Latch Miss Sources for DB:
-> only latches with sleeps are shown
-> ordered by name, sleeps desc
```

Latch Name	Where	NoWait Misses	Sleeps	Waiter Sleeps
KCL lock element parent	kclulb	0	431	248
batching SCNs	kcsl01	0	3,836	3,099
batching SCNs	kcsl02	0	474	1,206
cache buffers chains	kcbgtcr: kslbegin	0	63,446	47,535
cache buffers chains	kcbgcur: kslbegin	0	9,820	7,603
cache buffers lru chain	kcbzgb: multiple sets nowa	0	4,859	0
enqueues	ksqdel	0	106,769	12,576
library cache	kglhdgn: child:	0	1,973,311	#######
library cache	kglpnal: child: alloc spac	0	279,254	#######
redo allocation	kcrfwr: redo allocation	0	942	1,032
redo allocation	kcrfwi: before write	0	191	53
redo allocation	kcrfwi: more space	0	2	39

Figures 14-17 and 14-18 show similar statistics with the AWR Report. Notice in Figure 14-18 that Oracle no longer displays/keeps the Sleep 1–3 statistics.

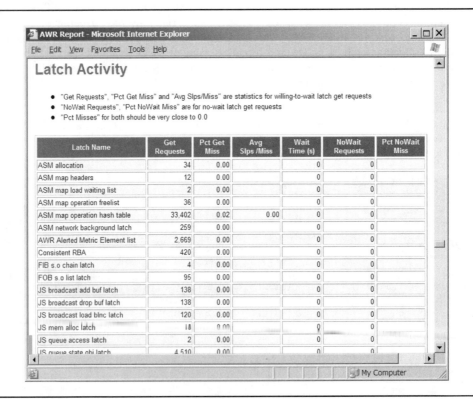

FIGURE 14-17. *The AWR Report latch activity*

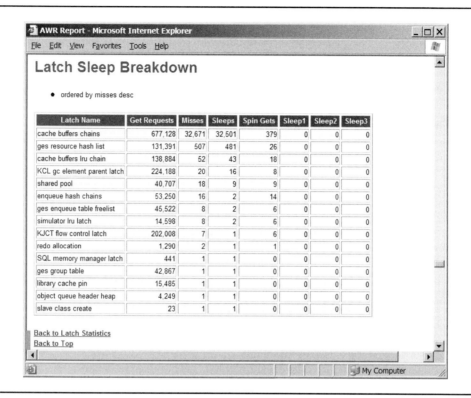

FIGURE 14-18. *The AWR Report latch sleep breakdown*

One thing to remember about processes that are sleeping: These processes may also be holding other latches that will not be released until the process is finished with them. This will cause even more processes to sleep, waiting for those latches. So, you can see how important it is to reduce contention as much as possible. The following table explains the columns in this part of the report:

Latch Name	The name of the latch.
Gets	The number of times a "willing to wait" request for a latch was requested and it was available.
Misses	The number of times a "willing to wait" request for a latch was initially requested but was not available.
Sleeps	The number of a "willing to wait request" for a latch failed over and over until the spin count was exceeded and the process went to sleep. The number of sleeps may be higher than the misses. Processes may sleep multiple times before obtaining the latch.
NoWait Misses	The number of times an immediate (not willing to wait) request for a latch was unsuccessful.

Following are some latches to look for and remember:

- **Latch free** When 'latch free' is high in the wait events section of the report, then there are problems that need to be investigated in the latch section of the report. This section will help you look for which latches are a problem. The problem could be a sleeping latch (couldn't get the latch and sleeping until the next try) or a spinning latch (waiting and retrying based on spin count).

- **Library cache and shared pool** The library cache is a hash table you access through an array of hash buckets (similar to the buffer cache). The memory for the library cache comes from the shared pool (the dictionary cache used for Oracle internal objects is also part of the shared pool). The library cache latch serializes access to objects in the library cache. Every time a SQL or PL/SQL procedure, package, function, or trigger is executed, this library cache latch is used to search the shared pool for the exact statement so that it can be reused. A single shared pool latch protected the allocation of memory in the library cache in Oracle 8i; as of Oracle 9i, there are 7 child latches for this. Contention for the 'shared pool,' 'library cache pin,' or 'library cache' latches primarily occurs when the shared pool is too small or when statements are not reused. Statements are not usually reused when bind variables are not used. Common but not exact SQL can flood the shared pool with statements. Increasing the size of the shared pool, at times, only makes the latch problem worse. You can also set the value of the initialization parameter CURSOR_SHARING=FORCE (or CURSOR_SHARING=SIMILAR) to help fix this issue and to reduce problems when bind variables are not used. CURSOR_SHARING=FORCE will substitute bind variables for literals. CURSOR_SHARING=SIMILAR will substitute bind variables for literals if the execution plan is guaranteed to be the same.

The shared pool latch and library cache latch issues also occur when space is needed in the library cache when the shared pool is too small for the number of SQL statements that need to be processed. A *hard* parse occurs when a new SQL statement is issued that does not exist in the shared pool currently, since it will have to be parsed. Oracle has to allocate memory for the statement from the shared pool, as well as check the statement syntactically and semantically. A hard parse is very expensive in both terms of CPU used and in the number of latch gets performed. A *soft* parse occurs when a session issues a SQL statement that is already in the shared pool *and* it can use an existing version of that statement. As far as the application is concerned, it has asked to parse the statement. While space is being freed up in order to load a SQL or PL/SQL statement, the shared pool latch (held for allocate and free) is being held exclusively and other users must wait. You can help to reduce contention by increasing the shared pool or by pinning large SQL and PL/SQL statements in memory using the DBMS_Shared_Pool.Keep procedures to avoid reloads. The number of library cache latches can be increased by setting _KGL_LATCH_ COUNT (the maximum is 66, see Appendix A for more information on the undocumented initialization parameters)

Note that a count of x$ksmsp will show how many shared pool pieces there are; each row in the table represents a piece of memory in the shared pool. Columns to note are ksmchcom (describes the piece of memory), ksmchptr (the physical address of the piece of memory), ksmchsiz (piece size), ksmchcls (the state/class of the piece of memory, including "recr," a recreatable piece currently in use that can be a candidate for flushing when the shared pool is low in available memory; "freeabl," a freeable piece of memory that is currently in use and not a candidate for flushing but can be freed; "free," a free unallocated piece of memory; and "perm," a permanently allocated piece of memory that can't be freed without deallocating the entire heap).

The shared pool architecture is similar to the buffer cache in that there are a fixed number of hash buckets (that grow to the next level as needed) protected by a fixed number of library cache latches (unless changed as noted earlier). The number of buckets and latches is always prime to avoid hashing anomalies. At startup, the database allocates 509 hash buckets and 2*CPU_count library cache latches rounded up to the nearest prime number. As the number of objects in the library cache increases, Oracle increases the number of hash buckets in the following order: 509, 1021, 2039, 4093, 8191, 16381, 32749, 65521, 131071, and 4292967293. You can set the number of hash buckets by setting _KGL_BUCKET_COUNT (the default is 0 to get 509 hash buckets, and the max is 8 to get 131,071). A single hash bucket can contain multiple SQL statements and potentially long hash chains, which explains why you can see long library cache latch hold times even when no space allocation was needed and no search of the LRU list is involved. Also note that a SQL hash value is not the only value used in determining which hash bucket is used; the initial tree starts with object handles, which include name, namespace (CURSOR is the main namespace—others include trigger, cluster), lock owner, lock waiter, pin owner, pin waiter, and other pre-SQL items. The object handle then points to the next level of the tree, the data heap itself (where the statement itself is for a cursor), which includes the type of heap, name (for example SCOTT.EMP), flags (things like wrapped, valid), tables (for example, privilege, dependencies) and data blocks (everything else—the SQL text). This means that we can have hundreds of identical SQL statements all referenced by different users and they will be distributed fairly evenly across the hash buckets with no super-long hash chains full of identical SQL, but we will need a larger shared pool. If the statement is *not* in the library cache, the library load lock latch is used to load it (the library cache latch and shared pool latch are also needed in this process).

If the preceding paragraphs are complex or confusing, just focus on this paragraph. The keys to limiting latch issues on the library cache or shared pool latch are the following: use bind variables, use cursor sharing, parse things once and execute them many times, use session_cached_ cursors to move the cursors from the shared pool to the PGA, and if you are sharing cursors and using bind variables, increase the shared pool (although if you are not sharing statements, reducing it may help).

NOTE
I've seen more 1G+ shared pools in Oracle 10g than ever before.

- **Redo copy** The redo copy latch is used to copy redo records from the PGA into the redo log buffer. The number of "redo copy" latches has a default of 2*CPU_COUNT, but this can be set using the _LOG_SIMULTANEOUS_COPIES initialization parameter. Increasing this parameter may help to reduce contention for the redo copy latch.

- **Redo allocation** The redo allocation latch (allocates the space in the redo log buffer) contention can be reduced by increasing the size of the log buffer (LOG_BUFFER) or by using the NOLOGGING feature, which will reduce the load on the redo log buffer. You should also try to avoid unnecessary commits.

- **Row cache objects** The "row cache objects" latch contention usually means that there is contention in the data dictionary. This may also be a symptom of excessive parsing of SQL statements that depend on public synonyms. Increasing the shared pool usually solves this latch problem. You usually increase the shared pool for a library cache latch problem well before this one is a problem. Also, according to MetaLink Note 166474.1, "Use Locally Managed tablespaces for your application objects, especially indexes. This will decrease Row Cache locks in a surprising fashion and consequently avoid common hanging problems."

■ **Cache buffers chains (CBC)** The "cache buffers chains" (CBC) latch is needed to scan the SGA buffer cache for database cache buffers. In Oracle 10g, the CBC can be shared, eliminating some of the contention. Tuning the code to use less of these is the best solution to eliminating problems with this latch. Also, reducing the popularity of the block will reduce the length of the hash chain (as discussed in the next item).

The CBC latches are used when searching for, adding, or removing a buffer from the buffer cache. Buffer hash table x$bh holds headers (on a hash chain protected by a CBC latch) that point to db_block buffers in memory. Buffers are "hashed to a chain," and the _db_block_hash_buckets define the number of chains (buckets) to which a buffer will hash. The more buckets (chains) that there are, the smaller the "chain" length will be with buffers hashed to the same chain (as long as it's a prime number). The CBC latches are used to protect a buffer list in the buffer cache. If _db_block_hash_buckets is not set to a prime number, you get many buffers hashed to one chain and none hashed to others (causing hot blocks to tie up other blocks on the chain) because of hashing anomalies. Contention on this latch could indicate a "hot block" or bad setting for _db_block_hash_buckets prior to 9i. Prior to version 8i, Oracle made this the prime number higher than db_block_buffers/4 and this worked pretty well, although multiple blocks still got hashed to the same chain. In 8i, Oracle made this db_block_buffers*2, but they forgot to make it prime (which, because it is a hashed value, caused many blocks to be hashed to the same chain); *many* users experienced severe problems with this latch (you can set _db_block_hash_buckets = next prime(db_block_buffers*2) to solve this issue in prior versions). In 9i and 10g, Oracle sets it correctly and there are enough "hash latches," as people often call them. You will access a *lot* of these, since you need one every time you access a block, but you *should not* have a miss ratio of over 1–2 percent on this latch.

■ **For a given block** Only one block is CURRENT and no more than five other CR versions of the block are allowed (as of V9), and all of them are located on the same doubly linked (can move both ways) hash chain. For DML, you need the CURRENT version (of which there is only *one* current version of any given block), and for a read query, you can use the CURRENT version if it is not being used and/or build a CONSISTENT READ (CR) version by applying and UNDO needed to CURRENT version of a changed block after cloning it. This may include reading the ITL, mapping to the UNDO HEADER (but the ITL also maps directly to the UNDO BLOCK), and applying the UNDO to get the correct CR version that you need. When there are multiple versions of a block (one current and a few CR versions) the hash chain gets longer and the CBC latch gets held longer scanning the hash chain. This is why Oracle now limits the number of clones (CR versions) of a block (limits the chain length). Although you can change this by setting _DB_BLOCK_MAX_CR_DBA, which is the maximum allowed number of CR buffers for a given DBA (data block address), it's a setting that performs well out of the box.

■ **Hot blocks** Blocks often accessed in the buffer cache cause "cache buffers chains" latch issues. Hot blocks may also be a symptom of poorly tuned SQL statements. A hot record creates a hot block that can cause issues for other records inside that block as

well as any block "hashed" to the same chain. To find the hot block, query v$latch_
children for the address and join it to v$bh to identify the blocks protected by this latch
(this will show all blocks that are affected by the hot block). You can identify the object
by querying DBA_EXTENTS according to the file# and dbablk found from v$bh. Using a
reverse key index, if the hot block is on an index, will move sequential records to other
blocks so that they are not locked up by the hot block in the chain. If the hot block is the
index root block, a reverse-key index won't help.

■ **Cache buffers LRU chain**   The "cache buffers lru chain" latch is used to scan the LRU
(least recently used) chain containing all of the blocks in the buffer cache. A small buffer
cache, excessive buffer cache throughput, many cache-based sorts, and the DBWR not
keeping up with the workload are all culprits that can cause this issue. Try to fix the
queries that are causing the excessive logical reads and/or use multiple buffer pools.

Some of the most common latch problems and potential solutions are described in the
following table:

Latch Problem	Potential Fix
Library cache	Use bind variables; adjust the shared_pool_size.
Shared pool	Use bind variables; adjust the shared_pool_size.
Redo allocation	Minimize redo generation and avoid unnecessary commits.
Redo copy	Increase the _log_simultaneous_copies.
Row cache objects	Increase the shared pool.
Cache buffers chain	Increase _DB_BLOCK_HASH_BUCKETS or make it prime.
Cache buffers lru chain	Use multiple buffer pools or fix queries causing excessive reads.

You should also configure LRU latches so that each buffer pool has *n*CPUs worth of latches.
For example, if the system has 8 CPUs, they should set

buffer_pool_keep = buffers:*XXXX*, lru latches=8

buffer_pool_recycle = buffers:*YYYY*, lru_latches=8

Here, *XXXX* and *YYYY* are the desired number of buffers in the keep and recycle pools
respectively. There is really no reason to have more LRU latches than the number of processes
that may be concurrently executing.

Some latch problems have often been bug related in the past, so make sure that you check
MetaLink for issues related to latches. Any of the latches that have a hit ratio below 99 percent should
be investigated. Some of the more common latches on the problem list were detailed in this article
and include the cache buffers chains, redo copy, library cache, and the cache buffers lru chain.

TIP
*Latches are like locks on pieces of memory (or memory buffers). If the
latch hit ratio is below 99 percent, there is a serious problem, since
not even the lock to get memory could be gotten.*

Tuning and Viewing at the Block Level (Advanced)

Infrequently, when you have a hot block or some other block-level issue, you may need to find the exact location of the block for a given object and the number of versions (as was discussed in the preceding section). I will briefly discuss some of the details of Oracle at the block level in this section.

CAUTION
This section should not be used by beginners.

An internal table called the buffer hash table (x$bh) holds block headers. There is a hash chain which blocks are linked to that are protected by a CBC latch (cache buffers chains latch). This links to the actual address located in memory (the memory set up with DB_CACHE_SIZE and/or SGA_TARGET, which is the cache used for data). For a given block in Oracle, only one version of a block is CURRENT and there are no more than five other CR versions of the block (as of V9). So there are only six versions of a given block (maximum) in memory at a time. Later in this section, I will tell you how to control this with an undocumented parameter. Oracle recommends that you not use the undocumented parameters unless you are directed by Oracle support or your database may not be supported.

When you perform a DML (Data Manipulation Lock) transaction, which is an INSERT, UPDATE, or DELETE, you always need the CURRENT version of a block. Oracle has something in Oracle 10g called "in-memory undo" (IMU), which can give you some hard-to-understand results when you are viewing information at the block level (whether it's dirty or not). IMU is new in 10g; what it means is that the undo records and redo records for some transactions are stored in memory until the transaction commits. When a CR block is needed, the database first checks to see if the undo records are stored in the memory pool; if so, it applies the undo and redo records from memory instead of retrieving them from the UNDO segments and redo logs/buffers (it's much faster to do this in memory). When you are querying a block for the first time, you always use the CURRENT version of a block. It the block is being used, you will build a CLONE of the block called a CONSISTENT READ (CR) version by applying any undo needed to the CURRENT version of the block to get it to a point in time that makes it useful to you (perhaps you need a version of the block before the DML was performed and not committed by another user). This complex, Oracle-patented process may include reading the ITL (interested transaction list, which is populated when someone does a DML on a block) and mapping the record to the UNDO HEADER, or else mapping it directly to the UNDO BLOCK and then applying the UNDO to get the correct CR version that you need. So, let's take a look at how this happens:

1. User 1 updates a record in block 777 (user 1 has not committed)

2. User 2 queries the same block and sees that the lock byte is set for a row being queried.

3. User 2 goes to the ITL portion of the block and gets the XID (transaction ID).

4. The XID (transaction ID) maps to the UNDO block, which holds the information before the update was done. If using IMU, then a check is done to see if the undo for this transaction is available in memory before going to the UNDO block.

5. A clone of the block is done (call it block 778).

6. The UNDO information is applied to the block, rolling it forward, but to where it used to be.

7. Block 777 is a CURRENT block.

8. Block 778 is a CONSISTENT READ block before the User 1 update occurred.

9. If another user wants to do a query before the commit, that user can also read the CR version.

Note *especially* the fact that the block is not *rolled back* to what it was, but it is *rolled forward* to what it used to be. While the result is the same, how Oracle performs this operation is *critical* to understanding how Oracle works. Oracle books are always moving forward in time (this is why the REDO works—it's always applying things forward sequentially). There are also links to all blocks for the LRU (least recently used) and LRU-W (least recently used—write) chains to help make buffer replacement and writing much faster. This is also maintained in the buffer headers.

Here are some nice (rarely found) queries to get block-level information.

Finding the block number (56650) for a given object (EMP1)

```
select  rowid,empno,
        dbms_rowid.rowid_relative_fno(rowid) fileno,
        dbms_rowid.rowid_block_number(rowid) blockno,
        dbms_rowid.rowid_row_number(rowid)   rowno, rownum,
        rpad(to_char(dbms_rowid.rowid_block_number(rowid), 'FM0xxxxxxx') || '.' ||
        to_char(dbms_rowid.rowid_row_number   (rowid), 'FM0xxx'   ) || '.' ||
        to_char(dbms_rowid.rowid_relative_fno(rowid), 'FM0xxx'   ), 18) myrid
from    emp1;

ROWID                  EMPNO    FILENO    BLOCKNO    ROWNO    ROWNUM              MYRID
------------------     -------  -------   --------   ------   ------   -----------------

AAAM4cAABAAAN1KAAA       7369       1      56650        0          1 0000dd4a.0000.0001
AAAM4cAABAAAN1KAAB       7499       1      56650        1          2 0000dd4a.0001.0001
... (output truncated)
AAAM4cAABAAAN1KAAN       7934       1      56650       13         14 0000dd4a.000d.0001

14 rows selected.
```

Finding the versions (1 Current and 5 CR versions) of a block for a given block number (56650)

```
select lrba_seq, state, dbarfil, dbablk, tch, flag, hscn_bas,cr_scn_bas,
       decode(bitand(flag,1), 0, 'N', 'Y') dirty,    /* Dirty bit */
       decode(bitand(flag,16), 0, 'N', 'Y') temp,    /* temporary bit */
       decode(bitand(flag,1536),0,'N','Y') ping,    /* ping (shared or null) bit */
       decode(bitand(flag,16384), 0, 'N', 'Y') stale, /* stale bit */
       decode(bitand(flag,65536), 0, 'N', 'Y') direct, /* direct access bit */
       decode(bitand(flag,1048576), 0, 'N', 'Y') new/* new bit */
from   x$bh
where  dbablk = 56650
order by dbablk;

LRBA_SEQ       STATE     DBARFIL      DBABLK        TCH       FLAG    HSCN_BAS
----------     --------  --------     --------   --------   --------  --------
CR_SCN_BAS D T P S D N
---------- - - - - - -
        0            3           1      56650          1     524416          0
```

```
4350120  N N N N N N
      0            3        1      56650        1      524416           0
4350105  N N N N N N
    365            1        1      56650        7    33562633     4350121
      0  Y N N N N N
      0            3        1      56650        1      524416           0
4350103  N N N N N N
      0            3        1      56650        1      524416           0
4350089  N N N N N N
      0            3        1      56650        1      524288           0
4350087  N N N N N N
```

NOTE
*In the preceding listing, state=1 is CURRENT and state=3 is CR; only
the CURRENT block is (can be) Dirty.*

Finding the setting for the maximum CR (consistent read) versions of a block

```
select a.ksppinm, b.ksppstvl, b.ksppstdf, a.ksppdesc
from   x$ksppi a, x$ksppcv b
where  a.indx = b.indx
and    substr(ksppinm,1,1) = '_'
and    ksppinm like '%&1%'
order  by ksppinm;

Enter a value for 1: db_block_max_cr_dba

KSPPINM        KSPPSTVL KSPPSTDF KSPPDESC
-----------------  -------- -=------ ----------------------------------------------
_db_block_max_cr_dba    6 TRUE    Maximum Allowed Number of CR buffers per dba
```

To dump what's inside the block for EMP1

```
SQL> select header_file, header_block, blocks from dba_segments
  2  where segment_name = 'EMP'
  3  and owner = 'SCOTT';

HEADER_FILE HEADER_BLOCK     BLOCKS
----------- ------------- ----------
          4            27          8


ALTER SYSTEM DUMP DATAFILE 4 BLOCK 28;
System Altered.
```

CAUTION
*Never go to the block level unless you absolutely have to go there.
The block level is a great place to find hot block and ITL issues, but
it takes a lot of time and energy on the part of an advanced DBA to
pinpoint problems at this level.*

Dictionary and Library Cache Statistics

The next two sections contain the dictionary and library cache information. Listed first is all of the data dictionary information. This data pertains to all of the objects in the database. This information is accessed for every SQL statement that gets parsed and again when the statement is executed. The activity in this area can be very heavy. Maintaining a good hit ratio is very important to prevent recursive calls back to the database to verify privileges. You can also evaluate the efficiency of the dictionary cache by querying the V$ROWCACHE view. The query that follows shows the information that the STATSPACK report lists for this section of the report:

```
Dictionary Cache Stats for DB: ORA10  Instance: ora10  Snaps: 1 -2
->"Pct Misses"  should be very low (< 2% in most cases)
->"Cache Usage" is the number of cache entries being used
->"Pct SGA"     is the ratio of usage to allocated size for that cache
```

Cache	Get Requests	Pct Miss	Scan Reqs	Pct Miss	Mod Reqs	FinalPct UsageSGA	
dc_constraints	0		0		0	0	0
dc_objects	170,317	1.0	0		4	841	77
dc_outlines	0		0		0	0	0
dc_profiles	175	0.0	0		0	1	14
dc_segments	451,486	0.3	0		33	1,525	100
dc_sequences	8,622	1.1	0		8,218	37	93
dc_synonyms	51,702	0.3	0		0	174	98
dc_tablespaces	40,925	0.1	0		0	22	76
dc_used_extents	33	60.6	0		33	7	64
dc_user_grants	18,533	0.0	0		0	25	66
dc_usernames	62,263	0.0	0		0	16	62

The second part of this section of the report deals with the performance of the library cache. These statistics are generated from the V$LIBRARYCACHE view. The library cache contains the Shared SQL and PL/SQL areas. These areas are represented by the BODY, SQL AREA, TABLE/ PROCEDURE, and TRIGGER values (these are values in the NAMESPACE column). They contain all of the SQL and PL/SQL statements that are cached in memory. The other names are areas that Oracle uses. If your "Pct Miss" value is high in this section of the report, you may need to improve cursor sharing in your application or increase the size of the shared pool (as discussed in the "Top Wait Events" section of this chapter). The following listing shows sample data for this section:

```
Library Cache Activity for DB: ORA10  Instance: ora10  Snaps: 1 -2
->"Pct Misses"  should be very low
```

Namespace	Get Requests	Pct Miss	Pin Requests	Pct Miss	Reloads	Invali- dations
BODY	102	2.0	104	4.8	3	0
CLUSTER	108	0.0	167	0.0	0	0
INDEX	3,586	1.9	2,327	3.1	0	0
OBJECT	0		0		0	0
PIPE	0		0		0	0
SQL AREA	924,407	5.4	27,307,859	0.3	3,621	61

TABLE/PROCEDURE	244,185	0.6	1,861,627	0.2	461	0
TRIGGER	173	4.6	173	7.5	5	0

Here is what the columns mean in this part of the report:

Namespace	The name of the library namespace.
Get Requests	The number of times the system requested a handle to an object in this namespace.
Pct Miss *(Get Miss Ratio)*	The number of gethits divided by the number of gets is the get hit ratio. The gethits are the number of times a request was made for an object and the object was already in the cache. The hit ratio should be as close to 0.99 as possible. The pct miss should be less than 1 percent.
Pin Requests	The number of times an item in the cache was executed. A high number is what you are after.
Pct Miss *(Pin Miss Ratio)*	The number of pinhits divided by the number of pins shows the hit ratio. Pinhits are the number of times that objects the system is pinning are already in the cache. This ratio should be as close to 1 as possible. The miss ratio should be less than 1 percent.
Reloads	The number of library cache misses on an execution step. The number of reloads divided by the number of pins should be around 0 percent. If the ratio between this is greater than 1 percent, you should probably increase the size of the shared pool.
Invalidations	The total number of times objects in this namespace were marked invalid because a dependent object was modified.

TIP
If the PINHITRATIO is less than 0.95 when the report is run for an extended period of time, the SHARED_POOL_SIZE is probably too small for your best system performance. If the reloads are greater than 1 percent, this also points to a SHARED_POOL_SIZE that is too small.

SGA Memory Statistics

Following an SGA memory summary (from V$SGA) and a listing of the memory changes during the snapshot interval, the report lists the database initialization parameters in use at the beginning and end of the report.

Taken as a whole, the report generates a significant amount of data, allowing you to develop a profile of the database and its usage. By drawing on the initialization, file I/O, and SGA data, you can develop an understanding of the major components in the database configuration. Here is a sample listing of this section of the report:

```
SGA Memory Summary for DB: ORA10   Instance: ORA10   Snaps: 164 -194
SGA regions                      Size in Bytes
-------------------------------- ----------------
```

```
Database Buffers              1,572,864,000
Fixed Size                          103,396
Redo Buffers                     41,959,424
Variable Size                 3,854,102,528
                              ---------------
sum                           5,469,029,348
        ----------------------------------------------------------------
```

```
SGA breakdown difference for DB: ORA10   Instance: ora10   Snaps: 1 -2
Pool   Name                         Begin value        End value    %Diff
------ ----------------------------  ----------------  ---------------  ------
java   free memory                    27,934,720        27,934,720     .00
java   memory in use                   5,619,712         5,619,712     .00
shared 1M buffer                       1,049,088         1,049,088     .00
shared Checkpoint queue                  141,152           141,152     .00
shared DML lock                          100,408           100,408     .00
shared FileIdentificatonBlock            323,292           323,292     .00
shared FileOpenBlock                     695,504           695,504     .00
shared KGK heap                            3,756             3,756     .00
shared KGLS heap                       1,325,688         1,355,676     .26
shared KSXR pending messages que         226,636           226,636     .00
shared KSXR receive buffers            1,060,000         1,060,000     .00
shared PL/SQL DIANA                    2,882,084         2,882,084     .00
shared PL/SQL MPCODE                     257,108           290,300    2.91
shared PLS non-lib hp                      2,068             2,068    0.00
shared VIRTUAL CIRCUITS                  266,120           266,120    0.00
shared character set object              315,704           315,704    0.00
shared db_handles                         93,000            93,000    0.00
shared dictionary cache                  925,680           938,100    1.34
shared enqueue                           171,860           171,860    0.00
shared errors                             64,344            64,344    0.00
shared event statistics per sess       1,356,600         1,356,600    0.00
shared fixed allocation callback              60                60    0.00
shared free memory                    23,924,812        21,787,064   -8.94
shared joxlod: in ehe                    317,060           317,060    0.00
shared joxlod: in phe                    114,024           114,024    0.00
shared joxs heap init                      4,220             4,220    0.00
shared ksm_file2sga region               148,652           148,652    0.00
shared library cache                   3,832,604         4,238,528    0.59
shared message pool freequeue            772,672           772,672    0.00
shared miscellaneous                   2,318,632         2,324,904    0.27
shared parameters                          8,228            13,904    8.98
shared processes                         127,800           127,800    0.00
shared sessions                          395,760           395,760    0.00
shared simulator trace entries            98,304            98,304    0.00
shared sql area                        2,626,452         4,269,888    2.57
shared table definiti                        952             1,792   88.24
shared transaction                       182,376           182,376    0.00
shared trigger defini                      2,324             2,324    0.00
shared trigger inform                      1,108             1,108    0.00
shared trigger source                      1,212             1,212    0.00
       db_block_buffers               25,165,824        25,165,824    0.00
       fixed_sga                         282,536           282,536    0.00
       log_buffer                        524,288           524,288    0.00
        ----------------------------------------------------------------
```

SGA Memory Statistics

Non-Default Initialization Parameters

This last section shows the parameters in the initialization file that are set to a value other than the default (see Figure 14-19). The list is generated by querying the V$PARAMETER view where the default column is equal to FALSE. This list can be used as a reference. While you are tuning the

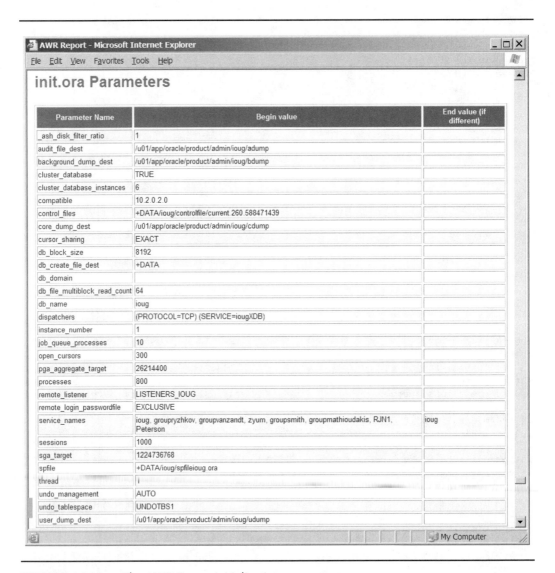

FIGURE 14-19. *The AWR Report initialization parameters*

database, these parameters can provide a record of how the database performed with certain values. The output that follows shows this section of the report:

```
init.ora Parameters for DB: ORA10  Instance: ora10  Snaps: 1 -2

                                                             End value
Parameter Name                  Begin value                  (if different)
-----------------------------   ------------------------------ --------------
background_dump_dest            f:\ora10\admin\ora10\bdump
compatible                      10.2.0.2
control_files                   f:\ora10\oradata\ora10\CONTROL01.
core_dump_dest                  f:\ora10\admin\ora10\cdump
db_block_size                   4096
db_cache_size                   25165824
db_create_file_dest            F:\ORA10\ORADATA\ORA10
db_domain                       world
db_name                         ora10
fast_start_mttr_target          300
instance_name                   ora10=
java_pool_size                  33554432
large_pool_size                 1048576
open_cursors                    300
processes                       150
remote_login_passwordfile       EXCLUSIVE
shared_pool_size                46137344
sort_area_size                  524288
timed_statistics                TRUE
undo_management                 AUTO
undo_tablespace                 UNDOTBS
user_dump_dest                  f:\ora10\admin\ora10\udump
-------------------------------------------------------------------
End of Report
```

Top 10 Things to Look for in AWR Report and STATSPACK Output

Many DBAs already know how to use STATSPACK but are not always sure what to check regularly. Remember to separate OLTP and Batch activity when you run STATSPACK, since they usually generate different types of waits. The SQL script "spauto.sql" can be used to run STATSPACK every hour on the hour. See the script in $ORACLE_HOME/rdbms/admin/spauto.sql for more information (note that JOB_QUEUE_PROCESSES must be set > 0). Since every system is different, this is only a general list of things you should *regularly* check in your STATSPACK output:

- Top 5 wait events (timed events)
- Load profile
- Instance efficiency hit ratios
- Wait events

- Latch waits

- Top SQL

- Instance activity

- File I/O and segment statistics

- Memory allocation

- Buffer waits

Managing the STATSPACK Data

You should manage the data generated by STATSPACK to guarantee that the space usage and performance of the STATSPACK application meets your requirements as the application data grows. Managing STATSPACK data includes the following steps:

1. Regularly analyze the STATSPACK data. At a minimum, you should analyze the STATSPACK schema prior to running the spreport.sql report:

   ```
   execute DBMS_UTILITY.ANALYZE_SCHEMA('PERFSTAT','COMPUTE');
   ```

2. Purge old data. Since you cannot generate valid interval reports across database shutdown/startup actions, data prior to the last database startup may not be as useful as the most current data. When the data is no longer needed, purge it from the tables. Oracle provides a script, sppurge.sql, to facilitate purges. The sppurge.sql script, located in the /rdbms/admin directory under the Oracle software home directory, lists the currently stored snapshots and prompts you for two input parameters: the beginning and ending snapshot numbers for the purge. The related records in the STATS$ tables will then be deleted. Due to the size of the transactions involved, databases using rollback segments should force the session to use a large rollback segment during the deletes:

   ```
   SQL> commit;
   SQL> set transaction use rollback segment roll_large;
   SQL> @sppurge
   ```

   The sppurge script prompts you to back up your old statistics before purging them. You can back up the data by exporting the PERFSTAT schema.

3. Truncate the STATSPACK tables when the data is not needed. Old statistical data may no longer be relevant, or you may have imported the old statistics during database migrations or creations. To truncate the old tables, execute the sptrunc.sql SQL*Plus script from within the PERFSTAT account. The script is located in the /rdbms/admin directory under the Oracle software home directory.

4. Include the STATSPACK tables in your backup scheme. If you are using Export, Oracle provides a parameter file named spuexp.par to assist you.

5. Include the STATSPACK tables in your space monitoring procedures.

Upgrading STATSPACK

To upgrade old STATSPACK data to a new version of the database, execute the scripts provided by Oracle. Oracle does not support upgrading STATSPACK directly from 8.1.6 to 9.0.1 or 9.2 to 10.2; you must go through multiple steps:

1. Upgrade from the 8.1.6 STATSPACK objects to 8.1.7 by executing the spup816.sql script.

2. Upgrade from the 8.1.7 STATSPACK objects to 9.0 by executing the spup817.sql script.

3. Upgrade from the 9.0 STATSPACK objects to 9.2 by executing the spup90.sql script.

4. Upgrade from the 9.2 STATSPACK objects to 10.1 by executing the spup92.sql script.

5. Upgrade from the 10.1 STATSPACK objects to 10.2 by executing the spup101.sql script.

Deinstalling STATSPACK

Since STATSPACK includes public synonyms as well as private objects, you should remove the application via a SYSDBA privileged account. Oracle provides a script, spdrop.sql, to automate the deinstallation process. From within the /rdbms/admin directory under the Oracle software home directory, log in to SQL*Plus and execute the script as shown in the following listing:

```
SQL> connect system/manager as SYSDBA
SQL> @spdrop
```

The spdrop.sql script calls scripts (spdtab.sql, spdusr.sql) that will drop the tables, the package, the public synonyms, and the PERFSTAT user. To reinstall STATSPACK, execute the spcreate.sql script as shown earlier in this chapter.

Quick Notes on the New ADDM Report

You can also use ADDM (Automatic Database Diagnostics Monitor) Report called addmrpt.sql to analyze a snapshot range. You run the addmrpt.sql script from SQL plus (the script is located in the $ORACLE_HOME/rdbms/admin directory). The script provides you with a list of snapshots from which you can generate the report (like STATSPACK or the AWR Report from SQL*Plus). You select a begin snapshot and an end snapshot, and finally, you define the name of the report that you want addmrpt.sql to create. Addmrpt.sql will then run the ADDM analysis on the snapshot pair you entered, and provide the output analysis report. Using ADDM through Enterprise Manager Grid Control (covered in Chapter 5) is much more detailed and is recommended. The resulting report contains a header and then detailed finding information. The header will look much like this example:

```
Specify the Report Name
~~~~~~~~~~~~~~~~~~~~~~~~~
The default report file name is addmrpt_1_3902_3903.txt. To use this name,
press <return> to continue, otherwise enter an alternative.
Enter value for report_name:
```

The New ADDM Report

```
Using the report name addmrpt_1_3902_3903.txt
Running the ADDM analysis on the specified pair of snapshots ...
Generating the ADDM report for this analysis ...

        DETAILED ADDM REPORT FOR TASK 'TASK_4152' WITH ID 4152
        ----------------------------------------------------------
              Analysis Period: 02-OCT-2006 from 09:33:40 to 11:00:51
         Database ID/Instance: 1071709215/1
       Database/Instance Names: ORCL/orcl
                    Host Name: RJNMOBILE2
             Database Version: 10.1.0.2.0
               Snapshot Range: from 3902 to 3903
                Database Time: 34 seconds
        Average Database Load: 0 active sessions
```

There is also a summary information section related to the ADDM analysis. Following the header and individual findings, the summary will be listed. An example of such a finding is seen here:

```
FINDING 1: 51% impact (309 seconds)
-----------------------------------
SQL statements consuming significant database time were found.
      ACTION: Run SQL Tuning Advisor on the SQL statement with SQL_ID
          "db78fxqxwxt7r".
          RELEVANT OBJECT: SQL statement with SQL_ID db78fxqxwxt7r and
          PLAN_HASH 3879501264
          SELECT a.emp, b.dname
          FROM EMP a, DEPT b
          WHERE a.deptno=b.deptno;
```

There are a few interesting things in this report. First of all, our first finding indicates that the problem identified had a 51 percent overall impact in the DB time. In other words, the ADDM report is sorting its findings according to those processes that are consuming the most database time. We see, looking at this finding further, that it is a SQL statement that is causing problems (usually the source of most issues), and ADDM suggests that we tune the statement. Oracle gives us the SQL address and hash value so that we can find the SQL statement in the SQL area. Note that the ACTION suggests that we run the SQL Tuning Advisor to generate some suggested tuning actions on the SQL statement in question. In Chapter 5, we look at the SQL Tuning Advisor and see just how it can help us to tune SQL statements in Oracle Database 10g.

If not enough work has been done on the instance or if not enough work is being done currently, instead of giving you suggestions, it will display the following:

```
~~~~~~~~~~~~~~~~~~~~~~~~~~~~~~~~~~~~~~~~~~~~~~~~~~~~~~~~~~~~~~~~~~~~~~~~~~~~~~~~
THERE WAS NOT ENOUGH INSTANCE SERVICE TIME FOR ADDM ANALYSIS.
~~~~~~~~~~~~~~~~~~~~~~~~~~~~~~~~~~~~~~~~~~~~~~~~~~~~~~~~~~~~~~~~~~~~~~~~~~~~~~~~
```

The ADDM report is a good start for getting tips for tuning. As with any new utility, it has room for improvement and growth in future releases of Oracle, and it is best used from the Enterprise Manager interface if possible. There are other aspects related to ADDM that we have not been able to address in this section, such as user-defined alerts and the SQL Tuning Advisor, which we looked at in Chapter 5.

TIP
*The ADDM Report can be a helpful Tuning Utility, but ADDM is
better used through Oracle's Grid Control for maximum benefits.*

Scripts 10gR2

Here is a list of scripts that you will find in 10gR2. Please refer to the documentation for a
complete description of each of these.

- **spcreate.sql**   Creates the STATSPACK environment by calling spcusr.sql, spctab.sql,
  and spcpkg.sql. This is run as with SYSDBA privileges.

- **spdrop.sql**   Drops the entire STATSPACK environment by calling spdtab.sql and
  spdusr.sql. This is run with SYSDBA. privileges.

- **spreport.sql**   This is the main script to generate the STATSPACK report. It is run by the
  PERFSTAT user.

- **sprepins.sql**   Generates a STATSPACK instance report for a database and instance
  specified.

- **sprepsql.sql**   Generates a STATSPACK SQL Report for the SQL hash value specified.

- **sprsqins.sql**   Generates a STATSPACK SQL Report for the SQL hash value specified for
  the database and instance specified.

- **spauto**   Automates STATSPACK statistics collection (snap) using DBMS_JOB.

- **sprepcon.sql**   Configuration file that configures SQL*Plus variable to set things like
  thresholds. This is called automatically as part of the STATSPACK instance report.

- **spurge.sql**   Purges a range of snapshot IDs for a given database instance (does not
  purge baseline snapshots).

- **sptrunc.sql**   Truncates all performance data in STATSPACK tables (CAREFUL!).

- **spuexp.par**   Exports parameter file for exporting the entire PERFSTAT user.

- **spup101.sql**   To upgrade to 10.2 from 10.1 (back up schema before upgrading).

- **spup92.sql**   To upgrade to 10.1 from 9.2 (back up schema before upgrading).

- **spup90.sql**   To upgrade from 9.0 to 9.2. (back up schema before upgrading).

- **spup817.sql**   To upgrade from 8.1.7 to 9.0 (back up schema before upgrading).

- **spup816.sql**   To upgrade from 8.1.6 to 8.1.7 (back up schema before upgrading).

NOTE
*You must use the specific version of STATSPACK with that version of
the database (for instance, you must use 10.2 schema of STATSPACK
with 10.2 of the database). Also note that spdoc.txt is the complete
instruction and documentation file for STATSPACK.*

Scripts 10gR2

Tips Review

- The files needed to create, manage, and drop the STATSPACK objects are all in the /rdbms/admin subdirectory under the Oracle software home directory, and all start with the letters 'sp'.

- Create a tablespace to hold the STATSPACK data apart from your application and SYSTEM objects.

- Change the PERFSTAT account's password and consider locking the account when it is no longer in use.

- Select the proper level for your reporting. In general, start with level 5 and use a higher level for further investigation.

- Avoid running STATSPACK reports for intervals that include database shutdowns.

- Actively manage the STATSPACK data, analyzing and purging it as needed. Monitor its space usage and include it in your backup and upgrade plans.

- If you choose to run *both*, ensure that you stagger the data collection of AWR from the collection for STATSPACK (by at least 30 minutes) to avoid a performance hit as well as conflicts.

- If you use Grid Control, you can run the AWR Report directly from Grid Control.

- Get to know your system by reviewing and knowing the regular Load Profile of your system. Significant changes to the Load Profile during what should be similar workloads or common times during the day may warrant further investigation.

- Hit ratios are a great barometer of the health of your system. A large increase or drop from day to day is an indicator of a major change that needs to be investigated.

- Generally, buffer and library cache hit ratios should be greater than 95 percent for OLTP, but they could be lower for a data warehouse that may do many full table scans.

- Tuning by wait events is one of the best possible reactive tuning methods.

- The top 5 wait events reveal to you the largest issues on your system at the macro level. Rarely do they point you to a specific problem. Other parts of STATSPACK will tell you why you are receiving the top 5 waits.

- Tuning the top 25 buffer get and top 25 physical get queries has yielded system performance gains of anywhere from 5 to 5000 percent. The SQL section of the STATSPACK report tells you which queries to potentially tune first.

- The top 10 percent of your SQL statements should not be more than 10 percent of your buffer gets or disk reads.

- If the free buffers inspected divided by the free buffer scans equals less than 1, the DB_CACHE_SIZE parameter may need to be increased.

- The "sorts (disk)" statistic divided by the "sorts (memory)" should not be above 1–5 percent. If it is, you should increase the PGA_AGGREGATE_TARGET (or SORT_

AREA_SIZE) parameter in the initialization file (given that physical memory is available to do this). Remember that the memory allocated for Sort_Area_Size is a per-user value and PGA_AGGREGATE_TARGET is across all sessions.

- Latches are like locks on pieces of memory (or memory buffers). If the latch hit ratio is below 99 percent, there is a serious problem, since not even the lock to get memory could be gotten.

- Segment statistics are a great way to pinpoint performance problem to a given table, index, or partition. Oracle 10gR2 contains many segment-level statistics in both the AWR Report and STATSPACK.

- If the PINHITRATIO is less than 95 percent when the report is run for an extended period of time, the SHARED_POOL_SIZE is probably too small for your best system performance. If the reloads are greater than 1 percent, this also points to a SHARED_POOL_SIZE that is too small.

- You do not set maxtrans in 10g (it defaults to 255).

- Never go to the block level unless you absolutely have to go there. The block level is a great place to find hot block and ITL issues, but it takes a lot of time and energy on the part of an advanced DBA to pinpoint problems at this level.

- The ADDM Report can be a helpful tuning utility, but ADDM is better used through Oracle's Grid Control for maximum benefits.

References

Connie Dialeris Green, Cecilia Gervasio, Graham Wood (guru), Russell Green, Patrick Tearle, Harald Eri, Stefan Pommerenk, and Vladimir Barriere, *Oracle 10g Server, Release 10.2,* (Production, Oracle Corporation)
Rich Niemiec, *Tuning Oracle9i & 10g using STATSPACK and AWR Report*
Robert Freeman, *Oracle 10g New Features* (Oracle Press)
Steve Adams, *Oracle8i Internal Services for Waits, Latches, Locks, and Memory* (excellent)
Connie Dialeris and Graham Wood, "Performance Tuning with STATSPACK" (White Paper, 2000)
Notes from Richard Powell, Cecilia Gervasio, Russell Green, and Patrick Tearle
Randy Swanson and Bob Yingst, "STATSPACK Checklist" (2002)
Rich Niemiec, "IOUG Masters Tuning Class" (2002)
Metalink Notes: 104937.1, 135223.1, 135223.1, 148511.1, 148511.1, 155971.1, 181306.1, 22908.1, 29787.1, 33567.1, 39017.1, 61998.1, 62172.1, 62160.1, and 62354.1

Special thanks to Robert Freeman, who contributed much of the AWR information. Thanks to Kevin Loney for the entire installation portion of this chapter written for the last version and some added notes. Thanks to Greg Pucka for the original chapter on estat/bstat. Rich Niemiec upgraded this chapter from 9i to 10g (painful!).

CHAPTER
15

Performing a Quick
System Review (DBA)

O racle 10g introduced many new features that can be leveraged for tuning. While some DBAs are great at planning and implementing a new version, few are good at evaluating and implementing the new features that will help their system. With the introduction of the Automatic Workload Repository (AWR) and the AWR Report (see Chapter 14 for differences with STATSPACK), you can monitor your system in different ways. And with the advent of the Tuning Advisor, comes different ways to fix your system. One of the keys to a good system review is checking to see if you've implemented the features that fit your needs and have a good return on the cost of the feature as well as the time it takes to implement it. While nobody seems to like tests or evaluations, simple evaluations can help to point out future performance problems and/or current issues.

One of the key approaches to achieving a focus on improving and maintaining excellent system performance requires a system review on at least an annual basis. This could be an internal or external review of your system performance. Many companies have come up with methods of measuring system performance and overall system speed that are tailored directly to their system. This chapter will not describe the six-month process that many of the more detailed evaluations propose, but it will serve as a very simple barometer of how your system rates compared to others in the industry. Variations in your business processes may cause your score to be higher or lower using this simple review. You will need to adjust these scales for your unique system. Tips covered in this chapter include the following:

- The Total Performance Index (TPI) and reasons you might want to use it
- How to get your Education Performance Index (EPI)
- How to get your System Performance Index (SPI)
- How to get your Memory Performance Index (MPI)
- How to get your Disk Performance Index (DPI)
- How to get your Total Performance Index (TPI)
- An overall system review example
- The Immediate Action Items list
- Gathering the System Information list
- Rating the DBA by a impartial expert

Total Performance Index (TPI)

I created the Total Performance Index (TPI) as a most basic tool for Oracle DBAs to measure their system and compare it to other systems, using a quick and simple scoring method as shown in the following table. This is only meant to be a barometer to see if improvements might be beneficial. Many systems differ in categories based on their business case and system use, but this system tells you how close or far your system is to or from others in the industry. There are four categories: Education, System, Memory, and Disk. This chapter will show how you can measure your TPI using several simple queries. For detailed information on a particular category, please refer to the chapter in this book related to that issue. To help identify how your system is progressing, use your TPI to compare future growth in the number of users or changes in hardware and software. You can also customize the index to conform to tools you use most often, such as Oracle Enterprise Manager (EM) or Automatic Database Diagnostics Monitor (ADDM).

Category Index	Maximum Score
Education Performance Index (EPI)	250
System Performance Index (SPI)	250
Memory Performance Index (MPI)	250
Disk Performance Index (DPI)	250
Total Performance Index (TPI)	**1000**

Education Performance Index (EPI)

This section measures the knowledge and education of your technical staff members. The following table illustrates how to receive a perfect EPI score. This rating system is not meant to be an all-encompassing benchmark of knowledge and education, but rather a barometer to see if educational improvements could be beneficial.

Category	Level Required	Maximum Score
DBAs required to tune database	Yes	30
Developers required to tune code written	Yes	30
DBAs last trained in tuning	Less than 1 year	30
Developers last trained in tuning	Less than 1 year	30
DBAs proficient in V$ views	Yes	30
DBAs proficient in ADDM or EM if used	Yes	20
DBAs trained in EXECUTION PLAN	Yes	20
Developers trained in EXECUTION PLAN	Yes	20
DBAs trained if using SQL Tuning Advisor	Yes	20
Developers trained if using SQL Tuning Advisor	Yes	20
Education Performance Index (EPI)	**Section Total**	**250**

Rate Your System

Are DBAs *required* to tune the database?	Yes	30 points
	No	0 points
	Score	30

Are developers *required* to tune the code that they write?	Yes No Score	30 points 0 points 0
When is the last time that your DBAs attended a training course that included tuning?	< 1 year 1–2 years > 2 years Score	30 points 20 points 0 points 20
When is the last time that your developers attended a training course that included tuning?	< 1 year 1–2 years > 2 years Score	30 points 20 points 0 points 20
Are DBAs proficient in using the V$ views?	Yes No Score	30 points 0 points 30
Are DBAs proficient in using ADDM, EM or an equivalent performance tool?	Yes No Score	20 points 0 points 20
Have DBAs been trained on use of EXECUTION PLAN? (See Chapter 6 on EXECUTION PLAN)	Yes No Score	20 points 0 points 20
Have developers been trained on use of EXECUTION PLAN?	Yes No Score	20 points 0 points 0
Have DBAs been trained on use of SQL Tuning Advisor?	Yes No Score	20 points 0 points 20
Have developers been trained on use of SQL Tuning Advisor?	Yes No Score	20 points 0 points 0
Example Education Performance Index (EPI)	**Total Score**	160 (Grade: B)

Grade Your System

EPI Grade	Comments	Score
A+	Top 10 percent of most systems	250
A	Top 20 percent of most systems	210–249
B	Top 40 percent of most systems	150–209
C	Top 70 percent of most systems	90–149
Needs help now	Bottom 30 percent of most systems	< 90

TIP
Measuring your EPI (Education Performance Index) can be helpful in identifying educational improvements that could be beneficial.

System Performance Index (SPI)

This section measures overall system issues. The following table illustrates how to receive a perfect SPI score. This rating system is not meant to be an all-encompassing benchmark of overall system issues; rather, it is a barometer to see if improvements could be beneficial.

Category	Level Required	Maximum Score
Inside party database review	< 1 year	50
Ran AWR or STATSPACK last	< 1 month	30
Users asked about performance issues	< 2 months	30
Backup tested for recovery speed	Yes	30
Outside party database review	< 1 year	30
Outside party operating system review	< 1 year	30
Statistics/AWR Frequency	AUTO	20
Design is strictly or partially denormalized	Partially Denormalized	20
Parallel query used or tested for gains	Yes	10
System Performance Index (SPI)	**Section Total**	**250**

Rate Your System

When is the last time that your database was reviewed by a business user?		
	< 1 year	50 points
	1–2 years	30 points
	> 2 years	0 points
	Score	50

System Performance Index

When is the last time that you ran *and* reviewed the results of AWR Report or STATSPACK? (See Chapter 14)	< 1 month 1–3 months 4–6 months > 6 months Score	30 points 20 points 10 points 0 points 20
When is the last time that users of your system were asked about system performance or where things could be improved?	< 2 months 3–6 months 7–12 months > 1 year Score	30 points 20 points 10 points 0 points 20
Has your backup plan been tested to determine the time that it will take to recover?	Yes No Score	30 points 0 points 30
When is the last time that your database was reviewed by an outside party?	< 1 year 1–2 years > 2 years Score	30 points 20 points 0 points 20
When is the last time that your operating system was reviewed by an outside party?	< 1 year 1–2 years > 2 years Score	30 points 20 points 0 points 30
Frequency of statistics collection?	AUTO Monthly Unsure Score	20 points 10 points 0 points 20
Do designers adhere *strictly* to 3rd normal form or higher in their design of the database?*	Yes Denormalize* No designer Score	10 points 20 points 0 points 20
Has parallel query been evaluated, and is it in use where advantageous?	Yes Not needed Not tested Score	10 points 10 points 0 points 10
Example System Performance Index (SPI)	**Total Score**	220 (A+)

*Denormalized only where needed.

Grade Your System

SPI Grade	Comments	Score
A+	Top 10 percent of most systems	> 210
A	Top 20 percent of most systems	180–210
B	Top 40 percent of most systems	140–179
C	Top 70 percent of most systems	80–139
Needs help now	Bottom 30 percent of most systems	< 80

TIP
Measuring your SPI (System Performance Index) can be helpful in identifying overall system improvements that could be beneficial.

Memory Performance Index (MPI)

This section measures memory use and allocation. The following table illustrates how to receive a perfect MPI score. This rating system is not meant to be an all-encompassing benchmark of memory use and allocation; rather, it is a barometer to see if memory use and allocation improvements could be beneficial.

Category	Level Required	Maximum Score
Buffer hit ratio	> 98 percent	30
Dictionary hit ratio	> 98 percent	30
Library hit ratio	> 98 percent	30
PGA sorts in memory	> 98 percent	30
Buffers in x$bh at state=0	10–25 percent	30
Top 10 statements memory use	< 5 percent	60
Top 25 (worst memory) statements tuned	Yes	30
Pin/cache frequently used objects	Yes	10
Memory Performance Index (MPI)	**Section Total**	**250**

Buffer Hit Ratio

The buffer cache hit ratio represents how often frequently requested blocks of data have been found in the memory structure without requiring disk access. Hit ratios are used more in third-party tuning products than ever before, and they are also being used more by Oracle than ever before, primarily because they are a great barometer. But, hit ratios can be misleading and should always be used as a barometer and indicator that you may want to look deeper. Nobody ever uses hit ratios as the sole way to tune a system as some people claim (I've asked this in very large sessions and nobody ever does). People that say that you shouldn't use them at all don't usually understand their value or how to use them. The DBAs who don't look at them can miss a *major* issue that could have been potentially fixed at a very low cost. Hit ratios are very rarely the indicator of good performance but often can be an indicator of bad performance. Their best use is as a barometer or an indicator of changing performance. This statistic is calculated by using the dynamic performance view V$SYSSTAT.

Query for buffer cache hit ratio

```
select    (1 - (sum(decode(name, 'physical reads',value,0)) /
          (sum(decode(name, 'db block gets',value,0)) +
          sum(decode(name, 'consistent gets',value,0)))))) * 100 "Hit Ratio"
from      v$sysstat;
```

Sample output

```
 Hit Ratio
----------
98.8249067
```

Rate Your OLTP System

What is your buffer hit ratio?		
	< 90%	0 points
	90–94%	10 points
	95–98%	20 points
	> 98%	30 points
	Score	30

You can also expand the preceding query to include the actual ratings in your result. The query that follows shows how this is accomplished using the DECODE function. You can also apply this to the remainder of the queries in this chapter if you would like the score in your results. At TUSC, we use a PL/SQL procedure to accomplish the results (we also display them graphically).

Query for hit ratio with rating

```
select (1 - (sum(decode(name, 'physical reads',value,0)) /
(sum(decode(name, 'db block gets',value,0)) +
sum(decode(name, 'consistent gets',value,0)))))) * 100 "Hit Ratio",
decode(sign((1-(sum(decode(name, 'physical reads',value,0)) /
(sum(decode(name, 'db block gets',value,0)) +
sum(decode(name, 'consistent gets',value,0)))))) * 100 - 98),1,30,
decode(sign((1-(sum(decode(name, 'physical reads',value,0)) /
(sum(decode(name, 'db block gets',value,0)) +
sum(decode(name, 'consistent gets',value,0)))))) * 100 - 95),1,20,
decode(sign((1-(sum(decode(name, 'physical reads',value,0)) /
(sum(decode(name, 'db block gets',value,0)) +
```

```
sum(decode(name, 'consistent gets',value,0))))) * 100 - 90),1,10,0)))
"Score"
from v$sysstat
/
```

Sample output

```
 Hit Ratio       Score
---------- ----------
99.8805856         30
```

The data in V$SYSSTAT reflects the statistics for logical and physical reads for all buffer pools. To derive the hit ratio for the buffer pools individually, query the V$BUFFER_POOL_STATISTICS dynamic performance view.

The buffer cache hit ratio can be used to validate physical I/O simulated in the dynamic performance view V$DB_CACHE_ADVICE. This dynamic performance view provides information that assists in sizing the cache by providing information that predicts the number of physical reads for each possible cache size. Included in the data is a physical read factor, which predicts the number of physical reads that are estimated to change if the buffer cache is resized to a given value. To use V$DB_CACHE_ADVICE, the parameter DB_CACHE_ADVICE should be set to ON, and a representative workload allowed to stabilize prior to querying the view. Query to validate physical I/O simulated by the buffer cache advisory:

Query to validate physical I/O

```
COLUMN size_for_estimate FORMAT 999,999,999,999 heading 'Cache Size in MB'
COLUMN buffers_for_estimate      FORMAT 999,999,999 heading 'Buffers'
COLUMN estd_physical_read_factor FORMAT 999.99 heading 'Estd Phys Read Fctr'
COLUMN estd_physical_reads       FORMAT 999,999,999 heading 'Estd Phys Reads'
SELECT size_for_estimate,
       buffers_for_estimate,
       estd_physical_read_factor,
       estd_physical_reads
FROM V$DB_CACHE_ADVICE
WHERE name = 'DEFAULT'
  AND block_size = (SELECT value FROM V$PARAMETER
                    WHERE  name = 'db_block_size')
  AND advice_status = 'ON'
/
```

Sample output

Cache Size in MB	Buffers	Estd Phys Read Fctr	Estd Phys Reads
4	501	1.36	11,130
8	1,002	1.27	10,427
12	1,503	1.19	9,743
16	2,004	1.00	8,205
20	2,505	.96	7,901
24	3,006	.84	6,856

Buffer Hit Ratio

```
        28          3,507                    .81              6,629
        32          4,008                    .76              6,249
(...Simplistic Listing Displayed)
```

Dictionary Cache Hit Ratio

The dictionary hit ratio displays the percentage of memory reads for the data dictionary and other objects.

Query for dictionary hit ratio

```
select    (1-(sum(getmisses)/sum(gets))) * 100 "Hit Ratio"
from      v$rowcache;
```

Sample output

```
Hit Ratio
95.4630137
```

Rate Your System

What is your dictionary cache hit ratio?	< 85%	0 points
	86–92%	10 points
	92–98%	20 points
	> 98%	30 points
	Score	20

Library Cache Hit Ratio

The library cache hit ratio reveals the percentage of memory reads for actual statements and PL/SQL objects. Note that a high hit ratio is not *always* good; see Chapter 4 for a detailed explanation.

Query for library hit ratio

```
select    Sum(Pins) / (Sum(Pins) + Sum(Reloads)) * 100   "Hit Ratio"
from      V$LibraryCache;
```

Sample output

```
 Hit Ratio
----------
99.9670304
```

The hit percentage is 99.97 percent, which means that only 0.03 percent of executions resulted in reparsing.

Rate Your System

What is your library cache hit ratio?	< 90%	0 points
	90–95%	10 points
	95–98%	20 points
	> 98%	30 points
	Score	<u> 30 </u>

PGA Memory Sort Ratio

Automatic PGA memory management simplifies the way PGA memory is allocated. By default, PGA memory management is enabled. When running in this mode, Oracle adjusts, dynamically, the size of the portion of the PGA memory dedicated to work areas, which is based on 20 percent of the SGA memory size. When running in automatic PGA memory management mode, sizing of work areas for all sessions is automatic. The total amount of PGA memory available to active work areas in the instance is automatically derived from the SORT_AREA_SIZE or the PGA_AGGREGATE_TARGET (preferred) initialization parameter. The objective is to have sort operations in the PGA performed in memory versus using the I/O subsystem (on disk) when possible. Statistics related to PGA memory sorts can be derived by the following query or from an AWR report, which reflects overall values for sorts in memory and disk, as well as the percentage of those in memory. The values reflect activity since the start of the instance. Values for a PGA Memory Sort Ratio greater than 98 percent are desired. Depending on the value of the initialization parameter PGA_AGGREGATE_TARGET (or SORT_AREA_SIZE for backward compatibility), user sorts may fit into memory or be performed on disk in a specified temporary tablespace if this initialization parameter is not high enough to hold the sort.

Query for PGA Memory Sort Ratio

You can receive specific sorting statistics (memory, disk, and rows) by running the following queries, or go to the AWR Report or STATSPACK output file (report.txt) to receive these statistics (see Chapter 14 for more information on STATSPACK and AWR Report).

Query to get PGA memory sort ratio

```
select    a.value "Disk Sorts", b.value "Memory Sorts",
          round((100*b.value)/decode((a.value+b.value),0,1,(a.value+b.value)),2)
          "Pct Memory Sorts"
from      v$sysstat a, v$sysstat b
where     a.name = 'sorts (disk)'
and       b.name = 'sorts (memory)';
```

Sample output

```
Disk Sorts    Memory Sorts  Pct Memory Sorts
        16           66977             99.98
```

Rate Your System

What percent of sorts are performed in memory?	< 90%	0 points
	90–94%	10 points
	95–98%	20 points
	> 98%	30 points
	Score	_____30_____

Percent of Data Buffers Still Free

When you start the Oracle database, users start using memory for their queries. Although this memory is reusable when the user's query is complete, when the following query runs on a system after two hours of processing, it is a good indication of how quickly the buffers are being used up (high-volume systems may need to vary the time frame to be much shorter). The number of free buffers divided by the total number of records in x$bh (which is the total data block buffers allocated) is the percentage. Also note that you have to run this query as SYS. Remember that having a lot of free buffers is not necessarily the best situation. See chapter 13 on queries to this table for more information.

Query for free data buffers

```
select    decode(state,0, 'FREE',
          1,decode(lrba_seq,0,'AVAILABLE','BEING USED'),
          3, 'BEING USED', state) "BLOCK STATUS",
          count(*)
from      x$bh
group by decode(state,0,'FREE',1,decode(lrba_seq,0,'AVAILABLE',
          'BEING USED'),3, 'BEING USED', state);
```

Sample output

BLOCK STATUS	COUNT(*)
AVAILABLE	7790
BEING USED	1540
FREE	1670

Rate Your System

What percent of buffers in x$bh are at a state=0 (free) after two hours of running in production?	< 5%	0 points
	5–10%	30 points
	10–25%	20 points
	> 25%	0 points
	Score	_____30_____

Note that the reason that you get 0 points for greater than 25 percent free is because the data buffers are probably oversized and potentially wasting memory. The scoring should be tailored to your individual system use. Remember that this is only a general guideline and one that definitely needs to be tailored to your system.

Top 10 "Memory Abusers" as a Percent of All Statements

I have found that the top 10 statements accessed on most systems when left untuned can make up over 50 percent of all memory reads of the entire system. This section measures how severe the most harmful memory using statements are, as a percentage of the entire system.

Script to retrieve this percentage

```
set serverout on
DECLARE
  CURSOR c1 is
   select    buffer_gets
   from      v$sqlarea
   order by buffer_gets DESC;
  CURSOR c2 is
   select    sum(buffer_gets)
   from      v$sqlarea;
  sumof10 NUMBER:=0;
  mybg NUMBER;
  mytotbg NUMBER;
BEGIN
  dbms_output.put_line('Percent');
  dbms_output.put_line('-------');
  OPEN c1;
  FOR i IN 1..10 LOOP
   FETCH c1 INTO mybg;
   sumof10 := sumof10 + mybg;
  END
LOOP;
  CLOSE c1;
  OPEN c2;
  FETCH c2 INTO mytotbg;
  CLOSE c2;
  dbms_output.put_line(sumof10/mytotbg*100);
END;
/
```

Sample output

```
Percent
-------
44.0708709707597476170181803062274565242

PL/SQL procedure successfully completed.
```

Top 10 "Memory Abusers"

Alternative SQL, which is faster (Oracle 9*i* and 10*g* only)

```
select  sum(pct_bufgets) "Percent"
from    (select rank() over ( order by buffer_gets desc ) as rank_bufgets,
            to_char(100 * ratio_to_report(buffer_gets) over (), '999.99') pct_bufgets
         from   v$sqlarea )
where   rank_bufgets < 11;

   Percent
----------
     44.03
```

Rate Your System

Take your top 10 memory read statements in the V$SQLAREA view. What percent are they of all memory reads?	> 25%	0 points
	20–25%	30 points
	5–19%	50 points
	< 5%	60 points
	Score	60

Top 25 "Memory Abusers" Statements Tuned

I have found that the top 25 statements accessed on most systems when left untuned make up over 75 percent of all memory and disk reads of the entire system. The code that follows lists and illustrates how to find the greatest 25 memory abusers.

Query to get the 25 worst memory abusers

```
set serverout on size 1000000
declare
 top25 number;
 text1 varchar2(4000);
 x number;
 len1 number;
cursor c1 is
  select buffer_gets, substr(sql_text,1,4000)
  from v$sqlarea
  order by buffer_gets desc;
begin
 dbms_output.put_line('Gets'||'    '||'Text');
 dbms_output.put_line('----------'||'  '||'----------------------');
 open c1;
 for i in 1..25 loop
  fetch c1 into top25, text1;
  dbms_output.put_line(rpad(to_char(top25),9)||' '||substr(text1,1,66));
  len1:=length(text1);
  x:=66;
  while len1 > x-1 loop
   dbms_output.put_line('"          '||substr(text1,x,66));
  x:=x+66;
  end loop;
```

```
  end loop;
end;
/
```

Sample partial output

```
SQL> @pl4

Gets    Text
16409    select f.file#, f.block#, f.ts#, f.length from fet$ f, ts$ t where
"        e t.ts#=f.ts# and t.dflextpct!=0
6868     select job from sys.job$  where next_date < sysdate  order by next
"        t_date, job
6487     SELECT BUFFER_GETS,SUBSTR(SQL_TEXT,1,3500)   FROM V$SQLAREA ORDER
"         BY BUFFER_GETS DESC
3450     SELECT BUFFER_GETS,SUBSTR(SQL_TEXT,1,4000)   FROM V$SQLAREA ORDER
"         BY BUFFER_GETS DESC
(...Simplistic Partial Listing Displayed)
```

Rate Your System

How many of your top 25	0	0 points
memory statements in the	1–5	10 points
V$SQLAREA view have you	6–15	20 points
attempted to tune?	16–25	30 points
	Score	30

Pinning/Caching Objects

Objects can be pinned into memory using DBMS_SHARED_POOL.KEEP if they are often-used objects, as shown in Chapter 10. Tables can also be pinned into memory by caching the table when it is created, or by using the ALTER command to cache a table. See Chapter 7 for more information on caching tables.

The recommended packages to consider for pinning are the following:

DBMS_ALERT	DBMS_DESCRIBE
DBMS_DDL	DBMS_LOCK
DBMS_OUTPUT	DBMS_PIPE
DBMS_SESSION	DBMS_SHARED_POOL
DBMS_STANDARD	DBMS_UTILITY
STANDARD	

Rate Your System

Do you pin PL/SQL objects or	Yes/no need	10 points
cache tables when needed?	No	0 points
	Score	10

Example Memory Performance   **Total Score**   <u>230</u>   **(A)**
Index (MPI)

Grade Your System

MPI Grade	Comments	Score
A+	Top 10 percent of most systems	> 230
A	Top 20 percent of most systems	200–230
B	Top 40 percent of most systems	160–199
C	Top 70 percent of most systems	100–159
Needs help now	Bottom 30 percent of most systems	< 100

TIP
Measuring your MPI (Memory Performance Index) can be helpful in identifying potential memory allocation and usage improvements that could be beneficial.

Disk Performance Index (DPI)

This section measures disk use. The following table illustrates how to receive a perfect DPI score. This rating system is not meant to be an all-encompassing benchmark of disk use; rather, it is a barometer to see if disk use improvements could be beneficial. With the advent of SANs and other disk and disk-caching technology, you may need to alter the rating system to be more appropriate for your system. Oracle features such as LMTs (Locally Managed Tablespaces) and ASSM (Automatic Segment Space Management) should be strongly considered. (See Chapter 4 for more information on these features.)

Category	Level Required	Maximum Score
Top 25 (worst disk) statements tuned	Yes	40
Top 10 statements disk use	< 5 percent	60
Tables/indexes collocated	No	30
Mission-critical table in LMTs w/ASSM	Yes	30
Redo logs/undo/Data Separated	Yes	30
Automatic UNDO Management	Yes	30
Disks used for temporary tablespaces	> 2	30
Disk Performance Index (DPI)	**Section Total**	**250**

Top 25 "Disk-Read Abuser" Statements Tuned

I have found that the top 25 statements accessed on most systems when left untuned can make up over 75 percent of all disk and/or memory reads of the entire system. This section lists the most intense 25 disk reading statements of the entire system. The example that follows shows a pretty well-tuned system where only data dictionary queries show up.

Query to get the 25 worst disk-read abusers

```
set serverout on size 1000000
declare
 top25 number;
 text1 varchar2(4000);
 x number;
 len1 number;
cursor c1 is
  select disk_reads, substr(sql_text,1,4000)
  from v$sqlarea
  order by disk_reads desc;
begin
 dbms_output.put_line('Reads'||'   '||'Text');
 dbms_output.put_line('----------'||' '||'----------------------');
 open c1;
 for i in 1..25 loop
  fetch c1 into top25, text1;
  dbms_output.put_line(rpad(to_char(top25),9)||' '||substr(text1,1,66));
  len1:=length(text1);
  x:=66;
  while len1 > x-1 loop
    dbms_output.put_line('"          '||substr(text1,x,66));
  x:=x+66;
  end loop;
 end loop;
end;
/
```

Sample partial output

```
Reads   Text
1156      select file#, block#, ts# from seg$ where type# = 3
122       select distinct d.p_obj#,d.p_timestamp from sys.dependency$ d, obj
"         j$ o where d.p_obj#>=:1 and d.d_obj#=o.obj# and o.status!=5
111       BEGIN sys.dbms_ijob.remove(:job); END;
(...Simplistic Partial Listing Displayed)
```

Rate Your System

How many of your top 25	0	0 points
disk read statements in the	1–5	10 points
V$SQLAREA view have you	6–15	20 points
attempted to tune?	16–25	40 points
	Score	40

Top 25 "Disk-Read Abuser" Statements Tuned

Top 10 Disk-Read Abusers as Percent of All Statements

This section measures how much of the system the top 10 heaviest disk reading statements are as a percentage of the entire system.

Script to retrieve this percentage

```
Set serverout on;
DECLARE
 CURSOR c1 is
  select    disk_reads
  from      v$sqlarea
  order by  disk_reads DESC;
 CURSOR c2 is
  select    sum(disk_reads)
  from      v$sqlarea;
 Sumof10 NUMBER:=0;
 mydr NUMBER;
 mytotdr NUMBER;
BEGIN
 dbms_output.put_line('Percent');
 dbms_output.put_line('--------');
 OPEN c1;
 FOR i IN 1..10 LOOP
  FETCH c1 INTO mydr;
  sumof10 := sumof10 + mydr;
 END LOOP;
 CLOSE c1;
 OPEN c2;
 FETCH c2 INTO mytotdr;
 CLOSE c2;
 dbms_output.put_line(sumof10/mytotdr*100);
END;
/
```

Sample output

```
Percent
5.5183036
```

Alternative/simple and fast SQL

```
select sum(pct_bufgets)
from ( select rank() over ( order by disk_reads desc ) as rank_bufgets,
       to_char(100 * ratio_to_report(disk_reads) over (), '999.99') pct_bufgets
       from    v$sqlarea )
where rank_bufgets < 11;


SUM(PCT_BUFGETS)
----------------
          68.59
```

Rate Your System

Take your top 10 disk read statements in the V$SQLAREA view. What percent are they of all disk reads?	> 25%	0 points
	20–25%	30 points
	5–19%	50 points
	< 5%	60 points
	Score	50

Tables/Indexes Separated

Tables and their corresponding indexes should be located on separate physical disks to decrease file I/O for a given disk. This is of course becoming harder to do, as DBAs are often unaware of where things are because of how a SAN may be managed. Chapter 3 covers this topic in great detail and provides queries to assist in this matter. Note that if you use ASM (also covered in Chapters 1 and 3), you should ensure that when you add new disks you follow the tips on rebalancing that are listed in Chapter 3.

Rate Your System

Are tables and their corresponding indexes located on the same physical disk or array?	Yes	0 points
	Disk array	20 points
	No	30 points
	Score	30

Mission-Critical Table Management

TUSC generally recommends managing mission-critical tables by storing them in locally managed tablespaces (LMTs) with automatic segment space management (ASSM) utilized. Also, row chaining (usually when tables are stored in dictionary-managed tablespaces) may require rebuilding some objects.

Tablespaces implemented using automatic segment-space management are sometimes referred to as bitmap tablespaces. These are locally managed tablespaces with bitmap segment space management. To use automatic segment-space management, create locally managed tablespaces, with the segment space management clause set to AUTO. Automatic segment-space management in locally managed tablespaces eliminates the need to specify the PCTUSED, FREELISTS, and FREELIST GROUPS parameters. If possible, switch from manual space management to automatic segment-space management.

When a table is updated and the block of the record updated does not have enough room to fit the changes, a record is "chained" to another block. In this situation a record spans more than one block and in most instances creates additional I/O. By analyzing a table for chained rows and querying the CHAINED_ROWS table, it is possible to identify tables that have records that are chained. The CHAINED_ROWS table is created using the script utlchain.sql, which resides in a file under the $ORACLE_HOME/rdbms/admin directory, where Oracle software is located (note that the exact name and location may vary depending on your platform). To populate the CHAINED_ROWS table, use the ANALYZE command. The ANALYZE command has an option to determine chained rows in a table as follows:

```
ANALYZE table TABLE_NAME list chained rows into chained_rows;

Table analyzed.
```

The command will place the output into a table called CHAINED_ROWS. The following query will select the most informative columns of the CHAINED_ROWS table:

```
SELECT OWNER_NAME,        /*owner of object*/
       TABLE_NAME,        /*Name of table*/
       CLUSTER_NAME,      /*Name of cluster if applicable*/
       HEAD_ROWID,        /*ID of the first part of the row*/
       ANALYZE_TIMESTAMP /*Timestamp associated with last analyze*/
FROM   CHAINED_ROWS;
```

Rate Your System

Are mission-critical tables stored in LMTs with ASSM, and do you address chaining issues?	No	0 points
	Yes	30 points
	Score	30

Key Oracle Files Separated

Separating often accessed Oracle data files from each other can help eliminate I/O bottlenecks as well as eliminate potential saturation of the disk's memory cache. Separating heavily written files (especially redo logs) will generally improve performance.

Rate Your System

Are redo logs on a different disks than database datafiles?	Yes	30 points
	Disk array	20 points
	No	0 points
	Score	20

Automatic UNDO Management

TUSC recommends using automatic undo management where possible. When configured in this manner, the database automatically determines how long undo data should be kept on the basis of the time queries take to run. Undo data preserved within this window of time is said to be in the unexpired state. After this time, the state of the undo data changes to expired. Undo data is a good candidate for overwriting only when it is in the expired state. The length of time that Oracle keeps undo data in the unexpired state depends on tablespace configuration. When creating a database with DBCA (Database Configuration Assistant), the undo tablespace is set by default to automatically extend itself to maintain unexpired undo for the longest-running query.

When using a fixed-sized undo tablespace, Oracle automatically keeps the undo data in the unexpired state for the longest possible time for the tablespace of the specified size. If the undo tablespace does not have adequate free or expired space to store active undo data generated by current transactions, then Oracle might be forced to overwrite the unexpired undo data. This situation might cause long-running queries to fail with an error and an alert.

In the event that it is not possible to use automatic undo management, auto-extension may be disabled, requiring adjustment of the size of the tablespace manually. In this case, ensure that the tablespace is large enough to meet the read-consistency requirements for the longest-running query.

Also, if using Flashback features, then make certain the tablespace is large enough to accommodate Flashback operations. The queries listed next estimate the number of bytes required when sizing the UNDO tablespace under different conditions.

The following information is appropriate for UNDO Query A, B, and C. Sizing an UNDO tablespace requires three pieces of information:

- **(UR)**   UNDO_RETENTION in seconds
- **(UPS)**   Number of undo data blocks generated per second
- **(DBS)**   Overhead varies based on extent and file size (db_block_size)

UndoSpace = (UR * (UPS * DBS) + DBS)

Or, when the guesstimate equates to zero, then add a multiplier (24) to the overhead (DBS) to derive more appropriate results:

UndoSpace = [UR * (UPS * DBS)] + (DBS * 24)

Two of the pieces of information can be obtained from the initialization file: UNDO_ RETENTION and DB_BLOCK_SIZE. The third piece of the formula requires a query against the database. The number of undo blocks generated per second can be acquired from V$UNDOSTAT as follows:

```
SELECT (SUM(undoblks))/ SUM ((end_time - begin_time) * 86400)
FROM    v$undostat;
```

To convert days to seconds, we multiply by 86400, the number of seconds in a day. The result of the query returns the number of undo blocks per second. This value needs to be multiplied by the size of an undo block, which is the same size as the database block defined in DB_BLOCK_SIZE.

The query that follows represents a point-in-time estimate based on the undo blocks per second at the time of execution. The query can be utilized when UNDO space has not been allocated. If this time frame is during high activity or a worst-case scenario for UNDO, then the results derived provide a good estimate.

UNDO query A

```
SELECT (UR * (UPS * DBS) + DBS) AS "Bytes"
FROM    (SELECT value AS UR
         FROM   v$parameter
         WHERE  name = 'undo_retention'),
        (SELECT (SUM(undoblks) / SUM( ((end_time - begin_time) * 86400))) AS UPS
         FROM   v$undostat),
        (SELECT value AS DBS
         FROM   v$parameter
WHERE   name = 'db_block_size');

    Bytes
----------
126630.554
```

If the results derived from UNDO Query A are low because of activity during the time frame, then UNDO Query B can be utilized to derive results as follows:

UNDO query B

```
SELECT (UR * (UPS * DBS)) + (DBS * 24) AS "Bytes"
FROM    (SELECT value AS UR
         FROM    v$parameter
         WHERE   name = 'undo_retention'),
         (SELECT (SUM(undoblks)/SUM(((end_time - begin_time)*86400))) AS UPS
         FROM    v$undostat),
         (SELECT value AS DBS
         FROM    v$parameter
WHERE   name = 'db_block_size');


     Bytes
----------
335717.434
```

The following query is valid when UNDO space has already been allocated and the database has been running for some period of time.

UNDO query C

```
SELECT /*+ ordered */ d.file_name, v.status,
       TO_CHAR((d.bytes / 1024 /1024), '99999990.000'),
       NVL(TO_CHAR(((d.bytes - s.bytes) / 1024 /1024), '99999990.000'),
       TO_CHAR((d.bytes / 1024 / 1024), '99999990.000')), d.file_id,
       d.autoextensible, d.increment_by, d.maxblocks
FROM sys.dba_data_files d, v$datafile v,
     (SELECT file_id, SUM(bytes) bytes
     FROM    sys.dba_free_space
     WHERE   tablespace_name ='NAME_OF_UNDO_TABLESPACE'
     GROUP   BY file_id) s
WHERE (s.file_id (+)= d.file_id)
AND    (d.tablespace_name = 'NAME_OF_UNDO_TABLESPACE')
AND    (d.file_name = v.name);
```

If you are capturing the peak for UNDO Query A, then UNDO Query C might be the same at that point (where the two will come together).

Ideally, undo segments should be separated from each other and, optimally, from the disks that hold the tables and indexes they are performing operations on. If your system is very small, then separating undo segments may not be possible. Also, the number of DML statements that users are executing should determine the true number of undo segments that are optimal. This varies greatly from those of others (please use whichever you feel is best for your system).

Query

```
select    segment_name, file_name
from      dba_data_files, dba_rollback_segs
where     dba_data_files.file_id = dba_rollback_segs.file_id;
```

Sample output (*Old* Rollback Segment Way)

```
SEGMENT_NAME   FILE_NAME
RBS1           /disk1/oracle/rbs1.dbf
RBS2           /disk2/oracle/rbs2.dbf
RBS3           /disk3/oracle/rbs3.dbf
RBS4           /disk4/oracle/rbs4.dbf
RBS5           /disk1/oracle/rbs1.dbf
RBS6           /disk2/oracle/rbs2.dbf
RBS7           /disk3/oracle/rbs3.dbf
RBS8           /disk4/oracle/rbs4.dbf
```

Sample output (*New* UNDO Tablespace Way)

```
SEGMENT_NAME   FILE_NAME
------------   ------------------------------------------------
SYSTEM         C:\ORACLE\PRODUCT\10.1.0\ORADATA\ORCL\SYSTEM01.DBF
_SYSSMU11$     C:\ORACLE\PRODUCT\10.1.0\ORADATA\ORCL\UNDOTBS01.DBF
_SYSSMU10$     C:\ORACLE\PRODUCT\10.1.0\ORADATA\ORCL\UNDOTBS01.DBF
_SYSSMU9$      C:\ORACLE\PRODUCT\10.1.0\ORADATA\ORCL\UNDOTBS01.DBF
_SYSSMU8$      C:\ORACLE\PRODUCT\10.1.0\ORADATA\ORCL\UNDOTBS01.DBF
_SYSSMU7$      C:\ORACLE\PRODUCT\10.1.0\ORADATA\ORCL\UNDOTBS01.DBF
_SYSSMU6$      C:\ORACLE\PRODUCT\10.1.0\ORADATA\ORCL\UNDOTBS01.DBF
_SYSSMU5$      C:\ORACLE\PRODUCT\10.1.0\ORADATA\ORCL\UNDOTBS01.DBF
_SYSSMU4$      C:\ORACLE\PRODUCT\10.1.0\ORADATA\ORCL\UNDOTBS01.DBF
_SYSSMU3$      C:\ORACLE\PRODUCT\10.1.0\ORADATA\ORCL\UNDOTBS01.DBF
_SYSSMU2$      C:\ORACLE\PRODUCT\10.1.0\ORADATA\ORCL\UNDOTBS01.DBF
_SYSSMU1$      C:\ORACLE\PRODUCT\10.1.0\ORADATA\ORCL\UNDOTBS01.DBF
```

Rate Your System

Automatic UNDO Management?	No	0 points
	Yes	30 points
	Score	_30_

Temporary Segment Balance

When the PGA_AGGREGATE_TARGET (or SORT_AREA_SIZE if used) specified in the init.ora is not sufficient for sorting, users will sort in their predefined temporary tablespace. If a large amount of sorting on disk is prevalent, you need to ensure that users are sorting efficiently. If you use TEMPFILES, then you must query DBA_TEMP_FILES instead of DBA_DATA_FILES to get this output. In 10g, you should be using TEMPFILES, which is another name for Locally Managed Temporary Tablespaces. A couple of the advantages of TEMPFILES include

- No need to check the data dictionary for freespace for a temporary tablespace, since TEMPFILES use Locally Managed Tablespaces (LMT).

- Locally managed extents are faster with TEMPFILES and automatically track adjacent free space so that coalescing is not necessary.

(Temporary Segment Balance — side tab)

- TEMPFILES are always set to NOLOGGING, you cannot rename a TEMPFILE, you cannot make a TEMPFILE *read only,* and you cannot create a TEMPFILE with the *alter database* command.

Query

```
select    username, file_name
from      dba_data_files, dba_users
where     dba_data_files.tablespace_name = dba_users.temporary_tablespace;
```

Sample output

```
USERNAME   FILE_NAME
SYS        /disk1/oracle/sys1orcl.dbf
TEDP       /disk1/oracle/tmp1orcl.dbf
SANDRA     /disk1/oracle/tmp1orcl.dbf
TEDR       /disk1/oracle/tmp2orcl.dbf
ROB        /disk1/oracle/tmp2orcl.dbf
DIANNE     /disk1/oracle/tmp2orcl.dbf
RICH       /disk1/oracle/tmp2orcl.dbf
DONNA      /disk1/oracle/tmp3orcl.dbf
DAVE       /disk1/oracle/tmp3orcl.dbf
ANDREA     /disk1/oracle/tmp3orcl.dbf
MIKE       /disk1/oracle/tmp3ora.dbf
```

Rate Your System

The users in your system can be altered to use different disks for sorting. How many disks are used for this?		
	All in system	0 points
	1	10 points
	2	20 points
	> 2	30 points
	Score	10

Example Disk Performance Index (DPI)	**Total Score**	**210** (A)

Grade Your System

DPI Grade	Comments	Score
A+	Top 10 percent of most systems	> 235
A	Top 20 percent of most systems	205–235
B	Top 40 percent of most systems	170–204
C	Top 70 percent of most systems	110–169
Needs help now	Bottom 30 percent of most systems	< 110

TIP

Measuring your DPI (Disk Performance Index) can be helpful in identifying potential disk improvements that could be beneficial.

Total Performance Index (TPI)

The Total Performance Index is the composite score of the memory, disk, education, and system indices, as shown here:

Category Index	Maximum Score
Education Performance Index (EPI)	250
System Performance Index (SPI)	250
Memory Performance Index (MPI)	250
Disk Performance Index (DPI)	250
Total Performance Index (TPI)	1000

Example Education Performance Index (EPI)	Total Score	150	(B)
Example System Performance Index (SPI)	Total Score	220	(A+)
Example Memory Performance Index (MPI)	Total Score	230	(A)
Example Disk Performance Index (DPI)	Total Score	210	(A)
Example Total Performance Index (SPI)	Total Score	810	(A)

Grade Your System

TPI Grade	Comments	Score
A+	Top 10 percent of most systems	> 925
A	Top 20 percent of most systems	795–924
B	Top 40 percent of most systems	620–794
C	Top 70 percent of most systems	380–619
Needs help now	Bottom 30 percent of most systems	< 380

TIP
Measuring your TPI (Total Performance Index) can be helpful in identifying bottlenecks; it is a simple barometer rating your overall system performance that may help find areas of improvement.

Overall System Review Example

The following is an example rating scale. You can use the rating results to generate a yearly review for your system. Some of the items (such as backup and recovery ratings) are not covered in depth. The objective of this section is to give you ideas of some of the areas you might consider reviewing. This is not an actual client system review but a slightly modified version of several reviews to help generate discussion items for your review template. The goal is to give you a "feel" of a review.

Overall System
Review Example

Rating System

Here is an example rating report that can be used as a guideline as you detail an overall review and ratings. Having a review that includes a rating for items that desperately need improvement or attention (where appropriate) is important in generating manager support. In many cases, a DBA needs managerial support to receive the time to address major issues with their system. At times, if the system is up and running, upper management may not realize that there is a need for change. This review can be a catalyst for needed change as issues are identified.

Grade	Ranking	Comments
A+	Top 5 percent of systems reviewed	Excellent
A	Top 10 percent	Very good to excellent
A–	Top 15 percent	Very good
B, B+, B–	Top 25 percent	Good/could be improved
C, C+, C–	Top 50 percent	Requires improvement
D, D+, D–	Bottom 50 percent	Desperately requires improvement
F	Bottom 10 percent	Immediately needs to be corrected

TIP

Have your system reviewed on an annual basis by an outside party or at the minimum by someone inside your company.

Example System Review Rating Categories

The following table summarizes the results of the system review. While some of the categories of the TPI are discussed, this section is an addition to the TPI that goes into greater depth. An overview of the recommended changes should follow this section, and the TPI rating could precede or follow this section. This section is more subjective, so an experienced person that you respect should make these evaluations. The ratings should include more detailed comments than those given here as an example. The recommended changes should be detailed with supporting documentation.

NOTE

This is an example, not an actual review.

Category	Grade	Comments
Overall review	C–	The system is running very poorly due to an insufficient amount of memory allocated for the data processing. Several areas need to be corrected immediately for substantially improved system performance, especially as additional users are added.

Category	Grade	Comments
Architecture	B	The overall architecture is good, but a review of the SAN and cache should be investigated to improve I/O distribution across available controllers.
Hardware sizing	A–	The hardware is well sized for the business activity, but the system is not tuned to take full advantage of the hardware.
Security	F	The passwords are never changed, even when employees leave the company. Several unprotected files have hard-coded passwords. The default accounts are not locked when unused. This is unacceptable! The security checklist that Oracle provides at otn.oracle.com/deploy/security has not been reviewed.
Memory allocation	B+	Of the 2G of memory, more of the memory can be allocated for the DB_CACHE_SIZE.
Database tuning	D–	The top 25 queries make up 98 percent of all resource usage. No effort has been made to tune these queries.
Disk configuration	B	Disk I/O is reasonably balanced but could be improved by partitioning a few of the hardest-hit tables and indexes.
Redo logs	B+	Redo logs are sized well, but you may want to add a few more of them for batch processing when they switch much faster.
Archived log files	A+	File systems containing the archive log files are independent of other Oracle file systems. Archives are archived to tape but also kept on disk for fast recoveries.
Rollback segments	A+	Automatic UNDO has been implemented and tuned.
Control files	A–	Multiple control files are located on different physical disks, but a backup of control file to TRACE does not exist.
Initialization parameters	A+	There is 2GB of SGA used on the system.
Table design	C–	There is no database-level referential integrity.
Tables	C–	Tables are not partitioned as they should be, and parallel should be set on some of the larger tables. Some of the smaller tables need to be altered so that they will be cached in memory.
Indexes	C–	Indexes should be partitioned more. Bitmap indexes are not being employed for the low-cardinality (few unique rows) columns of query-only tables.
Tablespaces	C+	Tablespaces are severely undersized for future growth.

Example System Review
Rating Categories

Items Requiring Immediate Action

Once you have reviewed your system, you need to make a comprehensive list of items that need to be addressed immediately. The following list is a summary (partial list only) of some of the issues that could warrant immediate action:

- Lock the default accounts when unused! Let's do it now.

- All other default passwords should be changed. Change all user passwords, as the security is currently compromised.

- DB_CACHE_SIZE needs to be increased immediately! This can be done with the system up in Oracle 10g if the SGA_MAX_SIZE is large enough. You can also use SGA_TARGET, so the DB_CACHE_SIZE is used only as a minimum (See Chapters 1 and 4 for more information).

- The top 25 queries causing disk and memory reads need to be tuned.

TIP
A system review should always include immediate action items. This ensures that the time needed for improvements will be allocated.

Other Items Requiring Action

The second list that you should make lists items needing attention, after the most pressing issues have been addressed. A summary example list is shown here. Your list should include more detail on how the action will be corrected:

- Monitor the items detailed in this document at least once per quarter with the current growth rate of the system.

- SYSTEM and SYS passwords in production should be different in development.

- Resize the database objects that are currently oversized and undersized.

- Change all passwords at least once per quarter.

- Fix file protection so that users are unable to delete Oracle software.

- Remove hard-coded passwords from scripts and backup jobs.

- Consider adding additional indexes for the top 25 worst disk read queries to improve query performance.

If initialization parameter changes are to be made, you should compile a list with both the current and suggested values. Refer to Appendix A for a complete list of init.ora parameters with descriptions. Last, make sure that you repeat the review after the changes have been made to ensure everything has been implemented correctly.

System Information List

This section describes some of the system information that you should gather and keep with the review. As you look back on a review, you need to know what the parameters of the system were at the time of the review. Any ratings of specific items (such as backup and recovery) could be placed in this section. I also have included a sample DBA review that illustrates some of the areas that may be reviewed. It is wise to have someone else rate your DBA skills so that you can continue to improve. This section has been greatly simplified for the book. It is a quick list designed to give a "picture" of the system as whole.

Memory-Related Values

The following are memory-related questions and answers about the system:

- What is the current memory for the hardware: **4GB**
- What is the current number of users: **500 total / 50 concurrent**
- What will be the future number of users: **100–150 concurrent in the next 3 months**
- What other software is used on the system: **None that is a major influence**
- Is the system client/server or browser/server: **browser/server**
- What response times are required: **Subsecond. OLTP transactions make up main mix**
- How large is the database: **Currently 9.5T with 100GB currently free in the database**
- How large are often-accessed tables: **One million rows is the average**
- Future software that will affect memory: **None**
- Implementing any other features/options: **Oracle Streams in 6 months. Oracle Grid in two years**

Disk-Related Values

The following are disk-related questions and answers:

- What is the maximum SAN capacity for the hardware: **twenty times current capacity**
- What disk sizes are available: **Unknown**
- What will be the size of the database in one year: **10% larger than current**
- Is there a RAID (striping) level for database files/OS: **Yes; RAID 1+0**
- Will there be multiplexed redo Logs: **Yes**
- All software that will be installed: **No additions in near future**
- System utilities that will be installed: **Quest Utilities, Veritas Storage Foundation**
- What transfers will happen nightly: **Bulk order transfers**

CPU-Related Values

The following are CPU-related questions and answers:

- Number of processors/maximum for the hardware: **6 currently/12 maximum**
- Is there a future upgrade path: **Yes; path to 64 processors**
- What is the transaction processing load: **60 percent CPU average/90 percent sustained maximum**
- What is the batch load: **Some heavy at night/okay during the day**
- Are hot backups employed: **RMAN backups are employed with archiving**
- Are batch processes running during the day: **None that are affecting performance**
- Will parallel query be used in the future: **Currently being used on some processes**
- Will there be a future distributed setup: **Yes, with Oracle Streams**

Backup- and Recovery-Related Information

The following are backup- and recovery-related questions and answers:

- Does the system require 7x24 use: **No, it is 6x24**
- How fast will recovery need to be made (On disk backup): **12-hour maximum**
- Are there "standby" disks in case of failure: **No, 4-hour turnaround from HP**
- How much data is "backed up"; is it being "tape-striped" with parity: **Unknown**
- Has the UPS been established: **Yes**
- Are export files also taken: **No**
- Cold backup procedures: **Not applicable**
- Export procedures: **Needs improvement**
- Hot backup procedures: **Excellent**
- Flash Recovery sized properly? **Yes**
- Disaster recovery procedures. **Needs improvement (Data Guard suggested)**

The following is an example of some of the areas you may evaluate in a backup and recovery rating. The *Oracle DBA Tips and Techniques* book goes into this rating in depth. The layout should be identical to your system review.

Category	Grade	Comments
Backup and recovery overall	A	A script to replace all of the backed up files should also be generated
Backup procedures	A	Excellent
Archiving procedures	A	Excellent
Recovery procedures	A–	Should have scripts ready to go for a recovery
Backup knowledge	A	Very good
Recovery knowledge	A	Very good
Disaster backup	A+	Excellent
Disaster recovery	A	Very good, rolling forward was still being worked on

Naming Conventions and/or Standards and Security Information

The following are naming convention, standards-, or security-related questions and answers:

- Review naming conventions used: **Excellent**
- Check file protections on key Oracle files: **Poor**
- Check database security procedures: **Poor**
- Check password procedures: **Poor**
- Review otn.oracle.com/deploy/security checklist: **Not Complete**

DBA Knowledge Rating

Having all DBAs reviewed by an impartial expert is paramount to identifying and improving the skills for a DBA. Often, the primary DBA is too busy to attend training sessions or improve his skills on new versions of Oracle. This area will help identify areas of strengths and weaknesses. This process will fail if this review is used against a person. It *must* be used with the goal of identifying and improving.

Category	Rating
DBA knowledge overall	A
Oracle architecture	A–
Oracle objects	B+

Category	Rating
Oracle internals	B+
Oracle initialization parameters	B+
Oracle query tuning	A
Oracle database tuning	A
Oracle backup	A
Oracle recovery	A
Oracle utilities	A
Operating system	B+

CAUTION
Reviewing a DBA's ability should only be done if the review will be used as a means of improving the skills of the DBA. Reviewing a person is a very sensitive issue and must be done by someone who has the goal of improvement first and foremost.

Other Items to Consider in Your TPI and System Review

As I stated earlier in this chapter, I was looking to give the most basic barometer as a starting guide. There are many things that may or may not be important to your specific system. Here are some items that I also think may be important to consider in your System Review that you develop and the TPI that you customize for your system:

- Are all of the Oracle Tools schema objects in the SYSAUX tablespace?

- Have you considered using ASM in your storage architecture?

- Are you fully using Transportable Tablespaces if you often move a lot of data?

- Do you have appropriate Flashback technology implemented as a means of accelerated recovery and high availability? No query is slower than the one accessing a system that is down!

- Are statistics being collected often enough? Are they being collected too often on tables that are generally static?

- Have you used AWR and ADDM (see Chapters 1, 5, and 14 for more information) to diagnose and fix potential problems?

- Has using Enterprise Manager Grid Control made you faster at deploying new nodes and diagnosing RAC issues?

■ Do you have a sufficient test and development system to ensure proper testing before moving code to production?

■ Have you considered using SGA_TARGET and Oracle's automatic tuning capabilities for smaller systems? If yes, have you set parameters that need minimum settings such as DB_CACHE_SIZE, SHARED_POOL_SIZE, and JAVA_POOL_SIZE?

■ Do you have an encrypted backup, or could your system potentially face downtime, causing severe delays in production performance? Once again, no query is slower than the one accessing a system that is down!

Tips Review

■ Measuring your EPI (Education Performance Index) can be helpful in identifying educational improvements that could be beneficial.

■ Measuring your SPI (System Performance Index) can be helpful in identifying overall system improvements that could be beneficial.

■ Measuring your MPI (Memory Performance Index) can be helpful in identifying potential memory allocation and usage improvements that could be beneficial.

■ Measuring your DPI (Disk Performance Index) can be helpful in identifying potential disk improvements that could be beneficial.

■ Measuring your TPI (Total Performance Index) can be helpful in identifying bottlenecks and is a simple barometer rating your overall system performance as it compares to others in the industry.

■ Have your system reviewed on an annual basis by an outside party or, at a minimum, by someone inside your company.

■ A system review should always include immediate action items. This ensures that the time needed for improvements will be allocated.

■ Reviewing a DBA's ability should only be done if the review will be used as a means of improving the skills of the DBA. Reviewing a person is a very sensitive issue and must be done by someone who has the goal of improvement first and foremost.

■ If you can't effectively monitor your own system, then contract someone who can. The cost of maintaining a database is usually far less than the cost of downtime when problems occur.

■ Include new 10*g* items (covered throughout this book) such as SYSAUX, Transportable Tablespaces, Flashback, AWR, ADDM, Grid Control, and Encrypted Backup in *your* items to review as needed.

References

Oracle10g SQL Language Reference Manual Versions (Oracle Corporation)
Memory Performance Index, Disk Performance Index, Education Performance Index,
Total Performance Index, MPI, DPI, EPI, SPI and TPI (Copyright TUSC 1998–2007)
Maurice Aelion, Dr. Oleg Zhooravlev, and Arie Yuster, *Tuning Secrets from the Dark Room*
of the DBA

Many thanks to Brad Nash for updating this chapter. Thanks to Randy Swanson, Judy Corley, Sean McGuire, and Greg Pucka of TUSC for their contributions to this chapter.

CHAPTER
16

Monitor the System Using Unix Utilities (DBA)

Part of being able to solve performance problems includes being able to effectively use operating system utilities. Using the correct utilities to find CPU, memory, and disk I/O issues is crucial to identifying where performance problems exist. Today's DBAs and system managers increasingly include performance management as part of their duties.

There are basically two main categories of activities needed for system management. The first, accounting and monitoring, consisting of tools such as accounting logs, software monitors, hardware monitors, or manual logs to monitor the system usage, workload, performance, availability, and reliability. This enables the system administrator to do load balancing and control resource usage. The second, performance analysis, consists of using the monitored data to determine what system tuning is required and by predicting future workload when upgrading is required. In a broad sense, system performance refers to how well the computer resources accomplish the work they are supposed to do. This chapter will give you the utilities you need to accomplish both of these objectives.

Unix/Linux Utilities

This chapter will focus on tips related to Unix and Linux utilities and shell scripts that can be used to find problems as well as gather statistics for monitoring. Tips covered in this chapter include

- Using the sar command to monitor CPU usage

- Finding the worst user on the system using the top command

- Using the uptime command to monitor the CPU load

- Using the mpstat command to identify CPU bottlenecks

- Combining ps with selected V$ views

- Using the sar command to monitor disk I/O problems

- Using iostat to identify disk I/O bottlenecks

- Using sar and vmstat to monitor paging/swapping

- Determining shared memory usage using ipcs

- Monitoring system load using vmstat

- Monitoring disk free space

- Monitoring network performance

Using the sar Command to Monitor CPU Usage

The sar command has many different switches that can be set to display different pieces of performance information. With the –u switch, sar can be used to monitor CPU utilization. The sar utility is an effective way to see a quick snapshot of how much the CPU is "bogged down" or utilized (100 percent is not a good thing). Run this utility on a regular basis to get a baseline for your system, enabling you to identify when your system is running poorly. The sar command has the following benefits:

- Provides great information that can be used for performance tuning and monitoring

- Logs to a disk file (but does not provide per process information)

- Requires low overhead to run

- Is found on most Unix and Linux platforms

The sar command has many different switches that can be set to display different pieces of performance information.

sar –u (Check for CPU Bogged Down)

With the –u switch, sar can be used to monitor CPU utilization. The sar utility is an effective way to see a quick snapshot of how the heavily the CPU is "bogged down." Run this utility on a regular basis to get a baseline for your system, enabling you to identify when your system is running poorly. Of the two numbers following the switch for sar (the switch is –u in the following example), the first displays the number of seconds between sar readings, and the second is the number of times you want sar to run. Here is a sample report showing CPU utilization (the default):

%usr	Percent of CPU running in user mode
%sys	Percent of CPU running in system mode
%wio	Percent of CPU running idle with a process waiting for block I/O
%idle	Percent of CPU that is idle

```
# sar -u 10 8

HP-UX sch1p197 B.10.20 E 9000/893     01/23/98

              usr     %sys    %wio    %idle
11:55:53      80      14       3       3
11:56:03      70      14      12       4
11:56:13      72      13      21       4
11:56:23      76      14       6       3
11:56:33      73      10      13       4
11:56:43      71       8      17       4
11:56:53      67       9      20       4
11:57:03      69      10      17       4

Average       73      11      13       4
```

A low %idle time could point to a CPU-intensive job or an underpowered CPU. Use the ps or top command (later in this chapter) to find a CPU-intensive job. A poorly written query requiring a large amount of disk access can also cause a large amount of CPU usage as well.

In the following sar output, the cause for concern is the large values being returned for %wio (waiting for block I/O) vs. actual heavy CPU usage:

```
# sar -u 5 4

              %usr    %sys    %wio    %idle
14:29:58      20      20      60       0
14:30:03      17      23      60       0
```

14:30:08	19	14	67	0
14:30:13	22	11	67	0
Average	21	16	64	0

This list shows a high %wio, waiting for I/O, time. This would point toward a disk contention problem. Iostat (discussed later in this chapter) can be used to pinpoint disk contention.

TIP
Use the sar –u command to see a quick snapshot of how much the CPU is "bogged down." Run sar on a regular basis to get a baseline for your system so that you can identify when your system is running poorly. However, at times low CPU idle time can also be an I/O issue, not a CPU issue.

Here are some things to look for in sar's output:

- Low CPU idle times.

- High percent of time spent waiting on I/O or '%wio> 10'.

- Bottlenecks with %sys > 15. This could indicate swapping, paging, or backups are causing a bottleneck.

- Abnormally high %usr. This could be due to applications not being tuned properly or over-utilizing the CPU.

The sar –d Command (Find I/O Problems)

The sar –d command is used to report the activity of block devices on the system for each disk or tape drive. This is usually used to help identify heavily accessed disks and imbalanced disk I/O. Disk-striping software frequently can help in cases where the majority of disk access goes to a handful of disks. Where a large amount of data is making heavy demands on one disk or one controller, striping distributes the data across multiple disks and/or controllers. When the data is striped across multiple disks, the accesses to it are averaged over all the I/O controllers and disks, thus optimizing overall disk throughput. Some disk-striping software also provides support for a Redundant Array of Inexpensive Disks (RAID) and the ability to keep one disk in reserve as a hot standby (that is, a disk that can be automatically rebuilt and used when one of the production disks fails). When thought of in this manner, this can be a very useful feature in terms of performance because a system that has been crippled by the failure of a hard drive will be viewed by your user community as having pretty bad performance.

This information may seem obvious, but it is important to the overall performance of a system. Frequently, the answer to disk performance simply rests on matching the disk architecture to the use of the system. Here are some examples using sar –d to find disk I/O and other issues:

```
# sar -d
```

09:34:54	device	%busy	avque	r+w/s	blks/s	avwait	avserv
09:34:59	c0t6d0	0.60	0.50	1	6	3.84	5.38
	c3t6d0	0.20	0.50	1	6	3.85	3.76

```
            c7t0d0     0.20     0.50      4      50     2.60     0.89
            c7t0d2     8.78    21.61    270    4315    10.39     1.77
            c7t0d3     8.78    21.82    267    4273    10.77     1.80
            c7t0d4    23.15     0.50    252   13019     5.06     1.51
            c7t0d5     0.60     0.50      1      19     6.15     6.48
09:35:04    c0t6d0     2.60     0.50     16     140     5.04     1.69
            c3t6d0     0.40     0.50      1       7     1.12     9.02
            c7t0d0     1.60     1.23     10     152     6.01     5.30
            c7t0d1     2.40     1.07     10     155     5.45     6.31
            c7t0d2     0.80    19.38     15     234    10.02     1.71
            c7t0d3     0.40    21.89     12     198    10.89     1.85
            c7t0d4    24.60     0.50    274   10357     5.04     1.22
```

Things to watch for with disk I/O (sar –d) include the following:

- %busy on a device that is greater than 50 percent

- avwait is greater than avserv

- Unbalanced load of disk I/O in the report indicates a serious imbalance of disk I/O

Here's an example of using sar with the –d switch that shows us a disk I/O bottleneck. This command, which lists the %busy, avque (average queue length), r+w/s (read and write activity), blks/s (#of blocks transferred), avwait, and avserv. A high %busy and high avque would indicate a big disk I/O bottleneck. Consider the following output, where disk sd17 is a big problem (it is 100 percent busy). If this condition persisted, an analysis of disk sd17 should lead to a reorganization of information from sd17 to a less-used disk. The sar command allows two significant numerical inputs (as shown next); the first is the number of seconds between running sar, and the second is how many times to run it (below 5 indicates a five-second interval and 2 indicates two repetitions).

```
# sar -d 5 2

            device  %busy  avque  r+w/s  blks/s  avwait  avserv
13:37:11    fd0       0     0.0     0       0      0.0     0.0
            sd1       0     0.0     0       0      0.0     0.0
            sd3       0     0.0     0       0      0.0     0.0
            sd6       0     0.0     0       0      0.0     0.0
            sd15      0     0.0     0       0      0.0     0.0
            sd16     13     0.1     5     537      0.0    26.4
            sd17    100     6.1    84    1951      0.0    72.4
            sd18      0     0.0     0       0      0.0     0.0
13:37:16    fd0       0     0.0     0       0      0.0     0.0
            sd1       0     0.0     0       0      0.0     0.0
            sd3       1     0.0     1      16      0.0    32.7
            sd6       0     0.0     0       0      0.0     0.0
            sd15      3     0.1     1      22      0.0    92.3
            sd17    100     6.1    85    1955      0.0    71.5
            sd18      0     0.0     0       0      0.0     0.0
Average     fd0       0     0.0     0       0      0.0     0.0
            sd1       0     0.0     0       0      0.0     0.0
            sd3       0     0.0     0       3      0.0    32.7
```

The sar –d Command

sd6	0	0.0	0	0	0.0	0.0
sd15	1	0.0	0	4	0.0	92.3
sd16	13	0.1	5	570	0.0	25.3
sd17	100	6.1	85	1962	0.0	71.2
sd18	0	0.0	0	0	0.0	0.0

Tuning Disk-Bound Systems

Conceptually, upgrading disk systems is fairly easy. Get faster disks, get faster controllers, and get more disks. The problem is predicting how much of an improvement one might expect from a given upgrade. If the system is truly spindle bound, and the load is parallelizable such that adding more disks is practical, this route is almost always the best way to go. When a straightforward upgrade path exists, there's no more likely or predictable way to improve a system's I/O than by increasing the number of disks. The problem is that a straightforward path for this sort of upgrade isn't always obvious.

As an example, assume we have one state-of-the-art disk on its own controller storing sendmail's message queue, and the system has recently started to slow down. There are two ways to effectively add a second disk to a sendmail system. First, we could add the disk as its own file system and use multiple queues to divide the load between the disks. This upgrade will work but will become more difficult to maintain and potentially unreliable if it is repeated too many times. Second, we could perform a more hardware-centric solution, upgrading to either create a hardware RAID system, install a software RAID system to stripe the two disks together, or add NVRAM (non-volatile RAM—retains its contents even when power is lost) to accelerate the disk's performance. With any of these solutions, upgrading the file system might also become necessary. None of these steps is a trivial task, and there's no way to be nearly as certain about the ultimate effect on performance with the addition of so many variables.

Obviously, we can't add disks without considering the potential effect on the I/O controller, and sometimes limits restrict the number of controllers that can be made available in a system. While we rarely push the limits of controller throughput with a small number of disks because e-mail operations are so small and random, it's possible to add so many disks on a system that we run out of chassis space in which to install controller cards.

Any time a system has I/O problems, it would be a mistake to quickly dismiss the potential benefits of running a high-performance file system. This solution is usually cheap and effective, and where available, it can offer the best bang for the buck in terms of speed improvement. If I am asked to specify the hardware for an e-mail server, in situations where I have complete latitude in terms of the hardware vendors, I know I can get fast disks, controllers, RAID systems, and processors for any operating system. The deciding factor for the platform then usually amounts to which high-performance file systems are supported. This consideration is that important.

If a RAID system is already in use, performance might potentially be improved by rethinking its setup. If the storage system is running out of steam using RAID 5 but has plenty of disk space, perhaps going to RAID 0+1 will give the box better performance and increase its hardware life. If the system is having problems with write bandwidth, lowering the number of disks per RAID group and thus having a larger percentage of the disk space devoted to parity may help. Using some of your unused space is certainly preferable to buying a new storage system. Changing the configuration of the storage system is especially worth consideration if it wasn't set up by someone who really understood performance tuning.

If a RAID system has been set up suboptimally, it may also be possible to improve its performance by upgrading it. Vendors often provide upgrade solutions to their RAID systems that can improve their throughput, both in terms of hardware components and the software that manages the system.

Last, to save money, the system might have originally included insufficient NVRAM or read cache. Performance might improve dramatically if you increase the NVRAM. See Chapter 3 for much more information on the topics in this section.

You can also use *tunefs* to help with disk issues. The tunefs command will list the current characteristics of a file system:

```
tunefs -v /dev/rdsk/c0txdx
```

To set minfree to 5 percent,

```
tunesfs -m 5 /dev/dsk/c2d5s0
```

To change rotational delay from 1 to 0,

```
tunesfs -d 0 /dev/rdsk/c0txd0
```

Refer to Chapter 3 for additional information on tuning disk I/O when it is at the database level.

The sar –b Command (Check the Buffer Cache)

The sar –b command reports on the system's buffer cache activities (*not* the Oracle buffer cache). It provides the number of transfers per second between system buffers and block devices. The main parameters to look for are as follows:

- Read cache: %rcache > 90%, indicating the potential for bad disk I/O
- Write cache: %wcache < 70%, likewise indicating the potential for bad disk I/O

```
sar -b

9:48:44     bread/s lread/s %rcache bwrit/s lwrit/s %wcache pread/s pwrit/s
09:48:49    437     422     0       404     113     2       0       0
09:48:54    604     858     30      617     630     2       0       0
09:48:59    359     451     20      431     479     10      0       0
09:49:04    678     750     10      671     633     0       0       0
09:49:09    369     577     36      473     511     7       0       0

Average     490     612     20      519     533     3       0       0
```

To look deeper into the buffer cache operation, consider a typical HP processor module. It consists of a CPU, a cache, a transaction look-aside buffer (TLB), and a coprocessor. These components are connected together with buses, and the processor module itself is connected to the system bus. The cache is a very high-speed memory unit. Typical access times are 10–20 ns (nanoseconds), compared to RAM, which is typically 80–90 ns. Cache can be accessed in one CPU cycle. Its contents and instructions and data that were recently used by the CPU or that are anticipated to be used by the CPU are stored here. The TLB is used to translate virtual addresses into physical addresses. It's a high-speed cache whose entries consist of pairs of recently used virtual addresses and their associated physical addresses. The coprocessor is a specialized piece of hardware that does complex mathematical numerical instructions. With memory management in Unix, *vhand* is the paging daemon. The buffer cache, as we see from the HP example, is a pool of memory designed to decrease file access time. These are some other noteworthy characteristics of the buffer cache:

- The buffer cache can have a fixed state.

- The default system uses dynamic size allocation.

- The buffer cache can increase performance of disk reads and writes

- Data is flushed from the buffer cache by the Sync process.

The sar –q Command (Check the Run Queue and Swap Queue Lengths)

The sar –q command reports on the system's run queue lengths and swap queue lengths. It gives the length of the run queue (runqsz), the percentage of time the run queue was occupied (%runocc), the length of the swap queue (swpq-sz), and the percentage of time the swap queue was occupied (%swpocc); the smaller these numbers, the better. We need to compare "sar –q" against "sar –w" data to see if the runq-sz is greater than 4 or the %swpocc is greater than 5, which would signal a potential issue.

```
sar -q

10:00:18 runq-sz %runocc swpq-sz %swpocc
10:00:23     0.0       0     0.0       0
10:00:28     0.0       0     0.0       0
10:00:33     0.0       0     0.0       0
10:00:38     0.0       0     0.0       0
10:00:43     1.0       5     0.0       0

Average      1.0       1     0.0       0
```

Using the sar and vmstat Commands to Monitor Paging/Swapping

A quick way to determine if there has been any swapping activity since the system started is to issue the command vmstat –S. Having a non-zero value in the swp/in and swp/out columns is a good indicator of a possible problem. You can delve into more detail using the sar command, which can also be used to check for system paging/swapping. Depending on the system, any paging and swapping could be a sign of trouble. In a virtual memory system, paging is when users that *are not* currently active are moved from memory to disk (a small issue). Swapping is when users that *are* currently active are moved to disk due to insufficient memory (very large issue). Swapping and paging could easily take an entire book due to the depth of the subject. Simple and fast commands to get a general picture of the state of your system will be covered in this section.

Using the –p Switch of sar to Report Paging Activities

The following table provides a description for the fields that are displayed with sar's –p swtich.

atch/s	Page faults per second that are satisfied by reclaiming a page currently in memory (per second)
pgin/s	Page-in requests per second
ppgin/s	Pages paged in per second
pflt/s	Page faults from protection errors per second (illegal access to page) or "copy-on-writes"
vflt/s	Address translation page faults per second (valid page not in memory)
slock/s	Faults per second caused by software lock requests requiring physical I/O

```
#sar -p 5 4

          atch/s   pgin/s   ppgin/s   pflt/s   vflt/s   slock/s
14:37:41   13.15    20.12    179.08    11.16     2.19     58.57
14:37:46   34.33    20.56    186.23     4.19     1.40     57.49
14:37:51   22.36    19.56    151.30     2.20     0.00     60.88
14:37:56   24.75    22.36    147.90     1.80     0.00     60.28
Average    27.37    20.11    161.81     7.58     8.14     60.85
```

The key statistic to look for is an inordinate amount of page faults of any kind. This usually indicates a high degree of paging. Remember that paging is not nearly as bad as swapping, but as paging increases, swapping will soon follow. You can review the daily reports over a period to see if paging is steadily increasing during a specific time frame. The command sar –p without any time intervals will show you the paging statistics from the entire day if you have enabled periodic automatic monitoring.

Using the –w Switch of sar to Report Swapping and Switching Activities

The –w switch of sar shows swapping activity. This command will display the swpin/s, swpot/s, bswin/s, and bswot/s fields, which are the number of transfers and number of 512-byte units transferred for swapins and swapouts (including initial loading of some programs). The field pswch/s shows context switches that occur per second. Pswch/s should be < 50. The swapping activity should be looked at closely if swpot/s rises above 0.

```
#sar -w 5 4

SunOS hrdev 5.5.1 Generic sun4m     08/05/98

          swpin/s   bswin/s   swpot/s   bswot/s   pswch/s
14:45:22    0.00       0.0      0.00       0.0       294
```

```
14:45:27     0.00      0.0      0.00      0.0       312
14:45:32     0.00      0.0      0.00      0.0       322
14:45:37     0.00      0.0      0.00      0.0       327
Average      0.00      0.0      0.00      0.0       315
```

A high count for process switching would point toward a memory deficiency, because actual process memory is being paged. There is no problem with swapping in the preceding example.

Using the –r Switch of sar to Report Free Memory and Free Swap

The following command line and output illustrate the sar command with the –r switch:

```
# sar -r 5 4

            freemem    freeswap
14:45:21    517        1645911
14:45:26    294        1645907
14:45:36    378        1645919
14:45:41    299        1642633
Average     367        1644597
```

When freemem (free memory—listed here in 512-byte blocks) falls below a certain level, the system will start to page. If it continues to fall, the system will then start to swap processes out. This is a sign of a rapidly degrading system. Look for processes taking an extreme amount of memory, or else an excessive number of processes.

Using the –g Switch of sar to Report Paging Activities

The following table gives a description for the fields that are displayed with sar's –g switch.

pgout/s	Page-out requests per second.
ppgout/s	Pages paged out per second.
pgfree/s	Pages per second placed on the free list by the page-stealing daemon.
pgscan/s	Pages per second scanned by the page-stealing daemon.
%ufs_ipf	The percentage of UFS inodes taken off the freelist by iget (a routine called to locate the inode entry of a file) that had reusable pages associated with them. These pages are flushed and cannot be reclaimed by processes. Thus, this is the percentage of igets with page flushes.

```
#sar -g

            pgout/s   ppgout/s   pgfree/s   pgscan/s   %ufs_ipf
14:58:34    2.40      74.40      132.80     466.40     0.00
14:58:39    1.80      55.69      90.62      263.87     0.00
14:58:44    2.20      62.32      98.00      298.00     0.00
```

```
14:58:49    4.59    142.32     186.43      465.07       0.00
14:58:54    0.80     24.75      24.15        0.00       0.00
```

A high ppgout (pages being moved out of memory) also points toward a memory deficiency.

Using the –wpgr Switch of sar

More information about the system's utilization of memory resources can be obtained by using sar –wpgr:

```
% sar -wpgr 5 5

07:42:30 swpin/s pswin/s swpot/s bswot/s pswch/s
         atch/s  pgin/s ppgin/s  pflt/s  vflt/s slock/s
         pgout/s ppgout/s pgfree/s pgscan/s %s5ipf
         freemem freeswp
07:42:35   0.00     0.0    0.00     0.0     504
           0.00    0.00    0.00    0.00    6.20   11.78
           0.00    0.00    0.00    0.00    0.00
          33139  183023
...
Average    0.00     0.0    0.00     0.0     515
Average    0.00    0.32    0.40    2.54    5.56   16.83
Average    0.00    0.00    0.00    0.00    0.00
Average   32926  183015
```

Check for page-outs (pgout/s means page-out requests per second; ppgout/s means page-out pages per second), and watch for their consistent occurrence. Look for a high incidence of address translation faults (vflt/s). Check for swap-outs (swpot/s). If they are occasional, it may not be a cause for concern, as some number of them is normal (for example, inactive jobs). However, consistent swap-outs are usually bad news, indicating that the system is very low on memory and is probably sacrificing active jobs. If you find evidence of memory shortages in any of these, you can use ps to look for memory-intensive jobs.

TIP

The sar command can be used to monitor and evaluate memory use and a potential need for additional memory. Paging is generally the movement of inactive processes from memory to disk. A high degree of paging is usually the predecessor to swapping. Swapping is the movement of active processes from memory to disk. If swapping starts to escalate, your system begins the downward "death spiral." Fixing memory hogs or adding memory is the correct solution.

What's a Good Idle Percentage for the CPU?

It really depends on the system size and variation in time accessed. For instance, a system that is accessed with heavy CPU usage for short periods of time may have an 80 percent average CPU idle time. In contrast, a system with very small jobs, but many of them, may have the same 80 percent average CPU idle time. The idle percentage is not as important as what is available when you run a job that must complete immediately (and is very important to the business). A 50 percent idle CPU may be a problem for the company with a large CPU-bound job that must complete quickly, while a 10 percent idle CPU may be more than enough for a company that has a very small job (requiring little CPU) that must complete quickly. Oracle will generally try to use the entire CPU available to complete a job.

I have found it helpful to run sar at regularly scheduled intervals throughout the day. The overhead of this is minimal, and it could be a great help in determining what was happening on your system last week when the problem actually started occurring. You have the ability to keep information in report format for thirty days by default. The following entries in root's crontab will produce a snapshot of the system state every twenty minutes during working hours:

```
20,40 8-17 * * 1-5 /usr/lib/sa/sa1
```

The next entry will report produce a report of important activities throughout the workday:

```
5 18 * * 1-5 /usr/lib/sa/sa2 -s 8:00 -e 18:01 -i 1200 –A
```

To access the report at any time, simply type **sar** with the appropriate switches and you will see output for each sampling period. For further information, see your man pages for "sar," "sa1," and "sa2."

CPU Scheduler and Context Switching

The goal in tuning is to keep the CPU as busy as possible to use all available resources allotted to get things done faster. There are five major process states:

- **SRUN**   The process is running or runnable.

- **SSLEEP**   The process is waiting for an event in memory or on the swap device.

- **SZOMB**   The process has released all system resources except for the process table. This is the final process state.

- **SIDL**   The process is being set up via fork and/or exec.

- **SSTOP**   The process has been stopped by job control or by process tracing and is waiting to continue.

The CPU scheduler handles context switches and interrupts. In multiprocessing environments, a *context switch* is when one process is suspended from execution on the CPU, its current state is recorded, and another process starts its execution. Obviously, in computer processing environments, the goal is good design of the CPU and the components of the computer system in order to reduce the context switch management overhead or to have a processing load that works more efficiently and does not require too many context switches. Context switching occurs when any of the following occur:

- A time slice expires.

- A process exits.

- A process puts itself to sleep.

- A process puts itself in a stopped state.

- A process returns from user mode from a system call but is no longer the most eligible process to run.

- A real-time priority process becomes ready to run.

Checking Oracle CPU Utilization Within Oracle

This section explains how to examine the processes running in Oracle. V$SYSSTAT shows Oracle CPU usage for all sessions. The statistic "CPU used by this session" actually shows the aggregate CPU used by all sessions. V$SESSTAT shows Oracle CPU usage per session. You can use this view to see which particular session is using the most CPU.

For example, if you have eight CPUs, then for any given minute in real time, you have eight minutes of CPU time available. On NT and Unix-based systems this can be either user time or time in system mode ("privileged" mode, in NT). If your process is not running, it is waiting. CPU utilized by all systems may thus be greater than one minute per interval.

At any given moment you know how much time Oracle has utilized *on* the system. So if eight minutes are available and Oracle uses four minutes of that time, then you know that 50 percent of all CPU time is used by Oracle. If your process is not consuming that time, then some other process is. Go back to the system and find out what process is using up the CPU. Identify it, determine why it is using so much CPU, and see if you can tune it.

The major areas to check for Oracle CPU utilization are

- Reparsing SQL statements

- Inefficient SQL statements

- Read consistency

- Scalability limitations within the application

- Latch contention

Finding the Worst User on the System Using the top Command

The top command shows a continuous display of the most active processes. DBAs and operations experts often run this (or similar utilities) at the first sign of system performance issues. This display will automatically update itself on the screen every few seconds. The first lines give general system information, while the rest of the display is arranged in order of decreasing current CPU usage (the worst user is on "top"). If your system does not have "top" installed, it is commonly available from sunfreeware.com or various other sources on the web. Simply do a web search for "top program download" and you should be rewarded with multiple locations from which to download the program.

```
# top

Cpu states:  0.0% idle, 81.0% user, 17.7% kernel,  0.8% wait,  0.5% swap
Memory: 765M real, 12M free, 318M swap, 1586M free swap
```

PID	USERNAME	PRI	NICE	SIZE	RES	STATE	TIME	WCPU	CPU	COMMAND
23626	psoft	-25	2	208M	4980K	cpu	1:20	22.47%	99.63%	oracle
15819	root	-15	4	2372K	716K	sleep	22:19	0.61%	3.81%	pmon
20434	oracle	33	0	207M	2340K	sleep	2:47	0.23%	1.14%	oracle
20404	oracle	33	0	93M	2300K	sleep	2:28	0.23%	1.14%	oracle
23650	root	33	0	2052K	1584K	cpu	0:00	0.23%	0.95%	top
23625	psoft	27	2	5080K	3420K	sleep	0:17	1.59%	0.38%	sqr
23554	root	27	2	2288K	1500K	sleep	0:01	0.06%	0.38%	br2.1.adm
15818	root	21	4	6160K	2416K	sleep	2:05	0.04%	0.19%	proctool
897	root	34	0	8140K	1620K	sleep	55:46	0.00%	0.00%	Xsun
20830	psoft	-9	2	7856K	2748K	sleep	7:14	0.67%	0.00%	PSRUN
20854	psoft	-8	2	208M	4664K	sleep	4:21	0.52%	0.00%	oracle
737	oracle	23	0	3844K	1756K	sleep	2:56	0.00%	0.00%	tnslsnr
2749	root	28	0	1512K	736K	sleep	1:03	0.00%	0.00%	lpNet
18529	root	14	10	2232K	1136K	sleep	0:56	0.00%	0.00%	xlock
1	root	33	0	412K	100K	sleep	0:55	0.00%	0.00%	init

The preceding display shows the top user to be psoft with a PID (Process ID) of 23626 (this output may be slightly different on your system). This user is using 99.63 percent of one CPU. If this output persisted for any length of time, it would be imperative to find out *who* this is and *what* they are doing. I will show how to link this back to an Oracle user using the ps command and querying the V$ views later in this chapter.

TIP
Use the top command to find the worst user on the system at a given point in time (the kill command usually follows for many DBAs). If the worst query only lasts a short period of time, it may not be a problem; but if it persists, additional investigation may be necessary.

Monitoring Tools

There are GUI monitoring tools available on most platforms that either come bundled with the software or are available on the Internet. The Task Manager process monitor is available on NT, sdtprocess and Management Console are available for later versions of Solaris (once again www.sunfreeware.com has a plethora of free tools), and tools like Superdome Support Management Station (SMS) and ServiceControl suite are available for HP. When using any tools remember to manage system performance with the following guidelines:

- Measure performance continuously.

- Assess systems and applications.

- Select the tool to use.

- Monitor.

- Troubleshoot issues that arise.

- Remove bottlenecks.

- Optimize applications.

- Plan for future workloads.

It's worth remembering to always use basic tuning guidelines:

- Do not tune at random except to solve an emergency.
- Measure before and after you tune.
- Tune one area at a time, and only change one thing at a time.
- Always use at least two tools when possible to base tuning decisions on.
- Know when to say stop.

Using the uptime Command to Monitor CPU Load

The uptime command is an excellent utility to find a quick 1-, 5-, and 15-minute CPU load of all jobs (including those currently running). You would want to look at the load average. This is the *number of jobs* in the CPU run queue for the last 1, 5, and 15 minutes. Note that this is not the percentage of CPU being used.

```
# uptime
  3:10pm  up 5 day(s), 19:04,  2 users,  load average: 2.10, 2.50, 2.20
```

I have found that a system with an average run queue of 2–3 is acceptable. If you add the following script to your cron table to run every hour, you will be mailed your average system load every two hours.

```
{uptime; sleep 120; uptime; sleep 120; uptime;} | mailx -s uptime
you@company.com
```

TIP
Use cron and uptime to get your system load mailed to you on a regular basis. See your Unix manual for any specific syntax when using these commands.

Using the mpstat Command to Identify CPU Bottlenecks

The mpstat command is a Sun Solaris tool that reports per-processor statistics in tabular form. Each row of the table represents the activity of one processor. The first table shows the summary of activity since boot time. Pay close attention to the smtx measurement. Smtx measures the number of times the CPU failed to obtain a mutex (mutual exclusion lock). Mutex stalls waste CPU time and degrade multiprocessor scaling. In the example that follows, there are four processors numbered 0–3, and a system that is heading toward disaster is displayed.

```
# mpstat 10 5

CPU minf mjf xcal intr ithr csw icsw migr smtx srw syscl usr sys wt  idl
0   1    0   0    110  9    75  2    2    9    0   302   4   4   11  81
```

CPU	minf	mjf	xcal	intr	ithr	csw	icsw	migr	smtx	srw	syscl	usr	sys	wt	idl
1	1	0	0	111	109	72	2	2	11	0	247	3	4	11	82
2	1	0	0	65	63	73	2	2	9	0	317	4	5	10	81
3	1	0	0	2	0	78	2	2	9	0	337	4	5	10	81
CPU	minf	mjf	xcal	intr	ithr	csw	icsw	migr	smtx	srw	syscl	usr	sys	wt	idl
0	2	8	0	198	12	236	113	35	203	60	1004	74	26	0	0
1	1	17	0	371	286	225	107	39	194	48	1087	60	40	0	0
2	0	22	0	194	82	267	127	38	227	49	1197	63	37	0	0
3	0	14	0	103	0	218	107	35	188	46	1075	71	29	0	0
CPU	minf	mjf	xcal	intr	ithr	csw	icsw	migr	smtx	srw	syscl	usr	sys	wt	idl
0	17	22	0	247	12	353	170	26	199	21	1263	54	46	0	0
1	8	14	0	406	265	361	165	27	200	25	1242	53	47	0	0
2	6	15	0	408	280	306	151	23	199	24	1229	56	44	0	0
3	10	19	0	156	0	379	174	28	163	27	1104	63	37	0	0
CPU	minf	mjf	xcal	intr	ithr	csw	icsw	migr	smtx	srw	syscl	usr	sys	wt	idl
0	0	19	0	256	12	385	180	24	446	19	1167	48	52	0	0
1	0	13	0	416	279	341	161	24	424	20	1376	45	55	0	0
2	0	13	0	411	290	293	144	22	354	15	931	54	46	0	0
3	0	14	0	140	0	320	159	22	362	14	1312	58	42	0	0
CPU	minf	mjf	xcal	intr	ithr	csw	icsw	migr	smtx	srw	syscl	usr	sys	wt	idl
0	23	15	0	264	12	416	194	31	365	25	1146	52	48	0	0
1	20	10	0	353	197	402	184	29	341	25	1157	41	59	0	0
2	24	5	0	616	486	360	170	30	376	20	1363	41	59	0	0
3	20	9	0	145	0	352	165	27	412	26	1359	50	50	0	0

TIP

If the smtx column for the mpstat output is greater than 200, you are heading toward CPU bottleneck problems.

Combining ps with Selected V$ Views

Which process is using the most CPU? The following ps Unix command will list the top nine CPU users (much like the top command earlier in this chapter).

```
ps -e -o pcpu,pid,user,args | sort -k 3 -r | tail
```

%CPU	PID	USER	COMMAND
0.3	1337	oracle	oraclePRD
0.3	4888	oracle	oraclePRD (LOCAL=NO)
0.4	3	root	fsflush
0.4	1333	psoft	PSRUN PTPUPRCS
0.4	3332	root	./pmon
0.4	4932	oracle	oraclePRD (LOCAL=NO)
0.4	4941	oracle	oraclePRD (LOCAL=NO)
2.6	4943	oracle	oraclePRD (LOCAL=NO)
16.3	4699	oracle	oraclePRD

This command lists the %CPU used, the PID, the Unix username, and the command that was executed. If the top user was an Oracle user, you could then get the information on the process from Oracle using the queries listed next. This is done by passing the system PID obtained from the ps command into the following queries:

```
ps_view.sql
col username format a15
col osuser    format a10
col program   format a20
set verify off
select    a.username, a.osuser, a.program, spid, sid, a.serial#
from      v$session a, v$process b
where     a.paddr  =  b.addr
and       spid     = '&pid';


ps_sql.sql
set verify off
column username format a15
column sql_text   format a60
undefine sid
undefine serial#
accept sid prompt 'sid: '
accept serial prompt 'serial#: '
select    'SQL Currently Executing: '
from      dual;


select    b.username, a.sql_text
from      v$sql a, v$session b
where     b.sql_address       = a.address
and       b.sql_hash_value = a.hash_value
and       b.sid      = &sid
and       b.serial# = '&serial';


select    'Open Cursors:'
from      dual;


select    b.username, a.sql_text
from      v$open_cursor a, v$session b
where     b.sql_address       = a.address
and       b.sql_hash_value = a.hash_value
and       b.sid      = &sid
and       b.serial# = '&serial';
```

In the following output, we're running an example (one step at a time):

```
$ ps -e -o pcpu,pid,user,args | sort -k 3 -r | tail

%CPU   PID    USER     COMMAND
0.4    650    nobody   /opt/SUNWsymon/sbin/sm_logscand
0.4    3242   oracle   ora_dbwr_DM6
0.4    3264   oracle   ora_dbwr_DMO
0.4    3316   oracle   ora_dbwr_CNV
0.4    4383   oracle   ora_dbwr_QAT
0.5    3      root     fsflush
0.8    654    root     /opt/SUNWsymon/sbin/sm_krd -i 10
1.7    652    root     /opt/SUNWsymon/sbin/sm_configd -i 10
```

```
3.6    4602    oracle    oracleCNV (LOCAL=NO)

$ sqlplus system/manager
SQL> @ps_view
Enter value for pid: 4602
```

Note that we use 4602 as the input, as it is the PID for the worst CPU from the ps command:

```
old   4:         and spid='&pid'
new   4:         and spid='4602'


USERNAME    OSUSER    PROGRAM              SPID    SID    SERIAL#
DBAENT      mag       sqlplus@hrtest       4602    10         105

SQL> @ps_sql
sid: 10
serial#: 105
```

Note that we use 10 as the SID and 105 as the serial #, as they were the values retrieved in the preceding query (ps_view.sql):

```
'SQLCURRENTLYEXECUTING:'
------------------------
SQL Currently Executing:
old   5: and b.sid=&sid
new   5: and b.sid=10
old   6: and b.serial#='&serial'
new   6: and b.serial#='105'


USERNAME    SQL_TEXT
DBAENT      select sum(bytes),sum(blocks) from dba_segments

'OPENCURSORS:'
Open Cursors:
old   5: and b.sid=&sid
new   5: and b.sid=10
old   6: and b.serial#='&serial'
new   6: and b.serial#='105'


USERNAME    SQL_TEXT
DBAENT      select sum(bytes),sum(blocks) from dba_segments
```

Putting it all together (setting headings off), you get

```
DBAENT      mag       sqlplus@hrtest       4602    10         105
SQL Currently Executing:
DBAENT      select sum(bytes),sum(blocks) from dba_segments
Open Cursors:
DBAENT      select sum(bytes),sum(blocks) from dba_segments
```

If we had a problem with users executing ad hoc queries and received problem queries that showed up in this result on a regular basis, we could add an automated kill command at the end to completely automate our job.

TIP
Combine operating system utilities with Oracle utilities to quickly and effectively find problematic users.

CPU/Memory Monitoring Tool on XP

Task Manager can be used for monitoring CPU and memory use under XP. The next screen shows a two-processor system under XP:

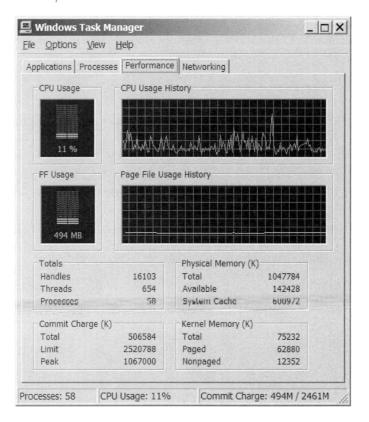

Using the iostat Command to Identify Disk I/O Bottlenecks

The iostat command can also be used to identify a disk bottleneck. The iostat command reports terminal and disk I/O activity, as well as CPU utilization. The first line of the output is for everything since booting the system, whereas each subsequent line shows only the prior interval specified.

Depending on the flavor of Unix, this command has several options (switches). The most useful switches are usually –d (transfers per second by disk), –x (extended statistics), –D (reads and writes per second by disk), –t (terminal or tty), and –c (cpu load).

```
Format:    iostat [option] [disk] [interval] [count]
```

Using the –d switch, we are able to list the number of kilobytes transferred per second for specific disks, the number of transfers per second, and the average service time in milliseconds. This displays I/O only; it doesn't distinguish between read and writes.

Using the –d Switch of iostat for Disk Drives sd15, sd16, sd17, and sd18

The output that follows shows that sd17 is severely overloaded compared to the other drives. Moving information from sd17 to one of the other drives would be a good idea if this information is representative of disk I/O on a consistent basis.

```
# iostat -d sd15 sd16 sd17 sd18 5 5
```

	sd15			sd16			sd17			sd18	
Kps	tps	serv	Kps	tps	serv	Kps	tps	serv	Kps	tps	serv
1	0	53	57	5	145	19	1	89	0	0	14
140	14	16	0	0	0	785	31	21	0	0	0
8	1	15	0	0	0	814	36	18	0	0	0
11	1	82	0	0	26	818	36	19	0	0	0
0	0	0	1	0	22	856	37	20	0	0	0

Using the –D Switch of iostat

The –D switch will report the reads per second, writes per second, and percentage disk utilization.

```
# iostat -D sd15 sd16 sd17 sd18 5 5
```

	sd15			sd16			sd17			sd18	
rps	wps	util	rps	wps	util	rps	wps	util	rps	wps	util
0	0	0.3	4	0	6.2	1	1	1.8	0	0	0.0
0	0	0.0	0	35	90.6	237	0	97.8	0	0	0.0
0	0	0.0	0	34	84.7	218	0	98.2	0	0	0.0
0	0	0.0	0	34	88.3	230	0	98.2	0	0	0.0
0	2	4.4	0	37	91.3	225	0	97.7	0	0	0.0

This shows that the activity on sd17 is completely read activity, while the activity on sd16 is strictly write activity. Both drives are at a peak level of utilization, and there may also be I/O problems. These statistics were gathered during a backup of sd17 to sd16. Your system should never look this bad!

Using the –x Switch of iostat

Using the –x switch will report extended disk statistics for all disks. This combines many of the switches previously discussed.

```
extended disk statistics
disk    r/s    w/s    Kr/s     Kw/s    wait    actv    svc_t    %w    %b
fd0     0.0    0.0    0.0      0.0     0.0     0.0     0.0      0     0
sd1     0.0    0.2    0.0      23.2    0.0     0.0     37.4     0     1
sd3     0.0    1.2    0.0      8.4     0.0     0.0     31.3     0     1
sd6     0.0    0.0    0.0      0.0     0.0     0.0     0.0      0     0
sd15    0.0    1.6    0.0      12.8    0.0     0.1     93.3     0     3
sd16    0.0    5.8    0.0      315.2   0.0     0.1     25.0     0     15
sd17    73.0   2.8    941.1    117.2   0.0     6.9     90.8     0     100
sd18    0.0    0.0    0.0      0.0     0.0     0.0     0.0      0     0

extended disk statistics
disk    r/s    w/s    Kr/s     Kw/s    wait    actv    svc_t    %w    %b
fd0     0.0    0.0    0.0      0.0     0.0     0.0     0.0      0     0
sd1     0.0    0.0    0.0      0.0     0.0     0.0     0.0      0     0
sd3     0.0    0.0    0.0      0.0     0.0     0.0     0.0      0     0
sd6     0.0    0.0    0.0      0.0     0.0     0.0     0.0      0     0
sd15    0.0    0.0    0.0      0.0     0.0     0.0     0.0      0     0
sd16    0.0    4.6    0.0      257.6   0.0     0.1     26.4     0     12
sd17    69.0   3.2    993.6    179.2   0.0     7.6     105.3    0     100
sd18    0.0    0.0    0.0      0.0     0.0     0.0     0.0      0     0
```

Once again, disks sd16 and sd17 are problems that need to be investigated and monitored further.

Combining –x Switch of iostat with Logic in a Shell Script

The script in this section will take the iostat –x output, sort it by the busy field (%b), and print out the 10 busiest disks for the listed interval. Some options for this script are listed here, followed by the script example and output:

- ■   This is the diskbusy script built on 1/1/2000.

- ■   The shell this example is running in is !/bin/ksh.

- ■   This script will get an iostat –x listing and sort it by the %busy field.

- ■   Change print $10 to sort by a different field.

- ■   Change to iostat –x 5 5 to get a different interval & count (5 seconds / 5 times).

- ■   Change tail to tail –20 to get the top 20 busiest disks only.

```
iostat -x | awk '/^disk/'
iostat -x 5 5|grep -v '^    ' |grep -v '^disk'| awk '{
        print $10 ", " $0
        }' $* |
sort -n |
awk -F, '{
        print $2
        }' |
tail
```

Running the preceding shell script, we receive this output:

```
# ./diskbusy

disk      r/s      w/s     Kr/s     Kw/s    wait     actv    svc_t     %w      %b
sd6       0.0      0.0      0.0      0.0     0.0      0.0      0.0      0       0
sd3       0.2      0.6      0.2      2.0     0.0      0.0      8.1      0       1
sd6       0.1      0.0      2.0      0.0     0.0      0.0    176.3      0       1
sd1       3.0      0.1     11.9     10.4     6.0      1.9   2555.3      3       3
sd17      3.4      0.7     37.4     17.2     0.0      0.2     54.6      0       4
sd16      4.1      0.8     38.6     26.0     0.0      0.6    129.5      0       6
sd17     99.0     14.2    790.8    795.2     0.0      3.6     31.4      0      99
sd17    100.0     14.0    798.8    784.0     0.0      3.5     30.8      0     100
sd17     95.0     14.2    760.0    772.8     0.0      3.6     32.7      0     100
sd17     95.5     14.0    764.3    762.7     0.0      3.5     31.6      0     100
```

In the preceding example, iostat is run five times and the top 10 busiest disks are displayed over all five runs. The disk sd17 is listed five times because it hits the combined top 10 all five times that iostat is run.

TIP
The sar and iostat commands can be used to find potential disk I/O problem areas. Utilizing the capabilities of shell scripting with these commands embedded can further enhance these commands.

Using the ipcs Command to Determine Shared Memory

Another helpful memory command that can be used to monitor the Oracle SGA is the ipcs command. The ipcs command will show the size of each shared memory segment for the SGA. If there is not enough memory for the entire SGA to fit in a contiguous piece of memory, the SGA will be built in noncontiguous memory segments. In the event of an instant crash, there is a possibility that the memory will not be released. If this happen to you, note that the ipcrm command will remove the segments (ipcrm –m for memory segments and ipcrm –s for semaphore segments).

```
# ipcs -b

Shared Memory:
m     204 0x171053d8 --rw-r-----   oracle     dba        65536
m     205 0x1f1053d8 --rw-r-----   oracle     dba    100659200
m     206 0x271053d8 --rw-r-----   oracle     dba      1740800
Semaphores:
s 393218 00000000   --ra-r-----    oracle     dba        300
```

In the preceding example, the SGA is built in three noncontiguous segments (making up the 100M+ SGA). The instance is then shut down and started with a smaller SGA (so that contiguous pieces of memory will make up the SGA). The SGA has been lowered to 70MB. The ipcs command is again issued.

```
# ipcs -b

Shared Memory:
m   4403 0x0f1053d8 --rw-r-----    oracle      dba 71118848
Semaphores:
s 393218 00000000   --ra-r-----    oracle      dba   300
```

It is usually preferable to have the entire SGA fit into a single shared memory segment because of the overhead that can be required to track more than one segment and the time required to switch back and forth between those segments. You can increase the maximum size of a single shared memory segment by increasing the SHMMAX setting in the /etc/system files. See the Oracle install documentation for more specific information for your platform.

TIP
Use the ipcs command to see if your SGA is built using multiple noncontiguous pieces of memory. A crash of your database can render this to be a problem with releasing the memory. Use the ipcrm command (only if the SGA pieces are not released after a database crash) to then remove the SGA pieces from memory. Do not issue the ipcrm command with a running database.

Using the vmstat Command to Monitor System Load

The vmstat command is a conglomeration of many of the other commands listed in this chapter. The advantage of vmstat is you get to see everything at once. The problem with vmstat is that you see everything at once and must evaluate it.

The vmstat command will show you these sets of procedures:

r	Processes that are currently running
b	Processes that are able to run, but are waiting on a resource
w	Processes that are able to run, but have been swapped out

It will additionally offer this information about CPU usage:

us	Percentage of user time for normal and priority processes
sy	Percentage of system time
id	Percentage of idle time

```
#vmstat 5 3

procs    memory          page         disk       faults     cpu
 r   b   w    swap     free    re  mf  pi    po  fr  de  sr  s0   s1  s6  s9
in     sy        cs      us     sy    id
19  5   0    1372992  26296    0   2     363   0   0   0   0   70  31  0   0    703
4846   662     64      36      0
```

```
23  3     0      1372952  27024   0   42   287   0   0   0   0   68  22  0    0    778
4619  780   63    37     0
16  4     0      1381236  36276   0   43   290   0   0   0   0   59  23  0    0    1149
4560  1393  56    44     0
```

Having any process in the *b* or *w* column is usually a sign of a problem system (the preceding system has a problem if this continues). If processes are blocked from running, the CPU is likely to be overwhelmed. The CPU idle time that is displayed in the preceding example is 0. Clearly the system is overwhelmed, as there are processes blocked and people are waiting to get CPU time. On the reverse side, if the idle time is high, you may not be using your system to its full capacity (not balancing activities efficiently) or the system may be oversized for the task. I like to see an idle time of 5–20 percent for a static (not adding new users) system.

Be aware that as the amount of time the system is waiting on IO requests increases, the amount of idle time on the CPU will decrease. This is because system resources have to be expended to track those waiting I/O requests. I mention this to make sure that you take a look at the whole picture before making your decisions. Eliminating an I/O bottleneck may free up significant amounts of CPU time. Time spent tracking I/O is reflected as 'sy' or system time in the output of vmstat.

In the CPU columns of the report, the vmstat command summarizes the performance of multiprocessor systems. If you have a two-processor system and the CPU load is reflected as 50 percent, that doesn't necessarily mean that both processors are equally busy. Rather, depending on the multiprocessor implementation, it can indicate that one processor is almost completely busy and the next is almost idle. The first column of vmstat output also has implications for multiprocessor systems. If the number of runnable processes is not consistently greater than the number of processors, it is less likely that you can get significant performance increases from adding more CPUs to your system.

The vmstat command is also used to view system paging and swapping. The po (page out) and pi (page in) values indicate the amount of paging that is occurring on your system. A small amount of paging is acceptable during a heavy usage cycle but should not occur for a prolonged period of time. On most systems, paging will occur during Oracle startup.

TIP
Use the vmstat command to find blocked processes (users waiting for CPU time) and also for paging or swapping problems. The vmstat command is a great way to see many of the sar options in one screen.

Monitoring Disk Free Space

Often it is important for DBAs, especially those without in-house system administrators, to closely monitor disk free space. For example, if the file system containing your archived redo logs fills, all activity on your database can instantly come to a halt! What follows is a script that allows you to easily monitor disk free space; it will e-mail you a message if there is an issue. I would schedule this script to run about every fifteen minutes. Scheduling a program to run at specified intervals is usually done through the cron process. You add or remove entries with the command crontab –e. This command should bring up your crontab file in a vi editor. An example that would check disk free space every fifteen minutes would look like this:

```
0,15,30,45 * * * * /usr/local/bin/diskfreespace.sh
```

This would run the diskfreespace.sh program every fifteen minutes, every day. For further information about scheduling programs via cron, refer to your systems man pages on "crontab." The command to see the man page (help page) for crontab would be to run man crontab from the Unix prompt.

Finally, here is an example script to check file system free space on your host and then e-mail you if there is less than 5 percent free space. You can edit this script for more or less free space by changing "$PERC –gt 95" to, for example, "$PERC –gt 90". This would alert you when the system has less than 10 percent free space. Note that this script is designed for Linux and will run unmodified on Solaris. To run it on HP, change the command "df –kl" to "df –kP."

```
#!/bin/sh
# script name: diskfreespace.sh
#
#
df -kl | grep -iv filesystem | awk '{ print $6" "$5}' | while read LINE; do
        PERC='echo $LINE | awk '{ print $2 }''
        if [ $PERC -gt 95 ]; then
           echo "'date' - ${LINE} space used on 'hostname' " | mailx -s "${LINE} on
'hostname' at ${CLIENT} is almost full" rich@tusc.com
        fi
        done
```

The df Command

One of the biggest and most frequent problems that systems have is running out of disk space, particularly in /tmp or /usr. There is no magic answer to the question "How much space should be allocated to these?" but a good rule of thumb is between 1500KB and 3000KB for /tmp and roughly twice that for /usr. Other file systems should have about 5 or 10 percent of the system's available capacity. The *df* command shows the free disk space on each disk that is mounted. The –k option displays the information about each file system in columns, with the allocations in KB.

```
% df -k
```

Filesystem	kbytes	used	avail	capacity	Mounted on
/dev/dsk/c0t0d0s0	38111	21173	13128	62%	/
/dev/dsk/c0t0d0s6	246167	171869	49688	78%	/usr
/proc	0	0	0	0%	/proc
fd	0	0	0	0%	/dev/fd
swap	860848	632	860216	0%	/tmp
/dev/dsk/c0t0d0s7	188247	90189	79238	53%	/home
/dev/dsk/c0t0d0s5	492351	179384	263737	40%	/opt
gs:/home/prog/met	77863	47127	22956	67%	/home/met

From this display you can see the following information (all entries are in KB):

Kbytes   Total size of usable space in file system (size is adjusted by allotted head room)

Used   Space used

Available	Space available for use
capacity	Percentage of total capacity used
mounted on	Mount point

The usable space has been adjusted to take into account a 10 percent reserve head room adjustment and thus reflects only 90 percent of the actual capacity. The percentage shown under capacity is therefore used space divided by the adjusted usable space.

Monitoring Network Performance

Occasionally, you will notice a performance drop that can only be attributed to network performance. You will know this because you will have tuned every other aspect of the system, and network problems are all that are left. I say this because network tuning can be very difficult with many variables. I usually consider it "tuning of last resort." That's not to say that the network settings "out of the box" cannot be improved upon for your environment—they can. But you will usually see a much larger percentage improvement by tuning your SQL statements than you will by tuning your TCP stack.

The settings that we will look at here are Solaris specific, but there are analogs in Linux, HP, and AIX. Any Unix-based system that communicates using the TCP protocol will use some or all of the settings in some way. Making any of these changes requires that you are the superuser, or "root." You can view them if you are not, but you cannot make any changes. Here's a simple Perl script to list /dev/tcp parameters and their current values:

```perl
#/!/usr/bin/perl
#get all tunable tcp parameters
use strict;
#get all of the possible parameters
my tcp= 'ndd /dev/tcp \?';
foreach (@tcp)
{
(my $parameter, my $junk)= split(/\(/, $_);
(my $parameter, my $junk2)= split(/ /, $parameter);
chomp ($junk);
chomp ($parameter);
#now disregard parameters that we cannot change
if ( $junk ne "read only)" && $junk ne "write only)" && parameter ne   \
"tcp_host_param" && $parameter ne "?")
{
(my $type, my $junk)=split(/_/, $parameter);
my $result = 'ndd /dev/tcp $parameter';
chomp ($result);
print "$parameter\t";
print "$result\n";
}
}
```

Now that you have a listing of your TCP settings, we can take a look at tuning some of them. First, you have to determine if anything actually needs to be tuned! The output of netstat –s will help you determine where your possible problems are. The normal output has been truncated to allow us to focus on certain areas.

```
TCP
        tcpRtoMax           = 60000     tcpMaxConn            =     -1
        tcpActiveOpens      =138398     tcpPassiveOpens       =157734
        tcpCurrEstab        =     96    tcpOutSegs            =761862710
        tcpOutDataSegs      =737025936  tcpOutDataBytes       =974079802
        tcpRetransSegs      = 56784     tcpRetransBytes       =16421938
        tcpOutAck           =24835587   tcpOutAckDelayed      =3487354
        tcpInInorderSegs    =95997710   tcpInInorderBytes     =3154946802
        tcpInUnorderSegs    = 54135     tcpInUnorderBytes     =3265601
        tcpListenDrop       =     11    tcpListenDropQ0       =     0
        tcpHalfOpenDrop     =      0    tcpOutSackRetrans     =   319
```

Here we see a relatively high muber of tcpActiveOpens and tcpPassiveOpens. I know that this number is high because I know that the system has only been up for 25 hours. Incoming calls are "'passive opens" and outgoing calls are "active opens." This would seem to indicate that there is a high amount of network traffic on this box. This is further reinforced by the size of tcpOutdataBytes. To determine if you are possibly reaching the maximum throughput on your network interface, the calculation is simple: TcpRetransBytes/tcpOutDataBytes=retransmission %.

If this number is greater than 10 percent, then you most likely have a serious throughput problem. You should almost definitely add more bandwidth or reduce the amount of traffic coming and going to the box. It is also important to remember that only a certain amount of traffic can go through a network card and only a certain number of users can be connected or establishing connections at one time. You can determine if you are having a problem with user connections by looking at tcpListenDrop. If you have a value greater than 0, that means that connections are being dropped and you need to increase the size of the listen queue. You can do that by increasing the parameter tcp_conn_req_max_q0. The default on Solaris is 1024. I usually recommend changing this to 10000 instead. Here's the command to make the change on a running system:

```
'ndd -set /dev/tcp /tcp_conn_req_max_q0 10000'
```

A simple way that you can drastically improve the efficiency of managing *active* TCP connections is to increase the tcp_connection_hash_size parameter. This will improve the efficiency of hash table lookups on your system quite a bit. Additional memory will be required to manage the increased size of the hash table, but if you are expecting many connections, it is well worth the cost. To make this point clearer, the system defaults to 512 and Sun engineers set this to 262144 when they are benchmarking their systems at times! There must quite a benefit if they change the default so drastically (but such a change should still be tested for your system)! Since this is a read-only parameter, it must be set in the /etc/system file and will require a system reboot.

Another interesting phenomenon is the "slow start" bug. This was intended to avoid congestion on the network by using a "delayed ACK." By using a delayed ACK, the application can piggyback its response onto the first response back to the server. This seems like a great idea, until . . . a sender request can't fit into a single packet. TCP will break the packet up before sending an ACK and send a partial packet. The receiver is waiting for the completion of the packet before sending any more data, which it will not do until it receives a full packet. But the "slow start" phase only allows *one* packet. The sender needs to send *more* than one packet. This deadlock eventually times out and the receiver will send the ACK that is needed to establish the connection. This problem doesn't normally show up, unless you have many short-lived connections that are experiencing this. For example, a web server may have serious performance problems due to this issue. On Solaris, as of 2.6, a parameter was added to bypass this problem. This is the tcp_slow_start_initial parameter. It defaults to 1, which is the normal behavior mentioned previously. I recommend that you consider changing this to either 2 or 4. It is important to note that as of Solaris 8, this changes to 4 for the default, so no action should be needed.

```
ndd -set /dev/tcp tcp_slow_start_initial 4
```

Several timers can be set to improve performance as well. The most important one, in my opinion, is the tcp_keep_alive_interval. This sets how long the system will wait to verify that a connection is still valid. On a web server, which can have many short-lived connections, this setting can be critical. This defaults to 7200000. On a busy web server, you want to clean up dead connection much faster than that.

```
ndd -set /dev/tcp tcp_keep_alive_interval 10000
```

Sometimes the output of netstat will show a lot of connections that are in "FIN_WAIT_2." This is a connection that is, essentially, "waiting to die." If an application does not close a connection actively or a browser crashes (that never happens!), a connections will end up in FIN_WAIT_2, using up resources that should be allocated to new connections. The default tcp_fin_wait_2_flush_interval is 675000. Ten percent of that seems to be a much more reasonable amount of time to wait before cleaning up the connections.

```
ndd -set /dev/tcp tcp_fin_wait_2_flush_interval 67500
```

TIP
Use the ndd and netstat to tune network performance issues.

Monitoring Using the spray Command

The *spray* command is a Unix command used to deliver a burst of data packets to another machine and report how many of the packets made the trip successfully and how long it took. Similar in scope to its little brother ping, spray can be used more effectively to monitor performance than ping because it can send more data. The results of the command, shown next, will let you know whether the other machine was able to successfully receive all of the packets you sent. In the example shown here, a burst of data packets is being sent from the source machine (pacland) to the destination machine (galaxian).

```
pacland % spray galaxian
sending 1162 packets of lnth 86 to galaxian ...
        no packets dropped by galaxian
5917 packets/sec, 508943 bytes/sec
```

In the preceding example, the destination machine (galaxian) successfully returned all of the data sent to it by the source machine (pacland). If galaxian were under heavy load, caused by either network traffic or other intense activity, some of the data packets would not have been returned by galaxian. The spray command defaults to sending 1162 86-byte packets. Spray supports several command-line parameters that you can use to modify the count of packets sent, the length of each packet, and the number of buffers to use on the source machine. These parameters can be helpful in running tests that are more realistic. The listing that follows shows the spray command used with the –c option, which delivers 1000 packets, and the –l option, which sets each packet to 4096 bytes.

```
pacland % spray -c 1000 -d 20 -l 4096 galaxian

sending 1000 packets of lnth 4096 to galaxian ...
        no packets dropped by galaxian
95 packets/sec, 392342 bytes/sec
```

Simulating network data transmissions with spray can be made more realistic by increasing the number of packets and the length of each packet. The –c option will let you increase the total count of packets that is sent, and the –l option lets you set the length of each packet. This can be helpful in mimicking certain transmission protocols. The –d option is used to set the delay between the transmission of each packet. This can be useful so that you do not overrun the network buffers on the source machine. The listing that follows shows what a problem might look like. In this case, the source machine (pacland) overwhelms the destination machine (millipede) with data. This does not immediately indicate that a networking problem exists, but that the destination machine (millipede) might not have enough available processing power to handle the network requests.

```
pacland % spray -l 4096 millipede

sending 1162 packets of lnth 4096 to millipede ...
        415 packets (35.714%) dropped by millipede
73 packets/sec, 6312 bytes/sec
```

In the event that your tests with spray result in packet loss, your next step would be to take a closer look at the destination machine you have been testing. First, look for a heavy process load, memory shortage, or other CPU problems. Anything on that system that might be bogging it down can cause degraded network performance. In the event that you cannot find anything wrong with your test system that might be causing a delayed network response, sending a similar test back to your initial test machine might indicate a larger network problem. At that point, it is time to start checking your routing hardware and your infrastructure with the analysis hardware. Here is an example of how to use netstat to monitor individual packet and error rates for each network interface.

```
pacland % netstat -i

Name Mtu   Network    Address       Ipkts      Ierrs   Opkts      Oerrs   Coll
ec3  1500  207.221.40 pacland       45223252   0       953351793  0       21402113
lo0  8304  loopback   localhost 2065169 0 2065169 0 0
```

The table that follows shows the values of the output from the netstat command.

Value	Data
Name	The name of the network interface (naming conventions vary among Unix versions)

Value	Data
MTU	The maximum packet size of the interface
Net/Dest	The network that the interface connects to
Address	The resolved Internet name of the interface
Ipkts	The number of incoming packets since the last time the system was rebooted
Ierrs	The number of incoming packet errors since the last time the system was rebooted
Opkts	The number of outgoing packets since the last time the system was rebooted
Oerrs	The number of outgoing packet errors since the last time the system was rebooted
Collis	The number of detected collisions

Monitoring Network Performance with nfsstat –c

Systems running NFS can skip spray and instead use nfsstat –c. The –c option specifies the client statistics, and –s can be used for server statistics. As the name implies, client statistics summarize this system's use of another machine as a server. The NFS service uses synchronous procedures called RPCs (remote procedure calls). This means that the client waits for the server to complete the file activity before it proceeds. If the server fails to respond, the client retransmits the request. Just as with collisions, the worse the condition of the communication, the more traffic that is generated. The more traffic that is generated, the slower the network and the greater the possibility of collisions. So if the retransmission rate is large, you should look for servers that are under heavy loads, high collision rates that are delaying the packets en route, or Ethernet interfaces that are dropping packets.

```
% nfsstat -c

Client rpc:
calls      badcalls retrans  badxid   timeout  wait     newcred  timers
74107      0        72       0        72       0        0        82

Client nfs:
calls      badcalls   nclget     nclcreate
73690      0          73690      0
null       getattr    setattr    root       lookup     readlink   read
0  0%      4881  7%    1  0%      0  0%      130  0%     0  0%      465  1%
wrcache    write      create     remove     rename     link       symlink
0  0%      68161 92%   16  0%     1  0%      0  0%      0  0%       0  0%
mkdir      rmdir      readdir    statfs
0  0%      0  0%       32  0%     3  0%
```

The following fields are shown here:

Calls	The number of calls sent
badcalls	The number of calls rejected by the RPC
retrans	The number of retransmissions
Badxid	The number of duplicated acknowledgments received
timeout	The number of time-outs
Wait	The number of times no available client handles caused waiting
newcred	The number of refreshed authentications
Timers	The number of times the time-out value is reached or exceeded
readlink	The number of reads made to a symbolic link

If the time-out ratio is high, the problem can be unresponsive NFS servers or slow networks that are impeding the timely delivery and response of the packets. In the example, there are relatively few time-outs compared to the number of calls (72/74107 or about 1/10 of 1 percent) that do retransmissions. As the percentage grows toward 5 percent, system administrators begin to take a closer look at it. If badxid is roughly the same as retrans, the problem is probably an NFS server that is falling behind in servicing NFS requests, since duplicate acknowledgments are being received for NFS requests in roughly the same numbers as the retransmissions that are required. The same thing is true if badxid is roughly the same as timeout. However, if badxid is a much smaller number than retrans and timeout, then it follows that the network is more likely to be the problem.

Monitoring Network Performance with netstat

One way to check for network loading is to use netstat without any parameters:

```
% netstat

TCP
    Local Address         Remote Address     Swind Send-Q Rwind Recv-Q  State
-------------------   -------------------   ----- ------ ----- ------  -------
AAA1.1023             bbb2.login             8760      0  8760      0 ESTABLISHED
AAA1.listen           Cccc.32980             8760      0  8760      0 ESTABLISHED
AAA1.login            Dddd.1019              8760      0  8760      0 ESTABLISHED
AAA1.32782            AAA1.32774            16384      0 16384      0 ESTABLISHED
...
```

In the report, the important field is the Send-Q field, which indicates the depth of the send queue for packets. If the numbers in Send-Q are large and increasing in size across several of the connections, the network is probably bogged down.

Corrective Network Actions

If you suspect that there are problems with the integrity of the network itself, you must try to determine where the faulty piece of equipment is. If the problem is that the network is extremely busy, thus increasing collisions, time-outs, retransmissions, and so on, you may need to redistribute the workload more appropriately. By partitioning and segmenting the network nodes into subnetworks that more clearly reflect the underlying workloads, you can maximize the overall performance of the network. This can be accomplished by installing additional network interfaces in your gateway and adjusting the addressing on the gateway to reflect the new subnetworks. Altering your cabling and implementing some of the more advanced intelligent hubs may be needed as well. By reorganizing your network, you will maximize the amount of bandwidth that is available for access to the local subnetwork. Make sure that systems that regularly perform NFS mounts of each other are on the same subnetwork.

If you have an older network and are having to rework your network topology, consider replacing the older coax-based networks with the more modern twisted-pair types, which are generally more reliable and flexible. Make sure that the workload is on the appropriate machine(s). Use the machine with the best network performance to do its proper share of network file service tasks. Check your network for diskless workstations. These require large amounts of network resources to boot up, swap, page, etc. With the cost of local storage descending constantly, it is getting harder to believe that diskless workstations are still cost-effective when compared to regular workstations. Consider upgrading the workstations so that they support their users locally, or at least minimize their use of the network.

If your network server has been acquiring more clients, check its memory and its kernel buffer allocations for proper sizing. If the problem is that I/O-intensive programs are being run over the network, work with the users to determine what can be done to make that requirement a local, rather than a network, one. Educate your users to make sure they understand when they are using the network appropriately and when they are being wasteful with this valuable resource.

Displaying Current Values of Tunable Parameters

To display a list of the current values assigned to the tunable kernel parameters, you can use the sysdef –i command:

```
% sysdef -i

... (portions of display are deleted for brevity)
*
* System Configuration
*
swapfile           dev  swaplo blocks    free
/dev/dsk/c0t3d0s1  32,25     8 547112   96936
*
* Tunable Parameters
*
 5316608   maximum memory allowed in buffer cache (bufhwm)
    4058   maximum number of processes (v.v_proc)
      99   maximum global priority in sys class (MAXCLSYSPRI)
    4053   maximum processes per user id (v.v_maxup)
      30   auto update time limit in seconds (NAUTOUP)
      25   page stealing low water mark (GPGSLO)
       5   fsflush run rate (FSFLUSHR)
      25   minimum resident memory for avoiding deadlock (MINARMEM)
      25   minimum swapable memory for avoiding deadlock (MINASMEM)
```

```
*
* Utsname Tunables
*

     5.3   release (REL)
    DDDD   node name (NODE)
   SunOS   system name (SYS)
Generic_101318-31  version (VER)
*
* Process Resource Limit Tunables (Current:Maximum)
*

Infinity:Infinity    cpu time
Infinity:Infinity    file size
7ffff000:7ffff000    heap size
  800000:7ffff000    stack size
Infinity:Infinity    core file size
      40:     400    file descriptors
Infinity:Infinity    mapped memory
*
* Streams Tunables
*

       9     maximum number of pushes allowed (NSTRPUSH)
   65536     maximum stream message size (STRMSGSZ)
    1024     max size of ctl part of message (STRCTLSZ)
*
* IPC Messages
*

     200     entries in msg map (MSGMAP)
    2048     max message size (MSGMAX)
   65535     max bytes on queue (MSGMNB)
      25     message queue identifiers (MSGMNI)
     128     message segment size (MSGSSZ)
     400     system message headers (MSGTQL)
    1024     message segments (MSGSEG)
     SYS     system class name (SYS_NAME)
```

As stated earlier, over the years many enhancements have been tried to minimize the complexity of the kernel configuration process. As a result, many of the tables that were once allocated in a fixed manner are now allocated dynamically, or else linked to the value of the maxusers field. The next step in understanding the nature of kernel tables is to look at the maxusers parameter and its impact on Unix system configuration.

Modifying the Configuration Information File

SunOS uses the /etc/system file for modification of kernel-tunable variables. The basic format is this:

```
set parameter = value
```

It can also have this format:

```
set [module:]variablename = value
```

The /etc/system file can also be used for other purposes (for example, to force modules to be loaded at boot time, to specify a root device, and so on). The /etc/system file is used for permanent changes to the operating system values. Temporary changes can be made using adb kernel debugging tools. The system must be rebooted for the changes to become active using /etc/system. Once you have made your changes to this file, you can recompile to make a new Unix kernel. The command is mkkernel –s system. This new kernel, called vmunix.test, is placed in the /stand/build directory. Next, you move the present stand/system file to /stand/system.prev; then you can move the modified file /stand/build/system to /stand/system. Then you move the currently running kernel /stand/vmunix to /stand/vmunix.prev, and then move the new kernel, /stand/build/vmunix.test, into place in /stand/vmunix (i.e., mv /stand/build/vmunix.test /stand/vmunix). The final step is to reboot the machine to make your changes take effect.

Other Factors That Affect Performance

Good performance is difficult to define. There are two common but different and not necessarily equivalent measures used for performance. Response time is the time between the instant the user hits the ENTER key and the time the system provides a response. Throughput is the number of transactions accomplished in a fixed period of time. Of the two measures throughput is the better measure of how much work is actually getting accomplished. Response time is more visible and therefore used more frequently; it is a better measurement for meeting business objectives of the system. Some people don't look at everything when tuning. Remember to check

- **All hardware**   Are the CPUs fast enough and are there enough of them? How much memory is there; is it enough?

- **Operating system and application software**   Is the system configured correctly for the current environment?

- **People**   Are people trained sufficiently on the system and applications to optimize their productivity?

- **Changes**   What changes in workload and user requirements can be expected to occur?

A resource is a bottleneck if the size of a request exceeds the available resource. A bottleneck is a limitation of system performance due to the inadequacy of the hardware or software component or the system's organization.

Tuning a CPU-Bound System

- Upgrade to faster or more processors.

- Upgrade the system with a larger data/instruction cache.

- Spread applications across multiple systems.

- Run long batch jobs during off-peak hours whenever possible.

- Use the nice command (changes the priority of a process) for unimportant applications.

- Lock frequently used processes in memory.

- Turn off system accounting.

- Optimize the applications.

Tuning Memory-Bound Systems

- Add physical memory.
- Use diskless workstations rather than X-Terms.
- Reduce maxdsiz.
- Reduce the use of memory locking.
- Identify programs with memory leaks.
- Tune the applications.
- Reduce the size of the kernel drivers and subsystems.
- Reduce the size of the buffer cache.

Disk Tuning

- Add disk drives.
- Add disk channels.
- Use faster disks.
- Use striping.
- Use mirroring.
- Balance I/O across multiple spindles.
- Dedicate a disk section to an application.
- Use raw disk I/O.
- Increase the system buffer cache.
- Increase the kernel table sizes.
- Use the tunefs command.

Volume Manager Factors That Can Affect Performance

- File system parameters
- Fragmentation
- Mirroring
- Scheduling
- Spindles
- Strictness
- Striping
- Workload
- Work type

Other Factors That Affect Performance

Tips Review

- Use the sar –u command to see a quick snapshot of how the much the CPU is "bogged down."

- Use the top command to find the worst user on the system at a given point in time.

- Use cron and uptime to get your system load mailed to you on a regular basis.

- If the smtx column for the mpstat output is greater than 200, you are heading toward CPU bottleneck problems.

- Combine operating system utilities with Oracle V$ views.

- The sar and iostat commands can be used to find potential disk I/O problem areas. These commands are further enhanced by utilizing the capabilities of shell scripting.

- Paging is generally the movement of inactive processes from memory to disk. A high degree of paging is usually the predecessor to swapping. Swapping is the movement of active processes from memory to disk. If swapping starts to escalate, your system begins the downward "death spiral." Fixing memory hogs or adding memory is the correct solution.

- Use the ipcs command to see if your SGA is built using multiple noncontiguous pieces of memory. A crash of your database can render this to be a problem with releasing the memory.

- Use the ipcrm command (only if the SGA pieces are not released after a database crash) to then remove the SGA pieces from memory. Do *not* issue the ipcrm command with a running database.

- Use the vmstat command to find blocked processes (users waiting for CPU time) and also for paging or swapping problems. The vmstat command is a great way to see many of the sar options in one screen.

- Use the ndd and netstat commands to tune network performance issues. Use spray to simulate network traffic.

References

Mark Gurry & Peter Corrigan, *Oracle Performance Tuning* (O'Reilly, 2001)
Adrian Cockcroft, *Sun Performance and Tuning* (Sun Microsystems Press, 1998)
Andy Johnston and Robin Anderson, *UNIX Unleashed, System Administrator's Edition* (Sams, 2001)
Performance and Tuning (Hewlett-Packard)

Many thanks to Mike Gallagher, who updated this chapter and added a lot of new information, and also to Judy Corley and Jon Vincenzo, who updated the last version that we built upon.

APPENDIX A

Key Initialization Parameters (DBA)

There are 257 different documented and 1124 different undocumented initialization (init.ora/spfile.ora) parameters in Oracle 10g Release 2 (10gR2). This means there are a total of 1381 initialization parameters to play with; you can do a count(*) of x$ksppi for the total number of parameters both documented and undocumented (you need to be SYS to access the x$ tables). A count of V$PARAMETER will give you a count of only the documented parameters. When I refer to the undocumented parameters, I am referring to parameters that start with an underscore (_), although some of them are actually even documented. There are also several of the parameters that I call documented (no "_" in front of them, but they are not really documented, only externalized or available for use, usually for backward compatibility). Even these numbers vary slightly on different versions of Oracle and platforms. The initialization parameters vary (in both name and number) according to the database version and release used. Run the queries listed at the end of this appendix (accessing the V$PARAMETER view and the x$ksppi table) on your version of the database to get the number of parameters and details for your specific version. Tips covered in this chapter:

- Desupported and deprecated initialization parameters

- Top 25 documented initialization parameters with descriptions and suggested settings

- Top 10 documented initialization parameters that you better not forget (option dependent)

- Top 13 undocumented initialization parameters (Shhh!)

- Complete list of documented initialization parameters (there are 257 in 10gR2)

- Query for undocumented initialization parameters (there are 1124 in 10gR2)

Since every system is set up differently, my top 25 may not be the same as your top 25 (so feel free to write in this book as if it were yours). Hopefully, this will give you a place to start until someone writes the 1000-page book on *all* of the initialization parameters. Please refer to Chapter 4 for a detailed look at the most important initialization parameters.

Desupported Initialization Parameters

These are Oracle 10gR2 desupported initialization parameters. This means that these are gone, although they sometimes become undocumented parameters, which means that they have an underscore (_) in front of them (these I note in parentheses as of 10.2.0.1).

- ENQUEUE_RESOURCES (undocumented in 10gR2)

- DBLINK_ENCRYPT_LOGIN

- HASH_JOIN_ENABLED (undocumented parameter)

- LOG_PARALLELISM (undocumented parameter)

- MAX_ROLLBACK_SEGMENTS

- MTS_CIRCUITS (this is replaced by CIRCUITS)

- MTS_DISPATCHERS (this is replaced by DISPATCHERS)

- MTS_LISTENER_ADDRESS

- MTS_MAX_DISPATCHERS (this is replaced by MAX_DISPATCHERS)

- MTS_MAX_SERVERS (this is replaced by MAX_SHARED_SERVERS)

- MTS_MULTIPLE_LISTENERS

- MTS_SERVERS (this is replaced by SHARED_SERVERS)

- MTS_SERVICE

- MTS_SESSIONS (this is replaced by SHARED_SERVER_SESSIONS)

- OPTIMIZER_MAX_PERMUTATIONS (undocumented parameter)

- ORACLE_TRACE_COLLECTION_NAME

- ORACLE_TRACE_COLLECTION_PATH

- ORACLE_TRACE_COLLECTION_SIZE

- ORACLE_TRACE_ENABLE

- ORACLE_TRACE_FACILITY_NAME

- ORACLE_TRACE_FACILITY_PATH

- PARTITION_VIEW_ENABLED (undocumented parameter)

- PLSQL_NATIVE_C_COMPILER

- PLSQL_NATIVE_LINKER

- PLSQL_NATIVE_MAKE_FILE_NAME

- PLSQL_NATIVE_MAKE_UTILITY

- ROW_LOCKING (undocumented parameter)

- SERIALIZABLE (undocumented parameter)

- TRANSACTION_AUDITING (undocumented parameter)

- UNDO_SUPPRESS_ERRORS

Deprecated Initialization Parameters

The following are Oracle 10gR2 deprecated initialization parameters. This means that you can use them for backward compatibility, but they are probably going away in the future.

- LOGMNR_MAX_PERSISTENT_SESSIONS (Oracle Streams uses it)

- MAX_COMMIT_PROPAGATION_DELAY

- REMOTE_ARCHIVE_ENABLE

- SERIAL_REUSE

- SQL_TRACE

- BUFFER_POOL_KEEP [replaced by DB_KEEP_CACHE_SIZE]

Initialization Parameters

- BUFFER_POOL_RECYCLE [replaced by DB_RECYCLE_CACHE_SIZE]

- GLOBAL_CONTEXT_POOL_SIZE

- LOCK_NAME_SPACE

- LOG_ARCHIVE_START

- MAX_ENABLED_ROLES

- PARALLEL_AUTOMATIC_TUNING

- PLSQL_COMPILER_FLAGS [replaced by PLSQL_CODE_TYPE and PLSQL_DEBUG]

Top 25 Initialization Parameters

The following list is *my* list of the top 25 most important initialization parameters, in order of importance. Your top 25 may vary somewhat from my top 25, since everyone has a unique business, applications, and experiences.

1. DB_CACHE_SIZE   Initial memory allocated to data cache or memory used for data itself.

2. SGA_TARGET   If you use Oracle's Automatic Shared Memory Management, this parameter is used to automatically determine the size of your data cache, shared pool, large pool, and Java pool (see Chapter 1 for more information). Setting this to 0 disables it.

3. PGA_AGGREGATE_TARGET   Soft memory cap for total of all users' PGAs.

4. SHARED_POOL_SIZE   Memory allocated for data dictionary and for SQL and PL/SQL.

5. SGA_MAX_SIZE   Maximum memory that the SGA can dynamically grow to.

6. OPTIMIZER_MODE   CHOOSE, RULE, FIRST_ROWS, FIRST_ROWS_*n,* or ALL_ROWS. Although RULE is definitely desupported and obsolete and people are often scolded for even talking about it, I was able to set the mode to RULE in 10g. Consider the following error I received when I set OPTIMIZER_MODE to a mode that doesn't exist (SUPER_FAST):

```
SQL> alter system set optimizer_mode=super_fast

ERROR:
ORA-00096: invalid value SUPER_FAST for parameter optimizer_mode, must be from
among first_rows_1000, first_rows_100, first_rows_10, first_rows_1, first_rows,
all_rows, choose, rule
```

7. CURSOR_SHARING   Converts literal SQL to SQL with bind variables, reducing parse overhead.

8. OPTIMIZER_INDEX_COST_ADJ   Coarse adjustment between the cost of an index scan and the cost of a full table scan. Set between 1 and 10 to force index use more frequently. Setting this parameter to a value between 1 and 10 would pretty much guarantee index use, even when not appropriate, so be careful, since it is highly dependent on the index design and implementation being correct. Please note that if you are using Applications 11*i*: Setting OPTIMIZER_INDEX_COST_ADJ to any value other than the default (100) is not supported (see Metalink Note 169935.1). Also, see bug 4483286.

9. QUERY_REWRITE_ENABLED   Used to enable Materialized View and Function-Based-Index capabilities and other features in some versions.

10. DB_FILE_MULTIBLOCK_READ_COUNT   For full table scans to perform I/O more efficiently, this reads the given number of blocks in a single I/O.

11. LOG_BUFFER   Buffer for uncommitted transactions in memory (set in pfile).

12. DB_KEEP_CACHE_SIZE   Memory allocated to keep pool or an additional data cache that you can set up outside the buffer cache for very important data that you don't want pushed out of the cache.

13. DB_RECYCLE_CACHE_SIZE   Memory allocated to recycle pool or an additional data cache that you can set up outside the buffer cache and in addition to the keep cache described in Item 12. Usually, DBAs set this up for ad hoc user query data that has queries that are poorly written.

14. DBWR_IO_SLAVES (also DB_WRITER_PROCESSES if you have async I/O)   Number of writers from SGA to disk for simulated async I/O. If you have async I/O, then you use DB_WRITER_PROCESSES to set up multiple writers to more quickly write out dirty blocks during a database write (DBWR).

15. LARGE_POOL_SIZE   Total blocks in the large pool allocation for large PL/SQL and a few other Oracle options less frequently used.

16. STATISTICS_LEVEL   Used to enable advisory information and optionally keep additional O/S statistics to refine optimizer decisions. TYPICAL is the default.

17. JAVA_POOL_SIZE   Memory allocated to the JVM for JAVA stored procedures.

18. JAVA_MAX_SESSIONSPACE_SIZE   Upper limit on memory that is used to keep track of user session state of JAVA classes.

19. MAX_SHARED_SERVERS   Upper limit on shared servers when using shared servers.

20. WORKAREA_SIZE_POLICY   Used to enable automatic PGA size management.

21. FAST_START_MTTR_TARGET   Bounds time to complete a crash recovery. This is the time (in seconds) that the database will take to perform crash recovery of a single instance. If you set this parameter, LOG_CHECKPOINT_INTERVAL should *not* be set to 0. If you don't set this parameter, you can still see your estimated MTTR (mean time to recovery) by querying V$INSTANCE_RECOVERY for ESTIMATED_MTTR.

22. LOG_CHECKPOINT_INTERVAL   Checkpoint frequency (in OS blocks—most OS blocks are 512 bytes) at which Oracle performs a database write of all dirty (modified) blocks to the datafiles in the database. Oracle will also perform a checkpoint if more than one-quarter of the data buffers are dirty in the db cache and also on any log switch. The LGWR (log writer) also updates the SCN in the control files and datafiles with the SCN of the checkpoint.

23. OPEN_CURSORS   Specifies the size of the private area used to hold (open) user statements. If you get "ORA-01000: maximum open cursors exceeded," you may need to increase this parameter, but make sure you are *closing* cursors that you no longer need. Prior to 9.2.0.5, these open cursors were also cached and at times caused issues

(ORA-4031) if OPEN_CURSORS was set too high. In 9.2.05, SESSION_CACHED_CURSORS now controls the setting of the PL/SQL cursor cache. Do *not* set the parameter SESSION_CACHED_CURSORS as high as you set OPEN_CURSORS, or you may experience ORA-4031 or ORA-7445 errors.

24. **DB_BLOCK_SIZE**   Default block size for the database. A smaller block size will reduce contention by adjacent rows, but a larger block size will lower the number of I/Os needed to pull back more records. A larger block size will also help in range scans where the blocks desired are sequentially stored.

25. **OPTIMIZER_DYNAMIC_SAMPLING**   Controls the number of blocks read by the dynamic sampling query. Very useful with systems that are using Global Temporary Tables.

TIP
Setting certain initialization parameters correctly could be the difference between a report taking two seconds and two hours. Test changes on a test system thoroughly before implementing those changes in a production environment.

Top 10 Initialization Parameters Not to Forget

This section details some other important initialization parameters. On the other hand, these parameters may be important only in certain cases or only if you are using a certain feature or version of Oracle:

- CONTROL_FILES   This is the location of your control files.

- COMPATIBLE   Set this to the correct version, or you'll miss things in the new version.

- OPTIMIZER_FEATURES_ENABLE   If this is not set, you are missing out on new features.

- UNDO_MANAGEMENT   Set this to AUTO for automatic UNDO management.

- UNDO_TABLESPACE   Set this to the tablespace to use for UNDO management.

- UNDO_RETENTION   The undo retention time in seconds.

- JOB_QUEUE_PROCESSES   If you want to use DBMS_JOB, you must set this parameter. Note that DBMS_JOB has been replaced by the Scheduler in 10g, but it uses the same parameter.

- UTL_FILE_DIR   This must be set to use the UTL_FILE package.

- RECOVERY_PARALLELISM   Recover using the Parallel Query Option, a faster recovery.

- LICENSE_MAX_SESSIONS and LICENSE_MAX_USERS   These limit concurrent and named users.

- LICENSE_SESSIONS_WARNING   Here, you specify at which session+1 you get a license warning.

TIP
There are some excellent options within Oracle. Unfortunately, some of them do not work unless you have the initialization parameter set correctly.

Top 13 Undocumented Initialization Parameters (As I See It)

The following list is *my* list of the top 13 undocumented initialization parameters, in order of importance. Your top 13 may vary somewhat, depending on your need for one of these parameters. While the following warning describes well the risks associated with using these parameters, I will note that the fastest RAC TPC (Transaction Processing Council) benchmark uses 17 undocumented parameters, as do many of the TPC benchmarks that I've seen.

CAUTION
These 13 parameters are not supported by Oracle, nor do I recommend them on a production system. Use them only if directed by Oracle Support and you have thoroughly tested them on your crash-and-burn system (and your closest friend has been using them for years). Undocumented initialization parameters can lead to database corruption (although some of them can get your database back up when you have corruption).

1. _ALLOW_RESETLOGS_CORRUPTION This saves you when you have corrupted redo logs. It allows the database to open with the datafiles at different SCN synchronization levels. This means some datafiles may contain changes that other datafiles do not (like the RBS or UNDO tablespace). This parameter may allow you to get to your data, but there is no easy way to determine if the data that is available after using these parameters is logically consistent. Regardless of data consistency, the DBA will have to rebuild the database afterward. Failure to do so results in multiple ORA-600s occurring within the database at a later time.

2. _CORRUPTED_ROLLBACK_SEGMENTS This can be a means of last resort when you have corrupted rollback segments that you can list with this parameter to skip. The _CORRUPTED_ROLLBACK_SEGMENTS parameter can force the database open after a failed recovery, but at a very high cost. _CORRUPTED_ROLLBACK_SEGMENTS allows the database to open by assuming every transaction in the rollback segments is a complete, committed transaction. This leads to logical corruption throughout the database and can easily corrupt the data dictionary. An example would be where you transfer money from one bank to another. The transaction would only be complete if you can verify that all parts of it are complete. In Oracle, when creating a table, think of all the individual dictionary objects that are updated: fet$, uet$, tab$, ind$, col$, etc. By setting this parameter, you allow the table creation to succeed, even if only fet$ was updated, but not uet$, or tab$ was updated, but not col$. Use it when there is no other means of recovery and export/import/rebuild soon after.

CAUTION
These first two parameters do not always work or may corrupt the database so badly that an export cannot be taken once the database is open. If they are used and do not work, then there is nothing support can do to salvage the database if the DBA breaks down and calls support, but there are things that can be done before using these parameters that will allow other recovery methods to be used afterward. So, if you must use these parameters, please ensure that you use them with the help of Oracle Support. One good reason to use Oracle Support in this effort is the fact that the _ALLOW_RESETLOGS_ CORRUPTION parameter is problematic, often requiring an event to be set as well, in order to get the database open.

3. _HASH_JOIN_ENABLED   Enables/disables hash joining if you have the memory needed.

4. _INIT_SQL_FILE (where the SQL.BSQ file is)   File that executes upon database creation.

5. _TRACE_FILES_PUBLIC   This allows users to see the trace output without giving them major privileges elsewhere.

6. _FAST_FULL_SCAN_ENABLED   This allows index fast full scans if only the index is needed.

7. _KSMG_GRANULE_SIZE   This is the multiple for SGA pieces of memory such as SHARED_POOL_SIZE and DB_CACHE_SIZE.

8. _HASH_MULTIBLOCK_IO_COUNT   Number of blocks that a hash join will read/write at once.

9. _INDEX_JOIN_ENABLED   Used to enable/disable the use of index joins.

10. _OPTIMIZER_ADJUST_FOR_NULLS   Adjust selectivity for null values.

11. _TRACE_FILE_SIZE   Maximum size of trace file (default is 65536).

12. _TRACE_EVENTS   Trace events enabled at startup.

13. _UNNEST_SUBQUERY   Unnesting of correlated subquery.

TIP
Undocumented initialization parameters can corrupt your database! Some of them can help you salvage a corrupted database. Try to use these only when all other choices have failed and with the help of Oracle Support.

Four additional initialization parameters used for latch contention are

- _KGL_LATCH_COUNT   Number of library cache latches (set this to the next prime number higher than 2*CPU). Setting this parameter too high (>66) will cause ORA-600 errors (Bug 1381824).

- _LOG_SIMULTANEOUS_COPIES   The number of redo copy latches (or simultaneous copies allowed into the redo log buffer). Redo records are written to the redo log buffer requiring the redo copy latch when changes are made. This can be used to reduce the contention on multi-CPU systems.

■ _DB_BLOCK_HASH_BUCKETS   Must be prime (set to next prime number higher than 2 * Cache buffers) in version 9*i* and 10*g* (look for an algorithm change in 11*g*). This should not be a problem or need to be set in 10*g*.

■ _SPIN_COUNT   How often the processor will take a new request (reduce CPU time-outs). This determines how many times a process will try to get a latch until it goes to sleep (when it is a willing-to-wait latch). Many processes spinning to get a latch can cost a lot of CPU, so be careful if you increase this value. In Oracle 7, this parameter was called the _LATCH_SPIN_COUNT.

The hidden parameters are used mainly by the development group at Oracle. The implementation of hidden parameters can change from release to release, even when you only applied a patch to your database. Because they are not documented and not supported, they may not work as you expect, or as is described here. For a query that will give you a complete listing of all undocumented parameters, their default values, and descriptions, see the section "Listing of Undocumented Initialization Parameters (x$ksppi/x$ksppcv)" later in this appendix.

Listing of Documented Initialization Parameters (V$PARAMETER)

The following query will retrieve the listing that follows on 10*g*R2 (257 rows returned). This particular query was run on 10.2.0.1.

```
Col name format a25
Col value for a10
Col ismodified for a5
Col description for a35
select     name, value, ismodified,  description
from       v$parameter
order by   name;
```

The following table contains the output for this query and includes the parameter names, values, whether the parameter can be modified, and a brief description.

Parameter Name	Value	Is Modified	Description
O7_DICTIONARY_ACCESSIBILITY	FALSE	FALSE	Version 7 Dictionary Accessibility Support
active_instance_count		FALSE	Number of active instances in the cluster database
aq_tm_processes	0	FALSE	Number of AQ Time Managers to start
Archive_lag_target	0	FALSE	Maximum number of seconds of redos the standby could lose
asm_diskgroups		FALSE	Disk groups to mount automatically

Parameter Name	Value	Is Modified	Description
asm_diskstring		FALSE	Disk set locations for discovery
asm_power_limit	1	FALSE	Number of processes for disk rebalancing
audit_file_dest	F:\...ORCL\ADUMP	FALSE	Directory in which auditing files are to reside
audit_sys_operations	FALSE	FALSE	Enable sys auditing
audit_trail	NONE	FALSE	Enable system auditing
background_core_dump	partial	FALSE	Core size for background processes
background_dump_dest	F:\...\ORCL\BDUMP	FALSE	Detached process dump directory
backup_tape_io_slaves	FALSE	FALSE	BACKUP tape I/O slaves
bitmap_merge_area_size	1048576	FALSE	Maximum memory allow for BITMAP MERGE
blank_trimming	FALSE	FALSE	Blank trimming semantics parameter
buffer_pool_keep		FALSE	Number of database blocks/latches in keep buffer pool
buffer_pool_recycle		FALSE	Number of database blocks/latches in recycle buffer pool
circuits		FALSE	Max number of circuits
cluster_database	FALSE	FALSE	If TRUE startup in cluster database mode
cluster_database_instances	1	FALSE	Number of instances to use for sizing cluster DB SGA structures
cluster_interconnects		FALSE	Interconnects for RAC use
commit_point_strength	1	FALSE	Bias this node has toward not preparing in a two-phase commit
commit_write		FALSE	Transaction commit log write behavior
compatible	10.2.0.1.0	FALSE	Database will be completely compatible with this software version
control_file_record_keep_time	7	FALSE	Control file record keep time in days
control_files	F:\... ORCL\CONTROL01.CTL,...	FALSE	Control file names list
core_dump_dest	F:\...\ORCL\CDUMP	FALSE	Core dump directory
cpu_count	1	FALSE	Number of CPUs for this instance

Parameter Name	Value	Is Modified	Description
create_bitmap_area_size	8388608	FALSE	Size of create bitmap buffer for bitmap index
create_stored_outlines		FALSE	Create stored outlines for DML statements
cursor_sharing	EXACT	FALSE	Cursor sharing mode
cursor_space_for_time	FALSE	FALSE	Use more memory in order to get faster execution
db_16k_cache_size	0	FALSE	Size of cache for 16K buffers
db_2k_cache_size	0	FALSE	Size of cache for 2K buffers
db_32k_cache_size	0	FALSE	Size of cache for 32K buffers
db_4k_cache_size	0	FALSE	Size of cache for 4K buffers
db_8k_cache_size	0	FALSE	Size of cache for 8K buffers
db_block_buffers	0	FALSE	Number of database blocks cached in memory
db_block_checking	FALSE	FALSE	Header checking and data and index block checking
db_block_checksum	TRUE	FALSE	Store checksum in DB blocks and check during reads
db_block_size	8192	FALSE	Size of database block in bytes
db_cache_advice	ON	FALSE	Buffer cache sizing advisory
db_cache_size	0	FALSE	Size of DEFAULT buffer pool for standard block size buffers
db_create_file_dest		FALSE	Default database location
db_create_online_log_dest _1		FALSE	Online log/controlfile destination #1
db_create_online_log_dest _2		FALSE	Online log/controlfile destination #2
db_create_online_log_dest _3		FALSE	Online log/controlfile destination #3
db_create_online_log_dest _4		FALSE	Online log/controlfile destination #4
db_create_online_log_dest _5		FALSE	Online log/controlfile destination #5
db_domain		FALSE	Directory part of global database name stored with CREATE DATABASE
db_file_multiblock_read_count	16	FALSE	DB block to be read each I/O
db_file_name_convert		FALSE	Datafile name convert patterns and strings for standby/clone db
db_files	200	FALSE	Max allowable # db files

Initialization Parameters

Parameter Name	Value	Is Modified	Description
db_flashback_retention_target	1440	FALSE	Maximum flashback database log retention time in minutes
db_keep_cache_size	0	FALSE	Size of KEEP buffer pool for standard block size buffers
db_name	orcl	FALSE	Database name specified in CREATE DATABASE
db_recovery_file_dest	F:\...flash _recovery_ area	FALSE	Default database recovery file location
db_recovery_file_dest_size	2147483648	FALSE	Database recovery files size limit
db_recycle_cache_size	0	FALSE	Size of RECYCLE buffer pool for standard block size buffers
db_unique_name	orcl	FALSE	Database Unique Name
db_writer_processes	1	FALSE	Number of background database writer processes to start
dbwr_io_slaves	0	FALSE	DBWR I/O slaves
ddl_wait_for_locks	FALSE	FALSE	Disable NOWAIT DML lock acquisitions
dg_broker_config_file1	F:\...\DR1ORCL.DAT	FALSE	Data guard broker configuration file #1
dg_broker_config_file2	F:\...\DR2ORCL.DAT	FALSE	Data guard broker configuration file #2
dg_broker_start	FALSE	FALSE	Start Data Guard broker framework (DMON process)
disk_asynch_io	TRUE	FALSE	Use asynch I/O for random access devices
dispatchers	(PROTOCOL= TCP) (SERV ICE=orclXD B)	FALSE	Specifications of dispatchers
distributed_lock_timeout	60	FALSE	Number of seconds a distributed transaction waits for a lock
dml_locks	748	FALSE	DML locks—one for each table modified in a transaction
drs_start	FALSE	FALSE	Start DG Broker monitor (DMON process)
event		FALSE	Debug event control—default null string
fal_client		FALSE	FAL client
fal_server		FALSE	FAL server list
fast_start_io_target	0	FALSE	Upper bound on recovery reads

Parameter Name	Value	Is Modified	Description
fast_start_mttr_target	0	FALSE	MTTR target of forward crash recovery in seconds
fast_start_parallel_rollback	LOW	FALSE	Max number of parallel recovery slaves that may be used
file_mapping	FALSE	FALSE	Enable file mapping
fileio_network_adapters		FALSE	Network adapters for file I/O
filesystemio_options		FALSE	I/O operations on file system files
fixed_date		FALSE	Fixed SYSDATE value
gc_files_to_locks		FALSE	Mapping between file numbers and global cache locks
gcs_server_processes	0	FALSE	Number of background GCS server processes to start
global_context_pool_size		FALSE	Global application context pool size in bytes
global_names	FALSE	FALSE	Enforce that database links have same name as remote database
hash_area_size	131072	FALSE	Size of in-memory hash work area
hi_shared_memory_address	0	FALSE	SGA starting address (high-order 32 bits on 64-bit platforms)
hs_autoregister	TRUE	FALSE	Enable automatic server DD updates in HS agent self-registration
ifile		FALSE	Include file in init.ora
instance_groups		FALSE	List of instance group names
instance_name	orcl	FALSE	Instance name supported by the instance
instance_number	0	FALSE	Instance number
instance_type	RDBMS	FALSE	Type of instance to be executed
java_max_sessionspace_size	0	FALSE	Max allowed size in bytes of a Java session space
java_pool_size	0	FALSE	Size in bytes of java pool
java_soft_sessionspace_limit	0	FALSE	Warning limit on size in bytes of a Java session space
job_queue_processes	10	FALSE	Number of job queue slave processes
large_pool_size	0	FALSE	Size in bytes of large pool
ldap_directory_access	NONE	FALSE	RDBMS's LDAP access option

Parameter Name	Value	Is Modified	Description
license_max_sessions	0	FALSE	Maximum number of non-system user sessions allowed
license_max_users	0	FALSE	Maximum number of named users that can be created in the database
license_sessions_warning	0	FALSE	Warning level for number of non-system user sessions
local_listener		FALSE	Local listener
lock_name_space		FALSE	Lock name space used for generating lock names for standby/clone database
lock_sga	FALSE	FALSE	Lock entire SGA in physical memory
log_archive_config		FALSE	Log archive config parameter
log_archive_dest		FALSE	Archival destination text string
log_archive_dest_1		FALSE	Archival destination #1 text string
log_archive_dest_10		FALSE	Archival destination #10 text string
log_archive_dest_2		FALSE	Archival destination #2 text string
log_archive_dest_3		FALSE	Archival destination #3 text string
log_archive_dest_4		FALSE	Archival destination #4 text string
log_archive_dest_5		FALSE	Archival destination #5 text string
log_archive_dest_6		FALSE	Archival destination #6 text string
log_archive_dest_7		FALSE	Archival destination #7 text string
log_archive_dest_8		FALSE	Archival destination #8 text string
log_archive_dest_9		FALSE	Archival destination #9 text string
log_archive_dest_state_1	enable	FALSE	Archival destination #1 state text string
log_archive_dest_state_10	enable	FALSE	Archival destination #10 state text string
log_archive_dest_state_2	enable	FALSE	Archival destination #2 state text string
log_archive_dest_state_3	enable	FALSE	Archival destination #3 state text string

Parameter Name	Value	Is Modified	Description
log_archive_dest_state_4	enable	FALSE	Archival destination #4 state text string
log_archive_dest_state_5	enable	FALSE	Archival destination #5 state text string
log_archive_dest_state_6	enable	FALSE	Archival destination #6 state text string
log_archive_dest_state_7	enable	FALSE	Archival destination #7 state text string
log_archive_dest_state_8	enable	FALSE	Archival destination #8 state text string
log_archive_dest_state_9	enable	FALSE	Archival destination #9 state text string
log_archive_duplex_dest		FALSE	Duplex archival destination text string
log_archive_format	ARC%S_%R.% T	FALSE	Archival destination format
log_archive_local_first	TRUE	FALSE	Establish EXPEDITE attribute default value
log_archive_max_processes	2	FALSE	Maximum number of active ARCH processes
log_archive_min_succeed_dest	1	FALSE	Minimum number of archive destinations that must succeed
log_archive_start	FALSE	FALSE	Start archival process on SGA initialization
log_archive_trace	0	FALSE	Establish archive log operation tracing level
log_buffer	2899456	FALSE	Redo circular buffer size
log_checkpoint_interval	0	FALSE	# redo blocks checkpoint threshold
log_checkpoint_timeout	1800	FALSE	Maximum time interval between check points in seconds
log_checkpoints_to_alert	FALSE	FALSE	Log checkpoint begin/end to alert file
log_file_name_convert		FALSE	Log file name convert patterns and strings for standby/clone DB
logmnr_max_persistent_sessions	1	FALSE	Maximum number of threads to mine
max_commit_propagation_delay	0	FALSE	Max age of new snapshot in 0.01 seconds
max_dispatchers		FALSE	Max number of dispatchers
max_dump_file_size	UNLIMITED	FALSE	Maximum size (blocks) of dump file
max_enabled_roles	150	FALSE	Max number of roles a user can have enabled

Initialization Parameters

Parameter Name	Value	Is Modified	Description
max_shared_servers		FALSE	Max number of shared servers
nls_calendar		FALSE	NLS calendar system name
nls_comp		FALSE	NLS comparison
nls_currency		FALSE	NLS local currency symbol
nls_date_format		FALSE	NLS Oracle date format
nls_date_language		FALSE	NLS date language name
nls_dual_currency		FALSE	Dual currency symbol
nls_iso_currency		FALSE	NLS ISO currency territory name
nls_language	AMERICAN	FALSE	NLS language name
nls_length_semantics	BYTE	FALSE	Create columns using byte or char semantics by default
nls_nchar_conv_excp	FALSE	FALSE	NLS, raise an exception instead of allowing implicit conversion
nls_numeric_characters		FALSE	NLS numeric characters
nls_sort		FALSE	NLS linguistic definition name
nls_territory	AMERICA	FALSE	NLS territory name
nls_time_format		FALSE	Time format
nls_time_tz_format		FALSE	Time with time zone format
nls_timestamp_format		FALSE	Time stamp format
nls_timestamp_tz_format		FALSE	Time stamp with time zone format
object_cache_max_size_percent	10	FALSE	Percentage of maximum size over optimal of the user session's object cache
object_cache_optimal_size	102400	FALSE	Optimal size of the user session's object cache in bytes
olap_page_pool_size	0	FALSE	Size of the OLAP page pool in bytes
open_cursors	300	FALSE	Max # cursors per session
open_links	4	FALSE	Max # open links per session
open_links_per_instance	4	FALSE	Max # open links per instance
optimizer_dynamic_sampling	2	FALSE	Optimizer dynamic sampling
optimizer_features_enable	10.2.0.1	FALSE	Optimizer plan compatibility parameter
optimizer_index_caching	0	FALSE	Optimizer percent index caching

Parameter Name	Value	Is Modified	Description
optimizer_index_cost_adj	100	FALSE	Optimizer index cost adjustment
optimizer_mode	ALL_ROWS	FALSE	Optimizer mode
optimizer_secure_view_merging	TRUE	FALSE	Optimizer secure view merging and predicate pushdown/movearound
os_authent_prefix	OPS$	FALSE	Prefix for auto-logon accounts
os_roles	FALSE	FALSE	Retrieve roles from the operating system
parallel_adaptive_multi_user	TRUE	FALSE	Enable adaptive setting of degree for multiple user streams
parallel_automatic_tuning	FALSE	FALSE	Enable intelligent defaults for parallel execution parameters
parallel_execution_message_size	2148	FALSE	Message buffer size for parallel execution
parallel_instance_group		FALSE	Instance group to use for all parallel operations
parallel_max_servers	20	FALSE	Maximum parallel query servers per instance
parallel_min_percent	0	FALSE	Minimum percent of threads required for parallel query
parallel_min_servers	0	FALSE	Min parallel query servers per instance
parallel_server	FALSE	FALSE	If TRUE start up in parallel server mode
parallel_server_instances	1	FALSE	Number of instances to use for sizing OPS SGA structures
parallel_threads_per_cpu	2	FALSE	Number of parallel execution thread s per CPU
pga_aggregate_target	96468992	FALSE	Target size for the aggregate PGA memory consumed by the instance
plsql_ccflags		FALSE	PL/SQL ccflags
plsql_code_type	INTERPRETED	FALSE	PL/SQL code-type
plsql_compiler_flags	INTERPRETED, NON_DEBUG	FALSE	PL/SQL compiler flags
plsql_debug	FALSE	FALSE	PL/SQL debug
plsql_native_library_dir		FALSE	PL/SQL native library dir
plsql_native_library_subdir_count	0	FALSE	PL/SQL native library number of subdirectories

Initialization Parameters

Parameter Name	Value	Is Modified	Description
plsql_optimize_level	2	FALSE	PL/SQL optimize level
plsql_v2_compatibility	FALSE	FALSE	PL/SQL version 2.x compatibility flag
plsql_warnings	DISABLE:ALL	FALSE	PL/SQL compiler warnings settings
pre_page_sga	FALSE	FALSE	Pre-page SGA for process
processes	150	FALSE	User processes
query_rewrite_enabled	TRUE	FALSE	Allow rewrite of queries using materialized views if enabled
query_rewrite_integrity	enforced	FALSE	Perform rewrite using materialized views with desired integrity
rdbms_server_dn		FALSE	RDBMS's distinguished name
read_only_open_delayed	FALSE	FALSE	If TRUE delay opening of read-only files until first access
recovery_parallelism	0	FALSE	Number of server processes to use for parallel recovery
recyclebin	on	FALSE	Recycle bin processing
remote_archive_enable	true	FALSE	Remote archival enable setting
remote_dependencies_mode	TIMESTAMP	FALSE	Remote-procedure-call dependencies mode parameter
remote_listener		FALSE	Remote listener
remote_login_passwordfile	EXCLUSIVE	FALSE	Password file usage parameter
remote_os_authent	FALSE	FALSE	Allow non-secure remote clients to use auto-logon accounts
remote_os_roles	FALSE	FALSE	Allow non-secure remote clients to use OS roles
replication_dependency_tracking	TRUE	FALSE	Tracking dependency for replication parallel propagation
resource_limit	FALSE	FALSE	Master switch for resource limit
resource_manager_plan		FALSE	Resource mgr top plan
resumable_timeout	0	FALSE	Set resumable_timeout
rollback_segments		FALSE	Undo segment list
serial_reuse	disable	FALSE	Reuse the frame segments
service_names	orcl	FALSE	Service names supported by the instance

Parameter Name	Value	Is Modified	Description
session_cached_cursors	20	FALSE	Number of cursors to cache in a session
session_max_open_files	10	FALSE	Maximum number of open files allowed per session
sessions	170	FALSE	User and system sessions
sga_max_size	293601280	FALSE	Max total SGA size
sga_target	293601280	FALSE	Target size of SGA
shadow_core_dump	partial	FALSE	Core size for shadow processes
shared_memory_address	0	FALSE	SGA starting address (low-order 32 bits on 64-bit platforms)
shared_pool_reserved_size	4194304	FALSE	Size in bytes of reserved area of shared pool
shared_pool_size	0	FALSE	Size in bytes of shared pool
shared_server_sessions		FALSE	Max number of shared server sessions
shared_servers	1	FALSE	Number of shared servers to start up
skip_unusable_indexes	TRUE	FALSE	Skip unusable indexes if set to TRUE
smtp_out_server		FALSE	utl_smtp server and port configuration parameter
sort_area_retained_size	0	FALSE	Size of in-memory sort work area retained between fetch calls
sort_area_size	65536	FALSE	Size of in-memory sort work area
spfile	F:\ORACLE\ PRODUCT\10 .2.0\DB_1\ DBS\ SPFILE ORCL.ORA	FALSE	Server parameter file
sql92_security	FALSE	FALSE	Require select privilege for searched update/delete
sql_trace	FALSE	FALSE	Enable SQL trace
sql_version	NATIVE	FALSE	SQL language version parameter for compatibility issues
sqltune_category	DEFAULT	FALSE	Category qualifier for applying hintsets
standby_archive_dest	%ORACLE_ HO ME%\RDBMS	FALSE	Standby database archive log destination text string
standby_file_management	MANUAL	FALSE	If auto then files are created/dropped automatically on standby

Initialization Parameters

Parameter Name	Value	Is Modified	Description
star_transformation_enabled	FALSE	FALSE	Enable the use of star transformation
statistics_level	TYPICAL	FALSE	Statistics level
streams_pool_size	0	FALSE	Size in bytes of the streams pool
tape_asynch_io	TRUE	FALSE	Use asynch I/O requests for tape devices
thread	0	FALSE	Redo thread to mount
timed_os_statistics	0	FALSE	Internal OS statistic gathering interval in seconds
timed_statistics	TRUE	FALSE	Maintain internal timing statistics
trace_enabled	TRUE	FALSE	Enable KST tracing
tracefile_identifier		FALSE	Trace file custom identifier
transactions	187	FALSE	Max number of concurrent active transactions
transactions_per_rollback _segment	5	FALSE	Number of active transactions per rollback segment
undo_management	AUTO	FALSE	Instance runs in SMU mode if TRUE, else in RBU mode
undo_retention	900	FALSE	Undo retention in seconds
undo_tablespace	UNDOTBS1	FALSE	Use/switch undo tablespace
use_indirect_data_buffers	FALSE	FALSE	Enable indirect data buffers (very large SGA on 32-bit platforms)
user_dump_dest	F:\...\ORCL\UDUMP	FALSE	User process dump directory
utl_file_dir		FALSE	utl_file accessible directories list
workarea_size_policy	AUTO	FALSE	Policy used to size SQL working areas (MANUAL/AUTO)

Listing of Undocumented Initialization Parameters (x$ksppi/x$ksppcv)

Using these parameters is not supported by Oracle, nor do I recommend them on a production system. Use them only if you are directed to use them by Oracle Support *and* have thoroughly tested them on your crash-and-burn system. Undocumented initialization parameters can lead to database corruption (although a few of them can get your database back up when you have corruption). Use at your own risk.

The following query retrieves the undocumented parameters. No output is displayed because of space considerations.

```
select     a.ksppinm, b.ksppstvl, b.ksppstdf, a.ksppdesc
from       x$ksppi a, x$ksppcv b
where      a.indx = b.indx
and        substr(ksppinm,1,1) = '_'
order      by ksppinm;
```

TIP
Undocumented initialization parameters often show a glimpse of things coming in the next version of Oracle. However, some of them don't work or cause severe problems.

Oracle Applications 11*i* Recommendations (Note: 216205.1)

The Oracle Applications Development Team wrote a note on Metalink (Note: 216205.1) that shows the initialization parameters that should be used (or not used) with various versions of Oracle Applications. I always review the settings that the Oracle Applications Development team recommends, as they often are dealing with large systems and they've learned some nice tricks. While I do feel a bit cautious about using SGA_TARGET and removing DB_CACHE_SIZE (mainly because SGA_TARGET is so new), the other things listed are very helpful in my opinion. SGA_TARGET has been around since 10*g*R1, and is also a 10*g*R2 RAC Best Practice from Oracle. There were some bugs in 10*g*R1, but 10*g*R2 seems to be solid. There are also some nice descriptions listed here.

The release-specific database initialization parameters for 10*g*R2 (10.2.*x*) are shown here:

```
###################################################################
#
# Oracle Applications 11i - database initialization parameters
#
# This file contains the release specific database
# initialization parameters for 10gR2. Oracle Applications
# 11i certification requires a minimum of 10.2.0.2.


#########
#
# Compatible
#
# Compatibility should be set to the current release.
#
#########
compatible = 10.2.0      #MP
#########
#
# Cache Sizes
#
# For 10g, the automatic SGA tuning option is required.
# This avoids the need to individually tune the different
# SGA caches such as the buffer cache, shared pool, large
```

```
# pool, etc.. The automatic SGA tuning option improves
# overall performance and improves manageability.
#
# SGA target refers to the total size of the SGA including
# all the sub-caches such as the buffer cache,
# shared pool, large pool, etc. Refer to the sizing table
# in the section Database Initialization Parameter Sizing for
# sizing recommendations for sga_target.
#
# Also, it is recommended to use a Server Parameter file
# (i.e. SPFILE) to store the initialization parameter
# values when sga_target is being used. The Automatic
# SGA tuning option (sga_target) dynamically sizes the
# individual caches such as the buffer cache and shared pool.
# Using an SPFILE allows the dynamically adjusted values to
# persist across restarts. Please refer to the
# Database Administrator's Guide for information on how
# to create and maintain an SPFILE.
#
#
########
sga_target = 1G


########
#
# Shared Pool
#
# It is important to tune the shared pool so as to minimize
# contention for SQL and PL/SQL objects. A value of 400M is a
# reasonable starting point for 11i, and automatic SGA
# tuning will adjust the caches as per the workload.
# The values below for the shared pool related caches
# are simply minimum values (i.e., starting values).
#
########
shared_pool_size = 400M
shared_pool_reserved_size = 40M


#########
#      _kks_use_mutex_pin
#
#      Enables use of more efficient mutex mechanism for
#      implementing library cache pins.
#
#########

_kks_use_mutex_pin=TRUE


#########
#
# NLS and character sets.
```

```
#
#
#########

nls_length_semantics = BYTE        #MP

#########
#
# Rollback segments
#
# As of 9i, Oracle Applications requires the use of System
# Managed Undo. System Managed Undo is much more efficient, and
# reduces the chances of snapshot too old errors. In addition,
# it is much easier to manage and administer system managed undo
# than manually managing rollback segments.
#
########

undo_management = AUTO             #MP
undo_tablespace = APPS_UNDOTS1    #MP

########
#
# Private memory areas
#
# The automatic memory manager is being used to manage
# the PGA memory. This avoids the need to manually tune
# the sort_area_size and the hash_area_size.
#
# Auto. Memory Manager also improves performance and scalability
# as the memory is released to the OS.
#
########

pga_aggregate_target = 1G
workarea_size_policy = AUTO        #MP
olap_page_pool_size = 4194304

########
#
# Cursor related settings.
#
# 10g changed the default behavior for the server side PL/SQL
# cursor cache. Prior to 10g, PL/SQL (server side) used
# open_cursors as the upper limit for caching PL/SQL
# (server side) cursors. In 10g, the upper limit is now
# controlled by the parameter session_cached_cursors.
# For 10g environments, the parameters open_cursors and
# session_cached_cursors should be set as follows in accordance
# with this change in behavior.
#
```

```
########

open_cursors = 600
session_cached_cursors = 500

########
#
# Events
#
# Events should not be set unless directed by Oracle Support,
# or by instruction as per the Applications documentation.
#
########

#########
#
# PL/SQL Parameters
#
# The following parameters are used to enable the PL/SQL
# global optimizer as well as native compilation.
#
# Oracle Applications recommends the use of PL/SQL native
# compilation for 10g based Apps environments. The
# parameter (plsql_native_library_dir) should be set
# to the directory path, which will be used to store
# the shared libraries generated as part of native
# compilation. Interpreted mode is supported and
# can be used with Oracle Applications, however, native
# compilation is recommended in order to maximize runtime
# performance and scalability.

# Compiling PL/SQL units with native compilation does
# take longer than interpreted mode due to the generation
# and compilation of the native shared libraries.
#
#
#########

plsql_optimize_level = 2        #MP
plsql_code_type = native        #MP
plsql_native_library_dir = ?/prod11i/plsql_nativelib
plsql_native_library_subdir_count = 149

#########
#
# Optimizer
#
# Release 11i uses the Cost Based Optimizer (CBO). The
# following optimizer parameters MUST be set as below, and should
# not be changed.
#
```

```
#########
_b_tree_bitmap_plans = FALSE            #MP
optimizer_secure_view_merging = FALSE   #MP
```

The Oracle Applications note also recommends that you remove the following initialization parameters from your database initialization parameters file for 10*g*R2 (if they exist).

CAUTION
Do not do this without testing and investigating the ramifications.

```
_always_anti_join
_always_semi_join
_complex_view_merging
_index_join_enabled
_new_initial_join_orders
_optimizer_cost_based_transformations
_optimizer_cost_model
_optimizer_mode_force
_optimizer_undo_changes
_or_expand_nvl_predicate
_ordered_nested_loop
_push_join_predicate
_push_join_union_view
_shared_pool_reserved_min_alloc
_sortmerge_inequality_join_off
_table_scan_cost_plus_one
_unnest_subquery
_use_column_stats_for_function
always_anti_join
always_semi_join
db_block_buffers
db_cache_size
enqueue_resources
event="10932 trace name context level 32768"
event="10933 trace name context level 512"
event="10943 trace name context forever, level 2"
event="10943 trace name context level 16384"
event="38004 trace name context forever, level 1"
hash_area_size
java_pool_size
job_queue_interval
large_pool_size
max_enabled_roles
optimizer_dynamic_sampling
optimizer_features_enable
optimizer_index_caching
optimizer_index_cost_adj
optimizer_max_permutations
optimizer_mode
optimizer_percent_parallel
```

```
plsql_compiler_flags
query_rewrite_enabled
row_locking
sort_area_size
undo_retention
undo_suppress_errors
```

Top 10 Reasons *Not* to Write a Book

1. You like sleep and caffeine-enhanced water clogs your coffee maker.

2. You have enough trouble getting the time to read books, let alone write one.

3. You enjoy getting together with your family from time to time.

4. You're tired of being the first one in the office (actually, you've been there all night).

5. You hobby is golf and you never play.

6. You enjoy noticing the world around you rather than feeling a "purple haze all through your mind."

7. Kevin Loney will write on that subject eventually . . . you'll wait for his book.

8. You don't want to "show off" how much you know . . . you're far too humble.

9. Your PC is out of disk space already, although you've just loaded Windows 99.1415926.

10. You just got your *life* back after the last Oracle upgrade—No way!

TIP
Retirement is a good time to write a book, not during one of the fastest tech growth cycles in history (not as fast as pre-2000, yet). Perhaps when the 2000-year bull market ends somewhere between 2018 and 2020 (good time to get out of the market, in my opinion) that might be a better time.

Tips Review

■ Setting certain initialization parameters correctly could be the difference between a report taking two seconds and two hours. Try changes out on a test system thoroughly *before* implementing those changes in a production environment!

■ There are some excellent options within Oracle. Unfortunately, some of them do *not* work unless the initialization parameter is set correctly.

■ Undocumented initialization parameters can corrupt your database! Some of them can also salvage a corrupted database. Try to use these only when all other choices have failed and use them with the help of Oracle Support.

- Undocumented initialization parameters often show a glimpse of things coming in the next version of Oracle, but some of them don't work at all.

- Retirement is a good time to write a book. Writing a book during the largest growth period in history followed by the most painful economic conditions since 1929 is *not*.

References

Oracle Server Tuning (Oracle Corporation)
Oracle9i, Oracle10g Performance Tuning (Oracle Corporation)
Kevin Loney, *Oracle Database 10g DBA Handbook* (McGraw-Hill, 2005)
Metalink Notes: 22908.1, 216205.1, 316889.1

Thanks to Brad Brown, Joe Trezzo, Randy Swanson, Sean McGuire, Greg Pucka, Mike Broullette, and Kevin Loney for their contributions to this chapter.

APPENDIX

B

The V$ Views (DBA and Developer)

T he V$ views are very helpful in analyzing database issues. This appendix lists all views and creation scripts used to actually build the V$ and GV$ views. The V$ views vary in structure and number, depending on the database version and release used. Run the queries on your version of the database to get the number of views and structure for your specific version. The topics covered in this appendix include the following:

- Creation of V$ and GV$ views and x$ tables
- A list of all Oracle 10gR2 GV$ and V$ views
- Oracle 10g script listing of the x$ tables used in the creation of the V$ views

NOTE
V$ to X$ and X$ to V$ cross-references can be found in Appendix C.

Creation of V$ and GV$ Views and X$ Tables

To obtain an understanding of the creation of x$ tables, V$ and data dictionary views can be crucial to fully comprehend the intricacies of Oracle. While knowledge of the views and tables is critical to your career, their creation has remained somewhat of a vexing mystery. Figure B-1 illustrates the creation of the underlying tables and the data dictionary views, while Figure B-2 illustrates the creation of the x$ tables and the V$ views.

A List of Oracle 10g (10.2.0.1) GV$ and V$ Views

NOTE
The Oracle 10g V$ views are the same as the GV$ views, minus the instance ID.

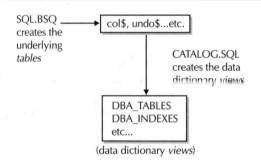

FIGURE B-1. *Creation of the data dictionary views*

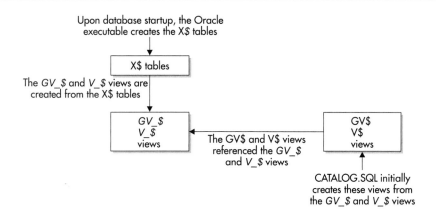

FIGURE B-2. *Creation of the x$ tables and the V$ views*

Here is the Oracle 10*g* query to get this listing (372 views):

```
set pagesize 1000

select    name
from      v$fixed_table
where     name like 'GV%'
order by  name;
```

The listing itself follows:

GV$ACCESS	GV$ACTIVE_INSTANCES
GV$ACTIVE_SERVICES	GV$ACTIVE_SESSION_HISTORY
GV$ACTIVE_SESS_POOL_MTH	GV$ADVISOR_PROGRESS
GV$ALERT_TYPES	GV$AQ1
GV$ARCHIVE	GV$ARCHIVED_LOG
GV$ARCHIVE_DEST	GV$ARCHIVE_DEST_STATUS
GV$ARCHIVE_GAP	GV$ARCHIVE_PROCESSES
GV$ASM_ALIAS	GV$ASM_CLIENT
GV$ASM_DISK	GV$ASM_DISKGROUP
GV$ASM_DISKGROUP_STAT	GV$ASM_DISK_STAT
GV$ASM_FILE	GV$ASM_OPERATION
GV$ASM_TEMPLATE	GV$AW_AGGREGATE_OP
GV$AW_ALLOCATE_OP	GV$AW_CALC
GV$AW_LONGOPS	GV$AW_OLAP
GV$AW_SESSION_INFO	GV$BACKUP
GV$BACKUP_ASYNC_IO	GV$BACKUP_CORRUPTION
GV$BACKUP_DATAFILE	GV$BACKUP_DEVICE
GV$BACKUP_PIECE	GV$BACKUP_REDOLOG
GV$BACKUP_SET	GV$BACKUP_SPFILE

V$ Views

GV$BACKUP_SYNC_IO
GV$BH
GV$BSP
GV$BUFFERED_QUEUES
GV$BUFFER_POOL
GV$CIRCUIT
GV$CLASS_PING
GV$CLUSTER_INTERCONNECTS
GV$CONTEXT
GV$CONTROLFILE_RECORD_SECTION
GV$CR_BLOCK_SERVER
GV$DATABASE
GV$DATABASE_INCARNATION
GV$DATAFILE_COPY
GV$DATAGUARD_CONFIG
GV$DATAPUMP_JOB
GV$DBFILE
GV$DB_CACHE_ADVICE
GV$DB_PIPES
GV$DELETED_OBJECT
GV$DISPATCHER_CONFIG
GV$DLM_ALL_LOCKS
GV$DLM_CONVERT_REMOTE
GV$DLM_LOCKS
GV$DLM_RESS
GV$ENABLEDPRIVS
GV$ENQUEUE_STAT
GV$EVENTMETRIC
GV$EVENT_NAME
GV$FAST_START_SERVERS
GV$FILEMETRIC
GV$FILESPACE_USAGE
GV$FILE_CACHE_TRANSFER
GV$FILE_PING
GV$FIXED_VIEW_DEFINITION
GV$FLASHBACK_DATABASE_LOGFILE
GV$GCSHVMASTER_INFO
GV$GC_ELEMENT
GV$GES_BLOCKING_ENQUEUE
GV$GLOBALCONTEXT
GV$GLOBAL_TRANSACTION
GV$HS_PARAMETER
GV$HVMASTER_INFO
GV$INSTANCE
GV$INSTANCE_LOG_GROUP
GV$JAVAPOOL
GV$JAVA_POOL_ADVICE

GV$BGPROCESS
GV$BLOCKING_QUIESCE
GV$BUFFERED_PUBLISHERS
GV$BUFFERED_SUBSCRIBERS
GV$BUFFER_POOL_STATISTICS
GV$CLASS_CACHE_TRANSFER
GV$CLIENT_STATS
GV$CONFIGURED_INTERCONNECTS
GV$CONTROLFILE
GV$COPY_CORRUPTION
GV$CURRENT_BLOCK_SERVER
GV$DATABASE_BLOCK_CORRUPTION
GV$DATAFILE
GV$DATAFILE_HEADER
GV$DATAGUARD_STATUS
GV$DATAPUMP_SESSION
GV$DBLINK
GV$DB_OBJECT_CACHE
GV$DB_TRANSPORTABLE_PLATFORM
GV$DISPATCHER
GV$DISPATCHER_RATE
GV$DLM_CONVERT_LOCAL
GV$DLM_LATCH
GV$DLM_MISC
GV$DLM_TRAFFIC_CONTROLLER
GV$ENQUEUE_LOCK
GV$ENQUEUE_STATISTICS
GV$EVENT_HISTOGRAM
GV$EXECUTION
GV$FAST_START_TRANSACTIONS
GV$FILEMETRIC_HISTORY
GV$FILESTAT
GV$FILE_HISTOGRAM
GV$FIXED_TABLE
GV$FLASHBACK_DATABASE_LOG
GV$FLASHBACK_DATABASE_STAT
GV$GCSPFMASTER_INFO
GV$GC_ELEMENTS_WITH_COLLISIONS
GV$GES_ENQUEUE
GV$GLOBAL_BLOCKED_LOCKS
GV$HS_AGENT
GV$HS_SESSION
GV$INDEXED_FIXED_COLUMN
GV$INSTANCE_CACHE_TRANSFER
GV$INSTANCE_RECOVERY
GV$JAVA_LIBRARY_CACHE_MEMORY
GV$LATCH

GV$LATCHHOLDER

GV$LATCH_CHILDREN

GV$LATCH_PARENT

GV$LIBRARY_CACHE_MEMORY

GV$LOADISTAT

GV$LOCK

GV$LOCKS_WITH_COLLISIONS

GV$LOCK_ELEMENT

GV$LOG

GV$LOGHIST

GV$LOGMNR_CONTENTS

GV$LOGMNR_DICTIONARY_LOAD

GV$LOGMNR_LOGFILE

GV$LOGMNR_PARAMETERS

GV$LOGMNR_REGION

GV$LOGMNR_STATS

GV$LOGSTDBY

GV$LOGSTDBY_PROGRESS

GV$LOGSTDBY_STATS

GV$LOG_HISTORY

GV$MAP_COMP_LIST

GV$MAP_EXT_ELEMENT

GV$MAP_FILE_EXTENT

GV$MAP_LIBRARY

GV$MAX_ACTIVE_SESS_TARGET_MTH

GV$METRICGROUP

GV$METRIC_HISTORY

GV$MUTEX_SLEEP

GV$MVREFRESH

GV$NLS_PARAMETERS

GV$OBJECT_DEPENDENCY

GV$OFFLINE_RANGE

GV$OPTION

GV$PARALLEL_DEGREE_LIMIT_MTH

GV$PARAMETER2

GV$PGASTAT

GV$PGA_TARGET_ADVICE_HISTOGRAM

GV$PQ_SLAVE

GV$PQ_TQSTAT

GV$PROCESS_MEMORY

GV$PROCESS_MEMORY_DETAIL_PROG

GV$PROPAGATION_SENDER

GV$PROXY_DATAFILE

GV$PX_BUFFER_ADVICE

GV$PX_PROCESS_SYSSTAT

GV$PX_SESSTAT

GV$QUEUEING_MTH

GV$LATCHNAME

GV$LATCH_MISSES

GV$LIBRARYCACHE

GV$LICENSE

GV$LOADPSTAT

GV$LOCKED_OBJECT

GV$LOCK_ACTIVITY

GV$LOCK_TYPE

GV$LOGFILE

GV$LOGMNR_CALLBACK

GV$LOGMNR_DICTIONARY

GV$LOGMNR_LATCH

GV$LOGMNR_LOGS

GV$LOGMNR_PROCESS

GV$LOGMNR_SESSION

GV$LOGMNR_TRANSACTION

GV$LOGSTDBY_PROCESS

GV$LOGSTDBY_STATE

GV$LOGSTDBY_TRANSACTION

GV$MANAGED_STANDBY

GV$MAP_ELEMENT

GV$MAP_FILE

GV$MAP_FILE_IO_STACK

GV$MAP_SUBELEMENT

GV$METRIC

GV$METRICNAME

GV$MTTR_TARGET_ADVICE

GV$MUTEX_SLEEP_HISTORY

GV$MYSTAT

GV$NLS_VALID_VALUES

GV$OBSOLETE_PARAMETER

GV$OPEN_CURSOR

GV$OSSTAT

GV$PARAMETER

GV$PARAMETER_VALID_VALUES

GV$PGA_TARGET_ADVICE

GV$PQ_SESSTAT

GV$PQ_SYSSTAT

GV$PROCESS

GV$PROCESS_MEMORY_DETAIL

GV$PROPAGATION_RECEIVER

GV$PROXY_ARCHIVEDLOG

GV$PWFILE_USERS

GV$PX_PROCESS

GV$PX_SESSION

GV$QUEUE

GV$RECOVERY_FILE_STATUS

V$ Views

GV$RECOVERY_LOG
GV$RECOVERY_STATUS
GV$REPLPROP
GV$REQDIST
GV$RESOURCE
GV$RESTORE_POINT
GV$RFS_THREAD
GV$RMAN_ENCRYPTION_ALGORITHMS
GV$RMAN_STATUS_CURRENT
GV$ROWCACHE
GV$ROWCACHE_SUBORDINATE
GV$RSRC_CONSUMER_GROUP_CPU_MTH
GV$RSRC_PLAN
GV$RSRC_PLAN_HISTORY
GV$RULE
GV$RULE_SET_AGGREGATE_STATS
GV$SEGMENT_STATISTICS
GV$SEGSTAT_NAME
GV$SERVICEMETRIC_HISTORY
GV$SERVICE_EVENT
GV$SERVICE_WAIT_CLASS
GV$SESSION
GV$SESSION_CURSOR_CACHE
GV$SESSION_LONGOPS
GV$SESSION_WAIT
GV$SESSION_WAIT_HISTORY
GV$SESSTAT
GV$SESS_TIME_MODEL
GV$SGA
GV$SGASTAT
GV$SGA_DYNAMIC_COMPONENTS
GV$SGA_RESIZE_OPS
GV$SHARED_POOL_ADVICE
GV$SHARED_SERVER
GV$SORT_SEGMENT
GV$SPPARAMETER
GV$SQLAREA
GV$SQLSTATS
GV$SQLTEXT_WITH_NEWLINES
GV$SQL_BIND_METADATA
GV$SQL_JOIN_FILTER
GV$SQL_PLAN
GV$SQL_PLAN_STATISTICS_ALL
GV$SQL_SHARED_CURSOR
GV$SQL_WORKAREA
GV$SQL_WORKAREA_HISTOGRAM
GV$STANDBY_LOG

GV$RECOVERY_PROGRESS
GV$RECOVER_FILE
GV$REPLQUEUE
GV$RESERVED_WORDS
GV$RESOURCE_LIMIT
GV$RESUMABLE
GV$RMAN_CONFIGURATION
GV$RMAN_OUTPUT
GV$ROLLSTAT
GV$ROWCACHE_PARENT
GV$RSRC_CONSUMER_GROUP
GV$RSRC_CONS_GROUP_HISTORY
GV$RSRC_PLAN_CPU_MTH
GV$RSRC_SESSION_INFO
GV$RULE_SET
GV$SCHEDULER_RUNNING_JOBS
GV$SEGSTAT
GV$SERVICEMETRIC
GV$SERVICES
GV$SERVICE_STATS
GV$SERV_MOD_ACT_STATS
GV$SESSION_CONNECT_INFO
GV$SESSION_EVENT
GV$SESSION_OBJECT_CACHE
GV$SESSION_WAIT_CLASS
GV$SESSMETRIC
GV$SESS_IO
GV$SES_OPTIMIZER_ENV
GV$SGAINFO
GV$SGA_CURRENT_RESIZE_OPS
GV$SGA_DYNAMIC_FREE_MEMORY
GV$SGA_TARGET_ADVICE
GV$SHARED_POOL_RESERVED
GV$SHARED_SERVER_MONITOR
GV$SORT_USAGE
GV$SQL
GV$SQLAREA_PLAN_HASH
GV$SQLTEXT
GV$SQL_BIND_DATA
GV$SQL_CURSOR
GV$SQL_OPTIMIZER_ENV
GV$SQL_PLAN_STATISTICS
GV$SQL_REDIRECTION
GV$SQL_SHARED_MEMORY
GV$SQL_WORKAREA_ACTIVE
GV$STANDBY_APPLY_SNAPSHOT
GV$STATISTICS_LEVEL

GV$STATNAME	GV$STREAMS_APPLY_COORDINATOR
GV$STREAMS_APPLY_READER	GV$STREAMS_APPLY_SERVER
GV$STREAMS_CAPTURE	GV$STREAMS_POOL_ADVICE
GV$STREAMS_TRANSACTION	GV$SUBCACHE
GV$SYSAUX_OCCUPANTS	GV$SYSMETRIC
GV$SYSMETRIC_HISTORY	GV$SYSMETRIC_SUMMARY
GV$SYSSTAT	GV$SYSTEM_CURSOR_CACHE
GV$SYSTEM_EVENT	GV$SYSTEM_PARAMETER
GV$SYSTEM_PARAMETER2	GV$SYSTEM_WAIT_CLASS
GV$SYS_OPTIMIZER_ENV	GV$SYS_TIME_MODEL
GV$TABLESPACE	GV$TEMPFILE
GV$TEMPORARY_LOBS	GV$TEMPSTAT
GV$TEMP_CACHE_TRANSFER	GV$TEMP_EXTENT_MAP
GV$TEMP_EXTENT_POOL	GV$TEMP_HISTOGRAM
GV$TEMP_PING	GV$TEMP_SPACE_HEADER
GV$THREAD	GV$THRESHOLD_TYPES
GV$TIMER	GV$TIMEZONE_FILE
GV$TIMEZONE_NAMES	GV$TRANSACTION
GV$TRANSACTION_ENQUEUE	GV$TRANSPORTABLE_PLATFORM
GV$TSM_SESSIONS	GV$TYPE_SIZE
GV$UNDOSTAT	GV$VERSION
GV$VPD_POLICY	GV$WAITCLASSMETRIC
GV$WAITCLASSMETRIC_HISTORY	GV$WAITSTAT
GV$WALLET	GV$XML_AUDIT_TRAIL
GV$_LOCK	GV$_LOCK1
GV$_RESUMABLE2	GV$_SEQUENCES

V$ Views

The Oracle 10g (10.2.0.1) V$ Views

Here is the Oracle 10g query to get this listing (396 views):

```
set pagesize 1000
```

```
select     name
from       v$fixed_table
where      name like 'V%'
order by   name;
```

The listing itself follows:

V$ACCESS	V$ACTIVE_INSTANCES
V$ACTIVE_SERVICES	V$ACTIVE_SESSION_HISTORY
V$ACTIVE_SESS_POOL_MTH	V$ADVISOR_PROGRESS
V$ALERT_TYPES	V$AQ1
V$ARCHIVE	V$ARCHIVED_LOG
V$ARCHIVE_DEST	V$ARCHIVE_DEST_STATUS
V$ARCHIVE_GAP	V$ARCHIVE_PROCESSES
V$ASM_ALIAS	V$ASM_CLIENT

V$ASM_DISK	V$ASM_DISKGROUP
V$ASM_DISKGROUP_STAT	V$ASM_DISK_STAT
V$ASM_FILE	V$ASM_OPERATION
V$ASM_TEMPLATE	V$AW_AGGREGATE_OP
V$AW_ALLOCATE_OP	V$AW_CALC
V$AW_LONGOPS	V$AW_OLAP
V$AW_SESSION_INFO	V$BACKUP
V$BACKUP_ARCHIVELOG_DETAILS	V$BACKUP_ARCHIVELOG_SUMMARY
V$BACKUP_ASYNC_IO	V$BACKUP_CONTROLFILE_DETAILS
V$BACKUP_CONTROLFILE_SUMMARY	V$BACKUP_COPY_DETAILS
V$BACKUP_COPY_SUMMARY	V$BACKUP_CORRUPTION
V$BACKUP_DATAFILE	V$BACKUP_DATAFILE_DETAILS
V$BACKUP_DATAFILE_SUMMARY	V$BACKUP_DEVICE
V$BACKUP_PIECE	V$BACKUP_PIECE_DETAILS
V$BACKUP_REDOLOG	V$BACKUP_SET
V$BACKUP_SET_DETAILS	V$BACKUP_SET_SUMMARY
V$BACKUP_SPFILE	V$BACKUP_SPFILE_DETAILS
V$BACKUP_SPFILE_SUMMARY	V$BACKUP_SYNC_IO
V$BGPROCESS	V$BH
V$BLOCKING_QUIESCE	V$BLOCK_CHANGE_TRACKING
V$BSP	V$BUFFERED_PUBLISHERS
V$BUFFERED_QUEUES	V$BUFFERED_SUBSCRIBERS
V$BUFFER_POOL	V$BUFFER_POOL_STATISTICS
V$CIRCUIT	V$CLASS_CACHE_TRANSFER
V$CLASS_PING	V$CLIENT_STATS
V$CLUSTER_INTERCONNECTS	V$CONFIGURED_INTERCONNECTS
V$CONTEXT	V$CONTROLFILE
V$CONTROLFILE_RECORD_SECTION	V$COPY_CORRUPTION
V$CR_BLOCK_SERVER	V$CURRENT_BLOCK_SERVER
V$DATABASE	V$DATABASE_BLOCK_CORRUPTION
V$DATABASE_INCARNATION	V$DATAFILE
V$DATAFILE_COPY	V$DATAFILE_HEADER
V$DATAGUARD_CONFIG	V$DATAGUARD_STATS
V$DATAGUARD_STATUS	V$DATAPUMP_JOB
V$DATAPUMP_SESSION	V$DBFILE
V$DBLINK	V$DB_CACHE_ADVICE
V$DB_OBJECT_CACHE	V$DB_PIPES
V$DB_TRANSPORTABLE_PLATFORM	V$DELETED_OBJECT
V$DISPATCHER	V$DISPATCHER_CONFIG
V$DISPATCHER_RATE	V$DLM_ALL_LOCKS
V$DLM_CONVERT_LOCAL	V$DLM_CONVERT_REMOTE
V$DLM_LATCH	V$DLM_LOCKS
V$DLM_MISC	V$DLM_RESS
V$DLM_TRAFFIC_CONTROLLER	V$ENABLEDPRIVS
V$ENQUEUE_LOCK	V$ENQUEUE_STAT
V$ENQUEUE_STATISTICS	V$EVENTMETRIC
V$EVENT_HISTOGRAM	V$EVENT_NAME

V$EXECUTION	V$FAST_START_SERVERS
V$FAST_START_TRANSACTIONS	V$FILEMETRIC
V$FILEMETRIC_HISTORY	V$FILESPACE_USAGE
V$FILESTAT	V$FILE_CACHE_TRANSFER
V$FILE_HISTOGRAM	V$FILE_PING
V$FIXED_TABLE	V$FIXED_VIEW_DEFINITION
V$FLASHBACK_DATABASE_LOG	V$FLASHBACK_DATABASE_LOGFILE
V$FLASHBACK_DATABASE_STAT	V$FLASH_RECOVERY_AREA_USAGE
V$GCSHVMASTER_INFO	V$GCSPFMASTER_INFO
V$GC_ELEMENT	V$GC_ELEMENTS_WITH_COLLISIONS
V$GES_BLOCKING_ENQUEUE	V$GES_ENQUEUE
V$GLOBALCONTEXT	V$GLOBAL_BLOCKED_LOCKS
V$GLOBAL_TRANSACTION	V$HS_AGENT
V$HS_PARAMETER	V$HS_SESSION
V$HVMASTER_INFO	V$INDEXED_FIXED_COLUMN
V$INSTANCE	V$INSTANCE_CACHE_TRANSFER
V$INSTANCE_LOG_GROUP	V$INSTANCE_RECOVERY
V$JAVAPOOL	V$JAVA_LIBRARY_CACHE_MEMORY
V$JAVA_POOL_ADVICE	V$LATCH
V$LATCHHOLDER	V$LATCHNAME
V$LATCH_CHILDREN	V$LATCH_MISSES
V$LATCH_PARENT	V$LIBRARYCACHE
V$LIBRARY_CACHE_MEMORY	V$LICENSE
V$LOADISTAT	V$LOADPSTAT
V$LOCK	V$LOCKED_OBJECT
V$LOCKS_WITH_COLLISIONS	V$LOCK_ACTIVITY
V$LOCK_ELEMENT	V$LOCK_TYPE
V$LOG	V$LOGFILE
V$LOGHIST	V$LOGMNR_CALLBACK
V$LOGMNR_CONTENTS	V$LOGMNR_DICTIONARY
V$LOGMNR_DICTIONARY_LOAD	V$LOGMNR_LATCH
V$LOGMNR_LOGFILE	V$LOGMNR_LOGS
V$LOGMNR_PARAMETERS	V$LOGMNR_PROCESS
V$LOGMNR_REGION	V$LOGMNR_SESSION
V$LOGMNR_STATS	V$LOGMNR_TRANSACTION
V$LOGSTDBY	V$LOGSTDBY_PROCESS
V$LOGSTDBY_PROGRESS	V$LOGSTDBY_STATE
V$LOGSTDBY_STATS	V$LOGSTDBY_TRANSACTION
V$LOG_HISTORY	V$MANAGED_STANDBY
V$MAP_COMP_LIST	V$MAP_ELEMENT
V$MAP_EXT_ELEMENT	V$MAP_FILE
V$MAP_FILE_EXTENT	V$MAP_FILE_IO_STACK
V$MAP_LIBRARY	V$MAP_SUBELEMENT
V$MAX_ACTIVE_SESS_TARGET_MTH	V$METRIC
V$METRICGROUP	V$METRICNAME
V$METRIC_HISTORY	V$MTTR_TARGET_ADVICE
V$MUTEX_SLEEP	V$MUTEX_SLEEP_HISTORY

V$ Views

V$MVREFRESH	V$MYSTAT
V$NLS_PARAMETERS	V$NLS_VALID_VALUES
V$OBJECT_DEPENDENCY	V$OBSOLETE_PARAMETER
V$OFFLINE_RANGE	V$OPEN_CURSOR
V$OPTION	V$OSSTAT
V$PARALLEL_DEGREE_LIMIT_MTH	V$PARAMETER
V$PARAMETER2	V$PARAMETER_VALID_VALUES
V$PGASTAT	V$PGA_TARGET_ADVICE
V$PGA_TARGET_ADVICE_HISTOGRAM	V$PQ_SESSTAT
V$PQ_SLAVE	V$PQ_SYSSTAT
V$PQ_TQSTAT	V$PROCESS
V$PROCESS_MEMORY	V$PROCESS_MEMORY_DETAIL
V$PROCESS_MEMORY_DETAIL_PROG	V$PROPAGATION_RECEIVER
V$PROPAGATION_SENDER	V$PROXY_ARCHIVEDLOG
V$PROXY_ARCHIVELOG_DETAILS	V$PROXY_ARCHIVELOG_SUMMARY
V$PROXY_COPY_DETAILS	V$PROXY_COPY_SUMMARY
V$PROXY_DATAFILE	V$PWFILE_USERS
V$PX_BUFFER_ADVICE	V$PX_PROCESS
V$PX_PROCESS_SYSSTAT	V$PX_SESSION
V$PX_SESSTAT	V$QUEUE
V$QUEUEING_MTH	V$RECOVERY_FILE_DEST
V$RECOVERY_FILE_STATUS	V$RECOVERY_LOG
V$RECOVERY_PROGRESS	V$RECOVERY_STATUS
V$RECOVER_FILE	V$REPLPROP
V$REPLQUEUE	V$REQDIST
V$RESERVED_WORDS	V$RESOURCE
V$RESOURCE_LIMIT	V$RESTORE_POINT
V$RESUMABLE	V$RFS_THREAD
V$RMAN_BACKUP_JOB_DETAILS	V$RMAN_BACKUP_SUBJOB_DETAILS
V$RMAN_BACKUP_TYPE	V$RMAN_CONFIGURATION
V$RMAN_ENCRYPTION_ALGORITHMS	V$RMAN_OUTPUT
V$RMAN_STATUS	V$ROLLSTAT
V$ROWCACHE	V$ROWCACHE_PARENT
V$ROWCACHE_SUBORDINATE	V$RSRC_CONSUMER_GROUP
V$RSRC_CONSUMER_GROUP_CPU_MTH	V$RSRC_CONS_GROUP_HISTORY
V$RSRC_PLAN	V$RSRC_PLAN_CPU_MTH
V$RSRC_PLAN_HISTORY	V$RSRC_SESSION_INFO
V$RULE	V$RULE_SET
V$RULE_SET_AGGREGATE_STATS	V$SCHEDULER_RUNNING_JOBS
V$SEGMENT_STATISTICS	V$SEGSTAT
V$SEGSTAT_NAME	V$SERVICEMETRIC
V$SERVICEMETRIC_HISTORY	V$SERVICES
V$SERVICE_EVENT	V$SERVICE_STATS
V$SERVICE_WAIT_CLASS	V$SERV_MOD_ACT_STATS
V$SESSION	V$SESSION_CONNECT_INFO
V$SESSION_CURSOR_CACHE	V$SESSION_EVENT
V$SESSION_LONGOPS	V$SESSION_OBJECT_CACHE
V$SESSION_WAIT	V$SESSION_WAIT_CLASS

V$SESSION_WAIT_HISTORY	V$SESSMETRIC
V$SESSTAT	V$SESS_IO
V$SESS_TIME_MODEL	V$SES_OPTIMIZER_ENV
V$SGA	V$SGAINFO
V$SGASTAT	V$SGA_CURRENT_RESIZE_OPS
V$SGA_DYNAMIC_COMPONENTS	V$SGA_DYNAMIC_FREE_MEMORY
V$SGA_RESIZE_OPS	V$SGA_TARGET_ADVICE
V$SHARED_POOL_ADVICE	V$SHARED_POOL_RESERVED
V$SHARED_SERVER	V$SHARED_SERVER_MONITOR
V$SORT_SEGMENT	V$SORT_USAGE
V$SPPARAMETER	V$SQL
V$SQLAREA	V$SQLAREA_PLAN_HASH
V$SQLSTATS	V$SQLTEXT
V$SQLTEXT_WITH_NEWLINES	V$SQL_BIND_DATA
V$SQL_BIND_METADATA	V$SQL_CURSOR
V$SQL_JOIN_FILTER	V$SQL_OPTIMIZER_ENV
V$SQL_PLAN	V$SQL_PLAN_STATISTICS
V$SQL_PLAN_STATISTICS_ALL	V$SQL_REDIRECTION
V$SQL_SHARED_CURSOR	V$SQL_SHARED_MEMORY
V$SQL_WORKAREA	V$SQL_WORKAREA_ACTIVE
V$SQL_WORKAREA_HISTOGRAM	V$STANDBY_APPLY_SNAPSHOT
V$STANDBY_LOG	V$STATISTICS_LEVEL
V$STATNAME	V$STREAMS_APPLY_COORDINATOR
V$STREAMS_APPLY_READER	V$STREAMS_APPLY_SERVER
V$STREAMS_CAPTURE	V$STREAMS_POOL_ADVICE
V$STREAMS_TRANSACTION	V$SUBCACHE
V$SYSAUX_OCCUPANTS	V$SYSMETRIC
V$SYSMETRIC_HISTORY	V$SYSMETRIC_SUMMARY
V$SYSSTAT	V$SYSTEM_CURSOR_CACHE
V$SYSTEM_EVENT	V$SYSTEM_PARAMETER
V$SYSTEM_PARAMETER2	V$SYSTEM_WAIT_CLASS
V$SYS_OPTIMIZER_ENV	V$SYS_TIME_MODEL
V$TABLESPACE	V$TEMPFILE
V$TEMPORARY_LOBS	V$TEMPSTAT
V$TEMP_CACHE_TRANSFER	V$TEMP_EXTENT_MAP
V$TEMP_EXTENT_POOL	V$TEMP_HISTOGRAM
V$TEMP_PING	V$TEMP_SPACE_HEADER
V$THREAD	V$THRESHOLD_TYPES
V$TIMER	V$TIMEZONE_FILE
V$TIMEZONE_NAMES	V$TRANSACTION
V$TRANSACTION_ENQUEUE	V$TRANSPORTABLE_PLATFORM
V$TSM_SESSIONS	V$TYPE_SIZE
V$UNDOSTAT	V$UNUSABLE_BACKUPFILE_DETAILS
V$VERSION	V$VPD_POLICY
V$WAITCLASSMETRIC	V$WAITCLASSMETRIC_HISTORY
V$WAITSTAT	V$WALLET
V$XML_AUDIT_TRAIL	V$_LOCK
V$_LOCK1	V$_SEQUENCES

V$ Views

Oracle 10g Scripts of the x$ Tables Used to Create the V$ Views

Because of the number of views in 10g, it's no longer possible to list all queries in this book. I have, however, listed several that pertain primarily to performance tuning. You can run your own query to see a specific one. There are several new SQL_ID and HASH_VALUE columns as well as other nice surprises. Here is the Oracle 10g query to get a listing of *all* x$ queries for the V$ views:

```
select 'View Name:
'||view_name,substr(view_definition,1,(instr(view_definition,'from')
      -1)) def1,substr(view_definition,(instr(view_definition,'from')))||';' def2
from    v$fixed_view_definition
order   by view_name;
```

View Name: GV$BH

```
select bh.inst_id,file#,dbablk,class,decode(state,0,'free',1,'xcur',2,'scur',
      3,'cr',4,'read',5,'mrec',6,'irec',7,'write',8,'pi',9,'memory',10, 'mwrite',

11,'donated'),0,0,0,bh.le_addr,name,le_class,decode(bitand(flag,1),0,'N','Y'),
      decode(bitand(flag,16),0,'N','Y'),decode(bitand(flag,1536),0,'N','Y'),
      decode(bitand(flag,16384),0,'N','Y'),decode(bitand(flag,65536),0,'N','Y'),
      'N',obj,ts#
from    x$bh bh, x$le le
where   bh.le_addr = le.le_addr (+);
```

View Name: V$BH

```
select
file#,block#,class#,status,xnc,forced_reads,forced_writes,lock_element_addr,

lock_element_name,lock_element_class,dirty,temp,ping,stale,direct,new,objd,ts#
from    gv$bh
where   inst_id = USERENV('Instance');
```

View Name: GV$BUFFER_POOL

```
select inst_id,bp_id,bp_name,bp_blksz,decode(bp_state, 0, 'STATIC',1,'ALLOCATING',
      2,'ACTIVATING',3,'SHRINKING'),bp_currgrans * bp_gransz,bp_size,bp_tgtgrans *
      bp_gransz,bp_tgtgrans * bp_bufpergran,bp_prevgrans * bp_gransz,bp_prevgrans *
      bp_bufpergran,0,0,bp_lo_sid,bp_hi_sid,bp_set_ct
from    x$kcbwbpd
where   bp_id > 0 and bp_currgrans > 0 and bp_tgtgrans > 0;
```

View Name: V$BUFFER_POOL

```
select id,name,block_size,resize_state,current_size,buffers,target_size,

target_buffers,prev_size,prev_buffers,lo_bnum,hi_bnum,lo_setid,hi_setid,
      set_count
from    gv$buffer_pool
where   inst_id = USERENV('Instance');
```

View Name: **GV$BUFFER_POOL_STATISTICS**

```
select kcbwbpd.inst_id,kcbwbpd.bp_id,kcbwbpd.bp_name,kcbwbpd.bp_blksz,
       sum(kcbwds.cnum_set),sum(kcbwds.cnum_repl),sum(kcbwds.cnum_write),
       sum(kcbwds.cnum_set),sum(kcbwds.buf_got),sum(kcbwds.sum_wrt),
       sum(kcbwds.sum_scn),sum(kcbwds.fbwait),sum(kcbwds.wcwait),
       sum(kcbwds.bbwait),sum(kcbwds.fbinsp),sum(kcbwds.dbinsp),
       sum(kcbwds.dbbchg),sum(kcbwds.dbbget),sum(kcbwds.conget),sum(kcbwds.pread),
       sum(kcbwds.pwrite)
from   x$kcbwds kcbwds,x$kcbwbpd kcbwbpd
where  kcbwds.set_id >= kcbwbpd.bp_lo_sid and kcbwds.set_id <= kcbwbpd.bp_hi_sid
       and kcbwbpd.bp_size != 0 group by kcbwbpd.inst_id,kcbwbpd.bp_id,
       kcbwbpd.bp_name,kcbwbpd.bp_blksz;
```

View Name: **V$BUFFER_POOL_STATISTICS**

```
select id,name,block_size,set_msize,cnum_repl,cnum_write,cnum_set,buf_got,
       sum_write,sum_scan,free_buffer_wait,write_complete_wait,buffer_busy_wait,

free_buffer_inspected,dirty_buffers_inspected,db_block_change,db_block_gets,
       consistent_gets,physical_reads,physical_writes
from   gv$buffer_pool_statistics
where  inst_id = USERENV('Instance');
```

View Name: **GV$DATABASE**

```
select di.inst_id, di.didbi, di.didbn,to_date(di.dicts,'MM/DD/RR HH24:MI:SS',
       'NLS_CALENDAR=Gregorian'),to_number(di.dirls),to_date(di.dirlc,
       'MM/DD/RR HH24:MI:SS','NLS_CALENDAR=Gregorian'),to_number(di.diprs),
       to_date(di.diprc,'MM/DD/RR HH24:MI:SS','NLS_CALENDAR=Gregorian'),
       decode(bitand(di.diflg,1),0,'NOARCHIVELOG','ARCHIVELOG','MANUAL'),
       to_number(di.discn),to_number(di.difas),decode(bitand(di.diflg,256),256,'CREATED',
       decode(bitand(di.diflg,1024),1024,'STANDBY',decode(bitand(di.diflg,32768),
       32768,'CLONE',decode(bitand(di.diflg,4096),4096,'BACKUP','CURRENT')))),
       to_date(di.dicct,'MM/DD/RR HH24:MI:SS','NLS_CALENDAR=Gregorian'),
       di.dicsq,to_number(di.dickp_scn),to_date(di.dickp_tim,'MM/DD/RR HH24:MI:SS',
       'NLS_CALENDAR=Gregorian'),decode(bitand(di.diflg,4),4,'REQUIRED',decode(di.diirs,0,
       'NOT ALLOWED','ALLOWED'))),to_date(di.divts,'MM/DD/RR HH24:MI:SS',
       'NLS_CALENDAR=Gregorian'),decode(di.didor,0,'MOUNTED',decode(di.didor,1,
       'READ WRITE','READ ONLY')),decode(bitand(di.diflg,65536),65536,'MAXIMUM
       PROTECTION',decode(bitand(di.diflg,128),128,'MAXIMUM AVAILABILITY',
       decode(bitand(di.diflg,134217728),134217728,'RESYNCHRONIZATION',
       decode(bitand(di.diflg,8),8,'UNPROTECTED','MAXIMUM PERFORMANCE')))),
       decode(di.diprt,1,'MAXIMUM PROTECTION',2,'MAXIMUM AVAILABILITY',3,
       'RESYNCHRONIZATION',4,'MAXIMUM PERFORMANCE',5,'UNPROTECTED','UNKNOWN'),
       decode(dirae,0,'DISABLED',1,'SEND',2,'RECEIVE',3,'ENABLED','UNKNOWN'),
       to_number(diacid),decode(bitand(di.diflg,33554432),33554432,'LOGICAL STANDBY',
       decode(bitand(di.diflg,1024),1024,'PHYSICAL STANDBY','PRIMARY')),to_number(di.diars),
       decode(di.disos,0,'IMPOSSIBLE',1,'NOT ALLOWED',2,'SWITCHOVER LATENT',3,
       'SWITCHOVER PENDING',4,'TO PRIMARY',5,'TO STANDBY',6,'RECOVERY NEEDED',7,
       'SESSIONS ACTIVE',8,'PREPARING SWITCHOVER',9,'PREPARING DICTIONARY',10,
       TO LOGICAL STANDBY','UNKNOWN'),decode(di.didgd,0,'DISABLED','ENABLED'),
       decode(bitand(di.diflg,1048576),1048576,'ALL',decode(bitand(di.diflg,2097152),
       2097152,'STANDBY','NONE')),decode(bitand(diflg,1073741824),1073741824,
       'YES', decode(bitand(diflg, 131072 + 262144 + 524288),0,
       decode(bitand(difl2,2), 0,'NO','IMPLICIT'),'IMPLICIT')),
```

```
              decode(bitand(di.diflg,131072),131072,'YES','NO'),
              decode(bitand(di.diflg,262144),262144,'YES','NO'),
              decode(bitand(di.diflg,268435456),268435456,'YES','NO'),
              di.diplid, di.dipln, di2.di2rdi, di2.di2inc,to_number(di.dicur_scn),
              decode(bitand(di2.di2flag,1),1,'YES',
              decode(di2.di2rsp_oldest,0,'NO','RESTORE POINT ONLY')),
              decode(bitand(diflg,524288),524288,'YES','NO'),
              decode(bitand(difl2,2),2,'YES','NO'),di.didbun, to_number(di2.di2actiscn),
              decode(di.difsts,0,'DISABLED',1,'BYSTANDER',2,'SYNCHRONIZED',
              3,'UNSYNCHRONIZED',4,'SUSPENDED',5,'STALLED',6,'LOADING DICTIONARY',
              7,'PRIMARY UNOBSERVED',8,'REINSTATE REQUIRED',9,'REINSTATE IN PROGRESS',
              10,'REINSTATE FAILED',''), di.diftgt, di.difths,
              decode(di.difopr,1,'YES',2,'NO',3,'UNKNOWN',''), di.difobs
from     x$kccdi di, x$kccdi2 di2;
```

View Name: V$DATABASE

```
select  DBID,NAME,CREATED,RESETLOGS_CHANGE#,RESETLOGS_TIME,PRIOR_RESETLOGS_CHANGE#,
        PRIOR_RESETLOGS_TIME,LOG_MODE,CHECKPOINT_CHANGE#,ARCHIVE_CHANGE#,

CONTROLFILE_TYPE,CONTROLFILE_CREATED,CONTROLFILE_SEQUENCE#,CONTROLFILE_CHANGE#,
        CONTROLFILE_TIME,OPEN_RESETLOGS,VERSION_TIME,OPEN_MODE,PROTECTION_MODE,
        PROTECTION_LEVEL,REMOTE_ARCHIVE,ACTIVATION#,SWITCHOVER#,DATABASE_ROLE,
        ARCHIVELOG_CHANGE#, ARCHIVELOG_COMPRESSION, SWITCHOVER_STATUS,
        DATAGUARD_BROKER, GUARD_STATUS, SUPPLEMENTAL_LOG_DATA_MIN,
        SUPPLEMENTAL_LOG_DATA_PK, SUPPLEMENTAL_LOG_DATA_UI, FORCE_LOGGING,
        PLATFORM_ID, PLATFORM_NAME, RECOVERY_TARGET_INCARNATION#,
        LAST_OPEN_INCARNATION#, CURRENT_SCN, FLASHBACK_ON,SUPPLEMENTAL_LOG_DATA_FK,
        SUPPLEMENTAL_LOG_DATA_ALL, DB_UNIQUE_NAME, STANDBY_BECAME_PRIMARY_SCN,
        FS_FAILOVER_STATUS, FS_FAILOVER_CURRENT_TARGET, FS_FAILOVER_THRESHOLD,
        FS_FAILOVER_OBSERVER_PRESENT, FS_FAILOVER_OBSERVER_HOST
from    GV$DATABASE
where   inst_id = USERENV('Instance');
```

View Name: GV$DATAFILE

```
select /*+ rule */ fe.inst_id,fe.fenum,to_number(fe.fecrc_scn),to_date
        (fe.fecrc_tim,'MM/DD/RR HH24:MI:SS','NLS_CALENDAR=Gregorian'),
        fe.fetsn,fe.ferfn,decode(fe.fetsn,0,decode(bitand(fe.festa,2),0,
        'SYSOFF','SYSTEM'),decode(bitand(fe.festa,18),0,'OFFLINE',2,
        'ONLINE','RECOVER')),decode(fe.fedor,2,'READ ONLY',
        decode(bitand(fe.festa, 12),0,'DISABLED',4,'READ ONLY',12,'READ WRITE',
        'UNKNOWN')),to_number(fe.fecps),to_date(fe.fecpt,'MM/DD/RR HH24:MI:SS',
        'NLS_CALENDAR=Gregorian'),to_number(fe.feurs),to_date(fe.feurt,
        'MM/DD/RR HH24:MI:SS','NLS_CALENDAR=Gregorian'),to_number(fe.fests),
        decode(fe.fests,NULL,to_date(NULL),to_date(fe.festt,'MM/DD/RR HH24:MI:SS',
        'NLS_CALENDAR=Gregorian')),to_number(fe.feofs),to_number(fe.feonc_scn),
        to_date(fe.feonc_tim,'MM/DD/RR HH24:MI:SS','NLS_CALENDAR=Gregorian'),
        fh.fhfsz*fe.febsz,fh.fhfsz,fe.fecsz*fe.febsz,fe.febsz,fn.fnnam,fe.fefdb,
        fn.fnbof,decode(fe.fepax, 0,'UNKNOWN', 65535,'NONE',fnaux.fnnam),
        to_number(fh.fhfirstunrecscn),
        to_date(fh.fhfirstunrectime,'MM/DD/RR HH24:MI:SS','NLS_CALENDAR=Gregorian')
from    x$kccfe fe,x$kccfn fn,x$kccfn fnaux,x$kcvfh fh
where   ((fe.fepax!=65535 and fe.fepax!=0 and fe.fepax=fnaux.fnnum) or
        ((fe.fepax=65535 or fe.fepax=0) and fe.fenum=fnaux.fnfno and fnaux.fntyp=4
```

```
      and fnaux.fnnam is not null bitand(fnaux.fnflg, 4) != 4
      and fe.fefnh=fnaux.fnnum))

      and fn.fnfno=fe.fenum and fn.fnfno=fh.hxfil and fe.fefnh=fn.fnnum
      and fe.fedup!=0 and fn.fntyp=4 and fn.fnnam is not null
      and bitand(fn.fnflg, 4) != 4;
```

View Name: V$DATAFILE

```
select FILE#,CREATION_CHANGE#,CREATION_TIME,TS#,RFILE#,STATUS,ENABLED,

CHECKPOINT_CHANGE#,CHECKPOINT_TIME,UNRECOVERABLE_CHANGE#,UNRECOVERABLE_TIME,
       LAST_CHANGE#,LAST_TIME,OFFLINE_CHANGE#,ONLINE_CHANGE#,ONLINE_TIME,

BYTES,BLOCKS,CREATE_BYTES,BLOCK_SIZE,NAME,PLUGGED_IN,BLOCK1_OFFSET,AUX_NAME,
       FIRST_NONLOGGED_SCN, FIRST_NONLOGGED_TIME
from   GV$DATAFILE
where  inst_id = USERENV('Instance');
```

View Name: GV$DB_CACHE_ADVICE

```
select   A.inst_id,A.bpid,B.bp_name,A.blksz,decode (A.status,2,'ON','OFF'),A.poolsz,
         round((A.poolsz / A.actual_poolsz),4),A.nbufs,decode(A.base_preads,0,
         to_number(null),round((A.preads / A.base_preads),4)),decode(A.base_preads,0,
         A.preads,round((A.preads * (A.actual_preads / A.base_preads)),0))
from     x$kcbsc A, x$kcbwbpd B
where    A.bpid = B.bp_id and A.inst_id = B.inst_id
order by A.inst_id,A.bpid,A.poolsz;
```

View Name: V$DB_CACHE_ADVICE

```
select id,name,block_size,advice_status,size_for_estimate,size_factor,
       buffers_for_estimate,estd_physical_read_factor,estd_physical_reads
from   gv$db_cache_advice
where  inst_id = userenv('instance');
```

View Name: GV$DB_OBJECT_CACHE

```
select inst_id,kglnaown,kglnaobj,kglnadlk,decode(kglhdnsp,0,'CURSOR',1,
     'TABLE/PROCEDURE',2,'BODY',3,'TRIGGER',4,'INDEX',5,'CLUSTER',6,'OBJECT',13,
     'JAVA SOURCE',14,'JAVA RESOURCE',15,'REPLICATED TABLE OBJECT',16,
     'REPLICATION INTERNAL PACKAGE',17,'CONTEXT POLICY',18,'PUB_SUB',19,
     'SUMMARY',20,'DIMENSION',21,'APP CONTEXT',22,'STORED OUTLINE',23,'RULESET',24,
     'RSRC PLAN',25,'RSRC CONSUMER GROUP',26,'PENDING RSRC PLAN',27,
     'PENDING RSRC CONSUMER GROUP',28,'SUBSCRIPTION',29,'LOCATION',30,
     'REMOTE OBJECT',31,'SNAPSHOT METADATA',32,'JAVA SHARED DATA',33,
     'SECURITY PROFILE','INVALID NAMESPACE'),decode(bitand(kglobflg,3),0,
     'NOT LOADED',2,'NON-EXISTENT',3,'INVALID STATUS',decode(kglobtyp,0,'CURSOR',1,
     'INDEX',2,'TABLE',3,'CLUSTER',4,'VIEW',5,'SYNONYM',6,'SEQUENCE',7,
     'PROCEDURE',8,'FUNCTION',9,'PACKAGE',10,'NON-EXISTENT',11,
     'PACKAGE BODY',12,'TRIGGER',13,'TYPE',14,'TYPEBODY',15,'OBJECT',16,
     'USER',17,'DBLINK',18,'PIPE',19,'TABLE PARTITION',20,'INDEX PARTITION',21,
     'LOB',22,'LIBRARY',23,'DIRECTORY',24,'QUEUE',25,'INDEX-ORGANIZED TABLE',26,
     'REPLICATION OBJECT GROUP',27,'REPLICATION PROPAGATOR',28,'JAVA SOURCE',29,
     'JAVA CLASS',30,'JAVA RESOURCE',31,'JAVA JAR',32,'INDEX TYPE',33,'OPERATOR',34,
```

V$ Views

```
        'TABLE SUBPARTITION',35,'INDEX SUBPARTITION',36,'REPLICATED TABLE OBJECT',37,
        'REPLICATION INTERNAL PACKAGE',38,'CONTEXT POLICY',39,'PUB_SUB',40,
        'LOB PARTITION',41,'LOB SUBPARTITION',42,'SUMMARY',43,'DIMENSION',44,
        'APP CONTEXT',45,'STORED OUTLINE',46,'RULESET',47,'RSRC PLAN',48,
        'RSRC CONSUMER GROUP',49,'PENDING RSRC PLAN',50,'PENDING RSRC CONSUMER GROUP',51,
        'SUBSCRIPTION',52,'LOCATION',53,'REMOTE OBJECT',54,'SNAPSHOT METADATA',55,
        'IFS',56,'JAVA SHARED DATA',57,'SECURITY PROFILE','INVALID TYPE')),
        kglobhs0+kglobhs1+kglobhs2+kglobhs3+kglobhs4+kglobhs5+kglobhs6,
        kglhdldc,kglhdexc,kglhdlkc,kglobpc0,decode(kglhdkmk,0,'NO','YES'),kglhdclt,
        kglhdivc
from    x$kglob;
```

View Name: V$DB_OBJECT_CACHE

```
select
OWNER,NAME,DB_LINK,NAMESPACE,TYPE,SHARABLE_MEM,LOADS,EXECUTIONS,LOCKS,PINS,KEPT,
      CHILD_LATCH, INVALIDATIONS
from    GV$DB_OBJECT_CACHE
where   inst_id = USERENV('Instance');
```

View Name: GV$DLM_ALL_LOCKS

```
select USERENV('Instance'),HANDLE,GRANT_LEVEL,REQUEST_LEVEL,RESOURCE_NAME1,

RESOURCE_NAME2,PID,TRANSACTION_ID0,TRANSACTION_ID1,GROUP_ID,OPEN_OPT_DEADLOCK,

OPEN_OPT_PERSISTENT,OPEN_OPT_PROCESS_OWNED,OPEN_OPT_NO_XID,CONVERT_OPT_GETVALUE,
      CONVERT_OPT_PUTVALUE,CONVERT_OPT_NOVALUE,CONVERT_OPT_DUBVALUE,
      CONVERT_OPT_NOQUEUE,CONVERT_OPT_EXPRESS,CONVERT_OPT_NODEADLOCKWAIT,
      CONVERT_OPT_NODEADLOCKBLOCK,WHICH_QUEUE,STATE,AST_EVENT0,OWNER_NODE,BLOCKED,
      BLOCKER
from    V$GES_ENQUEUE;
```

View Name: V$DLM_ALL_LOCKS

```
select LOCKP,GRANT_LEVEL,REQUEST_LEVEL,RESOURCE_NAME1,RESOURCE_NAME2,PID,
      TRANSACTION_ID0,TRANSACTION_ID1,GROUP_ID,OPEN_OPT_DEADLOCK,OPEN_OPT_PERSISTENT,
      OPEN_OPT_PROCESS_OWNED,OPEN_OPT_NO_XID,CONVERT_OPT_GETVALUE,CONVERT_OPT_PUTVALUE,
      CONVERT_OPT_NOVALUE,CONVERT_OPT_DUBVALUE,CONVERT_OPT_NOQUEUE,CONVERT_OPT_EXPRESS,
      CONVERT_OPT_NODEADLOCKWAIT,CONVERT_OPT_NODEADLOCKBLOCK,WHICH_QUEUE,LOCKSTATE,
      AST_EVENT0,OWNER_NODE,BLOCKED,BLOCKER
from    GV$DLM_ALL_LOCKS
where   INST_ID = USERENV('Instance');
```

View Name: GV$DLM_LATCH

```
select
USERENV('Instance'),addr,latch#,level#,name,gets,misses,sleeps,immediate_gets,
      immediate_misses,waiters_woken,waits_holding_latch,spin_gets,sleep1,sleep2,
      sleep3,sleep4,sleep5,sleep6,sleep7,sleep8,sleep9,sleep10,sleep11,wait_time
from    V$LATCH
where   NAME like 'ges %' or NAME like 'gcs %';
```

View Name: V$DLM_LATCH

```
select addr,latch#,level#,name,gets,misses,sleeps,immediate_gets,immediate_misses,
       waiters_woken,waits_holding_latch,spin_gets,sleep1,sleep2,sleep3,sleep4,sleep5,
       sleep6,sleep7,sleep8,sleep9,sleep10,sleep11,wait_time
from   GV$DLM_LATCH
where  INST_ID = USERENV('Instance');
```

View Name: GV$DLM_LOCKS

```
select USERENV('Instance'),HANDLE,GRANT_LEVEL,REQUEST_LEVEL,RESOURCE_NAME1,
       RESOURCE_NAME2,PID,TRANSACTION_ID0,TRANSACTION_ID1,GROUP_ID,OPEN_OPT_DEADLOCK,
       OPEN_OPT_PERSISTENT,OPEN_OPT_PROCESS_OWNED,OPEN_OPT_NO_XID,CONVERT_OPT_GETVALUE,
       CONVERT_OPT_PUTVALUE,CONVERT_OPT_NOVALUE,CONVERT_OPT_DUBVALUE,
       CONVERT_OPT_NOQUEUE,CONVERT_OPT_EXPRESS,CONVERT_OPT_NODEADLOCKWAIT,
       CONVERT_OPT_NODEADLOCKBLOCK,WHICH_QUEUE,STATE,AST_EVENT0,OWNER_NODE,BLOCKED,
       BLOCKER
from   V$GES_BLOCKING_ENQUEUE;
```

View Name: V$DLM_LOCKS

```
select LOCKP,GRANT_LEVEL,REQUEST_LEVEL,RESOURCE_NAME1,RESOURCE_NAME2,PID,
       TRANSACTION_ID0,TRANSACTION_ID1,GROUP_ID,OPEN_OPT_DEADLOCK,OPEN_OPT_PERSISTENT,
       OPEN_OPT_PROCESS_OWNED,OPEN_OPT_NO_XID,CONVERT_OPT_GETVALUE,CONVERT_OPT_PUTVALUE,
       CONVERT_OPT_NOVALUE,CONVERT_OPT_DUBVALUE,CONVERT_OPT_NOQUEUE,CONVERT_OPT_EXPRESS,
       CONVERT_OPT_NODEADLOCKWAIT,CONVERT_OPT_NODEADLOCKBLOCK,WHICH_QUEUE,LOCKSTATE,
       AST_EVENT0,OWNER_NODE,BLOCKED,BLOCKER
from   GV$DLM_LOCKS
where  INST_ID = USERENV('Instance');
```

View Name: GV$ENQUEUE_LOCK

```
select s.inst_id,l.addr,l.ksqlkadr,s.ksusenum,r.ksqrsidt,r.ksqrsid1,
       r.ksqrsid2, l.ksqlkmod, l.ksqlkreq,l.ksqlkctim,l.ksqlklblk
from   x$ksqeq l,x$ksuse s,x$ksqrs r
where  l.ksqlkses=s.addr
and    bitand(l.kssobflg,1)!=0
and    (l.ksqlkmod!=0 or l.ksqlkreq!=0)
and    l.ksqlkres=r.addr;
```

View Name: V$ENQUEUE_LOCK

```
select ADDR,KADDR,SID,TYPE,ID1,ID2,LMODE,REQUEST,CTIME,BLOCK
from   GV$ENQUEUE_LOCK
where  inst_id = USERENV('Instance');
```

View Name: GV$ENQUEUE_STAT

```
select inst_id, ksqsttyp, sum(ksqstreq), sum(ksqstwat), sum(ksqstsgt),
       sum(ksqstfgt), sum(ksqstwtm)
from   X$KSQST
group by inst_id, ksqsttyp having sum(ksqstreq) > 0;
```

V$ Views

View Name: V$ENQUEUE_STAT

```
select INST_ID,EQ_TYPE,TOTAL_REQ#,TOTAL_WAIT#,SUCC_REQ#,FAILED_REQ#,CUM_WAIT_TIME
from    GV$ENQUEUE_STAT
where   inst_id = USERENV('Instance');
```

View Name: GV$EVENT_NAME

```
select inst_id, indx, ksledhash, kslednam, ksledp1, ksledp2, ksledp3,
       ksledclassid, ksledclass#, ksledclass
from   x$ksled;
```

View Name: V$EVENT_NAME

```
select event#, event_id, name,parameter1,parameter2,parameter3,
       wait_class_id, wait_class#, wait_class
from   gv$event_name
where  inst_id = USERENV('Instance');
```

View Name: GV$EXECUTION

```
select inst_id,pid,val0,func,decode(id,1,'call',2,'return',3,'longjmp'),nvals,val2,
       val3,seqh,seql
from   x$kstex where op=10;
```

View Name: V$EXECUTION

```
select PID,DEPTH,FUNCTION,TYPE,NVALS,VAL1,VAL2,SEQH,SEQL
from    GV$EXECUTION
where   inst_id = USERENV('Instance');
```

View Name: GV$FILESTAT

```
select
k.inst_id,k.kcfiofno,k.kcfiopyr,k.kcfiopyw,k.kcfiopbr,k.kcfiopbw,k.kcfiosbr,
       k.kcfioprt,k.kcfiopwt,k.kcfiosbt,k.kcfioavg,k.kcfiolst,k.kcfiomin,
       k.kcfiormx,k.kcfiowmx
from   x$kcfio k,x$kccfe f
where  f.fedup <> 0
and    f.fenum=k.kcfiofno;
```

View Name: V$FILESTAT

```
select  FILE#,PHYRDS,PHYWRTS,PHYBLKRD,PHYBLKWRT,SINGLEBLKRDS,READTIM,WRITETIM,
       SINGLEBLKRDTIM,AVGIOTIM,LSTIOTIM,MINIOTIM,MAXIORTM,MAXIOWTM
from   GV$FILESTAT
where  inst_id = USERENV('Instance');
```

View Name: GV$FILE_CACHE_TRANSFER

```
select x.inst_id, kcfiofno, 0, 0, 0, 0, 0, 0, 0, 0, 0, 0, 0, 0, 0, 0, 0
from   x$kcfio x, x$kccfe fe
where  x.kcfiofno = fe.fenum;
```

View Name: **V$FILE_CACHE_TRANSFER**

```
select file_number,x_2_null,x_2_null_forced_write,x_2_null_forced_stale,x_2_s,
       x_2_s_forced_write,s_2_null,s_2_null_forced_stale,rbr,rbr_forced_write,
       rbr_forced_stale,null_2_x,s_2_x,null_2_s,cr_transfers,cur_transfers
from   gv$file_cache_transfer
where  inst_id = USERENV('Instance');
```

View Name: **GV$FIXED_TABLE**

```
select inst_id,kqftanam,kqftaobj,'TABLE',indx
from   x$kqfta union all
          select inst_id,kqfvinam,kqfviobj,'VIEW',65537
          from   x$kqfvi union all
             select inst_id,kqfdtnam, kqfdtobj, 'TABLE', 65537
             from   x$kqfdt;
```

View Name: **V$FIXED_TABLE**

```
select NAME,OBJECT_ID,TYPE,TABLE_NUM
from   GV$FIXED_TABLE
where  inst_id = USERENV('Instance');
```

View Name: **GV$FIXED_VIEW_DEFINITION**

```
select i.inst_id,kqfvinam,kqftpsel
from   x$kqfvi i,x$kqfvt t
where  i.indx = t.indx;
```

View Name: **V$FIXED_VIEW_DEFINITION**

```
select VIEW_NAME,VIEW_DEFINITION
from   GV$FIXED_VIEW_DEFINITION
where  inst_id = USERENV('Instance');
```

View Name: **GV$GES_BLOCKING_ENQUEUE**

```
select USERENV('Instance'),HANDLE,GRANT_LEVEL,REQUEST_LEVEL,RESOURCE_NAME1,
       RESOURCE_NAME2,PID,TRANSACTION_ID0,TRANSACTION_ID1,GROUP_ID,
       OPEN_OPT_DEADLOCK,OPEN_OPT_PERSISTENT,OPEN_OPT_PROCESS_OWNED,OPEN_OPT_NO_XID,
       CONVERT_OPT_GETVALUE,CONVERT_OPT_PUTVALUE,CONVERT_OPT_NOVALUE,
       CONVERT_OPT_DUBVALUE,CONVERT_OPT_NOQUEUE,CONVERT_OPT_EXPRESS,
       CONVERT_OPT_NODEADLOCKWAIT,CONVERT_OPT_NODEADLOCKBLOCK, WHICH_QUEUE,
       STATE,AST_EVENT0,OWNER_NODE,BLOCKED,BLOCKER
from   V$GES_ENQUEUE
where (REQUEST_LEVEL != 'KJUSERNL')
and   (BLOCKED = 1 or BLOCKER = 1);
```

View Name: **V$GES_BLOCKING_ENQUEUE**

```
select HANDLE,GRANT_LEVEL,REQUEST_LEVEL,RESOURCE_NAME1,RESOURCE_NAME2,PID,
       TRANSACTION_ID0,TRANSACTION_ID1,GROUP_ID,OPEN_OPT_DEADLOCK,
```

```
        OPEN_OPT_PERSISTENT,OPEN_OPT_PROCESS_OWNED,OPEN_OPT_NO_XID,
        CONVERT_OPT_GETVALUE,CONVERT_OPT_PUTVALUE,CONVERT_OPT_NOVALUE,
        CONVERT_OPT_DUBVALUE,CONVERT_OPT_NOQUEUE,CONVERT_OPT_EXPRESS,
        CONVERT_OPT_NODEADLOCKWAIT,CONVERT_OPT_NODEADLOCKBLOCK,WHICH_QUEUE,STATE,
        AST_EVENT0,OWNER_NODE,BLOCKED,BLOCKER
from    GV$GES_BLOCKING_ENQUEUE
where   INST_ID = USERENV('Instance');
```

View Name: GV$GES_ENQUEUE

```
select inst_id,kjilkftlkp,kjilkftgl,kjilkftrl,kjilkftrn1,kjilkftrn2,kjilkftpid,
       kjilkftxid0,kjilkftxid1,kjilkftgid,kjilkftoodd,kjilkftoopt,kjilkftoopo,
       kjilkftoonxid,kjilkftcogv,kjilkftcopv,kjilkftconv,kjilkftcodv,kjilkftconq,
       kjilkftcoep,kjilkftconddw,kjilkftconddb,kjilkftwq,kjilkftls,kjilkftaste0,
       kjilkfton,kjilkftblked,kjilkftblker
from   x$kjilkft union all
           select inst_id, kjbllockp, kjblgrant, kjblrequest,kjblname,
                  kjblname2,0,0,0,0,0,1,0,1,0,0,0,0,0,0,0,0,kjblqueue,kjbllockst,0,
                  kjblowner,kjblblocked,kjblblocker
           from   x$kjbl;
```

View Name: V$GES_ENQUEUE

```
select HANDLE,GRANT_LEVEL,REQUEST_LEVEL,RESOURCE_NAME1,RESOURCE_NAME2,PID,
       TRANSACTION_ID0,TRANSACTION_ID1,GROUP_ID,OPEN_OPT_DEADLOCK,
       OPEN_OPT_PERSISTENT,OPEN_OPT_PROCESS_OWNED,OPEN_OPT_NO_XID,
       CONVERT_OPT_GETVALUE,CONVERT_OPT_PUTVALUE,CONVERT_OPT_NOVALUE,
       CONVERT_OPT_DUBVALUE,CONVERT_OPT_NOQUEUE,CONVERT_OPT_EXPRESS,
       CONVERT_OPT_NODEADLOCKWAIT,CONVERT_OPT_NODEADLOCKBLOCK,WHICH_QUEUE,STATE,
       AST_EVENT0,OWNER_NODE,BLOCKED,BLOCKER
from   GV$GES_ENQUEUE
where   INST_ID = USERENV('Instance');
```

View Name: GV$GLOBAL_BLOCKED_LOCKS

```
select USERENV('instance'),addr,kaddr,sid,type,id1,id2,lmode,request,ctime
from    v$lock l
where exists
  (select *
   from    v$dlm_locks d
   where   substr(d.resource_name2,1,instr(d.resource_name2, ',',1,1)-1) = id1
   and     substr(d.resource_name2,instr(d.resource_name2,',',1,1)+1,
           instr(d.resource_name2, ',',1,2)-instr(d.resource_name2,',',1,1)-1) = id2
   and     substr(d.resource_name2,instr(d.resource_name2,',',-1,1)+1,2) = type);
```

View Name: V$GLOBAL_BLOCKED_LOCKS

```
select ADDR,KADDR,SID,TYPE,ID1,ID2,LMODE,REQUEST,CTIME
from    gv$global_blocked_locks
where   inst_id = userenv('instance');
```

View Name: GV$GLOBAL_TRANSACTION

```
select  inst_id,K2GTIFMT,K2GTITID_EXT,K2GTIBID,K2GTECNT,K2GTERCT,K2GTDPCT,
        decode (K2GTDFLG,0,'ACTIVE',1,'COLLECTING',2,'FINALIZED',4,'FAILED',8,
        'RECOVERING',16,'UNASSOCIATED',32,'FORGOTTEN',64,'READY FOR RECOVERY',
        'COMBINATION'),K2GTDFLG,decode (K2GTETYP,0,'FREE',1,'LOOSELY COUPLED',2,
        'TIGHTLY COUPLED')
from    X$K2GTE2;
```

View Name: V$GLOBAL_TRANSACTION

```
select  FORMATID,GLOBALID,BRANCHID,BRANCHES,REFCOUNT,PREPARECOUNT,STATE,FLAGS,
        COUPLING
from    GV$GLOBAL_TRANSACTION
where   INST_ID = USERENV('Instance');
```

View Name: GV$INDEXED_FIXED_COLUMN

```
select  c.inst_id,kqftanam,kqfcoidx,kqfconam,kqfcoipo
from    x$kqfco c,x$kqfta t
where   t.indx = c.kqfcotab
and     kqfcoidx != 0;
```

View Name: V$INDEXED_FIXED_COLUMN

```
select  TABLE_NAME,INDEX_NUMBER,COLUMN_NAME,COLUMN_POSITION
from    GV$INDEXED_FIXED_COLUMN
where   inst_id = USERENV('Instance');
```

View Name: GV$INSTANCE

```
select ks.inst_id,ksuxsins,ksuxssid,ksuxshst,ksuxsver,ksuxstim,
       decode(ksuxssts,0,'STARTED',1,'MOUNTED',2,'OPEN',3,'OPEN MIGRATE','UNKNOWN'),
       decode(ksuxsshr,0,'NO',1,'YES',2,NULL),ksuxsthr,
       decode(ksuxsarc,0,'STOPPED',1,'STARTED','FAILED'),
       decode(ksuxslsw,0,NULL,2,'ARCHIVE LOG',3,'CLEAR LOG',4,'CHECKPOINT',
       5,'REDO GENERATION'),
       decode(ksuxsdba,0,'ALLOWED','RESTRICTED'),
       decode(ksuxsshp,0,'NO','YES'),
       decode(kvitval,0,'ACTIVE',2147483647,'SUSPENDED','INSTANCE RECOVERY'),
       decode(ksuxsrol,1,'PRIMARY_INSTANCE',2,'SECONDARY_INSTANCE','UNKNOWN'),
       decode(qui_state,0,'NORMAL',1,'QUIESCING',2,'QUIESCED','UNKNOWN'),
       decode(bitand(ksuxsdst, 1), 0, 'NO', 1, 'YES', 'NO')
from   x$ksuxsinst ks, x$kvit kv, x$quiesce qu
where  kvittag = 'kcbwst';
```

View Name: V$INSTANCE

```
select
INSTANCE_NUMBER,INSTANCE_NAME,HOST_NAME,VERSION,STARTUP_TIME,STATUS,PARALLEL,
       THREAD#,ARCHIVER,LOG_SWITCH_WAIT,LOGINS,SHUTDOWN_PENDING,DATABASE_STATUS,
```

```
        INSTANCE_ROLE,ACTIVE_STATE, BLOCKED
from    GV$INSTANCE
where   inst_id = USERENV('Instance');
```

View Name: GV$LATCH

```
select d.inst_id,d.kslldadr,la.latch#,d.kslldlvl,d.kslldnam,d.kslldhsh,la.gets,
       la.misses,la.sleeps,la.immediate_gets,la.immediate_misses,la.waiters_woken,
       la.waits_holding_latch,la.spin_gets,la.sleep1,la.sleep2, la.sleep3,la.sleep4,
       la.sleep5,la.sleep6,la.sleep7,la.sleep8,la.sleep9,la.sleep10,la.sleep11,
       la.wait_time
from   x$kslld d,
       (select kslltnum latch#,sum(kslltwgt)gets,sum(kslltwff)misses,
       sum(kslltwsl) sleeps,sum(kslltngt) immediate_gets,
       sum(kslltnfa) immediate_misses,sum(kslltwkc) waiters_woken,
       sum(kslltwth) waits_holding_latch,sum(ksllthst0) spin_gets,
       sum(ksllthst1) sleep1,sum(ksllthst2) sleep2,sum(ksllthst3) sleep3,
       sum(ksllthst4) sleep4,sum(ksllthst5) sleep5, sum(ksllthst6) sleep6,
       sum(ksllthst7) sleep7,sum(ksllthst8) sleep8,sum(ksllthst9) sleep9,
       sum(ksllthst10) sleep10,sum(ksllthst11) sleep11,sum(kslltwtt) wait_time
       from  x$ksllt group by kslltnum) la
       where  la.latch# = d.indx;
```

View Name: V$LATCH

```
select
addr,latch#,level#,hash,name,gets,misses,sleeps,immediate_gets,immediate_misses,
       waiters_woken,waits_holding_latch,spin_gets,sleep1,sleep2,sleep3,sleep4,
       sleep5,sleep6,sleep7,sleep8,sleep9,sleep10,sleep11,wait_time
from   gv$latch
where  inst_id = USERENV('Instance');
```

View Name: GV$LATCHHOLDER

```
select  inst_id,ksuprpid,ksuprsid,ksuprlat,ksuprlnm,ksulagts
from    x$ksuprlat;
```

View Name: V$LATCHHOLDER

```
select  PID,SID,LADDR,NAME,GETS
from    GV$LATCHHOLDER
where   inst_id = USERENV('Instance');
```

View Name: GV$LATCHNAME

```
select  inst_id,indx,kslldnam,kslldhsh
from    x$kslld;
```

View Name: V$LATCHNAME

```
select  latch#,name,hash
from    gv$latchname
where   inst_id = userenv('Instance');
```

View Name: GV$LATCH_CHILDREN

```
select  t.inst_id,t.addr,t.kslltnum,t.kslltcnm,n.kslldlvl,n.kslldnam,n.kslldhsh,
        t.kslltwgt,t.kslltwff,t.kslltwsl,t.kslltngt,t.kslltnfa,t.kslltwkc,t.kslltwth,
        t.kslltthst0,t.kslltthst1,t.kslltthst2,t.kslltthst3,t.kslltthst4,t.kslltthst5,
        t.kslltthst6,t.kslltthst7,t.kslltthst8,t.kslltthst9,t.kslltthst10,t.kslltthst11,
        t.kslltwtt
from    x$ksllt t,x$kslld n
where   t.kslltcnm > 0
and     t.kslltnum = n.indx;
```

View Name: V$LATCH_CHILDREN

```
select  ADDR,LATCH#,CHILD#,LEVEL#,NAME,HASH,GETS,MISSES,SLEEPS,IMMEDIATE_GETS,
        IMMEDIATE_MISSES,WAITERS_WOKEN,WAITS_HOLDING_LATCH,SPIN_GETS,SLEEP1,SLEEP2,
        SLEEP3,SLEEP4,SLEEP5,SLEEP6,SLEEP7,SLEEP8,SLEEP9,SLEEP10,SLEEP11,
        WAIT_TIME
from    GV$LATCH_CHILDREN
where   inst_id = USERENV('Instance');
```

View Name: GV$LATCH_MISSES

```
select  t1.inst_id,t1.ksllasnam,t2.ksllwnam,t1.kslnowtf,t1.kslsleep,t1.kslwscwsl,
        t1.kslwsclthg,t2.ksllwnam
from    x$ksllw t2,x$kslwsc t1
where   t2.indx = t1.indx;
```

View Name: V$LATCH_MISSES

```
select  PARENT_NAME,LOCATION,NWFAIL_COUNT,SLEEP_COUNT,WTR_SLP_COUNT,LONGHOLD_COUNT,
        LOCATION
from    GV$LATCH_MISSES
where   inst_id = USERENV('Instance');
```

View Name: GV$LATCH_PARENT

```
select  t.inst_id,t.addr,t.kslltnum,n.kslldlvl,n.kslldnam,n.kslldhsh,t.kslltwgt,

t.kslltwff,t.kslltwsl,t.kslltngt,t.kslltnfa,t.kslltwkc,t.kslltwth,t.kslltthst0,
        t.kslltthst1,t.kslltthst2,t.kslltthst3,t.kslltthst4,t.kslltthst5,t.kslltthst6,
        t.kslltthst7,t.kslltthst8,t.kslltthst9,t.kslltthst10,t.kslltthst11,t.kslltwtt
from    x$ksllt t,x$kslld n
where   t.kslltcnm = 0
and     t.kslltnum = n.indx;
```

View Name: V$LATCH_PARENT

```
select
ADDR,LATCH#,LEVEL#,NAME,HASH,GETS,MISSES,SLEEPS,IMMEDIATE_GETS,IMMEDIATE_MISSES,
        WAITERS_WOKEN,WAITS_HOLDING_LATCH,SPIN_GETS,SLEEP1,SLEEP2,SLEEP3,SLEEP4,
        SLEEP5,SLEEP6,SLEEP7,SLEEP8,SLEEP9,SLEEP10,SLEEP11,WAIT_TIME
from    GV$LATCH_PARENT
where   inst_id = USERENV('Instance');
```

V$ Views

View Name: GV$LIBRARYCACHE

```
select inst_id,decode(indx,0,'SQL AREA',1,'TABLE/PROCEDURE',2,'BODY',3,
       'TRIGGER',4,'INDEX',5,'CLUSTER',6,'OBJECT',7,'PIPE',13,'JAVA SOURCE',14,
       'JAVA RESOURCE',32,'JAVA DATA','?'),kglstget,kglstght,
       decode(kglstget,0,1,kglstght/kglstget),kglstpin,kglstpht,
       decode(kglstpin,0,1,kglstpht/kglstpin),kglstrld,kglstinv,kglstlrq,
       kglstprq,kglstprl,kglstirq,kglstmiv
from   x$kglst
where  indx<8 or indx=13 or indx=14 or indx=32;
```

View Name: V$LIBRARYCACHE

```
select NAMESPACE,GETS,GETHITS,GETHITRATIO,PINS,PINHITS,PINHITRATIO,RELOADS,
       INVALIDATIONS,DLM_LOCK_REQUESTS,DLM_PIN_REQUESTS,DLM_PIN_RELEASES,
       DLM_INVALIDATION_REQUESTS,DLM_INVALIDATIONS
from   GV$LIBRARYCACHE
where  inst_id = USERENV('Instance');
```

View Name: GV$LIBRARY_CACHE_MEMORY

```
select inst_id,decode(kglsim_namespace,0,'SQL AREA',1,'TABLE/PROCEDURE',2,
       'BODY',3,'TRIGGER',4,'INDEX',5,'CLUSTER',6,'OBJECT',7,'PIPE',13,
       'JAVA SOURCE',14,'JAVA RESOURCE',32,'JAVA DATA','?'),kglsim_pincnt,
       kglsim_pinmem,kglsim_unpincnt,kglsim_unpinmem
from   x$kglmem
where  kglsim_namespace<8
or     kglsim_namespace=13
or     kglsim_namespace=14
or     kglsim_namespace=32
union
select inst_id,'OTHER/SYSTEM',sum(kglsim_pincnt)sum_pincnt,
       sum(kglsim_pinmem)sum_pinmem,sum(kglsim_unpincnt) sum_unpincnt,
       sum(kglsim_unpinmem) sum_unpinmem
from   x$kglmem
where  not (kglsim_namespace<8
or     kglsim_namespace=13
or     kglsim_namespace=14
or     kglsim_namespace=32)
group  by   inst_id;
```

View Name: V$LIBRARY_CACHE_MEMORY

```
select lc_namespace,lc_inuse_memory_objects,lc_inuse_memorysize,
       lc_freeable_memory_objects,lc_freeable_memory_size
from   gv$library_cache_memory
where  inst_id = USERENV('Instance');
```

View Name: GV$LOCK

```
select  s.inst_id,l.laddr,l.kaddr,s.ksusenum,r.ksqrsidt,r.ksqrsid1,
        r.ksqrsid2,l.lmode,l.request,l.ctime,decode(l.lmode,0,0,l.block)
from    v$_lock l,x$ksuse s,x$ksqrs r
where   l.saddr=s.addr
and     l.raddr=r.addr;
```

View Name: V$LOCK

```
select  ADDR,KADDR,SID,TYPE,ID1,ID2,LMODE,REQUEST,CTIME,BLOCK
from    GV$LOCK
where   inst_id = USERENV('Instance');
```

View Name: GV$LOCKED_OBJECT

```
select  x.inst_id,x.kxidusn,x.kxidslt,x.kxidsqn,l.ktadmtab,s.indx,s.ksuudlna,
        s.ksuseunm,s.ksusepid,l.ksqlkmod
from    x$ktcxb x,x$ktadm l,x$ksuse s
where   x.ktcxbxba = l.kssobown
and     x.ktcxbses = s.addr;
```

View Name: V$LOCKED_OBJECT

```
select  xidusn,xidslot,xidsqn,object_id,session_id,oracle_username, os_user_name,
        process,locked_mode
from    gv$locked_object
where   inst_id = USERENV('Instance');
```

View Name: GV$LOCKS_WITH_COLLISIONS

```
select    USERENV('Instance'),lock_element_addr
from      v$bh
where     (forced_writes + forced_reads) > 10
group by lock_element_addr having count(*) >= 2;
```

View Name: V$LOCKS_WITH_COLLISIONS

```
select    lock_element_addr
from      v$bh
where     (forced_writes + forced_reads) > 10
group by lock_element_addr having count(*) >= 2;
```

View Name: GV$LOCK_ACTIVITY

```
Select    0, 'NULL', 'S', 'Lock buffers for read', 0
from      dual;
```

V$ Views

View Name: V$LOCK_ACTIVITY

```
select FROM_VAL,TO_VAL,ACTION_VAL,COUNTER
from   GV$LOCK_ACTIVITY
where  INST_ID = USERENV('INSTANCE');
```

View Name: GV$LOCK_ELEMENT

```
select inst_id,le_addr,indx,le_class,name,le_mode,le_blks,le_rls,le_acq,0,le_flags
from   x$le;
```

View Name: V$LOCK_ELEMENT

```
select lock_element_addr,indx,class,lock_element_name,mode_held,block_count,
       releasing,acquiring,invalid,flags
from   gv$lock_element
where  inst_id = USERENV('Instance');
```

View Name: GV$MTTR_TARGET_ADVICE

```
select distinct inst_id,mttr_v,decode(status,0,'OFF',4,'ON','READY'),
       decode(dirty_limit,0,to_number(NULL),dirty_limit),
       decode(factored_sim_writes,-1,to_number(NULL),factored_sim_writes),
       decode(base_real_nondirect_writes,0,to_number(NULL),
       decode(factored_sim_writes,-1,to_number(NULL),
       round((factored_sim_writes / base_real_nondirect_writes),4))),
       decode(total_writes,-1,to_number(NULL),total_writes),
       decode(base_total_writes,0,to_number(NULL),
       decode(total_writes,-1,to_number(NULL),
       round((total_writes / base_total_writes),4))),
       decode(total_ios,-1,to_number(NULL),total_ios),
       decode(base_total_ios,0,to_number(NULL),
       decode(total_ios,-1,to_number(NULL),round((total_ios / base_total_ios), 4)))
from   x$kcbmmav;
```

View Name: V$MTTR_TARGET_ADVICE

```
select mttr_target_for_estimate,advice_status,dirty_limit,estd_cache_writes,
       estd_cache_write_factor,estd_total_writes,estd_total_write_factor,
       estd_total_ios, estd_total_io_factor
from   gv$mttr_target_advice
where  inst_id = userenv('instance');
```

View Name: GV$MVREFRESH

```
select       inst_id,sid_knst,serial_knst,currmvowner_knstmvr,currmvname_knstmvr
from         x$knstmvr x
where        type_knst=6
and exists   (select 1
                from   v$session s
                where  s.sid=x.sid_knst
                and    s.serial#=x.serial_knst);
```

View Name: **V$MVREFRESH**

```
select SID,SERIAL#,CURRMVOWNER,CURRMVNAME
from   GV$MVREFRESH;
```

View Name: **GV$MYSTAT**

```
select inst_id,ksusenum,ksusestn,ksusestv
from   x$ksumysta
where  bitand(ksspaflg,1)!=0
and    bitand(ksuseflg,1)!=0
and    ksusestn<
          (select ksusgstl
            from x$ksusgif);
```

View Name: **V$MYSTAT**

```
select SID,STATISTIC#,VALUE
from   GV$MYSTAT
where  inst_id = USERENV('Instance');
```

View Name: **GV$OBSOLETE_PARAMETER**

```
select inst_id,kspponm,decode(ksppoval,0,'FALSE','TRUE')
from   x$ksppo;
```

View Name: **V$OBSOLETE_PARAMETER**

```
select NAME,ISSPECIFIED
from   GV$OBSOLETE_PARAMETER
where  inst_id = USERENV('Instance');
```

View Name: **GV$OPEN_CURSOR**

```
select inst_id,kgllkuse,kgllksnm,user_name,kglhdpar,kglnahsh,kgllksqlid,kglnaobj
from   x$kgllk
where  kglhdnsp = 0
and    kglhdpar != kgllkhdl;
```

View Name: **V$OPEN_CURSOR**

```
select SADDR,SID,USER_NAME,ADDRESS,HASH_VALUE,SQL_ID,SQL_TEXT
from   GV$OPEN_CURSOR
where  inst_id = USERENV('Instance');
```

View Name: **GV$OPTION**

```
select inst_id,parameter,value
from   x$option;
```

V$ Views

View Name: V$OPTION

```
select PARAMETER,VALUE
from   GV$OPTION
where  inst_id = USERENV('Instance');
```

View Name: GV$PARAMETER

```
select x.inst_id,x.indx+1,ksppinm,ksppity,ksppstvl, ksppstdvl, ksppstdf,
       decode(bitand(ksppiflg/256,1),1,'TRUE','FALSE'),
       decode(bitand(ksppiflg/65536,3),1,'IMMEDIATE',2,'DEFERRED',
       3,'IMMEDIATE','FALSE'),decode(bitand(ksppiflg,4),4,'FALSE',
       decode(bitand(ksppiflg/65536,3), 0, 'FALSE', 'TRUE')),
       decode(bitand(ksppstvf,7),1,'MODIFIED',4,'SYSTEM_MOD','FALSE'),
       decode(bitand(ksppstvf,2),2,'TRUE','FALSE'),
       decode(bitand(ksppilrmflg/64, 1), 1, 'TRUE', 'FALSE'),
       ksppdesc, ksppstcmnt, ksppihash
from   x$ksppi x, x$ksppcv y
where  (x.indx = y.indx)
and    ((translate(ksppinm,'_','#') not like '##%')
and    ((translate(ksppinm,'_','#') not like '#%')
or     (ksppstdf = 'FALSE') or (bitand(ksppstvf,5) > 0)));
```

View Name: V$PARAMETER

```
select NUM,NAME,TYPE,VALUE,DISPLAY_VALUE,ISDEFAULT,ISSES_MODIFIABLE,
       ISSYS_MODIFIABLE,ISINSTANCE_MODIFIABLE,ISMODIFIED,ISADJUSTED,
       ISDEPRECATED, DESCRIPTION, UPDATE_COMMENT, HASH
from   GV$PARAMETER
where  inst_id = USERENV('Instance');
```

View Name: GV$PARAMETER2

```
select  x.inst_id,kspftctxpn,ksppinm,ksppity,kspftctxvl,kspftctxdvl, kspftctxdf,
        decode(bitand(ksppiflg/256,1),1,'TRUE','FALSE'),
        decode(bitand(ksppiflg/65536,3),1,'IMMEDIATE',2,'DEFERRED',
        3,'IMMEDIATE','FALSE'),
        decode(bitand(ksppiflg,4),4,'FALSE',
        decode(bitand(ksppiflg/65536,3), 0, 'FALSE', 'TRUE')),
        decode(bitand(kspftctxvf,7),1,'MODIFIED',4,'SYSTEM_MOD','FALSE'),
        decode(bitand(kspftctxvf,2),2,'TRUE','FALSE'),
        decode(bitand(ksppilrmflg/64, 1), 1, 'TRUE', 'FALSE'),
        ksppdesc, kspftctxvn, kspftctxct
from    x$ksppi x, x$ksppcv2 y
where   ((x.indx+1) = kspftctxpn)
and     ((translate(ksppinm,'_','#') not like '##%')
and     ((translate(ksppinm,'_','#') not like '#%')
or      (kspftctxdf = 'FALSE') or (bitand(kspftctxvf,5) > 0)));
```

View Name: **V$PARAMETER2**

```
select NUM,NAME,TYPE,VALUE,DISPLAY_VALUE,ISDEFAULT,ISSES_MODIFIABLE,
       ISSYS_MODIFIABLE,ISINSTANCE_MODIFIABLE,ISMODIFIED,ISADJUSTED,
       ISDEPRECATED, DESCRIPTION,ORDINAL,UPDATE_COMMENT
from   GV$PARAMETER2
where  inst_id = USERENV('Instance');
```

View Name: **GV$PGASTAT**

```
select INST_ID,QESMMSGANM,
       decode(QESMMSGAUN,3,(QESMMSGAVL*QESMMSGAMU)/100,QESMMSGAVL*QESMMSGAMU),
       decode(QESMMSGAUN,0,'bytes',1,'microseconds',3,'percent','')
from   X$QESMMSGA
where  QESMMSGAVS = 1;
```

View Name: **V$PGASTAT**

```
select NAME,VALUE,UNIT
from   GV$PGASTAT
where  INST_ID = USERENV('Instance');
```

View Name: **GV$PGA_TARGET_ADVICE**

```
select INST_ID,PAT_PRED * 1024,round(PAT_PRED/PAT_CURR,4),
       decode(status,0,'OFF','ON'),BYTES_PROCESSED * 1024,
       EXTRA_BYTES_RW * 1024,round(decode(BYTES_PROCESSED+EXTRA_BYTES_RW,0,0,
       (BYTES_PROCESSED*100)/(BYTES_PROCESSED+EXTRA_BYTES_RW))), OVERALLOC
from   X$QESMMAPADV;
```

View Name: **V$PGA_TARGET_ADVICE**

```
select
PGA_TARGET_FOR_ESTIMATE,PGA_TARGET_FACTOR,ADVICE_STATUS,BYTES_PROCESSED,
       ESTD_EXTRA_BYTES_RW,ESTD_PGA_CACHE_HIT_PERCENTAGE,ESTD_OVERALLOC_COUNT
from   GV$PGA_TARGET_ADVICE
where  INST_ID = USERENV('Instance');
```

View Name: **GV$PGA_TARGET_ADVICE_HISTOGRAM**

```
select INST_ID,PAT_PRED * 1024,round(PAT_PRED/PAT_CURR, 4),
       decode(status,0,'OFF','ON'),LOWBND * 1024,(HIBND * 1024)-1,
       OPTIMAL,ONEPASS,MPASS,MPASS+ONEPASS+OPTIMAL,IGNORED
from   X$QESMMAHIST;
```

View Name: **V$PGA_TARGET_ADVICE_HISTOGRAM**

```
select PGA_TARGET_FOR_ESTIMATE,PGA_TARGET_FACTOR,ADVICE_STATUS,LOW_OPTIMAL_SIZE,
       HIGH_OPTIMAL_SIZE,ESTD_OPTIMAL_EXECUTIONS,ESTD_ONEPASS_EXECUTIONS,
```

V$ Views

```
        ESTD_MULTIPASSES_EXECUTIONS,ESTD_TOTAL_EXECUTIONS,IGNORED_WORKAREAS_COUNT
from    GV$PGA_TARGET_ADVICE_HISTOGRAM
where   INST_ID = USERENV('Instance');
```

View Name: GV$PROCESS

```
select inst_id,addr,indx,ksuprpid,ksuprunm,ksuprser,ksuprtid,ksuprpnm,ksuprtfi,
       decode(bitand(ksuprflg,2),0,null,1), decode(ksllawat,hextoraw('00'),
       null,ksllawat),decode(ksllaspn,hextoraw('00'),null,ksllaspn),
       ksuprpum,ksuprpnam+ksuprpram,ksuprpfm,
case
  when ksuprpnam+ksuprpram > ksuprpmm
  then ksuprpnam+ksuprpram
  else ksuprpmm end
from   x$ksupr
where  bitand(ksspaflg,1)!=0;
```

View Name: V$PROCESS

```
select addr,pid,spid,username,serial#,terminal,program,traceid,background,latchwait,
       latchspin,pga_used_mem,pga_alloc_mem,pga_freeable_mem,pga_max_mem
from   gv$process
where  inst_id = USERENV('Instance') ;
```

View Name: GV$QUEUE

```
select inst_id,kmcqspro,decode(indx,0,'COMMON','DISPATCHER'),kmcqsncq,kmcqswat,
       kmcqstnc
from   x$kmcqs
where  indx=0 or kmcqspro!=hextoraw('00');
```

View Name: V$QUEUE

```
select PADDR,TYPE,QUEUED,WAIT,TOTALQ
from   GV$QUEUE
where  inst_id = USERENV('Instance');
```

View Name: GV$ROLLSTAT

```
select inst_id,kturdusn,kturdlat,kturdext,kturdsiz,kturdwrt,kturdnax,kturdget,
       kturdwat,decode(kturdopt, -1,to_number(null),kturdopt),kturdhwm,kturdnsh,
       kturdnwp,kturdnex,kturdash,kturdaae,
       decode(bitand(kturdflg,127),0,'ONLINE',2,'PENDING OFFLINE',3,'OFFLINE',4,
       'FULL','UNKNOWN'),kturdcex, kturdcbk
from   x$kturd
where  kturdsiz != 0
and    bitand(kturdflg,127) != 3;
```

View Name: V$ROLLSTAT

```
select USN,LATCH,EXTENTS,RSSIZE,WRITES,XACTS,GETS,WAITS,OPTSIZE,HWMSIZE,SHRINKS,
WRAPS,EXTENDS,AVESHRINK,AVEACTIVE,STATUS,CUREXT,CURBLK
```

```
from    GV$ROLLSTAT
where   inst_id = USERENV('Instance');
```

View Name: GV$ROWCACHE

```
select inst_id,kqrstcid,decode(kqrsttyp,1,'PARENT','SUBORDINATE'),
decode(kqrsttyp,2,kqrstsno,null),kqrsttxt,kqrstcsz,kqrstusg,kqrstfcs,
       kqrstgrq,kqrstgmi,kqrstsrq,kqrstsmi,kqrstsco,kqrstmrq,kqrstmfl,
       kqrstilr,kqrstifr,kqrstisr

   from    x$kqrst;
```

View Name: V$ROWCACHE

```
select cache#,type,subordinate#,parameter,count,usage,fixed, gets,getmisses,scans,
scanmisses,scancompletes,modifications,flushes,dlm_requests,dlm_conflicts,
       dlm_releases
from    gv$rowcache
where   inst_id = USERENV('Instance');
```

View Name: GV$ROWCACHE_PARENT

```
select inst_id,indx,kqrfphsh,kqrfpadd,kqrfpcid,kqrfpcnm,
decode(bitand(kqrfpflg,1),0,'Y','N'),kqrfpmod,kqrfpreq,kqrfptxn,kqrfpses,
       kqrfpirq, kqrfpirl,kqrfpity, kqrfpii1,kqrfpii2,kqrfpkey
from    x$kqrfp;
```

View Name: V$ROWCACHE_PARENT

```
select indx,hash,address,cache#,cache_name,existent,lock_mode,lock_request,
txn,saddr,inst_lock_request,inst_lock_release,inst_lock_type,inst_lock_id1,
       inst_lock_id2,key
from    gv$rowcache_parent
where   inst_id = USERENV('Instance');
```

View Name: GV$ROWCACHE_SUBORDINATE

```
select inst_id,indx,kqrfshsh,kqrfsadd,kqrfscid,kqrfssid,kqrfssnm,
       decode(bitand(kqrfsflg,1),0,'Y','N'),kqrfspar,kqrfskey
from x$kqrfs;
```

View Name: V$ROWCACHE_SUBORDINATE

```
select indx,hash,address,cache#,subcache#,subcache_name,existent,parent,key
from    gv$rowcache_subordinate
where   inst_id = USERENV('Instance');
```

View Name: GV$SEGMENT_STATISTICS

```
select s.inst_id,u.name,o.name,o.subname,ts.name,s.fts_tsn, o.obj#,o.dataobj#,
decode(o.type#,0,'NEXT OBJECT',1,'INDEX',2,'TABLE',3,'CLUSTER',4,'VIEW',5,
```

V$ Views

```
         'SYNONYM',6,'SEQUENCE',7,'PROCEDURE',8,'FUNCTION',9,'PACKAGE',11,
         'PACKAGE BODY',12,'TRIGGER',13,'TYPE',14,'TYPE BODY',19,'TABLE PARTITION',20,
         'INDEX PARTITION',21,'LOB',22,'LIBRARY',23,'DIRECTORY',24,'QUEUE',28,
         'JAVA SOURCE',29,'JAVA CLASS',30,'JAVA RESOURCE',32,'INDEXTYPE',33,
         'OPERATOR',34,'TABLE SUBPARTITION',35,'INDEX SUBPARTITION',40,
         'LOB PARTITION',41,'LOB SUBPARTITION',42,'MATERIALIZED VIEW',43,
         'DIMENSION',44,'CONTEXT',47,'RESOURCE PLAN',48,'CONSUMER GROUP',51,
         'SUBSCRIPTION',52,'LOCATION',55,'XML SCHEMA',56,'JAVA DATA',57,
         'SECURITY PROFILE','UNDEFINED'),s.fts_statnam,s.fts_statid,s.fts_staval
from   obj$ o,user$ u,x$ksolsfts s,ts$ ts
where  o.owner# = u.user#
and    s.fts_inte = 0
and    s.fts_objn = o.obj#
and    s.fts_tsn = ts.ts#
and    s.fts_objd = o.dataobj#
and    o.linkname is null
and    (o.type# not in (1  /* INDEX - handled below */,10 /* NON-EXISTENT */)
or     (o.type# = 1
and     1 =
   (select 1
    from   ind$  i
    where  i.obj# = o.obj#
    and    i.type# in (1,2,3,4,6,7,9))))
    and    o.name != '_NEXT_OBJECT'
    and    o.name != '_default_auditing_options_'
union all
select s.inst_id,u.name,o.name,o.subname,ts.name,s.fts_tsn,t.ktssoobjn,t.ktssoobjd,
        decode(o.type#,0,'NEXT OBJECT',1,'INDEX',2,'TABLE',3,'CLUSTER',4,'VIEW',5,
        'SYNONYM',6,'SEQUENCE',7,'PROCEDURE',8,'FUNCTION',9,'PACKAGE',11,
        'PACKAGE BODY',12,'TRIGGER',13,'TYPE',14,'TYPE BODY',19,'TABLE PARTITION',20,
        'INDEX PARTITION',21,'LOB',22,'LIBRARY',23,'DIRECTORY',24,'QUEUE',28,
        'JAVA SOURCE',29,'JAVA CLASS',30,'JAVA RESOURCE',32,'INDEXTYPE',33,
        'OPERATOR',34,'TABLE SUBPARTITION',35,'INDEX SUBPARTITION',40,
        'LOB PARTITION',41,'LOB SUBPARTITION',42,'MATERIALIZED VIEW',43,
        'DIMENSION',44,'CONTEXT',47,'RESOURCE PLAN',48,'CONSUMER GROUP',51,
        'SUBSCRIPTION',52,'LOCATION',55,'XML SCHEMA',56,'JAVA DATA',57,
        'SECURITY PROFILE','UNDEFINED'),s.fts_statnam,s.fts_statid,s.fts_staval
from   obj$ o, user$ u, x$ksolsfts s,x$ktsso t, ts$ ts
where  o.owner# = u.user#
and    s.fts_inte = 0
and    s.fts_objn = o.obj#
and    s.fts_tsn  = t.ktssotsnum
and    s.fts_objn = t.ktssoobjn
and    s.fts_objd = t.ktssoobjd
and    s.fts_tsn  = ts.ts#
and    t.ktssotsn = ts.name
and    o.linkname is null
and    (o.type# not in (1  /* INDEX - handled below */,10 /* NON-EXISTENT */)
or     (o.type# = 1
and     1 =
   (select 1
    from   ind$  i
    where  i.obj# = o.obj#
    and    i.type# in (1,2,3,4,6,7,9))))
    and    o.name != '_NEXT_OBJECT'
    and    o.name != '_default_auditing_options_';
```

View Name: V$SEGMENT_STATISTICS

```
select owner,object_name,subobject_name,tablespace_name,ts#,obj#,dataobj#,
object_type,statistic_name,statistic#,value
```

```
from    gv$segment_statistics
where   inst_id = userenv('instance');
```

View Name: GV$SEGSTAT

```
select inst_id,fts_tsn,fts_objn,fts_objd,fts_statnam,fts_statid,fts_staval
from    x$ksolsfts
where   fts_inte = 0;
```

View Name: V$SEGSTAT

```
select ts#,obj#,dataobj#,statistic_name,statistic#,value
from    gv$segstat
where   inst_id = userenv('instance');
```

View Name: GV$SEGSTAT_NAME

```
select inst_id,st_statid,st_name,decode(bitand(st_flag,1),0,'NO',1,'YES')
from    x$ksolsstat where bitand(st_flag, 2) <> 2;
```

View Name: V$SEGSTAT_NAME

```
select statistic#,name,sampled
from    gv$segstat_name
where   inst_id = userenv('instance');
```

View Name: GV$SESSION

```
select s.inst_id,s.addr,s.indx,s.ksuseser,s.ksuudses,s.ksusepro,s.ksuudlui,
       s.ksuudlna,s.ksuudoct,s.ksusesow,
        decode(s.ksusetrn,hextoraw('00'),null,s.ksusetrn),
        decode(s.ksqpswat,hextoraw('00'),null,s.ksqpswat),
        decode(bitand(s.ksuseidl,11),1,'ACTIVE',0,
        decode(bitand(s.ksuseflg,4096),0,'INACTIVE','CACHED'),
        2,'SNIPED',3,'SNIPED','KILLED'),
        decode(s.ksspatyp,1,'DEDICATED',2,'SHARED',3,'PSEUDO','NONE'),
        s.ksuudsid,s.ksuudsna,s.ksuseunm,s.ksusepid,s.ksusemnm,s.ksusetid,s.ksusepnm,
        decode(bitand(s.ksuseflg,19),17,'BACKGROUND',1,'USER',2,'RECURSIVE','?'),
        s.ksusesql, s.ksusesqh, s.ksusesqi,
        decode(s.ksusesch, 65535, to_number(null), s.ksusesch),  s.ksusepsq,
        s.ksusepha, s.ksusepsi,
        decode(s.ksusepch, 65535, to_number(null), s.ksusepch),  s.ksuseapp,
        s.ksuseaph, s.ksuseact, s.ksuseach, s.ksusecli, s.ksusefix, s.ksuseobj,
        s.ksusefil, s.ksuseblk, s.ksuseslt, s.ksuseltm, s.ksusectm,
        decode(bitand(s.ksusepxopt, 12),0,'NO','YES'),
        decode(s.ksuseft, 2,'SESSION', 4,'SELECT',8,'TRANSACTIONAL','NONE'),
        decode(s.ksusefm,1,'BASIC',2,'PRECONNECT',4,'PREPARSE','NONE'),
        decode(s.ksusefs, 1, 'YES', 'NO'),s.ksusegrp,
        decode(bitand(s.ksusepxopt,4),4,'ENABLED',
        decode(bitand(s.ksusepxopt,8),8,'FORCED','DISABLED')),
        decode(bitand(s.ksusepxopt,2),2,'FORCED',
        decode(bitand(s.ksusepxopt,1),1,'DISABLED','ENABLED')),
        decode(bitand(s.ksusepxopt,32),32,'FORCED',
        decode(bitand(s.ksusepxopt,16),16,'DISABLED','ENABLED')),s.ksusecqd,s.ksuseclid,
        decode(s.ksuseblocker,4294967295,'UNKNOWN',294967294,'UNKNOWN',
```

```
      4294967293,'UNKNOWN',4294967292,'NO HOLDER',  4294967291,
      'NOT IN WAIT','VALID'),decode(s.ksuseblocker, 4294967295,
      to_number(null),4294967294,to_number(null), 4294967293,to_number(null),
      4294967292,to_number(null),4294967291,
      to_number(null),bitand(s.ksuseblocker, 2147418112)/65536),
      decode(s.ksuseblocker, 4294967295,to_number(null),4294967294,
      to_number(null), 4294967293,to_number(null), 4294967292,to_number(null),
      4294967291,  to_number(null),bitand(s.ksuseblocker, 65535)),s.ksuseseq,
      s.ksuseopc,e.kslednam, e.ksledp1, s.ksusep1,s.ksusep1r,e.ksledp2,
      s.ksusep2,s.ksusep2r,e.ksledp3,s.ksusep3,s.ksusep3r,e.ksledclassid,
      e.ksledclass#, e.ksledclass, decode(s.ksusetim,0,0,-1,-1,-2,-2,
      decode(round(s.ksusetim/10000),0,-1,round(s.ksusetim/10000))), s.ksusewtm,
      decode(s.ksusetim, 0,'WAITING',-2,'WAITED UNKNOWN TIME',-1,'WAITED SHORT TIME',
      decode(round(s.ksusetim/10000),0,'WAITED SHORT TIME','WAITED KNOWN TIME')),
      s.ksusesvc, decode(bitand(s.ksuseflg2,32),32,'ENABLED','DISABLED'),
      decode(bitand(s.ksuseflg2,64),64,'TRUE','FALSE'),
      decode(bitand(s.ksuseflg2,128),128,'TRUE','FALSE')
from  x$ksuse s, x$ksled e
where bitand(s.ksspaflg,1)!=0
and bitand(s.ksuseflg,1)!=0
and s.ksuseopc=e.indx;
```

View Name: V$SESSION

```
select SADDR,SID,SERIAL#,AUDSID,PADDR,USER#,USERNAME,COMMAND,OWNERID,TADDR,
       LOCKWAIT,STATUS,SERVER,SCHEMA#,SCHEMANAME,OSUSER,PROCESS,MACHINE,TERMINAL,
       PROGRAM,TYPE,SQL_ADDRESS,SQL_HASH_VALUE, SQL_ID, SQL_CHILD_NUMBER,
       PREV_SQL_ADDR,PREV_HASH_VALUE,PREV_SQL_ID, PREV_CHILD_NUMBER,
       MODULE,MODULE_HASH,ACTION,ACTION_HASH,CLIENT_INFO,FIXED_TABLE_SEQUENCE,
       ROW_WAIT_OBJ#,ROW_WAIT_FILE#,ROW_WAIT_BLOCK#,ROW_WAIT_ROW#,LOGON_TIME,
       LAST_CALL_ET,PDML_ENABLED,FAILOVER_TYPE,FAILOVER_METHOD,FAILED_OVER,
       RESOURCE_CONSUMER_GROUP,PDML_STATUS,PDDL_STATUS,PQ_STATUS,
       CURRENT_QUEUE_DURATION,CLIENT_IDENTIFIER,BLOCKING_SESSION_STATUS,
       BLOCKING_INSTANCE,BLOCKING_SESSION,SEQ#,EVENT#,EVENT,P1TEXT,P1,P1RAW,
       P2TEXT,P2,P2RAW, P3TEXT,P3,P3RAW,WAIT_CLASS_ID, WAIT_CLASS#,WAIT_CLASS,
       WAIT_TIME, SECONDS_IN_WAIT,STATE,SERVICE_NAME, SQL_TRACE, SQL_TRACE_WAITS,
       SQL_TRACE_BINDS
from   GV$SESSION
where  inst_id = USERENV('Instance');
```

View Name: GV$SESSION_CONNECT_INFO

```
select inst_id,ksusenum,decode(ksuseaty,0,'DATABASE',1,'OS',2,'NETWORK',3,
       'PROXY',4,'SERVER',5,'PASSWORD',6,'EXTERNAL ADAPTERS',7,'INTERNAL',8,
       'GLOBAL',9,'EXTERNAL',10,'PASSWORD BASED GLOBAL USER','?'),ksuseunm,ksuseban
from   x$ksusecon
where  bitand(ksuseflg,1)!=0
and bitand(ksuseflg,16)=0;
```

View Name: V$SESSION_CONNECT_INFO

```
select sid,authentication_type,osuser,network_service_banner
from   gv$session_connect_info
where  inst_id = USERENV('Instance');
```

View Name: GV$SESSION_CURSOR_CACHE

```
select  inst_id,kgiccmax,kgicccnt,kgiccopd,kgiccope,kgiccopn,kgicchit,
        decode(kgiccopn,0,1,kgicchit/kgiccopn)
from    x$kgicc;
```

View Name: V$SESSION_CURSOR_CACHE

```
select  MAXIMUM,COUNT,OPENED_ONCE,OPEN,OPENS,HITS,HIT_RATIO
from    GV$SESSION_CURSOR_CACHE
where   inst_id = USERENV('Instance');
```

View Name: GV$SESSION_EVENT

```
select  s.inst_id,s.kslessid,d.kslednam,s.ksleswts,s.kslestmo,
round(s.kslestim / 10000),round(s.kslestim / (10000 * s.ksleswts)),
        round(s.kslesmxt / 10000),s.kslestim
from    x$ksles s, x$ksled d
where   s.ksleswts != 0 and s.kslesenm = d.indx;
```

View Name: V$SESSION_EVENT

```
select
sid,event,total_waits,total_timeouts,time_waited,average_wait,max_wait,
time_waited_micro,event_id, wait_class_id,wait_class#, wait_class
from    gv$session_event
where   inst_id = USERENV('Instance');
```

View Name: GV$SESSION_LONGOPS

```
select  inst_id,ksulosno,ksulosrn,ksulopna,ksulotna,ksulotde,ksulosfr,ksulotot,
        ksulouni,to_date(ksulostm,'MM/DD/RR HH24:MI:SS','NLS_CALENDAR=Gregorian'),
        to_date(ksulolut,'MM/DD/RR HH24:MI:SS','NLS_CALENDAR=Gregorian'),
        to_date(ksuloinft, 'MM/DD/RR HH24:MI:SS','NLS_CALENDAR=Gregorian'),
        decode(ksulopna, 'Advisor', ksuloif2,
        decode(sign(ksulotot-ksulosfr),-1,to_number(NULL),
        decode(ksulosfr,0,to_number(NULL),
        round(ksuloetm*((ksulotot-ksulosfr)/ksulosfr)))))),ksuloetm,ksuloctx,ksulomsg,
        ksulounm,ksulosql,ksulosqh,ksulosqi,ksuloqid
from    x$ksulop;
```

View Name: V$SESSION_LONGOPS

```
select  SID,SERIAL#,OPNAME,TARGET,TARGET_DESC,SOFAR,TOTALWORK,UNITS,START_TIME,
LAST_UPDATE_TIME,TIME_STAMP, TIME_REMAINING,ELAPSED_SECONDS,CONTEXT,MESSAGE,USERNAME,
        SQL_ADDRESS,SQL_HASH_VALUE,SQL_ID,QCSID
from    GV$SESSION_LONGOPS
where   inst_id = USERENV('Instance');
```

View Name: GV$SESSION_OBJECT_CACHE

```
select  inst_id,kocstpin,kocsthit,kocsttht,decode(kocstpin,0,1,kocsthit/kocstpin),
        decode(kocstpin,0,1,kocsttht/kocstpin),kocstorf,kocstrfs,kocstofs,
```

```
        kocstfls,kocstshr,kocstcnt,kocstpnd,kocstsiz,kocstopt,kocstmax
from    x$kocst;
```

View Name: V$SESSION_OBJECT_CACHE

```
select pins,hits,true_hits,hit_ratio,true_hit_ratio,object_refreshes,
       cache_refreshes,object_flushes,cache_flushes,cache_shrinks,
       cached_objects,pinned_objects,cache_size,optimal_size,maximum_size
from gv$session_object_cache
where inst_id=userenv('Instance');
```

View Name: GV$SESSION_WAIT

```
select s.inst_id,s.indx,s.ksussseq,e.kslednam, e.ksledp1,s.ksussp1,
       s.ksussp1r,e.ksledp2,s.ksussp2,s.ksussp2r,e.ksledp3,s.ksussp3,s.ksussp3r,
       e.ksledclassid, e.ksledclass#, e.ksledclass,
       decode(s.ksusstim,0,0,-1,-1,-2,-2,
       decode(round(s.ksusstim/10000),0,-1,round(s.ksusstim/10000))),
       s.ksusewtm, decode(s.ksusstim,0,'WAITING',-2,'WAITED UNKNOWN TIME',-1,
       'WAITED SHORT TIME','WAITED KNOWN TIME',
       decode(round(s.ksusstim/10000),0,'WAITED SHORT TIME','WAITED KNOWN TIME'))
from x$ksusecst s, x$ksled e
where bitand(s.ksspaflg,1)!=0
and bitand(s.ksuseflg,1)!=0
and s.ksussseq!=0
and s.ksussopc=e.indx;
```

View Name: V$SESSION_WAIT

```
select sid,seq#,event,p1text,p1,p1raw,p2text,p2,p2raw,p3text, p3,p3raw,
       wait_class_id, wait_class#,wait_class,wait_time,
       seconds_in_wait,state
from   gv$session_wait
where  inst_id = USERENV('Instance');
```

View Name: GV$SESSION_WAIT_CLASS

```
select s.inst_id,s.kslcssid,s.kslcsser,s.kslcsclsid,s.kslcscls,s.kslcsclsname,
       s.kslcswts, round(s.kslcstim / 10000)
from   x$kslcs s
where  s.kslcswts != 0;
```

View Name: V$SESSION_WAIT_CLASS

```
select sid,serial#,wait_class_id, wait_class#,wait_class,total_waits, time_waited
from   gv$session_wait_class
where  inst_id = USERENV('Instance');
```

View Name: GV$SESSION_WAIT_HISTORY

```
select s.inst_id,s.ksusehsnum,s.ksusehwnum,s.ksusehopc, s.ksusehname,
       s.ksusehp1text,s.ksusehp1,s.ksusehp2text, s.ksusehp2,s.ksusehp3text,
```

```
        s.ksusehp3, round(s.ksusehwtm/10000), s.ksusehcnt
from    x$ksuseh s;
```

View Name: **V$SESSION_WAIT_HISTORY**

```
select sid,seq#,event#,event,p1text,p1,p2text,p2,p3text,p3,wait_time,wait_count
from   gv$session_wait_history
where  inst_id = USERENV('Instance');
```

View Name: **GV$SESSTAT**

```
select inst_id,ksusenum,ksusestn,ksusestv
from   x$ksusesta
where  bitand(ksspaflg,1)!=0
and    bitand(ksuseflg,1)!=0
and    ksusestn<
   (select ksusgstl
    from x$ksusgif);
```

View Name: **V$SESSTAT**

```
select SID,STATISTIC#,VALUE
from   GV$SESSTAT
where  inst_id = USERENV('Instance');
```

View Name: **GV$SESS_IO**

```
select inst_id,indx,ksusesbg,ksusescg,ksusespr,ksusesbc,ksusescc
from   x$ksusio
where  bitand(ksspaflg,1)!=0
and    bitand(ksuseflg,1)!=0;
```

View Name: **V$SESS_IO**

```
select SID,BLOCK_GETS,CONSISTENT_GETS,PHYSICAL_READS,BLOCK_CHANGES,
       CONSISTENT_CHANGES
from   GV$SESS_IO
where  inst_id = USERENV('Instance');
```

View Name: **GV$SGA**

```
select inst_id,ksmsdnam,ksmsdval
from   x$ksmsd;
```

View Name: **V$SGA**

```
select NAME,VALUE
from   GV$SGA
where  inst_id = USERENV('Instance');
```

V$ Views

View Name: GV$SGASTAT

```
select inst_id,'',ksmssnam,ksmsslen
from    x$ksmfs
where   ksmsslen>1
union all
select inst_id,'shared pool',ksmssnam,sum(ksmsslen)
from x$ksmss
where ksmsslen>1
group by inst_id,'shared pool',ksmssnam

union all
select inst_id,'large pool',ksmssnam, sum(ksmsslen)
from x$ksmls
where ksmsslen>1
group by inst_id, 'large pool', ksmssnam
union all
select inst_id,'java pool',ksmssnam, sum(ksmsslen)
from    x$ksmjs
where   ksmsslen>1
group by inst_id, 'java pool', ksmssnam

union all
select inst_id,'streamspool',ksmssnam, sum(ksmsslen)
from    x$ksmstrs
where   ksmsslen>1
group by inst_id, 'streams pool', ksmssnam;
```

View Name: V$SGASTAT

```
select  POOL,NAME,BYTES
from     GV$SGASTAT
where    inst_id = USERENV('Instance');
```

View Name: GV$SHARED_POOL_ADVICE

```
select inst_id,sp_size,round(sp_size / basesp_size, 4),kglsim_size,kglsim_objs,
        kglsim_timesave,decode(kglsim_basetimesave,0,to_number(null),
        round(kglsim_timesave / kglsim_basetimesave,4)), kglsim_parsetime,
        decode(kglsim_baseparsetime,0,to_number(null),
        round(kglsim_parsetime / kglsim_baseparsetime, 4)),kglsim_hits
from    x$kglsim;
```

View Name: V$SHARED_POOL_ADVICE

```
select  shared_pool_size_for_estimate,shared_pool_size_factor,estd_lc_size,
        estd_lc_memory_objects,estd_lc_time_saved,estd_lc_time_saved_factor,
        estd_lc_load_time,  estd_lc_load_time_factor, estd_lc_memory_object_hits
from    gv$shared_pool_advice
where   inst_id = USERENV('Instance');
```

V$ Views

View Name: **GV$SHARED_POOL_RESERVED**

```
select p.inst_id, p.free_space, p.avg_free_size, p.free_count,
p.max_free_size, p.used_size, p.avg_used_size, p.used_count, p.max_used_size,
s.requests, s.request_misses, s.last_miss_size, s.max_miss_size,
s.request_failures, s.last_failure_size, s.aborted_request_threshold,
s.aborted_requests, s.last_aborted_size
from (select avg(x$ksmspr.inst_id) inst_id,
             sum(decode(ksmchcls,'R-free',ksmchsiz,0)) free_space,
             avg(decode(ksmchcls,'R-free',ksmchsiz,0)) avg_free_size,
             sum(decode(ksmchcls,'R-free',1,0)) free_count,
             max(decode(ksmchcls,'R-free',ksmchsiz,0)) max_free_size,
             sum(decode(ksmchcls,'R-free',0,ksmchsiz)) used_size,
             avg(decode(ksmchcls,'R-free',0,ksmchsiz)) avg_used_size,
             sum(decode(ksmchcls,'R-free',0,1)) used_count,
             max(decode(ksmchcls,'R-free',0,ksmchsiz)) max_used_size
     from   x$ksmspr
     where  ksmchcom not like '%reserved sto%') p,
            (select sum(kghlurcn) requests, sum(kghlurmi) request_misses,
                    max(kghlurmz) last_miss_size,
                    max(kghlurmx) max_miss_size,
                    sum(kghlunfu) request_failures,
                    max(kghlunfs) last_failure_size,
                    max(kghlumxa) aborted_request_threshold,
                    sum(kghlumer) aborted_requests,
                    max(kghlumes) last_aborted_size
             from x$kghlu) s;
```

View Name: **V$SHARED_POOL_RESERVED**

```
select FREE_SPACE,AVG_FREE_SIZE,FREE_COUNT,MAX_FREE_SIZE,USED_SPACE,AVG_USED_SIZE,
       USED_COUNT,MAX_USED_SIZE,REQUESTS,REQUEST_MISSES,LAST_MISS_SIZE,
       MAX_MISS_SIZE,REQUEST_FAILURES,LAST_FAILURE_SIZE,ABORTED_REQUEST_THRESHOLD,
       ABORTED_REQUESTS,LAST_ABORTED_SIZE
from   GV$SHARED_POOL_RESERVED
where  inst_id = USERENV('Instance');
```

View Name: **GV$SORT_SEGMENT**

```
select inst_id,tablespace_name,segment_file,segment_block,extent_size,
       current_users,total_extents,total_blocks,used_extents,used_blocks,
       free_extents,free_blocks,added_extents,extent_hits,freed_extents,
       free_requests,max_size,max_blocks,max_used_size,max_used_blocks,
       max_sort_size,max_sort_blocks,relative_fno
from   x$ktstssd;
```

View Name: **V$SORT_SEGMENT**

```
select TABLESPACE_NAME,SEGMENT_FILE,SEGMENT_BLOCK,EXTENT_SIZE,CURRENT_USERS,
       TOTAL_EXTENTS,TOTAL_BLOCKS,USED_EXTENTS,USED_BLOCKS,FREE_EXTENTS,FREE_BLOCKS,
```

```
        ADDED_EXTENTS,EXTENT_HITS,FREED_EXTENTS,FREE_REQUESTS,MAX_SIZE,MAX_BLOCKS,
        MAX_USED_SIZE,MAX_USED_BLOCKS,MAX_SORT_SIZE,MAX_SORT_BLOCKS,RELATIVE_FNO
from    GV$SORT_SEGMENT
where   inst_id = USERENV('Instance');
```

View Name: GV$SORT_USAGE

```
select x$ktsso.inst_id,username,username,ktssoses,ktssosno,prev_sql_addr,

prev_hash_value,prev_sql_id,ktssotsn,decode(ktssocnt,0,'PERMANENT',1,'TEMPORARY'),
       decode(ktssosegt,1,'SORT',2,'HASH',3,'DATA',4,'INDEX',5,
       'LOB_DATA',6,'LOB_INDEX','UNDEFINED'),ktssofno,ktssobno,ktssoexts,
       ktssoblks,ktssorfno
from    x$ktsso,v$session
where   ktssoses = v$session.saddr
and     ktssosno = v$session.serial#;
```

View Name: V$SORT_USAGE

```
select USERNAME,"USER",SESSION_ADDR,SESSION_NUM,SQLADDR,SQLHASH,SQL_ID,
       TABLESPACE,CONTENTS,SEGTYPE,SEGFILE#,SEGBLK#,EXTENTS,BLOCKS,SEGRFNO#
from    GV$SORT_USAGE
where   inst_id = USERENV('Instance');
```

View Name: GV$SPPARAMETER

```
select INST_ID, KSPSPFFTCTXSPSID, KSPSPFFTCTXSPNAME, KSPSPFFTCTXSPVALUE,
       KSPSPFFTCTXSPDVALUE, KSPSPFFTCTXISSPECIFIED, KSPSPFFTCTXORDINAL,
       KSPSPFFTCTXCOMMENT
from    x$kspspfile
WHERE   ((translate(KSPSPFFTCTXSPNAME,'_','#') not like '##%')
and     ((translate(KSPSPFFTCTXSPNAME, '_', '#') not like '#%')
OR      KSPSPFFTCTXISSPECIFIED = 'TRUE'));
```

View Name: V$SPPARAMETER

```
select SID,NAME,VALUE,DISPLAY_VALUE,ISSPECIFIED,ORDINAL,UPDATE_COMMENT
from    GV$SPPARAMETER
where   INST_id = USERENV('Instance');
```

View Name: GV$SQL

```
select inst_id,kglnaobj,kglfnobj,kglobt03, kglobhs0+kglobhs1+kglobhs2+
       kglobhs3+kglobhs4+kglobhs5+kglobhs6+kglobt16, kglobt08+kglobt11,
       kglobt10, kglobt01, decode(kglobhs6,0,0,1), decode(kglhdlmd,0,0,1),
       kglhdlkc, kglobt04, kglobt05, kglobt48, kglobt35, kglobpc6, kglhdldc,
       substr(to_char(kglnatim,'YYYY-MM-DD/HH24:MI:SS'),1,19), kglhdivc,
       kglobt12, kglobt13, kglobwdw, kglobt14, kglobwap, kglobwcc,
       kglobwcl, kglobwui, kglobt42, kglobt43, kglobt15, kglobt02,
       decode(kglobt32,0,'NONE',1,'ALL_ROWS',2,'FIRST_ROWS',3,'RULE',
```

```
      4,'CHOOSE','UNKNOWN'), kglobtn0, kglobcce, kglobcceh, kglobt17,
      kglobt18, kglobts4, kglhdkmk, kglhdpar, kglobtp0, kglnahsh, kglobt46,
      kglobt30, kglobt09, kglobts5, kglobt48, kglobts0, kglobt19, kglobts1,
      kglobt20, kglobt21, kglobts2, kglobt06, kglobt07,
      decode(kglobt28, 0, to_number(NULL), kglobt28), kglhdadr, kglobt29,
      decode(bitand(kglobt00,64),64, 'Y', 'N'), decode(kglobsta,
      1,'VALID',2,'VALID_AUTH_ERROR',3,'VALID_COMPILE_ERROR',
      4,'VALID_UNAUTH',5,'INVALID_UNAUTH',6,'INVALID'), kglobt31,
      substr(to_char(kglobtt0,'YYYY-MM-DD/HH24:MI:SS'),1,19),
      decode(kglobt33, 1, 'Y', 'N'),  kglhdclt, kglobts3, kglobt44,
      kglobt45, kglobt47, kglobt49, kglobcla,  kglobcbca
from   x$kglcursor_child;
```

View Name: V$SQL

```
select SQL_TEXT,SQL_FULLTEXT, SQL_ID,SHARABLE_MEM,PERSISTENT_MEM,RUNTIME_MEM,SORTS,
      LOADED_VERSIONS,OPEN_VERSIONS,USERS_OPENING,FETCHES,EXECUTIONS, PX_SERVERS_EXECUTIONS,
      END_OF_FETCH_COUNT,USERS_EXECUTING,LOADS,FIRST_LOAD_TIME,INVALIDATIONS,PARSE_CALLS,
      DISK_READS , DIRECT_WRITES , BUFFER_GETS , APPLICATION_WAIT_TIME,
      CONCURRENCY_WAIT_TIME, CLUSTER_WAIT_TIME, USER_IO_WAIT_TIME, PLSQL_EXEC_TIME,
      JAVA_EXEC_TIME, ROWS_PROCESSED , COMMAND_TYPE , OPTIMIZER_MODE , OPTIMIZER_COST,
      OPTIMIZER_ENV, OPTIMIZER_ENV_HASH_VALUE, PARSING_USER_ID , PARSING_SCHEMA_ID,
      PARSING_SCHEMA_NAME, KEPT_VERSIONS , ADDRESS , TYPE_CHK_HEAP , HASH_VALUE,
      OLD_HASH_VALUE, PLAN_HASH_VALUE, CHILD_NUMBER, SERVICE, SERVICE_HASH, MODULE,
      MODULE_HASH , ACTION , ACTION_HASH ,  SERIALIZABLE_ABORTS , OUTLINE_CATEGORY,
      CPU_TIME, ELAPSED_TIME, OUTLINE_SID, CHILD_ADDRESS, SQLTYPE, REMOTE,
      OBJECT_STATUS, LITERAL_HASH_VALUE, LAST_LOAD_TIME, IS_OBSOLETE, CHILD_LATCH,
      SQL_PROFILE, PROGRAM_ID,PROGRAM_LINE#, EXACT_MATCHING_SIGNATURE,
      FORCE_MATCHING_SIGNATURE, LAST_ACTIVE_TIME, BIND_DATA
from   GV$SQL
where  inst_id = USERENV('Instance');
```

View Name: GV$SQLAREA

```
select inst_id, kglnaobj, kglfnobj, kglobt03, kglobhs0+kglobhs1+
      kglobhs2+kglobhs3+kglobhs4+kglobhs5+kglobhs6, kglobt08+kglobt11,
      kglobt10, kglobt01, kglobccc, kglobclc, kglhdlmd, kglhdlkc, kglobt04,
      kglobt05, kglobt48, kglobt35, kglobpc6, kglhdldc,
      substr(to_char(kglnatim,'YYYY-MM-DD/HH24:MI:SS'),1,19), kglhdivc,
      kglobt12, kglobt13, kglobwdw, kglobt14, kglobwap, kglobwcc, kglobwcl,
      kglobwui, kglobt42, kglobt43, kglobt15, kglobt02, decode(kglobt32, 0,
      'NONE',1,'ALL_ROWS',2,'FIRST_ROWS',3,'RULE',4, 'CHOOSE', 'UNKNOWN'),
      kglobtn0, kglobcce, kglobcceh, kglobt17, kglobt18, kglobts4, kglhdkmk,
      kglhdpar, kglnahsh, kglobt46, kglobt30, kglobts0, kglobt19, kglobts1,
      kglobt20, kglobt21, kglobts2, kglobt06, kglobt07,
      decode(kglobt28, 0, NULL, kglobt28), kglhdadr,
      decode(bitand(kglobt00,64),64, 'Y', 'N'),
      decode(kglobsta,1,'VALID',2,'VALID_AUTH_ERROR',3, 'VALID_COMPILE_ERROR',
      4,'VALID_UNAUTH',5,'INVALID_UNAUTH',6,'INVALID'), kglobt31, kglobtt0,
      decode(kglobt33, 1, 'Y', 'N'),  kglhdclt, kglobts3, kglobt44, kglobt45,
      kglobt47, kglobt49,  kglobcla,  kglobcbca
from   x$kglcursor_child_sqlid
where  kglobt02 != 0;
```

View Name: **V$SQLAREA**

```
select  SQL_TEXT,SHARABLE_MEM,PERSISTENT_MEM,RUNTIME_MEM,SORTS,VERSION_COUNT,
        LOADED_VERSIONS,OPEN_VERSIONS,USERS_OPENING,FETCHES,EXECUTIONS,
        USERS_EXECUTING,LOADS,FIRST_LOAD_TIME,INVALIDATIONS,PARSE_CALLS,DISK_READS,
        BUFFER_GETS,ROWS_PROCESSED,COMMAND_TYPE,OPTIMIZER_MODE,PARSING_USER_ID,
        PARSING_SCHEMA_ID,KEPT_VERSIONS,ADDRESS,HASH_VALUE,MODULE,MODULE_HASH,
        ACTION,ACTION_HASH,SERIALIZABLE_ABORTS,CPU_TIME,ELAPSED_TIME,IS_OBSOLETE,
        CHILD_LATCH
from    GV$SQLAREA
where   inst_id = USERENV('Instance');
```

View Name: **GV$SQLAREA_PLAN_HASH**

```
select  inst_id, kglnaobj, kglfnobj, kglhdpar, kglobt46, kglobt03, kglobt30,
        kglobccc, kglhdadr, kglobhs0+kglobhs1+kglobhs2+kglobhs3+kglobhs4+
        kglobhs5+kglobhs6, kglobt08+kglobt11, kglobt10, kglobt01, kglobclc,
        kglhdlmd, kglhdlkc, kglobpc6, kglobt04, kglobt05, kglobt50, kglobt35,
        kglhdldc, kglnatim, kglobtt0, kglobcla, kglhdivc, kglobt12, kglobt13,
        kglobwdw, kglobt14, kglobt06, kglobt07, kglobwap, kglobwcc, kglobwcl,
        kglobwui, kglobt42, kglobt43, kglobt15, kglobt02,
        decode(kglobt32, 0, 'NONE', 1, 'ALL_ROWS',2, 'FIRST_ROWS',3, 'RULE',
        4, 'CHOOSE', 'UNKNOWN'), kglobtn0, kglobcce, kglobcceh, kglobt17,
        kglobt18, kglobts4, kglhdkmk, kglobts0, kglobt19, kglobts1, kglobt20,
        kglobt21, kglobts2, decode(kglobt28, 0, NULL, kglobt28),
        decode(bitand(kglobt00,64),64, 'Y', 'N'), decode(kglobsta, 1, 'VALID',
        2, 'VALID_AUTH_ERROR', 3, 'VALID_COMPILE_ERROR', 4, 'VALID_UNAUTH',
        5, 'INVALID_UNAUTH', 6, 'INVALID'), kglobt31, kglobts3, kglobt44,
        kglobt45, kglobt47,  kglobt49,  kglobcbca
from    x$kglcursor_child_sqlidph;
```

View Name: **V$ SQLAREA_PLAN_HASH**

```
select  inst_id,kglhdadr,kglnahsh, kglnasqlid, kgloboct,piece,name
select   SQL_TEXT, SQL_FULLTEXT, ADDRESS, HASH_VALUE, SQL_ID, PLAN_HASH_VALUE,
        VERSION_COUNT, LAST_ACTIVE_CHILD_ADDRESS, SHARABLE_MEM, PERSISTENT_MEM,
        RUNTIME_MEM, SORTS, LOADED_VERSIONS, OPEN_VERSIONS,USERS_OPENING,
        USERS_EXECUTING, FETCHES, EXECUTIONS, PX_SERVERS_EXECUTIONS,
        END_OF_FETCH_COUNT, LOADS, FIRST_LOAD_TIME, LAST_LOAD_TIME,
        LAST_ACTIVE_TIME, INVALIDATIONS, PARSE_CALLS, DISK_READS,
        DIRECT_WRITES, BUFFER_GETS, CPU_TIME, ELAPSED_TIME,
        APPLICATION_WAIT_TIME, CONCURRENCY_WAIT_TIME, CLUSTER_WAIT_TIME,
        USER_IO_WAIT_TIME, PLSQL_EXEC_TIME, JAVA_EXEC_TIME, ROWS_PROCESSED,
        COMMAND_TYPE, OPTIMIZER_MODE, OPTIMIZER_COST, OPTIMIZER_ENV,
        OPTIMIZER_ENV_HASH_VALUE, PARSING_USER_ID, PARSING_SCHEMA_ID,
        PARSING_SCHEMA_NAME, KEPT_VERSIONS, MODULE, MODULE_HASH, ACTION,
        ACTION_HASH, SERIALIZABLE_ABORTS, OUTLINE_CATEGORY, OUTLINE_SID,
        REMOTE, OBJECT_STATUS, LITERAL_HASH_VALUE, SQL_PROFILE, PROGRAM_ID,
        PROGRAM_LINE#, EXACT_MATCHING_SIGNATURE, FORCE_MATCHING_SIGNATURE,
        BIND_DATA
from    GV$SQLAREA_PLAN_HASH
where    inst_id = USERENV('Instance');
```

View Name: GV$SQLSTATS

```
select INST_ID, SQL_TEXT, SQL_FULLTEXT, SQL_ID, LAST_ACTIVE_TIME,
       LAST_ACTIVE_CHILD_ADDRESS, PLAN_HASH_VALUE, PARSE_CALLS, DISK_READS,
       DIRECT_WRITES, BUFFER_GETS, ROWS_PROCESSED, SERIALIZABLE_ABORTS,
       FETCHES, EXECUTIONS, END_OF_FETCH_COUNT, LOADS, VERSION_COUNT,
       INVALIDATIONS, PX_SERVERS_EXECUTIONS, CPU_TIME, ELAPSED_TIME,
       APPLICATION_WAIT_TIME,CONCURRENCY_WAIT_TIME, CLUSTER_WAIT_TIME,
       USER_IO_WAIT_TIME, PLSQL_EXEC_TIME, JAVA_EXEC_TIME, SORTS,
       SHARABLE_MEM, TOTAL_SHARABLE_MEM
FROM   x$kkssqlstat;
```

View Name: V$SQLSTATS

```
select SQL_TEXT, SQL_FULLTEXT, SQL_ID,LAST_ACTIVE_TIME, LAST_ACTIVE_CHILD_ADDRESS,
       PLAN_HASH_VALUE, PARSE_CALLS, DISK_READS, DIRECT_WRITES, BUFFER_GETS,
       ROWS_PROCESSED, SERIALIZABLE_ABORTS, FETCHES, EXECUTIONS,
       END_OF_FETCH_COUNT, LOADS, VERSION_COUNT, INVALIDATIONS,
       PX_SERVERS_EXECUTIONS, CPU_TIME, ELAPSED_TIME, APPLICATION_WAIT_TIME,
       CONCURRENCY_WAIT_TIME, CLUSTER_WAIT_TIME, USER_IO_WAIT_TIME,
       PLSQL_EXEC_TIME, JAVA_EXEC_TIME, SORTS, SHARABLE_MEM, TOTAL_SHARABLE_MEM
FROM   gv$sqlstats
where inst_id=USERENV('Instance');
```

View Name: GV$SQLTEXT

```
select inst_id,kglhdadr,kglnahsh, kglnasqlid, kgloboct,piece,name
from   x$kglna where kgloboct != 0;
```

View Name: V$SQLTEXT

```
select ADDRESS,HASH_VALUE,SQL_ID,COMMAND_TYPE,PIECE,SQL_TEXT
from   GV$SQLTEXT
where  inst_id = USERENV('Instance');
```

View Name: GV$SQLTEXT_WITH_NEWLINES

```
select inst_id,kglhdadr,kglnahsh,kglnasqlid,kgloboct,piece,name
from   x$kglna1 where kgloboct != 0;
```

View Name: V$SQLTEXT_WITH_NEWLINES

```
select ADDRESS,HASH_VALUE,SQL_ID,COMMAND_TYPE,PIECE,SQL_TEXT
from   GV$SQLTEXT_WITH_NEWLINES
where  inst_id = USERENV('Instance');
```

View Name: GV$SQL_BIND_CAPTURE

```
select INST_ID, KQLFBC_PADD, KQLFBC_HASH, KQLFBC_SQLID, KQLFBC_CADD, KQLFBC_CHNO,
     substr(KQLFBC_NAME, 1, 30), KQLFBC_POS,
```

V$ Views

```
       to_number(decode(KQLFBC_DUPPOS, 65535, NULL, KQLFBC_DUPPOS)),
       KQLFBC_OACDTY, substr(KQLFBC_DTYSTR, 1, 15),
       decode(KQLFBC_OACCSI, 0, to_number(null), KQLFBC_OACCSI),
       decode(KQLFBC_OACPRE, 0, to_number(null), KQLFBC_OACPRE),
       decode(KQLFBC_OACSCL, 0, to_number(null), KQLFBC_OACSCL),KQLFBC_OACMXL,
       decode(KQLFBC_WCAP, 0, 'NO', 'YES'),
       decode(KQLFBC_WCAP, 0, to_date(NULL), KQLFBC_LCAP), KQLFBC_STRVAL,
       decode(KQLFBC_WCAP, 0, NULL,
       sys.sys$rawtoany(KQLFBC_BINVAL, KQLFBC_OACDTY,KQLFBC_OACCSF, KQLFBC_OACCSI))
from   x$kqlfbc;
```

View Name: V$SQL_BIND_CAPTURE

```
select ADDRESS, HASH_VALUE, SQL_ID, CHILD_ADDRESS, CHILD_NUMBER, NAME,
       POSITION, DUP_POSITION, DATATYPE, DATATYPE_STRING, CHARACTER_SID,
       PRECISION, SCALE, MAX_LENGTH, WAS_CAPTURED, LAST_CAPTURED, VALUE_STRING,
       VALUE_ANYDATA
from   go$sql_bind_capture
where  inst_id = USERENV('Instance');
```

View Name: GV$SQL_BIND_DATA

```
select inst_id,kxsbdcur,kxsbdbnd,kxsbddty,kxsbdmxl,kxsbdpmx,kxsbdmal,kxsbdpre,
       kxsbdscl,kxsbdofl,kxsbdof2,kxsbdbfp,kxsbdbln,kxsbdavl,kxsbdbfl,kxsbdind,
       kxsbdval
from   x$kxsbd;
```

View Name: V$SQL_BIND_DATA

```
select CURSOR_NUM,POSITION,DATATYPE,SHARED_MAX_LEN,PRIVATE_MAX_LEN,ARRAY_SIZE,
       PRECISION,SCALE,SHARED_FLAG,SHARED_FLAG2,BUF_ADDRESS,BUF_LENGTH,VAL_LENGTH,
       BUF_FLAG,INDICATOR,VALUE
from   GV$SQL_BIND_DATA
where  inst_id = USERENV('Instance');
```

View Name: GV$SQL_BIND_METADATA

```
select inst_id,kglhdadr,position,kkscbndt,kkscbndl,kkscbnda,kksbvnnam
from   x$kksbv;
```

View Name: V$SQL_BIND_METADATA

```
select ADDRESS,POSITION,DATATYPE,MAX_LENGTH,ARRAY_LEN,BIND_NAME
from   GV$SQL_BIND_METADATA
where  inst_id = USERENV('Instance');
```

View Name: GV$SQL_CURSOR

```
select inst_id,kxscccur,kxscccfl,
       decode(kxsccsta,0,'CURNULL',1,'CURSYNTAX',2,'CURPARSE',3,'CURBOUND',4,
       'CURFETCH',5,'CURROW','ERROR'),kxsccphd,kxscccplk, kxsccclk, kxscccpn,
       kxscctbm,kxscctwm,kxscctbv,kxscctdv,kxsccbdf,kxsccflg,kxsccfl2,kxsccchd
from   x$kxscc;
```

View Name: **V$SQL_CURSOR**

```
select CURNO,FLAG,STATUS,PARENT_HANDLE,PARENT_LOCK,CHILD_LOCK,CHILD_PIN,
       PERS_HEAP_MEM,WORK_HEAP_MEM,BIND_VARS,DEFINE_VARS,BIND_MEM_LOC,INST_FLAG,
       INST_FLAG2,CHILD_HANDLE
from   GV$SQL_CURSOR
where  inst_id = USERENV('Instance');
```

View Name: **GV$SQL_JOIN_FILTER**

```
SELECT  INST_ID, QCSID, QCINSTID, SQLHASHV, LEN, NSET, FLT, TOT, ACTIVE
FROM    X$QESBLSTAT;
```

View Name: **V$SQL_JOIN_FILTER**

```
SELECT qc_session_id, qc_instance_id, sql_plan_hash_value, length,
       bits_set, filtered, probed, active
FROM   GV$SQL_JOIN_FILTER
WHERE  inst_id = USERENV('INSTANCE');
```

View Name: **GV$SQL_OPTIMIZER_ENV**

```
select INST_ID, KQLFSQCE_PHAD, KQLFSQCE_HASH, KQLFSQCE_SQLID, KQLFSQCE_HADD,
       KQLFSQCE_CHNO, KQLFSQCE_PNUM, KQLFSQCE_PNAME,
       decode(bitand(KQLFSQCE_FLAGS, 2), 0, 'NO', 'YES'), KQLFSQCE_PVALUE
from   X$KQLFSQCE
where  bitand(KQLFSQCE_FLAGS, 8) = 0
and    (bitand(KQLFSQCE_FLAGS, 4)= 0
or     bitand(KQLFSQCE_FLAGS, 2) = 0);
```

View Name: **V$SQL_OPTIMIZER_ENV**

```
select ADDRESS, HASH_VALUE, SQL_ID, CHILD_ADDRESS, CHILD_NUMBER, ID, NAME,
       ISDEFAULT, VALUE
from   GV$SQL_OPTIMIZER_ENV
where  INST_ID = USERENV('Instance');
```

View Name: **GV$SQL_PLAN**

```
select inst_id,kqlfxpl_phad,kqlfxpl_hash,kqlfxpl_sqlid,kqlfxpl_plhash,
       kqlfxpl_hadd,kqlfxpl_chno,kqlfxpl_timestamp,substr(kqlfxpl_oper, 1, 30),
       substr(kqlfxpl_oopt, 1, 30),substr(kqlfxpl_tqid, 1, 40),
       to_number(decode(kqlfxpl_objn, 0, NULL, kqlfxpl_objn)),
       kqlfxpl_objowner,kqlfxpl_objname,kqlfxpl_alias,
       substr(kqlfxpl_objtype, 1, 20),substr(kqlfxpl_opti, 1, 20),
       kqlfxpl_opid,to_number(decode(kqlfxpl_opid,0,NULL,kqlfxpl_paid)),
       kqlfxpl_depth,to_number(decode(kqlfxpl_pos, 0,
       decode(kqlfxpl_cost,4294967295,NULL,kqlfxpl_cost),kqlfxpl_pos)),
       kqlfxpl_scols,to_number(decode(kqlfxpl_cost, 4294967295, NULL,
       kqlfxpl_cost)), to_number(decode(kqlfxpl_card, 0, NULL, kqlfxpl_card)),
       to_number(decode(kqlfxpl_size, 0, NULL, kqlfxpl_size)),
```

```
         substr(kqlfxpl_otag, 1, 35),substr(kqlfxpl_psta, 1, 5),
         substr(kqlfxpl_psto, 1, 5),
         to_number(decode(kqlfxpl_pnid, 0, NULL, kqlfxpl_pnid)),
         kqlfxpl_other,substr(kqlfxpl_dist, 1, 20),
         to_number(decode(kqlfxpl_cpuc, 4294967295, NULL, kqlfxpl_cpuc)),
         to_number(decode(kqlfxpl_ioct, 4294967295, NULL, kqlfxpl_ioct)),
         to_number(decode(kqlfxpl_temp, 0, NULL, kqlfxpl_temp)),kqlfxpl_keys,
         kqlfxpl_filter, kqlfxpl_proj,
         to_number(decode(kqlfxpl_time, 0, NULL, kqlfxpl_time)),
         kqlfxpl_qblock, kqlfxpl_remark, kqlfxpl_other_xml
from     x$kqlfxpl p ;
```

View Name: V$SQL_PLAN

```
select ADDRESS, HASH_VALUE, SQL_ID, PLAN_HASH_VALUE, CHILD_ADDRESS,
       CHILD_NUMBER, TIMESTAMP, OPERATION, OPTIONS, OBJECT_NODE, OBJECT#,
       OBJECT_OWNER, OBJECT_NAME, OBJECT_ALIAS, OBJECT_TYPE, OPTIMIZER,
       ID, PARENT_ID, DEPTH, POSITION, SEARCH_COLUMNS, COST, CARDINALITY,
       BYTES, OTHER_TAG, PARTITION_START, PARTITION_STOP, PARTITION_ID, OTHER,
       DISTRIBUTION, CPU_COST, IO_COST, TEMP_SPACE, ACCESS_PREDICATES,
       FILTER_PREDICATES, PROJECTION, TIME, QBLOCK_NAME, REMARKS, OTHER_XML
from   GV$SQL_PLAN
where  inst_id = USERENV('Instance');
```

View Name: GV$SQL_PLAN_STATISTICS

```
select inst_id,PHADD_QESRS,HASHV_QESRS,SQLID_QESRS,PLHASH_QESRS,HADDR_QESRS,
       CHILDNO_QESRS,OPERID_QESRS,EXECS_QESRS,LSTARTS_QESRS,STARTS_QESRS,
       LOUTROWS_QESRS,OUTROWS_QESRS,LCRGETS_QESRS,CRGETS_QESRS,LCUGETS_QESRS,
       CUGETS_QESRS,LDREADS_QESRS,DREADS_QESRS,LDWRITES_QESRS,DWRITES_QESRS,
       LELAPTIME_QESRS,ELAPTIME_QESRS
from   X$QESRSTAT;
```

View Name: V$SQL_PLAN_STATISTICS

```
select ADDRESS, HASH_VALUE, SQL_ID, PLAN_HASH_VALUE, CHILD_ADDRESS,
       CHILD_NUMBER,OPERATION_ID,EXECUTIONS,LAST_STARTS,STARTS,
       LAST_OUTPUT_ROWS,OUTPUT_ROWS,LAST_CR_BUFFER_GETS,CR_BUFFER_GETS,
       LAST_CU_BUFFER_GETS,CU_BUFFER_GETS,LAST_DISK_READS,DISK_READS,
       LAST_DISK_WRITES,DISK_WRITES,LAST_ELAPSED_TIME,ELAPSED_TIME
from   GV$SQL_PLAN_STATISTICS
where  inst_id = USERENV('Instance');
```

View Name: GV$SQL_PLAN_STATISTICS_ALL

```
select inst_id, PHADD_QESRS, HASHV_QESRS, SQLID_QESRS, PLHASH_QESRS,
       HADDR_QESRS,  CHILDNO_QESRS, TIMESTAMP_QESRS, substr(oper_qesrs, 1, 30),
       substr(oopt_qesrs, 1, 30), substr(tqid_qesrs, 1, 40),
       to_number(decode(objn_qesrs, 0, NULL, objn_qesrs)), objowner_qesrs,
       objname_qesrs,  alias_qesrs, substr(objtype_qesrs, 1, 20),
       substr(opti_qesrs, 1, 20), opid_qesrs,
       to_number(decode(opid_qesrs, 0, NULL, paid_qesrs)), depth_qesrs,
       to_number(decode(pos_qesrs,0,decode(cost_qesrs,4294967295,NULL,cost_qesrs),
```

```
        pos_qesrs)),  scols_qesrs, to_number(decode(cost_qesrs, 4294967295,
        NULL, cost_qesrs)),  to_number(decode(card_qesrs, 0, NULL, card_qesrs)),
        to_number(decode(size_qesrs, 0, NULL, size_qesrs)),
        substr(otag_qesrs, 1, 35), substr(psta_qesrs, 1, 5),
        substr(psto_qesrs, 1, 5), to_number(decode(pnid_qesrs, 0, NULL, pnid_qesrs)),
        other_qesrs,  substr(dist_qesrs, 1, 20),
        to_number(decode(cpuc_qesrs, 4294967295, NULL, cpuc_qesrs)),
        to_number(decode(ioct_qesrs, 4294967295, NULL, ioct_qesrs)),
        to_number(decode(temp_qesrs, 0, NULL, temp_qesrs)),  KEYS_QESRS,
        FILTER_QESRS,PROJ_QESRS,to_number(decode(time_qesrs, 0, NULL, time_qesrs)),
        QBLOCK_QESRS,   REMARK_QESRS,   OTHER_XML_QESRS,   EXECS_QESRS,
        to_number(decode(LSTARTS_QESRS, 4294967295, NULL, LSTARTS_QESRS)),
        to_number(decode(LSTARTS_QESRS, 4294967295, NULL, STARTS_QESRS)),
        to_number(decode(LSTARTS_QESRS, 4294967295, NULL, LOUTROWS_QESRS)),
        to_number(decode(LSTARTS_QESRS, 4294967295, NULL, OUTROWS_QESRS)),
        to_number(decode(LSTARTS_QESRS, 4294967295, NULL, LCRGETS_QESRS)),
        to_number(decode(LSTARTS_QESRS, 4294967295, NULL, CRGETS_QESRS)),
        to_number(decode(LSTARTS_QESRS, 4294967295, NULL, LCUGETS_QESRS)),
        to_number(decode(LSTARTS_QESRS, 4294967295, NULL, CUGETS_QESRS)),
        to_number(decode(LSTARTS_QESRS, 4294967295, NULL, LDREADS_QESRS)),
        to_number(decode(LSTARTS_QESRS, 4294967295, NULL, DREADS_QESRS)),
        to_number(decode(LSTARTS_QESRS, 4294967295, NULL, LDWRITES_QESRS)),
        to_number(decode(LSTARTS_QESRS, 4294967295, NULL, DWRITES_QESRS)),
        to_number(decode(LSTARTS_QESRS, 4294967295, NULL, LELAPTIME_QESRS)),
        to_number(decode(LSTARTS_QESRS, 4294967295, NULL, ELAPTIME_QESRS)),
        substr(SIZEPOLICY_QESRS, 1, 10),
        to_number(decode(OPTIMAL_QESRS, 0, NULL, OPTIMAL_QESRS * 1024)),
        to_number(decode(OPTIMAL_QESRS, 0, NULL, ONEPASS_QESRS * 1024)),
        to_number(decode(OPTIMAL_QESRS, 0, NULL, LASTMEM_QESRS * 1024)),
        decode(OPTIMAL_QESRS, 0, NULL,
        substr(decode(LASTPASS_QESRS, 0, 'OPTIMAL',
        to_char(LASTPASS_QESRS)||' PASS'||decode(LASTPASS_QESRS, 1, '', 'ES')),1,10)),
        to_number(decode(LASTDOP_QESRS, 0, NULL, LASTDOP_QESRS)),
        to_number(decode(OPTIMAL_QESRS, 0, NULL, (OPTACTS_QESRS + SPAACTS_QESRS
        + MPAACTS_QESRS))),to_number(decode(OPTIMAL_QESRS,0,NULL,OPTACTS_QESRS)),
        to_number(decode(OPTIMAL_QESRS, 0, NULL, SPAACTS_QESRS)),
        to_number(decode(OPTIMAL_QESRS, 0, NULL, MPAACTS_QESRS)),
        to_number(decode(OPTIMAL_QESRS, 0, NULL, ATIME_QESRS)),
        to_number(decode(MAXTSEG_QESRS, 0, NULL, MAXTSEG_QESRS)),
        to_number(decode(LASTTSEG_QESRS, 0, NULL, LASTTSEG_QESRS))
from    X$QESRSTATALL p
where   p.haddr_qesrs != p.phadd_qesrs;
```

View Name: V$SQL_PLAN_STATISTICS_ALL

```
select ADDRESS, HASH_VALUE, SQL_ID, PLAN_HASH_VALUE, CHILD_ADDRESS,
       CHILD_NUMBER, TIMESTAMP, OPERATION, OPTIONS, OBJECT_NODE,
       OBJECT#, OBJECT_OWNER, OBJECT_NAME, OBJECT_ALIAS, OBJECT_TYPE,
       OPTIMIZER,ID, PARENT_ID, DEPTH, POSITION, SEARCH_COLUMNS, COST,
       CARDINALITY, BYTES, OTHER_TAG, PARTITION_START, PARTITION_STOP,
       PARTITION_ID, OTHER, DISTRIBUTION, CPU_COST, IO_COST, TEMP_SPACE,
       ACCESS_PREDICATES, FILTER_PREDICATES, PROJECTION,TIME, QBLOCK_NAME,
       REMARKS, OTHER_XML, EXECUTIONS, LAST_STARTS, STARTS, LAST_OUTPUT_ROWS,
       OUTPUT_ROWS, LAST_CR_BUFFER_GETS, CR_BUFFER_GETS, LAST_CU_BUFFER_GETS,
       CU_BUFFER_GETS, LAST_DISK_READS, DISK_READS, LAST_DISK_WRITES,
       DISK_WRITES, LAST_ELAPSED_TIME, ELAPSED_TIME, POLICY,
       ESTIMATED_OPTIMAL_SIZE, ESTIMATED_ONEPASS_SIZE, LAST_MEMORY_USED,
       LAST_EXECUTION, LAST_DEGREE, TOTAL_EXECUTIONS, OPTIMAL_EXECUTIONS,
       ONEPASS_EXECUTIONS, MULTIPASSES_EXECUTIONS, ACTIVE_TIME,
```

```
        MAX_TEMPSEG_SIZE, LAST_TEMPSEG_SIZE
from    GV$SQL_PLAN_STATISTICS_ALL
where   inst_id = USERENV('Instance');
```

View Name: GV$SQL_REDIRECTION

```
select c.inst_id,c.kglhdadr,c.kglhdpar,c.kglnahsh,C.kglobt03,c.kglobt09,
       c.kglobt17,c.kglobt18, c.kglobt02,
       decode(r.reason,1,'INVALID OBJECT',2,'ROWID',3,'QUERY REWRITE','READ ONLY'),
       r.error_code,r.position,r.sql_text_piece,r.error_msg
from   x$kglcursor c, x$kkssrd r
where  c.kglhdpar = r.parAddr
and    c.kglhdadr = r.kglhdadr;
```

View Name: V$SQL_REDIRECTION

```
select ADDRESS,PARENT_HANDLE,HASH_VALUE,SQL_ID,CHILD_NUMBER,PARSING_USER_ID,
       PARSING_SCHEMA_ID,COMMAND_TYPE,REASON,ERROR_CODE,POSITION,SQL_TEXT_PIECE,
       ERROR_MESSAGE
from   GV$SQL_REDIRECTION
where  inst_id = USERENV('Instance');
```

View Name: GV$SQL_SHARED_CURSOR

```
select inst_id, sql_id, kglhdpar, kglhdadr, childno,
       decode(bitand(bitvector,POWER(2,0)),POWER(2,0),'Y','N'),
       decode(bitand(bitvector,POWER(2,1)),POWER(2,1),'Y','N'),
       decode(bitand(bitvector,POWER(2,2)),POWER(2,2),'Y','N'),
       decode(bitand(bitvector,POWER(2,3)),POWER(2,3),'Y','N'),
       decode(bitand(bitvector,POWER(2,4)),POWER(2,4),'Y','N'),
       decode(bitand(bitvector,POWER(2,5)),POWER(2,5),'Y','N'),
       decode(bitand(bitvector,POWER(2,6)),POWER(2,6),'Y','N'),
       decode(bitand(bitvector,POWER(2,7)),POWER(2,7),'Y','N'),
       decode(bitand(bitvector,POWER(2,8)),POWER(2,8),'Y','N'),
       decode(bitand(bitvector,POWER(2,9)),POWER(2,9),'Y','N'),
       decode(bitand(bitvector,POWER(2,10)),POWER(2,10),'Y','N'),
       decode(bitand(bitvector,POWER(2,11)),POWER(2,11),'Y','N'),
       decode(bitand(bitvector,POWER(2,12)),POWER(2,12),'Y','N'),
       decode(bitand(bitvector,POWER(2,13)),POWER(2,13),'Y','N'),
       decode(bitand(bitvector,POWER(2,14)),POWER(2,14),'Y','N'),
       decode(bitand(bitvector,POWER(2,15)),POWER(2,15),'Y','N'),
       decode(bitand(bitvector,POWER(2,16)),POWER(2,16),'Y','N'),
       decode(bitand(bitvector,POWER(2,17)),POWER(2,17),'Y','N'),
       decode(bitand(bitvector,POWER(2,18)),POWER(2,18),'Y','N'),
       decode(bitand(bitvector,POWER(2,19)),POWER(2,19),'Y','N'),
       decode(bitand(bitvector,POWER(2,20)),POWER(2,20),'Y','N'),
       decode(bitand(bitvector,POWER(2,21)),POWER(2,21),'Y','N'),
       decode(bitand(bitvector,POWER(2,22)),POWER(2,22),'Y','N'),
       decode(bitand(bitvector,POWER(2,23)),POWER(2,23),'Y','N'),
       decode(bitand(bitvector,POWER(2,24)),POWER(2,24),'Y','N'),
       decode(bitand(bitvector,POWER(2,25)),POWER(2,25),'Y','N'),
       decode(bitand(bitvector,POWER(2,26)),POWER(2,26),'Y','N'),
       decode(bitand(bitvector,POWER(2,27)),POWER(2,27),'Y','N'),
       decode(bitand(bitvector,POWER(2,28)),POWER(2,28),'Y','N'),
```

```
        decode(bitand(bitvector,POWER(2,29)),POWER(2,29),'Y','N'),
        decode(bitand(bitvector,POWER(2,30)),POWER(2,30),'Y','N'),
        decode(bitand(bitvector,POWER(2,31)),POWER(2,31),'Y','N'),
        decode(bitand(bitvector,POWER(2,32)),POWER(2,32),'Y','N'),
        decode(bitand(bitvector,POWER(2,33)),POWER(2,33),'Y','N'),
        decode(bitand(bitvector,POWER(2,34)),POWER(2,34),'Y','N'),
        decode(bitand(bitvector,POWER(2,35)),POWER(2,35),'Y','N'),
        decode(bitand(bitvector,POWER(2,36)),POWER(2,36),'Y','N'),
        decode(bitand(bitvector,POWER(2,37)),POWER(2,37),'Y','N'),
        decode(bitand(bitvector,POWER(2,38)),POWER(2,38),'Y','N'),
        decode(bitand(bitvector,POWER(2,39)),POWER(2,39),'Y','N'),
        decode(bitand(bitvector,POWER(2,40)),POWER(2,40),'Y','N'),
        decode(bitand(bitvector,POWER(2,41)),POWER(2,41),'Y','N'),
        decode(bitand(bitvector,POWER(2,42)),POWER(2,42),'Y','N'),
        decode(bitand(bitvector,POWER(2,43)),POWER(2,43),'Y','N'),
        decode(bitand(bitvector,POWER(2,44)),POWER(2,44),'Y','N'),
        decode(bitand(bitvector,POWER(2,45)),POWER(2,45),'Y','N'),
        decode(bitand(bitvector,POWER(2,46)),POWER(2,46),'Y','N'),
        decode(bitand(bitvector,POWER(2,47)),POWER(2,47),'Y','N'),
        decode(bitand(bitvector,POWER(2,48)),POWER(2,48),'Y','N'),
        decode(bitand(bitvector,POWER(2,49)),POWER(2,49),'Y','N'),
        decode(bitand(bitvector,POWER(2,50)),POWER(2,50),'Y','N'),
        decode(bitand(bitvector,POWER(2,51)),POWER(2,51),'Y','N'),
        decode(bitand(bitvector,POWER(2,52)),POWER(2,52),'Y','N')
from    x$kkscs;
```

View Name: **V$SQL_SHARED_CURSOR**

```
select SQL_ID, ADDRESS, CHILD_ADDRESS, CHILD_NUMBER, UNBOUND_CURSOR,
       SQL_TYPE_MISMATCH, OPTIMIZER_MISMATCH, OUTLINE_MISMATCH, STATS_ROW_MISMATCH,
       LITERAL_MISMATCH, SEC_DEPTH_MISMATCH,  EXPLAIN_PLAN_CURSOR,
       BUFFERED_DML_MISMATCH, PDML_ENV_MISMATCH, INST_DRTLD_MISMATCH,
       SLAVE_QC_MISMATCH, TYPECHECK_MISMATCH, AUTH_CHECK_MISMATCH, BIND_MISMATCH,
       DESCRIBE_MISMATCH, LANGUAGE_MISMATCH,    TRANSLATION_MISMATCH,
       ROW_LEVEL_SEC_MISMATCH, INSUFF_PRIVS, INSUFF_PRIVS_REM,
       REMOTE_TRANS_MISMATCH, LOGMINER SESSION MISMATCH, INCOMP LTRL MISMATCH,
       OVERLAP_TIME_MISMATCH, SQL_REDIRECT_MISMATCH, MV_QUERY_GEN_MISMATCH,
       USER_BIND_PEEK_MISMATCH, TYPCHK_DEP_MISMATCH, NO_TRIGGER_MISMATCH,
       FLASHBACK_CURSOR, ANYDATA_TRANSFORMATION, INCOMPLETE_CURSOR,
       TOP_LEVEL_RPI_CURSOR, DIFFERENT_LONG_LENGTH, LOGICAL_STANDBY_APPLY,
       DIFF_CALL_DURN, BIND_UACS_DIFF, PLSQL_CMP_SWITCHS_DIFF,
       CURSOR_PARTS_MISMATCH, STB_OBJECT_MISMATCH, ROW_SHIP_MISMATCH,
       PQ_SLAVE_MISMATCH, TOP_LEVEL_DDL_MISMATCH, MULTI_PX_MISMATCH,
       BIND_PEEKED_PQ_MISMATCH, MV_REWRITE_MISMATCH, ROLL_INVALID_MISMATCH,
       OPTIMIZER_MODE_MISMATCH, PX_MISMATCH, MV_STALEOBJ_MISMATCH,
       FLASHBACK_TABLE_MISMATCH, LITREP_COMP_MISMATCH
from   GV$SQL_SHARED_CURSOR
where  inst_id = USERENV('Instance');
```

View Name: **GV$SQL_SHARED_MEMORY**

```
select /*+use_nl(h,c)*/ c.inst_id,kglnaobj,kglfnobj,kglnahsh, kglobt03,kglobhd6,
       rtrim(substr(ksmchcom,1,instr(ksmchcom, ':', 1, 1) - 1)),
       ltrim(substr(ksmchcom,-(length(ksmchcom) - (instr(ksmchcom,':',1,1)))),
       (length(ksmchcom) - (instr(ksmchcom,':',1,1)) + 1))),ksmchcom,ksmchptr,
```

```
        ksmchsiz,ksmchcls,ksmchtyp,ksmchpar
from    x$kglcursor c, x$ksmhp h
where   ksmchds = kglobhd6
and     kglhdadr != kglhdpar;
```

View Name: V$SQL_SHARED_MEMORY

```
select  SQL_TEXT,SQL_FULLTEXT,HASH_VALUE,SQL_ID,HEAP_DESC,STRUCTURE,FUNCTION,
        CHUNK_COM,CHUNK_PTR,CHUNK_SIZE,ALLOC_CLASS,CHUNK_TYPE,SUBHEAP_DESC
from    GV$SQL_SHARED_MEMORY
where   inst_id = USERENV('Instance');
```

View Name: GV$SQL_WORKAREA

```
SELECT INST_ID,PHADD_QKSMM, HASHV_QKSMM, SQLID_QKSMM, CHILDNO_QKSMM, WADDR_QKSMM,
      substr(OPERTYPE_QKSMM, 1, 20),
      to_number(decode(OPERTID_QKSMM, 65535, NULL, OPERTID_QKSMM)),
      substr(SIZEPOLICY_QKSMM, 1, 10),OPTIMAL_QKSMM * 1024, ONEPASS_QKSMM * 1024,
      LASTMEM_QKSMM * 1024,substr(decode(LASTPASS_QKSMM, 0, 'OPTIMAL',
      to_char(LASTPASS_QKSMM) || 'PASS' || decode(LASTPASS_QKSMM,1,'','ES')),1,10),
      LASTDOP_QKSMM, (OPTACTS_QKSMM + SPAACTS_QKSMM + MPAACTS_QKSMM),OPTACTS_QKSMM,
      SPAACTS_QKSMM,MPAACTS_QKSMM,ATIME_QKSMM,
      to_number(decode(MAXTSEG_QKSMM,0,NULL,MAXTSEG_QKSMM*1024)),
      to_number(decode(LASTTSEG_QKSMM,0,NULL,LASTTSEG_QKSMM*1024))
from  X$QKSMMWDS;
```

View Name: V$SQL_WORKAREA

```
select ADDRESS,HASH_VALUE,SQL_ID,CHILD_NUMBER,WORKAREA_ADDRESS,OPERATION_TYPE,
       OPERATION_ID,POLICY,ESTIMATED_OPTIMAL_SIZE,ESTIMATED_ONEPASS_SIZE,
       LAST_MEMORY_USED,LAST_EXECUTION,LAST_DEGREE,TOTAL_EXECUTIONS,OPTIMAL_EXECUTIONS,
       ONEPASS_EXECUTIONS,MULTIPASSES_EXECUTIONS,ACTIVE_TIME,MAX_TEMPSEG_SIZE,
       LAST_TEMPSEG_SIZE
from   GV$SQL_WORKAREA
where  inst_id = USERENV('Instance');
```

View Name: GV$SQL_WORKAREA_ACTIVE

```
select INST_ID,SQLHASHV,SQLID,WADDR,substr(OPER_TYPE,1,20),
       to_number(decode(OPID,65535,NULL,OPID)),
       substr(decode(bitand(MEM_FLAGS,1),0,'MANUAL','AUTO'),1,6),SID,
       to_number(decode(QCINSTID,65535,NULL,QCINSTID)),
       to_number(decode(QCSID,65535,NULL,QCSID)),ATIME,WA_SIZE * 1024,
       to_number(decode(bitand(MEM_FLAGS,1),0,NULL,EXP_SIZE*1024)),
       ACTUAL_MEM * 1024,MAX_MEM * 1024,PASSES,
       to_number(decode(KTSSOTSN,'',NULL,KTSSOSIZE*1024)),
       decode(KTSSOTSN,'',NULL,KTSSOTSN),
       to_number(decode(KTSSOTSN,'',NULL,KTSSORFNO)),
       to_number(decode(KTSSOTSN,'',NULL,KTSSOBNO))
from   x$qesmmiwt;
```

View Name: **V$SQL_WORKAREA_ACTIVE**

```
select SQL_HASH_VALUE,SQL_ID,WORKAREA_ADDRESS,OPERATION_TYPE,OPERATION_ID,POLICY,SID,
       QCINST_ID,QCSID,ACTIVE_TIME,WORK_AREA_SIZE,EXPECTED_SIZE,ACTUAL_MEM_USED,
       MAX_MEM_USED,NUMBER_PASSES,TEMPSEG_SIZE,TABLESPACE,SEGRFNO#,SEGBLK#
from   GV$SQL_WORKAREA_ACTIVE
where  INST_ID = USERENV('Instance');
```

View Name: **GV$STATISTICS_LEVEL**

```
select inst_id,name,description,
       decode(session_status,0,'DISABLED',1,'ENABLED','UNKNOWN'),
       decode(system_status,0,'DISABLED',1,'ENABLED', 'UNKNOWN'),
       decode(activation_level,0,'BASIC',1,'TYPICAL','ALL'),
       view_name,decode(session_changeable,0,'NO','YES')
from   x$prmsltyx;
```

View Name: **V$STATISTICS_LEVEL**

```
select statistics_name,description,session_status,system_status,activation_level,
       statistics_view_name,session_settable
from   gv$statistics_level
where  inst_id = USERENV('Instance');
```

View Name: **GV$SUBCACHE**

```
select inst_id,kglnaown,kglnaobj,kglobtyp,kqlfshpn,kqlfscid,kqlfsscc,kqlfsesp,
       kqlfsasp, kqlfsusp
from   x$kqlset;
```

View Name: **V$SUBCACHE**

```
select OWNER_NAME,NAME,TYPE,HEAP_NUM,CACHE_ID,CACHE_CNT,HEAP_SZ,HEAP_ALOC,HEAP_USED
from   GV$SUBCACHE
where  inst_id = USERENV('Instance');
```

View Name: **GV$SYSSTAT**

```
select inst_id,indx,ksusdnam,ksusdcls,ksusgstv,ksusdhsh
from   x$ksusgsta;
```

View Name: **V$SYSSTAT**

```
select STATISTIC#,NAME,CLASS,VALUE,STAT_ID
from   GV$SYSSTAT
where  inst_id = USERENV('Instance');
```

View Name: **GV$SYSTEM_CURSOR_CACHE**

```
select inst_id,kgicsopn,kgicshit,decode(kgicsopn,0,1,kgicshit/kgicsopn)
from   x$kgics;
```

V$ Views

View Name: V$SYSTEM_CURSOR_CACHE

```
select  OPENS,HITS,HIT_RATIO
from    GV$SYSTEM_CURSOR_CACHE
where   inst_id = USERENV('Instance');
```

View Name: GV$SYSTEM_EVENT

```
select  d.inst_id,d.kslednam,s.ksleswts,s.kslestmo,round(s.kslestim / 10000),
        round(s.kslestim / (10000 * s.ksleswts),2),s.kslestim,
        d.ksledhash, d.ksledclassid, d.ksledclass#, d.ksledclass
where   s.ksleswts != 0
and     s.indx = d.indx;
```

View Name: V$SYSTEM_EVENT

```
select  event,total_waits,total_timeouts,time_waited,average_wait,time_waited_micro,
        event_id, wait_class_id, wait_class#, wait_class
from    gv$system_event
where   inst_id = USERENV('Instance');
```

View Name: GV$SYSTEM_PARAMETER

```
select  x.inst_id,x.indx+1,ksppinm,ksppity,ksppstvl, ksppstdvl,ksppstdf,
        decode(bitand(ksppiflg/256,1),1,'TRUE','FALSE'),
        decode(bitand(ksppiflg/65536,3),1,'IMMEDIATE',
        2,'DEFERRED', 3,'IMMEDIATE','FALSE'),
        decode(bitand(ksppiflg,4),4,'FALSE', decode(bitand(ksppiflg/65536,3),
        0, 'FALSE', 'TRUE')), decode(bitand(ksppstvf,7),1,'MODIFIED','FALSE'),
        decode(bitand(ksppstvf,2),2,'TRUE','FALSE'),
        decode(bitand(ksppilrmflg/64, 1), 1, 'TRUE', 'FALSE'),
        ksppdesc, ksppstcmnt, ksppihash
from    x$ksppi x, x$ksppsv y
where   (x.indx = y.indx)
and     ((translate(ksppinm,'_','#') not like '##%')
and     ((translate(ksppinm,'_','#') not like '#%')
or      (ksppstdf = 'FALSE')
or      (bitand(ksppstvf,5) > 0)));
```

View Name: V$SYSTEM_PARAMETER

```
select  NUM,NAME,TYPE,VALUE,DISPLAY_VALUE,ISDEFAULT,ISSES_MODIFIABLE,
        ISSYS_MODIFIABLE,ISINSTANCE_MODIFIABLE,ISMODIFIED,ISADJUSTED,
        ISDEPRECATED,DESCRIPTION,UPDATE_COMMENT,HASH
from    GV$SYSTEM_PARAMETER
where   inst_id = USERENV('Instance');
```

View Name: GV$SYSTEM_PARAMETER2

```
select  x.inst_id,kspftctxpn,ksppinm,ksppity,kspftctxvl,  kspftctxdvl, kspftctxdf,
        decode(bitand(ksppiflg/256,1),1,'TRUE','FALSE'),  decode(bitand
        (ksppiflg/65536,3),1,'IMMEDIATE',2,'DEFERRED', 3,'IMMEDIATE','FALSE'),
```

```
        decode(bitand(ksppiflg,4),4,'FALSE',
        decode(bitand(ksppiflg/65536,3), 0, 'FALSE', 'TRUE')),
        decode(bitand(kspftctxvf,7),1,'MODIFIED','FALSE'),
        decode(bitand(kspftctxvf,2),2,'TRUE','FALSE'),
        decode(bitand(ksppilrmflg/64, 1), 1, 'TRUE', 'FALSE'),
        ksppdesc, kspftctxvn, kspftctxct
from    x$ksppi x, x$ksppsv2 y
where  ((x.indx+1) = kspftctxpn)
and    ((translate(ksppinm,'_','#') not like '##%')
and    (translate(ksppinm,'_','#') not like '#%'
or     (kspftctxdf = 'FALSE')
or     (bitand(kspftctxvf,5) > 0)));
```

View Name: V$SYSTEM_PARAMETER2

```
select NUM,NAME,TYPE,VALUE,DISPLAY_VALUE,ISDEFAULT,ISSES_MODIFIABLE,
       ISSYS_MODIFIABLE,ISINSTANCE_MODIFIABLE,ISMODIFIED,ISADJUSTED,ISDEPRECATED,
       DESCRIPTION,ORDINAL,UPDATE_COMMENT
from   GV$SYSTEM_PARAMETER2
where  inst_id = USERENV('Instance');
```

View Name: GV$TABLESPACE

```
select inst_id,tstsn,tsnam,decode(bitand(tsflg, 1+2), 1, 'NO', 2,'NO','YES'),
       decode(bitand(tsflg, 4), 4, 'YES','NO'),
       decode(bitand(tsflg, 8), 8,'NO','YES'),
       decode(bitand(tsflg, 16+32), 16, 'ON', 32, 'OFF', to_char(null))
from   x$kccts
where  tstsn != -1;
```

View Name: V$TABLESPACE

```
select TS#,NAME,INCLUDED_IN_DATABASE_BACKUP,BIGFILE,FLASHBACK_ON,ENCRYPT_IN_BACKUP
from   GV$TABLESPACE
where  inst_id = USERENV('Instance');
```

View Name: GV$TEMPFILE

```
select tf.inst_id,tf.tfnum,to_number(tf.tfcrc_scn),to_date(tf.tfcrc_tim,
       'MM/DD/RR HH24:MI:SS','NLS_CALENDAR=Gregorian'),tf.tftsn,tf.tfrfn,
       decode(bitand(tf.tfsta,2),0,'OFFLINE',2,'ONLINE','UNKNOWN'),
       decode(bitand(tf.tfsta, 12), 0,'DISABLED',4,'READ ONLY',12,'READ WRITE',
       'UNKNOWN'),fh.fhtmpfsz*tf.tfbsz,fh.fhtmpfsz,tf.tfcsz*tf.tfbsz,tf.tfbsz,
       fn.fnnam
from   x$kcctf tf,x$kccfn fn,x$kcvfhtmp fh
where  fn.fnfno=tf.tfnum |
and    fn.fnfno=fh.htmpxfil
and    tf.tffnh=fn.fnnum
and    tf.tfdup!=0
and    bitand(tf.tfsta, 32) <> 32
and    fn.fntyp=7
and    fn.fnnam is not null;
```

V$ Views

View Name: V$TEMPFILE

```
select FILE#,CREATION_CHANGE#,CREATION_TIME,TS#,RFILE#,STATUS,ENABLED,BYTES,BLOCKS,
       CREATE_BYTES,BLOCK_SIZE,NAME
from   GV$TEMPFILE
where  inst_id = USERENV('Instance');
```

View Name: GV$TEMPSTAT

```
select k.inst_id,k.kcftiofno,k.kcftiopyr,k.kcftiopyw,k.kcftiopbr,k.kcftiopbw,
       k.kcftiosbr,k.kcftioprt,k.kcftiopwt,k.kcftiosbt,k.kcftioavg,k.kcftiolst,
       k.kcftiomin,k.kcftiormx,k.kcftiowmx
from   x$kcftio k,x$kcctf f
where  f.tfdup <> 0
and    f.tfnum=k.kcftiofno;
```

View Name: V$TEMPSTAT

```
select FILE#,PHYRDS,PHYWRTS,PHYBLKRD,PHYBLKWRT,SINGLEBLKRDS,READTIM,WRITETIM,
       SINGLEBLKRDTIM,AVGIOTIM,LSTIOTIM,MINIOTIM,MAXIORTM,MAXIOWTM
from   GV$TEMPSTAT
where  inst_id = USERENV('Instance');
```

View Name: GV$TEMP_CACHE_TRANSFER

```
select x.inst_id, kcftiofno, 0, 0, 0, 0, 0, 0, 0, 0, 0, 0, 0, 0
from   x$kcftio x, x$kcctf tf
where  x.kcftiofno = tf.tfnum;
```

View Name: V$TEMP_CACHE_TRANSFER

```
select file_number,x_2_null, x_2_null_forced_write,x_2_null_forced_stale,x_2_s,
       x_2_s_forced_write,s_2_null,s_2_null_forced_stale,rbr,rbr_forced_write,
       null_2_x, s_2_x, null_2_s
from   gv$temp_cache_transfer
where  inst_id = USERENV('Instance');
```

View Name: GV$TEMP_EXTENT_MAP

```
select /*+ ordered use_nl(me) */ me.inst_id,ts.name,me.ktftmetfno,me.ktftmebno,
       me.ktftmeblks*ts.blocksize,me.ktftmeblks,me.ktftmeinst,me.ktftmefno
from   ts$ ts,x$ktftme me
where  ts.contents$ = 1
and    ts.bitmapped <> 0
and    ts.online$ = 1
and    ts.ts# = me.ktftmetsn;
```

View Name: V$TEMP_EXTENT_MAP

```
select TABLESPACE_NAME,FILE_ID,BLOCK_ID,BYTES,BLOCKS,OWNER,RELATIVE_FNO
from   GV$TEMP_EXTENT_MAP
where  inst_id = USERENV('Instance');
```

View Name: **GV$TEMP_EXTENT_POOL**

```
select /*+ ordered use_nl(fc) */ fc.inst_id,ts.name,fc.ktstfctfno,fc.ktstfcec,
       fc.ktstfceu,fc.ktstfcbc,fc.ktstfcbu,fc.ktstfcbc*ts.blocksize,
       fc.ktstfcbu*ts.blocksize,fc.ktstfcfno
from   ts$ ts,x$ktstfc fc
where  ts.contents$ = 1
and    ts.bitmapped <> 0
and    ts.online$ = 1
and    ts.ts# = fc.ktstfctsn;
```

View Name: **V$TEMP_EXTENT_POOL**

```
select TABLESPACE_NAME,FILE_ID,EXTENTS_CACHED,EXTENTS_USED,BLOCKS_CACHED,
       BLOCKS_USED,BYTES_CACHED,BYTES_USED,RELATIVE_FNO
from   GV$TEMP_EXTENT_POOL
where  inst_id = USERENV('Instance');
```

View Name: **GV$TEMP_PING**

```
select x.inst_id, kcftiofno,0, 0, 0, 0, 0, 0, 0, 0,   0, 0, 0, 0, 0, 0, 0, 0,
       0, 0, 0, 0, 0, 0, 0, 0, 0
from   x$kcftio x,x$kcctf tf
where  x.kcftiofno = tf.tfnum;
```

View Name: **V$TEMP_PING**

```
select file_number,frequency,x_2_null,x_2_null_forced_write, x_2_null_forced_stale,
       x_2_s, x_2_s_forced_write,x_2_ssx,x_2_ssx_forced_write,s_2_null,
       s_2_null_forced_stale,ss_2_null,ss_2_rls,wrb,wrb_forced_write,rbr,
       rbr_forced_write,rbr_forced_stale,cbr,cbr_forced_write,null_2_x, s_2_x,
       ssx_2_x, null_2_s, null_2_ss, op_2_ss
from   gv$temp_ping
where  inst_id = USERENV('Instance');
```

View Name: **GV$TEMP_SPACE_HEADER**

```
select /*+ ordered use_nl(hc) */ hc.inst_id,ts.name,hc.ktfthctfno,
       (hc.ktfthcsz - hc.ktfthcfree)*ts.blocksize,(hc.ktfthcsz - hc.ktfthcfree),
       hc.ktfthcfree*ts.blocksize, hc.ktfthcfree, hc.ktfthcfno
from   ts$ ts, x$ktfthc hc
where  ts.contents$ = 1
and    ts.bitmapped <> 0
and    ts.online$ = 1
and    ts.ts# = hc.ktfthctsn
and    hc.ktfthccval = 0;
```

View Name: **V$TEMP_SPACE_HEADER**

```
select TABLESPACE_NAME,FILE_ID,BYTES_USED,BLOCKS_USED,BYTES_FREE,BLOCKS_FREE,
       RELATIVE_FNO
from   GV$TEMP_SPACE_HEADER
where  inst_id = USERENV('Instance');
```

View Name: GV$THREAD

```
select  rt.inst_id,rtnum,decode(bitand(rtsta,1),1,'OPEN','CLOSED'),
        decode(bitand(rtsta,6),0,'DISABLED',2,'PRIVATE',6,'PUBLIC','UNKNOWN'),
        rtnlf,tirsid,to_date(rtots,'MM/DD/RR HH24:MI:SS','NLS_CALENDAR=Gregorian'),
        rtcln,rtseq, to_number(rtckp_scn),
        to_date(rtckp_tim,'MM/DD/RR HH24:MI:SS','NLS_CALENDAR=Gregorian'),
        to_number(rtenb),to_date(rtets,'MM/DD/RR HH24:MI:SS','NLS_CALENDAR=Gregorian'),
        to_number(rtdis),to_date(rtdit,'MM/DD/RR HH24:MI:SS','NLS_CALENDAR=Gregorian'),
        cpodr_seq, cpodr_bno, to_number(cpods),
        to_date(cpodt,'MM/DD/RR HH24:MI:SS','NLS_CALENDAR=Gregorian')
from    x$kccrt rt, x$kcctir tr, x$kcccp
where   rtnlf != 0
and     tr.inst_id = rt.inst_id
and     tirnum = rtnum
and     cptno = rtnum;
```

View Name: V$THREAD

```
select  THREAD#,STATUS,ENABLED,GROUPS,INSTANCE,OPEN_TIME,CURRENT_GROUP#,SEQUENCE#,
        CHECKPOINT_CHANGE#,CHECKPOINT_TIME,ENABLE_CHANGE#,ENABLE_TIME,
        DISABLE_CHANGE#,DISABLE_TIME,LAST_REDO_SEQUENCE#,LAST_REDO_BLOCK,
        LAST_REDO_CHANGE#, LAST_REDO_TIME
from    GV$THREAD
where   inst_id = USERENV('Instance');
```

View Name: GV$TRANSACTION

```
select  inst_id,ktcxbxba,kxidusn,kxidslt,kxidsqn,ktcxbkfn,kubablk,kubaseq,kubarec,
        decode(ktcxbsta,0,'IDLE',1,'COLLECTING',2,'PREPARED',3,'COMMITTED',4,
        'HEURISTIC ABORT',5,'HEURISTIC COMMIT',6,'HEURISTIC DAMAGE',7,'TIMEOUT',9,
        'INACTIVE',10,'ACTIVE',11,'PTX PREPARED',12,'PTX COMMITTED','UNKNOWN'),
        ktcxbstm,ktcxbssb,ktcxbssw,ktcxbsen,ktcxbsfl,ktcxbsbk,ktcxbssq,ktcxbsrc,
        ktcxbses,ktcxbflg, decode(bitand(ktcxbflg,16),0,'NO','YES'),
        decode(bitand(ktcxbflg,32),0,'NO','YES'),decode(bitand(ktcxbflg,64),0,
        'NO','YES'),  decode(bitand(ktcxbflg,8388608),0,'NO','YES'),ktcxbnam,
        ktcxbpus,ktcxbpsl,ktcxbpsq,ktcxbpxu,ktcxbpxs,ktcxbpxq,ktcxbdsb,ktcxbdsw,
        ktcxbubk,ktcxburc,ktcxblio,ktcxbpio,ktcxbcrg,ktcxbcrc,
        to_date(ktcxbstm,'MM/DD/RR HH24:MI:SS','NLS_CALENDAR=Gregorian'),
        ktcxbdsb, ktcxbdsw,  ktcxbssc, ktcxbdsc, ktcxbxid, ktcxbpid, ktcxbpxi
from    x$ktcxb
where   bitand(ksspaflg,1)!=0
and     bitand(ktcxbflg,2)!=0;
```

View Name: V$TRANSACTION

```
select  ADDR,XIDUSN,XIDSLOT,XIDSQN,UBAFIL,UBABLK,UBASQN,UBAREC,STATUS,START_TIME,
        START_SCNB,START_SCNW,START_UEXT,START_UBAFIL,START_UBABLK,START_UBASQN,
        START_UBAREC,SES_ADDR,FLAG,SPACE,RECURSIVE,NOUNDO,PTX,NAME,PRV_XIDUSN,
        PRV_XIDSLT,PRV_XIDSQN,PTX_XIDUSN,PTX_XIDSLT,PTX_XIDSQN,"DSCN-B","DSCN-W",
        USED_UBLK,USED_UREC,LOG_IO,PHY_IO,CR_GET,CR_CHANGE, START_DATE, DSCN_BASE,
        DSCN_WRAP, START_SCN, DEPENDENT_SCN, XID, PRV_XID, PTX_XID
from    gv$transaction
where   inst_id = USERENV('Instance');
```

View Name: **GV$TRANSACTION_ENQUEUE**

```
select  s.inst_id,l.ktcxbxba,
        l.ktcxblkp,s.ksusenum,r.ksqrsidt,r.ksqrsid1,r.ksqrsid2,l.ksqlkmod,l.ksqlkreq,
        l.ksqlkctim,l.ksqlklblk
from    x$ktcxb l,x$ksuse s,x$ksqrs r
where   l.ksqlkses=s.addr
and     bitand(l.ksspaflg,1)!=0
and     (l.ksqlkmod!=0)
or      l.ksqlkreq!=0)
and     l.ksqlkres=r.addr;
```

View Name: **V$TRANSACTION_ENQUEUE**

```
select  ADDR,KADDR,SID,TYPE,ID1,ID2,LMODE,REQUEST,CTIME,BLOCK
from    GV$TRANSACTION_ENQUEUE
where   inst_id = USERENV('Instance');
```

View Name: **GV$UNDOSTAT**

```
select  inst_id,
        to_date(KTUSMSTRBEGTIME,'MM/DD/RR HH24:MI:SS','NLS_CALENDAR=Gregorian'),
        to_date(KTUSMSTRENDTIME,'MM/DD/RR HH24:MI:SS','NLS_CALENDAR=Gregorian'),
        KTUSMSTTSN, KTUSMSTUSU, KTUSMSTTCT, KTUSMSTMQL, KTUSMSTRMQI, KTUSMSTMTC,
        KTUSMSTUAC, KTUSMSTUBS, KTUSMSTUBR, KTUSMSTXAC, KTUSMSTXBS,  KTUSMSTXBR,
        KTUSMSTSOC, KTUSMSTOOS, KTUSMSTABK, KTUSMSTUBK, KTUSMSTEBK,  KTUSMSTTUR
from    X$KTUSMST;
```

View Name: **V$UNDOSTAT**

```
select  to_date(KTUSMSTRBEGTIME,'MM/DD/RR HH24:MI:SS','NLS_CALENDAR=Gregorian'),
        to_date(KTUSMSTRENDTIME,'MM/DD/RR HH24:MI:SS','NLS_CALENDAR=Gregorian'),
        KTUSMSTTSN, KTUSMSTUSU, KTUSMSTTCT, KTUSMSTMQL, KTUSMSTRMQI, KTUSMSTMTC,
        KTUSMSTUAC, KTUSMSTUBS, KTUSMSTUBR, KTUSMSTXAC, KTUSMSTXBS,  KTUSMSTXBR,
        KTUSMSTSOC, KTUSMSTOOS, KTUSMSTABK, KTUSMSTUBK, KTUSMSTEBK,  KTUSMSTTUR
from    X$KTUSMST
where   INST_ID = userenv('instance');
```

View Name: **GV$VERSION**

```
select  inst_id,banner
from    x$version;
```

View Name: **V$VERSION**

```
select  BANNER
from    GV$VERSION
where   inst_id = USERENV('Instance');
```

View Name: **GV$WAITSTAT**

```
select inst_id,decode(indx,1,'data block',2,'sort block',3,'save undo block',4,
       'segment header',5,'save undo header',6,'free list',7,'extent map',8,
```

```
        '1st level bmb',9,'2nd level bmb',10,'3rd level bmb', 11,'bitmap block',12,
        'bitmap index block',13,'file header block',14,'unused',15,
        'system undo header',16,'system undo block', 17,'undo header',18,
        'undo block'), count,time
from   x$kcbwait
where  indx!=0;
```

View Name: V$WAITSTAT

```
select class,count,time
from   gv$waitstat
where  inst_id = USERENV('Instance');
```

View Name: GV$_LOCK

```
select USERENV('Instance'),laddr,kaddr,saddr,raddr,lmode,request,ctime,block
from   v$_lock1
union all
select inst_id,addr,ksqlkadr,ksqlkses,ksqlkres,ksqlkmod,ksqlkreq,ksqlkctim,ksqlklblk
from   x$ktadm
where  bitand(kssobflg,1)!=0
and    (ksqlkmod!=0 or ksqlkreq!=0)
union all
select inst_id,addr,ksqlkadr,ksqlkses,ksqlkres,ksqlkmod,ksqlkreq,ksqlkctim,ksqlklblk
from   x$ktatrfil
where  bitand(kssobflg,1)!=0
and    (ksqlkmod!=0 or ksqlkreq!=0)
union all
select inst_id,addr,ksqlkadr,ksqlkses,ksqlkres,ksqlkmod,ksqlkreq,ksqlkctim,ksqlklblk
from   x$ktatrfsl
where  bitand(kssobflg,1)!=0
and    (ksqlkmod!=0 or ksqlkreq!=0)
union all
select inst_id,addr,ksqlkadr,ksqlkses,ksqlkres,ksqlkmod,ksqlkreq,ksqlkctim,ksqlklblk
from   x$ktatl
where  bitand(kssobflg,1)!=0
and    (ksqlkmod!=0 or ksqlkreq!=0)
union all
select inst_id,addr,ksqlkadr,ksqlkses,ksqlkres,ksqlkmod,ksqlkreq, ksqlkctim,ksqlklblk
from   x$ktstusc
where  bitand(kssobflg,1)!=0
and    (ksqlkmod!=0 or ksqlkreq!=0)
union all
select inst_id,addr,ksqlkadr,ksqlkses,ksqlkres,ksqlkmod,ksqlkreq, ksqlkctim,ksqlklblk
from   x$ktstuss
where  bitand(kssobflg,1)!=0
and    (ksqlkmod!=0 or ksqlkreq!=0)
union all
select inst_id,addr,ksqlkadr,ksqlkses,ksqlkres,ksqlkmod,ksqlkreq,ksqlkctim,ksqlklblk
from   x$ktstusg
where  bitand(kssobflg,1)!=0
and (ksqlkmod!=0 or ksqlkreq!=0)
union all
select inst_id,ktcxbxba,ktcxblkp,ksqlkses,ksqlkres,ksqlkmod,ksqlkreq,ksqlkctim,ksqlklblk
from   x$ktcxb
where  bitand(ksspaflg,1)!=0
and    (ksqlkmod!=0 or ksqlkreq!=0);
```

View Name: V$_LOCK

```
select  LADDR,KADDR,SADDR,RADDR,LMODE,REQUEST,CTIME,BLOCK
from    GV$_LOCK
where   inst_id = USERENV('Instance');
```

View Name: GV$_LOCK1

```
select inst_id,addr,ksqlkadr,ksqlkses,ksqlkres,ksqlkmod,ksqlkreq,ksqlkctim,ksqlklblk
from   x$kdnssf
where  bitand(kssobflg,1)!=0
and    (ksqlkmod!=0 or ksqlkreq!=0)
union all
select inst_id,addr,ksqlkadr,ksqlkses,ksqlkres,ksqlkmod,ksqlkreq,ksqlkctim,ksqlklblk
from   x$ksqeq
where  bitand(kssobflg,1)!=0
and    (ksqlkmod!=0 or ksqlkreq!=0);
```

View Name: V$_LOCK1

```
select  LADDR,KADDR,SADDR,RADDR,LMODE,REQUEST,CTIME,BLOCK
from    GV$_LOCK1
where   inst_id = USERENV('Instance');
```

View Name: GO$SQL_BIND_CAPTURE

```
select INST_ID, KQLFBC_PADD, KQLFBC_HASH, KQLFBC_SQLID, KQLFBC_CADD, KQLFBC_CHNO,
       substr(KQLFBC_NAME, 1, 30), KQLFBC_POS,
       to_number(decode(KQLFBC_DUPPOS, 65535, NULL, KQLFBC_DUPPOS)),
       KQLFBC_OACDTY, substr(KQLFBC_DTYSTR, 1, 15),
       decode(KQLFBC_OACCSI, 0, to_number(null), KQLFBC_OACCSI),
       decode(KQLFBC_OACPRE, 0, to_number(null), KQLFBC_OACPRE),
       decode(KQLFBC_OACSCL, 0, to_number(null), KQLFBC_OACSCL),KQLFBC_OACMXL,
       decode(KQLFBC_WCAP, 0, 'NO', 'YES'),
       decode(KQLFBC_WCAP, 0, to_date(NULL), KQLFBC_LCAP), KQLFBC_STRVAL,
       decode(KQLFBC_WCAP, 0, NULL,
       sys.sys$rawtoany(KQLFBC_BINVAL, KQLFBC_OACDTY,KQLFBC_OACCSF, KQLFBC_OACCSI))
from   x$kqlfbc;
```

View Name: O$SQL_BIND_CAPTURE

```
select ADDRESS, HASH_VALUE, SQL_ID, CHILD_ADDRESS, CHILD_NUMBER, NAME,
       POSITION, DUP_POSITION, DATATYPE, DATATYPE_STRING, CHARACTER_SID,
       PRECISION, SCALE, MAX_LENGTH, WAS_CAPTURED, LAST_CAPTURED, VALUE_STRING,
       VALUE_ANYDATA
from   go$sql_bind_capture
where  inst_id = USERENV('Instance');
```

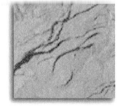

APPENDIX
C

The X$ Tables (DBA)

The X$ tables are usually not mentioned or talked about in many Oracle books or even in the Oracle user community. For this reason, I am including them in this book as one of the few references available. There are 613 X$ tables in 10gR2 (10.2.0.1) compared to only 394 in Oracle 9i Release 2 (9.2.0.1.0). The X$ tables vary in structure and number, depending on the database version and release used. Run the queries on your version of the database to get the number of views and structure for your specific version. Areas covered in this appendix include

- A list of all Oracle 10g (10.2.0.1) X$ tables (613 total)

- A list of all Oracle 10g (10.2.0.1) X$ indexed columns (440 total)

- The Oracle 10g (10.2.0.1) V$ views cross-referenced to the X$ tables

- A listing of Oracle 10g (10.2.0.1) X$ tables *not* referenced by a V$ or GV$ view (285 total)

Oracle 10g X$ Tables Ordered by Name

This is the Oracle 10g query to get the following listing:

```
select     name
from       v$fixed_table
where      name like 'X%'
order by   name;
```

The following table contains the entire 613 Oracle 10gR2 10.2.0.10 X$ tables (ordered by name):

X$ABSTRACT_LOB	X$ACTIVECKPT	X$ASH
X$BH	X$BUFFER	X$BUFFER2
X$BUFFERED_PUBLISHERS	X$BUFFERED_QUEUES	X$BUFFERED_SUBSCRIBERS
X$CKPTBUF	X$CONTEXT	X$DUAL
X$ESTIMATED_MTTR	X$GLOBALCONTEXT	X$HOFP
X$HS_SESSION	X$INSTANCE_CACHE_TRANSFER	X$JOXFC
X$JOXFD	X$JOXFM	X$JOXFR
X$JOXFS	X$JOXFT	X$JSKJOBQ
X$JSKSLV	X$K2GTE	X$K2GTE2
X$KAUVRSTAT	X$KCBBES	X$KCBBF
X$KCBBHS	X$KCBFWAIT	X$KCBKPFS
X$KCBKWRL	X$KCBLDRHIST	X$KCBLSC
X$KCBMMAV	X$KCBOBH	X$KCBOQH
X$KCBSC	X$KCBSDS	X$KCBSH
X$KCBSW	X$KCBVBL	X$KCBWAIT
X$KCBWBPD	X$KCBWDS	X$KCBWH
X$KCCAGF	X$KCCAL	X$KCCBF

X$KCCBI	X$KCCBL	X$KCCBP
X$KCCBS	X$KCCCC	X$KCCCF
X$KCCCP	X$KCCDC	X$KCCDFHIST
X$KCCDI	X$KCCDI2	X$KCCDL
X$KCCFC	X$KCCFE	X$KCCFLE
X$KCCFN	X$KCCIC	X$KCCIRT
X$KCCLE	X$KCCLH	X$KCCNRS
X$KCCOR	X$KCCPA	X$KCCPD
X$KCCRDI	X$KCCRM	X$KCCRS
X$KCCRSP	X$KCCRSR	X$KCCRT
X$KCCSL	X$KCCTF	X$KCCTIR
X$KCCTS	X$KCFIO	X$KCFIOHIST
X$KCFTIO	X$KCFTIOHIST	X$KCKCE
X$KCKFM	X$KCKTY	X$KCLCRST
X$KCLCURST	X$KCLFH	X$KCLFI
X$KCLFX	X$KCLLS	X$KCLQN
X$KCLRCVST	X$KCPXPL	X$KCRFDEBUG
X$KCRFSTRAND	X$KCRFWS	X$KCRFX
X$KCRMF	X$KCRMT	X$KCRMX
X$KCRRALG	X$KCRRARCH	X$KCRRASTATS
X$KCRRDEST	X$KCRRDGC	X$KCRRDSTAT
X$KCRRLNS	X$KCRRMS	X$KCRRNHG
X$KCRRPTDGSTATS	X$KCRRPVRS	X$KCTICW
X$KCTLAX	X$KCVFH	X$KCVFHALL
X$KCVFHMRR	X$KCVFHONL	X$KCVFHTMP
X$KDLT	X$KDNSSF	X$KDXHS
X$KDXST	X$KEACMDN	X$KEAOBJT
X$KEHECLMAP	X$KEHEVTMAP	X$KEHF
X$KEHOSMAP	X$KEHPRMMAP	X$KEHR
X$KEHRP	X$KEHR_CHILD	X$KEHSQT
X$KEHSYSMAP	X$KEHTIMMAP	X$KELRSGA
X$KELRTD	X$KELRXMR	X$KELTGSD
X$KELTOSD	X$KELTSD	X$KEWAM
X$KEWASH	X$KEWECLS	X$KEWEFXT
X$KEWESMAS	X$KEWESMS	X$KEWMAFMV
X$KEWMDRMV	X$KEWMDSM	X$KEWMEVMV
X$KEWMFLMV	X$KEWMGSM	X$KEWMRSM

X$KEWMRWMV	X$KEWMSEMV	X$KEWMSMDV
X$KEWMSVCMV	X$KEWRATTRNEW	X$KEWRATTRSTALE
X$KEWRSQLCRIT	X$KEWRSQLIDTAB	X$KEWRTB
X$KEWRTOPTENV	X$KEWRTSEGSTAT	X$KEWRTSQLPLAN
X$KEWRTSQLTEXT	X$KEWSSESV	X$KEWSSMAP
X$KEWSSVCV	X$KEWSSYSV	X$KEWXOCF
X$KEWX_LOBS	X$KEWX_SEGMENTS	X$KFALS
X$KFBH	X$KFCBH	X$KFCCE
X$KFCLLE	X$KFDAT	X$KFDPARTNER
X$KFDSK	X$KFDSK_STAT	X$KFFIL
X$KFFXP	X$KFGMG	X$KFGRP
X$KFGRP_STAT	X$KFKID	X$KFKLIB
X$KFNCL	X$KFTMTA	X$KGHLU
X$KGICC	X$KGICS	X$KGLAU
X$KGLBODY	X$KGLCLUSTER	X$KGLCURSOR
X$KGLCURSOR_CHILD	X$KGLCURSOR_CHILD_SQLID	X$KGLCURSOR_CHILD_SQLIDPH
X$KGLDP	X$KGLINDEX	X$KGLJMEM
X$KGLJSIM	X$KGLLC	X$KGLLK
X$KGLMEM	X$KGLNA	X$KGLNA1
X$KGLOB	X$KGLPN	X$KGLRD
X$KGLSIM	X$KGLSN	X$KGLST
X$KGLTABLE	X$KGLTR	X$KGLTRIGGER
X$KGLXS	X$KGSKASP	X$KGSKCFT
X$KGSKCP	X$KGSKDOPP	X$KGSKPFT
X$KGSKPP	X$KGSKQUEP	X$KGSKSCS
X$KGSKTE	X$KGSKTO	X$KGSKVFT
X$KJBL	X$KJBLFX	X$KJBR
X$KJBRFX	X$KJCTFR	X$KJCTFRI
X$KJCTFS	X$KJDRHV	X$KJDRMAFNSTATS
X$KJDRMHVSTATS	X$KJDRMREQ	X$KJDRPCMHV
X$KJDRPCMPF	X$KJICVT	X$KJILLFT
X$KJILKFT	X$KJIRFT	X$KJISFT
X$KJITRFT	X$KJLEQFP	X$KJMDDP
X$KJMSDP	X$KJREQFP	X$KJXM
X$KKSAI	X$KKSBV	X$KKSCS
X$KKSSQLSTAT	X$KKSSRD	X$KLCIE
X$KLPT	X$KMCQS	X$KMCVC
X$KMGSBSADV	X$KMGSCT	X$KMGSOP

X$KMGSTFR	X$KMMDI	X$KMMDP
X$KMMRD	X$KMMSG	X$KMMSI
X$KNGFL	X$KNGFLE	X$KNLAROW
X$KNLASG	X$KNSTACR	X$KNSTASL
X$KNSTCAP	X$KNSTMVR	X$KNSTRPP
X$KNSTRQU	X$KNSTTXN	X$KOCST
X$KQDPG	X$KQFCO	X$KQFDT
X$KQFOPT	X$KQFP	X$KQFSZ
X$KQFTA	X$KQFVI	X$KQFVT
X$KQLFBC	X$KQLFSQCE	X$KQLFXPL
X$KQLSET	X$KQRFP	X$KQRFS
X$KQRPD	X$KQRSD	X$KQRST
X$KRBAFF	X$KRBMROT	X$KRBMRST
X$KRBMSFT	X$KRBZA	X$KRCBIT
X$KRCCDE	X$KRCCDR	X$KRCCDS
X$KRCEXT	X$KRCFBH	X$KRCFDE
X$KRCFH	X$KRCGFE	X$KRCSTAT
X$KRFBLOG	X$KRFGSTAT	X$KRFSTHRD
X$KRVSLV	X$KRVSLVAS	X$KRVSLVPG
X$KRVSLVS	X$KRVSLVST	X$KRVSLVTHRD
X$KRVXDKA	X$KRVXSV	X$KRVXTHRD
X$KRVXTX	X$KRVXWNMESG	X$KSBDD
X$KSBDP	X$KSBFT	X$KSBTABACT
X$KSFMCOMPL	X$KSFMELEM	X$KSFMEXTELEM
X$KSFMFILE	X$KSFMFILEEXT	X$KSFMIOST
X$KSFMLIB	X$KSFMSUBELEM	X$KSFQDVNT
X$KSFQP	X$KSFVQST	X$KSFVSL
X$KSFVSTA	X$KSIMAT	X$KSIMAV
X$KSIMSI	X$KSIRESTYP	X$KSIRGD
X$KSKPLW	X$KSLCS	X$KSLECLASS
X$KSLED	X$KSLEI	X$KSLEMAP
X$KSLES	X$KSLHOT	X$KSLLCLASS
X$KSLLD	X$KSLLT	X$KSLLW
X$KSLPO	X$KSLSCS	X$KSLSESHIST
X$KSLWSC	X$KSMDD	X$KSMDUT1
X$KSMFS	X$KSMFSV	X$KSMGE
X$KSMHP	X$KSMJCH	X$KSMJS
X$KSMLRU	X$KSMLS	X$KSMMEM

X$KSMNIM	X$KSMNS	X$KSMPGDP
X$KSMPGDST	X$KSMPGST	X$KSMPP
X$KSMSD	X$KSMSGMEM	X$KSMSP
X$KSMSPR	X$KSMSP_DSNEW	X$KSMSP_NWEX
X$KSMSS	X$KSMSST	X$KSMSTRS
X$KSMUP	X$KSOLSFTS	X$KSOLSSTAT
X$KSPPCV	X$KSPPCV2	X$KSPPI
X$KSPPO	X$KSPPSV	X$KSPPSV2
X$KSPSPFH	X$KSPSPFILE	X$KSPVLD_VALUES
X$KSQDN	X$KSQEQ	X$KSQEQTYP
X$KSQRS	X$KSQST	X$KSRCCTX
X$KSRCDES	X$KSRCHDL	X$KSRMPCTX
X$KSRMSGDES	X$KSRMSGO	X$KSTEX
X$KSUCF	X$KSUCPUSTAT	X$KSULL
X$KSULOP	X$KSULV	X$KSUMYSTA
X$KSUPGP	X$KSUPGS	X$KSUPL
X$KSUPR	X$KSUPRLAT	X$KSURLMT
X$KSURU	X$KSUSD	X$KSUSE
X$KSUSECON	X$KSUSECST	X$KSUSEH
X$KSUSESTA	X$KSUSEX	X$KSUSGIF
X$KSUSGSTA	X$KSUSIO	X$KSUSM
X$KSUTM	X$KSUVMSTAT	X$KSUXSINST
X$KSWSASTAB	X$KSWSCLSTAB	X$KSWSEVTAB
X$KSXAFA	X$KSXPIA	X$KSXRCH
X$KSXRCONQ	X$KSXRMSG	X$KSXRREPQ
X$KSXRSG	X$KTADM	X$KTATL
X$KTATRFIL	X$KTATRFSL	X$KTCNREG
X$KTCSP	X$KTCXB	X$KTFBFE
X$KTFBHC	X$KTFBUE	X$KTFTHC
X$KTFTME	X$KTIFB	X$KTIFF
X$KTIFP	X$KTIFV	X$KTRBHIST
X$KTPRXRS	X$KTPRXRT	X$KTRSO
X$KTSKSTAT	X$KTSPSTAT	X$KTSSO
X$KTSTFC	X$KTSTSSD	X$KTSTUSC
X$KTSTUSG	X$KTSTUSS	X$KTTEFINFO
X$KTTVS	X$KTUGD	X$KTUQQRY
X$KTURD	X$KTURHIST	X$KTUSMST
X$KTUSMST2	X$KTUSUS	X$KTUXE

X$KUPVA	X$KUPVJ	X$KVII
X$KVIS	X$KVIT	X$KWDDEF
X$KWQBPMT	X$KWQPD	X$KWQPS
X$KWQSI	X$KWRSNV	X$KXFPBS
X$KXFPCDS	X$KXFPCMS	X$KXFPCST
X$KXFPDP	X$KXFPNS	X$KXFPPFT
X$KXFPSDS	X$KXFPSMS	X$KXFPSST
X$KXFPYS	X$KXFQSROW	X$KXSBD
X$KXSCC	X$KZDOS	X$KZEKMFVW
X$KZRTPD	X$KZSPR	X$KZSRO
X$KZSRT	X$LCR	X$LE
X$LOGMNR_ATTRIBUTE$	X$LOGMNR_CALLBACK	X$LOGMNR_COL$
X$LOGMNR_COLTYPE$	X$LOGMNR_CONTENTS	X$LOGMNR_DICT$
X$LOGMNR_DICTIONARY	X$LOGMNR_DICTIONARY_LOAD	X$LOGMNR_ENCRYPTED_OBJ$
X$LOGMNR_ENCRYPTION_PROFILE$	X$LOGMNR_IND$	X$LOGMNR_INDPART$
X$LOGMNR_LATCH	X$LOGMNR_LOG	X$LOGMNR_LOGFILE
X$LOGMNR_LOGS	X$LOGMNR_OBJ$	X$LOGMNR_PARAMETERS
X$LOGMNR_PROCESS	X$LOGMNR_REGION	X$LOGMNR_ROOT$
X$LOGMNR_SESSION	X$LOGMNR_TAB$	X$LOGMNR_TABCOMPART$
X$LOGMNR_TABPART$	X$LOGMNR_TABSUBPART$	X$LOGMNR_TS$
X$LOGMNR_TYPE$	X$LOGMNR_USER$	X$MESSAGES
X$MUTEX_SLEEP	X$MUTEX_SLEEP_HISTORY	X$NLS_PARAMETERS
X$NSV	X$OBJECT_AFFINITY_STATISTICS	X$OPERATORS
X$OPTION	X$PRMSLTYX	X$QESBLSTAT
X$QESMMAHIST	X$QESMMAPADV	X$QESMMIWH
X$QESMMIWT	X$QESMMSGA	X$QESRSTAT
X$QESRSTATALL	X$QKSCESES	X$QKSCESYS
X$QKSMMWDS	X$QUIESCE	X$RFMP
X$RFMTE	X$RULE	X$RULE_SET
X$SKGXPIA	X$TARGETRBA	X$TEMPORARY_LOB_REFCNT
X$TIMEZONE_FILE	X$TIMEZONE_NAMES	X$TRACE
X$TRACE_EVENTS	X$UGANCO	X$VERSION
X$VINST	X$XML_AUDIT_TRAIL	X$XSAGGR
X$XSAGOP	X$XSAWSO	X$XSLONGOPS
X$XSOBJECT	X$XSOQMEHI	X$XSOQOJHI
X$XSOQOPHI	X$XSOQOPLU	X$XSOQSEHI
X$XSSINFO		

X$ Tables

Oracle 10g X$ Indexes

This is the Oracle 10g query to get the following listing:

```
select    table_name, column_name, index_number
from      v$indexed_fixed_column
order by  table_name, index_number;
```

Following are the Oracle 10gR2 X$ indexed columns ordered by table name (440 total):

TABLE_NAME	COLUMN_NAME	INDEX_NUMBER
X$ASH	SAMPLE_ID	1
X$ASH	SAMPLE_ADDR	1
X$BUFFER	OBJNO	1
X$BUFFER2	OBJNO	1
X$DUAL	ADDR	1
X$DUAL	INDX	2
X$JOXFM	OBN	1
X$JOXFT	JOXFTOBN	1
X$KAUVRSTAT	ADDR	1
X$KAUVRSTAT	INDX	2
X$KCBBES	ADDR	1
X$KCBBES	INDX	2
X$KCBBF	INDX	1
X$KCBBHS	ADDR	1
X$KCBBHS	INDX	2
X$KCBFWAIT	ADDR	1
X$KCBFWAIT	INDX	2
X$KCBKWRL	ADDR	1
X$KCBKWRL	INDX	2
X$KCBLDRHIST	ADDR	1
X$KCBLDRHIST	INDX	2
X$KCBLSC	ADDR	1
X$KCBLSC	INDX	2
X$KCBSDS	ADDR	1
X$KCBSDS	INDX	2

TABLE_NAME	COLUMN_NAME	INDEX_NUMBER
X$KCBSW	ADDR	1
X$KCBSW	INDX	2
X$KCBWAIT	ADDR	1
X$KCBWAIT	INDX	2
X$KCBWBPD	ADDR	1
X$KCBWBPD	INDX	2
X$KCBWDS	ADDR	1
X$KCBWDS	INDX	2
X$KCBWH	ADDR	1
X$KCBWH	INDX	2
X$KCCAL	ALRID	1
X$KCCBF	BFRID	1
X$KCCBI	BIRID	1
X$KCCBL	BLRID	1
X$KCCBP	BPRID	1
X$KCCBS	BSRID	1
X$KCCCC	CCRID	1
X$KCCCP	CPTNO	1
X$KCCDC	DCRID	1
X$KCCDFHIST	DFHRID	1
X$KCCDL	DLRID	1
X$KCCFC	FCRID	1
X$KCCFE	FENUM	1
X$KCCFLE	FLENUM	1
X$KCCFN	FNNUM	1
X$KCCIC	ICRID	1
X$KCCLE	LENUM	1
X$KCCLH	LHRID	1
X$KCCOR	ORRID	1
X$KCCPA	PCRID	1
X$KCCPD	PCRID	1

X$ Tables

TABLE_NAME	COLUMN_NAME	INDEX_NUMBER
X$KCCRM	RMRNO	1
X$KCCRSR	RSRRID	1
X$KCCRT	RTNUM	1
X$KCCTF	TFNUM	1
X$KCCTIR	TIRNUM	1
X$KCCTS	TSRNO	1
X$KCFIO	INDX	1
X$KCFTIO	INDX	1
X$KCLCRST	ADDR	1
X$KCLCRST	INDX	2
X$KCLCURST	ADDR	1
X$KCLCURST	INDX	2
X$KCLRCVST	ADDR	1
X$KCLRCVST	INDX	2
X$KCPXPL	ADDR	1
X$KCPXPL	INDX	2
X$KCRFDEBUG	ADDR	1
X$KCRFDEBUG	INDX	2
X$KCRFWS	ADDR	1
X$KCRFWS	INDX	2
X$KCVFH	HXFIL	1
X$KCVFHTMP	HTMPXFIL	1
X$KDNSSF	ADDR	1
X$KDNSSF	INDX	2
X$KDXHS	ADDR	1
X$KDXHS	INDX	2
X$KDXST	INDX	1
X$KEACMDN	ADDR	1
X$KEACMDN	INDX	2
X$KEAOBJT	ADDR	1
X$KEAOBJT	INDX	2
X$KEHF	ADDR	1

TABLE_NAME	COLUMN_NAME	INDEX_NUMBER
X$KEHF	INDX	2
X$KEHR	ADDR	1
X$KEHR	INDX	2
X$KEHRP	ADDR	1
X$KEHRP	INDX	2
X$KEHSQT	ADDR	1
X$KEHSQT	INDX	2
X$KELRSGA	ADDR	1
X$KELRSGA	INDX	2
X$KELRTD	ADDR	1
X$KELRTD	INDX	2
X$KELRXMR	HNUM	1
X$KELTGSD	ADDR	1
X$KELTGSD	INDX	2
X$KELTOSD	ADDR	1
X$KELTOSD	INDX	2
X$KELTSD	ADDR	1
X$KELTSD	INDX	2
X$KEWAM	ADDR	1
X$KEWAM	INDX	2
X$KEWECLS	CLSPOS	1
X$KEWESMAS	STATPOS	1
X$KEWESMS	STATPOS	1
X$KEWMAFMV	GROUPID	1
X$KEWMDRMV	GROUPID	1
X$KEWMEVMV	GROUPID	1
X$KEWMFLMV	GROUPID	1
X$KEWMGSM	ADDR	1
X$KEWMGSM	INDX	2
X$KEWMRWMV	GROUPID	1
X$KEWMSEMV	GROUPID	1
X$KEWMSMDV	GROUPID	1

X$ Tables

TABLE_NAME	COLUMN_NAME	INDEX_NUMBER
X$KEWMSVCMV	GROUPID	1
X$KEWRTB	ADDR	1
X$KEWRTB	INDX	2
X$KEWSSESV	KSUSENUM	1
X$KEWSSESV	KEWSNUM	2
X$KEWSSMAP	EXTID	1
X$KEWSSVCV	SVCHSH	1
X$KEWSSVCV	KEWSOFF	2
X$KEWSSYSV	ADDR	1
X$KEWSSYSV	INDX	2
X$KFALS	GROUP_KFALS	1
X$KFALS	ENTNUM_KFALS	2
X$KFALS	REFER_KFALS	3
X$KFALS	PARENT_KFALS	4
X$KFDAT	GROUP_KFDAT	1
X$KFDAT	NUMBER_KFDAT	2
X$KFDAT	COMPOUND_KFDAT	3
X$KFDPARTNER	GRP	1
X$KFDPARTNER	DISK	2
X$KFDPARTNER	COMPOUND	3
X$KFDSK	GRPNUM_KFDSK	1
X$KFDSK	NUMBER_KFDSK	2
X$KFDSK	COMPOUND_KFDSK	3
X$KFDSK_STAT	GRPNUM_KFDSK	1
X$KFDSK_STAT	NUMBER_KFDSK	2
X$KFDSK_STAT	COMPOUND_KFDSK	3
X$KFFIL	GROUP_KFFIL	1
X$KFFIL	NUMBER_KFFIL	2
X$KFFIL	COMPOUND_KFFIL	3
X$KFFXP	GROUP_KFFXP	1
X$KFFXP	NUMBER_KFFXP	2
X$KFFXP	COMPOUND_KFFXP	3

TABLE_NAME	COLUMN_NAME	INDEX_NUMBER
X$KFGMG	NUMBER_KFGMG	1
X$KFGRP	NUMBER_KFGRP	1
X$KFGRP_STAT	NUMBER_KFGRP	1
X$KFTMTA	GROUP_KFTMTA	1
X$KFTMTA	ENTRY_KFTMTA	2
X$KFTMTA	COMPOUND_KFTMTA	3
X$KGICC	ADDR	1
X$KGICC	INDX	2
X$KGICS	ADDR	1
X$KGICS	INDX	2
X$KGLDP	KGLNAHSH	1
X$KGLLC	ADDR	1
X$KGLLC	INDX	2
X$KGLLK	KGLNAHSH	1
X$KGLLK	KGLLKSQLID	2
X$KGLNA	KGLNAHSH	1
X$KGLNA	KGLNASQLID	2
X$KGLNA1	KGLNAHSH	1
X$KGLNA1	KGLNASQLID	2
X$KGLOB	KGLNAHSH	1
X$KGLOB	KGLOBT03	2
X$KGLRD	KGLNACHV	1
X$KGLST	ADDR	1
X$KGLST	INDX	2
X$KGSKASP	ADDR	1
X$KGSKASP	INDX	2
X$KGSKCP	ADDR	1
X$KGSKCP	INDX	2
X$KGSKDOPP	ADDR	1
X$KGSKDOPP	INDX	2
X$KGSKPP	ADDR	1
X$KGSKPP	INDX	2

X$ Tables

TABLE_NAME	COLUMN_NAME	INDEX_NUMBER
X$KGSKQUEP	ADDR	1
X$KGSKQUEP	INDX	2
X$KGSKTE	ADDR	1
X$KGSKTE	INDX	2
X$KGSKTO	ADDR	1
X$KGSKTO	INDX	2
X$KJDRMAFNSTATS	ADDR	1
X$KJDRMAFNSTATS	INDX	2
X$KJDRMHVSTATS	ADDR	1
X$KJDRMHVSTATS	INDX	2
X$KJMDDP	ADDR	1
X$KJMDDP	INDX	2
X$KJMSDP	ADDR	1
X$KJMSDP	INDX	2
X$KKSCS	SQL_ID	1
X$KKSSQLSTAT	SQL_ID	1
X$KMMDI	ADDR	1
X$KMMDI	INDX	2
X$KMMDP	INDX	1
X$KMMRD	ADDR	1
X$KMMRD	INDX	2
X$KMMRD	KMMRDBUC	3
X$KMMSG	ADDR	1
X$KMMSG	INDX	2
X$KMMSI	ADDR	1
X$KMMSI	INDX	2
X$KNSTACR	ADDR	1
X$KNSTACR	INDX	2
X$KNSTASL	ADDR	1
X$KNSTASL	INDX	2
X$KNSTCAP	ADDR	1
X$KNSTCAP	INDX	2

TABLE_NAME	COLUMN_NAME	INDEX_NUMBER
X$KNSTMVR	ADDR	1
X$KNSTMVR	INDX	2
X$KNSTRPP	ADDR	1
X$KNSTRPP	INDX	2
X$KNSTRQU	ADDR	1
X$KNSTRQU	INDX	2
X$KOCST	ADDR	1
X$KOCST	INDX	2
X$KQDPG	ADDR	1
X$KQDPG	INDX	2
X$KQFDT	ADDR	1
X$KQFDT	INDX	2
X$KQFOPT	ADDR	1
X$KQFOPT	INDX	2
X$KQFP	ADDR	1
X$KQFP	INDX	2
X$KQFSZ	ADDR	1
X$KQFSZ	INDX	2
X$KQFTA	ADDR	1
X$KQFTA	INDX	2
X$KQFVI	ADDR	1
X$KQFVI	INDX	2
X$KQFVT	ADDR	1
X$KQFVT	INDX	2
X$KQLFBC	KQLFBC_HASH	1
X$KQLFBC	KQLFBC_SQLID	2
X$KQLFSQCE	KQLFSQCE_HASH	1
X$KQLFSQCE	KQLFSQCE_SQLID	2
X$KQLFXPL	KQLFXPL_HADD	1
X$KQLFXPL	KQLFXPL_PHAD	2
X$KQLFXPL	KQLFXPL_HASH	3
X$KQLFXPL	KQLFXPL_SQLID	4

X$ Tables

TABLE_NAME	COLUMN_NAME	INDEX_NUMBER
X$KQRFP	KQRFPHSH	1
X$KQRFS	KQRFSHSH	1
X$KQRPD	ADDR	1
X$KQRPD	INDX	2
X$KQRSD	ADDR	1
X$KQRSD	INDX	2
X$KQRST	ADDR	1
X$KQRST	INDX	2
X$KRBAFF	FNO	1
X$KRCSTAT	ADDR	1
X$KRCSTAT	INDX	2
X$KRVXDKA	ADDR	1
X$KRVXDKA	INDX	2
X$KSBDD	ADDR	1
X$KSBDD	INDX	2
X$KSBDP	INDX	1
X$KSBFT	ADDR	1
X$KSBFT	INDX	2
X$KSFMIOST	FILE_IDX	1
X$KSFQP	SID	1
X$KSIMAT	ADDR	1
X$KSIMAT	INDX	2
X$KSIRESTYP	ADDR	1
X$KSIRESTYP	INDX	2
X$KSLCS	KSLCSSID	1
X$KSLECLASS	ADDR	1
X$KSLECLASS	INDX	2
X$KSLED	ADDR	1
X$KSLED	INDX	2
X$KSLEI	ADDR	1
X$KSLEI	INDX	2
X$KSLEMAP	ADDR	1

TABLE_NAME	COLUMN_NAME	INDEX_NUMBER
X$KSLEMAP	INDX	2
X$KSLES	KSLESSID	1
X$KSLHOT	ADDR	1
X$KSLHOT	INDX	2
X$KSLLCLASS	ADDR	1
X$KSLLCLASS	INDX	2
X$KSLLW	ADDR	1
X$KSLLW	INDX	2
X$KSLPO	ADDR	1
X$KSLPO	INDX	2
X$KSLWSC	ADDR	1
X$KSLWSC	INDX	2
X$KSMDD	INDX	1
X$KSMDUT1	ADDR	1
X$KSMDUT1	INDX	2
X$KSMDUT1	ARR1_INDX	3
X$KSMFSV	ADDR	1
X$KSMFSV	INDX	2
X$KSMHP	KSMCHDS	1
X$KSMMEM	ADDR	1
X$KSMMEM	INDX	2
X$KSMSP_DSNEW	ADDR	1
X$KSMSP_DSNEW	INDX	2
X$KSOLSFTS	FTS_OBJD	1
X$KSPVLD_VALUES	PARNO_KSPVLD_VALUES	1
X$KSQDN	ADDR	1
X$KSQDN	INDX	2
X$KSQEQ	ADDR	1
X$KSQEQ	INDX	2
X$KSQEQTYP	ADDR	1
X$KSQEQTYP	INDX	2
X$KSQRS	ADDR	1

X$ Tables

TABLE_NAME	COLUMN_NAME	INDEX_NUMBER
X$KSQRS	INDX	2
X$KSQST	ADDR	1
X$KSQST	INDX	2
X$KSRCCTX	ADDR	1
X$KSRCCTX	INDX	2
X$KSRCDES	ADDR	1
X$KSRCDES	INDX	2
X$KSRMPCTX	ADDR	1
X$KSRMPCTX	INDX	2
X$KSRMSGDES	ADDR	1
X$KSRMSGDES	INDX	2
X$KSUCF	ADDR	1
X$KSUCF	INDX	2
X$KSUCF	KSUPLSTN	3
X$KSUPL	ADDR	1
X$KSUPL	INDX	2
X$KSUPL	KSUPLSTN	3
X$KSUPR	INDX	1
X$KSURU	INDX	1
X$KSURU	KSURIND	3
X$KSUSE	INDX	1
X$KSUSECST	INDX	1
X$KSUSEH	KSUSEHSNUM	1
X$KSUSESTA	KSUSENUM	1
X$KSUSESTA	KSUSESTN	2
X$KSUSEX	SID	1
X$KSUSGIF	ADDR	1
X$KSUSGIF	INDX	2
X$KSUSIO	INDX	1
X$KSUSM	INDX	1
X$KSUTM	ADDR	1
X$KSUTM	INDX	2

TABLE_NAME	COLUMN_NAME	INDEX_NUMBER
X$KSXRCH	ADDR	1
X$KSXRCH	INDX	2
X$KSXRCONQ	ADDR	1
X$KSXRCONQ	INDX	2
X$KSXRMSG	ADDR	1
X$KSXRMSG	INDX	2
X$KSXRREPQ	ADDR	1
X$KSXRREPQ	INDX	2
X$KSXRSG	ADDR	1
X$KSXRSG	INDX	2
X$KTADM	ADDR	1
X$KTADM	INDX	2
X$KTATL	ADDR	1
X$KTATL	INDX	2
X$KTATRFIL	ADDR	1
X$KTATRFIL	INDX	2
X$KTATRFSL	ADDR	1
X$KTATRFSL	INDX	2
X$KTFBFE	KTFBFETSN	1
X$KTFBHC	KTFBHCAFNO	1
X$KTFBUE	KTFBUESEGFNO	1
X$KTFBUE	KTFBUESEGBNO	1
X$KTFBUE	KTFBUESEGTSN	1
X$KTFTHC	KTFTHCTFNO	1
X$KTFTHC	KTFTHCTSN	2
X$KTFTME	KTFTMETSN	1
X$KTIFP	KTIFPNO	1
X$KTIFV	KTIFVPOOL	1
X$KTSKSTAT	KTSKSTATOBJD	1
X$KTSTFC	KTSTFCTSN	1
X$KTSTUSC	ADDR	1
X$KTSTUSC	INDX	2

X$ Tables

TABLE_NAME	COLUMN_NAME	INDEX_NUMBER
X$KTSTUSG	ADDR	1
X$KTSTUSG	INDX	2
X$KTSTUSS	ADDR	1
X$KTSTUSS	INDX	2
X$KTTVS	ADDR	1
X$KTTVS	INDX	2
X$KTUGD	ADDR	1
X$KTUGD	INDX	2
X$KTUQQRY	XID	1
X$KTUSUS	KTUSUSTSN	1
X$KTUXE	KTUXEUSN	1
X$KVII	ADDR	1
X$KVII	INDX	2
X$KVIS	ADDR	1
X$KVIS	INDX	2
X$KVIT	ADDR	1
X$KVIT	INDX	2
X$KWDDEF	ADDR	1
X$KWDDEF	INDX	2
X$KWQSI	KWQSIQID	1
X$KWRSNV	ADDR	1
X$KWRSNV	INDX	2
X$KXFPCDS	ADDR	1
X$KXFPCDS	INDX	2
X$KXFPCMS	ADDR	1
X$KXFPCMS	INDX	2
X$KXFPCST	ADDR	1
X$KXFPCST	INDX	2
X$KXFPSDS	ADDR	1
X$KXFPSDS	INDX	2
X$KXFPSMS	ADDR	1
X$KXFPSMS	INDX	2

TABLE_NAME	COLUMN_NAME	INDEX_NUMBER
X$KXFPSST	ADDR	1
X$KXFPSST	INDX	2
X$KZDOS	ADDR	1
X$KZDOS	INDX	2
X$KZRTPD	KZRTPDPH	1
X$KZSRO	ADDR	1
X$KZSRO	INDX	2
X$MESSAGES	ADDR	1
X$MESSAGES	INDX	2
X$OPERATORS	ADDR	1
X$OPERATORS	INDX	2
X$QESMMIWH	ADDR	1
X$QESMMIWH	INDX	2
X$QESRSTAT	HADDR_QESRS	1
X$QESRSTAT	PHADD_QESRS	2
X$QESRSTAT	HASHV_QESRS	3
X$QESRSTAT	SQLID_QESRS	4
X$QESRSTATALL	HADDR_QESRS	1
X$QESRSTATALL	PHADD_QESRS	2
X$QESRSTATALL	HASHV_QESRS	3
X$QESRSTATALL	SQLID_QESRS	4
X$QKSMMWDS	HASHV_QKSMM	1
X$QKSMMWDS	SQLID_QKSMM	2
X$QUIESCE	ADDR	1
X$QUIESCE	INDX	2
X$RFMP	ADDR	1
X$RFMP	INDX	2
X$SKGXPIA	ADDR	1
X$SKGXPIA	INDX	2
X$XSAWSO	ADDR	1
X$XSAWSO	INDX	2
X$XSOBJECT	AW_XSOBJFT	1

X$ Tables

Oracle 10g V$ Views Cross-Referenced to the X$ Tables

The Oracle 10g V$ views are the same as the GV$ views without the instance_id. I am showing the X$ table mapped back to the V$ view. Because of the number of views in 10g, it's no longer possible to list all cross-references here. I have, however, listed several that pertain primarily to performance tuning. You can run your own query to see a specific query associated with the GV$ or V$ views as shown in Appendix B. You must go through the GV$ view to make this inference. Here are the referenced X$ tables, ordered by the selected V$ view names:

FixedView	Underlying Base X$ Tables and/or Fixed Views
V$BH	xbh, xle
V$BUFFER_POOL	x$kcbwbpd
V$BUFFER_POOL_STATISTICS	x$kcbwds, x$kcbwbpd
V$DATABASE	x$kccdi, x$kccdi2
V$DATAFILE	x$kccfe, x$kccfn, x$kccfn, x$kcvfh
V$DB_CACHE_ADVICE	x$kcbsc, x$kcbwbpd
V$DB_OBJECT_CACHE	x$kglob
V$DLM_ALL_LOCKS	V$GES_ENQUEUE
V$DLM_LATCH	V$LATCH
V$DLM_LOCKS	V$GES_BLOCKING_ENQUEUE
V$ENQUEUE_LOCK	x$ksqeq, x$ksuse, x$ksqrs
V$ENQUEUE_STAT	x$ksqst
V$EVENT_NAME	x$ksled
V$EXECUTION	x$kstex
V$FILESTAT	x$kcfio, x$kccfe
V$FILE_CACHE_TRANSFER	x$kcfio, x$kccfe
V$FIXED_TABLE	x$kqfta, x$kqfvi, x$kqfdt
V$FIXED_VIEW_DEFINITION	x$kqfvi, x$kqfvt
V$GES_BLOCKING_ENQUEUE	V$GES_ENQUEUE
V$GES_ENQUEUE	x$kjilkft, x$kjbl
V$GLOBAL_BLOCKED_LOCKS	v$lock, v$dlm_locks
V$GLOBAL_TRANSACTION	x$k2gte2
V$INDEXED_FIXED_COLUMN	x$kqfco, x$kqfta
V$INSTANCE	x$ksuxsinst, x$kvit, x$quiesce
V$LATCH	x$ksllt, x$kslld

FixedView	Underlying Base X$ Tables and/or Fixed Views
V$LATCHHOLDER	x$ksuprlat
V$LATCHNAME	x$kslld
V$LATCH_CHILDREN	x$ksllt, x$kslld
V$LATCH_MISSES	x$ksllw, x$kslwsc
V$LATCH_PARENT	x$ksllt, x$kslld
V$LIBRARYCACHE	x$kglst
V$LIBRARY_CACHE_MEMORY	x$kglmem
V$LOCK	v$_lock, x$ksuse, x$ksqrs
V$LOCKED_OBJECT	x$ktcxb, x$ktadm, x$ksuse
V$LOCKS_WITH_COLLISIONS	v$bh
V$LOCK_ACTIVITY	Dual
V$LOCK_ELEMENT	x$le
V$MTTR_TARGET_ADVICE	x$kcbmmav
V$MVREFRESH	x$knstmvr, v$session
V$MYSTAT	x$ksumysta, x$ksusgif
V$OBSOLETE_PARAMETER	x$ksppo
V$OPEN_CURSOR	x$kgllk
V$OPTION	x$option
V$PARAMETER	x$ksppi, x$ksppcv
V$PARAMETER2	x$ksppi, x$ksppcv2
V$PGASTAT	x$qesmmsga
V$PGA_TARGET_ADVICE	x$qesmmapadv
V$PGA_TARGET_ADVICE_HISTOGRAM	x$qesmmahist
V$PROCESS	x$ksupr
V$QUEUE	x$kmcqs
V$ROLLSTAT	x$kturd
V$ROWCACHE	x$kqrst
V$ROWCACHE_PARENT	x$kqrfp
V$ROWCACHE_SUBORDINATE	x$kqrfs
V$SEGMENT_STATISTICS	obj$, user$, x$ksolsfts, ts$, ind$
V$SEGSTAT	x$ksolsfts
V$SEGSTAT_NAME	x$ksolsstat

X$ Tables

FixedView	Underlying Base X$ Tables and/or Fixed Views
V$SESSION	x$ksuse, x$ksled
V$SESSION_CONNECT_INFO	x$ksusecon
V$SESSION_CURSOR_CACHE	x$kgicc
V$SESSION_EVENT	x$ksles, x$ksled
V$SESSION_LONGOPS	x$ksulop
V$SESSION_OBJECT_CACHE	x$kocst
V$SESSION_WAIT	x$ksusecst, x$ksled
V$SESSION_WAIT_CLASS	x$kslcs
V$SESSION_WAIT_HISTORY	x$ksuseh
V$SESSTAT	x$ksusesta, x$ksusgif
V$SESS_IO	x$ksusio
V$SGA	x$ksmsd
V$SGASTAT	x$ksmfs, x$ksmss, x$ksmls, x$ksmjs, x$ksmstrs
V$SHARED_POOL_ADVICE	x$kglsim
V$SHARED_POOL_RESERVED	x$ksmspr, x$kghlu
V$SORT_SEGMENT	x$ktstssd
V$SORT_USAGE	x$ktsso, v$session
V$SPPARAMETER	x$kspspfile
V$SQL	x$kglcursor_child
V$SQLAREA	x$kglcursor_child_sqlid
V$SQLAREA_PLAN_HASH	x$kglcursor_child_sqlidph
V$SQLSTATS	x$kkssqlstat
V$SQLTEXT	x$kglna
V$SQLTEXT_WITH_NEWLINES	x$kglna1
V$SQL_BIND_CAPTURE	x$kqlfbc
V$SQL_BIND_DATA	x$kxsbd
V$SQL_BIND_METADATA	x$kksbv
V$SQL_CURSOR	x$kxscc
V$SQL_JOIN_FILTER	x$qesblstat
V$SQL_OPTIMIZER_ENV	x$kqlfsqce
V$SQL_PLAN	x$kqlfxpl

FixedView	Underlying Base **X$** Tables and/or Fixed Views
V$SQL_PLAN_STATISTICS	x$qesrstat
V$SQL_PLAN_STATISTICS_ALL	x$qesrstatall
V$SQL_REDIRECTION	x$kglcursor, x$kkssrd
V$SQL_SHARED_CURSOR	x$kkscs
V$SQL_SHARED_MEMORY	x$kglcursor, x$ksmhp
V$SQL_WORKAREA	x$qksmmwds
V$SQL_WORKAREA_ACTIVE	x$qesmmiwt
V$STATISTICS_LEVEL	x$prmsltyx
V$SUBCACHE	x$kqlset
V$SYSSTAT	x$ksusgsta
V$SYSTEM_CURSOR_CACHE	x$kgics
V$SYSTEM_EVENT	x$kslei, x$ksled
V$SYSTEM_PARAMETER	x$ksppi, x$ksppsv
V$SYSTEM_PARAMETER2	x$ksppi, x$ksppsv2
V$TABLESPACE	x$kccts
V$TEMPFILE	x$kcctf, x$kccfn, x$kcvfhtmp
V$TEMPSTAT	x$kcftio, x$kcctf
V$TEMP_CACHE_TRANSFER	x$kcftio, x$kcctf
V$TEMP_EXTENT_MAP	ts$, x$ktftme
V$TEMP_EXTENT_POOL	ts$,x$ktstfc
V$TEMP_PING	x$kcftio, x$kcctf
V$TEMP_SPACE_HEADER	ts$, x$ktfthc
V$THREAD	x$kccrt, x$kcctir, x$kcccp
V$TRANSACTION	x$ktcxb
V$TRANSACTION_ENQUEUE	x$ktcxb, x$ksuse, x$ksqrs
V$UNDOSTAT	x$ktusmst
V$VERSION	x$version
V$WAITSTAT	x$kcbwait
V$_LOCK	v$_lock1, x$ktadm, x$ktatrfil, x$ktatrfsl, x$ktatl, x$ktstusc, x$ktstuss, x$ktstusg, x$ktcxb,
V$_LOCK1	x$kdnssf, x$ksqeq
O$SQL_BIND_CAPTURE	x$kqlfbc

X$ Tables

Oracle 10g X$ Tables *Not Referenced* by a GV$ View

This is the Oracle 10g query to get the following listing:

```
select     name
from       v$fixed_table ft
where      not exists
    (select    'x'
     from      v$fixed_view_definition fv
     where     instr(fv.view_definition,lower(ft.name)) > 0)
and name like 'X%'
order by name;
```

These are the table names, ordered by x$ (285 total):

X$ABSTRACT_LOB	X$ACTIVECKPT	X$BUFFER2
X$CKPTBUF	X$ESTIMATED_MTTR	X$HOFP
X$HS_SESSION	X$JOXFC	X$JOXFD
X$JOXFM	X$JOXFR	X$JOXFS
X$JOXFT	X$JSKJOBQ	X$K2GTE
X$K2GTE2	X$KAUVRSTAT	X$KCBBES
X$KCBBF	X$KCBBHS	X$KCBFWAIT
X$KCBKPFS	X$KCBKWRL	X$KCBLDRHIST
X$KCBLSC	X$KCBOBH	X$KCBOQH
X$KCBSDS	X$KCBSH	X$KCBSW
X$KCBVBL	X$KCBWH	X$KCCDFHIST
X$KCCIRT	X$KCCRM	X$KCKCE
X$KCKFM	X$KCKTY	X$KCLFH
X$KCLFI	X$KCLFX	X$KCLLS
X$KCLQN	X$KCLRCVST	X$KCRFDEBUG
X$KCRFSTRAND	X$KCRMT	X$KCRRASTATS
X$KCRRLNS	X$KCRRNHG	X$KCTICW
X$KCVFHALL	X$KDLT	X$KDXHS
X$KDXHT	X$KEACMDN	X$KEAOBJT
X$KEHECLMAP	X$KEHEVTMAP	X$KEHF
X$KEHOSMAP	X$KEHPRMMAP	X$KEHR
X$KEHRP	X$KEHR_CHILD	X$KEHSQT
X$KEHSYSMAP	X$KEHTIMMAP	X$KELRSGA
X$KELRXMR	X$KEWAM	X$KEWEFXT
X$KEWMAFMV	X$KEWMRSM	X$KEWMRWMV

X$KEWRATTRNEW	X$KEWRATTRSTALE	X$KEWRSQLCRIT
X$KEWRSQLIDTAB	X$KEWRTB	X$KEWRTOPTENV
X$KEWRTSEGSTAT	X$KEWRTSQLPLAN	X$KEWRTSQLTEXT
X$KEWX_LOBS	X$KEWX_SEGMENTS	X$KFBH
X$KFCBH	X$KFCCE	X$KFCLLE
X$KFDAT	X$KFDPARTNER	X$KFFXP
X$KFKLIB	X$KGLAU	X$KGLBODY
X$KGLCLUSTER	X$KGLINDEX	X$KGLLC
X$KGLPN	X$KGLRD	X$KGLSN
X$KGLTABLE	X$KGLTR	X$KGLTRIGGER
X$KGLXS	X$KGSKTE	X$KGSKTO
X$KJBLFX	X$KJBRFX	X$KJCTFR
X$KJCTFRI	X$KJCTFS	X$KJDRMAFNSTATS
X$KJDRMHVSTATS	X$KJDRMREQ	X$KJILFT
X$KJLEQFP	X$KJMDDP	X$KJMSDP
X$KJREQFP	X$KJXM	X$KKSAI
X$KMGSTFR	X$KNGFL	X$KNGFLE
X$KNLASG	X$KQDPG	X$KQFOPT
X$KQFP	X$KQLFSQCE	X$KQRPD
X$KQRSD	X$KRBAFF	X$KRBMSFT
X$KRCBIT	X$KRCCDE	X$KRCCDR
X$KRCCDS	X$KRCEXT	X$KRCFBH
X$KRCFDE	X$KRCGFE	X$KRCSTAT
X$KRVSLVTHRD	X$KRVXDKA	X$KRVXTHRD
X$KRVXWNMESG	X$KSBFT	X$KSBTABACT
X$KSFVQST	X$KSFVSL	X$KSFVSTA
X$KSIMAT	X$KSIMAV	X$KSIRESTYP
X$KSIRGD	X$KSLECLASS	X$KSLEMAP
X$KSLHOT	X$KSLLCLASS	X$KSLPO
X$KSMDD	X$KSMDUT1	X$KSMFSV
X$KSMLRU	X$KSMMEM	X$KSMNIM
X$KSMNS	X$KSMPP	X$KSMSP_DSNEW
X$KSMSP_NWEX	X$KSMSST	X$KSMUP
X$KSPSPFH	X$KSPVLD_VALUES	X$KSQDN
X$KSQEQTYP	X$KSQST	X$KSRCCTX
X$KSRCDES	X$KSRCHDL	X$KSRMPCTX
X$KSRMSGDES	X$KSRMSGO	X$KSUCF

X$KSUCPUSTAT	X$KSUPGP	X$KSUPGS
X$KSUPL	X$KSURU	X$KSUSEX
X$KSUVMSTAT	X$KSXAFA	X$KSXPIA
X$KSXRCH	X$KSXRCONQ	X$KSXRMSG
X$KSXRREPQ	X$KSXRSG	X$KTCNREG
X$KTCSP	X$KTFBFE	X$KTFBHC
X$KTFBUE	X$KTIFB	X$KTIFF
X$KTIFP	X$KTIFV	X$KTPRHIST
X$KTSKSTAT	X$KTSPSTAT	X$KTTEFINFO
X$KTTVS	X$KTUGD	X$KTUQQRY
X$KTUSMST	X$KTUSMST2	X$KTUSUS
X$KTUXE	X$KVII	X$KVIS
X$KWQBPMT	X$KWQSI	X$KXFPBS
X$KXFPCDS	X$KXFPCMS	X$KXFPCST
X$KXFPPFT	X$KXFPSDS	X$KXFPSMS
X$KZDOS	X$KZEKMFVW	X$KZSRO
X$LCR	X$LOGMNR_ATTRIBUTE$	X$LOGMNR_COL$
X$LOGMNR_COLTYPE$	X$LOGMNR_DICT$	X$LOGMNR_ENCRYPTED_OBJ$
X$LOGMNR_ENCRYPTION_PROFILE$	X$LOGMNR_IND$	X$LOGMNR_INDPART$
X$LOGMNR_OBJ$	X$LOGMNR_ROOT$	X$LOGMNR_TAB$
X$LOGMNR_TABCOMPART$	X$LOGMNR_TABPART$	X$LOGMNR_TABSUBPART$
X$LOGMNR_TS$	X$LOGMNR_TYPE$	X$LOGMNR_USER$
X$MESSAGES	X$MUTEX_SLEEP	X$MUTEX_SLEEP_HISTORY
X$NSV	X$OBJECT_AFFINITY_STATISTICS	X$OPERATORS
X$QESBLSTAT	X$QESMMAHIST	X$QESMMAPADV
X$QESMMIWH	X$QESMMSGA	X$QESRSTAT
X$QESRSTATALL	X$QKSCESES	X$QKSCESYS
X$QKSMMWDS	X$RFMP	X$RFMTE
X$SKGXPIA	X$TARGETRBA	X$TEMPORARY_LOB_REFCNT
X$TIMEZONE_FILE	X$TIMEZONE_NAMES	X$TRACE
X$TRACE_EVENTS	X$VINST	X$XML_AUDIT_TRAIL
X$XSOBJECT	X$XSOQMEHI	X$XSOQOJHI
X$XSOQOPHI	X$XSOQOPLU	X$XSOQSEHI

Index

References to figures are in italics.

<> operators, 40
!= operators, 40
80/20 Rule, 321–322

A

access methods, hints, 283
active transaction management, 475–476
ADDM. *See* Automatic Database
    Diagnostic Monitor (ADDM)
alerts, server-generated, 6–7
aliases, and hints, 287
ALL_ROWS hint, 289
allocation units (AUs), 93
APPEND hint, 304
Applications database, sizing, 156–157
AS COMPRESSED BACKUPSET
    argument, 15
ASM. *See* Automatic Storage Management
    (ASM)
ASM instances, 5, 79–80
ASMB, 91
ASMLib, 83
ASMM. *See* Automatic Shared Memory
    Management (ASMM)
ASSM. *See* Automatic Segment Space
    Management (ASSM)
associative arrays, 464–467

Automatic Database Diagnostic Monitor
    (ADDM), 8–10, 759–761
Automatic Segment Space Management
    (ASSM), 76, 108
Automatic Shared Memory Management
    (ASMM), 11–13
Automatic SQL Tuning, 338–342
Automatic Storage Management (ASM), 5
    allocation units (AUs), 93
    ASM instances, 5, 79–80
    ASMLib, 83
    and bigfile, 91
    Cluster Synchronization Services, 89
    database consolidation and
        clustering, 90
    and database deployment best
        practices, 92
    and database instances, 89–90
    database processes to support ASM,
        90–91
    diskgroups, 84–86
    disks, 82–83
    and Enterprise Manager, 230–231
    failure groups, 87–88
    init.ora parameters, 80, 91–92
    installation, 80
    and multipathing, 83–84
    overview, 78–79
    parameters and SGA sizing, 81
    and privileges, 81
    rebalance and redistribution, 93–95

GET YOUR FREE SUBSCRIPTION
TO ORACLE MAGAZINE

Oracle Magazine is essential gear for today's information technology professionals. Stay informed and increase your productivity with every issue of *Oracle Magazine*. Inside each free bimonthly issue you'll get:

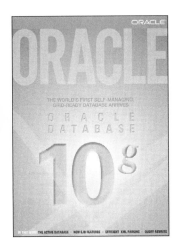

- Up-to-date information on Oracle Database, Oracle Application Server, Web development, enterprise grid computing, database technology, and business trends
- Third-party vendor news and announcements
- Technical articles on Oracle and partner products, technologies, and operating environments
- Development and administration tips
- Real-world customer stories

IF THERE ARE OTHER ORACLE USERS AT YOUR LOCATION WHO WOULD LIKE TO RECEIVE THEIR OWN SUBSCRIPTION TO ORACLE MAGAZINE, PLEASE PHOTOCOPY THIS FORM AND PASS IT ALONG.

Three easy ways to subscribe:

① Web
Visit our Web site at otn.oracle.com/oraclemagazine. You'll find a subscription form there, plus much more!

② Fax
Complete the questionnaire on the back of this card and fax the questionnaire side only to +1.847.763.9638.

③ Mail
Complete the questionnaire on the back of this card and mail it to P.O. Box 1263, Skokie, IL 60076-8263

FREE SUBSCRIPTION

○ **Yes, please send me a FREE subscription to *Oracle Magazine*.**   ○ **NO**

To receive a free subscription to *Oracle Magazine*, you must fill out the entire card, sign it, and date it (incomplete cards cannot be processed or acknowledged). You can also fax your application to +1.847.763.9638.
Or subscribe at our Web site at otn.oracle.com/oraclemagazine

○ From time to time, Oracle Publishing allows our partners exclusive access to our e-mail addresses for special promotions and announcements. To be included in this program, please check this circle.

○ Oracle Publishing allows sharing of our mailing list with selected third parties. If you prefer your mailing address not to be included in this program, please check here. If at any time you would like to be removed from this mailing list, please contact Customer Service at +1.847.647.9630 or send an e-mail to oracle@halldata.com.

signature (required)   date

X

name   title

company   e-mail address

street/p.o. box

city/state/zip or postal code   telephone

country   fax

YOU MUST ANSWER ALL TEN QUESTIONS BELOW.

① WHAT IS THE PRIMARY BUSINESS ACTIVITY OF YOUR FIRM AT THIS LOCATION? (check one only)
- □ 01 Aerospace and Defense Manufacturing
- □ 02 Application Service Provider
- □ 03 Automotive Manufacturing
- □ 04 Chemicals, Oil and Gas
- □ 05 Communications and Media
- □ 06 Construction/Engineering
- □ 07 Consumer Sector/Consumer Packaged Goods
- □ 08 Education
- □ 09 Financial Services/Insurance
- □ 10 Government (civil)
- □ 11 Government (military)
- □ 12 Healthcare
- □ 13 High Technology Manufacturing, OEM
- □ 14 Integrated Software Vendor
- □ 15 Life Sciences (Biotech, Pharmaceuticals)
- □ 16 Mining
- □ 17 Retail/Wholesale/Distribution
- □ 18 Systems Integrator, VAR/VAD
- □ 19 Telecommunications
- □ 20 Travel and Transportation
- □ 21 Utilities (electric, gas, sanitation, water)
- □ 98 Other Business and Services

② WHICH OF THE FOLLOWING BEST DESCRIBES YOUR PRIMARY JOB FUNCTION? (check one only)
Corporate Management/Staff
- □ 01 Executive Management (President, Chair, CEO, CFO, Owner, Partner, Principal)
- □ 02 Finance/Administrative Management (VP/Director/ Manager/Controller, Purchasing, Administration)
- □ 03 Sales/Marketing Management (VP/Director/Manager)
- □ 04 Computer Systems/Operations Management (CIO/VP/Director/ Manager MIS, Operations)
IS/IT Staff
- □ 05 Systems Development/ Programming Management
- □ 06 Systems Development/ Programming Staff
- □ 07 Consulting
- □ 08 DBA/Systems Administrator
- □ 09 Education/Training
- □ 10 Technical Support Director/Manager
- □ 11 Other Technical Management/Staff
- □ 98 Other

③ WHAT IS YOUR CURRENT PRIMARY OPERATING PLATFORM? (select all that apply)
- □ 01 Digital Equipment UNIX
- □ 02 Digital Equipment VAX VMS
- □ 03 HP UNIX

- □ 04 IBM AIX
- □ 05 IBM UNIX
- □ 06 Java
- □ 07 Linux
- □ 08 Macintosh
- □ 09 MS-DOS
- □ 10 MVS
- □ 11 NetWare
- □ 12 Network Computing
- □ 13 OpenVMS
- □ 14 SCO UNIX
- □ 15 Sequent DYNIX/ptx
- □ 16 Sun Solaris/SunOS
- □ 17 SVR4
- □ 18 UnixWare
- □ 19 Windows
- □ 20 Windows NT
- □ 21 Other UNIX
- □ 98 Other
- □ 99 None of the above

④ DO YOU EVALUATE, SPECIFY, RECOMMEND, OR AUTHORIZE THE PURCHASE OF ANY OF THE FOLLOWING? (check all that apply)
- □ 01 Hardware
- □ 02 Software
- □ 03 Application Development Tools
- □ 04 Database Products
- □ 05 Internet or Intranet Products
- □ 99 None of the above

⑤ IN YOUR JOB, DO YOU USE OR PLAN TO PURCHASE ANY OF THE FOLLOWING PRODUCTS? (check all that apply)
Software
- □ 01 Business Graphics
- □ 02 CAD/CAE/CAM
- □ 03 CASE
- □ 04 Communications
- □ 05 Database Management
- □ 06 File Management
- □ 07 Finance
- □ 08 Java
- □ 09 Materials Resource Planning
- □ 10 Multimedia Authoring
- □ 11 Networking
- □ 12 Office Automation
- □ 13 Order Entry/Inventory Control
- □ 14 Programming
- □ 15 Project Management
- □ 16 Scientific and Engineering
- □ 17 Spreadsheets
- □ 18 Systems Management
- □ 19 Workflow

Hardware
- □ 20 Macintosh
- □ 21 Mainframe
- □ 22 Massively Parallel Processing
- □ 23 Minicomputer
- □ 24 PC
- □ 25 Network Computer
- □ 26 Symmetric Multiprocessing
- □ 27 Workstation
Peripherals
- □ 28 Bridges/Routers/Hubs/Gateways
- □ 29 CD-ROM Drives
- □ 30 Disk Drives/Subsystems
- □ 31 Modems
- □ 32 Tape Drives/Subsystems
- □ 33 Video Boards/Multimedia
Services
- □ 34 Application Service Provider
- □ 35 Consulting
- □ 36 Education/Training
- □ 37 Maintenance
- □ 38 Online Database Services
- □ 39 Support
- □ 40 Technology-Based Training
- □ 98 Other
- □ 99 None of the above

⑥ WHAT ORACLE PRODUCTS ARE IN USE AT YOUR SITE? (check all that apply)
Oracle E-Business Suite
- □ 01 Oracle Marketing
- □ 02 Oracle Sales
- □ 03 Oracle Order Fulfillment
- □ 04 Oracle Supply Chain Management
- □ 05 Oracle Procurement
- □ 06 Oracle Manufacturing
- □ 07 Oracle Maintenance Management
- □ 08 Oracle Service
- □ 09 Oracle Contracts
- □ 10 Oracle Projects
- □ 11 Oracle Financials
- □ 12 Oracle Human Resources
- □ 13 Oracle Interaction Center
- □ 14 Oracle Communications/Utilities (modules)
- □ 15 Oracle Public Sector/University (modules)
- □ 16 Oracle Financial Services (modules)
Server/Software
- □ 17 Oracle9*i*
- □ 18 Oracle9*i* Lite
- □ 19 Oracle8*i*
- □ 20 Other Oracle database
- □ 21 Oracle9*i* Application Server
- □ 22 Oracle9*i* Application Server Wireless
- □ 23 Oracle Small Business Suite

Tools
- □ 24 Oracle Developer Suite
- □ 25 Oracle Discoverer
- □ 26 Oracle JDeveloper
- □ 27 Oracle Migration Workbench
- □ 28 Oracle9*i* AS Portal
- □ 29 Oracle Warehouse Builder
Oracle Services
- □ 30 Oracle Outsourcing
- □ 31 Oracle Consulting
- □ 32 Oracle Education
- □ 33 Oracle Support
- □ 98 Other
- □ 99 None of the above

⑦ WHAT OTHER DATABASE PRODUCTS ARE IN USE AT YOUR SITE? (check all that apply)
- □ 01 Access
- □ 02 Baan
- □ 03 dbase
- □ 04 Gupta
- □ 05 IBM DB2
- □ 06 Informix
- □ 07 Ingres
- □ 08 Microsoft Access
- □ 09 Microsoft SQL Server
- □ 10 PeopleSoft
- □ 11 Progress
- □ 12 SAP
- □ 13 Sybase
- □ 14 VSAM
- □ 98 Other
- □ 99 None of the above

⑧ WHAT OTHER APPLICATION SERVER PRODUCTS ARE IN USE AT YOUR SITE? (check all that apply)
- □ 01 BEA
- □ 02 IBM
- □ 03 Sybase
- □ 04 Sun
- □ 05 Other

⑨ DURING THE NEXT 12 MONTHS, HOW MUCH DO YOU ANTICIPATE YOUR ORGANIZATION WILL SPEND ON COMPUTER HARDWARE, SOFTWARE, PERIPHERALS, AND SERVICES FOR YOUR LOCATION? (check only one)
- □ 01 Less than $10,000
- □ 02 $10,000 to $49,999
- □ 03 $50,000 to $99,999
- □ 04 $100,000 to $499,999
- □ 05 $500,000 to $999,999
- □ 06 $1,000,000 and over

⑩ WHAT IS YOUR COMPANY'S YEARLY SALES REVENUE? (please choose one)
- □ 01 $500, 000, 000 and above
- □ 02 $100, 000, 000 to $500, 000, 000
- □ 03 $50, 000, 000 to $100, 000, 000
- □ 04 $5, 000, 000 to $50, 000, 000
- □ 05 $1, 000, 000 to $5, 000, 000

100103